THE CRB COMMODITY YEARBOOK 2001

Bridge Commodity Research Bureau, Inc.

John Wiley & Sons, Inc.
New York • Chichester • Weinheim • Brisbane • Singapore • Toronto

Bridge Commodity Research Bureau, Inc.
30 South Wacker Drive, Suite 1810
Chicago, IL 60606
312-454-1801
800-621-5271
http://www.crbindex.com
E-mail: crbinfo@bridge.com

ISBN 0-471-41267-8

Printed in the United States of America.

10 9 8 7 6 5 4 3 2 1

TABLE OF CONTENTS

In Memoriam

Terrance J. Lown
1950-2001

In 1979, John Burrell and his four partners, all local traders on the Chicago Board of Trade, were looking for somebody to take on the responsibility of coordinating the production of the weekly commodity chart book their company produced. The publication was known as Commodity Perspective (CP), and in those days anyone involved in the futures markets in Chicago was a weekly subscriber to CP. John asked his brother-in-law, Terry Lown, if he would like to move to Chicago from his home in Iowa and take on the role of Production and Technical Coordinator of CP. Terry agreed to take the position, although nearly a full year of weekly commuting to Chicago from Iowa elapsed before Terry actually moved his full-time residence to Chicago. Under Terry's supervision, Commodity Perspective became the standard for quality and excellence in commodity chart books.In 1985, Commodity News Service, whom had previously acquired Commodity Perspective, finalized the acquisition of Commodity Research Bureau and its chart book, Commodity Chart Service, thereby combining the two preeminent commodity chart publications under the new corporate entity, Knight-Ridder Financial Publishing (KRFP). Terry continued to perform the duties of Production and Technical Coordinator at KRFP and oversaw the weekly production and distribution of both weekly chart books until they were merged into CRB Futures Perspective in 1995.

In 1996, Bridge Information Systems purchased KRFP and changed the name of the unit to Bridge/CRB. Terry assumed the title of Systems and Database Director, although all of us close to him knew him better as the Person In Charge Of Just About Everything.

On February 25, 2001, Terrance Joseph Lown suddenly and unexpectedly passed away. All of us at Bridge Commodity Research Bureau would like to thank Terry Lown for his immeasurable contributions to the success of Bridge/CRB. His absence leaves a void in our hearts and in our office that will never be filled.

Milton W. Jiler
1908-2000

It was 1933, the country was in the depth of the Depression, and the United States had just gone off the gold standard. Milton W. Jiler, a young reporter for the New York American, was covering commodity exchanges and doing freelance public relations work for some of the exchanges to supplement his income. Gregarious by nature, Jiler soon became known among the exchanges' commodity traders. He was quick to realize that unless one was actually on the floor of the exchanges, price and volume information was difficult to come by. Although The Wall Street Journal covered the stock market quite thoroughly, there was little if any price information available for commodity futures.

Milton Jiler had a simple idea. If no one was providing information about the commodities markets, trading was limited to those people with direct access to the floor. What he saw was the need for a medium that would bring information about the futures markets to interested parties on a timely basis. With that in mind, he founded the Commodity Research Bureau, with the Futures Market Service as its first publication. The Commodity Research Bureau became profitable within its first year of existence. Its success was due in large part to its ability to provide information that was not readily available to traders.

On August 7, 2000, Milton W. Jiler passed away peacefully in the presence of his wife and son. All of us, at Bridge Commodity Research Bureau, would like to thank Milton W. Jiler for his foresight and contributions to the success of Commodity Research Bureau.

ACKNOWLEDGEMENTS

The editors wish to thank the following for source material:

Agricultural Marketing Service (AMS)
Agricultural Research Service (ARS)
American Bureau of Metal Statistics, Inc. (ABMS)
American Forest & Paper Association (AF & PA)
The American Gas Association (AGA)
American Iron and Steel Institute (AISI)
American Metal Market (AMM)
Bureau of the Census
Bureau of Economic Analysis (BEA)
Bureau of Labor Statistics (BLS)
Chicago Board of Trade (CBT)
Chicago Mercantile Exchange (CME / IMM / IOM)
Coffee, Sugar & Cocoa Exchange (CSCE)
Commodity Credit Corporation (CCC)
Commodity Futures Trading Commision (CFTC)
The Conference Board
Economic Research Service (ERS)
Edison Electric Institute (EEI)
E D & F Man Cocoa Ltd
Farm Service Agency (FSA)
Federal Reserve Bank of St. Louis
Fiber Economics Bureau, Inc.
Florida Department of Citrus
Food and Agriculture Organization of
    the United Nations (FAO)

Foreign Agricultural Service (FAS)
Futures Industry Association (FIA)
International Cotton Advisory Committee (ICAC)
International Rubber Study Group (IRSG)
Johnson Matthey
Kansas City Board of Trade (KCBT)
Leather Industries of America
MidAmerica Commodity Exchange (MidAm)
Minneapolis Grain Exchange (MGE)
National Agricultural Statistics Service (NASS)
National Coffee Association of U.S.A., Inc. (NCA)
New York Cotton Exchange (NYCE / NYFE / FINEX)
New York Mercantile Exchange (NYMEX)
    Commodity Exchange, Inc. (COMEX)
Oil World
The Organisation for Economic Co-Operation
    and Development (OECD)
Random Lengths
The Silver Institute
The Society of the Plastics Industry, Inc. (SPI)
United Nations (UN)
United States Department of Agriculture (USDA)
United States Geological Survey (USGS)
Wall Street Journal (WSJ)
Winnipeg Commodity Exchange (WCE)

THE COMMODITY PRICE TREND

In 2000, the Bridge Commodity Research Bureau's Futures Price Index closing value of 227.83 was 11.06 percent higher than the 1999 close of 205.14, and marked the second consecutive yearly increase. In 1999, the Index rose 7.28 percent.

For the year, 11 of the 17 component commodities finished higher paced by the startling 319.71 percent rise in the natural gas price. Five of the six Bridge/CRB Futures Price Sub-indices posted gains, ranging from 60.99 to 5.49 percent. Only the imported group finished the year in minus territory, down 9.07 percent.

Energy

The Energy Sub-index rose 60.99 percent in 2000, led by an amazing 319.71 percent gain in the price of natural gas from $2.3299 per MMBtu at the end of 1999 to $9.775 per MMBtu at the end of 2000. Heating oil rose 31.33 percent on the year and crude oil posted a 4.69 percent year-on-year increase. For the first time ever, the Bridge/CRB energy group markets posted back-to-back annual gains in excess of 60 percent.

The price of natural gas skyrocketed in 2000 making headlines across the United States and adversely impacting on the finances of households, businesses, and even California power producers. Amazingly, the lowest natural gas price of the year was set in the first week of 2000, and the highest price was reached in the last week of 2000. The rally was fueled by concerns that natural gas storage supplies were inadequate and was exacerbated by an unusually harsh start to the winter of 2000.

Crude oil prices continued in the uptrend that had originated in 1998, finally peaking at $37.00 per barrel in October, 2000. Yielding to pressure from the U.S. administration, the Organization of Petroleum Exporting Countries (OPEC) began increasing oil production in mid-2000 to combat the rising price trend. By November, crude oil prices began a decline that reached below $27.00 per barrel by year-end.

Grains

The Grains sub-index registered a gain of 11.36 percent for the year 2000, recovering from the 28-year low set at year-end 1999. All three component commodities rallied led by a 13.33 percent rise in corn. Wheat rose 12.47 percent for the year and soybeans rose 8.18 percent.

The year 2000 began with rising price trends in soybeans, corn, and wheat, undoubtedly responding to strong global economies and expectations of rising demand and consumption. However, the uptrends aprubtly ended in May and by August both corn and soybeans were trading at new lows for the year. Prices then began a mild recovery that reached the January 2000 level by year-end. Wheat prices never did reach new yearly lows in August, and by the end of December they had recovered all of the summer losses, benefit-ting from declining global supplies and a poor start for the U.S. winter wheat crop.

Industrials

The Industrial sub-index rose 9.39 percent in 2000, building on the 4.09 percent gain it had registered in 1999. Cotton prices gained 22.74 percent, recovering from the 13-year lows registered at the end of 1999. Copper prices declined 4.87 percent for the year, trending primarily sideways in an apparent consolidation of the 28.42 percent gain in 1999.

With the exception of a sharp decline begining in late May and carrying through June, cotton prices spent most of the year in a steady advance due to increased global demand and diminished expectations for the U.S. crop.

Livestock

The Livestock subindex rose 5.82 percent in 2000, the second consecutive annual rise but far short of the 28.34 gain registered in 1999.

Live cattle prices spent the first eight months of the year in a dull, sideways pattern before moving sharply higher in the September-December period. At year-end they were up 11.95 percent. Lean hogs began the year by strongly advancing from 54.00 cents per pound up to 78.00 cents by late April. A price collapse followed with the market down to 50.00 by October.

Precious Metals

The Precious Metals subindex rose 5.49 percent in 2000, ending the year at the highest level since 1995. A strong gain of 41.70 percent in platinum was countered by a 5.52 percent decline in gold and a 15.92 percent fall in silver.

For the second consecutive year, irregular exports from Russia of platinum and palladium combined with strong demand from the automative industry sparked sharp gains in both markets. Gold and silver continued to languish as paper assets continued to grab the attention of investors.

Imported

The Imported subindex fell by 9.07 percent in 2000, the third consecutive annual decline in this group and the lowest close since year-end 1992. Three of the four components declined. Coffee fell 47.93 percent, orange juice fell 16.13 percent and cocoa fell 9.44 percent. Sugar prices rose 66.67 percent for the year.

Large supplies resulting from new sources of production plagued the coffee, orange juice, and cocoa markets. Sugar prices rallied sharply as a result of a severe drought that reduced the Brazilian crop and a cyclone that severely damaged the sugar cane fields in Australia.

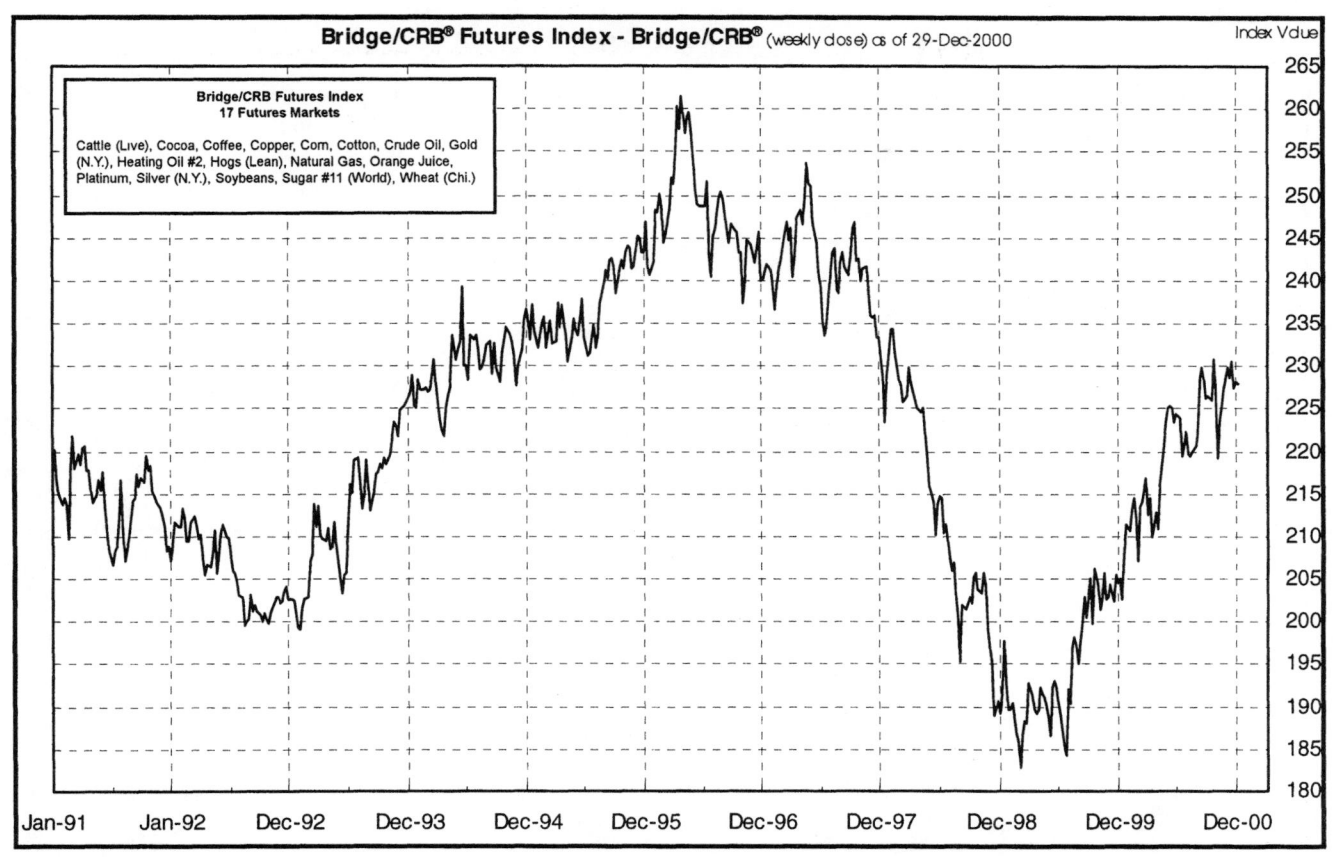

Bridge/CRB® Futures Index - Bridge/CRB® (weekly close) as of 29-Dec-2000

Bridge/CRB Futures Index
17 Futures Markets

Cattle (Live), Cocoa, Coffee, Copper, Corn, Cotton, Crude Oil, Gold (N.Y.), Heating Oil #2, Hogs (Lean), Natural Gas, Orange Juice, Platinum, Silver (N.Y.), Soybeans, Sugar #11 (World), Wheat (Chi.)

Monthly Bridge/CRB Futures Index   High, Low and Close (1967=100)

Year		Jan.	Feb.	Mar.	Apr.	May	June	Jule	Aug.	Sept.	Oct.	Nov.	Dec.	Range
1991	High	222.80	215.60	221.80	222.20	217.00	217.70	214.10	216.50	217.60	219.80	218.60	213.90	222.80
	Low	214.10	209.70	217.30	216.20	214.10	208.40	205.90	204.70	211.90	216.20	213.30	207.20	204.70
	Close	214.10	215.60	218.50	216.20	215.40	208.40	214.10	211.80	215.60	218.20	213.30	208.10	----
1992	High	212.20	215.30	212.90	210.30	211.70	212.90	209.10	204.90	203.50	202.90	203.60	204.30	215.30
	Low	206.90	207.20	208.60	204.50	204.90	208.00	203.00	198.20	199.30	199.10	199.20	201.20	198.20
	Close	211.20	209.60	209.80	204.80	208.00	209.30	203.10	201.00	200.40	199.90	203.10	202.80	----
1993	High	203.20	204.90	214.30	213.90	211.80	210.00	219.70	223.50	217.80	220.60	223.80	226.80	226.80
	Low	199.30	198.40	203.40	207.80	207.40	202.60	207.20	212.10	211.90	216.60	217.40	218.40	198.40
	Close	199.50	202.90	212.50	210.90	208.70	207.10	219.30	217.20	216.10	218.40	218.00	226.30	----
1994	High	229.80	229.20	231.00	227.80	239.20	239.70	234.70	235.40	234.40	235.20	234.70	237.18	239.70
	Low	226.20	225.70	227.40	227.80	225.20	235.90	230.40	228.00	228.60	227.00	228.80	226.97	225.20
	Close	225.60	227.60	227.70	225.00	235.50	230.40	233.70	231.90	229.90	233.30	229.20	236.64	----
1995	High	237.96	236.16	236.89	237.70	237.12	238.00	235.90	240.27	245.81	242.67	244.49	246.47	246.47
	Low	232.58	230.97	231.07	233.16	229.55	232.18	229.31	231.71	239.38	238.32	240.85	240.93	229.31
	Close	232.78	234.25	232.94	235.30	232.72	233.38	233.23	239.97	241.73	242.22	241.84	243.18	----
1996	High	247.56	251.21	253.50	263.79	261.24	252.92	251.90	252.04	250.35	249.59	247.08	246.85	263.79
	Low	238.63	245.62	242.72	250.19	251.79	246.64	240.09	242.83	243.10	237.78	235.99	238.12	235.99
	Close	247.53	248.77	251.40	256.09	254.07	248.67	241.99	249.46	245.63	237.83	243.36	239.61	----
1997	High	244.30	243.91	248.01	249.00	254.79	249.98	243.38	245.30	244.50	247.62	243.52	238.39	254.79
	Low	238.93	236.14	241.64	237.64	245.54	238.52	232.01	236.69	240.03	238.34	235.27	228.84	228.84
	Close	238.99	242.41	245.17	248.29	250.96	239.42	242.75	241.98	243.06	240.04	235.92	229.14	----
1998	High	235.36	236.08	231.74	229.09	226.67	216.75	216.75	207.48	205.03	206.57	206.73	197.29	236.08
	Low	221.56	223.97	223.04	223.42	214.03	208.42	205.99	195.18	196.31	201.34	195.18	187.89	187.89
	Close	234.28	227.65	228.88	223.99	215.90	214.63	206.00	195.68	203.30	203.28	195.42	191.22	----
1999	High	198.96	191.45	193.28	192.89	193.99	193.43	192.91	199.59	209.41	209.91	207.54	206.20	209.91
	Low	187.18	182.76	183.38	187.14	185.05	185.07	182.67	190.14	199.03	199.66	202.23	200.74	182.67
	Close	189.74	182.95	191.83	192.39	186.72	191.54	190.36	199.35	205.19	201.52	204.07	205.14	----
2000	High	213.70	215.29	217.88	214.15	226.12	227.29	225.69	228.02	232.20	234.38	231.46	233.37	234.38
	Low	201.43	206.74	209.61	207.61	211.86	222.23	217.42	217.76	224.74	218.38	220.93	225.46	201.43
	Close	210.46	208.78	214.37	211.03	222.27	223.93	218.61	227.41	226.57	219.28	229.79	227.83	----

Source: Bridge/Commodity Research Bureau (CRB)

9T

Bridge/CRB Indices

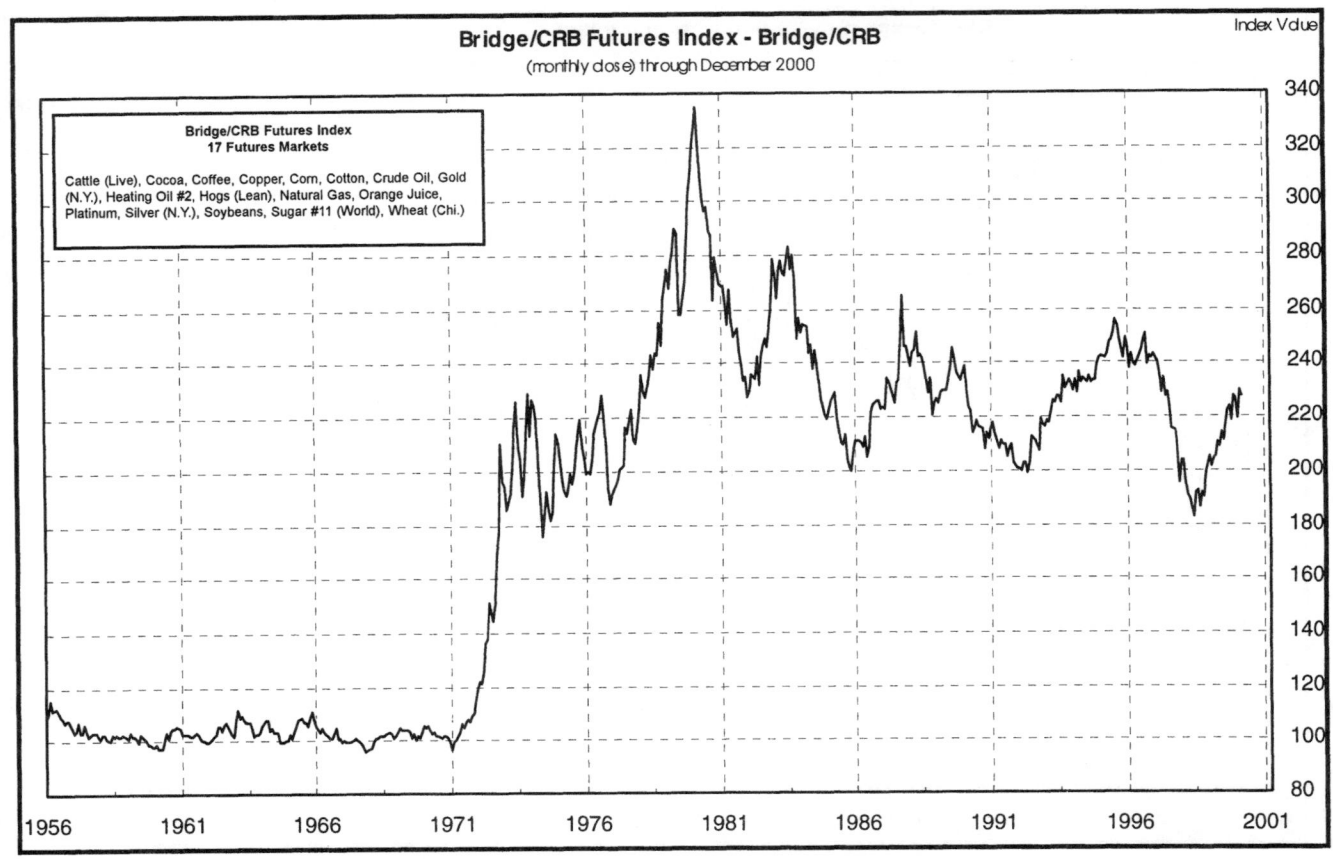

Bridge/CRB Futures Index - Bridge/CRB
(monthly close) through December 2000

Index Value

Bridge/CRB Futures Index
17 Futures Markets

Cattle (Live), Cocoa, Coffee, Copper, Corn, Cotton, Crude Oil, Gold (N.Y.), Heating Oil #2, Hogs (Lean), Natural Gas, Orange Juice, Platinum, Silver (N.Y.), Soybeans, Sugar #11 (World), Wheat (Chi.)

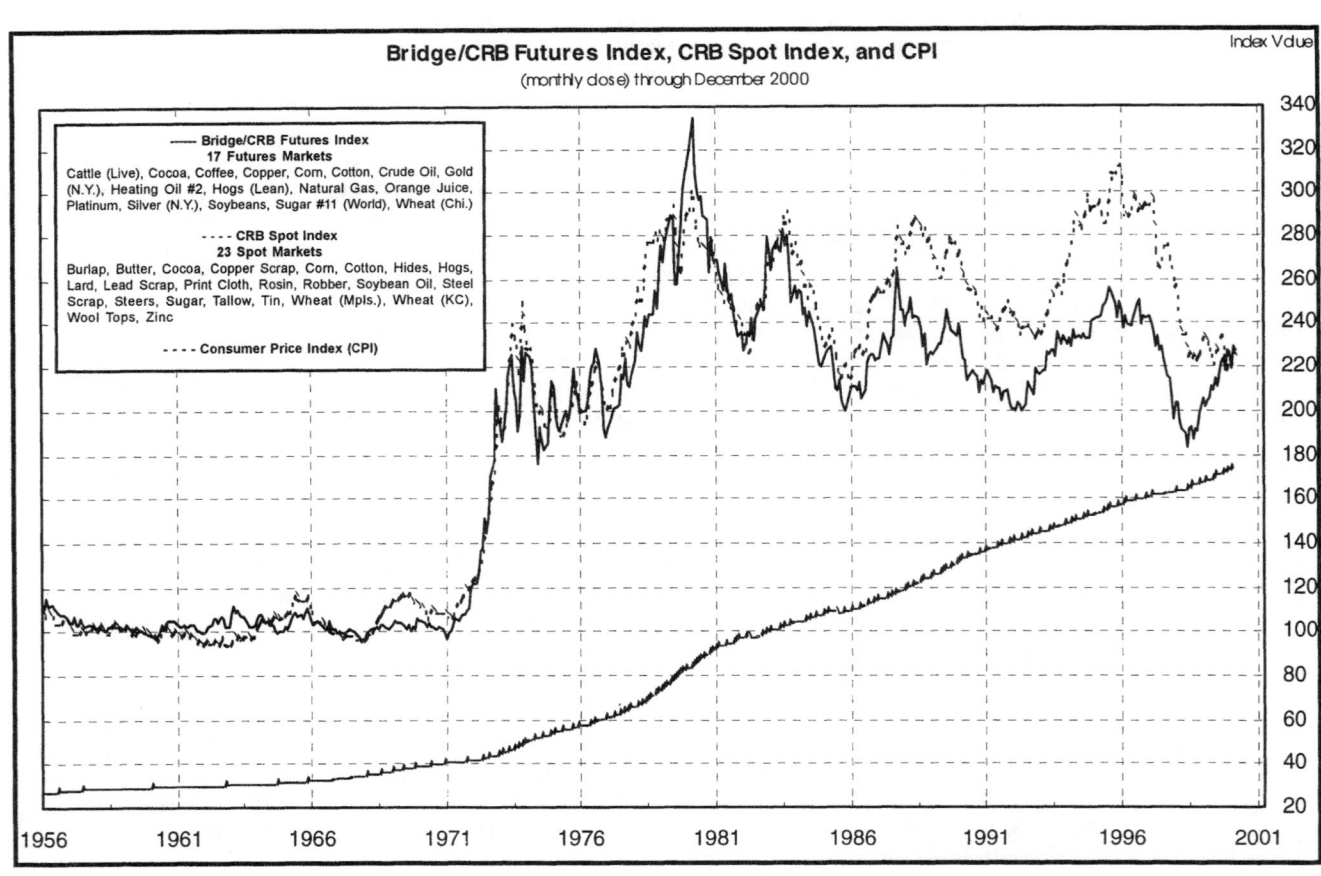

Bridge/CRB Futures Index, CRB Spot Index, and CPI
(monthly close) through December 2000

Index Value

——— **Bridge/CRB Futures Index**
17 Futures Markets
Cattle (Live), Cocoa, Coffee, Copper, Corn, Cotton, Crude Oil, Gold (N.Y.), Heating Oil #2, Hogs (Lean), Natural Gas, Orange Juice, Platinum, Silver (N.Y.), Soybeans, Sugar #11 (World), Wheat (Chi.)

- - - - **CRB Spot Index**
23 Spot Markets
Burlap, Butter, Cocoa, Copper Scrap, Corn, Cotton, Hides, Hogs, Lard, Lead Scrap, Print Cloth, Rosin, Robber, Soybean Oil, Steel Scrap, Steers, Sugar, Tallow, Tin, Wheat (Mpls.), Wheat (KC), Wool Tops, Zinc

- - - - **Consumer Price Index (CPI)**

Bridge/CRB Futures Index vs. 30-year T-Bond Yield - 12-month Rate of Change
(monthly close) through December 2000
Bridge/CRB Futures Index
30-year T-Bond Yield
100%
90%
80%
70%
60%
50%
40%
30%
20%
10%
0%
-10%
-20%
-30%
-40%
1957
1962
1967
1972
1977
1982
1987
1992
1997

Bridge/CRB Futures Index vs. CPI - 12-month Rate of Change
(monthly close) through December 2000
Bridge/CRB Futures Index
Consumer Price Index (CPI)
100%
90%
80%
70%
60%
50%
40%
30%
20%
10%
0%
-10%
-20%
-30%
1957
1962
1967
1972
1977
1982
1987
1992
1997

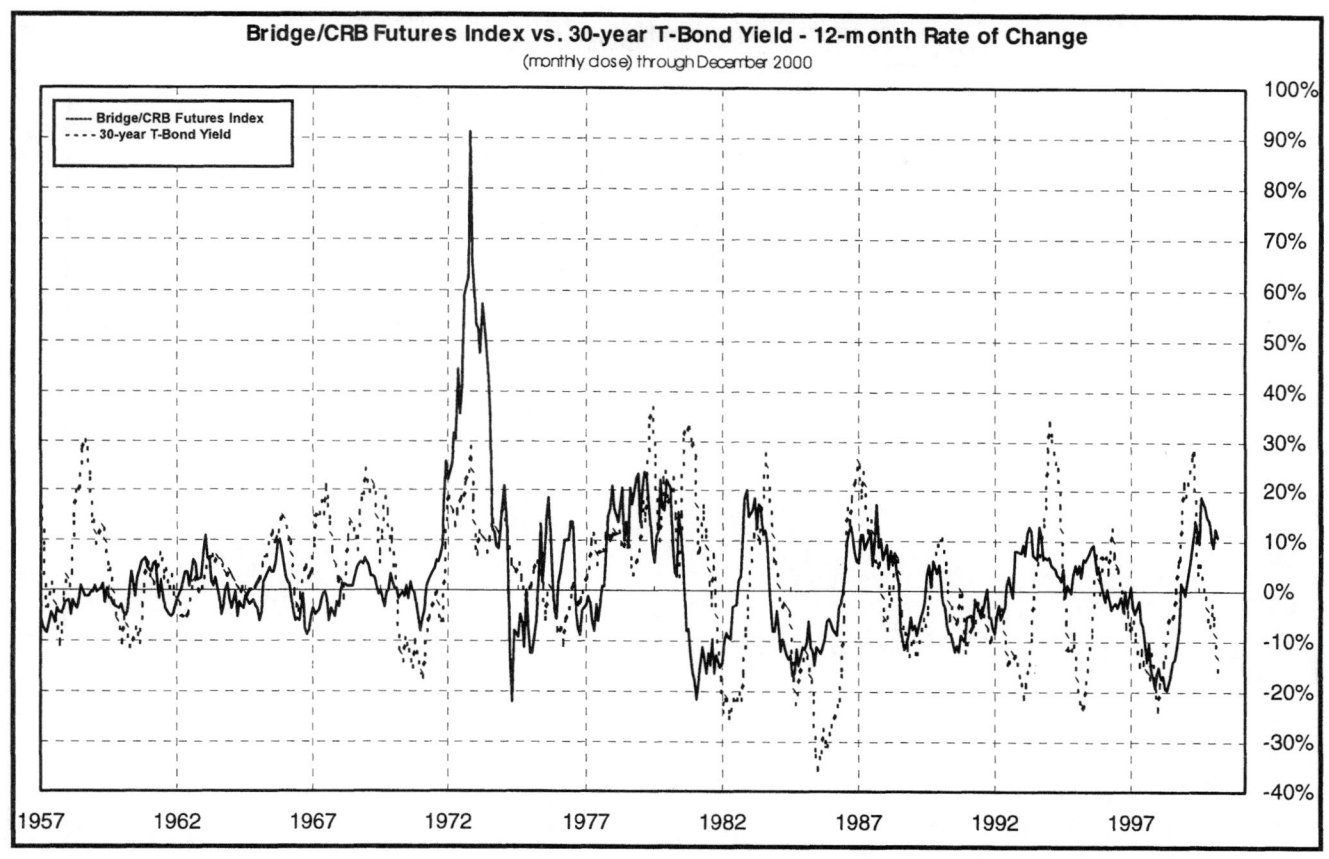

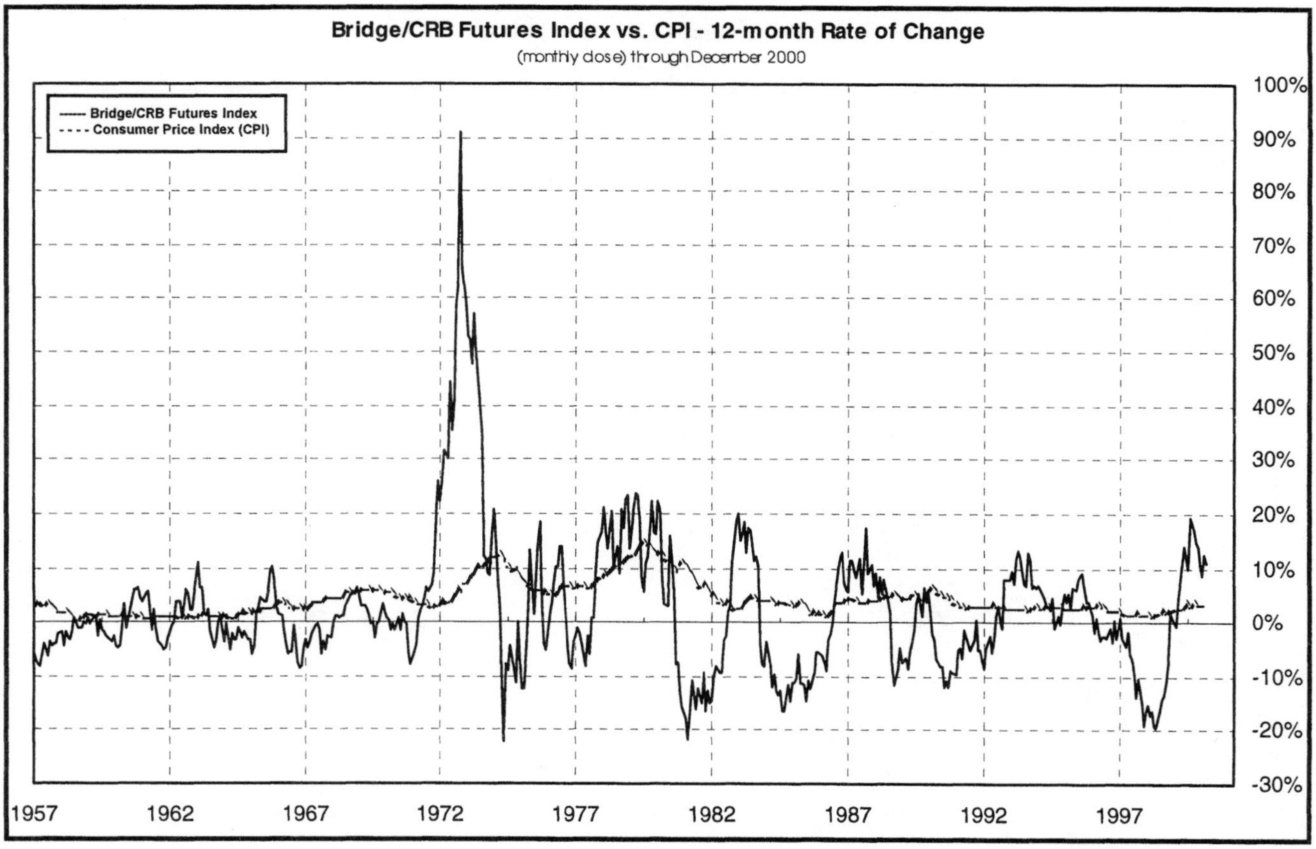

Bridge/CRB Indices

Bridge/CRB® Total Return Index (weekly close) as of 29-Dec-2000

Bridge/CRB Total Return Index

(monthly close) through December 2000

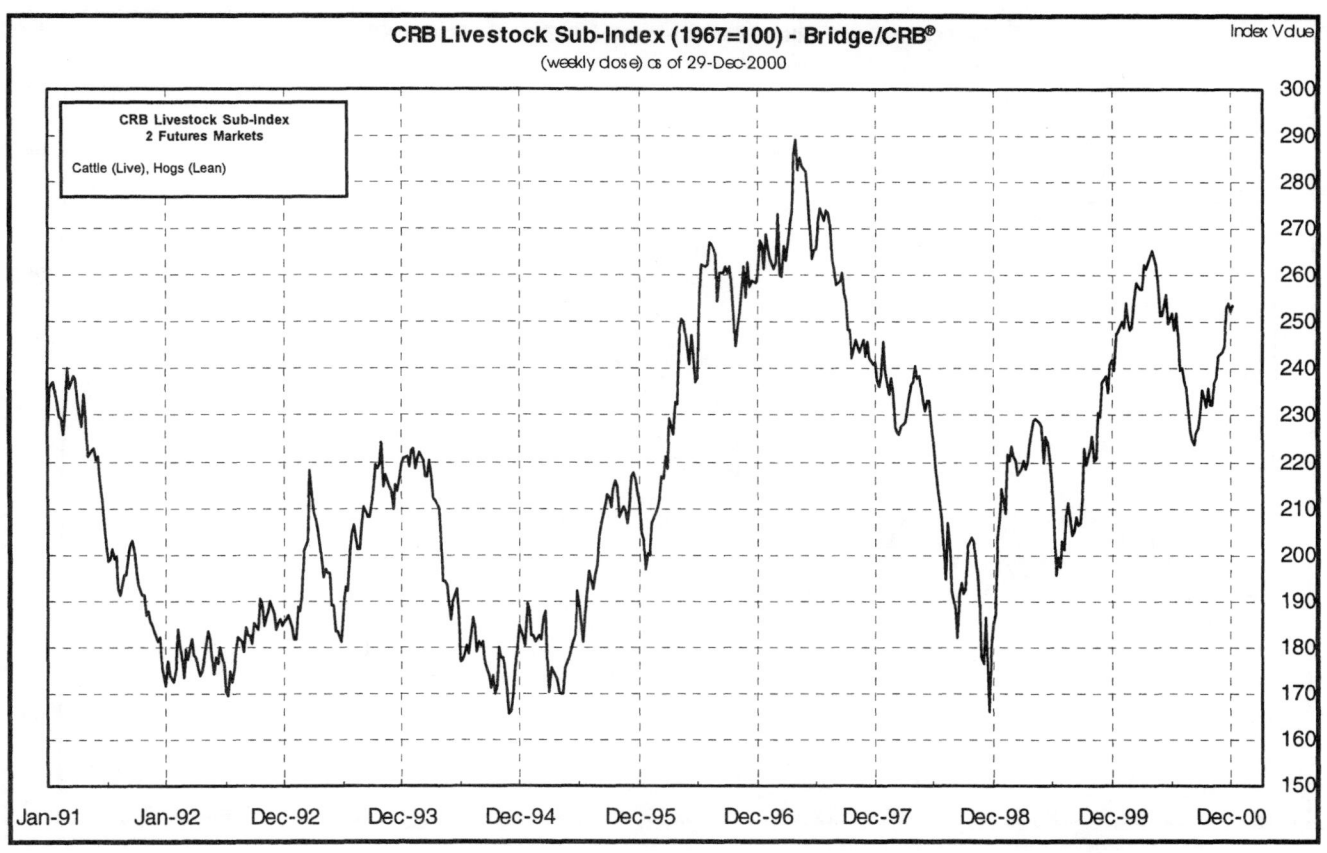

CRB Livestock Sub-Index (1967=100) - Bridge/CRB®
(weekly close) as of 29-Dec-2000
Index Value
CRB Livestock Sub-Index
2 Futures Markets
Cattle (Live), Hogs (Lean)
300
290
280
270
260
250
240
230
220
210
200
190
180
170
160
150
Jan-91 Jan-92 Dec-92 Dec-93 Dec-94 Dec-95 Dec-96 Dec-97 Dec-98 Dec-99 Dec-00

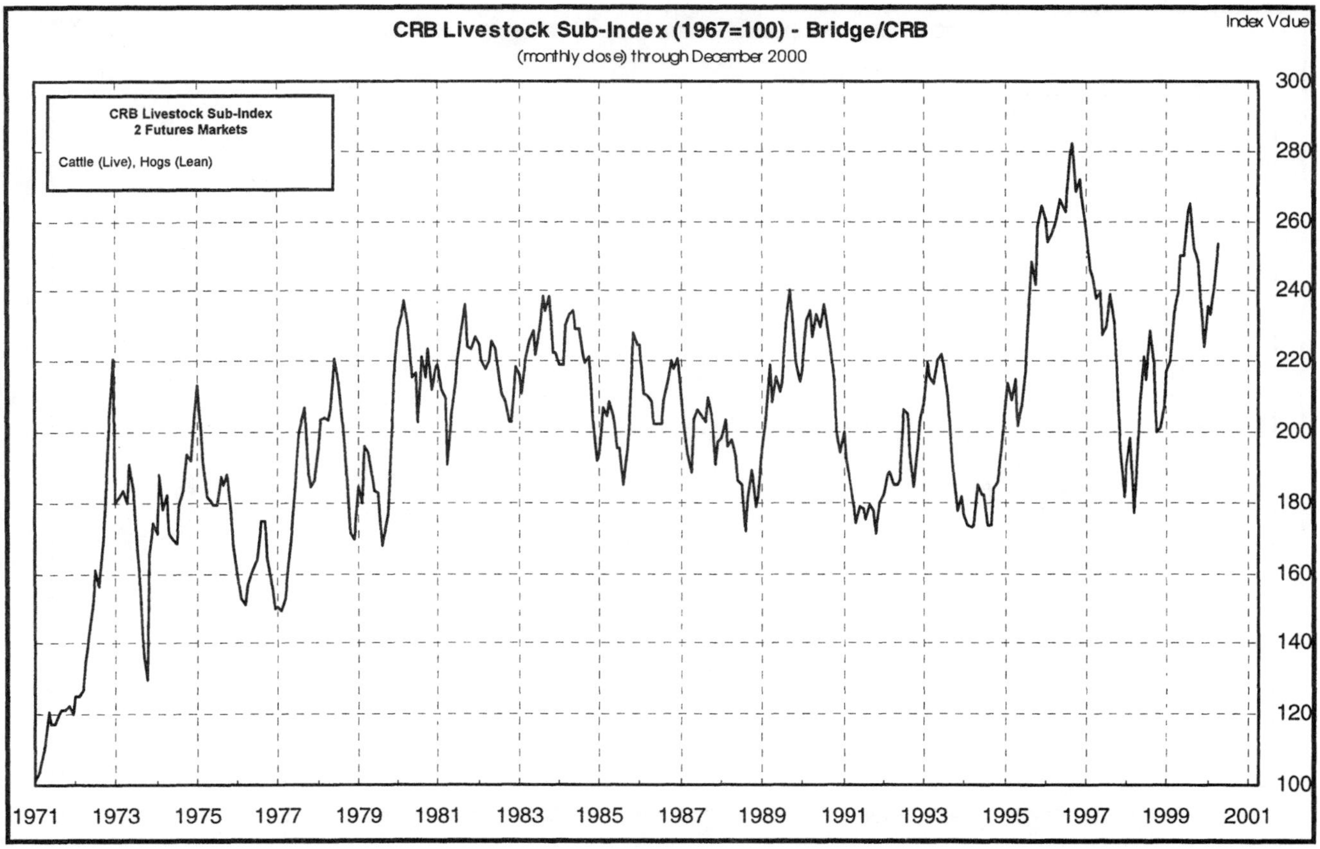
CRB Livestock Sub-Index (1967=100) - Bridge/CRB
(monthly close) through December 2000
Index Value
CRB Livestock Sub-Index
2 Futures Markets
Cattle (Live), Hogs (Lean)
300
280
260
240
220
200
180
160
140
120
100
1971 1973 1975 1977 1979 1981 1983 1985 1987 1989 1991 1993 1995 1997 1999 2001

Bridge/CRB Indices

CRB Grains and Oilseeds Sub-Index (1967=100) - Bridge/CRB®
(weekly close) as of 29-Dec-2000

Index Value

CRB Grains and Oilseeds Sub-Index
3 Futures Markets

Corn, Soybeans, Wheat (Chi.)

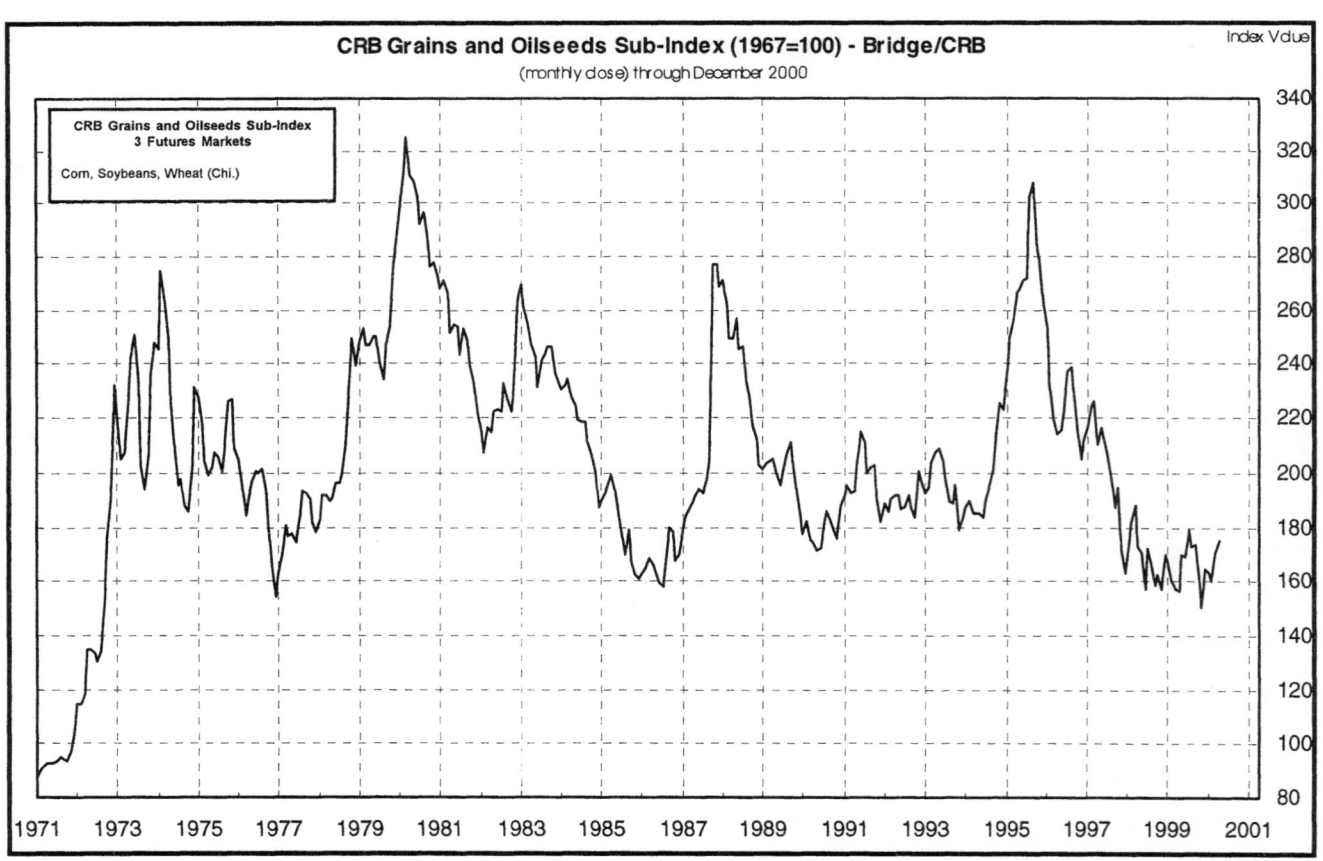

CRB Grains and Oilseeds Sub-Index (1967=100) - Bridge/CRB
(monthly close) through December 2000

Index Value

CRB Grains and Oilseeds Sub-Index
3 Futures Markets

Corn, Soybeans, Wheat (Chi.)

CRB Softs Sub-Index (1967=100) - Bridge/CRB®
(weekly close) as of 29-Dec-2000

Index Value

CRB Softs Sub-Index
4 Futures Markets

Cocoa, Coffee, Orange Juice, Sugar #11 (World)

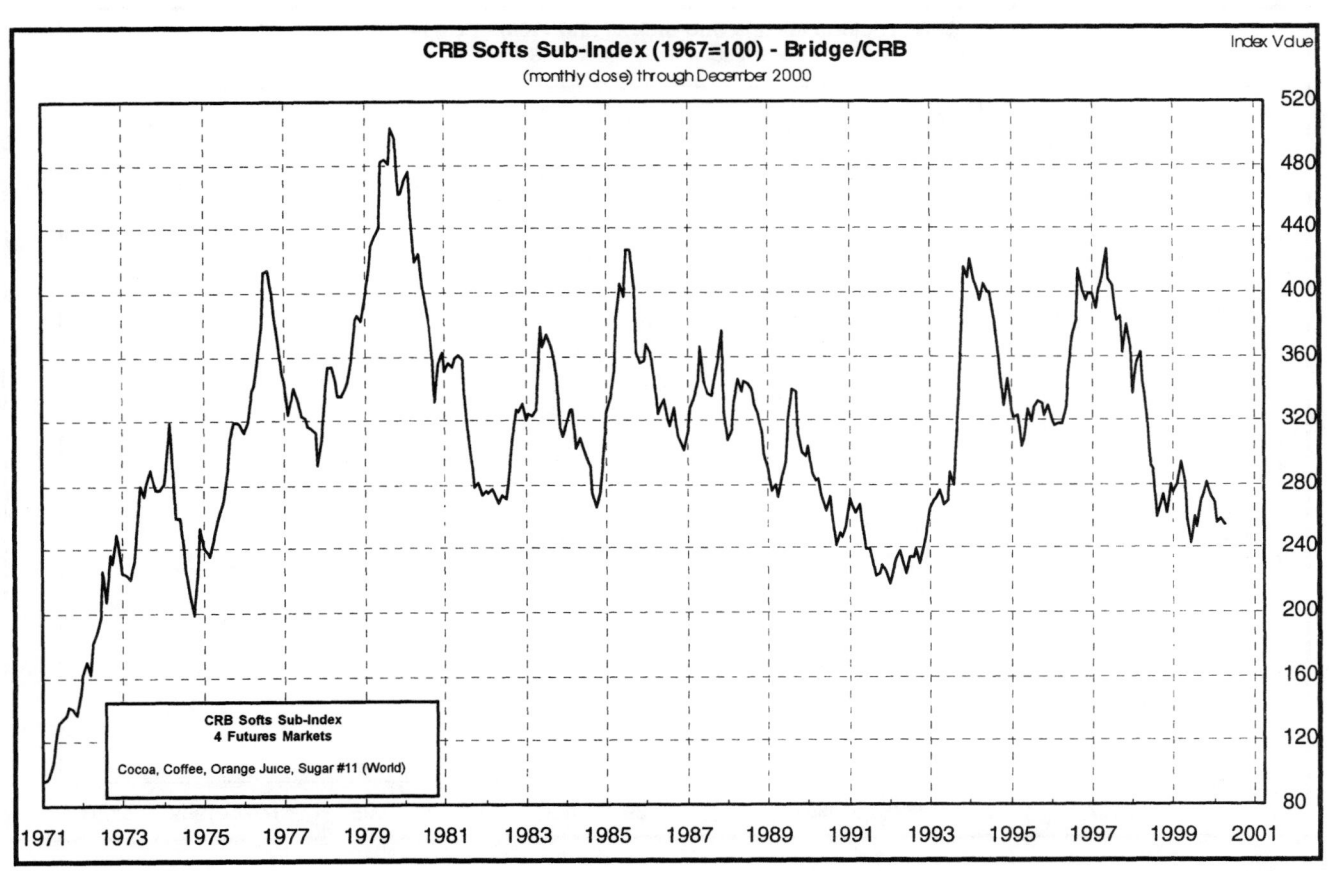

CRB Softs Sub-Index (1967=100) - Bridge/CRB
(monthly close) through December 2000

Index Value

CRB Softs Sub-Index
4 Futures Markets

Cocoa, Coffee, Orange Juice, Sugar #11 (World)

Bridge/CRB Indices

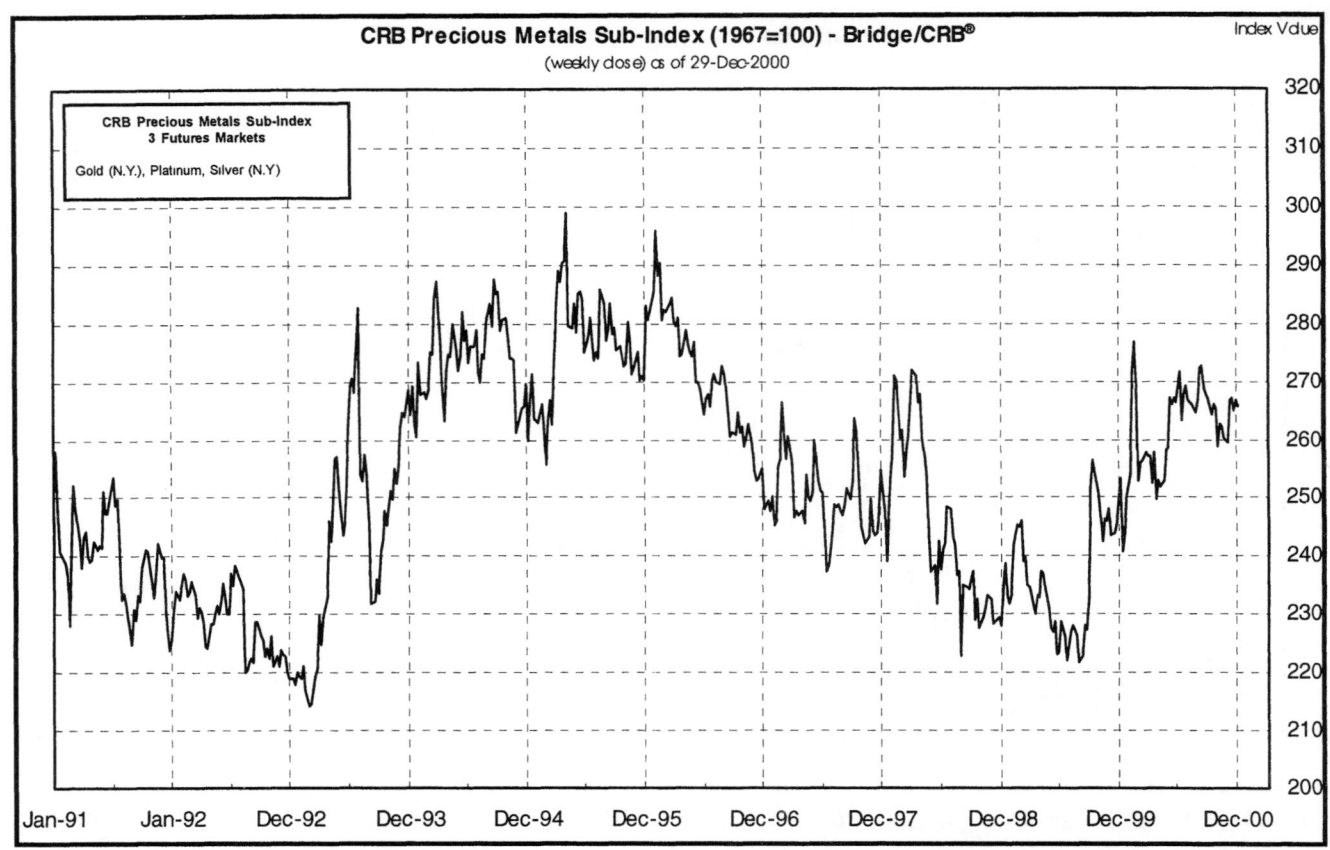

CRB Precious Metals Sub-Index (1967=100) - Bridge/CRB®

(weekly close) as of 29-Dec-2000

Index Value

CRB Precious Metals Sub-Index
3 Futures Markets

Gold (N.Y.), Platinum, Silver (N.Y)

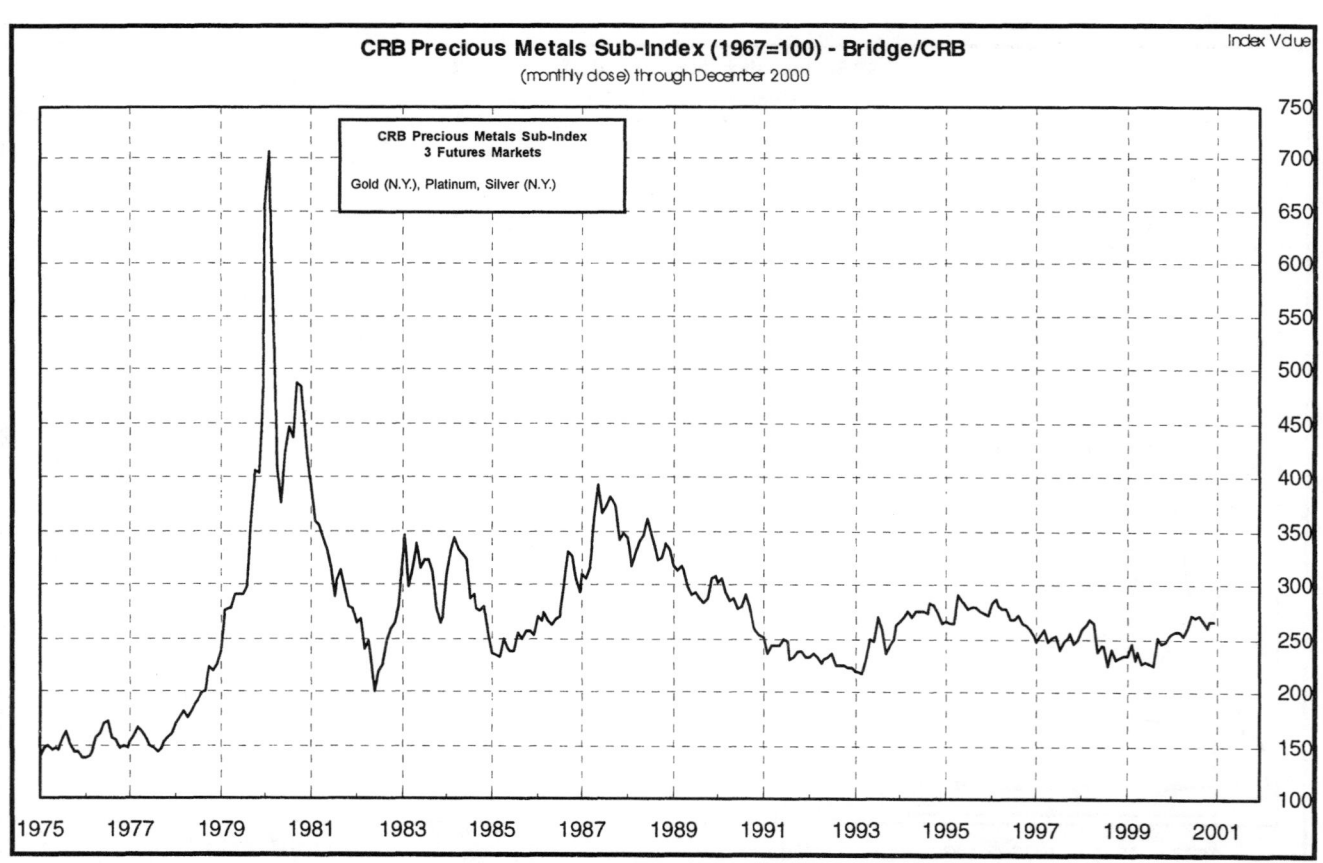

CRB Precious Metals Sub-Index (1967=100) - Bridge/CRB

(monthly close) through December 2000

Index Value

CRB Precious Metals Sub-Index
3 Futures Markets

Gold (N.Y.), Platinum, Silver (N.Y.)

CRB Industrials Sub-Index (1967=100) - Bridge/CRB®
(weekly close) as of 29-Dec-2000

CRB Industrials Sub-Index
2 Futures Markets

Copper, Cotton

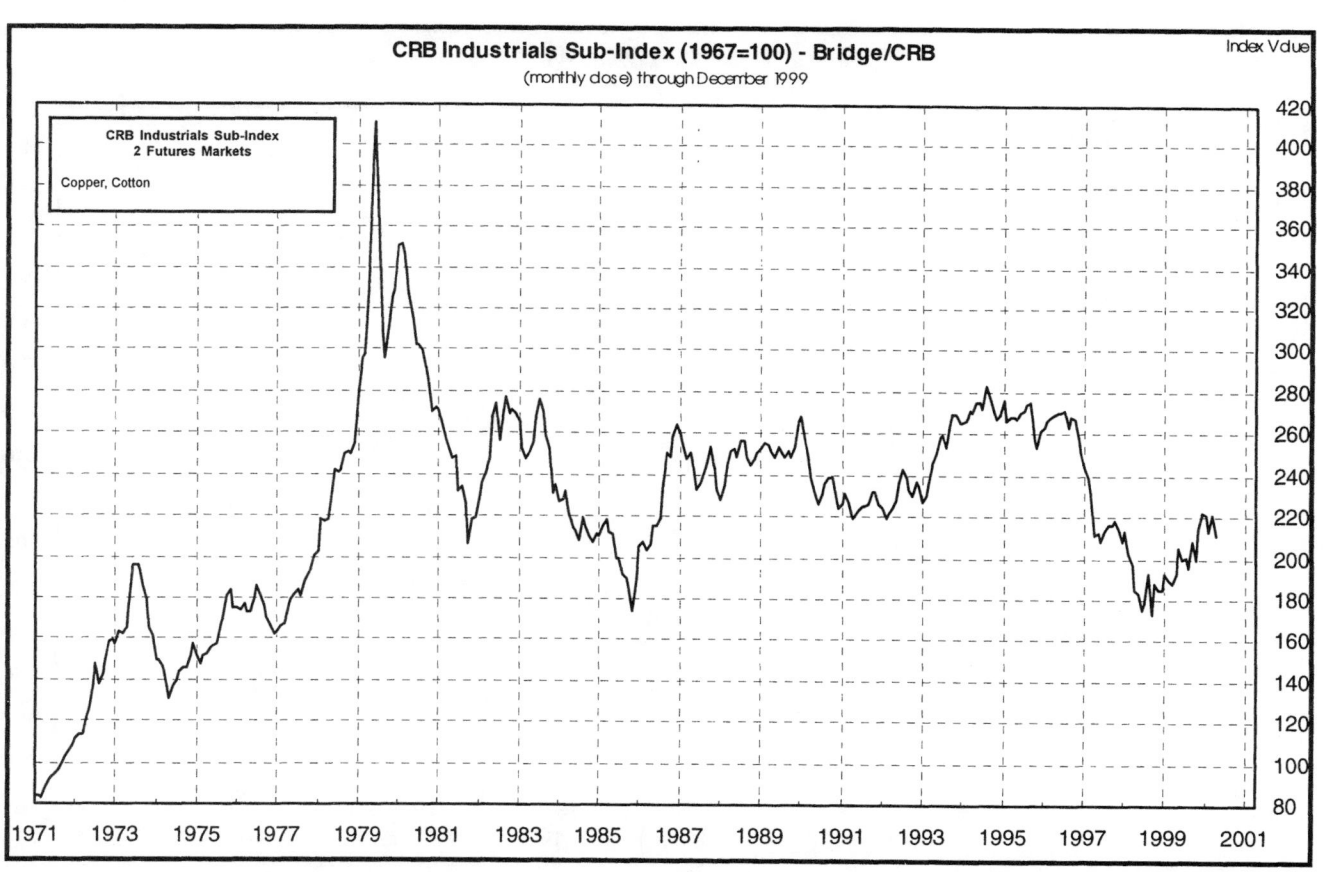

CRB Industrials Sub-Index (1967=100) - Bridge/CRB
(monthly close) through December 1999

CRB Industrials Sub-Index
2 Futures Markets

Copper, Cotton

Bridge/CRB Indices

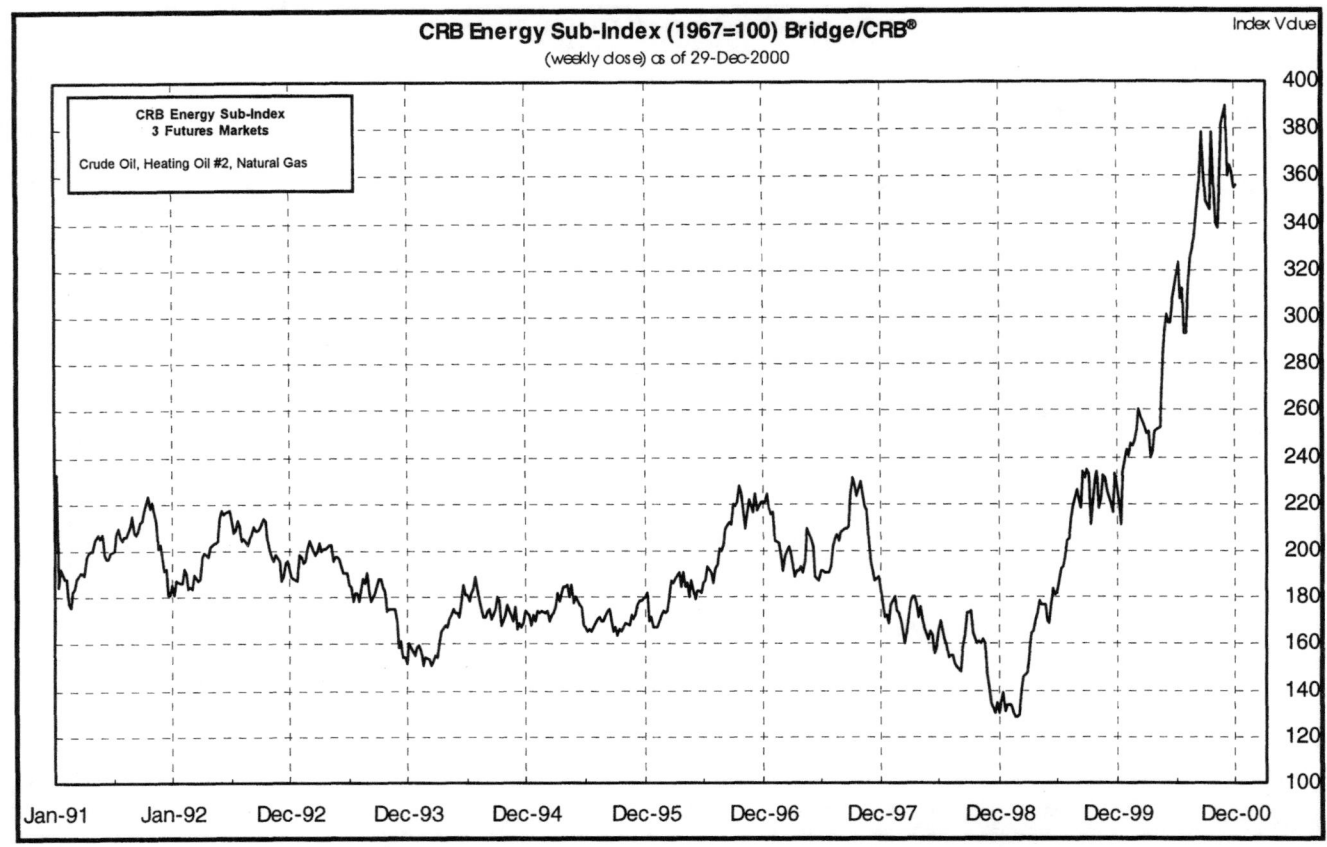

CRB Energy Sub-Index (1967=100) Bridge/CRB®
(weekly close) as of 29-Dec-2000

Index Value

CRB Energy Sub-Index
3 Futures Markets

Crude Oil, Heating Oil #2, Natural Gas

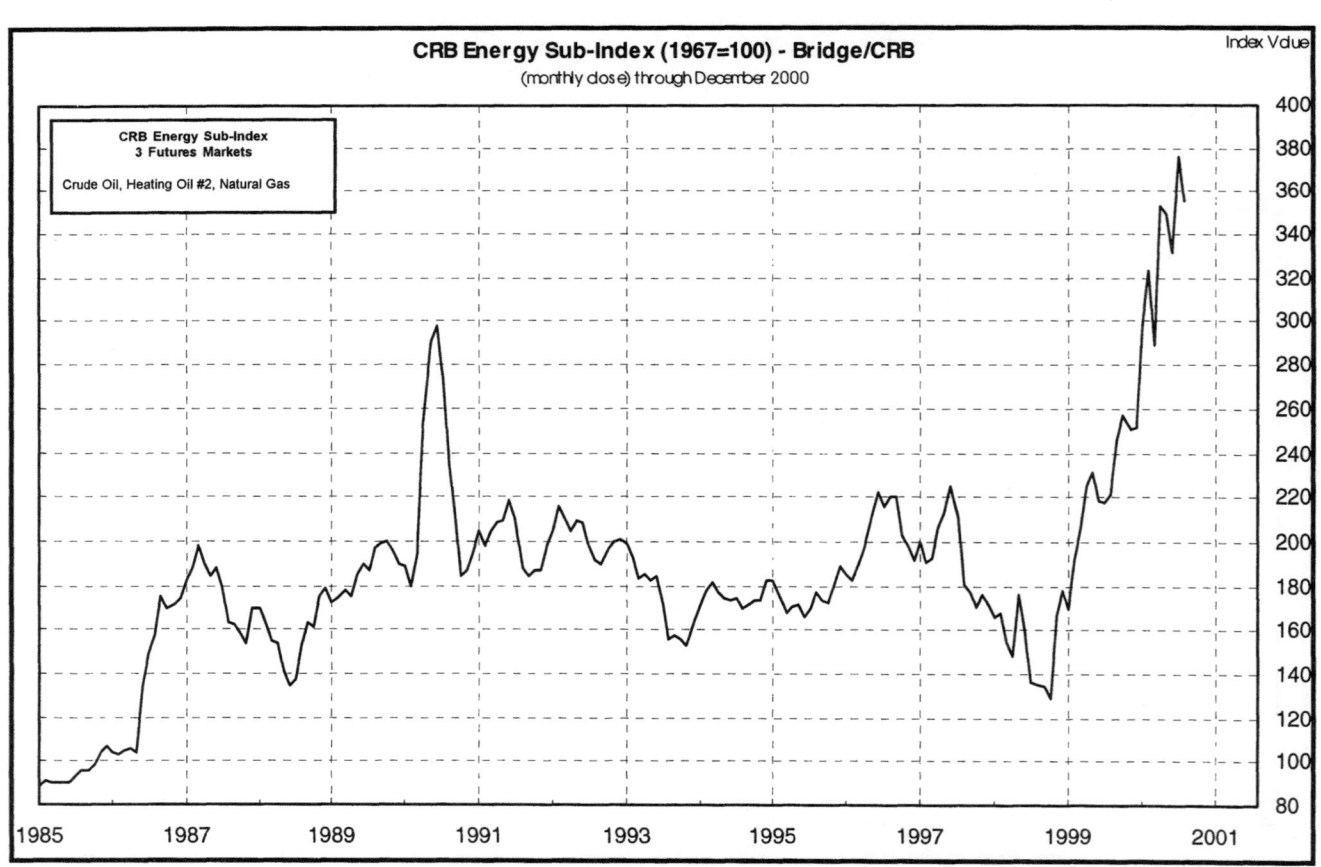

CRB Energy Sub-Index (1967=100) - Bridge/CRB
(monthly close) through December 2000

Index Value

CRB Energy Sub-Index
3 Futures Markets

Crude Oil, Heating Oil #2, Natural Gas

CRB Interest Rates Index (1977=100) Bridge/CRB®

(weekly close) as of 29-Dec-2000

Index Value

CRB Interest Rates Index (1977)
3 Futures Markets

3-month T-Bills, 10-year T-Notes, 30-year T-Bonds

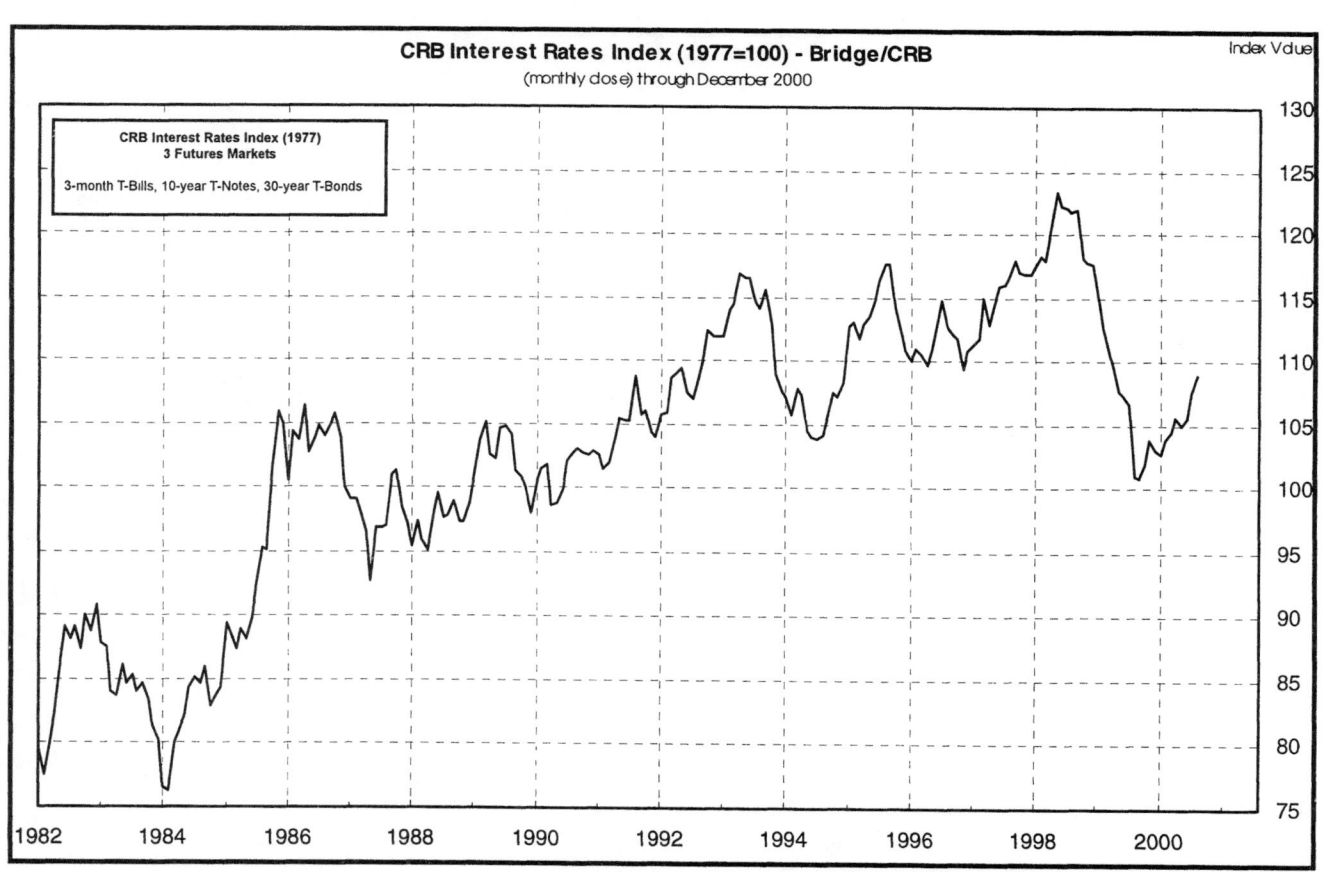

CRB Interest Rates Index (1977=100) - Bridge/CRB

(monthly close) through December 2000

Index Value

CRB Interest Rates Index (1977)
3 Futures Markets

3-month T-Bills, 10-year T-Notes, 30-year T-Bonds

Bridge/CRB Indices

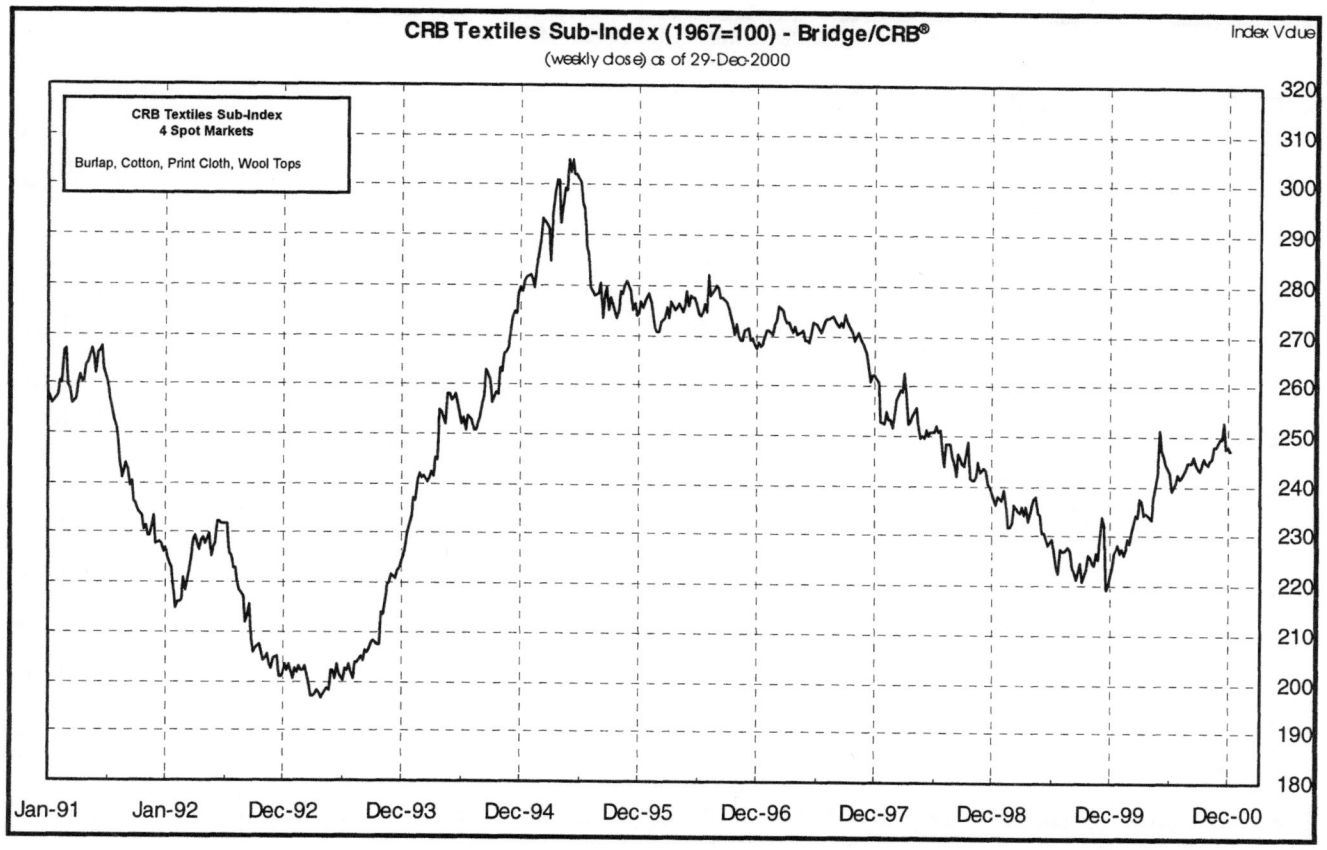

CRB Textiles Sub-Index (1967=100) - Bridge/CRB®
(weekly close) as of 29-Dec-2000
Index Value
CRB Textiles Sub-Index
4 Spot Markets
Burlap, Cotton, Print Cloth, Wool Tops
320
310
300
290
280
270
260
250
240
230
220
210
200
190
180
Jan-91
Jan-92
Dec-92
Dec-93
Dec-94
Dec-95
Dec-96
Dec-97
Dec-98
Dec-99
Dec-00

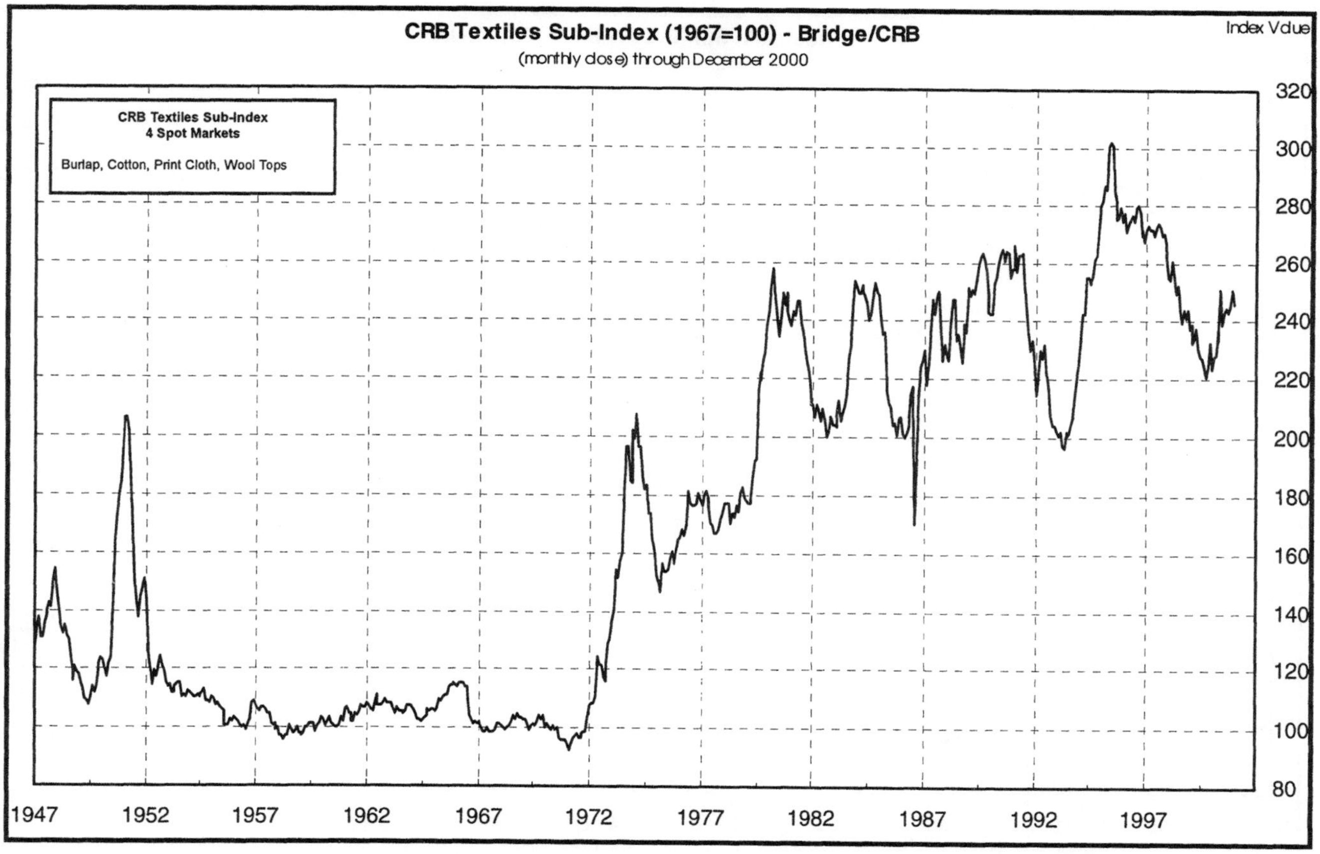

CRB Textiles Sub-Index (1967=100) - Bridge/CRB
(monthly close) through December 2000
Index Value
CRB Textiles Sub-Index
4 Spot Markets
Burlap, Cotton, Print Cloth, Wool Tops
320
300
280
260
240
220
200
180
160
140
120
100
80
1947
1952
1957
1962
1967
1972
1977
1982
1987
1992
1997

Bridge/CRB Indices

CRB Raw Industrials Sub-Index (1967=100) - Bridge/CRB®
(weekly close) as of 29-Dec-2000

Index Value

CRB Raw Industrials Sub-Index
13 Spot Markets

Burlap, Copper Scrap, Cotton, Hides, Lead Scrap, Print Cloth, Rosin,
Rubber, Steel Scrap, Tallow, Tin, Wool Tops, Zinc

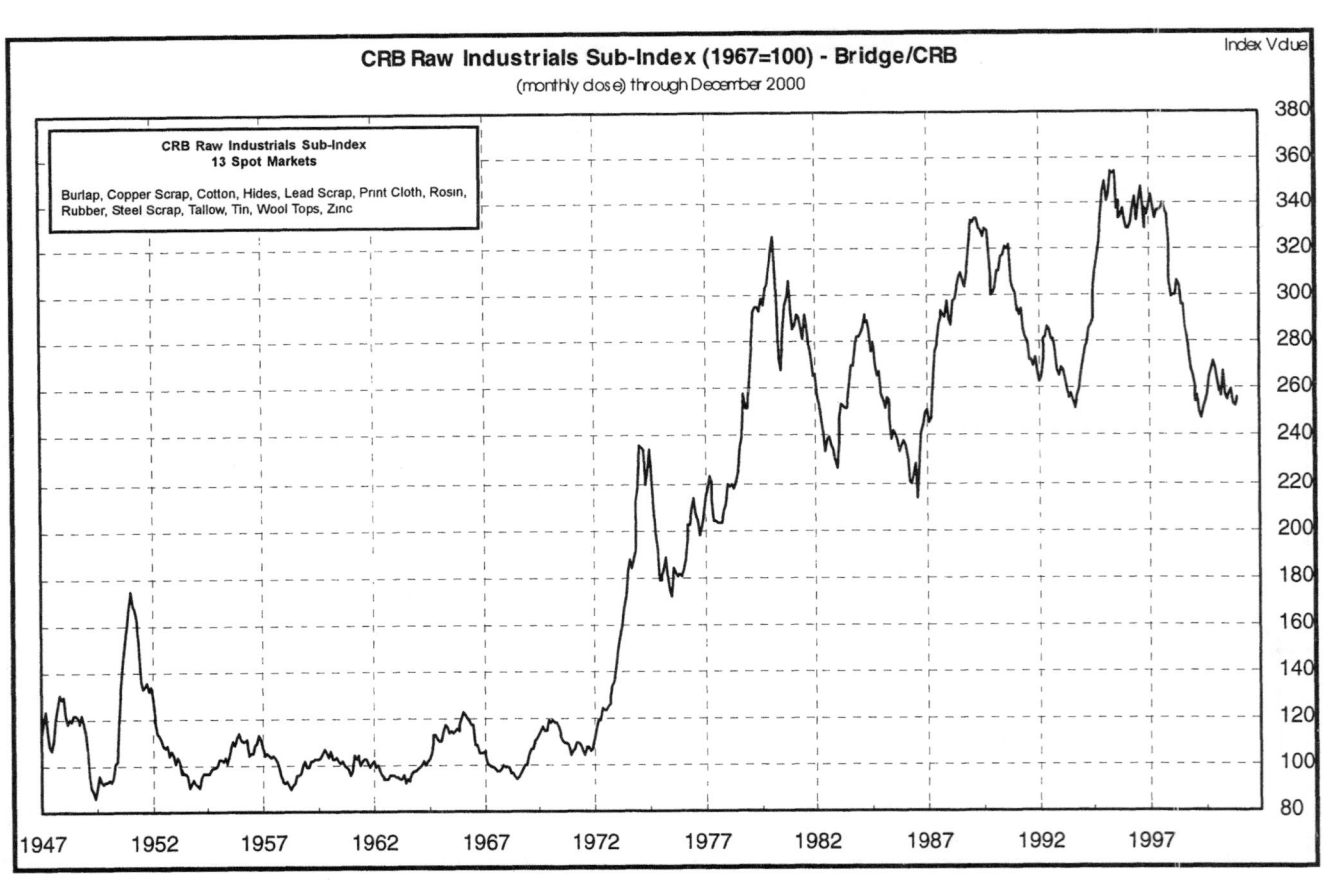

CRB Raw Industrials Sub-Index (1967=100) - Bridge/CRB
(monthly close) through December 2000

Index Value

CRB Raw Industrials Sub-Index
13 Spot Markets

Burlap, Copper Scrap, Cotton, Hides, Lead Scrap, Print Cloth, Rosin,
Rubber, Steel Scrap, Tallow, Tin, Wool Tops, Zinc

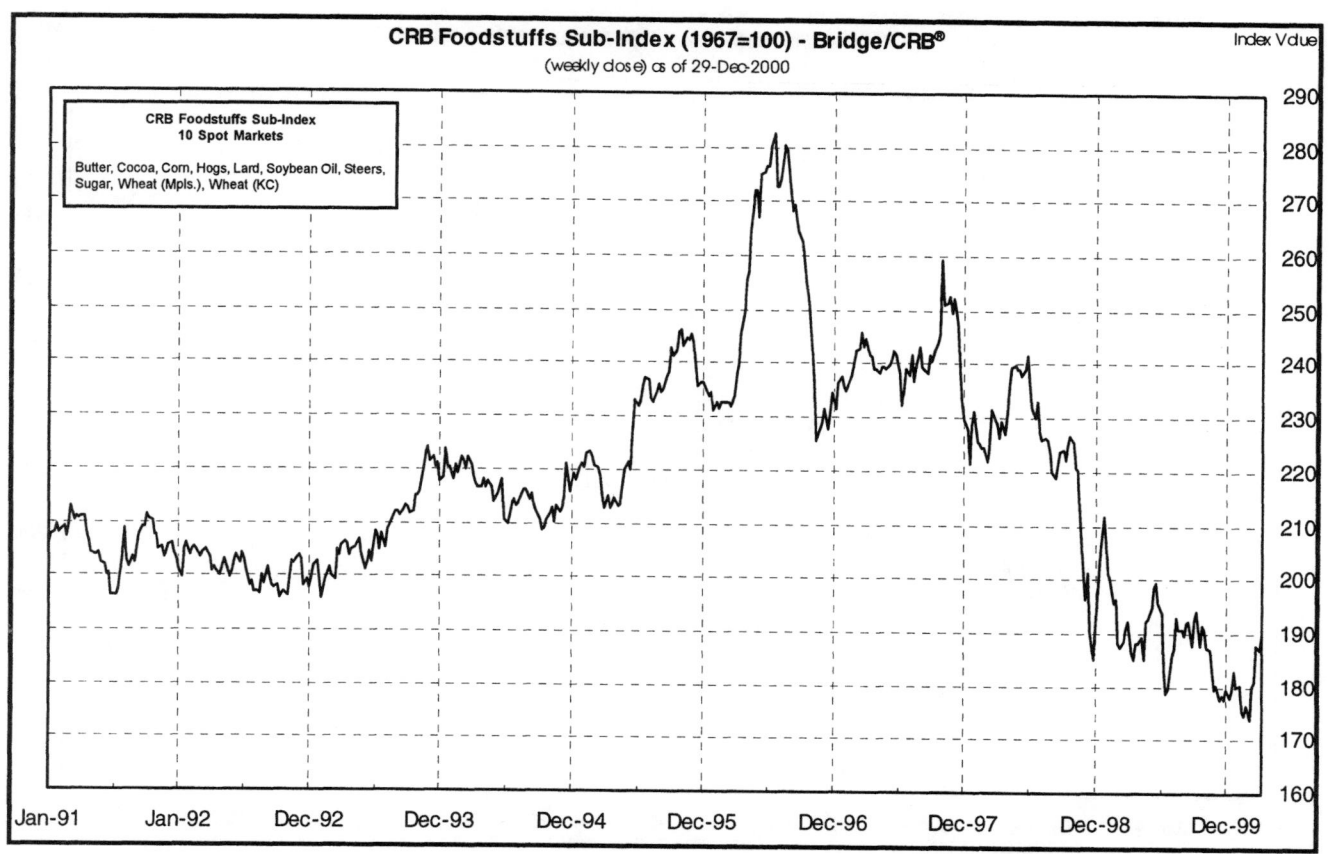

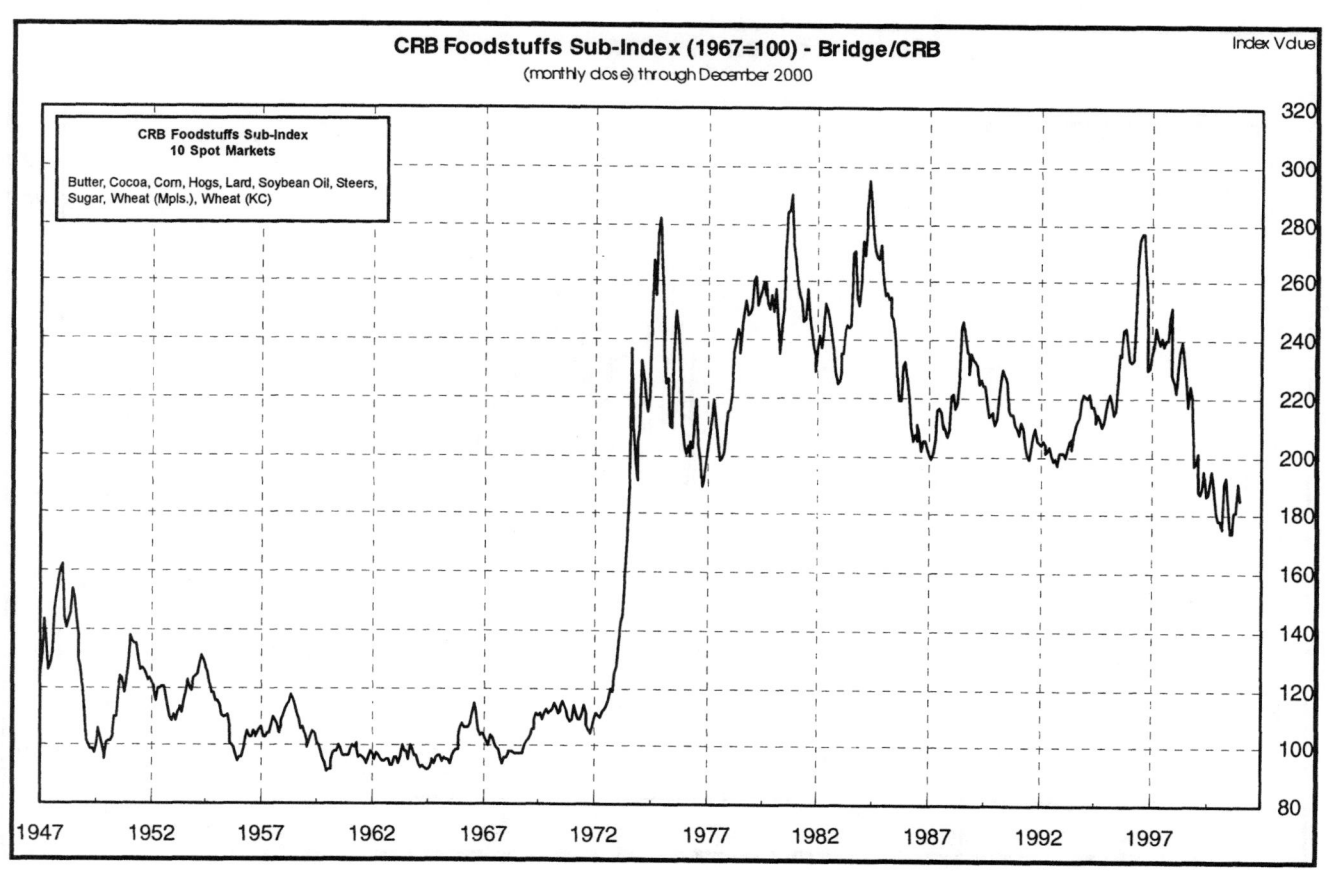

Bridge/CRB Indices

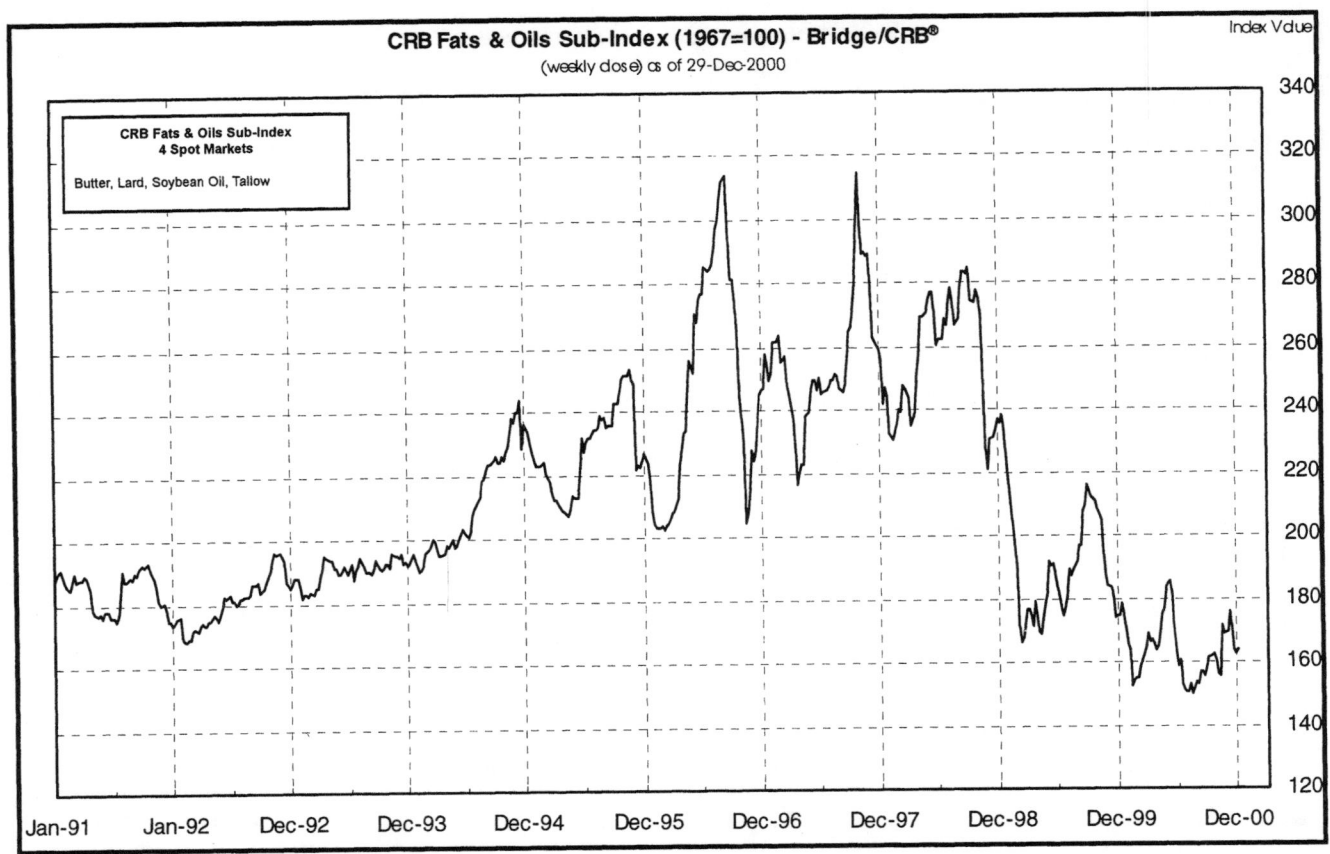

CRB Fats & Oils Sub-Index (1967=100) - Bridge/CRB®
(weekly close) as of 29-Dec-2000

Index Value

CRB Fats & Oils Sub-Index
4 Spot Markets

Butter, Lard, Soybean Oil, Tallow

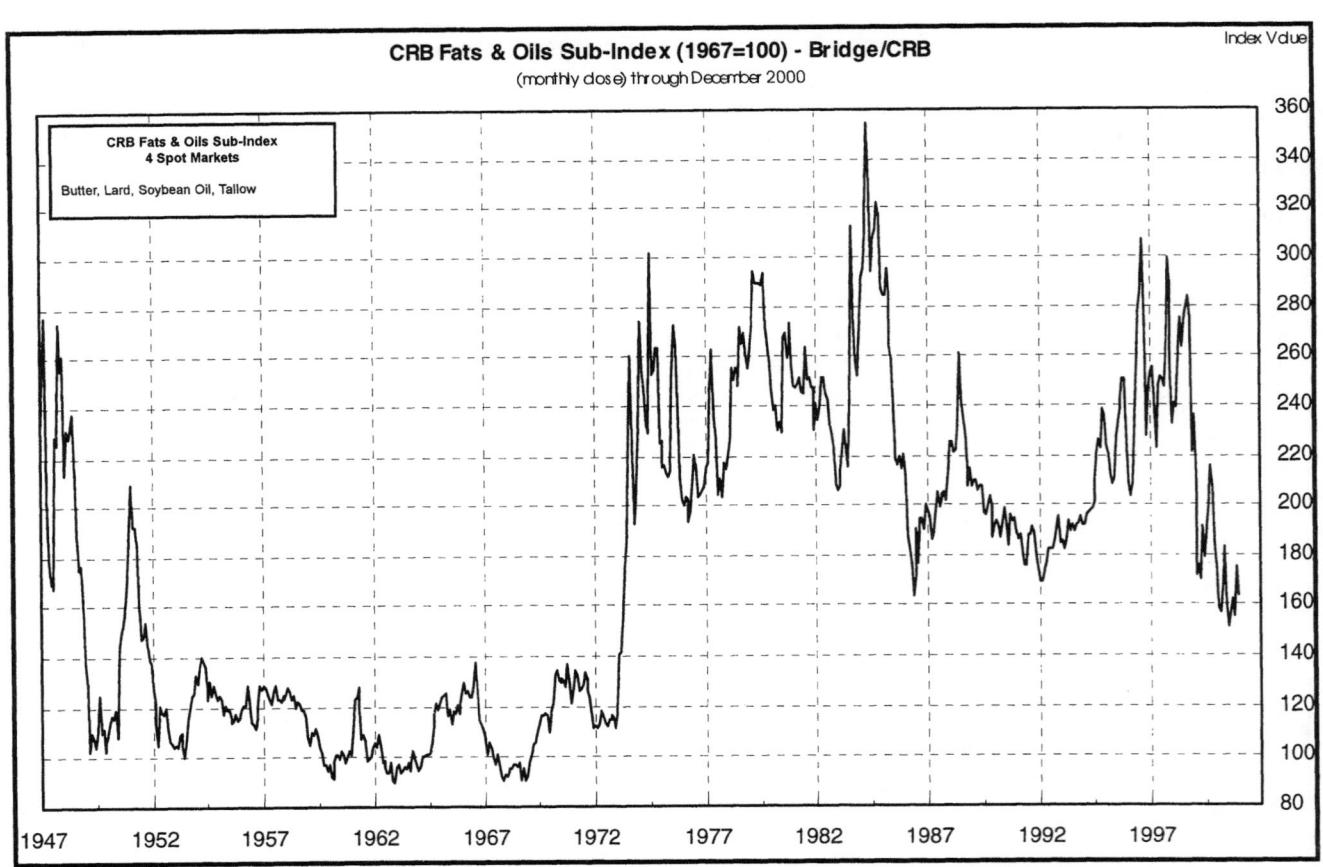

CRB Fats & Oils Sub-Index (1967=100) - Bridge/CRB
(monthly close) through December 2000

Index Value

CRB Fats & Oils Sub-Index
4 Spot Markets

Butter, Lard, Soybean Oil, Tallow

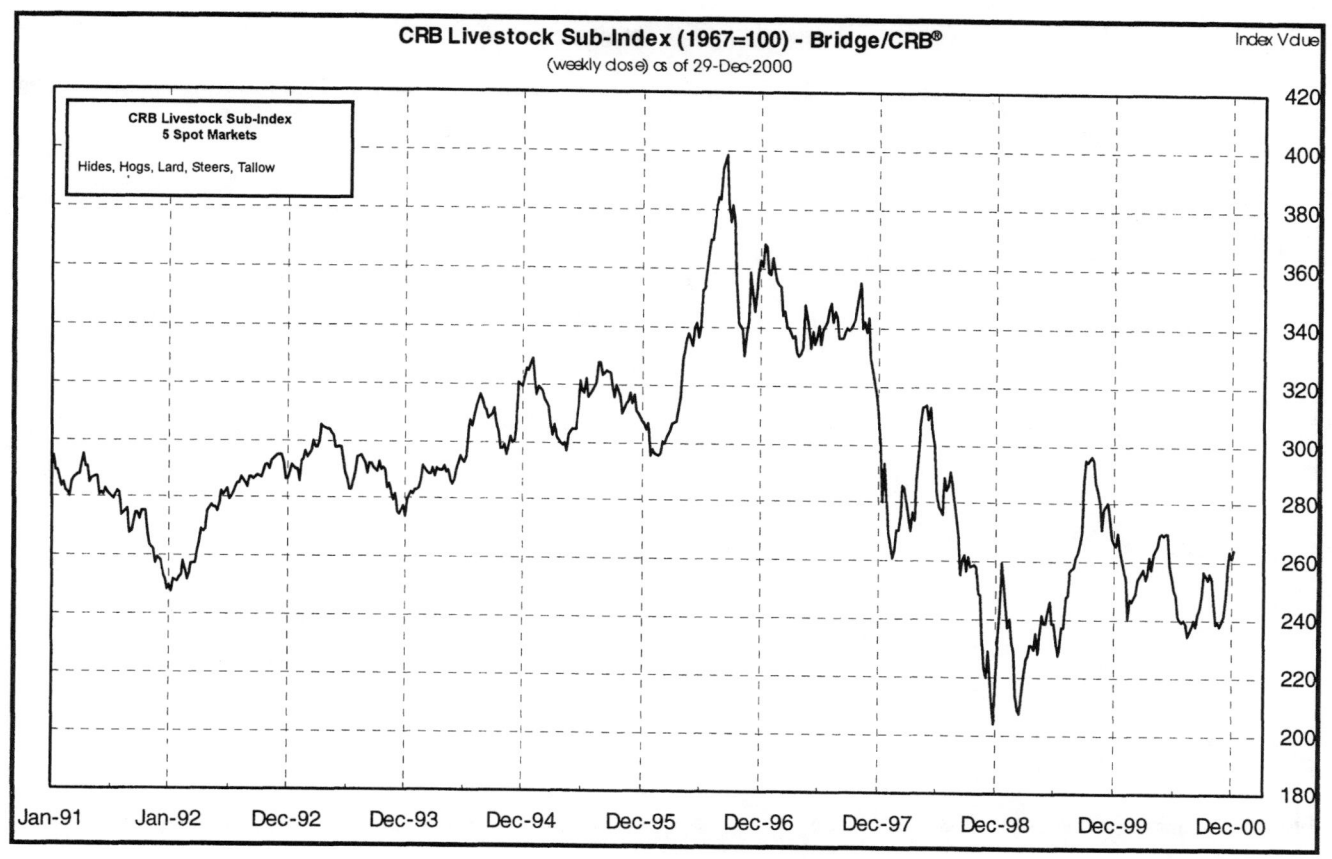

CRB Livestock Sub-Index (1967=100) - Bridge/CRB®
(weekly close) as of 29-Dec-2000
Index Value
CRB Livestock Sub-Index
5 Spot Markets
Hides, Hogs, Lard, Steers, Tallow
420
400
380
360
340
320
300
280
260
240
220
200
180
Jan-91
Jan-92
Dec-92
Dec-93
Dec-94
Dec-95
Dec-96
Dec-97
Dec-98
Dec-99
Dec-00

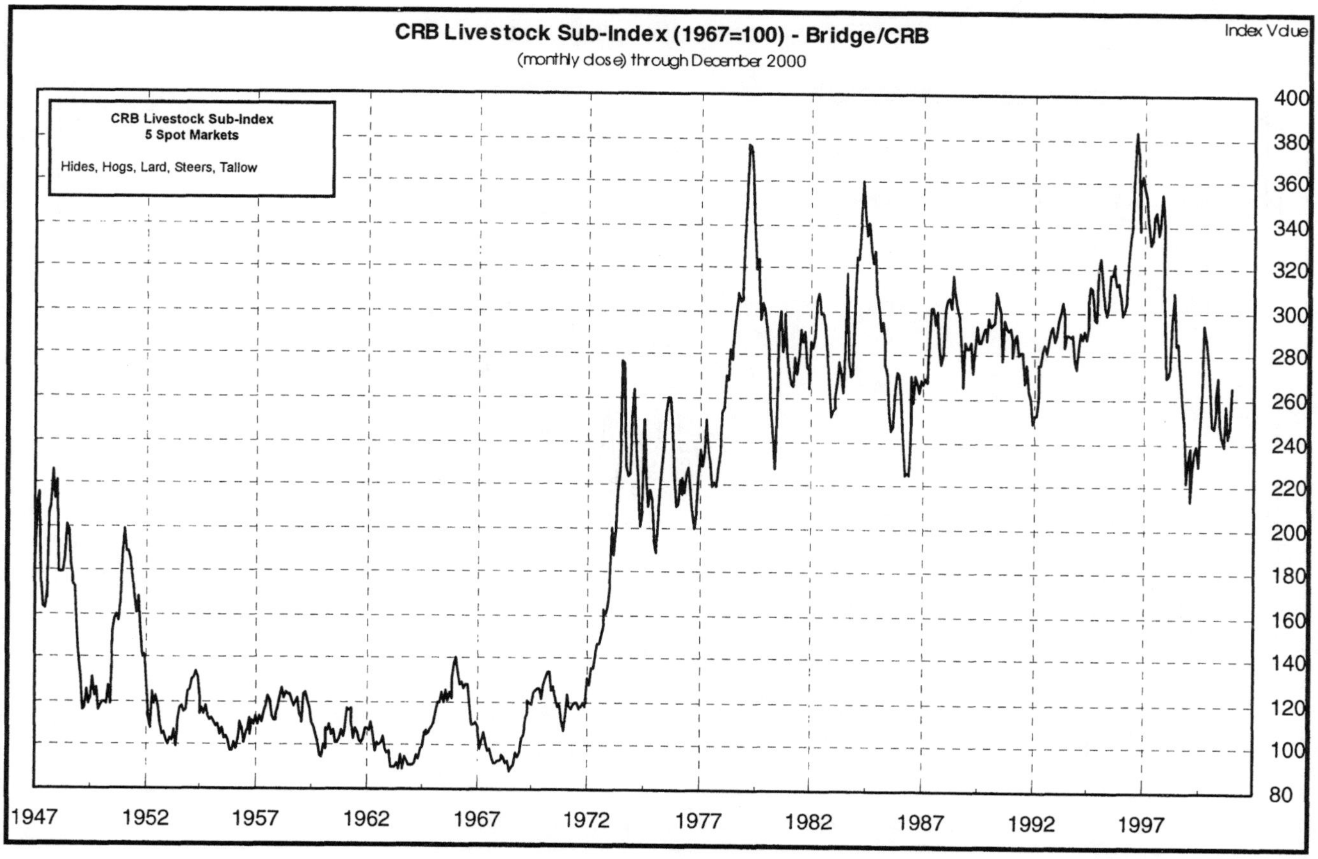
CRB Livestock Sub-Index (1967=100) - Bridge/CRB
(monthly close) through December 2000
Index Value
CRB Livestock Sub-Index
5 Spot Markets
Hides, Hogs, Lard, Steers, Tallow
400
380
360
340
320
300
280
260
240
220
200
180
160
140
120
100
80
1947
1952
1957
1962
1967
1972
1977
1982
1987
1992
1997

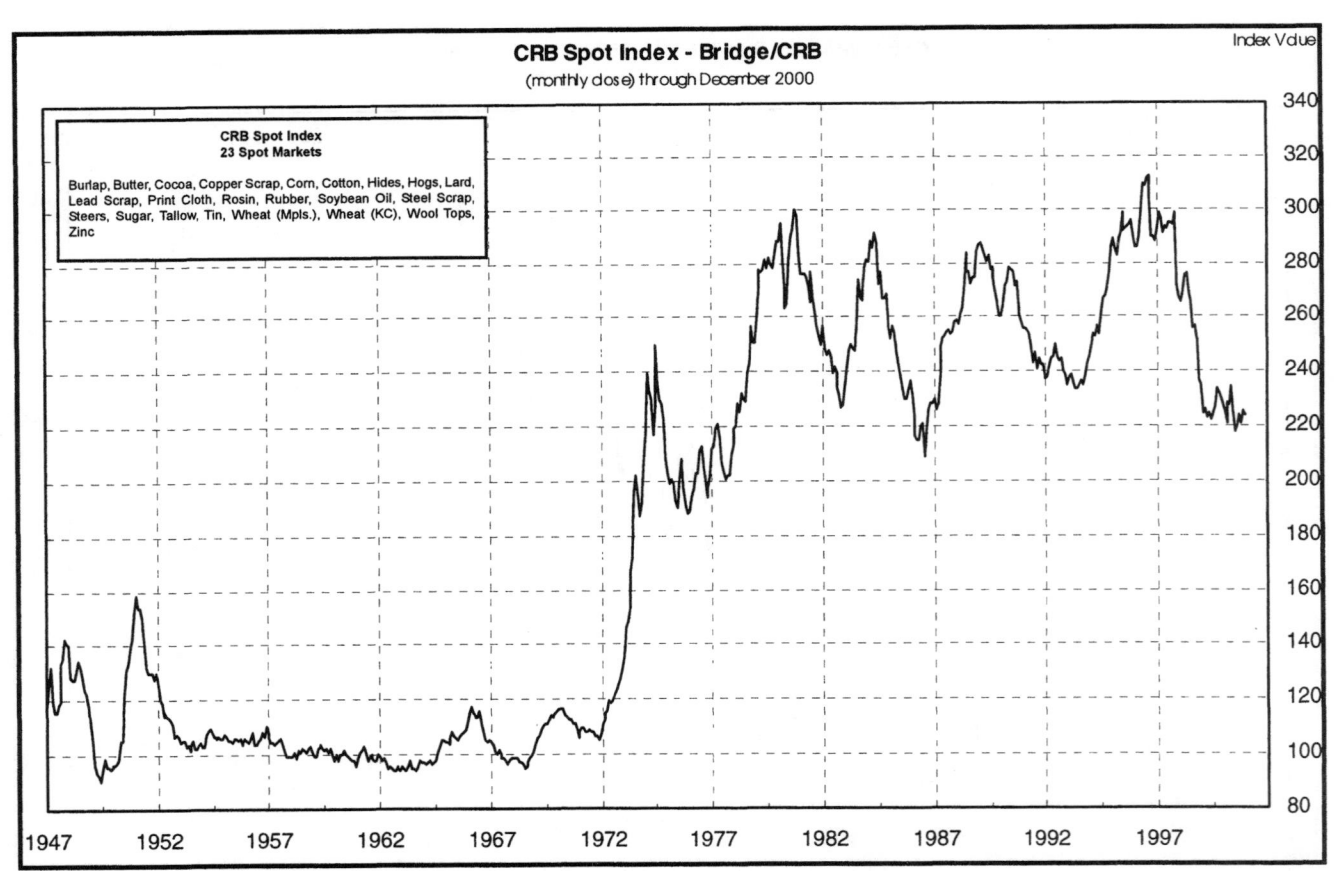

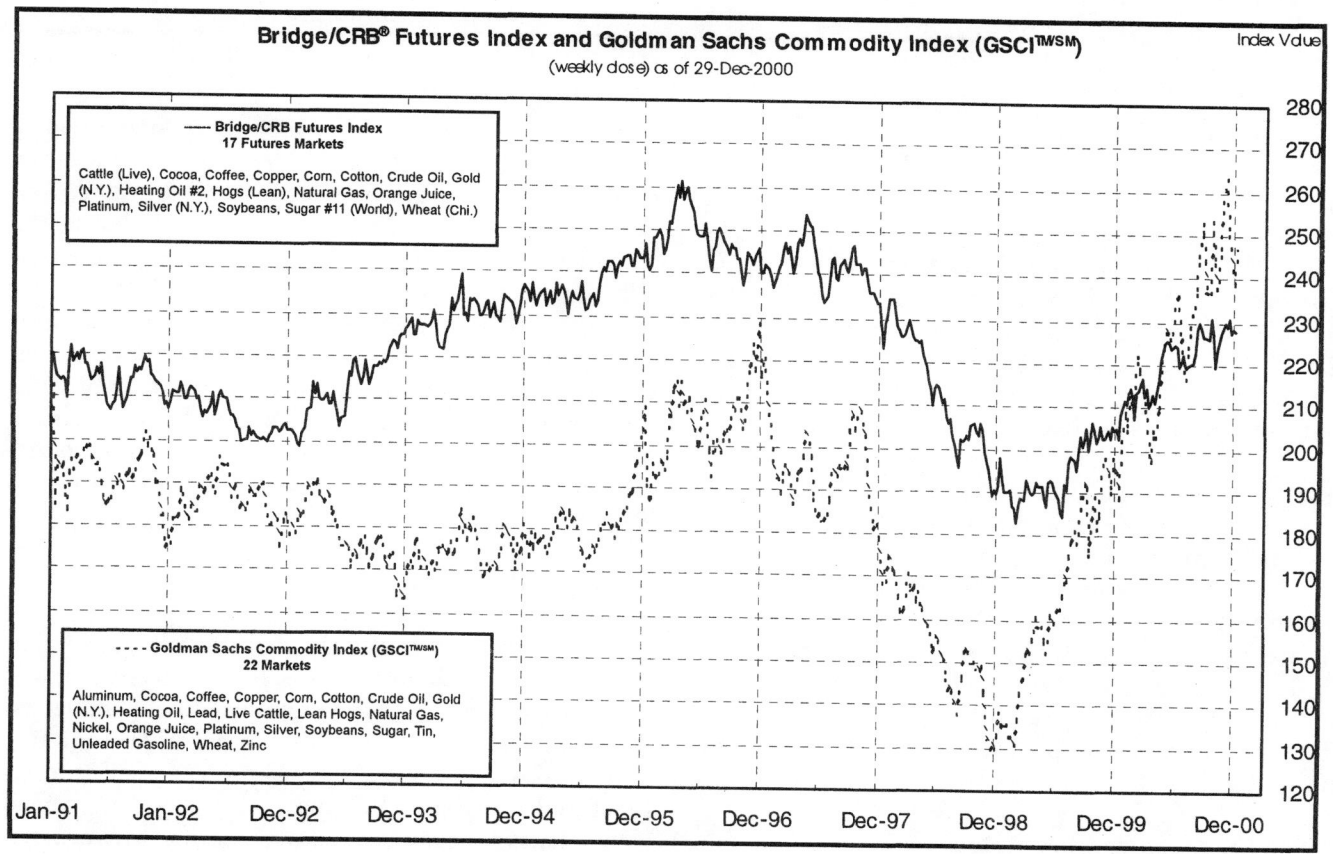

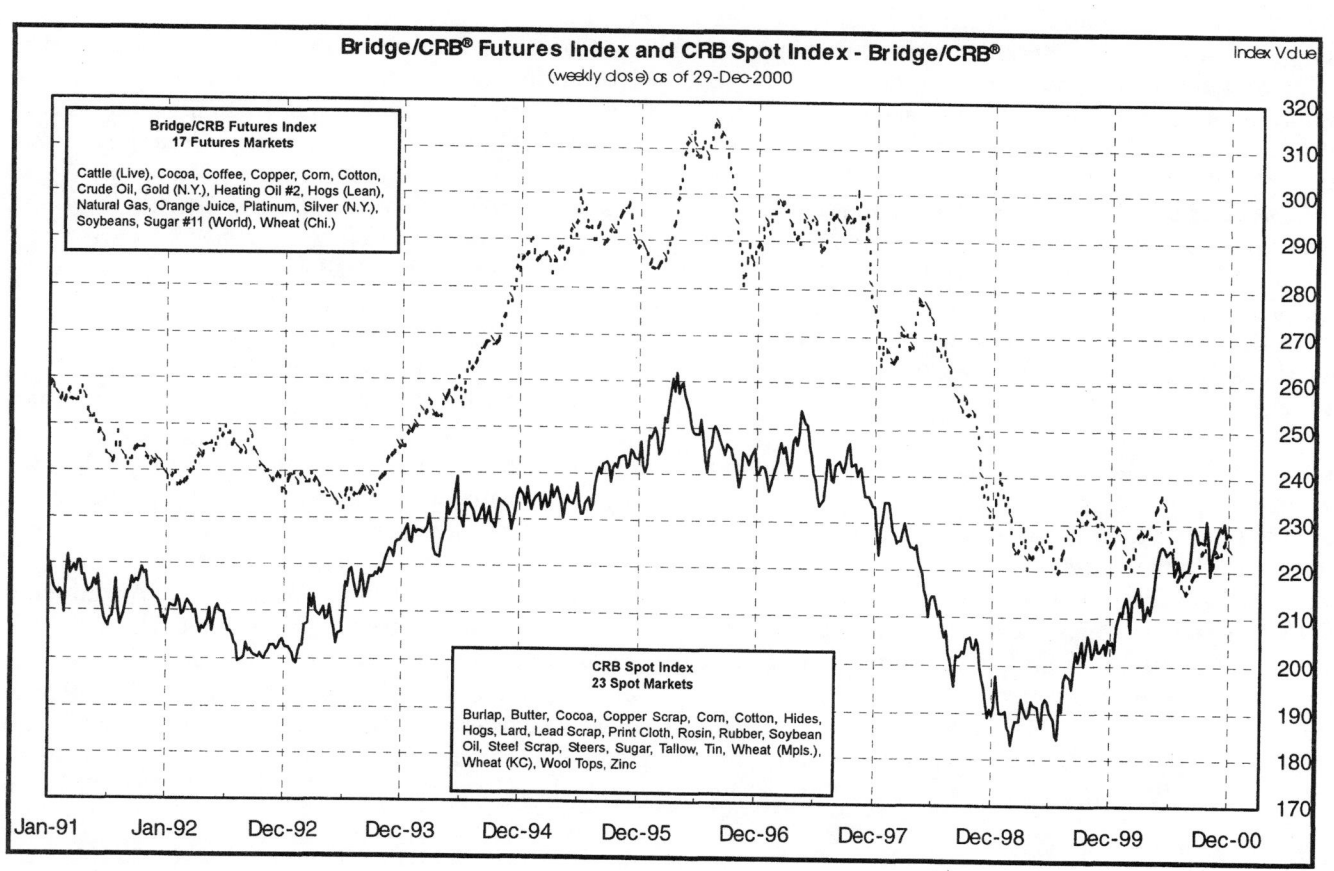

UNDERSTANDING AND ANALYZING THE COCOA MARKET

by Walter Spilka

Introduction

Cocoa, and its derived product chocolate, is a most familiar product to consumers. Cocoa has a long history extending back several thousand years. It is thought that the first cocoa trees were found in the reaches of the upper Amazon Basin. From there, Indians likely transported the seeds into Venezuela, Central America, and Mexico. It was in these areas that cocoa was first cultivated.

Spanish settlers encountered cocoa several hundred years ago, by which time cocoa had also spread into the Caribbean. On a voyage to the New World, Christopher Columbus encountered cocoa beans and brought them back to Spain. Spanish traders carried the beans to Indonesia where cultivation followed. Production started in Malaysia later. In Europe, the consumption of cocoa spread slowly in part due to its high price. From Europe, cocoa reached the U.S. in the 1700s.

Maybe the most significant development in the history of cocoa production was its migration into West Africa. In the 1870s, cocoa was introduced into the British colonies of Nigeria and Ghana and from there it moved to the French colonies of Cameroon and the Ivory Coast. In the mid 1800s, commercial production of cocoa started in Brazil, shifting later into the Bahia region. Cocoa production also developed in Ecuador. It is of interest that large-scale commercial production often developed later. While Brazil was a large producer in the 1800s, commercial production in West Africa developed around 1900. Ghana emerged as a leader, though production declined due to disease. In the 1920s, production in West Africa was over one-half of the world total. At the same time, production in the Bahia region in Brazil was on the increase. In the 1900s, Malaysia was engaged in large-scale commercial production of cocoa.

To some extent, the rise and fall of cocoa production in various regions has been determined by the prevalence of various diseases that can kill the cocoa tree. Disease in Ghana caused a production shift into other parts of West Africa. A serious disease problem in Brazil in recent years has caused widespread damage, moving that country from being a major exporter of cocoa to an importer.

Cocoa is of the species Theobroma cacao, of the genus Theobroma. While there are a number of other species, Theobroma cacao is the one that is commercially produced today. There are three general varieties or types: Criollo or native, Trinitario or Trinidad, and Forastero or foreign. The largest portion of the world's cocoa production is of the Forastero variety. The Criollo variety is considered to have a delicate flavor, though production is very limited as the trees are susceptible to disease. Trinitario is a mix between Criollo and Forastero, and its production is somewhat limited. Forastero is considered more of a base cocoa. The Forastero tree is hardy, is less susceptible to disease, and has higher yields. West Africa produces the Forastero variety.

Cocoa Production

Cocoa is a tropical crop. Almost all world production can be found in a zone that runs from 15 degrees north to 15 degrees south of the equator. Most production in West Africa lies within 10 degrees of the equator and is close to sea level. The cocoa tree itself is long-lived and can reach 100 years old. The tree comes into economic production at about 5-6 years and can remain in production for many years, though the amount of cocoa produced will decline with age. The most productive period is from 5-20 years of age. This necessitates replacing the trees on a periodic basis.

Tree age is a consideration in determining the amount of cocoa that can be produced. The tree in its natural state can grow to 40 feet, but is normally pruned to 20 feet or so for harvesting accessibility. Production takes place mostly on small plots or farms of a few acres. In some countries like Malaysia and Brazil, there are large plantations of cocoa trees. The trees are sometimes intermixed with shade trees like bananas, with the idea the trees do better with less direct sunlight.

The cocoa tree itself is in an almost continuous state of flowering throughout the year. At certain times there are more flowers, leading to the eventual development of more cocoa pods and a harvest. A given tree in the course of a year will have several thousand flowers but relatively few will develop and mature into cocoa pods. The flowers are pollinated by insects, resulting in the fruit of the trees, the pod. An unusual characteristic of the tree is that some of the pods will grow out of the trunk. The pods themselves are elongated with a length of about 10 inches and change in color from green to yellow or reddish at maturity. The inside of the pod is full of pulp in which are imbedded the seeds or beans. A pod can have from 20 to as many as 50 seeds. A tree can carry 30 pods or more as a main crop.

There are many factors that go into determining how large a cocoa crop will be. One important factor that differentiates one country from another is the climatic pattern and in particular, the rainfall pattern. There is great variance in rainfall patterns between countries and this affects the overall world pattern of cocoa production. In some countries like Brazil, the rainfall pattern is more equally distributed between months. This leads to a more even flow of production. In Ecuador, rainfall is not even at all. Heavy rains fall from January to April, after which it becomes very dry. In Cameroon, there are rains from March until November. In Ghana, the pattern is again different. There are heavy rains in March through June, after which the rains slow, only to increase again in September and October. In terms of cocoa production, these rainfall patterns are important. For one, the amount of rain that falls will affect the subsequent crop, though there is some difference of opinion among experts on how significant this is. Below-average rains can lead to fewer flowers and less of a pod set. If the rains are late in arriving, the crop may be late in maturing. The pattern, which can vary some, is for the periods of heavy rain to lead to a flushing of the trees (a period of heavy vegetative growth and flower development). Some flowers are pollinated and the pods start to develop. The time to maturity can be 5-6 months.

The rains in Ghana from March to June lead to a main crop ready for harvest in September through December, with the harvest season extending into March. A similar pattern holds for the neighboring Ivory Coast. In Brazil, with a more normally distributed rainfall pattern, the main crop season is from September into January. Most countries also harvest a smaller mid-crop. In Ghana, the heavy rains of September and October lead to a smaller harvest in April extending into June and July. The Ghana mid-crop is small compared to the main crop, while in the Ivory Coast the mid-crop tends to be larger. In Brazil, the mid-crop occurs from May into August, and because of the evenly distributed rainfall pattern, this crop can be larger than the main crop. Therefore, an analysis of cocoa production needs to consider the onset of rains and their amounts.

Another climatic factor to be monitored in West Africa is the very dry and hot harmattan winds which originate in the Sahara. These occur in the December to March period, and the combination of wind and extreme dryness can cause damage to the cocoa tree if it persists for weeks. One advantage in West African cocoa production is the fact that there is a dry season when the crop is harvested, fermented, and dried using the sun. Other countries must use artificial drying methods.

Another factor to monitor in determining cocoa production is the prevalence of disease. Because of the tropical locations and the spread of disease by insects, cocoa trees can suffer extensive damage and loss of productivity from any of a number of diseases. Among the diseases to watch for are black pod, a fungal disease which occurs in many cocoa regions. Some countries have very little of this disease, which is much more prevalent in Cameroon and Ghana. A humid climate seems to promote black pod disease, which can attack various parts of the tree and pods. Treatment with chemical sprays is effective but expensive. Swollen shoot is a virus found largely in Ghana and Nigeria. In the past, swollen shoot has caused a great deal of damage in Ghana. Transmission of the disease is by insect and the only treatment is removal of the infected trees. Witches' broom is a fungal disease found in the Western Hemisphere. This disease is named for the shoots that grow out of the infected bud. The disease has caused damage in South America and especially in Brazil, where a great deal of production has been lost from it. There are a number of controls to the disease, including removing the tree, spraying, and the replanting of new disease resistant trees. This later approach is being used in Brazil to stave off further destruction.

Cocoa Processing

The path from the flowering of the cocoa tree to the final production of chocolate and cocoa products is a long one. Generally, the path is as follows:

> Rains in the cocoa-producing countries lead to a flushing of the trees and the development of flowers. In a 5-6 month period after some flowers are successfully pollinated, pods develop and ripen. The color of the pods changes from green to orange-red. At maturity, the pods are harvested with a knife and opened. During the main crop season, the trees may be harvested several times with intervals of a few weeks. The pods are opened and the seeds removed and placed in trays or boxes for fermentation. This is an important step, as the beans start to undergo the various biochemical processes that eventually result in cocoa's unique flavor and color. During fermentation, the pulp around the bean liquifies and is drained away. To aid the process, the beans are turned or mixed. Fermentation can take about six days. After this, the beans are removed and spread in an open space for dry-

ing. In parts of West Africa with a dry season this is done by the sun, while other areas use driers. After several days of drying to obtain a moisture level of 8 percent which prevents mold, the beans are bagged for shipment.

Some beans are processed in the countries where they are grown, while most are shipped to processors primarily in the U.S. and Europe. At the processor, the beans are cleaned and roasted at temperatures up to 350 degrees. This is an important step that allows more development of flavor while also softening the shell. After this, the beans are rolled or cracked to break the shell and winnowed to separate the shells from the particles of the crushed cocoa bean, called the nibs. The nibs of various beans may be blended together to get a desired mix of flavor and may also be further treated. The nibs are milled or processed to obtain cocoa liquor which consists of cocoa particles suspended in the bean's cocoa butter, a vegetable fat. The cocoa butter content is over 50 percent. As the cocoa liquor cools down, it hardens. It is then pressed to remove some of the cocoa butter. The resulting cocoa liquor can be molded into bars to form unsweetened or baking chocolate. The cocoa liquor can be pulverized into cocoa powder and used to add chocolate flavor to products like milk and ice cream. The cocoa liquor can have cocoa butter and sugar added to it to form sweet chocolate. Whole milk solids can be added to form milk chocolate.

The International Cocoa Organization estimates that it takes 2.35 tonnes of cocoa beans to produce a metric tonne of cocoa powder, and 2.67 tonnes of beans to produce a tonne of cocoa butter. An excellent reference book on cocoa is G.A.R. Wood's *Cocoa*, London: Longman (1975) Third Edition.

The 2000/01 Cocoa Season

About three-fourths of the world's cocoa production is harvested between October and March. The cocoa season for statistical purposes begins in October. The 1999/00 world season was one in which production was very large, with trade estimates averaging about 2.9 million metric tonnes. The International Cocoa Organization (ICCO) placed the crop at just over 3 million tonnes, while a U.S.D.A. estimate made early in the season was 2.9 million tonnes. Crops in individual countries are very difficult to estimate, making the total crop difficult to forecast. The world crop for 2000/01 has been initially estimated at about 2.8 million tonnes by the ICCO, though that is subject to change as more crops come in. There are still large crops to be harvested later in the season in Indonesia and Brazil, as well as a potentially large Ivory Coast mid-crop. Given current trends, global production could well be lower than 2.8 million tonnes. The new season has already seen a great deal of uncertainty about the cocoa supply, and that could eventually translate into less production.

The world's largest producer and exporter of cocoa is the Ivory Coast, and developments in that country weigh heavy in any analysis of production. The Ivory Coast produces about 40 percent of the world crop. The 2000/01 season got underway in the Ivory Coast with world prices trending lower, partly in response to large production in 1999/00, ample global stocks of cocoa, and no apparent weather threats in the major production regions.

It appeared in October 2000 that the new season would see another large crop and a potential buildup in stocks. By December 2000, cocoa prices had slipped to multi-year lows, with cocoa at the Coffee, Sugar & Cocoa Exchange, Inc. (CSCE) division of the New York Board of Trade, priced at just under $700 per tonne. At that point, prices started to strengthen, staging a very strong rally in January and February 2001 that carried prices to over $1200 per tonne. Most of the reasons for the rally could be found in the Ivory Coast. A military government that had stood for election was voted out of office. While this was seen as positive politically, the nation was also seeing festering ethnic tensions related in part to resentment on the part of natives toward immigrants. Previous governments had managed to keep these tensions under control, but now they started to bubble to the surface. An attempted coup against the elected government in January led to another round of ethnic problems spurred by ideas the coup attempt was plotted outside the country.

As far as the cocoa was concerned, one problem was that many of the immigrants from the north worked in the cocoa areas. These tensions drove some of them back out of the country leading the trade to question who would be there to harvest, ferment, and dry the cocoa. Another question that arose concerned the long-term stability of the government in a part of the world where instability seemed to be spreading. There were concerns about the movement of the main crop to the export facilities in Abidjan and San Pedro. Data on arrival of the cocoa to the ports was not very accurate, but indicated the movement was slow. This led to further increases in price. There were a number of reasons why the crop was slow in moving, including a late-developing crop, and the possibility that cocoa had been hoarded at low prices, as well as because the ethnic unrest prevented the normal movement. The other possibility was that crop was not as large as expected. The main crop had been expected to be about one million tonnes, but now looks like it will

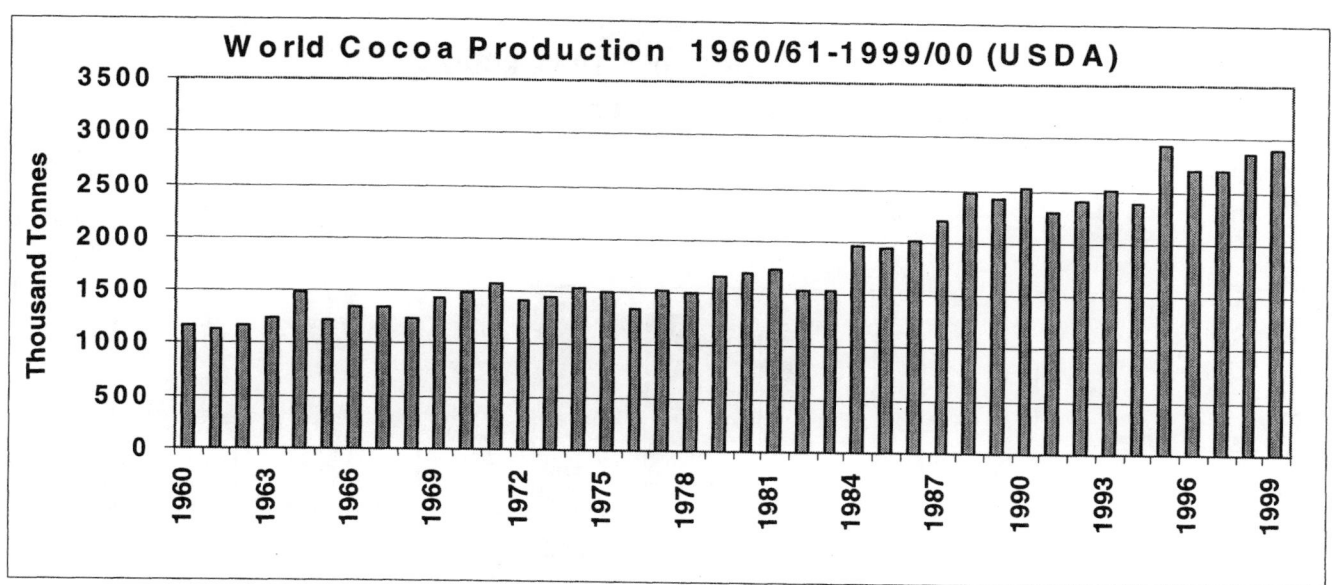

World Cocoa Production 1960/61-1999/00 (USDA)

come in as much as 50,000 tonnes under that level. The mid-crop is expected to be somewhat less than 200,000 tonnes. It now looks like the total crop will range between 1.1 million and 1.2 million tonnes. This compares with the 1999/00 record crop estimated at 1.3 million tonnes.

In the Ivory Coast, another important fact is that the cocoa industry has been liberalized or freed from the influence of the government. In the past, a government board set prices which acted to provide a minimum price that growers would be paid for their crop. That is no longer the case, and the low prices seen early in the season were partly blamed on the fact that the buyers of cocoa were now in a stronger financial position than the sellers. There has been no move to change this, though the fact that cocoa production is such a large part of the Ivory Coast economy may put pressure on the government to do something to protect growers from very low prices. As the 2000/01 season progresses, the market will be carefully watching the mid-crop harvest and for signs of renewed social tensions.

Ghana is the second largest producer and exporter of cocoa. The main crop is of high quality and is considered the standard by which other crops are measured. As such, how the crop develops and its size are important factors affecting the market. The main crop is harvested between October and March, with a smaller mid-crop following. Ghana also held an election, but there was a peaceful transfer of power. The weather for this year's crop appeared to be good, though the pattern of rainfall appeared to favor a late-developing crop. In Ghana, the Ghana Cocoa Board authorizes buyers to go out and purchase the crop. The purchases that are made each week are announced and totaled, providing a good measure of harvest progress. Generally, the purchases start in October and carry through March for the main crop. In 1999-00, purchases started the week ending October 21 and ended the week of March 16, for a total of just over 396,000 tonnes. The mid-crop was about 50,000 tonnes, for a total crop of 450,000 tonnes. In 1998-99, the purchases were 324,000 tonnes of main crop. The 2000-01 season purchases through the week of February 1, 2001 totaled 373,083 tonnes. This was some 9 percent less than the prior year, though the total crop was expected to be larger than a year ago. E.D.&F. Man estimated the crop at 460,000 tonnes in total. The U.S.D.A. agricultural attache estimated the crop at 475,000 tonnes, with 430,000 tonnes of main crop and 45,000 tonnes of mid-crop. The buying season may be extended, and it appears the crop could still reach 440,000 to 460,000 tonnes. The government of Ghana has indicated that they intend to produce 500,000 tonnes of cocoa by 2005, and 700,000 tonnes by 2010. The crop in Nigeria was estimated by E.D.&F. Man at 170,000 tonnes, while the U.S.D.A. sees the crop at 180,000 tonnes. The Cameroon crop looks to be about 120,000 tonnes.

In Asia, the two major producers are Malaysia and Indonesia. Malaysia had been a very large producer of cocoa, with 1990 production estimated at 247,000 tonnes. Since then there has been a steady decline in production, as producers have switched to palm oil production. Palm oil trees are planted, and when they come into production the cocoa trees are removed. Production in the 2000-01 season is expected to be about 80,000 tonnes, though the Malaysian Cocoa Board indicated that production could be 90,000 tonnes. This has put the local cocoa processing industry in somewhat of a bind, and Malaysia is now in a position of importing cocoa from neighboring Indonesia. For its part, Indonesia has been trying to

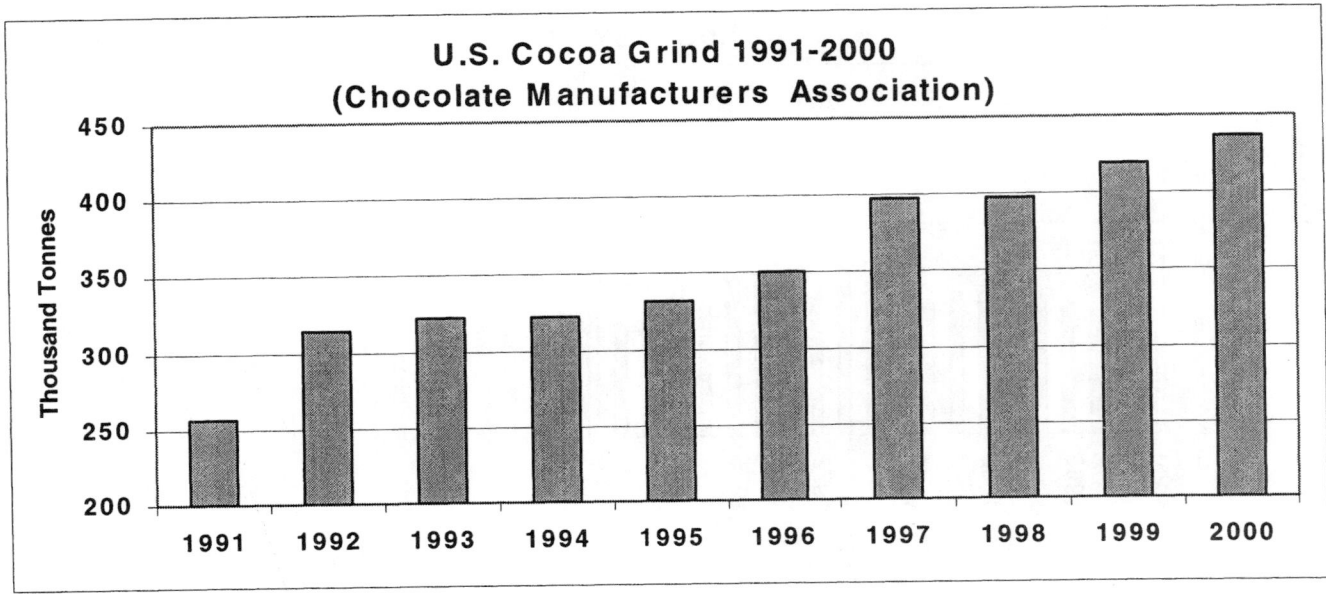

U.S. Cocoa Grind 1991-2000
(Chocolate Manufacturers Association)

increase production, perhaps in anticipation of increased exports into China, which has a very low per-capita consumption rate. Indonesia has been plagued by weather problems, as well as insect infestation. Accurate estimates of production are difficult, with wide variations in forecasts but the crop looks to be in the 400,000 tonne area.

One of the big questions in the cocoa trade is what will happen to production in Brazil, as production there has been devastated by witches' broom disease. A major effort has been underway to replace trees with genetically improved plants that are resistant to the disease. A Cocoa Bioplant in the major growing state of Bahia is producing the plants, and there are some signs that production is leveling off. As recently as 1994-95, the U.S.D.A. estimated production at just over 228,000 tonnes. Based on cocoa arrival data, the 2000-01 crop looks like it will be similar to the 1999-00 crop, which is estimated at about 125,000 tonnes. Brazil has a large cocoa-processing industry, and because of the decline in production has had to import cocoa. Ecuador is expected to have a crop of about 90,000 tonnes. In 1997-98, Ecuador suffered extensive damage from El Nino, which the U.S.D.A. estimated reduced the crop to 25,500 tonnes.

Consumption and Stocks

Cocoa consumption is less variable than production, due to the lack of weather as an influence. Cocoa consumption is measured in terms of the grind or the amount of cocoa processed. The demand for cocoa beans is derived from the demand for the major products, cocoa butter and cocoa powder. In the last two years, there has been an increase in cocoa butter stocks, which appears partly due to the increased use

of less expensive non-cocoa vegetable fats in the making of chocolate. This is an issue in the industry, as the use of these fats in effect reduces the need for cocoa beans. One result is that cocoa powder prices have increased relative to cocoa butter prices, and the grind has been more for powder.

The major grinders are the U.S., the Netherlands, the U.K., and Germany, as well as the cocoa-producing countries like Brazil, Malaysia, and the Ivory Coast. Data on the grind has become more limited, as the countries of Europe have started to consolidate their grind data into one statistic with no current history to measure against. The U.S. did report that the grind in calendar 2000 was 436,510 tonnes, up 4.2 percent from 1999. Germany reported the 2000 grind at 224,538 tonnes, up 14.7 percent from 1999. Overall, it appears that for 2000/01, the world cocoa grind will increase about 2 percent, to between 2.95 and 3 million tonnes. The I.C.C.O. forecasts the grind at 3.01 million tonnes.

The key to the cocoa market as the 2000/01 season progresses will be the size of the West African cocoa crop and the Ivory Coast's in particular. With an overall decline in West African production of possibly 150,000 tonnes compared to 1999/00, and some increase in world consumption, global ending stocks could decline as much as 100,000 to 200,000 tonnes. A lingering problem for the cocoa market has been large world stocks particularly relative to use. By September 2001, those stocks should see a decline to 1.14 to 1.18 million tonnes. The I.C.C.O. estimate is 1.18 million tonnes. While still large, it is a step in the right direction and would argue that cocoa prices should remain above the December lows. Any unrest or problems in the Ivory Coast could lead to a rally in

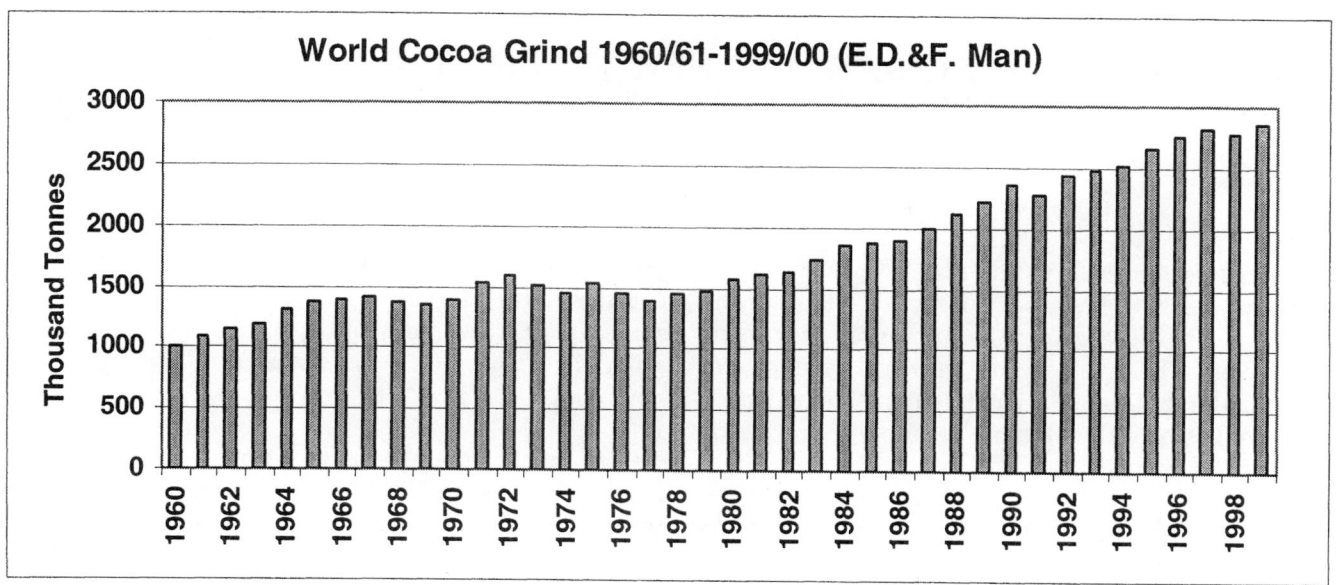

World Cocoa Grind 1960/61-1999/00 (E.D.&F. Man)

prices, and the market is likely to keep a close eye on events in that country over the next several months.

Cocoa Futures Markets

There are two primary futures and options markets for cocoa. The London International Financial Futures Exchange (LIFFE) has traded cocoa since 1928. The unit of trading is 10 metric tonnes, with delivery months of March, May, July, September, and December. Pricing is in pounds sterling, with delivery warehouses in a number of locations including Amsterdam, Bremen, Hamburg, Liverpool, London, and Rotterdam. Cocoa that is smoky or hammy is not tenderable. Other delivery specifications include the number of defects and size. For price and delivery purposes, the various cocoa beans trade at par or are discounted. Trading at par are beans from Ghana, the Ivory Coast, Nigeria, and Cameroon, among others. Trading at a discount are beans from Papua New Guinea and Sri Lanka, and at a steeper discount are cocoa beans from Brazil, Ecuador, and Malaysia.

Cocoa futures also trade at the Coffee, Sugar and Cocoa Exchange, Inc., a division of the New York Board of Trade. Trading is in dollars, with a trading unit of 10 metric tonnes. (Prior to December, 1980, New York cocoa futures were priced in cents per pound.) The delivery months are March, May, July, September, and December. The contract specifications call for the delivery of "the growth of any country or clime, including new or yet unknown growths" as long as it meets Food and Drug Administration standards for importation. There are accepted standards for, among other things, defects, size, and bean count. There are three delivery points at warehouses in the Port of New York District, Delaware River Port District, and the Port of Hampton Roads. There are three grouping of cocoa beans for delivery. Group A is deliverable at a premium of $160 per tonne and includes the main crops of Ghana, the Ivory Coast, and Nigeria among others; Group B is deliverable at a premium of $80 per tonne and includes Bahia Brazilian cocoa among others, while Group C is deliverable at par and includes Malaysian cocoa among others.

*   *   *

Walter Spilka is a cocoa analyst at Salomon Smith Barney in New York. He was formerly an analyst with the U.S.D.A., and has been a cocoa trader. He received a doctorate in agricultural economics from the Virginia Polytechnic Institute.

TECHNOTRADING:
NEW MARKETS, NEW RULES, AND NEW TECHNOLOGY

by Philip Gotthelf

As technology moves forward at breakneck speed, investment markets have been forced to structurally change. Such changes mark monumental alterations in our lives. The invention of the wheel, gunpowder, railroad, automobile, aviation, telephone, television... the list of structurally altering technology has a long history with many entries.

The term, "structural change," identifies developments or events that permanently modify the way things are done. Obvious inventions like the automobile or telephone changed the way we communicate, conduct commerce, and live. Financial markets undergo structural change that is equally profound, although not as commonly recognized. The abandonment of the Gold Standard is one example. Deregulating oil and the banking industry may be viewed as others. Synthetic investments or "derivatives" changed financial market strategies and objectives.

Few structural events have had more impact upon financial or investment markets than the personal computer and Internet. Since 1980, the PC has completely altered the standards by which investment decisions are generally made. The PC has placed tremendous investigative power into the general public's hands. Equally important, the PC, combined with the Internet and television coverage, creates an entirely new environment that smashes old rules and approaches. However, we are just beginning to find replacements for the "old," and therein lies our most exciting and potentially rewarding challenge.

The New Definition of Risk

Our perception of "risk" is, perhaps, the first casualty of our New Age of Investing. The strict risk definition is associated with probability; the chance for profit or loss. We know that a fair coin flip has a 50/50 probability of being heads or tails. Thus, a bet on a coin toss has a 0.5 "risk" of being correct or wrong. This narrow view is an essential foundation for understanding new risk concepts and parameters.

Understanding the probabilistic aspect of risk, we add the element of exposure. Simply put, exposure is the amount we place at risk. For example, most of us might bet a dime on a coin flip to have fun. The expected outcome over many flips would be 50% multiplied by our bet of ten cents ... a nickel. But, would you bet $1 million on the same flip? The probability is the same; 50/50. Obviously, loss exposure has dramatically risen. The expected outcome becomes 0.5 times $1 million.

Having touched upon probability and exposure, the next frontier is speed. The dissemination of information through various media and mediums has condensed reaction times. This increase in volatility over time represents a major structural change we can link to television, cell phones, and the Internet. Consider that within approximately two decades, television coverage has expanded by more than 100 times ... 1,000%. From 24-hour by 7-day weather coverage to a bird's eye view of Congress, we have these channels in real time. CNBC, CNN, and FOX News exemplify the speed and (perhaps) accuracy of public information resources. Add the Internet and analysis programs labeled "analytics," to round out a potential decision-making package. Suddenly, assessments become near instantaneous. This does not suggest more accuracy, but simply more speed.

Many experts believe the speed of information is the direct cause of higher volatility. Some may recall when a 3 to 5 tick move (3/32 – 5/32) in Treasury Bonds was a big change for a single session. Former FED Chairman Volker swiftly altered that perception when he incited the first limit move of two full points (64/32) in T-bond futures during his "inflation adjustments." The world of bond volatility was forever changed.

Coming off fixed currency exchange rates seemed like a long process. Yet, the transition from gold to floating parity took less than a decade. Today, we see the U.S. Dollar move as much as 2% against the Euro Currency in a day. This is historically unprecedented during peacetime. The point, of course, is that major moves take place in shorter periods. When such volatility exists, risk perception increases and an investor's accuracy becomes paramount.

Certainly, 1999 through 2001 will be noted as a pivotal period ... a shift from raging bull to painful correction. As this Yearbook goes to press, the final outcome of a stock market meltdown remains unknown. In approximately one year, 65% of the Nasdaq Index evaporated. More than $4 trillion in value disappeared. Therein is another aspect of risk perception that may be considered a structural alteration. Stocks have finally entered their last frontier, completing the leap from asset-oriented investment to pure trading vehicle. The Nasdaq is every bit as speculative (if not, more so) as commodities.

Why is this element of risk perception so vital? The public was lured into a false sense of security when it plunged billions into the final 1999 high-tech rally. It was "safe" because it was stocks. The market axiom brought a rude awakening; the greater the return, the higher the risk. In spite of this market law, investors acquired an insatiable taste for high yields ... big returns ... huge gains. This appetite is fed by new "trading instruments," including traditional commodity futures and options.

The fact that Generation X had not experienced a bear market until the demise of 2000/01 created a sense of risk appreciation rather than risk aversion. This is the generation of the X-Games and extreme sports. This is the generation of high-tech and big risks. This is the generation of lightning speed communication and assimilation.

My heavens! Commodity speculation has become fashionable!

New Tools For The Job

Clearly, a new market environment based upon structural changes requires new methodologies. The very developments leading to structural change like the PC, Internet, and diversified television represent tools for constructing investment strategies. Information access is being homogenized. This is to say that all information is likely to become available on the Internet and its relatives, like linked cell phones, palm devices, and pagers. All information will be accessible from all brands of personal computers hooked into high-speed lines like DSL, cable modems, satellite dishes and wireless. The delivery system will be homogeneous. Hardware will adhere to a standard.

In addition to information delivery, order entry, tracking, and execution has turned electronic. Before the first decade of the new Millennium ends, open outcry pits could be dinosaurs. Investors will "trade" everything online. Central computers match the bid and ask. That's simply the way it must be.

Since computers don't sleep and the world rotates through a 24-hour day and a dateline, there will be no opening or closing bell. Expect full volume 24-hour trading to be commonplace. It is possible exchanges will become "global." The delineation between Chicago, New York, London, and Tokyo will blur, or even disappear. The question most individual investors will ask is, "Am I ready?"

The fact is that *you must be ready*. There simply is no choice. This is the future, and wealth accumulation will depend upon a careful balance between speculation and investment ... risk and exposure ... short-term achievements and long-term goals. You must adapt to the new risk-conscious markets. Proof lies in the damage done by the 2001 bear market continuation. Retirement accounts were decimated just as the leading edge of Baby Boomers expected to retire or pay for college education. There is a need to earn it back. But, the words of the familiar Paine Webber commercial take on new meaning in the new market environment ..."We make money the old fashioned way. We earn it!"

Earning investment returns means being prepared for opportunity. Opportunity comes in sectors, waves, and cycles. This means that sectors like computers, biotechnology, energy, mining, industrials, utilities and more become hot. Bull and bear market volatility moves in waves. The economy oscillates in cycles. Each of these market phenomenon is statistically identifiable with modern trading tools. First and foremost are the new full-featured market information systems. These include quote vendors like Bridge, Quotron, Reuters, Bloomberg, Data Transmission Network (DTN) and others listed in directories for financial market services.

These systems are being offered through the homogeneous Internet as either browser-based like Bridge Channel, or proprietary like FutureSource Market Professional. Software that is easily downloaded from quote vendor Internet sites can be up and operational in less than an hour. Exchange quote permission is obtained via a faxed contract and BINGO, you're online with live quotes, charts, and analytics.

Once you have your market information resources, there are two ways to place trades. Conventionally, you would call your broker and give your buy, sell, and stop requests by phone. Your broker reduces your request to an order ticket, time stamps the ticket, and calls his order desk... or, perhaps he enters the trade through his or her workstation. But, convention has changed. Now, you have the same access to electronic order entry that generally includes live quotes, bid/ask, time & sales, along with a host of other information. Examples of electronic order entry include ManTrade offered by E D & F Man International, Iowa Grain's system, Rosenthal Collins' system, and a host of others. These systems can be previewed by visiting the web-site of the brokerage company of your choice.

For example, www.equidex.com provides demonstrations of several trading systems offered by futures commission merchants (FCMs). EQUIDEX Brokerage Group, Inc., is a self-guaranteed introducing broker (IB) that allows customers to trade through a variety of different FCMs and electronic systems.

Moving up the ladder, there are proprietary systems that are leased for direct interface with electronic exchanges. These systems represent even more power and flexibility because you are directly linked to the trade-matching computers. These systems include names like PATS, Yes Trader, Trade Technologies, and Easy System. Many of these "front-ends" are also available for preview at www.equidex.com. The trend in electronic trading suggests that quote vendors, themselves, may add order entry/execution and tracking capability. All you'll do is designate the clearing firm and/or introducing broker carrying your account.

Advantages range from ease, speed, accuracy, and risk management to inexpensive commissions. The elimination of middlemen saves money. The computer interface allows you to check orders against open positions and stops so that the chance of a double-entry error is substantially reduced. You can sit at your home or office computer and trade futures, options, and related instruments just as the professionals do ... with unbelievable POWER! And, these systems are not unique to commodities. Stock trading is possible on E*Trade, Datek Online, Scottrade.com, DLJ Direct, Merrill Lynch ... again, just naming a few.

Perhaps the most exciting for die-hard, in-your-veins traders is the introduction of cash currency trading via electronic InterBank. These systems were just being released in March, 2001, and allow *individual investors* to trade leveraged *unregulated* currencies ... all of them. Clearly, profit potentials in cash currencies are huge. There are rumors about currency schemes and systems that can turn $100 U.S. into millions ... secret societies that covet their secret methods. Back to reality, daily swings in currency parity represent more than $1.5 trillion per day! There is no bigger market. Not Stocks. Not Bonds. Not Commodities! However, the availability of currency futures and options makes this new investment prospect even more enticing.

Among firms on the cutting edge of electronic cash currency trading is a division of REFCO. A front-end to the REFCO system is also available through a TurboSystem™ to make this new market particularly attractive. Of course, what's a TurboSystem?

This is where technology becomes interesting for the full spectrum of traders. Certainly, an advantage to homogeneous Internet access is the ability to turn your existing home, office, or notebook PC into a trading station. Virtually every information vendor allows access through existing hardware ... leaving them free from being in the hardware business. Unquestionably, the "average" PC bought within the past two years can handle quote software and a browser-based order entry/tracking interface. However, requirements for running simultaneous quotes, analytics, order entry, news, and on-screen television generally bump up the necessary horsepower. Trading is considered "mission critical." Further, some proprietary functions require specific "static" IP addresses. Without becoming too technical, a static IP (Internet Protocol) address is set in the "network" function of Windows. If you are running multiple applications requiring unique IP addresses, you will need several network cards and a multi-port hub.

From a practical standpoint, traders who want to move into the full-featured electronic forum are discovering that it is more efficient to purchase a "trading-specific" system that can run other functions rather than try to fit trading-specific utilities onto a PC that is not uniquely configured for such a purpose. The line of TurboSystems was the first to appear in 2000 with trade-specific designs. Professional TurboSystem configurations range from multiple 60-inch plasma wall displays that service an entire trading floor to multi-screen flat panel individual workstations. Advantages are obvious.

TurboSystems are only modestly more costly than similarly configured Dells, Gateways, Microns, IBMs, and the like. The difference is that none of these standard vendors offer *the same configurations*. As of 2001, the "top-of-the-line" TurboSystem Black Stallion is an eye-popping 3-screen monster machine based upon the AMD Athlon® gigahertz (plus) processor. A 4-port custom video card with an onboard processor and 128 megabytes of RAM supports up to four flat-panel screens in a single seamless ground. The standard configuration sports a pitch-black 18-inch high resolution flat-panel TFT centerpiece with built-in stereo speakers. An optional television function is available. Two 15-inch black monitors flank the centerpiece to provide an ergonomically comfortable panorama. Since flat panel screens emit no radiation and very little heat, they address health concerns as well as space-saving efficiency and sharp design.

Why three screens? For the professional trader or the serious individual, the Black Stallion gives news, quotes, graphics, analytics, order entry, and order tracking in distinct "grounds;" two background and the main foreground. Each function is appropriately separated for maximum efficiency and trading safety.

There is no popping into and out of windows. All information is there all the time. Under pressure, this environment makes a noticeable difference. Those who have sampled the Black Stallion admit feeling markedly more relaxed during an active trading session.

When they invented the expression, "Black is beautiful," this TurboSystem was not in mind. But, the black screens are complimented by all-black components including a DVD/CD-Rom, ZIP-drive, and battery backup. These systems also address data integrity and preservation issues with a built-in 4-disk striped and mirrored RAID that permits an instant disk swap in the event of any failure.

Multiple network cards accommodate several network interfaces so that quotes, order entry, and internal networks operate independently. As long as the main line is operational, the loss of one service will not affect the other functions.

In addition to the Black Stallion, there is the Black Beauty that features the same essential horsepower without the multiple screens. If black is not "cool" enough to justify the higher price, there are standard cream-colored systems, too. Configurations go all the way to a portable notebook unit and range from approximately $15,000 for the Stallion down to a few thousand for the Workhorse and Mustang models.

Even memory is above standard. These units boast double data rate RAM (DDR) to take full advantage of processor speed. Yet, with prices of high-end Dells, Compaqs, and Gateways well under $15,000, why would anyone consider such an expensive system? The answer is time, effort, and utility. First, a comparable vendor brand machine isn't much less expensive. More importantly, the TurboSystem runs *trading systems*. Other systems can require endless tinkering to bring them up to speed ... if you can ever get them to run smoothly.

There are other reasons to add on horsepower. Analysis is increasingly sophisticated and complex. During the 1970s and 1980s, basic statistical analysis required large main frames or powerful mini computers to examine narrow market sectors and limited data. Database technology and scope was limited and difficult to manipulate. The huge increase in PC power impacted analytical techniques and database management. Consider that analysis has been renamed "analytics." Implementation of market analysis is a science and process encompassed by this new term. Developments like the Commodity Research Bureau Infotech CD-Rom brings enormous historical trading data to all who sport a CD reader. This is only one example of the massive research and development resources that are available.

Multiple analytic passes of huge data require extreme speed. That's another reason why traders opt for the "latest and greatest" hardware. Step back and consider that systems like Omega's TradeStation can cull diverse systems from back-testing this data. From moving averages to Market Profile®, no approach is beyond today's modestly priced technology.

Although 2000 and 2001 may be remembered for tragic stock market performance, commodity traders enjoyed some of the most spectacular trends in more than a dozen previous years. The key to achieving impressive profit potentials was a blend of traditional market analysis and leading-edge technology. While there are some "all new" approaches to trading, recent studies reveal that implementation was, and remains, as valuable as the method. Thus, "neural networks" and "genetic models" representing the latest leading-edge trading systems did not necessarily outperform traditional technical and fundamental analysis.

One example is the simple moving average system. As crude as some may consider a moving average crossover system, high-tech has given this approach new life with new meaning. First, statistical packages allow you to analyze *the probability of success* related to technical events like a 10-day crossing a 20-day average ... or the price crossing a 5-day average. Once historical probabilities are measured, highly sophisticated models can be derived, which anticipate crossovers and follow-through. Consider that a price crossing the 5-day average may exhibit a 30% probability of success. A 10-over-the-20 may provide an independent 40% success. The combined events can have a "joint probability" that can be correlated with other events to produce *multiple probabilities analytics* (sometimes called probit).

The COMMODEX® System uses correlations of price, volume, and open interest changes to identify "accumulation" and "distribution" patterns in futures. Its theory is that increased volume and open interest change relative to price forecasts immediate price direction. COMMODEX has been published daily since 1959, and was the first "automatic trading system" of its kind. Today, the system remains the oldest and most consistently profitable daily futures trading system in the world, however, even this impressive claim cannot guarantee a subscriber will achieve profitable results. COMMODEX tracks up to fifty U.S. futures markets. This wide diversification across varying market sectors is not accessible to modestly capitalized traders.

But, modern technology has moved systems like COMMODEX into the 21st Century. Spreadsheet programs automatically import COMMODEX daily bulletins, parse a portfolio that matches capital constraints, and can even print out time-stamped order tickets. More intriguing is the application of "neural network" programs like BrainMaker and NeuroShell to portfolio design and money management. Using COMMODEX historical data from the web site (www.commodex.com), investors can optimize a portfolio by back-testing a neural network model. Thus, a $10,000 account could theoretically perform as well or better than a multi-million dollar account on a rate-of-return basis.

The real clincher is technologically advanced system implementation is made possible by multi-function trading systems like the TurboSystem line of computers. These systems run "leading edge" software that actually conducts the analysis in real-time and generates "micro-trades" in time to profit. Historically, it has been difficult to take small bites from fast-moving futures markets. By the time analysis was complete, the decision made, and the trade called in, the profit potential could be gone. This is not so with the leading-edge systems. Multiple traditional techniques can be calculated in "near real-time" with decisions derived at lightning speeds.

For example, quote vendor software like BridgeStation, FutureSource Professional, Quotron, ILX, Reuters, Bloomberg, and Signal® (to name a few) use Windows features called Dynamic Data Exchange (DDE) and OLE to move data streams into analytical programs ranging from Excel to neural networks or custom models. With electronic order entry side-by-side, the analysis is instantly fed into PATS, ManTrade, or another order-entry system. Suddenly, it becomes possible for *the average trader* to successfully scalp! This process has become so efficient that even former local traders feel comfortable moving "upstairs."

There is no doubt that this is a trading revolution ... or, more appropriately called an *evolution* that defines the new Century and Millennium. Theoretically, this evolution should contain seeds of its own destruction. Perhaps you are familiar with the "Efficient Market Theory," postulating that markets are so prompt and accurate in conducting price discovery that scalping should not be possible. Of course, theory flies in the face of reality since hundreds (if not thousands) of scalpers earn hefty livings year after year. The concern is that increased participation will increase efficiency and lower the chance for success. Profit increments will shrink to the point where costs exceed gains.

Yet, another evolution derived from technological advances and structural change is a rapidly declining transaction cost. Using electronic markets and order entry, *individual traders* with modest volumes and account equity can enjoy very low execution fees. In turn, this justifies smaller and smaller profit objectives. From a historical perspective, trading is becoming microscopic. The smallest trends within trends or cycles within cycles are eyed as potential.

Hardware and software development in conjunction with the Internet and associated technologies expand profit horizons further with "financial engineering." Although it is not a new industry term, the engineering of financial services and products is rapidly expanding as new markets and their interrelationships are evaluated by computer systems. Consider the introduction of the European Currency Unit. Originally named the ECU, the consolidated or unified currency of Western Europe appeared as the Euro Currency and bounced against the U.S. Dollar like an Olympic ping-pong match. Suddenly, cross-parity took on new meaning as linkage between the Swiss Franc, Deutschmark, British Pound, and other currencies blended. The world seeks currency consolidation and the new Millennium may bring about several changes to global valuation models.

The world tested the Euro in 2000 and 2001. Its potential was probed and Iraq expressed confidence in a unified Europe by demanding Euros in lieu of U.S. Dollars for settling oil payments. Within a blink of this decision, traders constructed cross parity models with oil in the middle. Suddenly, there was opportunity in differentials between oil priced in Dollars and oil priced in Euros. This 3-way arbitrage is one more remarkable example of investor ingenuity. Assume crude oil remains static in U.S. Dollars while the Euro/Dollar parity declines. SNAP! You buy oil in the cheaper currency and resell in the higher.

Yes, the more participants, the narrower the spreads. Some will claim this arbitrage will fall victim to efficient market theory. Yet, it is this very arbitrage that has sustained professionals and even general investors. Some profit experiences are absolutely enormous! This 3-way arbitrage is not new nor unique to Iraq's decision to accept Euro payment. Coffee traded in London and New York pits Dollars against the Pound. Gold is priced in all currencies despite the fact that the London fix remains a focus. Silver, platinum, and palladium are candidates for cross-parity arbitrage. Combinations and permutations seem endless ... now that your PC can almost instantly perform the calculations, identify the trade, and place the order!

For those who remember the Bob Dylan song, *The Times They Are A Changing*, it is clear the time is now. Having been in the futures industry more than thirty years, and my father before me another fifty years, I can honestly say we are in the midst of the fastest and most profound market development and restructuring of the last century and, perhaps, this century. Looking forward, the world is challenged by "globalization" and its monetary consequences.

Change is truly breathtaking. How do I know? Watch a quote screen and trade a full spectrum portfolio on any given day. If you're like me, you'll be out of breath by noon ... if not sooner!

As a footnote, there are fringe participants who called for a high-tech market meltdown of "biblical proportions." They pointed out that the binary numeric representation of the first day of the Christian calendar was represented by 01/01/01; the base ten number 18. Divide 18 by the three components of month, day, and year and you have 18/3=6. This yields three 6's; the 666 sign of the "End Time." Since this prophecy was given in the binary language of digital computers, the conclusion is that the computer sector began an apocalyptic phase. Of course the NASDAQ composite declined by more than 60%. It was giving investors a "devil" of a time.

In every market there are two opinions that create a buyer and a seller. When confronted with this forecast of doom, another group pointed out that 18 is represented by the Hebrew letter ä. It represents "life" and is a symbol of good luck and good fortune to come.

As this edition of the CRB COMMODITY YEARBOOK sits on the shelf, time will tell who was right.

---

*   *   *

Philip Gotthelf publishes the COMMODEX® System and COMMODITY FUTURES FORECAST® Service. He is also President of EQUIDEX Incorporated (registered Commodity Trading Advisor) and EQUIDEX Brokerage Group, Inc. (registered Introducing Broker). Mr. Gotthelf is a graduate of Lehigh University with a B.S. in Economics and Finance and a minor in statistics.

He is known for extensive work in the futures industry and is the son of world renowned Edward B. Gotthelf, developer of the COMMODEX® trading methods. Philip Gotthelf's works have appeared in major industry publications including FUTURES MAGAZINE, INVESTING, STOCKS & COMMODITIES, TOP FARMER, PRO PRODUCER, BARRON'S, and ENERGY IN THE NEWS. He is quoted regularly in BARRON'S, THE WALL STREET JOURNAL, THE NEW YORK TIMES, FORTUNE, FORBES, U.S. NEWS & WORLD REPORT, MONEY, and has acted as consultant to major financial and consumer publications. He is a regular guest on CNBC, MS-NBC, The Cable News Network (CNN), and appeared on The NBC TODAY SHOW and NBC Nightly News. He has also been featured on THE WALL STREET JOURNAL REPORT, CBS, ABC, and FOX News.

As editor of the COMMODITY FUTURES FORECAST® Service, he has a reputation for uncanny accuracy. Among his notable forecasts were the October "Crash of '87," precise currency predictions since such futures opened in 1972, an exceptional record for interim and long-term interest rate moves, and exact calls on tops and bottoms in meats, grains, sugar, precious metals and coffee. His first book, TechnoFundamental Trading (Probus Press / McGraw Hill) provides a basic "from the ground up" education in commodity markets and uniquely links technical and fundamental analysis in clear, concise language and examples.

Mr. Gotthelf completed The New Precious Metals Market (McGraw Hill) in March, 1997, which was released in January, 1998. His predictions for declining gold and silver prices and rising platinum and palladium have been astoundingly accurate. Mr. Gotthelf has acted as an advocate for investors by warning about precious metals and related scams. In a CNBC appearance, Mr. Gotthelf warned about the claims made by the Canadian upstart, Bre-X, well in advance of the discovery of assay fraud.

Philip Gotthelf's "creative computer applications" have been used by substantial firms for developing proprietary trading models and hedging programs. In particular, Philip Gotthelf is known for developing "Inventory Income Enhancement Programs" (IIEPs) for energy companies, banks, money managers, farmers and institutional traders.

These programs are designed to increase revenues through scientific commodity options strategies. Mr. Gotthelf is also responsible for developing Yield Enhancement Programs (YEPs) for financial institutions (featured in INVESTING magazine, 1989).

He has been the primary speaker for the annual "Technical Analysis & Systems Trading of Energy Futures" seminars that have been sponsored by a variety of firms and educational institutions, and he is the contributing author of the Technical Analysis chapter of PennWell Books' ENERGY FUTURES text.

His COMMODEX System is the oldest daily futures trading system published in the world. The remarkable record spans more than 40 years. In independent surveys of COMMODEX performance, the system has been consistently rated in the top 5% of all available services. Therefore, COMMODEX has the most consistently profitable and time-proven record in the industry.

COMMODITY FUTURES FORECAST has an equally impressive record as a published service. Dating back to 1956, the forty-five year history has caught every major move since inception. The FORECAST combines highly accurate COMMODEX technical signals with fundamental analysis to produce a unique techno-fundamental approach to commodities. Both services have the distinction of being the first to successfully track financial futures, stock indices, and energy markets.

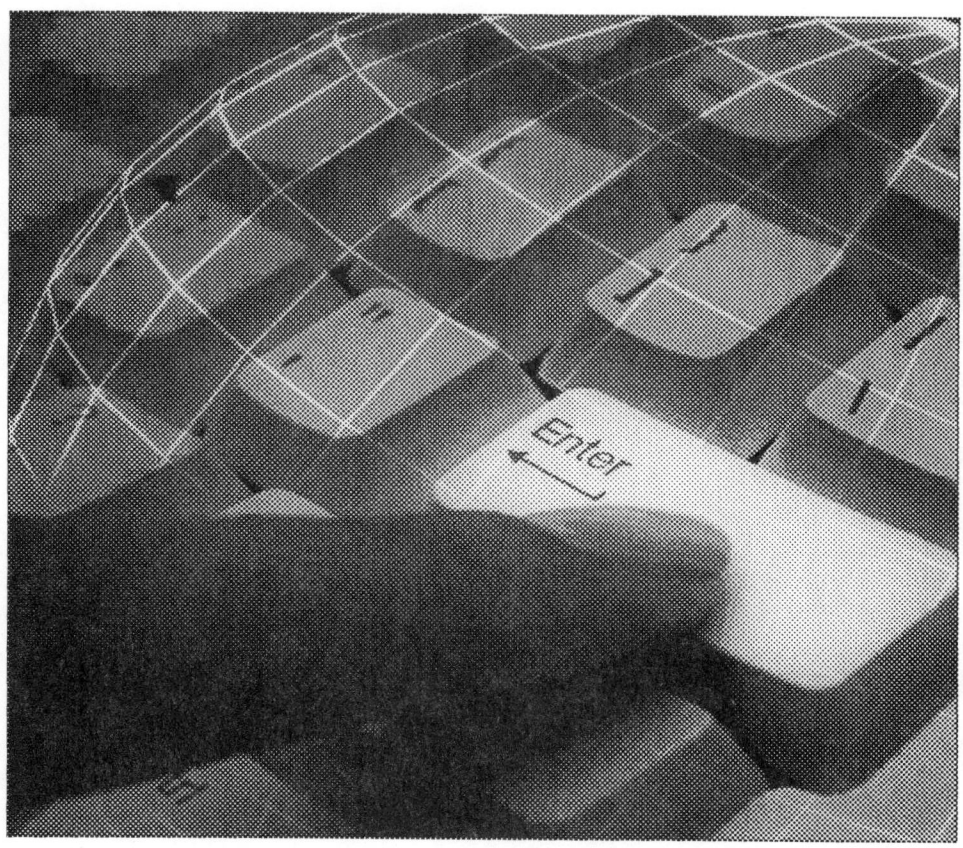

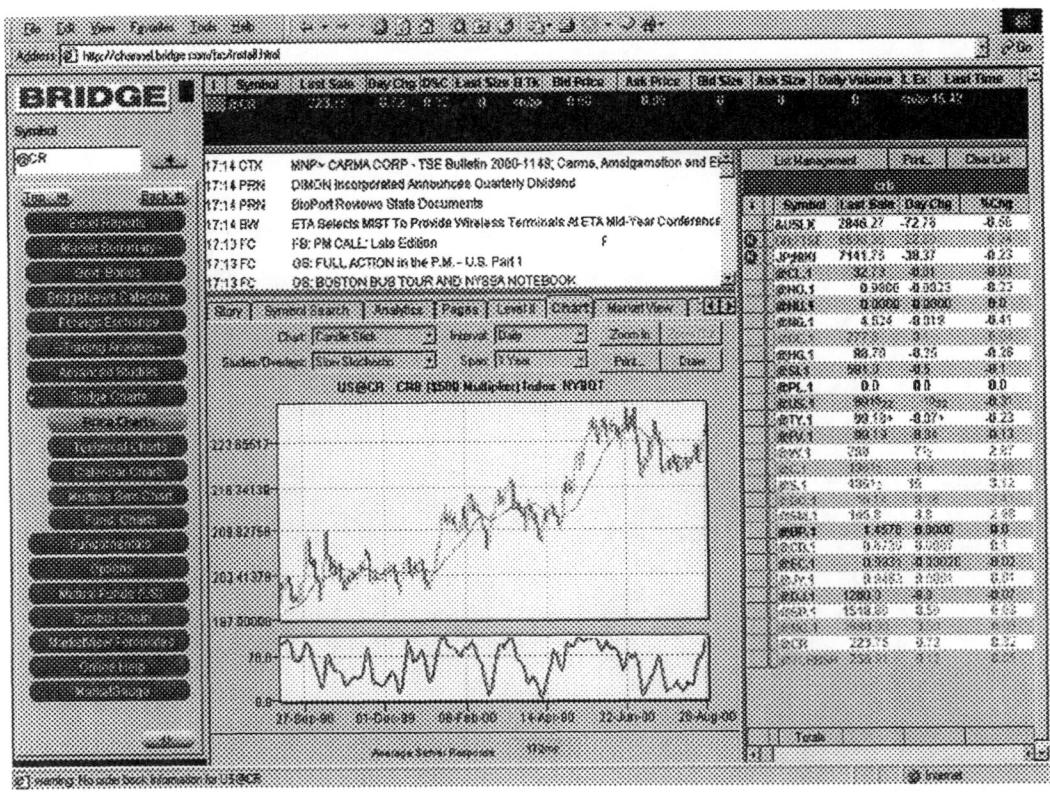

THE BLUE LINE

1-900-454-BLUE

Staying in Touch is Now only a Phone Call Away...

The **BLUE LINE** gives you both Pre-Opening market analysis and Mid-Day Updates (11:30 pm cst) keeping you informed on fast-paced, changing market events!

CALL 1-900-454-2583 PRE-OPENING AND NEW MID-DAY UPDATES

1. **Traders Update**
2. **Financial Market Forecast**
3. **Grain Market Forecast**
4. **Livestock Market Forecast**

5. **Metals & Energy Forecast**
6. **Softs Market Forecast**
7. **Technical Analysis**

The per minute cost is $1.33

The **BLUE LINE** is brought to you by Bridge/CRB®

Volume U.S.

U.S. Futures Volume Highlights
2000 in Comparison with 1999

2000 Rank	Top 50 Contracts Traded in 2000	2000 Contracts	%	1999 Contracts	%	1999 Rank
1	Eurodollar, CME	108,114,998	22.00%	93,418,498	19.55%	1
2	T-Bonds, CBT	62,750,843	12.77%	90,042,282	18.84%	2
3	T-Notes (10 Year), CBT	46,700,538	9.50%	34,045,758	7.12%	4
4	Crude Oil, NYMEX	36,882,692	7.50%	37,860,064	7.92%	3
5	T-Notes (5 Year), CBT	23,331,981	4.75%	16,983,812	3.55%	7
6	S&P 500 Index, CME	22,467,859	4.57%	27,003,387	5.65%	5
7	E Mini S&P 500 Index, CME	19,211,355	3.91%	10,953,551	2.29%	10
8	Natural Gas, NYMEX	17,875,013	3.64%	19,165,096	4.01%	6
9	Corn, CBT	17,185,442	3.50%	15,724,845	3.29%	8
10	Soybeans, CBT	12,627,950	2.57%	12,481,947	2.61%	9
11	E-Mini NASDAQ 100, CME	10,817,277	2.20%	682,059	0.14%	45
12	#2 Heating Oil, NYMEX	9,631,376	1.96%	9,200,703	1.93%	12
13	Unleaded Regular Gas, NYMEX	8,645,182	1.76%	8,701,216	1.82%	13
14	Gold (100 oz.), COMEX Div. of NYMEX	6,643,464	1.35%	9,575,788	2.00%	11
15	Wheat, CBT	6,407,531	1.30%	6,570,025	1.37%	14
16	Soybean Meal, CBT	6,317,988	1.29%	6,326,897	1.32%	15
17	Sugar #11, NYBOT	5,933,850	1.21%	5,911,299	1.24%	17
18	Soybean Oil, CBT	5,369,903	1.09%	5,663,895	1.19%	18
19	NASDAQ 100, CME	5,094,042	1.04%	2,360,938	0.49%	29
20	Euro FX	4,267,408	0.87%	3,002,453	0.63%	23
21	Japanese Yen, CME	3,965,377	0.81%	5,935,843	1.24%	16
22	Live Cattle, CME	3,681,512	0.75%	3,839,548	0.80%	22
23	Dow Jones Industrial Index, CBOT	3,572,428	0.73%	3,896,086	0.82%	21
24	Swiss Franc, CME	3,241,207	0.66%	4,114,824	0.86%	20
25	Silver (5,000 oz), COMEX Div. of NYMEX	3,117,017	0.63%	4,157,500	0.87%	19
26	High Grade Copper, COMEX Div. of NYMEX	2,778,124	0.57%	2,852,962	0.60%	24
27	Cotton, NYBOT	2,597,757	0.53%	2,448,087	0.51%	28
28	Canadian Dollar, CME	2,460,134	0.50%	2,573,762	0.54%	27
29	Wheat, KCBT	2,427,950	0.49%	2,321,059	0.49%	31
30	Coffee C, NYBOT	2,134,961	0.43%	2,659,233	0.56%	26
31	Lean Hogs, CME	2,111,807	0.43%	2,358,096	0.49%	30
32	Cocoa, NYBOT	2,110,048	0.43%	1,868,036	0.39%	32
33	British Pound, CME	2,029,542	0.41%	2,738,600	0.57%	25
34	T-Notes (2 Year), CBT	1,477,253	0.30%	1,047,348	0.22%	37
35	30 Day Federal Funds, CBT	1,443,665	0.29%	1,023,716	0.21%	38
36	Agency Debt (10 Year), CBT	1,334,340	0.27%			
37	Mexican Peso, CME	1,117,304	0.23%	1,143,641	0.24%	34
38	Euroyen, CME	1,079,074	0.22%	945,419	0.20%	39
39	Goldman Sachs Commodity Index, CME	1,002,673	0.20%	926,933	0.19%	40
40	Wheat, MGE	955,659	0.19%	1,119,812	0.23%	35
41	One Month LIBOR, CME	896,269	0.18%	843,054	0.18%	42
42	Australian Dollar, CME	749,555	0.15%	861,023	0.18%	41
43	Orange Juice (Frozen Conc.), NYCE	712,204	0.14%	793,882	0.17%	44
44	E-mini Feeder Cattle, CME	582,279	0.12%			
45	Soybeans, MIDAM	572,672	0.12%	651,268	0.14%	46
46	Municipal Bond Index, CBT	551,634	0.11%	798,597	0.17%	43
47	T-Bonds, MIDAM	550,714	0.11%	1,058,816	0.22%	36
48	Russell 2000, CME	508,726	0.10%			
49	Nikkei 225, CME	455,298	0.09%	513,848	0.11%	49
50	Oats, CBT	402,190	0.08%	371,406	0.08%	50
	Top 50 Contracts	486,896,065		469,536,912*		
	Contracts Below the Top 50	4,555,008	0.93%	8,382,396	1.75%	
	TOTAL	**491,451,073**	**100.00%**	**477,919,308**	**100.00%**	

* For 1999 Top 50 contracts totaled 472,251,640 including 3 contracts that are not among 2000's Top 50.

U.S. Futures Volume Highlights
2000 in Comparison with 1999

2000 Rank	Exchange	2000 Contracts	%	1999 Contracts	%	1999 Rank
1	Chicago Mercantile Exchange (CME)	195,106,383	39.70%	168,013,357	35.16%	2
2	Chicago Board of Trade (CBT)	189,662,407	38.59%	195,147,279	40.83%	1
3	New York Mercantile Exchange (NYMEX)	86,087,640	17.52%	92,415,006	19.34%	3
4	New York Board of Trade (NYBOT)*	15,214,528	3.10%	15,958,237	3.34%	4
5	Kansas City Board of Trade (KCBT)	2,446,607	0.50%	2,378,271	0.50%	6
6	MidAmerica Commodity Exchange	1,649,549	0.34%	2,433,894	0.51%	5
7	Minneapolis Grain Exchange (MGE)	958,420	0.20%	1,134,945	0.24%	7
8	Cantor Exchange (CE)	325,539	0.07%	438,068	0.09%	8
9	Philadelphia Board of Trade (PBOT)	0	0.00%	251	0.00%	9
	TOTAL	491,451,073	100.00%	477,919,308	100.00%	

* Includes the New York Futures Exchange, New York Cotton Exchange and Coffee, Sugar and Cocoa Exchange

U.S. Futures Volume 1996-2000

Cantor Exchange (CE)

Future	Contract Unit	2000	1999	1998	1997	1996
8% U.S. Treasury Bonds (30-year)	100,000 USD		299,094			
8% U.S. Treasury Notes (5-year)	100,000 USD		30,439			
8% U.S. Treasury Notes (10-year)	100,000 USD		101,510			
6% U.S. Treasury Bonds (30-year)	100,000 USD	24,577	5,135			
6% U.S. Treasury Notes (5-year)	100,000 USD	75,662	85			
6% U.S. Treasury Notes (10-year)	100,000 USD	223,610	1,805			
U.S. Agency Note (5-year)	100,000 USD	1,220				
U.S. Agency Note (10-year)	100,000 USD	470				
Total		325,539	438,068			

Chicago Board of Trade (CBT)

Future	Contract Unit	2000	1999	1998	1997	1996
Wheat	5,000 bu	6,407,531	6,570,025	5,681,569	5,058,645	5,385,967
Corn	5,000 bu	17,185,442	15,724,845	15,795,493	16,984,951	19,620,188
Oats	5,000 bu	402,190	371,406	442,874	397,332	501,858
Soybeans	5,000 bu	12,627,950	12,481,947	12,431,156	14,539,766	14,236,295
Soybean Oil	60,000 lbs	5,369,903	5,663,895	6,498,263	5,284,994	4,980,277
Soybean Meal	100 tons	6,317,988	6,326,897	6,553,846	6,424,945	5,955,977
Rice	200,000 lbs	169,133	139,592	157,764	171,973	119,900
Crop Yield	Crop yield est. X 10	41	115	337	1,472	1,343
TVA Hub Electricity	1,680 Mwh		22	184		
Silver	5,000 oz	66	125	7	61	110
Silver	1,000 oz	12,272	20,560	35,505	30,771	41,575
Gold	100 oz	3	4	204	138	335
Gold	Kilo	7,173	10,247	13,363	13,620	17,687
T-Bonds (30-year)	100,000 USD	62,750,843	90,042,282	112,224,081	99,827,659	84,725,128
T-Notes (10-year)	100,000 USD	46,700,538	34,045,758	32,482,576	23,961,819	21,939,725
T-Notes (5-year)	100,000 USD	23,331,981	16,983,812	18,060,048	13,488,725	11,463,640
T-Notes (2-year)	200,000 USD	1,477,253	1,047,348	1,347,575	1,018,545	643,845
Agency Debt (10-year)	100,000 USD	1,334,340				
30-Day Federal Funds	5,000,000 USD	1,443,665	1,023,716	844,408	910,474	608,308
Municipal Bond Index	1,000 USD x Index	551,634	798,597	1,002,075	983,877	883,901
Dow Jones Industrial Index	10 USD x Index	3,572,428	3,896,086	3,567,512	755,476	
Dow Jones Transportation Index	20 USD x Index	4				
Dow Jones Utility Index	200 USD x Index	22				
Dow Jones Composite Index	20 USD x Index	7		910,474	608,308	643,717
Total		189,662,407	195,147,279	217,138,928	190,056,287	171,134,185

Volume U.S.

Chicago Mercantile Exchange (CME)

Future	Contract Unit	2000	1999	1998	1997	1996
Lean Hogs	40,000 lbs	2,111,807	2,358,096	2,136,282	2,100,909	311,347
E-mini Lean Hogs	10,000 lbs	14,445				
Pork Bellies, Frozen	40,000 lbs	309,576	368,309	481,252	595,319	612,649
Pork Bellies, Fresh	40,000 lbs		195	4,922		
Boneless Beef	20,000 lbs 90% lean		105	3,433	4,245	
Butter	40,000 lbs	5,366	3,354	667	2,805	273
Cheddar Cheese	40,000 lbs		8	1,540	533	
Dry Whey	44,000 lbs	4				
Fluid MIlk	50,000 lbs	45,527	45,753	30,734	4,188	2,336
Class IV Milk	200,000 lbs	4,868				
Live Cattle	40,000 lbs	3,681,512	3,839,548	4,216,506	3,919,642	3,926,192
Stocker Cattle	25,000 lbs	865	906	411		
Feeder Cattle	44,000 lbs	582,279	650,071	738,567	837,165	772,222
E-mini Feeder Cattle	10,000 lbs	627				
Pork Cutout	40,000 lbs	1	847			
Orient Strand Board Lumber	100,000 bd ft	532	535	505	1,115	235
Random Lumber	80,000 bd ft	221,168	287,856	249,847	260,318	277,781
T-Bills (90-day)	1,000,000 USD	16,763	41,260	104,180	199,084	251,353
Eurodollar (3-month)	1,000,000 USD	108,114,998	93,418,498	109,472,507	99,770,237	88,883,119
Euroyen	1,000,000,000 JPY	1,079,074	945,419	962,574	1,119,827	503,104
Federal Funds Turn	45,000,000 USD		373	370		
One Month LIBOR	3,000,000 USD	896,269	843,054	1,108,454	1,504,230	1,190,652
Agency Note (5-year)	100,000 USD	35,579				
Agency Note (10-year)	100,000 USD	51,032				
Brazilian EL Bond	500 USD x Bond		822	3,150		253
Japanese Government Bond	50,000,000 JPY		73			
Mexican CETES	2,000,000		1	343	8,598	
Mexican TIIE	6,000,000		2		1,897	
British Pound	62,500	2,029,542	2,738,600	2,645,017	2,664,401	2,961,782
Brazilian Real	100,000	2,067	59,104	79,509	49,092	87,323
Canadian Dollar	100,000	2,460,134	2,573,762	2,396,300	2,542,102	1,932,729
Deutschemark	125,000	21,076	1,497,389	6,884,026	7,044,783	5,979,464
Euro Canada	1,000,000		50	12,311		
Japanese Yen	12,500,000	3,965,377	5,935,843	7,065,266	6,034,565	5,101,819
Mexican Peso	500,000	1,117,304	1,143,641	1,353,867	1,707,706	850,040
Swiss Franc	125,000	3,241,207	4,114,824	3,974,163	4,222,268	3,929,225
Australian Dollar	100,000	749,555	861,023	664,563	595,573	461,084
French Franc	250,000	44	6,745	72,562	112,520	67,835
New Zealand Dollar	100,000	32,862	42,646	16,580	3,506	
South African Rand	500,000	40,701	51,762	12,766	6,287	
Russian Ruble	500,000	71	43	21,766		
Euro FX	125,000	4,267,408	3,002,453	17		
E-Mini Euro FX	62,500	29,942	1,775			
E-Mini Japanese Yen	6,250,000	6,166	1,072			
Euro / British Pound	125,000 x Euro	973	3,332			
Euro / Japanese Yen	125,000 x Euro	4,289	2,018			
Eyro / Swiss Franc	125,000 x Euro	2	398			
EuroYen LIBOR	100,000,000 JPY	7,924	3,869			
Nikkei 225	5 USD x Index	455,298	513,848	479,248	417,541	502,072
E-Mini S&P	50 USD x S&P Index	19,211,355	10,953,551	4,466,032	885,825	
S&P 500 Index	500 USD x Index	22,467,859	27,003,387	31,430,523	21,294,584	19,899,999
S&P 500 Barra Growth Index	500 USD x Index	16,733	11,015	9,816	6,196	3,400
S&P 500 Barra Value Index	500 USD x Index	31,121	26,698	21,245	11,203	7,531
S&P MidCap 400 Index	500 USD x Index	332,438	326,117	310,008	262,017	289,989
Fortune E-50 Index	20 USD x Index	19,838				
NASDAQ 100 Index	500 USD x Index	5,094,042	2,360,938	1,063,328	807,604	380,963
E-Mini NASDAQ 100 Index	20 USD x Index	10,817,277	682,059			
Russell 2000	500 USD x Index	508,726	363,041	276,662	182,717	78,353
Goldman Sachs Commodity Index	250 USD x Index	1,002,673	926,933	854,264	773,088	446,186
Atlanta HDD	100 x HDD	23	197			
Chicago HDD	100 x HDD	39	20			
Cincinnati HDD	100 x HDD	3	70			
New York HDD	100 x HDD	2	49			
Dallas CDD	100 x CDD	5				
Tucson CDD	100 x CDD	5				
Des Moines CDD	100 x CDD	5				
Las Vegas CDD	100 x CDD	5				
Total		195,106,383	168,013,357	183,627,443	159,975,955	141,600,469

Volume U.S.

Kansas City Board of Trade (KCBT)

Future	Contract Unit	2000	1999	1998	1997	1996
Wheat	5,000 bu	2,427,950	2,321,059	2,006,779	1,937,140	1,830,276
Western Natural Gas	10,000 MMBtu	1	18,382	77,350	86,723	89,706
Western Natural Gas Index	10,000 MMBtu		3			
Value Line Index	500 USD x Index	9,954	1,264	4,485	14,047	28,663
Mini Value Line	100 USD x Index	3,962	31,377	76,345	154,784	135,848
ISDEX	100 USD x Index	4,740	3,186			
Total		**2,446,607**	**2,378,271**	**2,164,959**	**2,192,694**	**2,084,493**

MidAmerica Commodity Exchange (MidAm)

Future	Contract Unit	2000	1999	1998	1997	1996
Wheat	1,000 bu	77,477	132,392	133,200	130,968	151,755
Corn	1,000 bu	270,890	291,186	314,815	432,461	462,318
Oats	1,000 bu	2,711	3,509	5,451	4,916	8,449
Soybeans	1,000 bu	572,672	651,268	767,858	1,026,830	976,134
Soybean Meal New	20 tons	7,961	15,914	18,371	23,773	11,638
Soybean Oil	30,000 lbs	5,266	23,955	27,923	37,962	14,248
Live Cattle	20,000 lbs	8,326	16,285	18,883	16,316	20,983
Lean Hogs	20,000 lbs	16,047	31,827	18,597	1,312	
New York Silver	1,000 oz	15,970	23,493	14,999	8,928	8,398
New York Gold	33.2 oz	10,637	23,662	14,060	15,161	15,876
Platinum	25 oz	1,038	1,162	1,582	4,248	6,949
T-Bonds	50,000 USD	550,714	1,058,816	1,537,286	1,513,925	1,281,967
T-Bills	500,000 USD	68	117	315	461	753
T-Notes (10 Year)	50,000 USD	9,183	33,364	39,458	49,700	41,849
T-Notes (5 Year)	50,000 USD	225	29	96	479	383
Eurodollars	500,000 USD	9,411	5,745	5,347	5,997	8,893
Australian Dollar	50,000	573	846	1,205	585	266
British Pound	12,500	12,078	17,871	23,929	28,094	21,424
Swiss Franc	62,500	34,532	29,039	33,599	47,504	48,027
Deutschemark	62,500	1,746	17,764	36,674	84,344	79,093
Japanese Yen	6,250,000	28,958	41,167	47,821	48,585	42,085
Canadian Dollar	50,000	9,905	13,865	18,358	14,090	7,104
Euro Currency	62,500	3,161	618		7,104	11,970
Total		**1,649,549**	**2,433,894**	**3,081,181**	**3,500,791**	**3,229,710**

Minneapolis Grain Exchange (MGE)

Future	Contract Unit	2000	1999	1998	1997	1996
Wheat	5,000 bu	955,659	1,119,812	1,092,964	1,024,523	996,780
White Wheat	5,000 bu	1,495	4,786	15,209	14,284	14,602
Durum Wheat	5,000 bu	559	9,818	15,997		
Cottonseed	120 Tons	447				
White Shrimp	5,000 lbs	29	164	679	737	56
Black Tiger Shrimp	5,000 lbs	26	115	291	598	529
Twin Cities Electricity - On Peak	736 Mwh	180	250	54		
Twin Cities Electricity - Off Peak	736 Mwh	25				
Total		**958,420**	**1,134,945**	**1,125,194**	**1,040,594**	**1,012,598**

New York Board of Trade (NYBOT)*

Future	Contract Unit	2000	1999	1998	1997	1996
Coffee C	37,500 lbs	2,134,961	2,659,233	2,095,030	2,294,181	2,039,576
Sugar #11	112,000 lbs	5,933,850	5,911,299	5,524,111	5,284,971	4,751,852
Sugar #14	112,000 lbs	122,976	138,661	157,987	158,431	182,393
Cocoa	10 metric tons	2,110,048	1,868,036	1,810,580	2,274,509	2,121,576
BFP Milk		588	5,385	6,222	7,084	
BFP Milk, Large		307	3,156			
Cotton #2	50,000 lbs	2,597,757	2,448,087	3,200,830	2,837,280	2,373,855
Orange Juice Frozen Concentrate	15,000 lbs	712,204	793,882	914,614	1,029,861	654,937
Orange Juice Frozen Concentrate - 2	15,000 lbs	202	82			
Orange Juice Frozen Concentrate - Diff		1,003	886			
Deutsche Mark / British Pound	125,000 GBP		7,399	123,043	86,166	87,757
Deutsche Mark / Japanese Yen	125,000 DEM		12,568	301,555	172,612	167,093
Deutsche Mark / Italian Lira	250,000 DEM		207	119,667	137,077	74,997
Deutsche Mark / Swiss Franc	125,000 DEM		4,980	220,117	121,303	37,566
Deutsche Mark / Swedish Krona	125,000 DEM		864	121,203	63,685	8,378
British Pound / Swiss franc	125,000 GBP	11,061	28,789	29,902	5,699	
British Pound / Japanese Yen	125,000 GBP	85,530	69,207	46,584	9,629	
Swiss Franc / Japanese Yen	200,000 CHF	13,662	20,988	6		
U.S. Dollar / Deutsche Mark	125,000 DEM		200	43,331	33,917	32,441
U.S. Dollar / Canadian Dollar	200,000 USD	2,825	3,406	3,726	830	

Volume U.S.

New York Board of Trade (NYBOT)* (Continued)

Future	Contract Unit	2000	1999	1998	1997	1996
U.S. Dollar / Swedish Krona	200,000 USD	2,423				
U.S. Dollar / Norwegian Krone	200,000 USD	58				
U.S. Dollar / Swiss Franc	200,000 USD	16,671	25,523	18,224	4,282	4,098
U.S. Dollar / Japanese Yen	200,000 USD	30,353	41,632	23,828	9,060	9,037
U.S. Dollar / British Pound	125,000 GBP	14,202	16,571	7,795	6,375	2,290
U.S. Dollar / South Arican Rand	100,000 USD	9,984	10,859	3,165	4,683	
Canadian Dollar / Japanese Yen	200,000 CAD	5,380				
Australian Dolar - New Zealand Dollar	200,000 AUD	15,333	26,088			
U.S. Dollar / Australian Dollar	100,000 AUD	44,307	40,711	7,310	5,393	
Australian Dollar / Canadian Dollar	200,000 AUD	2,064				
Australian Dollar / Japanese Yen	200,000 AUD	32,390	18,538			
U.S. Dollar / New Zealand Dollar	100,000 NZD	23,866	70,717	30,622	9,499	
Euro		97,032	85,211	1,325		
Euro / US Dollar, Small		6,508	2,337			
Euro / US Dollar	100,000 EUR	213				
Euro / Australian Dollar	100,000 EUR	7,674				
Euro / Canadian Dollar	100,000 EUR	8,183				
Euro / Japanese Yen	100,000 EUR	278,119	192,987	356		
Euro / Swedish Krona	100,000 EUR	54,076	101,605	89		
Euro / Norwegian	100,000 EUR	2,461	10,452			
Euro / British Pound	100,000 EUR	159,862	200,560	50		
Euro / Swiss Franc	100,000 EUR	69,538	147,650	199		
U.S. Dollar Index	1,000 USD x Index	297,745	356,544	469,291	485,481	509,067
T-Note (5 Year)	100,000 USD	8,482	8,503	13,088	18,040	45,064
NYSE Composite Index	500 USD x Index	130,984	334,222	590,327	916,716	791,325
Russell 1000 Index	500 USD x Index	94,736	161,114			
PSE Tech 100	500 USD x Index	11,304	40,402	9,814	9,848	8,663
PSE Tech 100	100 USD x Index	112		10,950		
Commodity Research Bureau Index	500 USD x Index	63,494	88,696	58,993	71,482	81,113
Total*		**15,214,528**	**15,958,237**	**16,049,651**	**16,223,662**	**14,069,205**

New York Mercantile Exchange (NYMEX)

COMEX Division

Future	Contract Unit	2000	1999	1998	1997	1996
High Grade Copper	25,000 lbs	2,778,124	2,852,962	2,483,610	2,356,170	2,311,919
Silver	5,000 oz	3,117,017	4,157,500	4,094,616	4,893,520	4,870,808
Gold	100 oz	6,643,464	9,575,788	8,990,094	9,541,904	8,902,179
Eurotop 100 Index	100 USD x Price	4,800	25,181	50,619	47,427	38,925
Eurotop 300 Index	200 USD x Price	36,863	6,279			
Aluminum	44,000 lbs	46,099	27,978			
Total		**12,626,367**	**16,645,688**	**15,618,939**	**16,839,021**	**16,123,831**

NYMEX Division

Future	Contract Unit	2000	1999	1998	1997	1996
Palladium	100 oz	50,766	75,394	131,250	238,716	205,610
Platinum	50 oz	320,924	567,268	528,269	698,597	802,468
No. 2 Heating Oil, NY	1,000 bbl	9,631,376	9,200,703	8,863,764	8,370,964	8,341,877
Unleaded Gasoline, NY	1,000 bbl	8,645,182	8,701,216	7,992,269	7,475,145	6,312,339
Natural Gas	10,000 MMBTU	17,875,013	19,165,096	15,978,286	11,923,628	8,813,867
Palo Verde Electricity	736 Mwh	21,477	51,852	139,738	155,977	17,548
California Oregon Border Electricity	736 Mwh	7,060	52,032	128,423	120,896	52,340
Cinergy Electricity	736 Mwh	461	34,367	48,483		
Entergy Electricity	736 Mwh	34	20,528	42,580		
PJM Electricity	736 Mwh	188	3,254			
Propane	42,000 gal	26,075	37,544	43,868	40,255	53,903
Sour Crude Oil	1,000 bbl	25		1		
Crude Oil	1,000 bbl	36,882,692	37,860,064	30,495,647	24,771,375	23,487,821
Total		**73,461,273**	**75,769,318**	**64,392,578**	**53,795,678**	**48,099,460**
Total**		**86,087,640**	**92,415,006**	**80,011,517**	**70,634,699**	**64,223,291**

Philadelphia Board of Trade (PBOT)

Future	Contract Unit	2000	1999	1998	1997	1996
Australian Dollar	100,000		20	148	1,270	2,532
British Pound	62,500		92	235	2,543	1,761
Canadian Dollar	100,000		27		80	91
ECU	125,000		28		158	616
Deutschemark	125,000			909	12,510	23,904
Swiss Franc	125,000		39	445	3,913	4,723
French Franc	500,000			101	3,489	3,704
Japanese Yen	12,500,000		45	734	5,112	10,871
Total		**0**	**251**	**2,572**	**29,075**	**48,202**
Total Futures		**491,451,073**	**477,919,308**	**503,201,445**	**443,653,757**	**397,402,153**
Percent Change		**2.83%**	**-5.02%**	**13.42%**	**11.64%**	**0.53%**

* Includes the New York Futures Exchange, New York Cotton Exchange and Coffee, Sugar and Cocoa Exchange.

** In August 1994, the Commodity Exchange and the New York Mercantile Exchange merged and is now listed as one exchange.

Options Traded on U.S. Futures Exchanges Volume Highlights
2000 in Comparison with 1999

2000 Rank	Exchange	2000 Contracts	%	1999 Contracts	%	1999 Rank
1	Chicago Board of Trade (CBT)	43,866,151	42.56%	59,413,936	51.66%	1
2	Chicago Mercantile Exchange (CME)	36,007,913	34.94%	32,723,766	28.46%	2
3	New York Mercantile Exchange (NYMEX)	17,987,598	17.45%	17,123,825	14.89%	3
4	New York Board of Trade (NYBOT) *	4,922,626	4.78%	5,519,619	4.80%	4
5	Kansas City Board of Trade (KCBT)	218,062	0.21%	146,105	0.13%	5
6	Minneapolis Grain Exchange (MGE)	42,658	0.04%	53,870	0.05%	6
7	MidAmerica Commodity Exchange (MidAm)	20,368	0.02%	18,969	0.02%	7
	Total	**115,000,090**	**100.00%**	**115,000,090**	**100.00%**	

* Includes the New York Futures Exchange, New York Cotton Exchange and Coffee, Sugar and Cocoa Exchange

Options Volume on U.S. Futures Exchange 1995-1999
Chicago Board of Trade (CBT)

Option	Contract Unit	1999	1998	1997	1996	1995
Corn	5000 bu	4,205,325	4,267,274	4,963,603	6,602,010	3,783,446
Soybeans	5000 bu	4,792,245	3,845,804	5,339,936	5,135,124	3,149,635
Oats	5000 bu	56,418	51,852	21,654	45,037	35,250
Wheat	5000 bu	1,516,037	1,346,272	1,698,969	1,886,909	1,243,567
Soybean Oil	60,000 lbs	801,367	752,627	381,193	285,274	232,635
Soybean Meal	100 tons	709,194	889,462	716,079	593,165	304,835
Rice	200,000 lbs	48,515	33,602	37,769	14,658	14,336
Diammonium Phosphate	100 tons				50	
Crop Yield	Crop yield est. X 10	25	841	165	1,061	3,519
Silver	1,000 oz	38	154	68	515	1,476
Eastern Catastrophe Insurance	Loss/EP x 25,000 USD				66	3,274
Midwest Catastrophe Insurance	Loss/EP x 25,000 USD					50
PCS Castastrophe Insurance		561	7,753	15,706	14,688	1,064
U.S. Treasury Bonds (30-year)	100,000 USD	34,680,068	39,941,672	30,805,885	25,930,661	25,639,950
U.S. Treasury Notes (10 Year)	100,000 USD	9,738,808	9,296,742	6,032,088	7,907,650	6,887,102
U.S. Treasury Notes (5 Year)	100,000 USD	2,537,044	3,184,609	2,105,792	2,723,525	3,619,462
U.S. Treasury Notes (2 Year)	200,000 USD	1,780	2,780	4,268	2,806	13,189
German Bund	250,000 USD			15,620		
Muni Bonds	1,000 USD x Index	33,754	100,739	210,990	43,219	13,018
Brady Bond Index	1,000 USD x Index				440	
Yield Curve Spread	25,000 USD x 100 YCS			360	3,284	
Flexible U.S. T-Bonds		54,454	68,043	118,895	94,453	59,804
Flexible T-Notes (10 Year)		6,150	10,520	15,910	12,735	36,425
Flexible T-Notes (5 Year)		2,593	4,364	1,350	6,990	14,730
Flexible T-Notes (2 Year)				200		100
Dow Jones Industrial Index	10 USD x Index	229,560	245,398	156,132		
Total		**59,413,936**	**64,050,508**	**52,642,632**	**51,304,320**	**45,056,867**

Volume U.S.

Chicago Mercantile Exchange (CME)

Option	Contract Unit	1999	1998	1997	1996	1995
Live Hogs	40,000 lbs				169,214	137,435
Lean Hogs	40,000 lbs	231,273	206,014	210,429	35,831	
Live Cattle	40,000 lbs	545,709	685,606	540,804	539,523	463,455
Stocker Cattle	25,000 lbs	41				
Fluid Milk	40,000 lbs				307	
Boneless Beef	20,000 lbs 90% lean		425	997		
Boneless Beef Trimmings	20,000 lbs 50% lean		134	1,054		
Butter	50,000 lbs	752	595	479	92	
Cheddar Cheese	40,000 lbs		168	54		
Fluid Milk	200,000 lbs	12,604	16,680	4,078		
Mini BFP Milk	50,000 lbs	607	304			
Mini BFP Milk	100,000 lbs	387				
Pork Bellies, Frozen	40,000 lbs	16,780	21,545	29,324	52,040	21,156
Pork Bellies, Fresh	40,000 lbs		19			
Feeder Cattle	44,000 lbs	130,410	170,857	161,100	174,518	109,096
Lumber	160,000 bd ft				1,753	14,433
Orient Strand Board	100,000 bd ft		40	489	86	
Random Lumber	80,000 bd ft	24,745	18,928	19,826	26,922	491
One Month LIBOR	3,000,000 USD	1,916	5,541	28,809	16,031	54,219
Brazilian C Bond	500 USD x Index				30	
Mexican PAR Bond	500 USD x Index				130	
Mexican TIIE	6,000,000		35	110		
Eurodollar (3-month)	1,000,000 USD	24,884,494	33,147,148	29,595,246	22,234,888	22,363,853
Eurodollar 5-year Bundle			64			
Euroyen	100,000,000 JPY	41,073	38,208	41,577		
T-Bill (90-day)	1,000,000 USD				80	3,594
British Pound	62,500	208,921	241,720	986,950	2,886,041	1,668,624
Brazilian Real	100,000		14,397	114,464	74,106	3,700
Deutschemark	125,000	140,522	734,678	1,411,110	1,822,649	2,642,904
Euro Canada	1,000,000		2,109			
Mexican Peso	500,000	8,133	25,948	186,594	13,466	1,114
Swiss Franc	125,000	178,433	281,354	591,509	753,418	630,016
Japanese Yen	12,500,000	1,100,130	1,942,417	1,661,417	1,734,186	2,141,043
Canadian Dollar	100,000	121,933	278,730	253,075	197,741	259,857
New Zealand Dollar	100,000		46	32		
Australian Dollar	100,000	9,509	9,133	25,465	5,785	9,892
French Franc	250,000		38	1,884	2,149	4,935
Euro FX	125,000 x EUR	167,078				
Deutsche Mark / Japanese Yen	250,000 DEM	58				
Euro / British Pound	125,000 x EUR	200				
Nikkei 225	5 USD x Index	6,007	7,725	7,834	5,722	8,986
Mexican IPC Index	25 USD x Index				75	
S&P 500 Index	500 USD x Index	4,603,946	4,986,687	4,734,950	4,636,236	4,568,232
E-Mini S&P	50 USD x Index	54,480	20,629	8,661		
S&P 500 Barra Value Index	500 USD x Index		40	1,791	4,765	30
S&P 500 Barra Growth Index	500 USD x Index		82	962	2,960	
S&P MidCap 400 Index	500 USD x Index	3,841	1,899	3,272	2,201	5,435
Major Market	500 USD x Index			20	729	289
NASDAQ 100 Index	500 USD x Index	225,981	127,532	108,922	23,992	
Dow Jones Taiwan Index	250 USD x Index			146		
Russell 2000	500 USD x Index	1,230	2,656	2,849	2,089	1,532
Goldman Sachs Commodity Index	250 USD x GSCI	2,573	1,257	2,190	1,971	28,028
Total		**32,723,766**	**42,991,388**	**40,738,473**	**35,421,726**	**35,142,349**

Kansas City Board of Trade (KCBT)

Option	Contract Unit	1999	1998	1997	1996	1995
Wheat	5,000 bu	143,974	112,825	99,092	65,190	75,849
Western Natural Gas	10,000 MMBtu		55	240	1,850	2,546
Mini Value Line	100 USD x Index	2,094	1,662	4,547	1,439	3,014
ISDEX	100 USD x Index	37				
Total		**146,105**	**114,542**	**103,879**	**68,479**	**81,409**

MidAmerica Commodity Exchange (MidAm)

Option	Contract Unit	1999	1998	1997	1996	1995
Soybeans	1,000 bu	10,705	44,603	19,594	13,689	11,908
Soybean Oil	30,000 lbs	6	7	3		5
Soft Red Winter Wheat	5,000 bu	1,813	3,121	4,491	3,422	2,425
Corn	1,000 bu	4,325	8,348	8,904	9,753	7,296
T-Bonds	50,000 USD	2,095	2,646	1,282	530	721
Gold	33.2 oz	25	3	63	137	772
Total		**18,969**	**25,728**	**34,337**	**27,531**	**23,127**

Minneapolis Grain Exchange (MGE)

Option	Contract Unit	1999	1998	1997	1996	1995
American Spring Wheat	5,000 bu	53,246	41,702	40,383	21,126	26,893
European Spring Wheat	5,000 bu		153	88	44	184
White Wheat	5,000 bu	205	1,772	6,320	5,175	5,333
Durum Wheat	5,000 bu	154	97			
Barley	180,000 lbs				8	
White Shrimp	5,000 lbs	118	337	180	7	118
Black Tiger Shrimp	5,000 lbs	147	278	739	531	138
Total		**53,870**	**44,339**	**47,710**	**26,891**	**32,666**

New York Board of Trade (NYBOT)**

Option	Contract Unit	1999	1998	1997	1996	1995
Sugar #11	112,000 lbs	2,275,704	2,113,369	1,369,465	1,094,879	1,203,779
Flexible Sugar		5,200	9,930	155		
Coffee	37,500 lbs	1,369,021	974,690	1,272,767	856,710	867,303
Cocoa	10 metric tons	364,450	326,221	399,408	335,173	319,513
Cheddar Cheese	40,000 lbs				4	76
Non Fat Dry Milk	44,000 lbs				21	
BFP Milk		13,177	12,193	1,364		
BFP Milk, Large		2,682				
Butter	10,000 lbs			77		
Milk	50,000 lbs			379	963	103
Cotton	50,000 lbs	706,589	1,127,326	648,154	816,550	1,416,054
Orange Juice Frozen Concentrate	15,000 lbs	351,763	464,773	457,143	316,469	171,209
Potato	85,000 lbs			14	26	
U.S. Dollar Index	500 USD x Index	11,654	21,575	22,539	50,461	23,987
Deutsche Mark / British Pound	125,000 GBP		10,687	3,484	9,247	116
Deutsche Mark / French Franc	500,000 DEM			105	1,473	570
Deutsche Mark / Japanese Yen	125,000 DEM	50	884	458	2,010	160
Deutsche Mark / Swiss Franc	125,000 DEM	4,278	6,926	675	7,313	33
Deutsche Mark / Swedish Krona	125,000 DEM		37			
Deutsche Mark / Italian Lira	250,000 DEM		3,500	1,637	367	354
British Pound / Swiss Franc	125,000 GBP	361				
British Pound / Japanese Yen	125,000 GBP	291	20			
New Zealand Dollar / U.S. Dollar	200,000 NZD		2			
Swiss Franc / Japanese Yen	200,000 CHF	321				
Euro		7,137				
Euro / Bristish Pound	100,000 EUR	2,228				
Euro / Japanese Yen	100,000 EUR	5,200				
U.S. Dollar / Deutsche Mark	125,000 DEM		3,974	912	266	
U.S. Dollar / British Pound	125,000 GBP	280	6	32	22	
U.S. Dollar / South African Rand	100,000 USD	910	11			
U.S. Dollar / Swiss Franc	200,000 USD	300				
U.S. Dollar / Japanese Yen	12,500,000 JPY	2,431	1,811	1,225	1,209	
NYSE Composite Index	500 USD x Index	112,052	93,343	81,038	48,714	26,457
Russell 1000 Index	500 USD x Index	69,990				
PSE Tech 100 Index	500 USD x Index	204,682	37,339	8,801	2,211	
PSE Tech 100 Index	100 USD x index		37,827			
Bridge/CRB Futures Index	500 USD x Index	8,868	5,844	5,835	4,771	6,384
Total**		**5,519,619**	**5,252,288**	**4,275,667**	**3,548,859**	**4,036,098**

Volume U.S.

New York Mercantile Exchange (NYMEX)*

COMEX Division

Option	Contract Unit	1999	1998	1997	1996	1995
Gold	100 oz	2,815,831	1,945,366	2,064,883	2,079,663	2,006,695
5 Day Gold	100 oz				150	688
Silver	5,000 oz	722,885	818,053	842,923	949,239	1,146,513
5 Day Silver	5,000 oz				96	221
High Grade Copper	25,000 lbs	160,857	153,332	133,603	150,339	134,212
5 Day Copper	25,000 lbs					34
Aluminum	44,000 lbs	642				
Total		**3,703,215**	**2,916,751**	**3,041,409**	**3,179,487**	**3,288,363**

NYMEX Division

Option	Contract Unit	1999	1998	1997	1996	1995
No. 2 Heating Oil	42,000 gal	695,558	669,725	1,147,034	1,108,935	703,388
Crude Oil	1,000 bbl	8,161,976	7,448,095	5,790,333	5,271,456	3,975,611
Unleaded Gasoline	1,000 bbl	600,009	730,421	1,033,778	655,965	766,557
Natural Gas	10,000 MMBTU	3,849,454	3,115,765	2,079,607	1,234,691	921,520
Alberta Natural Gas	10,000 MMBTU				15	
Gas-Crude Oil Spread	1,000 bbl	46,281	22,575	41,867	31,743	64,285
Heating Oil-Crude Oil Spread	1,000 bbl	46,482	36,615	18,657	45,920	72,969
Palo Verde Electricity	736 Mwh	4,419	28,597	19,328	3,964	
California Oregon Border Electricity	736 Mwh	3,761	19,989	13,495	7,650	
Cintergy Electricity	736 Mwh	1,419	2,597			
Entergy Electricity	736 Mwh	105	1,855			
Platinum	50 oz	11,146	14,183	31,139	36,175	43,601
Total		**13,420,610**	**12,090,417**	**10,175,238**	**8,396,514**	**6,547,931**
Total*		**17,123,825**	**15,007,168**	**13,216,647**	**11,576,001**	**9,836,294**
Total Options		**115,000,090**	**127,485,961**	**111,059,345**	**101,973,807**	**94,208,810**
Percent Change		**-9.79%**	**14.79%**	**8.91%**	**8.24%**	**-6.61%**

* In August 1994, the Commodity Exchange and the New York Mercantile Exchange merged and is now listed as one exchange.

** Includes the New York Futures Exchange, New York Cotton Exchange and Coffee, Sugar and Cocoa Exchange.

Volume Worldwide

Agricultural Futures Markets (AFM), Netherlands

	2000	1999	1998	1997	1996
Live Hogs	32,020	43,051	45,705	57,069	49,986
Piglets	738	1,172	2,531	2,610	2,529
Eggs	300				
Potatoes	63,184	67,663	114,601	76,646	75,046
Potatoes Options	8,863	10,967	16,394		
Hogs Options	495				
Total	**105,600**	**122,853**	**179,231**	**136,325**	**128,097**

Amsterdam Exchanges (AEX), Netherlands

(formerly European Options Exchange (EOE))	2000	1999	1998	1997	1996
AEX Stock Index (FTI)	2,674,824	2,925,385	3,484,558	2,554,776	2,426,699
Light AEX Stock Index (FTIL)	20,700	12,445			
Dutch Top 5 Index (FT5)		101	14,412	58,891	70,873
Amsterdam Information Technology Index (FIA)	10	25			
Amsterdam Financial Sector Index (FFA)	8	1,345			
Amsterdam MidCap Index (FTM)	1,914	263			
FTSE sStars (FTES)	13	32			
FTSE Eurotop 100 Index (FETI)	2,112	292			
Euro / U.S. Dollar (FED)	989	167			
U.S. Dollar/Euro (FDE)	3,656	1,241	4,411	2,987	
All Futures on Individual Equities	773				
Gold Options	10,284	35,627	29,562	59,871	89,779
Silver Options	520	2,640	4,435	4,320	7,799
Euro / U.S. Dollar (EDX) Options	30,835	17,398			
U.S. Dollar / Euro Options	63,560	87,249	273,455	270,088	
Dutch Government Bond Options	22,515	77,619	208,994	286,808	474,525
EOE Stock Index Options	4,953,037	5,527,137	7,864,884	8,232,719	6,039,984
Light AEX Stock Index (AEXL) Options	37,782	38,872			
Eurotop 100 Options		19,763	33,586	12,127	5,090
FTSE sStars (STAR) Options	384	1,137			
FTSE Eurotop 100 Index (ETI) Options	9,940	11,017			
Amsterdam Information Technology Index (AIS) Options	1,573	514			
Amsterdam Financial Sector Index (AFS) Options	284	16,069			
Amsterdam MidCap Index (MID) Options	2,517	743			
Eurotop Bank Sector Index (EBS) Options	182	35			
Eurotop Information Technology Sector Index (EIS)	213	57			
Dutch Top 5 Index Options		446	86,454	414,956	861,025
Equity Options Options	50,345,697	40,653,520	52,741,082	36,340,078	18,754,623
Total	**58,184,322**	**49,431,139**	**64,756,919**	**48,669,669**	**29,299,550**

Wiener Borse - Derivatives Market of Vienna, Austria

(formerly the Austrian Futures & Options Exchange)	2000	1999	1998	1997	1996
Austrian Government Bond		180	35,865	107,421	151,633
ATX Index	431,048	598,981	618,358	566,459	412,047
CeCe (5 Eastern European Indices)	227,829	203,421	472,077	464,480	
ATX Index Options	205,286	395,323	557,463	572,644	960,513
ATX LEOs (Long-term Equity) Options	2,154	7,971	11,421	4,693	43,990
CeCe (5 Eastern European Indices) Options	10,659	24,157	75,709	43,424	
Equity Options		802,924	1,201,197	1,346,990	1,266,960
Total	**876,976**	**2,032,957**	**2,972,090**	**3,111,523**	**2,841,978**

Belgian Futures and Options Exchange (BELFOX), Belgium

	2000	1999	1998	1997	1996
Euribor 3-month (ERF)		98			
Mini Bel 20 Index (MBEL)	23,814,060	4,888,140			
Mini Dow Jones Euro Stoxx 50 (MEUR)	5,704,990				
Bel 20 Index	780,301	823,244	664,360	551,044	326,542
Bel 20 Index Options	911,275	1,151,862	978,341	954,238	1,170,948
USO (Dollar/Belgian Franc) Options	1,240	9,684	81,806	119,251	128,548
Gold Index Options	1,720	8,793	34,611	61,269	82,442
Equity Options	589,218	530,389	364,885	402,547	378,034
Total	**31,802,804**	**7,412,210**	**2,175,033**	**2,527,665**	**2,635,945**

Volume Worldwide

Bolsa de Mercadorias & Futuros (BM&F), Brazil

	2000	1999	1998	1997	1996
Arabica Coffee	390,513	317,722	198,547	114,521	116,071
Live Cattle	149,795	123,442	88,054	109,261	117,395
Sugar Crystal	52,552	33,764	30,080	8,330	6,212
Cotton	306	5,115	17,007	13,689	2,339
Corn	8,084	10,432	15,949	18,907	3,696
Soybean Futures	2,257	13,424	13,489	16,082	20,274
Gold Forward	1,520	25	10		
Gold Spot	95,494	155,947	132,747	173,752	278,476
Anhydrous Fuel Alcohol	53,963				
Bovespa Stock Index Futures	7,000,335	5,551,918	9,926,890	14,914,692	15,122,751
Interest Rate	37,626,151	22,235,992	35,150,416	36,466,961	49,541,598
Interest Rate Swap	6,656,112	8,224,534	8,562,215	11,660,972	6,313,852
Interesst Rate x Stock Basket Swap		18,586			
Interest Rate x Exchange Rate Swap	2,216,247	2,440,318	2,499,084	3,504,600	2,069,329
Interest Rate x Reference Rate Swap	33,753	80,140	83,256	139,929	161,159
Interest Rate x Inflation Index Swap (formerly Inflation)	67,468	17,163	4,496	10,324	6,486
Interest Rate x Basic Financial Rate Swap		18,985	16,187		
Interest Rate x Ibovespa Swap	33	42	4,113		1
ID x U.S. Dollar Spread Futures	5,059,141	2,126,164	3,013,081	52,587	99,631
ID Long-term Futures	78,340				
ID Forward with Reset	370,747				
C-Bond	983	646	6,581	296,758	608,798
EI-Bond	1,617	2,074	703	4,060	1,850
U.S. Dollar	20,208,454	11,420,923	18,573,100	40,387,111	45,132,135
Mini U.S. Dollar		110			
Exchange Rate Swap			6,333	71,713	58,885
Price Index x Exchange Rate			9	773	564
Gold on Actuals Options	119,512	283,221	88,932	141,880	363,089
Gold Exercise Options	34,114	35,634	41,928	81,542	150,144
U.S. $ Denominated Arabica Coffee Options	8,137	42,918	17,921	3,210	14,767
U.S. $ Denominated Arabica Coffee Exercise Options	1,041	4,856	1,103	1,256	29,249
Corn Options		10	122		
Corn Exercise Options		26			
Soybean Options		22	82		
Soybean Exercise Options		3			
Live Cattle Options	1,533		308	392	5,882
Bovespa Stock Options	5,365	26,020	103,860	359,846	201,757
Bovespa Stock Exercise Options	2,885	210	2,810	31,971	15,722
Interest Rate Options				375,435	761,541
Interest Rate (IDI) Exercise Options	134,920	22,461	57,015	57,390	30,550
Interbank Deposit Rate Index Options	584,398	908,004	1,605,106	348,990	
Fexible Bovespa Stock Index Options	116,976	257,870	333,582	618,424	167,918
U.S. Dollar on Actuals Options	1,328,215	694,483	3,405,413	7,211,258	5,180,578
U.S. Dollar Exercise Options	75,685	50,741	86,963	974,381	142,710
Flexible Currency Options	458,631	807,153	2,818,616	3,809,659	7,662,050
Total	**82,945,277**	**55,931,098**	**87,015,050**	**122,179,393**	**134,611,376**

Budapest Commodity Exchange (BCE), Hungary

	2000	1999	1998	1997	1996
Milling Wheat		3,785	35,164	108,431	65,454
Corn	41,956	48,918	37,941	77,992	44,253
Euro Wheat		747	17,254	2,263	
Feed Wheat	726	48	858	13,693	6,179
Feed Barley	1,369	2,518	2,139	10,330	5,982
Wheat	21,345	65,823	2,011		
Black Seed	845	7,351	9,623	4,448	2,580
Rapeseed	129	121			
Soybean	55	19			
TAX	17	2			
Ammonium Nitrate	67				
Europe I Live Hogs	106	198	198	249	191
Europe II Live Hogs	120	194	40	101	322
Deutsche Mark		200,027	5,823,625	2,731,592	751,130
U.S. Dollar	486,860	470,550	1,730,165	1,097,502	871,174
Japanese Yen	232,844	101,884	183,118	852,629	916,857
EUR	1,306,688	596,258			
British Pound	42,380	17,103	42,454	201,974	304,872
Swiss Franc	38,901	72,500	389,118	849,185	419,885
Czech Crown	72	1		2	
Corn Options	697	1,665	290		
Milling Wheat Options		250	360		
Black Seed Options	143	270			
Wheat Options	19	3,464	525		
Total	**2,175,339**	**1,593,696**	**8,454,122**	**6,573,857**	**5,427,393**

Budapest Stock Exchange (BSE), Hungary

	2000	1999	1998	1997	1996
3-Year Hungarian Government Bond	500	12,230			
Budapest Stock Index (BUX) Futures	839,978	1,555,939	1,993,353	1,208,388	136,920
DEM / HUF		5,975	503,539	183,470	25,429
EUR / HUF	22,536	33,527	1		
CHF / HUF	7,064	120	1,004		
GBP / HUF	1,000	150	1,602		
USD / HUF	74,790	25,106	144,368	55,116	20,439
All Futures on Individual Equities	456,510	181,031	71,158		
Budapest Stock Index (BUX) Options	8,516				
All Options on Individual Equities	1,218				
Total	**1,412,112**	**1,814,078**	**2,772,821**	**1,464,628**	**242,766**

EUREX, Frankfurt, Germany

(formerly Deutsche Terminborse (DTB))

	2000	1999	1998	1997	1996
DAX	11,524,330	12,876,982	6,937,139	6,623,287	5,452,505
MDAX		4,040	58,013	180,668	47,865
FOX	109,822	741			
NEMAX 50	702,873				
DJ Nordic STOXX 30		1			
DJ Euro STOXX 50	14,315,518	5,341,864	366,435		
DJ STOXX 50	355,801	326,136	94,771		
BUND		22,846,162	89,877,840	31,337,633	16,496,809
Euro-BUND	151,326,295	121,311,878	2		
Medium Term Notional Bond (BOBL)		6,473,320	31,683,256	24,299,906	18,269,169
Euro-BOBL	62,502,582	45,481,843			
1-Month Euribor	1,896	64,019	10,418		
3-Month Euribor	1,224,877	3,031,138	378,420		
3-Month Euromark	330	6,236	400,168	964,096	
Euro-BUXL		226	625		
Euro-SCHATZ	42,822,290	17,748,784			
SCHATZ		1,898,555	10,043,087	4,805,755	
Rollover BUND Mar/FGBL Jun		105,682			
Rollover BOBL Mar/FGBM Jun		50,005			
Rollover SHAZ Mar/FGBS Jun		12,761			
FEU3-LIB3 Rollover Facility		98			
SHAZ-FGBS Rollover Facility		1,970			
BOBL-FGBM Rollover Facility		857			
BUND FGBL Rollover Facility		10,660			
DAX Odd Lot**		68,670			
MDAX Odd Lot**		37			
DAX Options	31,941,562	32,613,783	29,948,503	31,521,286	26,042,463
FOX Options	50,926	652			
NEMAX 50 Options	473,297				
DJ Euro STOXX 50 Options	8,197,999	3,791,738	122,951		
DJ STOXX 50 Options	61,530	80,254	73,779		
BUND Options		1,799,617	6,827,203	702,882	205,520
Euro-BUND Options	26,291,123	24,940,113	5,000		
SCHATZ Options		35,546	378,448		
Euro-SCHATZ Options	1,954,183	450,836			
3-Month Euribor Options		2,966	900		
Euro-BOBL Options	2,436,491	1,787,840			
Medium Term Notional Bond (BOBL) Options		94,638	1,077,939	1,640,211	663,502
NEMAX 50 Component Equities Options	4,536,186	111,332			
DJ Euro STOXX 50 Component Equities Options	294,917				
All Options on German Equities	9,905				
All Options on Individual Equities	48,748,287	36,123,317	30,853,782	9,667,248	10,024,170
DAX Odd Lot** Options	17	319,632			
Total	**409,883,037**	**339,814,929**	**209,550,981**	**112,164,106**	**77,314,480**

* Odd lots are a result of the Euro conversion and are not included in the total volume figures.

EUREX, Zurich, Switzerland

(formerly SOFFEX)

	2000	1999	1998	1997	1996
Swiss Market Index (SMI)	4,586,219	6,515,036	4,445,396	1,810,698	1,720,053
Swiss Government Bond (CONF)	479,350	577,030	722,066	638,638	913,466
Medium Term Swiss Government Bond (COMI)		80	1,534	20,055	42,007
Swiss Market Index (SMI) Options	3,474,369	3,669,386	3,394,098	4,316,384	8,018,333
Swiss Government Bond (CONF) Options		1,650	3,423	5,289	26,446
Equity Options*	35,648,521	28,570,528	30,104,988	3,334,251	28,802,225
Total	**44,188,459**	**39,333,710**	**38,671,505**	**10,125,315**	**39,522,530**

* 1998 data reflects different contract size introduced in July. Not comparable with 1997 data.

Volume Worldwide

Helsinki Exchanges, Finland
(formerly the Finnish Options Market Exchange(FOM))

	2000	1999	1998	1997	1996
Finnish Government Bond		7,234	156,455	374,214	291,658
STOX Stock Future	853,872	820,574	811,834	640,268	275,172
FOX Index	20,990	273,808	236,220	246,907	203,138
FOX Index Options	7,628	270,133	267,959	684,704	404,161
All Options on Individual Equitites (STOX)	324,526	1,263,363	693,310	1,699,591	1,143,787
Total	**1,207,016**	**2,635,112**	**2,814,089**	**5,513,479**	**3,491,471**

FUTOP Clearing Centre, Denmark

	2000	1999	1998	1997	1996
Danish Government Bonds 8% 2003		658	9,042	422	
Danish Government Bonds 7% 2004	775	4,774		18,962	4,789
Danish Government Bonds 7% 2007		7,113	68,535	49,768	
Danish Government Bonds 6% 2009 (G09)	28,775	17,984			
Danish Government Bonds 5% 2005 (G05)	1,142				
6% 2026 Mortgage Bonds (A26)	50		38,234	44,395	58,590
6% 2029 Mortgage Bonds (A29)	2,693	10,842	15,722		
KFX Stock Index	995,934	1,093,917	289,424	252,571	303,856
Danish Government Bonds 6% 2009 (G09) Options	2,388	4,519			
Danish Government Bonds 7% 2007 Options		2,617	23,170	7,859	
KFX Stock Index Options	10,277	18,128	4,073	31,638	42,586
All Options on Individual Options	3,838	2,656	4,152	34,306	44,810
Total	**1,045,872**	**1,163,208**	**454,019**	**681,466**	**747,723**

International Petroleum Exchange (IPE), United Kingdom

	2000	1999	1998	1997	1996
Crude Oil	17,297,974	15,982,355	13,674,664	10,301,918	10,675,389
Gasoil	7,115,435	6,150,912	4,974,171	4,031,608	4,361,062
Fuel Oil		1,935			
Natural Gas - Seasons	50				
Natural Gas - Quarters	1,465				
Natural Gas BOM	2,555	4,270			
Natural Gas Daily (NBP)	5,440	12,000	3,160		
Natural Gas Monthly (NBP)	515,305	290,750	328,350	81,445	
Crude Oil Options	452,284	495,798	337,999	250,176	374,233
Gasoil Options	100,631	104,813	104,523	68,195	110,226
Total	**25,491,139**	**23,042,833**	**19,422,867**	**14,733,342**	**15,520,910**

Italian Derivatives Market of the Italian Stock Exchange, Italy

	2000	1999	1998	1997	1996
MIB 30 Index	4,260,085	5,094,312	5,896,238	4,463,034	2,675,238
Mini FIB 30 Index	358,439				
MIDEX	2,044	5,144	30,072		
MIB 30 Index Options	2,843,986	2,236,241	1,616,635	1,159,059	476,138
Equity Options	5,875,138	1,947,931	1,296,791	2,444,424	
Total	**13,339,692**	**9,283,628**	**8,839,736**	**8,066,517**	**3,151,376**

London Metal Exchange (LME), United Kingdom

	1999	1998	1997	1996	1995
High Grade Primary Aluminum	22,211,729	20,091,765	22,484,144	14,552,878	14,060,243
Aluminum Alloy	740,955	498,839	389,558	292,429	210,787
Copper - Grade A	16,789,674	15,699,702	15,099,842	18,484,367	17,530,263
Standard Lead	3,310,109	2,420,777	2,352,731	2,202,864	1,758,742
Primary Nickel	5,396,342	4,676,526	4,627,929	3,104,514	3,319,697
Special High Grade Zinc	7,341,620	5,742,948	7,390,436	4,852,942	5,241,931
Silver	1,773				
Tin	1,770,807	1,429,115	1,119,776	1,121,836	1,275,718
High Grade Primary Aluminum Options	1,502,276	909,526	1,659,879	1,030,703	1,241,596
Aluminum Alloy Options	1,037	1,031	535	242	96
Copper - Grade A Options	1,156,929	1,052,239	1,732,509	1,623,575	2,212,821
Standard Lead Options	114,498	36,862	34,531	30,992	22,262
Primary Nickel Options	250,823	119,406	60,645	54,646	83,637
Special High Grade Zinc Options	520,942	204,479	285,453	126,094	177,005
Tin Options	147,615	61,132	13,005	8,925	15,532
Primary Aluminum TAPOS	299,167	115,626	47,447		
Copper TAPOS	41,261	15,108	74,080		
Total	**61,597,557**	**53,075,081**	**57,372,500**	**47,487,007**	**47,150,330**

Korea Stock Exchange (KSE), Korea

	2000	1999	1998	1997	1996
KOPSI 200	19,666,518	17,200,349	17,893,592	3,252,060	715,621
KOPSI 200 Index Options	193,829,070	79,936,658	32,310,812	4,528,424	
Total	**213,495,588**	**97,137,007**	**50,204,404**	**7,780,484**	**715,621**

Korea Futures Exchange (KFE), Korea

	2000	1999
Korea Treasury Bonds	1,538,507	295,833
CD Interest Rate	2,801	349,812
U.S. Dollar	1,355,730	259,249
Gold	62,936	40,509
U.S. Dollar Options	16,705	61,398
Total	**2,976,679**	**1,006,801**

London International Financial Futures Exchange (LIFFE), United Kingdom

(LCE merged with LIFFE in 1996)

	2000	1999	1998	1997	1996
3-Month Short Sterling	22,606,948	27,272,559	33,750,746	20,370,846	15,793,775
3-Month Euromark		3,785,667	54,559,028	43,326,030	36,231,178
3-Month Eurolira		70,207	15,592,396	14,894,163	6,936,873
3-Month Euroswiss	4,621,559	5,956,797	7,381,809	4,746,234	3,299,058
3-Month ECU	5,249	739,667	262,997	534,457	602,518
3-Month Euribor	58,016,852	35,657,690	1,269		
3-Month Euroyen TIBOR	13,958	27,006	39,240	162,686	242,413
3-Month Euroyen LIBOR		15			
10-Year Euro EFB	4	3,897	14,190		
5-Year Euro EFB	4	1,487	8,185		
Long Gilt	5,350,705	8,421,533	16,185,316	19,651,565	15,408,010
5-Year Gilt	5	78	113,372		
Euro BTP	13,072	1,180,170			
Euro Bund		1			
Italian Government Bond		574,034	8,213,552	15,260,072	12,603,754
Japanese Government Bond	379,541	465,727	692,404	813,241	816,059
FTSE 100 Index	10,142,828	8,704,574	6,955,096	3,698,368	3,627,044
Mini FTSE 100 Index	29,765				
FTSE 100 techMARK	143				
FTSE Eurotop 100 Index	153,792	139,552	42,058		
FTSE Eurotop 300 Index		1,780			
FTSE Eurotop 300 Index ex. UK		15,070			
FTSE Estars Index	268	1,862			
FTSE Eurobloc 100 Index	2,099	1,750			
MSCI Euro Index	77,140	41,746			
MSCI Pan-Euro Index	166,135	22,172			
FTSE Mid 250 Index	8,706	47,663	65,219	68,280	34,068
Barley	3,567	6,526	11,142	15,325	17,892
BIFFEX (Baltic Freight Index)	3,244	16,085	23,595	45,059	60,577
Cocoa #7	1,636,322	1,862,119	1,786,090	1,857,065	1,688,921
Robusta Coffee	1,470,980	1,565,708	1,290,049	1,544,193	1,182,528
Potatoes in Bulk	15,045	15,850	24,697	22,933	21,330
Wheat	87,387	100,127	98,501	128,411	115,869
White Sugar	907,399	990,595	945,896	686,302	579,463
3-Month Short Sterling Options	4,167,648	6,451,680	7,348,877	2,662,716	2,213,494
3-Month Sterling Mid-curve Options	127,080	112,735	35,480		
3-Month Euromark Options		656,429	5,878,551	4,225,874	4,888,942
3-Month Euroswiss Options	68,922	89,777	154,477	31,390	45,568
3-Month Euribor Options	7,900,121	4,819,366			
3-Month Euribor Mid Curve Options	432,445	3,200			
3-Month Euro LIBOR Options Options	192	338,037			
Long Gilt Options	4,923	159,713	1,644,323	1,799,660	1,361,344
FTSE 100 Index (ESX) Options	6,285,819	4,858,373	3,512,173	7,188,349	6,738,955
FTSE 100 Index (SEI) Options	531,389	843,100	1,001,428		
FTSE Eurotop 100 Index Options	3,010				
FTSE Estar Index Options		1			
MSCI Pan-Euro Index Options		51			
FTSE 100 Index FLEX Options	71,898	58,878	27,855	32,985	65,701
Barley Options	157	280	40	206	22
BIFFEX (Baltic Freight Index) Options		862	1,350	149	728
Cocoa Options	7,119	22,758	25,317	27,838	57,094
U.S. Dollar Coffee Options	119,200	186,155	159,557	184,975	129,844
Potatoes Options	15	171	35	5	35
Wheat Options	15,610	41,436	10,784	9,326	8,758
White Sugar Options	121,671	105,932	97,949	21,062	13,268
Equity Options	5,484,873	3,601,383	3,307,913	4,295,877	4,298,010
Total	**131,054,809**	**120,040,031**	**194,394,159**	**209,425,578**	**170,806,206**

Volume Worldwide

Commodity and Monetary Exchange of Malaysia, Malaysia
(formerly the Kuala Lumpur Commodity Exchange)

	2000	1999	1998	1997	1996
Crude Palm Oil	308,622	388,105	353,545	935,595	498,118
3-Month KLIBOR	44,812	28,670			
Total	353,434	416,775	353,545	935,595	498,118

Kuala Lumpur Options & Financial Futures Exchange, Malaysia

	2000	1999	1998	1997	1996
KLSE Composite Index	366,942	436,678	771,244	382,974	71,278
Total	366,942	436,678	771,244	382,974	71,278

Marche a Terme International de France (MATIF), France

	2000	1999	1998	1997	1996
Notional Bond	43,317,155	6,130,969	23,284,475	33,752,483	35,321,843
Euro 5-Year		114,946	2,825,479	2,100,683	
Euro 2-Year		3,968			
30-Year Euro Bond		754	3,932		
3-Month Pibor	195,169	2,968,774	5,305,778	14,417,310	14,133,278
Sugar		4,614	86,762	144,849	193,024
Wheat #2	33,038	43,193	41,091		
Corn	27,677	7,158			
European Rapeseed Meal	212	132			
Rapeseed Oil	127				
Rapeseed	115,840	137,244	102,897	74,387	60,148
Euro Notional Bond Options	11,536	135,742	3,302,799	8,376,474	8,894,196
Euribor Options		31,990	484,057	2,788,126	3,107,113
Euro 5-Year Options		5,950	91,936	70,416	
Rapeseed Options	5,313	3,332			
Total	43,706,067	9,588,766	35,595,438	62,147,396	62,440,066

Marche des Options Negociables de Paris (MONEP), France

	2000	1999	1998	1997	1996
CAC 40 Stock Index 1 Euro		4,201,673			
CAC 40 Stock Index 10 Euro	18,249,903	20,973,911			
DJ Euro STOXX 50	999,596	437,447			
DJ STOXX 50	23,603	103,160			
DJ STOXX Sector Indices	6,243	1,131			
CAC 40 Odd Lot**		501,809			
CAC 40 Index (Short Term) Options		7,728,661	5,108,041	6,250,090	2,465,497
CAC 40 Index (Long Term) Options	84,036,775	75,652,724	2,752,536	3,285,383	2,126,001
DJ STOXX 50 Options	4,761	4,031	14,536		
DJ STOXX Sector Indices Options	339	215			
Euro STOXX 50 Options	38,356	131,106	106,457		
Equity Options*	89,434,383	68,095,743	28,953,142	5,565,057	3,980,856
CAC 40 Index (Short Term) Odd Lot** Options		186,197			
CAC 40 Index (Long Term) Odd Lot** Options		477,598			
Total	192,793,959	178,495,406	53,377,988	21,561,838	14,425,526

** Odd lots are a result of the Euro conversion and are not included in the total volume figures.

MEFF Renta Fija (RF), Spain

	2000	1999	1998	1997	1996
90-Day MIBOR Plus	68	12,980	1,886,299	2,462,893	1,275,222
360-Day MIBOR Plus		464	32,523	80,555	61,702
Euribor	306	11,321			
5-Year Notional Bond		37	44,893	9,731	
10-Year Notional Bond	1,094,548	3,614,750	15,662,560	21,046,078	18,535,566
30-Year Notional Bond		96	55,047		
10-Year Notional Bond Options	13,282	1,106	1,078,904	2,563,370	3,372,235
Euribor Options	127				
90-Day MIBOR Plus Options	42	2,400	150,683	400,311	249,806
Total	1,108,373	3,643,154	18,917,159	26,585,419	23,931,008

MEFF Renta Variable (RV), Spain

	2000	1999	1998	1997	1996
IBEX 35 Plus	4,183,028	5,101,588	8,627,374	6,053,283	
IBEX 35 Plus Options	766,078	861,255	1,681,205	1,411,101	
Equity Options	16,580,519	8,091,728	2,695,206	1,485,074	951,271
Total	21,529,625	14,054,571	13,003,785	8,949,458	4,739,599

Mercado a Termino de Buenos Aires, Argentina

	2000	1999	1998	1997	1996
Wheat	52,293	54,271	48,558	49,492	
Corn	46,672	39,475	42,486	42,125	
Sunflowerseed	26,910	34,080	23,576	19,312	
Soybean	53,672	43,882	29,069	26,934	
Wheat Options	18,240	26,930	20,567	24,490	
Corn Options	8,993	9,787	15,045	20,679	
Sunflowerseed Options	1,807	6,104	9,957	9,805	
Soybean Options	27,475	17,736	10,920	9,905	
Total	**236,062**	**232,265**	**200,178**	**202,742**	

Mercato Italiano Futures (MIF), Italy

	2000	1999	1998	1997	1996
10-Year BTP	1,786	188,650	1,293,408	2,851,585	2,240,085
30-Year BTP		70			
Euribor	180	20,890			
10-Year BTP Options			45,150	140,597	130,307
Total	**1,966**	**209,610**	**1,485,693**	**3,296,778**	**2,569,396**

Montreal Exchange (ME), Canada

	2000	1999	1998	1997	1996
3 Month Bankers Acceptance	4,992,957	6,047,542	6,803,028	4,139,777	2,415,563
10 Year Canadian Government Bond	1,501,264	1,598,463	1,836,937	1,272,970	1,072,111
5 Year Canadian Government Bond	222	23,768	45,113	50,944	35,649
S&P Canada 60 Index	1,272,244	262,058			
5 Year Canadian Government Bond Options		2,667	2,797	933	703
3 Month Bankers Acceptance Options	249,976	168,903	210,850	155,308	75,224
10 Year Canadian Government Bond Options	8,877	9,190	18,533	23,175	30,159
S&P Canada 60 Index Options	88,923	40,650			
i60 Index (XIU) Options	120,556				
Equity Options	4,753,495	1,439,476	1,375,274	1,016,945	660,962
Total	**12,988,514**	**9,592,717**	**10,292,532**	**6,660,052**	**4,290,685**

New Zealand Futures Exchange (NZFOE), New Zealand

	2000	1999	1998	1997	1996
3-Year Government Stock	3,867	2,356	18,240	43,967	14,356
10-Year Government Stock	8,024	2,853	9,948	17,265	8,565
90-Day Bank Bill	781,074	816,931	1,236,944	1,019,686	655,270
NZSE-10 Captial Share Price Index	1,087	1,842	2,138	3,038	5,686
New Zealand Electricity	450	1,564	3,092	4,596	
90-Day Bank Bill Options	22,906	11,600	410	1,810	8,845
Equity Options	65,390	24,621	71,847	117,669	144,207
Total	**882,798**	**861,767**	**1,342,892**	**1,208,078**	**836,982**

OM Stockholm (OMS), Sweden

	2000	1999	1998	1997	1996
Interest Rate	5,371,720	8,002,707	9,356,221	12,704,397	15,642,920
OMX Index	11,477,162	11,931,352	9,265,510	2,163,560	1,625,391
NOX Index	60	234			
All Futures on Individual Equities	2,144,767	1,129,453	533,508	288,841	272,514
Interest Rate Options	15,500	100	2,727	5,846	32,825
OMX Index Options	4,167,448	5,733,106	4,947,486	3,545,967	5,399,227
NOX Index Options	40	1,554			
Equity Options	30,691,587	26,824,117	20,589,273	19,485,816	12,920,145
Total	**53,868,284**	**53,622,623**	**44,694,725**	**38,194,473**	**35,896,860**

Oslo Stock Exchange (OSE), Norway

	2000	1999	1998	1997	1996
OBr10	10,960	21,116	36,423	58,518	55,376
OBr5	2,521	8,224	31,332	33,422	50,673
Forwards	260,521	170,950	57,938	1,630	
OBX	750,264	675,240	354,602	135,284	36,366
OBX Options	1,025,027	978,014	828,445	926,646	512,460
Equity Options	2,062,350	2,580,178	883,045	1,086,171	815,396
Total	**4,111,643**	**4,433,722**	**2,192,785**	**2,241,671**	**1,470,271**

Volume Worldwide

Shangai Metal Exchange (SME), China

	2000	1999	1998	1997	1996
Copper	2,674,016	2,559,687	2,772,124	1,299,520	
Aluminum	455,206	256,485	60,656	73,077	
Rubber	1,000,299	318,096	391,009		
Total	**4,129,521**	**3,134,268**	**3,223,797**	**1,372,671**	

Singapore Exchange (SGX), Singapore

	2000	1999	1998	1997	1996
Eurodollar	10,083,633	8,999,879	9,837,115	7,400,058	8,184,887
Singapore Dollar Interest Rate	61,300	18,725			
Nikkei 225 Index	4,484,978	5,429,843	5,537,558	4,844,495	4,887,912
Nikkei 300 Index	38,304	34,273	95,255	129,695	156,482
Straits Times Index	47,106				
S&P CNX Nifty Index	20,403				
Dow Jones Thailand Index	950	1,347	721		
MSCI Hong Kong Index		2,597	6,124		
MSCI Singapore Index	479,486	291,527	27,727		
MSCI Taiwan Index	3,390,153	2,362,385	1,842,977	677,295	
Brent Crude Oil	3,980	18,853	32,600	33,067	63,535
Euroyen TIBOR	7,149,469	6,777,548	8,757,516	9,624,680	8,162,548
Euroyen LIBOR	326,849	374,198			
Japanese Government Bond	718,353	168,829	194,373	132,104	138,471
Euroyen Options	57,095	234,630	661,008	481,138	208,363
Japanese Government Bond Options	299	1,962	2,211	11,658	18,709
MSCI Taiwan Index Options	1,107	8,828	20,521	7,550	
Nikkei 225 Index Options	708,498	1,137,716	838,891	628,222	586,660
Total	**27,571,963**	**25,863,140**	**27,861,162**	**24,090,285**	**22,568,545**

South African Futures Exchange (SAFEX), Africa

	2000	1999	1998	1997	1996
All Share Index	5,817,231	6,037,573	4,620,298	2,599,489	1,943,973
Industrial Index	3,303,760	2,838,168	2,709,146	1,960,260	1,493,987
Financial Index (FINI)	25,788	80,497	80,229		
Mining Index		1,260	3,210		
RESI	460	14,120			
3-Month Bank Bill		1,029	92	106	1,360
Johannesburg Interbank Rate (JBAR)	2,350	6,092			
R 150	1,600	1,723	8,375	8,489	39,640
R 153	1,063	1,026	8,394	5,924	101
All Futures on Individual Equities	29,991	82,901			
All Share Index Options	12,137,585	8,511,293	7,915,791	4,873,560	3,759,424
Industrial Index Options	1,063,434	973,633	713,337	1,282,555	913,342
Financial Index (FINI) Options	10,734	123,585	56,924		
Mining Index Options		3,200			
RESI Options		4,000			
R 150 Options		955	5,294	10,467	26,682
R 153 Options	3,099	2,720	5,957	20,085	2,060
Equity Options	1,992,579	82,576	152,960	75,360	
Total	**24,389,674**	**18,766,351**	**16,366,570**	**11,583,654**	**9,824,673**

Taiwan Futures Exchange, Taiwan

	2000	1999	1998	1997	1996
TAIEX	1,339,908	971,578	277,909		
Taiwan Stock Exchange Electronic Sector Index	409,706	87,156			
Taiwan Stock Exchange Bank & Insurance Sector Index	177,175	18,938			
Total	**1,926,789**	**1,077,672**	**277,909**		

Toronto Futures Exchange (TFE), Canada

(All trading has been moved to the Montreal Exchange)	2000	1999	1998	1997	1996
TSE 35 Index		374,525	440,851	317,408	155,652
TSE 100 Index		7,624	16,900	19,317	8,135
TSE 35 Options		250,960	388,273	431,623	254,199
Total		**633,109**	**846,024**	**768,399**	**418,831**

Sydney Futures Exchange (SFE), Australia

	2000	1999	1998	1997	1996
All Ordinaries Share Price Index	3,678,706	3,819,800	3,678,151	3,204,266	2,675,754
SPI 200	146,154				
DJ AP/ELS Australian Index		68			
90-Day Bank Bills	7,700,381	7,184,423	7,735,231	5,918,447	4,977,945
3-Year Treasury Bonds	12,372,147	10,787,444	10,485,750	10,378,357	9,209,228
10-Year Treasury Bonds	4,990,883	5,345,640	5,640,716	5,819,677	5,315,845
NSW Electricity	832	4,670	6,797	1,191	
NSW Peak Period Electricity	617	846			
VIC Electricity	421	2,130	4,615	1,129	
VIC Peak Period Electricity	448	557			
Wheat	6,110	8,017	9,692	7,937	6,482
Fine Wool	3,063	4,106	2,041		
Broad Wool	417	699	496		
Barley	161				
Canola	971				
Sorghum	2,188				
Greasy Wool	11,126	16,108	11,507	10,127	7,554
All Futures on Individual Equities	8,817	8,658	9,026	29,157	54,463
All Ordinaries Share Price Index Options	1,028,665	1,237,294	847,375	896,340	896,880
SPI 200 Options	70,254				
90-Day Bank Bills Options	326,638	453,048	770,229	984,363	911,005
Overnight 90-Day Bank Bills Options	1,003				
3-Year Treasury Bond Options	319,383	289,196	223,842	418,081	457,808
Overnight 3-Year Treasury Bond Options	477,192	217,959	64,394	43,540	42,461
10-Year Treasury Bonds Options	104,948	242,732	354,311	545,359	845,571
Overnight 10-Year Treasury Bond Options	47,373	169,347	90,015	149,817	128,426
Wheat Options	120	561	2,040	1,740	788
Greasy Wool Options	3	30	47	11	41
Total	**31,299,021**	**29,793,333**	**29,936,275**	**28,409,539**	**25,530,251**

Winnipeg Commodity Exchange (WCE), Canada

	2000	1999	1998	1997	1996
Wheat	164,981	106,378	146,713	197,619	206,120
Oats	503	375	3,970	3,205	3,496
Flaxseed	101,216	78,433	115,552	140,756	99,889
Canola (Rapeseed)	1,858,773	1,685,756	1,557,358	1,387,675	1,345,952
Feed Peas		70	3,286	14,247	17,979
Field Peas	15	4,520			
Western Barley	266,077	211,377	238,994	284,614	334,809
Wheat Options	210	115	537	250	355
Flaxseed Options	6,437	3,295	1,093	66	466
Western Barley Options	6,656	1,648	553	959	3,166
Canola Options	63,641	61,476	23,310	31,810	61,233
Total	**2,468,509**	**2,153,443**	**2,091,366**	**2,061,201**	**2,073,465**

Hong Kong Futures Exchange (HKFE), Hong Kong

	2000	1999	1998	1997	1996
Hang Seng Index	4,023,138	5,132,332	6,969,708	6,446,696	4,656,084
Mini Hang Seng Index	120,165				
Hang Seng 100 Index	30,991	66,822	15,450		
Hang Seng Properties Sub-Index		341			
Red Chip Index	3,801	30,753	170,385	143,078	
Rolling Forex	3,279	9,042	17,146	251,226	195,355
1-Month HIBOR	12,075	9,726	4,405		
3-Month HIBOR	325,155	308,646	502,982	87,819	
All Futures on Individual Equities	3,322	5,696	4,082	4,453	
Hang Seng Index Options	544,047	714,309	798,712	1,147,374	1,093,871
Hang Seng 100 Index Options	5,893	51,393	4,610		
Hang Seng Properties Sub-Index Options	2	2,330			
Equity Options	4,188,702	2,197,972			
Total	**9,260,570**	**8,529,372**	**8,506,788**	**8,333,106**	**6,140,665**

Volume Worldwide

Kanmon Commodity Exchange (KCE), Japan

	2000	1999	1998	1997	1996
Red Beans	37,689	92,622	200,215	95,982	118,438
Imported Soybeans	307,676	498,795	572,570	1,382,063	496,376
Non-GMO Soybeans	1,284,179				
Refined Sugar	1,443	1,421	1,433	1,421	1,438
Corn	2,357,240	2,897,402	2,951,184	5,069,142	4,346,586
Broiler	2,443,593	1,203,656			
Total	**6,431,820**	**4,693,896**	**3,725,402**	**6,548,608**	**4,962,838**

Kansai Agricultural Commodities Exchange (KANEX), Japan

	1999	1998	1997	1996	1995
Red Beans	177,039	450,610	483,330	877,474	1,723,230
Imported Soybeans	1,245,358	1,513,589	4,022,023	2,656,174	1,695,414
Refined Sugar	2,842	2,866	2,842	2,876	2,886
Raw Sugar	462,427	558,075	643,742	577,641	730,582
Raw Silk (formerly at Kobe Raw Silk Exchange)	178,114	231,376	327,009	458,243	591,922
Kansai International Grain Index	376,660	60,008			
Raw Sugar Options	30,363	70,561	47,189	71,145	79,365
Total	**2,472,803**	**2,887,085**	**5,526,135**	**4,643,553**	**4,823,399**

Central Japan Commodity Exchange (CJCE), Japan

(formerly CCE, NGSE, NTE, and TDCE)	2000	1999	1998	1997	1996
Red Beans	45,297	147,511	188,937	241,008	287,220
Imported Soybeans	372,475	348,567	505,345	1,010,201	620,703
Non-GMO Soybeans	65,642				
Refined Sugar	1,443	1,421	1,433	1,421	1,438
Dried Cocoon	146,737	240,841	277,944	684,141	1,202,536
Cotton Yarn (40S)	344,006	183,945	114,877	126,684	296,455
Staple Fiber Yarn (Dull)		1,913	9,194	9,948	10,001
Wool Yarn	482	12,351	33,973	35,315	27,277
Hen Egg	590,274	390,475			
Gasoline	11,048,071				
Kerosene	8,714,440				
Total	**21,328,867**	**1,327,024**	**1,131,738**	**2,108,766**	**2,445,678**

Osaka Securities Exchange(OSE), Japan

	2000	1999	1998	1997	1996
Nikkei 225 Index	7,426,478	9,067,883	8,191,130	7,484,182	7,043,977
Nikkei 300 Index	1,281,029	1,470,954	1,531,004	1,526,538	1,872,983
High-Tech Index	115	457	3,794		
Financial Index	115	471	3,576		
Consumer Index	116	459	2,626		
Nikkei 225 Index Options	5,715,856	5,753,760	5,230,046	4,910,359	3,924,543
Nikkei 300 Index Options	674	652	2,577	7,798	44,254
Financial Index Options		1	86		
Equity Options Options	103,556	683,778	363,901	222,094	
Total	**14,527,939**	**16,978,415**	**15,328,802**	**14,150,971**	**12,885,757**

Osaka Mercantile Exchange (OME), Japan

(formerly KRE and OTE)	2000	1999	1998	1997	1996
Staple Fiber Yarn (Dull)		705	4,338	4,952	2,928
Wool Yarn	184	8,062	15,677	22,589	18,624
Cotton Yarn (20S)	183,568	189,240	583,851	1,245,452	1,109,607
Cotton Yarn (40S)	83,508	34,378	42,993	147,444	254,828
Rubber (RSS3)	1,404,451	1,546,297	2,835,126	1,200,850	2,232,827
Rubber (TSR20)	213,758				
Rubber Index	1,561,707	1,355,731	672,582	382,913	373,879
Aluminum	1,695,737	2,218,159	1,107,266	160,060	
Total	**5,142,913**	**5,352,572**	**5,261,833**	**3,164,947**	**3,995,802**

Tokyo Commodity Exchange (TOCOM), Japan

	2000	1999	1998	1997	1996
Gold	7,841,692	16,011,962	9,373,909	8,871,965	9,510,941
Silver	558,770	966,838	1,679,647	792,844	752,995
Platinum	13,577,201	13,277,043	16,944,343	10,839,577	6,895,464
Palladium	1,007,307	5,832,649	5,194,391	3,817,892	434,163
Aluminum	543,015	710,782	305,436	567,175	
Gasoline	14,370,266	3,973,668			
Kerosene	6,741,173	1,441,163			
Rubber	6,195,440	6,193,292	9,975,520	4,758,390	9,085,709
Cotton Yarn	17,018	33,986	110,645	524,717	874,052
Woolen Yarn		778	5,832	5,789	6,830
Total	**50,851,882**	**48,442,161**	**43,589,723**	**30,178,349**	**27,560,154**

Tokyo Grain Exchange (TGE), Japan

	2000	1999	1998	1997	1996
American Soybeans	2,355,163	3,279,175	3,820,850	9,966,257	7,120,741
Non-GMO Soybeans	2,875,667				
Arabic Coffee	4,231,369	3,508,798	831,163		
Red Beans	680,751	1,378,169	1,953,638	2,542,760	2,847,511
Corn	8,341,227	8,107,879	7,267,045	13,840,721	16,034,716
Refined Sugar	2,886	2,842	2,886	2,842	2,876
Robusta Coffee	729,618	699,153	305,160		
Raw Sugar	1,561,657	1,042,427	789,778	1,279,550	1,045,438
American Soybean Options	84,819	79,955	97,599	263,990	275,269
Corn Options	113,888	141,578	201,269	44,220	
Raw Sugar Options	85,957	153,285	143,434	186,698	182,724
Total	**21,063,002**	**18,393,261**	**15,412,822**	**28,127,038**	**27,509,275**

Tokyo International Financial Futures Exchange (TIFFE), Japan

	2000	1999	1998	1997	1996
3-Month Euroyen TIBOR	17,077,791	14,572,255	21,162,012	25,523,583	29,334,830
3-Month Euroyen LIBOR	8,255	57,479			
U.S. Dollar /Japanese Yen	3,900	28,681	46,949	63,755	44,194
3-Month Euroyen Options	98,281	271,487	500,002	535,895	567,793
Total	**17,188,227**	**14,929,902**	**21,708,963**	**26,123,233**	**29,970,017**

Tokyo Stock Exchange (TSE), Japan

	2000	1999	1998	1997	1996
5-Year Government Yen Bond	112,226	111,975	195,207	118,447	220,955
10-Year Government Yen Bond	9,909,127	9,727,855	10,784,966	11,873,549	12,450,925
TOPIX Stock Index	4,148,776	3,157,441	2,727,070	3,035,724	2,857,272
Electric Appliance Index	2,610	182	2,671		
Transportation Equipment Index	31,064	239	429		
Bank Index	50,545	25,719	1,127		
TOPIX Options	2,630	2,030	583	9,356	13,444
10-Year Government Yen Bond Options	1,271,887	1,137,319	1,848,851	2,002,357	1,975,274
Total	**15,528,865**	**14,162,760**	**15,563,087**	**17,072,250**	**17,551,142**

Yokohama Commodity Exchange (YCE), Japan

(formerly Maebashi Dried Cocoon & Yokohama Raw Silk Ex.)	2000	1999	1998	1997	1996
Raw Silk	789,795	704,657	371,732	658,176	1,083,386
Internaional Raw Silk	387,081				
Dried Cocoon	208,119	191,048	520,698	565,423	864,703
Total	**1,384,995**	**895,705**	**892,430**	**1,223,599**	**1,948,089**

	2000	1999	1998	1997	1996
Total Futures	952,604,313	781,797,938	798,107,856	750,548,594	703,482,637
Percent Change	21.85%	-2.82%	6.29%	7.54%	-1.68%
Total Options	722,927,902	523,145,631	344,862,103	275,602,274	271,860,316
Percent Change	38.19%	51.02%	25.14%	-1.22%	-26.70%
Total	1,675,532,215	1,296,397,321	1,142,969,959	1,026,150,868	975,342,953
Percent Change	28.40%	13.42%	11.35%	5.10%	-8.03%

Conversion Factors

Commonly Used Agricultural Weights and Measurements

Bushel Weights:
wheat and soybeans = 60 lbs.
corn, sorghum and rye = 56 lbs.
barley grain = 48 lbs.
barley malt = 34 lbs.
oats = 32 lbs.

Bushels to tonnes:
wheat and soybeans = bushels X 0.027216
barley grain = bushels X 0.021772
corn, sorghum and rye = bushels X 0.0254
oats = bushels X 0.014515

1 tonne (metric ton) equals:
2204.622 lbs.
1,000 kilograms
22.046 hundredweight
10 quintals

1 tonne (metric ton) equals:
36.7437 bushels of wheat or soybeans
39.3679 bushels of corn, sorghum or rye
45.9296 bushels of barley grain
68.8944 bushels of oats
4.5929 cotton bales (the statistical bale used by the USDA and ICAC contains a net weight of 480 pounds of lint)

Area Measurements:
1 acre = 43,560 square feet = 0.040694 hectare
1 hectare = 2.4710 acres = 10,000 square meters
640 acres = 1 square mile = 259 hectares

Yields:
wheat: bushels per acre X 0.6725 = quintals per hectare
rye, corn: bushels per acre X 0.6277 = quintals per hectare
barley grain: bushels per acre X 0.538 = quintals per hectare
oats: bushels per acre X 0.3587 = quintals per hectare

Commonly Used Weights

The troy, avoirdupois and apothecaries' grains are identical in U.S. and British weight systems, equal to 0.0648 gram in the metric system. One avoirdupois ounce equals 437.5 grains. The troy and apothecaries' ounces equal 480 grains, and their pounds contain 12 ounces.

Troy weights and conversions: 100 kilograms = 1 quintal
24 grains = 1 pennyweight
20 pennyweights = 1 ounce
12 ounces = 1 pound
1 troy ounce = 31.103 grams
1 troy ounce = 0.0311033 kilogram
1 troy pound = 0.37224 kilogram
1 kilogram = 32.1507 troy ounces
1 tonne = 32,151 troy ounces

Avoirdupois weights and conversions:
27 11/32 grains = 1 dram
16 drams = 1 ounce
16 ounces = 1 lb.
1 lb. = 7,000 grains
14 lbs. = 1 stone (British)
100 lbs. = 1 hundredweight (U.S.)
112 lbs. = 8 stone = 1 hundredweight (British)
2,000 lbs. = 1 short ton (U.S. ton)
2,240 lbs. = 1 long ton (British ton)
160 stone = 1 long ton
20 hundredweight = 1 ton
1 lb. = 0.4536 kilogram
1 hundredweight (cwt.) = 45.359 kilograms
1 short ton = 907.18 kilograms
1 long ton = 1,016.05 kilograms

Metric weights and conversions:
1,000 grams = 1 kilogram

1 tonne = 1,000 kilograms = 10 quintals
1 kilogram = 2.204622 lbs.
1 quintal = 220.462 lbs.
1 tonne = 2204.6 lbs.
1 tonne = 1.102 short tons
1 tonne = 0.9842 long ton

U.S. dry volumes and conversions:
1 pint = 33.6 cubic inches = 0.5506 liter
2 pints = 1 quart = 1.1012 liters
8 quarts = 1 peck = 8.8098 liters
4 pecks = 1 bushel = 35.2391 liters
1 cubic foot = 28.3169 liters

U.S. liquid volumes and conversions:
1 ounce = 1.8047 cubic inches = 29.6 milliliters
1 cup = 8 ounces = 0.24 liter = 237 milliliters
1 pint = 16 ounces = 0.48 liter = 473 milliliters
1 quart = 2 pints = 0.946 liter = 946 milliliters
1 gallon = 4 quarts = 231 cubic inches = 3.785 liters
1 milliliter = 0.033815 fluid ounce
1 liter = 1.0567 quarts = 1,000 milliliters
1 liter = 33.815 fluid ounces
1 imperial gallon = 277.42 cubic inches = 1.2 U.S. gallons = 4.546 liters

ENERGY CONVERSION FACTORS

U.S. Crude Oil (average gravity)
1 U.S. barrel = 42 U.S. gallons
1 short ton = 6.65 barrels
1 tonne = 7.33 barrels

Barrels per tonne for various origins

Abu Dhabi	7.624
Algeria	7.661
Angola	7.206
Australia	7.775
Bahrain	7.335
Brunei	7.334
Canada	7.428
Dubai	7.295
Ecuador	7.58
Gabon	7.245
Indonesia	7.348
Iran	7.37
Iraq	7.453
Kuwait	7.261
Libya	7.615
Mexico	7.104
Neutral Zone	6.825
Nigeria	7.41
Norway	7.444
Oman	7.39
Qatar	7.573
Romania	7.453
Saudi Arabia	7.338
Trinidad	6.989
Tunisia	7.709
United Arab Emirates	7.522
United Kingdom	7.279
United States	7.418
Former Soviet Union	7.35
Venezuela	7.005
Zaire	7.206

Barrels per tonne of refined products:

Product	Barrels per tonne
aviation gasoline	8.9
motor gasoline	8.5
kerosene	7.75
jet fuel	8
distillate, including diesel	7.46

(continued above)

Product	Barrels per tonne
residual fuel oil	6.45
lubricating oil	7
grease	6.3
white spirits	8.5
paraffin oil	7.14
paraffin wax	7.87
petrolatum	7.87
asphalt and road oil	6.06
petroleum coke	5.5
bitumen	6.06
LPG	11.6

Approximate heat content of refined products:
(Million Btu per barrel, 1 British thermal unit is the amount of heat required to raise the temperature of 1 pound of water 1 degree F.)

Petroleum Product	Heat Content
asphalt	6.636
aviation gasoline	5.048
butane	4.326
distillate fuel oil	5.825
ethane	3.082
isobutane	3.974
jet fuel, kerosene	5.67
jet fuel, naptha	5.355
kerosene	5.67
lubricants	6.065
motor gasoline	5.253
natural gasoline	4.62
pentanes plus	4.62

Petrochemical feedstocks:

naptha less than 401*F	5.248
other oils equal to or greater than 401*F	5.825
still gas	6
petroleum coke	6.024
plant condensate	5.418
propane	3.836
residual fuel oil	6.287
special napthas	5.248
unfinished oils	5.825
unfractionated steam	5.418
waxes	5.537

Source: U.S. Department of Energy

Natural Gas Conversions

Although there are approximately 1,031 Btu in a cubic foot of gas, for most applications, the following conversions are sufficient:

Cubic Feet			MMBtu		
1,000	(one thousand cubic feet)	=	1 Mcf	=	1
1,000,000	(one million cubic feet)	=	1 MMcf	=	1,000
10,000,000	(ten million cubic feet)	=	10 MMcf	=	10,000
1,000,000,000	(one billion cubic feet)	=	1 Bcf	=	1,000,000
1,000,000,000,000	(one trillion cubic feet)	=	1 Tcf	=	1,000,000,000

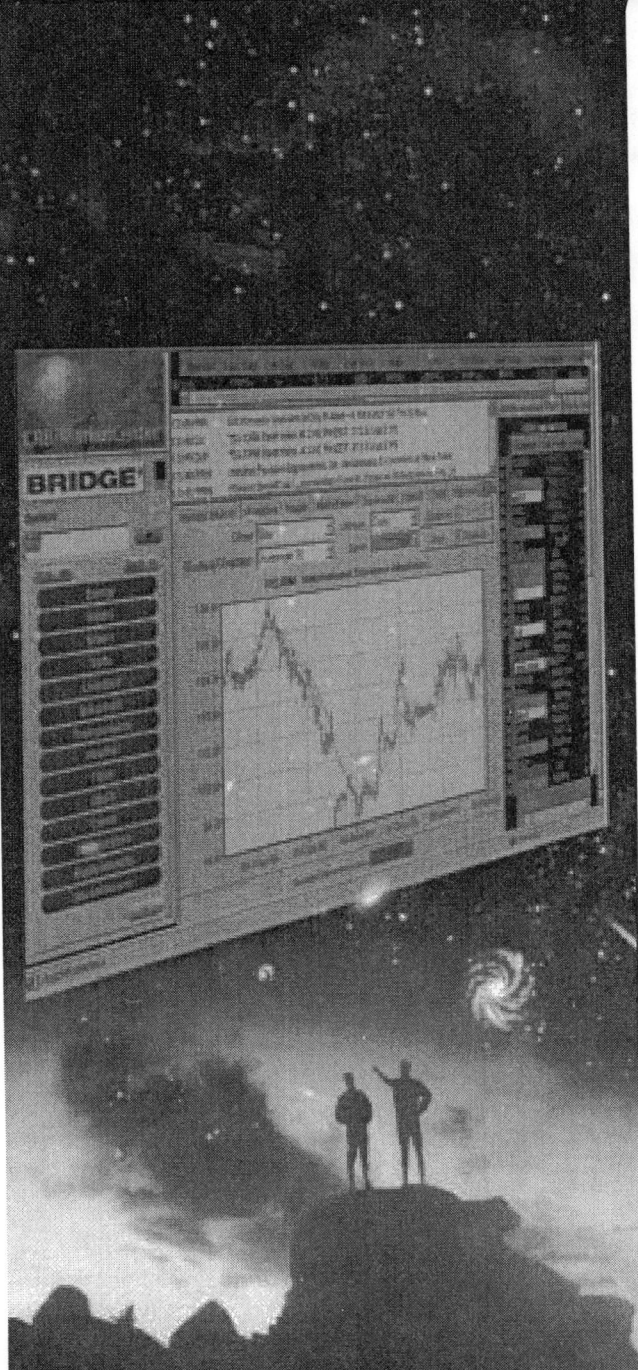

Aluminum

The U.S. Geological Survey reported that world smelter production of aluminum in 1999 was 22.7 million metric tonnes, up 3 percent from the previous year. The U.S. was the world's largest producer of aluminum with production in 1999 estimated to be 3.8 million tonnes, up 2 percent from the previous year. The next largest producer was Russia with 1999 output estimated at 3.1 million tonnes, up 3 percent from 1998. Production by Canada in 1999 was estimated at 2.38 million tonnes, about the same as in 1998. Other large aluminum producers include China, Australia, Brazil, and Norway. World production capacity in 1999 was estimated to be 25.4 million tonnes, up 1 percent from 1998. U.S. production capacity was 4.26 million tonnes, while Russia had capacity of 3.19 million tonnes. Other countries with large production capacity include China, Canada, and Australia.

In the U.S. in 1999, 12 domestic companies operated 23 primary aluminum reduction plants which produced almost 3.8 million tonnes of aluminum metal. Most of the production occurs in Montana, Oregon, and Washington. The transportation and the container and packaging industries were the largest markets for aluminum products in 1999. The transportation industry accounted for 37 percent of domestic consumption, while container and packaging took 24 percent. The building and construction industry took 15 percent of aluminum products, while consumer durables used 8 percent, and electrical 7 percent. The remainder used 9 percent.

U.S. primary production of aluminum in August 2000 was 296,000 tonnes, down 9 percent from the same month a year earlier. In the first eight months of 2000, U.S. primary production of aluminum was 2.5 million tonnes, virtually the same as in 1999. For all of 1999, production was 3.8 million tonnes.

There is substantial recovery of aluminum from secondary sources. In August 2000, secondary recovery of aluminum totaled 308,000 tonnes. Of the total, 181,000 tonnes came from new sources, while 126,000 tonnes came from old sources. In the January-August 2000 period, aluminum recovered from the secondary sources totaled 2.48 million tonnes, with 1.49 million tonnes from new sources and 987,000 tonnes from old sources. For all of 1999, secondary recovery of aluminum totaled 3.75 million tonnes, of which 59 percent came from new sources and 41 percent from old.

U.S. imports for consumption of aluminum crude metals and alloys, in July 2000, were 250,000 tonnes, up 2 percent from the previous month. In the January-July 2000 period, imports totaled 1.59 million tonnes. For all of 1999, metal and alloy imports totaled 2.65 million tonnes. Imports of aluminum plates, sheets, and bars in July 2000 totaled 73,000 tonnes, up 16 percent from the previous month. In the January-July 2000 period, imports of plates, sheets, and bars were 472,000 tonnes, while for all of 1999 they were 735,000 tonnes. Total aluminum imports for consumption in July 2000 were 323,000 tonnes, while in the first seven months of 2000 they were 2.07 million tonnes. In 1999, imports totaled 3.39 million tonnes. The total new supply (primary production, secondary recovery, and imports for consumption) in July 2000 was 920,000 tonnes. The total supply in the January-July period was 6.44 million tonnes, while for all of 1999 it was 10.9 million tonnes.

Futures Markets

Aluminum futures and options are listed on the London Metals Exchange (LME), the New York Mercantile Exchange (NYMEX), the Shangai Metal Exchange (SME), and the Tokyo Commodity Exchange (TOCOM).

World Production of Primary Aluminum   In Thousands of Metric Tons

Year	Australia	Brazil	Canada	China	France	Germany	Norway	Russia[3]	Spain	United Kingdom	United States	Venezuela	World Total
1991	1,228	1,140	1,822	963	286	690	833	3,251	355	294	4,121	601	19,700
1992	1,236	1,193	1,972	1,100	418	603	838	2,700	359	244	4,042	561	19,500
1993	1,381	1,172	2,308	1,220	426	552	887	2,820	364	239	3,695	568	19,800
1994	1,317	1,185	2,255	1,450	437	505	857	2,670	338	231	3,299	585	19,200
1995	1,297	1,188	2,172	1,680	372	575	847	2,724	361	238	3,375	630	19,700
1996	1,372	1,195	2,283	1,770	380	576	863	2,874	362	240	3,577	629	20,700
1997	1,495	1,200	2,327	1,960	399	572	919	2,906	360	248	3,603	634	21,600
1998[1]	1,627	1,208	2,374	2,340	424	612	996	3,005	362	258	3,713	585	22,500
1999[2]	1,718	1,250	2,390	2,450	400	600	1,034	3,146	360	272	3,779	570	23,100

[1] Preliminary.   [2] Estimate.   [3] Formerly part of the U.S.S.R.; data not reported separately until 1992.   Source: U.S. Geological Survey (USGS)

Production of Primary Aluminum (Domestic and Foreign Ores) in the U.S.   In Thousands of Metric Tons

Year	Jan.	Feb.	Mar.	Apr.	May	June	July	Aug.	Sept.	Oct.	Nov.	Dec.	Total
1991	349	317	352	340	353	343	354	350	336	347	337	343	4,121
1992	344	320	343	330	342	330	339	340	330	343	335	347	4,042
1993	335	292	323	313	325	315	316	302	291	303	287	294	3,695
1994	293	261	286	269	277	268	275	274	267	277	270	280	3,299
1995	281	253	280	272	285	277	288	286	280	289	285	299	3,375
1996	301	283	303	293	303	293	301	302	292	304	295	305	3,577
1997	305	277	307	295	304	296	305	304	294	307	298	310	3,603
1998	309	280	312	305	316	307	319	318	309	315	307	317	3,713
1999	315	287	320	309	319	310	319	324	310	323	316	328	3,779
2000[1]	329	308	327	316	327	299	296	296	291	300			3,707

[1] Preliminary.   Source: U.S. Geological Survey (USGS)

1

ALUMINUM

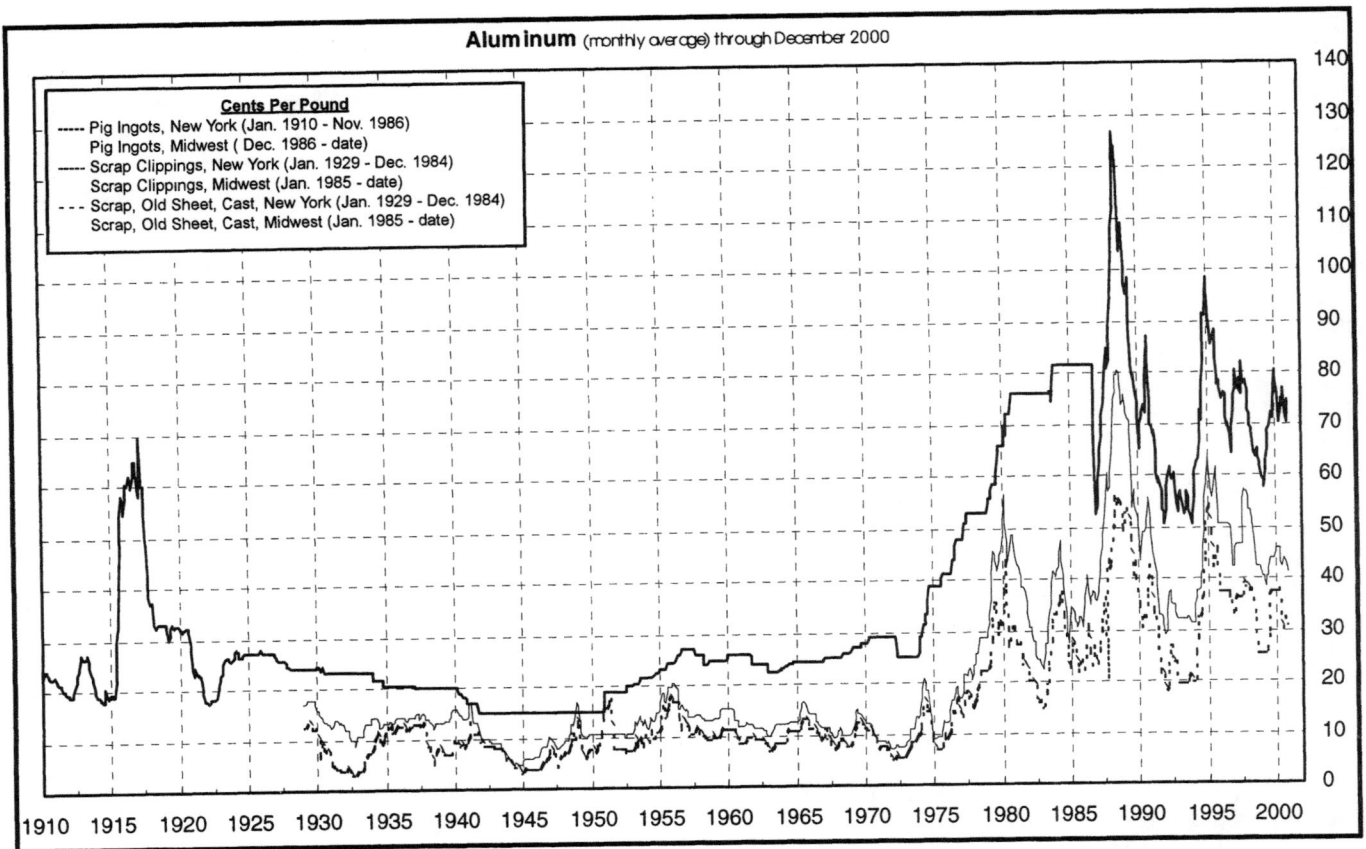

Aluminum (monthly average) through December 2000

Cents Per Pound
- ---- Pig Ingots, New York (Jan. 1910 - Nov. 1986)
- Pig Ingots, Midwest (Dec. 1986 - date)
- ---- Scrap Clippings, New York (Jan. 1929 - Dec. 1984)
- Scrap Clippings, Midwest (Jan. 1985 - date)
- --- Scrap, Old Sheet, Cast, New York (Jan. 1929 - Dec. 1984)
- Scrap, Old Sheet, Cast, Midwest (Jan. 1985 - date)

Salient Statistics of Aluminum in the United States   In Thousands of Metric Tons

| | | | | | | | | | Net Shipments[5] by Producers | | | | | | | |
| | | | | | | | | | Wrought Products | | | | Castings | | | Total |
Year	Net Import Reliance as a % of Apparent Consumption	Production Primary	Production Second-ary	Primary Ship-ments	Recovery from Scrap OLd	Recovery from Scrap New	Apparent Con-sumption	Plate, Sheet, Foil	Rolled Structural Shapes[3]	Ex-truded Shapes[4]	All	Perma-nent Mold	Die	Sand	All	All Net Ship-ments
1990	E	4,048	2,390	6,590	1,360	1,030	5,260	3,799	301	1,211	5,425	208	620	103	968	6,393
1991	E	4,121	2,290	6,400	1,320	969	5,040	3,787	311	1,096	5,300	168	575	97	864	6,156
1992	1	4,042	2,760	6,810	1,610	1,140	5,730	4,097	303	1,186	5,691	198	595	99	804	6,609
1993	19	3,695	2,940	7,300	1,630	1,310	6,600	4,030	297	1,300	5,770	225	645	103	994	6,770
1994	30	3,299	3,090	8,160	1,500	1,580	6,880	4,810	296	1,420	6,690	247	551	208	1,050	7,740
1995	23	3,375	3,190	8,260	1,510	1,680	6,300	4,900	526	1,540	7,130	442	627	207	1,440	8,580
1996	22	3,577	3,310	8,330	1,570	1,730	6,610	4,430	350	1,540	6,480	473	612	180	1,390	7,860
1997	23	3,603	3,550	8,880	1,530	2,020	6,720	4,710	315	1,610	6,800	468	670	153	1,410	8,210
1998	25	3,713	3,440	9,260	1,500	1,950	7,090	4,760	551	1,560	7,040	511	584	134	1,350	8,390
1999[1]	30	3,779	3,750	9,840	1,550	2,200	7,740	5,040	573	1,620	7,410	NA	NA	NA	NA	NA

[1] Preliminary.   [2] To domestic industry.   [3] Also rod, bar & wire.   [4] Also rod, bar, tube, blooms & tubing.   [5] Consists of total shipments less shipments to other mills for further fabrication.   NA = Not available.   E = Net exporter.   *Source: U.S. Geological Survey (USGS)*

Supply and Distribution of Aluminum in the United States   In Thousands of Metric Tons

Year	Apparent Consump-tion	Production Primary	Production From Old Scrap	Imports	Exports	Inventories December 31 Private	Inventories December 31 Govern-ment[2]	Year	Apparent Consump-tion	Production Primary	Production From Old Scrap	Imports	Exports	Inventories December 31 Private	Inventories December 31 Govern-ment[2]
1988	5,373	3,944	1,045	1,620	1,247	1,883	2	1994	6,880	3,299	1,500	3,380	1,370	2,070	57
1989	4,957	4,030	1,011	1,470	1,615	1,822	2	1995	6,300	3,375	1,510	2,980	1,610	2,000	57
1990	5,260	4,048	1,360	1,514	1,659	1,820	2	1996	6,610	3,577	1,570	2,810	1,500	1,860	57
1991	5,040	4,121	1,320	1,490	1,762	1,780	2	1997	6,720	3,603	1,530	3,080	1,570	1,860	[4]
1992	5,730	4,042	1,610	1,725	1,453	1,880	57	1998[1]	7,090	3,713	1,500	3,550	1,590	1,930	----
1993	6,600	3,695	1,630	2,540	1,210	1,980	57	1999[2]	7,740	3,779	1,550	4,000	1,640	1,870	----

[1] Preliminary.   [2] Estimate.   [3] National Defense Stockpile.   [4] Less than 1/2 unit.   Source: U.S. Geological Survey (USGS)

Aluminum Products Distribution of End-Use Shipments in the United States In Thousands of Metric Tons

Year	Building & Construction	Consumer Durables	Containers & Packaging	Electrical	Exports	Machinery & Equipment	Trans-portaion	Other	Total
1990	1,208	509	2,157	594	1,131	452	1,388	261	7,700
1991	1,052	472	2,210	579	1,357	426	1,414	241	7,752
1992	1,144	523	2,259	587	1,236	448	1,591	256	8,045
1993	1,240	563	2,180	609	1,090	477	1,970	259	8,390
1994	1,400	647	2,270	682	1,200	572	2,310	276	9,360
1995	1,220	621	2,310	657	1,310	570	2,610	279	9,570
1996	1,330	655	2,180	671	1,290	569	2,640	291	9,610
1997	1,320	694	2,220	708	1,360	626	2,990	318	10,200
1998	1,390	725	2,270	714	1,260	629	3,250	273	10,500
1999[1]	1,470	760	2,320	739	1,330	661	3,600	293	11,200

[1] Preliminary.   Source: U.S. Geological Survey (USGS)

World Consumption of Primary Aluminum   In Thousands of Metric Tons

Year	Brazil	Canada	China	France	Germany	India	Italy	Japan	Rep. of Korea	Russia	United Kingdom	United States	World Total
1990	341.2	387.2	861.0	723.0	1,295.4	433.3	652.0	2,414.3	368.9	2,790.0	453.7	4,330.4	19,275.4
1991	354.2	408.2	938.0	725.9	1,360.9	430.2	670.0	2,431.6	383.5	2,409.0	412.4	4,137.2	18,778.2
1992	377.1	420.4	1,253.8	730.5	1,457.1	414.3	660.0	2,271.6	397.0	1,242.0	550.0	4,616.9	18,529.5
1993	378.9	492.5	1,339.9	667.2	1,150.7	475.3	554.0	2,138.3	524.8	657.0	540.0	4,877.1	18,122.6
1994	414.1	559.0	1,500.1	736.3	1,370.3	475.0	660.0	2,344.8	603.9	470.0	570.0	5,407.1	19,670.8
1995	500.6	611.9	1,941.6	743.8	1,491.3	581.0	665.4	2,335.6	675.4	476.0	620.0	5,054.8	20,480.9
1996	497.0	619.9	2,135.3	671.7	1,355.4	584.8	585.1	2,392.6	674.3	443.8	600.0	5,348.0	20,627.3
1997	478.6	628.2	2,260.3	724.2	1,558.4	553.4	671.0	2,434.3	666.3	469.2	619.1	5,390.0	21,760.5
1998	521.4	733.5	2,425.4	744.2	1,580.0	566.5	673.5	2,079.9	505.7	489.2	668.3	5,813.6	21,894.8
1999[1]	463.1	773.7	2,945.8	735.4	1,430.7	554.0	746.2	2,099.7	814.0	480.0	499.3	6,203.3	23,073.0

[1] Preliminary.   Source: American Metal Market (AMM)

Salient Statistics of Recycling Aluminum in the United States

Year	Percent Recycled	New Scrap[1]	Old Scrap[2]	Recycled Metal[3]	Apparent Supply	New Scrap[1]	Old Scrap[2]	Recycled Metal[3]	Apparent Supply
		In Thousands of Metric Tons				Value in Millions of Dollars			
1990	38	1,034	1,359	2,393	6,298	1,688	2,218	3,906	10,280
1991	38	969	1,320	2,290	6,010	1,270	1,730	3,000	7,880
1992	40	1,140	1,610	2,760	6,870	1,450	2,040	3,500	8,710
1993	37	1,310	1,630	2,940	7,920	1,540	1,920	3,460	9,300
1994	36	1,580	1,500	3,090	8,460	2,480	2,360	4,840	13,300
1995	40	1,680	1,510	3,190	7,980	3,190	2,850	6,040	15,100
1996	40	1,730	1,570	3,310	8,340	2,730	2,480	5,200	13,100
1997	41	2,020	1,530	3,550	8,740	3,430	2,590	6,020	14,800
1998	38	1,950	1,500	3,440	9,040	2,810	2,160	4,970	13,100
1999	38	2,200	1,550	3,750	9,940	3,180	2,240	5,420	14,400

[1] Scrap that results from the manufacturing process.   [2] Scrap that results from consumer products.   [3] Metal recovered from new plus old scrap.
Source: U.S. Geological Survey (USGS)

Producer Prices for Aluminum Used Beverage Can Scrap   In Cents Per Pound

Year	Jan.	Feb.	Mar.	Apr.	May	June	July	Aug.	Sept.	Oct.	Nov.	Dec.	Average
1990	48.50	45.50	47.55	50.50	50.77	50.50	49.71	51.13	57.53	52.15	48.00	44.67	49.71
1991	49.00	49.11	48.67	42.09	37.86	37.00	39.79	37.50	37.50	35.76	35.18	34.50	40.33
1992	35.38	38.32	40.73	43.91	44.40	41.50	41.50	41.69	39.93	38.07	38.00	38.68	40.18
1993	41.00	41.00	38.04	36.63	35.00	35.00	37.52	37.59	36.50	34.19	33.60	34.78	36.74
1994	38.45	43.08	42.50	46.60	45.50	48.98	56.40	56.00	56.00	62.64	70.40	71.00	53.13
1995	74.85	72.24	65.00	65.00	65.00	65.00	65.00	67.98	64.80	58.45	57.00	58.50	64.91
1996	57.73	56.00	56.24	58.90	59.00	49.70	47.50	49.25	50.20	48.50	49.03	53.50	52.96
1997	56.98	59.00	59.00	58.27	58.05	58.05	58.32	59.60	59.50	59.13	59.00	57.12	58.50
1998	54.53	57.00	57.00	52.95	49.85	47.09	45.50	44.50	46.21	44.50	44.50	46.14	49.15
1999	44.50	44.50	44.20	45.68	47.45	46.50	48.40	49.00	49.00	53.79	55.50	57.64	48.84

Source: American Metal Market (AMM)

ALUMINUM

Average Price of Cast Aluminum Scrap (Crank Cases) in Chicago   In Cents Per Pound

Year	Jan.	Feb.	Mar.	Apr.	May	June	July	Aug.	Sept.	Oct.	Nov.	Dec.	Average
1991	33.50	32.00	32.00	30.64	28.45	22.40	21.50	21.50	21.13	19.00	18.11	18.00	24.85
1992	18.71	23.00	26.91	27.00	24.45	24.00	24.00	24.00	21.21	19.50	19.50	19.50	22.65
1993	19.50	19.50	19.50	19.50	19.50	19.50	20.79	21.00	20.62	20.00	20.00	20.00	19.95
1994	20.00	25.79	28.33	32.50	32.50	33.18	35.90	36.50	41.07	44.45	50.50	53.50	36.19
1995	53.53	54.08	49.02	48.50	44.41	42.50	43.76	45.80	45.05	39.27	37.50	37.50	45.08
1996	37.50	37.50	37.50	37.50	37.50	37.50	37.50	36.50	35.40	33.80	33.50	33.50	36.27
1997	36.09	36.50	36.50	36.50	36.50	36.50	36.50	39.36	38.60	38.50	38.50	38.07	37.34
1998	37.50	37.50	37.50	35.95	35.50	31.59	25.50	25.50	25.50	25.50	25.50	25.50	30.71
1999	25.50	25.50	25.50	25.50	26.45	29.23	36.83	37.50	37.50	37.50	37.50	37.50	31.87
2000	37.50	37.50	37.50	35.55	31.09	30.32	30.30	32.00	32.00	31.09	31.00	31.00	33.07

Source: American Metal Market (AMM)

Aluminum Exports of Crude Metal and Alloys from the United States   In Thousands of Metric Tons

Year	Jan.	Feb.	Mar.	Apr.	May	June	July	Aug.	Sept.	Oct.	Nov.	Dec.	Total
1991	61.1	54.8	46.7	82.8	56.4	71.3	69.0	80.1	54.6	68.0	80.7	67.3	792.8
1992	50.8	43.8	49.7	38.6	33.6	39.8	50.0	50.3	40.4	82.1	50.5	73.5	603.1
1993	54.8	38.6	41.7	26.3	38.6	30.7	33.9	24.5	27.9	31.7	24.1	27.6	400.4
1994	22.1	18.3	28.3	17.9	37.5	30.5	30.6	38.3	40.3	24.8	26.1	24.1	338.9
1995	26.1	32.7	25.4	31.1	31.4	20.7	26.6	39.2	38.9	33.0	30.4	33.6	369.1
1996	23.1	27.9	31.2	34.3	46.2	54.3	36.3	33.7	30.2	40.3	33.2	26.2	416.9
1997	31.0	25.5	22.5	33.0	24.1	34.9	23.9	33.2	34.4	26.5	33.0	30.0	352.0
1998	21.2	21.4	21.8	17.4	22.6	21.8	20.9	21.5	28.0	23.9	20.4	24.7	265.6
1999	18.6	26.7	23.9	22.7	25.2	27.7	23.7	27.5	26.1	31.4	30.3	34.8	318.6
2000[1]	18.7	27.2	30.2	21.9	24.4	22.4	20.5	24.2	20.5				280.0

[1] Preliminary.   *Source: U.S. Geological Survey (USGS)*

Aluminum General Imports of Crude Metal and Alloys into the United States   In Thousands of Metric Tons

Year	Jan.	Feb.	Mar.	Apr.	May	June	July	Aug.	Sept.	Oct.	Nov.	Dec.	Total
1991	79.5	79.4	84.3	88.2	85.1	75.9	97.3	89.0	86.6	90.4	81.0	88.0	1,024.7
1992	100.7	93.1	97.1	94.6	96.3	87.8	82.4	103.4	94.3	108.4	100.5	96.8	1,155.4
1993	120.8	123.9	165.8	172.0	152.1	152.6	125.1	162.7	173.5	149.4	182.9	155.6	1,836.4
1994	200.2	157.8	282.0	206.9	251.9	179.3	202.8	198.3	160.0	183.4	240.1	222.2	2,484.9
1995	214.0	168.0	204.0	195.0	184.0	172.0	136.0	134.0	117.0	137.0	139.0	133.0	1,933.0
1996	158.0	150.0	148.0	188.0	176.0	169.0	139.0	149.0	136.0	170.0	147.0	180.0	1,910.0
1997	145.0	147.0	209.0	196.0	198.0	167.0	157.0	152.0	150.0	175.0	146.0	222.0	2,060.0
1998	220.0	204.0	202.0	200.0	189.0	243.0	170.0	204.0	198.0	198.0	189.0	177.0	2,394.0
1999	191.0	200.0	240.0	311.0	281.0	258.0	213.0	219.0	178.0	202.0	178.0	180.0	2,651.0
2000[1]	246.0	213.0	206.0	211.0	233.0	234.0	250.0	206.0	189.0				2,650.7

[1] Preliminary.   *Source: U.S. Geological Survey (USGS)*

Average Open Interest of Aluminum Futures in New York   In Contracts

Year	Jan.	Feb.	Mar.	Apr.	May	June	July	Aug.	Sept.	Oct.	Nov.	Dec.
1999	----	----	----	----	1,032	1,461	1,875	1,984	1,767	1,244	625	615
2000	794	580	254	326	965	2,035	3,938	4,803	4,580	4,598	3,587	2,046

Source: New York Mercantile Exchange (NYMEX), COMEX Division

Volume of Trading of Aluminum Futures in New York   In Contracts

Year	Jan.	Feb.	Mar.	Apr.	May	June	July	Aug.	Sept.	Oct.	Nov.	Dec.	Total
1999	----	----	----	----	6,179	5,875	5,275	3,373	3,114	2,801	639	722	27,978
2000	1,224	2,394	1,664	1,901	3,859	3,566	6,295	3,767	5,993	6,365	5,055	4,016	46,099

Source: New York Mercantile Exchange (NYMEX), COMEX Division

Antimony

Antimony is primarily a byproduct of the mining, smelting, and refining of lead and silver-copper ores. In the U.S., one silver mine in Idaho produced antimony as a byproduct. Primary antimony metal and oxide was produced by five companies at processing plants that used foreign feedstock and a small amount of domestic feed materials. Antimony is used in the production of flame retardants, ceramics, glass, ammunition, and chemicals.

The U.S. Geological Survey reported that world mine production of antimony in 1999 was 138,000 metric tonnes, a decline of 1 percent from 1998. By far the largest producer of antimony was China with 1999 mine production estimated at 120,000 tonnes, unchanged from the previous year. Other producers of antimony include Bolivia with 5,000 tonnes, Russia with 3,000 tonnes, and South Africa with 3,000 tonnes. U.S. production of antimony was estimated at 480 tonnes in 1999. World antimony reserves in 1999 were estimated at 2.1 million tonnes. Most reserves are located in China with other significant reserves in Russia, Bolivia, and South Africa.

U.S. production of primary smelter antimony in second quarter 2000 was 5,100 tonnes, nearly all of which was antimony trioxide. For all of 1999, primary smelter production of antimony was 23,800 tonnes. Secondary production of antimony in second quarter 2000 was 617 tonnes, down 19 percent from the first quarter. For all of 1999, secondary production of antimony was 8,220 tonnes.

U.S. imports for consumption of antimony in the April-May 2000 period were 6,310 tonnes. For 1999, antimony imports totaled 36,800 tonnes. Antimony ore and concentrate imports in April-May 2000 were 349 tonnes, while for all of 1999 they were 2,870 tonnes. Antimony metal imports in April-May 2000 were 3,350 tonnes, and for all of 1999 they were 14,800 tonnes. Antimony oxide imports in April-May 2000 were 2,620 tonnes, while for all of 1999 they were 19,100 tonnes.

Exports of antimony products in April-May 2000 were 759 tonnes. For all of 1999, they were 3,660 tonnes. Exports of metal, alloys, and scrap in April-May 2000 totaled 162 tonnes and in 1999 totaled 473 tonnes. Antimony oxide exports in April-May 2000 were 597 tonnes. For 1999, antimony oxide exports were 3,190 tonnes.

Consumption of primary antimony in second quarter 2000 was 3,550 tonnes and in 1999 totaled 12,800 tonnes.

World Mine Production of Antimony (Content of Ore)   In Metric Tons

Year	Australia	Bolivia	Canada	China[2]	Guatemala	Kyrgyzstan	Mexico[3]	Peru[4]	Russia	South Africa	Thailand	Turkey	World Total
1996	1,800	6,488	1,716	129,000	880	1,200	983	460	6,000	5,137	70	285	155,000
1997	1,900	5,999	529	131,000	880	1,200	1,909	460	6,000	3,415	60	31	155,000
1998[1]	1,800	4,735	428	97,400	440	150	1,301	460	4,000	4,243	200	30	117,000
1999[2]	1,800	4,800	566	100,000	440	100	1,500	460	4,000	6,000	190	30	122,000

[1] Preliminary.   [2] Estimate.   [3] Includes antimony content of miscellaneous smelter products.   [4] Recoverable.   W = Withheld proprietary data; not included in total.   *Source: U.S. Geological Survey (USGS)*

Salient Statistics of Antimony in the United States   In Metric Tons

Year	Avg. Price cents/lb. CIF U.S. Ports	Production[3] Primary[2] Mine	Production[3] Primary[2] Smelter	Production[3] Secondary (Alloys)[2]	Imports for Consumption Ore Gross Weight	Imports for Consumption Ore Antimony Content	Imports for Consumption Oxide (Gross Weight)	Exports (Oxide)	Industry Stocks, December 31[3] Metallic	Industry Stocks, December 31[3] Oxide	Industry Stocks, December 31[3] Sulfide	Industry Stocks, December 31[3] Other	Industry Stocks, December 31[3] Total[4]
1996	146.5	242	25,600	7,780	1,610	1,000	22,100	3,990	3,520	4,420	W	3,060	11,000
1997	97.8	356	26,400	7,550	1,530	1,300	27,900	3,230	3,070	4,530	W	3,240	10,800
1998[1]	71.8	498	24,000	7,710	2,640	2,020	23,000	3,270	2,920	4,610	W	3,060	10,600
1999[2]	62.7	449	23,800	8,220	3,590	2,870	23,100	3,190	2,430	5,550	W	2,720	10,700

[1] Preliminary.   [2] Estimate.   [3] Antimony content.   [4] Including primary antimony residues & slag.   W = Withheld proprietary data.
Source: U.S. Geological Survey (USGS)

Industrial Consumption of Primary Antimony in the United States   In Metric Tons (Antimony Content)

Year	Metal Products Ammunition	Metal Products Antimonial Lead	Metal Products Sheet & Pipe	Metal Products Bearing Metal & Bearings	Metal Products Solder	Metal Products Total All Metal Products	Non-Metal Products Flame Retardants Plastics	Non-Metal Products Flame Retardants Total	Non-Metal Products Ceramics & Glass	Non-Metal Products Pigments	Non-Metal Products Plastics	Non-Metal Products Total	Grand Total
1996	W	1,760	W	44	256	3,110	6,850	7,770	1,030	450	1,080	2,690	13,600
1997	W	1,180	W	45	226	2,600	6,610	7,560	1,080	824	1,230	3,310	13,500
1998	W	1,710	W	33	153	2,580	5,460	6,190	1,110	1,130	1,460	3,910	12,700
1999[1]	W	1,760	W	32	135	2,440	5,640	6,410	1,120	1,020	1,580	3,940	12,800

[1] Preliminary.   [2] Estimated coverage based on 77% of the industry.   W=Withheld proprietary data.   *Source: U.S. Geological Survey (USGS)*

Average Price of Antimony[1] in the United States   In Cents Per Pound

Year	Jan.	Feb.	Mar.	Apr.	May	June	July	Aug.	Sept.	Oct.	Nov.	Dec.	Average
1997	127.50	127.50	115.95	106.50	106.50	106.50	105.27	93.00	94.90	98.00	98.00	86.00	105.47
1998	80.00	80.00	80.00	80.00	74.38	71.25	66.25	61.50	62.50	65.00	65.00	65.00	70.91
1999	65.00	65.00	65.00	65.55	66.50	66.50	66.50	66.50	66.50	66.50	66.50	66.50	66.05
2000	66.50	66.50	66.50	66.50	66.50	66.50	68.38	69.00	84.40	91.00	91.00	91.00	74.48

[1] Prices are for antimony metal (99.65%) merchants, minimum 18-ton containers, c.i.f. U.S. Ports.   *Source: American Metal Market (AMM)*

Apples

The U.S.D.A. reported that apple bearing acreage in 1999 was estimated at 461,500 acres, down 1 percent from the 1998 total. The yield per acre was estimated at 11.5 tons. Apple production in 1999 was 10.58 billion pounds, including harvested and unharvested fruit, down 9 percent from 1998 production of 11.65 billion pounds. Utilization of apples in 1999 was 10.39 billion pounds, down 3 percent from 1998. In terms of utilization, the fresh market consumed 5.96 billion pounds of apples, down 7 percent from the previous year. Utilization of apples for processing totaled 4.43 billion pounds in 1999, up 2 percent from the previous year.

In terms of the processed apple market, apples used for canning in 1999 were 1.35 billion pounds, up 15 percent from the previous year. Use of apples for the making of juice and cider totaled 2.46 billion pounds, down 1 percent from the previous season. Apples used for frozen products were 215 million pounds, down 19 percent from the previous year, while dried apples used 278 million pounds.

In the 1999/2000 (Aug.-Sept.) season, U.S. imports of fresh apples were 376 million pounds, up 9 percent from 1998. Exports were 1.18 billion pounds. Total fresh apple consumption was 5.17 billion pounds; per capita consumption was 18.84 pounds.

World Production of Apples[3], Fresh (Dessert & Cooking)   In Thousands of Metric Tons

Year	Argentina	Canada	France	Germany	Hungary	Italy	Japan	Netherlands	South Africa	Spain	Turkey	United States	World Total
1990-1	950	540	1,895	2,222	945	2,102	1,053	431	542	635	1,900	4,398	21,224
1991-2	1,043	513	1,236	1,165	859	1,869	760	223	605	517	1,900	4,413	18,250
1992-3	947	564	2,398	3,228	666	2,394	1,039	640	633	1,095	2,100	4,798	35,443
1993-4	1,006	488	2,079	1,719	819	2,145	1,011	670	638	891	2,080	4,847	36,505
1994-5	1,146	554	2,166	2,080	610	2,153	989	590	577	739	2,095	5,217	37,712
1995-6	1,254	608	2,089	1,373	353	1,889	963	595	703	843	2,100	4,801	36,443
1996-7	1,300	513	2,047	1,878	552	2,025	899	490	639	894	2,200	4,714	40,825
1997-8	1,202	503	2,027	1,465	500	2,014	993	470	671	880	2,550	4,683	40,564
1998-9[1]	1,275	523	1,794	2,077	450	2,243	879	507	660	700	2,450	5,165	43,349
1999-00[2]	----	515	2,080	1,837	420	2,293	941	575	----	819	2,500	4,791	40,795

[1] Preliminary.   [2] Estimate.   [3] Commercial crop.   *Source: Foreign Agricultural Service, U.S. Department of Agriculture (FAS-USDA)*

Salient Statistics of Apples[2] in the United States

| | Production | | Growers Prices | | Utilization of Quantities Sold | | | | | | | Foreign Trade[4] | | | Fresh |
| | | | | | | | Processed[5] | | | | | | Domestic | | | Per Capita |
Year	Total	Utilized	Fresh cents/lb.	Processing $/ton	Fresh	Canned	Dried	Frozen	Juice & Cider	Other[3]	Avg. Farm Price cents /lb.	Farm Value Million $	Exports Fresh	Dried[5] & Dried[5]	Imports Fresh & Dried[5]	Consumption Lbs.
					Millions of Pounds								Metric Tons			
1990	9,657	9,618	20.9	144.0	5,515	1,378	270	304	2,077	74	15.1	1,447.7	371.3	55.5	122.0	19.6
1991	9,707	9,637	25.1	171.0	5,447	1,311	299	286	2,194	100	17.9	1,727.0	530.1	44.2	143.9	18.2
1992	10,569	10,463	19.5	130.0	5,767	1,498	324	247	2,472	155	13.6	1,428.0	487.8	22.1	139.3	19.3
1993	10,685	10,574	18.4	107.0	6,124	1,335	366	282	2,382	85	12.9	1,363.8	662.9	19.2	130.9	19.2
1994	11,501	11,333	18.6	114.0	6,366	1,406	415	304	2,707	133	12.9	1,466.9	663.1	25.1	171.7	19.6
1995	10,578	10,384	24.0	159.0	5,840	1,292	334	305	2,538	78	17.0	1,767.0	565.0	24.6	202.9	18.9
1996	10,382	10,330	20.8	171.0	6,207	1,294	317	268	2,185	61	15.9	1,641.5	689.7	20.4	187.5	19.0
1997	10,324	10,254	22.1	130.0	5,815	1,499	267	349	2,145	180	15.4	1,575.4	656.8	18.0	158.7	18.4
1998	11,646	10,763	17.3	94.6	6,413	1,174	330	266	2,485	95	12.2	1,322.3	559.1		142.0	19.4
1999[1]	10,580	10,392	21.2	121.0	5,964	1,348	278	215	2,460	126	14.8	1,678.9	610.8		164.2	18.8

[1] Preliminary.   [2] Commercial crop.   [3] Mostly crushed for vinegar, jam, etc.   [4] Year beginning July.   [5] Fresh weight basis.
Source: Economic Research Service, U.S. Department of Agriculture (ERS-USDA)

Price of Apples Received by Growers (for Fresh Use) in the United States   In Cents Per Pound

Year	Jan.	Feb.	Mar.	Apr.	May	June	July	Aug.	Sept.	Oct.	Nov.	Dec.	Average
1991	20.1	20.5	20.3	20.2	22.5	23.2	24.6	23.2	26.4	23.8	25.1	25.7	23.0
1992	24.6	24.8	24.3	24.1	25.0	25.2	28.6	33.3	27.1	21.2	19.4	19.9	24.8
1993	18.3	16.7	14.5	14.3	14.9	16.1	17.8	24.4	24.1	21.1	19.3	18.6	18.3
1994	18.7	17.8	16.6	15.5	14.3	13.5	19.4	29.0	20.8	19.2	16.4	19.2	18.4
1995	19.5	18.3	18.2	16.6	15.4	15.6	17.5	24.5	26.0	25.1	23.5	24.0	20.4
1996	25.4	24.2	25.1	22.6	21.9	21.9	23.3	25.2	30.2	24.6	23.2	22.6	24.2
1997	22.5	20.3	17.6	15.6	14.3	13.7	14.6	19.2	25.9	25.3	23.0	23.3	19.6
1998	21.9	20.8	20.5	19.4	17.8	16.3	12.7	13.8	22.6	22.1	17.5	14.9	18.4
1999	15.8	15.0	15.3	14.1	13.3	12.7	16.3	22.7	21.6	24.3	22.9	23.2	18.1
2000[1]	21.8	21.1	20.5	19.7	18.2	16.1	16.2	19.5	23.3	21.8	18.5	18.1	19.6

[1] Preliminary.   Source: Economic Research Service, U.S. Department of Agriculture (ERS-USDA)

Arsenic

The U.S. Geological Survey reported that no arsenic was removed from domestic ores in the United States in 1999. All arsenic metals and compounds used in the U.S. are imported. More than 95 percent of the arsenic consumed is in compound form, mostly as arsenic trioxide which in turn is converted into arsenic acid. Production of chromated copper arsenate, a wood preservative, accounts for over 90 percent of the domestic consumption of arsenic trioxide. Chromated copper arsenate is manufactured by three companies in the U.S., while another company uses arsenic acid to produce arsenical herbicide. Arsenic metal is used to produce nonferrous alloys, primarily lead-acid batteries.

One area where arsenic does seem to have a future is in the semiconductor industry. Very high-purity arsenic is used in the production of gallium arsenide. High speed and high frequency integrated circuits that use gallium arsenide have better signal reception and lower power consumption. It is estimated that 15 tonnes per year of high-purity arsenic is used in the production of semiconductor materials.

The largest market for arsenic in the U.S. is the production of arsenical wood preservatives. Demand for arsenic is therefore highly related to the home construction industry. The U.S. Geological Survey reports that the U.S. is probably the world's largest consumer of arsenic. Demand for arsenic in the U.S. in 1999 was estimated to be 22,000 metric tonnes. Three companies in the Unites States account for the largest end use of arsenic trioxide in the production of wood preservatives.

Arsenic metal is used as an additive to improve corrosion resistance and tensile strength in copper alloys and as an additive to increase the strength of posts and grids in some lead-acid storage batteries. Arsenic also finds use in herbicides for weed control.

World production of arsenic trioxide in 1999 was estimated to be 41,500 metric tonnes, up 2 percent from 1998. The largest producer of arsenic trioxide is China with 1999 output of 16,000 tonnes. Other large producers include Chile, Ghana, Belgium, Mexico, France, and Kazakhstan. It is estimated that world resources of copper and lead contain about 11 million tonnes of arsenic. Substantial resources of arsenic occur in copper ores in northern Peru and the Philippines, and in copper-gold ores in Chile.

U.S. imports of arsenic metal in 1999 were 1,300 tonnes, an increase of 30 percent from 1998. Imports in 1997 were 909 tonnes, while in 1996 they were 252 tonnes. Imports of arsenic compounds in 1999 were 22,100 tonnes, while in 1998 they were 29,300 tonnes. Total U.S. imports in 1999 were 23,400 tonnes. U.S. exports of arsenic metal in 1999 were 1,350 tonnes compared to 177 tonnes in 1998 and 61 tonnes in 1997. U.S. apparent demand in 1999 was 22,000 tonnes compared to 30,100 tonnes in 1997.

Of the 22,000 tonnes of arsenic compounds demanded, some 19,000 went for wood preservatives, down 30 percent from 1998. Nonferrous alloys and electronics took 1,300 tonnes compared to 1,000 tonnes in 1998. Glass manufacturing consumed 700 tonnes, the same as in 1998.

U.S. imports of arsenic trioxide in 1999 were 29,100 tonnes, down 25 percent from 1998. The major supplier was China. Imports of arsenic acid in 1999 were four tonnes. The major supplier of arsenic acid was France.

World Production of White Arsenic (Arsenic Trioxide)   In Metric Tons

Year	Belgium	Bolivia	Canada[4]	Chile	China	France	Germany	Mexico	Namibia[3]	Peru	Phillip-pines	Russia[5]	World Total
1992	2,000	633	250	6,020	15,000	2,000	300	4,293	2,456	644	5,000	2,500	45,800
1993	2,000	663	250	6,200	14,000	3,000	300	4,447	2,290	391	2,000	2,000	42,100
1994	2,000	341	250	4,050	18,000	6,000	300	4,400	3,047	286	----	1,500	46,800
1995	2,000	362	250	4,076	21,000	5,000	250	3,620	1,661	285	----	1,500	47,000
1996	2,000	255	250	8,000	15,000	3,000	250	2,942	1,559	111	----	1,500	42,900
1997	2,000	282	250	8,350	15,000	2,500	250	2,999	1,297	103	----	1,500	41,600
1998[1]	1,500	284	250	8,400	15,500	2,000	200	2,573	175	122	----	1,500	40,000
1999[2]	1,500	280	250	8,000	16,000	1,000	200	2,500	----	120	----	1,500	38,800

[1] Preliminary.   [2] Estimate.   [3] Output of Tsumeb Corp. Ltd. only.   [4] Includes low-grade dusts that were exported to the U.S. for further refining.
[5] Formerly part of the U.S.S.R.; not reported separately until 1992.   *Source: U.S. Geological Survey (USGS)*

Salient Statistics of Arsenic in the United States   In Metric Tons (Arsenic Content)

	---------------- Supply ----------------				-- Distribution --	------------------ Estimated Demand Pattern ------------------						-- Average Price --			
	---- Imports ----		Industry Stocks Jan. 1			Industry Stocks Dec.31	Agricul-tural Chemicals	Glass	Wood Preserv-atives	Non-Ferrous Alloys & Electric	Other		Trioxide Mexican	Metal Chinese		
Year	Metal	Com-pounds		Total	Apparent Demand							Total	-- Cents/Pound --		Imports Trioxide[3]	Exports
1992	740	23,300	----	24,040	23,900	----	3,900	900	17,900	800	400	23,900	29	56	30,671	94
1993	767	20,900	----	21,667	21,300	----	3,000	900	16,200	800	400	21,300	33	44	27,500	364
1994	1,330	20,300	----	21,630	21,500	----	1,200	700	18,000	1,300	300	21,500	32	40	26,800	79
1995	557	22,100	----	22,657	22,300	----	1,000	700	19,600	600	400	22,300	33	66	29,000	430
1996	252	21,200	----	21,452	21,400	----	950	700	19,200	250	300	21,400	33	40	28,000	36
1997	909	22,800	----	23,709	23,700	----	1,400	700	20,000	900	300	23,700	31	32	30,000	61
1998[1]	997	29,300	----	30,297	30,100	----	1,500	700	27,000	1,000	300	30,100	30	40	38,600	177
1999[2]	1,300	22,100	----	23,400	22,000	----	1,100	700	19,000	1,300	300	22,000	----	----	29,100	1,350

[1] Preliminary.   [2] Estimate.   [3] For Consumption.   Source: U.S. Geological Survey (USGS)

Barley

The persistent slide in world barley production during the 1990's was halted in 2000/01, but the rebound was marginal with production estimated at 132.2 million metric tonnes vs. 127.6 million in 1999/00. World production in the 1990's averaged about 160 million tonnes. The decline largely reflects less planted acreage. Collectively, the E.U. is the largest producing area with 51.6 million tonnes forecast in 2000/01 vs. 48.9 million in 1999/00, with Germany the largest producer within the E.U. and, recently, the global leader as well. Russia's crop rebounded to 13 million tonnes in 2000/01 from 10.6 million in 1999/00, but still nearly half the crop size often grown in the 1990's. Canada's 2000/01 crop of 13 million tonnes fell short of initial forecasts by about 1 million tonnes and compares with 13.1 million in 1999/00. In the U.S., barley is the third largest produced feed grain; on a worldwide basis U.S. production accounts for only 5 percent of the total. World barley usage of 134.5 million tonnes in 2000/01 compares with 132.8 million in 1999/00. The 2000/01 world carryover of 22.8 million tonnes, the lowest since the mid-1990's, compares with 25.1 million at yearend 1999/00, most of which is in the European Union.

The U.S. barley crop year begins June 1. Production peaked in the 1980's and has since declined sharply as producers found returns more favorable from wheat and sunflower crops. Barley production in 2000/01 of 318 million bushels compares with the record low 282 million bushels a year earlier. Planted acreage for the 2000 crop totaled 5.8 million acres vs. 5.2 million in 1999, and an annual average of 7 million in the mid-1990's. North Dakota and Montana are the largest producing states.

U.S. disappearance in 2000/01 of 357 million bushels compares with a record low 338 million in 1999/00. Feed and residual usage were estimated at 145 million bushels, up 9 million from a year earlier, while industrial usage, mostly for beer and alcohol, was forecast at 172 million bushels, unchanged from 1999/00. Exports of 40 million bushels were up 10 million from 1999/00, while imports of 30 million bushels compare with 28 million, respectively, and mostly consist of malting quality barley from Canada. Carryover stocks on May 31, 2001, were estimated at only 102 million bushels vs. 111 million a year earlier.

World barley trade was forecast at 17.8 million tonnes in 2000/01 vs. 18.1 million in 1999/00. The European Union exports at least half of the total, with Canada and Australia much of the balance. Importing countries are more numerous, with Saudi Arabia the largest importer.

U.S. farm prices were forecast to average $2.10-2.40 per bushel in 2000/01 vs. $2.13 in 1999/00.

Futures Markets

Barley futures and options are traded on the Winnipeg Commodity Exchange (WCE) and are quoted in Canadian dollars per ton. Futures are traded on the London International Financial Futures and Options Commodity Exchange (LIFFE) and on the Budapest Commodity Exchange.

World Barley Supply and Demand   In Thousands of Metric Tons

| | Exports | | | | | Imports | | | | Utilization | | | Ending Stocks | | |
Year	Aus-tralia	Can-ada	EC-15	Total Non-US	U.S.	Total Exports	Saudi Arabia	Unac-ounted	Total Imports	Russia	U.S.	Total Util-ization	Canada	U.S.	Total Stocks
1991-2	1,951	3,379	15,356	23,250	2,088	25,338	6,590	77	22,051	23,454	8,734	166,353	2,615	2,800	33,364
1992-3	2,600	2,859	11,543	20,501	1,610	22,111	3,431	807	19,024	27,357	7,916	166,027	3,271	3,292	33,155
1993-4	4,232	3,789	10,055	20,414	1,550	21,964	4,308	384	20,285	26,824	9,053	168,997	3,376	3,023	33,236
1994-5	1,356	2,551	9,570	18,451	1,355	19,806	4,235	99	19,167	24,087	8,726	165,684	1,820	2,451	28,470
1995-6	3,375	2,596	8,654	18,347	1,182	19,529	3,876	214	19,172	17,566	7,635	150,925	1,749	2,168	19,650
1996-7	3,967	3,442	11,279	21,798	1,214	23,012	5,887	737	22,342	16,435	8,459	149,424	2,919	2,383	23,761
1997-8	2,838	1,897	7,587	16,431	1,066	17,497	4,052	578	17,073	16,494	6,879	145,956	2,459	2,596	32,292
1998-9	4,241	1,185	13,281	22,081	600	22,681	6,061	793	22,010	12,900	7,208	138,901	2,737	3,084	30,151
1999-00[1]	2,870	1,767	15,031	22,015	839	22,854	4,800	879	21,809	11,300	6,707	133,150	3,071	2,424	25,092
2000-1[2]	3,600	2,200	14,056	21,906	750	22,656	4,800	890	21,275	11,800	6,793	135,026	2,611	2,225	22,748

[1] Preliminary.   [2] Estimate.   Source: Foreign Agricutural Service, U.S. Department of Agriculture (FAS-USDA)

World Production of Barley   In Thousands of Metric Tons

Year	Aus-tralia	Canada	China	Den-mark	France	Ger-many	India	Russia	Spain	Tur-key	United Kingdom	United States	World Total
1991-2	4,606	11,617	4,622	5,041	10,789	14,494	1,640	22,174	9,141	6,800	7,700	10,110	169,801
1992-3	5,460	11,032	4,665	2,974	10,580	12,196	1,700	26,989	6,105	6,500	7,350	9,908	166,068
1993-4	6,956	12,972	4,327	3,369	8,981	11,000	1,510	26,900	9,520	6,500	6,040	8,666	169,078
1994-5	2,913	11,690	4,411	3,446	7,646	10,902	1,310	27,000	7,596	6,900	5,945	8,162	160,918
1995-6	5,823	13,035	4,089	3,864	7,739	11,891	1,730	15,800	5,200	6,833	7,824	142,105	
1996-7	6,696	15,562	4,000	3,953	9,540	12,074	1,510	15,900	9,600	7,200	7,780	8,544	153,535
1997-8	6,482	13,527	4,000	3,887	10,181	13,399	1,462	20,800	8,600	7,300	7,828	7,835	154,487
1998-9	5,680	12,709	3,500	3,565	10,591	12,512	1,680	9,800	10,902	7,500	6,630	7,667	136,760
1999-00[1]	5,043	13,196	3,000	3,620	9,550	13,301	1,470	10,600	7,434	6,600	6,580	6,103	128,091
2000-1[2]	5,400	13,500	3,000	4,100	10,000	12,100	1,500	13,000	10,800	7,400	6,700	6,921	132,682

[1] Preliminary.   [2] Estimate.   Source: Foreign Agricutural Service, U.S. Department of Agriculture (FAS-USDA)

Barley Acreage and Prices in the United States

Year Begin-ning June 1	Acreage ----- 1,000 Acres ----- Planted	Harvested for Grain	Yield Per Harvested Acre -- Bushels --	Received by Farmers[3] All	Feed[4]	Malting[4]	Portland No. 2 Western	National Average Loan Rate	Target Price	Put Under Support (mil. Bu.)	% of Pro-duction
							Dollars per Bushel				
1992-3	7,762	7,285	62.5	2.04	2.11	2.37	2.57	1.40	2.36	42.9	9.4
1993-4	7,786	6,753	58.9	1.99	2.05	2.48	2.40	1.40	2.36	37.7	9.5
1994-5	7,159	6,667	56.2	2.03	2.02	2.75	2.51	1.54	2.36	28.2	7.5
1995-6	6,689	6,279	57.3	2.89	2.67	3.69	3.51	1.54	2.36	14.9	4.1
1996-7	7,094	6,707	58.5	2.74	2.29	3.18	3.07	1.55	NA	28.7	NA
1997-8	6,706	6,198	58.1	2.38	1.91	2.50	2.49	1.57	NA	32.8	NA
1998-9[1]	6,337	5,864	60.0	1.98	1.23	2.30	1.96	1.56	NA	NA	NA
1999-00[2]	5,223	4,758	59.2	2.13	1.65	2.43		1.59	NA	NA	NA

Seasonal Prices; Government Price Support Operations

[1] Preliminary. [2] Estimate. [3] Excludes support payments. [4] Duluth through May 1998. *Source: Economic Research Service, U.S. Department of Agriculture (ERS-USDA)*

Salient Statistics of Barley in the United States   In Millions of Bushels

Year Begin-ning June 1	Beginning Stocks	Produc-tion	Imports	Total Supply	Food & Acohol Beverages	Seed	Feed & Residual	Total	Exports	Total Disap-pearance	Gov't Owned	Privately Owned[3]	Total Stocks
1993-4	151.2	398.0	71.5	620.7	162.9	11.9	243.7	415.8	66.1	481.8	5.2	133.7	138.9
1994-5	138.9	374.9	65.9	579.6	163.8	11.1	228.1	400.8	66.2	467.0	5.0	107.6	112.6
1995-6	112.6	359.4	40.7	512.7	160.1	11.7	178.9	350.7	62.4	413.1	4.2	95.4	99.6
1996-7	99.6	392.4	36.8	528.8	160.9	11.1	216.5	388.5	30.8	419.3	0	109.5	109.5
1997-8	109.5	360.0	40.3	509.6	161.6	10.4	144.0	316.0	74.4	390.3	0	119.2	119.2
1998-9	119.2	359.9	29.8	501.2	161.4	8.6	161.1	331.1	28.5	359.5	0.3	141.4	141.7
1999-00[1]	141.7	352.1	25.0	448.5	162.5	9.5	136.0	308.0	30.0	338.0	0	111.0	111.0
2000-1[2]	111.0	318.0	30.0	459.0			130.0		50.0	352.0	0	107.0	107.0

Disappearance — Domestic Use; Supply; Ending Stocks

[1] Preliminary. [2] Estimate. [3] Uncommitted inventory. [4] Includes quantity under loan & farmer-owned reserve. *Source: Economic Research Service, U.S. Department of Agriculture (ERS-USDA)*

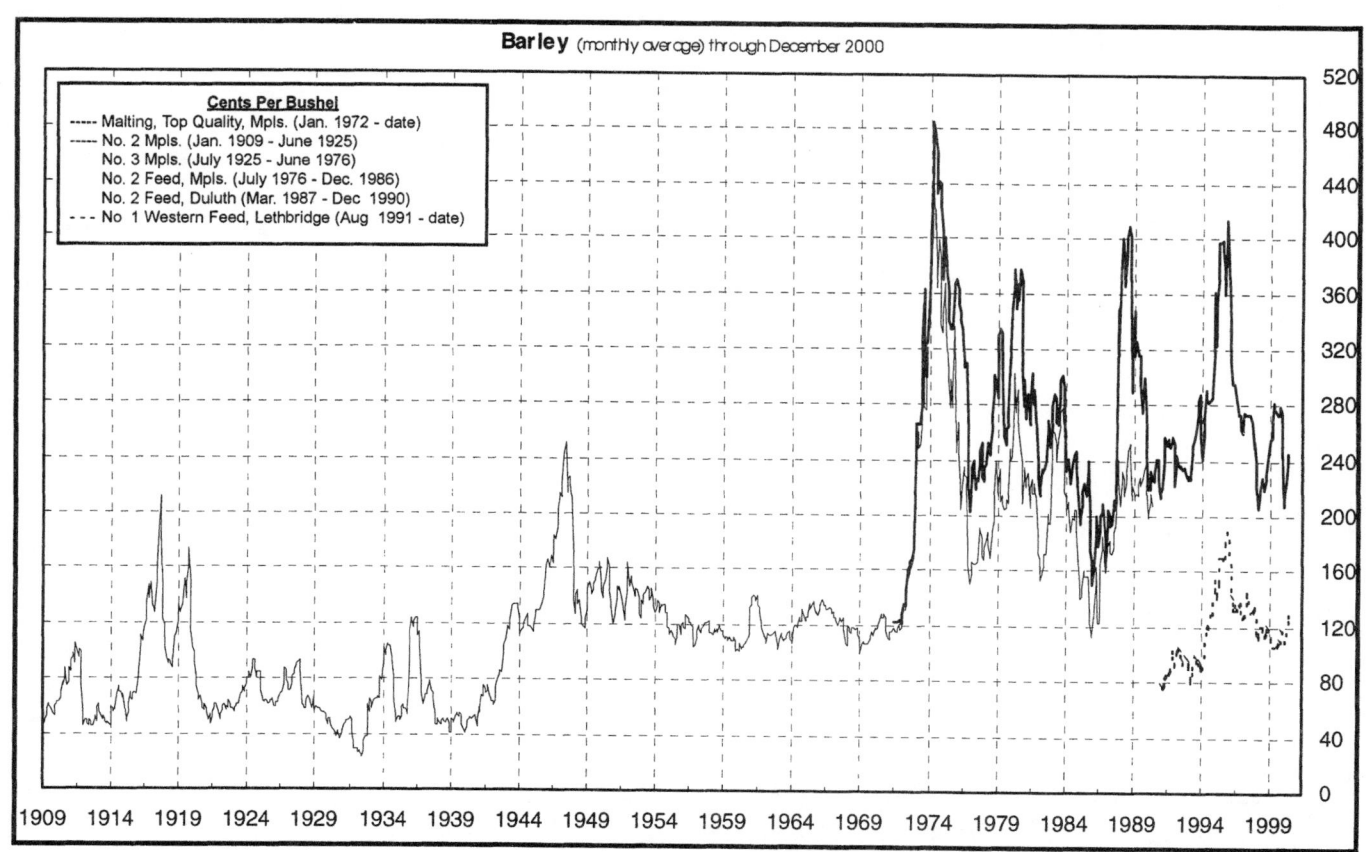

Barley (monthly average) through December 2000

Cents Per Bushel
----- Malting, Top Quality, Mpls. (Jan. 1972 - date)
----- No. 2 Mpls. (Jan. 1909 - June 1925)
No. 3 Mpls. (July 1925 - June 1976)
No. 2 Feed, Mpls. (July 1976 - Dec. 1986)
No. 2 Feed, Duluth (Mar. 1987 - Dec 1990)
- - - No 1 Western Feed, Lethbridge (Aug 1991 - date)

BARLEY

Average Price Received by Farmers for Feed[2] Barley in the United States   In Cents Per Bushel

Year	June	July	Aug.	Sept.	Oct.	Nov.	Dec.	Jan.	Feb.	Mar.	Apr.	May	Average
1996-7	322	279	260	234	210	190	196	195	201	222	233	245	232
1997-8	231	204	210	229	205	198	166	158	156	151	142	NQ	186
1998-9	182	162	149	140	146	147	155	158	160	149	154	162	155
1999-00	155	148	150	164	161	166	164	163	168	178	168	193	165
2000-1[1]	173	171	151	155	170	185	170	185					170

[1] Preliminary.   [2] Duluth No. 2 through May 1998.   NQ = No quote.   *Source: Economic Research Service, U.S. Department of Agriculture (ERS-USDA)*

Average Price Received by Farmers for All Barley in the United States   In Cents Per Bushel

Year	June	July	Aug.	Sept.	Oct.	Nov.	Dec.	Jan.	Feb.	Mar.	Apr.	May	Average
1996-7	355	318	299	278	269	265	267	252	245	237	229	231	270
1997-8	226	227	235	238	244	261	243	242	240	213	216	213	233
1998-9	193	201	207	201	191	205	203	189	190	200	178	182	195
1999-00	170	204	237	203	196	214	225	204	213	223	209	219	210
2000-1[1]	207	270	230	182	193	212	219	209					215

[1] Preliminary.   *Source: National Agricultural Statistical Service, U.S. Department of Agriculture (NASS-USDA)*

Average Open Interest of Western Feed Barley Futures in Winnipeg   In Contracts

Year	Jan.	Feb.	Mar.	Apr.	May	June	July	Aug.	Sept.	Oct.	Nov.	Dec.
1996	13,803	12,979	15,746	18,022	19,045	18,502	15,504	14,190	16,647	20,143	21,233	24,590
1997	22,718	19,290	15,080	14,620	14,385	12,291	10,023	13,641	12,909	13,147	14,473	13,576
1998	15,789	17,337	18,039	14,706	12,666	10,847	9,915	10,384	11,420	11,460	11,338	8,622
1999	8,231	10,635	10,579	9,713	8,333	8,993	10,348	11,959	13,206	15,014	15,662	15,031
2000	16,709	20,500	21,100	22,501	20,299	17,402	15,128	15,095	15,885	14,921	17,192	19,605

Source: Winnipeg Commodity Exchange (WCE)

Volume of Trading of Western Barley Futures in Winnipeg   In Contracts

Year	Jan.	Feb.	Mar.	Apr.	May	June	July	Aug.	Sept.	Oct.	Nov.	Dec.	Total
1996	24,789	14,762	22,492	29,326	25,659	22,968	33,908	24,878	25,456	50,745	33,702	26,124	334,809
1997	30,608	30,298	25,910	23,511	17,228	18,912	15,615	21,993	23,291	29,418	31,629	16,201	284,614
1998	23,954	23,472	23,904	23,553	17,395	20,273	21,011	18,101	16,097	21,330	21,589	8,315	238,994
1999	15,463	17,539	13,853	17,179	8,911	16,294	17,936	15,837	29,141	16,662	26,445	16,117	211,377
2000	23,371	22,402	21,563	23,631	19,816	24,298	15,230	11,981	23,105	23,447	42,529	14,508	265,881

Source: Winnipeg Commodity Exchange (WCE)

Western Barley Futures - Winnipeg Commodity Exchange (weekly close) as of 29-Dec-2000   CAD Per MetricTon

Bauxite

Bauxite is a naturally occurring, heterogeneous material comprised of one or more aluminum hydroxide minerals plus various mixtures of silica, iron oxide, titania, aluminosilicates, and other impurities in trace amounts.

Bauxite is the only raw material used in the production of alumina on a commercial scale in the United States. Bauxite is classified according to the intended commercial application, such as abrasive, cement, chemical, metallurgical, and refractory. Of all the bauxite mined, about 85 percent is converted to alumina for the production of aluminum metal, with an additional 10 percent going to nonmetal uses as various forms of specialty alumina. The remaining 5 percent is used in nonmetallurgical bauxite applications. The bulk of the bauxite produced in the world goes to the production of alumina which is further processed into aluminum metal. Quantities of bauxite are also used to produce aluminum chemicals and in the steel industries.

The U.S. Geological Survey reported that 1999 world mine production of bauxite was 123 million metric tonnes, 1 percent more that in 1998. The largest producer of bauxite was Australia with production of 46.5 million tonnes, an increase of 4 percent from 1998. The next largest producer was Guinea with output of 15 million tonnes. Production by Jamaica was 11.6 million tonnes, with Brazil at 11.8 million tonnes. Estimated world reserves of bauxite, in 1999, were 25 billion tonnes. The largest reserves are in Guinea, with 7.4 billion tonnes, followed by Brazil with 3.9 billion tonnes, and Australia with 3.2 billion tonnes.

Nearly all bauxite used in the U.S. came from imported sources. Domestic ore was mined by one company from surface mines in Alabama and Georgia. Virtually all of this production was used in nonmetallurgical products such as abrasives, chemicals, and refractories. Of the bauxite that is imported into the U.S., about 95 percent was converted to alumina. The U.S. also imports about half of the alumina that is needed. U.S. bauxite import sources are Guinea, Jamaica, Brazil, and Guyana, while sources for imported alumina are Australia, Suriname, and Jamaica.

U.S. imports of crude and dried bauxite in second quarter 2000 were 2.22 million tonnes. Imports in the first quarter were 2.17 million tonnes. For all of 1999, imports were 9.89 million tonnes. In 1999, imports from Guinea were 4.06 million tonnes, with imports from Jamaica 2.8 million tonnes. U.S. exports of crude and dried bauxite, in the second quarter of 2000, were 44,500 tonnes. In the first quarter exports were 36,600 tonnes. For all of 1999, exports were 11,500 tonnes. The major export destination in 1999 was Canada with 98,900 tonnes. Mexico took 11,400 tonnes.

U.S. imports of calcined bauxite in second quarter 2000 were 91,500 tonnes. For all of 1999, imports were 299,000 tonnes. U.S. exports of calcined bauxite in second quarter 2000 were 3,351 tonnes. The major destinations were Japan, Canada, and Mexico. U.S. exports of crude and dried bauxite in the second quarter of 2000 were 44,500 tonnes. For all of 1999, exports were 115,000 tonnes. The major market was Canada, with Mexico taking a smaller amount.

World Production of Bauxite   In Thousands of Metric Tons

Year	Australia	Brazil	China	Greece	Guinea	Guyana[2]	Hungary	India	Jamaica[3]	Russia[34]	Sierra Leone	Suriname	World Total
1990	41,391	9,678	2,400	2,496	15,772	1,424	2,559	4,852	10,921	5,500	1,430	3,283	113,000
1991	40,510	10,365	2,600	2,133	15,466	2,204	2,037	4,735	11,552	5,000	1,288	3,198	111,000
1992	39,746	9,366	2,700	2,078	13,800	2,376	1,721	4,898	11,302	4,578	1,250	3,250	105,000
1993	41,320	10,001	3,500	2,205	15,300	2,125	1,561	5,277	11,307	4,260	1,165	3,421	110,000
1994	41,733	8,673	3,700	2,196	13,300	1,732	836	4,809	11,564	3,000	735	3,772	106,000
1995	42,655	10,214	5,000	2,200	15,800	2,028	1,015	5,240	10,857	3,100	----	3,530	112,000
1996	43,063	10,998	6,200	2,452	15,600	2,475	1,044	5,757	11,863	3,300	----	3,695	117,000
1997	44,465	11,671	8,000	1,877	16,400	2,467	743	6,019	11,987	3,350	----	3,877	122,000
1998[1]	44,553	11,961	8,200	1,823	15,000	2,600	908	6,102	12,646	3,450	----	4,000	122,000
1999[2]	48,416	12,880	8,500	1,883	15,000	3,300	1,000	6,200	11,688	3,750	----	4,000	127,000

[1] Preliminary. [2] Estimate. [3] Dry Bauxite equivalent of ore processed. [4] Formerly part of the U.S.S.R.; data not reported separately until 1992.

Source: U.S. Geological Survey (USGS)

Salient Statistics of Bauxite in the United States   In Thousands of Metric Tons

Year	Net Import Reliance as a % of Apparent Consumption	Average Price FOB Mine $ per Ton	Total	Alumina	Abrasive	Chemical	Refractory	Dry Equivalent Imports[3] (for Consumption)	Exports[3]	Consumption	Producers & Consumers	Government	Total
1990	98	15-20	12,042	11,064	276	212	387	12,144	74	12,042	2,318	18,477	20,795
1991	100	15-18	12,204	11,383	204	218	328	11,871	51	12,204	2,620	18,477	21,097
1992	100	15-18	11,873	11,066	223	190	334	10,939	63	11,873	2,319	17,805	20,124
1993	100	15-24	11,917	11,002	203	225	429	11,621	90	12,200	1,590	16,938	18,500
1994	99	15-24	11,200	10,400	197	192	350	10,700	129	11,200	1,560	17,200	18,800
1995	99	15-18	10,900	10,100	133	201	394	10,100	108	10,900	1,730	16,300	18,100
1996	100	15-18	11,000	10,300	117	W	380	10,200	132	11,000	1,930	15,700	17,600
1997	100	15-18	11,500	10,700	98	W	466	10,700	85	11,500	2,260	14,300	16,500
1998[1]	100		12,700	12,000	135	W	332	11,000	99	12,700	1,860	11,000	12,800
1999[2]	100		11,700	11,100	113	W	251	9,890	149	11,700	1,440	6,800	8,250

[1] Preliminary. [2] Estimate. [3] Including concentrates. W = Withheld to avoid disclosing company proprietary data.

Source: U.S. Geological Survey (USGS)

Bismuth

Bismuth finds a wide variety of uses ranging from pharmaceutical compounds, to glass ceramics, to chemicals and pigments. Bismuth is found in household pharmaceuticals and is used to treat stomach ulcers. There have been several new uses for bismuth as a nontoxic substitute for lead in various applications. These have included the use of bismuth in brass plumbing fixtures, ceramic glazes, crystalware, lubricating greases, pigments, and solders. Of environmental interest has been the use of bismuth as a replacement for lead used in shot for waterfowl hunting and in fishing sinkers. Another new use has been in galvanizing to improve the drainage characteristics of galvanizing alloys. Zinc-bismuth alloys have the same drainage properties as zinc-lead alloys. Bismuth has the advantage of being as durable as lead without being as hazardous.

The U.S. Geological Survey reports that there is no domestic refinery production of primary bismuth in the U.S. now. Some forty-four companies accounted for about three-fourths of the bismuth consumed in 1999. About 42 percent of the bismuth is used in pharmaceuticals and chemicals; 39 percent in the fusible alloys, solders, and cartridges; 17 percent in metallurgical additives; and 2 percent in other uses.

World mine production of bismuth in 1999 was estimated at 3,310 metric tonnes, down 15 percent from the previous year. The largest producer of bismuth was Peru with 710 tonnes, down 9 percent from the previous year. Production by China was 700 tonnes, up 17 percent from 1998. Other large producers include Bolivia, Mexico,

Canada, and Japan. World reserves of bismuth in 1999 were estimated to be 110,000 tonnes. World reserves are usually associated with lead deposits except in China where bismuth is found with tungsten ores and Australia where it is found with copper-gold ores. Bismuth mineral is rarely found in sufficient quantities to be mined as the principal product, except in Bolivia and possibly China.

Bismuth metal consumed in the U.S. in the second quarter of 2000 totaled 506,000 kilograms. Consumption in the first quarter was 509,000 kilograms. For all of 1999, bismuth consumption in the U.S. was 2.05 million kilograms. In 1999, bismuth metal use in chemicals, cosmetics, and pharmaceuticals was 855,000 kilograms. For the first half of 2000, this same use consumed 429,000 kilograms. In 1999, bismuth alloy production consumed 823,000 kilograms of bismuth metal, while in the first half of 2000 it consumed 408,000 kilograms. Production of metallurgical additives consumed 340,000 kilograms in 1999, while in the first six months of 2000 bismuth metal consumed was 162,000 kilograms. Consumption for other products in 1999 was 31,000 kilograms, while in the first half of 2000 it was 14,500 kilograms.

U.S. imports for consumption of bismuth metal in May 2000 were 137,000 kilograms, down 37 percent from April. In the first five months of 2000, imports were 831,000 kilograms. For all of 1999, imports were 2.11 million kilograms. U.S. exports of bismuth metal in May 2000 were 9,550 kilograms. In January-May 2000, exports were 157,000 kilograms.

World Production of Bismuth   In Metric Tons (Mine Output=Metal Content)

| | Mine Output, Metal Content | | | | | | Refined Metal | | | | | | |
Year	Canada	China	Japan	Mexico	Peru	Total	Belgium	China	Kazak-hastan[3]	Japan	Mexico	Peru	Total
1990	87	1,060	133	733	555	3,440	1,000	1,060	80	442	549	521	4,190
1991	65	1,040	138	651	610	3,230	800	1,260	70	461	500	377	3,820
1992	224	820	159	807	550	2,870	800	1,060	170	530	550	419	3,710
1993	144	740	149	908	1,300	3,550	950	1,050	180	497	650	937	4,390
1994	129	610	152	1,047	1,210	3,410	900	850	85	505	836	877	4,180
1995	187	740	177	995	900	3,430	800	800	33	591	924	581	3,840
1996	150	610	169	1,070	1,000	3,430	800	750	50	562	957	939	4,180
1997	183	550	165	1,642	1,000	4,150	800	760	50	550	990	774	4,070
1998[1]	219	240	144	1,204	1,000	3,330	700	820	50	479	1,030	868	4,080
1999[2]	311	400	135	1,250	1,000	3,620	700	1,300	55	450	600	760	4,000

[1] Preliminary.   [2] Estimate.   [3] Formerly part of the U.S.S.R.; data not reported separately until 1992.   *Source U.S. Geological Survey (USGS)*

Salient Statistics of Bismuth in the United States   In Metric Tons

| | Bismuth Consumed, By Uses | | | | | | | Imports from | | | | |
| | Metallurgical Additives | Other Alloys & Uses | Fusible Alloys | Chemicals[3] | Total Consumption | Consumer Stocks Dec. 31 | Exports of Metal & Alloys | Metallic Bismuth from | | | | Dealer Price $ Per |
Year								Belgium	Mexico	Peru	Total	Pound
1990	424	24	249	577	1,274	331	122	668.1	404.8	262.7	1,612	3.56
1991	341	26	271	789	1,427	247	75	345.1	535.0	169.8	1,411	3.00
1992	381	33	278	758	1,450	272	90	467.4	550.5	75.7	1,621	2.66
1993	232	59	256	750	1,300	323	70	275.1	479.1	117.2	1,330	2.50
1994	306	26	276	841	1,450	402	160	512.0	665.0	114.9	1,660	3.25
1995	257	27	544	1,320	2,150	390	261	636.0	444.0	10.9	1,450	3.85
1996	231	35	401	855	1,520	122	151	584.0	453.0	19.5	1,490	3.65
1997	252	31	593	655	1,530	213	206	691.0	601.0	163.0	2,170	3.50
1998[1]	335	32	741	884	1,990	175	245	739.0	807.0	68.8	2,720	3.60
1999[2]	340	31	823	855	2,050	121	257	742.0	277.0	6.8	2,110	3.85

[1] Preliminary.   [2] Estimate.   [3] Includes pharmaceuticals.   *Source: U.S. Geological Survey (USGS)*

Broilers

Federally inspected U.S. broiler production set new year-to-year highs during the 1990's and the upward trend is expected to persist, although at a slower percentile pace of perhaps only 3 percent in 2000 and 2001. Production in calendar year 2000, of a record 30.6 billion pounds, compares with 29.7 billion in 1999, and a forecast of 31.6 billion in 2001. In the early 1990's, production averaged 20 billion pounds. Third quarter 2000 broiler production of 7.6 billion pounds was only 1.5 percent above a year earlier and, at the end of the quarter, the number of chicks placed for growout was averaging between 1 and 2 percent higher than in 1999, reflecting weak broiler returns to growers and strong competition in export markets. U.S. per capita consumption, however, shows few signs of slowing, averaging 77.1 pounds in 1999, 77.9 in 2000, and an estimated 80.4 pounds in 2001.

The 12-city 1999 average broiler price of 58.10 cents per pound is forecast to slip to 55.50 cents in 2000, and dip further to 52.00-56.00 cents in 2001. However, whole bird prices can be misleading; leg prices, in the third quarter of 2000, strengthened substantially due to strong export demand, but breast prices slipped based on slower domestic demand.

A key factor for the steady gains in U.S. broiler production is strong foreign demand, notably for leg quarters. Exports in 2000, of a record large 5.26 billion pounds, compares with 4.9 billion a year earlier, and are forecast at 5.3 billion in 2001. The major importers are Russia, Hong Kong, Japan, and Mexico. However, U.S. exports are likely to face increasing supply competition, notably from Brazil, but inexpensive feed grain prices and an efficient industry will help keep U.S. broilers export prices competitive.

Broiler Supply and Prices in the United States

Year & Quarters	Number (Millions)	Average Weight (Pounds)	Liveweight Pounds (Mil. Lbs.)	Certified RTC Weight (Mil. Lbs.)	Total Production RTC[3] (Mil. Lbs.)	Per Capita Consumption RTC Basis (Mil. Lbs.)	Farm	Geogia Dock[4]
							Cents per Pound	
1995	7,371	4.66	34,348	25,021	24,827	79.2	34.68	54.73
1996	7,546	4.78	36,034	36,336	26,124	81.4	38.67	61.09
1997	7,714	4.81	39,098	27,271	27,271	71.9	37.35	59.96
1998	7,825	4.86	38,016	27,832	27,863	72.6	39.81	59.81
1999[1]	8,103	4.99	40,402	29,709	29,674	77.5	36.88	58.75
2000[2]	8,257	4.98	41,111	30,239	31,150	81.6	35.95	58.14
I	2,046	5.01	10,259	7,547	7,650	20.3	34.47	56.56
II	2,097	4.98	10,438	7,669	7,900	20.8	36.83	56.72
III	2,050	4.95	10,135	7,463	7,800	20.3	37.17	59.07
IV							35.33	60.22

[1] Preliminary. [2] Estimate. [3] Total production equals federal inspected slaughter plus other slaughter minus cut-up & further processing condemnation. [4] Ready-to-cook basis. *Source: Economic Research Service, U.S. Department of Agriculture (ERS-USDA)*

Salient Statistics of Broilers in the United States

Year	Commercial Production Number (Mil. Lbs.)	Commercial Production Liveweight (Mil. Lbs.)	Average Liveweight Per Bird (Pounds)	Average Price (Cents/Lb.)	Value of Production (Mil. $)	Federally Inspected	Other Chickens	Total	Storage Stocks January 1	Exports	Broiler Feed Ratio (Pounds)	Consumption Total (Mil. Lbs.)	Consumption Per Capita[4] (Pounds)
						In Millions of Pounds							
1993	6,694	30,618	4.56	34.0	10,417	22,178	36	22,015	368	1,966	5.3	20,059	68.50
1994	7,018	32,529	4.64	35.0	11,372	23,846	38	23,666	358	2,876	5.2	20,690	69.50
1995	7,326	34,222	4.66	34.4	11,762	25,021	39	24,827	458	3,894	5.1	20,832	68.80
1996	7,598	36,483	4.80	38.1	13,903	26,336	38	26,124	560	4,420	4.4	21,626	70.40
1997	7,764	37,541	4.84	37.7	14,159	27,271	35	27,041	641	4,664	4.7	22,416	71.90
1998[1]	7,934	38,554	4.86	39.3	15,145	27,863	26	27,612	607	4,673	6.3	22,841	72.60
1999[2]	8,146	40,830	5.01	37.1	15,129	29,446	27	29,175	711	4,512	7.4	24,629	77.60

[1] Preliminary. [2] Estimate. [3] Ready-to-cook. [4] Retail weight basis. *Source: Economic Research Service, U.S. Department of Agriculture (ERS-USDA)*

Average Wholesale Broiler[1] Prices RTC (Ready-to-Cook) (In Cents Per Pound)

Year	Jan.	Feb.	Mar.	Apr.	May	June	July	Aug.	Sept.	Oct.	Nov.	Dec.	Average
1994	52.67	55.22	57.56	57.80	61.39	60.71	57.36	54.65	55.80	54.02	50.50	50.87	55.71
1995	51.14	51.73	52.32	51.51	52.94	55.88	58.76	61.74	61.48	58.79	61.08	58.87	56.35
1996	59.00	55.31	54.31	56.01	61.71	65.52	64.58	64.07	64.01	62.64	64.37	63.50	61.25
1997	61.99	59.53	58.41	59.77	58.53	59.05	63.04	63.25	59.86	55.39	54.62	52.25	58.81
1998	54.66	56.40	58.10	58.52	60.08	64.26	68.53	72.13	70.53	68.04	64.13	60.45	62.99
1999	59.33	58.23	56.79	55.08	60.02	60.33	59.46	57.65	57.15	54.87	59.52	58.42	58.07
2000[2]	55.43	53.84	54.48	55.39	55.71	56.01	56.61	55.47	58.35	57.22	58.22	57.23	56.16

[1] 12-city composite wholesale price. [2] Preliminary. *Source: Economic Research Service, U.S. Department of Agriculture (ERS-USDA)*

Butter

U.S. butter production in the second half of the 1990's showed little growth, averaging about 530,000 metric tons annually, however, production has since rebounded, estimated at 600,000 tons in 2000, the highest output since the record large 619,000 tons in 1992. Most of the increase is due to the surge in milk supplies available for butter production. Despite the expected increase in butter output, strong demand in 1999 and 2000 had the effect of keeping prices over a $1/pound. U.S. annual butter consumption fell during much of the 1990's, totaling only 505,000 tons in 1997, but has since rebounded sharply, to 555,000 tons in 1998, followed by 595,000 in 1999 and 597,000 tons in 2000. During the latter three years, consumption either exceeded or about equaled production. There is a definite production seasonality: January is the highest producing month and August the lowest. U.S. butter stocks, once mostly government owned, dropped sharply in the 1990's; from a high at year-end 1991 of 249,000 tons to 6,000 at year end 1996, although since then have increased moderately with ending 2000 stocks forecast at 25,000 tons. In the late 1990's annual U.S. per capita butter averaged near 2 kilograms.

Butter production is derived directly from milk production. Butter manufacture is the third largest use of milk production, the first being milk as a fluid and then its conversion into cheese. California was the largest producing state in 2000 followed by Wisconsin and Washington.

World butter production in 2000 of 5.6 million metric tons compares with 5.4 million in 1999 and the 1990's low of 5.1 million in 1997. The U.S. is the world's largest producer followed by France and Germany, the three countries combined generally accounting for almost a third of global production. India's 2000 output of record large 1.95 million tons compares with 1.75 million in 1999, but their product is mostly Ghee, a butter like substance which is consumed almost entirely in India. Russia's production of 270,000 tons in 2000 was up marginally from 1999, but about half their output ten years earlier. World consumption has increased since the mid-1990's, forecast at 5.2 million tons in 2000 vs. 5 million in 1999. Among foreign nations, but exclusive of India, the world's largest consumer in 2000 with nearly 2 million tons, was Germany with 540,000 tons followed by France with 510,000. Russia, once the largest consumer now ranks third: 322,000 tons in 2000 vs. 570,000 tons five years earlier.

Global trade in butter is small. Exports were forecast at 618,000 tons in 2000 vs. 579,000 in 1999, almost two-thirds of which come from New Zealand and Australia. U.S. exports and imports are insignificant. Not too long ago, the EU relied heavily on Russia to absorb its surplus butterfat, but Russia's economic crisis has cut deeply into their butter imports, estimated at only 60,000 tons in 2000 vs. 250,0000 tons in 1997 owing in part to an almost commensurate decline in Russia's (and the Ukraine) per capita butter consumption.

U.S. wholesale butter prices, basis grade AA-Chicago in 1999 averaged $1.252/lb. vs. $1.776 in 1998. World butter prices at the start of 2000 were near $1450 per metric ton and by mid-year averaging near $1300 vs. mid-1999 prices of about $1400/ton, basis Northern Europe.

Supply and Distribution of Butter in the United States   In Millions of Pounds

Year	Supply — Production	Supply — Cold Storage Stocks[3] Jan. 1[5]	Supply — Imports	Supply — Total Supply	Distribution — Domestic Disappearance — Total	Distribution — Domestic Disappearance — Per Capita (Pounds)	Distribution — Exports	Distribution — Dept. of Agriculture — Jan. 1 Stocks[4]	Distribution — Dept. of Agriculture — Dec. 31 Stocks[4]	Distribution — Dept. of Agriculture — Removed by USDA Programs	Distribution — Total Use	93 Score AA Wholesale Price — California $ per Pound	93 Score AA Wholesale Price — Chicago $ per Pound
1990	1,302	275	4.798	1,582	1,095	4.4	68	223	373	400.3	1,165	1.3050	1.0346
1991	1,337	417	4.740	1,759	1,101	4.4	107	373	511	442.8	1,209	1.2856	1.0182
1992	1,365	550	4.153	1,919	1,114	4.4	307	511	430	439.5	1,464	1.1386	.8427
1993	1,315	455	4.374	1,774	1,209	4.7	320	430	229	288.8	1,530	1.0612	.7693
1994	1,296	244	3.340	1,543	1,255	4.8	207	229	67	204.3	1,463	.9581	.7068
1995	1,264	80	1.536	1,348	1,186	4.5	140	67	----	78.5	1,329	----	.7068
1996	1,174	19	10.544	1,204	1,148	4.3	41	----	----	0	1,190	----	.8188
1997	1,151	14	24.153	1,177	1,116	4.2	39	----	----	1	1,156	----	1.0824
1998[1]	1,168	21	66.138	1,243	1,208	4.5	6	----	----	----	1,217	----	1.1625
1999[2]	1,275	26	22.046	1,337	1,305	4.8	4	----	----	----	1,312	----	1.7764
													1.7760

[1] Preliminary.   [2] Estimates.   [3] Includes butter-equivalent.   [4] Includes butteroil.   [5] Includes stocks held by USDA.
Source: Economic Research Service, U.S. Department of Agriculture (ERS-USDA)

Commercial Disappearance of Creamery Butter in the United States   In Millions of Pounds

Year	First Quarter	Second Quarter	Third Quarter	Fourth Quarter	Total	Year	First Quarter	Second Quarter	Third Quarter	Fourth Quarter	Total
1989	188.3	145.6	228.8	291.3	854.1	1995	335.7	269.0	261.2	304.9	1,186.0
1990	197.5	218.1	218.1	281.8	915.2	1996	325.6	301.8	237.5	310.3	1,180.0
1991	186.8	184.0	255.6	276.5	903.5	1997	302.7	250.7	265.8	287.6	1,109.0
1992	214.6	216.6	236.8	276.2	944.3	1998	289.0	276.3	255.3	308.6	1,137.0
1993	224.6	231.5	271.9	312.7	1,040.6	1999	299.3	316.4	318.3	374.8	1,308.8
1994	261.7	254.9	285.0	298.3	1,097.3	2000[1]	320.7	280.3	336.6	409.4	1,347.0

[1] Preliminary.   Source: Economic Research Service, U.S. Department of Agriculture (ERS-USDA)

BUTTER

World (Total) Butter[3] Production   In Thousands of Metric Tons

Year	Aus-tralia	France	Germany	India	Ireland	Nether-lands	New Zealand	Poland	Russia	Uk-raine	United Kingdom	United States	World Total
1991	111	496	555	1,020	146	196	269	220	729	376	132	606	5,667
1992	116	454	474	1,060	142	191	268	180	762	303	127	619	5,470
1993	131	444	480	1,110	135	184	276	180	732	312	152	596	5,493
1994	147	444	461	1,200	136	159	297	160	488	254	154	588	5,221
1995	138	453	486	1,300	150	132	280	163	419	219	130	573	5,173
1996	153	462	480	1,400	150	122	309	160	290	163	129	533	5,094
1997	147	466	442	1,470	145	134	307	178	280	109	139	522	5,073
1998	154	463	426	1,600	145	149	343	183	270	113	137	530	5,253
1999[1]	175	448	427	1,750	143	140	316	181	260	105	142	578	5,424
2000[2]	184	450	410	1,950	146	135	320	185	270	90	141	600	5,640

[1] Preliminary.   [2] Forecast.   [3] Factory (including creameries and dairies) & farm.   *Source: Foreign Agricultural Service, U.S. Department of Agriculture (FAS-USDA)*

Production of Creamery Butter in Factories in the United States   In Millions of Pounds

Year	Jan.	Feb.	Mar.	Apr.	May	June	July	Aug.	Sept.	Oct.	Nov.	Dec.	Total
1991	142.1	126.3	131.6	133.7	126.0	98.3	88.9	85.0	84.7	105.2	108.5	130.1	1,360.4
1992	156.0	132.0	129.9	119.7	118.2	103.0	97.8	86.7	96.6	101.6	98.3	119.8	1,365.2
1993	147.3	127.2	131.6	121.8	116.4	102.3	86.2	80.7	86.3	97.8	97.3	120.3	1,315.2
1994	135.3	118.4	118.0	119.4	118.2	99.2	84.2	88.2	91.2	101.8	100.7	121.4	1,295.9
1995	135.6	121.7	127.3	120.6	119.4	98.4	85.0	76.0	80.2	93.5	90.5	112.4	1,260.7
1996	132.4	114.7	111.9	109.3	100.9	72.7	75.2	73.2	80.7	96.6	95.3	111.3	1,174.5
1997	127.6	108.6	105.4	118.3	102.7	82.0	80.0	68.8	79.3	83.3	89.1	106.0	1,151.3
1998	117.8	105.7	106.7	107.1	92.6	69.9	63.8	64.3	68.2	88.5	91.1	106.3	1,081.9
1999[1]	123.3	111.5	113.7	106.4	104.7	86.0	75.8	66.1	78.8	93.0	90.4	117.2	1,166.8
2000[2]	142.3	130.3	122.5	115.4	111.2	91.8	87.0	85.6	91.6	106.2	105.8		1,297.8

[1] Preliminary.   [2] Estimate.   *Source: Economic Research Service, U.S. Department of Agriculture (ERS-USDA)*

Cold Storage Holdings of Creamery Butter on First of Month in the United States   In Millions of Pounds

Year	Jan.	Feb.	Mar.	Apr.	May	June	July	Aug.	Sept.	Oct.	Nov.	Dec.
1991	416.1	470.8	524.8	555.9	620.5	646.7	662.7	659.8	629.4	597.2	567.1	539.4
1992	539.4	565.4	624.8	645.3	678.7	712.6	747.0	755.8	705.7	608.1	541.7	487.6
1993	447.7	489.1	492.5	515.6	552.7	559.0	569.0	516.4	473.3	395.4	341.1	276.3
1994	234.7	251.0	243.2	253.5	265.7	281.4	275.1	245.9	206.6	163.4	124.6	84.5
1995	79.5	89.9	88.3	74.8	79.1	81.3	79.2	68.3	50.2	32.8	23.6	15.7
1996	18.6	25.5	33.7	48.7	39.8	34.0	29.7	31.7	27.3	21.4	20.5	17.6
1997	13.7	23.2	36.0	50.3	86.8	104.2	93.7	85.6	69.5	43.9	26.6	15.4
1998	20.8	34.2	44.2	55.9	67.4	72.7	60.6	51.0	41.1	34.1	31.2	28.7
1999	25.9	60.8	95.0	108.4	125.5	136.6	120.6	123.6	90.7	71.5	64.2	30.2
2000[1]	25.1	72.9	88.9	97.8	126.8	138.1	144.9	136.8	101.2	84.9	58.0	27.2

[1] Preliminary.   *Source: Agricultural Statistics Board, U.S. Department of Agriculture (ASB-USDA)*

Wholesale Price of 92 Score Creamery (Grade A) Butter, Central States[1]   In Cents Per Pound

Year	Jan.	Feb.	Mar.	Apr.	May	June	July	Aug.	Sept.	Oct.	Nov.	Dec.	Average
1991	97.3	97.3	97.3	97.3	97.3	98.6	98.9	98.9	100.7	106.3	104.6	98.4	99.3
1992	94.9	86.3	86.3	86.3	83.8	76.6	76.6	76.6	81.7	82.2	80.7	78.6	82.5
1993	75.3	75.3	75.3	75.3	75.3	76.2	73.5	74.6	74.3	74.2	73.6	69.7	74.4
1994	64.0	64.0	65.5	65.5	64.5	65.1	66.9	71.5	71.5	71.5	71.5	67.0	67.4
1995	64.0	65.5	66.5	66.5	66.5	69.9	74.5	79.5	80.9	95.4	103.5	74.4	75.6
1996	75.4	66.4	65.5	69.0	87.8	129.3	145.3	145.5	145.5	128.6	74.1	71.9	100.4
1997	81.9	98.4	106.3	95.6	86.1	105.5	102.7	102.5	101.6	135.3	148.8	120.1	116.2
1998	109.2	139.8	134.1	136.4	153.2	186.7	203.1	216.6	273.1	242.3	187.9	140.8	177.6
1999	144.4	133.1	130.3	103.9	111.0	147.7	134.7	141.4	135.8	113.8	109.6	94.2	125.0
2000	91.6	92.9	99.7	108.7	122.2	128.6	120.3	120.3	119.1	116.9	151.7	150.0	118.5

[1] Data prior to June 1998 are for Grade AA in Chicago.   *Source: Economic Research Service, U.S. Department of Agriculture (ERS-USDA)*

Cadmium

Cadmium is a rare chemical element that is the byproduct of the refining and smelting of zinc ores. The most common cadmium mineral is greenockite, which is almost always associated with the zinc ore mineral, sphalerite. It is estimated that at least 80 percent of the global cadmium output is the result of being a byproduct of primary zinc production. The remaining 20 percent comes from secondary sources and recycling of cadmium products. Because of low prices, the processing of many wastes for cadmium recovery is not economically viable. Cadmium is used primarily in iron and steel plating to protect them from corrosion. Due to the cost of waste disposal and problems with toxicity, the use of electroplating has decreased.

The U.S. Geological Survey reported that refinery production of cadmium in 1999 was estimated at 19,900 metric tonnes, up 2 percent from 1998. The largest producers of cadmium were Japan and Canada. Production by Japan in 1999 was estimated to be 2,300 tonnes, down 2 percent from 1998. Cadmium production by Canada in 1999 was also 2,300 tonnes, the same as in 1998. Other large producers of cadmium in 1999 were China with 2,100 tonnes, the U.S. with 1,800 tonnes, and Belgium with 1,300 tonnes.

Most of the cadmium used by Western countries goes into the manufacture of batteries. It is estimated that about 60 percent of the cadmium consumed by Western countries is for battery production. About 75 percent of the batteries produced by Western manufactures are for cellular telephones and other cordless electronic equipment. The remainder is for industrial purposes like emergency power supplies. Because of environmental concerns, some nickel-cadmium batteries are being replaced by lithium-ion.

U.S. production of primary and secondary cadmium metal in 1999 was estimated to be 1,190 metric tonnes, 4 percent lower than in 1998. Shipments of cadmium metal by producers in 1999 were estimated at 440 tonnes, down 27 percent from 1998. U.S. apparent consumption of cadmium metal in 1999 was estimated at 1,300 tonnes, down 36 percent from 1998. Government stocks of cadmium metal at the end of 1999 were 1,740 tonnes, the same as at the end of 1998. Industry stocks of metal at the end of 1999 were 893 tonnes, up 22 percent from the end of 1998. 1999 stocks at metal producers were 800 tonnes, while stocks at compound manufacturers were 93 tonnes.

U.S. imports of cadmium metal in 1999 were 294,000 kilograms, down 43 percent from 1998. The major supplier of cadmium metal to the U.S. was Canada with 98,200 kilograms, down from 304,000 kilograms in 1998. Other large suppliers were Australia, Belgium, and Peru.

U.S. imports of cadmium sulfide in 1999 were 18,400 kilograms, up 95 percent from 1998. The major supplier of cadmium sulfide to the U.S. was Japan with 13,800 kilograms, followed by the U.K. with 4,640 kilograms.

U.S. exports of cadmium metal in 1999 were 20,400 kilograms with the major destinations being Canada, France, Mexico, and Japan. 1999 exports of cadmium sulfide were 107,000 kilograms, mostly to Japan and Canada.

World Refinery Production of Cadmium   In Metric Tons

Year	Australia	Belgium	Canada	China	Finland	Germany	Italy	Japan	Kazakhstan[4]	Mexico	United Kingdom	United States[3]	World Total
1990	638	1,960	1,470	1,100	569	990	691	2,450	2,800	882	438	1,680	20,200
1991	1,076	1,807	1,829	1,200	593	1,048	658	2,889	2,500	688	449	1,680	20,900
1992	1,001	1,549	1,963	1,150	590	961	742	2,986	1,000	602	383	1,620	19,800
1993	951	1,573	1,944	1,160	785	1,056	517	2,832	800	797	458	1,090	18,400
1994	910	1,556	2,173	1,280	548	1,145	475	2,629	1,097	646	469	1,010	18,200
1995	838	1,710	2,349	1,450	539	1,150	308	2,652	794	689	549	1,270	20,100
1996	639	1,579	2,537	1,570	648	1,150	296	2,344	800	784	541	1,530	18,900
1997	632	1,420	1,272	1,980	540	1,145	287	2,473	1,000	1,223	455	2,060	19,500
1998[1]	600	1,318	1,361	2,130	520	1,020	328	2,337	1,450	1,275	440	1,240	19,100
1999[2]	600	1,400	1,390	2,200	520	1,100	350	2,600	1,061	1,300	500	1,190	19,100

[1] Preliminary.   [2] Estimate.   [3] Primary and secondary metal.   [4] Formerly part of the U.S.S.R.; data not reported separately until 1992.
Source: U.S. Geological Survey (USGS)

Salient Statistics of Cadmium in the United States   In Metric Tons of Contained Cadmium

Year	Net Import Reliance as a % of Apparent Consumption	Production (Metal)	Producer Shipments	Cadmium Sulfide Production	Production Other Compounds	Imports of Cadmium Metal[3]	Exports[4]	Apparent Consumption	Industry Stocks Dec. 31[5]	New York Dealer Price $ per Pound
1990	46	1,680	1,860	228	1,144	1,740	385	2,800	653	3.38
1991	50	1,680	1,740	263	1,089	2,040	448	3,080	835	2.01
1992	50	1,620	2,080	270	1,073	1,960	213	3,330	868	.91
1993	64	1,090	1,320	303	731	1,420	38	2,940	579	.45
1994	3	1,010	1,290	170	898	1,110	1,450	1,040	423	1.13
1995	E	1,270	1,280	105	936	848	1,050	1,160	990	1.84
1996	32	1,530	1,310	119	720	843	201	2,250	1,140	1.24
1997	16	2,060	1,370	113	607	790	554	2,510	1,090	.51
1998[1]	20	1,240	600	125	638	514	180	2,030	729	.28
1999[2]	19	1,190	440	64	604	294	20	1,300	893	.14

[1] Preliminary.   [2] Estimate.   [3] For consumption.   [4] Cadmium metal, alloys, dross, flue dust.   [5] Metallic, Compounds, Distributors (including in compounds from 1985)   [6] Sticks & Balls in 1 to 5 short ton lots.   E = Net exporter.   *Source: U.S. Geological Survey (USGS)*

Canola (Rapeseed)

Following a steady increase in production during the 1990's, the world canola (or rapeseed, the terms are interchangeable) crop in 2000/01 declined about 10 percent from the previous season. Still, canola is the second largest oilseed in crop size, although production is only about 25 percent that of soybeans. Production in 2000/01 of 38.6 million metric tonnes trailed initial forecasts and compares with a record large 42.6 million tonnes in 1999/00, and a mid-1990's average of about 30 million tonnes. On a protein meal basis, rapeseed has been the world's second largest meal product for some time, production of which totaled a near record large 22 million tonnes in 2000/01 vs. a record 22.7 million in 1999/00. For oil, however, rapeseed ranks third (after soybean and palm) with production of 13.35 million tonnes in 2000/01 vs. a record large 13.8 million in 1999/00. For both meal and oil, 2000/01 production marginally exceeded initial estimates.

World rapeseed supplies in 2000/01 of 41.4 million tonnes compares with 43.9 million in 1999/00, which includes relatively small carryover stocks of about 2 million tonnes for each crop year. The world 2000/01 (July/June) crush of 36.5 million tonnes compares with the previous year's record 32.8 million metric tonnes.

Collectively, the European Union is the largest producer with 9.3 million tonnes in 2000/01 vs. a record large 11.3 million in 1999/00, with Germany the largest producer within the E.U. China is the largest single producer: production in 2000/01 of a record large 11 million tonnes compares with 10.1 million in 1999/00; Canada then follows with 6.9 million and 8.8 million, respectively. Although China continues to increase rapeseed acreage, average yield has failed to show much improvement and is at least 50 percent less than the yield realized in Western Europe.

In terms of protein meal consumption, the E.U.'s 2000/01 meal consumption of a near record large 6 million tonnes is about one-fifth that of soybean meal. E.U. estimated rapeseed oil usage, however, in 2000/01 of 3 million tonnes is nearly twice that of soybean oil. Between the two products, oil has shown the greater percentile growth in recent years. Foreign trade in rapeseed is second only to soybeans: exports of 9.9 million tonnes in 2000/01 compare with a record large 11 million in 1999/00.

U.S. production of canola seed is small in absolute terms, but percentagewise increased rapidly in the 1990's.

The crop is grown mostly in the Northern Plains states. Production in 2000/01 (June/May) of a record large 2 billion pounds compares with 1.4 billion in 1999/00, and crops of less than 100 million pounds prior to the 1990's. Acreage is also growing, almost doubling from year-to-year at times during the 1990's. Contributing to the gains in U.S. production include: (1) government incentives to increase acreage; (2) development of better varieties that can be grown in the U.S.; and (3) the wider acceptance of canola oil in cooking due to its lower content of saturated fats. Canola oil is said to be 94 percent saturated fat free, the lowest of any leading edible oil. Demand for canola meal has also grown sharply as a livestock feed.

U.S. canola oil production in 2000/01 (October/September) of a record large 585 million pounds compares with 562 million in 1999/00. The U.S. imports even more oil, 1.2 billion pounds in 2000/01 vs. less than a billion pounds until the mid-1990's. Domestic use in 2000/01 of a record 1.5 billion pounds compares with 1.4 billion a year earlier, and about one half billion pounds at the start of the 1990's. The U.S. is forecast to export about 261 million pounds in 2000/01 vs. 225 million in 1999/00. There were virtually no yearly U.S. exports until early in the 1990's.

Canola meal production in 2000/01 of 462,000 short tons compares with 444,000 in 1999/00; imports totaled 1.3 millions tons vs. 1.2 million tons, respectively. Domestic usage of a record large 1.7 million tons compares with 1.6 million the year before. U.S. exports of canola meal are minimal, as are carryover stocks.

The average price received by farmers for canola seed in 2000/01 was forecast to range between $6.90-8.50/cwt. vs. $7.80 a year earlier and a high during the 1990's of $12.90 in 1996/97. Canola oil's price was forecast at 16.80-19.80 cents per pound in 2000/01 vs. 17.80 cents in 1999/00, while meal's price of $93.00-123.00 per short ton in 2000/01 compares with $118.00 in 1999/00.

Futures Markets

Canola futures and options are traded on the Winnipeg Commodity Exchange (WCE) and quoted in Canadian dollars per ton. Rapeseed futures are traded on the Marche a Terme International de France (MATIF).

World Production of Canola (Rapeseed)   In Thousands of Metric Tons

Year	Austrlia	Canada	China	Czecho-slovakia	France	Germany	India	Pakistan	Poland	Sweden	United Kingdom	Former USSR	World Total
1989-90	78	3,209	5,435	387	1,748	1,893	4,125	233	1,586	370	953	401	21,891
1990-1	99	3,266	6,958	380	1,937	2,090	5,229	228	1,206	367	1,200	426	25,045
1991-2	170	4,224	7,436	445	2,270	3,030	5,863	219	1,043	252	1,300	313	28,214
1992-3	179	3,872	7,653	375	1,810	2,617	4,872	243	758	247	1,150	329	25,284
1993-4	305	5,480	6,940	377	1,550	2,848	5,390	225	594	313	1,136	211	26,734
1994-5	309	7,233	7,492	452	1,800	2,837	5,884	225	756	214	1,298	244	30,309
1995-6	561	6,436	9,777	662	2,700	3,127	6,000	255	1,377	215	1,330	252	34,438
1996-7	641	5,062	9,200	521	2,870	2,150	6,942	255	449	139	1,410	226	31,546
1997-8	860	6,392	9,578	575	3,400	2,867	4,935	286	595	118	1,523	223	33,226
1998-9[1]	1,761	7,643	8,300	680	3,700	3,388	4,900	292	1,099	124	1,569	366	35,918
1999-00[2]	2,426	8,798	10,132	931	4,400	4,212	5,500	282	1,132	180	1,733	500	42,678
2000-1[3]	1,600	7,119	11,000	850	3,600	3,550	4,400	260	900	120	1,200	610	37,641

[1] Preliminary.   [2] Estimate.   [3] Forecast.   *Source: Economic Research Service, U.S. Department of Agriculture (ERS-USDA); The Oil World*

CANOLA

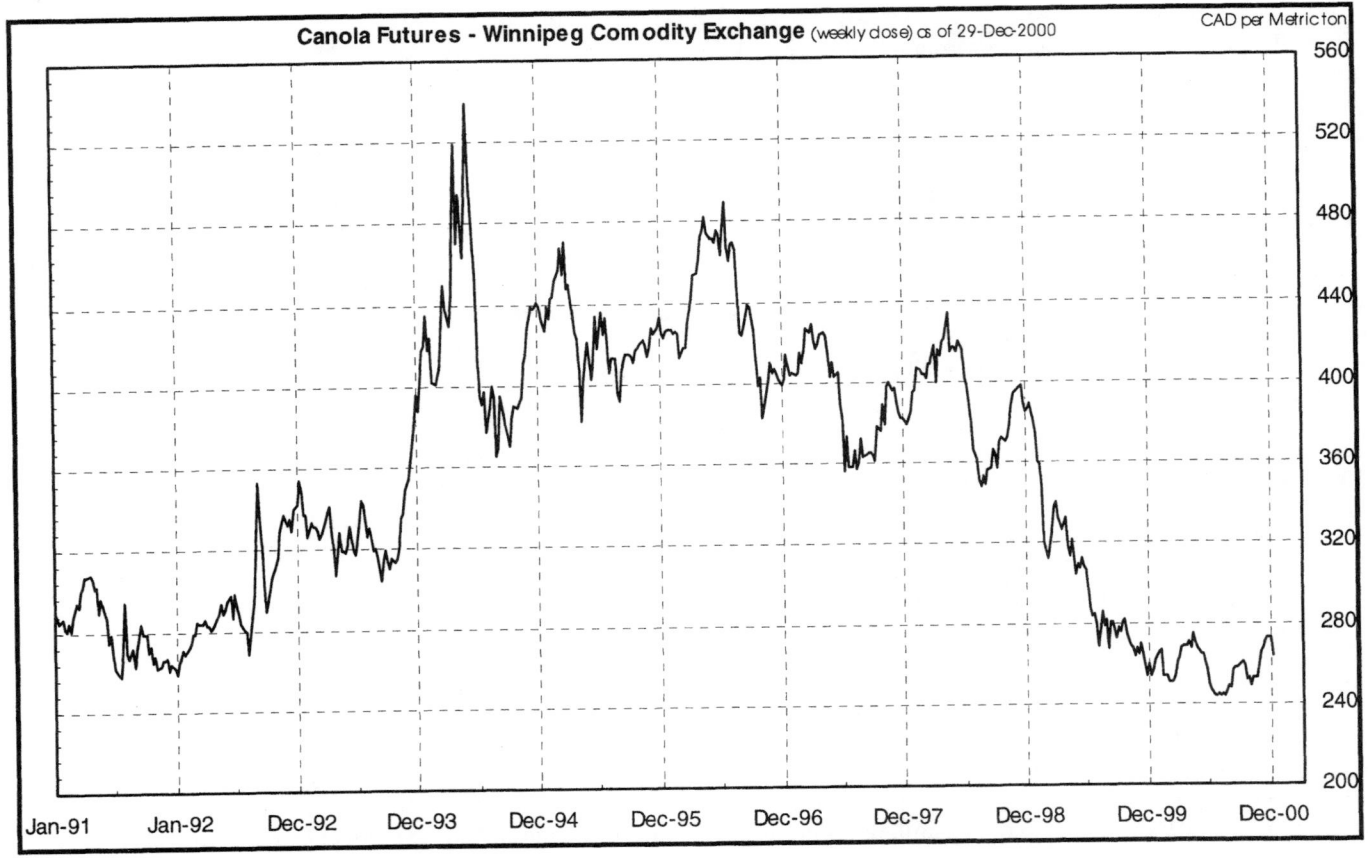

Canola Futures - Winnipeg Comodity Exchange (weekly close) as of 29-Dec-2000

CAD per Metric ton

Volume of Trading of Canola Futures in Winnipeg   In Contracts

Year	Jan.	Feb.	Mar.	Apr.	May	June	July	Aug.	Sept.	Oct.	Nov.	Dec.	Total
1991	67,489	59,380	64,193	67,572	68,849	59,270	90,575	65,541	76,966	75,457	53,660	66,421	815,373
1992	57,429	54,546	57,174	38,674	87,638	75,018	50,157	72,971	79,034	93,692	99,577	73,805	839,715
1993	73,411	74,362	63,737	73,358	61,996	70,117	94,286	77,325	56,377	73,953	107,485	112,377	938,784
1994	119,691	103,517	85,125	100,923	111,962	79,307	83,903	95,712	54,893	87,350	101,727	96,797	1,120,907
1995	75,068	87,113	86,340	67,937	95,447	85,126	94,576	70,904	94,794	126,210	84,991	107,177	1,075,683
1996	99,542	95,034	76,704	128,169	148,189	103,892	135,652	87,896	108,490	161,894	90,105	110,453	1,346,020
1997	121,433	133,056	131,473	148,647	117,219	116,117	80,867	72,602	93,967	150,065	97,984	124,245	1,387,675
1998	100,926	144,309	110,708	140,789	130,551	121,829	107,816	89,457	121,573	181,002	127,120	181,278	1,557,358
1999	129,758	59,772	132,732	143,282	102,838	134,179	94,256	113,913	130,505	184,973	157,428	179,798	1,563,434
2000	137,528	63,180	163,038	169,807	168,164	152,358	79,071	91,762	146,890	208,639	154,727	204,045	1,739,209

Source: Winnipeg Commodity Exchange (WCE)

Average Open Interest of Canola Futures in Winnipeg   In Contracts

Year	Jan.	Feb.	Mar.	Apr.	May	June	July	Aug.	Sept.	Oct.	Nov.	Dec.
1991	22,000	22,829	24,815	26,637	30,072	28,240	28,288	27,547	27,558	29,079	23,880	20,117
1992	15,943	17,556	20,559	21,410	23,727	28,885	26,013	25,674	28,049	32,724	35,693	37,375
1993	34,098	37,658	36,715	38,210	38,231	29,743	39,763	43,844	50,616	55,107	54,998	54,475
1994	50,335	55,280	54,899	58,012	60,567	55,434	54,733	57,044	57,049	54,375	55,045	49,475
1995	47,579	43,662	36,530	32,580	38,361	42,961	43,607	42,828	51,067	57,638	46,640	45,444
1996	42,646	43,808	45,126	47,989	54,228	52,176	49,387	40,619	42,242	52,273	53,121	54,323
1997	48,681	48,281	50,815	50,025	49,212	43,941	35,496	30,039	25,255	36,674	38,702	42,510
1998	35,864	46,678	49,161	48,683	56,163	60,285	57,627	51,462	53,919	56,651	51,426	60,663
1999	57,958	64,014	57,851	57,351	51,808	53,039	49,273	41,819	53,425	67,244	63,780	64,286
2000	59,057	65,545	65,296	66,253	65,855	59,673	46,813	51,367	59,342	72,618	64,862	65,170

Source: Winnipeg Commodity Exchange (WCE)

World Supply and Distribution of Canola and Products   In Thousands of Metric Tons

Year	Canola Production	Exports	Imports	Crush	Ending Stocks	Meal Production	Exports	Imports	Consumption	Ending Stocks	Oil Production	Exports	Imports	Consumption	Ending Stocks
1991-2	28,214	4,675	4,734	25,557	1,045	15,662	3,367	3,389	15,569	445	9,314	2,076	2,049	9,194	468
1992-3	25,284	4,055	4,241	22,988	1,045	14,067	3,374	3,412	14,097	453	8,392	1,729	1,694	8,424	401
1993-4	26,734	5,153	5,317	24,636	838	15,085	3,346	3,509	15,254	447	9,119	2,239	2,203	9,064	420
1994-5	30,309	5,836	5,900	27,178	1,001	16,525	3,718	3,661	16,448	467	10,016	2,654	2,779	10,236	325
1995-6	34,438	5,978	5,795	30,397	1,681	18,467	4,322	4,108	18,138	582	11,129	2,596	2,563	10,971	450
1996-7	31,546	5,673	5,967	29,768	1,037	18,125	4,361	4,023	17,859	510	10,860	2,625	2,547	10,842	390
1997-8	33,226	6,902	6,757	30,571	761	18,439	4,581	4,417	18,351	434	11,248	3,024	2,718	10,887	445
1998-9[1]	35,918	9,154	9,101	32,592	1,297	19,552	3,842	3,764	19,695	313	12,074	2,873	2,606	11,780	472
1999-00[2]	42,678	11,039	11,024	37,971	2,838	22,791	4,620	4,541	22,598	427	13,831	2,973	2,694	13,354	670
2000-1[3]	37,641	9,963	9,983	35,698	1,610	21,444	4,125	4,162	21,590	318	13,128	2,875	2,863	13,168	618

[1] Preliminary.   [2] Estimate.   [3] Forecast.   Source: Economic Research Service, U.S. Department of Agriculture (ERS-USDA); The Oil World

Salient Statistics of Canola and Canola Oil in the United States   In Thousands of Metric Tons

Year	Canola Stocks June 1	Production	Imports	Total	Crush	Exports	Total[3]	Oil Stocks June 1	Production	Imports	Total	Domestic	Exports	Total
1991-2	15	94	1	110	57	44	101	20	14	374	408	367	7	374
1992-3	6	72	12	90	35	47	82	34	24	396	454	415	7	422
1993-4	5	118	351	474	389	35	424	32	186	412	630	532	35	567
1994-5	43	209	286	538	413	103	516	63	137	430	630	535	70	605
1995-6	16	250	253	519	409	62	.471	25	162	497	684	582	67	649
1996-7	40	219	259	518	395	79	474	35	155	502	692	529	133	662
1997-8	36	355	355	746	589	126	715	30	205	504	739	529	158	687
1998-9	19	710	310	1,039	698	246	944	52	250	503	805	603	123	726
1999-00[1]	77	621	242	940	722	136	858	79	274	534	887	662	129	791
2000-1[2]	50	872	165	1,087	718	250	968	96	273	537	906	693	122	815

[1] Preliminary.   [2] Forecast.   [3] Includes planting seed and residual.   Source: Economic Research Service, U.S. Department of Agriculture

Wholesale Price of Canola Oil, Refined (Denatured), in Tanks in New York   In Cents Per Pound

Year	Jan.	Feb.	Mar.	Apr.	May	June	July	Aug.	Sept.	Oct.	Nov.	Dec.	Average
1991	82.25	82.25	82.25	82.25	82.25	82.25	82.25	82.25	82.25	82.25	82.25	82.25	82.30
1992	82.25	82.25	82.25	82.25	82.25	82.25	82.25	82.25	67.25	62.25	62.25	62.25	76.00
1993	62.25	62.25	62.25	62.25	55.88	53.75	53.25	53.00	53.00	52.00	52.50	50.00	56.00
1994	53.75	53.75	53.75	53.75	53.75	53.75	53.75	53.75	53.75	53.75	53.75	53.75	53.75
1995	53.75	53.75	53.75	53.75	53.15	50.75	50.75	50.75	50.75	50.75	50.75	50.75	51.95
1996	50.75	50.75	50.75	50.75	50.75	50.75	50.75	50.75	50.75	60.56	90.00	90.00	58.11
1997	90.00	90.00	90.00	90.00	90.00	90.00	90.00	90.00	90.00	82.00	82.00	82.00	88.00
1998	90.00	90.00	90.00	90.00	90.00	90.00	90.00	90.00	90.00	90.00	90.00	90.00	90.00
1999	80.00	80.00	80.00	80.00	80.00	80.00	80.00	80.00	80.00	80.00	80.00	80.00	80.00
2000[1]	90.00	90.00	90.00	90.00	90.00	90.00	90.00	90.00	90.00	90.00			90.00

[1] Preliminary.   Source: Economic Research Service, U.S. Department of Agriculture (ERS-USDA)

Average Price of Canola in Vancouver   In Canadian Dollars Per Tonne

Year	Jan.	Feb.	Mar.	Apr.	May	June	July	Aug.	Sept.	Oct.	Nov.	Dec.	Average
1991	285.01	280.36	291.50	298.57	293.83	277.25	258.12	269.40	275.00	270.30	262.90	261.60	276.99
1992	264.15	273.35	282.70	276.85	288.08	292.35	272.20	282.26	320.62	302.10	327.22	331.57	292.79
1993	344.22	329.26	328.67	325.06	318.85	319.23	331.29	322.85	311.29	311.66	331.44	366.37	328.35
1994	408.60	413.10	422.23	454.90	481.44	484.95	388.63	382.54	381.70	379.99	401.38	432.35	419.32
1995	431.85	440.41	456.13	425.40	404.27	414.31	426.49	405.94	405.89	413.29	416.03	423.77	421.98
1996	424.07	422.60	417.55	443.94	473.04	469.28	470.38	453.86	453.53	444.01	432.30	439.79	445.36
1997	441.96	441.68	457.95	448.09	446.00	428.47	395.58	400.68	390.38	398.81	419.12	410.21	423.24
1998	416.48	428.88	434.68	441.44	450.56	443.11	404.86	387.05	389.34	400.40	412.17	417.41	418.87
1999	402.74	368.17	363.24	362.16	353.21	356.53	317.36	305.73	302.93	302.68	297.76	287.62	335.01
2000	286.09	277.92	280.97	287.34	284.59	274.12	265.32	262.24	269.17	265.32	267.75	278.59	274.95

Source: Winnipeg Commodity Exchange (WCE)

Cassava

Cassava, or tapioca root, is used primarily as an animal feed and as a foodstuff in tropical countries. Cassava has been viewed as a food that could be the solution to the hunger problems that exist in less developed countries. Technological advances have held the promise that there will be substantial increases in yields in the future. New strains of cassava root are being developed in Africa that could eventually be used in the fight against world hunger.

Cassava is grown in countries with tropical climates. It is a popular crop to produce since it is resistant to drought and relatively easy to grow. Cassava is a diet staple in many countries. In countries where the price of imported foodstuffs has risen there has been increased demand for locally produced foods like cassava.

For 2000, the Food and Agricultural Organization of the United Nations reported that world production of cassava was 170.6 million metric tonnes, up 1 percent from 1999. World harvested acreage was estimated at 16.6 million hectares. Cassava production has been increasing. In the 1995-1997 period, world production averaged 165.3 million tonnes.

The world's largest producer of cassava is Nigeria with 2000 production estimated at 32.7 million tonnes or 19 percent of the world total. In Nigeria, root crops like cassava are diet staples.

The next largest producer of cassava is Brazil. Production in year 2000 was estimated at 21.8 million tonnes, up 4 percent from the previous year and some 11 percent more than 1998 production which totaled 19.7 million tonnes. Brazil's harvested acreage was estimated at 1.57 million hectares.

Another large producer of cassava is Thailand which is also the largest exporter. Thailand exports of cassava have exceeded 4 million tonnes or over 90 percent of the world total. Most exports go to European countries. Thailand's cassava production in 2000 was estimated at 18.5 million tonnes, up 12 percent from the previous year. Production by Indonesia in 2000 was estimated to be 15.4 million tonnes. Production by the Congo in 2000 was estimated to be 16 million tonnes, down 3 percent from the previous year. Other large producers are Ghana, India, Mozambique, and Tanzania.

World Cassava Production — In Thousands of Metric Tons

Year	Brazil	China	Ghana	India	Indo-nesia	Mozam-bique	Nigeria	Para-guay	Tan-zania	Thailand	Uganda	Zaire	World Total
1991	24,538	3,310	3,600	5,416	15,954	3,690	20,000	2,585	7,460	20,356	3,229	19,500	153,562
1992	21,919	3,357	4,000	5,469	16,516	3,239	21,320	2,591	7,112	20,356	2,896	20,210	153,058
1993	21,837	3,403	4,500	5,413	16,799	3,511	29,900	2,656	6,833	20,203	3,139	20,835	163,002
1994	24,464	3,501	6,025	5,784	15,729	3,352	31,005	2,518	7,209	19,091	2,080	18,051	163,514
1995	25,423	3,501	6,612	5,929	15,442	4,178	31,404	3,054	5,969	17,388	2,224	17,500	165,436
1996	24,584	3,501	7,111	5,979	17,003	4,734	31,418	2,649	5,992	18,084	2,245	18,000	165,650
1997[1]	24,354	3,501	6,800	5,979	16,103	5,337	30,409	3,155	6,444	18,000	2,291	----	164,751

[1] Estimate.   Source: Food and Agriculture Organization of the United Nations (FAO-UN)

Prices of Tapioca, Hard Pellets, F.O.B. Rotterdam — U.S. Dollars Per Tonne

Year	Jan.	Feb.	Mar.	Apr.	May	June	July	Aug.	Sept.	Oct.	Nov.	Dec.	Average
1993	160	150	140	149	145	133	130	131	136	127	120	125	137
1994	122	123	128	133	138	141	147	154	158	161	161	161	144
1995	164	170	180	178	174	176	183	176	178	184	182	178	177
1996	167	160	155	158	163	154	149	154	146	139	140	133	152
1997	133	118	112	108	114	110	100	97	100	102	102	100	108
1998	96	100	98	104	106	104	105	106	112	122	124	109	107
1999	104	102	101	102	108	104	99	102	100	99	100	97	102
2000	94	90	88	92	85	88	88	81	78	74	76	79	84

Source: The Oil World

World Trade in Tapioca — In Thousands of Metric Tons

Year	Exports					Imports						
	China	Indonesia	Thailand	Viet Nam	Total World Exports	China	EC-12[2]	Japan	Rep. of Korea	United States	Former USSR	Total World Imports
1993	269	936	6,707	29	8,090	149	6,449	151	658	60	8	8,376
1994	77	686	4,703	28	5,645	92	5,441	94	132	18	----	6,076
1995	10	481	3,297	1	3,860	362	2,924	16	140	----	----	3,590
1996	11	389	3,607	1	4,052	75	3,321	22	554	----	----	4,174
1997	11	247	4,155	26	4,477	242	3,413	15	455	----	----	4,475
1998	10	221	3,199	----	3,468	250	2,620	19	347	----	----	3,440
1999[1]	10	340	4,341	1	4,740	381	3,905	18	90	----	----	4,630

[1] Estimate.   [2] Intra-EU trade is excluded.   Source: The Oil World

Castor Beans

Castorseed beans are used to produce castor oil. The beans contain about 35 percent to 55 percent oil. The oil is obtained by pressing or solvent extraction. Castor oil finds use in many products. It is used in paint varnish and for making platicizers and dibasic acids. Castor oil and derivatives like dehydrated castor oil find use in cosmetics, hair oils, printing inks, nylon plastics, greases and hydraulic fluids, dyeing acids, and in textile finishing materials.

World production of castorseed beans in the 1999/2000 season was forecast to be just over a million tonnes. In recent seasons, production has averaged about 1.11 million tonnes per year. In the 1994/95 and the 1995/96 seasons, production increased to average 1.22 million tonnes.

The largest producer of castorseed beans is India. Most of India's castor beans are produced in the western state of Gujarat which accounts for about three-fourths of India's

castorseed production. The 1999/00 crop was estimated at 680,000 tonnes, down 16 percent from the previous year. A drought in the August-September 1999 period damaged the crop. India is also the largest exporter of castor oil.

The next largest producer of castorseed beans is China. The 1999/00 crop was estimated at 210,000 tonnes, up 11 percent from the previous season. Brazil is the third largest producer of castorseeds with the 1999/00 crop estimated at 45,000 tonnes. Other producers include Paraguay and Thailand.

The U.S. is the largest user of castor oil. U.S. castor oil (in inedible products like plastics) consumption has averaged about 53 million pounds per year. In January 2000, U.S. stocks were 44.3 million pounds, up 24 percent from a year earlier.

World Production of Castorseed Beans   In Thousands of Metric Tons

Crop Year	Brazil	China	Ecuador	India	Mexico	Paraguay	Pakistan	Philippines	Sudan	Tanzania	Thailand	Former U.S.S.R.	World Total
1993-4	45	280	13	700	1	15	7	7	6	3	22	4	1,135
1994-5	53	230	7	850	1	10	5	7	4	3	15	8	1,226
1995-6	33	165	5	930	1	9	9	7	2	3	16	3	1,214
1996-7	43	220	4	770	1	15	5	4	1	2	15	3	1,117
1997-8[1]	96	180	4	800	2	16	5	4	1	3	14	3	1,162
1998-9[2]	14	210	4	810	1	19	7	4	1	3	12	3	1,122
1999-00[3]	32	215	4	730	1	18	7	4	1	3	8	3	1,060

[1] Preliminary.   [2] Estimate.   [3] Forecast.   Sources: Foreign Agricultural Service, U.S.Department of Agriculture (FAS-USDA); The Oil World

Castor Oil Consumption[2] in the United States   In Thousands of Pounds

Year	Oct.	Nov.	Dec.	Jan.	Feb.	Mar.	Apr.	May	June	July	Aug.	Sept.	Total
1994-5	5,032	4,204	5,092	6,001	5,179	4,911	4,722	3,740	5,067	4,891	6,452	4,834	60,125
1995-6	5,228	5,463	6,232	5,794	6,979	5,545	3,369	5,864	5,469	5,439	4,332	3,818	63,532
1996-7	3,921	4,460	4,555	3,738	4,679	4,256	4,476	4,006	3,851	3,855	3,763	5,050	50,610
1997-8	3,276	4,353	4,367	4,409	3,035	4,389	4,218	3,645	4,651	4,350	3,489	4,210	48,392
1998-9	2,348	3,579	3,740	3,323	4,197	5,004	5,218	4,639	4,396	4,471	4,465	4,494	49,874
1999-00	4,281	3,917	4,682	3,819	4,328	5,346	4,135	3,341	4,268	3,884	4,257	4,573	50,831
2000-1[1]	2,694	4,601	2,432										38,908

[1] Preliminary.   [2] In inedible products (Resins, Plastics, etc.).   Source: Bureau of the Census, U.S. Department of Commerce

Castor Oil Stocks in the United States, on First of Month   In Thousands of Pounds

Year	Oct.	Nov.	Dec.	Jan.	Feb.	Mar.	Apr.	May	June	July	Aug.	Sept.
1994-5	21,066	23,484	23,357	21,132	29,245	20,986	10,387	5,492	22,765	33,557	37,542	42,516
1995-6	27,143	35,329	43,189	51,713	45,746	37,210	29,718	36,829	55,687	43,954	37,802	25,535
1996-7	23,831	38,785	41,016	31,755	23,630	15,157	7,200	24,164	14,166	27,754	17,426	20,656
1997-8	25,098	24,188	25,425	17,543	12,736	7,138	2,804	18,897	15,386	24,682	16,586	29,862
1998-9	40,018	46,809	36,881	35,668	31,961	22,252	13,771	11,950	5,568	13,952	34,956	25,944
1999-00	44,427	34,180	31,191	44,315	36,632	26,885	25,486	27,605	39,038	38,118	42,934	31,015
2000-1[1]	32,585	35,858	30,058	24,732								

[1] Preliminary.   Source: Bureau of the Census, U.S. Department of Commerce

Average Wholesale Price of Castor Oil No. 1, Brazilian Tanks in New York   In Cents Per Pound

Year	Jan.	Feb.	Mar.	Apr.	May	June	July	Aug.	Sept.	Oct.	Nov.	Dec.	Average
1994	44.00	41.75	41.00	41.00	46.00	45.00	45.00	45.00	45.00	45.00	45.00	45.00	44.06
1995	45.00	45.00	45.00	45.00	45.00	45.00	45.00	45.00	45.00	45.00	45.00	45.00	45.00
1996	43.50	41.50	41.50	41.50	41.50	41.50	41.50	41.50	41.50	41.50	41.50	41.50	41.67
1997	41.50	41.50	41.50	41.50	41.50	41.50	41.50	41.50	41.50	41.50	41.50	41.50	41.50
1998	41.50	41.50	41.50	41.50	41.50	48.00	48.00	48.00	48.00	48.00	48.00	48.00	45.29
1999	48.00	48.00	48.00	48.00	48.00	48.00	48.00	48.00	48.00	48.00	48.00	48.00	48.00
2000	47.00	47.00	47.00	47.00	47.00	47.00	47.00	48.00	48.00	48.00			47.30

Source: Foreign Agricultural Service, U.S.Department of Agriculture (FAS-USDA)

Cattle and Calves

Cattle disease outbreaks were probably the major story in 2000. Foot and Mouth Disease (FMD) occurrences broke out in Argentina and Brazil, the impact of which suspended their shipments of fresh beef to the U.S. and the resultant ban could continue into 2001. In Europe, meanwhile, renewed consumer fears of Mad Cow Disease resurfaced in late 2000, possibly leading to the forced destruction of two million head of older cattle among the 15 members of the European Union.

The world cattle inventory showed relatively little growth during the late 1990's; the January 1, 2000, total of 1,030 million head compares with 1,025 million a year earlier, and a forecast of 1,036 million as of early 2001. However, some large changes have occurred, notably the steady decline in cattle numbers in the former U.S.S.R. and the increase in China. The combined Russian and Ukraine cattle inventory in early 2000 was estimated at only 38 million head vs. 40 million in 1999, and an estimate of less than 36 million head in early 2001. In contrast, China's January 1, 2000, inventory of a record high 127 million head compares with 124 million a year earlier and 130 million early in 2001. India, which held 30 percent of the world's total cattle inventory on January 1, 2000, about 312 million head, appears to be slowly increasing its inventory following little expansion in the first half of the decade, with a projected total of 314 million head in early 2001. Brazil had the second largest inventory in early 2000 with 146 million head vs. 144 million in 1999. Brazil is projecting 151 million head in early 2001.

The U.S. cattle inventory apparently peaked in the 1980's at 110 million head, then sliding to 96 million by early 1990. A moderate cyclical expansion followed that carried the inventory to 103 million head by early 1996. The cyclical downturn that followed the expansion does not yet appear over although it may be slowing. The January 1, 2000, inventory of 98 million head compares with 99.1 million a year earlier, and 97 million in early 2001. The three largest cattle inventory states are generally Texas, Kansas, and Nebraska.

World beef consumption in 2000 proved stable; usage was estimated at 48.6 million metric tonnes vs. 48.2 million in 1999, and an estimated 48.6 million in 2001. European Union usage in 2000 of 7.3 million tonnes was about unchanged from 1999, and it may prove no higher, if not lower, in 2001 depending upon the depth of consumer fears

towards possible contaminated beef. China beef consumption in 2000 of a record high 5.3 million tonnes compares with 5 million in 1999, and an estimated 5.7 million in 2001. In the former U.S.S.R., consumption in 2000 fell to 2.8 million tonnes from 3.4 million in 1999, but is forecast to hold at 2.8 million in 2001.

U.S. commercial cattle slaughter in 2000 (through October) of 30.6 million head compares with 30.3 million in the like 1999 period. Dressed slaughter weights in late 2000 averaged a record large 757 pounds. U.S. beef production in 2000 of 26.8 billion pounds compares with 26.4 billion in 1999, and is estimated at 25.5 billion in 2001. U.S. per capita beef consumption had shown little growth in recent years as consumers opt for less red meat in their diet; per capita use in 2000 of 69.7 pounds (retail weight) compares with 69 pounds in 1999, and a 2001 estimate of only 66 pounds. However, a more positive consumer attitude towards beef seemed to take hold in 1999-2000 reflecting the strong U.S. economy and greater disposable income, and a change in the industry's advertising that stressed beef's high protein nutritional value. Demand in 2001 could be checked if the economy cools as it seemed to be doing in late 2000.

U.S. beef (and veal) exports in 2000 of 2.5 billion pounds compares with 2.4 billion in 1999, and is forecast to slip under 2.5 billion in 2001, possibly due to the U.S. dollar's strength. U.S. beef imports in 2000 of 3 billion pounds compare with 2.9 billion in 1999, and a 3.1 billion estimate for 2001. Australia, New Zealand, and Canada are the largest beef suppliers to the U.S. Live cattle is imported from Canada and Mexico.

Choice steer prices, basis Nebraska, in 2000 averaged $68.84 per cwt. vs. $65.56 in 1999. Prices are forecast between $71.00-$77.00/cwt. in 2001. On the retail level, choice beef prices in mid-2000 averaged around $3.10/lb., about 10 cents above the a year earlier level.

Futures Markets

Live cattle futures and options on futures are traded on the Chicago Mercantile Exchange (CME), the Bolsa de Mercadorias & Futures (BM&F), and the Midamerica Commodity Exchange (MidAm). Feeder cattle futures are traded on the CME and the BM&F, and feeder cattle options are traded on the CME.

World Cattle and Buffalo Numbers as of January 1   In Thousands of Head

Year	Argentina	Australia	Brazil	China	Colombia	France	Germany	India	Mexico	Russia	Ukraine	United States	World Total (Mil. Head)
1992	55,229	25,857	141,800	104,592	16,008	20,970	17,134	271,200	30,232	54,677	23,728	97,556	1,032
1993	55,577	25,182	149,000	107,840	16,391	20,383	16,207	271,255	30,649	52,226	22,457	99,176	1,031
1994	54,875	25,758	149,100	113,157	16,614	20,112	15,897	291,973	30,702	48,914	21,607	100,974	1,053
1995	54,207	25,736	149,315	123,317	17,556	20,524	15,962	293,922	30,191	43,296	19,624	102,785	1,058
1996	53,569	26,500	149,228	104,000	18,478	20,662	15,890	296,462	28,140	39,700	17,558	103,548	1,029
1997	51,696	26,780	146,110	110,318	19,038	20,557	15,760	299,802	26,822	35,800	15,313	101,656	1,026
1998	49,238	26,710	144,670	121,757	19,507	20,154	15,227	303,030	25,628	31,500	12,579	99,744	1,026
1999	49,437	26,578	143,893	124,419	20,621	20,097	14,942	306,967	24,859	28,600	11,722	99,115	1,025
2000[1]	49,832	26,600	146,272	126,986	21,700	20,194	14,657	312,572	23,716	27,000	10,627	98,048	1,030
2001[2]	50,052	27,050	150,853	130,000	22,663	20,150	14,220	313,774	22,441	25,800	10,000	96,909	1,036

[1] Preliminary.   [2] Forecast.   *Source: Foreign Agricultural Service, U.S. Department of Agriculture (FAS-USDA)*

Cattle Supply and Distribution in the United States   In Thousands of Head

Year	Cattle & Calves on Farms January 1	Imports	Calves Born	Total Supply	Federally Inspected	Other[3]	All Commercial	Farm	Total Slaughter	Deaths on Farms	Exports	Total Disappearance
1991	96,393	1,939	38,583	139,861	33,285	841	34,126	242	34,368	4,247	311	38,927
1992	97,556	2,255	38,933	141,104	33,428	817	34,245	242	34,489	4,366	322	39,177
1993	99,176	2,499	39,369	142,750	33,752	767	34,519	233	34,746	4,630	153	39,529
1994	100,974	2,083	40,105	143,799	34,719	745	25,464	227	35,691	4,254	231	40,176
1995	102,755	2,786	40,264	145,805	36,272	798	37,069	225	37,294	4,382	95	41,771
1996	103,548	1,965	39,823	145,336	37,435	917	38,351	225	38,575	4,572	174	43,321
1997	101,656	2,046	38,961	142,663	37,101	792	37,893	224	38,111	4,676	282	43,069
1998	99,744	2,034	38,812	140,590	36,209	714	36,923	218	38,111	4,220	285	41,643
1999[1]	99,115	1,945	38,710	139,770	35,486	664	36,150	215	37,138		329	
2000[2]	98,048	2,150			35,631	616	36,247	210	37,642		485	

[1] Preliminary.   [2] Estimate.   [3] Wholesale and retail.   Source: Economic Research Service, U.S. Department of Agriculture (ERS-USDA)

Beef Supply and Utilization in the United States

Year/ Quarter	Beginning Stocks	Production Commercial	Production Total	Imports	Total Supply	Exports	Ending Stocks	Total Disappearance	Per Capita Disappearance Carcass Weight	Per Capita Disappearance Retail Weight
			Million Pounds						Pounds	
1996	519	25,419	25,525	2,073	28,117	1,877	377	25,863	97.4	67.7
I	519	6,303	6,340	508	7,367	452	461	6,454	24.4	17.0
II	461	6,642	6,658	526	7,645	544	406	6,695	25.2	17.5
III	406	6,390	6,406	555	7,367	436	414	6,517	24.5	17.0
IV	414	6,084	6,121	484	7,019	445	377	6,197	23.2	16.2
1997	377	25,384	25,490	2,343	28,210	2,136	465	25,609	96.7	67.2
I	377	6,112	6,149	536	7,062	455	387	6,220	23.3	16.2
II	387	6,419	6,435	716	7,538	513	425	6,600	24.7	17.1
III	425	6,603	6,636	576	7,741	600	430	6,811	25.4	17.6
IV	430	6,258	6,187	515	7,152	568	400	6,302	23.4	16.3
1998	465	25,653	27,134	2,642	29,775	2,171	465	25,536	94.5	68.1
I	465	6,215	6,680	644	7,324	500	375	6,317	23.4	16.7
II	375	6,463	6,838	682	7,520	537	316	6,451	23.9	17.2
III	316	6,638	6,954	685	7,639	563	323			17.5
IV	323	6,339	6,662	630	7,292	571	465			16.7
1999[1]	296	26,386	27,579	2,874	30,453	2,329	302			67.4
I	296	6,399	6,695	628	7,323	564	309			16.7
II	309	6,627	6,936	812	7,748	557	293			17.7
III	293	6,838	7,131	742	7,873	593	294			17.2
IV	294	6,522	6,816	692	7,508	615	302			15.8
2000[2]	314	26,777	28,244	3,015	31,259	2,350	402			69.4
I	314	6,653	6,967	720	7,687	540	369			17.2
II	367	6,699	7,066	820	7,886	565	374			17.5
III	380	6,914	7,294	775	8,069	625	378			18.0
IV	406	6,511	6,917	700	7,617	620	412			16.7

[1] Preliminary.   [2] Forecast.   Source: Economic Research Service, U.S. Department of Agriculture (ERS-USDA)

United States Cattle on Feed in 13 States   In Thousands of Head

Year/ Quarter	Number on Feed[3]	Placed on Feed	Marketings	Other Disappearance	Year/ Quarter	Number on Feed[3]	Placed on Feed	Marketings	Other Disappearance
1997	10,558	24,271	22,774	930	1999[1]	10,667	25,172	23,480	894
I	10,558	5,605	5,563	239	I	10,667	5,742	5,819	206
II	10,391	4,856	6,014	275	II	10,384	5,501	6,064	266
III	8,958	7,135	5,975	155	III	9,555	6,999	6,119	169
IV	9,963	6,675	5,222	261	IV	10,276	6,930	5,478	253
1998	11,155	19,476	18,878	712	2000[2]	11,475	25,348	24,100	925
I	11,155	4,931	5,706	262	I	11,475	6,107	6,150	250
II	10,118	1,563	2,033	72	II	11,182	5,656	6,187	262
III	9,161	6,606	5,857	163	III	10,389	7,043	6,269	147
IV	9,781	6,376	5,282	215	IV	11,016	6,542	5,494	266

[1] Preliminary.   [2] Estimate.   [3] Beginning of period.   Source: Economic Research Service, U.S. Department of Agriculture (ERS-USDA)

CATTLE AND CALVES

Live Cattle (monthly average) through December 2000

Cents Per Pound
- - - - All Grades, Chicago (Jan. 1909 - Dec. 1947)
Good, Chicago (Jan. 1948 - Dec. 1964)
Choice, Chicago (Jan. 1965 - July 1971)
Choice, Average, Omaha (Aug. 1971 - Aug. 1987)
Average, Texas-Oklahoma (Sept. 1987 - date)

United States Cattle on Feed in 7 States, on First of Month   In Thousands of Head

Year	Jan.	Feb.	Mar.	Apr.	May	June	July	Aug.	Sept.	Oct.	Nov.	Dec.
1991	9,082	9,133	9,044	9,111	8,740	8,740	8,027	7,533	7,199	7,306	8,053	8,477
1992	8,397	8,223	8,195	8,058	7,868	7,876	7,377	7,050	7,018	7,565	8,704	8,984
1993	9,163	9,140	8,851	8,781	8,409	8,393	7,973	7,703	7,794	8,224	9,096	9,397
1994	8,256	8,139	7,981	7,960	7,772	7,511	6,910	6,841	6,949	7,295	7,988	8,198
1995	8,031	8,119	8,227	8,328	8,233	8,182	7,734	7,391	7,189	7,722	8,420	8,685
1996	8,667	8,304	8,152	8,286	7,758	7,253	6,578	6,337	6,612	7,486	8,534	9,003
1997	8,943	8,813	8,769	8,904	8,484	8,231	7,679	7,536	7,850	8,558	9,390	9,718
1998	9,455	9,180	8,835	8,607	8,295	8,289	7,825	7,706	7,750	8,376	9,190	9,404
1999	9,021	8,917	8,878	8,899	8,583	8,547	8,183	7,889	8,185	8,793	9,789	10,020
2000[1]	9,752	9,885	9,695	9,573	9,361	9,411	8,959	8,812	8,972	9,502	10,192	10,213

[1] Preliminary.   *Source: Economic Research Service, U.S. Department of Agriculture (ERS-USDA)*

United States Cattle Placed on Feedlots in 7 States   In Thousands of Head

Year	Jan.	Feb.	Mar.	Apr.	May	June	July	Aug.	Sept.	Oct.	Nov.	Dec.	Total
1991	1,776	1,490	1,723	1,447	1,837	1,137	1,342	1,479	1,826	2,514	1,902	1,456	19,929
1992	1,565	1,502	1,516	1,425	1,724	1,319	1,432	1,641	2,189	2,688	1,813	1,694	20,508
1993	1,641	1,262	1,626	1,326	1,801	1,430	1,513	1,865	2,148	2,494	1,878	1,490	20,474
1994	1,416	1,256	1,518	1,310	1,359	1,113	1,520	1,761	1,915	2,244	1,642	1,345	18,399
1995	1,631	1,532	1,681	1,403	1,673	1,356	1,404	1,653	2,173	2,278	1,804	1,446	20,034
1996	1,312	1,441	1,666	1,150	1,242	1,068	1,483	1,965	2,267	2,536	1,953	1,423	19,506
1997	1,663	1,552	1,694	1,296	1,612	1,224	1,751	2,111	2,278	2,454	1,826	1,304	20,765
1998	1,492	1,290	1,421	1,358	1,740	1,314	1,677	1,773	2,254	2,396	1,732	1,250	19,697
1999	1,681	1,563	1,741	1,443	1,733	1,515	1,565	2,085	2,345	2,629	1,823	1,408	21,531
2000[1]	1,931	1,606	1,716	1,450	1,998	1,413	1,674	2,091	2,286	2,387	1,678	1,440	21,670

[1] Preliminary.   *Source: Economic Research Service, U.S. Department of Agriculture (ERS-USDA)*

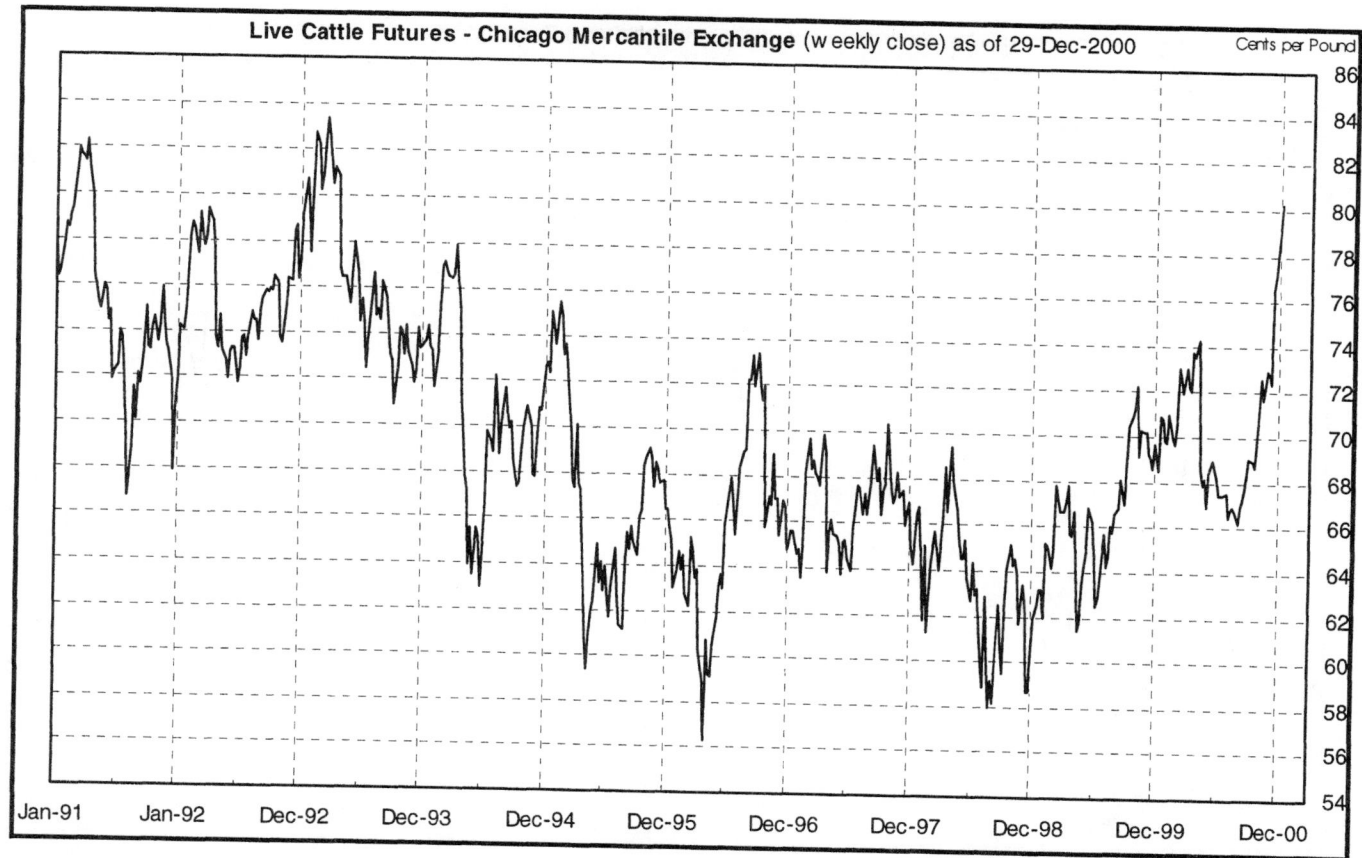

United States Cattle Marketings in 7 States   In Thousands of Head

Year	Jan.	Feb.	Mar.	Apr.	May	June	July	Aug.	Sept.	Oct.	Nov.	Dec.	Total
1991	1,607	1,466	1,519	1,690	1,696	1,736	1,744	1,746	1,633	1,690	1,396	1,443	19,366
1992	1,640	1,410	1,536	1,490	1,594	1,702	1,674	1,592	1,581	1,473	1,442	1,414	18,548
1993	1,534	1,441	1,585	1,572	1,681	1,743	1,702	1,692	1,652	1,546	1,469	1,431	19,048
1994	1,481	1,357	1,467	1,430	1,542	1,632	1,550	1,602	1,525	1,504	1,370	1,432	17,892
1995	1,484	1,372	1,513	1,437	1,667	1,754	1,698	1,815	1,594	1,529	1,478	1,412	18,753
1996	1,626	1,541	1,476	1,613	1,747	1,696	1,678	1,653	1,342	1,431	1,418	1,415	18,636
1997	1,728	1,554	1,497	1,648	1,785	1,732	1,852	1,755	1,528	1,545	1,429	1,499	19,552
1998	1,689	1,579	1,580	1,609	1,681	1,727	1,755	1,687	1,577	1,537	1,455	1,564	19,440
1999	1,738	1,560	1,668	1,681	1,696	1,835	1,816	1,747	1,682	1,570	1,530	1,601	20,124
2000[1]	1,747	1,749	1,764	1,591	1,863	1,828	1,784	1,895	1,708	1,647	1,568	1,440	20,584

[1] Preliminary.   *Source: Economic Research Service, U.S. Department of Agriculture (ERS-USDA)*

Quarterly Trade of Live Cattle in the United States   In Head

	Imports					Exports				
Year	First Quarter	Second Quarter	Third Quarter	Fourth Quarter	Annual	First Quarter	Second Quarter	Third Quarter	Fourth Quarter	Annual
1991	599,398	551,390	225,710	562,556	1,939,054	49,497	62,134	103,866	95,465	310,962
1992	599,255	505,568	389,417	801,025	2,255,265	97,683	100,282	74,827	48,998	321,790
1993	672,447	635,341	469,439	721,819	2,499,046	50,733	33,286	22,049	47,348	153,416
1994	569,466	540,845	386,596	585,597	2,082,504	51,803	43,115	62,729	73,144	230,791
1995	868,694	804,686	488,515	624,350	2,786,245	26,597	18,441	19,794	29,716	94,548
1996	605,648	467,059	391,633	501,108	1,965,448	33,906	42,796	42,757	54,848	174,307
1997	494,637	500,052	423,838	627,825	2,046,352	63,217	58,153	81,095	79,879	282,344
1998	538,018	503,547	373,451	618,993	2,034,009	69,824	63,459	53,145	98,781	285,209
1999	549,847	424,182	313,211	657,836	1,945,076	51,830	59,195	47,049	171,245	329,319
2000[1]	580,174	537,009	346,087	761,810	2,225,080	117,889	67,895	72,028	279,951	537,763

[1] Preliminary.   *Source: Economic Research Service, U.S. Department of Agriculture (ERS-USDA)*

CATTLE AND CALVES

Feeder Cattle (monthly average) through December 2000

Cents Per Pound
----- Oklahoma City (Jan 1971 - date)

Average Slaughter Steer Price, Choice 2-4, Texas, 1100-1300 Lb.   In Dollars Per 100 Pounds

Year	Jan.	Feb.	Mar.	Apr.	May	June	July	Aug.	Sept.	Oct.	Nov.	Dec.	Average
1994	72.88	73.03	75.41	75.48	68.12	63.60	66.58	68.04	66.79	66.51	69.43	69.35	69.60
1995	73.60	73.79	70.64	67.54	64.27	63.91	61.81	61.95	63.80	64.89	67.94	66.14	66.69
1996	64.63	63.00	61.77	59.85	59.78	61.37	64.07	67.15	71.12	70.95	70.70	66.30	65.06
1997	65.07	65.35	67.44	67.66	67.36	63.53	63.80	65.19	66.04	66.93	67.66	65.91	66.00
1998	64.57	60.77	64.52	65.00	64.52	63.85	60.28	60.00	57.93	61.54	62.23	59.97	62.10
1999	61.46	63.17	64.75	65.34	65.00	66.15	64.51	65.29	66.05	69.63	70.28	69.01	65.89
2000	69.07	68.88	71.74	73.13	71.28	69.41	67.22	65.02	65.43	68.51	72.19	76.41	69.86

Source: Economic Research Service, U.S. Department of Agriculture (ERS-USDA)

Average Price of Steers (Feeder) in Oklahoma City   In Dollars Per 100 Pounds

Year	Jan.	Feb.	Mar.	Apr.	May	June	July	Aug.	Sept.	Oct.	Nov.	Dec.	Average
1994	90.90	91.88	94.34	93.18	87.21	83.45	85.48	85.97	79.77	77.88	80.99	82.58	86.14
1995	83.41	83.05	79.50	76.62	73.69	72.89	70.09	69.62	66.71	68.60	63.45	64.44	72.67
1996	61.38	60.16	60.03	57.20	57.06	61.66	60.56	64.79	64.33	63.45	66.33	68.26	62.10
1997	71.52	76.77	79.66	81.60	85.43	87.04	91.67	88.69	87.23	85.66	84.37	85.25	83.74
1998	85.58	86.53	87.87	89.46	86.84	79.54	74.13	72.72	71.13	71.85	74.24	75.71	79.63
1999	79.49	80.92	83.21	84.44	81.80	84.37	86.80	83.84	85.24	84.75	89.13	95.92	84.99
2000	96.49	97.21	101.16	99.01	95.88	97.01	102.11	99.05	93.41	90.84	96.19	97.40	97.15

Source: The Wall Street Journal

Federally Inspected Slaughter of Cattle in the United States   In Thousands of Head

Year	Jan.	Feb.	Mar.	Apr.	May	June	July	Aug.	Sept.	Oct.	Nov.	Dec.	Total
1994	2,679	2,501	2,799	2,656	2,780	2,984	2,770	3,001	2,885	2,878	2,744	2,806	33,483
1995	2,802	2,524	2,890	2,591	3,064	3,187	2,878	3,160	3,019	2,982	2,897	2,741	34,735
1996	3,046	2,855	2,834	3,039	3,257	3,078	3,080	3,148	2,693	3,074	2,801	2,800	35,721
1997	3,169	2,726	2,795	2,998	3,125	3,003	3,127	3,050	2,909	3,156	2,698	2,811	35,567
1998	2,977	2,691	2,838	2,872	2,906	3,050	2,987	2,987	2,938	2,991	2,717	2,834	34,787
1999	2,904	2,665	2,990	2,916	2,947	3,154	3,037	3,099	3,045	3,033	2,882	2,814	35,486
2000[1]	2,878	2,883	3,078	2,735	3,128	3,191	2,918	3,211	2,984	3,082	2,879	2,665	35,631

[1] Preliminary.   *Source: National Agricultural Statistics Board, U.S. Department of Agriculture (NASS-USDA)*

Feeder Cattle Futures - Chicago Mercantile Exchange (weekly close) as of 29-Dec-2000   Cents per Pound

Average Open Interest of Live Cattle Futures in Chicago   In Contracts

Year	Jan.	Feb.	Mar.	Apr.	May	June	July	Aug.	Sept.	Oct.	Nov.	Dec.
1991	74,392	79,695	84,574	83,322	78,284	70,107	67,868	68,359	74,483	70,395	75,788	74,687
1992	79,638	97,500	97,222	90,823	83,112	68,135	67,828	62,656	61,783	60,761	63,945	67,125
1993	78,481	79,256	88,113	78,144	72,183	68,287	66,617	66,560	70,275	70,559	73,571	76,042
1994	87,923	87,578	83,949	70,287	72,851	75,470	76,663	72,988	73,391	67,924	74,152	68,600
1995	80,306	78,793	76,821	64,763	61,460	56,783	58,077	55,511	58,319	62,222	69,495	69,065
1996	72,870	83,064	91,348	97,315	97,911	96,320	96,547	93,557	92,804	88,467	88,062	87,305
1997	97,014	103,437	108,157	98,354	99,640	96,279	99,042	98,590	94,137	93,579	100,368	102,741
1998	105,559	102,036	101,264	88,257	88,167	87,493	86,776	86,874	95,013	102,636	108,263	106,156
1999	115,254	115,283	115,410	104,482	103,290	101,078	96,843	101,858	121,305	123,466	126,040	120,204
2000	128,918	123,980	123,925	122,596	117,834	106,196	116,266	120,526	123,945	123,517	131,773	132,239

Source: Chicago Mercantile Exchange (CME)

Volume of Trading of Live Cattle Futures Chicago   In Thousands of Contracts

Year	Jan.	Feb.	Mar.	Apr.	May	June	July	Aug.	Sept.	Oct.	Nov.	Dec.	Total
1991	344.2	252.1	288.9	300.4	247.2	254.8	311.2	406.1	321.2	386.3	327.7	352.8	3,792.9
1992	375.6	322.5	353.8	319.1	275.9	263.9	268.9	231.0	196.0	227.9	203.8	246.7	3,319.6
1993	328.8	294.2	363.4	263.5	199.7	255.4	269.3	226.0	269.5	297.6	248.4	291.1	3,307.0
1994	280.8	291.8	262.4	264.2	372.9	363.9	318.2	317.1	270.0	308.9	275.9	291.1	3,307.0
1995	289.7	259.2	391.7	287.2	285.7	290.2	245.3	266.8	233.4	220.1	246.7	254.6	3,580.9
1996	312.0	275.4	333.2	457.5	385.9	303.1	319.8	299.5	278.1	339.4	312.6	241.1	3,257.1
1997	361.6	352.2	312.1	331.9	285.9	303.4	387.5	324.9	316.8	374.6	238.0	309.7	3,926.2
1998	355.7	400.2	327.2	400.6	296.7	321.4	334.4	369.6	370.3	373.2	318.2	330.6	3,919.6
1999	298.8	342.6	338.1	320.5	296.5	342.9	287.6	266.5	371.7	345.3	318.2	349.1	4,216.5
2000	347.3	323.5	356.3	236.5	302.0	244.8	248.4	293.5	277.9	294.0	397.9	253.2	3,839.5
													3,681.5

Source: Chicago Mercantile Exchange (CME)

CATTLE AND CALVES

Beef Steer-Corn Price Ratio in the United States

Year	Jan.	Feb.	Mar.	Apr.	May	June	July	Aug.	Sept.	Oct.	Nov.	Dec.	Average
1993	38.8	39.8	38.8	37.8	37.8	37.1	33.8	33.4	33.7	31.8	29.8	27.0	35.0
1994	27.1	26.2	27.5	28.5	26.8	24.8	28.4	31.6	30.2	32.1	34.4	31.9	29.1
1995	32.6	32.3	30.5	28.2	26.3	25.2	23.5	23.5	23.0	22.3	22.7	21.1	25.9
1996	20.3	18.1	17.2	15.1	13.9	14.2	14.0	15.0	19.1	23.6	25.8	24.9	18.4
1997	24.2	24.6	24.3	24.3	25.4	25.4	27.0	26.6	26.6	26.5	27.1	26.5	25.7
1998	25.8	24.8	25.2	27.5	28.3	28.3	27.9	31.6	32.2	32.1	32.3	30.0	28.8
1999	30.2	31.0	31.8	32.4	32.8	33.9	37.5	37.8	38.3	41.5	41.7	38.9	35.7
2000[2]	37.5	36.0	36.2	37.0	34.9	37.4	42.9	44.4	42.6	40.5	39.7	39.0	39.0

[1] Bushels of corn equal in value to 100 pounds of steers and heifers.   [2] Preliminary.   *Source: Economic Research Service, U.S. Department of Agriculture*

Farm Value, Income and Wholesale Prices of Cattle and Calves in the United States

			Gross Income From C & C[2] Million $	At Ohama[3]				Feeder Heifers at Oklahoma City[5]	Cows, Boning Utility Sioux Falls[6]	Cows, Com-mercial Sioux Falls	Wholesale Prices, Central U.S.		
	January 1			Steers[3]		Heifers					Choice	Select	Cow[6],
Year	Per Head Dollars	Total Million $		Choice	Select	Select	Choice				700-850 lb.	700-850 lb.	Canner[7]
							Dollars per 100 Pounds						
1993	649	64,436	39,877	76.23	74.09	73.77	76.01	82.79	47.52	56.47	117.71	113.53	95.43
1994	659	66,513	36,604	67.60	66.33	66.14	67.93	74.55	42.51	48.28	106.73	102.08	84.39
1995	615	63,185	34,349	65.64	63.94	63.69	65.46	64.43	35.58	39.03	106.09	98.45	68.67
1996	503	52,056	31,251	74.50	61.83	61.22	64.18	57.21	30.45	33.70	102.01	95.70	58.16
1997	525	53,383	36,322	65.92	63.85	63.36	65.66	70.48	35.00	37.13	102.38	96.96	65.39
1998	603	60,193	34,030	60.07	56.17	55.17	59.23						
1999[1]	594	58,834		65.64			65.68						

[1] Preliminary.   [2] Excludes interfarm sales & Gov't. payments. Cash receipts from farm marketings + value of farm home consumption.   [3] 1,000 to 1,100 lb.   [4] 1,000 to 1,200 lb.   [5] 1992 to date are 700 to 750 lb., 1987 thru 1991 are 600 to 700 lb.   [6] All weights.   [7] & Cutter.
Source: Economic Research Service, U.S. Department of Agriculture (NASS-USDA)

Average Price Received by Farmers for Beef Cattle in the United States   In Dollars Per 100 Pounds

Year	Jan.	Feb.	Mar.	Apr.	May	June	July	Aug.	Sept.	Oct.	Nov.	Dec.	Average
1993	75.10	75.80	77.20	77.30	77.10	74.50	72.50	72.70	71.40	69.10	69.30	68.50	73.40
1994	69.90	70.10	72.30	72.00	67.20	62.70	62.90	65.90	63.50	62.90	64.40	64.40	66.50
1995	67.50	68.70	66.90	63.80	60.80	60.90	59.50	59.40	59.10	58.80	60.70	60.60	62.20
1996	59.10	57.90	56.80	54.90	54.70	56.40	59.10	61.30	63.80	63.30	63.40	61.00	59.30
1997	61.40	61.90	64.80	64.80	65.10	62.30	62.80	63.90	63.60	63.30	63.30	62.90	63.30
1998	62.50	60.40	61.30	63.00	63.00	61.80	58.40	57.40	56.10	58.00	58.10	56.80	59.70
1999	59.00	60.60	62.40	62.70	62.10	63.70	62.60	63.50	63.80	66.20	66.20	66.60	63.28
2000[1]	67.80	67.60	69.80	71.30	69.40	68.50	67.50	65.50	65.30	66.70	69.10	71.90	68.37

[1] Preliminary.   *Source: National Agricultural Statistics Service, U.S. Department of Agriculture (NASS-USDA)*

Average Price Received by Farmers for Calves in the United States   In Dollars Per 100 Pounds

Year	Jan.	Feb.	Mar.	Apr.	May	June	July	Aug.	Sept.	Oct.	Nov.	Dec.	Average
1993	94.70	96.00	98.60	99.60	99.20	99.10	96.90	95.10	93.50	93.90	91.60	92.80	95.90
1994	93.90	94.90	97.60	95.80	89.40	84.80	83.80	84.40	80.00	78.20	81.00	81.90	87.10
1995	85.00	86.90	84.40	81.80	77.00	76.90	72.00	70.90	68.50	66.20	64.00	63.30	74.70
1996	61.80	60.20	59.40	55.10	54.40	55.10	56.80	59.30	61.00	60.10	61.20	61.80	58.90
1997	68.10	74.90	80.00	82.20	84.30	85.40	86.90	88.00	86.90	84.30	82.90	83.30	82.30
1998	86.60	88.70	89.80	90.80	88.90	81.70	76.60	76.90	74.10	75.70	77.50	80.20	82.30
1999	83.20	86.90	87.30	88.20	87.60	89.00	89.20	89.60	90.90	91.90	93.00	98.60	89.62
2000[1]	103.00	105.00	109.00	111.00	107.00	104.00	106.00	106.00	103.00	102.00	106.00	106.00	105.67

[1] Preliminary.   *Source: National Agricultural Statistics Board, U.S. Department of Agriculture (NASS-USDA)*

Federally Inspected Slaughter of Calves and Vealers in the United States   In Thousands of Head

Year	Jan.	Feb.	Mar.	Apr.	May	June	July	Aug.	Sept.	Oct.	Nov.	Dec.	Total
1993	101	97	116	96	82	91	90	95	94	94	101	103	1,159
1994	99	94	112	92	90	98	93	106	106	112	114	121	1,237
1995	121	104	118	96	114	115	111	121	119	124	125	125	1,393
1996	140	140	141	128	133	131	156	153	146	159	139	149	1,715
1997	143	122	128	126	114	115	131	123	133	137	121	142	1,534
1998	125	111	125	107	99	115	131	122	132	121	109	127	1,422
1999	103	98	115	95	87	102	109	115	117	102	100	110	1,252
2000[1]	91	92	97	75	86	91	92	98	91	95	91	90	1,088

[1] Preliminary.   *Source: Crop Reporting Board, U.S. Department of Agriculture (CRB-USDA)*

Cement

The U.S. Geological Survey reported that world production of cement in 1999 was 1.56 billion metric tonnes, up 3 percent from 1998. Cement is the binding agent in concrete and mortar, two construction materials. The production and consumption of cement is directly related to the level of activity in the construction industry. Hydraulic cements are those that set and harden in water and they are the dominant form of cement produced in the U.S. and the world.

By far the largest producer of cement in the world is China with 1999 output estimated at 520 million tonnes, up 1 percent from a year ago. The U.S. is the second largest producer of cement with 1999 output of 87.3 million tonnes, up 2 percent from 1998. India was the next largest producer with 1999 production of 87 million tonnes, up 2 percent from the prior year. Production of cement by Japan in 1999 was 80 million tonnes, down 2 percent from 1998. Other large cement producers include South Korea, Brazil, Germany, Italy, Turkey, and Mexico.

U.S. shipments of Portland and blended cement in August 2000 were 9.1 million tonnes, up 15 percent from July and some 12 percent more than a year ago. For all of 1999,

shipments were 83.5 million tonnes. Masonry cement shipments in August 2000 were 415,121 tonnes, up 13 percent from July. Shipments in August were up 4 percent from a year ago. For all of 1999, masonry cement shipments were 4.3 million tonnes.

Clinker production in August 2000 was 6.95 million tonnes. In the January-August 2000 period production was 51.5 million tonnes. In the first eight months of 2000, southern California produced the most clinker with 5.2 million tonnes. They were followed by northern Texas with 3 million tonnes and eastern Pennsylvania with 2.9 million tonnes. Imports of clinker in July 2000 were 462,986 tonnes, while for the January-July 2000 period imports were 2.52 million tonnes. In this period, the largest supplier of clinker to the U.S. was Thailand with 1.5 million tonnes, followed by Canada, Turkey, and Colombia. Hydraulic cement and clinker imported into the U.S. in July 2000 were 3.3 million tonnes. In January-July 2000, imports were 17 million tonnes. White cement imported into the U.S. in July 2000 totaled 82,887 tonnes, while for the first seven months of 2000 white cement imports were 494,942 tonnes.

World Production of Hydraulic Cement   In Thousands of Short Tons

Year	Brazil	China	France	Germany	India	Italy	Japan	Rep. of Korea	Russia	Spain	Turkey	United States	World Total
1993	24,843	367,880	20,464	36,649	53,812	33,771	88,046	47,313	49,900	22,878	31,241	75,117	1,290,905
1994	25,230	421,180	21,296	36,130	57,000	32,713	91,624	50,730	37,200	25,150	29,493	79,353	1,370,000
1995	28,256	475,910	19,692	33,302	62,000	33,715	90,474	55,130	36,500	26,423	33,153	78,320	1,445,000
1996	34,597	491,190	19,514	31,533	75,000	33,327	94,492	58,434	27,800	25,157	35,214	80,818	1,495,000
1997	38,096	511,730	19,780	35,945	80,000	33,721	91,938	60,317	26,700	27,632	36,035	84,255	1,547,000
1998[1]	39,942	536,000	19,500	36,610	85,000	35,512	81,328	46,091	26,000	27,943	38,200	85,522	1,545,000
1999[2]	40,270	573,000	19,527	38,099	90,000	36,000	80,120	48,157	28,400	30,800	34,403	87,777	1,606,000

[1] Preliminary.   [2] Estimate.   Source: U.S. Geological Survey (USGS)

Salient Statistics of Cement in the United States

Year	Net Import Reliance as a % of Apparent Consumption	Production Portland	Production Others[3]	Production Total	Capacity Used at (Portland Mills) %	Shipments From Mills Total Mil. Tons	Shipments From Mills Value[4] Mil. $	Average Value (F.O.B. Mill) $ per ton	Stocks at Mills Dec. 31	Exports	Apparent Consumption	Imports for Consumption[5] by Country Canada	Imports for Consumption[5] by Country Japan	Imports for Consumption[5] by Country Mexico	Imports for Consumption[5] by Country Spain	Imports for Consumption[5] by Country Total
		Thousand Tons							Million Tons			Thousands of Short Tons				
1993	7	70,845	2,962	73,807	79.1	72,770	4,175	55.65	4,788	625	79,198	3,629	43	783	597	7,060
1994	10	74,335	3,613	77,948	82.3	79,087	4,845	61.26	4,701	633	86,476	4,268	14	640	1,342	11,303
1995	11	73,303	3,603	76,906	81.2	78,518	5,329	67.87	5,814	759	86,003	4,886	[6]	850	1,501	13,848
1996	12	75,797	3,469	79,266	83.4	83,963	5,952	70.89	5,488	803	90,355	5,351	[6]	1,272	1,595	14,154
1997	14	78,948	3,634	82,582	84.7	90,359	6,637	73.46	5,784	791	96,018	5,350	----	995	1,845	17,596
1998[1]	19	79,942	3,989	83,931	84.9	96,857	7,404	76.45	5,393	743	103,457	5,957	----	1,280	2,204	24,086
1999[2]	23	81,577	4,375	85,952	83.6	103,271	8,083	78.27	6,367	694	108,862	5,511	----	1,286	1,900	29,351

[1] Preliminary.   [2] Estimate.   [3] Masonry, natural & pozzolan (slag-line).   [4] Value received F.O.B. mill, excluding cost of containers.   [5] Hydraulic & clinker cement for consumption.   [6] Less than 1/2 unit.   Source: U.S. Geological Survey (USGS)

Shipments of Finished Portland Cement from Mills in the United States   In Thousands of Metric Tons

Year	Jan.	Feb.	Mar.	Apr.	May	June	July	Aug.	Sept.	Oct.	Nov.	Dec.	Total
1995	3,685.2	3,959.7	5,556.6	5,668.6	6,720.6	7,336.8	6,748.1	7,660.9	7,177.0	7,736.3	6,238.3	4,667.7	73,155.6
1996	3,913.3	4,312.7	5,234.1	6,801.6	7,621.3	7,395.1	7,749.4	8,193.4	7,178.3	8,276.7	6,011.4	4,763.3	77,550.0
1997	4,111.3	4,487.1	5,739.1	7,009.5	7,489.3	7,733.7	7,749.4	8,186.1	8,678.9	6,108.6	5,471.9	81,064.3	
1998	4,552.0	4,559.7	5,867.4	7,009.7	7,420.2	8,095.1	8,295.6	7,963.3	8,089.5	8,404.6	6,640.5	6,059.4	82,956.8
1999	4,499.4	5,149.1	6,399.4	7,128.9	7,424.0	8,109.6	7,784.3	8,133.9	7,652.7	8,204.2	7,453.4	5,959.1	83,841.5
2000[1]	4,765.5	5,343.1	7,196.2	6,927.0	8,451.3	8,389.8	7,934.7	9,089.2	7,956.5	8,572.3	6,706.1		88,725.4

[1] Preliminary.   Source: U.S. Geological Survey (USGS)

Cheese

World cheese production set consecutive new year-to-year highs during the 1990's, and the trend is continuing with a total production estimate of 12.8 million metric tonnes in 2000 vs. 12.5 million in 1999, and about 10 million in 1991. U.S. production accounted for 3.7 million, 3.4 million, and 2.7 million tonnes, respectively. France produces one-half the U.S. total to rank in second place globally, followed by Germany and Italy.

World consumption is keeping up with the new supply, totaling a record 12.4 million tonnes in 2000 vs. 12.2 million in 1999, with U.S. usage of 3.87 million and 3.71 million tonnes, respectively. France's annual usage in recent years has averaged 1.35 million tons and Italy's about 1.17 million. Most of the world's cheese is consumed where it is produced. However, record per capita cheese consumption in the U.S. of almost 14 kilograms pales relative to Europe where use tops 20 kg. in some countries, notably France.

World foreign trade of cheese is biased towards exports, with slightly more than one million tonnes in 2000, marginally higher than in 1999, but still a new high; imports in both years hovered around 755,000 tonnes. New Zealand was the single largest exporter in 2000 with 245,000 tonnes, while collectively the European Union countries exported nearly one half the world total with 409,000 tonnes. However, E.U. cheese exports showed little growth in the sec-ond half of the 1990's, whereas Oceania's exports nearly doubled. U.S. exports are small, averaging 38,000 tonnes in 1998-00. Importwise, the U.S. vies with Japan as the largest importer with 175,000 tonnes to the U.S. in 2000 vs. Japan's 190,000 tonnes. Ending 2000 world stocks of 1.73 million tonnes compares with 1.88 million a year earlier, with Italy accounting for 785,000 tonnes of the 2000 carryover, and the U.S. 275,000 tonnes.

Cheese is an $11 billion industry in the U.S. with American and cheddar cheeses accounting for the largest individual varieties of both production and consumption. However, other varieties, mostly Italian, now have a combined production that easily exceeds American cheese with 3.6 billion pounds of American in 1999 vs. over 6.0 billion pounds of Italian cheeses. Per capita consumption of American cheese slipped during the 1990's, while other cheese usage rose. The combined per capita total in now almost 25 pounds.

Wholesale American cheese prices (40-pound blocks, Wisconsin) averaged about $1.42 per pound in 1999 with the lowest prices seen as calendar 2000 neared. Northern European monthly average cheddar prices (40 pound blocks) in 1999 ranged from $2100 per metric tonne in January to $1775 in December.

World Production of Cheese   In Thousands of Metric Tons

Year	Argentina	Australia	Brazil	Canada	Denmark	France	Germany	Italy	Nether-lands	New Zealand	United Kingdom	United States	World Total
1992	310	197	296	262	290	1,489	783	890	634	142	324	2,943	10,931
1993	350	211	310	271	321	1,509	821	885	637	145	331	2,961	10,895
1994	385	234	330	282	286	1,541	855	913	648	192	326	3,054	11,194
1995	370	241	360	277	311	1,579	875	942	680	197	354	3,138	11,345
1996	390	268	385	289	298	1,594	947	950	688	230	364	3,274	11,059
1997	415	285	405	329	290	1,645	990	985	693	240	368	3,325	11,388
1998	407	305	421	330	289	1,648	1,008	1,003	638	266	358	3,398	11,562
1999	446	320	434	331	285	1,658	1,006	969	643	245	361	3,603	11,826
2000[1]	432	367	445	329	305	1,680	1,046	1,000	690	270	330	3,775	12,232
2001[2]	420	395	460	337	315	1,685	1,060	1,000	690	283	350	3,900	12,500

[1] Preliminary.   [2] Estimate.   Source: Foreign Agricultural Service, U.S. Department of Agriculture (FAS-USDA)

Supply and Distribution of All Cheese in the United States   In Millions of Pounds

Year	Production Whole Milk[2]	Production All Cheese[3]	Commercial Stocks January 1	Imports[4]	Total Supply	Cheese 40-lb. Blocks Wisconsin Assembly Points cents/lb.	Exports & Shipments[5]	Gov't - Stocks Dec. 31	American Cheese Removed by USDA Programs	Total Disappearance	American Cheese Donated	Domestic Disappearance Total	Per Capita
1990	2,894	6,059	329	302	6,685	136.69	75	8.2	21.5	6,231	21	6,156	24.64
1991	2,769	6,055	458	301	6,806	124.41	72	23.1	76.9	6,393	60	6,321	25.01
1992	2,937	6,488	416	286	7,167	131.91	78	16.5	14.4	6,720	0	6,642	26.01
1993	2,957	6,528	470	321	7,303	131.52	87	2.2	8.3	6,853	0	6,766	26.24
1994	2,974	6,735	466	345	7,546	131.45	55	.9	6.9	7,094	0	6,994	26.82
1995	3,131	6,917	437	337	7,691	132.77	65	----	6.1	7,279	0	7,174	27.30
1996	3,281	7,218	412	338	7,968	149.14	71	----	4.6	7,478	0	7,364	27.70
1997	3,286	7,330	487	312	8,129	132.40	84	----	11.3	7,647	0	7,511	28.00
1998	3,326	7,502	480	344	8,326	158.10	82	----		7,807	0	7,673	28.40
1999[1]	3,577	7,944	517	419	8,880	142.30	86	----					

[1] Preliminary.   [2] Whole milk American cheddar.   [3] All types of cheese except cottage, pot and baker's cheese.   [4] Imports for consumption.
[5] Commercial.   Source: Economic Research Service, U.S. Department of Agriculture (ERS-USDA)

Production of Cheese in the United States   In Millions of Pounds

	American			Swiss, Including Block	Munster	Brick	Lim-burger	Cream & Neufchatel Cheese	Italian Varieties	Blue Mond	All Other Varieties	Total of All Cheese[2]	Cottage Cheese		
Year	Whole Milk	Part Skim	Total										Lowfat	Curd[3]	Creamed[4]
1990	2,894	0.8	2,895	261.1	100.2	17.3	.8	430.8	2,207.0	36.4	110.7	6,059	301.8	493.5	530.6
1991	2,769	0.8	2,770	234.5	106.4	15.3	.7	446.7	2,328.6	34.3	118.5	6,055	321.1	490.9	497.9
1992	2,937	1.2	2,938	237.3	116.4	15.5	1.0	516.7	2,508.6	33.3	121.9	6,488	329.5	502.4	457.3
1993	2,957	3.7	2,961	231.4	117.5	12.5	.9	539.9	2,494.5	33.3	137.2	6,528	317.0	471.4	430.5
1994	2,974	24.7	2,999	221.2	113.6	12.2	.8	573.4	2,625.7	36.5	152.1	6,735	321.1	463.3	410.0
1995	3,131	24.0	3,155	221.7	109.1	10.4	.9	543.8	2,674.4	36.6	164.6	6,917	325.9	458.9	384.9
1996	3,281	NA	3,281	219.0	106.8	10.6	.7	574.7	2,812.4	38.3	106.7	7,218	329.9	448.3	360.4
1997	3,286	NA	3,286	207.6	100.2	8.5	.7	614.9	2,881.4	42.8	119.8	7,330	346.7	458.5	359.5
1998	3,315	NA	3,315	206.4	94.6	7.6	.9	621.3	3,004.7	5	166.0	7,492	361.2	465.8	366.8
1999[1]	3,577	NA	3,577	220.5	80.1	8.1	.6	646.9	3,142.6	5	182.0	7,944	360.3	465.5	361.6

[1] Preliminary.   [2] Excludes full-skim cheddar and cottage cheese.   [3] Includes cottage, pot, and baker's cheese with a butterfat content of less than 4%.
[4] Includes cheese with a butterfat content of 4 to 19 %.   [5] Included in All Other Varieties.   *Source: Economic Research Service, U.S. Department of Agriculture ERS-USDA)*

Wholesale Price of Cheese, 40-lb. Blocks, Wisconsin Assembly Points[2]   In Cents Per Pound

Year	Jan.	Feb.	Mar.	Apr.	May	June	July	Aug.	Sept.	Oct.	Nov.	Dec.	Average
1991	111.4	111.5	111.5	111.7	115.0	121.4	128.4	136.1	139.7	140.2	135.8	130.2	124.4
1992	125.4	119.0	119.8	131.9	140.0	141.3	141.8	142.0	136.9	132.4	129.4	123.2	131.9
1993	119.3	118.6	124.3	140.8	141.8	133.7	126.3	124.8	137.4	138.9	138.7	133.7	131.5
1994	132.2	134.2	140.0	143.3	125.7	120.2	129.1	132.2	135.6	135.4	127.9	121.3	131.5
1995	124.5	130.4	131.1	122.8	122.1	126.9	126.7	132.2	141.3	145.0	145.8	144.6	132.8
1996	139.3	139.3	140.9	145.1	151.8	151.5	158.2	167.6	145.5	162.3	133.9	126.0	146.8
1997	127.9	132.3	134.0	125.6	116.5	117.9	123.3	137.6	141.4	142.4	143.8	146.1	132.4
1998	144.5	144.7	138.8	129.7	123.0	151.3	162.6	166.9	171.0	183.5	188.7	192.5	158.1
1999	162.4	131.5	134.0	133.6	124.8	138.1	159.7	189.0	167.3	134.0	117.3	115.7	142.3
2000[1]	114.6	111.6	112.2	110.7	110.6	120.0	125.2	125.5	133.4	109.4	107.5	113.0	116.1

[1] Preliminary.   *Source: Economic Research Service, U.S. Department of Agriculture (ERS-USDA)*

Production[2] of Cheese in the United States   In Millions of Pounds

Year	Jan.	Feb.	Mar.	Apr.	May	June	July	Aug.	Sept.	Oct.	Nov.	Dec.	Total
1991	501.7	458.0	530.1	515.4	532.3	509.0	499.5	498.2	485.0	521.0	502.3	533.7	6,061
1992	514.1	497.1	542.7	534.7	550.9	549.8	541.8	534.6	528.3	558.2	547.5	571.6	6,488
1993	517.3	492.5	563.2	561.4	576.9	563.2	537.9	525.8	531.1	560.0	540.1	558.9	6,528
1994	538.3	505.8	591.8	554.3	590.4	558.7	550.7	562.4	565.5	574.5	559.3	578.3	6,730
1995	559.3	523.3	596.0	559.6	595.3	579.2	556.5	550.8	571.3	588.6	584.7	618.4	6,883
1996	590.0	576.0	625.4	606.0	636.5	595.8	582.2	589.5	584.5	612.2	595.5	623.9	7,218
1997	598.1	577.1	638.0	598.5	642.0	623.4	613.2	596.5	604.3	615.5	594.5	627.9	7,329
1998	617.4	574.1	646.6	639.1	652.6	642.1	610.1	598.6	584.1	632.1	636.6	668.5	7,502
1999	634.0	592.7	697.4	669.7	675.0	669.4	649.8	648.5	641.3	671.9	688.5	705.8	7,944
2000[1]	686.9	645.6	717.9	693.5	737.1	697.7	690.0	686.5	655.1	691.6	671.9	690.0	8,264

[1] Preliminary.   [2] Excludes cottage cheese.   *Source: National Agricultural Statistics Service, U.S. Department of Agriculture (NASS-USDA)*

Cold Storage Holdings of All Varieties of Cheese in the United States, on First of Month   Millions of Pounds

Year	Jan.	Feb.	Mar.	Apr.	May	June	July	Aug.	Sept.	Oct.	Nov.	Dec.
1991	457.8	483.9	475.1	492.4	510.3	512.1	521.5	511.5	494.1	477.9	429.3	409.0
1992	415.4	440.9	445.9	449.0	449.7	455.9	465.2	496.2	487.3	449.7	441.1	462.0
1993	462.0	476.1	454.4	460.0	453.6	480.5	541.2	533.3	517.7	500.1	471.9	462.4
1994	465.2	495.2	473.6	473.3	487.9	513.4	521.4	506.3	474.7	453.0	448.3	434.2
1995	436.9	449.7	448.7	458.8	466.1	465.8	473.6	482.4	458.1	428.5	418.7	393.6
1996	412.1	441.3	466.4	490.9	525.5	541.8	542.8	536.6	506.9	495.8	494.6	480.2
1997	487.0	501.5	494.6	517.0	555.4	584.3	604.8	604.9	582.3	543.7	505.0	474.4
1998	480.4	509.3	521.5	533.1	557.6	568.5	583.7	595.8	576.8	553.0	522.7	494.5
1999	517.2	622.4	635.9	645.1	688.7	741.3	728.4	748.7	694.7	651.3	622.0	591.7
2000[1]	621.3	668.1	708.4	726.7	748.6	763.4	782.3	834.7	800.0	744.6	681.8	687.1

Quantities are given in net weight.   [1] Preliminary.   *Source: National Agricultural Statistics Service, U.S. Department of Agriculture (NASS-USDA)*

Chromium

Chromite is the ore mineral of chromium. Chromium finds a wide variety of uses in metals, chemicals, and refractories. Chromium enhances hardenability and resistance to corrosion and oxidation in iron, steel, and nonferrous alloys. Two of its applications are in the production of stainless steel and nonferrous alloys. It is also used in alloy steel, plating of metals, pigments, leather processing, surface treatments, catalysts, and refractories.

According to the U.S. Geological Survey, the U.S. consumes about 14 percent of world chromite ore production in various forms of imported materials (chromite ore, chromium chemicals, chromium ferroalloys and chromium metals). In the U.S., imported chromite was consumed by two chemical firms and two refractory firms to produce chromium chemicals and chromite-containing refractories, respectively. Consumption of chromium ferroalloys and metal was mostly for the production of stainless and heat-resisting steel and superalloys, respectively.

World mine production of chromium in 1999 was estimated at 12.8 million metric tonnes, an increase of 100,000 tonnes from 1998. The world's largest producer of chromium was South Africa with 5.6 million tonnes, an increase of 2 percent from 1998. Other large producers include Turkey with 1999 output of 1.6 million tonnes, the same as in 1998. Kazakhstan produced 1.6 million tonnes, also unchanged from 1998. Production by India in 1999 was 1.4 million tonnes, up 3 percent from 1998. Other producers include Zimbabwe, Finland and Brazil. World reserves of chromium are estimated at 3.6 million tonnes.

U.S. stainless steel production in January-August 2000 was 1.6 million tonnes. For all of 1999, production was 2.19 million tonnes. U.S. stainless steel scrap receipts in January-August 2000 were 605,000 tonnes. For all of 1999 they were 696,000 tonnes. U.S. stainless steel scrap consumption in the same period of 2000 was 878,000 tonnes, while for all of 1999 it was 1.14 million tonnes. U.S. imports for consumption of chromite ore in January-August 2000 were 171,000 tonnes, while in 1999 they were 252,000 tonnes. Imports of high-carbon ferrochromium in the first eight months of 2000 were 296,000 tonnes, while for all of 1999 they were 565,000 tonnes. In 1999, medium-carbon ferrochromium imports were 3,000 tonnes, imports of low-carbon ferrochromium were 39,000 tonnes, and ferrochromium silicon imports were 36,000 tonnes. Total ferroalloy imports in January-August 2000 were 314,000 tonnes, while for 1999 they totaled 640,000 tonnes.

Imports of chromium metal in the first eight months of 2000 were 6,380 tonnes, while in 1999 they totaled 9,030 tonnes. Stainless steel imports in January-August 2000 were 649,000 tonnes and in 1999 they were 941,000 tonnes. 1999 imports of stainless steel scrap totaled 66,100 tonnes.

The government stockpile of chromite ore in August 2000 was 712,000 tonnes. The stockpile of chromium ferroalloys in August 2000 was 954,000 tonnes, while the stockpile of chromium metal was 7,720 tonnes. At the end of 1999, government stocks of chromite ore were 820,000 tonnes. Stocks of chromium ferroalloys were 973,000 tonnes.

World Mine Production of Chromite   In Thousands of Metric Tons (Gross Weight)

Year	Albania	Brazil	Cuba	Finland	India	Iran	Kazakhstan[3]	Madagascar	Philippines	South Africa	Turkey	Zimbabwe	World Total
1990	950	263	50	504	1,050	77	3,800	151	183	4,620	836	573	13,200
1991	587	340	50	473	940	90	3,800	149	191	5,100	940	564	13,300
1992	322	449	50	499	1,082	130	3,500	161	66	3,363	759	522	11,100
1993	115	308	15	511	1,000	124	2,900	144	62	2,838	767	252	9,300
1994	118	360	20	573	909	354	2,020	90	76	3,599	1,270	517	10,200
1995	160	448	31	598	1,536	371	2,417	106	111	2,086	2,080	707	14,000
1996	143	408	37	574	1,363	130	1,190	137	107	2,078	1,279	697	11,600
1997	106	300	44	589	1,363	169	1,798	140	88	6,162	1,703	670	13,600
1998[1]	86	360	49	611	1,311	212	1,603	104	54	6,480	1,404	605	13,500
1999[2]	85	350	36	610	1,300	255	2,405	105	20	6,817	770	650	14,000

[1] Preliminary.   [2] Estimate.   [3] Formerly part of the U.S.S.R.; data not reported separately unitl 1992.   *Source: U.S. Geological Survey (USGS)*

Salient Statistics of Chromite in the United States   In Thousands of Metric Tons (Gross Weight)

Year	Net Import Reliance as a % of Apparent Consumption	Production of Ferrochromium	Exports	Imports for Consumption	Reexports	Consumption by Primary Conumer Groups - Total	Metallurgical & Chemical	Refractory	Consumer Stocks, Dec. 31 -- Metallurgical & Chemical	Refractory	Total Stocks	$ per Metric Ton - South Africa[3]	Turkish[4]
1990	79	109	6	347	4	405	361	44	333	21	355	55	135
1991	73	68	9	310	----	375	339	36	310	11	321	50	130
1992	73	61	7	324	----	362	335	27	308	13	321	60	110
1993	81	63	10	329	2	337	314	23	259	16	275	60	110
1994	75	67	33	273	----	322	302	20	250	17	266	60	110
1995	80	73	27	416	----	W	W	W	194	11	205	80	230
1996	79	37	51	362	----	W	W	W	165	8	173	80	230
1997	75	61	30	350	----	W	W	W	167	8	175	75	150
1998[1]	80	W	62	381	----	W	W	W	W	W	159	68	145
1999[2]	80	W	23	429	----	W	W	W	W	W	130	63	145

[1] Preliminary.   [2] Estimate.   [3] Cr_2O_3, 44% (Transvaal).   [4] 48% Cr_2O_3.   W = Withheld.   *Source: U.S. Geological Survey (USGS)*

Coal

U.S. coal production in the January-March 2000 quarter was 274.1 million short tons. In the April-June period, production was 260.5 million tons. For all of 1999, production was 1.09 billion tons. In the April-June quarter, coal production east of the Mississippi River was 127.6 million tons, down 2 percent from the same quarter in 1999. Production west of the Mississippi River in second quarter 2000 was 132.9 million tons, down 1 percent from 1999. In the second quarter 2000, the largest producing coal state was Wyoming with 80.3 million tons, up 1 percent from the year before. The next largest producing state was West Virginia, which in the second quarter 2000 produced 40.3 million tons, up 1 percent from the year before. Production in Kentucky was 32.6 million tons, down 3 percent from 1999.

U.S. exports of coal in the second quarter of 2000 were 14.4 million tons, while exports in first quarter 2000 were 13.6 million tons. In the first half of 2000, U.S. coal exports were 28 million tons. The major export market for U.S. coal in second quarter 2000 was Canada, which took 5.76 million tons, down 1 percent from a year ago. For the first half of 2000, exports to Canada were 8.29 million tons, up almost 8 percent from 1999. Exports to Brazil in second quarter 2000 were 1.29 million tons, up almost 7 percent from the year before. Coal exports to Japan totaled 810,906 tons in the second quarter.

U.S. coal consumption in the second quarter of 2000 was 249.4 million tons. Electric utilities consumed 202.1 million tons, while other power producers took 23.6 million tons. Electric utility coal usage in the first quarter of 2000 was 214.1 million tons, while in the second quarter it was 213.8 million tons. The states that are the major users of coal for utilities are Texas, Indiana and Ohio.

World Production[3] of Coal (Monthly Average)   In Thousands of Metric Tons

Year	Australia	Canada	China	Czech-Rep.[4]	Germany	India	Indonesia	Kazakhstan[5]	Poland	Russia[5]	Ukraine[5]	United Kingdom	United States
1991	13,720	3,326	88,212	1,623	6,063	18,905	1,143	----	11,698	33,769	----	8,028	68,755
1992	14,594	2,693	91,278	1,532	6,013	19,490	1,760	10,546	10,960	16,123	----	7,273	75,413
1993	14,746	2,943	96,177	1,532	5,347	20,503	2,300	9,323	10,873	16,200	9,545	5,683	71,473
1994	14,721	3,054	103,325	1,448	4,802	20,974	2,603	8,298	11,094	14,730	7,608	4,149	78,131
1995	15,921	3,216	113,394	1,431	4,905	22,131	3,460	6,626	11,349	14,743	6,796	4,420	78,091
1996	16,120	3,336	116,417	1,378	4,428	23,782	3,945	6,086	11,425	13,875	6,178	4,183	80,426
1997	17,235	3,435	114,402	1,339	4,267	24,688	4,340	6,268	11,427	13,317	6,293	4,041	82,398
1998	20,677	3,190	94,806	1,343	3,776	24,805	5,027	5,672	9,644	12,779	6,431	3,431	84,484
1999[1]	24,826	3,102	80,200	1,193	3,657	24,349	5,892	4,644	9,301	13,799	6,804	3,116	82,704
2000[2]	24,231		67,950	1,294	3,183	26,095	5,624	5,496	8,575	14,217	6,838	2,760	84,048

[1] Preliminary.   [2] Estimate.   [3] All grades of anthracite and bituminous coal, but excludes recovered slurries, lignite and brown coal.   [4] Formerly part of Czechoslovakia; data not reported separately until 1993.   [5] Formerly part of the U.S.S.R.; data not reported separately until 1992. NA = Not avaliable.   Source: United Nations

Production of Bituminous & Lignite Coal in the United States   In Thousands of Short Tons

Year	Alabama	Colorado	Illinois	Indiana	Kentucky	Montana	Ohio	Pennsylvania	Texas	Virginia	West Virginia	Wyoming	Total
1991	27,269	17,834	60,258	31,468	158,980	38,237	30,569	61,936	53,825	41,954	167,352	193,854	995,984
1992	25,796	19,226	59,857	30,466	161,068	38,889	30,403	65,498	55,071	43,024	162,164	190,172	997,545
1993	24,768	21,886	41,098	29,295	156,299	35,917	28,816	55,394	54,567	39,317	130,525	210,129	945,424
1994	23,266	25,304	52,797	30,927	161,642	41,640	29,897	62,237	52,346	37,129	161,776	237,092	1,033,504
1995	24,640	25,710	48,180	26,007	153,739	39,451	26,118	61,576	52,684	34,099	162,997	263,822	1,032,974
1996	24,637	24,886	46,656	29,670	152,425	37,891	28,572	67,942	55,164	35,590	170,433	278,440	1,063,856
1997	24,468	27,449	41,159	35,497	155,853	41,005	29,154	76,198	53,328	35,837	173,743	281,881	1,089,932
1998	23,224	30,825	38,182	36,297	145,609	42,092	28,600	76,519	53,578	34,059	175,794	313,983	1,109,768
1999[1]	19,504	29,989	40,417	34,004	139,626	41,102	22,480	76,368	53,071	32,181	157,919	337,119	1,095,474
2000[2]	19,736	28,992	34,525	27,696	135,333	38,794	22,229	78,512	50,398	31,605	155,820	347,442	1,082,307

[1] Preliminary.   [2] Estimate.   Source: Energy Information Administration, U.S. Department of Energy (EIA-DOE)

Production[2] of Bituminous Coal in the United States   In Thousands of Short Tons

Year	Jan.	Feb.	Mar.	Apr.	May	June	July	Aug.	Sept.	Oct.	Nov.	Dec.	Total
1991	85,810	82,592	85,012	79,324	79,917	76,896	79,745	88,851	81,533	90,307	81,730	79,383	991,100
1992	87,979	82,102	85,835	82,364	80,197	79,968	80,768	84,401	83,555	86,265	80,240	83,021	996,695
1993	80,508	76,341	84,782	79,329	73,759	80,949	70,771	76,209	79,705	80,628	79,404	79,905	942,290
1994	76,578	81,569	95,969	87,534	82,105	86,223	77,421	93,881	88,346	85,085	86,317	87,856	1,028,884
1995	88,351	83,893	93,020	80,092	83,291	84,210	79,511	88,035	89,052	90,573	86,779	81,292	1,032,974
1996	83,013	83,671	90,392	88,158	88,562	83,824	88,331	94,664	87,388	94,195	86,400	86,493	1,059,104
1997	92,425	88,028	92,265	87,909	94,296	86,382	88,666	89,319	92,298	94,562	83,344	94,913	1,085,254
1998	97,012	86,167	95,091	91,735	90,397	92,099	90,497	91,212	95,442	96,723	90,544	94,567	1,106,128
1999	90,928	92,015	98,672	88,630	84,436	89,734	87,759	92,600	92,248	89,146	90,885	92,450	1,089,503
2000[1]	87,459	87,121	99,420	87,528	94,958	97,031	93,411	99,092	91,457	96,530	94,035	87,272	1,115,314

[1] Preliminary.   [2] Includes small amount of lignite.   Source: Energy Information Administration, U.S. Department of Energy (EIA-DOE)

COAL

Production[2] of Pennsylvania Anthracite Coal   In Thousands of Short Tons

Year	Jan.	Feb.	Mar.	Apr.	May	June	July	Aug.	Sept.	Oct.	Nov.	Dec.	Total
1991	248	243	259	230	224	235	253	313	285	346	299	238	3,173
1992	247	257	279	296	274	287	305	337	311	322	321	306	3,542
1993	272	266	290	175	305	358	222	277	351	603	315	271	3,705
1994	318	335	415	380	375	379	346	457	412	453	452	395	4,717
1995	304	304	372	332	335	353	307	396	428	445	388	347	4,682
1996	302	349	367	371	361	335	367	418	385	557	505	434	4,751
1997	351	366	492	374	351	390	407	423	415	448	384	415	4,678
1998	306	305	309	405	384	388	525	454	452	533	167	167	4,612
1999	355	369	389	354	459	402	343	436	479	414	407	406	4,808
2000[1]	340	355	404	362	398	405	378	412	385	434	402	366	4,664

[1] Preliminary.   [2] Represents production in Pennsylvania only.   Source: Energy Information Administration, U.S. Department of Energy (EIA-DOE)

Salient Statistics of Coal in the United States   In Thousands of Short Tons

Year	Production	Imports	Consumption	Exports Brazil	Exports Canada	Exports Europe	Exports Asia	Exports Total	Total Ending Stocks[2]	Losses & Unaccounted For[3]
1990	1,029,076	2,699	895,480	5,847	15,511	58,382	22,725	105,804	201,629	3,949
1991	995,984	3,390	887,621	7,052	11,178	65,520	21,788	108,969	200,682	3,731
1992	997,545	3,803	907,655	6,370	15,140	57,255	20,540	102,516	197,685	-5,826
1993	945,424	7,309	944,081	5,197	8,889	37,575	19,500	74,519	120,458	-13,924
1994	1,033,504	7,584	951,461	5,482	9,193	35,825	17,957	71,359	136,139	-5,348
1995	1,032,974	7,201	962,039	6,351	9,427	48,620	19,095	88,547	134,639	-10,136
1996	1,063,856	7,126	1,005,573	6,540	12,029	47,193	17,980	90,473	122,979	-7,608
1997	1,089,932	7,487	1,030,453	7,455	14,975	41,331	14,498	83,545	106,401	-4,101
1998	1,117,535	8,724	1,038,972	6,475	19,901	33,773	12,311	77,295	128,072	-17,493
1999[1]	1,093,993	9,089	1,038,512	4,442	19,826	22,508	9,157	58,476	136,011	-1,675

[1] Preliminary.   [2] Producer & distributor and consumer stocks, excludes stocks held by retail dealers for consumption by the residential and commercial sector.   [3] Equals production plus imports minus the change in producer & distributor and consumer stocks minus consumption minus exports.
Source: Energy Information Administraion, U.S. Department of Energy (EIA-DOE)

Consumption and Stocks of Coal in the United States   In Thousands of Short Tons

Year	Consumption Electric Utilities Anthracite	Bituminous	Lignite	Total	Industrial Coke Plants	Other Industrial[2]	Residential and Commercial	Total	Stocks, Dec. 31[3] Consumer Electric Utilities	Coke Plants	Other Industrials	Producers and Distributors
1990	1,031	694,317	78,201	773,549	38,877	76,330	6,724	895,480	156,166	3,329	8,716	33,418
1991	994	691,275	79,999	772,268	33,854	75,405	6,094	887,621	157,876	2,773	7,061	32,971
1992	986	698,626	80,248	779,860	32,366	74,042	6,153	907,655	154,130	2,597	6,965	33,993
1993	951	732,736	79,821	813,508	31,323	74,892	6,221	944,081	111,341	2,401	6,716	25,284
1994	1,123	737,102	79,045	817,270	31,740	75,179	6,013	951,461	126,897	2,657	6,585	33,219
1995	978	749,951	78,078	829,007	33,011	73,055	5,807	962,039	126,304	2,632	5,702	34,444
1996	1,009	795,252	78,421	874,681	31,706	70,941	6,006	1,005,573	114,623	2,667	5,688	28,648
1997	1,014	821,823	77,524	900,361	30,203	70,599	6,463	1,029,228	98,826	1,978	5,597	33,973
1998	867	832,094	77,906	910,867	28,189	68,119	4,856	1,038,972	120,501	2,026	5,545	36,530
1999[1]	686	815,909	77,525	894,120	28,108	65,478	4,856	1,038,512	128,493	1,943	5,575	36,400

[1] Preliminary.   [2] Including transportation.   [3] Excludes stocks held at retail dealers for consumption by the residential and commercial sector.
Source: Energy Information Administration, U.S. Department of Energy (EIA-DOE)

Average Prices of Coal in the United States   In Dollars Per Short Ton

Year	End-Use-Sector Electric Utilities	Coke Plants	Other Industrial[3]	Imports[4]	Exports Steam	Metallurgical	Total Average[4]	Year	End-Use-Sector Electric Utilities	Coke Plants	Other Industrial[3]	Imports[4]	Exports Steam	Metallurgical	Total Average[4]
1990	30.45	47.73	33.59	34.45	36.81	46.51	42.63	1995	27.01	47.34	32.42	34.13	34.51	44.30	40.27
1991	30.02	48.88	33.54	33.12	36.91	46.15	42.39	1996	26.45	47.33	32.32	33.45	34.09	45.49	40.76
1992	29.36	47.92	32.78	33.46	35.73	45.41	41.34	1997	26.16	47.36	32.40	34.32	32.45	45.47	40.59
1993	28.58	47.44	32.23	29.89	36.03	44.11	41.41	1998	25.64	46.06	32.26	32.29	30.27	44.53	38.92
1994	28.03	46.56	32.55	30.21	34.34	42.77	39.93	1999[1]	24.75	45.86	31.60	30.76	30.20	41.83	36.69

[1] Preliminary.   [2] Estimate.   [3] Manufacturing plants only.   [4] Based on the free alongside ship (F.A.S.) value.   NA = Not available.
Source: Energy Information Administration, U.S. Department of Energy (EIA-DOE)

Trends in Bituminous Coal, Lignite and Pennsylvania Anthracite in the U.S.   In Thousands of Short Tons

	---------- Bituminous Coal and Lignite ----------				---- Labor Productivity ----			------ Pennsylvania Anthracite ------					All Mines
	------ Production ------				Under-ground	Surface	Average	Under-ground	Surface	Total	Miners[1] Employed	Labor Product. Short Tons Miner/Hr.	Labor Product. Short Tons Miner/Hr.
Year	Under-gound	Surface	Total	Miners[1] Employed	Short Tons Per Miner Per Hour								
1989	393,322	584,058	977,381	131,497	2.46	5.61	3.70	513	2,835	3,348	1,394	1.12	3.70
1990	424,119	601,449	1,025,570	131,310	2.54	5.94	3.83	427	3,080	3,506	1,687	1.03	3.83
1991	406,901	585,638	992,539	120,602	2.69	6.38	4.09	324	3,121	3,445	1,161	1.39	4.09
1992	406,815	587,248	994,062	110,196	2.93	6.59	4.36	424	3,058	3,483	1,217	1.33	4.36
1993	350,637	590,482	941,119	101,322	2.95	7.23	4.70	416	3,889	4,306	1,124	1.85	4.70
1994	399,103	634,401	1,033,504	97,500	3.19	7.67	4.98	343	4,278	4,621	1,183	1.93	4.98
1995	396,249	636,725	1,032,974	90,252	3.39	8.48	5.38	428	4,254	4,682	1,069	2.08	5.38
1996	409,849	654,007	1,063,856	83,462	3.57	9.05	5.69	391	4,360	4,751	1,171	1.92	5.69
1997	420,657	669,274	1,089,932	81,516	3.83	9.46	6.04	419	4,259	4,678	1,287	1.76	6.04
1998	417,728	699,807	1,117,535	81,257	3.84	9.85	6.22	408	4,823	5,231	1,185	1.75	6.22

[1] Excludes miners employed at mines producing less than 10,000 tons.   *Source: Energy Information Administration, U.S. Department of Energy (EIA-DOE)*

Average Mine Prices of Coal in the United States   In Dollars Per Short Ton

	----- Average Mine Price by Method -----			-------------- Average Mine Prices by Rank --------------				Bituminous & Lignite FOB Mines[2]	Anthracite FOB Mines[2]	All Coal CIF[3] Electric Utility Plants
Year	Under-ground	Surface	Total	Lignite	Sub-bituminous	Bituminous	Anthracite[1]			
1989	28.44	17.38	21.82	9.91	10.16	27.40	42.93	21.76	42.93	30.15
1990	28.58	16.98	21.76	10.13	9.70	27.43	39.40	21.71	39.40	30.45
1991	28.56	16.60	21.49	10.89	9.68	27.49	36.34	21.45	36.34	30.02
1992	27.83	16.34	21.03	10.81	9.68	26.78	34.24	20.98	34.24	29.36
1993	26.92	15.67	19.85	11.11	9.33	26.15	32.94	20.56	37.80	28.58
1994	26.39	15.02	19.41	10.77	8.37	25.68	36.07	25.68	36.07	28.03
1995	26.18	14.25	18.83	10.83	8.10	25.56	39.78	25.56	39.78	27.01
1996	25.96	13.82	18.50	10.92	7.87	25.17	36.78	25.17	36.78	26.45
1997	25.68	13.39	18.14	10.91	7.42	24.64	35.12	24.64	35.12	26.16
1998	25.64	12.92	17.67	10.80	6.96	24.87	42.91	24.87	42.91	25.64

[1] Produced in Pennsylvania.   [2] FOB = free on board.   [3] CIF = cost, insurance and freight.   W = Withheld data.

Source: Energy Information Adminstration, U.S. Department of Energy (EIA-DOE)

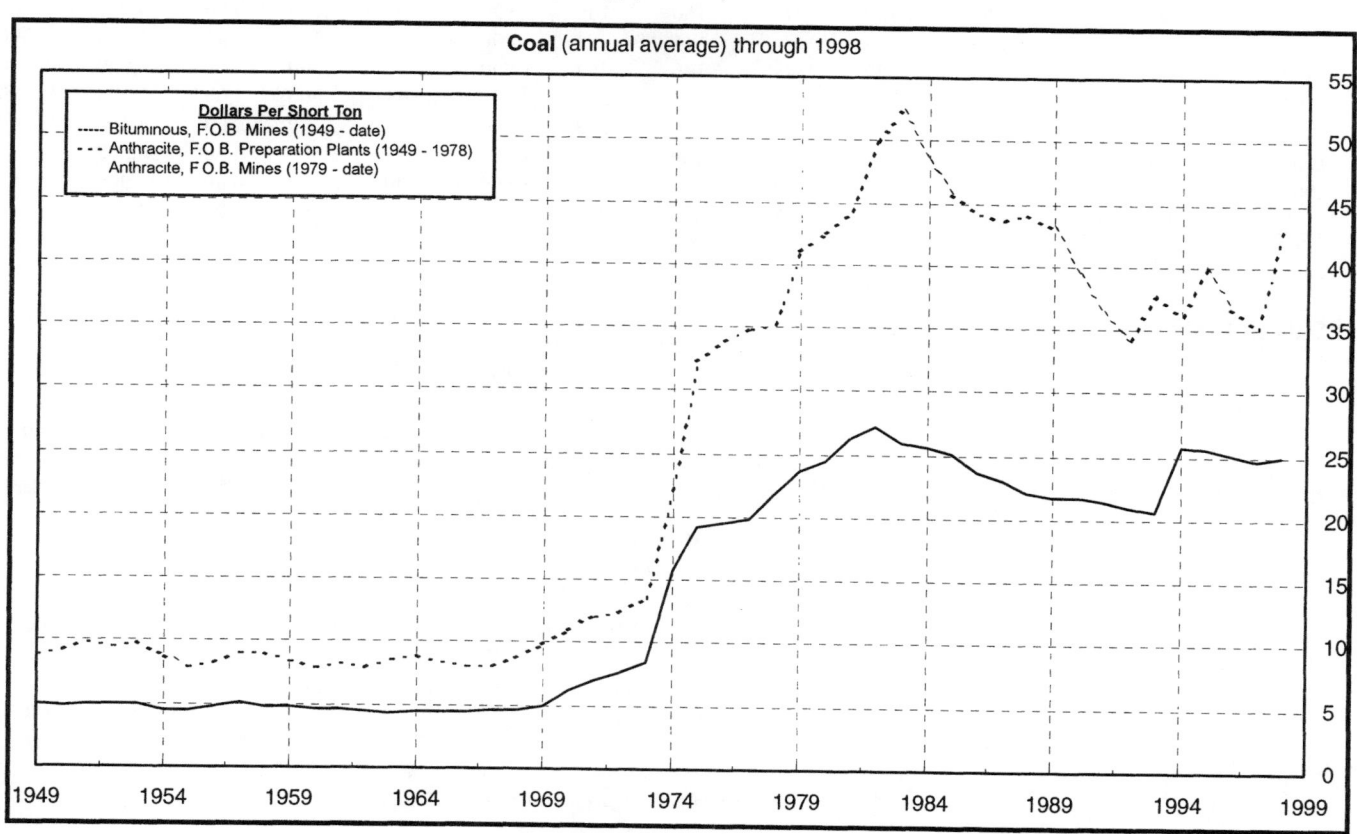

Coal (annual average) through 1998

Dollars Per Short Ton
- Bituminous, F.O.B Mines (1949 - date)
- Anthracite, F.O.B. Preparation Plants (1949 - 1978)
- Anthracite, F.O.B. Mines (1979 - date)

Cobalt

Cobalt is a strategic and critical metal with a variety of uses in industrial and military applications. It is found in the ores of iron and copper. Cobalt's largest usage is in superalloys that are used in the manufacture of gas turbine aircraft engines. It is also used to make magnets, cemented carbides and diamond tools, catalysts for the petroleum and chemical industries, drying agents for paints, ground coats for porcelain enamels, pigments, battery electrodes, steel-belted radial tires, and magnetic recording media.

The U.S. Geological Survey reported that world mine production of cobalt in 1999 was 28,300 metric tonnes, up 8 percent from the previous year. The world's largest producer of cobalt was Zambia with 1999 production of 7,000 tonnes, unchanged from 1998. The next largest producer was Canada with 5,900 tonnes, down 2 percent from the previous year. Other large producers of cobalt include Australia, Russia, the Congo, and Cuba. World cobalt production is expected to increase in the next few years as production in Australia should increase. Cobalt can be recovered from a number of sources including stockpiled tailings, slags, and concentrates. The cobalt supply is expected to increase faster than demand for cobalt.

World reserves of cobalt are estimated to be 4.5 million tonnes. The largest reserves are located in the Congo with 2 million tonnes. Reserves in Cuba are estimated to be one million tonnes. Other countries with reserves include Australia, Zambia, and New Caledonia. The cobalt reserves of the U.S. are estimated to be about 1.3 million tonnes. Most of these resources are located in Minnesota with other deposits in Alaska, California, Idaho, Missouri, and Oregon. Outside of resources in Idaho, cobalt production is the result of a by-product of the mining of another metal.

U.S. reported consumption of cobalt materials in August 2000 was 640 tonnes. Total consumption of cobalt materials in the January-August 2000 period was 5,290 tonnes. Consumption of cobalt metal and metal powder in August 2000 was 277 tonnes, down 2 percent from a year ago. In the January-August 2000 period, consumption of metal was 2,220 tonnes. For all of 1999, consumption was 3,780 tonnes. Consumption of cobalt oxide and other cobalt chemical compounds in August 2000 were 136 tonnes, down 11 percent from a year earlier. In the first eight months of 2000, consumption totaled 1,250 tonnes, while for all of 1999 it was 1,910 tonnes. Consumption of cobalt scrap in August 2000 was 227 tonnes. In January-August 2000, consumption of cobalt scrap was 1,820 tonnes, while for all of 1999 it was 2,720 tonnes.

U.S reported stocks of cobalt materials in August 2000 were 641 tonnes, down 5 percent from a year ago. Stocks of cobalt metal in August 2000 were 305 tonnes, while oxide and other chemical stocks of scrap were 144 tonnes. U.S. government metal stocks were 11,600 tonnes.

World Mine Production of Cobalt   In Metric Tons (Cobalt Content)

Year	Australia	Bots-wana	Canada	Cuba	Finland (Refinery)	France (Refinery)	Japan (Refinery)	New Caledonia	Norway (Refinery)	Russia[3]	Congo[4]	Zambia	World Total
1990	1,200	205	5,470	1,460	1,300	150	199	800	1,830	5,500	19,000	7,000	42,300
1991	1,400	208	5,274	1,100	1,503	123	185	800	1,983	5,800	9,900	6,994	33,300
1992	1,600	208	5,102	1,150	2,100	150	105	800	2,293	4,000	5,700	6,910	27,800
1993	1,900	205	5,108	1,061	2,200	144	191	800	2,414	3,500	2,459	4,840	21,900
1994	2,300	225	4,265	972	3,000	146	161	1,000	2,823	3,000	826	3,600	18,000
1995	2,500	271	5,339	1,591	3,610	161	227	1,100	2,804	3,500	1,647	5,908	24,500
1996	2,800	408	5,714	2,011	4,160	174	258	1,100	3,098	3,300	2,000	6,959	26,200
1997	3,000	334	5,709	2,082	5,000	159	264	1,000	3,417	3,300	3,500	6,037	27,100
1998[1]	3,300	335	5,861	2,200	10,600	300	480	1,000	4,500	3,200	6,000	11,900	35,300
1999[2]	4,100	335	5,324	2,160	10,000	300	480	1,100	4,500	3,300	7,000	4,700	29,900

[1] Preliminary.   [2] Estimate.   [3] Formerly part of the U.S.S.R.; data not reported separately until 1992.   [4] Formerly Zaire.
Source: U.S. Geological Survey (USGS)

Salient Statistics of Cobalt in the United States   In Metric Tons (Cobalt Content)

Year	Net Import Reliance as a % of Apparent Consumption	Cobalt Secondary Production	Processors and Consumer Stocks Dec. 31	Imports for Consumption	Ground Coat Frit	Stainless & Heat Resisting	Cata-lysts	Super-alloys	Tool Steel	Mag-netic Alloys	Pig-ments	Drier in Paints, etc.[3]	Cutting & Wear-Resistant Material	Welding Materials	Total Apparent Uses	Price $ Per Pound[4]
1990	84	1,225	1,853	6,530	357	41	W	3,345	123	710	W	751	541	180	7,512	10.09
1991	80	1,578	1,622	6,920	W	51	W	3,066	W	713	W	781	525	135	7,240	16.92
1992	76	1,613	840	5,760	257	26	949	2,697	47	670	197	745	522	128	6,590	22.93
1993	79	1,566	819	5,950	W	41	935	2,530	59	569	193	732	569	171	7,350	13.79
1994	81	1,570	914	6,780	W	41	871	2,810	84	698	198	809	723	312	8,730	24.66
1995	79	1,860	818	6,440	196	38	732	2,940	146	757	172	770	748	287	8,970	29.21
1996	76	2,280	770	6,710	391	38	652	3,360	95	719	191	733	722	347	9,380	25.50
1997	76	2,750	763	8,430	490	38	734	4,170	112	879	201	556	789	342	11,200	23.34
1998[1]	73	3,080	750	7,670	W	38	W	4,060	96	771	W	W	844	421	11,500	21.43
1999[2]	73	2,720	739	8,150	W	W	W	3,830	W	794	W	W	755	291	10,700	17.02

[1] Preliminary.   [2] Estimate.   [3] Or related usage.   [4] Annual spot for cathodes.   W = Withheld proprietary data.
Source: U.S. Geological Survey (USGS)

Cocoa

After an extended decline which carried prices to new 20-year lows, cocoa prices bottomed in December 2000 and then staged a powerful rally. Prices at the CSCE division of the New York Board of Trade moved from close to $700 per metric tonne to over $1000 per tonne. There were a number of reasons but the primary one was a growing concern in the trade about the stability of the new government in the Ivory Coast, the largest producer of cocoa. There was also concern about the new crop in Ghana and the possibility that it would not be as large as expected.

Cocoa is a tropical crop found mostly in a zone that extends about 15 degrees north and 15 degrees south of the equator. Cocoa trees reach maturity at 5-6 years and can live 50 years or more. A mature cocoa pod is six to ten inches long and can contain 20-50 seeds or beans. During the season, the tree will produce thousands of flowers but only a few pods. Typically, there is a large crop or main crop followed by a smaller or midcrop.

The largest production area for cocoa is West Africa where about 60 percent of the world's cocoa is produced. The four major West African producers are the Ivory Coast, Ghana, Nigeria, and Cameroon. The Ivory Coast is by far the largest producer with about 40 percent of the world total. Ghana is the next largest producer with about 15 percent of the total. Outside of West Africa, the other major producers are Indonesia, Brazil, Malaysia, Ecuador, and the Dominican Republic. A number of cocoa producers, such as Ghana and Indonesia, have been making concerted efforts to increase production. Other countries, such as Malaysia, have been switching to other crops. Brazil, which in the past was a major producer and exporter of cocoa, has seen its production reduced by disease. Brazil is now importing cocoa. In the 1999/2000 season, world cocoa crops had recovered from the effects of El Nino. As the new 2000/01 (October-September) season got underway, there were no serious weather problems in the major production regions.

The 2000/01 season is underway with the harvest of main crops in West Africa. Harvesting occurs from October to March. The International Cocoa Organization (ICCO) has estimated the 1999/00 world crop at 3.003 million tonnes, a downward revision from 3.025 million tonnes. In 1998/99, world production was estimated at 2.808 million tonnes. The U.S.D.A. estimated 1999/00 world production at 2.895 million tonnes which compared to 2.864 million tonnes in 1998/99. It is expected that 2000/01 world production will be somewhat less than 3 million tonnes.

By far the most dominant producer and exporter of cocoa is the Ivory Coast. The years 1999 and 2000 marked a period of change in the Ivory Coast on two fronts. The political situation was turbulent as there was an election to replace the military government which led to increased social unrest. There were ethnic tensions, particularly among many people involved in cocoa production. The other development of importance was the fact that the government influence and control over the cocoa industry had been removed or liberalized. The result was that market forces came into play. As cocoa prices moved to multiyear lows, this liberalization was often cited as one reason for the decline. It was pointed out that pricing power in cocoa had shifted from the sellers of cocoa to the buyers of cocoa. Add to this a record crop in 1999/00 and large world stocks and the result was a decline in prices. As the new 2000/01 season got underway, the political situation remained tense. Arrivals of the new main crop have been running behind a year ago. The main crop had been expected to be about one million tonnes though it was late to develop and some cocoa may be held back because of the political uncertainties. The rainfall pattern favored the midcrop which could turn out to be a large one.

The U.S.D.A. forecast the 1999/00 Ghana cocoa crop at 450,000 tonnes, up from 430,000 tonnes the previous year. Weather for the crop appeared favorable initially with ideas in the trade that the crop would exceed 450,000 tonnes. About midway through the purchasing season, the Ghana Cocoa Board indicated that the crop looked like it would be smaller than expected. Nigeria produced 170,000 tonnes in 1999/00 based on U.S.D.A. estimates. The new crop is late to develop and may be about the same as in 1999/00. Indonesia's crop in 1999/00 was about 348,000 tonnes.

World consumption of cocoa in 1999/00 was estimated by the ICCO at 2.948 million tonnes, up 6 percent from the previous year. Consumption in 2000/01 should be around 3.1 million tonnes. World stocks of cocoa remain large with the ICCO estimating 1999/00 stocks at 1.3 million tonnes.

Futures Markets

Cocoa futures and options are traded on the CSCE Division of the New York Board of Trade (NYBOT) and on the London International Financial Futures and Options Exchange (LIFFE).

World Supply and Demand Cocoa   In Thousands of Metric Tons

Crop Year Beginning October	Stocks Oct. 1	Net World Production	Total Availability	Seasonal Grindings	Closing Stocks	Stock Change	Crop Year Beginning October	Stocks Oct. 1	Net World Production	Total Availability	Seasonal Grindings	Closing Stocks	Stock Change
1985-6	531	1,962	2,474	1,877	597	65	1993-4	1,334	2,502	3,811	2,485	1,326	-8
1986-7	597	1,988	2,565	1,896	669	72	1994-5	1,326	2,386	3,688	2,507	1,181	-145
1987-8	669	2,194	2,841	2,003	838	169	1995-6	1,181	2,907	4,059	2,650	1,409	228
1988-9	838	2,460	3,273	2,118	1,155	317	1996-7	1,409	2,693	4,075	2,753	1,321	-87
1989-90	1,155	2,425	3,556	2,212	1,343	188	1997-8	1,321	2,644	3,939	2,802	1,137	-185
1990-1	1,343	2,510	3,828	2,351	1,476	133	1998-9[1]	1,194	2,803	3,969	2,758	1,211	17
1991-2	1,476	2,269	3,723	2,284	1,439	-38	1999-00[2]	1,211	2,937	4,119	2,924	1,195	-16
1992-3	1,439	2,360	3,775	2,441	1,334	-105	2000-1[3]	1,195	2,920	4,086	2,924	1,162	-33

[1] Preliminary.   [2] Estimate.   [3] Forecast.   [4] Obtained by adjusting the Gross World Crop for one percent loss in weight.
Source: E D & F Man Cocoa Ltd.

COCOA

World Production of Cocoa Beans — In Thousands of Metric Tons

Crop Year Beginning October	Brazil	Came-roon	Colom-bia	Domin-ican Republic	Ecuador	Ghana	Indo-nesia	Ivory Coast	Mal-aysia	Mexico	Nigeria	Papua New Guinea	World Total
1991-2	310	108	47	48	83	243	169	748	217	51	110	41	2,269
1992-3	305	99	54	52	70	312	234	697	219	51	130	39	2,360
1993-4	280	97	49	59	79	255	251	887	204	39	142	31	2,473
1994-5	230	109	48	57	83	310	238	862	120	43	144	29	2,367
1995-6	235	117	45	55	103	404	284	1,265	116	30	163	35	2,952
1996-7	170	121	45	47	101	323	327	1,130	102	35	157	28	2,702
1997-8	168	114	46	60	28	409	331	1,113	57	30	165	26	2,658
1998-9[1]	130	121	39	24	72	398	393	1,175	79	25	202	35	2,803
1999-00[2]	128	120	40	35	93	440	396	1,300	50	22	165	39	2,937
2000-1[3]	123	120	40	45	95	450	420	1,225	45	30	180	37	2,920

[1] Preliminary. [2] Estimate. [3] Forecast. *Source: Foreign Agricultural Service, U.S. Department of Agriculture (FAS-USDA)*

World Consumption of Cocoa[4] — In Thousands of Metric Tons

Year	Belgium	Brazil	Cote d'Ivoire	France	Germany	Italy	Malaysia	Nether-lands	Singa-pore	United Kingdom	United States	Former U.S.S.R.	World Total
1990-1	45	275	115	70	295	56	77	268	52	145	272	83	2,351
1991-2	46	216	108	67	306	62	87	294	51	153	307	25	2,284
1992-3	47	218	100	80	310	58	99	309	47	169	326	95	2,421
1993-4	50	220	110	95	310	65	103	331	52	170	317	90	2,480
1994-5	53	189	108	108	280	69	101	350	52	154	331	80	2,497
1995-6	54	183	135	111	270	73	96	385	56	191	345	80	2,645
1996-7	55	180	150	106	255	71	103	402	57	172	394	85	2,748
1997-8[1]	55	188	205	107	240	72	94	425	55	174	399	85	2,811
1998-9[2]	55	200	221	124	200	72	109	415	50	166	406	55	2,758
1999-00[3]	55	214	245	140	200	70	115	437	50	167	438	65	2,924

[1] Preliminary. [2] Estimate. [3] Forecast. [4] Figures represent the grindings of cocoa beans in each country. *Source: Foreign Agricultural Service, U.S. Department of Agriculture (FAS-USDA)*

Raw Cocoa Grindings in Selected Countries — In Metric Tons

Year	Total	First Quarter	Second Quarter	Third Quarter	Fourth Quarter	Total	First Quarter	Second Quarter	Third Quarter	Fourth Quarter
			Germany[2]					Netherlands		
1990	281,855	69,125	64,613	70,994	77,123	247,590	62,243	58,817	58,702	67,828
1991	290,703	73,172	72,396	70,934	73,661	274,741	64,299	71,643	63,973	74,826
1992	319,251	78,661	73,797	80,111	86,682	293,157	77,954	71,537	69,871	73,795
1993	298,681	74,119	69,805	74,010	80,747	320,060	78,338	75,548	81,183	84,991
1994	296,219	80,242	68,033	67,706	80,238	334,384	83,963	78,055	84,249	88,117
1995	258,817	69,441	56,478	61,523	71,375	355,492	91,314	85,248	85,311	93,619
1996	251,070	69,520	59,471	65,824	56,255	388,412	100,866	90,724	99,549	97,273
1997	245,244	61,379	57,402	65,233	61,230	407,340	102,338	100,132	101,817	103,053
1998	217,442	62,154	47,565	55,267	52,456	427,393	104,936	108,101	108,580	105,776
1999[1]	195,732	48,486	48,605	47,321	51,320	415,250	107,189	102,933	98,828	106,300
			United Kingdom					United States[3]		
1990	124,791	32,116	29,322	29,419	33,934	216,740	51,559	51,683	58,278	55,220
1991	148,191	32,902	36,016	41,863	37,410	255,781	51,191	64,365	66,544	73,681
1992	159,284	39,831	37,903	37,120	44,430	313,921	70,335	74,515	84,109	84,962
1993	171,343	44,575	41,975	37,496	47,297	321,905	78,968	77,720	84,593	80,624
1994	163,170	44,131	39,063	39,591	40,385	322,629	71,398	78,805	86,247	86,179
1995	159,877	43,410	35,348	34,431	46,688	338,401	78,835	78,886	87,360	93,320
1996	189,037	50,500	44,535	48,855	45,147	351,042	79,044	82,713	93,933	95,352
1997	173,522	44,059	42,702	41,180	45,581	397,895	95,435	97,223	105,984	99,253
1998	171,773	45,787	42,338	40,047	43,601	397,389	99,189	96,341	104,359	97,500
1999[1]	167,556	42,557	39,758	40,238	45,003	418,996	98,218	102,488	107,568	110,722

[1] Preliminary. [2] Beginning October 1990, includes former East Germany. [3] Data incomplete January 1984-March 1991, excludes one major processor. *Source: Foreign Agricultural Service, U.S. Department of Agriculture (FAS-USDA)*

Imports of Cocoa Butter in Selected Countries   In Metric Tons

Year	Australia	Austria	Belgium	Canada	France	Germany	Italy	Japan	Nether-Lands	Sweden	Switzer-land	United Kingdom	United States
1990	10,025	6,047	22,125	8,830	28,539	49,999	6,187	15,686	34,529	5,855	16,306	34,604	92,165
1991	11,218	5,171	24,795	8,682	28,628	54,452	7,813	15,245	29,729	6,299	16,544	26,876	90,004
1992	10,697	5,249	31,836	10,706	28,560	44,906	8,431	15,835	29,999	5,885	17,422	26,300	99,509
1993	13,129	5,417	28,989	10,225	30,611	37,269	9,851	16,422	51,559	6,390	16,711	26,300	85,400
1994	13,030	5,410	34,061	11,551	36,698	59,170	9,173	15,937	43,192	7,079	17,242	35,453	54,550
1995	12,150	7,425	26,185	11,146	40,245	69,928	12,027	12,898	38,300	7,078	17,835	30,654	57,210
1996	14,316	7,124	23,771	12,166	47,349	69,298	11,178	16,096	39,193	5,698	18,690	32,781	68,761
1997	14,896	6,922	34,222	16,782	46,516	71,094	9,706	16,609	29,023	6,937	19,058	37,021	87,687
1998	16,305	5,984	25,722	16,941	43,610	76,057	8,957	15,363	28,523	7,403	19,857	32,951	65,306
1999[1]	22,573	5,363	42,278	17,323	49,722	70,323	8,281	17,824	35,602	6,884	21,278	39,648	80,475

[1] Preliminary.   Sources: E D & F Man Cocoa Limited

Imports of Cocoa Liquor and Cocoa Powder in Selected Countries   In Metric Tons

Year	Cocoa Liqour						Cocoa Powder						
	France	Germany	Nether-lands	Japan	United Kingdom	United States	Denmark	France	Germany	Italy	Japan	Nether-lands	United States
1990	35,146	1,860	9,875	3,123	1,713	25,047	3,014	12,244	21,294	11,418	6,284	6,446	58,280
1991	40,251	3,242	7,443	2,057	1,918	25,320	3,583	12,215	25,315	12,189	6,557	6,239	55,636
1992	45,056	2,540	7,130	2,246	3,611	24,255	3,291	14,896	27,745	14,469	6,067	9,412	56,089
1993	41,999	1,694	15,543	2,468	1,490	31,641	3,402	16,773	25,732	13,221	5,771	5,626	66,533
1994	42,392	2,682	14,913	2,312	4,443	26,846	3,625	19,215	28,806	12,884	6,461	10,078	67,207
1995	46,570	5,083	6,822	1,832	5,030	19,192	3,229	17,081	32,247	15,265	6,310	10,048	66,075
1996	62,938	7,437	9,926	2,133	5,069	15,357	3,711	18,398	36,211	15,006	13,069	6,678	68,658
1997	61,148	10,299	8,401	1,393	5,860	17,850	4,189	19,555	35,069	15,872	8,941	4,424	71,024
1998	70,883	9,121	12,534	1,144	3,813	21,894	3,865	19,533	32,479	17,122	8,779	3,746	84,211
1999[1]	74,721	13,833	25,639	1,421	4,396	12,823	3,676	19,342	33,404	16,464	9,779	NA	84,975

[1] Preliminary.   NA = Not available.   Source: E D & F Man Cocoa Limited

Imports of Cocoa and Products in the United States   In Thousands of Metric Tons

Year	Jan.	Feb.	Mar.	Apr.	May	June	July	Aug.	Sept.	Oct.	Nov.	Dec.	Total
1991	70	53	51	74	62	66	65	59	53	NA	NA	73	761
1992	83	66	62	55	50	60	52	60	67	67	64	69	755
1993	67	57	56	61	58	61	77	58	59	71	71	98	801
1994	67	68	56	61	49	51	49	58	58	61	45	48	672
1995	68	54	44	48	47	48	48	51	53	49	54	79	643
1996	90	87	90	80	55	49	62	53	53	60	60	86	821
1997	80	47	77	71	64	54	59	47	64	61	56	88	768
1998	86	105	90	71	55	65	65	62	72	63	54	77	865
1999	100	79	81	93	51	60	77	62	68	67	82	102	922
2000[1]	111	128	101	91	70	67	70	70	86	76			1,044

[1] Preliminary.   NA = Not available.   Source: Foreign Agricultural Service, U.S. Department of Agriculture (FAS-USDA)

Visible Stocks of Cocoa in Port of Hampton Road Warehouses[1], at End of Month   In Thousands of Bags

Year	Jan.	Feb.	Mar.	Apr.	May	June	July	Aug.	Sept.	Oct.	Nov.	Dec.
1991	946.5	953.3	910.1	946.0	906.1	1,036.6	1,174.5	1,291.2	1,386.2	1,429.0	1,426.0	1,502.9
1992	1,588.3	1,892.1	2,233.1	2,236.2	2,236.9	2,204.8	2,150.8	2,087.4	1,982.4	2,018.6	2,043.9	2,188.5
1993	2,209.9	2,497.3	2,443.9	2,676.8	2,771.8	2,689.7	2,920.0	2,708.6	2,740.1	2,418.7	2,328.3	2,356.9
1994	2,329.6	2,441.1	2,443.9	2,522.9	2,533.1	2,460.2	2,445.4	2,335.0	2,308.4	2,360.2	2,306.9	2,253.7
1995	2,152.7	2,098.6	2,195.7	2,212.3	2,120.2	2,016.0	1,919.8	1,786.6	1,713.1	1,598.2	1,463.9	1,470.3
1996	1,439.8	1,492.8	1,458.0	1,549.6	1,561.7	1,493.9	1,412.3	1,315.4	1,239.6	1,338.9	1,108.1	1,116.2
1997	1,128.3	1,132.1	1,133.0	1,094.0	1,010.5	970.2	872.4	840.1	727.3	763.9	695.7	704.8
1998	726.5	693.4	841.9	842.5	811.6	764.7	714.3	712.3	795.4	801.9	705.9	673.0
1999	661.6	693.2	642.5	579.7	536.9	500.7	489.0	472.7	473.4	451.8	438.9	421.2
2000	469.7	448.4	571.7	583.4	711.1	672.4	720.3	925.2	921.4	839.7	762.9	816.0

[1] Licensed and unlicensed warehouses approved by the CSCE.   Source: New York Board of Trade (NYBOT)

COCOA

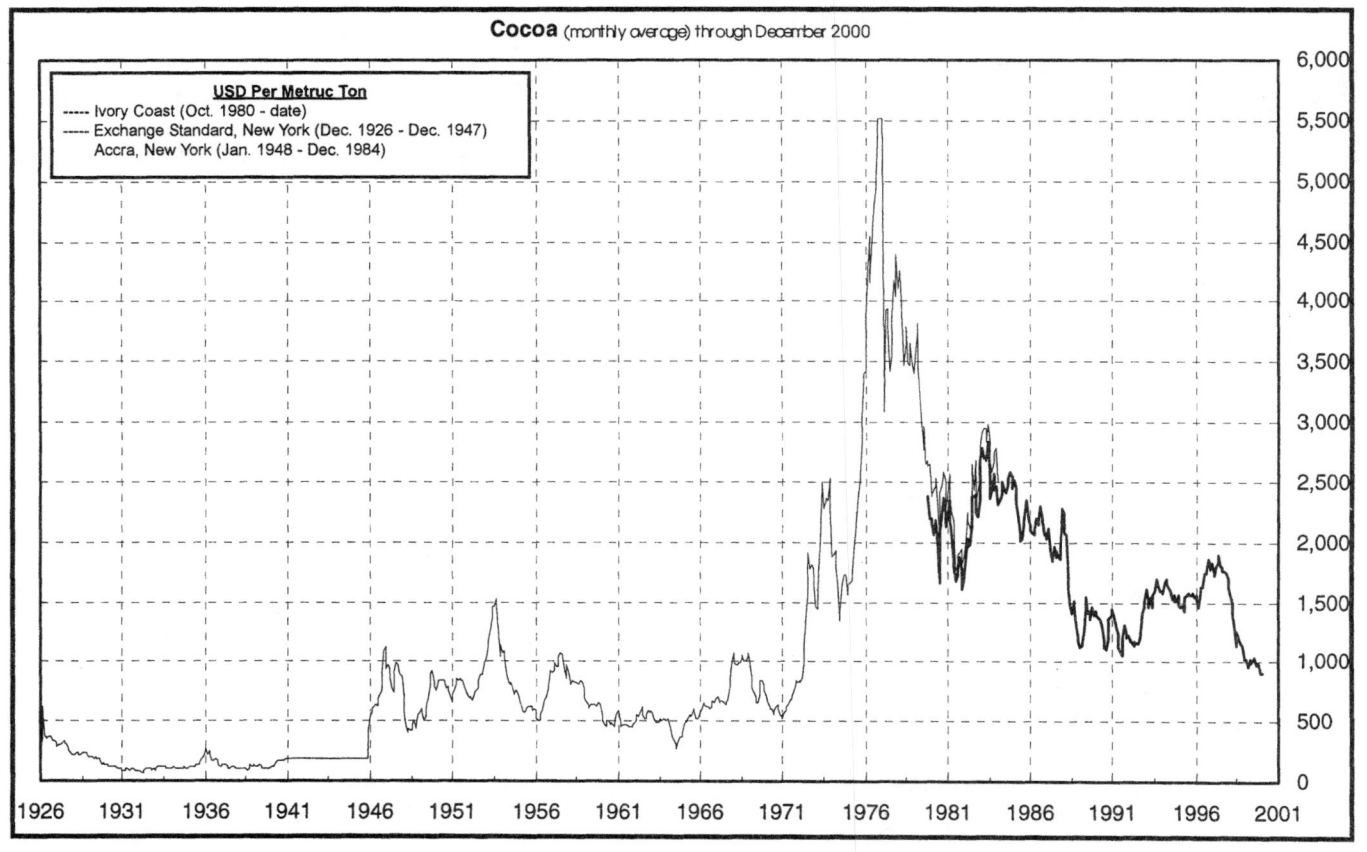

Cocoa (monthly average) through December 2000

USD Per Metric Ton
----- Ivory Coast (Oct. 1980 - date)
----- Exchange Standard, New York (Dec. 1926 - Dec. 1947)
Accra, New York (Jan. 1948 - Dec. 1984)

Visible Stocks of Cocoa in Philadelphia (Del. River) Warehouses[1], at End of Month   In Thousands of Bags

Year	Jan.	Feb.	Mar.	Apr.	May	June	July	Aug.	Sept.	Oct.	Nov.	Dec.
1991	216.2	226.9	249.3	254.9	309.2	376.8	382.8	376.8	375.5	355.1	280.5	282.7
1992	344.6	345.5	412.1	547.6	576.7	632.0	637.7	654.0	616.4	606.0	565.8	612.4
1993	562.2	589.8	603.9	606.0	653.1	678.0	665.7	648.9	600.6	611.5	685.2	781.8
1994	831.5	937.7	1,004.2	1,010.9	1,055.4	1,095.2	1,076.0	1,029.8	968.5	857.1	843.9	818.9
1995	807.5	1,034.3	1,038.9	1,020.2	963.7	924.3	860.7	759.2	852.2	727.0	666.0	735.6
1996	960.2	1,005.2	1,205.6	1,658.8	1,871.3	1,851.7	1,969.1	1,816.2	1,851.1	1,705.1	1,671.7	1,696.5
1997	1,753.0	1,634.4	1,579.6	1,641.0	1,578.7	1,625.9	1,696.2	1,637.6	1,530.9	1,491.8	1,414.2	1,394.0
1998	1,420.3	1,435.7	1,592.6	1,555.3	1,398.5	1,287.8	1,279.8	1,376.9	1,373.7	1,260.6	1,406.7	1,637.1
1999	1,763.0	1,832.8	1,982.7	2,217.8	2,019.4	1,999.6	2,084.6	2,133.4	2,144.1	2,015.5	1,774.4	1,608.5
2000	1,619.0	1,801.7	2,466.4	2,582.0	2,581.6	2,363.7	2,168.3	2,101.6	2,105.1	2,039.1	1,697.4	1,589.4

[1] Licensed and unlicensed warehouses approved by the CSCE.   *Source: New York Board of Trade (NYBOT)*

Visible Stocks of Cocoa in New York Warehouses[1], at End of Month   In Thousands of Bags

Year	Jan.	Feb.	Mar.	Apr.	May	June	July	Aug.	Sept.	Oct.	Nov.	Dec.
1991	355.6	219.6	295.9	294.1	250.4	292.6	313.3	317.1	271.5	253.9	292.9	282.4
1992	321.2	303.7	278.7	302.6	273.4	287.8	329.7	301.5	280.5	252.3	212.7	183.3
1993	150.9	144.1	122.0	125.0	119.8	119.8	119.8	119.8	119.8	118.6	132.4	187.7
1994	271.0	275.0	280.8	296.6	358.6	394.1	447.5	447.5	467.3	427.3	407.2	556.1
1995	560.5	634.5	559.2	539.4	510.4	561.1	579.3	595.4	459.9	598.7	679.7	598.7
1996	667.6	646.1	632.7	627.2	656.1	633.5	1,191.7	1,154.2	1,121.4	973.2	950.1	919.0
1997	984.7	981.3	945.0	1,250.0	1,574.4	1,524.7	1,512.8	1,348.0	1,217.3	1,073.7	1,020.0	980.4
1998	973.9	1,342.7	1,271.3	1,675.7	1,552.3	1,516.7	1,404.6	1,293.1	1,300.1	1,126.4	989.2	1,031.6
1999	1,085.0	1,089.3	1,083.1	1,134.1	1,139.4	1,114.3	1,093.5	974.5	941.9	821.7	847.5	1,573.1
2000	1,633.7	1,689.5	1,926.9	2,049.9	1,926.7	1,789.6	1,632.2	1,383.7	1,323.7	1,234.8	1,100.0	1,019.4

[1] Licensed and unlicensed warehouses approved by the CSCE.   *Source: New York Board of Trade (NYBOT)*

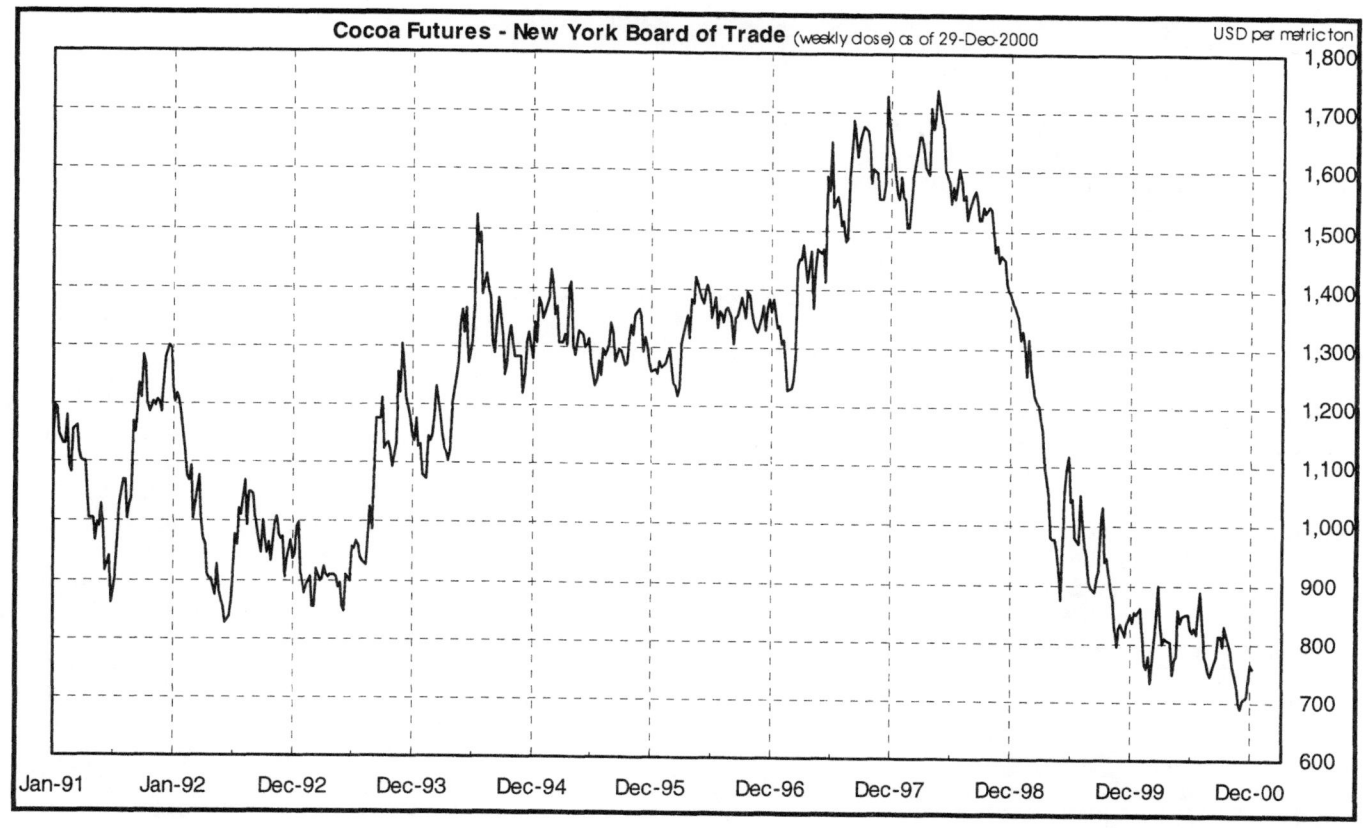

Cocoa Futures - New York Board of Trade (weekly close) as of 29-Dec-2000   USD per metric ton

Average Open Interest of Cocoa Futures in New York   In Contracts

Year	Jan.	Feb.	Mar.	Apr.	May	June	July	Aug.	Sept.	Oct.	Nov.	Dec.
1991	42,446	38,205	40,198	45,250	47,764	49,111	53,153	53,886	53,974	54,854	53,390	53,412
1992	54,464	54,797	52,110	49,904	48,076	47,690	49,924	50,532	51,706	56,101	57,426	60,521
1993	64,886	68,307	69,464	68,533	71,802	71,792	87,011	83,057	88,000	94,844	96,507	91,573
1994	89,174	87,349	91,715	82,500	82,970	72,288	72,249	69,614	73,436	74,163	72,232	75,995
1995	78,873	80,786	82,299	78,435	80,547	75,496	74,975	65,794	68,547	72,758	76,680	79,844
1996	90,478	93,533	98,049	95,390	96,346	88,232	80,873	77,134	77,942	79,572	77,139	78,592
1997	86,960	90,589	96,771	96,956	94,651	97,385	101,815	101,138	106,487	108,263	99,544	97,009
1998	90,574	82,205	78,022	73,237	79,294	74,347	74,295	73,975	71,978	74,139	74,127	73,480
1999	77,067	72,324	69,221	65,856	71,990	75,195	70,787	69,939	74,572	79,770	89,035	92,609
2000	100,540	110,316	106,056	102,382	113,239	111,948	112,864	117,260	123,463	138,523	139,141	138,266

Source: New York Board of Trade (NYBOT)

Volume of Trading of Cocoa Futures in New York   In Contracts

Year	Jan.	Feb.	Mar.	Apr.	May	June	July	Aug.	Sept.	Oct.	Nov.	Dec.	Total
1991	94,609	92,450	104,973	99,176	76,435	104,327	96,840	146,379	104,136	135,677	106,888	72,629	1,234,519
1992	122,576	119,375	94,131	116,804	66,185	135,373	104,660	145,815	113,589	109,888	137,815	95,024	1,397,235
1993	145,378	139,932	111,751	149,771	82,961	189,474	225,901	215,044	240,371	217,697	229,752	183,352	2,128,384
1994	178,303	190,804	205,623	188,004	267,188	251,300	193,883	241,340	142,589	183,975	210,635	164,917	2,417,006
1995	197,032	183,784	191,328	208,707	169,061	199,211	140,789	205,169	120,433	149,810	211,171	113,603	2,090,098
1996	177,720	226,701	213,189	242,988	164,749	183,544	159,070	164,719	107,634	167,227	185,226	128,809	2,121,576
1997	180,669	172,510	219,896	235,020	130,041	251,471	186,280	200,707	168,981	204,394	180,805	143,735	2,274,509
1998	175,844	145,311	171,333	192,120	143,602	183,719	131,642	156,737	115,066	125,320	155,280	114,606	1,810,580
1999	136,109	155,090	141,090	180,837	130,019	230,925	125,360	144,290	147,124	143,335	209,608	124,249	1,868,036
2000	156,812	231,562	232,803	186,837	147,072	267,470	124,906	191,849	111,740	174,216	186,515	98,266	2,110,048

Source: New York Board of Trade (NYBOT)

Coconut Oil and Copra

The U.S.D.A. lists copra as a major oilseed despite the fact that production consistently totals less than 2 percent of total global oilseed production. Copra, dried coconut meat, is crushed or processed to yield coconut oil and copra meal. Coconut oil, an important ingredient in cosmetics and soap, is also used as food ingredient. As an edible oil, however, foodstock use is shrinking, especially in the U.S. as the oil has a very high level of saturated fat at 92 percent. U.S. coconut oil imports are mostly processed into inedible products.

Most of the world's copra crop is processed into oil. Copra production in 2000/01, almost all of which was crushed, totaled 5.15 million metric tonnes. This compares with 5.03 million metric tonnes in 1999/00, and a high for the 1990's of 5.5 million in 1995. From the two most recent crops, 2000/01 and 1999/00, 3.13 million tonnes and 3.08 million tonnes, respectively, of coconut oil were obtained. Copra meal output of 1.67 million tonnes in 2000/01 compares with 1.61 million in 1999/00. Percentagewise, coconut oil accounts for only about 3-4 percent of the world's vegetable and marine oil, and coconut meal less than 1 percent.

The Philippines and Indonesia account for about two-thirds of world copra output, production of which is not only dependent on the weather but also on the belief that a well entrenched biological cycle triggers relatively sharp swings in output. Indonesia's output since the mid-1990's has trended irregularly higher, with 1.3 million tonnes from the 2000 crop vs. less than 1 million tonnes the previous two crop years. Philippine output, however, while up in 2000 to about 2 million tonnes from 1.3 million in 1999, compares with 1995's record production of 2.5 million tonnes. India, the third largest producer, has seen production rise from a first half 1990's annual average of about 528,000 tonnes to over 720,000 tonnes in the second half of the decade.

Foreign trade in copra products is small. Coconut oil exports in 2000/01 of 1.7 million tonnes are unchanged from 1999/00; meal exports were a shade under one million tonnes in both years.

World carryover stocks of both products are also minimal. The 2000/01 coconut oil carryover of 120,000 tonnes compares to 160,000 tonnes the previous year, while meal totals are 125,000 tonnes and 190,000 tonnes, respectively.

U.S. crude coconut oil prices, basis tankcars, New York, have averaged under 40 cents per pound in recent years, but U.S. processors are not adverse to switching to palm oil should coconut oil develop a wider than acceptable premium to palm oil. World copra meal prices, basis Rotterdam, in 1999/00 (October through September) of $91 per metric tonne compare with $108 in 1998/99, and the 1988/89-1997/98 average of $125 per tonne. Rotterdam oil prices in 1999/00 averaged $539 per metric tonne vs. $748 a year earlier, and the ten-year average of $499 per tonne. Average copra seed prices of $357 per tonne in 1999/00 compare with $468 in 1998/99, and the ten-year average of $371 per tonne.

World Production of Copra   In Thousands of Metric Tons

Year	India	Indonesia	Ivory Coast	Malaysia	Mexico	Mozam-bique	New Guinea	Philip-pines	Sri Lanka	Thailand	Vanuatu	Vietnam	World Total
1992	440	1,110	65	82	200	72	117	1,845	70	65	24	220	4,624
1993	515	1,100	60	65	173	73	120	1,980	50	60	28	225	4,776
1994	592	1,270	65	60	216	74	104	1,930	104	100	27	210	5,072
1995	655	1,080	72	66	217	74	125	2,500	113	103	30	208	5,544
1996	720	1,155	75	60	204	75	178	1,725	75	61	33	210	4,880
1997	720	1,300	45	60	215	76	159	2,210	67	62	34	96	5,363
1998	735	970	43	52	200	76	150	2,270	95	90	37	123	5,147
1999[1]	720	860	42	52	153	73	146	1,250	90	87	35	100	3,878
2000[2]	660	1,200	45	55	140	73	160	2,000	95	90		102	4,955
2001[3]	740	1,300			135		162	2,180				100	5,313

[1] Preliminary.   [2] Estimate.   [3] Forecast.   *Source: The Oil World*

World Supply and Distribution of Coconut Oil   In Thousands of Metric Tons

Year	India	Indo-nesia	Mal-aysia	Philip-pines	Total	Exports	Imports	European Union	India	Indo-nesia	Philip-pines	United States	Total	Philip-pines	United States	Total
		Production							**Consumption**						**Ending Stocks**	
1991-2	274	701	33	1,110	2,848	1,343	1,321	513	285	380	257	409	2,880	115	85	420
1992-3	299	691	29	1,294	3,035	1,667	1,583	516	312	441	249	491	3,007	38	114	364
1993-4	343	704	32	1,242	3,009	1,361	1,437	547	346	337	294	483	2,962	181	74	457
1994-5	383	638	36	1,564	3,312	1,775	1,760	660	384	492	309	491	3,325	99	74	430
1995-6	397	612	35	1,206	2,912	1,374	1,405	606	396	373	306	427	3,005	100	38	368
1996-7	421	756	35	1,257	3,152	1,751	1,695	692	429	213	315	504	3,081	92	68	382
1997-8	439	652	40	1,628	3,451	2,122	2,117	777	437	185	302	540	3,230	32	178	598
1998-9[1]	432	458	52	780	2,352	1,039	1,166	580	447	113	293	461	2,762	56	69	311
1999-00[2]	397	674	50	1,152	2,923	1,550	1,564	605	424	157	313	478	2,875	75	70	373
2000-1[3]	445	760	47	1,331	3,244	1,767	1,761	660	465	206	341	527	3,133	95	86	478

[1] Preliminary.   [2] Estimate.   [3] Forecast.   *Source: The Oil World*

Supply and Distribution of Coconut Oil in the United States   In Millions of Pounds

Year	Rotterdam Copra Tonne ($ U.S.)	Rotterdam Coconut Oil, CIF ($ U.S.)	Imports For Consumption	Stocks Oct. 1	Total Supply	Exports	Disappearance Total Domestic	Disappearance Edible Products	Disappearance Inedible Products	Production of Coconut Oil (Refined) Total	Production Oct.-Dec.	Production Jan.-Mar.	Production April-June	Production July-Sept.
1990-1	247	364	946	279	1,225	51	897	169	742	754.6	196.8	150.8	141.8	265.2
1991-2	397	605	838	277	1,115	22	906	164	699	733.9	145.3	158.8	159.3	270.5
1992-3	292	446	1,162	187	1,349	15	1,082	202	692	650.5	156.0	158.8	166.6	169.1
1993-4	388	564	999	251	1,250	20	1,067	234	716	536.2	155.6	129.0	131.8	119.8
1994-5	432	656	1,100	163	1,263	18	1,082	247	694	546.8	137.5	142.7	144.3	122.3
1995-6	487	746	873	163	1,036	11	941	221	453	445.0	127.5	118.4	132.8	66.4
1996-7	452	693	1,188	83	1,271	11	1,111	120	471	324.2	77.0	61.5	101.5	84.2
1997-8	391	587	1,440	149	1,589	7	1,190	141	472	397.8	113.4	103.6	100.4	80.4
1998-91	468	748	820	392	1,212	7	1,140	144	380	363.2	89.6	82.9	99.3	91.4
1999-00[2]	357	539	1,202	66	1,268	11	1,157	221	371	442.3	69.1	117.0	129.6	126.7

[1] Preliminary.   *Source: Bureau of Census, U.S. Department of Commerce*

Consumption of Coconut Oil in End Products (Edible and Inedible) in the U.S.   In Millions of Pounds

Year	Jan.	Feb.	Mar.	Apr.	May	June	July	Aug.	Sept.	Oct.	Nov.	Dec.	Total
1991	----	137.6	----	----	150.6	----	----	134.4	----	----	122.1	----	544.7
1992	72.5	70.6	76.5	70.7	78.7	74.8	65.2	70.6	77.4	75.8	76.2	66.4	875.4
1993	74.4	75.9	81.3	77.6	72.1	71.0	73.6	78.2	72.6	85.9	90.9	84.6	938.1
1994	74.4	77.4	77.5	80.4	86.6	88.8	76.0	88.4	65.1	74.6	85.1	95.0	969.3
1995	78.2	79.5	86.5	81.0	79.7	82.0	76.5	71.4	61.6	62.1	59.8	59.9	878.0
1996	47.0	54.3	60.1	60.2	68.6	54.6	55.1	47.9	44.9	49.6	50.3	47.9	640.7
1997	44.1	44.8	52.8	46.1	41.9	49.4	49.9	48.3	66.9	53.4	43.9	48.0	589.5
1998	51.5	48.1	59.4	54.3	54.5	47.0	49.3	50.3	53.7	49.4	50.0	42.1	609.6
1999	39.9	44.7	50.8	43.0	41.4	45.4	36.9	33.3	46.2	41.5	43.6	38.8	505.5
2000[1]	49.4	44.0	52.7	54.6	51.4	56.5	49.1	56.2	54.7	44.1	44.3	43.1	600.1

[1] Preliminary.   *Source: Bureau of Census, U.S. Department of Commerce*

Stocks of Coconut Oil (Crude and Refined) in the U.S., on First of Month   In Millions of Pounds

Year	Jan.	Feb.	Mar.	Apr.	May	June	July	Aug.	Sept.	Oct.	Nov.	Dec.
1991	NA	NA	359.0	NA	NA	364.3	NA	NA	279.3	NA	NA	298.0
1992	NA	266.3	274.2	239.7	211.2	173.7	178.3	141.1	187.1	187.7	225.1	278.8
1993	355.7	406.7	418.9	348.7	338.3	305.2	257.2	233.8	321.4	250.8	335.0	299.1
1994	291.7	316.5	284.5	251.5	237.6	199.9	151.4	163.7	156.0	164.1	166.2	152.9
1995	155.6	173.6	168.1	163.7	148.5	183.5	163.8	136.9	124.1	162.9	199.7	187.7
1996	164.7	229.1	200.4	217.7	173.6	175.9	171.5	116.7	113.8	84.0	78.6	65.0
1997	125.9	147.4	141.1	204.5	174.5	161.3	143.8	143.4	154.3	149.6	162.1	194.2
1998	274.2	332.4	344.5	337.4	318.8	300.6	366.3	424.6	434.4	392.6	431.8	447.3
1999	401.7	446.5	387.5	366.3	309.8	240.5	134.7	197.5	191.8	152.0	106.4	142.2
2000[1]	93.6	123.6	100.1	99.6	102.3	104.0	137.7	163.6	161.4	136.4	178.1	161.6

[1] Preliminary.   NA = Not available.   *Source: Bureau of Census, U.S. Department of Commerce*

Average Price of Coconut Oil (Crude) Tank Cars in New York   In Cents Per Pound

Year	Jan.	Feb.	Mar.	Apr.	May	June	July	Aug.	Sept.	Oct.	Nov.	Dec.	Average
1991	20.22	20.31	20.50	19.38	19.69	21.69	26.19	25.63	25.63	28.50	31.50	32.38	24.30
1992	39.33	36.00	34.57	34.63	33.56	32.13	29.63	27.31	27.88	26.95	27.00	25.50	31.21
1993	24.94	24.37	23.65	23.13	24.13	24.95	25.35	25.61	24.44	23.88	26.69	34.25	25.45
1994	30.30	29.69	27.31	28.19	29.45	30.25	29.56	30.35	30.63	30.60	34.19	33.69	30.35
1995	32.50	32.00	31.13	31.00	30.50	35.00	37.90	35.63	35.00	36.00	37.88	33.69	34.02
1996	35.80	36.63	36.75	38.75	39.50	42.25	41.80	42.80	47.20	48.00	49.50	50.00	42.42
1997	44.20	44.00	42.88	42.50	42.50	35.00	36.50	36.50	37.00	37.25	37.25	37.25	39.40
1998	37.25	37.25	37.25	37.25	37.25	37.00	36.50	35.50	36.50	39.00	37.50	38.50	37.23
1999	35.38	35.00	34.00	34.06	38.25	42.13	39.83	36.08	46.00	35.02	40.73	41.43	38.16
2000[1]	40.85	37.70	29.70	29.26	26.86	23.82	20.92	18.85	17.13	17.48	19.10	16.90	24.88

[1] Preliminary.   *Source: Economic Research Service, U.S. Department of Agriculture (ERS-USDA)*

Coffee

Coffee prices staged a strong rally in the fourth quarter of 1999 as drought struck the Brazilian coffee crop. The coffee trees flower in the September-October period and the drought caused the flowering to be poor. This led to forecasts in the trade that the 2000-2001 crop in Brazil would be small. That crop is harvested starting in May. Because Brazil is by far the largest producer and exporter of coffee, any problems with the crop were discounted in the form of higher prices. A poor flowering just about guaranteed that the crop would be below average leading to lower exports. At the end of 1999, rains returned to Brazil leading to a decline in prices. That decline developed into a persistent trend that extended for all of 2000. There was a brief interruption in July when frost occurred in Brazil leading to a sharp runup in prices. An initial assessment indicated that losses might not be severe leading to a quick retreat in prices back into the downtrend. In early 2001, coffee prices posted new multi-year lows.

Brazil is by far the world's largest producer and exporter of coffee. Production in Brazil follows a biennial cycle. Large crops are followed by small crops which in turn are followed by large crops. The U.S.D.A. estimated the 1996/97 Brazilian crop at 28 million bags. The 1997/98 crop declined to 23.5 million bags, while the 1998/99 crop was large at 35.6 million bags. The U.S.D.A. estimated the 1999/00 Brazilian crop at 30.8 million bags, down 13 percent from the previous year. The 2000/01 crop was estimated to be 32.6 million bags. In late December, the Brazilian government released an estimate of the 2000/01 crop of 31.1 million bags which was up from a previous estimate of 28.9 million bags. Brazil's initial estimate of the 2001-02 crop was 26.7 million bags, a forecast generally below trade estimates. Of the total, some 19.4 million bags would be arabica coffee and 7.3 million bags would be robusta coffee. Brazil indicated that the reasons for the low estimate were the lingering effects of the drought along with the frost in July.

The U.S.D.A.'s estimate of the new 2000/01 (October-September) crop in Colombia was 12 million bags, up 26 percent from the previous year. That crop had been damaged by rains from La Nina. Colombia is the second largest exporter of arabica coffee. Another large arabica coffee producer is Mexico with the current crop estimated by the U.S.D.A. at 5.8 million bags, down 3 percent from the 1999/00 crop of 6 million bags. Mexico is a major exporter of coffee to the United States. Guatemala is also a large exporter of arabica coffee with the crop this year estimated at 4.5 million bags, up 3 percent from the previous year.

There are a number of large robusta coffee producers. The largest is Vietnam which has seen a substantial increase in its coffee output. The current 2000/01 crop is estimated at 11.2 million bags, up 2 percent from the previous crop. In 1995/96 the crop was 3.9 million bags. At the current rate of increase, Vietnam is poised to pass Colombia to become the second largest coffee producer. The other large Asian robusta coffee producer is Indonesia which in 2000/01 is forecast by the U.S.D.A. to have a crop of 7.3 million bags, up 2 percent from the previous year. Among the African producers, the Ivory Coast crop was forecast to be 4.3 million bags, well below the 5.7 million bag crop of 1999/00. Uganda's crop in 2000/01 was forecast at 3.2 million bags. The U.S.D.A. forecast world coffee production at a record 115.1 million bags, up less than 1 percent from the 1999/00 output of 114 million bags.

A major development in the market in 2000 was the decision by the Association of Coffee Producing Countries (ACPC) to begin withholding coffee from the market in an attempt to increase prices. In effect, members agreed to withhold or retain 20 percent of their exports until prices increased a set amount. Among the members of the ACPC are Brazil and Colombia. While this type of retention agreement has been tried before with limited success, this agreement had more widespread support. Countries that were not members of the ACPC, like Vietnam and Mexico, offered to support the agreement by limiting exports to some extent. Mexico indicated that it would spread out its exports over a longer period. While the trade remained skeptical about the success of the plan and the ability of members to hold together, the fact that coffee was being removed from the market was a positive development for prices.

The U.S.D.A. estimated world coffee consumption in 1999/00 at 109.6 million bags, an increase of 3 percent from 1998/00. Consumption in coffee importing countries was estimated to be 84.3 million bags, while consumption in exporting countries was 25.3 million bags. With low prices, coffee consumption is expected to increase again in 2000/01. In terms of per capita coffee consumption, the largest users are countries in the north. The U.S.D.A. estimated that for 1999, per capita use in Finland was 11.4 kilograms. Per capita consumption in Norway was 10.4 kilograms. Per capita use in Denmark was 9.6 kilograms. In the U.S., per capita use of coffee in 1999 was 4 kilograms, down 2 percent from the previous year. Per capita use in Japan was 2.9 kilograms, while in Germany it was 7.1 kilograms. In Ireland, per capita consumption was only 1.8 kilograms. While world consumption of coffee has been trending higher, it appears that on a per capita basis it has trended somewhat lower in importing countries.

Futures Markets

Coffee futures are traded on the Bolsa de Mercadorias & Futuros (BM&F), the Tokyo Grain Exchange (TGE), the London International Financial Futures Exchange (LIFFE), and the CSCE Division of the New York Board of Trade (NYBOT). Options are traded on the BM&F, the LIFFE and the CSCE.

COFFEE

World Supply and Distribution of Coffee   In Thousands of 60 Kilogram Bags (132.276 Lbs. Per Bag)

Crop Year	Beginning Stocks	Production	Imports	Supply	Total Exports	Bean Exports	Rst/Grn Exports	Soluble Exports	Domestic Use	Ending Stocks
1991-2	45,096	104,064	291	149,451	80,887	77,844	53	2,990	22,266	46,298
1992-3	46,298	92,959	713	139,970	77,869	73,881	117	3,871	21,579	40,522
1993-4	40,522	92,406	585	133,513	76,284	71,779	108	4,397	22,928	34,301
1994-5	34,301	97,042	1,070	132,413	68,672	64,432	230	4,010	22,526	41,215
1995-6	41,215	88,946	1,079	131,240	74,103	69,021	231	4,851	24,049	33,088
1996-7	33,088	103,788	1,091	137,967	84,509	79,919	195	4,395	24,326	29,132
1997-8	29,132	97,485	1,220	127,837	78,076	73,390	193	4,493	25,170	24,591
1998-9[1]	24,591	108,740	1,090	134,421	84,803	80,584	211	4,008	25,596	24,022
1999-00[2]	24,022	114,004	1,242	139,268	91,706	87,113	218	4,375	25,306	22,256
2000-1[3]	22,256	115,053	1,148	138,457	86,547	81,953	240	4,354	26,547	25,363

[1] Preliminary.   [2] Estimate.   [3] Forecast.   Source: Foreign Agricultural Service, U.S. Department of Agriculture (FAS-USDA)

World Production of Green Coffee   In Thousands of 60 Kilogram Bags (132.276 Lbs. Per Bag)

Crop Year	Brazil	Cameroon	Colombia	Costa Rica	El Salvador	Ethiopia	Guatemala	India	Indonesia	Ivory Coast	Mexico	Uganda	World Total
1991-2	28,500	1,920	17,980	2,530	2,357	3,000	3,549	3,200	7,100	3,967	4,620	2,900	103,731
1992-3	24,000	837	14,950	2,620	2,894	3,500	3,584	2,700	7,350	2,500	4,180	2,800	92,894
1993-4	28,500	676	11,400	2,475	2,361	3,700	3,078	3,465	7,400	2,700	4,200	2,700	92,319
1994-5	28,000	401	13,000	2,492	2,314	3,800	3,500	3,060	6,400	3,733	4,030	3,100	97,024
1995-6	16,800	663	12,939	2,595	2,325	3,800	3,827	3,717	5,800	2,900	5,400	4,200	88,946
1996-7	28,000	1,432	10,779	2,376	2,498	3,800	4,141	3,417	7,900	5,333	5,300	4,297	103,788
1997-8	23,500	889	12,043	2,455	2,040	3,833	4,200	3,805	7,000	4,080	4,950	3,032	97,485
1998-9[1]	35,600	1,334	10,868	2,459	1,860	3,867	4,300	4,415	6,950	2,217	5,010	3,640	108,740
1999-00[2]	30,800	1,300	9,512	2,650	2,612	3,833	4,364	4,870	7,170	5,700	6,000	3,640	114,004
2000-1[3]	32,600	1,100	12,000	2,400	2,112	3,767	4,494	4,900	7,300	4,333	5,800	3,200	115,053

[1] Preliminary.   [2] Estimate.   [3] Forecast.   Source: Foreign Agricultural Service, U.S. Department of Agriculture (FAS-USDA)

World Exportable[4] Production of Green Coffee   In Thousands of 60 Kilogram Bags (132.276 Lbs. Per Bag)

Crop Year	Brazil	Cameroon	Colombia	Costa Rica	El Salvador	Ethiopia	Guatemala	Indonesia	Ivory Coast	Kenya	Mexico	Uganda	World Total
1991-2	19,500	1,895	16,580	2,270	2,173	1,400	3,239	5,550	3,929	1,483	3,170	2,845	81,729
1992-3	15,500	812	13,647	2,365	2,677	2,000	3,274	5,570	2,461	1,195	2,880	2,745	71,726
1993-4	19,100	611	9,700	2,225	2,131	2,200	2,777	5,535	2,661	1,208	2,900	2,640	69,678
1994-5	18,300	371	11,564	2,252	2,079	2,300	3,220	4,440	3,687	1,562	3,030	3,040	74,957
1995-6	6,300	563	11,439	2,360	2,055	2,300	3,527	3,750	2,852	1,789	4,340	4,140	65,393
1996-7	17,000	1,332	9,279	2,130	2,268	2,300	3,856	5,820	5,282	1,115	4,450	4,217	79,817
1997-8	12,000	789	10,483	2,150	1,805	2,250	3,850	5,360	4,025	1,005	3,955	2,952	72,793
1998-9[1]	23,100	1,234	9,418	2,154	1,633	2,234	3,900	5,350	2,159	1,125	4,050	3,580	83,463
1999-00[2]	18,000	1,200	7,982	2,335	2,445	2,200	3,964	5,490	5,640	1,656	5,000	3,120	88,823
2000-1[3]	19,500	995	10,440	2,075	1,944	2,100	4,069	5,610	4,270	1,098	4,700	3,119	88,686

[1] Preliminary.   [2] Estimate.   [3] Forecast.   [4] Marketing year begins in October in some countries and April or July in others. Exportable production represents total harvested production minus estimated domestic consumption.   Source: Foreign Agricultural Service, U.S. Department of Agriculture

Green Coffee Imports in the United States   In Thousands of 60 Kilogram Bags (132.276 Lbs. Per Bag)

Year	Brazil	Colombia	Costa Rica	Dominican Republic	Ecuador	El Salvador	Ethiopia	Guatemala	Indonesia	Mexico	Peru	Venezuela	Grand Total
1990	3,633	2,771	403	445	876	843	234	1,871	830	3,305	473	222	19,566
1991	5,335	3,048	603	343	785	868	31	1,489	536	2,993	610	108	18,849
1992	4,253	4,852	662	254	753	1,344	23	1,812	581	3,042	526	104	21,673
1993	3,376	2,957	437	213	671	1,274	192	1,815	542	2,947	158	444	18,023
1994	2,850	2,372	325	207	969	376	215	1,403	558	2,516	249	295	14,913
1995	2,302	2,485	388	266	745	284	109	1,637	513	2,887	621	89	15,886
1996	1,852	3,011	482	255	665	401	137	1,748	1,246	3,734	441	445	17,947
1997	2,331	3,179	608	150	431	500	308	1,921	1,325	2,935	652	65	18,848
1998	2,688	3,410	771	164	347	501	183	1,563	1,273	2,471	771	146	18,998
1999[1]	4,659	3,359	684	35	419	550	77	2,148	724	3,182	762	372	20,559

[1] Preliminary.   Source: Bureau of Census, U.S. Department of Commerce

45

COFFEE

Monthly Green Coffee Imports in the United States   In Thousands of 60 Kilogram Bags[2]

Year	Jan.	Feb.	Mar.	Apr.	May	June	July	Aug.	Sept.	Oct.	Nov.	Dec.	Total
1991	2,106	1,946	1,590	1,748	1,556	984	1,056	1,335	1,424	1,368	1,616	2,122	18,849
1992	2,262	1,944	2,125	1,698	1,534	1,795	1,806	1,692	1,644	1,615	1,508	2,050	21,673
1993	1,782	1,663	2,012	1,481	1,631	1,253	1,442	1,344	1,374	1,464	1,018	1,561	18,023
1994	1,538	1,152	1,409	1,077	1,082	1,151	1,195	1,560	1,266	1,127	1,103	1,213	14,872
1995	1,469	1,253	1,702	1,221	1,190	1,240	1,117	1,094	1,220	1,326	1,492	1,563	15,886
1996	1,824	1,657	1,753	1,395	1,444	1,236	1,329	1,341	1,364	1,279	1,485	1,828	17,936
1997	1,582	1,837	1,966	1,792	1,738	1,583	1,783	1,391	1,147	1,215	1,184	1,629	18,848
1998	1,747	1,893	1,827	1,587	1,540	1,412	1,386	1,478	1,369	1,499	1,423	1,837	18,998
1999	1,742	1,866	2,243	1,787	1,602	1,691	1,488	1,639	1,491	1,470	1,639	1,903	20,561
2000[1]	2,094	2,012	2,317	1,922	2,079	1,858	1,793	1,699	1,496	1,480	1,431	1,445	21,625

[1] Preliminary.   [2] 132.276 pounds per bag.   *Source: Bureau of the Census, U.S. Department of Commerce*

Average Price of Brazilian[1] Coffee in New York   In Cents Per Pound

Year	Jan.	Feb.	Mar.	Apr.	May	June	July	Aug.	Sept.	Oct.	Nov.	Dec.	Average
1991	75.59	79.39	83.83	81.58	75.56	72.44	69.24	68.15	75.08	65.91	66.03	62.14	72.91
1992	62.03	58.05	59.60	54.94	51.11	49.08	48.53	46.40	49.43	59.64	64.64	74.39	56.49
1993	67.13	66.34	62.60	54.92	57.26	55.70	65.76	73.25	75.58	71.65	74.20	74.51	66.58
1994	71.42	80.14	84.72	87.14	118.37	136.43	211.81	192.38	212.73	191.21	172.83	159.73	143.24
1995	162.81	161.07	171.48	166.54	161.72	145.22	139.68	149.54	130.26	127.23	125.33	110.46	145.95
1996	127.54	144.05	140.99	132.92	134.76	125.44	106.93	108.28	103.10	105.77	103.76	103.71	119.77
1997	127.28	160.21	179.75	183.73	209.62	184.21	158.52	158.25	167.77	152.12	149.07	171.12	166.80
1998	179.83	177.78	154.84	141.11	124.89	104.09	96.04	101.92	92.76	91.32	96.67	100.28	121.81
1999	99.43	91.72	88.90	86.14	96.29	91.69	78.13	76.67	70.43	78.74	98.41	109.47	88.84
2000	97.68	91.51	89.93	86.46	87.23	78.32	79.89	70.57	71.14	72.28	68.95		81.27

[1] And other Arabicas.   *Source: Coffee Publications, Inc.*

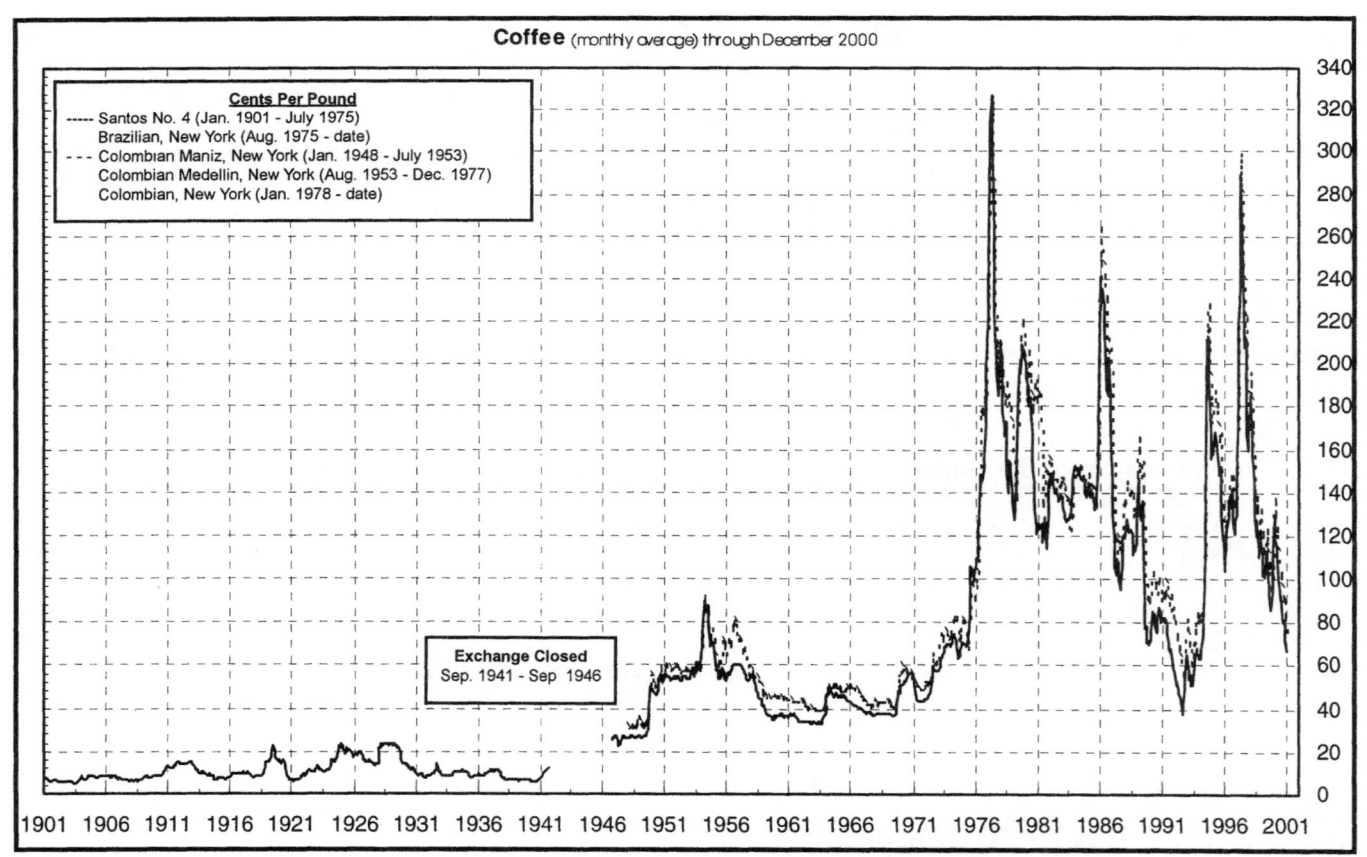

Coffee (monthly average) through December 2000

Cents Per Pound
----- Santos No. 4 (Jan. 1901 - July 1975)
     Brazilian, New York (Aug. 1975 - date)
- - - Colombian Maniz, New York (Jan. 1948 - July 1953)
     Colombian Medellin, New York (Aug. 1953 - Dec. 1977)
     Colombian, New York (Jan. 1978 - date)

Exchange Closed
Sep. 1941 - Sep. 1946

Average Monthly Retail [1] Price of Coffee in the United States   In Cents Per Pound

Year	Jan.	Feb.	Mar.	Apr.	May	June	July	Aug.	Sept.	Oct.	Nov.	Dec.	Average
1993	235.2	245.2	246.2	247.7	251.4	253.3	254.8	250.0	249.3	241.5	243.3	248.0	247.2
1994	253.0	252.9	251.5	251.6	253.5	259.8	334.1	448.0	445.8	445.0	448.2	438.2	340.1
1995	439.8	423.4	410.8	408.4	406.7	405.9	402.7	405.1	399.6	386.5	381.4	375.2	401.8
1996	357.7	359.0	355.0	352.7	344.4	343.8	338.0	339.0	333.3	334.4	328.3	330.7	343.0
1997	330.0	331.6	351.2	389.4	410.9	442.8	462.8	466.9	461.7	439.2	430.3	416.1	411.1
1998	402.5	397.3	403.3	395.9	387.8	378.6	377.1	370.4	362.0	350.3	348.2	344.6	376.5
1999	343.5	342.8	347.6	346.6	349.5	342.1	342.0	342.8	339.3	348.2	333.7	349.7	344.0
2000	365.4	367.7	363.3	358.4	353.1	343.1	344.6	344.4	333.9	331.7	324.3		348.2

[1] Roasted in 13.1 to 20 ounce cans.   *Source: Coffee Publications, Inc.*

Average Price of Colombian Mild Arabicas[1] in the United States   In Cents Per Pound

Year	Jan.	Feb.	Mar.	Apr.	May	June	July	Aug.	Sept.	Oct.	Nov.	Dec.	Average
1993	71.61	72.45	67.07	59.77	67.35	68.13	76.40	84.18	86.58	83.02	85.56	87.33	75.79
1994	85.85	93.04	93.23	97.53	133.90	151.85	222.75	210.57	231.52	206.07	186.96	173.94	157.27
1995	177.23	175.07	185.75	180.30	177.18	170.87	157.22	163.21	141.49	132.08	129.09	110.47	158.33
1996	119.08	134.94	160.60	134.31	142.56	133.25	135.39	137.68	123.30	127.77	129.41	126.41	133.73
1997	146.18	188.62	212.96	199.22	318.50	227.15	190.57	193.46	196.29	169.40	161.38	183.32	198.92
1998	184.21	190.59	166.07	158.17	146.33	135.83	125.03	129.45	117.56	115.01	121.74	123.96	142.83
1999	123.07	116.92	117.05	114.02	123.95	121.45	107.05	105.28	97.77	103.69	126.76	140.35	116.45
2000	130.13	124.73	119.51	112.67	110.31	100.30	101.67	91.87	89.98	90.25	84.01		105.04

[1] ICO monthly and composite indicator prices on the New York Market, 1979 ICA Agreement basis.   *Source: Coffee Publications, Inc.*

Average Price of Other Mild Arabicas[1] in the United States   In Cents Per Pound

Year	Jan.	Feb.	Mar.	Apr.	May	June	July	Aug.	Sept.	Oct.	Nov.	Dec.	Awerage
1993	68.66	67.46	62.77	56.88	61.48	61.61	71.46	76.56	79.87	75.05	77.07	80.00	69.91
1994	77.21	82.69	85.57	89.23	121.97	142.57	217.67	198.07	220.10	199.06	180.76	167.47	148.53
1995	171.74	168.71	178.22	172.81	168.63	151.56	143.83	151.41	131.87	125.38	123.23	103.99	149.28
1996	109.38	122.71	119.05	122.01	128.56	124.46	120.47	122.49	114.05	120.62	119.90	115.01	119.89
1997	131.83	167.20	193.82	204.43	264.50	212.55	186.52	185.17	184.38	161.45	154.15	174.25	185.02
1998	175.04	175.87	154.82	147.08	134.35	121.56	113.86	119.89	108.07	107.07	113.84	115.54	132.25
1999	110.99	103.24	103.23	99.69	109.10	104.21	90.85	87.64	81.06	92.22	112.74	123.56	101.54
2000	109.17	101.17	98.26	92.76	91.76	84.10	85.20	74.52	73.83	75.43	70.47		86.97

[1] ICO monthly and composite indicator prices on the New York Market, 1979 ICA Agreement basis.   *Source: Coffee Publications, Inc.*

Average Price of Robustas 1976[1] in the United States   In Cents Per Pound

Year	Jan.	Feb.	Mar.	Apr.	May	June	July	Aug.	Sept.	Oct.	Nov.	Dec.	Average
1993	48.13	48.25	46.86	45.51	46.91	47.65	50.39	59.29	63.44	60.05	62.53	62.90	53.49
1994	60.91	62.25	66.46	72.64	96.05	113.31	164.65	162.68	182.95	170.09	154.19	130.48	119.72
1995	132.26	135.22	146.83	145.47	141.89	129.53	120.89	131.28	116.41	114.15	112.79	94.72	126.79
1996	91.99	98.99	91.99	91.45	92.10	86.46	78.14	80.16	74.83	72.97	70.51	63.08	82.72
1997	67.66	76.65	81.31	78.48	95.74	91.94	82.52	76.92	77.43	76.90	78.20	84.65	80.70
1998	86.03	85.79	84.67	90.60	92.64	84.55	78.40	79.98	80.88	80.36	80.40	82.82	83.93
1999	81.65	77.68	72.70	68.89	68.28	66.20	62.28	63.80	60.44	59.25	64.10	66.40	67.64
2000	53.62	49.41	47.26	45.21	45.19	43.72	41.93	38.94	39.47	36.55	33.34		43.15

[1] ICO monthly and composite indicator prices on the New York Market, 1979 ICA Agreement basis.   *Source: Coffee Publications, Inc.*

Average Price of Composite 1979[1] in the United States   In Cents Per Pound

Year	Jan.	Feb.	Mar.	Apr.	May	June	July	Aug.	Sept.	Oct.	Nov.	Dec.	Average
1993	58.14	57.32	54.76	51.38	54.18	54.54	60.61	67.69	71.64	67.78	70.03	71.53	61.63
1994	69.17	72.37	76.11	81.19	108.42	127.91	191.44	181.53	202.39	185.64	168.12	149.14	134.45
1995	152.08	152.24	162.73	159.59	155.96	141.66	132.71	141.70	124.75	120.02	117.99	99.57	138.42
1996	100.33	110.50	105.89	107.09	110.24	105.79	99.97	102.73	96.52	98.56	97.14	90.04	102.07
1997	100.03	121.89	137.47	142.20	180.44	155.38	135.04	132.63	132.51	121.09	118.16	130.02	133.91
1998	130.61	130.78	119.93	119.66	114.23	103.84	97.32	101.25	95.82	95.01	98.26	100.73	108.95
1999	97.63	92.36	89.41	85.72	89.51	85.41	78.21	77.22	71.94	76.36	88.22	95.63	85.64
2000	82.15	76.15	73.49	69.53	69.23	64.56	64.09	57.59	57.31	56.40	52.18		65.70

[1] ICO monthly and composite indicator prices on the New York Market, 1979 ICA Agreement basis.   *Source: Coffee Publications, Inc.*

COFFEE

Average Open Interest of Coffee 'C' Futures in New York   In Contracts

Year	Jan.	Feb.	Mar.	Apr.	May	June	July	Aug.	Sept.	Oct.	Nov.	Dec.
1991	42,320	41,326	39,948	39,410	41,726	43,717	42,037	40,661	42,126	43,940	41,819	40,628
1992	47,042	51,183	48,961	51,979	59,275	58,304	59,096	58,401	56,446	59,808	57,527	58,257
1993	59,193	54,249	53,618	55,578	51,797	50,918	53,871	48,541	47,649	49,809	46,901	48,812
1994	54,796	50,230	53,713	57,226	58,574	54,589	43,056	35,052	35,800	34,258	31,046	31,134
1995	34,455	35,391	36,925	34,387	34,615	34,462	30,156	27,448	27,800	28,408	24,505	26,412
1996	28,430	28,224	28,127	28,793	28,394	25,096	26,188	25,799	23,929	26,202	27,599	27,201
1997	38,516	42,888	39,092	32,644	30,324	22,552	21,497	19,818	22,788	25,109	23,636	28,577
1998	30,042	30,539	30,211	32,617	36,345	36,651	37,531	30,074	30,429	32,940	31,677	32,816
1999	36,194	36,693	41,294	43,846	45,947	45,675	45,411	46,725	46,255	47,956	46,271	46,764
2000	47,829	50,620	50,565	53,662	49,692	50,293	45,513	40,177	40,133	42,906	43,187	45,086

Source: New York Board of Trade (NYBOT)

Volume of Trading of Coffee 'C' Futures in New York   In Contracts

Year	Jan.	Feb.	Mar.	Apr.	May	June	July	Aug.	Sept.	Oct.	Nov.	Dec.	Total
1991	138,642	174,688	188,842	153,436	103,344	135,887	107,058	170,113	180,017	148,640	159,099	112,882	1,772,648
1992	153,332	199,420	174,662	188,232	156,944	164,586	177,493	182,741	163,214	108,707	211,678	199,374	2,152,383
1993	290,120	214,771	183,354	209,607	176,559	197,761	193,002	233,479	202,363	187,763	217,947	182,486	2,489,223
1994	188,508	219,455	208,113	284,734	380,119	304,542	210,479	196,685	159,574	177,424	184,172	142,713	2,658,073
1995	169,250	191,352	213,326	156,191	163,248	186,550	162,562	161,076	165,337	152,959	157,240	123,923	2,003,014
1996	203,369	186,526	152,797	197,442	137,454	158,929	171,800	196,991	136,054	196,696	135,305	166,213	2,039,576
1997	242,719	280,014	267,369	223,330	219,214	186,227	135,664	136,807	142,610	151,171	145,610	163,446	2,294,181
1998	155,774	194,435	186,712	194,732	157,935	189,768	165,868	189,047	156,556	172,956	197,776	133,471	2,095,030
1999	216,810	201,670	252,841	243,630	237,968	243,164	187,019	232,817	151,724	270,013	244,258	177,309	2,659,223
2000	158,962	232,174	166,970	224,266	177,753	218,467	198,975	175,868	119,304	163,399	187,230	111,593	2,134,961

Source: New York Board of Trade (NYBOT)

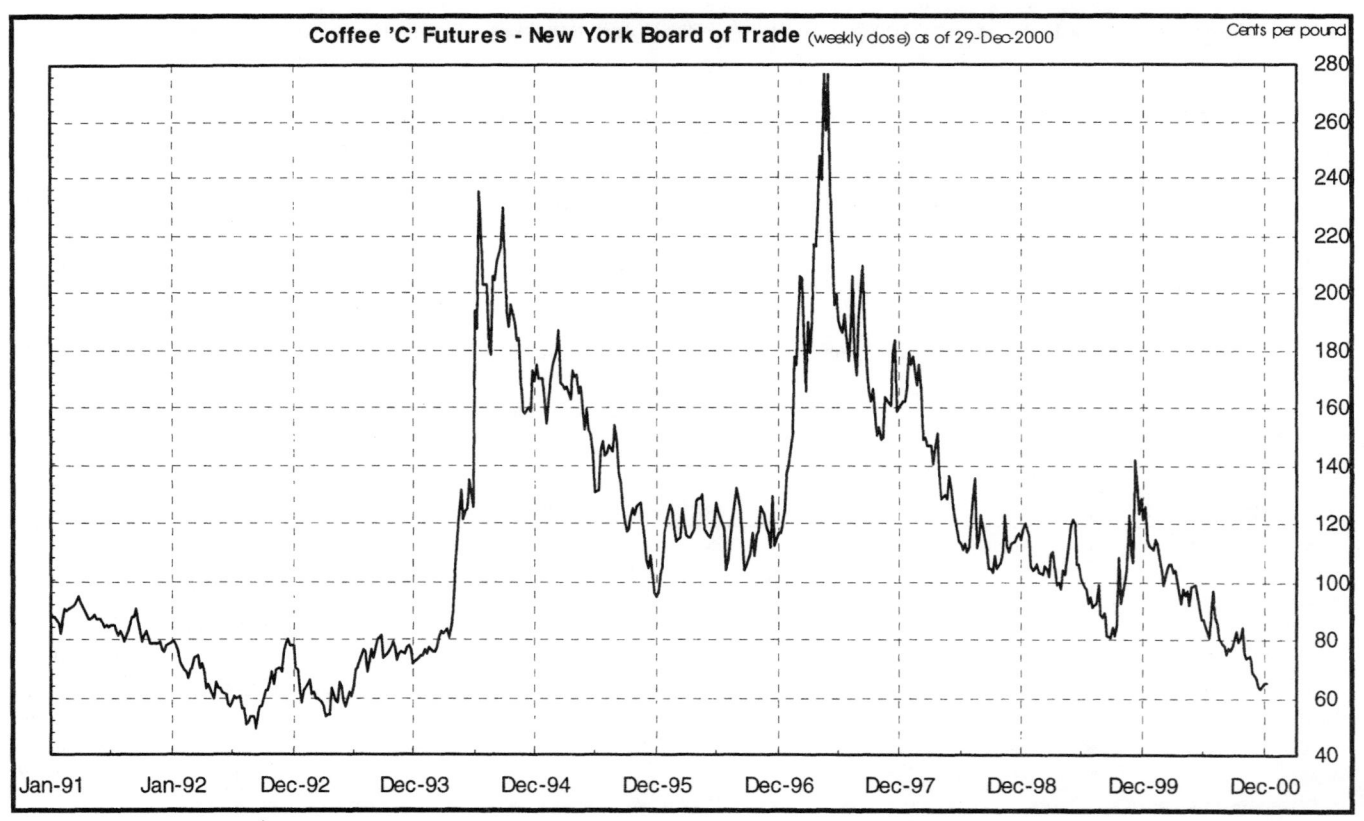

Coffee 'C' Futures - New York Board of Trade (weekly close) as of 29-Dec-2000   Cents per pound

Coke

U.S. production of coke in the April-June 2000 period was 5.4 million short tons. Production in the same quarter of 1999 was 5 million tons. In the first quarter of 2000, production was 5.1 million tons. For all of 1999, production was 20 million tons, about the same as in 1998.

Producer and distributor stocks of coke at the end of the second quarter of 2000 were 940,000 tons, up 11 percent from the end of the first quarter. The year before, stocks were 990,000 tons at the end of the second quarter. Consumption of coke in the April-June 2000 quarter was 6.05 million tons, up 3 percent from the first quarter of 2000.

For the entire year of 1999, consumption was 22.4 million tons.

U.S. coke exports in the second quarter of 2000 were 284,477 tons, up 35 percent from the first quarter. The year before, exports were 224,998 tons. Virtually all of the coke exports go to North American markets.

Imports of coke in the second quarter of 2000 were 1.02 million tons, up 12 percent from the first quarter and up 28 percent from a year ago. In the first half of 2000, imports were 1.92 million tonnes, up 22 percent from the same period in 1999.

Salient Statistics of Coke in the United States   In Thousands of Short Tons

| | Coke and Breeze Production at Coke Plants | | | | | | | | Producer and Distributor Stocks | Exports | | Imports | |
| | By Census Division | | | | | | | | | | | | |
Year	Middle Atlantic	East North Central	East South Central	Other	Total	Coke Total	Breeze Total	Consumption[2]	Stocks Dec. 31	Canada	Total	Japan	Total
1994	7,766	5,842	2,440	8,030	24,078	22,686	1,392	25,563	936	371	660	956	1,612
1995	7,751	6,490	2,465	8,506	25,212	23,749	1,463	25,895	1,302	579	750	1,019	1,816
1996	7,729	5,863	2,445	8,440	24,477	23,075	1,402	23,974	1,323	491	1,121	811	1,111
1997	8,994	8,882	3,393	2,080	23,349	22,116	1,233	24,017	1,294	498	832	1,018	1,565
1998	6,371	9,224	2,922	2,766	21,283	20,041	1,242	23,029	933	830	1,129	2,062	3,834
1999[1]	5,869	10,115	2,821	2,448	21,253	20,016	1,237	22,435	852	686	898	2,012	3,224

[1] Preliminary.   [2] Equal to production plus imports minus the change in producer and distributor stocks minus exports.
Source: Energy Information Administration, U.S. Department of Energy (EIA-DOE)

Production of Petroleum Coke in the United States   In Thousands of Barrels

Year	Jan.	Feb.	Mar.	Apr.	May	June	July	Aug.	Sept.	Oct.	Nov.	Dec.	Total
1994	19,170	16,873	18,695	18,454	19,748	19,325	20,008	19,473	17,868	18,753	18,995	19,697	227,059
1995	19,079	17,117	18,556	18,519	19,774	19,949	19,527	19,722	19,184	19,292	19,349	19,887	229,955
1996	19,536	18,706	21,015	20,663	20,426	19,927	19,836	20,328	20,124	20,558	20,447	21,389	242,955
1997	19,798	17,594	20,603	21,274	22,210	21,052	21,619	22,229	21,630	21,782	20,313	21,827	251,931
1998	20,929	18,968	21,998	21,834	21,790	20,856	21,790	22,469	21,526	21,234	20,837	22,258	256,489
1999	22,312	20,084	22,148	21,444	21,410	20,943	21,741	22,180	21,249	22,166	20,837	22,258	256,489
2000[1]	21,502	20,017	21,654	21,161	21,785	22,095	23,321	22,835	22,455	22,121	22,628		263,535

[1] Preliminary.   *Source: Energy Information Administration, U.S. Department of Energy (EIA-DOE)*

Coal Receipts and Average Prices at Coke Plants in the United States

| | Coal Receipts at Coke Plants | | | | | Average Price of Coal Receipts at Coke Plants | | | | |
| | By Census Division, In Thousands of Short Tons | | | | | By Census Division, In Dollars per Short Ton | | | | |
Year	Middle Atlantic	East North Central	East South Central	Other	Total	Middle Atlantic	East North Central	East South Central	Other	Total
1994	10,776	8,087	3,242	9,614	31,719	46.25	46.46	47.45	----	46.56
1995	10,959	8,489	3,183	10,405	33,036	46.11	47.47	48.42	----	47.34
1996	10,562	7,654	3,213	10,243	31,672	45.17	48.46	49.37	----	47.33
1997	11,555	10,825	4,290	2,880	29,550	47.05	49.12	47.72	----	47.61
1998	8,430	12,442	3,777	3,705	28,354	44.16	48.39	46.43	----	46.06
1999[1]	7,784	13,524	3,571	3,276	28,155	44.33	47.74	45.28	----	45.85

[1] Preliminary.   *Source: Energy Information Administration, U.S. Department of Energy (EIA-DOE)*

Coal Carbonized and Coke and Breeze Stocks at Coke Plants in the U.S.   In Thousands of Short Tons

| | Coal Carbonized at Coke Plants | | | | | Stocks at Coke Plants, Dec. 31 | | | | | | |
| | By Census Division | | | | | By Census Division | | | | | | |
Year	Middle Atlantic	East North Central	East South Central	Other	Total	Middle Atlantic	East North Central	East South Central	Other	Total	Coke Total	Breeze Total
1994	10,849	11,356	3,253	6,282	31,740	216	371	83	421	1,091	986	105
1995	10,858	12,345	3,257	6,551	33,011	191	589	81	577	1,438	1,302	136
1996	10,689	11,414	3,247	6,356	31,706	197	400	138	749	1,484	1,323	161
1997	11,655	11,366	4,299	2,883	30,203	297	509	159	465	1,430	1,294	135
1998	8,401	12,311	3,736	3,741	28,189	160	526	176	215	1,077	933	144
1999[1]	7,799	13,404	3,584	3,321	28,108	69	500	157	277	1,003	852	150

[1] Preliminary.   *Source: Energy Information Administration, U.S. Department of Energy (EIA-DOE)*

Copper

Copper metals and copper alloys have considerable commercial importance due to their electrical, mechanical, and physical properties. Copper is used in alloys such as brass which is composed of copper and zinc. Copper for commercial purposes is obtained by the reduction of copper compounds in ores and by electrolytic refining.

The U.S. Geological Survey reported that world mine production of copper in 1999 was 12.6 million metric tonnes, up 3 percent from 1998. The largest producer by far is Chile with 1999 production of 4.36 million tonnes, up 18 percent from 1998. The U.S. is the second largest producer. Indonesia's 1999 production was estimated at 765,000 tonnes, down 2 percent from 1998. Australia's output was estimated to be 730,000 tonnes. Other large producers include Canada, Peru, Russia, and China.

U.S. mine production of copper in July 2000 was 118,000 tonnes, down from 120,000 tonnes in June. In the January-July 2000 period, mine production totaled 852,000 tonnes. For all of 1999, it was 1.6 million tonnes. Refinery production of copper in July 2000 was 123,000 tonnes, down 6 percent from June. In the January-July 2000 period, refinery production was 935,000 tonnes, while for all of 1999 it was 1.89 million tonnes. In the first seven months of 2000, electrolytic production of copper was 605,800 tonnes. For all of 1999, electrolytic refining totaled 1.31 million tonnes of copper. Copper production using the electrowon method in January-July 2000 totaled 330,000 tonnes, while in 1999 it was 586,000 tonnes. Secondary recoverable copper production by refineries in July 2000 was 11,700 tonnes, down 24 percent from June. In January-July 2000, production was 136,000 tonnes, while for all of 1999 it was 243,000 tonnes. Secondary recoverable copper production by brass and wire-rod mills in July 2000 was 66,600 tonnes, down 5 percent from June. In January-July 2000, production was 494,000 tonnes, while for all of 1999 it was 830,000 tonnes. Smelter production of copper in July 2000 was 77,200 tonnes, up 6 percent from June. For the first seven months of 2000, smelter production was 578,000 tonnes, and for all of 1999 it was 1.19 million tonnes.

U.S. apparent consumption of copper in June 2000 was 257,000 tonnes, while for all of 1999 it was 3.12 million tonnes. Consumption of refined copper in July 2000 was 252,000 tonnes. Of the total, copper cathodes took 228,000 tonnes with ingots and ingot bars taking 6,940 tonnes. In January-July 2000, refined copper consumption was 1.75 million tonnes. Wire rod mills used 1.29 million tonnes, while brass mills took 427,000 tonnes and other plants such as ingot makers took 33,500 tonnes.

U.S. stocks of refined copper at the end of July 2000 were 368,000 tonnes, down 11 percent from June. Stocks at the end of 1999 were 566,000 tonnes. Blister copper stocks at the end of July 2000 were 99,900 tonnes compared to 94,000 tonnes at the end of June. Stocks at the end of 1999 were 138,000 tonnes.

Futures Markets

Copper futures and options are traded on the London Metals Exchange (LME) and the New York Mercantile Exchange, COMEX Division. Copper futures are traded on the Shanghai Futures Exchange (SHFE).

World Mine Production of Copper (Content of Ore)   In Thousands of Metric Tons

Year	Australia	Canada[3]	Chile	China	Indonesia	Mexico	Peru	Poland	Russia[4]	South Africa	United States[3]	Zambia	World Total
1990	330.0	793.7	1,588.4	285	164.1	293.9	339.3	330.0	950	178.7	1,588	421.0	8,950
1991	320.0	811.1	1,814.3	304	211.7	292.1	357.2	320.0	900	184.6	1,531	390.6	9,090
1992	378.0	768.6	1,932.7	334	280.8	279.0	345.6	331.9	699	176.1	1,760	429.5	9,470
1993	402.0	732.6	2,055.4	345	298.6	301.2	355.0	382.6	584	166.3	1,800	396.2	9,430
1994	415.6	616.8	2,219.9	396	322.2	294.7	395.9	378.0	573	160.1	1,820	373.2	9,490
1995	397.8	726.3	2,488.6	445	443.6	333.6	409.7	384.2	525	161.6	1,850	316.0	10,000
1996	547.3	688.4	3,115.8	439	507.5	340.7	484.2	421.9	523	152.6	1,920	334.0	11,000
1997	558.0	659.5	3,392.0	496	529.1	390.5	506.5	414.8	505	153.1	1,940	352.9	11,400
1998[1]	607.0	705.8	3,686.8	486	780.8	384.6	483.3	436.2	500	166.0	1,860	315.0	12,200
1999[2]	735.0	614.2	4,382.6	500	739.7	361.8	536.3	461.0	530	144.3	1,600	260.0	12,600

[1] Preliminary.   [2] Estimate.   [3] Recoverable.   [4] Formerly part of the U.S.S.R.; data not reported separately until 1992.

Source: U.S. Geological Survey (USGS)

Commodity Exchange Inc. Warehouse Stocks of Copper, on First of Month   In Thousands of Short Tons

Year	Jan.	Feb.	Mar.	Apr.	May	June	July	Aug.	Sept.	Oct.	Nov.	Dec.
1991	20.2	14.7	16.4	30.2	30.9	25.0	25.1	35.9	33.6	24.4	26.8	29.3
1992	33.7	34.8	29.5	28.2	30.3	32.4	31.8	36.0	40.4	51.7	70.1	73.8
1993	105.9	124.0	114.8	107.6	110.8	108.3	105.5	113.8	100.1	94.1	96.6	80.5
1994	74.0	56.7	49.8	37.2	31.6	30.4	36.0	37.4	28.5	17.9	20.3	21.5
1995	26.7	18.7	17.7	9.0	11.5	7.0	13.1	16.7	16.5	11.2	6.0	5.0
1996	23.7	12.1	12.4	13.9	20.7	13.2	7.6	17.7	22.1	21.7	30.8	36.2
1997	29.3	18.4	24.8	43.3	48.9	42.6	44.7	30.0	46.5	61.5	68.0	82.3
1998	91.9	101.8	113.7	112.6	106.5	83.0	62.5	55.7	56.1	67.7	70.7	75.8
1999	93.9	102.0	114.2	123.4	132.6	131.7	133.7	119.5	108.1	97.5	90.9	90.9
2000	92.3	95.7	95.9	95.9	85.7	75.0	73.6	72.0	62.8	62.3	63.4	64.9

Source: New York Mercantile Exchange (NYMEX), COMEX division

Salient Statistics of Copper in the United States   In Thousands of Metric Tons

Year	Mines	Smelters	Refineries	From Foreign Ores[3]	Total New	Secondary Recovered[4]	Imports[3] Unmanufactured	Imports[3] Refined	Exports Ore, Concentrate[6]	Exports Refined[7]	Stocks Dec 31 COMEX	Stocks Dec 31 Primary Producers (Refined)	Stocks Dec 31 Blister & Material in Solution	Apparent Consumption Refined Copper (Reported)	Apparent Consumption Primary & Old Copper[8]
1990	1,590	1,160	1,110	75	1,577	537	512	262	258	211	18	101	119	2,150	2,168
1991	1,630	1,120	1,060	77	1,577	518	512	289	253	263	31	132	135	2,048	2,105
1992	1,760	1,180	1,110	96	1,710	555	593	289	266	177	96	205	166	2,178	2,311
1993	1,800	1,270	1,210	89	1,790	543	637	343	227	217	67	153	146	2,360	2,510
1994	1,850	1,310	1,280	64	1,840	500	763	470	261	157	24	119	167	2,680	2,690
1995	1,850	1,250	1,300	91	1,930	443	825	429	239	217	22	163	171	2,530	2,540
1996	1,920	1,300	1,290	147	2,010	428	961	543	195	169	27	146	173	2,610	2,830
1997	1,940	1,440	1,370	113	2,070	498	999	632	127	93	83	314	180	2,790	2,950
1998[1]	1,860	1,490	1,290	238	2,140	466	1,190	683	37	86	85	532	160	2,890	3,020
1999[2]	1,600	1,090	1,110	196	1,890	381	1,280	837	48	25	83	564	138	2,990	3,130

[1] Preliminary. [2] Estimate. [3] Also from matte, etc., refinery reports. [4] From old scrap only. [5] For consumption. [6] Blister (copper content). [7] Ingots, bars, etc. [8] Old scrap only. Source: U.S. Geological Survey (USGS)

Consumption of Refined Copper[3] in the United States   In Thousands of Metric Tons

Year	Cathodes	Wire Bars	Ingots & Ingot Bars	Cakes & Slabs	Billets	Other[4]	Wire Rod Mills	Brass Mills	Chemical Plants	Ingot Makers	Foundries	Miscellaneous[5]	Total Consumption
1990	1,922.4	6.6	50.5	57.9	W	113.0	1,653.5	445.2	1.1	4.5	14.6	31.6	2,150.4
1991	1,854.9	W	24.7	33.3	W	135.4	1,591.8	458.5	0.9	3.4	12.7	25.3	2,048.3
1992	1,974.9	W	20.0	43.7	W	139.6	1,675.0	458.5	0.9	3.0	15.0	25.8	2,178.2
1993	2,130.0	W	37.7	55.5	W	136.0	1,819.1	503.0	0.9	2.2	10.2	27.6	2,360.0
1994	2,410.0	W	37.3	73.2	W	164.0	2,060.0	568.0	1.1	4.5	11.1	30.4	2,680.0
1995	2,250.0	W	31.3	75.9	W	181.0	1,950.0	533.0	1.1	7.7	15.6	31.4	2,530.0
1996	2,320.0	W	26.8	80.8	W	181.0	1,980.0	588.0	1.1	3.6	15.8	28.6	2,610.0
1997	2,490.0	W	29.4	81.1	W	194.0	2,140.0	597.0	1.0	4.2	16.6	29.9	2,790.0
1998[1]	2,600.0	W	30.7	76.2	W	184.0	2,170.0	659.0	1.1	5.4	19.2	31.8	2,890.0
1999[2]	2,710.0	W	31.8	79.3	W	166.0	2,230.0	691.0	1.2	4.5	28.6	29.8	2,990.0

[1] Preliminary. [2] Estimate. [3] Primary & secondary. [4] 1991 to date include Wirebars and Billets. [5] Includes iron and steel plants, primary smelters producing alloys other than copper, consumers of copper powder and copper shot, and other manufacturers. W - Withheld proprietary data.
Source: U.S. Geological Survey (USGS)

London Metals Exchange Warehouse Stocks of Copper, at End of Month   In Thousands of Metric Tons

Year	Jan.	Feb.	Mar.	Apr.	May	June	July	Aug.	Sept.	Oct.	Nov.	Dec.
1991	189.0	202.8	213.9	237.9	275.0	264.9	266.5	307.1	308.4	291.7	308.3	332.3
1992	308.6	302.7	296.4	279.7	265.4	259.1	246.8	275.2	299.7	317.8	327.0	315.8
1993	313.5	333.1	365.8	403.5	429.1	446.9	464.3	521.7	600.7	612.3	590.9	599.5
1994	597.6	554.5	504.3	446.4	379.0	350.9	338.9	367.8	359.3	333.1	318.4	302.2
1995	309.9	280.9	239.9	204.9	197.9	166.5	151.5	163.1	178.2	193.6	222.2	364.8
1996	355.1	348.4	322.3	303.9	309.7	263.0	227.6	275.5	240.7	122.1	96.1	119.6
1997	194.2	216.2	177.2	145.8	133.0	128.3	234.9	278.7	332.8	344.6	338.8	337.8
1998	365.7	376.0	339.5	262.3	261.8	249.3	260.9	307.7	414.2	460.6	511.9	590.1
1999	646.9	695.9	722.2	748.2	776.6	754.8	769.6	789.0	774.0	793.8	779.7	790.5
2000[1]	807.3	824.1	755.4	697.8	605.7	553.4	487.8	449.2	401.5	380.9		

[1] Preliminary. Source: American Bureau of Metal Statistics (ABMS)

Copper Refined from Scrap in the United States   In Thousands of Metric Tons

Year	Jan.	Feb.	Mar.	Apr.	May	June	July	Aug.	Sept.	Oct.	Nov.	Dec.	Total
1991	35.4	32.8	40.5	39.6	38.2	35.7	32.6	33.0	28.5	37.3	32.1	32.6	417.7
1992	27.8	34.1	39.8	34.8	36.7	39.4	27.8	35.4	39.8	40.0	34.3	35.8	433.2
1993	38.1	45.9	38.9	37.8	36.4	41.1	35.0	37.6	37.4	43.0	34.3	35.8	459.8
1994	33.3	28.3	37.9	30.7	37.1	28.7	26.9	33.0	38.7	27.0	34.3	32.2	391.7
1995	30.9	30.6	36.0	32.7	33.7	28.2	18.7	25.1	25.4	25.0	26.2	24.4	319.0
1996	25.0	23.7	25.5	22.5	26.8	30.9	24.4	25.0	26.8	30.6	25.9	26.3	333.0
1997	35.9	30.0	36.4	32.6	35.4	30.8	26.4	28.4	34.3	36.5	24.6	29.3	383.0
1998	25.9	28.6	23.7	31.0	17.8	21.4	24.2	23.9	23.8	31.8	23.2	26.3	336.0
1999	20.1	21.8	23.7	17.6	16.2	17.5	21.2	18.2	21.3	21.0	17.7	20.0	243.0
2000[1]	19.4	18.6	25.8	22.5	22.1	15.4	11.7	19.7	14.1				225.7

[1] Preliminary. Source: U.S. Geological Survey (USGS)

COPPER

Copper Futures - New York Mercantile Exchange, COMEX Division (weekly close) as of 29-Dec-2000   Cents per pound

Average Open Interest of Copper Futures in New York   In Contracts

Year	Jan.	Feb.	Mar.	Apr.	May	June	July	Aug.	Sept.	Oct.	Nov.	Dec.
1991	34,927	35,978	35,026	34,096	44,153	39,879	33,100	33,333	40,347	42,028	41,618	44,283
1992	47,109	47,929	48,700	45,114	39,986	48,129	47,065	38,397	37,041	41,658	44,927	45,541
1993	47,433	48,707	48,220	51,217	52,762	56,856	54,861	54,571	54,929	57,406	63,632	69,311
1994	65,518	65,446	66,177	59,346	63,825	60,383	51,616	46,855	56,344	59,060	59,158	51,078
1995	52,632	50,770	47,267	47,793	50,089	48,200	40,968	37,744	33,709	36,476	38,475	35,996
1996	47,771	45,706	42,732	46,771	47,284	52,558	56,564	56,549	55,408	58,124	61,031	55,807
1997	54,468	56,022	58,205	50,574	56,740	56,774	47,767	44,632	49,612	54,912	67,026	67,502
1998	69,607	72,302	67,154	68,670	65,033	66,002	63,271	61,116	60,520	62,944	67,984	76,846
1999	76,861	73,109	75,318	70,534	76,341	70,842	75,640	70,084	80,188	72,240	69,179	69,819
2000	82,289	73,778	68,026	75,520	69,531	63,786	71,389	79,565	83,546	73,609	74,161	70,349

Source: New York Mercantile Exchange (NYMEX), COMEX division

Volume of Trading of Copper Futures in New York   In Contracts

Year	Jan.	Feb.	Mar.	Apr.	May	June	July	Aug.	Sept.	Oct.	Nov.	Dec.	Total
1991	159,621	131,044	108,191	150,390	148,777	139,207	110,025	149,702	132,354	125,757	153,910	135,132	1,643,310
1992	145,245	168,015	105,003	157,473	77,722	182,091	138,225	177,581	137,423	121,392	146,062	117,931	1,674,163
1993	152,387	148,388	132,705	212,086	160,751	181,427	165,727	169,428	222,099	133,364	203,729	182,538	2,064,629
1994	197,959	233,016	231,239	207,963	247,143	297,393	188,644	242,393	219,788	208,957	290,585	178,887	2,737,967
1995	242,760	267,883	232,229	242,302	195,554	274,587	167,836	213,110	169,689	181,945	185,141	146,378	2,519,414
1996	184,431	173,689	157,553	210,836	200,469	255,172	150,445	174,351	166,537	250,420	227,800	160,216	2,311,919
1997	193,543	221,504	190,000	218,607	164,728	238,918	191,609	198,156	197,746	202,615	203,376	135,368	2,356,170
1998	172,133	223,117	197,652	264,061	175,956	217,316	202,596	213,541	196,355	195,255	250,986	174,642	2,483,610
1999	159,147	288,394	230,716	296,162	224,221	319,157	244,567	267,325	220,958	193,628	231,399	177,288	2,852,962
2000	220,488	276,374	195,668	261,971	232,971	241,854	187,453	283,328	171,080	243,342	266,051	197,544	2,778,124

Source: New York Mercantile Exchange (NYMEX), COMEX division

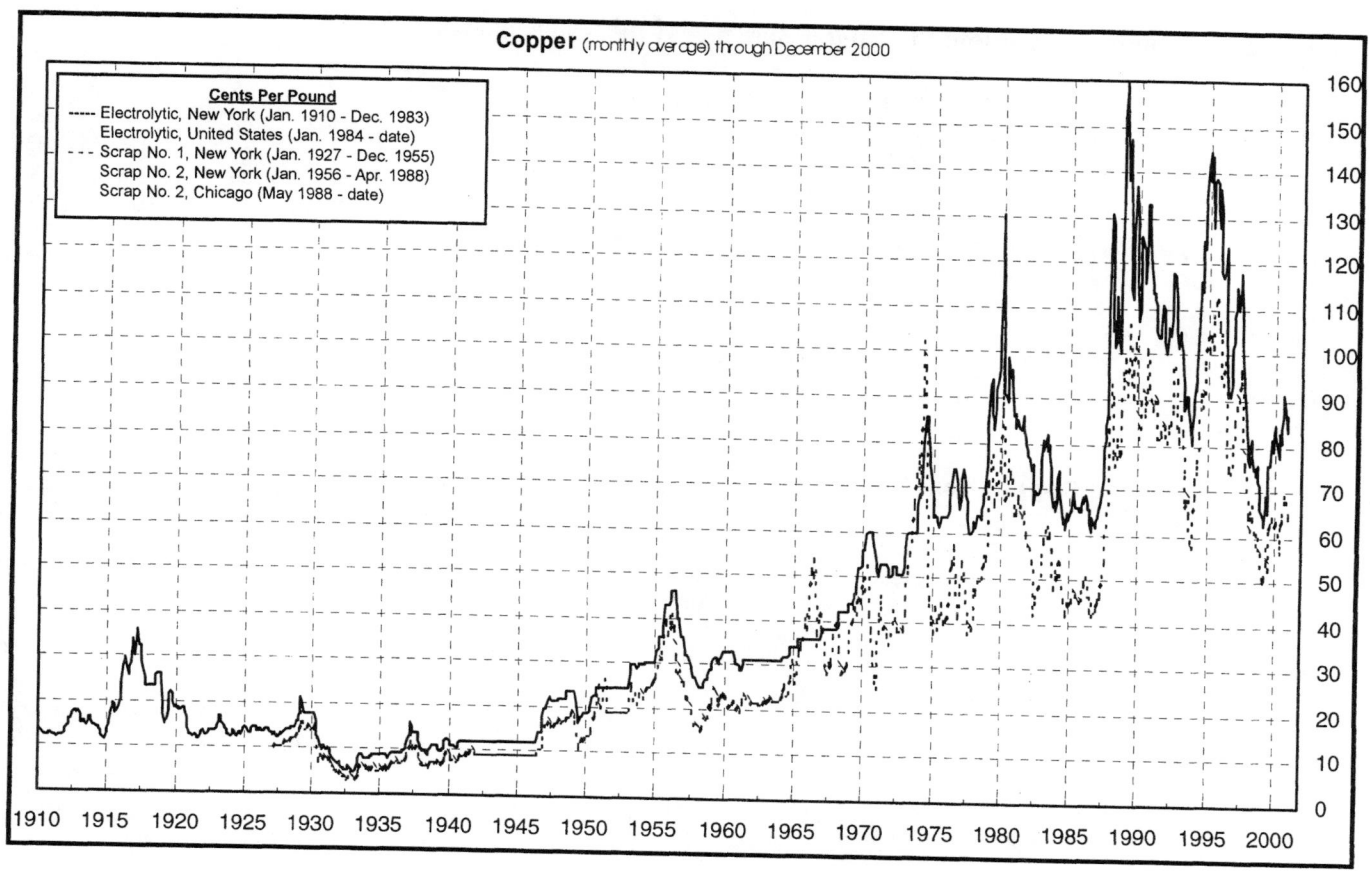

Copper (monthly average) through December 2000

Cents Per Pound
----- Electrolytic, New York (Jan. 1910 - Dec. 1983)
Electrolytic, United States (Jan. 1984 - date)
- - - Scrap No. 1, New York (Jan. 1927 - Dec. 1955)
Scrap No. 2, New York (Jan. 1956 - Apr. 1988)
Scrap No. 2, Chicago (May 1988 - date)

Producers' Price of Electrolytic (Wirebar) Copper, Delivered to U.S. Destinations   In Cents Per Pound

Year	Jan.	Feb.	Mar.	Apr.	May	June	July	Aug.	Sept.	Oct.	Nov.	Dec.	Average
1991	122.59	122.73	121.24	120.35	133.11	111.72	111.90	113.48	118.92	118.90	117.26	110.31	116.88
1992	108.16	112.52	113.56	112.35	112.56	116.74	125.66	124.30	119.39	112.09	108.23	111.13	114.72
1993	112.57	110.26	107.80	99.03	92.35	94.98	97.94	97.06	92.36	85.82	86.07	91.08	96.76
1994	95.65	99.13	101.76	99.87	112.30	120.58	123.68	121.38	132.53	130.91	141.92	148.86	119.05
1995	151.91	146.00	151.14	146.00	139.80	149.51	150.00	149.77	144.14	140.00	148.48	143.78	146.74
1996	130.09	128.75	130.20	131.29	135.33	116.55	103.63	104.14	102.51	101.80	112.58	114.78	117.86
1997	120.29	121.02	126.50	121.70	127.25	129.57	121.94	114.11	107.14	105.08	99.53	91.39	115.55
1998	88.88	87.52	91.69	93.54	90.02	86.90	87.37	85.30	87.62	84.26	83.51	78.30	87.09
1999	77.07	75.96	74.50	78.79	81.07	77.23	88.02	87.88	92.89	91.26	91.10	93.35	84.09
2000	96.83	94.41	91.63	89.32	94.80	92.74	95.81	98.67	103.49	99.63	95.25	98.92	95.96

Source: American Metal Market (AMM)

Dealers' Buying Price of No. 2 Heavy Copper Scrap in Chicago[1]   In Cents Per Pound

Year	Jan.	Feb.	Mar.	Apr.	May	June	July	Aug.	Sept.	Oct.	Nov.	Dec.	Average
1991	83.00	79.50	82.21	82.50	78.66	72.40	71.00	71.00	72.05	75.39	75.08	74.50	76.44
1992	73.21	73.37	75.23	75.16	74.00	74.27	77.18	78.38	75.38	70.27	69.00	67.18	73.55
1993	67.95	67.00	67.00	62.95	55.12	53.59	56.33	54.18	52.67	49.10	47.00	48.00	56.74
1994	50.80	56.11	59.61	62.00	64.86	72.32	76.40	74.30	75.69	76.45	78.10	82.95	69.13
1995	89.48	90.79	89.39	91.75	85.91	88.73	92.32	92.65	92.70	90.64	92.00	92.00	90.70
1996	87.17	82.90	83.24	83.29	82.95	71.48	61.43	62.00	62.00	63.00	64.84	66.00	72.53
1997	68.73	71.63	77.50	79.18	77.33	78.19	72.64	70.24	65.67	63.74	61.31	58.43	70.38
1998	53.26	52.58	53.09	54.00	52.60	49.64	48.00	47.71	46.00	44.00	40.00	40.00	48.41
1999	36.32	36.00	36.00	36.00	39.60	41.77	41.00	45.09	46.19	48.00	48.00	48.67	41.90
2000	50.00	50.00	50.00	49.15	49.00	49.00	49.30	52.65	54.60	55.00	52.65	51.00	51.03

Source: American Metal Market (AMM)

COPPER

Imports of Refined Copper into the United States   In Thousands of Metric Tons

Year	Jan.	Feb.	Mar.	Apr.	May	June	July	Aug.	Sept.	Oct.	Nov.	Dec.	Total
1991	22.7	27.1	21.7	30.9	17.5	23.6	23.7	17.4	22.9	36.3	26.8	18.0	288.6
1992	22.6	24.5	31.9	25.2	25.3	26.1	24.7	25.3	24.0	19.6	20.3	20.8	289.1
1993	21.8	25.6	28.2	35.9	29.5	26.9	30.6	28.3	22.5	31.6	32.2	30.5	343.4
1994	28.7	33.6	49.8	36.8	36.1	46.8	35.6	34.4	34.7	62.4	35.9	36.2	470.0
1995	34.9	30.0	37.1	36.9	36.5	37.9	31.5	31.8	28.7	38.7	44.4	40.3	429.0
1996	43.1	41.2	48.2	49.6	56.8	44.6	53.8	64.8	62.3	46.1	61.8	47.2	543.0
1997	55.4	48.0	43.6	43.6	61.0	42.0	53.1	73.3	53.8	55.0	53.4	42.0	632.0
1998	62.8	49.6	59.9	64.7	57.6	52.8	45.0	51.7	71.1	52.7	62.0	63.4	683.0
1999	64.7	53.2	68.1	59.9	62.3	63.8	73.0	84.5	90.3	81.0	59.0	77.5	837.0
2000[1]	84.9	67.8	85.5	92.1	83.6	84.5	89.4	83.0					1,006.2

[1] Preliminary.   *Source: U.S. Geological Survey (USGS)*

Exports of Refined Copper from the United States   In Thousands of Metric Tons

Year	Jan.	Feb.	Mar.	Apr.	May	June	July	Aug.	Sept.	Oct.	Nov.	Dec.	Total
1991	33.6	21.4	37.4	16.8	31.5	23.9	20.6	20.9	17.9	13.4	15.4	17.9	270.7
1992	21.7	18.4	10.8	12.3	11.7	12.0	9.3	13.0	13.6	24.1	14.1	16.1	176.9
1993	14.0	24.9	23.6	16.3	15.4	13.1	10.7	10.1	19.5	19.5	14.9	14.5	216.7
1994	13.0	10.2	10.7	6.8	14.8	9.1	15.6	10.9	15.4	15.9	13.1	21.1	157.0
1995	11.1	24.0	25.6	18.2	23.4	38.9	16.3	16.6	12.1	9.0	12.5	9.5	217.0
1996	13.7	16.5	12.7	12.3	10.8	10.7	15.7	17.7	14.5	16.4	12.8	16.0	170.0
1997	11.1	9.8	6.5	6.5	71.9	8.2	6.9	7.5	6.3	7.4	8.2	8.5	93.3
1998	6.2	12.1	12.2	7.5	7.8	6.4	7.5	6.4	5.8	5.0	3.6	6.2	86.2
1999	2.4	1.1	1.8	1.3	1.6	4.2	1.6	1.5	1.2	1.4	3.7	3.3	25.2
2000[1]	1.6	5.3	22.0	12.2	18.1	12.8	6.7	4.4					124.7

[1] Preliminary.   *Source: U.S. Geological Survey (USGS)*

Stocks of Refined Copper in the United States, on First of Month   In Thousands of Short Tons

Year	Jan.	Feb.	Mar.	Apr.	May	June	July	Aug.	Sept.	Oct.	Nov.	Dec.
1991	72.3	72.8	53.2	68.6	63.2	52.8	52.4	71.4	64.4	48.5	48.3	63.1
1992	75.3	76.3	67.2	69.7	75.9	65.0	62.2	71.2	87.1	99.5	110.3	107.1
1993	135.4	152.7	144.3	132.3	146.0	153.6	137.1	151.0	128.4	117.2	124.6	107.1
1994	103.0	87.7	83.6	72.8	70.7	70.4	73.3	81.1	74.6	66.5	52.7	53.6
1995[2]	55.8	39.6	37.0	22.6	33.1	30.8	27.0	50.0	60.6	71.1	69.4	73.4
1996	120.0	131.4	125.5	123.1	126.3	107.9	102.8	106.2	104.7	68.0	76.0	77.5
1997	88.2	98.8	104.4	116.0	117.9	121.7	122.9	148.8	177.1	197.9	227.6	253.3
1998	281.5	282.2	312.7	315.7	304.5	308.6	306.2	319.0	334.1	367.4	407.2	444.6
1999	562.6	593.1	614.6	653.5	676.6	687.8	668.4	657.2	639.7	611.2	626.5	608.2
2000[1]	619.2	620.8	619.5	582.9	537.0	508.8	467.8	417.4	401.0	394.3		

Recoverable copper content.   [1] Preliminary.   [2] New reporting method beginning January 1995, includes Comex, London Metal Exchange, and Refiners. Beginning January 1999, includes Consumers.   *Source: American Bureau of Metal Statistics (ABMS)*

Stocks of Refined Copper Outside the United States, on First of Month   In Thousands of Short Tons

Year	Jan.	Feb.	Mar.	Apr.	May	June	July	Aug.	Sept.	Oct.	Nov.	Dec.
1991	439.5	464.2	447.1	501.1	559.5	595.4	593.1	605.4	664.7	653.5	644.9	676.9
1992	640.4	718.1	704.2	715.7	714.9	723.2	726.4	737.9	816.5	822.5	873.8	896.1
1993	757.1	765.9	789.6	817.2	885.1	912.2	910.4	943.8	1,040.3	1,124.3	1,133.9	1,106.1
1994	1,075.0	1,095.5	1,046.8	984.9	913.7	859.5	843.7	839.7	874.6	870.7	835.1	818.4
1995[2]	611.6	655.8	622.2	577.9	537.0	525.6	494.9	464.7	465.7	467.7	481.4	503.5
1996	560.2	566.0	552.5	517.5	498.7	563.9	507.9	476.6	544.4	499.5	391.8	362.0
1997	405.4	469.5	476.3	445.7	413.5	402.4	408.3	489.6	550.9	607.7	574.5	553.3
1998	580.8	512.4	487.3	438.1	371.1	368.0	335.7	324.0	387.2	468.0	506.9	509.0
1999	922.6	944.3	960.3	963.0	990.5	1,008.3	993.3	990.0	1,017.0	996.9	1,001.5	992.0
2000[1]	983.8	1,034.9	1,040.7	1,011.4	988.6	880.9	866.0	857.9	834.4	809.0		

Recoverable copper content.   [1] Preliminary.   [2] New reporting method beginning January 1995, includes London Metal Exchange and Refiners. Beginning January 1999, also includes Shanghai Metal Exchange, Consumers and Other.   *Source: American Bureau of Metal Statistics (ABMS)*

Production of Refined Copper in the United States   In Thousands of Short Tons

Year	Jan.	Feb.	Mar.	Apr.	May	June	July	Aug.	Sept.	Oct.	Nov.	Dec.	Total
1991	129.0	127.7	134.9	119.7	137.1	124.8	136.8	142.7	135.6	153.1	141.0	149.7	1,632
1992	139.9	135.6	150.6	142.8	123.0	138.5	140.3	150.1	146.9	155.3	156.8	153.7	1,734
1993	153.9	153.8	173.2	166.0	160.3	177.0	151.4	153.7	160.2	157.3	157.2	166.2	1,930
1994	160.9	150.1	167.8	157.2	165.5	160.4	148.9	165.6	162.1	157.3	153.3	159.8	2,360
1995	202.7	185.5	204.8	194.6	210.0	198.3	193.8	208.8	199.0	206.5	211.3	208.1	2,423
1996	210.8	197.6	209.7	212.4	213.5	193.4	206.1	199.5	198.8	223.1	199.3	212.0	2,476
1997	206.0	192.0	204.0	202.0	198.0	179.0	207.0	203.0	213.0	222.0	205.0	212.0	2,470
1998	214.0	204.0	216.0	209.0	197.0	188.0	197.0	203.0	201.0	217.0	207.0	217.0	2,490
1999	185.0	178.0	220.0	198.0	186.0	175.0	163.0	161.0	172.0	172.0	158.0	164.0	2,130
2000[1]	158.0	150.0	174.0	145.0	162.0	147.0	135.0	149.0	140.0				1,813

Recoverable copper content.   [1] Preliminary.   *Source: U.S. Geological Survey (USGS)*

Production of Refined Copper Outside North America   In Thousands of Short Tons

Year	Jan.	Feb.	Mar.	Apr.	May	June	July	Aug.	Sept.	Oct.	Nov.	Dec.	Total
1991	416.5	381.1	427.7	405.5	425.3	404.5	375.1	378.7	411.4	411.8	409.2	424.5	4,871
1992	441.2	412.6	447.0	418.0	438.7	449.5	418.5	425.8	418.7	438.9	431.3	426.1	5,166
1993	429.2	405.6	475.1	426.2	440.9	447.5	421.6	449.4	448.0	425.9	447.2	436.5	5,253
1994	432.5	390.8	432.7	400.6	432.9	421.1	387.8	413.8	421.5	416.3	437.4	428.8	5,016
1995[2]	817.5	797.6	868.4	858.2	859.4	844.8	849.7	825.7	819.8	865.2	833.8	872.2	10,112
1996	903.2	869.3	929.3	922.2	916.3	918.3	908.3	931.1	938.2	972.9	935.8	992.4	11,137
1997	962.5	936.0	981.1	1,007.9	1,032.8	1,021.5	1,024.0	1,008.2	990.0	1,023.4	1,011.7	1,028.3	12,053
1998	1,073.1	1,012.8	1,066.3	1,039.4	1,057.2	1,027.6	1,027.9	1,031.9	1,069.7	1,072.8	1,050.1	1,139.1	12,668
1999	1,192.3	1,252.1	1,240.7	1,303.4	1,364.9	1,413.8	1,404.9	1,393.2	1,377.8	1,334.3	1,363.2	1,331.7	15,972
2000[1]	1,178.5	1,120.6	1,204.2	1,177.1	1,226.4	1,187.6	1,197.2	1,204.8	1,214.5	1,391.4			14,523

Recoverable copper content.   [1] Preliminary.   [2] New reporting method beginning January 1995, includes crude production. Data through December 1998 are Outside the United States.   NA = Not avaliable.   *Source: American Bureau of Metal Statistics (ABMS)*

Deliveries of Refined Copper to Fabricators in the United States   In Thousands of Short Tons

Year	Jan.	Feb.	Mar.	Apr.	May	June	July	Aug.	Sept.	Oct.	Nov.	Dec.	Total
1991	128.4	153.3	125.3	126.7	152.7	115.0	125.4	152.8	135.6	167.7	130.4	132.9	1,684
1992	144.9	159.0	165.9	155.5	149.4	161.4	145.8	144.1	146.9	150.4	166.2	130.0	1,813
1993	142.9	165.3	201.6	170.4	162.5	209.6	144.8	191.4	178.9	164.3	194.8	182.7	2,109
1994	193.3	168.6	204.6	178.3	187.8	171.9	154.3	194.6	188.2	188.7	167.5	175.1	2,173
1995[2]	233.8	209.2	239.1	200.9	230.0	210.5	187.1	208.8	202.9	224.7	222.4	175.5	2,545
1996	221.6	227.2	240.0	242.2	270.7	222.1	233.8	246.8	277.5	239.7	240.6	231.9	2,896
1997	246.3	234.5	240.6	247.4	254.9	228.1	241.1	258.2	252.3	259.2	256.0	236.6	2,959
1998	284.5	248.4	288.1	289.2	278.7	258.0	252.4	242.1	260.7	232.0	251.9	220.0	3,106
1999	199.6	202.8	235.0	221.4	206.3	201.9	188.0	186.8	193.7	182.3	182.4	175.2	2,375
2000[1]	166.8	161.3	176.3	157.0	173.7	161.3	145.2	148.7	149.5	154.9			1,914

Recoverable copper content.   [1] Preliminary.   [2] New reporting method beginning January 1995, includes crude copper deliveries.
Source: American Bureau of Metal Statistics (ABMS)

Deliveries of Refined Copper to Fabricators Outside the United States   In Thousands of Short Tons

Year	Jan.	Feb.	Mar.	Apr.	May	June	July	Aug.	Sept.	Oct.	Nov.	Dec.	Total
1990	419.9	466.3	436.7	392.9	408.3	466.7	303.7	373.5	370.8	448.9	469.1	420.7	4,972
1991	405.0	404.4	391.5	361.2	406.3	433.5	368.5	323.4	420.7	499.1	391.4	483.4	4,807
1992	453.7	408.9	441.8	416.4	413.4	432.4	410.4	364.7	432.6	403.5	406.1	461.3	5,045
1993	427.9	392.9	452.3	361.7	422.2	442.6	384.4	347.9	387.5	414.8	463.4	458.5	4,956
1994	399.8	429.5	481.2	466.5	468.9	428.1	387.9	369.2	423.5	448.9	457.1	436.0	5,197
1995[2]	758.5	810.1	892.8	882.2	853.0	867.3	863.7	814.1	803.4	835.1	796.6	726.2	9,903
1996	875.2	859.4	934.3	907.2	816.7	950.7	908.3	817.4	911.5	1,056.0	922.7	918.3	10,878
1997	862.2	889.7	977.9	1,007.1	991.1	982.7	897.8	873.9	886.2	1,009.0	980.4	966.6	11,349
1998	1,091.7	973.8	1,062.0	1,055.5	995.7	1,014.8	986.8	924.8	913.3	987.9	982.1	1,023.0	12,011
1999[1]	314.5	745.5											6,360

Recoverable copper content.   [1] Preliminary.   [2] New reporting method beginning January 1995, includes crude copper deliveries.
Source: American Bureau of Metal Statistics (ABMS)

Corn

U.S. corn prices in calendar 2000 witnessed a collapse in mid-spring from a high of nearly $2.50 per bushel in early May to less than $1.75 by mid-summer, basis nearby futures. However, by the end of the year, prices had recovered to $2.25 per bushel in a nearly straight line rally from the summer lows. Although prices were moving higher toward year-end, the bearish bias resurfaced in early 2001. The weakness largely reflected anticipated record supplies for the 2000/01 marketing year, but a late dampening factor on prices was the recall of a genetically engineered variety of corn that was thought to possibly contaminate other varieties as well. The result was a costly disruption to the nation's grain handling system, if not also the fear that the effect could last for some time.

The U.S. 2000/01 crop was estimated at 10.1 billion bushels (258.8 million metric tonnes), the second highest on record and comparing to 9.44 billion in 1999/00. Harvested acreage in 2000 of a record 73 million acres compared with 70.5 million in 1999. Average yield of 137.7 bushels per acre proved less than expected, but still up from 133.8 bushels in 1999. Three states, Iowa, Illinois, and Nebraska, generally account for more than one-third of U.S. production. In 2000, the three states produced 4.4 billion bushels. The large crop, however, was not seen as burdensome if domestic and export demand reach expectations.

Total domestic demand in 2000/01 of 7.8 billion bushels compares with 7.6 billion in 1999/00, while exports were put at 2.20 billion and 1.93 billion, respectively. Carryover stocks as of August 31, 2001, of 1.75 billion bushels compares with the year earlier 1.72 billion. The stock-to-use ratio in 2000/01 was forecast at about 16 percent vs. the previous season's 18 percent and the very low 5 percent ratio of 1995/96. Typically, the higher the ratio, the greater the downward pressure on prices.

In 2000/01, the average price received by farmers was forecast to range between $1.70-2.10 per bushel vs. the 1999/00 average of $1.80, and the 1995/96 record high of $3.24. If a less than $1.80 per bushel average is realized in 2000/01, it would be the lowest average price of the last decade.

Corn is the leading U.S. feed grain with sorghum a very distant second. The crop year encompasses September/August, but the international trade year is October/September. Animal feed usage in 2000/01 of 5.85 billion bushels compares with 5.67 billion in 1999/00. Food, seed, and industrial use (FSI) were estimated at a record high 1.97 billion bushels in 2000/01 vs. 1.91 billion in 1999/00. The increases in FSI use during the past few years are not surprising considering that industrial demand for corn processed into the sweetener high fructose corn syrup (HFCS) continues to quicken. 2000/01 recorded another record high in corn used for HFCS of 550 million bushels, up from 540 million in 1999/00, and less than 500 million in the mid-1990's. Corn used to make fuel (ethanol) was estimated at a record high 600 million bushels in 2000/01 vs. 566 million in 1999/00.

The U.S. is the world's largest corn exporter with Argentina a distant second. World importers are numerous, but the leaders are generally in Asia, paced by Japan, South Korea, and Taiwan. U.S. exports in 2000/01, of a projected record 2.3 billion bushels (47.5 million tonnes), compare with 1.9 billion in 1999/00. The 2000/01 estimate, however, could prove optimistic as exports to Japan, the largest purchaser of U.S. corn, have apparently sagged due to concerns about gene-altered corn.

U.S. corn imports are minimal, on average about 12 million bushels. World foreign trade in corn in 2000/01 of a near record 72.6 million metric tonnes is about 1.6 million tons more than initially forecast, and compares with the record large 72.8 million tonnes in 1999/00, of which the U.S. accounted for about two-thirds in both years. In the mid-1990's, the U.S. supplied about 80 percent of world exports. Argentina now exports about 12 percent of the world total vs. about 10 percent in the mid-1990's. Japan's imports have hovered around 16.2 million tonnes for some time. South Korea tends to be the second largest importer with 8.0 million tonnes in 2000/01 vs. 8.5 million in 1999/00. China imports relatively little corn, generally less than one million tonnes, and is the third largest exporter. In 2000/01, Chinese exports were 4 million tonnes vs. 10 million in 1999/00.

World corn production in 2000/01, of 587 million metric tonnes, trailed initial forecasts by 5 million tonnes and compares with the near record 605 million tonnes in 1999/00. China, the world's second largest producer since 1987/88, output 105 million tonnes in 2000/01 vs. a near record 128 million in 1999/00, and a record 133 million tonnes in 1998/99. The 2000/01 decline reflected a decrease in both acreage and average yield. Still, China's corn output has increased sharply from the 1980's when annual production averaged less than 100 million tonnes. The U.S. and China are forecast to produce 62 percent of the world's corn in 2000/01, while Brazil and Mexico combined should produce about 9 percent. The gains seen in China's production over the past decade reflect increases in per capita income and meat consumption, and the need for more corn as a livestock feed.

Global usage in 2000/01, of a record large 612 million tonnes compares with 603 million in 1999/00. China's usage of 120 million tonnes compares with 117 million in 1999/00, and marks the sixth consecutive year that China has used more than 100 million tonnes. The U.S. is the largest consumer with almost one-third of the total, 199 million tonnes in 2000/01 vs. 193 million in 1999/00. Brazil is in third place at 35 million tonnes. Ending world corn stocks are forecast to decrease during 2000/01 to 104 million tonnes from 125 million a year earlier, with almost one-half the total in the U.S. and one-third in China.

U.S. #2 yellow corn prices vary with the location. Typically, Gulf port prices are about 30¢ per bushel higher than prices in Central Illinois, while quotes at St. Louis run about 10¢-12¢ higher than Illinois prices. In mid- summer 2000, #2 yellow corn in Central Illinois averaged $1.50 per bushel vs. $1.75 a year earlier; for the Gulf ports the average was $1.91 per bushel vs. $2.15, respectively.

Futures Markets

Corn futures are traded on the Bolsa de Mercadorias & Futuros (BM&F) in Brazil, the Budapest Commodity Exchange, the Marche a Terme International de France (MATIF), the Mercado a Termino de Buenos Aires in Argentina, the Kanmon Commodity Exchange (KCE) in Korea, the Tokyo Grain Exchange (TGE), the Chicago Board of Trade (CBOT), and the Mid-American Commodity Exchange (MidAm).

World Production of Corn or Maize   In Thousands of Metric Tons

Crop Year	Argentina	Brazil	Canada	China	France	India	Italy	Mexico	Romania	South Africa	United States	Yugo-slavia	World Total
1991-2	10,600	30,800	7,413	98,770	12,928	8,060	6,238	14,689	10,500	3,277	189,868	11,500	491,360
1992-3	10,200	29,200	4,883	95,380	14,872	9,992	7,413	18,631	6,829	9,997	240,719	6,650	538,665
1993-4	10,000	32,934	6,501	102,700	14,843	9,600	8,029	19,141	8,000	13,275	160,986	6,420	476,214
1994-5	11,360	37,440	7,043	99,280	12,640	8,884	7,320	17,005	8,500	4,866	255,295	7,500	560,373
1995-6	11,100	32,480	7,271	112,000	12,394	9,530	8,454	17,780	9,923	10,171	187,970	8,375	517,204
1996-7	15,500	35,700	7,380	127,470	14,432	10,612	9,547	18,922	9,610	10,136	234,518	8,300	592,179
1997-8	19,360	30,100	7,180	104,309	16,754	10,852	10,005	16,934	12,680	7,693	233,864	10,500	576,136
1998-9[1]	13,500	32,350	8,952	132,954	15,204	10,680	8,600	17,788	8,000	7,724	247,882	8,700	605,567
1999-00[2]	16,700	31,600	9,096	128,086	15,630	11,470	10,000	19,000	10,500	10,584	239,719	8,700	605,224
2000-1[3]	15,500	37,000	6,800	105,000	16,300	12,000	10,800	19,000	4,000	8,500	255,382	5,500	587,800

[1] Preliminary.   [2] Estimate.   [3] Forecast.   Source: Foreign Agricultural Service, U.S. Department of Agriculture (FAS-USDA)

World Supply and Demand of Course Grains   In Millions of Metric Tons/Hectares

Crop Year Beginning Oct.1	Area Harvested	Yield	Pro-duction	World Trade	Total Con-sumption	Ending Stocks	Stocks as % of Con-sumption[3]
1991-2	322.8	2.51	810.7	95.9	810.1	135.8	16.8
1992-3	326.0	2.67	871.8	92.8	843.4	164.1	19.5
1993-4	318.7	2.51	798.9	85.8	838.7	124.3	14.8
1994-5	324.0	2.69	871.3	98.0	858.4	137.1	16.0
1995-6	313.9	2.56	802.9	87.8	839.3	100.8	12.0
1996-7	322.7	2.82	908.5	94.1	873.1	136.2	15.6
1997-8	311.2	2.84	883.9	85.6	873.0	147.1	16.8
1998-9	307.9	2.89	890.0	96.2	867.6	169.5	19.5
1999-00[1]	302.5	2.90	877.0	104.2	881.2	165.2	18.8
2000-1[2]	300.6	2.86	859.7	101.8	882.7	142.3	16.1

[1] Preliminary.   [2] Estimate.   [3] Represents the ratio of marketing year ending stocks to total consumption.   Source: Foreign Agricultural Service, U.S. Department of Agriculture (FAS-USDA)

Acreage and Supply of Corn in the United States   In Millions of Bushels

Crop Year Beginning Sept. 1[3]	Planted	Harvested For Grain	Harvested For Silage	Yield Per Harvested Acre Bushels	Carry-over, Sept. 1 On Farms	Carry-over, Sept. 1 Off Farms	Supply Beginning Stocks	Supply Pro-duction	Supply Imports	Total Supply
1991-2	75,957	68,822	6,101	108.6	691.2	830.0	1,521	7,475	20	9,016
1992-3	79,311	72,077	6,069	131.5	605.0	494.8	1,100	9,477	7	10,584
1993-4	73,235	62,921	6,831	100.7	1,070.7	1,042.0	2,113	6,338	21	8,472
1994-5	79,175	72,887	5,601	138.6	395.4	454.7	850	10,051	10	10,910
1995-6	71,245	64,995	5,295	113.5	740.9	816.9	1,558	7,400	16	8,974
1996-7	79,229	72,644	5,607	127.1	196.6	229.3	426	9,233	13	9,672
1997-8	79,537	72,671	6,054	126.7	475.0	408.2	883	9,207	9	10,099
1998-9	80,165	72,589	5,913	134.4	640.0	667.8	1,308	9,759	19	11,088
1999-00[1]	77,386	70,487	6,037	133.8	797.0	990.0	1,787	9,431	15	11,239
2000-1[2]	79,545	72,732	5,868	137.1	793.0	922.2	1,715	9,968	10	11,779

(In Thousands of Acres for Planted, For Grain, For Silage columns)

[1] Preliminary.   2 Estimate.   Source: Economic Research Service, U.S. Department of Agriculture (ERS-USDA)

Production of Corn (For Grain) in the United States, by State   In Million of Bushels

Year	Illinois	Indiana	Iowa	Kansas	Michigan	Minnesota	Missouri	Nebraska	Ohio	South Dakota	Texas	Wisconsin	Total
1991	1,177.0	510.6	1,427.4	206.3	253.0	720.0	213.4	999.6	326.4	240.5	165.0	380.8	7,475.5
1992	1,646.5	877.6	1,903.7	259.5	241.5	741.0	324.0	1,066.5	507.7	277.2	202.5	306.8	9,476.7
1993	1,300.0	712.8	880.0	216.0	225.5	322.0	166.5	785.2	360.8	160.7	212.8	306.8	6,336.5
1994	1,786.2	858.2	1,930.4	304.6	260.9	915.9	273.7	1,153.7	486.5	367.2	238.7	216.2	10,102.7
1995	1,130.0	598.9	1,402.2	244.3	249.6	731.9	149.9	854.7	375.1	193.6	216.6	437.1	7,373.9
1996	1,468.8	670.4	1,711.2	357.2	211.5	868.8	340.4	1,179.8	310.8	365.0	198.2	347.7	9,232.6
1997	1,425.5	701.5	1,642.2	371.8	255.1	851.4	299.0	1,135.2	475.7	326.4	241.5	333.0	9,206.8
1998	1,473.5	760.4	1,769.0	419.0	227.6	1,032.8	285.0	1,239.8	470.9	429.6	185.0	402.6	9,758.7
1999	1,491.0	748.4	1,758.2	420.2	253.5	990.0	247.4	1,153.7	403.2	367.3	228.3	404.2	9,437.3
2000[1]	1,690.7	815.9	1,752.0	416.0	241.8	976.8	413.3	1,006.3	491.7	426.6	236.8	363.0	10,053.9

[1] Preliminary.   Source: National Agricultural Statistics Service, U.S. Department of Agriculture (NASS-USDA)

CORN

Supply and Disappearance of Corn in the United States   In Millions of Bushels

Crop Year Beginning Sept. 1	Beginning Stocks	Pro-duction	Imports	Total Supply	Food, Alcohol & Industrial	Seed	Feed & Residual	Total	Exports	Total Disap-pearance	Gov't Owned[3]	Privately Owned[4]	Total
1996-7	426	9,233	13.3	9,672	1,672	20.3	5,299	6,991	1,797	8,789	2	881	883
Sept.-Nov.	426	9,233	3.4	9,662	383	0	1,890	2,272	487	2,759	30	6,873	6,903
Dec.-Feb.	6,903	----	2.4	6,905	394	0	1,492	1,887	525	2,411	30	4,464	4,494
Mar.-May	4,494	----	3.7	4,498	445	19.7	1,103	1,568	433	2,001	10	2,486	2,497
June-Aug.	2,497	----	3.8	2,500	449	.6	814	1,264	353	1,617	2	881	883
1997-8	883	9,207	8.8	10,099	1,784	20.4	5,482	7,287	1,504	8,791	4	1,304	1,308
Sept.-Nov.	883	9,207	2.2	10,092	435	0	2,030	2,465	380	2,845	2	7,245	7,247
Dec.-Feb.	7,247	----	1.0	7,248	425	0	1,503	1,928	380	2,308	2	4,938	4,940
Mar.-May	4,940	----	3.6	4,944	450	19.7	1,084	1,553	350	1,904	2	3,038	3,040
June-Aug.	3,040	----	2.0	3,042	474	.7	865	1,340	394	1,734	4	1,304	1,308
1998-9	1,308	9,759	18.8	11,085	1,826	19.8	5,472	7,318	1,981	9,298	12	1,775	1,787
Sept.-Nov.	1,308	9,759	4.0	1,171	11,071	0	2,119	13,189	450	3,019	13	8,039	8,052
Dec.-Feb.	8,052	----	5.7	8,058	434	0	1,460	1,894	465	2,359	15	5,684	5,698
Mar.-May	5,698	----	7.2	5,706	476	19.0	1,097	1,592	497	2,089	15	3,602	3,616
June-Aug.	3,616	----	1.8	3,618	467	.8	795	1,263	568	1,831	12	1,775	1,787
1999-00[1]	1,787	9,431	15.0	11,232	1,913	19.9	5,664	7,597	1,937	9,515	15	1,744	1,718
Sept.-Nov.	1,787	9,431	3.5	11,221	459	0	2,189	2,648	534	3,182	19	8,005	8,039
Dec.-Feb.	8,039	----	3.0	8,043	447	0	1,526	1,973	468	2,441	15	5,590	5,602
Mar.-May	5,602	----	6.0	5,607	512	0	1,059	1,571	451	2,021			3,586
June-Aug.	3,586	----	2.0	3,588	496	0	890	1,386	485	1,871			1,718
2000-1[2]	1,718	9,668	10.0	11,696	1,980		5,775	7,755	2,050	9,805			1,891
Sept.-Nov.	1,718	9,968	1.0	11,687	768		2,196	2,964	506	3,170			8,518

[1] Preliminary.   [2] Estimate.   [3] Uncommitted inventory.   [4] Includes quantity under loan and farmer-owned reserve.

Source: Economic Research Service, U.S. Department of Agriculture (ERS-USDA)

Corn Production Estimates and Cash Price in the United States

Year	Aug. 1	Sept. 1	Oct. 1	Nov. 1	Final	St. Louis No. 2 Yellow	Omaha No. 2 Yellow	Gulf Ports No. 2 Yellow	Kansas City No. 2 White	Chicago No. 2 Yellow	Average Farm Price[2]	Value of Pro-duction (Million Dollars)
	In Thousands of Bushels					Dollars Per Bushel						
1992-3	8,762,060	7,873,436	8,592,821	9,328,850	9,476,698	2.25	2.10	2.46	2.49	2.22	2.07	19,723
1993-4	7,423,142	7,229,427	6,961,902	6,503,237	6,336,470	2.67	2.56	2.85	2.78	2.68	2.50	16,032
1994-5	9,214,420	9,257,170	9,602,340	10,010,310	10,102,735	2.51	2.33	2.78	2.91	2.43	2.26	22,992
1995-6	8,121,520	7,832,140	7,541,400	7,373,700	7,373,876	4.06	3.87	4.30	4.14	3.97	3.24	24,118
1996-7	8,694,628	8,803,928	9,012,148	9,265,288	9,293,435	2.90	2.70	3.07	3.09	2.84	2.71	25,149
1997-8	9,275,870	9,267,655	9,311,705	9,359,485	9,206,832	2.60	2.36	2.78	2.93	2.56	2.43	22,352
1998-9	9,592,089	9,737,949	9,743,399	9,836,069	9,758,685	2.15	1.88	2.35	2.51	2.06	1.94	18,922
1999-00	9,560,919	9,380,947	9,466,977	9,537,137	9,437,337	2.06	1.80	2.28	2.03	1.99	1.80	17,950
2000-1[1]	10,369,369	10,362,374	10,191,817	10,053,942	9,968,358	----	----	----	----	----	1.70-2.10	

[1] Preliminary.   [2] Season-average price based on monthly prices weighted by monthly marketings.   *Source: Economic Research Service, U..S. Department of Agriculture (ERS-USDA)*

Distribution of Corn in the United States   In Millions of Bushels

Crop Year Beginning Sept. 1	HFCS	Glucose & Dextrose	Starch	Fuel	Beve-rage[3]	Seed	Cereal & Other Products	Total	Livestock Feed[4]	Exports (Including Grain Equiv. of Products)	Domestic Disap-pearance	Total Utilization
1992-3	414	214	238	426	83	19	117	1,493	5,252	1,663	6,808	8,471
1993-4	444	223	223	458	106	20	118	1,571	4,680	1,328	6,293	7,621
1994-5	465	231	226	533	100	18	132	1,686	5,460	2,178	7,175	9,352
1995-6	482	237	219	396	125	20	133	1,592	4,693	2,228	6,321	8,548
1996-7	504	246	229	429	130	20	135	1,672	5,277	1,797	6,991	8,789
1997-8	513	229	246	481	133	20	182	1,784	5,482	1,504	7,287	8,791
1998-9	531	219	240	526	127	20	184	1,826	5,472	1,981	7,318	9,298
1999-00[1]	540	222	251	566	130	20	185	1,893	5,650	1,900	7,580	9,480
2000-1[2]	550	220	255	600	130		190	1,945	5,625	1,800	7,485	9,285

[1] Preliminary.   [2] Estimate.   [3] Also includes nonfuel industrial alcohol.   [4] Feed and waste (residual, mostly feed).   *Source: Economic Research Service, U.S. Department of Agriculture (ERS-USDA)*

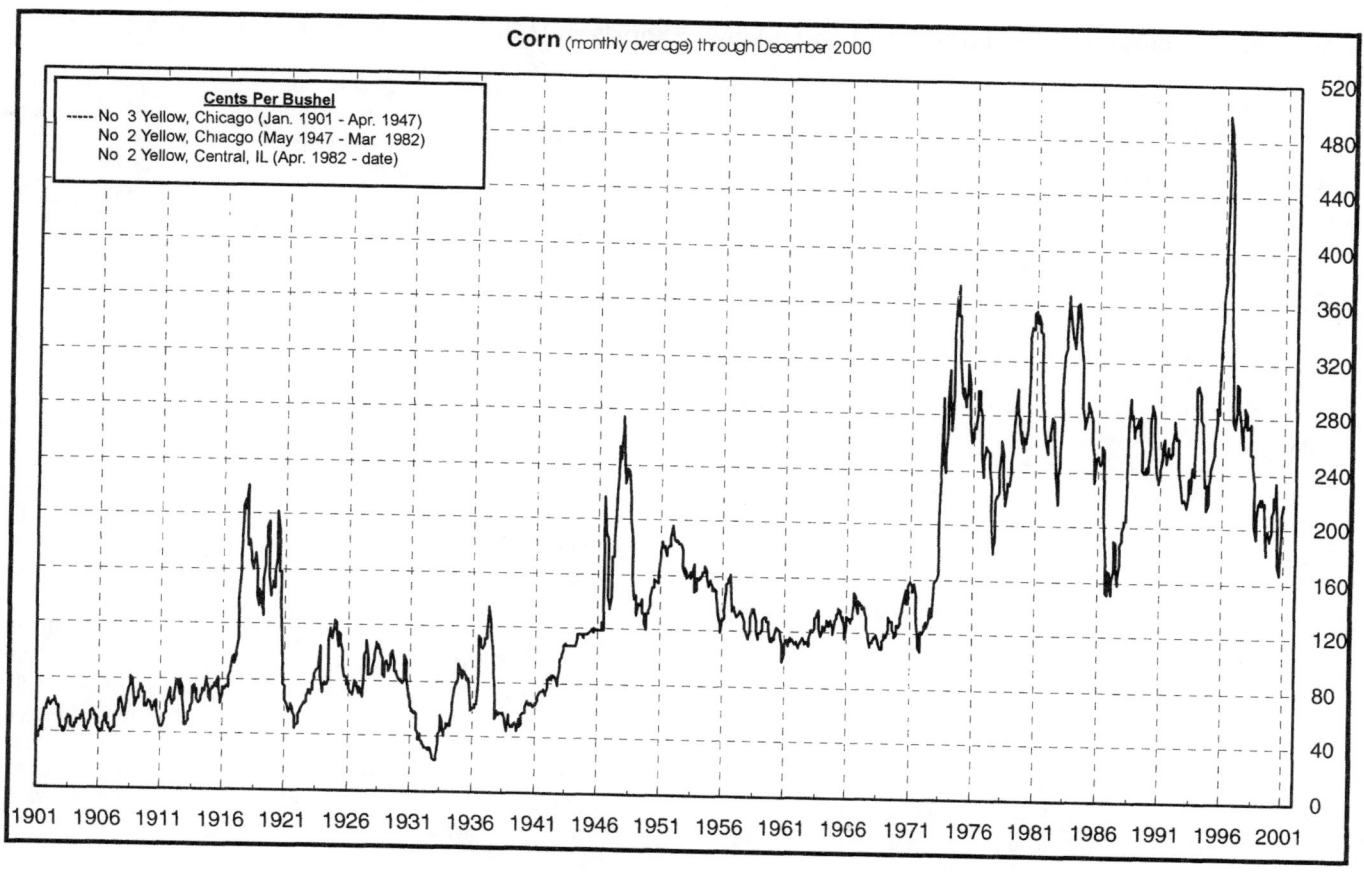

Corn (monthly average) through December 2000

Cents Per Bushel
----- No 3 Yellow, Chicago (Jan. 1901 - Apr. 1947)
No 2 Yellow, Chicago (May 1947 - Mar 1982)
No 2 Yellow, Central, IL (Apr. 1982 - date)

Average Cash Price of Corn, No. 2 Yellow in Central Illinois — In Dollars Per Bushel

Year	Sept.	Oct.	Nov.	Dec.	Jan.	Feb.	Mar.	Apr.	May	June	July	Aug.	Average
1991-2	2.39	2.41	2.41	2.42	2.49	2.58	2.64	2.50	2.51	2.51	2.31	2.17	2.45
1992-3	2.13	1.97	1.99	2.05	2.07	2.05	2.16	2.23	2.20	2.09	2.25	2.27	2.12
1993-4	2.22	2.27	2.63	2.81	2.89	2.83	2.76	2.61	2.58	2.61	2.19	2.13	2.54
1994-5	2.08	1.92	2.03	2.16	2.22	2.27	2.36	2.41	2.50	2.65	2.79	2.68	2.34
1995-6	2.83	3.12	3.22	3.36	3.53	3.71	3.92	4.47	4.86	4.74	4.70	4.48	3.91
1996-7	3.39	2.81	2.63	2.62	2.62	2.71	2.90	2.87	2.74	2.59	2.44	2.60	2.74
1997-8	2.61	2.66	2.70	2.60	2.60	2.58	2.59	2.41	2.37	2.29	2.16	1.86	2.45
1998-9	1.78	1.94	2.09	2.08	2.07	2.05	2.09	2.05	2.03	1.99	1.67	1.84	1.97
1999-00	1.81	1.72	1.82	1.84	1.95	2.03	2.08	2.09	2.15	1.83	1.53	1.49	1.86
2000-1[1]	1.58	1.81	1.96										1.78

[1] Preliminary.   Source: Economic Research Service, U.S. Department of Agriculture (ERS-USDA)

Average Cash Price of Corn, No. 2 Yellow at Gulf Ports[2] — In Dollars Per Bushel

Year	Sept.	Oct.	Nov.	Dec.	Jan.	Feb.	Mar.	Apr.	May	June	July	Aug.	Average
1991-2	2.76	2.76	2.72	2.71	2.70	2.89	2.96	2.77	2.77	2.80	2.61	2.48	2.74
1992-3	2.50	2.40	2.42	2.39	2.39	2.40	2.48	2.55	2.50	2.36	2.59	2.55	2.46
1993-4	2.57	2.68	2.94	3.08	3.22	3.14	3.05	2.88	2.81	2.85	2.51	2.44	2.85
1994-5	2.48	2.44	2.43	2.61	2.72	2.72	2.79	2.79	2.84	3.04	3.23	3.21	2.78
1995-6	3.32	3.57	3.63	3.76	4.00	4.18	4.34	4.80	5.17	4.99	5.07	4.73	4.30
1996-7	3.69	3.27	2.97	2.97	3.02	3.08	3.25	3.17	3.01	2.86	2.69	2.86	3.07
1997-8	2.88	3.05	2.98	2.89	2.90	2.88	2.89	2.71	2.69	2.64	2.55	2.24	2.78
1998-9	2.18	2.43	2.47	2.42	2.48	2.40	2.45	2.39	2.35	2.36	2.12	2.20	2.35
1999-00	2.21	2.17	2.17	2.21	2.36	2.42	2.42	2.43	2.43	2.13	1.91	1.91	2.23
2000-1[1]	2.03	2.15	2.26										2.15

[1] Preliminary.   [2] Barge delivered to Louisiana Gulf.   Source: Economic Research Service, U.S. Department of Agriculture (ERS-USDA)

CORN

Weekly Outstanding Export Sales and Cumulative Exports of U.S. Corn   In Thousands of Metric Tons

Marketing Year 1998/99 Week Ending	1998/99 Out-standing Sales	Cumu-lative Exports	Marketing Year 1999/00 Week Ending	1999/00 Out-standing Sales	Cumu-lative Exports	Marketing Year 2000-01 Week Ending	2000-01 Out-standing Sales	Cumu-lative Exports
Sept. 3, 1998	7,776	208	Sept. 2, 1999	8,647	475	Sept. 7, 2000	7,856	825
10	7,783	601	9	8,841	1,333	14	7,509	1,848
17	7,831	1,630	16	8,558	2,508	21	7,767	2,959
24	8,168	2,230	23	8,224	3,543	28	6,994	4,390
Oct. 1	7,907	3,097	30	8,037	4,398	Oct. 5	6,640	5,713
8	7,649	3,882	Oct. 7	7,682	5,355	12	6,812	6,591
15	7,796	4,840	14	7,769	6,322	19	6,923	7,408
22	8,252	5,654	21	8,270	7,455	26	7,087	8,056
29	8,202	6,536	28	8,418	8,627	Nov. 2	6,671	9,087
Nov. 5	8,206	7,312	Nov. 4	8,508	9,266	9	6,622	9,650
12	8,713	8,315	11	8,756	10,254	16	6,366	10,563
19	9,014	9,281	18	8,836	11,180	23	6,224	11,144
26	8,675	10,263	25	8,387	12,191	30	6,146	12,159
Dec. 3	8,699	11,108	Dec. 2	8,356	13,225	Dec. 7	6,664	12,954
10	8,472	12,570	9	8,351	14,278	14	6,726	13,853
17	8,515	13,690	16	8,645	15,227	21	6,547	14,820
24	8,193	14,673	23	8,220	16,191	28	6,697	15,269
31	7,779	15,501	30	7,894	17,010	Jan. 4, 2001	6,253	15,898
Jan. 7, 1999	7,870	16,080	Jan. 6, 2000	7,360	17,826	11	5,936	16,826
14	7,813	16,920	13	7,487	18,825	18	6,654	17,667
21	8,070	17,562	20	7,737	19,709	25	7,071	18,382
28	8,433	18,441	27	7,579	20,689	Feb. 1	7,569	18,913
Feb. 4	8,485	19,411	Feb. 3	7,771	21,479	8	7,585	20,055
11	8,500	20,266	10	7,408	22,367	15		
18	8,415	21,168	17	7,423	23,246	22		
25	8,539	22,175	24	7,517	24,282	Mar. 1		
Mar. 4	8,151	23,320	Mar. 2	8,148	25,022	8		
11	7,759	24,514	9	7,952	25,993	15		
18	7,275	25,468	16	7,537	26,940	22		
25	7,078	26,310	23	7,316	27,941	29		
Apr. 1	7,142	27,073	30	7,249	28,833	Apr. 5		
8	7,129	28,194	Apr. 6	7,132	29,674	12		
15	7,367	29,040	13	7,258	30,602	19		
22	7,408	30,029	20	7,405	31,698	26		
29	7,565	31,145	27	6,877	32,640	May 3		
May 6	8,246	31,807	May 4	6,817	33,432	10		
13	8,236	32,560	11	6,941	34,082	17		
20	7,534	33,825	18	6,979	34,970	24		
27	7,972	34,755	25	6,889	35,817	31		
June 3	8,373	35,737	June 1	7,063	36,584	June 7		
10	8,086	36,874	8	7,125	37,517	14		
17	7,668	38,119	15	7,250	38,348	21		
24	7,335	39,126	22	7,161	39,112	28		
July 1	6,956	40,286	29	7,227	39,854	July 5		
8	7,148	41,070	July 6	6,820	40,818	12		
15	7,104	42,207	13	6,716	41,731	19		
22	6,850	43,096	20	6,478	42,565	26		
29	6,145	44,348	27	6,116	43,477	Aug. 2		
Aug. 5	5,651	45,500	Aug. 3	5,766	44,337	9		
12	4,833	46,606	10	5,388	44,949	16		
19	3,625	47,536	17	4,296	46,181	23		
26	2,435	48,832	24	3,372	47,318	30		
			31	2,006	48,760			

Source: Foreign Agricultural Service, U.S. Department of Agriculture (FAS-USDA)

Average Price Received by Farmers for Corn in the United States   In Dollars Per Bushel

Year	Sept.	Oct.	Nov.	Dec.	Jan.	Feb.	Mar.	Apr.	May	June	July	Aug.	Average
1991-2	2.33	2.31	2.29	2.33	2.40	2.46	2.49	2.48	2.49	2.47	2.33	2.15	2.37
1992-3	2.16	2.05	1.98	1.97	2.03	2.00	2.10	2.16	2.14	2.09	2.22	2.25	2.07
1993-4	2.21	2.28	2.45	2.67	2.70	2.79	2.74	2.65	2.60	2.61	2.29	2.16	2.50
1994-5	2.19	2.06	1.99	2.13	2.19	2.23	2.30	2.36	2.41	2.51	2.63	2.63	2.26
1995-6	2.69	2.79	2.87	3.07	3.09	3.37	3.51	3.85	4.14	4.20	4.43	4.30	3.53
1996-7	3.55	2.89	2.66	2.63	2.69	2.65	2.79	2.80	2.69	2.56	2.42	2.50	2.74
1997-8	2.52	2.54	2.51	2.52	2.56	2.55	2.54	2.41	2.34	2.28	2.19	1.89	2.40
1998-9	1.83	1.91	1.93	2.00	2.06	2.05	2.06	2.04	1.99	1.97	1.74	1.75	1.94
1999-00	1.75	1.69	1.70	1.82	1.91	1.98	2.03	2.03	2.10	1.91	1.64	1.53	1.84
2000-1[1]	1.61	1.74	1.86	1.97	1.96								1.83

[1] Preliminary.   Source: Economic Research Service, U.S. Department of Agriculture (ERS-USDA)

Corn Price Support Data in the United States

Crop Year Beginning Sept. 1	National Average Loan Rate[3] --- Dollars Per Bushel ---	Target Price	Placed Under Loan	% of Pro-duction	Acquired by CCC	Owned by CCC Aug. 31	CCC Owned	Under CCC Loan	Quantity Pledged (Thousands of Bushels)	Face Amount (Thousands of Dollars)
					---------------- Millions of Bushels ----------------		CCC Inventory ------ As of Dec. 31 ------			
1990-1	1.57	2.75	1,071	13.5	285	371	214	1,071	1,071,040	1,616,948
1991-2	1.62	2.75	1,006	13.5	291	113	265	678	26,636	45,609
1992-3	1.72	2.75	1,646	17.4	0	56	125	1,021	15,245	28,947
1993-4	1.72	2.75	618	9.7	0	45	54	812	13,697	26,052
1994-5	1.89	2.75	2,002	19.8	0	-----	44	1,598	26,318	53,474
1995-6	1.89	2.75	970	9.2	0	-----	42	579	677,115	1,232,669
1996-7	1.89	NA	561	-----	0	-----	30	756	-----	-----
1997-8	1.89	NA	1,132	-----	19	-----	2	81	-----	-----
1998-9[1]	1.89	NA	823	-----	0	-----	-----	-----	-----	-----
1999-00[2]	1.89	-----	-----	-----	-----	-----	-----	-----	-----	-----

[1] Preliminary.   [2] Estimate.   [3] Findley or announced loan rate.   Source: National Agricultural Statistics Service, U.S. Department of Agriculture (NASS-USDA)

U.S. Exports[1] of Corn (Including Seed), By Country of Destination   In Thousands of Metric Tons

Year Beginning Oct. 1	Algeria	Canada	Egypt	Irael	Japan	Mexico	Rep. of Korea	Russia[3]	Saudi Arabia	Spain	Taiwan	Vene-zuela	Total
1988-9	973	896	1,014	304	13,016	3,113	4,591	15,573	616	1,280	3,625	0	50,676
1989-90	1,146	637	1,135	250	13,885	4,585	5,680	16,371	707	1,712	5,009	593	59,854
1990-1	1,328	302	1,756	299	13,639	1,901	1,982	9,077	725	1,434	5,086	321	44,497
1991-2	827	314	1,058	369	13,481	1,041	1,508	6,533	602	1,273	4,998	552	40,693
1992-3	1,224	1,189	1,543	539	14,235	396	1,021	3,380	787	1,075	5,450	777	41,766
1993-4	1,182	640	1,437	268	12,032	1,678	631	2,337	851	1,116	4,955	751	33,057
1994-5	846	1,135	2,608	671	16,107	3,166	8,921	9	864	2,497	6,210	886	58,645
1995-6	567	751	2,106	625	14,900	6,268	7,426	58	844	1,156	5,600	479	52,681
1996-7	929	879	2,364	556	15,482	3,141	5,452	88	1,025	1,080	5,609	730	46,638
1997-8[2]	829	1,397	1,951	-----	13,994	4,373	3,364	-----	928	-----	3,488	651	37,697

[1] Excludes exports of corn by-products.   [2] Preliminary.   [3] Formerly part of the U.S.S.R.; data not reported separately until 1992.   Source: Economic Research Service, U.S. Department of Agriculture (ERS-USDA)

Stocks of Corn (Shelled and Ear) in the United States   In Millions of Bushels

Year	On Farms Mar. 1	June 1	Sept. 1	Dec. 1	Off Farms Mar. 1	June 1	Sept. 1	Dec. 1	Total Stocks Mar. 1	June 1	Sept. 1	Dec. 1
1991	3,064.5	1,755.0	691.2	4,294.5	1,724.5	1,237.0	830.0	2,246.6	4,789.0	2,992.0	1,521.2	6,541.1
1992	2,610.2	1,517.5	605.5	5,736.9	1,950.8	1,221.1	494.8	2,169.5	4,561.0	2,738.6	1,100.3	7,906.4
1993	3,630.0	2,216.5	1,070.7	3,803.0	2,048.2	1,492.9	1,042.3	2,133.5	5,678.2	3,709.4	2,113.0	5,936.5
1994	2,210.0	1,203.0	395.4	5,417.5	1,785.5	1,156.9	454.7	2,663.0	3,995.7	2,359.9	850.1	8,080.5
1995	3,502.0	2,072.0	740.9	3,960.0	2,089.7	1,342.9	816.9	2,145.8	5,591.7	3,414.9	1,557.8	6,105.8
1996	2,000.2	780.1	196.6	4,800.0	1,799.3	937.8	229.3	2,103.7	3,799.5	1,717.9	425.9	6,903.7
1997	2,870.0	1,501.0	475.0	4,822.0	1,624.1	995.6	408.2	2,424.8	4,494.1	2,496.6	883.2	7,246.8
1998	2,975.0	1,830.0	640.0	5,320.0	1,964.9	1,209.8	667.8	2,731.8	4,939.9	3,039.8	1,307.8	8,051.8
1999	3,570.0	2,257.0	797.0	5,195.0	2,128.4	1,359.2	990.0	2,844.4	5,698.4	3,616.2	1,787.0	8,039.4
2000[1]	3,300.0	2,029.8	793.0	5,550.0	2,301.9	1,556.1	924.5	2,967.6	5,601.9	3,585.9	1,717.5	8,517.6

[1] Preliminary.   Source: National Agricultural Statistics Service, U.S. Department of Agriculture (NASS-USDA)

CORN

Corn Futures - Chicago Board of Trade (weekly close) as of 29-Dec-2000   Cents per bushel

Volume of Trading of Corn Futures in Chicago   In Thousands of Contracts

Year	Jan.	Feb.	Mar.	Apr.	May	June	July	Aug.	Sept.	Oct.	Nov.	Dec.	Total
1991	846.8	696.8	932.6	1,041.0	845.4	1,012.8	1,253.6	1,097.2	692.4	884.0	907.8	632.2	10,852.8
1992	901.2	1,002.6	952.2	868.6	938.2	1,015.2	865.6	795.0	688.6	688.4	996.2	644.4	10,356.6
1993	517.6	636.4	774.0	894.8	688.0	1,047.4	1,395.6	1,014.2	896.0	1,036.0	1,574.4	988.2	10,539.4
1994	1,251.4	1,035.6	1,045.6	1,108.8	1,079.2	1,455.0	747.6	601.8	615.0	703.0	1,025.4	861.4	11,529.8
1995	787.2	832.4	973.7	987.7	1,213.7	1,759.5	1,293.7	1,318.6	1,220.2	1,613.2	1,743.1	1,356.0	15,105.1
1996	1,992.2	1,819.6	1,607.6	2,655.2	2,085.2	1,545.1	1,590.5	1,144.6	1,183.4	1,435.7	1,514.7	1,046.3	19,620.2
1997	1,160.6	1,483.0	1,693.3	1,780.1	1,291.7	1,347.5	1,527.7	1,318.3	1,060.2	1,700.2	1,434.4	1,188.0	16,985.0
1998	1,250.2	1,276.5	1,432.8	1,620.3	1,148.5	1,771.0	1,415.3	1,231.4	1,126.3	1,319.3	1,217.2	986.6	15,795.5
1999	955.1	1,374.2	1,440.1	1,420.6	975.1	1,597.4	1,708.0	1,669.8	1,131.9	1,096.2	1,500.9	855.6	15,724.8
2000	1,502.2	1,580.9	1,713.1	1,386.3	1,789.7	1,830.7	1,178.3	1,291.8	1,057.4	1,256.1	1,612.8	986.1	17,185.4

Source: Chicago Board of Trade (CBT)

Average Open Interest of Corn Futures in Chicago   In Contracts

Year	Jan.	Feb.	Mar.	Apr.	May	June	July	Aug.	Sept.	Oct.	Nov.	Dec.
1991	210,006	219,236	229,010	229,404	204,828	202,100	198,527	219,700	215,527	242,466	257,065	228,347
1992	254,195	294,957	285,429	260,527	230,359	232,189	211,221	219,796	208,613	239,888	262,345	244,803
1993	256,113	260,986	248,638	250,000	229,016	232,590	265,672	264,938	243,892	275,792	332,445	327,226
1994	346,077	336,342	327,539	305,722	262,621	246,308	215,081	208,990	212,983	243,678	262,849	250,646
1995	292,090	311,372	336,433	355,443	368,381	427,744	413,839	418,450	439,170	473,698	490,970	487,977
1996	500,837	508,496	469,697	453,707	403,118	350,066	304,265	298,894	302,170	326,373	332,809	306,256
1997	305,779	347,392	382,261	351,852	290,649	274,760	267,531	281,194	307,415	378,453	379,045	331,386
1998	328,020	341,444	358,221	366,657	337,703	327,237	297,894	318,162	321,992	332,337	342,868	322,157
1999	357,682	363,153	357,126	343,624	338,467	323,658	329,460	315,858	316,247	410,955	461,037	389,187
2000	445,999	478,892	482,080	487,758	476,891	445,018	391,967	387,289	356,583	397,966	454,920	414,851

Source: Chicago Board of Trade (CBT)

Corn Oil

U.S. corn oil production totaled a record high 2.48 billion pounds in 1999/00 (October/September) vs. the previous record of 2.37 billion in 1998/99. Production in the mid-1990's averaged about 2.1 billion pounds. Seasonally, production tends to peak between December and March, and then reaches a low in July. On a total usage basis, the gain in domestic use pales against the past decade's percentage growth in export demand.

Total 1999/00 disappearance of a record 2.46 billion pounds compares with 2.3 billion in 1998/99. Domestic usage of a record high 1.46 billion pounds in 1999/00 compares with 1.39 billion in 1998/99, and a mid-1990's average of 1.25 billion pounds. Corn oil is cholesterol-free which enhances its appeal among health conscious consumers.

Exports are expected to total a near record 1 billion pounds in 1999/00, marginally above both 1998/99 and the record 1.1 billion in 1997/98. Exports averaged about 800 million pounds in the mid-1990's. The European Union is a major importer of U.S. corn oil. U.S. imports are minimal, 27 million pounds in 1999/00. Carryover stocks vary considerably with estimated ending 1999/00 stocks of 177 million pounds comparing with 135 million in 1998/99.

Crude corn oil prices, basis wet/dry-milled Central Illinois, averaged 23.36 cents per pound in calendar 1999 (vs. a marketing year average of 25.30 cents). Calendar 1998 prices averaged near 30 cents/pound vs. a marketing year average of 28.94 cents. Seasonally, prices tend to be highest around March/April and lowest late in the calendar year.

Supply and Disappearance of Corn Oil in the United States   In Millions of Pounds

Crop Year Beginning Oct. 1	Supply Stocks Oct. 1	Supply Pro-duction	Supply Imports	Supply Total Supply	Baking and Frying Fats	Salad and Cooking Oil	Marg-arine	Total Edible Products	Domestic Disap-pearance	Exports	Total Disap-pearance
1994-5	118	2,227	10.0	2,356	100	446	W	636	1,250	865	2,115
1995-6	241	2,139	11.0	2,391	82	434	79	595	1,298	977	2,275
1996-7	116	2,230	13.5	2,361	73	386	68	527	1,244	988	2,232
1997-8	129	2,335	28.1	2,492	W	375	W	492	1,272	1,118	2,390
1998-9	102	2,374	42.4	2,518	W	384	W	496	1,394	989	2,383
1999-00[1]	135	2,554	17.5	2,714	W	498	W	586	1,500	950	2,450
2000-1[2]	264	2,625		2,917					1,602	1,050	2,652

[1] Preliminary.   [2] Estimate.   W = Withheld proprietary data.   *Source: Economic Research Service, U.S. Department of Agriculture (ERS-USDA)*

Production[2] of Crude Corn Oil in the United States   In Millions of Pounds

Year	Oct.	Nov.	Dec.	Jan.	Feb.	Mar.	Apr.	May	June	July	Aug.	Sept.	Total
1994-5	175.5	165.3	180.9	163.2	161.8	232.7	188.4	191.2	193.6	193.5	180.3	188.5	2,215
1995-6	179.5	173.8	184.5	180.6	160.4	192.9	192.1	175.9	178.4	147.1	162.2	171.2	2,099
1996-7	183.8	182.3	208.2	172.5	170.9	209.9	188.3	182.5	184.3	174.0	180.6	182.2	2,220
1997-8	199.2	207.5	202.0	171.4	162.7	201.0	203.9	201.2	201.4	192.8	202.8	188.9	2,335
1998-9	209.2	199.4	189.2	182.9	177.0	201.0	201.1	205.3	205.7	194.8	212.5	196.3	2,374
1999-00	204.3	212.3	218.6	214.8	199.0	214.9	210.5	213.6	204.3	226.4	225.3	201.9	2,546
2000-1[1]	208.6	192.7	190.4										2,367

[1] Preliminary.   [2] Not seasonally adjusted.   *Source: Bureau of the Census, U.S. Department of Commerce*

Consumption Corn Oil, in Refining, in the United States   In Millions of Pounds

Year	Oct.	Nov.	Dec.	Jan.	Feb.	Mar.	Apr.	May	June	July	Aug.	Sept.	Total
1994-5	103.5	107.2	116.9	100.7	92.3	109.9	97.3	95.6	108.9	97.2	78.2	95.5	1,203
1995-6	82.9	97.9	102.0	78.6	91.6	100.0	84.8	90.0	90.5	74.5	66.5	90.2	1,049
1996-7	82.0	83.0	84.7	69.7	71.0	79.5	71.4	76.1	80.4	86.9	90.8	58.5	934
1997-8	87.5	83.8	100.6	83.0	89.2	100.5	92.5	100.5	104.2	90.6	101.7	94.6	1,129
1998-9	106.6	104.4	105.0	82.0	W	102.0	94.6	101.7	104.3	90.1	97.0	103.5	1,190
1999-00	96.2	97.1	114.7	94.9	89.2	W	W	W	W	W	134.2	129.6	1,296
2000-1[1]	136.2	112.2	129.3										1,511

[1] Preliminary.   W = Withheld proprietary data.   *Source: Bureau of Census, U.S. Department of Commerce*

Average Corn Oil Price, Wet Mill in Chicago   In Cents Per Pound

Year	Oct.	Nov.	Dec.	Jan.	Feb.	Mar.	Apr.	May	June	July	Aug.	Sept.	Average
1994-5	24.73	24.75	24.75	28.01	27.26	28.17	27.30	26.42	26.61	27.38	26.35	25.93	26.47
1995-6	26.05	25.54	24.99	24.52	24.30	24.34	25.60	27.98	25.66	25.46	24.33	24.14	25.24
1996-7	22.67	21.96	22.27	23.39	23.97	24.38	24.60	24.66	24.82	25.34	25.36	25.15	24.05
1997-8	25.20	26.25	26.28	26.04	27.31	28.50	30.93	33.20	32.82	31.52	29.93	29.25	28.94
1998-9	29.46	29.65	29.88	29.15	26.58	23.01	23.08	22.96	22.95	22.43	22.41	22.08	25.30
1999-00	21.97	21.96	21.68	20.81	20.06	19.28	18.32	16.63	14.57	13.55	13.03	11.85	17.81
2000-1[1]	10.52	10.37	10.54	10.25									10.42

[1] Preliminary.   *Source: Economic Research Service, U.S. Department of Agriculture (ERS-USDA)*

Cotton

U.S. cotton production in the 2000/2001 (August-July) season was forecast by the U.S.D.A. at 17.4 million bales. This was an increase of 400,000 bales from the previous season. Production of upland cotton was forecast to be 17 million bales compared to 16.3 million bales in the 1999/00 season. Production of extra-long staple cotton was forecast at a five year low of 410,000 bales.

The U.S. Cotton Belt is divided into four regions. The U.S.D.A. indicated that upland cotton production was projected to increase in three of the four regions. The Southwest region was expected to be lower than a year ago. The Southwest crop was forecast to be 4.3 million bales, down about one million bales from last season. The crop was damaged by drought and the cotton yield in the Southwest was expected to be 410 pounds per harvested acre, the lowest yield since 1995.

In the Southeast region, upland cotton production was expected to increase 17 percent from the 1999/00 season to almost 4.2 million bales. The large producers are Georgia and North Carolina. Last season the North Carolina crop was severely damaged by a late season hurricane. The crop rebounded this season. The average yield in the Southeast in 2000/01 is expected to be 629 pounds, up 100 pounds from the previous season.

The Delta region was expected to produce 5.4 million bales of upland cotton, up 5 percent from 1999. The production increase was due to more acreage being harvested. The Delta yield was 662 pounds per harvested acre, below the five year average.

In the West, the upland cotton crop was estimated to be 3.1 million bales, the largest crop in three years. Acreage increased and the average yield was a record 1,305 pounds. One notable change in California was the decline in extra-long staple cotton production which fell 40 percent as acreage was shifted out.

U.S. planted cotton acreage in 2000/01 was 15.53 million acres, up 4 percent from the previous year. Harvested cotton acreage in 2000/01 was 13.5 million acres, up slightly from 13.42 million in 1999/00. In 2000/01, some 13 percent of the acreage was abandoned compared to 10 percent the previous year. The national average cotton yield was 619 pounds per harvested acre, up from 607 pounds in 1999/00. The five year average is 629 pounds. The largest cotton producing states are Texas, California, Mississippi, Georgia, Arkansas, and North Carolina.

For the 2000/01 season, the U.S.D.A. sully and use report for December indicated that cotton stocks at the beginning of the season were 3.92 million bales. These were virtually the same as a year ago. With the crop of 17.4 million bales and minimal imports of 80,000 bales, the total U.S. supply of cotton in 2000/01 was 21.4 million bales, some 400,000 bales more than a year ago.

The U.S.D.A. estimated domestic use of cotton in 2000/01 to be 9.9 million bales, down 3 percent from last season. Domestic use of cotton by textile mills is related to a number of fundamental factors. The overall strength and direction of the U.S. economy is the most important factor. Cotton is an industrial commodity and its use is closely related to the overall health of the national economy. When the U.S. economy is growing and is strong with prospects for further growth, use of cotton tends to increase. If the economy slows or is in recession, use of cotton declines. Another factor is the direction of interest rates which affect a host of industries. In 2001, interest rates could decline further which may stimulate the housing sector which would increase the use of cotton. Cotton finds much use in household goods like towels and sheets. A slowing economy is likely to reduce purchases of apparel which would work against the increased use of the natural fiber. The U.S. textile industry has been pressured by increased imports of cotton textile products. The North American Free Trade Agreement (NAFTA) has increased textile trade, but the strength of the dollar has increased shipments of textiles to the U.S. and the U.S.D.A. has estimated that calendar 2000 cotton textile imports into the U.S. would reach the equivalent of 16 million bales.

The U.S.D.A. forecast cotton exports at 7.6 million bales, an increase of 13 percent from 1999/00 exports of 6.75 million bales, and 75 percent higher than the 1998/99 season exports of 4.34 million bales. The 2000/01 season presents some opportunities for U.S. exporters as a number of cotton crops in foreign countries are smaller. The U.S.D.A. forecast world production of cotton at 86.6 million bales, down 1 percent from last season. The largest producer of cotton is China with the 2000/01 crop forecast at 18 million bales, some 2 percent more than last season. Pakistan's cotton output was estimated at 8.3 million bales, down 3 percent from last year. India's crop of 11.9 million bales was 3 percent less than in 1999/00. Uzbekistan's cotton crop was damaged by rain during the harvest and was estimated at 4.3 million bales, down 17 percent from the previous year. Other large producers are Turkey, Brazil, and Australia.

Total use of cotton (domestic and exports) by the U.S. in 2000/01 was forecast by the U.S.D.A to be 17.5 million bales, up 3 percent from last season. Projected ending stocks of cotton are 3.9 million bales, virtually the same as a year ago. In late December, the U.S. Census Bureau estimated that in the month of November U.S. textile mills used cotton at a seasonally adjusted daily rate of 33,665 bales, down from 35,073 bales in October. The National Cotton Council estimated that the seasonally adjusted annual rate of cotton use in November was 9.12 million bales. Mill use of cotton declined in part due to lower retail sales of cotton goods.

Futures Markets

Cotton futures and options are traded on the New York Cotton Exchange, a division of the New York Board of Trade. Cotton futures are traded on the Bolsa de Mercadorias & Futuros (BM&F). Cotton yarn futures are traded on the Chuba Commodity Exchange (CCOM), the Osaka Mercantile Exchange (OME), and the Tokyo Commodity Exchange (ToCom).

Supply and Distribution of All Cotton in the United States   In Thousands of 480-Pound Bales

Crop Year Beginning Aug. 1	Acre Planted (1,000 Acres)	Acre Harvested (1,000 Acres)	Yield Lbs./acre	Supply Beginning Stocks[3]	Supply Pro-duction[4]	Supply Imports	Supply Total	Disappearance Mill Use	Disappearance Exports	Disappearance Total	Unac-counted	Ending Stocks	Farm Price[5] -- Cents per Lb. --	"A" Index Price[6] -- Cents per Lb. --	Value of Pro-duction Million $
1991-2	14,052	12,960	652	2,344	17,614	13	19,971	9,613	6,646	16,259	-8	3,704	58.1	62.90	4,913.2
1992-3	13,240	11,143	699	3,704	16,219	1	19,923	10,250	5,201	15,451	190	4,662	54.9	56.87	4,273.9
1993-4	13,438	12,783	606	4,662	16,134	6	20,802	10,418	6,862	17,280	8	3,530	58.4	70.75	4,520.9
1994-5	13,720	13,322	708	3,530	19,662	20	23,212	11,198	9,402	20,600	38	2,650	72.0	92.66	6,796.7
1995-6	16,931	16,007	537	2,650	17,900	408	20,958	10,604	7,675	18,322	-27	2,609	76.5	85.61	6,574.6
1996-7	14,653	12,888	705	2,609	18,942	403	21,954	11,126	6,865	17,991	8	3,971	70.5	78.66	6,408.1
1997-8	13,898	13,406	673	3,971	18,793	13	22,777	11,349	7,500	18,849	-41	3,887	66.2	72.11	5,975.6
1998-9	13,393	10,684	625	3,887	13,918	443	18,248	10,401	4,344	14,745	436	3,939	61.7	58.97	4,119.9
1999-00[1]	14,874	13,425	607	3,939	16,968	97	21,004	10,240	6,750	16,990	-92	3,922	46.6	52.85	3,836.5
2000-1[2]	15,532	13,519	622	3,922	17,510	75	21,507	10,000	7,600	17,600	-7	3,900			4,780.7

[1] Preliminary.   [2] Estimate.   [3] Excludes preseason ginnings (adjusted to 480-lb. bale net weight basis).   [4] Includes preseason ginnings.
[5] Marketing year average price.   [6] Average of 5 cheapest types of SLM 1 3/32 staple length cotton *offered on the European market.*
Source: Economic Research Service, U.S. Department of Agriculture (ERS-USDA)

World Production of All Cotton   In Thousands of 480-Pound Bales

Crop Year Beginning Aug. 1	Argen-tina	Brazil	China	Egypt	India	Iran	Mexico	Pakistan	Sudan	Turkey	United States	Uzbek-istan	World Total
1991-2	1,148	3,445	26,100	1,338	9,291	542	898	10,000	386	2,578	17,614	6,628	95,752
1992-3	666	2,113	20,700	1,620	10,775	464	147	7,073	276	2,635	16,218	5,851	82,505
1993-4	1,079	1,860	17,200	1,909	9,800	418	122	6,282	216	2,766	16,134	6,067	77,049
1994-5	1,608	2,526	19,900	1,170	11,148	762	460	6,250	400	2,886	19,662	5,778	85,857
1995-6	1,929	1,791	21,900	1,088	13,250	800	974	8,200	490	3,911	17,900	5,740	93,063
1996-7	1,493	1,286	19,300	1,568	13,918	825	1,078	7,323	460	3,600	18,942	4,813	89,589
1997-8	1,406	1,745	21,100	1,532	12,337	600	984	7,175	400	3,651	18,793	5,228	91,570
1998-9	920	2,100	20,700	1,050	12,883	638	1,039	6,300	250	3,860	13,918	4,600	84,879
1999-00[1]	615	3,100	17,600	1,050	12,337	650	669	8,600	240	3,634	16,968	5,180	87,357
2000-1[2]	925	3,700	18,000	850	11,900	650	360	8,300	250	3,700	17,399	4,300	86,633

[1] Preliminary.   [2] Estimate.   *Source: Foreign Agricultural Service, U.S. Department of Agriculture (FAS-USDA)*

World Stocks and Trade of Cotton   In Thousands of 480-Pound Bales

Crop Year Beginning Aug. 1	Beginning Stocks United States	Beginning Stocks Uzbek-istan	Beginning Stocks China	Beginning Stocks World Total	Imports Indo-nesia	Imports Mexico	Imports Russia	Imports Turkey	Imports World Total	Exports United States	Exports Uzbek-istan	Exports China	Exports World Total
1991-2	2,344	1,555	5,956	27,796	1,873	300	3,900	420	29,095	6,646	5,200	602	28,225
1992-3	3,704	2,133	11,934	37,580	1,989	656	2,650	1,070	26,945	5,201	5,500	684	25,579
1993-4	4,662	1,534	9,692	34,713	2,039	794	3,000	545	27,728	6,862	5,800	749	26,816
1994-5	3,530	1,006	5,251	26,758	2,075	580	2,159	1,060	30,618	9,402	5,006	183	28,452
1995-6	4,028	956	8,828	29,884	2,139	695	1,100	574	27,529	7,675	4,524	21	27,359
1996-7	2,609	1,304	14,052	36,614	2,147	900	1,000	1,150	28,763	6,865	4,550	10	26,494
1997-8	3,971	822	16,655	40,059	1,923	1,600	1,225	1,450	26,488	7,500	4,570	34	26,590
1998-9	3,887	635	19,955	43,684	2,329	1,488	850	1,139	25,248	4,344	3,812	681	23,649
1999-00[1]	3,939	603	21,133	44,886	2,076	1,850	1,600	2,400	28,281	6,800	4,100	1,700	27,281
2000-1[2]	3,922	838	14,953	41,151	2,100	2,100	1,650	1,850	27,172	7,900	3,600	700	27,450

[1] Preliminary.   [2] Estimate.   *Source: Foreign Agricultural Service, U.S. Department of Agriculture (FAS-USDA)*

World Consumption of All Cottons in Specified Countries   In Thousands of 480-Pound Bales

Year	Brazil	China	Egypt	France	Ger-many	India	Italy	Japan	Mexico	Pakistan	United States	Uzbek-istan	World Total
1991-2	3,215	20,850	1,463	483	790	8,648	1,447	2,783	772	6,482	9,613	860	86,135
1992-3	3,445	21,900	1,641	463	788	9,808	1,432	2,301	736	6,634	10,250	950	86,061
1993-4	3,950	21,400	1,343	516	781	9,840	1,594	2,071	838	6,725	10,418	800	85,453
1994-5	3,996	20,200	1,140	532	660	10,545	1,539	1,754	890	6,750	11,198	827	84,758
1995-6	3,904	19,700	1,010	484	606	11,977	1,539	1,529	1,100	7,200	10,647	873	86,040
1996-7	3,900	20,300	919	536	640	13,120	1,562	1,401	1,600	7,000	11,126	750	88,021
1997-8	3,400	19,600	1,033	505	650	12,675	1,612	1,400	1,950	7,187	11,349	850	87,157
1998-9	3,900	19,200	950	495	575	12,620	1,400	1,250	2,150	7,000	10,401	825	85,350
1999-00[1]	4,100	22,200	850	500	650	13,500	1,300	1,280	2,400	7,650	10,240	850	91,896
2000-1[2]	4,350	22,500	800	485	675	13,400	1,400	1,150	2,300	8,000	9,900	900	92,256

[1] Preliminary.   [2] Estimate.   *Source: Foreign Agricultural Service, U.S. Department of Agriculture (FAS-USDA)*

COTTON

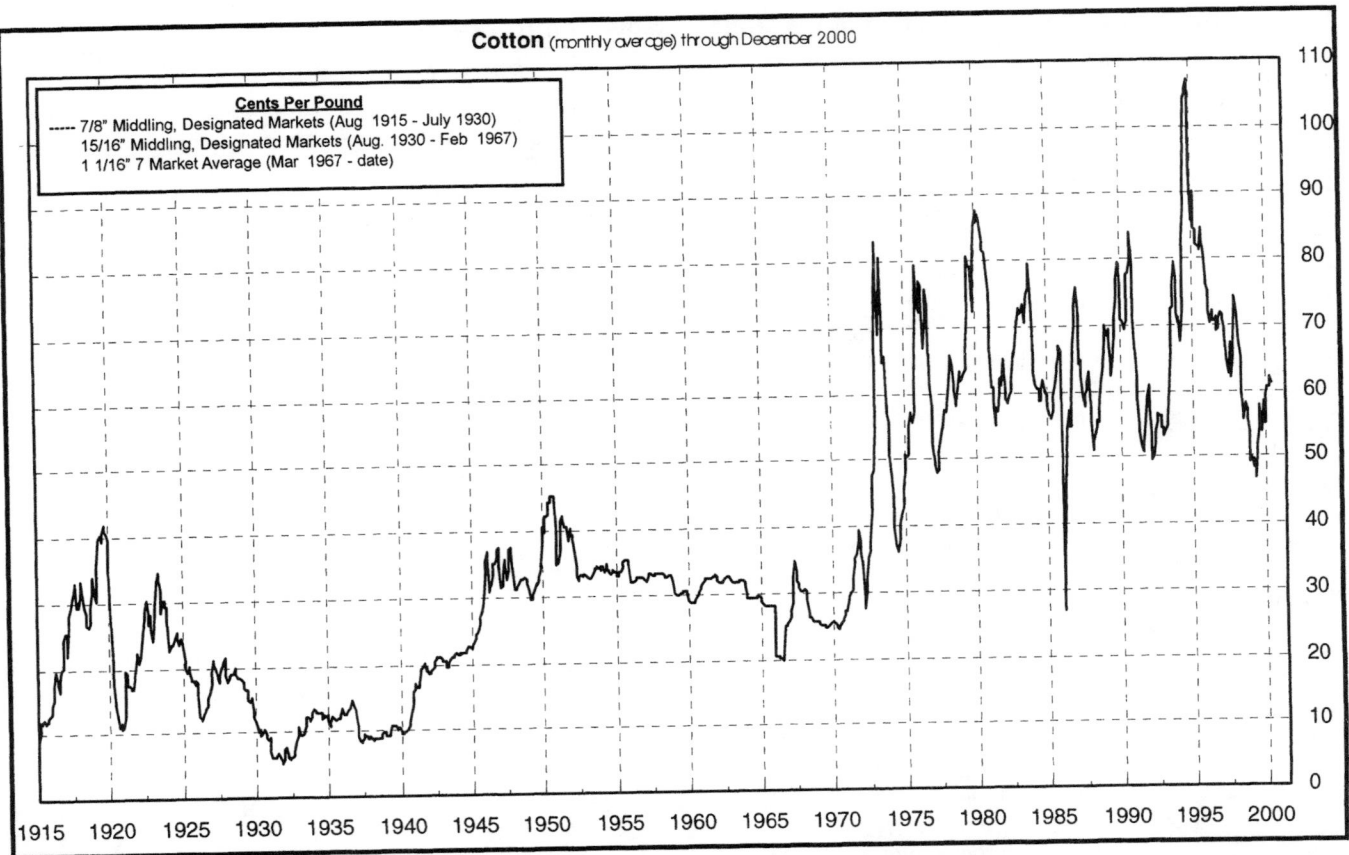

Cotton (monthly average) through December 2000

Cents Per Pound
----- 7/8" Middling, Designated Markets (Aug 1915 - July 1930)
15/16" Middling, Designated Markets (Aug. 1930 - Feb 1967)
1 1/16" 7 Market Average (Mar 1967 - date)

Average Spot Cotton Prices[2], C.I.F. Northern Europe   In U.S. Cents Per Pound

Crop Year Beginning Aug. 1	Argentina "C"[3] 1 1/16"	Australia M 1 3/32"	Cotlook Index A	Cotlook Index B	Egypt Giza[4] 81	Greece M 1 3/32"	Mexico[5] M 1 3/32"	Pakistan Sind/ Punjab[6]	Tanzania AR[7] Type 3	Turkey Izmir[8] 1 3/32"	U.S. Calif. ACALA SJV[9]	U.S. Memphis Terr.[10] M 1 3/32"	U.S. Orleans/ Texas[11] M 1 1/32"
1990-1	77.06	85.58	82.90	77.80	177.43	84.24	84.46	77.19	89.62	81.32	92.84	88.13	80.35
1991-2	55.08	65.97	63.05	58.50	128.10	65.90	68.19	58.14	68.90	74.66	74.47	66.35	63.41
1992-3	64.31	64.01	57.70	53.70	99.24	56.92	----	52.66	62.24	----	68.37	63.08	58.89
1993-4	80.20	72.81	70.60	67.30	88.35	58.81	----	54.42	69.83	59.80	77.55	72.80	69.78
1994-5	101.88	81.05	92.75	92.40	93.70	88.64	82.65	73.75	----	----	106.40	98.67	95.70
1995-6	82.98	93.75	85.61	81.06	----	84.95	94.94	81.86	96.20	90.38	103.49	94.71	90.37
1996-7	79.71	83.24	78.59	74.80	----	75.85	79.60	73.37	79.22	----	89.55	82.81	79.77
1997-8	69.96	77.49	72.19	70.69	----	72.03	81.70	72.93	84.04	----	85.11	78.12	74.74
1998-9	57.19	66.48	58.91	54.26	----	58.66	65.78	----	72.70	----	78.57	73.65	70.95
1999-00[1]	----	61.97	52.80	49.55	----	51.71	56.43	----	55.67	----	68.76	60.22	55.67

[1] Preliminary.   [2] Generally for prompt shipment.   [3] 1 1/32 prior to January 20, 1984; 1 1/16 since.   [4] Dendera until 1969/70; Giza 67 1969/70 until December 1983; Giza 69/75/81 until November 1990; Giza 81 since.   [5] S. Brazil Type 5, 1 1/32 prior to 1968-69; 1 1/16 until 1987/88; Brazilian Type 5/6, 1 1/16 since.   [6] Punjab until 1979/80; Sind SG until June 1984; Sind/Punjab SG until January 1985; Afzal 1 until January 1986; Afzal 1 1/32 since.   [7] No. 1 until 1978/79; No. 1/2 until February 1986; AR' Mwanza No. 3 until January 1992; AR' Type 3 since.   [8] Izmir ST 1 White 1 1/16 RG prior to 1981/82; 1 3/32 from 1981/82 until January 1987; Izmir/Antalya ST 1 White -3/32 RG since.   [9] SM 1 3/32 prior to 1975/76; SM 1 1/8 since.   [10] SM 1 1/16 prior to 1981/82; Middling 1 3/32 since.   [11] Middling 1 prior to 1988/89; Middling 1 1/32 since.   *Source: International Cotton Advisory Committee*

Average Producer Price Index of Gray Cotton Broadwovens   Index 1982 = 100

Year	Jan.	Feb.	Mar.	Apr.	May	June	July	Aug.	Sept.	Oct.	Nov.	Dec.	Average
1991	113.3	113.6	114.1	114.5	114.9	115.2	115.3	115.3	115.3	115.4	115.7	115.6	114.9
1992	116.9	116.8	116.7	116.7	116.8	117.5	117.3	117.3	117.2	116.9	117.1	117.2	117.0
1993	117.0	116.8	115.9	116.3	115.7	115.7	115.2	115.2	112.5	114.1	114.1	114.9	115.3
1994	109.9	110.8	115.4	115.7	114.9	114.9	115.0	117.5	117.6	118.9	117.2	118.0	116.2
1995	117.8	120.2	120.7	121.6	123.4	123.6	124.1	125.4	125.3	123.7	123.7	123.8	122.6
1996	123.6	123.7	122.0	122.0	121.1	120.7	120.7	119.9	119.7	120.4	120.0	121.2	121.2
1997	120.3	120.8	120.7	120.8	121.2	120.6	121.4	121.6	121.4	120.8	121.6	121.2	121.0
1998	122.8	122.0	122.1	121.5	121.8	120.8	120.0	119.1	118.8	118.1	117.3	117.8	120.2
1999	117.1	117.3	118.8	116.5	116.4	116.1	116.5	112.9	112.9	113.1	112.6	108.6	114.9
2000[1]	112.1	111.1	106.9	108.2	108.6	107.7	108.3	108.8	110.1	110.3	112.2	112.3	109.7

[1] Preliminary.   *Source: Bureau of Labor Statistics (0337-01), U.S. Department of Commerce*

Average Price of Strict Low Midd. 11/16,Cotton at Designated U.S. Mkts   In Cents Per Pound (Net Weight)

Year	Aug.	Sept.	Oct.	Nov.	Dec.	Jan.	Feb.	Mar.	Apr.	May	June	July	Average
1991-2	66.44	62.39	58.28	54.70	53.89	51.54	50.76	52.01	54.97	55.45	58.82	60.93	56.68
1992-3	57.56	53.49	49.47	49.98	51.85	53.72	55.38	56.45	56.17	56.37	54.38	54.35	54.10
1993-4	53.04	54.01	54.58	55.61	60.29	66.53	72.69	72.74	76.12	79.30	76.85	71.71	66.12
1994-5	70.32	71.10	67.58	72.00	81.92	88.11	91.89	104.20	104.94	105.38	106.96	93.26	88.14
1995-6	85.90	90.00	84.65	84.16	82.18	81.81	81.56	81.13	84.69	83.22	80.23	76.84	83.03
1996-7	76.15	75.24	72.21	70.12	71.98	70.53	70.53	71.12	69.09	69.30	71.03	71.83	71.59
1997-8	71.61	70.75	69.46	68.90	64.57	62.75	63.66	67.04	61.88	65.21	73.50	74.18	67.79
1998-9	71.87	71.75	67.61	64.95	59.88	56.20	55.46	58.17	57.01	55.54	53.74	49.23	60.12
1999-00	49.72	48.39	49.46	48.12	46.65	51.92	54.29	57.67	53.76	58.31	54.97	55.13	52.36
2000-1[1]	59.33	60.62	60.54	62.16	61.04	56.66							60.06

[1] Preliminary.   [2] Grade 41, leaf 4, staple 34, mike 35-36 and 43-49 , strength 23.5-26.4.   *Source: Agricultural Marketing Service, U.S. Department of Agriculture (AMS-USDA)*

Average Spot Cotton, 1 3/32 , Price (SLM) at Designated U.S. Markets   In Cents Per Pound (Net Weight)

Year	Aug.	Sept.	Oct.	Nov.	Dec.	Jan.	Feb.	Mar.	Apr.	May	June	July	Average
1991-2	68.24	64.18	59.74	55.57	54.62	52.39	51.84	53.11	56.30	56.90	60.26	62.35	57.96
1992-3	59.08	54.99	50.96	51.41	53.37	55.24	56.86	58.30	58.03	58.23	56.24	56.22	55.74
1993-4	54.89	55.90	56.46	57.34	61.76	67.97	73.99	74.15	77.55	80.42	78.01	72.97	67.62
1994-5	71.46	72.42	68.82	73.38	83.41	89.92	94.25	106.66	107.50	107.93	109.52	96.31	90.13
1995-6	88.31	92.71	87.06	86.43	84.25	84.32	84.04	83.65	87.25	85.90	82.71	78.86	85.46
1996-7	77.97	76.92	73.90	71.74	75.75	72.53	72.86	73.60	71.23	71.38	73.25	74.04	73.76
1997-8	73.69	72.64	71.13	70.35	66.30	64.55	65.78	69.25	64.31	67.66	76.02	76.63	69.86
1998-9	73.93	73.75	69.90	67.18	62.18	58.56	58.27	61.34	60.33	58.89	56.85	52.61	62.82
1999-00	52.90	51.27	52.43	51.51	49.73	55.02	57.38	61.02	57.52	63.09	59.28	58.80	55.83
2000-1[2]	62.60	63.62	63.13	65.08	64.73	60.18							63.22

[1] Preliminary.   *Source: Agricultural Marketing Service, U.S. Department of Agriculture (AMS-USDA)*

Average Spot Prices of U.S. Cotton[1], Base Quality (SLM) at Designated Markets   In Cents Per Pound

Crop Year Beginning Aug. 1	Dallas (East Tex.-Okl.)	Fresno (San Joaquin Valley)	Greenville (South-east)	Greenwood (South Delta)	Lubbock (West Texas)	Memphis (North Delta)	Phoenix Desert (South-west)	Average
1990-1	71.40	78.30	75.90	75.53	71.09	75.49	75.90	74.80
1991-2	55.63	57.50	57.70	56.21	55.79	56.18	57.77	56.68
1992-3	53.78	52.84	56.73	55.03	53.53	55.03	51.61	54.10
1993-4[2]	66.22	65.04	67.46	67.04	65.92	67.04	64.16	66.13
1994-5	86.96	93.73	87.17	87.25	86.66	87.25	87.96	88.14
1995-6	80.89	87.40	83.86	83.76	80.64	83.76	80.90	83.03
1996-7	70.29	74.47	72.33	72.11	69.89	72.11	69.88	71.58
1997-8	65.93	71.79	68.60	68.36	65.88	68.36	65.63	67.79
1998-9	57.66	63.78	62.06	61.82	57.76	61.82	55.92	60.12
1999-00[3]	50.49	56.67	53.81	53.34	50.12	53.34	48.79	52.36

[1] Prices are for mixed lots, net weight, uncompressed in warehouse.   [2] 1993 prices are for mixed lots, net weight, compressed, FOB car/truck.
[3] Preliminary.   *Source: Agricultural Marketing Service, U.S. Department of Agriculture (AMS-USDA)*

Average Price[1] Received by Farmers for Upland Cotton in the United States   In Cents Per Pound

Year	Aug.	Sept.	Oct.	Nov.	Dec.	Jan.	Feb.	Mar.	Apr.	May	June	July	Average
1991-2	66.3	64.9	62.9	61.2	55.7	51.7	49.8	50.3	53.1	53.2	58.0	56.3	56.8
1992-3	52.7	52.8	53.9	52.7	54.3	53.0	53.8	56.3	55.1	53.6	58.0	56.3	56.8
1993-4	52.4	51.4	52.4	53.3	56.5	62.7	65.7	66.6	67.5	69.0	63.3	58.7	58.1
1994-5	66.8	65.9	66.2	68.5	73.3	78.7	80.2	82.6	77.6	76.2	86.5	80.1	72.0
1995-6	72.2	74.8	74.2	75.0	75.7	76.4	75.7	76.8	78.9	76.7	76.9	73.6	75.4
1996-7	71.9	71.6	71.5	69.7	69.3	67.9	68.1	69.3	67.6	68.3	67.1	67.5	69.3
1997-8	67.0	69.6	69.4	67.9	63.8	61.1	62.5	63.9	63.6	63.5	69.7	68.0	65.2
1998-9	66.0	66.2	65.9	64.6	60.6	58.1	55.6	55.1	55.6	55.0	54.6	53.8	60.2
1999-00	53.0	46.2	45.9	44.7	43.0	43.1	45.9	47.9	46.0	47.3	46.4	49.1	44.9
2000-1[2]	51.3	50.6	55.9	58.0	58.0	53.8							54.6

[1] Weighted average by sales.   [2] Preliminary.   *Source: Agricultural Marketing Service, U.S. Department of Agriculture (AMS-USDA)*

COTTON

Purchases Reported by Exchanges in Designated U.S. Spot Markets[1]   In Running Bales

Crop Year Beginning Aug. 1	Aug.	Sept.	Oct.	Nov.	Dec.	Jan.	Feb.	Mar.	Apr.	May	June	July	Market Total
1991-2	50,469	55,637	179,671	347,393	776,233	1,043,190	1,063,959	699,026	302,102	110,764	134,500	105,795	4,868,739
1992-3	81,778	233,424	325,600	853,846	1,049,780	1,321,861	317,451	330,381	224,874	208,962	189,401	231,390	5,368,748
1993-4	143,237	173,896	321,119	1,071,518	1,213,655	500,246	602,766	318,008	234,331	318,244	83,083	40,699	5,020,802
1994-5	92,401	98,251	426,371	1,075,829	1,491,429	608,701	233,159	149,762	49,192	44,228	43,821	13,244	4,326,388
1995-6	60,442	38,855	73,857	209,279	381,943	765,502	153,758	241,197	225,797	73,459	59,042	31,324	2,314,455
1996-7	62,884	73,925	148,337	477,331	613,430	696,494	412,095	242,606	72,234	130,163	201,557	93,205	3,224,261
1997-8	48,504	106,503	323,400	367,010	617,470	655,432	482,625	396,946	92,072	210,906	105,139	39,647	3,445,654
1998-9	27,193	52,066	114,998	229,743	498,082	414,832	191,872	236,762	71,993	63,335	62,192	64,092	2,027,160
1999-00	83,564	95,241	195,370	320,434	517,579	744,400	294,843	189,460	89,473	129,879	49,012	33,942	2,743,197
2000-1	63,607	69,083	143,938	323,891	288,242	217,755							2,213,032

[1] seven markets.   *Source: Agricultural Marketing Service, U.S. Department of Agriculture (AMS-USDA)*

Production of Cotton (Upland and American-Pima) in the U.S.   In Thousands of 480-Pound Bales

Year	Ala-bama	Arizona	Arkan-sas	California	Georgia	Louis-iana	Missis-sippi	Missouri	North Carolina	South Carolina	Ten-nessee	Texas	Total American-Pima
1991	553	898	1,576	2,548	722	1,414	2,275	429	640	344	701	4,710	398.4
1992	621	725	1,681	2,817	744	1,299	2,131	541	468	226	834	3,265	508.3
1993	469	790	1,094	2,918	733	1,105	1,550	376	429	204	545	5,095	369.3
1994	726	862	1,772	2,902	1,537	1,512	2,132	615	829	393	885	4,968	337.7
1995	492	793	1,468	2,312	1,941	1,375	1,841	513	798	376	724	4,460	367.6
1996	789	778	1,636	2,390	2,079	1,286	1,876	591	1,002	455	675	4,345	528.5
1997	550	847	1,683	2,191	1,919	986	1,821	565	930	410	662	5,140	548.0
1998	553	608	1,209	1,146	1,542	641	1,444	350	1,026	350	546	3,600	442.3
1999[1]	625	716	1,428	1,580	1,567	901	1,731	472	816	281	595	5,050	674.3
2000[2]	540	760	1,450	2,200	1,640	910	1,730	540	1,440	380	715	3,950	397.5

[1] Preliminary.   [2] Forecasted.   *Source: Agricultural Statistics Board, U.S. Department of Agriculture (ASB-USDA)*

Cotton Production and Yield Estimates

Year	Forecast of Production (1,000 Bales of 480 Lbs.[1]) Aug. 1	Sept. 1	Oct. 1	Nov. 1	Dec. 1	Jan. 1	Actual Crop	Forecasts of Yield (Lbs. Per Harvested Acre) Aug. 1	Sept. 1	Oct. 1	Nov. 1	Dec. 1	Jan. 1	Actual Crop
1991	17,648	17,868	17,614	13,429	14,052	17,542	17,614	630	638	620	635	630	656	652
1992	16,533	16,943	15,885	16,204	16,259	16,260	16,219	696	685	694	698	696	700	699
1993	18,545	17,867	17,014	16,297	16,284	16,176	16,134	668	645	614	594	597	607	606
1994	19,195	19,025	19,303	19,453	19,573	19,728	19,662	690	690	690	695	699	710	708
1995	21,811	20,266	18,771	18,838	18,236	17,971	17,900	663	615	574	567	551	540	537
1996	18,577	17,900	18,189	18,594	18,738	18,951	18,942	686	661	673	698	704	709	705
1997	17,783	18,418	18,410	18,848	18,819	18,977	18,793	637	658	665	673	672	686	673
1998	14,263	13,563	13,288	13,231	13,452	----	13,918	640	614	616	612	621	----	625
1999	18,304	17,535	16,430	16,531	16,875	----	16,968	649	621	588	592	604	----	607
2000	19,159	18,315	17,485	17,510	17,399	----	17,220	648	622	620	622	619	----	631

[1] Net weight bales.   *Source: Agricultural Statistics Board, U.S. Department of Agriculture (ASB-USDA)*

Supply and Distribution of Upland Cotton in the United States   In Thousands of 480-Pound Bales

Crop Year Beginning Aug. 1	Area Planted (1,000 Acres)	Harvested (1,000 Acres)	Yield Lbs./Acre	Supply Beginning Stocks[3]	Pro-duction[4]	Imports	Total	Disappearance Mill Use	Exports	Total	Ending Stocks	Farm Price[5] Cents/Lb.
1991-2	13,802	12,716	650	2,262	17,216	13	19,491	9,548	6,348	15,896	3,583	56.8
1992-3	12,977	10,863	694	3,583	15,710	1	19,294	10,190	4,869	15,059	4,456	53.7
1993-4	13,248	12,594	601	4,456	15,764	6	20,226	10,346	6,555	16,901	3,303	58.4
1994-5	13,552	13,156	705	3,303	19,324	18	22,645	11,109	8,978	20,087	2,588	72.0
1995-6	16,717	15,796	533	2,588	17,532	400	20,520	10,538	7,375	17,913	2,543	75.4
1996-7	14,376	12,612	701	2,543	18,413	403	21,359	11,020	6,399	17,419	3,920	69.3
1997-8	13,648	13,157	666	3,920	18,245	13	22,178	11,234	7,060	18,294	3,822	65.2
1998-9	13,064	10,449	619	3,822	13,476	431	17,729	10,254	4,056	14,310	3,836	60.2
1999-00[1]	14,584	13,138	595	3,836	16,294	53	20,183	10,103	6,303	16,406	3,672	45.0
2000-1[2]	15,350	13,347	615	3,672	17,904	55	20,821	9,865	7,125	16,990	3,814	

[1] Preliminary.   [2] Estimate.   [3] Excludes preseason ginnings (adjusted to 480-lb. bale net weight basis).   [4] Includes preseason ginnings.   [5] Marketing year average price.   [6] Average of 5 cheapest types of SLM 1 3/32 staple length cotton offered on the European market.   *Source: Economic Research Service, U.S. Department of Agriculture (ERS-USDA)*

Cotton Futures - New York Board of Trade (weekly close) as of 29-Dec-2000

Cents per pound

Average Open Interest of No. 2 Cotton Futures in New York   In Contracts

Year	Jan.	Feb.	Mar.	Apr.	May	June	July	Aug.	Sept.	Oct.	Nov.	Dec.
1991	43,003	46,793	44,001	43,957	50,086	46,637	40,924	39,616	38,252	39,772	39,295	36,066
1992	38,097	40,095	38,592	36,228	37,839	36,861	35,891	42,241	46,168	46,577	40,425	38,487
1993	41,946	38,657	38,576	33,641	33,012	34,057	32,118	33,872	37,393	36,479	38,567	45,975
1994	54,424	55,558	53,724	54,670	52,830	51,001	52,357	50,597	50,955	51,561	53,563	59,065
1995	71,353	75,100	79,090	71,488	71,714	68,159	65,656	69,653	69,528	65,768	38,475	35,996
1996	58,001	60,231	57,542	61,795	64,555	62,342	61,921	60,182	58,168	58,415	57,397	47,652
1997	59,909	65,392	72,130	76,779	73,464	70,296	73,893	79,309	87,134	92,430	89,150	87,120
1998	89,358	86,739	81,236	85,505	84,562	90,178	81,652	78,571	85,378	88,970	88,917	77,873
1999	79,598	75,794	62,857	60,384	61,470	66,789	68,975	65,690	63,976	60,369	63,746	61,474
2000	63,987	67,720	69,788	56,038	54,058	48,024	53,621	63,069	73,735	67,767	65,017	62,931

Source: New York Board of Trade (NYBOT)

Volume of Trading of No. 2 Cotton Futures in New York   In Contracts

Year	Jan.	Feb.	Mar.	Apr.	May	June	July	Aug.	Sept.	Oct.	Nov.	Dec.	Total
1991	133,415	179,656	148,918	156,978	174,690	122,242	116,458	115,175	107,742	125,558	150,545	82,867	1,614,244
1992	134,531	134,184	149,711	167,778	173,128	153,194	105,534	142,323	144,844	129,680	161,194	105,157	1,701,258
1993	171,180	135,400	136,965	135,300	105,920	128,985	130,886	122,280	110,989	107,571	178,350	139,344	1,603,027
1994	210,011	207,421	210,363	252,614	179,591	208,945	161,688	128,879	140,574	179,604	205,936	203,021	2,289,998
1995	223,073	290,600	286,098	219,187	214,052	185,276	183,171	199,050	191,534	196,676	195,601	141,116	2,525,434
1996	215,882	196,225	147,393	251,786	236,684	264,047	131,183	177,430	166,629	229,305	229,281	128,010	2,373,855
1997	201,610	253,475	302,609	258,851	175,227	314,406	234,718	202,008	212,966	216,771	266,800	197,839	2,837,280
1998	221,308	289,222	310,075	362,688	218,595	407,922	226,138	230,752	195,690	303,849	272,775	161,816	3,200,830
1999	179,049	244,300	209,127	250,622	157,552	260,649	187,631	178,236	175,282	193,552	298,531	120,120	2,454,651
2000	270,792	279,566	248,017	220,222	232,947	272,023	147,878	175,707	154,735	172,875	242,013	180,982	2,597,757

Source: New York Board of Trade (NYBOT)

COTTON

Daily Rate of Upland Cotton Mill Consumption[2] on Cotton-System Spinning Spindles in the U.S.
In Thousands of Running Bales

Crop Year Beginning Aug. 1	Aug.	Sept.	Oct.	Nov.	Dec.	Jan.	Feb.	Mar.	Apr.	May	June	July	Average
1991-2	33.6	----	----	33.1	----	34.6	36.3	35.7	35.6	37.3	35.2	33.9	35.0
1992-3	38.5	37.8	39.7	37.6	31.5	39.1	39.5	38.8	38.7	39.4	37.8	34.5	37.8
1993-4	39.8	38.4	39.4	36.4	31.4	36.9	37.9	39.0	39.3	39.5	40.4	40.3	38.2
1994-5	41.0	41.4	41.1	41.8	41.7	42.6	42.1	42.4	41.1	40.2	39.2	37.2	41.0
1995-6	38.8	39.4	37.6	38.1	37.9	37.5	38.1	39.5	39.4	39.6	40.5	39.8	38.9
1996-7	40.5	40.7	40.5	41.5	41.1	41.3	40.4	39.4	41.0	41.0	40.9	42.5	40.9
1997-8	40.7	42.4	42.0	42.4	43.9	41.8	41.7	41.1	40.5	40.8	40.0	41.5	41.6
1998-9	39.3	38.7	39.9	37.4	37.5	38.6	38.2	37.9	37.8	37.5	37.7	36.8	38.1
1999-00	36.1	36.4	37.3	37.2	37.6	36.3	36.9	37.1	36.9	36.5	38.2	36.3	36.9
2000-1[1]	36.4	35.7	34.7	33.0	36.2								35.2

[1] Preliminary. [2] Not seasonally adjusted. Source: Bureau of the Census: U.S. Department of Commerce

Consumption of American and Foreign Cotton in the United States   In Thousands of Running Bales

Year	Aug.	Sept.	Oct.	Nov.	Dec.	Jan.	Feb.	Mar.	Apr.	May	June	July	Total
1991-2	2,215	----	----	2,199	----	870	730	898	718	752	885	682	9,949
1992-3	776	950	799	756	792	788	796	976	778	792	951	694	9,846
1993-4	801	965	792	731	790	743	785	999	806	830	1,032	744	10,019
1994-5	870	1,070	873	838	897	858	878	1,097	847	842	999	681	10,750
1995-6	829	1,020	798	761	801	744	787	1,029	810	824	1,040	731	10,216
1996-7	847	1,028	829	816	858	810	819	1,014	834	840	1,044	781	10,519
1997-8	868	1,100	872	855	951	848	861	1,068	839	854	1,017	770	10,902
1998-9	835	1,013	834	758	796	979	795	983	777	793	970	678	10,210
1999-00	762	949	793	757	801	736	769	966	772	771	990	670	9,735
2000-1[1]	766	929	741	663	762								9,269

[1] Preliminary. Source: Bureau of the Census, U.S. Department of Commerce

Exports of All Cotton[2] from the United States   In Thousands of Running Bales

Year	Aug.	Sept.	Oct.	Nov.	Dec.	Jan.	Feb.	Mar.	Apr.	May	June	July	Total
1991-2	219	126	239	396	674	961	725	791	787	535	430	466	6,349
1992-3	252	263	277	342	528	501	502	533	639	401	317	395	4,950
1993-4	287	248	345	405	571	738	512	743	761	854	770	626	6,860
1994-5	531	333	341	710	1,098	1,115	1,383	1,392	1,104	684	410	300	9,402
1995-6	315	245	452	733	1,230	1,262	1,295	777	576	343	263	183	7,675
1996-7	257	171	277	573	899	666	728	848	711	631	604	501	6,866
1997-8	458	299	400	581	774	734	777	888	669	477	574	571	7,202
1998-9	402	280	265	795	1,027	156	182	221	169	256	260	330	4,344
1999-00	254	146	167	455	654	658	736	978	708	659	508	479	6,402
2000-1[1]	430	336	382										4,592

[1] Preliminary. Source: Foreign Agricultural Service, U.S. Department of Agriculture (FAS-USDA)

U.S. Exports of American Cotton to Countries of Destination   In Thousands of 480-Pound Bales

Crop Year Beginning Aug. 1	Canada	China	Hong Kong	Indo-nesia	Italy	Japan	Rep. of Korea	Mexico	Philip-pines	Taiwan	Thai-land	United Kingdom	Total
1990-1	191	1,233	306	561	425	1,437	1,168	202	132	358	317	36	7,793
1991-2	181	792	335	739	240	1,107	1,024	213	181	380	368	60	6,646
1992-3	154	1	100	429	144	839	1,031	557	117	279	150	65	5,201
1993-4	165	1,183	314	653	96	790	976	653	168	356	277	65	6,862
1994-5	253	2,257	347	925	83	1,061	951	558	173	352	441	89	9,402
1995-6	294	1,847	223	794	115	940	769	618	144	255	331	85	7,675
1996-7	253	1,756	129	594	46	630	568	733	84	255	197	66	6,865
1997-8	288	737	151	464	85	637	712	1,447	53	376	220	13	7,202
1998-9[1]	281	71	245	241	29	421	382	1,355	58	251	82	6	4,328
1999-00[2]	245	146	318	573	61	424	307	1,503	71	474	256	4	6,402

[1] Preliminary. [2] Estimate. Source: Foreign Agricultural Service, U.S. Department of Agriculture (FAS-USDA)

Cotton[1] Government Loan Program in the United States

Crop Year Beginning Aug. 1	Support Price -- Cents Per Lb. --	Target Price	Put Under Support Ths Bales	% of Production	Acquired ----- Ths. Bales -----	Owned July 31	Crop Year Beginning Aug. 1	Support Price -- Cents Per Lb. --	Target Price	Put Under Support Ths Bales	% of Production	Acquired ----- Ths. Bales -----	Owned July 31
1990-1	50.27	72.9	3,205	21.1	1	4	1995-6	51.92	72.9	3,478	19.8	0	0
1991-2	50.77	72.9	6,312	36.6	8	3	1996-7	51.92	NA	3,340	18.1	0	0
1992-3	52.35	72.9	8,302	52.9	10	8	1997-8	51.92	NA	4,281	23.5	0	0
1993-4	52.35	72.9	7,721	49.0	3	14	1998-9	51.92	NA	4,724	35.1	4	2,571
1994-5	50.00	72.9	4,716	24.4	3	3	1999-00[2]	51.92	NA				

[1] Upland. [2] Preliminary. [3] Less than 500 bales. NA = Not applicable. Source: Economic Research Service, U.S. Department of Agriculture (ERS-USDA)

Production of Cotton Cloth[1] in the United States   In Millions of Square Yards

Year	First Quarter	Second Quarter	Third Quarter	Fourth Quarter	Total Year	Year	First Quarter	Second Quarter	Third Quarter	Fourth Quarter	Total Year
1991	1,081	1,148	1,082	1,093	4,404	1996	1,182	1,230	1,198	1,187	4,796
1992	1,154	1,172	1,130	1,144	4,600	1997	1,211	1,276	1,283	1,309	5,078
1993	1,150	1,144	1,071	1,039	4,403	1998	1,226	1,167	1,218	1,142	4,753
1994	1,073	1,125	1,131	1,143	4,473	1999	1,170	1,164	1,078	1,039	4,451
1995	1,169	1,137	1,090	1,093	4,488	2000[2]	1,075	1,129	1,113		4,423

[1] Cotton broadwoven goods over 12 inches in width. [2] Preliminary. Source: Bureau of Census, U.S. Department of Commerce

Cotton Ginnings[1] in the United States To: In Thousands of Running Bales

Crop Year	Aug. 1	Sept. 1	Sept. 15	Oct. 1	Oct. 15	Nov. 1	Nov. 15	Dec. 1	Dec. 15	Jan. 1	Jan. 15	Feb. 1	Total Crop
1991-2	NA	699	983	2,467	4,955	8,351	10,752	13,260	15,067	15,888	16,402	16,765	17,146
1992-3	14	446	740	1,664	4,046	7,584	10,296	12,597	14,083	14,944	15,311	15,527	15,786
1993-4	9	435	748	1,846	4,471	7,975	10,952	13,244	14,695	15,321	15,517	15,590	15,675
1994-5	113	680	943	2,324	5,002	8,878	12,479	15,587	17,465	18,438	18,842	19,028	19,127
1995-6	17	433	898	2,455	4,795	8,430	11,262	14,199	16,101	17,011	17,292	17,416	17,469
1996-7	48	342	637	2,146	4,780	8,876	11,906	14,623	16,528	17,681	18,101	18,308	18,439
1997-8	2	359	683	1,210	3,752	7,930	11,601	14,735	16,662	17,613	18,013	18,170	18,301
1998-9	146	523	739	2,056	4,265	7,359	9,366	11,310	12,558	13,160	13,376	13,458	13,534
1999-00	81	561	1,018	2,690	4,885	8,263	11,006	13,379	14,992	15,965	16,322	16,468	16,528
2000-1[2]	245	842	1,454	3,264	5,930	9,221	11,546	13,657	15,364	16,097	16,518	16,648	

[1] Excluding linters. [2] Preliminary. Source: National Agricultural Statistics Service, U.S. Department of Agriculture (NASS-USDA)

Fiber Prices in the United States   In Cents Per Pound

Year	Cotton[1] Actual	Raw[5] Equivalent	Rayon[2] Actual	Raw[5] Equivalent	Polyester[3] Actual	Raw[5] Equivalent	Price Ratios[4] in Percent Cotton/ Rayon	Cotton/ Polyester
1992	61.92	68.80	114.08	118.84	73.50	76.56	.58	.90
1993	62.43	69.37	111.42	116.06	72.50	75.52	.60	.92
1994	78.69	87.43	103.00	107.29	74.92	78.04	.82	1.12
1995	100.76	111.95	118.67	123.61	88.83	92.53	.91	1.21
1996	86.24	95.83	118.00	122.92	81.10	84.48	.78	1.14
1997	76.29	84.77	115.00	119.79	69.50	72.40	.71	1.17
1998	74.21	82.45	110.25	114.84	62.50	65.11	.72	1.29
1999	61.45	68.28	98.92	103.04	51.67	53.82	.66	1.27
2000[6]	64.06	71.17	97.58	101.65	57.08	59.46	.70	1.19
Jan.	58.52	65.02	97.00	101.04	53.00	55.21	.64	1.18
Feb.	61.67	68.52	97.00	101.04	55.00	57.29	.68	1.20
Mar.	64.76	71.96	97.00	101.04	55.00	57.29	.71	1.26
Apr.	61.04	67.82	97.00	101.04	55.00	57.29	.67	1.18
May	64.05	71.17	97.00	101.04	58.00	60.42	.70	1.18
June	62.10	69.00	98.00	102.08	58.00	60.42	.68	1.14
July	60.72	67.47	98.00	102.08	58.00	60.42	.66	1.12
Aug.	64.60	71.78	98.00	102.08	58.00	60.42	.70	1.19
Sept.	66.80	74.22	98.00	102.08	58.00	60.42	.73	1.23
Oct.	66.04	73.38	98.00	102.08	59.00	61.46	.72	1.12
Nov.	68.25	75.83	98.00	102.08	59.00	61.46	.74	1.23
Dec.	70.11	77.90	98.00	102.08	59.00	61.46	.76	1.27

[1] SLM-1 1/16 at group B Mill points, net weight. [2] 1.5 and 3.0 denier, regular rayon staples. [3] Reported average market price for 1.5 denier polyester staple for cotton blending. [4] Raw fiber equivalent. [5] Actual prices converted to estimated raw fiber equivalent as follows: cotton, divided by 0.90, rayon and polyester, divided by 0.96. [6] Preliminary. Source: Economic Research Service, U.S. Department of Agriculture (ERS-USDA)

Cottonseed and Products

Cottonseed production is directly related to the amount of cotton produced. Cottonseed is crushed to produce cottonseed meal and cottonseed oil. The meal is used as a feed ingredient for livestock, while the oil is used for cooking. For the U.S. in the 2000/2001 season, a large cotton crop was grown. Acreage planted to cotton increased by 4 percent to 15.5 million acres but the amount of acreage harvested was almost the same as the year before. The national average cotton yield was 619 pounds per acre, up 2 percent from the previous season. The crop was estimated at 17.4 million bales.

U.S. cottonseed production was estimated by the U.S.D.A. to be 5.91 million metric tonnes, up almost 3 percent from the 1999/00 production total of 5.76 million tonnes. World cottonseed production in 2000/01 was forecast to be 32.68 million tonnes, down less than 1 percent from the previous year. For 2000/01, the world's largest cottonseed producer was China with output of 7.05 million tonnes, up 2 percent from the year before. Following China and the U.S., the next largest producer of cottonseed is India with 2000/01 output of 5.05 million tonnes. Production of cottonseed by Pakistan was estimated to be 3.60 million tonnes, down 4 percent from last season. Uzbekistan cottonseed production was forecast to be 1.88 million tonnes, down 13 percent from the previous year.

U.S.D.A. export sales data through the week ended November 30, 2000, indicated outstanding export sales of cottonseed cake and meal were 2,100 metric tonnes, up from 400 tonnes a year earlier. All of the sales were to Mexico. Accumulated exports in the October-November 2000 period were 4,700 tonnes. Export sales of cottonseed oil were 1,700 tonnes, all of which was to Canada. Accumulated exports were 700 tonnes.

World Production of Cottonseed   In Thousands of Metric Ton

Crop Year	Argentina	Australia	Brazil	China	Egypt	Greece	India	Mexico	Pakistan	Turkey	United States	Former USSR	World Total
1992-3	275	528	800	8,024	571	410	4,740	50	3,080	905	5,652	3,557	31,914
1993-4	392	466	910	6,655	649	454	4,183	42	2,735	900	5,754	3,600	29,850
1994-5	638	474	980	7,727	411	574	4,709	187	2,959	930	6,898	3,380	33,129
1995-6	748	595	690	8,487	384	725	5,339	344	3,604	1,288	6,213	3,150	35,290
1996-7	564	859	568	7,481	560	540	5,890	421	3,230	1,259	6,480	2,561	34,490
1997-8	542	941	763	8,193	563	590	5,150	329	3,180	1,310	6,291	2,785	34,843
1998-9	337	1,012	924	8,012	379	665	5,420	363	2,990	1,284	4,867	2,577	32,818
1999-00[1]	241	983	1,144	6,817	375	730	5,500	220	3,500	1,360	5,764	2,950	33,500
2000-1[2]	310	1,045	1,200	6,300	310	640	5,300	110	3,100	1,340	6,380	2,900	32,860

[1] Preliminary.   [2] Estimate.   Source: The Oil World

Salient Statistics of Cottonseed in the United States   In Thousands of Short Tons

Crop Year Beginning Aug. 1	Supply — Stocks	Supply — Production	Supply — Total Supply	Disappearance — Crush	Disappearance — Exports	Disappearance — Other	Disappearance — Total Disappearance	Farm Price $/Ton	Value of Production Mil. $	Products Produced — Oil Million Lbs.	Products Produced — Meal Thousand Sh. Tons
1992-3	460	6,230	6,690	3,629	192	2,504	6,325	98	608.4	1,137	1,533
1993-4	365	6,343	6,708	3,470	157	2,649	6,276	113	714.4	1,119	1,563
1994-5	432	7,604	8,036	3,947	232	3,306	7,485	101	771.3	1,312	1,830
1995-6	551	6,849	7,399	3,882	114	2,886	6,882	106	731.0	1,229	1,748
1996-7	517	7,144	7,681	3,860	116	3,182	7,158	126	914.6	1,310	1,807
1997-8	523	6,935	7,553	3,885	149	2,957	6,990	121	835.4	1,224	1,769
1998-9	563	5,365	6,135	2,719	68	2,955	5,742	129	687.2	832	1,232
1999-00[1]	393	6,354	7,055	3,079	198	3,505	6,781	89	559.2	943	1,420
2000-1[2]	274	6,439	7,010	2,850	180	3,700	6,730		677.1	910	1,306

[1] Preliminary.   [2] Estimate.   Source: Economic Research Service, U.S. Department of Agriculture (ERS-USDA)

Average Wholesale Price of Cottonseed Meal (41% Solvent)[2] in Memphis   In Dollars Per Short Ton

Year	Jan.	Feb.	Mar.	Apr.	May	June	July	Aug.	Sept.	Oct.	Nov.	Dec.	Average
1992	156.25	140.10	124.25	121.25	127.50	132.50	133.75	146.90	163.00	154.40	157.50	174.50	144.33
1993	164.40	149.40	153.50	149.00	143.10	153.00	170.30	178.50	193.75	173.10	181.00	180.00	165.75
1994	170.30	173.10	174.00	166.25	157.75	154.10	152.50	144.50	145.00	134.40	120.50	114.20	150.55
1995	106.75	97.50	100.30	98.10	92.75	108.75	116.90	116.50	137.60	153.25	165.00	185.80	123.27
1996	208.80	202.80	195.60	220.00	191.25	192.20	201.56	193.10	193.10	183.25	196.60	224.50	200.23
1997	207.20	183.75	189.10	189.10	193.75	190.30	170.75	176.25	192.00	189.10	189.10	190.50	188.41
1998	153.10	139.10	128.70	116.25	105.00	129.40	146.65	130.30	115.60	106.50	107.90	119.75	124.85
1999	110.60	101.25	106.90	110.90	108.75	114.50	115.00	100.65	111.92	111.83	112.00	124.20	110.71
2000[1]	126.88	130.50	129.38	125.00	123.25	130.63	131.88	130.50	153.12	150.00	141.88	160.83	136.15

[1] Preliminary.   Source: Economic Research Service, U.S. Department of Agriculture (ERS-USDA)

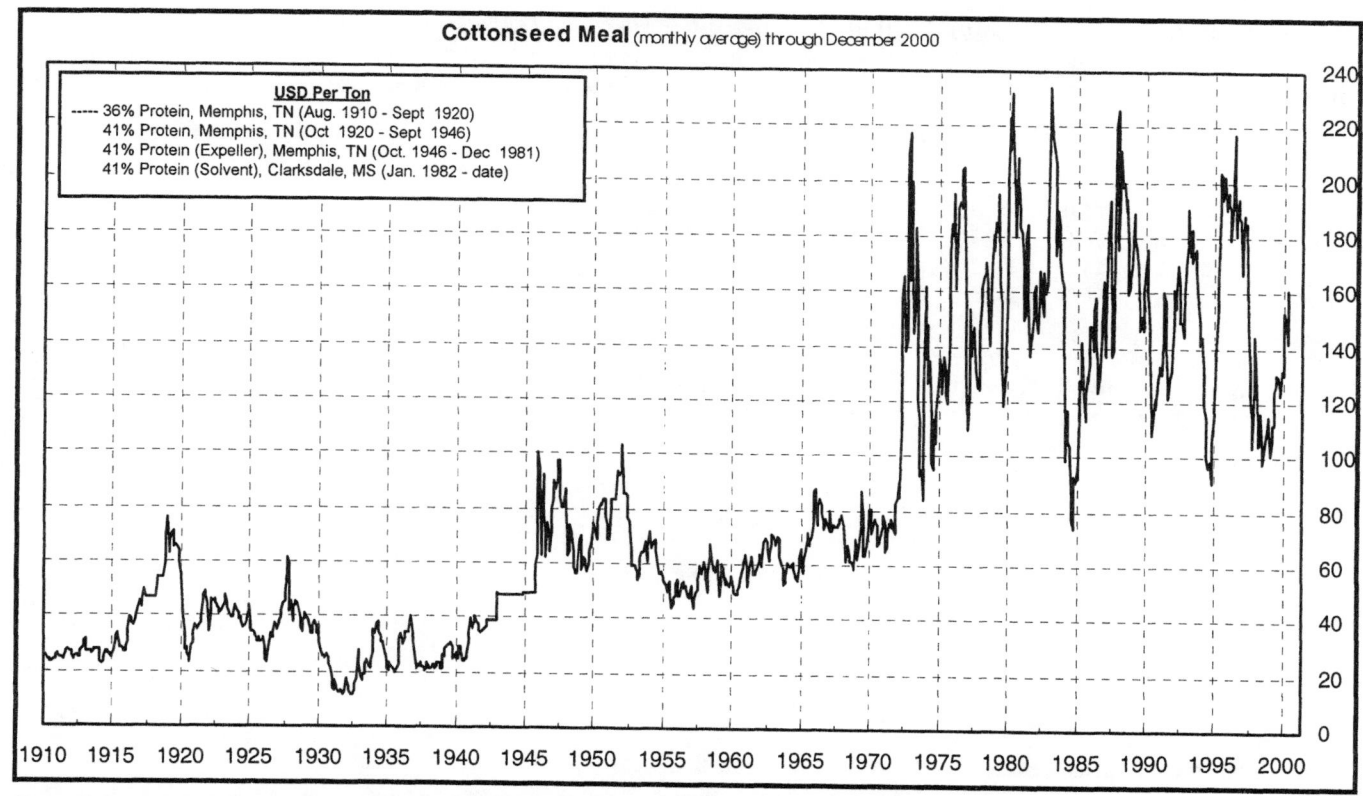

Cottonseed Meal (monthly average) through December 2000

USD Per Ton
- 36% Protein, Memphis, TN (Aug. 1910 - Sept 1920)
- 41% Protein, Memphis, TN (Oct 1920 - Sept 1946)
- 41% Protein (Expeller), Memphis, TN (Oct. 1946 - Dec 1981)
- 41% Protein (Solvent), Clarksdale, MS (Jan. 1982 - date)

Supply and Distribution of Cottonseed Oil in the United States   In Millions of Pounds

Crop Year Beginning Oct. 1	Supply				Disappearance			Per Capita Cunsump. of Salad & Cook Oils - In Lbs. -	Utilization Food Uses			Prices	
	Stocks	Pro-duction	Imports	Total Supply	Domestic	Exports	Total		Short-ening	Salad & Cooking Oils	Total	U.S.[3] (Crude) $/Met. Ton	Rott[4] (Cif)
1994-5	106	1,312	0	1,417	1,006	329	1,335	26	217	262	532	683	671
1995-6	82	1,229	.3	1,311	996	221	1,217	27	218	235	497	575	613
1996-7	94	1,216	.3	1,310	1,012	232	1,244	26	271	265	556	564	590
1997-8	66	1,224	.1	1,291	1,004	208	1,212	29	208	184	414	663	693
1998-9	79	832	48.2	958	772	111	882	28	170	262	457	633	632
1999-00[1]	76	943	8.1	1,027	837	141	978	29	W	251	520	474	496
2000-1[2]	49	910	8.3	967	770	145	915					383	454

[1] Preliminary. [2] Estimate. [3] Valley Points FOB; Tank Cars. [4] Rotterdam; US, PBSY, fob gulf. W = Withheld proprietary data.
Source: Economic Research Service, U.S. Department of Agriculture (ERS-USDA)

Consumption of Crude Cottonseed Oil in Refining in the United States   In Millions of Pound

Year	Oct.	Nov.	Dec.	Jan.	Feb.	Mar.	Apr.	May	June	July	Aug.	Sept.	Total
1994-5	81.9	97.2	109.8	107.7	87.1	96.2	87.2	72.8	73.4	76.0	83.3	71.6	1,044.4
1995-6	76.1	91.8	89.7	94.5	87.2	92.2	83.4	77.3	55.5	56.2	64.3	54.4	922.5
1996-7	67.2	85.1	85.1	88.7	83.3	80.8	77.4	79.2	58.4	55.3	59.0	39.2	858.7
1997-8	73.1	73.1	77.2	85.0	75.7	70.2	72.1	57.1	51.9	54.9	57.5	30.1	778.1
1998-9	52.9	49.6	50.2	46.6	48.9	50.7	36.4	28.3	28.4	30.5	46.2	43.5	512.3
1999-00	51.9	57.3	61.5	60.0	58.1	67.8	62.0	52.7	43.2	22.7	45.8	37.2	620.1
2000-1[1]	56.9	53.7	56.7										669.6

[1] Preliminary.   *Source: U.S. Bureau of Census, U.S. Department of Commerce*

Exports of Cottonseed Oil (Crude and Refined) from the United States   In Thousands of Pounds

Year	Jan.	Feb.	Mar.	Apr.	May	June	July	Aug.	Sept.	Oct.	Nov.	Dec.	Total
1994	32,011	11,093	21,156	26,595	34,921	11,583	24,303	24,644	25,265	17,487	33,385	36,613	299,056
1995	18,808	43,454	48,471	34,500	28,775	22,692	18,490	11,973	13,741	9,896	30,268	13,223	294,291
1996	26,407	8,103	38,597	24,628	16,052	14,135	7,827	21,197	10,903	12,526	10,345	13,145	203,865
1997	25,722	26,835	22,647	22,230	30,319	9,535	25,207	24,717	8,919	15,351	24,217	8,164	243,863
1998	24,003	15,077	16,150	22,874	20,791	22,994	15,348	14,392	8,818	11,056	7,610	11,447	190,560
1999	11,541	10,235	7,780	11,387	6,328	7,161	8,725	8,111	9,275	11,060	12,313	23,025	126,941
2000[1]	10,628	9,447	13,181	8,214	7,446	7,550	11,546	10,604	16,467	13,228	11,023		130,182

[1] Preliminary.   *Source: Economic Research Service, U.S. Department of Agriculture (ERS-USDA)*

COTTONSEED AND PRODUCTS

Cottonseed Crushed (Consumption) in the United States In Thousands of Short Tons

Year	Aug.	Sept.	Oct.	Nov.	Dec.	Jan.	Feb.	Mar.	Apr.	May	June	July	Total
1992-3	245.7	162.9	323.2	353.3	372.1	413.3	334.6	324.1	323.8	296.4	242.7	237.2	3,629
1993-4	182.9	162.6	300.4	391.4	375.0	391.0	335.2	358.6	265.7	257.7	239.4	210.2	3,470
1994-5	192.1	195.5	343.9	386.2	397.5	404.6	360.5	391.0	345.4	304.0	316.5	310.0	3,947
1995-6	264.4	245.5	337.1	386.7	362.4	402.3	373.5	381.4	349.6	325.2	223.7	209.2	3,861
1996-7	229.2	225.0	331.7	355.1	352.6	381.0	362.8	362.2	334.4	351.3	280.8	294.0	3,860
1997-8	244.4	178.6	329.7	374.5	371.3	428.4	352.3	370.8	359.1	309.1	278.8	277.6	3,875
1998-9	246.0	174.9	272.7	254.3	262.7	282.2	259.5	280.2	205.5	172.0	159.9	149.2	2,719
1999-00	166.8	230.7	281.6	302.5	296.4	297.7	300.1	301.8	265.5	250.8	227.7	156.9	3,079
2000-1[1]	170.5	141.6	264.1	253.4	248.7								2,588

[1] Preliminary. *Source: Economic Research Service, U.S. Department of Agriculture (ERS-USDA)*

Production of Cottonseed Cake and Meal in the United States In Thousands of Short Tons

Year	Aug.	Sept.	Oct.	Nov.	Dec.	Jan.	Feb.	Mar.	Apr.	May	June	July	Total
1992-3	111.2	76.0	143.7	150.2	160.5	176.2	146.6	136.4	140.9	126.1	103.0	101.0	1,572
1993-4	76.7	71.5	130.1	172.2	166.6	161.8	151.8	164.0	119.6	116.1	106.9	93.4	1,531
1994-5	90.6	89.4	154.2	171.5	176.9	184.1	162.2	174.3	154.2	137.4	143.9	137.2	1,776
1995-6	120.1	113.6	159.9	178.2	161.0	183.8	169.8	168.3	158.7	147.1	102.4	102.7	1,766
1996-7	100.9	99.1	146.1	161.5	158.2	174.5	164.6	162.1	152.2	160.7	128.6	123.2	1,732
1997-8	128.2	92.1	147.8	168.7	178.2	194.4	158.5	170.4	162.3	141.8	128.8	124.0	1,795
1998-9	114.7	77.1	118.7	115.9	122.5	130.2	114.8	127.2	90.6	75.6	75.6	71.0	1,234
1999-00	82.1	107.5	132.1	140.8	138.3	135.3	137.7	140.2	120.0	109.4	109.3	79.5	1,432
2000-1[1]	74.1	79.3	134.1	121.4	117.1								1,262

[1] Preliminary. *Source: Bureau of Census, U.S. Department of Commerce*

Production of Crude Cottonseed Oil[2] in the United States In Millions of Pounds

Year	Aug.	Sept.	Oct.	Nov.	Dec.	Jan.	Feb.	Mar.	Apr.	May	June	July	Total
1992-3	77.8	56.8	99.5	110.2	117.6	134.7	107.2	104.9	101.7	96.1	77.7	76.5	1,161
1993-4	59.1	51.7	93.5	122.2	117.5	124.7	99.9	119.6	85.3	85.2	78.4	69.8	1,107
1994-5	61.7	61.0	109.8	122.6	125.6	133.4	115.6	125.2	110.4	97.7	102.4	96.6	1,262
1995-6	87.8	84.3	105.2	121.6	111.6	130.9	121.4	125.6	110.4	101.9	73.3	76.7	1,251
1996-7	70.3	69.4	98.9	114.8	115.9	123.9	114.8	114.7	103.7	109.8	86.9	85.9	1,209
1997-8	80.6	66.0	97.8	120.3	119.6	136.4	111.1	115.5	112.7	96.1	87.3	88.8	1,232
1998-9	77.8	59.6	78.3	80.0	80.6	84.0	80.2	86.7	64.4	53.4	52.4	45.9	843
1999-00	56.1	69.6	88.3	95.4	94.2	93.4	93.2	93.8	82.6	75.7	70.2	49.2	962
2000-1[1]	55.1	52.1	84.3	76.8	73.5								820

[1] Preliminary. [2] Not seasonally adjusted. *Source: Bureau of Census, U.S. Department of Commerce*

Production of Refined Cottonseed Oil in the United States In Millions of Pounds

Year	Aug.	Sept.	Oct.	Nov.	Dec.	Jan.	Feb.	Mar.	Apr.	May	June	July	Total
1992-3	69.3	46.3	72.6	90.2	91.9	103.1	82.0	74.5	88.8	75.6	70.8	62.4	928
1993-4	65.1	54.6	79.4	109.1	100.6	107.2	93.4	107.8	66.9	71.6	70.0	72.2	998
1994-5	86.3	62.9	80.0	94.4	106.2	104.2	94.4	92.6	84.2	70.1	70.7	72.6	1,019
1995-6	80.5	69.0	74.0	89.5	86.9	91.7	84.6	89.8	81.7	75.0	53.8	54.5	931
1996-7	62.4	53.0	64.9	82.8	82.2	85.9	80.7	78.1	75.2	76.9	56.4	53.6	852
1997-8	57.4	38.1	48.3	71.0	74.8	82.2	73.1	68.2	69.8	55.2	50.3	53.0	741
1998-9	55.8	29.1	51.1	47.9	48.5	45.4	47.3	49.0	35.2	27.4	27.5	29.7	494
1999-00	44.8	42.4	50.4	55.6	59.5	58.3	56.7	65.8	60.0	51.0	41.9	22.0	608
2000-1[1]	44.4	36.2	55.1	52.2	55.1								583

[1] Preliminary. *Source: Bureau of the Census, U.S. Department of Commerce*

Stocks of Cottonseed Oil (Crude and Refined) in the U.S., at End of Month In Millions of Pounds

Year	Aug.	Sept.	Oct.	Nov.	Dec.	Jan.	Feb.	Mar.	Apr.	May	June	July
1992-3	94.3	81.0	93.1	101.7	123.2	148.4	152.6	167.1	157.0	159.2	144.8	143.8
1993-4	85.8	54.6	79.4	109.1	100.6	107.2	93.4	107.8	66.9	71.6	70.0	72.1
1994-5	112.4	105.6	103.5	117.0	114.7	122.2	150.5	129.9	120.8	95.7	96.9	92.2
1995-6	87.8	82.1	82.6	89.3	94.8	118.2	147.2	151.2	155.6	143.3	128.1	125.4
1996-7	101.2	94.1	97.5	102.5	106.0	120.9	133.7	137.5	131.7	116.1	103.4	85.9
1997-8	78.0	66.4	68.6	86.4	105.3	133.8	141.2	140.7	159.8	150.4	130.9	118.8
1998-9	97.3	78.6	89.1	110.0	85.5	109.5	113.3	125.3	126.0	112.0	100.7	83.7
1999-00	107.8	76.0	81.1	88.7	85.1	84.5	79.6	115.2	127.4	127.5	103.0	81.3
2000-1[1]	59.9	49.0	66.5	75.2	92.9							

[1] Preliminary. *Source: Bureau of Census, U.S. Department of Commerce*

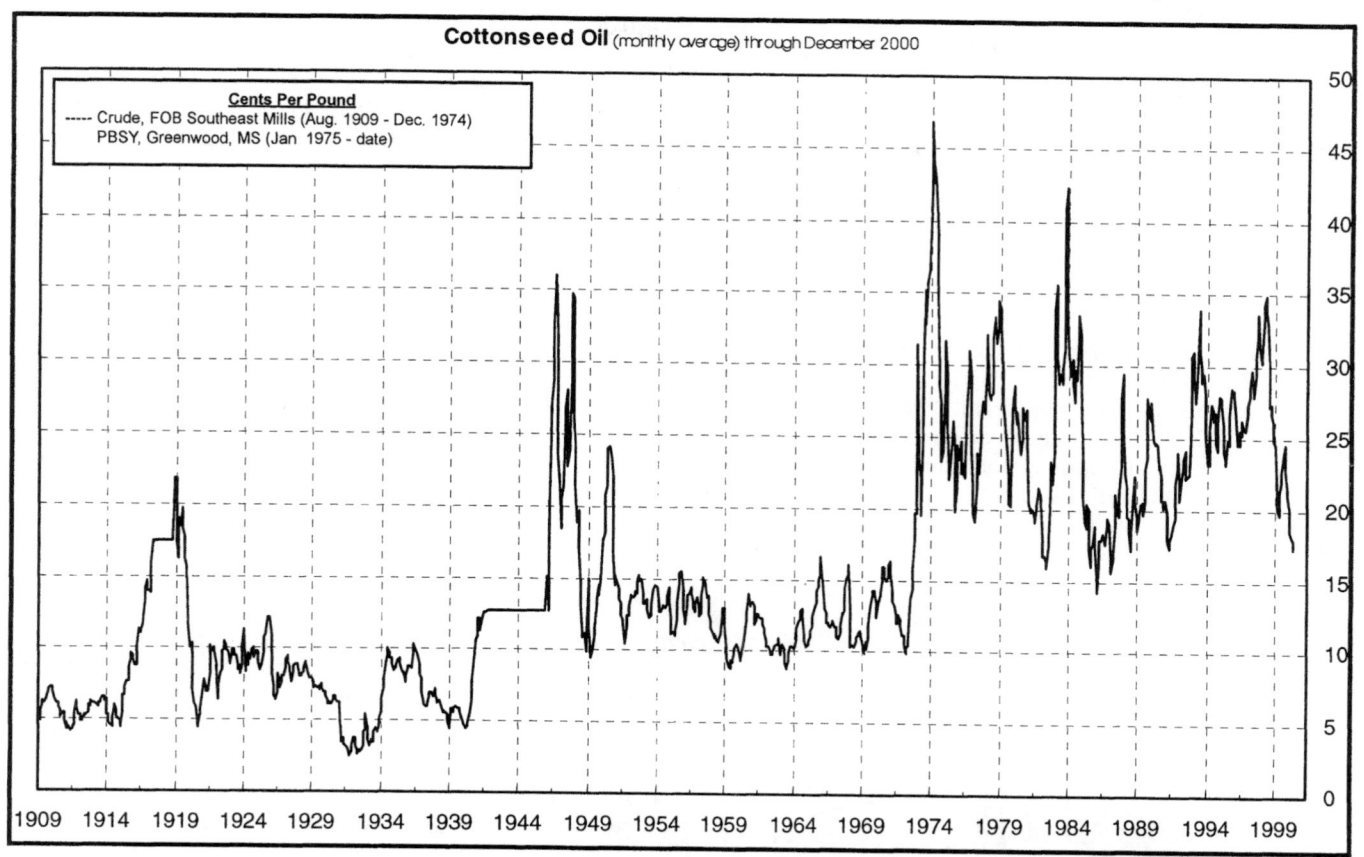

Cottonseed Oil (monthly average) through December 2000

Cents Per Pound
----- Crude, FOB Southeast Mills (Aug. 1909 - Dec. 1974)
PBSY, Greenwood, MS (Jan 1975 - date)

Average Price of Crude Cottonseed Oil, PBSY, Greenwood, MS.[1] in Tank Cars   In Cents Per Pound

Year	Jan.	Feb.	Mar.	Apr.	May	June	July	Aug.	Sept.	Oct.	Nov.	Dec.	Average
1991	23.75	22.88	23.00	22.13	20.67	20.31	20.50	21.00	19.88	17.98	17.41	18.07	20.63
1992	18.50	18.13	19.25	19.38	21.38	22.58	24.45	21.86	21.04	22.17	22.96	23.91	21.30
1993	24.09	22.03	22.24	22.55	22.70	26.76	30.74	30.45	28.98	24.79	26.69	30.39	26.03
1994	33.16	29.96	29.60	29.06	29.66	27.55	24.20	23.71	24.51	23.64	24.85	25.50	27.12
1995	28.70	29.95	27.14	27.61	27.51	30.04	30.63	30.26	28.61	27.61	26.27	26.10	26.36
1996	24.45	24.35	24.25	26.77	28.46	27.94	28.25	27.81	26.13	24.55	24.28	24.29	25.96
1997	25.21	25.44	26.18	25.10	25.19	25.01	26.53	27.11	28.03	28.47	29.11	26.78	26.51
1998	27.69	29.37	30.46	32.47	33.13	30.22	29.40	30.11	33.26	33.99	34.16	33.40	31.47
1999	31.72	28.21	26.27	24.39	24.25	25.19	24.70	21.39	20.22	20.15	19.69	21.25	23.95
2000	21.98	22.65	23.70	24.57	22.97	21.54	21.03	20.17	18.52	18.16	17.83	17.25	20.86

[1] Data prior to 1995 are F.O.B. Valley Points, Southeastern mills.   *Source: Economic Research Service, U.S. Department of Agriculture (ERS-USDA)*

Exports of Cottonseed Oil to Important Countries from the United States   In Thousands of Metric Tons

Year	Canada	Dominican Republic	Egypt	Guate-mala	Japan	Mexico	Nether-lands	Salvador	South Korea	Turkey	Vene-zuela	Total
1990	6.8	6.0	14.7	.4	36.7	1.4	2.9	21.0	36.0	----	9.2	136.3
1991	7.8	2.1	14.7	----	24.1	4.8	3.4	13.0	13.0	5.5	4.2	97.0
1992	11.3	1.0	8.2	3.2	15.3	8.5	17.4	26.5	10.9	7.0	3.7	123.3
1993	10.9	----	----	.5	17.6	5.8	.2	30.8	6.6	.5	1.5	83.1
1994	10.8	----	7.5	12.3	29.8	10.3	1.9	26.1	16.9	----	4.5	135.7
1995	12.0	----	10.3	1.9	17.9	5.7	1.5	37.8	19.2	----	2.8	133.7
1996	23.2	----	----	1.7	15.8	3.3	----	20.6	8.1	2.0	----	100.0
1997	28.1	----	----	.4	11.3	2.5	4.2	25.3	1.9	2.5	----	110.6
1998	37.6	----	----	----	6.0	6.1	----	16.1	1.5	----	----	86.3
1999[1]	37.5	----	----	----	4.2	5.4	.5	.8	.7	----	----	57.6

[1] Preliminary.   *Source: The Oil World*

Bridge/CRB Futures Index

The Bridge Commodity Research Bureau Futures Price Index was first calculated by Commodity Research Bureau, Inc. in 1957 and made its inaugural appearance in the 1958 CRB Commodity Year Book.

The Index originally consisted of two cash markets and 26 futures markets which were traded on exchanges in the U.S. and Canada. It included barley and flaxseed from the Winnipeg exchange; cocoa, coffee "B", copper, cotton, cottonseed oil, grease wool, hides, lead, potatoes, rubber, sugar #4, sugar #6, wool tops and zinc from New York exchanges; and corn, oats, wheat, rye, soybeans, soybean oil, soybean meal, lard, onions, and eggs from Chicago exchanges. In addition to those 26, the Index also included the spot New Orleans cotton and Minneapolis wheat markets.

Like the Bureau of Labor Statistics spot index, the Bridge/CRB Futures Price Index is calculated to produce an unweighted geometric mean of the individual commodity price relatives. In other words, a ratio of the current price to the base year average price. Currently, 1967 is the base year the Index is calculated against (1967 = 100).

The formula considers all future delivery contracts that expire on or before the end of the sixth calendar month from the current date, using up to a maximum of five contracts per commodity. However, a minimum of two contracts must be used to calculate the current price, even if the second contract is outside the six-month window. Contracts are excluded when in their delivery period.

The 2000 closing value of 227.83 was 11.06 percent higher than the 1999 close of 205.14, and marked the second consecutive yearly increase. 11 of the 17 component commodities finished higher for the year.

Futures Markets

Futures and options on the CRB Futures Price Index are traded on the New York Board of Trade (NYBOT).

Bridge/CRB Futures Index Component Commodities by Group

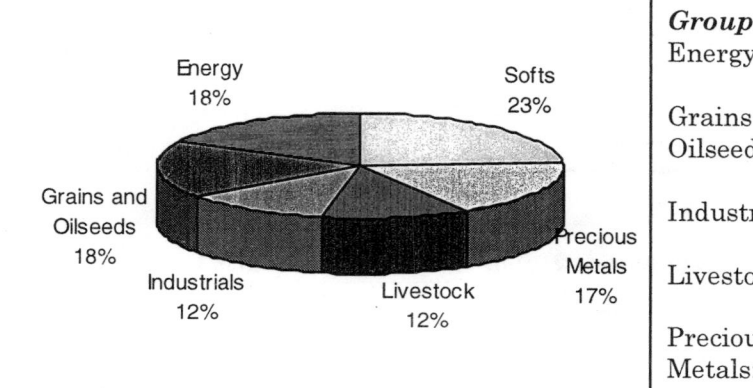

Groups:	Components
Energy:	Crude Oil, Heating Oil, Natural Gas
Grains and Oilseeds:	Corn, Soybeans, Wheat
Industrials:	Copper, Cotton
Livestock:	Live Cattle, Live Hogs
Precious Metals:	Gold, Platinum, Silver
Softs:	Cocoa, Coffee, Orange Juice, Sugar #11

The Bridge/CRB Futures Index is computed using a three-step process:

1) Each of the Index's 17 component commodities is arithmetically average using the prices for all of the designated contract months which expire on or before the end of the sixth calendar month from the current date, except that: a) no contract shall be included in the calculation whie in delivery; b) there shall be a minimum of two contract months for each component commodity (adding contracts beyond the six month window if necessary); c) there shall be a maximum of five contract months for each commodity (dropping the most deferred contracts to remain at five, if necessary). The result is that the Index extends six to seven months into the futures depending on where one is in the current month. For example, live cattle's average price on October 30, 1995 would be computed as follows:

$$\text{Cattle Average} = \frac{\text{Dec. '96} + \text{Feb. '97}}{2}$$

2) These 17 component averages are then geometrically average by multiplying all of teh number together and taking the 17th root.

$$\text{Geometric Average} = \sqrt[17]{\text{Crude Avg.} * \text{Heating Oil Avg.} * \text{Sugar Avg.} ....}$$

3) The resulting average is divided by 30.7766, the 1967 base-year average for these 17 commodities. That result is then multiplied by an adjustment factor of .8486. This adjustment factor is necessitated by the nine revisions to the Index since its inception in 1957. Finally, that result is multiplied by 100 in order to convert the Index into percentage terms:

$$\text{Bridge/CRB Futures Index} = \frac{\text{Current Geometric Average}}{\text{1967 Geometric Avg. (30.7766)}} * .8486 * 100$$

Bridge/CRB® Futures Index - New York Board of Trade (weekly close) as of 29-Dec-2000

Bridge/CRB Futures Index
17 Futures Markets
Cattle (Live), Cocoa, Coffee, Copper, Corn, Cotton, Crude Oil, Gold (NY), Heating Oil #2, Hogs (Lean), Natural Gas, Orange Juice, Platinum, Silver (NY), Soybeans, Sugar #11 (World), Wheat (Chi)

Average Open Interest of Bridge/CRB Futures Index in New York   In Contracts

Year	Jan.	Feb.	Mar.	Apr.	May	June	July	Aug.	Sept.	Oct.	Nov.	Dec.
1991	1,443	1,593	1,524	1,620	1,511	1,524	1,168	1,071	1,045	1,172	1,357	1,383
1992	1,435	1,472	1,185	1,347	1,311	1,087	951	1,179	1,075	1,226	1,283	1,406
1993	1,969	1,984	1,842	2,201	2,564	2,947	2,616	2,409	2,128	2,383	2,432	2,351
1994	2,607	3,146	2,680	2,691	2,339	2,698	3,838	5,146	4,562	4,942	4,535	2,800
1995	2,144	2,164	2,147	2,370	2,016	2,144	2,053	2,070	2,062	1,942	2,003	1,640
1996	1,934	1,826	1,753	2,355	1,881	1,890	1,562	1,345	1,596	1,853	1,861	1,866
1997	1,944	2,128	2,090	2,245	2,192	1,817	1,957	1,741	1,656	1,843	1,789	1,752
1998	1,679	1,557	1,626	1,509	1,641	1,895	1,832	1,719	1,839	2,162	2,639	2,787
1999	2,863	3,027	3,153	3,041	3,785	3,388	3,300	3,443	4,231	4,851	4,579	4,087
2000	3,487	3,525	3,271	3,117	3,155	2,737	2,104	1,640	1,551	1,632	1,544	1,438

Source: New York Board of Trade (NYBOT)

Volume of Trading of Bridge/CRB Futures Index in New York   In Contracts

Year	Jan.	Feb.	Mar.	Apr.	May	June	July	Aug.	Sept.	Oct.	Nov.	Dec.	Total
1991	5,835	5,391	6,715	6,432	3,671	5,557	4,853	5,876	4,414	3,766	4,132	4,543	61,185
1992	4,895	6,031	4,136	5,697	5,496	4,487	4,162	4,617	3,874	3,183	5,277	4,400	56,255
1993	3,620	5,720	8,050	7,340	8,680	10,722	12,418	8,590	6,192	4,350	8,535	6,954	91,171
1994	6,956	7,473	10,085	10,274	11,298	14,652	10,560	8,967	7,445	6,575	10,186	5,515	109,986
1995	6,151	5,545	5,763	7,955	7,877	7,573	6,875	10,094	7,376	5,030	5,865	5,309	81,413
1996	7,490	6,041	6,428	10,784	9,526	5,543	7,476	5,816	6,311	6,527	5,990	3,181	81,113
1997	6,645	4,942	5,245	8,600	8,156	7,776	6,248	7,685	4,537	4,588	3,468	3,592	71,482
1998	7,659	4,623	3,953	3,890	2,933	5,634	3,394	4,578	5,101	4,013	8,814	4,401	58,993
1999	7,606	7,766	7,556	7,808	4,986	8,404	4,378	12,053	6,660	8,063	9,497	3,932	88,709
2000	14,975	6,760	3,941	7,582	7,402	8,924	2,023	3,973	1,333	2,122	3,254	1,205	63,494

Source: New York Board of Trade (NYBOT)

Currencies

The fourth quarter of calendar year 2000 may have marked the end of the U.S. dollar's two year advance against the major currencies. Ironically, the shift away from the dollar was not indicative of deep concerns about the U.S. economy, which remains the world's most powerful, but a perception that other key economies were finally starting to show improvement. This may be particularly true of the European Union's Euro, which since its birth on 1/1/99 was in a virtual free-fall against the dollar. The Euro opened initially at $1.17, fell to $1.0066 by year-end 1999, continued down to a low of $0.8254 on 10/25/00, before recovering to $0.9373 at year-end. The break in the U.S. equity markets, notably the technology laden NASDAQ stocks, and the uncertain impact that value loss may have on the U.S. economy was a factor in the Euro's recovery. Prior to the collapse in equities, the U.S. had witnessed a huge net capital inflow that had overwhelmed efforts by the European Central Bank to shore up the Euro. Europe's central bank would seem to have more breathing room in 2001.

Historically, a currency's value is largely determined by three variables: interest rate differentials, economic differentials, and relative yield inside the country. For the U.S., the Federal Reserve's tight monetary policy during 2000 obviously enhanced the dollar's value, but the Fed's tightening may have gone too far as the policy reversed to one of easing in early 2001. Moreover, the fourth quarter appeared to highlight fears of a recession, although the more likely scenario is that the U.S. economy was simply experiencing a long awaited pause following torrid real growth during much of the 1990's. Adding further uncertainty to the outlook is a new presidential tenure and any fresh fiscal policy emphasis that might develop from the change in administration.

Trading in currencies now exceeds $2 trillion per day. Most of the trading is via electronic transfers for central banks and commercial banks, but a portion of the trading is done on organized exchanges where intraday price swings often have speculative based roots that can exaggerate short term price swings. Annual trading in the IMM's Japanese Yen futures contract is now about six million contracts. Not far behind with annual futures volume in excess of 4 million contracts is the Swiss Franc, the Euro, British Pound, and Canadian Dollar trade around 3 million per year. However, the U.S. dollar is the fulcrum from which the market value of many currencies is determined, a role that is not likely to diminish.

For the year, the B-pound lost 7.3 percent against the U.S. dollar. However, the C-dollar gained 3.5 percent, the Mexican peso gained 1.5 percent, South Korea's won and the Japanese yen gained about 11 percent.

Japan's economy once again appeared to be at a crossroad in late 2000, with most signs pointing to another slowdown in 2001. However, a return to a zero interest rate policy by the Bank of Japan appears unlikely so long as any economic downturn is viewed as simply cyclical. More likely, Japan will attempt to stimulate its economy with a series of fiscal policy incentives. For much of 2000, the J-yen traded within a narrow range, but in November, apparently taking a cue from the key European currencies, the yen strengthened against the dollar closing the year around 114 per dollar vs. 100 per dollar a year earlier. However, the flip side of a stronger yen is that it may dampen exports which are a major factor for Japan's economy, suggesting that the yen will have difficulty holding gains against the dollar in 2001. The U.S. overall trade deficit during the first ten months of 2000 was running at an annual rate of $363 billion vs. 1999's deficit of $265 billion. Japan typically has the largest trade imbalance with the U.S., but in October 2000, the U.S. deficit with China of $9.1 billion was the largest ever reached with one single country. The U.S. deficit with Canada, its largest trading partner, was a record $4.7 billion in October.

The Canadian dollar, which collapsed against the U.S. dollar in early fall, recovered about half the loss in November which again seemed to underscore a worldwide perception that the U.S. dollar's strength had finally peaked, or at a minimum suggesting that the U.S. dollar would stay on the defensive into early 2001.

The FINEX's U.S. Dollar Index, which rates the dollar against a basket of currencies, began the year at 100.19 and moved steadily higher to a peak of 119.07 on 10/26/00, before falling to 109.56 at year-end.

Futures Markets

The Chicago Mercantile Exchange's International Monetary Market (IMM) actively trades futures and options on the Australian dollar, British pound, Canadian dollar, Euro, Japanese yen, Mexican peso, and Swiss franc. Chicago's MidAmerica Exchange (MidAm) trades smaller futures contracts on many of the IMM's currencies. The FINEX division of the New York Board of Trade (NYBOT) trades futures and options on a composite dollar index and also offers crossrate contracts: D-mark/J-yen, D-mark/French Franc and D-Mark/B-pound. Many currency contracts are also traded in Europe and Asia.

CRB Currency Futures Index   1977 = 100

Year	Jan.	Feb.	Mar.	Apr.	May	June	July	Aug.	Sept.	Oct.	Nov.	Dec.	Average
1991	140.91	142.85	134.41	130.85	130.02	126.44	126.33	128.27	130.86	131.57	134.66	136.78	132.83
1992	136.15	133.37	129.33	129.78	132.13	135.42	139.83	142.26	140.65	136.30	129.70	129.91	134.57
1993	127.91	126.74	127.99	132.20	132.73	131.17	129.44	130.64	132.87	131.38	129.31	129.14	130.13
1994	128.54	129.57	130.89	130.57	132.23	134.18	137.60	137.51	139.78	141.94	140.29	137.85	135.08
1995	139.31	140.54	147.85	152.52	150.20	150.85	150.58	145.41	143.89	146.33	145.21	143.83	146.38
1996	141.69	141.01	141.12	139.61	138.11	138.37	139.53	140.52	139.51	138.74	139.92	137.47	139.63
1997	134.61	130.30	129.56	128.71	130.83	131.75	130.14	126.84	128.02	129.07	129.58	126.93	129.70
1998	125.06	126.10	125.65	124.96	124.33	122.86	121.89	120.65	126.18	130.98	128.86	130.69	125.68
1999	130.97	128.48	126.37	125.74	125.32	124.63	124.08	126.89	128.89	130.66	128.24	127.71	127.33
2000	127.65	124.37	124.01	123.43	119.42	122.54	121.59	119.04	117.11	115.99	114.89	117.55	120.63

Average.   *Source: Bridge Commodity Research Bureau (CRB)*

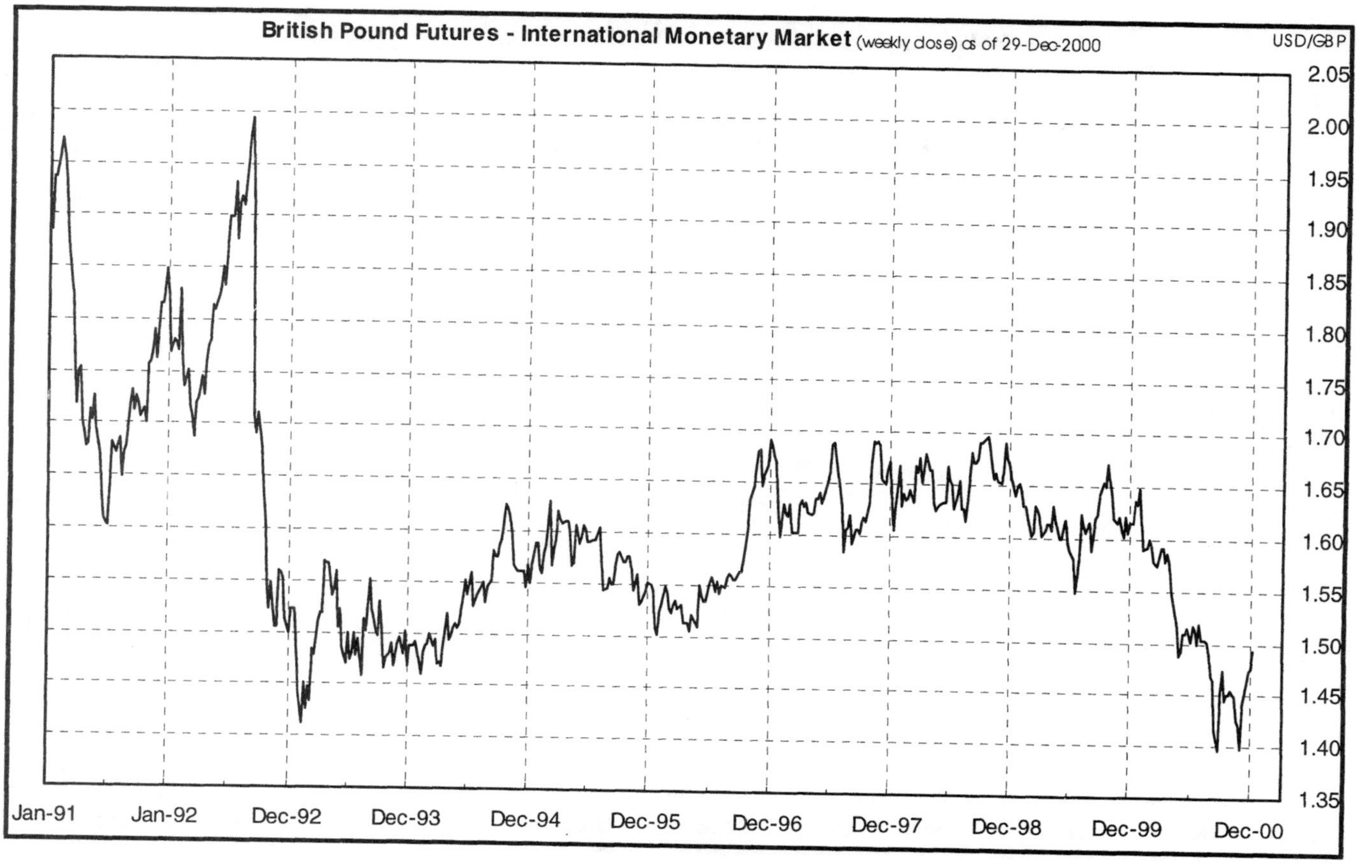
British Pound Futures - International Monetary Market (weekly close) as of 29-Dec-2000
USD/GBP
2.05
2.00
1.95
1.90
1.85
1.80
1.75
1.70
1.65
1.60
1.55
1.50
1.45
1.40
1.35
Jan-91
Jan-92
Dec-92
Dec-93
Dec-94
Dec-95
Dec-96
Dec-97
Dec-98
Dec-99
Dec-00

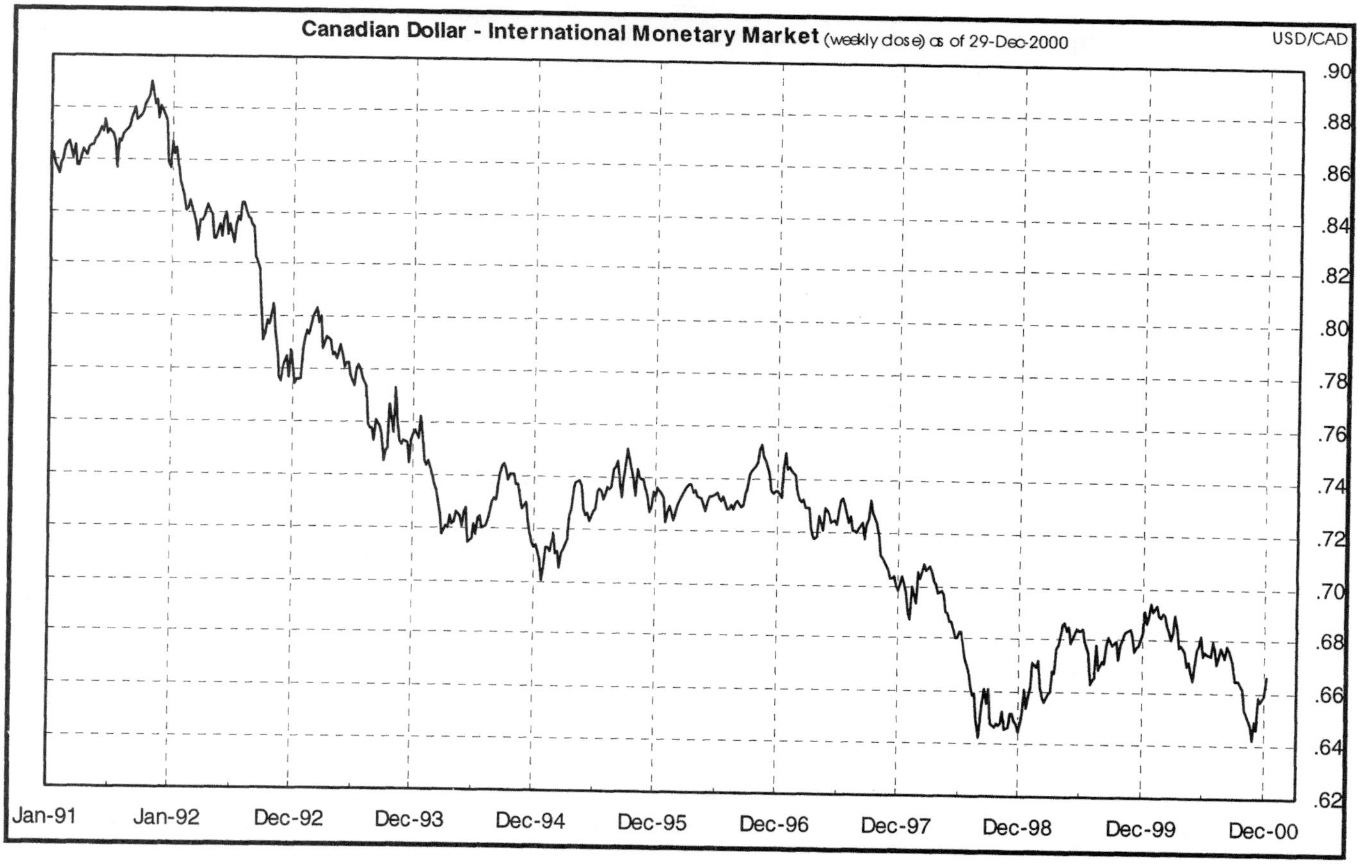
Canadian Dollar - International Monetary Market (weekly close) as of 29-Dec-2000
USD/CAD
.90
.88
.86
.84
.82
.80
.78
.76
.74
.72
.70
.68
.66
.64
.62
Jan-91
Jan-92
Dec-92
Dec-93
Dec-94
Dec-95
Dec-96
Dec-97
Dec-98
Dec-99
Dec-00

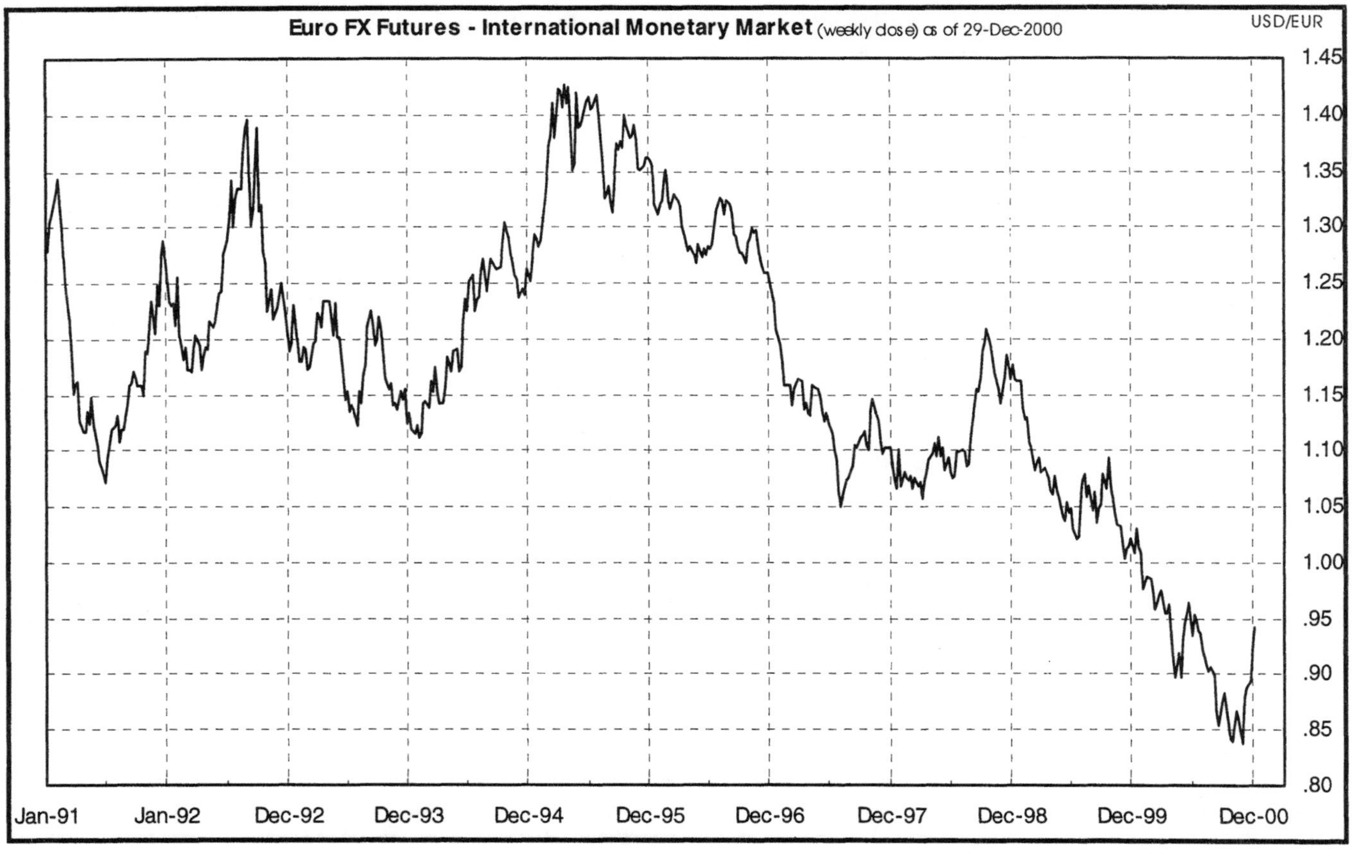

CURRENCIES

Euro FX Futures - International Monetary Market (weekly close) as of 29-Dec-2000

USD/EUR

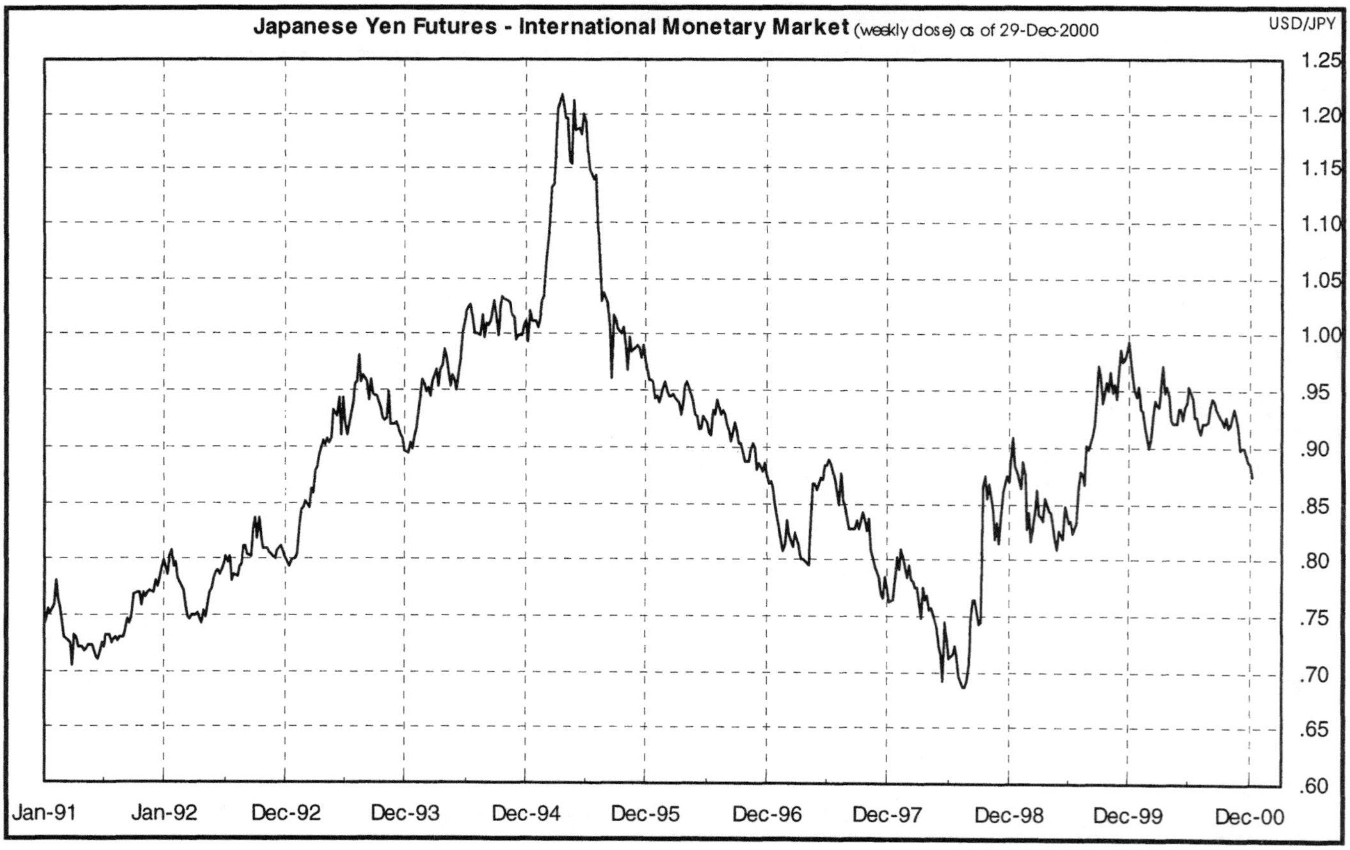

Japanese Yen Futures - International Monetary Market (weekly close) as of 29-Dec-2000

USD/JPY

Swiss Franc Futures - International Monetary Market (weekly close) as of 29-Dec-2000

USD/CHF

Jan-91   Jan-92   Dec-92   Dec-93   Dec-94   Dec-95   Dec-96   Dec-97   Dec-98   Dec-99   Dec-00

.92
.88
.84
.80
.76
.72
.68
.64
.60
.56
.52

CRB Currency Index (1977=100) (weekly close) as of 29-Dec-2000

Index Value

CRB Currency Index (1977 = 100)
5 Futures Markets
British Pound, Canadian Dollar, Euro FX,
Japanese Yen, Swiss Franc

Jan-91   Jan-92   Dec-92   Dec-93   Dec-94   Dec-95   Dec-96   Dec-97   Dec-98   Dec-99   Dec-00

156
152
148
144
140
136
132
128
124
120
116
112
108

CURRENCIES

Canadian Dollars per U.S. Dollar

Year	Jan.	Feb.	Mar.	Apr.	May	June	July	Aug.	Sept.	Oct.	Nov.	Dec.	Average
1992	1.1569	1.1827	1.1923	1.1871	1.1990	1.1955	1.1916	1.1906	1.2208	1.2440	1.2683	1.2711	1.2083
1993	1.2774	1.2595	1.2467	1.2616	1.2686	1.2788	1.2817	1.3078	1.3210	1.3253	1.3166	1.3307	1.2896
1994	1.3175	1.3419	1.3645	1.3821	1.3805	1.3831	1.3818	1.3777	1.3536	1.3495	1.3649	1.3896	1.3656
1995	1.4120	1.3995	1.4065	1.3749	1.3607	1.3772	1.3609	1.3550	1.3495	1.3449	1.3525	1.3685	1.3718
1996	1.3664	1.3753	1.3651	1.3591	1.3690	1.3649	1.3687	1.3717	1.3691	1.3501	1.3382	1.3621	1.3633
1997	1.3484	1.3555	1.3727	1.3947	1.3793	1.3844	1.3769	1.3894	1.3865	1.3863	1.4127	1.4272	1.3845
1998	1.4407	1.4335	1.4159	1.4294	1.4449	1.4647	1.4865	1.5344	1.5212	1.5430	1.5400	1.5429	1.4831
1999	1.5189	1.4971	1.5174	1.4868	1.4614	1.4691	1.4877	1.4921	1.4772	1.4767	1.4671	1.4713	1.4852
2000	1.4480	1.4499	1.4600	1.4681	1.4944	1.4762	1.4778	1.4819	1.4841	1.5119	1.5425	1.5219	1.4847

Average.   *Source: Bridge Information Systems, Inc.*

Euro per U.S. Dollar

Year	Jan.	Feb.	Mar.	Apr.	May	June	July	Aug.	Sept.	Oct.	Nov.	Dec.	Average
1992	1.2903	1.2634	1.2319	1.2433	1.2671	1.3029	1.3717	1.4064	1.3836	1.3205	1.2385	1.2383	1.2965
1993	1.2130	1.1856	1.1779	1.2214	1.2171	1.1828	1.1379	1.1253	1.1720	1.1587	1.1292	1.1285	1.1708
1994	1.1138	1.1183	1.1412	1.1390	1.1636	1.1819	1.2167	1.2182	1.2314	1.2559	1.2357	1.2129	1.1857
1995	1.2380	1.2536	1.3030	1.3292	1.3085	1.3196	1.3340	1.2939	1.2782	1.2987	1.2947	1.2757	1.2939
1996	1.2629	1.2543	1.2544	1.2430	1.2278	1.2386	1.2554	1.2686	1.2587	1.2532	1.2695	1.2416	1.2523
1997	1.2088	1.1592	1.1460	1.1396	1.1441	1.1309	1.0999	1.0694	1.0976	1.1190	1.1418	1.1114	1.1306
1998	1.0859	1.0896	1.0854	1.0931	1.1099	1.1015	1.0991	1.1041	1.1566	1.2015	1.1680	1.1746	1.1224
1999	1.1584	1.1202	1.0882	1.0700	1.0622	1.0385	1.0366	1.0603	1.0501	1.0705	1.0327	1.0117	1.0666
2000	1.0135	.9842	.9644	.9450	.9080	.9496	.9394	.9042	.8706	.8533	.8554	.9004	.9240

Average.   *Source: Bridge Information Systems, Inc.*

Japanese Yen per U.S. Dollar

Year	Jan.	Feb.	Mar.	Apr.	May	June	July	Aug.	Sept.	Oct.	Nov.	Dec.	Average
1992	125.24	127.65	132.79	133.51	130.61	126.72	125.69	126.10	222.58	121.23	123.80	123.94	134.99
1993	124.94	120.77	116.99	112.22	110.10	107.29	107.57	103.74	105.41	107.00	107.78	109.89	111.14
1994	111.33	106.22	105.00	103.36	103.76	102.37	98.65	99.88	98.78	98.36	98.08	100.08	102.16
1995	99.67	98.14	90.40	83.59	84.96	84.55	87.22	94.72	100.49	100.76	101.93	101.84	94.02
1996	105.66	105.57	105.90	107.23	106.42	108.91	109.21	107.84	109.87	112.40	112.35	114.01	108.78
1997	117.93	122.90	122.72	125.66	118.93	114.25	115.30	117.90	120.85	121.06	125.35	129.62	121.04
1998	129.39	125.71	129.04	131.79	135.01	140.40	140.75	144.51	134.45	120.49	120.41	117.01	130.75
1999	113.23	116.62	119.49	119.73	121.88	120.69	119.38	113.16	107.00	105.94	104.62	102.64	113.70
2000	105.29	109.49	106.34	105.65	108.19	106.15	108.03	108.06	106.79	108.39	108.94	112.18	107.79

Average.   *Source: Bridge Information Systems, Inc.*

Swiss Francs per U.S. Dollar

Year	Jan.	Feb.	Mar.	Apr.	May	June	July	Aug.	Sept.	Oct.	Nov.	Dec.	Average
1992	1.4045	1.4567	1.5072	1.5179	1.4895	1.4234	1.3322	1.2948	1.2763	1.3193	1.4276	1.4231	1.4060
1993	1.4775	1.5197	1.5199	1.4572	1.4471	1.4767	1.5138	1.4947	1.4158	1.4421	1.4966	1.4629	1.4770
1994	1.4707	1.4558	1.4295	1.4363	1.4120	1.3723	1.3256	1.3176	1.2895	1.2636	1.2974	1.3275	1.3665
1995	1.2865	1.2694	1.1691	1.1362	1.1678	1.1564	1.1542	1.1958	1.1868	1.1444	1.1440	1.1624	1.1811
1996	1.1810	1.1942	1.1945	1.2194	1.2546	1.2574	1.2324	1.2022	1.2333	1.2583	1.2757	1.3296	1.2361
1997	1.3925	1.4543	1.4622	1.4614	1.4298	1.4419	1.4810	1.5123	1.4702	1.4507	1.4057	1.4393	1.4501
1998	1.4756	1.4616	1.4896	1.5050	1.4782	1.4951	1.5126	1.4927	1.4002	1.3376	1.3856	1.3600	1.4495
1999	1.3856	1.4273	1.4656	1.4972	1.5078	1.5359	1.5472	1.5092	1.5251	1.4891	1.5541	1.5827	1.5022
2000	1.5888	1.6326	1.6624	1.6638	1.7151	1.6422	1.6503	1.7146	1.7564	1.7727	1.7772	1.6778	1.6878

Average.   *Source: Bridge Information Systems, Inc.*

U.S. Dollars per British Pound

Year	Jan.	Feb.	Mar.	Apr.	May	June	July	Aug.	Sept.	Oct.	Nov.	Dec.	Average
1992	1.8083	1.7776	1.7251	1.7562	1.8101	1.8555	1.9193	1.9445	1.8510	1.6547	1.5269	1.5497	1.7649
1993	1.5330	1.4383	1.4621	1.5465	1.5492	1.5090	1.4973	1.4928	1.5251	1.5027	1.4808	1.4904	1.5023
1994	1.4933	1.4787	1.4921	1.4832	1.5038	1.5261	1.5446	1.5421	1.5647	1.6073	1.5864	1.5582	1.5317
1995	1.5742	1.5727	1.6004	1.6087	1.5886	1.5960	1.5955	1.5668	1.5595	1.5782	1.5612	1.5411	1.5786
1996	1.5289	1.5376	1.5278	1.5159	1.5154	1.5417	1.5538	1.5501	1.5595	1.5863	1.6629	1.6660	1.5622
1997	1.6590	1.6258	1.6095	1.6285	1.6325	1.6457	1.6717	1.6044	1.6020	1.6331	1.6887	1.6606	1.6385
1998	1.6347	1.6402	1.6615	1.6720	1.6370	1.6509	1.6429	1.6355	1.6814	1.6933	1.6613	1.6713	1.6568
1999	1.6495	1.6269	1.6213	1.6085	1.6147	1.5957	1.5754	1.6051	1.6237	1.6570	1.6206	1.6131	1.6176
2000	1.6395	1.6007	1.5810	1.5807	1.5084	1.5102	1.5082	1.4885	1.4341	1.4509	1.4252	1.4657	1.5161

Average.   *Source: Bridge Information Systems, Inc.*

Average Open Interest of Canadian Dollar Futures in Chicago   In Contracts

Year	Jan.	Feb.	Mar.	Apr.	May	June	July	Aug.	Sept.	Oct.	Nov.	Dec.
1991	29,072	28,214	25,550	24,894	29,310	33,136	25,113	25,310	30,909	28,805	27,453	22,311
1992	19,724	24,020	24,118	21,354	24,020	22,860	24,773	27,665	28,221	27,827	28,025	24,923
1993	20,410	24,376	25,877	23,639	27,438	29,784	29,385	45,397	40,639	43,476	32,469	28,879
1994	28,277	38,157	48,411	42,730	44,363	42,845	35,370	39,582	49,312	40,706	42,353	59,763
1995	55,863	44,677	33,706	45,394	47,832	36,677	44,930	42,629	49,526	43,032	40,047	40,592
1996	31,028	37,674	38,551	41,411	46,470	37,141	37,522	42,063	44,014	68,674	82,817	72,586
1997	55,949	56,600	72,803	82,732	73,747	57,243	43,937	59,112	56,387	59,265	75,027	74,221
1998	63,300	67,862	61,528	58,938	64,859	74,027	71,313	75,193	60,863	51,967	61,318	50,271
1999	50,061	71,819	63,782	73,773	84,885	71,923	65,877	71,458	61,994	58,749	59,941	51,967
2000	66,374	64,528	58,621	60,389	76,444	69,033	67,198	65,370	65,779	81,995	77,746	65,452

Source: International Monetary Market (IMM), division of the Chicago Mercantile Exchange (CME)

Average Open Interest of Euro FX Futures in Chicago   In Contracts

Year	Jan.	Feb.	Mar.	Apr.	May	June	July	Aug.	Sept.	Oct.	Nov.	Dec.
1998	----	----	----	----	1	1	1	1	1	0	7	7
1999	8,261	30,546	37,837	37,881	46,446	50,615	46,777	55,858	49,352	57,380	58,846	65,346
2000	63,124	68,413	61,180	59,110	67,644	63,361	57,723	69,561	77,617	73,314	79,577	92,730

Source: International Monetary Market (IMM), division of the Chicago Mercantile Exchange (CME)

Average Open Interest of Japanese Yen Futures in Chicago   In Contracts

Year	Jan.	Feb.	Mar.	Apr.	May	June	July	Aug.	Sept.	Oct.	Nov.	Dec.
1991	43,552	64,694	57,115	49,060	52,964	55,727	53,045	56,496	66,174	74,353	74,585	64,219
1992	63,856	67,714	71,702	63,938	63,079	64,596	56,465	58,353	53,462	44,488	45,941	46,887
1993	50,066	70,195	81,979	76,696	82,028	81,103	72,186	80,780	73,002	83,097	84,812	95,817
1994	101,792	94,470	73,286	57,281	65,835	70,759	73,734	72,798	63,419	63,091	80,053	92,834
1995	86,569	86,852	77,649	63,379	67,644	56,285	48,680	63,463	73,830	67,336	73,335	70,268
1996	80,645	78,915	71,643	76,655	73,832	85,398	77,941	73,535	86,723	76,620	72,130	67,301
1997	73,391	82,542	78,466	81,117	85,984	73,322	62,488	82,369	96,468	90,080	130,606	121,001
1998	95,338	101,448	97,183	97,389	106,139	132,732	113,084	145,241	108,808	88,991	89,108	79,262
1999	78,767	81,859	96,271	87,829	118,819	120,681	118,329	136,826	115,884	82,657	87,869	87,595
2000	93,785	125,318	95,034	75,631	80,840	68,359	60,966	79,195	64,845	64,648	68,719	100,713

Source: International Monetary Market (IMM), division of the Chicago Mercantile Exchange (CME)

Average Open Interest of Swiss Franc Futures in Chicago   In Contracts

Year	Jan.	Feb.	Mar.	Apr.	May	June	July	Aug.	Sept.	Oct.	Nov.	Dec.
1991	31,489	36,483	49,061	40,026	38,601	43,476	36,031	35,881	29,833	24,949	32,342	32,439
1992	24,653	33,640	42,825	36,230	38,269	36,668	30,159	33,707	33,167	34,767	45,428	44,901
1993	52,713	49,472	48,002	43,514	47,832	42,343	40,703	44,329	60,446	49,320	58,406	49,670
1994	41,914	46,280	44,134	37,450	42,071	49,162	45,223	43,746	44,495	39,587	51,539	55,424
1995	39,726	44,364	39,358	30,270	30,586	26,766	23,121	30,267	34,228	34,889	38,033	44,741
1996	42,280	42,902	36,924	39,233	46,810	44,848	38,300	40,298	43,695	47,613	53,581	59,405
1997	51,652	54,114	51,121	45,725	48,651	42,530	55,279	58,098	49,296	43,585	51,822	48,560
1998	57,740	46,160	67,722	67,303	63,477	77,564	85,984	70,569	81,465	57,413	44,810	43,436
1999	39,434	58,279	66,250	66,530	73,322	75,322	66,603	71,060	60,214	65,020	67,936	64,507
2000	55,660	69,983	57,703	41,732	46,159	41,727	36,894	50,595	57,439	47,313	48,870	55,982

Source: International Monetary Market (IMM), division of the Chicago Mercantile Exchange (CME)

Average Open Interest of British Pound Futures in Chicago   In Contracts

Year	Jan.	Feb.	Mar.	Apr.	May	June	July	Aug.	Sept.	Oct.	Nov.	Dec.
1991	23,686	34,680	33,558	29,900	30,697	33,792	26,443	21,578	28,215	22,882	31,792	26,443
1992	21,578	28,215	22,882	31,595	36,426	35,529	27,160	28,041	30,137	30,330	33,121	27,935
1993	26,614	41,752	40,238	38,544	39,654	34,953	26,056	32,446	33,560	29,733	37,246	33,606
1994	39,223	43,878	35,554	44,725	46,577	41,801	37,633	34,988	40,751	42,648	49,684	65,834
1995	47,740	44,935	36,805	23,161	26,571	28,402	22,662	34,932	38,900	34,485	43,634	49,804
1996	40,315	50,106	52,349	54,954	52,573	61,461	55,080	50,862	53,868	51,934	62,128	47,652
1997	40,479	38,370	43,742	37,701	40,956	48,890	60,592	50,829	41,801	35,752	56,825	44,667
1998	33,616	31,282	38,712	41,256	47,303	55,511	39,156	49,645	63,756	53,458	54,004	53,578
1999	51,519	59,705	66,913	64,937	58,744	60,414	65,206	54,373	50,949	65,038	49,468	34,191
2000	37,192	45,329	51,645	41,488	51,965	43,009	30,766	36,320	42,781	30,978	34,627	32,913

Source: International Monetary Market (IMM), division of the Chicago Mercantile Exchange (CME)

CURRENCIES

United States Merchandise Trade Balance   In Millions of Dollars

Year	Jan.	Feb.	Mar.	Apr.	May	June	July	Aug.	Sept.	Oct.	Nov.	Dec.	Total
1991	-7,079	-4,201	-1,889	-3,411	-4,158	-3,948	-7,894	-7,450	-7,111	-8,735	-4,942	-5,908	-74,068
1992	-5,470	-2,178	-3,527	-5,772	-5,409	-6,718	-9,893	-10,218	-9,693	-9,706	-8,644	-7,276	-96,106
1993	-6,113	-5,905	-8,886	-8,428	-6,542	-11,749	-12,609	-11,949	-12,516	-12,638	-11,521	-9,115	-132,609
1994	-11,999	-13,573	-11,477	-13,405	-14,079	-14,009	-15,831	-14,232	-14,566	-14,926	-15,292	-13,272	-166,192
1995	-15,746	-14,221	-14,487	-16,051	-16,010	-15,862	-15,887	-13,415	-13,243	-13,108	-12,324	-12,600	-173,729
1996	-15,623	-12,911	-14,574	-15,897	-16,826	-14,839	-17,757	-16,759	-17,976	-15,320	-15,176	-17,695	-191,270
1997	-18,167	-16,780	-14,896	-16,505	-16,982	-15,610	-15,864	-16,909	-16,524	-16,270	-16,605	-16,962	-196,652
1998	-17,187	-18,331	-20,615	-20,860	-22,236	-20,404	-21,066	-22,291	-21,611	-20,990	-21,539	-21,059	-246,853
1999	-23,409	-25,233	-25,741	-25,851	-27,753	-30,381	-31,227	-30,518	-30,573	-31,576	-32,401	-32,255	-345,559
2000²	-34,049	-34,641	-37,148	-36,895	-36,474	-36,862	-38,523	-36,684	-39,328	-39,488			-444,110

¹ Not seasonally adjusted.   ² Preliminary.   *Source: Bureau of Economic Analysis, U.S. Department of Commerce (BEA)*

Index of Real Trade-Weighted Dollar Exchange Rates for Total Agriculture²   1990 = 100³

Year		Jan.	Feb.	Mar.	Apr.	May	June	July	Aug.	Sept.	Oct.	Nov.	Dec.
1993	U.S. Markets	78.2	78.4	78.3	77.0	77.3	76.0	77.1	76.8	76.0	76.6	77.4	77.9
	U.S. Competitors	78.3	78.6	79.1	78.4	78.9	77.7	78.5	78.7	78.0	78.3	78.6	78.1
1994³	U.S. Markets	77.0	77.0	97.1	97.4	97.0	96.9	95.3	95.2	94.3	93.8	94.2	96.7
	U.S. Competitors	78.3	78.3	107.3	107.6	105.7	104.5	101.5	101.2	100.1	98.4	99.1	100.5
1995	U.S. Markets	99.2	98.6	96.7	92.5	92.0	92.0	92.2	94.8	96.6	96.7	98.3	98.0
	U.S. Competitors	98.9	98.0	95.3	93.9	94.5	93.8	92.7	94.5	95.6	94.4	94.4	94.8
1996	U.S. Markets	99.4	99.2	99.4	99.4	99.4	100.1	100.4	99.4	100.1	101.1	100.8	101.5
	U.S. Competitors	96.0	96.0	96.3	97.0	97.9	97.5	96.7	96.2	96.8	97.4	96.5	97.8
1997	U.S. Markets	103.0	105.3	107.0	110.2	104.3	107.8	107.6	109.3	106.9	106.9	112.8	109.8
	U.S. Competitors	99.8	102.8	105.9	107.3	103.9	106.8	110.5	113.3	110.6	110.6	110.7	111.6
1998	U.S. Markets	115.9	114.6	117.1	115.2	115.1	117.6	117.5	119.8	118.5	113.8	114.9	118.6
	U.S. Competitors	117.2	115.6	115.5	114.2	114.8	116.3	117.1	116.3	112.3	109.0	113.9	117.9
1999	U.S. Markets	113.8	115.3	116.7	111.1	111.0	119.0	117.3	117.7	117.4	113.8	116.2	113.4
	U.S. Competitors	115.8	119.1	120.5	110.4	109.7	122.5	124.6	123.3	124.5	122.3	125.6	124.2
2000¹	U.S. Markets	117.0	118.7	116.4	116.4	117.5	118.9	118.3	119.4	118.9	120.7	122.7	
	U.S. Competitors	125.4	127.8	130.1	130.2	132.2	135.9	132.7	134.2	136.9	140.6	143.3	

¹ Preliminary.   ² Real indexes adjust nominal exchange rates for differences in rates of inflation, to avoid the distortion caused by high-inflation countries. A higher value means the dollar has appreciated. Federal Reserve Board Index of trade-weighted value of the U.S. dollar against 10 major currencies. Weights are based on relative importance in world financial markets.   ³ 1988 thru February 1994; 1985 = 100; March 1994 to date; 1990 = 100.   *Source: Economic Research Service, U.S. Department of Agriculture (ERS-USDA)*

United States Balance on Current Account¹   In Millions of Dollars

Year	First Quarter	Second Quarter	Third Quarter	Fourth Quarter	Annual
1991	17,838	4,653	-11,036	-7,171	6,616
1992	467	-10,809	-19,777	-20,509	-47,724
1993	-7,248	-19,867	-28,745	-29,425	-82,681
1994	-17,355	-27,813	-39,199	-37,313	-118,605
1995	-22,940	-32,213	-35,454	-22,959	-109,457
1996	-25,280	-29,878	-36,652	-31,515	-123,318
1997	-34,376	-29,985	-33,407	-42,772	-140,540
1998	-42,390	-51,475	-61,309	-61,965	-217,138
1999	-66,627	-78,982	-89,649	-96,223	-331,479
2000²	-101,505	-104,971	-113,773		-426,999

¹ Not seasonally adjusted.   ² Preliminary.   *Source: Bureau of Economic Analysis, U.S. Department of Commerce (BEA)*

Merchandise Trade and Current Account Balances   In Billions of Dollars

Year	Merchandise Trade Balance					Current Account Balance				
	Canada	Germany	Japan	Switzerland	U.K.	Canada	Germany	Japan	Switzerland	U.K.
1992	7.4	28.2	124.7	-1.0	-22.8	-21.1	-14.5	112.6	15.2	-17.8
1993	10.2	41.2	139.4	1.7	-20.0	-21.7	-9.7	131.9	19.5	-15.9
1994	14.8	50.9	144.1	1.6	-17.0	-13.0	-24.3	130.3	17.5	-2.1
1995	25.8	65.1	132.1	.9	-18.5	-4.4	-20.7	111.2	21.4	-5.9
1996	31.1	70.6	83.7	.9	-20.4	3.4	-7.9	65.8	21.9	-.8
1997	17.2	72.0	101.6	-.3	-19.5	-10.0	-3.1	94.3	25.5	10.8
1998	12.8	79.7	122.4	-1.7	-34.1	-11.0	-4.6	120.8	25.8	-.2
1999	22.8	73.1	123.1	-.3	-43.4	-2.3	-19.3	106.9	29.9	-17.8
2000¹	34.4	64.1	124.8	-1.8	-45.5	12.6	-17.7	127.6	30.3	-21.5
2001²	36.5	69.4	117.1	-2.6	-49.9	15.7	-10.6	126.5	29.6	-26.8

¹ Estimate.   ² Projection.   *Source: Organization for Economic Cooperation and Development (OECD)*

Euro / Swiss Franc
(weekly close) as of 29-Dec-2000

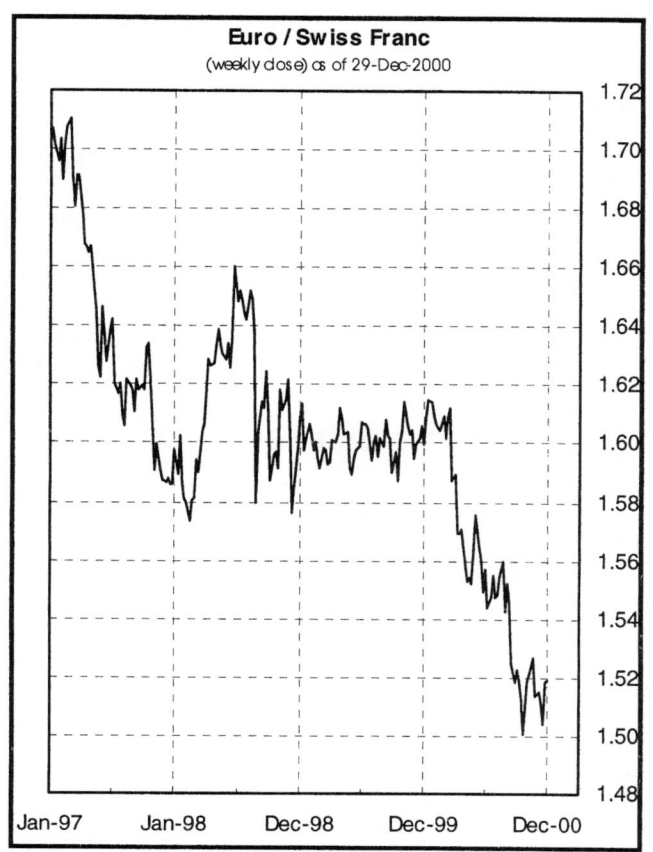

Euro / British Pound
(weekly close) as of 29-Dec-2000

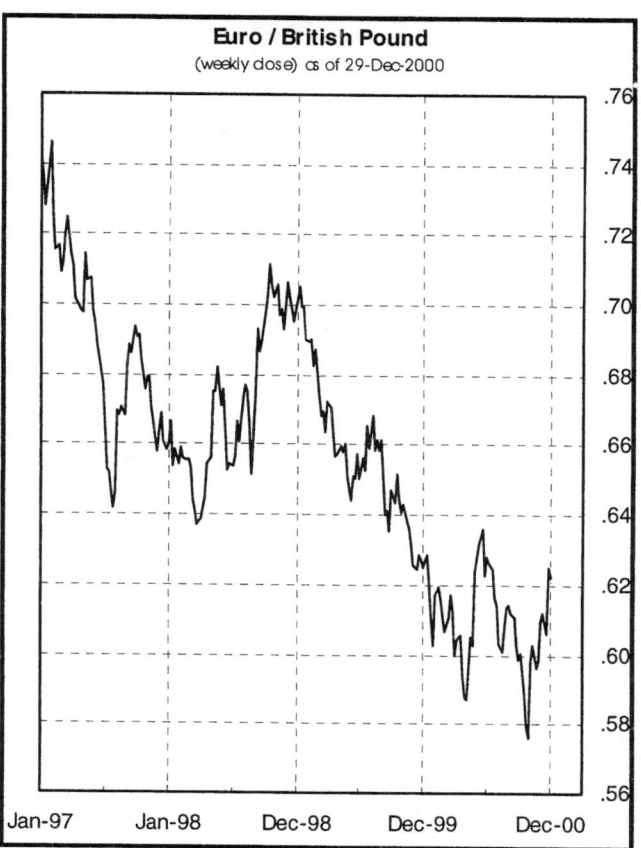

Japanese Yen / British Pound
(weekly close) as of 29-Dec-2000

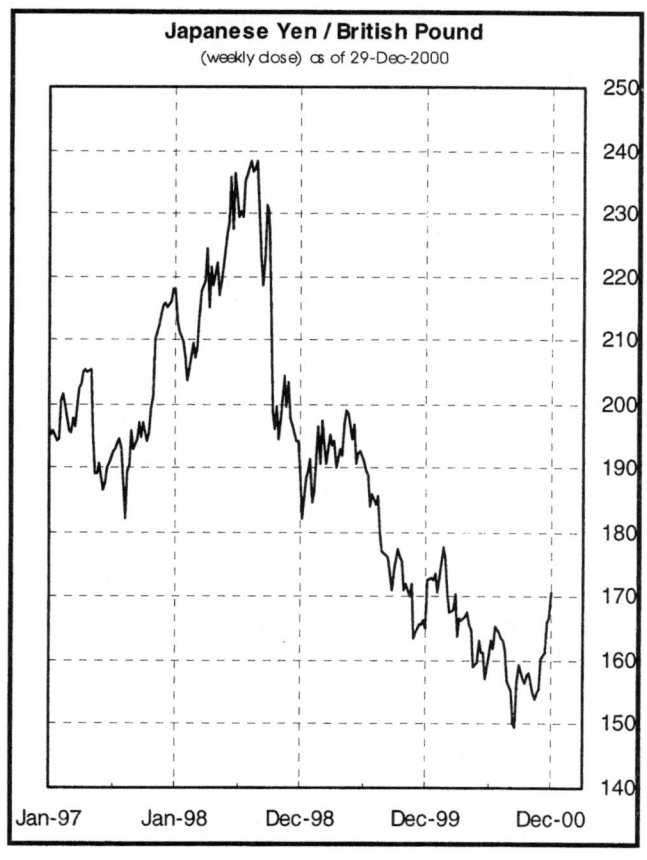

Euro / Japanese Yen
(weekly close) as of 29-Dec-2000

Diamonds

Diamonds have unique properties that give them value not only as gemstones but also as industrial materials. Diamonds are the strongest and hardest materials known and as such find use in grinding, drilling, cutting, and polishing applications. Diamonds that do not meet gem-quality standards for color, clarity, size, or shapes are used as industrial-grade diamonds. Though diamonds have higher costs, they are often more cost-effective because they can cut faster and last longer than rival abrasive materials.

The U.S. Geological Survey estimated 1999 world mine production of gem diamonds at 56.2 million carats, up 2 percent from 1998. The largest producer of gem diamonds was Australia with 18.5 million carats in 1999, up from 18.4 million in 1998. 1999 production in Botswana was 13.5 million carats and in Russia it was 10.5 million carats.

World mine production of natural industrial diamonds in 1999 was estimated at 60.5 million carats, up 1 percent from 1998. The largest producer was Australia with 22.5 million carats. Production by the Congo was 13.2 million carats. Russia produced 10.7 million carats. Other producers of industrial diamonds include Botswana, China, and Brazil. World reserves are estimated to be 580 million carats with the largest reserves in the Congo, Botswana, Australia, Russia, and South Africa.

World Production of Natural Gem Diamonds   In Thousands of Carats

Year	Angola	Australia	Botswana	Brazil	Central African Republic	China	Congo[3]	Ghana	Namibia	Russia	Sierra Leone	South Africa	World Total
1994	270	19,500	10,550	300	401	230	4,000	118	1,312	10,000	155	5,050	52,900
1995	2,600	18,300	11,500	676	400	230	4,000	126	1,382	10,500	113	5,070	55,700
1996	2,250	18,897	12,400	200	350	230	3,600	142	1,402	10,500	162	4,400	55,500
1997	1,110	18,100	15,100	300	400	230	3,000	664	1,345	10,500	300	4,500	56,600
1998[1]	2,400	18,400	14,800	300	330	230	3,300	649	1,394	11,500	200	4,300	58,900
1999[2]	1,080	13,403	15,000	300	400	230	3,500	649	1,995	11,500	225	4,000	55,600

[1] Preliminary.   [2] Estimate.   [3] Formerly Zaire.   *Source: U.S. Geological Survey (USGS)*

World Production of Natural Industrial Diamonds[4]   In Thousands of Carats

Year	Angola	Australia	Botswana	Brazil	Central African Republic	China	Congo[3]	Ghana	Russia	Sierra Leone	South Africa	Venezuela	World Total
1994	30	23,800	5,000	600	131	850	13,000	473	10,000	100	5,800	203	60,300
1995	300	22,400	5,300	600	130	900	13,000	505	10,500	101	5,880	66	60,100
1996	250	23,096	5,000	600	120	900	17,000	573	10,500	108	5,550	73	64,300
1997	124	22,100	5,000	600	100	900	17,600	166	10,500	100	5,540	90	63,400
1998[1]	364	22,500	5,000	600	200	900	18,900	160	11,500	50	6,460	150	67,300
1999[2]	120	16,381	5,000	600	150	920	14,500	160	11,500	75	6,000	150	56,300

[1] Preliminary.   [2] Estimate.   [3] Formerly Zaire.   *Source: U.S. Geological Survey (USGS)*

World Production of Synthetic Diamonds   In Thousands of Carats

Year	Belarus	China	Czech Republic	France	Greece	Ireland	Japan	Russia	South Africa	Sweden	Ukraine	United States	World Total
1994	25,000	15,500	5,000	3,500	1,000	65,000	32,000	80,000	60,000	25,000	8,000	104,000	434,000
1995	25,000	15,500	5,000	3,000	1,000	60,000	32,000	80,000	60,000	25,000	8,000	115,000	440,000
1996	25,000	15,500	5,000	3,000	750	60,000	32,000	80,000	60,000	25,000	8,000	114,000	439,000
1997	25,000	16,000	5,000	3,500	750	60,000	32,000	80,000	60,000	25,000	8,000	125,000	451,000
1998[1]	25,000	16,500	5,000	3,000	750	60,000	32,000	80,000	60,000	25,000	8,000	140,000	463,000
1999[2]	25,000	16,500	3,000	3,000	750	60,000	32,000	80,000		25,000	8,000	208,000	467,000

[1] Preliminary.   [2] Estimate.   *Source: U.S. Geological Survey (USGS)*

Salient Statistics of Industrial Diamonds in the United States   In Millions of Carats

	Bort, Grit & Powder & Dust — Natural and Synthetic								Stones (Natural)					
	Production													Net Import Reliance % of Consumption
Year	Manufactured Diamond	Secondary	Imports for Consumption	Exports & Reexports	In Manufactured Products	Gov't Sales	Apparent Consumption	Price Value of Imports $ Per Carat	Secondary Production	Imports for Consumption	Exports & Reexports	Gov't Sales	Apparent Consumption	Price Value of Imports $ Per Carat
1994	104.0	16.0	174.0	150.0	.4	2.0	146.0	.51	.1	2.8	.5	3.1	5.5	9.41	98
1995	115.0	26.1	188.0	98.0	----	.2	231.0	.43	.3	4.1	.5	.3	4.2	6.62	86
1996	114.0	20.0	218.0	105.0	----	1.0	248.0	.46	.4	2.9	.5	.5	3.3	7.54	88
1997	125.0	10.0	254.0	126.0	----	.7	264.0	.43	.5	2.8	.6	1.2	3.9	7.69	87
1998[1]	140.0	10.0	221.0	104.0	----	[3]	267.0	.44	.5	4.7	.8	.8	5.2	3.92	90
1999[2]	154.0	9.0	215.0	100.0	----	[3]	278.0	.42	.4	3.3	.7	.6	3.6	4.94	89

[1] Preliminary.   [2] Estimate.   [3] Less than 1/2 unit.   *Source: U.S. Geological Survey (USGS)*

Eggs

World egg production increased annually throughout the 1990's and the upward trend continued in 2000 with a record 773 billion eggs (64 billion dozen) produced vs. 762 billion in 1999. A further increase to 796 billion eggs is forecast for 2001.

China produces and consumes about one half of the world egg supply. Production of a record 372 billion eggs in 2000 compares with 365 billion in 1999, and forecasts of 390 billion in 2001. Year 2000 usage of 364 billion compares with 358 billion in 1999. China's egg production and usage doubled during the past decade.

The U.S. is the world's second largest egg producer with 2000 production estimated at a record 84.6 billion vs. 83 billion in 1999, and an 85.9 billion forecast for 2001. However, a major difference persists between China and the U.S. in respect to usage. Much of China's production is directly consumed as fresh brown eggs, whereas in the U.S. about one third of production is processed and white eggs are favored for table use. U.S. consumption of 71.4 billion eggs in 2000 compares with the 1996-99 average of 66 billion and forecasts of 72 billion in 2001. U.S. per capita egg consumption (including egg products) in 2000 was a record 260 vs. 256 in 1999. This is an increase of almost 20 eggs per person since 1997, a reflection of increased usage in the breaking egg market. However, no change in per capita use is expected in 2001.

U.S. consumer preference continues to show signs of shifting to egg products for which eggs are broken relative to whole table eggs, although per capita use is currently still biased towards the latter. Per capita use is much higher abroad: Japan is first at 346 eggs in 2000, followed by Taiwan at 338, Mexico at 327, and then China at 290. Except for France, European per capita usage runs lower than in the U.S.

Foreign egg trade is small and skewed towards exports. The E.U. generally accounts for about a third of world exports—2.8 billion in 2000 vs. the world total of 7.6 billion. Asia, paced by Japan and Hong Kong, imports 60 percent of the world total—3.5 billion in 2000 out of 5.3 billion. U.S. shell egg exports totaled 85 million dozen in 1999 vs. 102 million in 1998, with Canada the primary destination. Exports in the first eight months of 2000 were running ahead of the 1999 pace, but with less shipments to Canada.

There are definitive seasonal swings in U.S. egg production and table consumption. The table egg flocks typically reach a low in mid-summer when heat stress is greatest on the birds. The heat stress also reduces the size of eggs produced by hens from large down to medium. Larger egg production increases as the weather cools, reaching its average monthly high in the winter. However, table egg consumption tends to be highest in the summer when consumers have more time for leisurely meals. Thirty states account for most of U.S. production with Ohio, Iowa, and California the largest producers in 2000, with the bulk of total production as table eggs and the balance hatching eggs.

The New York wholesale market price in 2000 averaged 65.40 cents per dozen vs. 65.60 cents in 1999. Prices are forecast to range between 61-66 cents in 2001. Late summer 2000 retail prices averaged around 89 cents/dozen, basis grade A large, marginally lower than a year earlier.

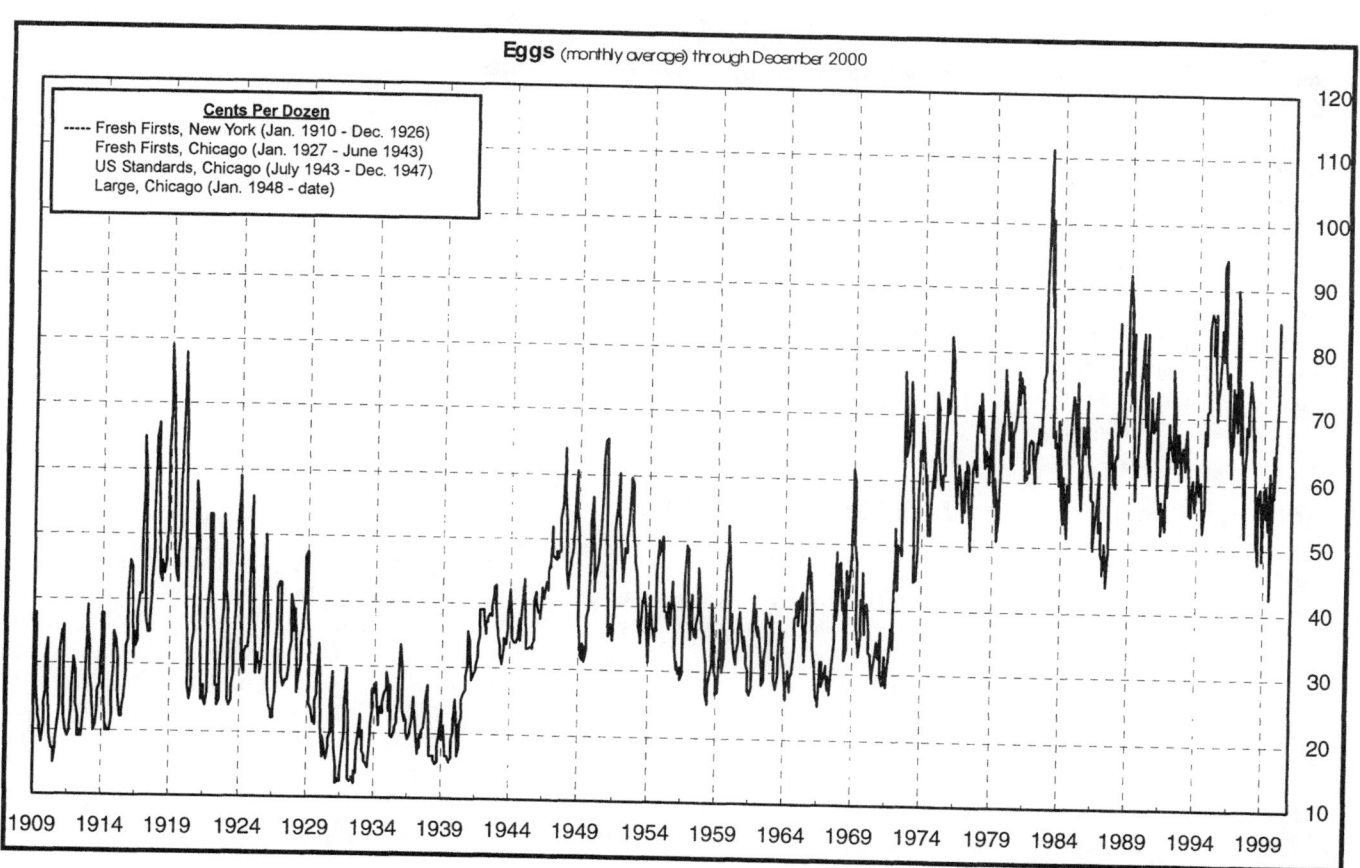

Eggs (monthly average) through December 2000

Cents Per Dozen
----- Fresh Firsts, New York (Jan. 1910 - Dec. 1926)
Fresh Firsts, Chicago (Jan. 1927 - June 1943)
US Standards, Chicago (July 1943 - Dec. 1947)
Large, Chicago (Jan. 1948 - date)

EGGS

World Production of Eggs — In Millions of Eggs

Year	Brazil	China	France	Germany	Italy	Japan	Mexico	Russia	Spain	Ukraine	United Kingdom	United States	World Total[3]
1992	14,190	230,980	15,375	15,165	11,454	42,911	19,650	42,900	8,675	13,445	10,699	70,860	541,859
1993	12,700	235,960	15,355	13,678	11,502	43,252	21,471	40,300	8,454	11,766	10,645	72,072	593,734
1994	13,460	281,010	16,370	13,960	11,599	43,047	25,896	37,400	9,670	10,145	10,620	74,136	643,045
1995	16,065	301,860	16,911	13,838	12,017	42,167	25,760	33,720	9,983	9,404	10,644	74,592	670,211
1996	15,932	253,680	16,500	13,922	11,923	42,786	26,045	31,500	8,952	8,763	10,668	76,536	631,846
1997	12,596	282,350	16,084	14,025	12,298	42,588	28,170	31,900	9,450	8,242	10,752	77,676	666,748
1998	13,636	307,760	16,900	14,164	12,433	42,117	29,898	33,000	9,084	8,269	10,812	79,896	695,281
1999	14,768	365,300	17,550	14,341	12,660	41,975	32,428	33,000	9,216	8,740	10,293	82,944	762,077
2000[1]	15,654	371,880	17,500	14,350	12,400	41,700	33,310	33,200	8,900	8,000	10,000	84,624	772,919
2001[2]	16,435	390,110	17,450	14,350	12,400	41,600	33,640	33,250	9,000	7,700	9,800	85,860	796,277

[1] Preliminary. [2] Forecast. [3] Selected countries. Source: Foreign Agricultural Service, U.S. Department of Agriculture (FAS-USDA)

Salient Statistics of Eggs in the United States

Year	Hens & Pullets On Farm Dec. 1[3] (Thousands)	Hens & Pullets Average Number During Year (Thousands)	Rate of Lay Per Layer During Year[4] (Number)	Eggs Total Produced (Millions)	Eggs Price in Cents Per Dozen	Value of Production[5] Million Dollars	Total Egg Production	Imports[6] (Million Dozen)	Exports[6] (Million Dozen)	Used for Hatching (Million Dozen)	Consumption Total	Consumption Per Capita Eggs[6] (Number)
1991	279,325	275,451	252	69,465	67.6	3,915	5,779	2.3	154.5	708.6	4,938	234.6
1992	282,034	278,824	254	70,749	57.6	3,397	5,885	4.3	157.0	732.0	5,020	235.9
1993	290,626	284,770	253	71,936	63.4	3,800	5,960	4.7	158.9	769.6	5,082	236.2
1994	298,509	291,018	254	73,911	61.4	3,780	6,177	3.7	187.6	803.0	5,186	238.7
1995	298,753	293,854	253	74,591	62.4	3,880	6,216	4.1	208.9	847.2	5,167	235.7
1996	303,754	297,958	256	76,281	74.9	4,762	6,378	5.4	253.1	863.8	5,269	238.0
1997	312,137	304,230	255	77,532	70.3	4,540	6,473	6.9	227.8	894.7	5,359	240.0
1998	321,718	312,035	255	79,754	66.8	4,439	6,659	5.8	218.8	921.8	5,523	245.2
1999[1]	329,305	322,354	257	82,715	62.7	4,323	6,831	4.6	187.8	963.5	5,688	250.3
2000[2]	332,205	327,908	257	84,412			6,980	4.0	200.0	1,010.0	5,774	252.0

[1] Preliminary. [2] Forecast. [3] All layers of laying age. [4] Number of eggs produced during the year divided by the average number of all layers of laying age on hand during the year. [5] Value of sales plus value of eggs consumed in households of producers. [6] Shell-egg equivalent of eggs and egg products. Source: National Agricultural Statistics Service, U.S. Department of Agriculture (NASS-USDA)

Average Wholesale Price of Shell Eggs (Large) Delivered, Chicago — In Cents Per Dozen

Year	Jan.	Feb.	Mar.	Apr.	May	June	July	Aug.	Sept.	Oct.	Nov.	Dec.	Average
1991	80.19	69.00	83.10	64.59	59.93	63.35	73.07	71.30	68.80	67.96	68.50	74.12	70.33
1992	59.16	55.68	55.73	57.17	52.00	56.05	52.82	57.86	64.83	58.14	69.30	68.05	58.90
1993	65.65	63.61	77.50	71.07	61.90	67.64	62.79	67.59	60.64	64.21	65.55	65.55	66.14
1994	62.07	64.89	68.28	58.34	55.12	55.05	58.75	60.63	59.21	55.93	61.50	62.88	60.22
1995	58.55	58.24	60.22	59.87	52.50	56.84	68.10	65.93	71.10	71.34	83.93	86.35	66.08
1996	85.25	80.00	86.12	78.88	69.77	73.00	74.73	80.59	83.80	79.13	93.68	94.60	81.63
1997	79.77	75.18	77.25	68.55	64.40	61.02	74.66	66.07	74.26	68.39	89.87	82.68	73.51
1998	75.20	64.92	74.68	63.64	51.91	61.86	65.00	68.76	67.76	71.45	75.85	75.27	68.03
1999	72.34	62.13	67.85	52.74	51.35	47.86	58.40	59.30	52.86	48.38	59.26	56.38	57.40
2000	54.97	59.65	52.93	61.71	42.59	55.18	52.80	64.39	58.08	66.45	74.26	84.90	60.66

Source: The Wall Street Journal

Total Egg Production in the United States — In Millions of Eggs

Year	Jan.	Feb.	Mar.	Apr.	May	June	July	Aug.	Sept.	Oct.	Nov.	Dec.	Total
1991	5,865	5,316	5,935	5,666	5,796	5,643	5,840	5,855	5,675	5,915	5,807	6,052	69,607
1992	5,951	5,558	6,042	5,832	5,918	5,693	5,908	5,919	5,753	6,019	5,920	6,163	70,860
1993	6,030	5,432	6,067	5,861	6,009	5,816	5,992	6,015	5,876	6,144	6,085	6,264	72,037
1994	6,186	5,598	6,320	6,073	6,189	5,992	6,205	6,272	6,125	6,377	6,265	6,516	74,121
1995	6,369	5,714	6,448	6,177	6,251	6,010	6,145	6,146	5,990	6,260	6,232	6,523	74,265
1996	6,398	5,954	6,495	6,243	6,340	6,169	6,440	6,447	6,235	6,495	6,409	6,696	76,321
1997	6,577	5,909	6,625	6,355	6,519	6,292	6,457	6,500	6,366	6,664	6,572	6,841	77,677
1998	6,766	6,109	6,869	6,603	6,665	6,456	6,720	6,694	6,480	6,791	6,723	7,047	79,923
1999[1]	6,979	6,281	7,052	6,784	6,941	6,742	6,903	6,971	6,860	7,131	7,016	7,279	82,939
2000[2]	7,157	6,648	7,234	7,013	7,104	6,801	7,061	7,104	6,854	7,130	7,027	7,279	84,412

[1] Preliminary. [2] Estimate. Source: National Agricultural Statistics Service, U.S. Department of Agriculture (NASS-USDA)

Per Capita Disappearance of Eggs⁴ in the United States   In Number of Eggs

Year	First Quarter	Second Quarter	Third Quarter	Fourth Quarter	Total	Total Consumption (Million Dozen)	Year	First Quarter	Second Quarter	Third Quarter	Fourth Quarter	Total	Total Consumption (Million Dozen)
1990	47.0	46.3	46.0	47.7	186.8	3,891	1996	44.5	42.1	43.4	45.0	175.0	3,893
1991	46.7	43.8	45.1	47.0	182.6	3,844	1997	59.0	59.3	59.7	62.1	240.1	3,894
1992	45.1	44.1	44.4	46.7	180.3	3,838	1998	60.5	60.5	61.1	63.2	244.9	3,993
1993	46.1	44.0	43.8	46.0	179.7	3,825	1999¹	62.7	62.8	63.8	66.2	255.7	4,070
1994	45.0	43.0	43.9	46.0	177.9	3,864	2000²	64.7	64.0	64.0	65.8	258.5	4,124
1995	44.0	43.1	42.7	45.0	174.9	3,834	2001³	64.3	63.6	63.9	66.4	258.2	

¹ Preliminary.   ² Estimate.   ³ Forecast   *Source: Economic Research Service, U.S. Department of Agriculture (ERS-USDA)*

Egg-Feed Ratio¹ in the United States

Year	Jan.	Feb.	Mar.	Apr.	May	June	July	Aug.	Sept.	Oct.	Nov.	Dec.	Average
1991	13.2	11.1	12.6	10.0	8.6	8.8	10.4	9.8	9.4	9.7	9.9	11.2	10.4
1992	8.4	7.8	7.4	7.6	6.7	7.0	7.3	8.1	9.6	9.3	11.2	11.1	8.4
1993	10.5	10.3	11.7	10.6	9.1	9.8	8.2	8.9	8.1	8.8	8.8	8.2	9.4
1994	7.9	8.0	8.4	7.7	7.2	7.0	8.0	9.0	9.2	8.9	10.3	9.9	8.5
1995	9.4	9.3	9.0	8.9	7.5	7.6	8.0	8.5	8.9	8.6	10.1	10.0	8.8
1996	9.8	8.7	9.1	7.9	6.5	6.7	6.3	6.9	8.1	9.3	11.3	12.5	8.6
1997	10.1	9.9	8.6	7.4	7.1	6.6	8.2	7.8	9.3	8.7	11.4	11.0	8.8
1998	10.1	8.3	9.4	8.5	6.7	8.0	7.9	10.8	10.7	11.3	12.6	12.8	9.7
1999	11.7	10.6	11.3	9.2	7.8	8.2	9.9	10.1	9.3	8.0	11.9	10.1	9.8
2000²	8.9	11.3	8.0	9.9	6.3	9.6	9.2	13.0	10.3	12.4	13.3	15.0	10.6

¹ Pounds of laying feed equivalent in value to one dozen eggs.   ² Preliminary.   *Source: Economic Research Service, U.S. Department of Agriculture (ERS-USDA)*

Total Eggs -- Supply and Distribution in the United States   In Millions of Dozen

Year & Quarters	Beginning Stocks	Production	Imports⁴	Total Supply	Exports⁴	Eggs Used for Hatching	Ending Stocks	Total	Per Capita (Number)
1994 I	10.7	1,509	1.0	1,520	40.2	195.3	12.1	1,273	58.8
II	12.1	1,521	1.1	1,535	45.5	205.3	11.9	1,272	58.6
III	11.9	1,550	1.0	1,563	49.3	202.8	13.8	1,297	59.6
IV	13.8	1,597	.6	1,611	52.6	199.6	14.9	1,344	61.6
1995 I	14.9	1,549	1.1	1,565	45.5	207.1	14.9	1,297	59.4
II	14.9	1,545	1.2	1,561	50.1	214.1	17.9	1,279	58.4
III	17.9	1,533	1.0	1,552	47.0	213.0	13.0	1,279	58.3
IV	13.0	1,589	.8	1,602	66.4	212.9	11.2	1,312	59.6
1996 I	11.2	1,571	1.5	1,583	59.3	217.4	9.8	1,297	58.8
II	9.8	1,563	1.6	1,574	65.6	217.2	9.6	1,282	58.0
III	9.6	1,594	1.2	1,604	66.0	215.8	11.9	1,311	59.1
IV	11.9	1,632	1.0	1,645	62.2	214.3	8.5	1,360	61.2
1997 I	8.5	1,593	1.9	1,603	61.7	221.1	6.5	1,314	59.0
II	6.5	1,597	1.5	1,605	50.3	227.2	6.3	1,321	59.3
III	6.3	1,610	1.6	1,618	51.6	225.1	8.2	1,333	59.7
IV	8.2	1,673	1.9	1,683	64.2	221.3	7.4	1,390	62.1
1998¹ I	7.4	1,645	1.7	1,654	61.7	226.5	7.9	1,358	60.5
II	7.9	1,644	1.2	1,653	51.5	233.3	7.7	1,360	60.5
III	7.7	1,658	1.2	1,667	53.3	230.6	6.3	1,377	61.1
IV	6.3	1,712	1.8	1,720	52.3	231.4	8.4	1,428	63.2
1999² I	8.4	1,691	1.6	1,701	39.8	233.5	7.0	1,421	62.7
II	7.0	1,702	2.3	1,712	37.3	241.2	8.6	1,425	62.8
III	8.6	1,727	1.9	1,737	39.8	236.5	6.4	1,455	64.2
IV	6.4	1,765	1.8	1,773	42.0	235.0	5.0	1,491	65.8
2000³ I	5.0	1,735	1.0	1,741	40.0	245.0	5.0	1,451	63.5
II	5.0	1,735	1.0	1,741	40.0	255.0	5.0	1,441	62.9
III	5.0	1,755	1.0	1,761	44.0	255.0	5.0	1,457	63.4
IV	5.0	1,805	1.0	1,811	46.0	250.0	5.0	1,510	65.6

¹ Preliminary.   ² Estimate.   ³ Forecast.   ⁴ Shell-egg equivalent of eggs and egg products.   *Source: Economic Research Service, U.S. Department of Agriculture (ERS-USDA)*

EGGS

Hens and Pullets of Laying Age (Layers) in the United States, on First of Month — In Thousands

Year	Jan.	Feb.	Mar.	Apr.	May	June	July	Aug.	Sept.	Oct.	Nov.	Dec.
1991	273,917	275,533	274,446	272,541	272,150	272,944	272,779	272,998	274,277	276,187	278,433	279,325
1992	280,697	279,274	279,117	279,009	276,757	275,645	275,179	275,091	274,010	279,233	280,183	282,034
1993	281,639	282,933	282,005	282,480	281,468	280,795	280,517	282,201	282,341	284,771	285,298	290,626
1994	290,413	289,625	290,416	290,979	289,125	288,398	287,454	288,484	292,116	294,576	295,719	298,509
1995	300,331	298,202	297,689	296,290	294,697	290,806	289,018	286,519	289,595	290,889	294,486	298,293
1996	299,261	298,320	298,348	298,029	295,123	293,740	294,044	296,612	296,911	298,433	299,910	303,754
1997	305,011	303,449	304,276	303,997	302,766	300,692	299,007	298,844	300,138	305,664	307,146	312,137
1998	311,593	312,111	314,322	313,833	309,945	309,235	309,049	308,747	309,706	312,807	316,840	321,718
1999	322,137	322,382	323,161	322,162	320,783	320,211	320,672	318,944	321,349	323,365	327,135	329,320
2000[1]	328,307	328,767	330,879	330,827	327,617	325,193	325,048	326,265	324,724	326,199	329,132	332,205

[1] Preliminary.   Source: National Agricultural Statistics Service, U.S. Department of Agriculture (NASS-USDA)

Eggs Laid Per Hundred Layers in the United States — In Number of Eggs

Year	Jan.	Feb.	Mar.	Apr.	May	June	July	Aug.	Sept.	Oct.	Nov.	Dec.	Average
1991	2,186	1,977	2,217	2,124	2,168	2,108	2,186	2,190	2,106	2,175	2,124	2,208	2,147
1992	2,176	2,036	2,216	2,148	2,186	2,110	2,196	2,204	2,125	2,200	2,140	2,226	2,164
1993	2,192	1,970	2,209	2,132	2,182	2,112	2,175	2,183	2,124	2,209	2,167	2,237	2,158
1994	2,199	1,987	2,246	2,160	2,204	2,142	2,222	2,230	2,152	2,227	2,180	2,176	2,177
1995	2,130	1,919	2,173	2,092	2,137	2,075	2,137	2,135	2,065	2,140	2,108	2,183	2,108
1996	2,141	1,996	2,178	2,105	2,153	2,099	2,180	2,172	2,094	2,171	2,124	2,199	2,134
1997	2,161	1,943	2,176	2,093	2,156	2,093	2,155	2,165	2,096	2,172	2,122	2,193	2,127
1998	2,169	1,950	2,187	2,117	2,153	2,088	2,175	2,165	2,082	2,157	2,109	2,190	2,129
1999	2,165	1,946	2,185	2,110	2,166	2,104	2,158	2,177	2,128	2,192	2,138	2,214	2,140
2000[1]	2,178	2,019	2,186	2,130	2,177	2,091	2,169	2,181	2,101	2,172	2,125	2,193	2,144

[1] Preliminary.   Source: National Agricultural Statistics Service, U.S. Department of Agriculture (NASS-USDA)

Egg-Type Chicks Hatched by Commercial Hatcheries in the United States — In Thousands

Year	Jan.	Feb.	Mar.	Apr.	May	June	July	Aug.	Sept.	Oct.	Nov.	Dec.	Total
1991	34,487	34,837	37,041	39,775	38,404	36,227	33,696	33,656	34,007	34,307	30,400	32,717	419,554
1992	32,496	31,950	36,490	35,755	38,513	34,568	32,265	28,349	28,760	32,843	27,718	31,612	391,319
1993	34,885	34,009	38,264	37,163	36,742	35,587	33,980	31,455	31,775	31,634	30,074	30,448	405,986
1994	33,236	31,086	33,489	35,657	35,322	31,985	29,613	31,295	31,587	32,066	26,075	30,166	381,577
1995	32,374	32,743	36,019	35,078	37,540	34,996	29,572	31,442	33,586	33,383	29,129	30,639	396,501
1996	31,580	34,608	36,890	35,740	38,028	33,017	31,920	31,782	31,930	32,319	30,947	32,879	401,640
1997	33,752	35,655	37,347	38,842	39,020	36,796	33,772	33,061	37,118	35,262	28,122	35,796	424,543
1998	37,168	34,597	40,604	39,057	39,206	39,323	35,576	33,398	37,959	34,667	31,217	35,501	438,273
1999	35,242	36,367	41,172	41,950	40,726	41,474	34,275	35,454	39,287	39,044	32,892	33,045	450,928
2000[1]	34,125	35,491	39,560	36,621	40,879	36,575	33,091	34,317	36,290	35,231	32,646	35,008	429,834

[1] Preliminary.   Source: National Agricultural Statistics Service, U.S. Department of Agriculture (NASS-USDA)

Cold Storage Holdings of Frozen Eggs in the United States, on First of Month — In Millions of Pounds[1]

Year	Jan.	Feb.	Mar.	Apr.	May	June	July	Aug.	Sept.	Oct.	Nov.	Dec.
1991	14.7	14.8	14.0	14.1	13.0	13.5	14.2	18.1	16.3	16.5	17.0	15.1
1992	16.0	20.0	19.2	19.7	18.8	18.9	21.1	19.5	20.2	20.0	21.7	18.7
1993	17.2	16.7	16.9	15.1	14.3	15.5	15.1	17.6	18.1	14.4	14.0	13.5
1994	13.7	14.8	15.8	15.6	16.3	15.2	15.4	19.0	19.7	17.8	20.0	19.1
1995	19.5	19.5	18.3	18.5	17.3	18.1	22.9	20.6	18.0	16.2	14.4	12.5
1996	13.8	15.6	16.2	12.4	11.5	11.4	11.7	13.5	15.0	14.9	12.6	10.4
1997	10.2	11.0	11.5	8.5	8.5	8.3	8.6	8.9	11.1	10.8	10.9	10.3
1998	9.7	12.0	12.3	10.4	9.2	12.9	10.2	11.8	9.0	8.2	9.0	9.3
1999	11.0	11.0	10.8	9.2	9.4	9.7	11.3	11.1	8.8	9.5	9.0	8.5
2000[2]	10.1	17.6	9.3	8.1	7.2	8.1	8.7	14.4	14.9	14.4	16.5	15.2

[1] Converted on basis 39.5 pounds frozen eggs equals 1 case.   [2] Preliminary.   Source: National Agricultural Statistics Service, U.S. Department of Agriculture (NASS-USDA)

90

Electric Power

U.S. net generation of electric power by electric utilities in the January-July 2000 period was 1.77 trillion kilowatt-hours. That represented a decline of 5 percent from the same period in 1999, and a 5 percent decline from 1998. In January-July 1999, U.S. generation of electric power was 1.86 trillion kilowatt-hours. In July 2000, electric power generated was 279 billion kilowatt-hours, up 4 percent from June. Electric power generation tends to be the highest in the months of July and August. Power generation in July 2000 was 12 percent less than in July 1999. For all of 1999, U.S. electric power generation was 3.17 trillion kilowatt-hours, down 1 percent from the 1998 total of 3.21 trillion kilowatt-hours.

Electric power production by nonutility power producers has been trending higher. For 1990, the total was 217 billion kilowatt-hours. For all of 1999, the total had risen to 517 billion kilowatt-hours. In January-July 2000, the total was 422 billion kilowatt-hours, up 53 percent from the same period in 1999. In July 2000, power production was 78 billion kilowatt-hours, up 18 percent from the previous month, and up 50 percent from July 1999.

Total U.S. electric power generation in July 2000 was 356 billion kilowatt-hours, down 4 percent from a year earlier. In January-July 2000, electric power generated was 2.19 trillion kilowatt-hours, up 2 percent from the same period in 1999. For all of 1999, the total was 3.69 trillion kilowatt-hours.

Most of the electric power in the U.S. was generated using coal as a fuel. In the January-July 2000 period coal generated 1.12 trillion kilowatt-hours of electric power, up almost 4 percent from the same period in 1999. For all of 1999, coal produced 1.88 trillion kilowatt-hours of power or 51 percent of the U.S. total.

Power generation using petroleum as a fuel in January-July 2000 was 57.4 billion kilowatt-hours, down 28 percent from the same period in 1999. For all of 1999, the total petroleum fuel power generation was 119 billion kilowatt-hours, 3 percent of the total.

Use of natural gas as a fuel generated 342.6 billion kilowatt-hours of power in 2000, up 10 percent from 1999. For all of 1999, power production was 555.9 billion kilowatt-hours, some 16 percent of the U.S. total.

Nuclear power in January-July 2000 generated 441.7 billion kilowatt-hours, up 7 percent from the same period in 1999. For all of 1999, nuclear power generated 728.2 billion kilowatt-hours, or 20 percent of the U.S. total.

Renewable energy sources generate smaller amounts of electric power. In 1999, conventional hydroelectric power generated 313.5 billion kilowatt-hours. Geothermal sources generated 14.2 billion kilowatt-hours of electric power in 1999. Wood fuel generated 42.9 billion kilowatt-hours in 1999. Wind power generated 4.8 billion kilowatt-hours in 1999.

World Electricity Production (Monthly Average) In Millions of Kilowatt Hours

Year	Australia	Canada	China	Germany	India	Italy	Japan	Rep. of Korea	Russia[3]	South Africa	Ukraine[3]	United Kingdom	United States
1991	13,071	42,326	55,918	44,949	23,893	18,503	74,007	9,885	136,156	14,026	----	26,900	254,818
1992	13,313	41,803	61,562	44,761	25,081	18,854	74,611	10,914	84,038	14,008	21,044	27,240	256,209
1993	13,646	42,591	67,723	37,722	26,961	18,566	75,559	12,036	79,716	14,548	19,159	26,834	266,410
1994	13,959	44,502	75,312	37,786	29,250	19,323	80,361	13,749	72,993	15,825	16,910	27,042	271,150
1995	14,449	44,868	81,979	38,207	31,675	20,228	82,490	15,388	71,669	16,016	16,193	27,970	279,820
1996	14,806	45,747	88,275	45,586	32,808	20,340	84,113	17,125	70,600	16,096	15,166	27,191	287,250
1997	15,256	46,151	91,277	45,133	35,105	20,898	86,676	18,704	69,511	16,108	14,834	27,012	291,185
1998	14,737	45,259	94,011	45,860	37,326	21,659	76,763	17,942	68,930	17,119	14,402	27,914	301,489
1999[1]	15,399	45,158	100,345	45,973	39,766	21,856	76,755	19,944	70,611	16,961	14,342	28,032	305,707
2000[2]	15,569	52,700	108,177	50,137	40,786	22,504	77,055	21,978	73,900	17,635	14,210	28,977	300,454

[1] Preliminary. [2] Estimate. [3] Formerly part of the U.S.S.R.; data not reported separately until 1992. *Source: United Nations*

Installed Capacity, Capability & Peak Load of the U.S. Electric Utility Industry In Millions of Kilowatt Hours

Year	Total Electric Utility Industry	Hydro	Gas, Turbine & Steam	Nuclear Power	Internal Combustion	Investor Owned	Cooperative	Subtotal Gov't	Municipal Utilities	State	Federal Projects	Capability at Winter Peak Load	Non-Coincident Winter Peak Load	Capacity Margin Non-Coincident Peak Load (%)	Total Electric Utility Industry Generation	Annual Peak Load Factor (%)
1990	735.1	87.2	531.1	108.0	8.7	568.8	26.3	139.9	40.1	65.4	34.4	696.8	484.0	20.4	2,808.2	60.4
1991	740.0	88.7	534.1	108.4	8.8	573.0	26.5	140.5	40.4	65.6	34.5	703.2	485.4	20.2	2,825.0	60.9
1992	741.7	89.7	534.5	107.9	9.6	572.9	26.0	142.7	41.6	66.1	35.0	707.8	493.0	21.1	2,797.2	61.1
1993	744.7	90.2	536.9	107.8	9.8	575.2	26.1	143.4	41.8	66.1	35.5	712.0	521.7	17.1	2,882.5	61.0
1994	746.0	90.3	537.9	107.9	9.9	574.8	26.4	144.7	42.0	66.3	36.4	715.1	518.3	16.7	2,910.7	61.2
1995	750.5	91.1	541.6	107.9	9.9	578.7	27.1	144.8	42.2	65.9	36.6	727.7	544.7	13.2	2,994.5	59.8
1996	756.5	91.0	546.6	109.0	9.9	582.2	27.2	147.1	43.0	67.2	36.9	740.5	545.1	14.9	3,073.1	61.0
1997	759.9	92.5	549.7	107.6	10.0	582.5	28.0	149.4	43.8	68.9	36.7	743.8	560.2	13.4	3,119.1	61.3
1998	728.3	91.2	522.1	104.8	10.2	531.3	32.5	164.5	50.5	68.7	45.3	835.3	652.4	12.0	3,212.2	62.0
1999[1]	678.0	89.8	476.3	102.3	9.6	483.7	34.6	159.6	50.2	68.7	40.7	848.9	656.3	10.3	3,173.7	61.2

[1] Preliminary. *Source: Edison Electric Institute (EEI)*

Available Electricity and Energy Sales in the United States — In Billions of Kilowatt Hours

	Net Generation — Electric Utility Industry									Sales to Ultimate Customers							
Year	Total²	Hydro	Natural Gas	Coal	Fuel Oil	Nu-clear	Other Source³	Total	Total Million $	Total	Resi-den-tial	Inter-depart-mental	Com-mercial	Indust-rial	Street & Highway Lighting	Other Public Auth.	Rail ways & Rail-roads
1986	2,487	290.8	248.5	1,386	136.6	414.0	11.5	2,599	152,481	2,360	820	5.2	629.0	819	15.0	61.9	4.7
1987	2,572	249.7	272.6	1,464	118.5	455.3	12.3	2,719	155,734	2,441	846	4.5	658.4	844	14.4	63.0	4.9
1988	2,704	222.9	252.8	1,541	148.9	527.0	12.0	2,879	162,449	2,561	886	4.2	697.8	882	14.6	64.6	5.1
1989	2,784	265.1	266.6	1,554	158.3	529.4	11.3	2,985	169,903	2,636	899	4.3	715.9	913	14.6	69.3	5.3
1990	2,808	279.9	264.1	1,560	117.0	576.9	10.7	3,041	176,929	2,705	916	4.2	738.9	932	15.2	72.8	5.3
1991	1,825	275.5	264.2	1,551	111.5	612.6	10.1	3,100	185,220	2,745	949	2.6	753.3	935	15.6	76.1	5.3
1992	2,797	239.6	263.9	1,576	88.9	618.8	10.2	3,107	187,399	2,744	929	2.6	755.7	949	15.8	77.2	5.2
1993	2,883	265.1	258.9	1,639	99.5	610.3	9.6	3,210	197,992	2,860	994	2.7	803.1	957	18.1	69.7	5.4
1994	2,911	243.7	291.1	1,635	91.0	640.4	8.9	3,283	202,597	2,936	1,008	3.0	833.5	990	18.5	70.6	5.8
1995	2,995	293.7	307.3	1,653	60.8	673.4	6.4	3,395	207,652	3,017	1,042	2.1	863.5	1,006	17.9	69.9	5.5
1996	3,073	324.5	262.3	1,737	67.0	674.7	7.2	3,473	212,390	3,103	1,082	2.5	887.1	1,028	18.0	70.3	5.3
1997	3,119	333.5	283.1	1,789	77.1	629.4	7.5	3,536	215,264	3,154	1,079	2.6	929.0	1,028	19.7	75.6	5.3
1998	3,212	304.4	309.2	1,807	110.2	673.7	7.2	3,726	218,491	3,256	1,128	NA	968.5	1,040	16.3	87.2	NA
1999¹	3,174	293.9	296.4	1,768	86.9	725.0	3.7	3,743	215,647	3,250	1,141	NA	970.6	1,018	15.9	90.9	NA

¹ Preliminary.   ² Includes internal combustion.   ³ Includes electricity produced from geothermal, wood, waste, wind, solar, etc.   NA = Not available.
Source: Edison Electric Institute (EEI)

Electric Power Production by Electric Utilities in the United States — In Millions of Kilowatt Hours

Year	Jan.	Feb.	Mar.	Apr.	May	June	July	Aug.	Sept.	Oct.	Nov.	Dec.	Total
1986	217,470	192,336	196,834	186,074	197,315	215,015	242,672	225,166	206,692	197,754	196,432	213,551	2,487,310
1987	222,749	194,034	201,849	189,496	206,074	225,589	247,915	247,645	213,008	203,009	200,258	220,500	2,572,127
1988	237,897	216,937	214,013	196,000	208,371	232,747	257,461	267,693	220,179	210,608	209,593	232,752	2,704,250
1989	232,747	219,826	226,742	208,042	220,124	235,689	257,050	258,687	227,150	219,910	219,300	259,038	2,784,304
1990	237,289	212,880	226,034	211,070	222,908	249,175	266,375	268,527	237,017	224,694	213,748	237,434	2,808,151
1991	248,455	210,821	221,400	209,004	234,373	248,427	271,976	268,115	233,885	223,430	221,377	233,760	2,825,023
1992	243,970	217,761	224,665	210,837	220,355	236,842	266,148	255,203	234,760	221,289	221,263	244,126	2,797,219
1993	245,782	224,617	234,801	211,374	222,396	249,633	282,292	279,132	236,603	223,629	225,855	246,412	2,882,525
1994	261,697	225,011	231,544	214,817	227,703	263,859	278,149	274,645	237,663	227,972	224,745	242,906	2,910,712
1995	253,077	228,127	233,675	217,381	236,381	256,083	292,827	304,709	245,574	234,409	234,117	258,170	2,994,529
1996	268,713	245,388	247,989	226,423	251,570	268,644	289,329	290,458	250,672	240,674	241,077	258,138	3,077,442
1997	273,410	233,907	244,659	230,512	243,143	266,588	304,628	294,557	266,649	253,267	243,726	267,477	3,122,522
1998	265,435	235,340	256,575	232,457	265,077	291,029	317,521	312,538	279,198	251,380	239,089	266,532	3,212,171
1999	275,094	239,532	258,738	238,922	254,233	280,472	317,766	308,325	261,924	243,786	235,792	259,089	3,173,674
2000¹	265,478	236,873	240,979	226,572	253,389	267,569	278,779	286,061	244,702	228,001			3,034,084

¹ Preliminary.   *Source: Energy Information Administration, U.S. Department of Energy (EIA-DOE)*

Use of Fuels for Electric Generation in the United States

	Consumption of Fuell			Total Fuel in Coal Equivalent³ (Thousand Short Tons)	Net Generation by Fuels4 (Million Kilowatthour)	Pounds of Coal Per Kilowatthour (Pounds)	Cost of Fossil-fuel at Elec. Util. Cents/MBTU	Average Cost of Fuel Per Kiliowatthour (Cents)	Heat Rate BTU Per kilowatthour	Cost Per Million BTU Consumed (Cents)
Year	Coal (Thousand Short Tons)	Fuel Oil (Thousand Barrels)²	Gas (Million Cubic Feet)							
1986	685,056	230,482	2,602,370	907,720	1,770,925	.989	175.0	1.92	10,423	184.5
1987	717,894	199,378	2,844,051	944,420	1,854,895	.981	170.6	1.84	10,354	177.7
1988	758,372	248,096	2,635,613	984,969	1,942,353	.984	164.3	1.76	10,328	170.7
1989	766,888	267,451	2,787,012	1,004,964	1,978,577	.987	167.5	1.79	10,312	174.0
1990	773,549	196,054	2,787,332	988,300	1,940,712	.997	168.9	1.80	10,366	174.1
1991	772,268	184,886	2,789,014	987,469	1,926,801	.996	160.3	1.75	10,322	169.6
1992	779,860	147,335	2,765,608	983,484	1,928,683	.990	159.0	1.72	10,340	166.6
1993	813,508	162,454	2,682,440	1,017,086	1,997,605	.993	159.5	1.72	10,351	166.6
1994	817,270	151,004	2,987,146	1,033,575	2,017,646	.999	152.6	1.59	10,425	152.6
1995	829,007	102,150	3,196,507	1,039,174	2,021,064	1.003	145.3	1.48	10,173	145.2
1996	874,681	113,274	2,732,107	1,063,755	2,066,666	1.007	151.9	1.55	10,176	151.9
1997	900,361	125,146	2,968,453	1,103,037	2,148,756	1.005	152.2	1.53	10,081	152.2
1998	910,867	178,614	3,258,054	1,147,317	2,226,860	.996	143.8	1.49	10,360	143.8
1999¹	894,120	143,830	3,113,419	1,113,614	2,150,989	1.012	144.2	1.48	10,301	144.1

¹ Preliminary.   ² 42-gallon barrels.   ³ Coal equivalents are calculated on the basis of Btu instead of generation data.   ⁴ Excludes wood & waste fuels.
Source: Edison Electric Institute (EEI)

Fertilizer

The three primary fertilizer chemicals used in the United States are nitrogen, phosphorus, and potassium. They provide basic nutrients to plants. The basic nitrogen fertilizer is ammonia which is comprised of nitrogen and natural gas. Nitrogen is required for proper nutrition and maturation of the plant. Phosphorus is produced from phosphate rock and is important in plant nutrition. Potash denotes a variety of mined and manufactured salts, all containing the element potassium in water soluble form. Potassium activates plant enzymes, aids photosynthesis in the leaves, and increases disease resistance.

The U.S. Geological Survey reported that in 1999, world production of ammonia was 101 million metric tonnes. This was down 5 percent from 1998. The largest producer was China with 1999 output of 28 million tonnes, up 6 percent from 1998. U.S. production of ammonia was 11 million tonnes, down 25 percent from the previous year. Low prices for ammonia, high natural gas prices, and large stocks led to reduced ammonia production in the United States. In the U.S. there were several plant closures that reduced production capacity. At the same time there was an increase in production capacity in other countries. It was expected that when economic activity in Asia increased there would be increased need for ammonia in fertilizer products. Other large producers of ammonia include India, Russia, Canada, Indonesia, and the Ukraine.

U.S. fixed nitrogen or synthetic anhydrous ammonia production (contained nitrogen) in 1999 was estimated to be 14.1 million tonnes, up 2 percent from 1998. For 1999, production of nitrogen fertilizer was 12.5 million tonnes, up 6 percent from the previous year, while nonfertilizer production was 1.6 million tonnes. In 1999, the major downstream nitrogen compounds produced in the U.S. were urea, 8.5 million tonnes; ammonium nitrate, 7.4 million tonnes; nitric acid, 8.2 million tonnes; and ammonium sulfate, 2.6 million tonnes.

U.S. apparent consumption of ammonia in 1999 was 16.7 million tonnes, down 2 percent from the previous year. U.S. nitrogen fertilizer consumption in 1999 was 11.3 million tonnes, the same as in 1998. Among the products, anhydrous ammonia consumption was 3.52 million tonnes, up 7 percent from 1998. Consumption of nitrogen solutions was 2.66 million tonnes, down 5 percent from the previous year. Consumption of urea in 1999 was 1.85 million tonnes, about the same as the year before. Ammonium nitrate consumption was 579,000 tonnes, down 3 percent from a year ago. Consumption of ammonium sulfate was 204,000 tonnes, while aqua ammonia consumption was 67,000 tonnes.

World mine consumption of phosphate rock in 1999 was estimated to be 138 million tonnes, down 5 percent from 1998. The world's largest producer was the U.S. followed by Morocco and Western Sahara, China, Russia, and Tunisia.

U.S. marketable production of phosphate rock in August 2000 was 3.66 million tonnes. In the January-August 2000 period, production was 26.5 million tonnes, while for all of 1999 it was 40.6 million tonnes. U.S. stocks of phosphate rock in August 2000 were 8.18 million tonnes. U.S. imports of phosphate rock in July 2000 were 68,000 tonnes. In the January-July 2000 period imports totaled 455,000 tonnes, while for all of 1999 they were 2.17 million tonnes.

World Production of Ammonia   In Thousands of Metric Tons of Contained Nitrogen

Year	Canada	China	France	Germany	India	Indonesia	Japan	Mexico	Netherlands	Poland	Russia[3]	United States	World Total
1991	3,016	18,000	1,604	2,123	7,132	2,706	1,553	2,221	3,033	1,531	17,100	12,803	93,800
1992	3,104	18,000	1,848	2,113	7,452	2,688	1,545	2,203	2,588	1,222	8,786	13,400	93,400
1993	3,410	19,000	1,871	2,100	7,176	2,888	1,471	1,758	2,472	1,163	8,138	12,600	91,600
1994	3,470	20,100	1,480	2,170	7,503	3,012	1,483	2,030	2,479	1,230	7,300	13,300	93,600
1995	3,773	22,600	1,470	2,518	8,287	3,336	1,584	1,992	2,580	1,726	7,900	13,000	100,000
1996	3,840	23,000	1,570	2,485	8,549	3,647	1,567	2,054	2,652	1,713	7,900	13,400	103,000
1997	4,081	25,000	1,757	2,470	9,328	3,770	1,589	1,448	2,480	1,824	7,150	13,300	103,000
1998[1]	3,900	26,500	1,570	2,512	10,240	3,600	1,460	1,418	2,350	1,683	6,500	13,300	104,000
1999[2]	4,135	28,400	1,570	2,406	10,376	3,700	1,378	1,003	2,430	1,474	7,633	14,100	109,000

[1] Preliminary.   [2] Estimate.   [3] Formerly part of the U.S.S.R.; data not reported separately until 1992.   *Source: U.S. Geological Survey (USGS)*

Salient Statistics of Nitrogen[3] (Ammonia) in the United States   In Thousands of Metric Tons

Year	Net Import Reliance as a % of Apparent Consumption	Production[3] (Fixed) Fertilizer	Non-fertilizer	Total	Imports[4] (Fixed)	Exports	Nitrogen[5] Compounds Produced	Con-sumption	Stocks, Dec. 31- Ammonia	Fixed Nitrogen Com-pounds	Ammonia Con-sumption (Apparent)	Urea FOB Gulf[6] Coast	FOB Corn Belt	Ammonium Nitrate: FOB Corn Belt	Ammonia FOB Gulf Coast
1992	14	12,000	1,349	13,349	2,690	354	10,404	10,448	1,059	1,789	15,600	142-146	149-160	138-149	106
1993	17	11,300	1,320	12,620	2,657	378	10,000	10,100	852	1,600	15,100	139-141	141-165	138-149	121
1994	19	11,600	1,750	13,350	3,450	215	10,000	11,700	956	1,650	16,500	219-226	204-215	165-176	211
1995	15	11,600	1,410	13,010	2,630	319	10,400	10,700	959	1,580	15,300	217-222	220-235	162-170	191
1996	19	11,500	1,720	13,220	3,390	435	11,502	11,100	881	1,390	16,400	188-190	197-210	160-170	190
1997	16	11,400	1,900	13,300	3,530	395	11,441	11,300	1,530	2,220	15,800	102-103	125-135	122-125	173
1998[1]	18	11,800	1,950	13,800	3,460	614	11,712	11,300	1,050	1,270	17,100	82-85	110-125	110-115	121
1999[2]	26	12,500	1,600	14,100	3,890	562	11,548	11,300	996	1,240	17,500	107-110	115-125	110-115	109

[1] Preliminary.   [2] Estimate.   [3] Anhydrous ammonia, synthetic.   [4] For consumption.   [5] Major downstream nitrogen compounds.   [6] *Granular.*
E = Net exporter.   *Source: U.S. Geological Survey (USGS)*

FERTILIZER

World Production of Phosphate Rock, Basic Slag & Guano   In Thousands of Metric Tons (Gross Weight)

Year	Brazil	China	Egypt	Israel	Jordan	Morocco	Russia[3]	Senegal	Syria	Togo	Tunisia	United States	World Total
1990	2,968	21,550	1,151	3,516	6,082	21,396	36,800	2,147	1,633	2,314	6,258	46,343	162,783
1991	3,280	22,000	1,652	3,370	4,433	17,900	28,400	1,741	1,359	2,965	6,352	48,096	150,731
1992	2,825	21,400	2,000	3,595	4,296	19,145	11,500	2,284	1,266	2,083	6,400	46,965	139,000
1993	3,419	21,200	1,585	3,680	4,129	18,193	9,400	1,667	931	1,794	5,500	35,494	119,000
1994	3,937	24,100	632	3,961	4,217	19,764	8,000	1,587	1,203	2,149	5,699	41,100	127,000
1995	3,888	19,300	765	4,063	4,984	20,684	9,000	1,500	1,551	2,570	7,241	43,500	131,000
1996	3,823	21,000	808	3,839	5,355	20,855	8,500	1,340	2,189	2,731	7,167	45,400	135,000
1997	4,270	24,500	900	4,047	5,896	23,084	9,900	1,565	2,392	2,631	6,941	45,900	143,000
1998[1]	4,421	25,000	1,058	4,050	5,967	23,587	10,000	1,478	2,496	2,250	7,901	44,200	144,000
1999[2]	4,100	25,100	1,050	4,100	6,000	24,000	11,100	1,800	2,100	1,700	8,000	40,600	141,000

[1] Preliminary.　[2] Estimate.　[3] Formerly part of the U.S.S.R.; data not reported separately until 1992.　*Source: U.S. Geological Survey (USGS)*

Salient Statistics of Phosphate Rock in the United States   In Thousands of Metric Tons

Year	Mine Production	Marketable Production	Value Million Dollars	Imports For Consumption	Exports	Apparent Consumption	Stocks, Dec. 31 (Producer)	Price - $ Avg. Per Metric Ton (FOB Mine)	Avg. Price of Florida & N. Carolina - $/Tonne - FOB Mine (-60% to +74%) - Domestic	Export	Average
1990	151,277	46,343	1,075	451	6,238	43,967	8,912	23.20	22.44	30.43	23.55
1991	154,485	48,096	1,109	552	5,082	40,177	10,168	23.06	22.67	31.69	23.69
1992	155,000	47,000	1,060	1,530	3,720	42,900	12,600	22.53	22.47	32.29	23.32
1993	107,000	35,500	759	534	3,200	38,300	9,220	21.38	21.26	28.51	21.89
1994	157,000	41,100	869	1,800	2,800	42,900	5,980	21.14	21.79	25.60	22.08
1995	165,000	43,500	947	1,800	2,760	42,700	5,710	21.75	21.29	28.35	21.75
1996	179,000	45,400	1,060	1,800	1,570	43,700	6,390	23.40	22.90	35.82	23.40
1997	166,000	45,900	1,080	1,830	335	43,600	7,910	24.50	24.40	34.80	24.50
1998[1]	170,000	44,200	1,130	1,760	378	45,000	7,920	25.87	25.46	42.70	25.87
1999[2]	161,000	40,600	1,240	2,170	272	43,500	6,920	31.49	30.56	41.96	31.49

[1] Preliminary.　[2] Estimate.　*Source: U.S. Geological Survey (USGS)*

World Production of Marketable Potash   In Thousands of Metric Tons (K$_2$O Equivalent)

Year	Belarus[3]	Brazil	Canada	China	France	Germany	Israel	Jordan	Russia[3]	Spain	United Kingdom	United States	World Total
1990	----	66	6,989	29	1,292	4,960	1,311	841	9,000	686	488	1,713	27,493
1991	----	101	7,406	32	1,129	3,855	1,320	818	8,560	585	495	1,749	26,136
1992	3,311	85	7,270	21	1,141	3,461	1,296	794	3,470	594	529	1,710	23,900
1993	1,947	168	3,836	25	890	2,861	1,309	822	2,628	661	555	1,510	20,400
1994	3,021	234	8,037	74	870	3,286	1,259	930	2,498	684	580	1,400	23,100
1995	3,211	215	9,066	80	799	3,278	1,330	1,075	2,800	760	582	1,480	24,800
1996	2,716	243	8,120	110	751	3,332	1,500	1,080	2,618	717	618	1,390	23,300
1997	3,248	280	8,989	115	725	3,423	1,488	868	3,400	640	565	1,400	25,200
1998[1]	3,400	326	9,201	120	656	3,581	1,500	910	3,500	585	608	1,300	25,700
1999[2]	3,600	350	8,329	125	300	3,600	1,750	1,100	4,200	550	500	1,200	25,700

[1] Preliminary.　[2] Estimate.　[3] Formerly part of the U.S.S.R.; data not reported separately until 1992.　*Source: U.S. Geological Survey (USGS)*

Salient Statistics of Potash in the United States   In Thousands of Metric Tons (K$_2$O Equivalent)

Year	Net Import Reliance as a % of Consumption	Production	Sales by Producers	Value Million Dollars	Imports For Consumption	Exports	Apparent Consumption	Producer Stocks Dec. 31	$ Per Ton Avg. Value Per Ton of Product ($)	Avg. Value of K$_2$O Equiv.	Avg. Price[3] $ Per Tonne
1990	68	1,713	1,716	303.3	4,164	470	5,410	303	89.46	176.80	130.00
1991	67	1,749	1,709	304.5	4,158	624	5,243	343	91.52	178.20	131.00
1992	68	1,710	1,770	334.0	4,250	663	5,350	283	96.45	189.36	134.00
1993	72	1,510	1,480	286.0	4,360	415	5,430	305	94.36	192.72	130.74
1994	76	1,400	1,470	284.0	4,800	464	5,810	234	95.93	193.50	125.34
1995	75	1,480	1,400	284.0	4,820	409	5,820	312	98.58	202.43	137.99
1996	77	1,390	1,430	299.0	4,940	481	5,890	265	101.08	208.57	134.07
1997	80	1,400	1,400	320.0	5,490	466	6,500	200	110.00	230.00	138.00
1998[1]	80	1,300	1,300	330.0	4,780	477	5,600	300	115.00	250.00	145.00
1999[2]	80	1,200	1,200	280.0	4,470	459	5,100	300	110.00	230.00	150.00

[1] Preliminary.　[2] Estimate.　[3] Unit of K$_2$O, standard 60% muriate F.O.B. mine.　*Source: U.S. Geological Survey (USGS)*

Fish

The U.S.D.A. reported that sales of catfish by growers to processors in 1999 were 597 million pounds. That represented an increase of 6 percent from the previous year. In August 2000, sales to processors were 53.2 million pounds, up nearly 6 percent from the same month in 1999. Catfish sold by processors in 1999 were 293 million pounds, up 4 percent from 1998. In August 2000, processors sold 25.8 million pounds of catfish, up 5 percent from the same month the year before. In the first eight months of 2000, processor sales were 206 million pounds. Processor sales of frozen catfish in August 2000 were 16 million pounds, up 8 percent from a year earlier. The processor inventory of catfish in August 2000 was 10.3 million pounds, up 37 percent from a year earlier. The inventory of fresh catfish in August 2000 was 892,000 pounds, up 21 percent from a year earlier. The inventory of frozen catfish in August 2000 was 9.37 million pounds, up 38 percent from last year.

Catfish growers indicated that on July 1, 2000, their stocks of broodfish were 1.27 million. The states surveyed were Alabama, Arkansas, Louisiana, and Mississippi. The broodfish inventory was up 9 percent from 1999. The inventory of fingerling/fry was 1.76 billion, about the same as a year earlier. The stocker inventory on July 1, 2000 was 762 million, down 2 percent from the previous year. The

inventory of small foodsize catfish was 231.4 million, down 4 percent from a year ago. The inventory of medium foodsize catfish was 52.1 million, down 8 percent from 1999. The inventory of large foodsize catfish was 4 million, down 20 percent from a year ago.

U.S. exports in January-June 2000 of fresh and frozen trout were 1.08 million pounds, up 8 percent from 1999. Exports of fresh Atlantic salmon in the first half of 2000 were 8.9 million pounds, up 39 percent from a year ago. Exports of fresh Pacific salmon were 4.79 million pounds, down 47 percent from a year ago. Exports of frozen Atlantic salmon were 154,000 pounds in the first half of 2000, up from 50,000 pounds a year before. Exports of frozen Pacific salmon were 34.3 million pounds, up 34 percent from a year ago.

U.S. imports of frozen shrimp in January-June 2000 were 246.9 million pounds, down 7 percent from 1999. Imports of fresh and prepared shrimp in the first half of 2000 were 43.8 million pounds, up 36 percent from a year ago. Imports of mussels were 23 million pounds, up 20 percent from 1999. Imports of oysters were 7.6 million pounds, up 7 percent from the year before. Imports of clams in first half 2000 were 4.6 million pounds.

Fishery Products -- Supply in the United States   In Millions of Pounds[2]

Year	Grand Total	For Human Food - Finfish	For Human Food - Shellfish[3]	For Industrial Use[4]	Domestic Catch Total	% of Grand Total	For Human Food - Finfish	For Human Food - Shellfish[3]	For Industrial Use[4]	Imports Total	% of Grand Total	For Human Food - Finfish	For Human Food - Shellfish[3]	For Industrial Use[4]
1989	15,485	9,735	2,533	3,217	8,463	54.7	4,897	1,307	2,259	7,022	45.3	4,838	1,226	958
1990	16,349	10,120	2,542	3,687	9,404	57.5	5,747	1,294	2,363	6,945	42.5	4,373	1,248	1,324
1991	16,364	10,186	2,834	3,344	9,484	58.0	5,564	1,467	2,453	6,879	42.0	4,622	1,367	890
1992	16,106	10,297	2,945	2,864	9,637	59.8	6,182	1,436	2,019	6,469	40.2	4,115	1,509	845
1993	20,334	10,796	3,025	6,513	10,467	51.5	6,770	1,444	2,253	9,867	48.5	4,026	1,581	4,260
1994	19,309	10,719	2,995	5,595	10,461	54.2	6,612	1,324	2,525	8,848	45.8	4,107	1,671	3,070
1995	16,484	10,692	2,891	2,900	9,788	59.4	6,414	1,252	2,121	6,696	40.6	4,278	1,639	779
1996	16,474	10,699	2,927	2,848	9,565	58.1	6,205	1,271	2,089	6,909	41.9	4,494	1,656	759
1997	17,133	10,580	3,160	3,393	9,843	57.5	5,969	1,277	2,598	7,290	42.5	4,612	1,883	795
1998[1]	16,898	10,837	3,338	2,723	9,194	54.4	5,935	1,238	2,021	7,704	45.6	4,901	2,100	702

[1] Preliminary.   [2] Live weight, except percent.   [3] For univalue and bivalues mollusks (conchs, clams, oysters, scallops, etc.) the weight of meats, excluding the shell is reported.   [4] Fish meal and sea herring.   *Source: Fisheries Statistics Division, U.S. Department of Commerce*

Fisheries -- Landings of Principal Species in the United States   In Millions of Pounds

Year	Fish Cod, Atlantic	Flounder	Halibut	Herring, Sea	Man-haden	Pollock	Salmon, Pacific	Tuna	Whiting	Shelfish Clams (Meats)	Crabs	Lobsters (American)	Oysters (Meats)	Scallops (Meats)	Shrimp
1989	78	202	75	209	1,989	2,385	786	89	39	138	458	53	30	41	352
1990	96	255	70	221	1,962	3,129	733	62	44	139	499	61	29	42	346
1991	93	405	66	230	1,977	2,873	783	36	37	134	650	63	32	40	320
1992	62	646	67	282	1,644	2,952	716	57	36	142	624	56	36	34	338
1993	51	599	63	216	1,983	3,258	888	55	36	148	604	57	34	19	293
1994	39	427	58	214	2,324	3,133	901	72	36	131	447	66	38	25	283
1995	30	423	45	265	1,847	2,853	1,137	14	34	134	364	66	40	20	307
1996	31	460	49	318	1,755	2,630	877	85	35	123	392	71	38	18	317
1997	29	566	70	348	2,028	2,522	568	83	83	114	430	84	40	15	290
1998[1]	25	391	73	272	1,706	2,729	644	85	85	108	553	80	34	13	278

[1] Preliminary.   *Source: National Marine Fisheries Service, U.S. Department of Commerce*

FISH

U.S. Fisheries: Quantity & Value of Domestic Catch & Consumption & World Fish Oil Production

Year	Fresh & Frozen	Canned	Cured	For Meal, Oil, Etc.	Total	For Human Food	For Industrial Products	Ex-vessel Value[3]	Average Price	Fish Per Capita Cunsumption	World[2] Fish Oil Production
	Millions of Pounds							- Million $ -	- Cents/Lb. -	- Pounds -	- 1,000 Tons -
1992	7,288	543	110	1,696	9,637	7,618	2,019	3,678	38.2	14.7	1,038
1993	7,744	649	115	1,959	10,467	8,214	2,253	3,471	33.2	14.9	1,184
1994	7,475	622	95	2,269	10,461	7,936	2,525	3,807	36.8	NA	1,470
1995	7,099	769	90	1,830	9,788	7,667	2,121	3,770	38.5	NA	1,302
1996	7,054	678	93	1,740	9,565	7,474	2,091	3,487	36.5	NA	1,337
1997	6,873	648	108	2,213	9,842	7,244	2,598	3,448	35.0	NA	1,214
1998[1]	6,870	516	129	1,679	9,194	7,173	2,021	3,128	34.0	NA	892

[1] Preliminary. [2] Crop years on a marketing year basis. [3] At the Dock Prices. *Source: Fisheries Statistics Division, U.S. Department of Commerce*

Imports of Seafood Products into the United States   In Thousands of Pounds

Year	Fresh Atlantic Salmon	Fresh Pacific Salmon	Fresh Shrimp	Frozen Trout	Frozen Atlantic Salmon	Frozen Pacific Salmon	Frozen Shrimp	Oysters[2]	Mussels[3]	Clams[4]	Canned Salmon	Prepared Shrimp[5]
1995	95,739	33,371	----	4,076	9,982	8,849	539,630	14,866	15,483	5,930	3,582	57,577
1996	116,606	43,962	----	4,552	10,752	8,514	507,823	14,222	21,241	6,596	4,182	74,648
1997	150,135	38,999	----	5,403	14,956	25,662	572,111	14,531	26,903	5,703	3,675	76,213
1998	190,131	38,486	----	5,670	19,092	17,134	599,466	18,049	34,099	6,541	3,430	95,942
1999	217,948	26,467	----	5,259	24,222	16,596	617,089	18,325	34,969	7,537	5,627	114,191
2000[1]	257,218	19,908	----	7,083	32,089	12,866	621,231	20,810	43,141	8,074	8,893	139,526

[1] Preliminary. [2] Oysters fresh or prepared. [3] Mussels fresh or prepared. [4] Clams, fresh or prepared. [5] Shrimp, canned, breaded or prepared.
NA = Not available. *Source: Bureau of the Census, U.S. Department of Commerce*

Exports of Seafood Products into the United States   In Thousands of Pounds

Year	Fresh Atlantic Salmon	Fresh Pacific Salmon	Fresh Shrimp	Frozen Trout	Frozen Atlantic Salmon	Frozen Pacific Salmon	Frozen Shrimp	Oysters[2]	Mussels[3]	Clams[4]	Canned Salmon	Prepared Shrimp[5]
1995	6,823	26,142	----	1,545	231	266,706	14,795	2,531	1,896	3,968	95,611	14,837
1996	7,280	42,999	----	1,867	322	223,346	11,180	2,097	1,603	5,126	94,842	17,665
1997	7,504	25,529	----	1,709	322	152,516	11,967	2,890	1,157	4,916	81,407	14,826
1998	7,978	34,645	----	1,453	243	105,869	11,323	2,496	1,347	5,375	77,201	13,882
1999	10,717	40,683	----	1,697	182	157,278	13,607	2,727	1,861	5,240	113,556	13,153
2000[1]	15,942	38,750	----	1,816	299	161,515	15,162	3,229	1,513	3,413	81,098	14,229

[1] Preliminary. [2] Oysters fresh or prepared. [3] Mussels fresh or prepared. [4] Clams, fresh or prepared. [5] Shrimp, canned, breaded or prepared.
NA = Not available. *Source: Bureau of the Census, U.S. Department of Commerce*

World Production of Fish Meal   In Thousands of Metric Tons

Year	Chile	Spain	Denmark	EU-12	FSU-12	Iceland	Japan	Norway	Peru	South Africa	Thailand	United States	World Total
1992-3	1,091.2	97.9	300.1	544.0	355.0	197.7	395.0	250.8	1,767.3	128.3	352.8	352.5	6,258.6
1993-4	1,526.1	65.1	352.7	558.6	295.0	190.5	343.0	216.8	2,254.4	92.9	373.2	447.8	7,216.7
1994-5	1,549.7	70.1	363.4	573.1	198.3	173.8	239.0	225.0	2,052.6	95.8	385.2	338.3	6,847.0
1995-6	1,387.6	76.4	322.9	532.5	209.8	271.0	195.0	233.8	1,702.7	49.6	380.9	331.1	6,332.9
1996-7	1,209.9	75.0	334.6	540.6	183.7	272.5	180.0	259.7	2,150.5	52.6	383.2	345.0	6,601.1
1997-8[1]	708.5	77.0	317.2	526.6	195.3	221.6	167.0	296.7	697.2	89.3	405.2	341.0	4,652.8
1998-9[2]	837.5	76.0	319.1	530.7	150.6	240.6	180.0	254.0	1,597.4	72.0	393.0	345.0	5,605.9
1999-00[3]	1,000.0	76.0	320.0	531.4	153.0	275.0	180.0	290.0	2,100.0	83.0	400.0	378.0	6,400.0

[1] Preliminary. [2] Estimate. [3] Forecast. *Source: The Oil World*

World Production of Fish Oil   In Thousands of Metric Tons

Year	Canada	Chile	China	Denmark	Iceland	Japan	Norway	Peru	South Africa	FSU-12	United States	World Total	Fish Oil CIF[4]
1992-3	11.8	165.3	9.4	90.3	86.0	107.4	112.3	250.9	17.0	71.6	119.0	1,150.4	375
1993-4	9.9	280.0	9.4	112.0	96.5	93.3	122.7	426.5	8.5	52.7	141.2	1,473.5	332
1994-5	10.1	323.1	9.9	118.3	85.0	57.7	94.1	388.1	7.5	48.5	109.6	1,371.6	405
1995-6	10.6	280.2	12.0	120.0	120.5	45.8	93.7	410.0	3.7	43.0	110.4	1,363.4	461
1996-7	10.5	192.6	12.0	129.5	134.6	51.2	86.4	407.1	4.1	41.0	110.0	1,293.8	502
1997-8[1]	10.5	91.4	12.6	106.4	107.0	54.0	89.0	74.0	7.8	39.5	116.0	826.2	722
1998-9[2]	10.0	173.0	9.0	135.0	92.0	59.0	81.0	377.0	7.0	7.0	142.0	1,225.0	408
1999-00[3]	11.0	143.0	11.0	135.0	92.0	60.0	88.0	695.0	8.0	8.0	92.0	1,475.0	268

[1] Preliminary. [2] Estimate. [3] Forecast. [4] Any origin, N.W. Europe. NA = Not available. *Source: The Oil World*

Monthly Production of Catfish--Round Weight Processed, in the US   In Thousands of Pounds (Live Weight)

Year	Jan.	Feb.	Mar.	Apr.	May	June	July	Aug.	Sept.	Oct.	Nov.	Dec.	Total
1992	36,200	39,228	45,048	41,177	39,111	36,813	36,128	37,958	37,857	39,212	35,073	33,562	457,367
1993	40,327	40,277	43,521	39,920	37,030	35,496	37,086	37,706	37,072	39,472	36,557	34,549	459,013
1994	36,714	35,035	40,446	34,494	34,163	34,595	35,901	39,813	38,716	39,072	36,054	34,266	439,269
1995	38,807	38,515	42,200	36,588	37,030	36,047	35,800	38,827	37,634	39,456	34,119	31,863	446,886
1996	38,475	38,004	46,376	38,557	39,583	36,810	39,025	40,463	38,807	42,070	37,210	36,874	472,254
1997	42,409	45,067	48,431	45,721	43,409	42,282	43,376	44,154	43,472	46,275	40,137	40,216	524,949
1998	46,723	47,606	53,761	49,393	45,218	46,244	46,383	47,739	46,579	47,904	43,224	43,581	564,355
1999	48,723	48,891	56,310	46,830	47,703	48,445	50,074	50,372	50,414	52,407	48,118	48,341	596,628
2000[1]	50,552	50,942	56,856	48,781	48,424	48,011	49,023	53,204	49,422	51,412	45,535	41,441	593,603

[1] Preliminary.   *Source: Economic Research Service, U.S. Department of Agriculture ERS-USDA)*

Average Price Paid to Producers for Farm-Raised Catfish in the US   In Cents Per Pound (Live Weight)

Year	Jan.	Feb.	Mar.	Apr.	May	June	July	Aug.	Sept.	Oct.	Nov.	Dec.	Average
1992	53.0	56.0	60.0	63.0	63.0	61.0	59.0	58.0	59.0	61.0	62.0	63.0	59.8
1993	63.0	67.0	70.0	71.0	72.0	72.0	72.0	73.0	73.0	73.0	73.0	73.0	71.0
1994	74.0	77.0	79.0	80.0	80.0	80.0	80.0	80.0	80.0	77.0	77.0	77.0	78.4
1995	78.0	79.0	79.0	79.0	79.0	79.0	79.0	79.0	78.0	78.0	78.0	78.0	78.6
1996	77.0	78.0	78.0	78.0	79.0	79.0	79.0	78.0	77.0	76.0	75.0	73.0	77.3
1997	73.0	73.0	73.0	73.0	73.0	72.0	71.0	70.0	69.0	69.0	69.0	69.0	71.2
1998	69.0	73.0	78.0	79.0	79.0	78.0	76.0	74.0	73.0	71.0	70.0	70.0	74.2
1999	70.3	71.4	73.2	75.6	77.7	77.5	76.8	74.3	72.8	71.6	71.3	71.6	73.7
2000[1]	74.4	78.8	78.9	78.9	78.5	78.6	76.0	74.1	72.7	71.0	69.6	68.2	75.0

[1] Preliminary.   *Source: Economic Research Service, U.S. Department of Agriculture (ERS-USDA)*

Sales of Fresh Catfish in the United States   In Thousands of Pounds

Year	Jan.	Feb.	Mar.	Apr.	May	June	July	Aug.	Sept.	Oct.	Nov.	Dec.	Total
Whole													
1997	3,402	3,632	4,133	3,770	3,456	3,447	3,481	3,284	3,370	3,598	3,002	3,051	41,626
1998	3,700	4,049	4,308	3,856	3,421	3,340	3,342	3,270	3,332	3,431	3,152	3,254	42,455
1999	3,650	3,957	4,467	3,459	3,492	3,380	3,471	3,271	3,583	3,561	3,209	3,313	42,813
2000[1]	3,496	3,396	4,031	3,655	3,483	3,581	3,491	3,545	3,246	3,504	2,971	2,993	41,392
Fillets[2]													
1997	3,627	4,272	4,531	4,084	4,126	3,894	4,033	4,135	4,009	4,464	3,623	3,543	48,341
1998	4,292	4,784	5,130	4,634	4,371	4,220	4,542	4,622	4,626	4,588	4,092	3,975	53,876
1999	4,581	5,030	5,768	4,897	4,918	4,707	4,846	5,002	4,550	4,811	4,171	4,142	57,423
2000[1]	4,686	4,853	5,957	5,206	5,099	4,792	4,650	4,899	4,650	5,283	4,355	4,099	58,529
Other[3]													
1997	1,287	1,497	1,562	1,530	1,430	1,307	1,385	1,332	1,358	1,498	1,212	1,147	16,545
1998	1,499	1,712	1,721	1,509	1,395	1,453	1,246	1,369	1,314	1,345	1,117	1,081	16,761
1999	1,243	1,614	1,724	1,153	1,227	1,126	1,305	1,495	1,354	1,676	1,299	1,227	16,443
2000[1]	1,429	1,437	1,685	1,547	1,364	1,299	1,340	1,438	1,332	1,473	1,271	1,198	16,813

[1] Preliminary.   [2] Includes regular, shank and strip fillets; excludes breaded products.   [3] Includes steaks, nuggets and all other products not reported.
Source: Economic Research Service, U.S. Department of Agriculture (ERS-USDA)

Prices of Fresh Catfish in the United States   In Dollars per Pound

Year	Jan.	Feb.	Mar.	Apr.	May	June	July	Aug.	Sept.	Oct.	Nov.	Dec.	Average
Whole													
1997	1.59	1.60	1.58	1.56	1.56	1.52	1.51	1.53	1.54	1.52	1.54	1.50	1.55
1998	1.52	1.57	1.63	1.61	1.65	1.60	1.60	1.63	1.59	1.59	1.56	1.52	1.59
1999	1.54	1.55	1.57	1.59	1.63	1.60	1.59	1.63	1.61	1.63	1.59	1.59	1.59
2000[1]	1.63	1.67	1.69	1.70	1.68	1.63	1.65	1.70	1.67	1.64	1.62	1.58	1.66
Fillets[2]													
1997	2.80	2.79	2.80	2.78	2.78	2.77	2.75	2.74	2.73	2.69	2.67	2.71	2.75
1998	2.71	2.75	2.85	2.86	2.86	2.85	2.84	2.82	2.78	2.78	2.75	2.73	2.80
1999	2.73	2.71	2.76	2.75	2.84	2.86	2.86	2.85	2.85	2.83	2.84	2.83	2.81
2000[1]	2.82	2.87	2.89	2.88	2.88	2.90	2.90	2.88	2.85	2.83	2.83	2.81	2.86
Other[3]													
1997	1.72	1.67	1.68	1.64	1.68	1.68	1.70	1.69	1.65	1.60	1.66	1.64	1.67
1998	1.61	1.65	1.72	1.78	1.78	1.76	1.79	1.71	1.72	1.69	1.73	1.69	1.72
1999	1.61	1.55	1.59	1.70	1.74	1.76	1.66	1.62	1.66	1.57	1.65	1.66	1.65
2000[1]	1.66	1.69	1.69	1.66	1.71	1.71	1.72	1.69	1.62	1.68	1.71	1.68	1.69

[1] Preliminary.   [2] Includes regular, shank and strip fillets; excludes breaded products.   [3] Includes steaks, nuggets and all other products not reported.
Source: Economic Research Service, U.S. Department of Agriculture (ERS-USDA)

Flaxseed and Linseed Oil

Flaxseed (from which linseed oil is derived) is considered a minor U.S. oilseed despite a relatively large gain in production, at least percentagewise, during the past few years. Planted acreage for the 1999/00 crop of 387,000 acres compares with 336,000 in 1998/99, and is the largest acreage since 1987. Average yield also increased to a record 20.6 bushels per acre in 1999, up from a 15 bushel per acre average ten years ago.

U.S. flaxseed production in 1999/00 (June/May) of 7.9 million bushels compares with 6.7 million the previous year and was the highest of the 1990's. The decade's low was 1.6 million bushels in 1996/97, whereas crops in excess of 10 million bushels were not uncommon in the 1970's and 1980's. The U.S. crop is produced mostly in the Northern Plains states. Imports of flaxseed, mostly from Canada, the world's largest producer with about one third of global production, were forecast at 4.1 million bushels in 1999/00 vs. 6 million in 1998/99, and a record 9.6 million in 1997/98. The U.S. has been a net importer of flaxseed since the late 1970's. Total 1999/00 supplies of 14.1 million bushels include a carry-in of 2.2 million bushels and compares to the previous crop year's total supply of 13.9 million. Disappearance in 1999/00 was forecast at 11.7 million bushels, marginally higher than the previous year, and will result in an ending carryover on May 31, 2000 of about 2.5 million bushels.

U.S. domestic demand for linseed oil in 1999/00 of 156 million pounds is marginally above the previous two seasons and compares with annual averages of 165 million pounds in the early 1990's. Exports were put at a near record 65 million pounds. The 1999/00 production of 214 million pounds is the highest since the early 1980's and compares with 212 million in 1998/99. Linseed oil is used as a drying agent in paint, but domestic use has at best stabilized in recent years due to the acceptance of water based latex paints. Carryover stocks as of June 1, 1999, of 48 million pounds were slightly larger than a year earlier and were expected to total the same at the season's end. Linseed meal production in 1999/00 of 198,000 short tons is also marginally over 1998/99. Meal usage in 1999/00 should about equal the total supply with carryover holding near 5,000 tons as it had for much of the 1990's.

The average price received by U.S. farmers for flaxseed in 1999/00 was estimated at $3.60-$4.40 per bushel vs. $5.05 in 1998/99. Linseed oil prices were projected at 36.0-38.0 cents per pound vs. 37.75 cents in 1998/99, basis Minneapolis. Linseed meal prices, basis Minneapolis, 34 percent protein, were forecast at $87.50-112.50 per short ton in 1999/00 vs. $91.58 in 1998/99.

Futures Markets

Flaxseed futures are traded on the Winnipeg Commodity Exchange (WCE). Prices are quoted in Canadian dollars per metric ton.

World Production of Flaxseed   In Thousands of Metric Tons

Year	Argen- tina	Aust- ralia	Bang- ladesh	Canada	China	Egypt	France	Hungary	India	Rom- ania	United States	Former USSR	World Total
1990-1	458	4	48	889	535	28	34	10	339	53	97	197	2,923
1991-2	341	5	55	635	410	24	26	13	292	23	158	140	2,458
1992-3	177	5	49	334	430	21	29	10	268	18	84	130	1,966
1993-4	112	8	49	627	410	22	27	4	330	28	88	120	2,191
1994-5	152	6	48	960	511	18	44	4	325	7	74	110	2,474
1995-6	149	15	49	1,105	420	16	27	4	308	5	56	113	2,518
1996-7	72	7	46	851	480	17	29	4	319	5	41	86	2,300
1997-8[1]	75	6	50	1,038	393	18	31	4	310	5	62	51	2,409
1998-9[2]	85	8	50	1,210	520	18	29	4	300	5	170	59	2,880
1999-00[3]	47	7	50	1,175	550	17	33	4	285	3	200	63	3,063

[1] Preliminary.   [2] Estimate.   [3] Forecast.   Source: The Oil World

Supply and Distribution of Flaxseed in the United States   In Thousands of Bushels

Crop Year Beginning June 1	Planted	Harvested	Yield Per Acre (Bushels)	Beginning Stocks	Pro- duction	Imports	Total Supply	Seed	Crush	Exports	Residual	Total Distribution
	------- 1,000 Acres -------			---------------------- Supply ----------------------				-------------------------------- Distribution --------------------------------				
1991-2	356	342	18.1	971	6,200	4,371	11,542	139	9,050	541	256	9,986
1992-3	171	165	19.9	1,556	3,288	6,035	10,879	167	8,600	230	337	9,334
1993-4	206	191	18.2	1,545	3,480	5,118	10,143	144	8,650	126	69	8,989
1994-5	178	171	17.1	1,155	2,922	6,005	10,082	134	8,550	72	156	8,912
1995-6	165	147	15.0	1,170	2,212	7,248	10,681	78	9,000	119	203	9,451
1996-7	96	92	17.4	1,230	1,602	8,390	11,222	122	10,000	144	503	10,769
1997-8	151	146	16.6	453	2,420	9,636	10,808	272	10,500	174	382	9,627
1998-9[1]	336	329	20.4	1,181	6,708	5,992	13,227	313	10,600	476	333	11,069
1999-00[2]	387	382	20.6	2,158	7,880	6,629	16,667	480	11,500	215	2,705	14,900
2000-1[3]	593	575	17.0	1,767	9,775	4,507	16,049	324	11,750	300	1,175	13,549

[1] Preliminary.   [2] Estimate.   [3] Forecast.   Source: Economic Research Service, U.S. Department of Agriculture

FLAXSEED AND LINSEED OIL

Production of Flaxseed in the United States, by States   In Thousands of Bushels

Crop Year	Minne-sota	North Dakota	South Dakota	Other States	Total	Crop Year	Minne-sota	North Dakota	South Dakota	Other States	Total
1991	640	4,860	578	122	6,200	1996	60	1,386	126	30	1,602
1992	220	2,730	322	16	3,288	1997	96	1,997	252	75	2,420
1993	170	2,886	323	101	3,480	1998	432	5,817	294	165	6,708
1994	126	2,450	304	42	2,922	1999	300	6,867	357	340	7,880
1995	171	1,725	260	55	2,211	2000[1]	198	9,975	361	196	10,730

[1] Preliminary.   Source: National Agricultural Statistics Service, U.S. Department of Agriculture (NASS-USDA)

Factory Shipments of Paints, Varnish and Lacquer in the United States   In Millions of Dollars

Year	First Quarter	Second Quarter	Third Quarter	Fourth Quarter	Total	Year	First Quarter	Second Quarter	Third Quarter	Fourth Quarter	Total
1991	2,498.4	3,158.7	3,123.0	2,611.2	11,707	1996	3,438.6	4,161.9	3,954.9	3,428.9	14,984
1992	2,852.3	3,464.1	3,308.7	2,816.4	12,441	1997	3,515.2	4,023.4	3,924.1	3,323.0	14,786
1993	2,894.1	3,600.5	3,448.9	2,993.7	12,937	1998	3,600.7	4,216.4	4,063.9	3,804.4	15,685
1994	3,039.8	3,783.0	3,736.2	3,240.8	13,800	1999	3,926.2	4,452.2	4,216.5	3,925.7	16,521
1995	3,330.3	3,838.0	3,814.5	3,423.4	14,406	2000[1]	4,169.8	4,690.3	4,184.2	3,557.0	16,601

[1] Preliminary.   Source: Bureau of the Census, U.S. Department of Commerce

Consumption of Linseed Oil (Inedible Products) in the United States   In Millions of Pounds

Year	July	Aug.	Sept.	Oct.	Nov.	Dec.	Jan.	Feb.	Mar.	Apr.	May	June	Total
1993-4	14.9	8.1	11.2	9.0	7.2	10.7	10.2	7.5	9.9	8.5	11.5	11.7	120.4
1994-5	10.7	10.8	12.3	12.2	9.0	10.0	12.6	8.2	11.4	8.1	10.0	9.7	124.9
1995-6	8.8	10.0	9.4	10.6	7.4	6.9	8.8	8.5	7.2	8.1	10.1	9.5	105.3
1996-7	9.0	10.8	7.8	6.0	6.7	6.1	6.7	7.1	6.3	8.3	8.9	8.5	92.3
1997-8	8.9	7.7	8.6	6.7	7.5	6.4	8.0	6.0	6.2	5.9	6.8	5.7	84.3
1998-9	7.2	6.8	6.4	5.6	4.6	6.6	5.9	4.7	6.8	6.4	5.6	7.9	74.6
1999-00	5.4	6.2	5.5	5.2	5.6	4.5	4.2	6.1	5.8	7.0	7.6	6.6	69.8
2000-1[1]	6.5	7.2	7.3	7.5	6.5	5.7	7.9						83.4

[1] Preliminary.   Source: Bureau of the Census, U.S. Department of Commerce

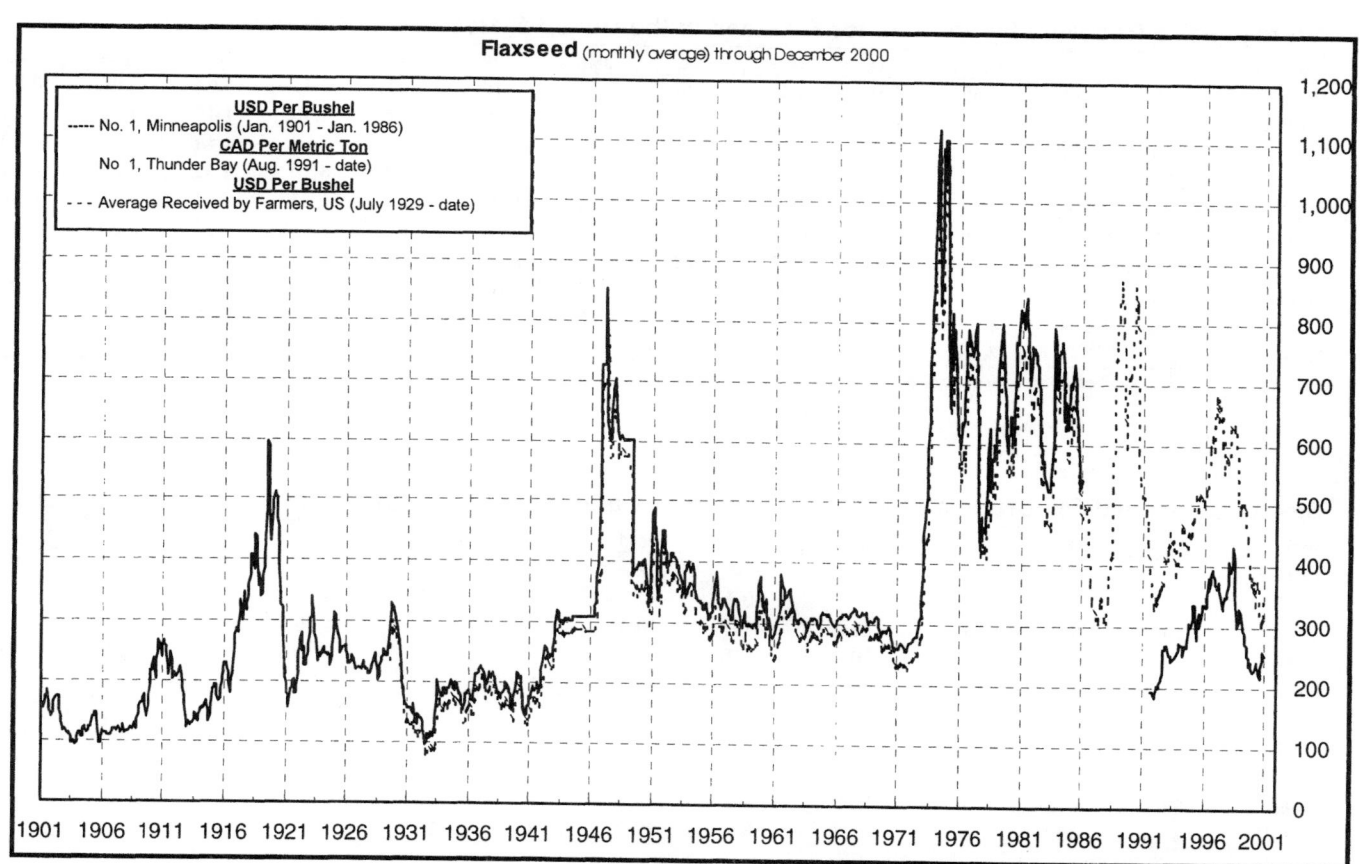

Flaxseed (monthly average) through December 2000

USD Per Bushel
----- No. 1, Minneapolis (Jan. 1901 - Jan. 1986)
CAD Per Metric Ton
No 1, Thunder Bay (Aug. 1991 - date)
USD Per Bushel
- - - Average Received by Farmers, US (July 1929 - date)

99

FLAXSEED AND LINSEED OIL

Supply and Distribution of Linseed Oil in the United States   In Millions of Pounds

Crop Year Beginning June 1	Supply			Disappearance			Average Price at Minneapolis Cents/Lb.
	Stocks June 1	Production	Total	Exports	Domestic	Total Disappearance	
1991-2	40	182	222	12	170	182	32.0
1992-3	40	172	212	8	150	158	31.5
1993-4	54	174	228	7	162	165	31.8
1994-5	63	171	235	24	166	190	33.7
1995-6	45	180	225	26	149	175	36.5
1996-7	50	200	250	66	149	215	36.0
1997-8	35	210	245	58	152	210	37.8
1998-9	35	212	247	63	139	202	37.5
1999-00[1]	45	230	275	76	150	226	37.8
2000-1[2]	49	235	284	75	163	238	26.0-29.0

[1] Preliminary.   [2] Forecast.   Source: Economic Research Service, U.S. Department of Agriculture (ERS-USDA)

World Production and Price of Linseed Oil   In Thousands of Metric Tons

Year	Argentina	Bangladesh	Belgium	China	Egypt	Germany	India	Japan	United Kingdom	United States	Former USSR	World Total	Rotterdam Ex-Tank $/Tonne
1990-1	141.5	12.0	12.2	126.9	12.3	57.5	94.2	34.7	16.8	84.0	10.1	685.8	502
1991-2	114.0	13.5	14.7	111.0	11.3	56.1	83.8	31.9	27.0	87.9	9.1	637.9	377
1992-3	62.3	12.6	25.5	117.0	8.1	56.8	78.0	28.4	27.2	80.0	9.6	570.0	450
1993-4	32.2	12.7	28.8	121.8	8.6	77.2	90.7	30.7	35.2	78.7	11.2	617.9	476
1994-5	46.8	13.0	35.2	137.4	8.2	104.0	91.4	29.2	41.4	81.7	10.6	697.5	657
1995-6	47.5	13.0	44.3	125.1	8.0	72.0	88.1	30.0	28.9	80.0	12.7	665.3	579
1996-7	17.1	12.5	52.1	142.5	9.6	52.2	88.8	31.0	34.1	97.9	10.2	670.4	560
1997-8	24.1	13.4	54.7	120.0	10.9	66.9	87.5	31.3	35.1	100.7	7.9	683.7	686
1998-9[1]	24.5	13.4	60.8	150.0	14.6	74.1	85.5	26.5	34.3	99.5	10.9	729.3	575
1999-00[2]	13.6	13.3	54.1	153.1	14.6	80.9	85.7	28.8	32.3	114.3	11.9	748.1	413

[1] Preliminary.   [2] Forecast.   Source: The Oil World

Average Price Received by Farmers for Flaxseed in the United States   In Dollars Per Bushel

Year	July	Aug.	Sept.	Oct.	Nov.	Dec.	Jan.	Feb.	Mar.	Apr.	May	June	Average
1991-2	3.92	3.69	3.55	3.39	3.31	3.46	3.39	3.43	3.51	3.53	3.61	3.66	3.54
1992-3	3.70	3.68	4.12	4.09	4.08	4.24	4.11	4.46	4.52	4.40	4.42	4.45	4.19
1993-4	4.29	3.79	4.24	4.09	4.05	4.18	4.38	4.61	4.64	4.60	4.43	4.25	4.30
1994-5	4.28	4.52	4.54	4.49	4.51	4.71	4.76	4.94	5.13	5.10	4.91	5.03	4.74
1995-6	5.11	5.21	5.11	5.11	5.17	5.03	5.26	5.21	5.28	5.31	6.13	5.90	5.32
1996-7	6.19	6.15	5.89	6.49	6.38	6.77	6.43	6.74	6.66	6.43	6.45	5.99	6.38
1997-8	6.07	5.53	5.72	5.81	5.71	5.72	5.82	6.27	6.26	6.23	6.33	6.17	5.97
1998-9	6.17	5.45	5.09	4.86	4.97	5.00	5.05	5.05	4.94	4.93	4.89	4.38	5.07
1999-00	4.40	3.86	4.00	3.76	3.66	3.61	3.75	3.43	3.70	3.65	3.75	3.64	3.77
2000-1[1]	3.25	3.05	3.10	3.17	3.42	3.47	3.47	3.50					3.30

[1] Preliminary.   Source: National Agricultural Statistics Service, U.S. Department of Agriculture (NASS-USDA)

Stocks of Linseed Oil (Crude and Refined) at Factories and Warehouses in the US   In Millions of Pounds

Year	July 1	Aug. 1	Sept. 1	Oct. 1	Nov. 1	Dec. 1	Jan. 1	Feb. 1	Mar. 1	Apr. 1	May 1	June 1
1991-2	----	60.6	----	----	64.2	----	73.1	51.2	62.3	45.6	45.7	41.4
1992-3	34.6	35.5	29.7	41.3	49.1	47.7	39.9	44.2	45.1	49.1	42.8	43.1
1993-4	45.2	39.0	42.1	47.0	27.9	19.3	22.5	38.0	42.0	49.4	52.0	62.6
1994-5	60.3	56.5	49.4	60.6	48.1	39.3	38.6	38.9	31.0	35.7	37.9	44.8
1995-6	39.5	44.6	37.4	46.0	48.0	44.5	45.3	58.9	64.0	62.0	60.6	47.2
1996-7	51.3	50.9	59.0	46.1	38.8	41.8	49.2	48.1	53.9	50.5	44.5	45.6
1997-8	39.9	35.2	40.3	33.3	38.6	40.3	46.9	60.8	55.8	63.1	54.6	49.4
1998-9	49.6	45.3	38.5	55.4	35.7	44.5	53.2	68.2	54.6	68.2	65.3	76.2
1999-00	68.7	65.5	68.9	74.0	92.4	69.6	72.0	69.5	65.7	53.9	49.1	44.2
2000-1[1]	39.5	42.5	41.3	54.3	58.7	87.0	61.6	50.1				

[1] Preliminary.   Source: Bureau of the Census, U.S. Department of Commerce

FLAXSEED AND LINSEED OIL

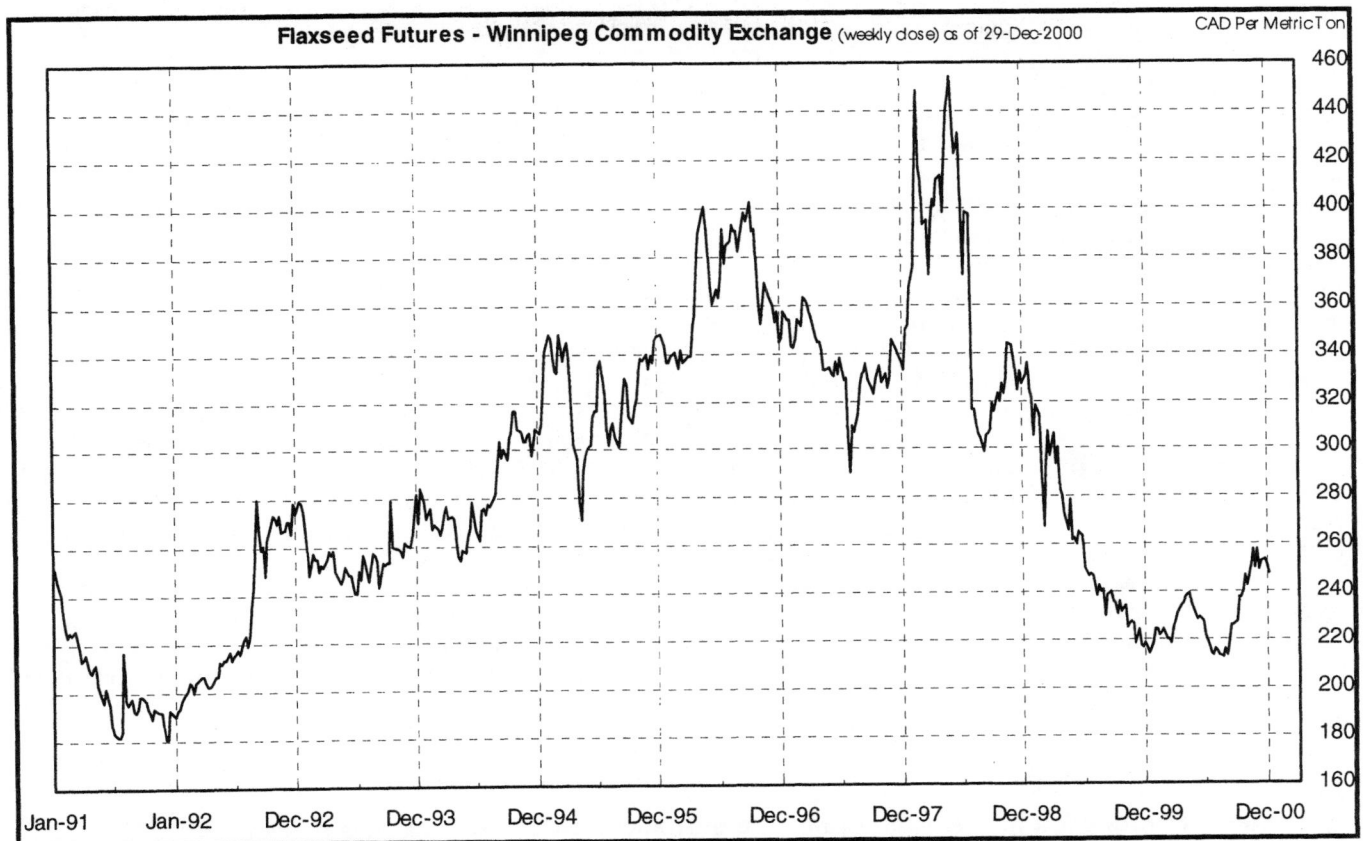

Flaxseed Futures - Winnipeg Commodity Exchange (weekly close) as of 29-Dec-2000   CAD Per Metric Ton

Wholesale Price of Raw Linseed Oil at Minneapolis in Tank Cars   In Cents Per Pound

Year	July	Aug.	Sept.	Oct.	Nov.	Dec.	Jan.	Feb.	Mar.	Apr.	May	June	Average
1991-2	36.00	36.00	36.00	30.00	30.00	30.00	30.00	30.00	30.00	30.00	30.00	30.00	31.50
1992-3	30.00	30.00	32.00	32.00	32.00	32.00	32.00	32.00	32.00	32.00	32.00	28.50	31.38
1993-4	32.00	32.00	32.00	32.00	32.00	32.00	32.00	32.00	32.00	32.00	32.00	32.00	32.00
1994-5	30.31	32.00	32.00	33.50	35.00	35.00	35.00	35.00	35.00	35.00	35.00	35.00	33.98
1995-6	35.00	35.50	37.00	37.00	37.00	37.00	37.00	37.00	37.00	37.00	37.00	37.00	36.71
1996-7	37.00	37.20	37.50	37.00	33.75	32.12	36.00	36.00	36.00	36.00	36.00	36.00	35.88
1997-8	36.00	36.00	36.00	37.00	37.00	37.00	36.00	36.00	36.00	36.00	37.00	37.00	36.42
1998-9	37.00	37.00	37.00	37.00	37.00	37.00	36.00	36.00	36.00	36.00	36.00	36.00	36.50
1999-00	36.00	36.00	36.00	36.00	36.00	36.00	36.00	36.00	36.00	36.00	36.00	36.00	36.00
2000-1[1]	36.00	36.00	36.00	36.00									36.00

[1] Preliminary.   *Source: Economic Research Service, U.S. Department of Agriculture (ERS-USDA)*

Average Open Interest of Flaxseed Futures in Winnipeg   In Contracts

Year	Jan.	Feb.	Mar.	Apr.	May	June	July	Aug.	Sept.	Oct.	Nov.	Dec.
1991	4,033	4,140	4,175	4,861	4,137	4,642	5,317	6,106	6,173	5,733	5,669	5,333
1992	5,620	6,772	7,864	7,984	7,786	7,321	6,299	6,553	5,623	4,860	6,734	5,979
1993	7,810	8,052	6,203	5,672	5,505	5,321	4,246	5,777	5,923	3,568	3,763	3,922
1994	6,118	6,201	5,946	5,519	4,683	3,945	4,301	4,654	4,997	3,077	4,888	5,251
1995	6,242	8,731	7,505	7,121	8,107	7,212	6,436	5,557	6,230	5,245	5,937	4,414
1996	6,059	6,056	4,402	5,192	6,970	4,435	3,102	2,989	3,257	3,438	4,326	5,119
1997	5,420	5,356	5,591	5,151	4,923	4,075	3,891	4,031	7,131	8,284	7,255	7,955
1998	10,059	10,190	9,707	8,540	6,480	6,874	6,030	6,767	7,421	7,221	7,564	5,828
1999	4,372	4,552	4,533	4,238	3,719	2,456	2,149	2,758	3,725	4,236	4,493	4,276
2000	4,365	4,907	5,588	6,218	5,066	3,696	3,152	3,585	3,936	4,666	4,922	4,914

Source: Winnipeg Commodity Exchange (WCE)

Fruits

The U.S. Department of Agriculture estimated U.S. sweet cherry production in 1999 at 229,120 short tons, up 8 percent from the previous season. Total utilization of sweet cherries in 1999 was estimated to be 227,760 tons, up 9 percent from 1998. Utilization of sweet cherries for fresh purposes was 131,910 tons in 1999, up 21 percent from the previous year. Utilization for processing was 95,850 tons, down 4 percent from 1998. In the 1999/00 (May-April) season, production of canned sweet cherries was 21.3 million pounds, down 19 percent from the previous season. Exports of canned sweet cherries totaled 9.9 million pounds, down 12 percent from the previous season. Total consumption was 12.2 million pounds, down 21 percent from 1998/99.

U.S. production of grapes in 1999 was estimated to be 6.23 million tons, up 7 percent from the previous year. Total utilization of grapes in 1999 was estimated to be 6.23 million tons. Fresh utilization of grapes in 1999 was estimated to be 887,000 tons, up 14 percent from 1998. Processed utilization was estimated to be 5.34 million tons, up 6 percent from the previous year. Grapes used for canned products in 1999 were 35,000 tons. Grapes used for juice totaled 502,100 tons, up 42 percent from 1998. Use of grapes for wine totaled 3.35 million tons, up 1 percent from a year ago. Use of grapes for dried products totaled 1.45 million tons, up 9 percent from a year ago.

The U.S.D.A. reported that based on data from Hawaii, there were 210 banana farms in 1999 compared to 200 in 1998. Banana acreage harvested was 1,420 acres, the same as the year before. The yield per acre was 17,300 pounds, up 17 percent from the year before. Utilized production of bananas in 1999 was 24.5 million pounds, up 17 percent from a year ago.

U.S. peach production in 1999 was estimated to be 2.53 billion pounds, up 5 percent from the previous year. Utilized production in 1999 was 2.43 billion pounds, up 5 percent from 1998. Fresh utilization was estimated at 1.1 billion pounds, with processed utilization 1.33 billion pounds. Use of peaches for canned products was 996 million pounds, up 1 percent from a year ago. Use of peaches for frozen purposes were 204 million pounds, up 10 percent from last season.

Pear production in 1999 was estimated to be 1.02 million tons, up 5 percent from a year ago. Utilized production of pears in 1999 was 1.02 million tons. Fresh pear utilization was 541,200 tons, with processed utilization of 477,300 tons.

Commerical Production for Selected Fruits in the United States · In Thousands of Short Tons

Year	Apples	Cherries[2]	Cran- berries	Grapes	Grape- fruit	Lemons	Nect- arines	Oranges	Peaches	Pears	Pine- apples	Prunes & Plums	Straw- berries	Tangelos	Tang- erines	Total All Fruits
1994	5,750	359	234	5,874	2,661	984	242	10,329	1,257	1,046	365	879	825	150	318	31,869
1995	5,293	363	210	5,922	2,912	897	176	11,432	1,151	948	345	744	804	142	287	32,140
1996	5,191	290	234	5,554	2,718	992	247	11,426	1,052	821	347	952	813	110	349	30,904
1997	5,162	372	275	7,291	2,885	962	264	12,692	1,312	1,043	324	899	814	178	425	35,507
1998	5,823	385	272	5,820	2,593	897	224	13,670	1,200	970	332	559	820	128	360	34,596
1999[1]	5,290	357	320	6,230	2,513	747	274	9,824	1,263	1,021	352	736	907	115	327	30,777

[1] Preliminary.　[2] Sweet and tart.　[3] Utilized production.　Source: Economic Research Service, U.S. Department of Agriculture (ERS-USDA)

Utilized Production for Selected Fruits in the United States · In Thousands of Short Tons

Year	Citrus[2]	Noncitrus	Tree Nuts[3]	Total	Citrus[2]	Noncitrus	Tree Nuts[3]	Total
	---------- Utilized Production ---------- In Thousands of Short Tons				---------- Value of Production ---------- In Thousands of Dollars			
1994	14,561	17,341	1,028	32,928	2,268,330	6,268,176	1,584,235	10,120,741
1995	15,799	16,358	811	32,958	2,328,915	6,815,962	1,714,547	10,859,424
1996	15,712	16,103	831	32,646	2,517,394	7,265,788	1,663,574	11,446,756
1997	17,271	18,363	1,210	36,844	2,582,767	8,158,095	2,093,697	12,834,559
1998	17,770	16,528	908	35,206	2,600,066	7,257,001	1,365,379	11,222,416
1999[1]	13,633	17,275	1,283	32,191	2,458,996	8,282,399	1,485,690	12,227,085

[1] Preliminary.　[2] Year harvest was completed.　[3] Tree nuts on an in-shell equivalent.
Source: Economic Research Service, U.S. Department of Agriculture (ERS-USDA)

Annual Average Retail Prices for Selected Fruits in the United States · In Dollars Per Pound

Year	Red Delicious Apples	Bananas	Anjou Pears	Thompson Seedless Grapes	Lemons	Grapefruit	Oranges Navel	Oranges Valen- cias
1994	.803	.462	.802	1.642	1.090	.513	.545	.587
1995	.835	.490	.774	1.551	1.136	.548	.625	.648
1996	.930	.490	.916	1.685	1.114	.574	.707	.703
1997	.907	.487	.985	1.712	1.154	.520	.592	.682
1998	.943	.494	1.089	1.589	1.198	.599	.565	.657
1999[1]	.897	.491	.950	1.841	1.236	.612	.843	.947

[1] Estimate.　Source: Economic Research Service, U.S. Department of Agriculture (ERS-USDA)

Utilization of Noncitrus Fruit Production, and Value in the U.S.   1,000 Short Tons (Fresh Equivalent)

Year	Utilized Production	Fresh	Processed							Value of utilized Production $1,000
			Canned	Dried	Juice	Frozen	Wine	Other	
1990	15,640	6,093	2,244	2,440	1,448	506	2,717	192	5,525,279
1991	15,740	6,215	2,119	2,417	1,583	501	2,739	167	6,021,210
1992	17,124	6,317	2,386	2,369	1,743	584	3,256	261	6,036,615
1993	16,554	6,391	2,042	2,339	1,749	627	3,029	181	6,130,119
1994	17,339	6,710	2,090	2,816	1,886	665	2,711	228	6,268,176
1995	16,348	6,285	1,753	2,400	1,857	647	2,992	205	6,815,962
1996	16,103	6,313	1,873	2,275	1,582	604	3,043	180	7,265,788
1997	18,363	6,643	2,130	2,660	1,675	699	4,035	247	8,158,095
1998	16,528	6,512	1,847	1,911	1,786	679	3,315	208	7,257,001
1999[1]	17,275	6,650	2,049	2,150	1,880	665	3,350	212	8,282,399

[1] Preliminary.   Source: Economic Research Service, U.S. Department of Agriculture (ERS-USDA)

Average Price Indexes for Fruits in the United States

Year	Index of all Fruit and Nut Prices Received by Growers (1990-92=100)	Producer Price Index				Consumer Price Index	
		Fresh Fruit	Dried Fruit	Canned Fruits and Juices	Frozen Fruits and Juices	Fresh Fruit	Processed Fruit
		1982 = 100				1982-84 = 100	
1990	97	118.1	107.0	126.9	138.9	170.9	136.6
1991	112	129.9	111.5	128.6	115.1	193.9	131.8
1992	99	84.0	114.3	134.6	125.7	184.2	137.7
1993	93	84.5	117.6	126.1	110.9	188.8	132.3
1994	90	82.7	120.9	126.0	111.9	201.2	133.1
1995	99	85.8	121.0	129.4	115.8	219.0	137.2
1996	118	100.8	124.2	137.5	123.9	234.4	145.2
1997	109	101.3	124.9	137.5	117.3	236.3	148.8
1998	111	90.5	124.4	138.6	----	246.5	101.9
1999[1]	114	103.2	122.0	130.0	----	266.3	105.4

[1] Estimate.   Source: Economic Research Service, U.S. Department of Agriculture (ERS-USDA)

Fresh Fruit: Per Capita Consumption[1] in the United States   In Pounds

Year	Citrus Fruit					Noncitrus Fruit					
	Oranges	Tangerines and Tangelos	Lemons	Grapefruit	Total	Apples	Apricots	Avacados	Bananas	Cherries	Cranberries
1990	12.38	1.31	2.60	4.43	21.37	19.60	.16	1.07	24.36	.39	.05
1991	8.46	1.38	2.60	5.87	19.07	18.18	.13	1.41	25.12	.40	.07
1992	12.91	1.94	2.54	5.95	24.36	19.25	.15	1.43	27.26	.53	.08
1993	14.24	1.87	2.65	6.23	25.97	19.17	.13	2.17	26.80	.43	.07
1994	13.06	2.11	2.68	6.12	24.96	19.58	.15	1.34	28.06	.53	.08
1995	11.97	2.01	2.87	6.07	24.12	18.94	.10	1.37	27.42	.29	.08
1996	12.77	2.19	2.90	5.93	24.95	18.97	.09	1.60	28.02	.41	.08
1997	14.16	2.57	2.80	6.28	26.98	18.42	.15	1.61	27.64	.61	.08
1998	14.91	2.21	2.51	6.05	27.11	19.38	.13	1.76	28.58	.58	.07
1999[2]	8.57	2.26	2.67	5.87	20.73	18.84	.13	1.55	31.40	.70	.09

[1] All data on calendar-year basis except for citrus fruits; apples, August; grapes and pears, July; grapefruit, September; lemons, August of prior year, all other citrus, November.   [2] Preliminary.   Source: Economic Research Service, U.S. Department of Agriculture (ERS-USDA)

Fresh Fruit: Per Capita Consumption[1] in the United States   In Pounds

Year	Noncitrus Fruit Continued										
	Grapes	Kiwifruit	Mangos	Nectarines & Peaches	Pears	Pineapples	Papaya	Plums & Prunes	Strawberries	Total Noncitrus	Total Fruit
1991	7.27	.45	.85	6.43	3.15	1.92	.17	1.42	3.58	70.55	89.62
1992	7.19	.39	.68	6.03	3.14	2.00	.24	1.78	3.61	73.75	98.11
1993	7.05	.60	.90	5.89	3.38	2.05	.28	1.28	3.64	73.84	99.81
1994	7.32	.57	.98	5.47	3.48	2.04	.30	1.62	4.09	75.62	100.59
1995	7.52	.56	1.13	5.39	3.40	1.93	.37	.94	4.16	73.59	97.72
1996	6.93	.55	1.36	4.44	3.10	1.92	.55	1.45	4.38	73.85	98.80
1997	8.04	.49	1.46	5.61	3.45	2.38	.48	1.54	4.17	76.13	103.11
1998	7.29	.57	1.52	4.70	3.36	2.81	.47	1.20	4.00	76.42	103.53
1999[2]	8.21	.56	1.58	5.25	3.44	3.10	.64	1.30	4.52	81.31	102.04

[1] All data on calendar-year basis except for citrus fruits; apples, August; grapes and pears, July; grapefruit, September; lemons, August of prior year; all other citrus, November.   [2] Preliminary.   Source: Economic Research Service, U.S. Department of Agriculture (ERS-USDA)

Gas

The year 2000 will be one for the history books in terms of energy. Prices for the various components of the energy sector soared. Crude oil, gasoline, heating oil, and natural gas prices all moved sharply higher. There were a number of reasons. Global stocks of petroleum declined which caused prices in the energy sector to strengthen. After two fairly mild winters, the winter of 2000/2001 was much colder especially in the Midwest where most natural gas is used to heat homes. There was a decline in exploration when prices were low and a lack of discovery of new large gas fields. There were significant drawdowns in gas stocks. In California, increased consumption of electricity which is generated by natural gas led to increased use. With the approach of winter, natural gas prices moved higher in August and September before a decline in October. Prices then exploded higher in November and December, doubling in two months.

The U.S. Energy Information Agency reported that in September 2000, dry natural gas production in the U.S. was estimated to be 1.54 trillion cubic feet, down 3 percent from the previous month, but some 1 percent higher than a year ago. In the January-September 2000 period, dry natural gas production was 14 trillion cubic feet, virtually the same as the year before, but down 1 percent from 1998. For all of 1999, dry natural gas production was 18.7 trillion cubic feet. Net imports of dry natural gas in September 2000 were 290 billion cubic feet, down 2 percent from the previous month. In the January-September 2000 period, net imports were 2.56 trillion cubic feet, up 1 percent from the same period in 1999, and 14 percent higher than in 1998. U.S. consumption of dry natural gas in September 2000 was 1.48 trillion cubic feet, down 7 percent from the previous month and about 1 percent more than a year ago. For the first nine months of 2000, dry natural gas consumption was 16.4 trillion cubic feet, up 2 percent from the same period in 1999, and some 3 percent more than in 1998. For all of 1998, dry natural gas production in the U.S. was 21.5 trillion cubic feet.

Gross withdrawals of natural gas in July 2000 were 2 billion cubic feet, up 1 percent from the previous month. For all of 1999, gross withdrawals were 24 trillion cubic feet. Natural gas repressuring in July 1999 was 286 billion cubic feet, down 1 percent from the previous month and 1 percent higher than a year ago. For all of 1999, natural gas repressuring was 3.53 trillion cubic feet.

Marketed production (wet) of natural gas in September 2000 was 1.62 trillion cubic feet, down 3 percent from the previous month. For all of 1999, marketed production was 19.6 trillion cubic feet.

Futures Markets

Natural gas futures and options are traded on the New York Mercantile Exchange (NYMEX) and the Kansas City Board of Trade (KCBT). Futures are traded on the International Petroleum Exchange (IPE).

World Production of Natural Gas (Monthly Average Marketed Production[3])   (In Terajoule[4])

Year	Aust-ralia	Canada	China	Germany	Indo-nesia	India	Italy	Mexico	Nether-lands	Romania	Rissia[5]	United Knigdom	Uinted States
1991	62,194	362,029	49,955	52,460	158,214	43,284	53,037	79,009	239,349	68,977	2,286,626	176,344	1,609,083
1992	67,696	397,229	50,052	51,911	165,761	43,297	57,117	95,688	240,043	61,470	1,743,167	176,661	1,614,941
1993	72,848	437,922	52,297	47,904	171,828	44,475	60,792	93,646	244,205	58,499	1,708,083	196,792	1,667,401
1994	87,178	480,577	57,036	52,911	190,775	55,355	64,122	95,250	207,317	51,720	1,657,151	214,710	1,703,771
1995	96,912	511,447	58,261	55,714	203,633	59,857	63,371	93,473	209,229	50,401	1,891,583	246,818	1,683,674
1996	99,461	530,891	72,609	60,925	248,574	85,092	63,436	106,214	236,803	48,023	1,844,954	293,536	1,706,758
1997	99,077	537,295	81,954	60,558	248,585	60,979	61,173	109,568	209,526	41,547	1,771,467	299,503	1,711,104
1998	95,265	538,273	72,074	59,072	274,281	64,262	60,242	179,213	198,554	32,932	1,665,726	314,506	1,693,542
1999[1]	95,468	558,779	79,523	62,651	280,711	62,786	57,161	182,610	186,672	38,952	1,807,313	345,506	1,689,378
2000[2]	94,238	571,502	86,733	54,848	NA	71,558	57,727	180,693	203,558	38,343	1,931,540	402,567	1,691,990

[1] Preliminary.   [2] Estimate.   [3] Compares all gas collected & utilized as fuel or as a chemical industry raw material, including gas used in oilfields and/or gasfields as a fuel by producers.   [4] Terajoule = 10 to the 12th power Joule = approximately 10 to the 9th power BTU.   [5] Formerly part os U.S.S.R., data not reported seperately until 1992.   NA = Not available.   *Source: United Nations*

Marketed Production of Natural Gas in the United States, by States   (In Million Cubic Feet)

Year	Alaska	California	Colorado	Kansas	Louisiana	Michigan	Mississippi	New Mexico	Oklahoma	Texas	Wyoming	Total
1990	402,907	362,748	242,997	573,603	5,241,989	172,151	94,616	965,104	2,258,471	6,343,146	735,728	18,593,792
1991	437,822	378,384	285,961	628,459	5,034,361	195,749	108,031	1,038,284	2,153,852	6,280,654	776,528	18,532,439
1992	443,597	365,632	323,041	658,007	4,914,300	194,815	91,697	1,268,863	2,017,356	6,145,862	842,576	18,711,808
1993	430,350	315,851	400,985	686,347	4,991,138	204,635	80,695	1,409,429	2,049,942	6,249,624	634,957	18,981,915
1994	555,402	309,427	453,207	712,730	5,169,705	222,657	63,448	1,557,689	1,934,864	6,353,844	696,018	19,709,525
1995	469,550	279,555	523,084	721,436	5,108,366	238,203	95,533	1,625,837	1,811,734	6,330,048	673,775	19,506,474
1996	480,828	286,494	572,071	712,796	5,240,747	245,740	103,263	1,554,087	1,734,887	6,449,022	666,036	19,750,793
1997	468,311	285,690	637,375	687,215	5,229,821	305,950	107,300	1,558,633	1,703,888	6,453,873	738,368	19,866,093
1998	466,648	315,277	696,321	603,586	5,287,870	278,076	108,068	1,501,098	1,644,531	6,318,754	761,313	19,645,554
1999[1]	457,363	365,945	742,284	555,446	5,474,842	278,202	111,022	1,598,128	1,604,156	6,200,786	779,369	19,609,959

[1] Preliminary.   *Source: Energy Information Administration, U.S. Department of Energy (EIA-DOE)*

World Production of Natural Gas Plant Liquids (Thousand Barrels per Day)

Year	Algeria	Canada	Mexico	Saudi Arabia	Russia	United States	Persian Gulf[2]	OAPEC[3]	OPEC[4]	World
1991	140	431	457	680	420	1,659	931	1,113	1,299	4,827
1992	140	460	454	713	230	1,697	1,003	1,185	1,364	4,974
1993	145	506	459	704	220	1,736	1,040	1,238	1,435	5,180
1994	140	529	461	698	200	1,727	1,071	1,267	1,465	5,292
1995	145	581	447	701	180	1,762	1,106	1,301	1,506	5,485
1996	150	596	423	697	185	1,830	1,082	1,295	1,501	5,576
1997	160	636	388	712	195	1,817	1,152	1,384	1,589	5,721
1998	155	651	424	755	220	1,759	1,225	1,449	1,662	5,866
1999	155	653	439	666	225	1,850	1,152	1,374	1,617	5,918
2000[1]	155	695	438	703	225	1,944	1,203	1,425	1,668	6,107

[1] Preliminary. [2] Bahrain, Iran, Iraq, Kuwait, Qatar, Saudi Arabia and the United Arab Emirates. [3] Organization of Arab Petroleum Exporting Countries. [4] Organization of Pertroleum Exporting Countries. [5] Through 1991; Former USSR. *Source: Energy Information Administration, U.S. Department of Energy (EIA-DOE)*

Recoverable Reserves and Deliveries of Natural Gas in the United States (in Billions of Cubic Feet)

Year	Gross Withdrawals	Recoverable Reserves of Natural Gas Dec. 31[2]	Deliveries Residential	Commercial	Electric Utility Plants[3]	Industrial	Total Deliveries	Consumption Lease & Plant Fuel	Used as Pipeline Fuel	Heating Value BTU per Cubic Foot
1990	21,523	169,346	4,391	2,623	2,786	7,018	16,819	1,236	660	1,031
1991	21,750	167,062	4,556	2,729	2,789	7,231	17,305	1,129	601	1,030
1992	22,132	165,015	4,690	2,803	2,766	7,527	17,786	1,171	588	1,030
1993	22,726	162,415	4,956	2,863	2,682	7,981	18,483	1,172	624	1,027
1994	23,581	163,837	4,848	2,897	2,987	8,167	18,899	1,124	685	1,028
1995	23,744	165,146	4,850	3,031	3,197	8,580	19,660	1,220	700	1,027
1996	24,114	166,474	5,241	3,158	2,732	8,870	20,006	1,250	711	1,027
1997	24,213	167,223	4,984	3,215	2,968	8,832	20,004	1,203	751	1,026
1998	24,096	NA	4,520	2,999	3,258	8,686	19,469	1,174	635	1,031
1999[1]	23,755	NA	4,724	3,049	3,113	8,990	19,882	1,077	735	1,027

[1] Preliminary. [2] Estimated proved recoverable reserves of dry natural gas. [3] Figures include gas other than natural (impossible to segregate); therefore, shown separately from other consumption. *Source: Energy Information Administration, U.S. Department of Energy (EIA-DOE)*

Gas Utility Sales in the United States by Types and Class of Service (In Trillions of BTUs)

Year	Total Utility Sales	Number of Customers (Millions)	Class by Service Residential	Commercial	Industrial	Electric Generation	Other	Total	Revenue - Million $ From Sales to Customers Residential	Commercial	industrial	Electric Generation	Other
1991	9,601	55.2	4,546	2,198	1,743	888	226	44,647	25,729	10,669	5,326	2,250	674
1992	9,907	56.1	4,694	2,209	1,959	813	231	46,178	26,702	10,865	5,837	2,077	698
1993	10,151	57.0	5,054	2,397	2,009	524	168	50,137	29,787	12,076	6,162	1,480	632
1994	9,248	57.9	4,845	2,253	1,690	420	159	49,852	30,552	12,276	5,529	1,170	597
1995	9,221	58.7	4,803	2,281	1,591	328	218	46,436	28,742	11,573	4,816	836	549
1996	9,532	59.8	5,198	2,395	1,519	271	148	51,115	32,021	12,726	5,039	783	545
1997	8,880	59.8	5,013	2,234	1,279	245	123	51,531	33,175	12,632	4,518	766	488
1998[1]	8,341	60.4	4,693	2,043	1,153	336	116	46,924	30,671	11,189	3,779	899	387

[1] Preliminary. [2] Estimate. *Source: American Gas Association (AGA)*

Salient Statistics of Natural Gas in the United States

Year	Supply Marketed Production	Extraction Loss	Dry Production	Storage Withdrawals	Imports (Consumed)	Total Supply	Disposition Consumption	Exports	Added to Storage	Total Disposition	Average Price Delivered to Consumers Wellhead Price	Imports	Exports	Residential	Commercial	Industrial	Electric Utilities
	In Billions of Cubic Feet										USD Per Thousand Cubic Feet						
1990	18,594	784	17,810	1,934	1,532	21,302	18,716	86	2,433	21,523	1.71	1.94	3.10	5.80	4.83	2.93	2.38
1991	18,532	835	17,698	2,689	1,773	21,836	19,035	129	2,608	21,750	1.64	1.82	2.59	5.82	4.81	2.69	2.18
1992	18,712	872	17,840	2,724	2,138	22,360	19,544	216	2,555	22,132	1.74	1.85	2.25	5.89	4.88	2.84	2.36
1993	18,982	886	18,095	2,717	2,350	23,578	20,279	140	2,760	23,578	2.04	2.03	2.59	6.16	5.22	3.07	2.61
1994	19,710	889	18,821	2,508	2,624	24,207	20,708	162	2,796	24,207	1.85	1.87	2.50	6.41	5.44	3.05	2.28
1995	19,506	908	18,599	2,974	2,841	24,837	21,581	154	2,566	24,837	1.55	1.49	2.39	6.06	5.05	2.71	2.02
1996	19,812	958	18,854	2,911	2,937	25,635	21,967	153	2,906	25,635	2.17	1.97	2.97	6.34	5.40	3.42	2.69
1997	19,866	964	18,902	2,824	2,994	25,502	21,959	157	2,800	25,502	2.32	2.17	3.02	6.94	5.80	3.59	2.78
1998[1]	19,809	938	18,871	2,377	3,152	24,859	21,279	159	2,904	24,859	1.95	1.97	2.45	6.82	5.48	3.14	2.40
1999[2]	19,596	951	18,695	2,772	3,586	25,055	21,694	163	2,598	25,055	2.17	2.24	2.61	6.69	5.33	3.10	2.62

[1] Preliminary. [2] Estimate. *Source: Energy Information Administration, U.S. Department of Energy (EIA-DOE)*

GAS

Average Open Interest of Natural Gas Futures in New York   In Contracts

Year	Jan.	Feb.	Mar.	Apr.	May	June	July	Aug.	Sept.	Oct.	Nov.	Dec.
1991	10,523	13,825	13,125	13,225	16,782	18,502	19,235	21,460	23,853	24,003	21,692	19,065
1992	24,718	28,661	29,851	33,626	41,456	49,642	49,829	57,346	68,306	77,034	80,349	74,569
1993	69,499	77,053	91,132	116,366	136,074	132,667	124,038	126,443	129,940	130,619	124,627	129,963
1994	127,254	128,336	118,480	119,908	120,894	120,956	111,044	135,652	156,238	145,766	139,471	139,054
1995	148,448	151,882	157,097	150,101	148,797	144,402	143,942	140,297	135,226	133,969	140,301	166,227
1996	155,024	150,521	149,809	159,132	147,616	156,959	151,913	135,191	138,657	144,944	147,854	151,498
1997	156,231	162,567	171,467	181,745	206,685	197,637	199,296	213,640	235,509	242,184	231,556	210,259
1998	192,652	198,853	203,402	251,344	255,837	264,517	255,878	273,350	275,868	252,827	236,292	240,832
1999	244,472	268,649	284,312	315,336	332,398	330,725	316,034	353,767	336,622	316,157	309,130	292,161
2000	262,845	266,826	295,176	313,739	342,455	347,353	330,604	339,025	373,654	369,448	389,363	377,470

Source: New York Mercantile Exchange (NYMEX)

Volume of Trading of Natural Gas Futures in New York   (In Thousands of Contracts)

Year	Jan.	Feb.	Mar.	Apr.	May	June	July	Aug.	Sept.	Oct.	Nov.	Dec.	Total
1991	29.2	14.9	22.8	20.3	28.7	51.2	37.0	33.1	42.3	46.6	49.0	50.2	425.3
1992	89.0	45.4	77.9	98.9	137.5	116.4	156.0	192.2	268.7	300.0	213.5	227.6	1,923.2
1993	194.3	274.4	318.8	443.0	471.5	365.9	335.6	353.3	459.6	417.1	449.7	613.9	4,697.1
1994	667.6	470.9	373.5	344.7	411.1	465.8	438.8	724.2	578.7	594.2	621.9	721.8	6,413.2
1995	733.0	557.8	676.1	524.5	621.3	622.5	641.8	745.6	548.3	664.4	763.0	988.5	8,086.7
1996	887.2	655.7	694.6	620.0	590.7	681.3	829.0	628.8	679.1	924.4	802.8	820.4	8,813.9
1997	922.8	693.6	664.7	836.3	945.4	803.7	812.9	1,313.8	1,377.1	1,394.0	1,104.8	1,054.6	11,923.6
1998	1,005.6	1,089.1	1,193.5	1,625.9	1,245.2	1,568.8	1,310.4	1,237.0	1,656.3	1,339.5	1,243.1	1,464.0	15,978.3
1999	1,296.7	1,158.6	1,788.5	1,655.8	1,465.3	1,474.2	1,865.8	1,892.1	1,978.6	1,676.5	1,552.3	1,360.7	19,165.1
2000	1,388.8	1,470.9	1,505.0	1,179.3	1,822.2	1,853.7	1,331.4	1,483.9	1,510.2	1,594.9	1,759.5	975.1	17,875.0

Source: New York Mercantile Exchange (NYMEX)

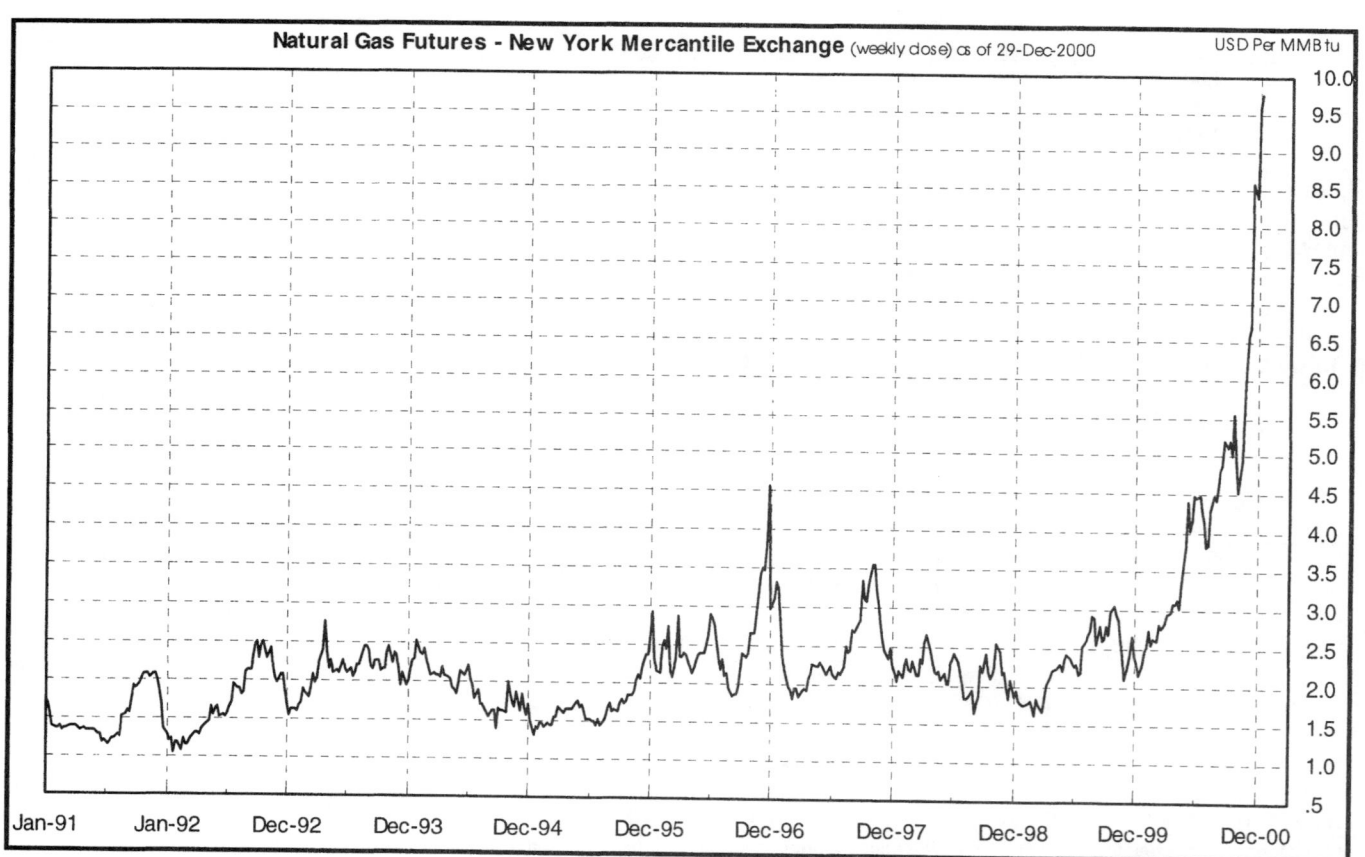

Gasoline

One of the major economic developments of the year 2000 was the substantial increase in the price of gasoline. There were a number of reasons associated with the rise in prices, the most prominent of which was the ability of the Organization of Petroleum Exporting Countries (OPEC) to adhere to production quota levels. Also, lower global stocks of petroleum fueled a surge in energy prices which included crude oil, gasoline, heating oil, and even spilled over into natural gas. At the height of the driving season in July, gasoline prices staged a huge rally that peaked in mid-October. Prices then declined as supplies increased. A decision by OPEC to increase petroleum output seemed to be the catalyst for an overall decline in energy prices while high prices were drawing more supply to the market and gasoline inventories were increasing. A positive for prices was the fact that gasoline demand remained strong.

Production of gasoline follows a seasonal pattern. As the summer driving season approaches, petroleum refineries increase production of gasoline to build inventories. At the end of the June-September driving season, refineries switch to more production of heating oil for the winter heating season. One feature of the market in late 2000 was that heating oil prices were trading at a premium to gasoline prices. That could mean that more heating oil and less gasoline will be produced.

U.S. production of finished motor gasoline in September 2000 was 8.24 million barrels per day. In September 1999, production was 8.19 million barrels per day. Over the January-September 2000 period, production of finished motor gasoline averaged 8.13 million barrels per day compared to 8.05 million barrels in the same period in 1999, and 8.04 million barrels in 1998.

U.S. imports of finished gasoline in September 2000 were 308,000 barrels per day, down from 338,000 in August. In September 1999, imports were 335,000 barrels. In the January-September 2000 period, imports of gasoline averaged 343,000 barrels, down 15 percent from the average in 1999, but 11 percent more than in 1998. For all of 1999, imports averaged 382,000 barrels per day, while in 1998 they averaged 311,000.

U.S. exports of motor gasoline in September 2000 averaged 118,000 barrels per day, down from 194,000 barrels in August. In the first nine months of 2000, exports averaged 120,000 barrels per day, up from 99,000 in 1999. Total gasoline supplied in January-September 2000 was 8.34 million barrels per day.

Finished motor gasoline stocks in September 2000 were 155 million barrels. In September 1999, stocks were 162 million barrels while in September 1998, stocks were 164 million barrels. Stocks of oxygenates in August 2000 were 13 million barrels which was down 7 percent from the previous year. In August 1998, oxygenate stocks were 13 million barrels.

Futures Markets

Unleaded gasoline futures and options are traded on the New York Mercantile Exchange (NYMEX).

Average Spot Price of Unleaded Gasoline in New York   In Cents Per Gallon

Year	Jan.	Feb.	Mar.	Apr.	May	June	July	Aug.	Sept.	Oct.	Nov.	Dec.	Average
1991	68.88	65.82	74.25	72.07	70.28	63.59	65.23	69.90	62.17	64.41	65.10	55.55	66.44
1992	53.04	55.14	54.10	59.75	63.48	64.51	59.94	62.06	61.63	60.81	58.22	53.24	58.83
1993	52.96	52.54	54.33	59.35	59.37	54.78	51.80	53.13	48.61	50.22	44.30	37.68	51.59
1994	42.40	43.75	44.04	48.98	50.62	52.84	54.52	55.61	46.53	51.14	52.32	46.87	49.14
1995	50.99	51.43	50.74	61.01	64.76	59.47	51.45	53.45	56.10	48.89	51.15	53.44	54.41
1996	50.70	53.26	58.56	69.17	65.10	58.03	61.65	61.17	62.43	65.52	69.23	68.58	61.95
1997	67.64	62.49	61.28	58.59	62.08	55.17	58.58	70.42	62.17	58.35	55.60	51.75	60.34
1998	47.85	45.14	44.13	46.98	48.26	43.95	42.29	40.14	42.70	43.71	36.78	30.92	42.74
1999	34.24	31.81	42.33	50.11	48.86	48.65	58.35	63.89	69.37	62.63	69.57	70.55	54.20
2000	70.43	81.30	89.11	73.15	89.06	96.18	86.76	86.97	96.04	94.71	93.94	73.66	85.94

Source: The Wall Street Journal

Average Open Interest of Unleaded Regular Gasoline Futures in New York   In Contracts

Year	Jan.	Feb.	Mar.	Apr.	May	June	July	Aug.	Sept.	Oct.	Nov.	Dec.
1991	54,807	75,337	81,393	74,801	71,900	73,633	74,503	87,073	90,680	100,606	111,745	125,578
1992	124,896	117,155	108,388	89,775	79,680	80,394	81,110	76,741	71,264	68,059	71,110	77,508
1993	80,610	93,630	100,657	96,607	88,311	94,926	104,260	103,371	100,921	107,339	126,649	150,359
1994	135,366	120,204	118,977	122,092	96,525	89,854	86,401	76,213	67,881	70,258	71,245	63,679
1995	61,015	67,631	65,201	76,323	76,269	69,676	64,379	58,426	62,089	58,782	57,902	70,098
1996	64,561	64,990	70,100	71,895	66,172	52,882	55,394	55,618	57,119	59,993	58,416	62,760
1997	68,188	84,693	92,520	97,619	90,407	78,492	83,082	103,538	103,250	94,602	92,852	103,497
1998	106,353	102,656	108,667	117,521	107,235	100,792	89,846	86,902	85,188	81,991	87,306	103,079
1999	105,532	113,683	111,449	110,531	107,644	102,927	113,619	120,468	120,328	111,758	109,428	96,652
2000	89,049	103,586	105,448	105,133	103,831	96,772	80,886	66,598	74,735	80,446	88,509	92,041

Source: New York Mercantile Exchange (NYMEX)

GASOLINE

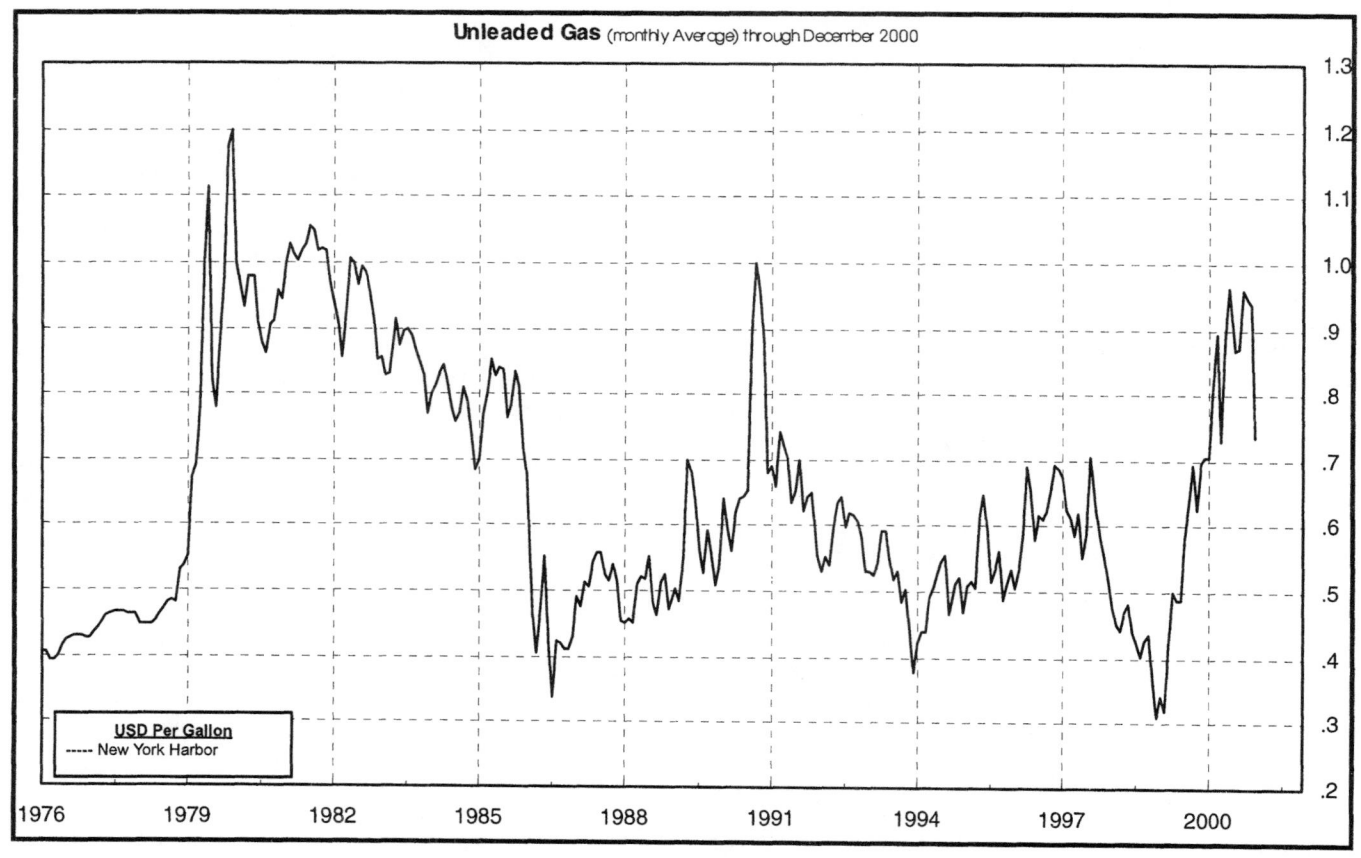

Unleaded Gas (monthly Average) through December 2000

USD Per Gallon
----- New York Harbor

Volume of Trading of Unleaded Regular Gasoline Futures in New York   In Contracts

Year	Jan.	Feb.	Mar.	Apr.	May	June	July	Aug.	Sept.	Oct.	Nov.	Dec.	Total
1991	366,772	351,188	525,432	541,073	482,943	446,350	396,429	562,085	386,421	477,111	537,834	529,940	5,603,578
1992	565,922	558,476	604,678	668,490	580,088	620,114	600,897	545,520	469,844	563,856	435,847	461,025	6,674,757
1993	531,780	558,770	584,899	539,785	571,860	611,951	594,740	721,852	642,959	629,733	674,814	729,717	7,392,860
1994	634,027	526,505	615,594	677,891	636,990	673,034	601,980	748,415	569,384	684,670	582,359	519,987	7,470,836
1995	592,329	506,640	736,704	663,743	780,568	680,792	565,655	556,589	573,551	473,014	480,507	461,695	7,071,787
1996	543,818	449,537	570,341	676,193	623,347	467,953	533,793	463,830	469,036	527,553	487,624	499,314	6,312,339
1997	590,066	563,180	605,121	623,169	618,312	555,543	721,386	795,404	664,906	613,557	509,893	614,608	7,475,145
1998	613,643	612,266	766,430	789,293	681,052	753,120	680,551	591,985	654,247	670,159	577,799	601,724	7,992,269
1999	561,493	619,704	876,350	741,511	721,122	737,690	821,991	800,399	751,305	705,144	748,839	615,668	8,701,216
2000	693,610	721,890	921,642	730,022	927,541	838,537	650,632	677,207	641,169	635,690	612,112	595,130	8,645,182

Source: New York Mercantile Exchange (NYMEX)

Production of Finished Motor Gasoline in the United States   In Thousand Barrels per Day

Year	Jan.	Feb.	Mar.	Apr.	May	June	July	Aug.	Sept.	Oct.	Nov.	Dec.	Average
1991	6,629	6,573	6,643	6,742	7,063	7,351	7,274	7,247	7,030	6,749	7,018	7,354	6,975
1992	7,013	6,726	6,683	6,954	7,092	7,198	7,195	6,817	7,071	7,198	7,323	7,411	7,058
1993	7,228	7,144	6,904	7,126	7,446	7,442	7,337	7,335	7,573	7,394	7,652	7,725	7,360
1994	7,097	6,790	6,760	7,195	7,348	7,455	7,380	7,432	7,385	7,151	7,849	7,867	7,312
1995	7,303	7,243	7,168	7,529	7,678	7,843	7,747	7,642	7,785	7,544	7,739	7,821	7,588
1996	7,333	7,303	7,242	7,475	7,724	7,820	7,811	7,696	7,585	7,496	7,835	7,784	7,593
1997	7,308	7,315	7,322	7,822	8,056	8,180	7,947	8,048	8,147	8,039	7,984	8,143	7,862
1998	7,749	7,485	7,591	8,029	8,057	8,372	8,287	8,200	8,029	7,995	8,263	8,395	8,041
1999	7,896	7,608	7,492	8,061	8,129	8,295	8,157	8,198	8,165	8,270	8,142	8,474	8,077
2000[1]	7,778	7,602	8,013	8,091	8,378	8,486	8,332	8,201	8,300	8,019	8,398	8,235	8,154

[1] Preliminary.   *Source: Energy Information Administration, U.S. Department of Energy (EIA-DOE)*

Disposition of Finished Motor Gasoline, Total Product Supplied in the U.S.   In Thousand Barrels per Day

Year	Jan.	Feb.	Mar.	Apr.	May	June	July	Aug.	Sept.	Oct.	Nov.	Dec.	Average
1991	6,645	6,838	7,017	7,137	7,437	7,456	7,561	7,528	7,083	7,281	7,008	7,224	7,188
1992	6,869	6,963	7,137	7,238	7,328	7,460	7,639	7,380	7,344	7,338	7,102	7,396	7,268
1993	6,639	7,112	7,389	7,435	7,585	7,700	7,785	7,864	7,607	7,382	7,533	7,661	7,476
1994	6,980	7,275	7,395	7,564	7,644	7,922	7,884	7,975	7,615	7,548	7,464	7,924	7,601
1995	7,163	7,481	7,788	7,651	7,894	8,220	7,888	8,187	7,786	7,781	7,866	7,742	7,789
1996	7,254	7,552	7,729	7,869	7,998	8,089	8,135	8,216	7,641	8,038	7,875	7,775	7,849
1997	7,312	7,651	7,808	8,067	8,128	8,260	8,471	8,195	8,004	8,166	7,955	8,093	8,007
1998	7,590	7,755	7,956	8,137	8,070	8,437	8,659	8,500	8,308	8,405	8,136	8,401	8,199
1999	7,630	8,091	8,081	8,389	8,233	8,752	8,783	8,583	8,350	8,528	8,249	8,843	8,378
2000[1]	7,498	8,222	8,232	8,229	8,505	8,663	8,600	8,762	8,416	8,364	8,297	8,573	8,364

[1] Preliminary.   Source: Energy Information Administration, U.S. Department of Energy (EIA-DOE)

Stocks of Finished Gasoline[2] on Hand in the United States, at End of Month   In Millions of Barrels

Year	Jan.	Feb.	Mar.	Apr.	May	June	July	Aug.	Sept.	Oct.	Nov.	Dec.
1991	189.1	182.7	174.4	171.9	173.7	178.5	173.5	172.8	179.1	168.3	173.3	183.3
1992	192.8	191.4	182.9	185.0	187.4	189.5	182.0	168.2	170.0	168.7	178.2	179.1
1993	197.8	201.9	189.0	184.0	186.8	184.2	176.8	166.7	171.2	175.6	182.6	187.1
1994	194.1	186.2	175.6	176.4	179.0	176.9	172.9	167.6	169.2	161.7	176.6	175.9
1995	182.7	180.0	167.8	167.1	167.1	163.5	166.0	154.6	158.9	155.6	155.6	161.3
1996	168.7	168.4	158.3	159.8	161.8	163.8	163.7	154.9	161.3	149.1	150.7	157.0
1997	164.9	161.3	153.8	152.0	157.8	163.9	150.6	149.6	158.1	158.0	161.1	166.1
1998	175.3	172.8	166.4	168.3	174.9	177.7	172.5	168.8	164.7	160.0	167.5	172.0
1999	185.2	178.4	167.8	168.9	176.5	172.3	163.6	158.6	159.2	158.8	160.5	151.6
2000[1]	165.7	156.1	157.7	161.6	163.5	165.4	164.9	151.9	154.4	147.5	157.4	

[1] Preliminary.   [2] Includes oxygenated and other finished.   Source: Energy Information Administration, U.S. Department of Energy (EIA-DOE)

Average Refiner Price of Finished Motor Gasoline to End Users[1] in the U.S.   In Cents Per Gallon

Year	Jan.	Feb.	Mar.	Apr.	May	June	July	Aug.	Sept.	Oct.	Nov.	Dec.	Average
1991	88.8	79.5	74.0	77.0	82.0	81.9	78.9	81.1	80.2	77.9	79.1	76.0	79.7
1992	71.2	70.2	71.0	74.6	80.3	84.0	83.5	82.3	82.3	81.3	81.4	78.5	78.4
1993	76.9	76.1	75.7	77.8	80.1	79.8	77.6	76.2	74.9	75.3	72.5	68.0	75.9
1994	66.8	67.6	67.3	69.5	71.1	74.1	77.0	81.5	79.6	76.9	77.5	75.1	73.8
1995	74.5	73.3	73.1	77.3	83.4	83.9	80.0	76.9	75.8	73.6	71.8	73.0	76.5
1996	74.6	74.8	79.8	88.1	92.7	90.3	87.5	84.9	84.4	84.4	86.7	85.9	84.7
1997	86.6	86.1	84.3	83.9	84.5	83.3	81.5	86.8	87.2	84.3	81.6	77.8	83.9
1998	73.3	69.0	65.6	67.4	71.0	70.4	69.4	66.7	65.4	66.4	64.0	60.0	67.3
1999	59.2	56.8	65.1	79.0	78.2	75.6	80.6	86.5	88.8	87.1	88.4	90.3	78.1
2000[2]	91.7	98.7	113.1	108.7	110.3	121.3	116.2	109.3	116.7	114.8	113.4		110.4

[1] Excludes aviation and taxes.   [2] Preliminary.   Source: Energy Information Administration, U.S. Department of Energy (EIA-DOE)

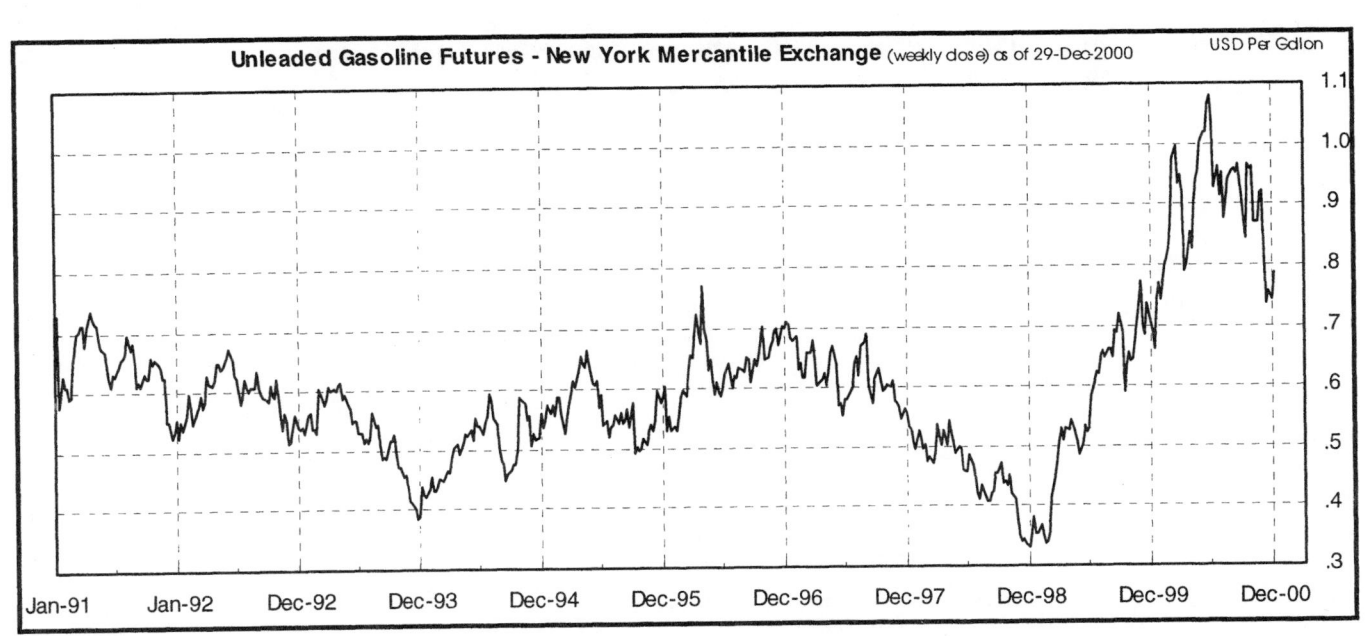

Unleaded Gasoline Futures - New York Mercantile Exchange (weekly close) as of 29-Dec-2000

GASOLINE

Average Retail Price of Unleaded Premium Motor Gasoline[2] in the United States   In Cents per Gallon

Year	Jan.	Feb.	Mar.	Apr.	May	June	July	Aug.	Sept.	Oct.	Nov.	Dec.	Average
1991	143.1	132.1	126.4	128.1	133.1	133.8	131.3	131.8	132.4	130.7	131.8	130.9	132.1
1992	126.7	124.8	125.0	126.8	131.7	135.9	136.3	134.8	134.6	134.5	135.1	133.0	131.6
1993	131.3	130.1	129.4	130.4	131.9	132.1	130.5	129.4	128.2	132.3	130.5	126.8	130.2
1994	124.0	124.5	124.3	126.0	127.4	130.0	132.7	136.7	136.4	134.5	135.4	133.7	130.5
1995	132.4	131.6	130.6	132.5	138.3	141.1	138.4	135.2	133.2	131.5	129.2	129.0	133.6
1996	131.7	131.1	134.8	143.1	150.7	148.1	145.3	142.1	141.7	140.8	142.8	143.8	141.3
1997	144.1	143.4	141.5	141.3	140.9	141.1	138.8	143.3	145.8	142.6	139.7	136.3	141.6
1998	131.9	127.1	122.9	123.7	127.5	127.9	126.8	124.4	123.0	123.6	122.5	118.7	125.0
1999	117.1	115.5	118.6	136.7	137.0	133.9	137.8	144.1	146.8	146.4	145.4	148.6	135.7
2000[1]	148.6	155.1	172.3	169.8	168.2	178.6	177.3	168.9	176.4	174.4	173.8	167.9	169.3

[1] Preliminary.   [2] Including taxes.   Source: Energy Information Administration, U.S. Department of Energy (EIA-DOE)

Average Retail Price of Unleaded Regular Motor Gasoline[2] in the United States   In Cents per Gallon

Year	Jan.	Feb.	Mar.	Apr.	May	June	July	Aug.	Sept.	Oct.	Nov.	Dec.	Average
1991	124.7	114.3	108.2	110.4	115.6	116.0	112.7	114.0	114.3	112.2	113.4	112.3	114.0
1992	107.3	105.4	105.8	107.9	113.6	117.9	117.5	115.8	115.8	115.4	115.9	113.6	112.7
1993	111.7	110.8	109.8	111.2	112.9	113.0	110.9	109.7	108.5	112.7	111.3	107.0	110.8
1994	104.3	105.1	104.5	106.4	108.0	110.6	113.6	118.2	117.7	115.2	116.3	114.3	111.2
1995	112.9	112.0	111.5	114.0	120.0	122.6	119.5	116.4	114.8	112.7	110.1	110.1	114.7
1996	112.9	112.4	116.2	125.1	132.3	129.9	127.2	124.0	123.4	122.7	125.0	126.0	123.1
1997	126.1	125.5	123.5	123.1	122.6	122.9	120.5	125.3	127.7	124.2	121.3	117.7	123.4
1998	113.1	108.2	104.1	105.2	109.2	109.4	107.9	105.2	103.3	104.2	102.8	98.6	105.9
1999	97.2	95.5	99.1	117.7	117.8	114.8	118.9	125.5	128.0	127.4	126.4	129.8	116.5
2000[1]	130.1	136.9	154.1	150.6	149.8	161.7	159.3	151.0	158.2	155.9	155.5	148.9	151.0

[1] Preliminary.   [2] Including taxes.   Source: Energy Information Administration, U.S. Department of Energy (EIA-DOE)

Average Retail Price of All-Types[2] Motor Gasoline[3] in the United States   In Cents per Gallon

Year	Jan.	Feb.	Mar.	Apr.	May	June	July	Aug.	Sept.	Oct.	Nov.	Dec.	Average
1991	130.4	119.8	113.8	115.9	120.9	121.4	118.5	119.6	119.9	118.0	119.3	118.2	119.6
1992	113.5	111.7	112.2	114.3	119.7	123.9	123.8	122.1	122.2	121.9	122.3	120.1	119.0
1993	118.2	117.2	116.3	117.5	119.3	119.4	117.4	116.3	115.1	119.3	117.8	113.6	117.3
1994	110.9	111.4	110.9	112.8	114.3	116.7	119.9	124.3	123.7	121.2	122.2	120.3	117.4
1995	119.0	118.1	117.3	119.7	125.6	128.1	125.2	122.2	120.6	118.5	116.1	116.0	120.5
1996	118.6	118.1	121.9	130.5	137.8	135.4	132.8	129.8	129.3	128.7	130.8	131.8	128.8
1997	131.8	131.2	129.3	128.8	128.4	128.6	126.3	131.0	133.4	130.0	127.1	123.6	129.1
1998	118.6	113.7	109.7	110.6	114.6	114.8	113.4	110.8	109.1	109.9	108.6	104.6	111.5
1999	103.1	101.4	104.8	123.2	123.3	120.4	124.4	130.9	133.4	132.9	131.9	135.3	122.1
2000[1]	135.6	142.2	159.4	156.1	155.2	166.6	164.2	155.9	163.5	161.3	160.8	154.4	156.3

[1] Preliminary.   [2] Also includes types of motor oil not shown separately.   [3] Including taxes.   Source: Energy Information Administration, U.S. Department of Energy (EIA-DOE)

Average Refiner Price of Finished Aviation Gasoline to End Users[2] in the U.S.   In Cents per Gallon

Year	Jan.	Feb.	Mar.	Apr.	May	June	July	Aug.	Sept.	Oct.	Nov.	Dec.	Average
1991	112.1	106.4	101.3	101.2	105.3	105.2	103.6	105.8	105.7	104.6	104.3	102.0	104.7
1992	98.5	98.5	98.0	99.1	102.4	106.4	106.8	105.7	104.9	104.3	103.4	101.3	102.7
1993	100.3	99.9	99.4	100.7	102.2	102.5	99.7	98.8	98.2	98.0	95.7	91.2	99.0
1994	88.6	88.4	89.0	91.3	92.3	95.6	95.9	101.7	101.1	100.0	100.0	99.2	95.6
1995	99.6	99.8	99.0	101.3	105.8	106.4	101.8	99.2	101.3	96.8	95.4	96.0	100.5
1996	97.6	100.6	105.0	111.2	114.4	113.5	113.7	114.4	114.3	115.0	115.1	115.3	111.6
1997	113.7	114.9	113.8	114.7	115.7	114.6	112.5	114.6	115.6	113.9	113.0	107.7	113.8
1998	104.3	101.1	98.2	98.6	99.9	99.0	98.4	95.9	94.1	95.1	93.2	88.5	97.2
1999	87.0	85.0	89.7	101.3	103.5	103.3	110.0	114.8	117.7	118.4	117.4	120.7	105.9
2000[1]	119.6	123.8	133.8	130.7	133.6	140.8	142.1	NA	138.2	134.9	134.9		133.2

[1] Preliminary.   [2] Excluding taxes.   Source: Energy Information Administration, U.S. Department Energy (EIA-DOE)

Gold

After a spectacular rally in February 2000 that saw gold prices move from $282 per ounce to just below $320 per ounce in a single week, prices trended lower the rest of the year, approaching $270 per ounce by the end of December. For most of the year 2000 gold prices edged lower. Part of the reason was currency related as the dollar strengthened against all of the major currencies, including those of the major gold producing nations, the Australian dollar, the Canadian dollar, and the South African rand. Gold prices tend to move higher if the dollar shows weakness against the currencies of gold producing countries. In late 2000, gold prices moved upwards some $10 per ounce in response to weakness in the U.S. Dollar, before settling back again as the year ended. If the dollar does weaken in 2001, gold prices could move higher. It is of some interest that different metal prices went different ways in 2000. Silver remained in a downtrend underperforming gold late in the year. By contrast, platinum and palladium prices moved to multiyear highs very early in 2001.

The U.S. Geological Survey reported that world mine production of gold in 1999 was 2,330 metric tonnes, down 5 percent from 1998. The world's largest producer of gold is South Africa with 1999 mine production estimated at 450 tonnes, down 3 percent from 1998. The U.S. is the next largest producer with 1999 mine output of 340 tonnes, down 7 percent from a year ago. Production by Australia was estimated to be 300 tonnes, down 4 percent from a year ago. Gold production by Canada in 1999 was estimated at 155 tonnes, down 7 percent from the previous year. China produced 150 tonnes, down 16 percent from a year earlier. Production by Russia was estimated to be 105 tonnes. Other gold producers include Uzbekistan and Brazil.

World reserves of gold are estimated to be 49,000 tonnes. About 20 percent of the gold is a byproduct of another metal. South Africa has by far the largest estimated reserves with 19,000 tonnes. It is estimated that 128,000 tonnes of gold have been mined in total, and about 15 percent of that has been lost, used up, or is unaccounted for. It is estimated that central banks hold gold stocks of 34,000 tonnes, and that 74,000 tonnes are held privately as bullion, coins, and jewelry.

U.S. mine production of gold in 1999 was estimated to be 340 tonnes and over the last five years gold production has averaged 342 tonnes per year. In the U.S., gold was produced at about 70 major lode mines, a dozen or more placer mines, and many smaller mines. Gold is also recovered as a byproduct of processing base metals, mostly cop-per. U.S. refinery production of secondary gold from new and old scrap was 150 tonnes in 1999, down 8 percent from a year ago. U.S. primary refinery production of gold in 1999 was 260 tonnes, down 6 percent. The estimated uses of gold were jewelry and arts, 79 percent; electronics, 4 percent; dental, 2 percent; and other, 15 percent.

In July 2000, production of gold in Nevada was 15,600 kilograms, down from 21,400 kilograms in June. In the January-July 2000 period, gold production in Nevada totaled 145,000 kilograms. For all of 2000, production totaled 257,000 kilograms. Gold production in Alaska in July 2000 was 1,190 kilograms, the same as the previous month. In the first seven months of 2000, production in Alaska was 8,280 kilograms, and for all of 1999 it was 15,700 kilograms. Gold production in California in July 2000 was 1,470 kilograms, unchanged from the previous month. In the January-July period, production was 9,830 kilograms, while for all of 1999 it was 17,500 kilograms.

U.S. imports for consumption of refined gold bullion in June 2000 were 10,400 kilograms. The major suppliers were Canada, Brazil, Colombia, and Chile. In the January-June 2000 period, refined bullion imports were 85,600 kilograms. For all of 1999, they were 196,000 kilograms. Imports of gold waste and scrap (gross weight) in June 2000 were 1,820 kilograms. In the first half of 2000, imports were 10,600 kilograms, and for all of 1999 they were 30,500 kilograms. Imports of gold metal powder in June 2000 were 600 kilograms. In January-June, they were 1,640 kilograms, while for all of 1999 they were 5,500 kilograms.

U.S. exports of refined bullion in June 2000 were 29,800 kilograms. In the first half of 2000, they were 209,000 kilograms, while for all of 1999 they were 435,000. Exports of gold waste and scrap in the first half of 2000 were 26,000 kilograms while for 1999 they were 40,000 kilograms. Exports of gold compounds in the January-June period were 275,000 kilograms.

Futures Markets

Gold futures are traded on the Bolsa de Mercadorias & Futuros (BM&F), the Tokyo Commodity Exchange (TOCOM), the Chicago Board of Trade (CBOT), the MidAmerica Commodity Exchange (MidAm), and the COMEX division of the New York Mercantile Exchange. Gold options are traded on the BM&F, The Amsterdam Exchanges (AEX-Optiebeurs), the MidAm, and the COMEX.

World Mine Production of Gold   In Kilograms (1 Kilogram = 32.1507 Troy Ounces)

Year	Australia	Brazil	Canada	Chile	China	Ghana	Indonesia	Papua N. Guinea	Russia[3]	South Africa	United States	Uzbekistan[3]	World Total
1990	244,137	101,913	169,412	27,503	100,000	16,840	11,158	31,938	302,000	605,100	294,189	----	2,180,000
1991	234,218	89,578	176,552	28,879	120,000	26,311	16,879	60,780	260,000	601,110	294,062	----	2,190,000
1992	243,400	85,862	161,402	33,774	125,000	31,032	37,983	71,190	146,000	614,071	330,212	70,000	2,260,000
1993	247,196	69,894	152,929	33,638	130,000	38,911	42,097	61,671	149,500	619,201	331,000	70,000	2,280,000
1994	256,188	72,397	146,428	38,786	132,000	43,478	42,600	59,286	146,600	580,201	327,000	65,000	2,250,000
1995	253,504	64,424	152,032	44,585	140,000	53,087	64,031	53,405	132,170	523,809	317,000	65,000	2,230,000
1996	289,530	60,011	166,378	53,174	145,000	49,211	83,564	51,119	123,000	496,846	326,000	72,000	2,300,000
1997	314,500	58,488	171,479	49,459	175,000	54,662	86,927	45,418	115,000	491,680	362,000	81,700	2,450,000
1998[1]	310,070	49,567	165,599	44,980	178,000	72,540	124,018	64,106	114,000	464,391	366,000	80,000	2,520,000
1999[2]	302,580	40,900	158,275	45,663	170,000	81,000	130,000	61,293	125,870	449,472	341,000	85,000	2,540,000

[1] Preliminary.   [2] Estimate.   [3] Formerly part of the U.S.S.R.; data not reported separately until 1992.   Source: U.S. Geological Survey (USGS)

GOLD

Gold (monthly average) through December 2000

USD Per Troy Ounce
- - - - U.S. Gov't Price Controls (1901 - 1933)($20.67)
U.S. Gov't Price Controls (1934 - 1939)($35.00)
London Market Prices (Jan 1940 - Feb 1968)
Handy & Harman, N.Y. (Mar. 1968 - May 1990)
Bridge Composite (June 1990 - date)

Salient Statistics of Gold in the United States   In Kilograms (1 Kilogram = 32.1507 Troy Ounces)

			Refinery Production				---------- Stocks, Dec. 31 ---------				-------------- Consumption --------------			
			Domestic Secondary		Exports	Imports	Treasury			Official					
	Mine	Value	& Foreign	(Old	(Excluding	for Con-	Depar	Futures		World				Jewelry	
Year	Production	Million $	Ores	Scrap)	Coinage)	sumption	tment[3]	Exchange	Industry	Reserves[4]	Dental	Industrial[5]	& Arts	Total
1990	294,189	3,640.8	225,183	43,980	296,397	97,519	8,146,432	50,881	37,065	35,572	8,700	30,996	78,514	118,216
1991	294,062	3,434.7	224,675	48,088	284,127	178,749	8,145,696	49,893	39,411	35,501	8,485	21,793	84,096	114,375
1992	330,212	3,662.4	283,951	53,396	368,851	174,341	8,145,000	46,453	36,713	35,100	6,543	20,360	83,508	110,410
1993	331,013	3,840.0	243,000	152,000	792,680	169,305	8,143,000	78,514	34,400	34,900	6,173	19,663	65,600	91,400
1994	327,000	4,050.0	241,000	148,000	471,000	114,000	8,142,000	49,100	32,700	34,800	5,430	17,013	53,700	76,100
1995	317,000	3,950.0	NA	NA	347,000	126,000	8,140,000	45,400	NA	34,600	NA	NA	NA	NA
1996	326,000	4,090.0	NA	NA	471,000	159,000	8,140,000	20,700	NA	34,400	NA	NA	NA	NA
1997	362,000	3,870.0	270,000	100,000	476,000	209,000	8,140,000	15,200	17,300	34,000	NA	NA	NA	NA
1998[1]	366,000	3,480.0	277,000	163,000	522,000	278,000	8,130,000	25,200	16,600	33,600	NA	NA	NA	NA
1999[2]	341,000	3,070.0	265,000	143,000	523,000	221,000	8,170,000	37,900	14,700	33,300	NA	NA	NA	NA

[1] Preliminary.   [2] Estimate.   [3] Includes gold in Exchange Stabilization Fund.   [4] Held by market economy country central banks and governments andinternational monetary orgainzations.   [5] Including space and defense.   *Source: U.S. Geological Survey (USGS)*

Monthly Average Gold Price (Handy & Harman) in New York   In Dollars Per Troy Ounce

Year	Jan.	Feb.	Mar.	Apr.	May	June	July	Aug.	Sept.	Oct.	Nov.	Dec.	Average
1991	383.60	363.80	363.40	358.40	356.80	366.70	367.50	356.20	348.80	358.70	359.50	361.10	362.18
1992	354.50	353.90	344.30	338.50	337.20	340.80	353.00	343.00	345.40	344.40	335.10	334.70	343.74
1993	329.00	329.40	330.10	341.90	366.70	371.90	392.40	378.50	354.90	364.20	373.50	383.70	359.67
1994	387.02	382.01	384.13	378.20	381.21	385.64	385.44	380.43	391.80	389.77	349.43	379.60	384.14
1995	378.55	376.51	382.12	391.11	385.46	387.56	386.40	383.63	382.22	383.14	385.53	387.42	384.22
1996	399.59	404.73	396.21	392.96	391.98	385.58	383.69	387.43	382.97	381.07	378.46	369.02	387.81
1997	355.10	346.71	351.67	344.47	343.75	340.75	324.08	324.03	322.74	324.87	307.10	288.65	331.16
1998	289.18	297.49	295.90	308.40	299.39	292.31	292.79	283.76	289.01	295.92	293.89	291.29	294.12
1999	287.05	287.22	285.96	282.45	276.94	261.31	255.81	256.56	265.23	310.72	292.74	283.69	278.81
2000[1]	284.26	299.60	286.39	279.75	275.10	285.73	281.01	274.44	273.53	270.00			280.98

[1] Preliminary.   *Source: U.S. Geological Survey (USGS)*

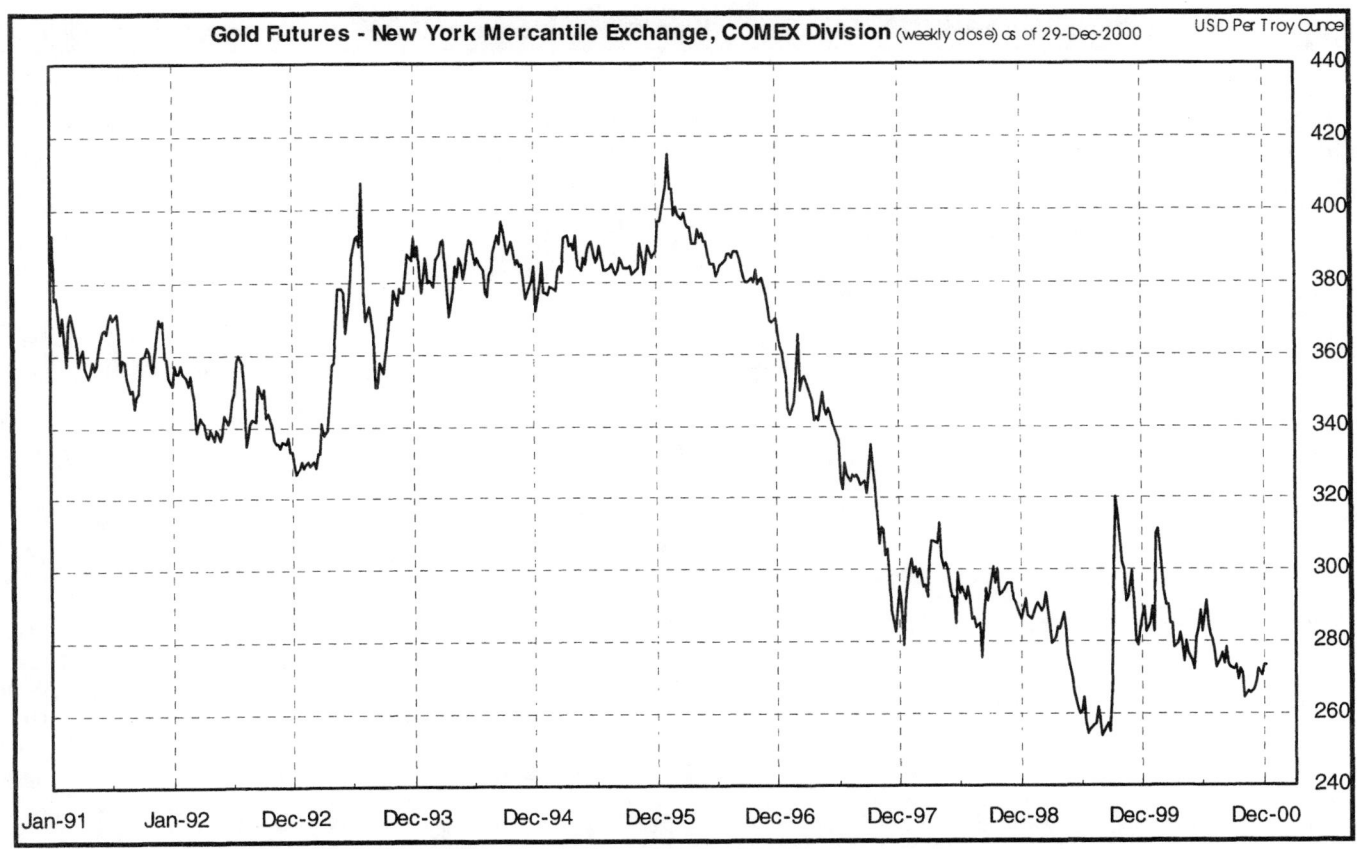

Average Open Interest of Gold in New York (NYMEX)   In Thousands of Contracts

Year	Jan.	Feb.	Mar.	Apr.	May	June	July	Aug.	Sept.	Oct.	Nov.	Dec.
1991	104,666	98,000	98,429	101,266	100,341	88,961	94,467	99,790	105,053	96,302	109,030	109,004
1992	106,110	103,319	109,796	106,485	109,947	98,127	111,039	102,239	102,376	102,232	109,965	100,328
1993	112,420	109,093	115,505	142,208	172,491	170,829	200,168	180,509	166,201	152,531	152,853	154,730
1994	156,045	139,354	146,269	144,386	147,738	146,255	148,915	155,641	167,981	166,041	166,536	178,998
1995	184,549	170,972	168,651	191,667	173,805	174,075	175,727	176,135	185,128	185,854	170,674	141,751
1996	210,695	226,160	203,968	201,826	203,056	192,423	185,374	159,435	185,907	192,606	187,145	185,994
1997	199,710	190,524	167,595	157,176	160,512	170,640	207,352	198,099	201,267	188,365	212,757	188,558
1998	180,994	171,507	183,358	180,267	158,157	172,250	169,180	192,623	183,351	186,680	164,304	153,063
1999	179,726	185,345	178,456	198,202	193,978	207,122	205,687	193,023	206,186	216,034	189,433	156,754
2000	149,606	158,026	160,325	155,188	162,516	144,099	133,087	126,893	132,731	132,546	134,630	113,830

Source: New York Mercantile Exchange (NYMEX), COMEX division

Volume of Trading of Gold Futures in New York (NYMEX)   In Thousands of Contracts

Year	Jan.	Feb.	Mar.	Apr.	May	June	July	Aug.	Sept.	Oct.	Nov.	Dec.	Total
1991	957.3	497.8	617.7	446.1	584.4	520.0	551.4	457.2	429.1	551.0	677.3	510.6	6,799.9
1992	729.8	388.4	607.3	425.4	485.4	427.2	734.6	500.2	465.3	414.1	504.1	320.1	6,001.9
1993	506.0	446.2	661.4	640.4	1,140.7	809.6	1,171.7	808.8	728.9	565.2	892.3	533.2	8,904.4
1994	981.8	584.0	889.5	589.2	922.6	740.2	723.8	626.0	645.6	651.2	687.8	461.5	8,503.2
1995	881.9	420.0	1,087.5	613.0	777.0	588.1	669.9	500.5	495.5	387.7	982.5	378.1	7,781.6
1996	1,384.7	987.5	943.6	647.1	858.5	582.1	749.8	541.9	541.9	528.5	795.2	458.8	8,694.5
1997	1,102.8	830.2	899.4	508.5	762.1	522.7	1,147.5	667.8	715.8	988.0	808.8	588.1	9,541.9
1998	1,078.2	534.2	877.2	698.1	845.2	718.7	712.4	680.0	851.7	769.6	705.6	519.0	8,990.1
1999	860.8	517.4	1,147.6	561.1	1,069.6	573.6	964.3	709.6	1,067.3	993.8	674.7	436.1	9,575.8
2000	616.4	833.5	767.7	362.2	701.5	625.5	532.5	374.4	403.2	424.9	625.7	349.0	6,643.5

Source: New York Mercantile Exchange (NYMEX), COMEX division

GOLD

Commodity Exchange, Inc. (COMEX) Depository Warehouse Stocks of Gold   In Thousands of Troy Ounces

Year	Jan. 1	Feb. 1	Mar. 1	Apr. 1	May 1	June 1	July 1	Aug. 1	Sept. 1	Oct. 1	Nov. 1	Dec. 1
1991	1,636	1,686	1,540	1,298	1,458	1,711	1,772	1,875	1,220	1,342	1,302	1,479
1992	1,605	1,362	1,435	1,411	1,591	1,618	1,605	1,733	1,688	1,947	1,766	1,524
1993	1,507	1,340	1,365	1,426	1,383	2,231	2,247	2,448	2,437	2,425	2,349	2,552
1994	2,524	2,955	2,958	2,862	2,802	2,434	2,665	2,574	2,030	1,904	1,843	1,867
1995	1,577	1,498	1,386	1,360	1,391	1,488	1,505	1,608	1,448	1,745	1,395	1,315
1996	1,460	1,869	1,412	1,429	1,335	1,711	1,263	1,273	1,402	1,283	1,060	1,104
1997	666	837	583	1,000	946	878	850	914	733	894	615	761
1998	488	446	481	720	658	1,077	1,055	1,092	911	958	827	819
1999	809	809	731	1,032	896	876	818	936	1,198	928	874	1,195
2000	1,219	1,393	1,374	1,967	1,966	1,893	1,890	2,013	1,958	1,918	1,865	1,864

Source: New York Mercantile Exchange (NYMEX), COMEX division

Central Gold Bank Reserves   In Millions of Troy Ounces

Year	Belgium	Canada	France	Germany	Italy	Japan	Netherlands	Switzerland	United Kingdom	United States	Industrial Total	Developing Oil	Developing Non-Oil	IMF[2]	Bank for Int'l Settlements	World Total
1990	30.2	14.8	81.9	95.2	66.7	24.2	43.9	83.3	18.9	261.9	889.4	41.5	101.7	103.4	7.8	1,143.8
1991	30.2	13.0	81.9	95.2	66.7	24.2	43.9	83.3	18.9	261.9	887.3	42.0	102.4	103.4	6.6	1,141.6
1992	25.0	9.9	81.9	95.2	66.7	24.2	43.9	83.3	18.6	261.8	877.4	42.0	100.3	103.4	6.8	1,129.9
1993	25.0	6.1	81.9	95.2	66.7	24.2	35.1	83.3	18.5	261.8	860.4	42.4	108.1	103.4	8.6	1,123.0
1994	25.0	3.9	81.9	95.2	66.7	24.2	34.8	83.3	18.4	261.7	856.9	42.4	106.6	103.4	7.0	1,116.2
1995	20.5	3.4	81.9	95.2	66.7	24.2	34.8	83.3	18.4	261.7	848.7	41.9	111.9	103.4	7.3	1,113.2
1996	15.3	3.1	81.9	95.2	66.7	24.2	34.8	83.3	18.4	261.7	840.1	42.5	115.5	103.4	6.6	1,108.2
1997	15.3	3.1	81.9	95.2	66.7	24.2	27.1	83.3	18.4	261.6	821.9	42.3	115.8	103.4	6.2	1,089.7
1998	9.5	2.5	102.4	119.0	83.4	24.2	33.8	83.3	23.0	261.6	809.0	40.6	115.7	103.4	6.4	1,075.1
1999[1]	8.0	2.1	97.0	111.5	79.0	24.2	32.5	83.3	23.0	261.7	815.3	40.5	113.9	103.4	6.4	1,079.6

[1] Preliminary.   [2] International Monetary Fund.   *Source: American Metal Market (AMM)*

Mine Production of Recoverable Gold in the United States   In Kilograms

Year	Arizona	California	Idaho	Montana	Nevada	Alaska	Colorado	South Dakota	New Mexico	Utah	Other States	Total
1990	5,000	29,607	W	13,012	179,078	3,232	2,357	17,870	888	W	43,145	294,189
1991	6,195	30,404	3,348	13,715	178,488	3,200	3,181	16,371	W	W	41,055	295,957
1992	6,656	33,335	4,037	13,994	203,393	5,003	3,763	18,681	W	W	40,262	329,124
1993	2,710	35,800	4,324	14,300	211,000	2,780	W	19,200	995	W	39,891	331,000
1994	2,050	30,100	3,610	12,600	214,000	5,660	4,420	W	W	W	33,560	306,000
1995	1,920	25,600	8,850	12,400	210,000	4,410	W	W	W	W	53,820	317,000
1996	1,740	23,800	7,410	9,110	213,000	5,020	W	W	W	W	57,920	318,000
1997	2,140	24,200	7,490	10,200	243,000	18,400	W	16,400	W	W	40,170	362,000
1998	1,840	18,700	W	8,200	273,000	18,300	W	12,100	W	W	33,860	366,000
1999[1]	786	17,500	W	7,570	257,000	15,700	W	9,940	W	W	32,504	341,000

[1] Preliminary.   W = Withheld proprietary data, included in Other States.   *Source: U.S. Geological Survey (USGS)*

Consumption of Gold, By End-Use in the United States   In Kilograms

Year	Jewelry and the Arts — Gold-Filled & Other	Electro-plating	Karat Gold	Total	Dental	Industrial — Gold-Filled & Other	Electro-plating	Karat Gold	Total	Grand Total
1987	9,256	3,133	58,635	71,024	6,944	21,010	12,343	1,892	35,245	113,319
1988	7,598	1,469	57,959	67,027	7,576	21,034	15,088	1,104	37,226	111,836
1989	7,364	1,283	60,877	69,524	7,927	15,723	20,684	1,215	37,621	115,078
1990	8,132	429	69,952	78,514	8,700	12,725	17,251	1,020	30,996	118,216
1991	3,848	373	79,875	84,096	8,485	8,102	12,624	1,068	21,793	114,375
1992	3,546	581	79,381	83,508	6,543	8,802	10,476	1,082	20,360	110,410
1993	3,530	373	61,700	65,600	6,170	9,470	9,090	1,100	19,700	91,400
1994	3,650	369	49,700	53,700	5,430	7,450	9,470	96	17,000	76,100
1995	NA	NA	NA	NA	NA	NA	NA	NA	NA	NA
1996	NA	NA	NA	NA	NA	NA	NA	NA	NA	NA

[1] Preliminary.   **Source: U.S. Geological Survey (USGS)**

114

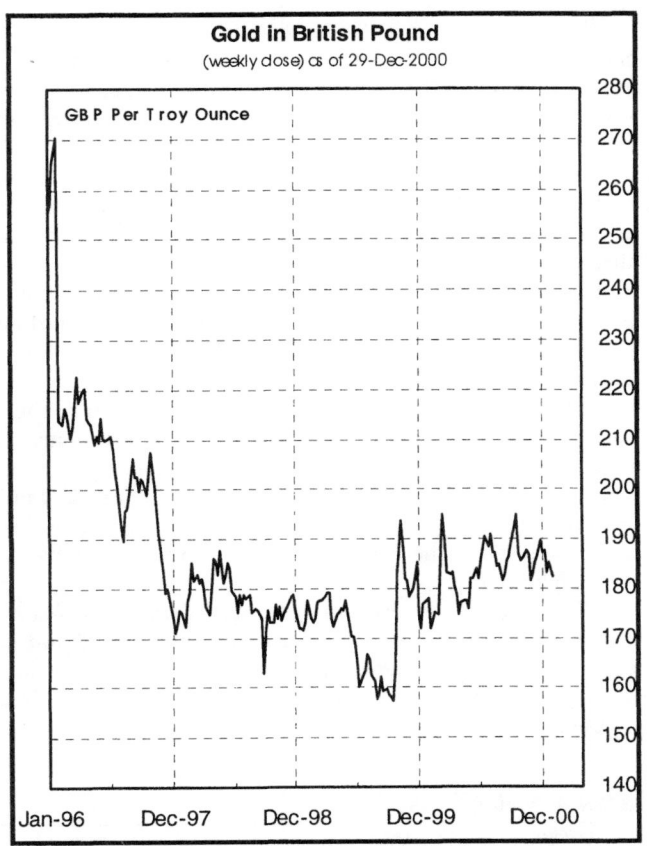

Gold in British Pound
(weekly close) as of 29-Dec-2000

GBP Per Troy Ounce

Gold in Euro
(weekly close) as of 29-Dec-2000

EUR Per Troy Ounce

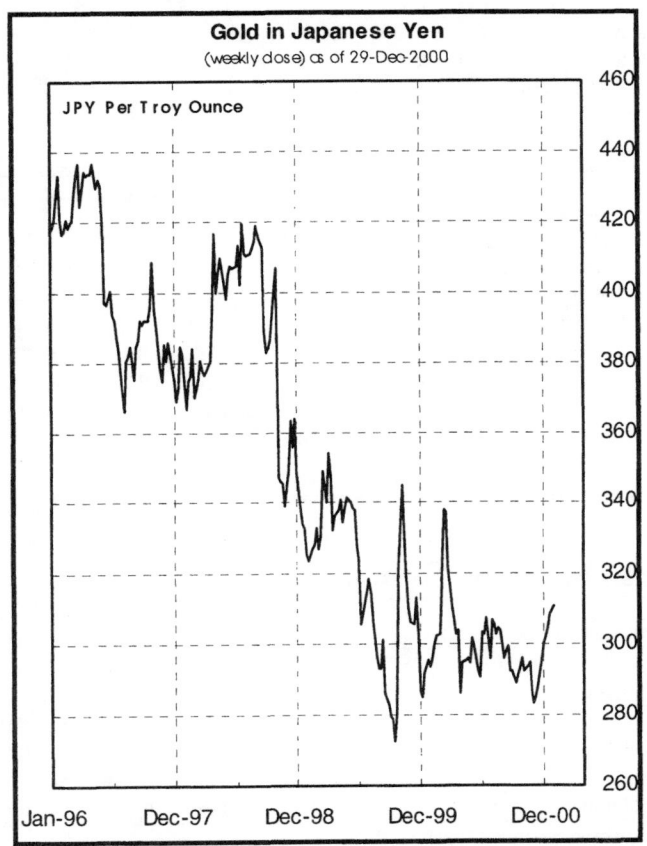

Gold in Japanese Yen
(weekly close) as of 29-Dec-2000

JPY Per Troy Ounce

Gold in Swiss Franc
(weekly close) as of 29-Dec-2000

CHF Per Troy Ounce

Grain Sorghum

The U.S. grain sorghum (milo) production has nearly been cut in half since the mid-1990's, but the U.S. is still the world's largest producer, followed by India. World production in 2000/01 of 55 million metric tonnes compares with initial estimates of 58 million tonnes, and 1999/00 production of 59 million. The U.S. produced nearly one-fifth of the total with 11.8 million tonnes. However, unlike most of the world's sorghum producing nations who consume their production domestically, the U.S. generally consumes about two-thirds and exports the balance.

India's estimated 2000/01 crop of 9 million tonnes compares with 1999/00 production of 8.65 million, and 11 plus million back in 1996/97. Significantly, India's sorghum acreage of 10.3 million hectares in 2000/01 accounts for about one-quarter of the world's sorghum acreage, but India's average yield is consistently among the world's lowest with 0.87 metric tonnes per hectare in 1999.00 vs. a world average of 1.35, and the U.S. average of 3.81. China's 2000/01 average yield was placed at 3.16 metric tonnes per hectare on acreage of less than 1 million hectare, yielding a crop of 3.0 million tonnes vs. a yield of 4.16 and a crop of almost 4 million tonnes in 1999/00.

World sorghum trade is small at about 6.0 million tonnes in 2000/01 vs. 7.6 million in 1999/00. The U.S. ac-counts for most of the exports with 5.0 million tonnes in 2000/01 vs. 6.2 million in 1999/00. The two largest importers are Japan and Mexico. Argentina is the second largest exporter with 600,000 tonnes in 2000/01. The world 2000/01 carryover is forecast at 4.0 million tonnes vs. 4.7 million a year earlier, almost one-third of which will be in the U.S.

The U.S. sorghum crop year begins September 1. The three major producing states are usually Kansas, Texas, and Nebraska. Total U.S. supplies in 2000/01 of 529 million bushels includes a record low production of 463 million bushels and a carry-in of 65 million. This compares to production of 595 million bushels in 1999/00 and a carry-in of 65 million bushels for a total supply of 660 million bushels. No sorghum is imported into the U.S. Total disappearance in 2000/01 of 480 million bushels includes exports of 200 million, feed and residual usage of 230 million (vs. 284 million in 1999/00), and other usage of 50 million, which if realized will leave the August 31, 2001 carryover at 49 million bushels.

Sorghum prices received by farmers during 2000/01 are forecast between $1.55-$1.95 per bushel vs. the 1999/00 average of $1.55. The average Kansas City price (#2 yellow) of sorghum grain has shown volatility in recent years, from $6.66/cwt. in 1995/96 to $3.29 in 1998/99.

World Supply and Demand Grain Sorghum — In Thousands of Metric Tons

Year	Exports Argentina	Exports Non-U.S.	Exports U.S.	Exports Total	Imports Japan	Imports Mexico	Imports Unaccounted	Imports Total	Total Production	Utilization China	Utilization Mexico	Utilization U.S.	Utilization Total	Ending Stocks Non-U.S.	Ending Stocks U.S.	Ending Stocks Total
1995-6	800	1,818	5,025	6,843	2,542	1,764	267	6,413	55,311	4,935	6,900	7,977	56,752	2,245	467	2,712
1996-7	798	1,430	5,217	6,647	2,774	2,091	206	6,188	69,549	5,379	8,500	14,246	67,667	3,388	1,206	4,594
1997-8	1,334	1,858	5,387	7,245	2,769	3,340	75	7,036	58,933	3,650	8,940	10,670	59,025	3,260	1,242	4,502
1998-9[1]	565	1,504	4,991	6,495	2,453	3,295	2	6,582	59,168	4,134	9,750	7,803	58,292	3,723	1,655	5,378
1999-00[2]	650	1,778	6,497	8,275	2,206	4,800	56	8,100	59,647	3,919	11,200	8,615	60,137	3,227	1,661	4,888
2000-1[3]	650	1,590	5,080	6,670	2,100	3,500	94	6,546	55,607	3,054	10,100	7,113	56,362	2,898	1,235	4,133

[1] Preliminary. [2] Estimate. [3] Forecast. *Source: Foreign Agricultural Service, U.S. Department of Agriculture (FAS-USDA)*

Salient Statistics of Grain Sorghum in the United States

Year	Acreage Planted[4] for All Purposes (1,000 Acres)	Acreage Harvested (1,000 Acres)	For Grain Production 1,000 Bushels	For Grain Yield Per Harvested Acre Bushels	For Grain Price in Cents Per Bushel	For Grain Value of Production Million $	For Silage Acreage Harvested 1,000 Acres	For Silage Production 1,000 Tons	For Silage Yield Per Harvested Acre	Sorghum Grain Stocks Dec. 1 On Farms	Sorghum Grain Stocks Dec. 1 Off Farms	Sorghum Grain Stocks June 1 On Farms	Sorghum Grain Stocks June 1 Off Farms
1995-6	9,454	8,278	460,373	55.6	319	1,395.4	368	3,652	9.9	79,090	222,186	13,955	56,433
1996-7	13,097	11,811	795,274	67.3	234	1,986.3	423	4,976	11.8	144,590	322,767	38,815	80,329
1997-8	10,052	9,158	633,545	69.2	221	1,408.9	412	5,385	13.1	96,625	274,244	27,200	68,907
1998-9[1]	9,626	7,723	519,933	67.3	166	905.5	308	3,526	11.4	95,900	239,416	27,400	88,680
1999-00[2]	9,288	8,544	595,166	69.7	157	937.4	320	3,716	11.6	90,300	259,136	27,300	99,606
2000-1[3]	9,195	7,723	470,070	60.9	175	822.6	265	2,223	10.8	74,300	187,287		

[1] Preliminary. [2] Estimate. [3] Forecast. NA = Not available. *Source: Economic Research Service, U.S. Department of Agriculture (ERS-USDA)*

Production of All Sorghum for Grain in the United States, by States — In Thousands of Bushels

Year	Arkansas	Colorado	Illinois	Kansas	Louisiana	Mississippi	Missouri	Nebraska	New Mexico	Oklahoma	South Dakota	Texas	Total
1995	13,135	4,620	11,730	173,600	5,880	2,665	35,770	56,840	3,380	12,800	4,800	129,600	460,373
1996	16,280	13,260	12,600	354,200	11,628	5,040	50,960	97,850	7,425	28,910	7,975	182,400	795,274
1997	11,100	6,000	10,465	265,200	6,600	2,475	36,800	60,750	9,988	22,500	11,360	185,850	633,545
1998	6,890	10,545	7,918	264,000	7,500	2,340	26,560	56,400	2,925	15,300	9,940	105,800	519,933
1999	9,750	8,610	9,215	258,400	19,270	4,872	22,010	42,770	7,425	18,000	4,640	185,850	595,166
2000[1]	9,940	6,510	8,075	188,800	17,845	6,708	24,840	35,000	1,625	13,680	5,880	143,350	470,070

[1] Preliminary. *Source: National Agricultural Statistics Service, U.S. Department of Agriculture (NASS-USDA)*

Grain Sorghum Quarterly Supply and Disappearance in the United States In Millions of Bushels

Crop Year Beginning Sept. 1	Beginning Stocks	Production	Imports	Total Supply	Food Alcohol & Industrial	Seed	Feed & Residual	Total	Export	Total	Gov't Owned[3]	Privately Owned[4]	Total Stocks
1997-8	47.5	633.5	0	681.0	53.9	1.2	364.9	420.0	212.1	632.1	.2	48.7	48.9
Sept.-Nov.	47.5	633.5	0	681.0	18.4	0	239.3	257.7	49.4	307.1	0	373.9	373.9
Dec.-Feb.	373.9	----	0	373.9	18.5	0	37.5	56.0	83.2	139.2	0	234.7	234.7
Mar.-May	234.7	----	0	234.7	11.3	.8	71.3	83.4	55.1	138.5	0	96.1	96.1
June-Aug.	96.1	----	0	96.1	5.7	.4	16.8	22.9	24.3	47.2	.2	48.7	48.9
1998-9	48.9	519.9	0	568.8	43.9	1.2	262.1	307.2	196.5	503.7	.3	64.9	65.2
Sept.-Nov.	48.9	519.9	0	568.8	15.0	0	178.0	193.0	40.5	233.5	.7	334.6	335.3
Dec.-Feb.	335.3	----	0	335.3	15.0	0	34.1	49.1	63.7	112.8	.7	221.7	222.4
Mar.-May	222.4	----	0	222.4	9.0	.6	45.4	55.0	51.4	106.4	.5	115.6	116.1
June-Aug.	116.1	----	0	116.1	4.9	.6	4.6	10.1	40.8	50.9	.3	64.9	65.2
1999-00[1]	65.0	595.2	0	660.0	55.0	1.1	284.0	595.0	256.0	851.0	1.0	44.3	65.0
Sept.-Nov.	65.0	595.2	0	660.0	18.0	0	228.0	311.0	65.0	376.0	.7	347.7	349.0
Dec.-Feb.	349.0	----	0	349.0	18.0	0	29.0	124.0	77.0	201.0	.5	224.6	226.0
Mar.-May	226.0	----	0	226.0	13.0		22.0	99.0	64.0	163.0			127.0
June-Aug.	127.0	----	0	127.0	6.0		6.0	62.0	50.0	112.0			65.0
2000-1[2]	65.0	470.0	0	535.0	50.0		240.0	490.0	200.0	690.0			45.0
Sept.-Nov.	65.0	470.0	0	535.0	16.0		193.0	274.0	64.0	338.0			262.0

[1] Preliminary. [2] Forecast. [3] Uncommitted inventory. [4] Includes quantity under loan & farmer-owned reserve. Source: *Economic Research Service, U.S. Department of Agriculture (ERS-USDA)*

Average Price of Sorghum Grain, No. 2, Yellow in Kansas City In Dollars Per Hundred Pounds (Cwt.)

Year	Sept.	Oct.	Nov.	Dec.	Jan.	Feb.	Mar.	Apr.	May	June	July	Aug.	Average
1993-4	3.89	4.03	4.60	4.91	4.93	4.81	4.64	4.33	4.38	4.43	3.79	3.73	4.37
1994-5	3.72	3.55	3.60	3.81	3.92	3.90	4.01	4.08	4.27	4.50	4.93	4.85	4.10
1995-6	5.08	5.45	5.68	6.19	6.39	6.58	6.81	7.79	8.17	7.79	7.24	6.74	6.66
1996-7	5.29	4.64	4.31	4.22	4.24	4.46	4.88	4.83	4.63	4.48	4.48	4.18	4.55
1997-8	4.13	4.36	4.30	4.26	4.33	4.36	4.40	4.10	4.09	4.03	4.03	3.74	4.18
1998-9	2.98	3.17	3.45	3.41	3.41	3.43	3.48	3.37	3.35	3.32	2.92	2.92	3.30
1999-00	2.97	2.71	2.75	2.87	3.20	3.28	3.51	3.53	3.75	3.18	2.71	2.76	3.10
2000-1[1]	2.67	3.14											2.91

[1] Preliminary. Source: *Economic Research Service, U.S. Department of Agriculture (ERS-USDA)*

Exports of Grain Sorghum, by Country of Destination from the United States In Metric Tons

Year Beginning Oct. 1	Canada	Ecuador	Ethiopia	Israel	Japan	Jordon	Mexico	South Africa	Spain	Sudan	Turkey	World Total
1992-3	1,795	9,501	0	217,110	1,933,012	0	3,970,069	56,186	188,893	4,287	132,182	6,651,528
1993-4	1,699	0	86,697	66,264	1,681,976	0	3,118,139	0	169,454	48,042	0	5,245,524
1994-5	3,713	0	0	214,073	1,987,738	0	2,543,696	0	398,339	12,304	0	5,652,585
1995-6	5,734	0	25,700	356,868	1,616,384	0	1,665,541	332	431,578	0	0	4,757,055
1996-7[1]	3,347	0	10,020	456,271	2,203,669	0	2,189,598	0	125,827	8,000	138,590	5,206,964
1997-8[2]					1,650,000		3,222,000					5,334,000
1998-9[2]					1,362,000		3,103,000					4,899,000

[1] Preliminary. [2] Estimate. Source: *Economic Research Service, U.S. Department of Agriculture (ERS-USDA)*

Grain Sorghum Price Support Program and Market Prices in the United States

Year	Price Support Quantity	% of Production	Aquired by CCC	Owned by CCC at Year End	Basic Loan Rate	Target Price	Findley Loan Rate	Effective Base[3] Million Acres	Participation Rate[4] % of Base	Kansas City	Texas High Plains	Los Angeles	Gulf Ports
	Million Cwt.				$ Per Bushel					$ Per Cwt.			
1992-3	27.2	5.5	0	2.2	1.91	2.61	1.63	13.6	78.6	3.74	4.06	5.11	4.27
1993-4	8.2	2.6	0	1.4	1.89	2.61	1.63	13.5	81.6	4.37	4.95	----	4.90
1994-5	25.2	6.9	0	.4	1.89	2.61	1.80	13.5	81.1	4.10	4.75	----	4.62
1995-6	4.0	1.6	0	0	1.84	2.61	1.80	13.3	76.9	6.66	7.30	----	7.19
1996-7	11.4	2.6	0	0	[5]	NA	1.81	13.2	98.8	4.55	5.02	----	5.03
1997-8[1]	9.8	2.8	.1	.1	[5]	NA	1.76	NA	98.8	4.18	4.72	----	4.76
1998-9[2]	12.0	4.1	.6	.2	[5]	NA	1.74	NA	98.8	3.30	3.78	----	3.97

[1] Preliminary. [2] Estimate. [3] National effective crop acreage base as determined by ASCS. [4] Percentage of effective base acres enrolled in acreage reduction programs. [5] Beginning with the 1996-7 marketing year, target prices are no longer applicable. Source: *Economic Research Service, U.S. Department of Agriculture (ERS-USDA)*

Hay

Total U.S. hay production in 2000 (marketing year, May to April) of 153 million short tons compares with the previous year's record 159 million tons. The all hay yield of 2.48 tons per acre in 2000 compares with 2.52 tons in 1999. The acreage harvested of all hay of 62 million acres compares with 63 million, respectively. Alfalfa production of 80 million tons in 2000 fell from 84 million in 1999, with average yield at 3.43 tons per acre vs. 3.5 tons in 1999. Hay is harvested in virtually all of the lower 48 states, but the top producing states are generally Texas, South Dakota, California, and Minnesota. Yields show wide variance among the major producing states with California's yield nearly twice that in Texas. Other hay production in 2000 totaled 66 million tons vs. 68 million in 1999. Hay farm stocks normally bottom in the spring and then peak following the fall harvest.

Roughage consuming animal units (RCAUs) in 2000/ 01 are estimated at 90 million vs. 89 million in 1999/00, and 88 million in 1998/99. Despite the greater animal units and lower production hay prices weakened during the 1999/ 00 marketing year with an average farm price of $80.20 per ton vs. $88.10 in 1998/99, and more than $100 per ton the previous year. However, farm prices in the initial months of 2000/01 showed signs of strengthening as the average alfalfa farm price during June through September of $85 per ton compared with $83 per ton in the like 1999 period.

Salient Statistics of All Hay in the United States

Crop Year Beginning May 1	Acres Harvested 1,000 Acres	Yield Per Acre Tons	Pro-duction	Carryover May 1	Disap-pearance	Supply Per Animal Unit	Disap-pearance	Animal Units Fed[3] Millions	Farm Price $ Per Ton	Farm Pro-duction Value Million $	Alfalfa (Certified)	Timothy	Red Clover	Sudan-Grass
			--- Millions of Tons ---			--- In Tons ---					--- Dollars Per Cwt. ---			
1995-6	59,629	2.59	154.2	20.8	154.2	2.24	1.97	78.1	82.2	11,042	274.00	71.00	134.00	51.80
1996-7	61,169	2.45	149.8	20.8	152.8	2.23	2.00	76.4	95.8	12,727	277.00	76.00	172.00	51.90
1997-8	61,084	2.50	152.5	17.4	148.1	2.27	1.98	74.9	100.0	13,250	282.00	73.00	184.00	51.40
1998-9	60,076	2.53	151.8	21.8	148.4	2.34	2.00	74.5	84.6	11,607	288.00	71.20	194.00	53.70
1999-00[1]	63,160	2.52	159.1	24.8	NA	2.51	NA	73.2	76.9	11,014	287.00	78.80	178.00	52.20
2000-1[2]	61,591	2.48	152.7						83.0	11,180				

[1] Preliminary. [2] Estimate. [3] Roughage-consuming animal units fed annually. NA = Not available. *Source: Economic Research Service, U.S. Department of Agriculture (ERS-USDA)*

Production of All Hay in the United States, by States   In Thousands of Tons

Year	California	Idaho	Iowa	Minnesota	Missouri	New York	North Dakota	Ohio	Oklahoma	South Dakota	Texas	Wisconsin	Total
1995	8,341	5,080	5,665	6,943	6,818	6,975	5,095	4,035	4,174	9,050	8,136	6,820	154,166
1996	8,008	4,760	5,310	5,998	7,270	7,455	4,825	3,400	4,940	8,200	7,815	6,050	149,779
1997	8,408	4,730	5,190	6,398	7,340	6,790	4,375	3,850	5,108	7,810	10,955	6,353	152,536
1998	8,554	5,549	5,332	7,110	7,703	7,680	4,190	3,875	3,380	8,160	6,870	6,370	151,780
1999	8,782	5,132	5,970	7,130	7,225	7,700	5,511	3,060	5,000	9,440	13,135	7,510	159,707
2000[1]	8,568	5,292	6,000	6,840	6,657	6,055	5,110	4,521	4,869	7,393	8,880	6,000	152,183

[1] Preliminary. *Source: Agricultural Statistics Board, U.S. Department of Agriculture (ASB-USDA)*

Hay Production and Farm Stocks in the United States   In Thousands of Short Tons

Year	Alfalfa & Mixtures	All Others	All Hay	Corn for Silage[1]	Sorghum Silage[1]	Farm Stocks May 1	Farm Stocks Dec. 1
1995	84,515	69,651	154,166	77,867	3,652	20,775	109,438
1996	79,139	70,640	149,779	86,581	4,976	20,739	105,179
1997	78,535	74,001	152,536	97,192	5,385	17,424	103,044
1998	82,310	69,470	151,780	95,479	3,526	21,827	112,066
1999	84,385	75,322	159,707	95,633	3,716	24,817	108,922
2000[2]	80,347	71,836	152,183	98,538	2,863	28,817	103,730

[1] Not included in all tame hay. [2] Preliminary. *Source: Agricultural Statistics Board, U.S. Department of Agriculture (ASB-USDA)*

Mid-Month Price Received by Farmers for All Hay (Baled) in the United States   In Dollars Per Ton

Year	May	June	July	Aug.	Sept.	Oct.	Nov.	Dec.	Jan.	Feb.	Mar.	Apr.	Average[2]
1995-6	90.4	83.9	80.6	81.1	80.3	83.0	81.0	80.3	81.7	81.2	83.4	90.3	82.2
1996-7	97.1	92.3	89.6	92.9	90.1	93.0	92.0	90.8	97.9	105.0	108.0	117.0	95.8
1997-8	118.0	108.0	98.4	99.0	103.0	103.0	101.0	97.7	98.1	97.2	97.5	101.0	100.0
1998-9	103.0	91.8	88.6	88.5	86.5	85.2	81.4	77.5	78.5	79.0	78.5	81.9	85.0
1999-00	91.6	81.7	78.4	77.4	74.5	73.7	74.0	71.1	71.8	72.6	74.8	80.7	76.9
2000-1[1]	89.4	82.5	80.2	80.5	82.7	85.2	85.0	85.1	84.9	86.8			84.2

[1] Preliminary. [2] Marketing year average. *Source: Economic Research Service, U.S. Department of Agriculture (ERS-USDA)*

Heating Oil

The year 2000 will be remembered as one in which prices of the various component products of the energy sector increased substantially. There were a host of reasons for this, all of which seemed to come together in late 2000. Perhaps most important for the energy sector and heating oil was the ability of the Organization of Oil Exporting Countries (OPEC) to adhere to production levels. In the past, various members of OPEC had in fact exceeded their production quotas allowing more crude oil onto the market. Lower global stocks of petroleum were the basic cause of higher prices in the sector. This, in turn, led to declines in stocks of various distillates. For heating oil, stocks declined substantially heading into the all important winter heating season in the Northeast United States. After the previous two winters where there were relatively mild temperatures in the Northeast, the forecasts for the winter of 2000/2001 were for a return to a more normal winter. That implied colder average temperatures and an increased use of heating oil. Heating oil inventories in 1998 and 1999 were large, but by 2000 they had dropped significantly.

The combination of a decline in heating oil stocks along with an expected increased in heating oil demand caused prices for heating oil to stage a very strong rally. Heating oil prices, as measured on the New York Mercantile Exchange, actually started to increase in May 2000 when they were about 63 cents per gallon. Prices rallied until mid-October 2000 when they peaked at about $1.10 per gallon, an increase of some 75 percent. The sharply higher prices were themselves a signal that the market required more heating oil production. Petroleum refineries produce both motor gasoline and heating oil. After the summer driving season, refineries ramp up production of heating oil for the winter season. The fact that heating oil prices maintained a premium to gasoline prices was a signal for still more heating oil production. Slowly, inventories of heating oil increased with imports helping to stem the shortfall. Despite the fact that in early 2001 the Northeast winter was colder, heating oil prices declined. Much of the coldest air was concentrated in the midsection of the U.S. which relies more on natural gas for heating.

U.S. distillate fuel oil production in September 2000 was 3.79 million barrels per day. The Energy Information Agency reported that this was some 3 percent more than in August. In September 1999, production averaged 3.48 million barrels per day. In the January-September 2000 period, daily production averaged 3.50 million barrels per day. This was some 3 percent more than in the same period in 1999. For all of 1999, production averaged 3.40 million barrels per day.

U.S. imports of distillate fuel oil in September 2000 were 240,000 barrels per day, up 16 percent from the previous month. In September 1999, imports were some 4 percent higher. In the January-September 2000 period, imports averaged 254,000 barrels per day, down 2 percent from the same period in 1999. For all of 1999, imports averaged 250,000 barrels per day.

U.S. exports of distillate fuel oil in September 2000 averaged 168,000 barrels per day, down 34 percent from the previous month. For the first nine months of 2000, exports averaged 163,000 barrels per day, up 7 percent from a year ago. In 1999, exports averaged 162,000 barrels per day.

U.S. ending stocks of distillate in September 2000 were 114 million barrels. This was down 21 percent from the stocks in September 1999 and represented a decline of 25 percent from stocks in 1998.

U.S. production of residual fuel oil in September 2000 averaged 753,000 barrels per day. In the January-September 2000 period, residual fuel oil production averaged 689,000 barrels per day, down 4 percent from the same period in 1999, and some 10 percent less than the same period in 1998. In 1999, production averaged 698,000 barrels per day.

U.S. imports of residual fuel oil in September 2000 averaged 242,000 barrels per day. For the first nine months of 2000, imports averaged 231,000 barrels per day, down 8 percent from a year ago. Stocks of residual fuel oil in September 2000 were 36 million barrels, down 12 percent from a year ago. At the end of 1998, stocks were 45 million barrels.

Futures Markets

Heating oil futures and options are traded on the New York Mercantile Exchange (NYMEX). In London, gasoil futures and options are listed on the International Petroleum Exchange (IPE).

Average Price of No. 2 Heating Oil   In Cents Per Gallon

Year	Jan.	Feb.	Mar.	Apr.	May	June	July	Aug.	Sept.	Oct.	Nov.	Dec.	Average
1991	74.96	70.80	61.92	56.36	55.04	53.67	57.74	60.48	61.54	66.58	64.33	53.35	61.31
1992	51.72	53.39	52.49	56.22	57.38	61.26	60.24	58.29	61.90	62.72	56.52	54.98	57.25
1993	53.14	56.02	58.13	55.49	54.53	52.62	49.74	50.70	51.96	54.00	50.30	43.47	52.51
1994	49.93	55.81	49.18	48.01	47.98	49.37	49.93	49.51	47.90	48.23	49.62	48.41	49.49
1995	47.98	47.64	45.95	49.40	50.31	47.75	46.65	49.14	50.21	48.89	51.89	57.76	49.46
1996	55.64	61.24	65.19	67.90	57.59	51.56	55.58	60.42	67.61	72.34	70.13	72.13	63.11
1997	69.90	61.15	54.83	57.74	56.31	52.32	53.11	54.02	53.19	57.24	56.23	51.09	56.43
1998	46.59	44.26	42.12	42.97	41.07	37.88	36.24	34.48	40.15	38.29	35.59	31.38	39.25
1999	33.41	30.48	38.74	43.07	41.68	43.36	50.02	54.81	60.27	58.34	64.89	67.36	48.87
2000	91.32	94.37	77.29	75.32	75.88	78.32	78.14	89.13	98.87	97.46	102.70	94.08	87.74

Source: The Wall Street Journal

HEATING OIL

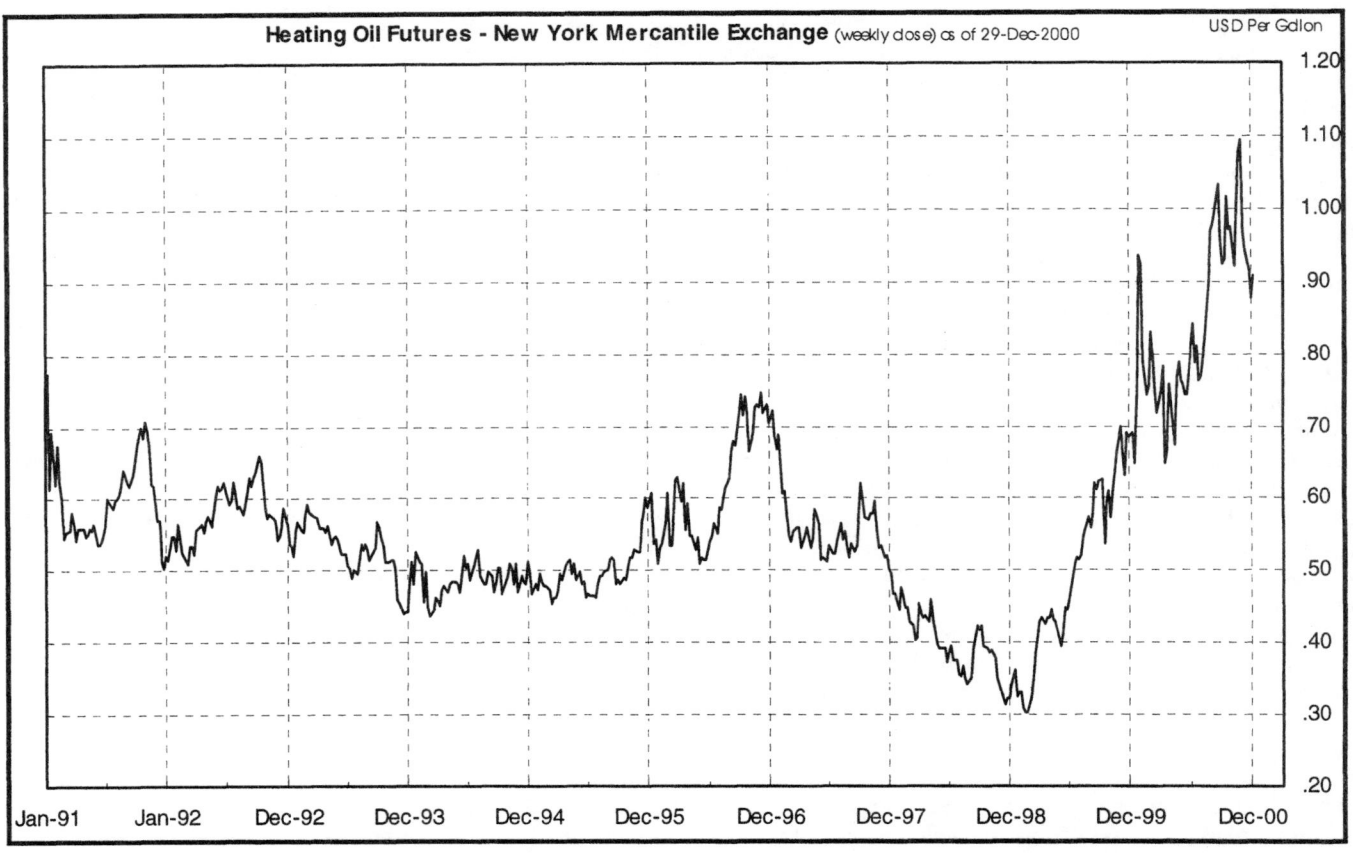

Heating Oil Futures - New York Mercantile Exchange (weekly close) as of 29-Dec-2000   USD Per Gallon

Average Open Interest of No. 2 Heating Oil Futures in New York   In Contracts

Year	Jan.	Feb.	Mar.	Apr.	May	June	July	Aug.	Sept.	Oct.	Nov.	Dec.
1991	74,216	81,742	81,103	82,419	89,482	102,887	115,896	125,463	135,804	144,026	128,330	117,182
1992	108,337	96,543	91,508	90,816	87,459	101,185	98,623	109,787	119,595	129,951	140,952	135,380
1993	130,536	125,603	130,438	107,363	102,708	113,898	131,816	142,054	166,253	172,940	175,781	199,299
1994	196,390	185,607	186,539	164,417	140,658	129,005	124,764	149,571	172,071	165,475	152,570	148,298
1995	128,664	112,508	118,700	121,974	115,501	122,163	136,722	140,214	149,934	152,244	139,232	138,596
1996	114,324	95,745	90,080	94,161	98,038	97,699	109,524	119,366	138,513	141,217	127,512	108,558
1997	100,333	105,223	122,149	139,981	135,523	141,864	151,403	149,243	151,407	141,008	126,528	145,153
1998	171,177	163,114	177,158	174,587	176,663	196,903	205,071	198,527	188,096	188,019	192,835	184,100
1999	167,686	160,388	166,472	172,127	170,842	168,307	182,383	188,726	192,883	179,040	165,334	146,997
2000	135,431	132,407	108,646	100,389	117,055	129,872	153,914	169,092	177,997	168,388	155,475	142,145

Source: New York Mercantile Exchange (NYMEX)

Volume of Trading of No. 2 Heating Oil Futures in New York   In Contracts

Year	Jan.	Feb.	Mar.	Apr.	May	June	July	Aug.	Sept.	Oct.	Nov.	Dec.	Total[1]
1991	603,683	523,870	392,484	387,232	399,919	425,082	507,755	595,913	538,240	689,143	781,291	835,559	6,680.2
1992	815,199	574,007	550,113	592,056	586,707	601,067	645,020	663,743	625,675	709,532	808,201	807,142	8,005.5
1993	829,034	660,546	747,299	537,543	481,957	543,356	632,168	721,852	833,800	761,764	886,565	988,871	8,625.1
1994	1,085,683	875,714	766,788	631,664	629,295	723,677	612,316	783,181	706,822	721,375	652,257	798,063	8,986.8
1995	779,827	608,691	715,968	622,810	729,753	618,812	612,683	563,605	714,239	650,809	659,518	990,068	8,266.8
1996	977,235	768,075	666,168	586,471	530,858	402,004	530,230	624,402	766,517	1,014,238	724,975	750,704	8,341.9
1997	794,382	719,006	588,604	710,143	591,958	679,426	679,612	694,656	828,320	742,680	619,301	722,876	8,371.0
1998	793,567	641,818	776,422	578,430	688,490	904,881	720,232	683,047	748,235	768,220	766,543	793,879	8,863.8
1999	738,909	662,334	973,273	706,258	768,142	802,661	770,367	707,858	720,061	819,625	818,562	712,653	9,200.7
2000	913,985	770,322	645,175	556,134	673,281	705,881	662,964	1,004,401	954,872	878,135	938,967	927,259	9,631.4

[1] In thousands of contracts.   *Source: New York Mercantile Exchange (NYMEX)*

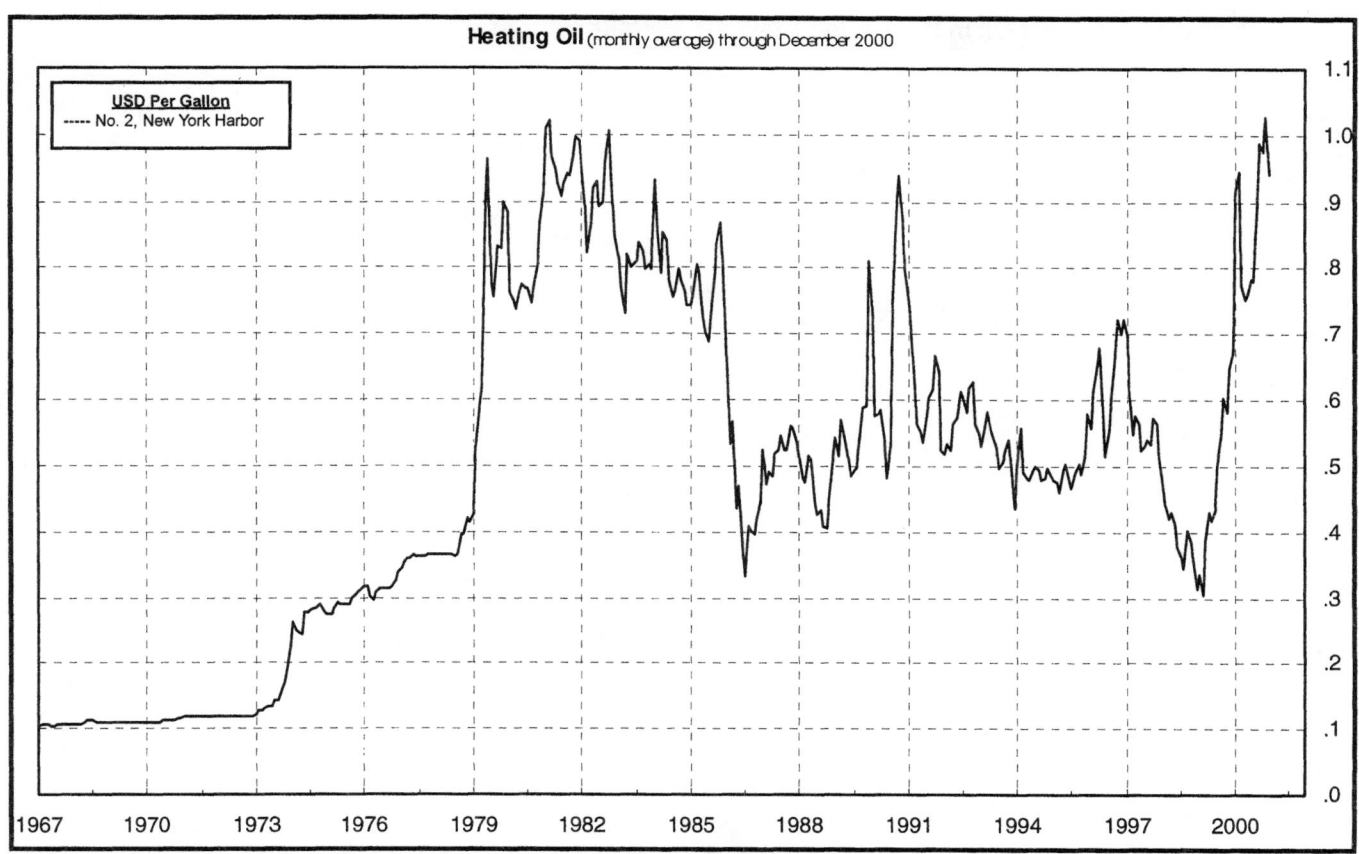

Heating Oil (monthly average) through December 2000

USD Per Gallon
----- No. 2, New York Harbor

Stocks of Distillate and Residual Fuel in the United States, on First of Month   In Millions of Barrels

Year	Jan.	Feb.	Mar.	Apr.	May	June	July	Aug.	Sept.	Oct.	Nov.	Dec.	Residual Fuel Oil Stocks Jan. 1	July 1
1991	112.1	111.7	101.6	98.2	102.9	106.9	113.7	124.7	131.4	140.1	138.3	144.5	47.6	43.7
1992	143.5	126.7	108.8	97.7	92.1	96.4	104.5	114.6	122.8	127.8	136.8	146.3	49.9	40.9
1993	140.6	130.7	110.4	97.3	99.5	102.8	110.0	120.7	128.2	131.3	145.3	149.2	42.6	45.7
1994	140.9	117.5	102.9	99.4	102.6	112.4	119.5	134.2	138.6	144.7	146.0	147.3	44.2	39.4
1995	145.2	140.2	122.1	115.4	114.6	118.3	114.7	125.0	130.9	131.7	131.4	135.4	41.9	36.0
1996	130.2	113.8	97.3	89.7	90.1	95.7	101.6	106.8	110.3	115.0	114.7	121.8	36.8	34.8
1997	126.7	111.3	105.9	101.8	97.5	108.4	118.2	123.0	132.9	138.9	136.2	140.5	45.9	39.2
1998	139.0	133.1	127.9	124.4	125.7	136.8	139.1	148.8	150.5	152.5	147.5	154.6	40.4	39.8
1999	156.2	147.9	142.3	125.7	125.3	134.8	133.2	138.1	142.0	145.2	137.6	140.6	44.9	42.5
2000[1]	124.1	106.7	105.2	96.0	100.1	105.4	106.4	112.9	111.0	115.3	116.5	121.1	35.8	37.1

[1] Preliminary.   *Source: Energy Information Administration; U.S. Department of Energy (EIA-DOE)*

Production of Distillate Fuel Oil in the United States   In Thousand Barrels per Day

Year	Jan.	Feb.	Mar.	Apr.	May	June	July	Aug.	Sept.	Oct.	Nov.	Dec.	Average
1991	2,845	2,870	2,865	2,819	2,929	2,941	2,998	2,961	3,055	3,040	3,103	3,107	2,962
1992	2,818	2,661	2,749	2,930	2,933	2,995	3,067	2,865	2,983	3,251	3,240	3,179	2,974
1993	2,914	2,815	2,919	3,047	2,994	3,093	3,186	3,100	3,205	3,432	3,474	3,382	3,132
1994	3,114	3,018	3,096	3,249	3,317	3,285	3,191	3,187	3,285	3,203	3,270	3,232	3,205
1995	3,054	2,954	3,157	3,126	3,111	3,109	3,056	3,145	3,287	3,169	3,341	3,344	3,155
1996	3,110	3,145	3,110	3,305	3,258	3,291	3,139	3,295	3,403	3,626	3,665	3,558	3,325
1997	3,119	3,089	3,258	3,291	3,525	3,517	3,362	3,427	3,452	3,488	3,543	3,578	3,389
1998	3,323	3,280	3,397	3,468	3,560	3,520	3,569	3,482	3,399	3,215	3,438	3,431	3,424
1999	3,176	3,253	3,183	3,407	3,458	3,374	3,521	3,419	3,482	3,506	3,608	3,401	3,399
2000[1]	3,124	3,354	3,342	3,533	3,651	3,481	3,520	3,677	3,848	3,776	3,768	3,876	3,579

[1] Preliminary.   *Source: Energy Information Administration, U.S. Department of Energy (EIA-DOE)*

HEATING OIL

Imports of Distillate Fuel Oil in the United States   In Thousand Barrels per Day

Year	Jan.	Feb.	Mar.	Apr.	May	June	July	Aug.	Sept.	Oct.	Nov.	Dec.	Average
1993	182	224	235	209	153	168	130	159	137	242	214	160	184
1994	161	276	318	226	202	182	164	211	193	159	166	187	203
1995	313	289	188	125	109	176	157	171	142	162	262	235	193
1996	243	271	253	258	215	185	194	195	187	246	192	253	224
1997	293	246	245	256	220	219	223	202	210	213	161	232	227
1998	195	213	237	209	185	202	229	181	203	239	179	245	210
1999	304	322	248	213	261	238	234	273	249	216	265	188	250
2000[1]	198	459	230	230	283	256	185	207	267	251	319	443	277

[1] Preliminary.   *Source: Energy Information Administration, U.S. Department of Energy (EIA-DOE)*

Exports of Distillate Fuel Oil in the United States   In Thousand Barrels per Day

Year	Jan.	Feb.	Mar.	Apr.	May	June	July	Aug.	Sept.	Oct.	Nov.	Dec.	Average
1993	287	301	154	241	355	158	296	196	267	237	342	453	274
1994	332	235	220	252	289	168	220	193	140	256	211	284	234
1995	141	212	216	172	202	137	148	84	116	238	236	298	183
1996	216	256	139	166	176	81	134	182	256	300	171	206	190
1997	133	107	120	166	153	174	151	185	160	133	149	192	152
1998	131	120	135	168	227	152	124	105	133	139	110	108	138
1999	117	116	159	191	187	180	123	130	162	192	170	212	162
2000[1]	132	112	211	178	127	149	132	253	194	255	191	135	173

[1] Preliminary.   *Source: Energy Information Administration, U.S. Department of Energy (EIA-DOE)*

Disposition of Distillate Fuel Oil, Total Product Supplied in the U.S.   In Thousand Barrels per Day

Year	Jan.	Feb.	Mar.	Apr.	May	June	July	Aug.	Sept.	Oct.	Nov.	Dec.	Average
1993	3,128	3,465	3,420	2,943	2,685	2,863	2,674	2,820	2,973	2,983	3,218	3,357	3,041
1994	3,698	3,581	3,307	3,116	2,912	3,062	2,663	3,063	3,133	3,066	3,180	3,203	3,162
1995	3,389	3,675	3,344	3,106	2,899	3,267	2,732	3,044	3,285	3,104	3,233	3,449	3,207
1996	3,681	3,722	3,453	3,385	3,118	3,194	3,046	3,184	3,178	3,575	3,460	3,434	3,368
1997	3,780	3,422	3,515	3,523	3,240	3,235	3,279	3,124	3,302	3,659	3,411	3,665	3,430
1998	3,566	3,598	3,606	3,465	3,268	3,574	3,294	3,446	3,377	3,547	3,320	3,484	3,461
1999	3,788	3,542	3,785	3,415	3,314	3,407	3,479	3,437	3,431	3,749	3,608	3,892	3,572
2000[1]	3,750	3,753	3,660	3,447	3,637	3,554	3,373	3,694	3,775	3,736	3,742	4,282	3,701

[1] Preliminary.   *Source: Energy Information Administration, U.S. Department of Energy (EIA-DOE)*

Production of Residual Fuel Oil in the United States   In Thousands Barrels per Day

Year	Jan.	Feb.	Mar.	Apr.	May	June	July	Aug.	Sept.	Oct.	Nov.	Dec.	Average
1993	820	840	818	896	908	795	762	752	822	841	899	869	835
1994	809	852	859	846	860	779	807	838	800	755	835	871	826
1995	903	776	778	789	748	746	797	801	811	724	705	874	788
1996	774	776	701	671	732	731	646	732	713	693	712	753	719
1997	800	789	639	617	618	727	645	643	688	711	786	810	705
1998	765	672	790	857	766	739	778	782	749	676	753	805	762
1999	775	726	683	679	725	706	736	701	702	658	596	690	698
2000[1]	654	643	651	627	662	701	746	763	702	756	783	780	706

[1] Preliminary.   *Source: Energy Information Administration U.S. Department of Energy (EIA-DOE)*

Supply and Disposition of Residual Fuel Oil in the United States

	Supply		Disposition			Ending Stocks	Average
	Total Production	Imports	Stock Change	Exports	Product Supplied	Million	Sales to End Users[3]
Year	Thousand Barrels Per Day					Barrels	Cents per Gallon
1993	835	373	4	123	1,080	44	33.7
1994	826	314	-6	125	1,021	42	35.2
1995	788	187	-13	136	852	37	39.2
1996	726	248	24	102	848	46	45.5
1997	708	194	-15	120	797	40	42.3
1998	762	275	12	138	887	45	30.5
1999	698	237	-25	129	830	36	37.4
2000[1]	706	267	[2]	139	834	36	

[1] Preliminary.   [2] Less than +500 barrels per day and greater than -500 barrels per day.   [3] Refiner price excluding taxes.
Source: Energy Information Administration, U.S. Department of Energy (EIA-DOE)

Hides and Leather

The major producers of bovine hides and skins are the U.S., Brazil, Argentina, and Russia. U.S. production of hides and skins is about 23 percent of the total world market. World production is close to 4 million metric tonnes. Production in the U.S. has been trending lower in recent years. After the U.S., the next largest producer is Brazil with production of over 650,000 tonnes. The production trend in Brazil has been higher over the last decade. Argentina is the third largest producer with about 7 percent of world output. The production trend there has been steady. Russia, which had been a large producer of hides and skins, has seen production decline significantly.

The U.S.D.A., in its report on U.S. exports through the week ended November 30, 2000, indicated that outstanding export sales of whole cattle hides (excluding wet blues) totaled 3.16 million pieces, up 15 percent from the year before. The marketing year is January to December. Sales to South Korea were 1.38 million pieces, up 13 percent from the year before. Sales to China were 702,300 pieces, up substantially from 273,600 pieces a year ago. Sales to Taiwan were 332,400 pieces, down 5 percent from a year ago, while sales to Mexico were 231,800 pieces. Cumulative exports of whole cattle hides in the January-November 2000 period were 20.5 million pieces, up 8 percent from 1999.

The major export destination was South Korea which had taken 9.13 million pieces or some 45 percent of total exports. Their total in 2000 was up 17 percent from 1999. The next largest importer was Taiwan with 2.88 million pieces, up 4 percent from the previous year. Other large importers of U.S. cattle hides included China, Mexico, and Japan.

U.S. export of calf skins (excluding wet blues) in the January-November 2000 period were 1.03 million pieces, down 5 percent from a year ago. By far the largest importer of U.S. calf skins is Italy, which in the first eleven months of 2000 took 937,600 pieces, down from 989,200 pieces a year ago. Japan was the next largest export destination taking 55,200 pieces, down 15 percent from a year ago. Other export destinations include the United Kingdom, France, Mexico, and Canada.

U.S. exports of kip skins (excluding wet blues) in January-November 2000 were 841,800 pieces, down 10 percent from the same period in 1999. The major destination was Italy which took 521,300 pieces, down 3 percent from 1999. The next largest importer of kip skins was Japan which took 236,500 pieces. Other importers of kip skins included Mexico, South Korea, France, Spain, China, and Chile.

World Production of Bovine Hides and Skins — In Thousands of Metric Tons

Year	Argentina	Australia	Brazil	Canada	Colombia	France	Germany	Italy	Mexico	Russia	United Kingdom	United States	World Total
1991	308	153	448	75	104	182	251	95	155	502	93	1,061	4,076
1992	298	162	442	77	88	180	205	98	160	466	88	1,073	3,983
1993	303	154	565	73	79	160	175	95	161	460	77	1,078	4,418
1994	305	152	573	74	77	151	158	93	166	350	81	942	4,073
1995	301	145	608	75	84	154	156	93	170	310	85	976	4,032
1996	306	145	615	81	88	158	164	92	160	280	90	994	4,072
1997	330	166	590	83	92	158	164	92	160	270	84	985	4,110
1998	285	171	622	83	93	148	152	90	170	235	86	987	4,116
1999[1]	300	162	637	88	92	145	149	90	170	210	85	1,002	4,130
2000[2]	295	152	667	89	92	148	139	91	175	200	83	993	4,139

[1] Preliminary. [2] Forecast. Source: Foreign Agricultural Service, U.S. Department of Agriculture (FAS-USDA)

Salient Statistics of Hides and Leather in the United States — In Thousands of Equivalent Hides

	New Supply of Cattle Hides				Wholesale Prices					Wholesale Leather				
	Domestic Slaughter				Cents Per Pound		Production		Value of Leather	Indexes		Footwear		
										Upper				
Year	Federally Inspected	Unin-spected[4]	Total Production	Net Exports	Heavy Native Cows[2]	Heavy Native Steers[3]	All U.S. Tanning	Cattle-hide	Exports $1,000	Men	Women	Pro-duction[5]	Exports	
	Thousands of Equivalent Hides						In 1,000 Equiv. Hides			1982 = 100		Million Pairs		
1990	32,391	851	33,242	20,920	92.58	92.0	14,820	13,018	750,836	132.8	118.8	184,568	15,174	
1991	31,887	803	32,690	18,636	76.92	78.9	14,800	13,021	680,348	136.9	120.7	167,386	18,109	
1992	32,094	780	32,874	17,810	81.71	75.9	15,900	14,474	705,038	140.5	124.2	168,451	21,401	
1993	32,593	731	33,324	17,117	82.16	78.9	18,057	16,931	764,120	142.8	126.9	171,733	20,700	
1994	33,483	713	34,196	16,259	94.99	87.3	18,842	18,117	811,951	144.7	127.2	163,000	22,505	
1995	34,879	760	35,639	18,336	93.89	87.6	18,092	17,480	870,247	150.1	129.0	147,550	20,571	
1996	36,583	177	36,760	18,626	92.15	86.4	18,769	18,135	950,510	152.4	132.1	127,315	23,726	
1997	35,567	925	36,492	17,562	90.99	86.1	19,592	18,930	1,145,664	156.4	132.2	124,444	21,958	
1998	34,787	850	35,637	15,937	75.45	69.5	20,297	19,706	1,289,547	157.0	133.0	109,194	19,009	
1999[1]	35,486	664	36,150	15,700	73.1		21,342	20,620	1,137,534	157.3	133.6	99,040	18,176	

[1] Preliminary. [2] Central U.S., heifers. [3] F.O.B. Chicago. [4] Includes farm slaughter; diseased & condemned animals & hides taken off fallen animals. [5] Other than rubber. Sources: Leather Industries of America (LIA); Bureau of Labor Statistics, U.S. Department of Commerce (BLS)

HIDES AND LEATHER

Production of All Footwear (Shoes, Sandals, Slippers, Athletic, Etc.) in the U.S.   In Millions of Pairs

Year	First Quarter	Second Quarter	Third Quarter	Fourth Quarter	Total	Year	First Quarter	Second Quarter	Third Quarter	Fourth Quarter	Total
1990	53.5	52.3	49.6	46.2	184.6	1995	37.2	38.3	34.8	36.7	147.0
1991	48.1	37.8	41.8	41.2	169.0	1996	33.2	31.8	29.7	33.2	128.0
1992	41.1	40.8	43.6	39.3	164.8	1997	31.4	33.1	28.6	30.6	123.7
1993	43.3	44.6	42.8	41.0	171.7	1998	32.8	31.8	29.3	28.6	122.5
1994	42.5	40.8	40.1	39.5	163.0	1999[1]	26.7	26.1	24.5	21.7	99.0

[1] Preliminary.   *Source: Bureau of the Census, U.S. Department of Commerce*

Average Factory Price[2] of Footwear in the United States   In Dollars Per Pair

Year	First Quarter	Second Quarter	Third Quarter	Fourth Quarter	Total	Year	First Quarter	Second Quarter	Third Quarter	Fourth Quarter	Total
1990	18.04	18.65	19.91	20.72	19.37	1995	19.61	21.46	25.37	21.26	21.79
1991	22.14	20.40	19.74	18.52	20.14	1996	23.65	22.78	22.14	20.38	22.07
1992	20.19	22.21	21.15	20.46	20.96	1997	22.42	21.56	22.21	22.24	22.11
1993	21.62	21.67	21.37	21.79	21.61	1998	24.39	24.21	20.27	19.78	21.84
1994	25.77	23.60	21.49	22.44	23.22	1999[1]	23.33	22.70	19.90	19.50	21.19

[1] Preliminary.   [2] Average value of factory shipments per pair.   *Source: Bureau of the Census, U.S. Department of Commerce*

Imports and Exports of All Cattle Hides in the United States   In Thousands of Hides

	Imports		U.S. Exports - by Country of Destination										
Year	Total	From Canada	Total	Canada	Italy	Japan	Rep. of Korea	Mexico	Portugal	Romania	Spain	Taiwan	Thailand
1990	661	678	21,582	674	136	6,802	9,839	1,438	29	253	175	1,476	91
1991	1,549	1,088	20,185	561	138	4,662	9,300	2,702	7	----	39	2,058	123
1992	1,536	1,457	19,347	684	107	4,647	8,589	2,729	100	4	30	1,823	160
1993	1,660	1,597	18,777	965	354	4,167	7,919	2,217	79	1	60	1,950	386
1994	1,731	----	17,990	995	309	3,133	7,472	1,553	168	72	141	2,491	332
1995	1,759	----	20,095	952	332	3,246	8,283	899	111	63	215	3,017	781
1996	1,702	----	20,328	1,149	522	2,372	7,956	2,123	64	171	189	2,871	455
1997	1,633	----	19,195	1,320	469	1,802	7,470	2,501	55	----	148	2,866	323
1998	1,930	----	17,867	1,126	1,164	1,407	4,897	2,846	91	----	440	2,701	336
1999[1]	1,921	----	17,621	829	738	1,252	6,038	2,723	46	----	262	2,863	343

[1] Preliminary.   *Source: Leather Industries of America*

Imports of Bovine Hides and Skins by Selected Countries   In Metric Tons

Year	Brazil	Canada	Hong Kong	Italy	Japan	Mexico	Portugal	Rep. of Korea	Spain	Taiwan	Turkey	United States	World Total
1992	11	17	80	131	188	71	32	385	26	91	28	65	1,266
1993	21	26	81	141	188	71	39	372	35	94	37	57	1,426
1994	16	28	95	243	139	60	56	356	29	112	17	49	1,556
1995	33	35	100	250	152	30	43	342	42	112	43	57	1,715
1996	20	34	79	263	123	71	42	341	33	124	50	60	1,692
1997	13	39	64	254	114	96	37	323	44	140	68	60	1,985
1998	10	42	71	249	96	110	39	229	44	142	45	59	1,876
1999[1]	8	34	91	215	95	115	42	254	29	142	55	57	2,002
2000[2]	8	36	93	220	95	115	43	260	30	142	60	57	2,058

[1] Preliminary.   [2] Forecast.   *Source: Foreign Agricultural Service, U.S. Department of Agriculture (FAS-USDA)*

Exports of Bovine Hides and Skins by Selected Countries   In Metric Tons

Year	Australia	Brazil	Canada	Germany	Hong Kong	Italy	Netherlands	New Zealand	Poland	Russia	United Kingdom	United States	World Total
1992	144	71	74	38	75	9	66	31	17	28	19	610	1,261
1993	142	76	87	40	76	7	35	21	5	150	25	581	1,374
1994	96	84	79	24	93	10	37	22	2	216	22	455	1,271
1995	85	148	90	34	100	10	47	22	2	195	22	510	1,351
1996	93	174	97	33	72	20	47	28	3	212	24	506	1,423
1997	115	216	97	35	60	16	48	27	3	210	25	473	1,475
1998	111	220	86	31	69	24	32	28	6	202	17	443	1,400
1999[1]	115	230	83	28	90	7	30	30	7	190	15	436	1,389
2000[2]	108	250	85	31	92	8	25	30	7	170	15	427	1,399

[1] Preliminary.   [2] Forecast.   *Source: Foreign Agricultural Service, U.S. Department of Agriculture (FAS-USDA)*

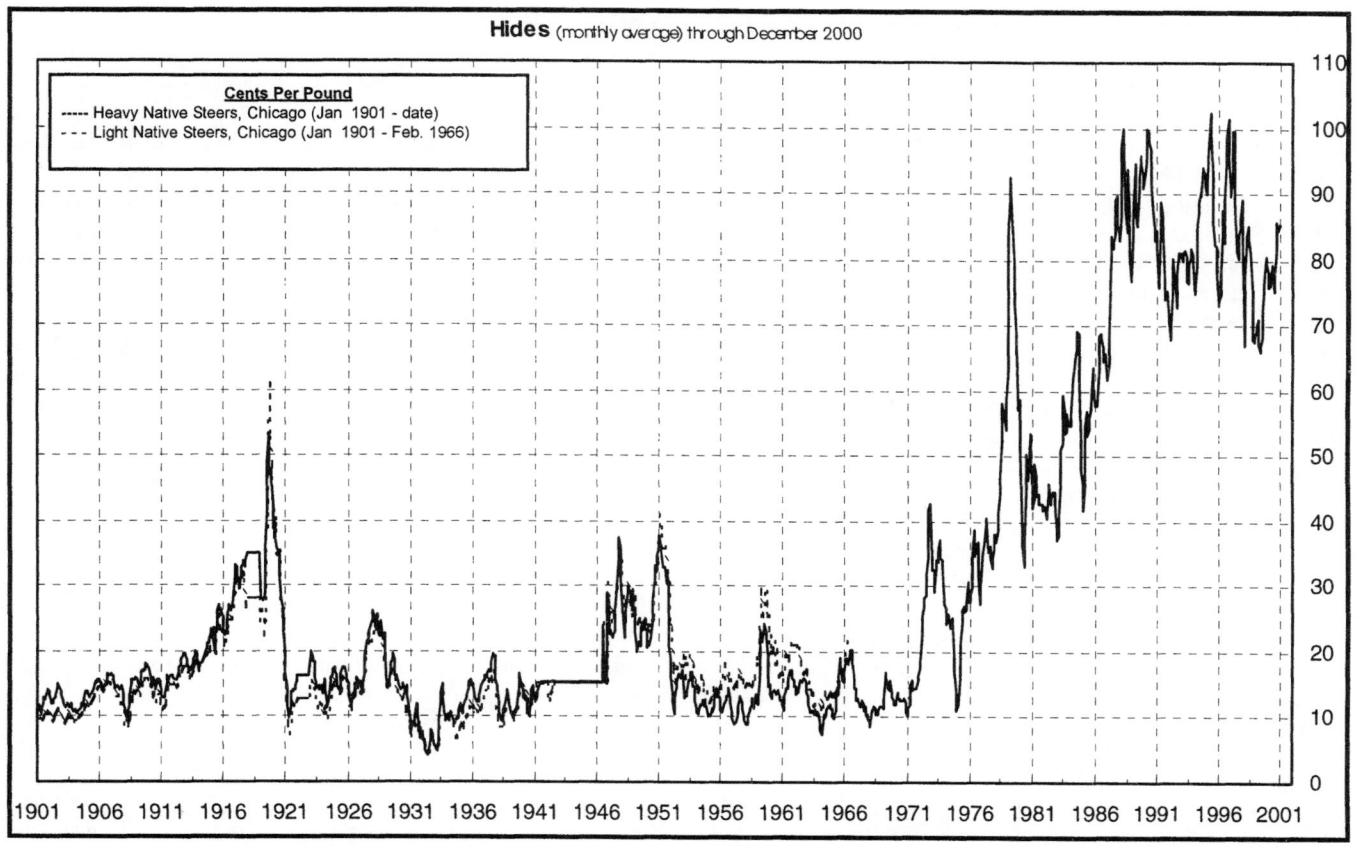

Hides (monthly average) through December 2000

Cents Per Pound
----- Heavy Native Steers, Chicago (Jan 1901 - date)
- - - Light Native Steers, Chicago (Jan 1901 - Feb. 1966)

Utilization of Bovine Hides and Skins by Selected Countries   In Metric Tons

Year	Argentina	Brazil	Colombia	Germany	Italy	Japan	Mexico	Rep. of Korea	Spain	Taiwan	Turkey	United States	World Total
1991	308	396	98	143	435	253	225	400	119	101	78	491	4,009
1992	298	382	97	129	435	229	231	400	98	91	90	528	3,977
1993	302	510	94	100	435	226	232	385	98	94	95	554	4,322
1994	304	505	96	83	550	200	226	374	94	112	85	536	4,282
1995	300	493	89	79	570	191	200	355	98	112	100	523	4,365
1996	308	461	91	80	615	165	230	353	95	124	110	548	4,332
1997	332	387	89	101	570	150	251	347	106	140	120	572	4,609
1998	285	412	91	100	540	135	275	265	108	142	100	603	4,584
1999[1]	300	415	89	102	500	130	280	280	104	142	110	623	4,707
2000[2]	285	425	89	103	505	130	285	283	108	142	120	623	4,774

[1] Preliminary.   [2] Forecast.   *Source: Foreign Agricultural Service, U.S. Department of Agriculture (FAS-USDA)*

Wholesale Price of Hides (Packer Heavy Native Steers) F.O.B. Chicago   In Cents Per Pound

Year	Jan.	Feb.	Mar.	Apr.	May	June	July	Aug.	Sept.	Oct.	Nov.	Dec.	Average
1991	81.64	75.84	76.50	86.32	88.77	86.60	84.05	77.18	74.05	75.30	75.30	71.29	79.40
1992	70.55	67.84	69.68	75.95	80.05	76.77	76.50	72.76	77.62	81.18	80.05	81.00	75.83
1993	79.82	81.05	81.48	81.44	80.35	76.95	76.62	79.27	80.52	81.76	80.81	79.83	79.99
1994	75.07	75.08	79.00	84.75	87.33	88.77	90.38	89.76	93.90	93.67	93.19	91.13	86.84
1995	90.10	91.42	97.99	102.32	99.64	92.45	85.74	82.46	82.45	82.16	78.02	73.02	88.15
1996	73.67	75.11	77.96	84.58	87.56	82.51	89.45	96.06	98.91	101.51	94.60	90.65	87.71
1997	89.77	93.47	99.44	99.40	89.44	81.45	80.20	83.92	84.86	86.35	89.20	82.61	88.34
1998	66.88	77.33	82.61	83.72	85.05	83.13	81.17	81.11	75.23	67.95	67.53	68.26	76.66
1999	69.42	69.97	70.84	67.36	65.96	66.89	68.17	72.41	77.52	80.43	79.67	78.00	72.22
2000	75.92	76.29	77.86	78.83	79.24	75.18	77.25	81.64	85.60	84.89	84.41	85.31	80.20

Source: The Wall Street Journal

Hogs

U.S. hog prices, basis nearest Chicago futures, spiked to a three-year high in mid-spring 2000, and then lost almost the entire bull move during the second half of the year. Still, prices for the year averaged in the mid-$40's per cwt., about $10-$11 higher than in the previous two years due to lower production and good domestic and foreign demand. However, the U.S. economy is expected to lose some of its buoyancy in 2001, which will likely trim consumer demand. Add to that an expected increase in hog production and the combined effect could pressure prices $2-$4 per cwt. lower, although a supporting factor is an expected 10 percent drop in beef production.

The world's hog inventory in 2000 of 765 million head compares with 762 million in 1999, and forecasts of a near record 773 million in 2001. World pork consumption set a new record high in 2000 at 81.4 million metric tonnes vs. 80.2 million in 1999, with an increase to 83.7 million forecast for 2001. On a world per capita basis, the 2000 estimate of 18.3 kilograms trails the 18.6 kg. of 1999, but a recovery is expected to 18.7 kg. in 2001.

China is the world's largest hog producer with more than one-half the total, leaving the U.S. a distant second. China's January 1, 2001 inventory of a near record 440 million head compares with 430 million in 2000. In the U.S., the early 2000 total of 59.3 million head compares with 62.2 million a year earlier and estimates of 60 million as of January 1, 2001. Germany's 2001 inventory, the largest in the European Union, was estimated at 25.8 million head vs. 26 million in 2000. The decade long slide in the Russian and Ukrainian inventory may have bottomed in 2000. Their combined January 1, 2001 total of almost 26 million head compares with 26.2 million in 2000, and over 50 million as recently as 1992.

The U.S. inventory on September 1, 2000, of 60.2 million head, was almost unchanged from a year earlier. Of the total, 6.9 million head were kept for breeding vs. 6.5 million, with the balance to be marketed. Farrowing intentions during the closing months of 2000, and into the first quarter of 2001, were forecast about 3 percent above the year earlier period. Although the 2000 U.S. hog inventory is only 8 percent of the world total, slaughter runs about 9.5 percent, with the total pork production percentage somewhat higher. U.S. per capita pork usage in 2000 of 52.4 pounds compares with 53.8 pounds in 1999, and a forecast of 53.2 pounds in 2001.

More than one-half of the inventory share of U.S. hog marketings now come from contract hog operations. In a contractual agreement, the contractor provides the hogs, feed, medication, and supplies, while the contractee provides the housing, utilities, and labor. Most hog production still occurs in Corn Belt states, but Southern states have seen a dramatic growth in contractual operations in recent years. Still, most U.S. producers continue to raise hogs in farrow-to-finish operations. As of September 1, 2000, the total number of hogs under contract owned by operations with over 5,000 head, but raised by contractees, accounted for 33 percent of the total U.S. inventory vs. 31 percent in 1999.

Commercial U.S. hog slaughter in the January-October 2000 period of 81.1 million head compares with 83.8 million in the like 1999 period, with an average dressed weight of about 191 pounds in both years. Pork production in 2000 of 18.9 billion pounds compares with 19.3 billion in 1999. Based upon the Fall 2000 hog inventory and breeding intentions, pork production in 2001 is forecast at 19.3 billion pounds.

The U.S. is the world's largest pork exporter with 569,000 metric tonnes in 2000 vs. 583,000 in 1999, and the world total of 3 million tonnes and 3.3 million, respectively. Denmark is second. Japan, Russia, Canada, and Mexico are generally the largest importers of U.S. pork. The U.S. imports pork products, mostly from Canada and Denmark, while live hogs are imported from Canada.

Midwest wholesale barrow and gilt hog prices during 2000 averaged about $44.51 per cwt. vs. $34.00 in 1999, and are forecast at $40.00-43.00 in 2001.

Futures Markets

Lean hog futures and options are traded on the Chicago Mercantile Exchange (CME) where futures settle to the CME lean hog Index. Their proprietary index tracks the value of lean pork at select U.S. packing plants.

Live hog futures are traded on the Mid-America Commodity Exchange (MidAm) and the Agricultural Futures Markets (AFM) in the Netherlands.

Salient Statistics of Pigs and Hogs in the United States

	Pig Crop						Value of Hogs		Hog	Quantity	Value	Hogs Slaughtered in Thousand Head				
	Spring[3]			Fall[4]			on Farms, Dec. 1		Marketings	Produced	of Pro-	Commercial				
	Sows Farrowed	Pig Crop	Pigs Per Litter	Sows Farrowed	Pig Crop	Pigs Per Litter	$ Per Head	Total Million $	Thousand Head	(Live Wt.) Mill. Lbs.	duction Mil. $	Federally Inspected	Other	Total	Farm	Total
Year	--- 1,000 Head ---			--- 1,000 Head ---												
1991	5,988	47,413	7.92	6,071	47,902	7.89	68.8	3,966	92,220	22,727	11,067	85,952	2,217	88,169	276	88,445
1992	6,260	50,466	8.06	6,012	48,676	8.10	71.2	4,147	98,589	23,947	9,854	92,611	2,278	94,889	268	95,157
1993	6,034	49,084	8.14	5,976	48,216	8.07	74.9	4,340	98,351	23,693	10,628	90,933	2,135	93,068	229	93,296
1994	6,257	51,217	8.18	6,139	50,262	8.19	53.2	3,178	100,747	24,437	9,692	93,435	2,261	95,696	208	95,905
1995	6,046	50,077	8.28	5,843	48,739	8.35	70.7	4,115	102,684	24,426	9,829	94,203	2,123	96,325	210	96,535
1996	5,648	47,887	8.46	5,449	46,571	8.55	94.0	5,281	101,852	23,267	12,013	90,534	1,860	92,394	175	92,569
1997	5,595	48,393	8.65	5,885	51,190	8.70	82.0	4,986	104,301	23,979	12,552	90,228	1,733	91,960	165	92,125
1998	6,015	52,469	8.73	6,047	52,536	8.69	44.0	2,766	117,240	25,715	8,674	99,285	1,745	101,029	163	101,192
1999[1]	5,877	51,519	8.77	5,764	50,835	8.82	72.0	4,269	121,187	25,600	7,660	99,739	1,816	101,555	141	101,696
2000[2]	5,688	50,132	8.81	5,774	51,222	8.87										

[1] Preliminary.　[2] Estimate.　[3] December-May.　[4] June-November.　*Source: Economic Research Service, U.S. Department of Agriculture (ERS-USDA)*

HOGS

World Hog Numbers in Specified Countries as of January 1   In Thousands of Head

Year	Brazil	Canada	China	Denmark	France	Germany	Philip-pines	Poland	Russia	Spain	Ukraine	United States	World Total
1992	33,050	10,498	369,646	9,767	12,067	26,063	8,022	20,725	35,384	17,209	17,839	57,469	728,789
1993	31,050	10,577	384,210	10,345	13,015	26,514	7,954	21,059	31,520	18,260	16,175	58,202	740,758
1994	31,200	10,534	393,000	10,870	14,791	26,075	8,227	17,422	28,600	18,234	15,298	57,940	743,930
1995	31,338	11,291	414,619	10,864	14,593	24,698	8,941	19,138	24,859	18,295	13,946	59,738	758,461
1996	32,068	11,588	345,848	10,709	14,523	23,737	9,023	20,343	22,630	18,600	13,144	58,201	782,425
1997	31,369	11,480	362,836	11,081	14,968	24,283	9,750	17,697	19,500	18,651	11,236	56,124	695,133
1998	31,427	11,985	400,348	11,442	15,473	24,845	10,210	18,498	16,579	18,970	9,479	61,158	731,575
1999	31,427	12,409	422,563	11,991	15,869	26,299	10,398	19,275	16,400	21,715	10,083	62,206	762,206
2000[1]	31,860	12,254	430,198	11,914	15,990	26,003	10,764	18,224	16,100	22,597	10,073	59,337	765,347
2001[2]	31,840	12,500	440,000	12,000	15,700	25,800	11,715	16,000	15,900	22,700	10,000	60,000	772,931

[1] Preliminary.   [2] Forecast.   *Source: Foreign Agricultural Service, U.S. Department of Agriculture (FAS-USDA)*

Hogs and Pigs on Farms in the United States on December 1   In Thousands of Head

Year	Georgia	Illinois	Indiana	Iowa	Kansas	Minne-sota	Missouri	Nebraska	North Carolina	Ohio	South Dakota	Wis-consin	Total
1991	1,130	5,900	4,600	15,000	1,430	4,900	2,700	4,500	3,650	1,925	1,950	1,180	57,684
1992	1,100	5,900	4,600	16,400	1,440	4,700	2,850	4,650	4,500	1,800	1,830	1,210	59,815
1993	1,000	5,450	4,300	15,000	1,350	4,750	3,000	4,300	5,400	1,630	1,750	1,170	57,904
1994	1,020	5,350	4,500	14,500	1,310	4,850	3,500	4,350	7,000	1,800	1,740	1,040	59,990
1995	900	4,800	4,000	13,400	1,230	4,950	1,100	4,050	8,200	1,800	1,450	900	58,264
1996	800	4,400	3,750	12,200	1,450	4,850	3,450	3,600	9,300	1,500	1,200	800	56,171
1997	520	4,700	3,950	14,600	1,530	5,700	3,550	3,500	9,600	1,700	1,400	740	61,158
1998	480	4,850	4,050	15,300	1,590	5,700	3,300	3,400	9,700	1,700	1,400	690	62,206
1999	480	4,050	3,250	15,400	1,460	5,500	3,150	3,000	9,500	1,480	1,260	570	59,342
2000[1]	380	4,200	3,400	15,400	1,570	5,800	2,900	3,100	9,400	1,510	1,360	620	59,848

[1] Preliminary.   *Source: National Agricultural Statistics Service, U.S. Department of Agriculture (NASS-USDA)*

Hog-Corn Price Ratio[1] in the United States

Year	Jan.	Feb.	Mar.	Apr.	May	June	July	Aug.	Sept.	Oct.	Nov.	Dec.	Average
1991	22.0	22.5	21.5	21.0	22.7	23.7	23.9	22.0	19.9	18.9	16.6	16.6	20.9
1992	15.3	16.3	15.7	16.5	18.1	18.9	19.1	20.5	19.5	20.5	20.8	21.2	18.5
1993	20.3	22.0	22.1	21.0	21.9	23.0	20.6	21.0	21.6	20.6	17.3	15.1	20.5
1994	16.1	17.2	16.2	16.1	16.4	16.4	18.4	19.4	16.2	15.4	14.1	14.5	16.4
1995	16.8	17.5	16.4	15.1	15.3	16.8	17.6	18.5	18.0	16.4	13.9	14.2	16.4
1996	13.8	13.8	13.9	12.9	13.7	13.4	13.2	13.9	15.4	19.3	20.5	21.1	15.4
1997	20.0	19.9	17.7	19.2	21.6	22.6	24.3	22.1	20.0	18.6	18.0	16.5	20.0
1998	14.1	14.1	13.7	14.8	18.1	18.6	16.8	18.6	16.1	14.6	9.7	7.3	14.7
1999	12.8	13.5	13.6	14.8	18.4	17.3	18.2	20.7	19.4	20.2	19.6	19.6	17.3
2000[2]	19.3	20.2	20.6	23.3	23.1	25.4	29.6	28.6	25.8	23.8	19.6	20.2	23.3

[1] Bushels of corn equal in value to 100 pounds of hog, live weight.   [2] Preliminary.   *Source: Economic Research Service, U.S. Department of Agriculture (ERS-USDA)*

Cold Storage Holdings of Frozen Pork[1] in the United States, on First of Month   In Millions of Pounds

Year	Jan.	Feb.	Mar.	Apr.	May	June	July	Aug.	Sept.	Oct.	Nov.	Dec.
1991	233.6	247.0	281.2	289.0	340.0	333.3	312.3	277.9	282.4	280.5	299.7	308.0
1992	311.1	341.2	364.0	372.2	362.6	344.9	319.0	307.0	266.7	297.3	306.8	316.7
1993	314.5	329.5	344.4	330.4	378.5	371.6	351.3	342.5	308.9	311.2	324.8	313.0
1994	299.2	348.8	356.9	393.1	429.7	437.6	410.8	393.7	364.0	352.7	385.4	383.2
1995	365.3	389.6	395.1	416.8	422.3	434.9	431.1	408.3	354.0	332.6	321.6	347.1
1996	334.8	382.2	385.5	352.9	385.5	381.3	351.8	322.7	322.9	340.3	333.3	316.4
1997	313.8	342.2	383.9	404.7	440.2	413.4	406.2	388.7	371.8	346.6	354.2	334.1
1998	346.4	446.1	464.5	458.8	487.0	477.4	426.8	414.6	392.6	388.9	411.9	443.4
1999	503.5	510.3	540.9	552.8	596.9	572.7	528.6	494.6	432.6	430.6	438.1	422.5
2000[2]	415.4	481.4	523.5	534.7	532.1	537.9	495.5	478.5	455.6	439.5	438.6	455.2

[1] Excludes lard.   [2] Preliminary.   *Source: Economic Research Service, U.S. Department of Agriculture (ERS-USDA)*

HOGS

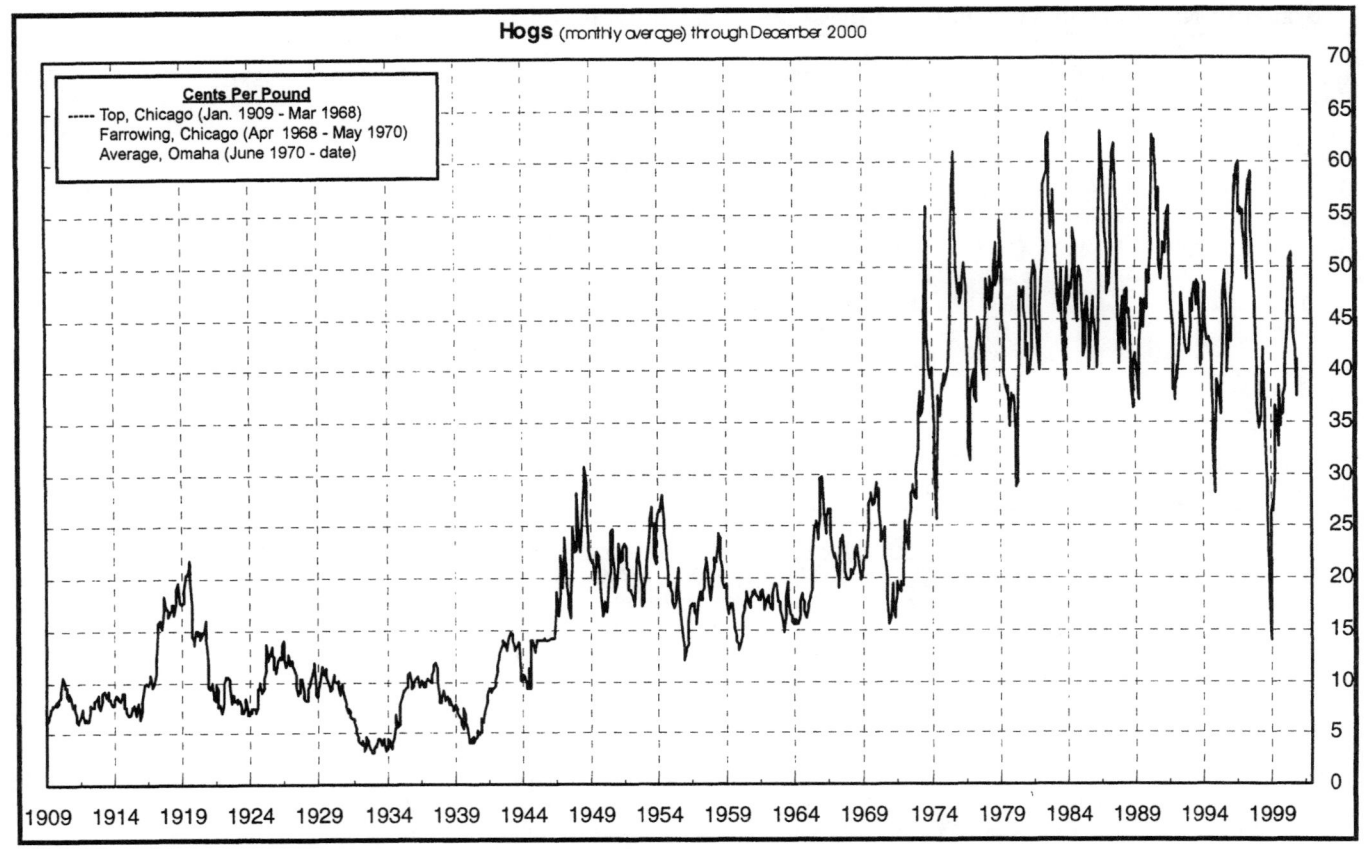

Hogs (monthly average) through December 2000

Cents Per Pound
----- Top, Chicago (Jan. 1909 - Mar 1968)
Farrowing, Chicago (Apr 1968 - May 1970)
Average, Omaha (June 1970 - date)

Average Wholesale Price of Hogs, Average (All Weights) in Sioux City In Dollars Per Hundred Pounds (Cwt.)

Year	Jan.	Feb.	Mar.	Apr.	May	June	July	Aug.	Sept.	Oct.	Nov.	Dec.	Average
1988	44.59	47.45	43.19	42.28	47.75	48.26	45.60	45.98	41.28	38.92	36.52	40.58	43.53
1989	41.64	41.11	39.88	37.22	42.40	46.24	47.26	47.04	44.58	47.49	47.21	49.65	44.31
1990	48.41	49.48	52.56	54.63	62.80	61.34	62.54	56.37	55.64	58.02	50.17	48.96	55.08
1991	51.32	52.31	51.92	51.42	54.83	54.79	55.74	51.11	46.76	43.51	38.29	38.93	49.24
1992	37.15	40.45	39.09	42.01	45.90	47.59	44.98	44.88	42.50	42.57	41.98	42.12	42.60
1993	41.66	44.57	46.76	45.46	47.10	48.52	46.38	48.67	48.40	47.27	42.76	40.38	45.66
1994	43.99	48.12	44.30	42.72	42.27	42.76	42.62	42.37	35.49	32.56	28.25	31.59	39.75
1995	37.82	39.09	37.94	35.88	37.35	43.03	47.18	49.46	48.67	45.42	40.02	43.80	42.14
1996	42.39	46.93	49.06	50.88	58.29	56.45	59.47	60.49	54.60	55.41	54.42	55.47	53.66
1997[1]	52.96	51.36	48.52	54.41	57.84	57.43	58.89	54.17	49.45	46.12	44.86	40.33	51.36

[1] Preliminary.   Source: Economic Research Service, U.S. Department of Agriculture (ERS-USDA)

Average Price Received by Farmers for Hogs in the United States   In Cents Per Pound

Year	Jan.	Feb.	Mar.	Apr.	May	June	July	Aug.	Sept.	Oct.	Nov.	Dec.	Average
1990	47.30	48.20	51.30	53.80	61.20	60.30	60.80	55.90	54.30	56.80	50.20	47.80	53.99
1991	50.00	52.20	51.50	50.90	54.10	54.70	54.20	51.20	46.40	43.60	38.00	38.60	48.78
1992	36.80	40.20	39.10	41.00	45.10	46.70	44.60	44.10	42.10	42.00	41.10	41.70	42.04
1993	41.20	44.00	46.50	45.40	46.90	48.10	45.70	47.30	47.80	46.90	42.50	40.40	45.23
1994	43.50	47.90	44.40	42.70	42.70	42.70	42.20	41.80	35.40	31.80	28.00	30.80	39.49
1995	36.90	39.10	37.80	35.70	37.20	42.30	46.30	48.60	48.40	45.70	39.90	43.50	41.78
1996	42.30	46.50	48.70	49.70	56.80	56.40	58.60	59.70	54.70	55.60	54.40	55.60	53.25
1997	53.80	52.80	49.40	53.80	58.20	57.80	58.90	55.30	50.40	47.30	45.10	41.60	52.03
1998	36.00	35.90	34.90	35.60	42.30	42.40	36.90	35.20	29.50	27.80	18.80	14.70	32.50
1999[1]	26.30	27.60	27.80	30.20	36.40	34.20	31.20	36.20	33.70	34.00	33.40	35.60	32.22

[1] Preliminary.   Source: Economic Research Service, U.S. Department of Agriculture (ERS-USDA)

Quarterly Hogs and Pigs Report in the United States, 10 States   In Thousands of Head

Year[2]	Inventory[3]	Breeding[3]	Market[3]	Farrowings	Pig Crop	Year[2]	Inventory[3]	Breeding[3]	Market[3]	Farrowings	Pig Crop
1991	42,900	5,257	37,643	9,516	75,330	1996	58,264	6,839	51,425	11,114	94,458
I	42,900	5,257	37,643	2,129	16,700	I	58,264	6,839	51,425	2,735	23,054
II	41,990	5,450	36,540	2,577	20,555	II	55,741	6,701	49,040	2,930	24,833
III	44,520	5,700	38,820	2,413	19,260	III	56,038	6,682	49,356	2,718	23,244
IV	46,950	5,685	41,265	2,433	18,551	IV	56,961	6,577	50,384	2,731	23,327
1992	45,735	5,610	40,125	10,202	82,497	1997	56,124	6,578	49,546	11,480	99,583
I	45,735	5,610	40,125	2,296	18,532	I	56,141	6,667	49,474	2,684	23,164
II	44,800	5,555	39,245	2,663	21,570	II	55,049	6,637	48,412	2,911	25,229
III	47,255	5,845	41,410	2,501	20,395	III	57,366	6,789	50,577	2,946	25,696
IV	49,175	5,840	43,335	2,398	19,351	IV	60,456	6,858	53,598	2,939	25,494
1993	58,202	7,109	51,093	11,982	97,050	1998	61,158	6,957	54,200	12,062	104,981
I	58,202	7,109	51,093	3,665	29,739	I	61,158	6,957	54,200	2,929	25,480
II	47,145	5,735	41,410	2,363	19,267	II	60,163	6,942	53,220	3,086	26,989
III	58,395	7,320	51,075	2,972	24,041	III	62,213	6,958	55,254	3,054	26,634
IV	59,030	7,130	51,900	2,982	24,003	IV	63,488	6,875	56,612	2,993	25,878
1994	57,904	7,130	50,739	12,376	101,400	1999	62,206	6,682	55,523	11,641	102,354
I	57,904	7,130	50,739	2,885	23,368	I	62,206	6,682	55,523	2,891	25,247
II	57,350	7,210	50,140	3,390	27,984	II	60,191	6,527	53,663	2,986	26,272
III	60,715	7,565	53,150	3,107	25,547	III	60,896	6,515	54,380	2,920	25,862
IV	62,320	7,415	54,905	2,997	24,517	IV	60,776	6,301	54,474	2,844	24,973
1995	59,990	7,060	52,930	11,847	98,516	2000[1]	59,342	6,234	53,109	11,462	101,354
I	59,990	7,060	52,930	2,886	23,851	I	59,342	6,234	53,109	2,798	24,522
II	58,465	6,998	51,467	3,170	26,373	II	57,782	6,190	51,593	2,890	25,610
III	59,560	7,180	52,380	2,976	24,813	III	59,137	6,234	52,904	2,899	25,686
IV	60,540	6,898	53,642	2,815	23,479	IV	60,065	6,246	53,820	2,875	25,536

[1] Preliminary.   [2] Quarters are Dec. preceding year-Feb.(I), Mar.-May(II), June-Aug.(III) and Sept.-Nov.(IV).   [3] Beginning of period.
Source: National Agricultural Statistics Service, U.S. Department of Agriculture (NASS-USDA)

Federally Inspected Hog Slaughter in the United States   In Thousands of Head

Year	Jan.	Feb.	Mar.	Apr.	May	June	July	Aug.	Sept.	Oct.	Nov.	Dec.	Total
1991	7,461	6,469	7,044	7,320	6,948	6,296	6,557	7,098	7,177	8,292	7,744	7,708	85,951
1992	8,144	7,153	7,934	7,610	6,897	7,166	7,461	7,494	8,217	8,599	7,796	8,142	92,613
1993	7,649	6,921	7,958	7,840	6,988	7,338	7,010	7,473	7,763	7,857	7,952	8,184	90,993
1994	7,285	6,783	8,148	7,609	7,383	7,452	6,941	7,997	8,192	8,585	8,516	8,547	93,435
1995	7,882	7,157	8,628	7,379	8,012	7,731	6,918	8,083	7,752	8,358	8,424	7,881	94,203
1996	8,129	7,506	7,549	7,886	7,485	6,395	7,187	7,509	7,541	8,423	7,469	7,455	90,534
1997	7,610	6,836	7,437	7,590	6,971	6,859	7,169	7,197	7,872	8,625	7,601	8,461	90,228
1998	8,454	7,590	8,335	8,198	7,443	7,596	8,130	8,024	8,443	9,192	8,650	9,231	99,285
1999	8,373	7,746	8,945	8,386	7,303	8,176	7,778	8,256	8,501	8,806	8,750	8,719	99,739
2000[1]	8,010	7,955	8,695	7,108	7,816	7,823	7,235	8,481	7,992	8,746	8,633	7,943	96,436

[1] Preliminary. *Source: National Agricultural Statistics Service, U.S. Department of Agriculture (NASS-USDA)*

Average Live Weight of all Hogs Slaughtered Under Federal Inspection   In Pounds Per Head

Year	Jan.	Feb.	Mar.	Apr.	May	June	July	Aug.	Sept.	Oct.	Nov.	Dec.	Average
1991	251	250	250	252	254	253	251	250	251	253	256	255	252
1992	255	253	252	253	254	254	251	250	252	252	255	255	253
1993	254	253	253	254	254	256	254	252	252	254	257	258	254
1994	254	254	254	256	255	256	252	252	255	259	261	260	256
1995	258	256	257	258	258	258	256	253	252	255	259	258	257
1996	257	254	255	255	255	256	251	250	250	255	258	257	254
1997	257	256	256	256	256	257	253	252	255	257	261	260	256
1998	259	258	257	257	256	255	252	252	253	257	262	261	257
1999	259	259	259	260	260	260	257	254	256	259	262	262	259
2000[1]	262	262	262	263	263	262	259	258	259	263	266	265	262

[1] Preliminary. *Source: Economic Research Service, U.S. Department of Agriculture (ERS-USDA)*

HOGS

Lean Hog Futures - Chicago Mercantile Exchange (weekly close) as of 29-Dec-2000
Cents Per Pound

Data Through December 1996 contract are for Live Hogs/ 74.
Adjusted to correspond to the Lean Hogs contract

Jan-91 Jan-92 Dec-92 Dec-93 Dec-94 Dec-95 Dec-96 Dec-97 Dec-98 Dec-99 Dec-00

Average Open Interest of Lean Hog¹ Futures in Chicago   In Contracts

Year	Jan.	Feb.	Mar.	Apr.	May	June	July	Aug.	Sept.	Oct.	Nov.	Dec.
1991	22,742	24,798	24,449	22,400	25,871	21,275	18,154	16,771	17,281	18,462	21,572	19,167
1992	23,854	31,545	32,441	32,430	30,947	26,362	24,935	24,535	27,535	32,555	32,738	30,468
1993	27,210	25,620	28,264	24,139	22,581	19,840	19,026	20,761	20,544	20,051	21,167	24,096
1994	31,899	32,123	31,012	31,713	30,889	27,327	26,414	25,335	28,957	32,077	36,304	33,516
1995	36,705	30,958	30,736	28,035	28,294	28,729	29,959	31,599	34,183	31,312	31,519	35,127
1996	35,253	34,823	38,730	42,900	41,916	36,620	35,616	32,541	32,591	34,329	33,148	32,163
1997	33,105	33,953	31,289	34,071	41,978	37,398	36,141	33,712	31,483	36,928	39,363	39,394
1998	45,908	42,241	38,965	33,610	34,257	32,456	32,085	31,199	34,165	34,051	42,224	45,241
1999	46,003	44,211	43,803	48,277	55,951	52,398	54,723	49,915	53,055	54,089	54,432	50,691
2000	49,209	54,094	57,472	68,535	64,938	54,208	45,730	38,233	38,802	38,254	40,075	45,141

¹ Data thru October 1995 are Live Hogs, November 1995 thru December 1996 are Live Hogs and Lean Hogs.
Source: Chicago Mercantile Exchange (CME)

Volume of Trading of Lean Hog¹ Futures in Chicago   In Contracts

Year	Jan.	Feb.	Mar.	Apr.	May	June	July	Aug.	Sept.	Oct.	Nov.	Dec.	Total²
1991	177,858	150,267	147,953	156,966	155,739	120,815	131,142	120,855	102,890	118,445	104,470	94,834	1,582.2
1992	135,226	136,997	140,411	138,248	116,738	131,209	148,754	102,165	116,565	149,458	117,023	123,298	1,556.1
1993	131,475	96,320	159,973	137,528	120,200	121,096	112,493	91,496	109,402	102,722	116,081	102,968	1,401.8
1994	144,701	96,736	146,934	93,105	127,381	144,373	116,181	122,058	110,697	128,980	150,744	172,132	1,554.0
1995	155,766	115,800	181,919	116,767	145,350	155,295	139,013	144,590	135,262	132,122	142,460	136,191	1,700.7
1996	177,299	138,002	150,117	216,476	208,696	177,359	185,872	157,540	158,077	203,789	170,586	152,098	2,095.9
1997	180,241	159,600	200,118	212,810	222,759	188,615	181,637	146,297	149,950	175,135	152,876	130,871	2,100.9
1998	180,241	182,698	174,752	132,952	155,737	167,767	185,427	157,973	164,964	173,163	218,950	241,767	2,136.3
1999	218,608	171,108	196,825	189,773	214,852	237,240	239,096	167,787	190,238	187,794	205,505	139,270	2,358.1
2000	175,399	186,352	231,532	158,765	218,222	235,036	172,725	145,849	146,240	142,240	153,043	146,404	2,111.8

¹ Data thru October 1995 are Live Hogs, November 1995 thru December 1996 are Live Hogs and Lean Hogs.   ² In thousands of contracts.
Source: Chicago Mercantile Exchange (CME)

Honey

The world's honey production declined steadily during the 1990's, and the downtrend appears likely to persist. The long-term decline largely reflects a contraction in the number of beekeepers and producing bee colonies. Also, the steady expansion of the more aggressive Africanized bees virtually erased honey production in some countries. On a shorter-term basis, weather can have a decisive impact on honey production if its effect harms the flowering plants that bees need to make honey.

China is the world's largest producer with more than one-third of total global production. Their annual production in the second half of the 1990's averaged 180,000 metric tonnes compared to the total world production of 467,000 tonnes. In the first half of the 1990's, total world production averaged over 600,000 tonnes. U.S. production currently ranks a distant second followed by Argentina and Mexico. The latter two nations increased output during the past decade, especially Argentina with a near 100 percent increase, while China's production declined about 5 percent during the same period.

U.S. honey production from producers with five or more colonies in 1999 totaled 205 million pounds, down 7 percent from 220 million pounds in 1998. The 1990's high was 231 million pounds set in 1993. There were 2.69 million producing colonies in 1999, up marginally from 1998, however, colonies are not counted if honey is not harvested. The annual yield per colony, which may be understated, shows wide variations averaging 76.3 pounds in 1999, vs. 83.7 pounds in 1998, and annual average during the 1990's of about 75 pounds. Producer honey stocks of 79.4 million pounds as of December 15, 1999, compares with 80.8 million a year earlier. Honey is produced is almost every state, but California is the leading producer with 30.3 million pounds in 1999 vs. 37.4 million in 1998. Other leading producing states include North and South Dakota, Florida, and Minnesota.

The U.S. imports honey, averaging more than 100 million pounds per year, whereas exports generally total less than 10 million pounds. Argentina is generally the largest exporter of honey to the U.S., followed by China at a distant second.

U.S. prices for the 1999 crop averaged 59.9 cents per pound, down 8 percent from 65.5 cents in 1998, and compared with a 1995-99 average of about 71 cents. Prices are based on retail sales by producers and sales to private processors and co-ops. At the state level prices reflect the portions of honey sold retail, co-op, and private. At the U.S. level, prices for each color, which range from white to amber, are derived by weighting quantities sold for each marketing channel. The total value of production in 1999 of $125 million compares with $147 million in 1998.

World Production of Honey   In Metric Tons

Year	Argentina	Australia	Brazil	Canada	China	Germany	Japan	Mexico	Russia	United States	Total[2]
1994	64,000	24,000	19,000	32,920	177,000	22,233	3,500	41,500	43,900	98,500	526,553
1995	70,000	24,000	19,200	30,575	178,000	36,685	3,500	49,228	44,000	95,490	550,678
1996	57,000	-----	-----	24,895	184,000	14,674	-----	47,997	-----	89,850	418,416
1997	70,000	-----	-----	30,021	207,000	15,069	-----	53,681	-----	89,148	464,919
1998	75,000	-----	-----	42,456	155,000	16,306	-----	56,061	-----	99,932	444,755
1999[1]	85,000	-----	-----	34,000	180,000	13,000	-----	57,500	-----	90,000	459,500

[1] Preliminary.   [2] Only for countries listed.   *Source: Foreign Agricultural Service, U.S. Department of Agriculture (FAS-USDA)*

Salient Statistics of Honey in the United States   In Millions of Pounds

Year	Number of Colonies (1,000)	Yield Per Colony Pounds	Stocks Jan. 1	Total U.S. Production	Imports for Consumption	Domestic Disappearance	Exports	Total Supply	Placed Under Loan	CCC Take Over	Net Gov't Expenditure[3] Mil. $	Domestic Avg. Price All Honey Cents Per Pound	National Avg. Price Support Cents Per Pound	Per Capita Consumption Pounds
1995	2,655	79.5	94.1	211.1	88.6	341.6	9.3	393.2	64.4	0	-9.3	68.5	50.0	1.0
1996	2,581	77.3	42.2	199.5	150.6	334.1	9.9	390.9	----	----	----	88.8	----	----
1997	2,631	74.7	47.0	196.5	167.4	328.8	8.9	406.8	----	----	----	75.2	----	----
1998	2,633	83.7	69.1	220.3	132.3	332.9	9.9	397.5	----	----	----	65.5	----	----
1999[1]	2,688	76.4	79.4	205.3										
2000[2]	2,634	83.9	86.2	221.0										

[1] Preliminary.   [2] Forecast.   [3] Fiscal year.   *Source: Economic Research Service, U.S. Department of Agriculture (ERS-USDA)*

Production and Yield of Honey in the United States

Year	Production in Thousands of Pounds						Value of Production $1,000	Yield per Colony in Pounds					
	California	Florida	Minnesota	North Dakota	South Dakota	Total		California	Florida	Minnesota	North Dakota	South Dakota	Average
1995	39,060	19,780	13,530	23,760	2,040	210,516	144,203	93	86	82	108	85	79.5
1996	27,300	25,200	11,550	19,780	23,280	198,197	175,999	70	105	77	86	97	77.3
1997	31,500	16,080	10,585	24,500	15,600	196,536	147,795	75	67	73	100	65	74.7
1998	37,350	22,540	11,060	29,440	21,375	220,316	147,254	83	98	79	128	95	83.7
1999	30,300	23,256	11,890	26,775	23,296	205,250	126,075	60	102	82	105	104	76.4
2000[1]	30,800	24,360	13,500	33,350	28,435	221,005	132,205	70	105	90	115	121	83.9

[1] Preliminary.   *Source: National Agricultural Statistics Service, U.S. Department of Agriculture (NASS-USDA)*

Interest Rates, U.S.

In late 1999, the Federal Reserve opted to adopt a preemptive stance against potential inflationary pressures and the tighter monetary policy carried into 2000. During the year plus period, short-term interest rates were raised six times. By year-end 2000, the marketplace consensus was that the Fed had overreacted to inflation fears, notwithstanding higher oil prices, and what was happening instead was a sharper than expected brake on the U.S. economy's growth. In the first half of 2000, the Gross Domestic Product was growing at more than 5 percent annually, by the fourth quarter the growth rate had fallen to less than 2 percent. During the year, real interest rates adjusted for inflation reached their highest level in fifteen years.

Moreover, the Fed's timing was questioned. In May, rates were raised 50 basis points after a sharp decline had occurred in the equities markets, the impact of which further cut into the wealth effect that the equities markets were thought to have given American consumers. By late 2000, the Fed's rachet tightening policy showed signs of backfiring, and at year-end the greater fear was that unless the Fed's policy was reversed in early 2001, the so-called soft landing could instead crash into a recession. Meanwhile, inflationary pressures in 2000, on both the producer and consumer levels, were largely benign, as they were in 1999.

The year 2000 also saw a switch in the market's benchmark rate from the 30-year Treasury bond to the 10-year Treasury Note due to a concerted Treasury effort to reduce the supply of 30-year paper. At yearend 2000, the 10-year T-note yield of 5.08 percent compared with 6.38 a year earlier; 3 month T-bills were at 5.71 percent vs. 5.05; fed funds were at 6.50 percent vs. 5.50; and the 30-year T-bond was at 5.42 percent vs. 6.44. The prime rate was at 9.50 percent, up from 7.75, and the discount rate was at 6.00 percent vs. 5.00 at year-end 1999. However, municipal bond rates fell during 2000, with the year-end yield of about 5.40 percent comparing with 6.22 a year earlier, and virtually a mirror image of 1999 when muni rates rose about a full point.

In the U.S. Treasury debt market major changes occurred, that over time are expected to shrink what was a $3.4 trillion market at year-end 2000. By mid-2001, if not earlier, the one-year T-bill is expected to be retired, the legislation making it possible approved in 2000. Also, the issuance of the popular two-year note will be reduced, possibly to $40 billion per year from $120 billion in 2000. In addition, the end of the 30-year T-bond may occur, the issuance of which was down to $15 billion of late, from as much as $47 billion in the year 1991. The Treasury is expected to repurchase as much as $40 billion of outstanding Treasury securities in 2001, vs. $30 billion bought in 2000. The rational behind the Treasury's moves is the expected U.S. governmental surplus, estimated at $268 billion for fiscal 2001, and $345 billion in fiscal 2002. These forecasts could prove optimistic considering the uncertainties for the economy in 2001, as well as the advent of a new administration and their preliminary policy objectives calling for tax cuts.

Futures Markets

A futures (and options) contract exists for almost every maturity on the yield curve, as well as for municipal and commercial credit risks. Major U.S. contracts include Eurodollars on Chicago's International Monetary Market (IMM), and T-bonds, 10-year T-notes, 5-year T-notes and 2-year T-notes on the Chicago Board of Trade (CBOT). Futures are also traded in Chicago on municipal bonds, 30-day fed funds, one-month LIBOR, and yield curve spreads. Smaller size contracts on some interest rate instruments are listed at the MidAmerica Commodity Exchange.

U.S. Producer Price Index[2] (Wholesale, All Commodities)   1982 = 100

Year	Jan.	Feb.	Mar.	Apr.	May	June	July	Aug.	Sept.	Oct.	Nov.	Dec.	Average
1992	115.6	116.0	116.1	116.3	117.2	118.0	117.9	117.7	118.0	118.1	117.8	117.6	117.2
1993	118.0	118.4	118.7	119.3	119.7	119.5	119.2	118.7	118.7	119.1	119.0	118.6	118.9
1994	119.1	119.3	119.7	119.7	119.9	120.5	120.7	121.2	120.9	120.9	121.5	121.9	120.4
1995	122.9	123.5	123.9	124.6	124.9	125.3	125.3	125.1	125.2	125.3	125.4	125.7	124.8
1996	126.3	126.2	126.4	127.4	128.1	128.0	128.0	128.3	128.2	128.0	128.2	129.1	127.7
1997	129.7	128.5	127.3	127.0	127.4	127.2	126.9	127.2	127.5	127.8	127.9	126.8	127.6
1998	125.4	125.0	124.7	124.9	125.1	124.8	124.9	124.2	123.8	124.0	123.6	122.8	124.4
1999	122.9	122.3	122.6	123.6	124.7	125.2	125.7	126.9	128.0	127.7	128.3	127.8	125.5
2000[1]	128.3	129.8	130.8	130.7	131.6	133.8	133.7	132.9	134.7	135.1	134.6	135.7	132.6

[1] Preliminary.   [2] Not seasonally adjusted.   *Source: Bureau of Labor Statistics, U.S. Department of Commerce (BLS)*

U.S. Consumer Price Index[2] (Retail Price Index for All Items: Urban Consumers)   1982-84 = 100

Year	Jan.	Feb.	Mar.	Apr.	May	June	July	Aug.	Sept.	Oct.	Nov.	Dec.	Average
1992	138.1	138.6	139.3	139.5	139.7	140.2	140.5	140.9	141.3	141.8	142.0	141.9	140.3
1993	142.6	143.1	143.6	144.0	144.2	144.4	144.4	144.8	145.1	145.7	145.8	145.8	144.5
1994	146.2	146.7	147.2	147.4	147.5	148.0	148.4	149.0	149.4	149.5	149.7	149.7	148.2
1995	150.3	150.9	151.4	151.9	152.2	152.5	152.5	152.9	153.2	153.7	153.6	153.5	152.4
1996	154.4	154.9	155.7	156.3	156.6	156.7	157.0	157.3	157.8	158.3	158.6	158.6	157.0
1997	159.1	159.6	159.8	160.0	160.1	160.4	160.6	160.9	161.3	161.6	161.8	161.9	160.6
1998	161.9	162.0	162.0	162.4	162.8	163.0	163.2	163.4	163.6	163.9	164.2	164.4	163.1
1999	164.6	164.8	165.1	166.2	166.2	166.2	166.7	167.2	167.8	168.1	168.4	168.8	166.7
2000[1]	169.2	170.1	171.3	171.3	171.5	172.4	172.8	172.7	173.6	173.9	174.2	174.5	172.3

[1] Preliminary.   [2] Not seasonally adjusted.   *Source: Bureau of Labor Statistics, U.S. Department of Commerce (BLS)*

Average Open Interest of 13 Week[1] Treasury Bill Futures in Chicago   In Thousands of Contracts

Year	Jan.	Feb.	Mar.	Apr.	May	June	July	Aug.	Sept.	Oct.	Nov.	Dec.
1991	55,371	53,484	38,259	43,538	53,941	51,178	55,514	55,999	47,509	50,865	57,680	51,750
1992	51,312	45,902	35,539	44,757	47,734	41,091	38,399	35,638	29,781	32,556	35,379	29,566
1993	32,544	35,756	32,556	39,115	40,724	34,614	30,895	34,177	28,983	30,121	33,800	30,996
1994	36,456	41,150	43,243	51,485	41,164	34,580	32,572	29,559	24,522	32,325	30,077	22,322
1995	21,065	26,289	33,420	35,873	34,608	25,930	20,534	19,195	18,929	16,781	16,384	11,279
1996	14,769	16,906	14,161	14,460	15,709	10,285	8,973	9,770	6,536	6,906	7,516	7,002
1997	8,114	9,793	9,968	10,390	10,048	8,949	8,425	9,760	7,899	9,497	11,223	10,679
1998	10,295	11,647	7,903	4,993	3,818	4,123	4,330	4,407	2,840	1,929	2,123	2,264
1999	2,179	2,998	2,720	1,523	2,367	1,586	690	909	471	476	1,033	2,321
2000	2,466	2,464	1,467	706	717	691	647	1,295	1,836	1,239	1,642	2,219

[1] 90-day U.S. Treasury Bill.   *Source: International Monetary Market (IOM), division of the Chicago Mercantile Exchange (CME)*

Volume of Trading of 13 Week[1] Treasury Bill Futures in Chicago   In Contracts

Year	Jan.	Feb.	Mar.	Apr.	May	June	July	Aug.	Sept.	Oct.	Nov.	Dec.	Total[2]
1991	252,890	193,880	166,801	163,962	187,955	173,255	141,651	222,919	110,978	110,297	139,435	141,642	2,012.1
1992	143,844	137,933	144,984	115,861	106,459	106,107	85,838	76,187	102,992	127,015	106,450	833,921	1,337.1
1993	86,062	100,444	97,041	65,612	103,198	105,960	71,711	75,685	89,276	69,060	87,350	65,951	1,017.4
1994	59,771	136,974	115,874	104,387	99,385	89,399	53,725	60,937	77,599	57,428	81,192	83,820	1,020.5
1995	72,240	79,970	90,311	37,388	58,707	49,932	28,081	41,495	44,396	36,904	46,582	34,219	620.2
1996	31,957	36,039	36,514	17,897	16,574	25,193	11,984	19,383	19,783	10,835	10,397	14,342	250.9
1997	10,603	19,432	20,602	11,552	16,633	14,916	11,540	15,418	19,045	20,437	16,775	22,131	199.1
1998	18,492	14,290	14,434	9,470	9,394	7,558	3,411	7,629	5,172	4,761	3,855	5,714	104.2
1999	4,837	6,085	6,499	2,892	3,566	3,173	1,934	2,019	590	829	2,075	6,761	41.3
2000	1,621	886	3,201	379	789	1,320	394	1,721	1,228	596	3,231	1,397	16.8

[1] 90-day U.S. Treasury Bill.   [2] In thousands of contracts.   *Source: International Monetary Market (IOM), division of the Chicago Mercantile Exchange*

INTEREST RATES, U.S.

30-Year Treasury Bond Futures - Chicago Board of Trade (weekly close) as of 29-Dec-2000 — Nominal Value

Average Open Interest of 30-year U.S. Treasury Bond Futures in Chicago   In Contracts

Year	Jan.	Feb.	Mar.	Apr.	May	June	July	Aug.	Sept.	Oct.	Nov.	Dec.
1991	257,229	279,378	250,028	283,473	279,443	254,983	273,774	325,303	310,110	304,198	317,445	301,604
1992	343,156	353,782	318,737	313,742	346,542	347,293	370,850	427,723	385,645	364,250	362,231	321,706
1993	336,327	375,435	361,675	362,404	370,485	349,285	361,393	396,411	388,188	360,859	359,739	337,575
1994	380,057	422,902	454,539	500,790	497,296	421,286	441,884	451,462	447,924	436,684	449,642	397,554
1995	384,356	389,908	369,989	367,964	399,500	421,234	438,267	381,237	361,394	395,346	447,409	426,384
1996	382,001	403,403	395,338	381,926	413,944	443,644	464,145	471,203	420,622	409,950	463,731	479,086
1997	497,539	545,775	509,573	493,511	554,418	480,669	530,011	608,474	624,231	723,321	719,186	737,703
1998	744,894	764,309	766,233	806,559	888,215	1,040,659	1,084,889	1,061,223	837,986	769,932	782,677	662,025
1999	657,180	801,115	664,131	618,453	717,453	674,225	672,983	748,974	647,816	621,816	637,656	561,919
2000	637,023	612,298	530,957	503,412	434,771	390,928	394,075	440,437	402,156	399,880	443,282	445,386

Source: Chicago Board of Trade (CBT)

Volume of Trading of 30-year U.S. Treasury Bond Futures in Chicago   In Thousands of Contracts

Year	Jan.	Feb.	Mar.	Apr.	May	June	July	Aug.	Sept.	Oct.	Nov.	Dec.	Total
1991	5,804.0	5,717.0	5,658.0	5,957.0	6,186.0	5,582.0	4,293.0	6,592.0	4,765.0	6,450.0	6,239.0	4,643.0	67,886.0
1992	7,523.4	6,270.1	6,793.4	4,810.1	5,417.7	4,828.8	6,081.0	6,085.5	5,953.3	6,870.7	5,287.8	4,083.0	70,004.8
1993	5,577.4	6,482.7	7,902.9	6,156.1	6,799.8	5,817.2	6,218.4	6,914.5	7,443.9	6,537.4	8,193.5	5,384.5	79,428.5
1994	7,287.8	8,430.2	10,836.7	9,557.4	9,999.0	9,804.0	6,987.0	7,910.0	7,913.0	7,004.0	8,533.0	5,699.0	99,960.0
1995	7,058.0	7,714.0	9,623.8	5,835.4	8,721.5	8,446.7	5,790.2	7,083.7	7,317.1	6,927.2	6,626.3	5,232.1	86,375.9
1996	7,528.6	8,781.4	7,199.3	6,010.6	7,932.3	6,520.6	6,422.1	6,625.8	6,926.1	6,772.4	7,297.7	6,708.4	84,725.1
1997	8,104.7	7,522.8	7,493.3	7,519.9	8,339.1	7,400.2	7,679.8	10,228.1	8,356.2	12,467.6	7,735.5	6,980.4	99,827.7
1998	9,595.3	9,368.1	9,763.9	8,516.7	9,054.1	10,208.6	8,070.9	12,024.8	11,159.2	10,698.1	8,155.0	5,609.2	112,224.1
1999	8,075.2	10,031.5	8,667.5	7,196.9	9,555.8	8,072.1	6,415.1	7,995.2	6,559.6	6,301.1	6,909.0	4,263.5	90,042.3
2000	7,966.4	8,157.4	5,378.6	5,282.3	5,972.9	4,458.6	3,080.0	4,709.9	4,529.2	4,460.4	5,072.8	3,682.3	62,750.8

Source: Chicago Board of Trade (CBT)

3-Month Eurodollar Futures - International Monetary Market (weekly close) as of 29-Dec-2000

Average Open Interest of 3-month Eurodollar Futures in Chicago   In Thousands of Contracts

Year	Jan.	Feb.	Mar.	Apr.	May	June	July	Aug.	Sept.	Oct.	Nov.	Dec.
1991	630.9	722.7	741.1	767.6	857.4	835.2	797.9	883.1	916.7	949.5	1,054.7	1,067.2
1992	1,129.8	1,213.7	1,244.6	1,269.1	1,377.2	1,382.7	1,434.1	1,549.9	1,537.0	1,537.6	1,547.0	1,418.7
1993	1,429.4	1,586.7	1,643.3	1,653.4	1,782.8	1,739.1	1,777.7	1,918.4	1,940.7	2,026.5	2,149.0	2,150.2
1994	2,300.5	2,529.5	2,568.1	2,627.3	2,734.3	2,565.2	2,599.1	2,703.8	2,699.6	2,561.2	2,660.3	2,606.3
1995	2,443.6	2,535.4	2,463.9	2,447.4	2,503.3	2,390.8	2,279.5	2,374.6	2,347.2	2,290.3	2,405.5	2,480.5
1996	2,519.4	2,638.6	2,511.4	2,483.5	2,571.8	2,590.1	2,504.4	2,485.5	2,392.4	2,349.7	2,378.2	2,225.7
1997	2,190.8	2,333.2	2,423.1	2,523.1	2,671.3	2,706.5	2,699.2	2,788.0	2,769.3	2,815.1	2,799.5	2,661.6
1998	2,713.4	2,821.5	2,797.9	2,892.6	3,089.0	3,093.9	3,027.7	3,223.0	3,359.9	3,303.4	3,297.4	3,000.1
1999	2,917.9	3,039.5	2,973.5	2,894.7	3,183.2	3,208.8	3,064.4	3,115.6	2,904.0	2,918.2	2,879.7	2,859.4
2000	2,971.3	3,261.4	3,138.7	3,156.6	3,331.7	3,272.1	3,160.3	3,225.7	3,181.8	3,067.2	3,201.1	3,349.7

Source: International Monetary Market (IOM), division of the Chicago Mercantile Exchange (CME)

Volume of Trading of 3-month Eurodollar Futures in Chicago   In Thousands of Contracts

Year	Jan.	Feb.	Mar.	Apr.	May	June	July	Aug.	Sept.	Oct.	Nov.	Dec.	Total
1991	2,859.0	2,635.0	3,445.0	3,208.0	2,458.0	2,972.0	2,629.0	4,035.0	3,000.0	3,505.0	3,301.0	3,196.0	37,243.0
1992	5,365.7	4,418.5	5,582.8	4,942.2	4,819.0	4,602.6	5,357.8	4,016.3	4,705.2	6,691.6	5,461.3	4,568.1	60,531.1
1993	5,556.8	5,003.8	6,013.8	4,059.4	5,977.8	5,672.9	5,656.7	4,494.2	6,340.6	4,888.4	6,269.8	4,477.3	64,411.4
1994	6,074.8	8,745.3	9,468.9	9,639.2	11,494.0	9,348.0	7,810.0	7,128.0	7,641.0	7,992.0	9,715.0	9,766.0	104,823.0
1995	10,341.1	10,429.3	9,549.0	6,069.2	9,897.1	10,104.7	6,669.9	7,013.5	7,171.1	6,477.9	6,055.2	5,952.1	95,730.0
1996	7,485.7	9,267.2	9,526.3	6,872.4	7,413.7	7,415.0	8,323.2	6,967.5	8,232.5	7,014.5	5,056.9	5,308.1	88,883.1
1997	7,903.4	6,918.0	8,936.4	9,351.7	8,447.4	8,049.7	7,291.6	9,295.4	7,634.7	12,569.7	6,314.1	7,058.2	99,770.2
1998	10,908.0	7,861.4	8,842.1	9,488.4	7,202.4	8,349.5	5,452.3	9,811.3	13,593.9	11,756.9	9,627.8	6,578.5	109,472.5
1999	7,470.9	7,674.5	8,718.6	7,346.5	8,957.0	9,649.8	7,746.3	8,898.0	7,629.1	7,500.6	6,223.2	5,604.0	93,418.5
2000	8,379.6	9,723.0	10,197.8	10,171.8	10,261.3	9,791.3	7,384.8	7,009.6	8,204.6	9,276.4	7,561.4	10,152.3	108,115.0

Source: International Monetary Market (IOM), division of the Chicago Mercantile Exchange (CME)

INTEREST RATES, U.S.

10-Year Treasury Note Futures - Chicago Board of Trade (weekly close) as of 29-Dec-2000 — Nominal Value

Average Open Interest of 10-year U.S. Treasury Note Futures in Chicago   In Contracts

Year	Jan.	Feb.	Mar.	Apr.	May	June	July	Aug.	Sept.	Oct.	Nov.	Dec.
1991	72,621	79,355	79,413	71,451	84,203	81,884	85,527	94,379	96,836	93,187	95,450	87,063
1992	119,739	114,521	106,497	102,862	112,666	126,228	143,924	158,831	179,045	191,725	199,990	195,705
1993	190,018	206,852	198,653	209,221	229,378	217,521	233,458	238,189	237,243	237,877	273,336	262,831
1994	264,848	258,643	300,080	328,821	294,091	254,612	232,373	253,233	273,564	277,313	301,000	271,992
1995	282,978	285,187	265,747	263,816	273,945	289,052	306,046	323,078	277,011	278,832	270,527	249,073
1996	260,374	297,850	285,501	319,234	331,032	293,416	302,330	326,391	291,208	284,581	313,298	303,702
1997	332,285	343,661	323,982	348,683	350,814	336,927	363,744	407,147	387,284	398,645	404,980	374,448
1998	430,335	507,986	474,916	494,417	533,214	513,369	512,173	604,862	555,268	482,928	508,299	503,533
1999	528,538	549,518	515,404	510,091	541,057	574,514	588,272	623,806	607,305	653,080	582,003	487,888
2000	595,180	653,822	571,932	615,618	621,361	583,900	608,358	602,068	547,582	564,606	555,189	508,888

Source: Chicago Board of Trade (CBT)

Volume of Trading of 10-year U.S. Treasury Note Futures in Chicago   In Thousands of Contracts

Year	Jan.	Feb.	Mar.	Apr.	May	June	July	Aug.	Sept.	Oct.	Nov.	Dec.	Total
1991	507.7	519.6	508.3	466.5	566.9	456.6	318.9	705.9	467.2	573.2	661.3	591.4	6,342.0
1992	929.6	866.4	824.9	531.2	758.9	683.3	859.4	1,047.7	1,138.5	1,300.2	1,225.8	1,052.1	11,218.0
1993	1,134.6	1,286.3	1,763.1	1,089.5	1,341.4	1,390.6	1,147.0	1,390.7	1,523.7	1,279.5	1,926.6	1,328.2	16,601.2
1994	1,484.3	1,935.7	2,572.4	2,213.5	2,399.4	2,250.2	1,621.8	2,028.7	1,932.9	1,635.1	2,253.6	1,750.2	24,078.0
1995	1,752.6	1,978.8	2,458.7	1,368.2	2,236.5	2,495.8	1,588.9	2,028.7	1,859.0	1,459.7	1,730.8	1,487.6	22,445.4
1996	1,649.1	2,313.1	2,075.8	1,632.1	2,211.3	1,715.6	1,556.3	1,865.7	1,810.4	1,494.7	1,904.5	1,711.2	21,939.7
1997	1,780.5	1,939.9	2,051.8	1,703.2	2,025.6	1,942.3	1,509.6	2,535.9	2,062.5	2,593.7	1,825.6	1,991.2	23,961.8
1998	2,393.5	2,748.7	2,817.5	2,342.1	2,695.9	2,681.9	1,704.1	3,632.2	3,560.3	2,882.7	2,912.2	2,111.5	32,482.6
1999	2,269.1	3,562.1	2,993.8	2,145.3	3,519.3	3,153.0	2,438.5	3,735.6	2,508.7	2,470.9	3,201.5	2,048.0	34,045.8
2000	3,557.0	4,974.7	3,750.4	3,529.7	4,711.6	3,706.0	2,580.9	4,459.8	3,779.5	3,824.3	4,513.6	3,313.1	46,700.5

Source: Chicago Board of Trade (CBT)

5-Year Treasury Note Futures - Chicago Board of Trade (weekly close) as of 29-Dec-2000   Nominal Value

Average Open Interest of 5-Year U.S. Treasury Note Futures in Chicago   In Contracts

Year	Jan.	Feb.	Mar.	Apr.	May	June	July	Aug.	Sept.	Oct.	Nov.	Dec.
1991	80,059	82,666	83,109	74,612	75,799	65,543	72,197	86,981	85,794	91,096	102,890	99,291
1992	116,322	121,667	125,155	130,826	135,111	144,386	143,928	143,203	127,418	122,113	129,548	127,690
1993	139,207	150,443	152,711	158,607	169,234	152,262	152,403	160,258	159,754	154,501	181,492	206,914
1994	200,812	213,037	200,626	185,083	192,659	186,026	189,828	182,027	181,518	181,578	176,322	205,150
1995	206,539	210,192	199,357	200,087	213,531	189,332	176,329	173,897	163,419	162,121	177,915	171,023
1996	163,026	184,523	200,253	191,690	179,951	177,370	174,484	179,599	154,764	138,246	155,820	154,764
1997	176,691	208,928	219,540	235,543	227,882	225,691	226,306	225,792	234,309	233,480	248,377	257,886
1998	257,094	270,048	282,327	277,540	274,145	257,193	264,756	389,118	382,855	383,809	353,399	326,860
1999	290,373	268,561	247,526	246,916	311,106	348,627	325,348	341,495	298,861	328,581	272,628	288,523
2000	387,008	475,464	420,789	417,929	428,239	379,628	402,658	405,087	372,779	373,698	381,432	380,248

Source: Chicago Board of Trade (CBT)

Volume of Trading of 5-Year U.S. Treasury Note Futures in Chicago   In Thousands of Contracts

Year	Jan.	Feb.	Mar.	Apr.	May	June	July	Aug.	Sept.	Oct.	Nov.	Dec.	Total
1991	220.5	318.5	252.3	181.4	307.6	232.4	179.7	385.4	243.9	291.5	419.9	353.1	1,064.5
1992	498.6	543.8	560.0	322.2	590.1	551.5	484.2	565.7	582.1	539.0	640.8	563.2	1,743.0
1993	539.5	673.1	886.0	447.6	755.9	753.8	506.4	711.3	753.8	472.6	908.0	715.8	2,096.4
1994	695.9	1,235.1	1,295.4	917.1	1,202.0	1,154.9	834.8	944.9	1,107.3	840.6	1,156.7	1,078.0	12,463.0
1995	988.5	1,296.2	1,386.9	783.4	1,291.1	1,402.9	828.6	1,100.5	1,008.7	769.6	996.0	784.7	12,637.1
1996	837.3	1,312.0	1,084.6	815.7	1,135.5	878.3	881.7	1,061.8	979.0	689.5	831.1	957.1	11,463.4
1997	927.5	1,156.7	1,271.1	984.4	1,190.6	1,143.8	761.4	1,244.6	1,243.7	1,314.1	1,068.1	1,182.8	13,488.7
1998	1,451.9	1,482.0	1,390.7	1,154.7	1,281.1	1,376.9	944.0	2,480.5	1,913.5	1,583.1	1,722.7	1,279.1	18,060.0
1999	1,119.7	1,553.6	1,336.6	1,115.0	1,906.4	1,543.9	1,166.4	2,163.6	1,034.1	1,245.2	1,606.6	1,192.8	16,983.8
2000	1,800.5	2,873.8	2,010.0	1,707.8	2,548.4	1,757.3	1,188.9	2,253.3	1,515.5	1,774.2	2,259.7	1,642.6	23,332.0

Source: Chicago Board of Trade (CBT)

137

INTEREST RATES, U.S.

Municipal Bond Futures - Chicago Board of Trade (weekly close) as of 29-Dec-2000

U.S. Federal Funds Rate   In Percent

Year	Jan.	Feb.	Mar.	Apr.	May	June	July	Aug.	Sept.	Oct.	Nov.	Dec.	Average
1991	6.91	6.25	6.12	5.91	5.78	5.90	5.82	5.66	5.45	5.21	4.81	4.43	5.69
1992	4.03	4.06	3.98	3.73	3.82	3.76	3.25	3.30	3.22	3.10	3.09	2.92	3.52
1993	3.02	3.03	3.07	2.96	3.00	3.04	3.06	3.03	3.09	2.99	3.02	2.96	3.02
1994	3.05	3.25	3.34	3.56	4.01	4.25	4.26	4.47	4.73	4.76	5.29	5.45	4.20
1995	5.53	5.92	5.98	6.05	6.01	6.00	5.85	5.74	5.80	5.76	5.80	5.60	5.84
1996	5.56	5.22	5.31	5.22	5.56	5.27	5.40	5.22	5.30	5.24	5.31	5.29	5.30
1997	5.25	5.19	5.39	5.51	5.50	5.56	5.52	5.54	5.54	5.50	5.52	5.50	5.46
1998	5.56	5.51	5.49	5.45	5.49	5.56	5.54	5.55	5.51	5.07	4.83	4.68	5.35
1999	4.63	4.76	4.81	4.74	4.74	4.76	4.99	5.07	5.22	5.20	5.42	5.30	4.97
2000	5.45	5.73	5.85	6.02	6.27	6.53	6.54	6.50	6.52	6.51	6.51	6.40	6.24

Source: Bureau of Economic Analysis, U.S. Department of Commerce (BEA)

U.S. Municipal Bond Yield[1]   In Percent

Year	Jan.	Feb.	Mar.	Apr.	May	June	July	Aug.	Sept.	Oct.	Nov.	Dec.	Average
1991	7.08	6.91	7.10	7.02	6.95	7.13	7.05	6.90	6.80	6.68	6.73	6.69	6.92
1992	6.54	6.74	6.76	6.67	6.57	6.49	6.13	6.16	6.25	6.41	6.36	6.22	6.44
1993	6.16	5.86	5.85	5.76	5.73	5.63	5.57	5.45	5.29	5.25	5.47	5.35	5.61
1994	5.31	5.40	5.91	6.23	6.19	6.11	6.23	6.21	6.28	6.52	6.97	6.80	6.18
1995	6.53	6.22	6.10	6.02	5.95	5.84	5.92	6.06	5.91	5.80	5.64	5.45	5.95
1996	5.43	5.43	5.79	5.94	5.98	6.02	5.92	5.76	5.87	5.72	5.59	5.64	5.76
1997	5.72	5.63	5.76	5.88	5.70	5.53	5.35	5.41	5.39	5.38	5.33	5.19	5.52
1998	5.06	5.10	5.21	5.23	5.20	5.12	5.14	5.10	4.99	4.93	5.03	4.98	5.09
1999	5.02	5.03	5.10	5.08	5.18	5.37	5.36	5.58	5.69	5.92	5.86	5.95	5.43
2000	6.08	6.00	5.83	5.75	6.00	5.80	5.63	5.51	5.56	5.59	5.54	5.22	5.71

[1] 20-bond average.   *Source: Bureau of Economic Analysis, U.S. Department of Commerce (BEA)*

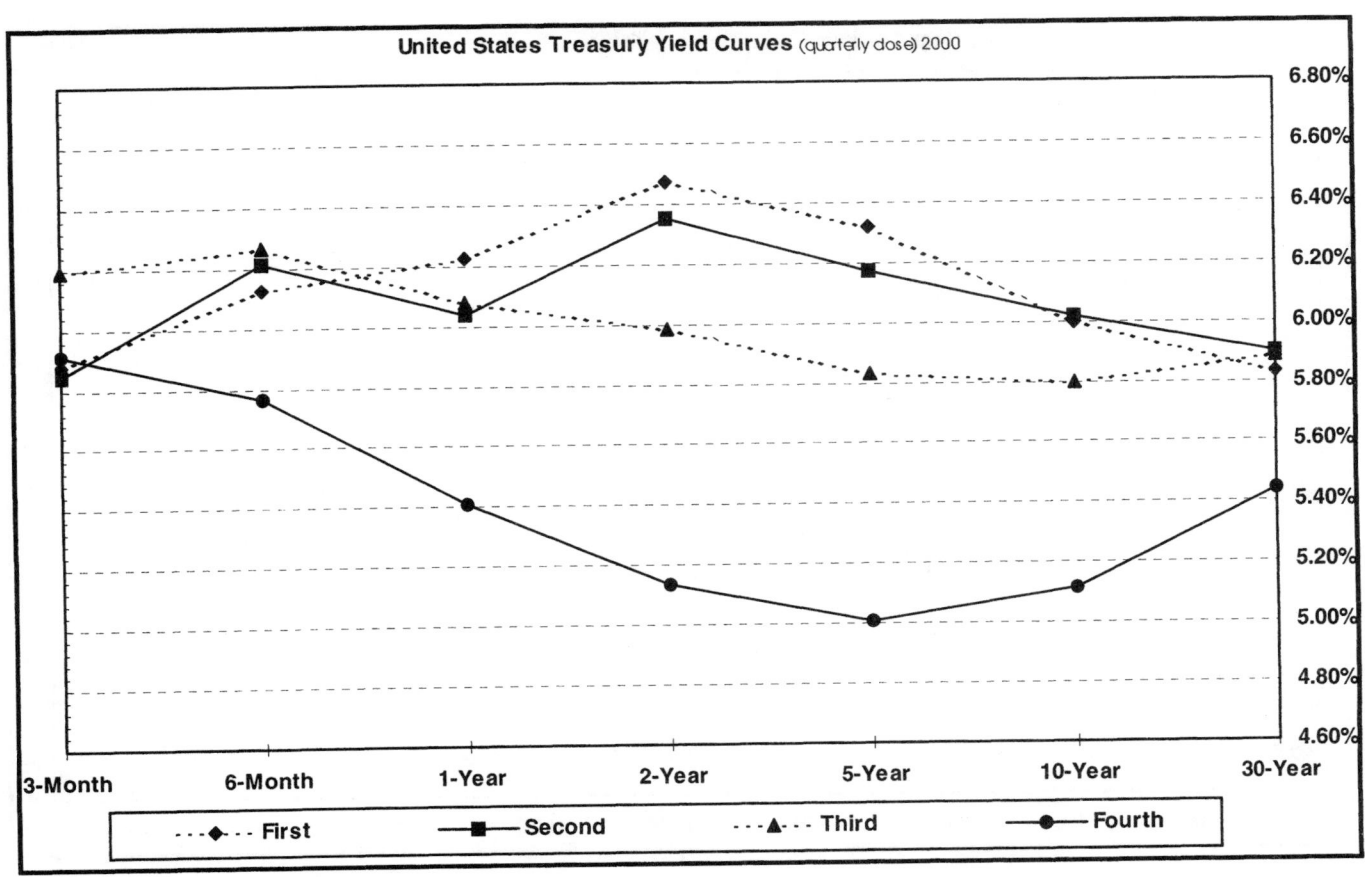

U.S. Industrial Production Index[1]   1992 = 100

Year	Jan.	Feb.	Mar.	Apr.	May	June	July	Aug.	Sept.	Oct.	Nov.	Dec.	Average
1991	96.7	95.9	95.0	95.3	96.0	97.2	97.2	97.4	98.3	98.2	98.1	97.4	96.9
1992	97.5	98.1	98.9	99.6	100.0	99.7	100.4	100.1	100.5	101.3	101.9	101.9	100.0
1993	102.3	102.8	102.8	103.2	102.6	102.8	103.1	102.8	103.9	104.1	104.6	105.4	103.4
1994	105.7	106.2	107.0	107.4	108.1	108.6	109.1	109.2	109.3	109.9	110.6	111.6	108.6
1995	111.9	111.6	111.7	111.4	111.5	111.7	111.7	112.6	113.0	112.5	112.7	112.8	114.5
1996	112.4	113.8	113.2	114.3	114.8	115.5	115.5	115.8	116.0	116.2	120.6	120.9	119.5
1997	121.3	122.1	122.5	123.1	123.3	123.5	124.5	125.2	125.6	129.3	129.9	130.3	127.0
1998	130.3	130.2	130.7	131.3	131.9	130.6	130.5	132.4	131.9	134.1	133.8	133.8	132.4
1999	134.1	134.5	135.1	135.5	136.2	136.6	137.4	137.7	138.1	139.1	141.9	142.8	137.0
2000[2]	143.6	144.3	145.2	146.3	147.2	147.9	147.6	148.7	149.0	148.5	148.1	147.3	147.0

[1] Total Index of the Federal Reserve Index of Quantity Output, seasonally adjusted.   [2] Preliminary.   *Source: Bureau of Economic Analysis,*
U.S. Department of Commerce (BEA)

U.S. Gross National Product, National Income, and Personal Income   In Billions of Constant Dollars[1]

	Gross Domestic Product					National Income					Personal Income				
Year	First Quarter	Second Quarter	Third Quarter	Fourth Quarter	Annual Average	First Quarter	Second Quarter	Third Quarter	Fourth Quarter	Annual Average	First Quarter	Second Quarter	Third Quarter	Fourth Quarter	Annual Average
1991	5,886	5,962	6,016	6,081	5,986	4,704	4,737	4,773	4,813	4,757	5,000	5,064	5,110	5,167	5,085
1992	6,184	6,277	6,346	6,470	6,319	4,935	4,996	4,952	5,097	4,995	5,277	5,352	5,391	5,542	5,390
1993	6,522	6,597	6,656	6,796	6,642	5,150	5,233	5,259	5,366	5,252	5,466	5,595	5,630	5,748	5,610
1994	6,888	7,016	7,096	7,218	7,054	5,373	5,525	5,609	5,720	5,557	5,714	5,861	5,935	6,042	5,888
1995	7,298	7,343	7,433	7,529	7,401	5,775	5,834	5,920	5,978	5,877	6,110	6,163	6,226	6,305	6,201
1996	7,630	7,783	7,859	7,981	7,813	6,067	6,178	6,255	6,343	6,210	6,405	6,509	6,597	6,678	6,547
1997	8,126	8,260	8,365	8,453	8,301	6,474	6,582	6,695	6,790	6,636	6,808	6,901	6,993	7,103	6,951
1998	8,611	8,684	8,798	8,948	8,790	6,887	6,979	7,090	7,199	7,038	7,195	7,296	7,414	7,531	7,391
1999	9,105	9,192	9,341	9,560	9,299	7,313	7,392	7,493	7,681	7,470	7,628	7,730	7,829	7,972	7,790
2000[2]	9,753	9,946	10,063		9,921	7,834	7,983			7,908	8,106	8,242	8,354		8,234

[1] Seasonally adjusted at annual rates.   [2] Preliminary.   *Source: Bureau of Economic Analysis, U.S. Department of Commerce (BEA)*

INTEREST RATES, U.S.

5-Year Treasury Note Yield (monthly average) through December 2000

U.S. Money Supply M1[2]   In Billions of Dollars

Year	Jan.	Feb.	Mar.	Apr.	May	June	July	Aug.	Sept.	Oct.	Nov.	Dec.	Average
1991	826.7	832.8	839.8	842.5	849.1	858.6	861.3	867.2	870.6	877.5	888.6	897.3	859.3
1992	910.0	926.2	936.8	944.3	952.4	954.2	963.2	975.4	988.2	1,003.9	1,016.7	1,025.0	966.4
1993	1,032.0	1,034.0	1,038.4	1,047.8	1,067.5	1,075.4	1,084.7	1,094.5	1,104.2	1,114.3	1,123.6	1,129.8	1,078.9
1994	1,132.8	1,137.3	1,140.1	1,142.4	1,143.5	1,144.7	1,150.9	1,149.7	1,150.8	1,150.4	1,150.4	1,150.7	1,145.3
1995	1,150.3	1,148.4	1,147.1	1,150.4	1,145.1	1,142.7	1,145.0	1,144.0	1,141.6	1,135.7	1,133.1	1,129.0	1,142.7
1996	1,122.2	1,119.8	1,126.2	1,123.5	1,117.1	1,115.5	1,108.8	1,099.8	1,093.3	1,080.3	1,080.1	1,081.1	1,106.1
1997	1,080.8	1,078.8	1,075.0	1,068.3	1,064.3	1,065.4	1,065.6	1,071.1	1,063.5	1,061.9	1,069.2	1,076.0	1,069.6
1998	1,073.8	1,076.0	1,080.6	1,082.1	1,078.2	1,077.8	1,075.4	1,072.2	1,074.7	1,080.4	1,089.3	1,093.7	1,080.9
1999	1,096.0	1,094.3	1,101.4	1,107.2	1,101.7	1,100.1	1,099.5	1,098.7	1,096.1	1,102.5	1,109.6	1,123.0	1,102.5
2000[1]	1,118.9	1,104.5	1,110.4	1,115.1	1,105.9	1,104.7	1,104.9	1,101.5	1,096.7	1,100.9	1,091.1	1,089.4	1,103.7

[1] Preliminary.   [2] M1 -- This measure is currency, travelers checks, plus deposits at commercial banks and interest-earning checkable deposits at all depository institutions.   *Source: Bureau of Economic Analysis, U.S. Department of Commerce (BEA)*

U.S. Money Supply M2[2]   In Billions of Dollars

Year	Jan.	Feb.	Mar.	Apr.	May	June	July	Aug.	Sept.	Oct.	Nov.	Dec.	Average
1991	3,293.4	3,311.1	3,329.4	3,337.9	3,348.0	3,359.1	3,361.0	3,360.5	3,360.0	3,363.9	3,372.5	3,379.6	3,348.0
1992	3,387.7	3,407.1	3,410.5	3,408.8	3,407.4	3,401.3	3,402.2	3,408.9	3,418.2	3,432.0	3,435.3	3,434.0	3,412.8
1993	3,431.3	3,424.0	3,420.4	3,423.6	3,447.6	3,452.9	3,452.7	3,456.8	3,463.6	3,469.7	3,480.2	3,486.6	3,450.8
1994	3,490.8	3,491.7	3,494.3	3,503.0	3,504.0	3,493.7	3,502.1	3,498.2	3,498.4	3,499.4	3,500.9	3,502.1	3,498.2
1995	3,506.3	3,506.1	3,506.7	3,519.1	3,534.9	3,562.9	3,583.1	3,604.4	3,620.1	3,629.8	3,639.3	3,655.0	3,572.3
1996	3,669.9	3,685.0	3,713.9	3,724.5	3,725.6	3,741.9	3,750.0	3,762.7	3,775.3	3,788.1	3,798.3	3,821.8	3,745.6
1997	3,840.7	3,853.3	3,868.9	3,890.0	3,892.5	3,908.0	3,922.5	3,954.8	3,979.3	3,999.3	4,023.6	4,046.4	3,931.5
1998	4,071.4	4,100.9	4,126.2	4,155.2	4,174.8	4,198.6	4,216.1	4,241.7	4,284.2	4,325.5	4,364.4	4,401.4	4,221.9
1999	4,422.4	4,538.5	4,463.4	4,490.4	4,513.0	4,530.9	4,552.8	4,570.5	4,590.0	4,608.8	4,614.6	4,643.7	4,538.5
2000[1]	4,668.8	4,682.0	4,720.1	4,762.3	4,761.0	4,776.5	4,790.9	4,721.3	4,857.5	4,876.0	4,886.9	4,933.1	4,786.4

[1] Preliminary.   [2] M2 -- This measure adds to M1 overnight repurchase agreements (RPs) issued by commercial banks and certain overnight Eurodollars (those issued by Caribbean branches of member banks) held by U.S. nonbank residents, general purpose and broker/dealer money market mutual funds shares (MMMF), and savings and small-denomination time deposits.   *Source: Bureau of Economic Analysis, U.S. Department of Commerce (BEA)*

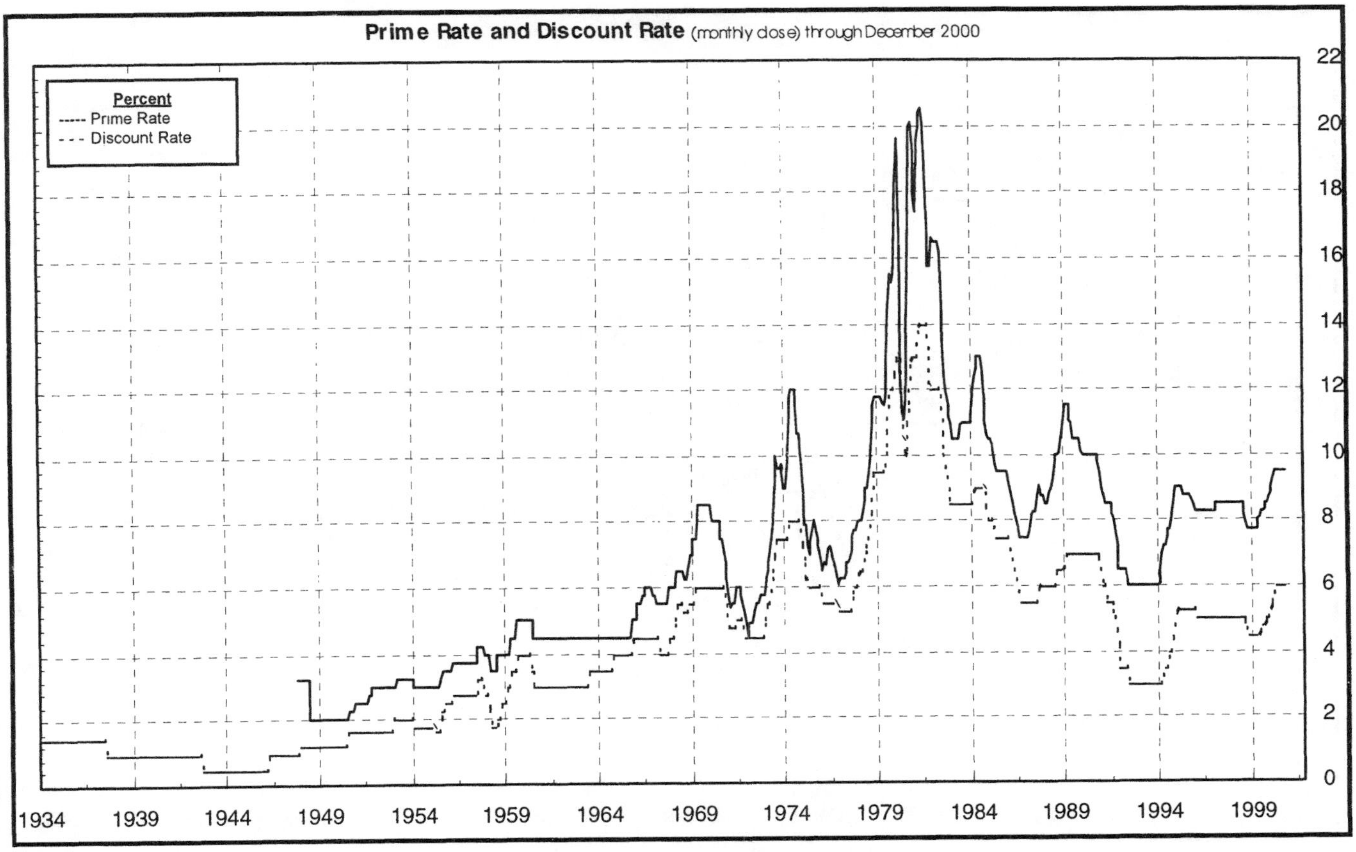
Prime Rate and Discount Rate (monthly close) through December 2000
Percent
----- Prime Rate
- - - Discount Rate
22
20
18
16
14
12
10
8
6
4
2
0
1934
1939
1944
1949
1954
1959
1964
1969
1974
1979
1984
1989
1994
1999

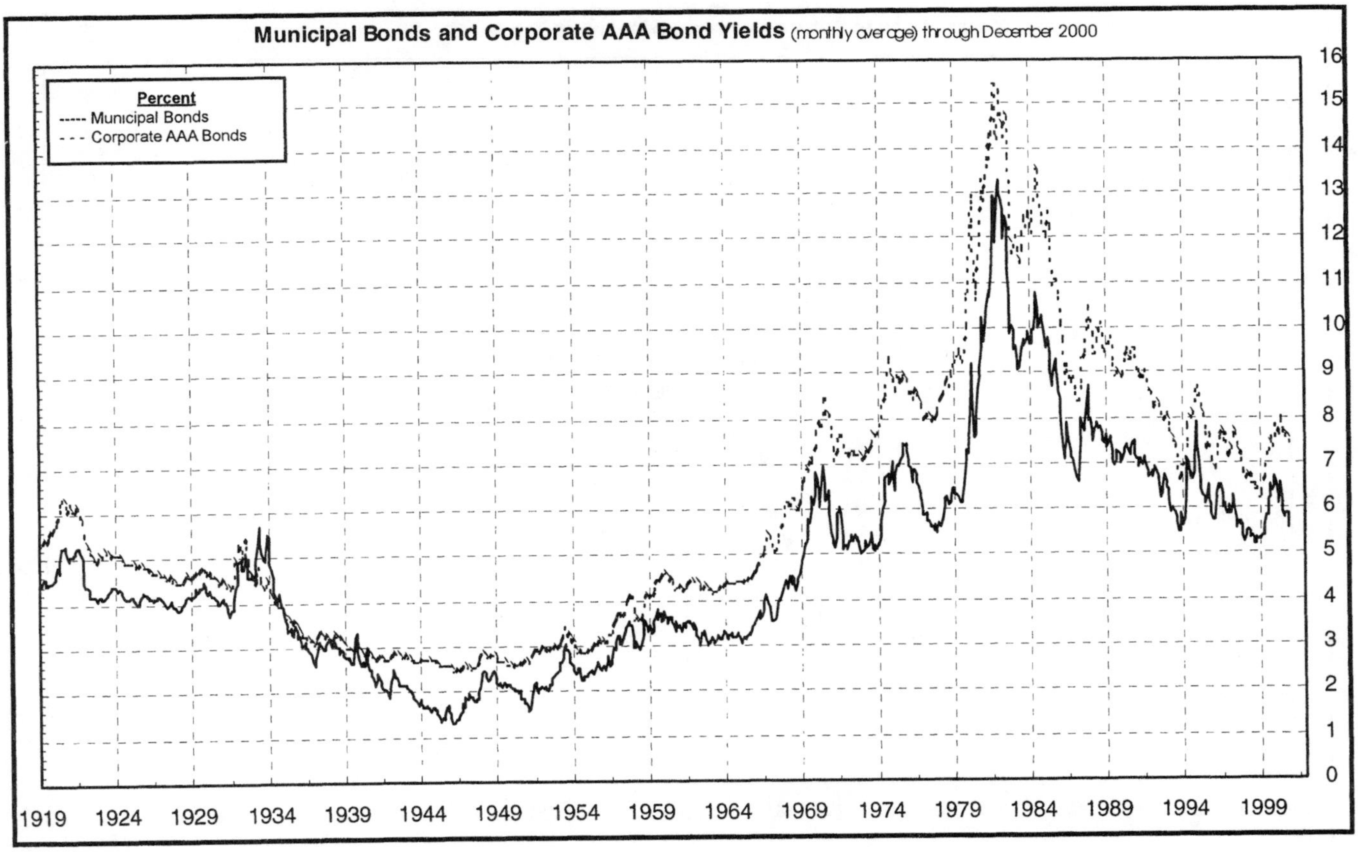
Municipal Bonds and Corporate AAA Bond Yields (monthly average) through December 2000
Percent
----- Municipal Bonds
- - - Corporate AAA Bonds
16
15
14
13
12
11
10
9
8
7
6
5
4
3
2
1
0
1919
1924
1929
1934
1939
1944
1949
1954
1959
1964
1969
1974
1979
1984
1989
1994
1999

INTEREST RATES, U.S.

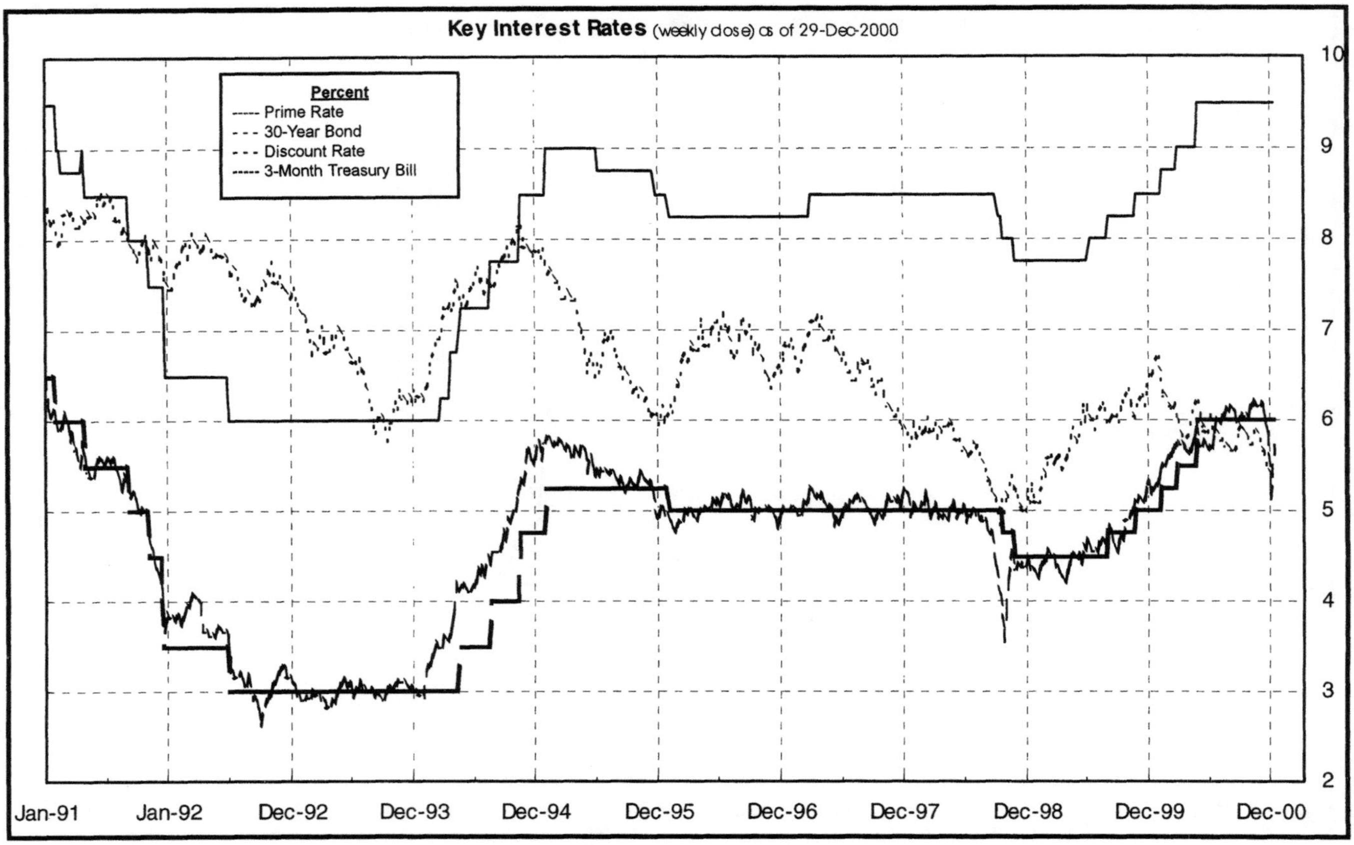

Key Interest Rates (weekly close) as of 29-Dec-2000
Percent
Prime Rate
30-Year Bond
Discount Rate
3-Month Treasury Bill
10
9
8
7
6
5
4
3
2
Jan-91
Jan-92
Dec-92
Dec-93
Dec-94
Dec-95
Dec-96
Dec-97
Dec-98
Dec-99
Dec-00

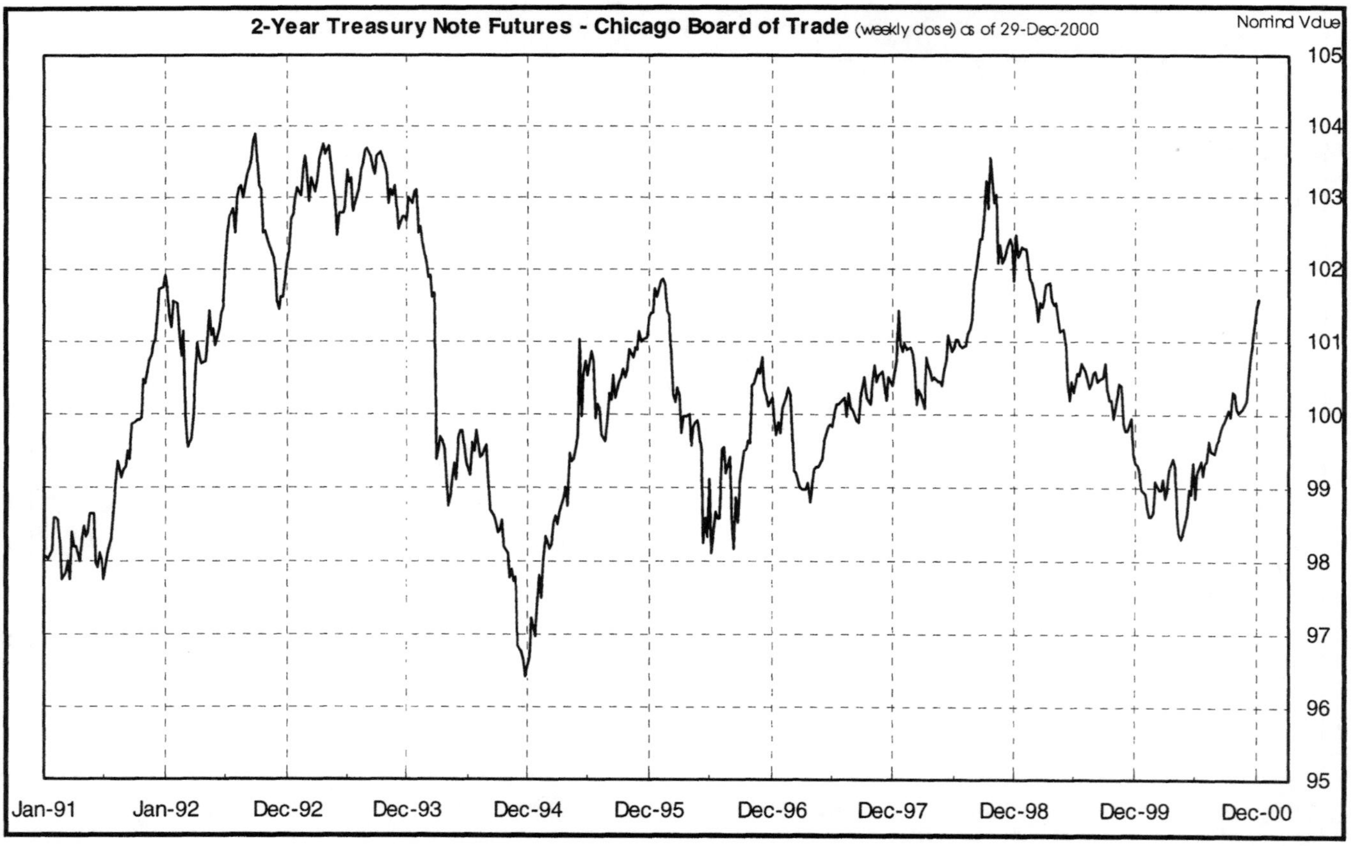

2-Year Treasury Note Futures - Chicago Board of Trade (weekly close) as of 29-Dec-2000
Nominal Value
105
104
103
102
101
100
99
98
97
96
95
Jan-91
Jan-92
Dec-92
Dec-93
Dec-94
Dec-95
Dec-96
Dec-97
Dec-98
Dec-99
Dec-00

Interest Rates, Worldwide

The world's major central banks basically maintained a tight monetary policy in 2000, which was an extension of their approach that began in the second half of 1999. However, while most nations opted to hold interest rates firm, the U.S. Federal Reserve tightened aggressively, but apparently by too much judging by the sharper than expected downturn in the U.S. To a lesser extent, the European Central Bank (E.C.B.) also tightened. The rational for the Fed's tightening was (1) the economy's continued strength, as measured by the Gross Domestic Product (G.D.P.), (2) a very tight labor market, and (3) the Fed's always present fear that the combination of strong growth and low unemployment would cause inflationary pressures to surface. The latter didn't happen, although it should have according to traditional economic theory. The Fed's six rate increases from mid-1999 into 2000 were largely preemptive, if not premature. It's becoming increasingly evident that the old economic rules may not apply to the burgeoning high-tech new economies, where increasing labor productivity is not necessarily prone to cost push inflation. Quite the contrary, increasing productivity may be deflationary.

As the new century unfolds, the role of the central banks are likely to prove a major issue. A century ago there were only 18 central banks, 16 of them in Europe. Now, there are almost 200, and they are generally inclined to claim independence from their national governments. The European Central Bank, as of early 2001, represents twelve of the fifteen European Union nations with a new degree of independence since no one government appoints all of its members.

In Europe, the E.C.B. raised its key rate six times during 2000 to a year ending 4.75 percent from 3.00 a year earlier; but it was still below comparable U.S. and U.K. levels, although well above Japan's key rate. However, the economic conditions that prompted the E.C.B. increases had largely diminished by year-end 2000, specifically, the euro was appreciating, the mid-2000 oil price hikes had backed off, and the European money-supply growth was slowing. Moreover, consumer and business confidence appeared to be strengthening. Thus, conditions were possibly right for the E.C.B. to moderate, if not reverse, its monetary policy in 2001. In the U.K., meanwhile, the Bank of England lifted its key rate only modestly during 2000, closing the year at 6 percent, a policy it may continue into 2001 due to strong domestic demand and a weakening pound.

Canada's central bank towards late 2000 was showing, for the first time in two years, a willingness to move independently from the actions of the U.S. Federal Reserve. During 1999 and 2000, Canada generally mirrored within a day the Fed's actions, but in December 2000, the Bank adopted a fixed schedule of meetings to announce changes in its rate, spacing the meetings at least one week apart from the Fed's meetings. This new approach became a reality in early 2001 when the Fed lowered its funds rate by 50 basis points and the Bank of Canada held its rate steady at 6 percent. The odds favor some easing later in 2001, but its apt to be less than the Fed's moves. Canada's economy was doing well at year-end, helped along with tax cutting fiscal policy stimulus in 2000.

The U.S. economy continues to dominate the world, a position it is not likely to lose. However, the Fed's rationale for its continued tight monetary policy in 2000 was that the economy was too strong for its own good. Still, the strong equity markets buoyed consumer spending and created a wealth effect that fed upon itself so long as the U.S. stock markets remained strong. The bullish setting in stocks, notably the high-tech oriented NASDAQ stocks, started to crack in March, 2000, after new record highs had been reached, but the Fed still saw reasons to be concerned and in May, 2000, lifted the funds rate 50 basis points, to 6.50 percent. That move may have been the straw that broke the camel's back. During the second half of the year, the economy slowed abruptly, and by Christmas consumer spending was well below earlier projections and the NASDAQ high-tech stocks had collapsed. For example, during the year's first quarter U.S. vehicle sales were running at an annual rate of over 18 million units, by the fourth quarter the rate was down to 16 million. Had the Fed overreacted? And what now was the driving force behind the economy, monetary policy or the stock market? By year-end 2000, the answers were elusive, but the Fed was under growing pressure to change course under the threat, realistic or not, of a recession taking hold in 2001. In early January 2001, the Fed reacted with a surprise 0.50 percent cut in the funds rate, the rationale for the move being greater concern for the economy's growth than inflationary fears. For the remainder of 2001, the odds favor further easing, perhaps a full point in the funds rate, notwithstanding the inflation fears that might arise from the new administration's push for fiscal stimulus, notably tax cuts, and the effect that a lower interest rate policy may have on the U.S. dollar.

In Japan, short-term interest rates stayed within an eyelash of zero during 2000, and a zero rate is not outside the realm of possibility in 2001. However, the latter would likely take an economic collapse and not just a cyclical downturn which the economy seemed to be experiencing toward year-end 2000. More likely would be an attempt to stimulate the economy with fiscal policy incentives rather than monetary.

Futures Markets

A number of actively traded interest rate futures markets are traded worldwide. The London International Financial Futures Exchange (LIFFE) trades contracts on 3-month Sterling prices and British long Gilts. LIFFE also offers futures on Euroswiss and Italian government bonds. The all-electronic Eurex exchange in Frankfurt trades a variety of Swiss and Euro government bonds as well as Euribors. Canadian Bankers Acceptances and 10-year Canadian government bonds are traded on the Montreal Exchange (ME). 3-year Australian Commonwealth T-bonds are traded on the Sydney Futures Exchange. Notional bond and PIBOR futures are traded on the Paris MATIF. Euroyen futures and Japanese yen government bonds are traded in Tokyo. Libor, eurodollars, and Brady Bonds are traded on Chicago's Mercantile Exchange. A Brady bond Index futures is traded on the CBOT. For a listing of other interest rate contracts see the volume section in the front of this Yearbook.

INTEREST RATES, WORLDWIDE

Long Gilt Futures - London International Financial Futures Exchange (weekly close) as of 29-Dec-2000   Nominal Value

9% through March 1998 contract
7% June 1998 contract to date

Jan-91   Jan-92   Dec-92   Dec-93   Dec-94   Dec-95   Dec-96   Dec-97   Dec-98   Dec-99   Dec-00

3-Month Sterling Futures - London International Financial Futures Exchange   Points of 100%
(weekly close) as of 29-Dec-2000

Jan-91   Jan-92   Dec-92   Dec-93   Dec-94   Dec-95   Dec-96   Dec-97   Dec-98   Dec-99   Dec-00

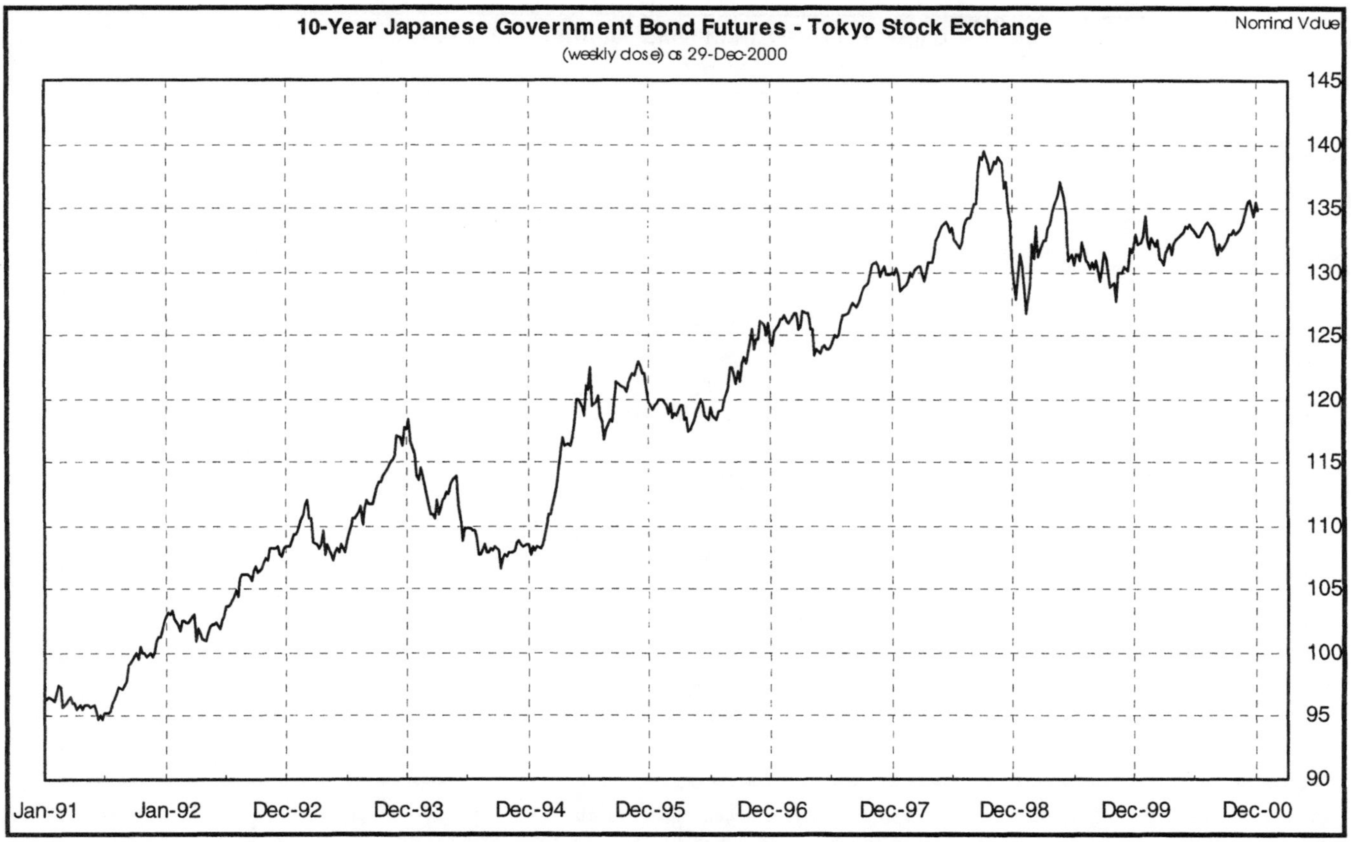

10-Year Japanese Government Bond Futures - Tokyo Stock Exchange
(weekly close) as 29-Dec-2000

Nominal Value

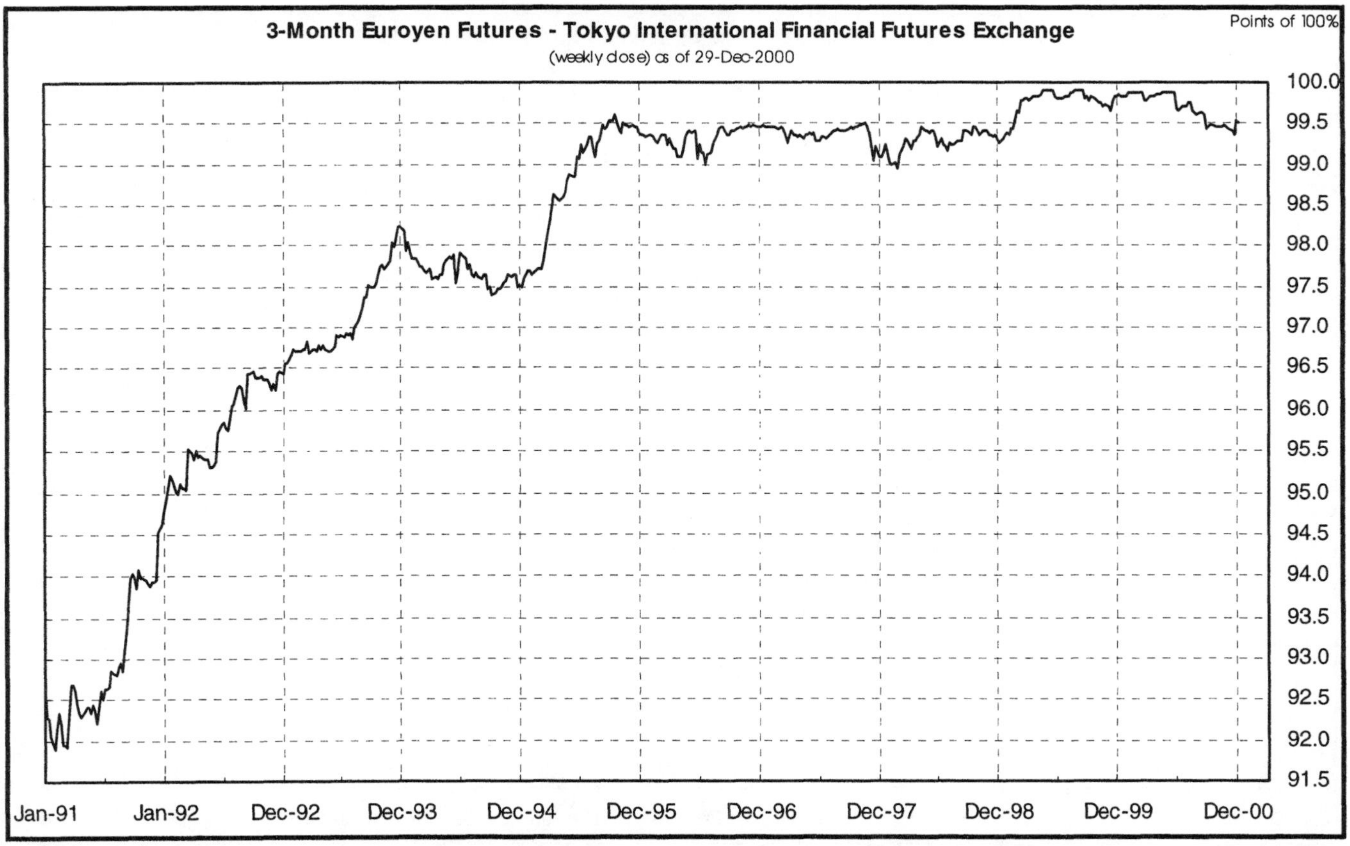

3-Month Euroyen Futures - Tokyo International Financial Futures Exchange
(weekly close) as of 29-Dec-2000

Points of 100%

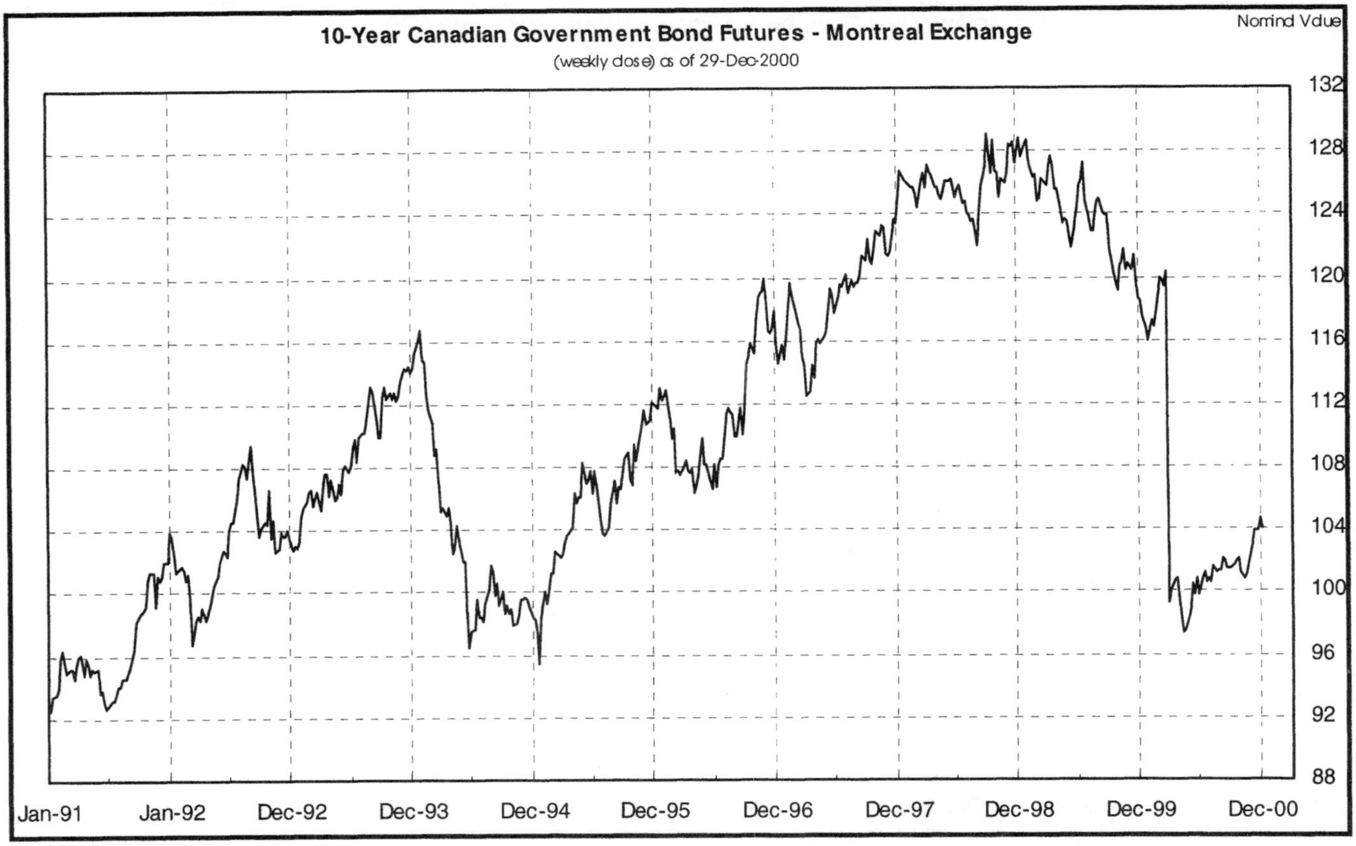

INTEREST RATES, WORLDWIDE

10-Year Canadian Government Bond Futures - Montreal Exchange
(weekly close) as of 29-Dec-2000

Nominal Value

3-Month Canadian Bankers' Acceptance Futures - Montreal Exchange
(weekly close) as of 29-Dec-2000

Points of 100%

146

Australia -- Economic Statistics   Percentage Change from Previous Period

Year	Real GDP	Nominal GDP	Real Private Consump-tion	Real Public Consump-tion	Grossed Fixed Invest-ment	Real Total Domestic Demand	Real Exports of Goods & Services	Real Imports of Goods & Services	Consumer Prices[1]	Unem-ployment Rate
1993	3.8	5.4	1.8	.3	4.9	3.0	8.0	4.2	1.8	10.9
1994	5.0	5.8	4.0	4.0	11.6	5.3	9.0	14.1	1.9	9.7
1995	4.4	6.0	5.0	3.6	3.2	4.8	5.1	8.1	4.6	8.5
1996	3.7	6.0	3.3	2.6	4.9	3.2	10.6	8.2	2.6	8.5
1997	3.8	5.4	3.9	1.6	11.0	3.4	11.5	10.3	.3	8.6
1998	5.6	5.7	4.6	4.0	7.5	7.0	-.3	5.9	.9	8.0
1999	4.7	5.7	5.2	5.3	6.5	5.7	4.6	9.5	1.5	7.2
2000[2]	4.2	7.8	3.7	6.0	3.6	4.0	10.8	9.9		6.6
2001[3]	3.7	6.6	3.5	3.3	4.8	3.9	8.5	6.8		6.3

[1] National accounts inplicit private consumption deflator.   [2] Estimate.   [3] Projection.   *Source: Organization for Economic Co-opertation and Development (OECD)*

Canada -- Economic Statistics   Percentage Change from Previous Period

Year	Real GDP	Nominal GDP	Real Private Consump-tion	Real Public Consump-tion	Grossed Fixed Invest-ment	Real Total Domestic Demand	Real Exports of Goods & Services	Real Imports of Goods & Services	Consumer Prices[1]	Unem-ployment Rate
1993	2.3	3.8	1.8	.1	-2.7	1.4	10.9	7.4	1.9	11.4
1994	4.7	5.9	3.1	-1.2	7.4	3.2	13.1	8.3	.2	10.3
1995	2.8	5.2	2.1	-.5	-1.9	1.7	9.0	6.2	2.2	9.4
1996	1.5	3.2	2.5	-1.4	5.8	1.4	5.9	5.8	1.6	9.6
1997	4.4	5.4	4.4	-1.2	15.4	6.2	8.8	15.1	1.6	9.1
1998	3.3	2.7	2.9	1.6	3.4	2.2	8.9	6.1	1.0	8.3
1999	4.5	6.2	3.5	1.3	10.1	4.2	10.0	9.4	1.7	7.6
2000[2]	4.8	8.3	3.6	2.0	11.8	5.4	11.6	13.3		6.7
2001[3]	3.4	5.8	2.8	1.7	6.4	3.4	7.5	7.8		6.7

[1] National accounts inplicit private consumption deflator.   [2] Estimate.   [3] Projection.   *Source: Organization for Economic Co-opertation and Development (OECD)*

France -- Economic Statistics   Percentage Change from Previous Period

Year	Real GDP	Nominal GDP	Real Private Consump-tion	Real Public Consump-tion	Grossed Fixed Invest-ment	Real Total Domestic Demand	Real Exports of Goods & Services	Real Imports of Goods & Services	Consumer Prices[1]	Unem-ployment Rate
1993	-.9	1.5	-.1	4.2	-6.5	-1.6	-.1	-3.8	2.1	11.7
1994	1.8	3.6	.6	.6	1.5	1.8	7.9	8.5	1.7	12.2
1995	1.8	3.6	1.6	-.1	2.1	1.8	7.8	7.8	1.7	11.6
1996	1.1	2.6	1.3	2.2	-.1	.7	3.1	1.5	2.0	12.3
1997	1.9	3.1	.1	2.1		.6	12.1	7.1	1.2	12.4
1998	3.2	4.0	3.4	.3	6.6	3.9	7.7	11.3	.8	11.8
1999	2.9	3.3	2.3	2.5	7.2	2.9	3.8	3.8	.5	11.1
2000[2]	3.3	4.2	2.6	1.3	6.0	3.0	12.8	12.5		9.7
2001[3]	2.9	4.6	2.3	1.3	4.6	2.5	8.7	8.1		8.8

[1] National accounts inplicit private consumption deflator.   [2] Estimate.   [3] Projection.   *Source: Organization for Economic Co-opertation and Development (OECD)*

Germany[2] -- Economic Statistics   Percentage Change from Previous Period

Year	Real GDP	Nominal GDP	Real Private Consump-tion	Real Public Consump-tion	Grossed Fixed Invest-ment	Real Total Domestic Demand	Real Exports of Goods & Services	Real Imports of Goods & Services	Consumer Prices[1]	Unem-ployment Rate
1993	-1.1	2.5	.1	.1	-4.5	-1.0	-5.5	-5.5	4.4	7.6
1994	2.3	4.9	1.0	2.4	4.0	2.3	7.6	7.4	2.8	8.2
1995	1.7	3.8	2.0	1.5	-.7	1.7	5.7	5.6	1.7	7.9
1996	.8	1.8	1.0	1.8	-.8	.3	5.1	3.1	1.4	8.6
1997	1.4	2.2	.7	-.9	.6	.6	11.3	8.4	1.9	9.5
1998	2.1	3.2	2.0	.5	3.0	2.4	7.0	8.6	.9	8.9
1999	1.6	2.5	2.6	-.1	3.3	2.4	5.1	8.1	.6	8.3
2000[3]	3.0	2.9	1.7	1.0	2.4	1.9	12.6	9.1		7.7
2001[4]	2.7	3.7	2.6	.5	2.8	2.1	9.3	7.7		6.9

[1] National accounts inplicit private consumption deflator.   [2] Data are for Western Germany only, except for foreign trade statistics.   [3] Estimate.
[4] Projection.   *Source: Organization for Economic Co-operation and Development (OECD)*

INTEREST RATES, WORLDWIDE

Italy -- Economic Statistics   Percentage Change from Previous Period

Year	Real GDP	Nominal GDP	Real Private Consump- tion	Real Public Consump- tion	Grossed Fixed Invest- ment	Real Total Domestic Demand	Real Exports of Goods & Services	Real Imports of Goods & Services	Consumer Prices[1]	Unem- ployment Rate
1993	-.9	3.0	-3.7	-.2	-10.9	-5.1	9.0	-10.9	4.6	10.2
1994	2.2	5.8	1.5	-.9	.1	1.7	9.8	8.1	4.1	11.2
1995	2.9	8.1	1.7	-2.2	6.0	2.0	12.6	9.7	5.2	11.7
1996	1.1	6.4	1.2	1.0	3.6	.9	.6	-.3	4.0	11.7
1997	1.8	4.3	3.0	.8	1.2	2.5	6.5	10.2	2.0	11.8
1998	1.5	4.2	2.3	.7	4.1	2.9	3.3	9.1	2.0	11.9
1999	1.4	2.9	1.7	.6	4.4	2.5	-.4	3.4	1.7	11.5
2000[2]	2.8	4.7	2.0	1.2	6.9	2.2	9.5	7.6		10.8
2001[3]	2.7	4.9	1.8	1.1	4.7	2.2	9.3	8.1		10.1

[1] National accounts inplicit private consumption deflator.   [2] Estimate.   [3] Projection.   *Source: Organization for Economic Co-opertation and Development (OECD)*

Japan -- Economic Statistics   Percentage Change from Previous Period

Year	Real GDP	Nominal GDP	Real Private Consump- tion	Real Public Consump- tion	Grossed Fixed Invest- ment	Real Total Domestic Demand	Real Exports of Goods & Services	Real Imports of Goods & Services	Consumer Prices[1]	Unem- ployment Rate
1993	.3	.9	1.2	2.4	-2.0	.1	1.3	-.3	1.2	2.5
1994	.6	.8	1.9	2.4	-.8	1.0	4.6	8.9	.7	2.9
1995	1.5	.8	2.1	3.3	1.7	2.3	5.4	14.2	-.1	3.1
1996	5.1	3.5	2.9	1.9	11.1	5.7	6.3	11.9	.1	3.4
1997	1.6	1.9	.5	1.5	-.8	.2	11.6	.5	1.7	3.4
1998	-2.5	-2.2	-.5	1.5	-7.4	-3.1	-2.5	-7.6	.6	4.1
1999	.2	-.7	1.2	1.3	-1.2	.5	1.9	5.3	-.3	4.7
2000[2]	1.9	.3	1.6	.2	.6	1.3	13.6	10.5		4.7
2001[3]	2.3	1.9	2.1	.5	2.8	2.4	5.5	6.4		4.6

[1] National accounts inplicit private consumption deflator.   [2] Estimate.   [3] Projection.   *Source: Organization for Economic Co-opertation and Development (OECD)*

Switzerland -- Economic Statistics   Percentage Change from Previous Period

Year	Real GDP	Nominal GDP	Real Private Consump- tion	Real Public Consump- tion	Grossed Fixed Invest- ment	Real Total Domestic Demand	Real Exports of Goods & Services	Real Imports of Goods & Services	Consumer Prices[1]	Unem- ployment Rate
1993	-.5	2.2	-.9	-.1	-2.7	-1.0	1.5	.1	3.3	4.5
1994	.5	2.2	1.0	2.0	6.5	2.7	1.8	7.9	.9	4.7
1995	.5	1.6	.6	-.1	1.8	1.8	1.6	5.1	1.8	4.2
1996	.3	.7	.7	2.0	-2.4	.4	2.5	2.7	.8	4.7
1997	1.7	1.5	1.4		1.5	1.3	8.6	7.6	.5	5.2
1998	2.3	2.6	2.2	.7	4.5	4.3	5.0	9.6		3.9
1999	1.5	2.1	2.2	-.4	1.8	1.4	5.9	5.5	.8	2.7
2000[2]	3.3	4.4	2.1	.3	6.2	2.6	9.9	8.2		2.0
2001[3]	2.4	4.0	2.0	.3	4.6	2.4	6.6	6.7		1.8

[1] National accounts inplicit private consumption deflator.   [2] Estimate.   [3] Projection.   *Source: Organization for Economic Co-opertation and Development (OECD)*

United Kingdom -- Economic Statistics   Percentage Change from Previous Period

Year	Real GDP	Nominal GDP	Real Private Consump- tion	Real Public Consump- tion	Grossed Fixed Invest- ment	Real Total Domestic Demand	Real Exports of Goods & Services	Real Imports of Goods & Services	Consumer Prices[1]	Unem- ployment Rate
1993	2.3	5.1	2.9	-.8	.8	2.2	3.9	3.2	1.6	10.3
1994	4.4	6.0	2.9	1.4	3.6	3.4	9.2	5.4	2.5	9.4
1995	2.8	5.4	1.7	1.6	2.9	1.8	9.5	5.5	3.4	8.5
1996	2.6	5.9	3.6	1.7	4.9	3.0	7.5	9.1	2.4	7.9
1997	3.5	6.5	3.9	-1.4	7.5	3.8	8.6	9.2	3.1	6.5
1998	2.6	5.7	4.0	1.1	10.1	4.6	2.6	8.8	3.4	5.9
1999	2.2	4.7	4.3	3.3	6.1	3.7	3.3	7.6	1.6	6.0
2000[2]	3.0	5.0	3.5	1.8	2.4	3.4	7.8	8.5		5.5
2001[3]	2.6	5.1	2.4	4.3	3.8	2.9	7.2	7.5		5.4

[1] National accounts inplicit private consumption deflator.   [2] Estimate.   [3] Projection.   *Source: Organization for Economic Co-opertation and Development (OECD)*

Iron and Steel

Iron is the least expensive and most widely used metal. Iron ore is used to make steel. In the U.S., about 97 percent of the iron ore produced is used in steelmaking. Iron ore is the basic raw material from which iron and steel are made. Scrap is used as a supplement in steelmaking but its use is limited because the supply of high quality scrap is limited. Iron and steel slags are the nonmetallic coproducts of many metallurgical processes. Iron and steel slags are coproducts of iron and steel production. Iron and steel slags have a wide range of uses from road construction to cement manufacturing to glass manufacturing.

The U.S. Geological Survey reported that world mine production of iron ore in 1999 was 992 million metric tonnes, down 3 percent from 1998. The world's largest producer of iron ore is China with 1999 production estimated at 205 million tonnes, down 2 percent from the previous year. Brazil was the next largest producer with 190 million tonnes, followed by Australia with 150 million tonnes. Other large producers include Russia, the U.S., India, and the Ukraine. U.S. mine production of iron ore in 1999 was estimated to be 57 million tonnes, down 10 percent from 1998. U.S. iron ore resources are mainly low-grade taconite-type ores from the Lake Superior district.

U.S. production of iron ore in August 2000 was 5.84 million tonnes, up 51 percent from a year ago. In the January-August 2000 period, production of iron ore was 42.7 million tonnes. Shipments of iron ore in August 2000 were 5.99 million tonnes, up almost 8 percent from a year ago. Shipments in the first eight months of 2000 were 38.3 million tonnes. U.S. imports of iron ore in July 2000 were 1.69 million tonnes, while in the January-July 2000 period imports were 9.59 million tonnes. In the same period of 1999, imports were 6.25 million tonnes. The major suppliers of iron ore to the U.S. were Canada and Brazil. U.S. imports of iron ore pellets in July 2000 were 922,000 tonnes, while for the first seven months of 2000 they were 6.39 million tonnes.

World production of pig iron in 1999 was estimated to be 541 million tonnes, up slightly from 539 million tonnes in 1998. World production of direct-reduced iron in 1999 was estimated to be 38.5 million tonnes, up 5 percent from the previous year. Global output of raw steel in 1999 was estimated to be 786 million tonnes, up 1 percent from 1998.

U.S. production of pig iron in 1999 was estimated to be 46.3 million tonnes, down 4 percent from the previous year. Imports for consumption in 1999 were 4.99 million tonnes, down 3 percent from the previous year. Raw steel production in 1999 was estimated at 97.4 million tonnes, down 1 percent from 1998.

World Production of Raw Steel (Ingots and Castings) In Thousands of Metric Tons

Year	Brazil	Canada	China	France	Germany	Italy	Japan	Rep. of Korea	Russia[3]	Ukraine[3]	United Kingdom	United States	World Total
1990	20,567	12,281	66,349	19,016	38,434	25,467	110,339	23,125	154,414	----	17,841	89,726	770,458
1991	22,617	12,987	71,000	18,434	42,169	25,112	109,649	26,001	77,093	45,002	16,474	79,738	733,592
1992	23,934	13,933	80,935	17,972	39,711	24,835	98,132	28,055	67,029	41,759	16,212	84,322	719,679
1993	25,207	14,387	89,539	17,106	37,625	25,720	99,623	33,026	58,346	32,609	16,625	88,793	727,548
1994	25,747	13,897	92,613	18,031	40,837	26,151	98,295	33,745	48,812	24,081	17,286	91,244	725,107
1995	25,076	14,415	95,360	18,100	42,051	27,766	101,640	36,772	51,589	22,309	17,604	95,191	752,260
1996	25,237	14,735	101,237	17,633	39,793	23,910	98,801	38,903	49,253	22,332	17,992	95,535	750,007
1997	26,153	15,554	108,911	19,767	45,007	25,842	104,545	42,554	48,502	25,629	18,489	98,486	798,842
1998[1]	25,760	15,930	114,588	20,126	44,046	25,714	93,548	39,896	43,822	24,445	17,315	98,658	777,385
1999[2]	24,996	16,235	123,709	20,200	42,062	24,908	94,195	41,042	51,510	27,453	16,284	97,284	787,733

[1] Preliminary. [2] Estimate. [3] Formerly part of the U.S.S.R.; data not reported separately until 1992. Source: U.S. Geological Survey (USGS)

Average Wholesale Prices of Iron and Steel in the United States

Year	No. 1 Heavy Melting Steel Scrap — Pittsburg	No. 1 Heavy Melting Steel Scrap — Chicago	Hot Rolled Sheet[2]	Sheet Bars — Hot Rolled	Sheet Bars — Cold Finished	Hot Rolled Strip	Carbon Steel Plates	Cold Rolled Strip	Galvanized Sheets	Railroad Steel Scrap[3]	Used Steel Cans[4]
	---- $ Per Gross Ton ----				Cents Per Pound					------ $ Per Gross Ton ------	
1990	106.61	108.62	22.25	20.43	25.37	22.10	23.75	37.24	33.55	131.59	77.16
1991	95.18	95.19	22.88	20.60	25.75	23.15	24.50	38.86	35.35	129.69	89.00
1992	88.72	88.52	19.13	17.48	24.03	23.50	24.50	39.40	30.88	117.40	88.73
1993	116.30	115.26	20.99	18.44	23.83	23.50	25.12	39.40	30.90	142.18	91.79
1994	136.76	131.91	22.93	NA	25.70	23.50	27.61	39.40	32.24	169.00	102.33
1995	142.34	143.17	25.32	NA	25.70	24.88	29.98	39.40	34.47	NA	126.32
1996	137.28	136.07	23.94	NA	26.46	25.00	31.16	NA	35.05	NA	121.27
1997	133.38	139.40	18.12	NA	25.65	NA	32.00	NA	28.62	NA	108.13
1998	110.10	118.76	15.57	NA	25.50	NA	33.24	NA	24.11	NA	109.44
1999[1]	97.86	102.49	14.74	NA	23.00	NA	33.50	NA	21.20	NA	68.94

[1] Preliminary. [2] 10 gauge; thru 1992, list prices; 1993 to date, market prices. [3] Specialties scrap. [4] Consumer buying prices.
NA = Not available. Source: American Metal Market (AMM)

IRON AND STEEL

Salient Statistics of Steel in the United States   In Thousands of Short Tons

Year	Pig Iron Production	Producer Price Index for Steel Mill Products (1982=100)	Raw Steel Production By Type of Furnace — Basic Oxygen	Open Hearth	Electric[2]	Stainless	Carbon	Alloy	Total	Net Shipments Steel Mill Products	Total Steel Products — Exports	Imports
1991	48,637	109.5	52,714	1,408	33,774	1,878	77,879	8,139	87,896	78,846	7,112	17,743
1992	52,224	106.4	57,642	----	35,308	1,993	82,458	8,498	92,949	82,241	5,016	19,033
1993	53,082	108.2	59,353	----	38,524	1,956	86,865	9,056	97,877	89,022	4,727	21,796
1994	54,426	113.4	61,028	----	39,551	2,022	89,535	9,022	100,579	95,084	4,852	32,705
1995	56,097	120.1	62,523	----	42,407	2,265	92,656	10,009	104,930	97,494	8,157	27,270
1996	54,485	115.7	60,433	----	44,876	2,061	93,649	9,599	105,309	100,878	6,168	32,115
1997	54,679	116.4	61,053	----	47,508	2,382	95,933	10,246	108,561	105,858	7,369	34,389
1998	53,164	113.8	59,686	----	49,067	2,214	97,054	9,484	108,752	102,420	5,520	41,520
1999	51,002	105.3	57,722	----	49,673	2,086	98,694	5,421	107,395	106,201	5,426	35,731
2000[1]	52,811	108.5	59,485	----	52,418	2,104	102,141	5,379	111,903	109,624	6,529	37,957

[1] Preliminary.   [2] Includes crucible steels.   *Sources: American Iron & Steel Institute (AISI); U.S. Geological Survey (USGS)*

Production of Steel Ingots, Rate of Capability Utilization[1] in the United States   In Percent

Year	Jan.	Feb.	Mar.	Apr.	May	June	July	Aug.	Sept.	Oct.	Nov.	Dec.	Average
1991	74.6	73.1	71.7	72.5	70.0	71.7	74.8	75.2	78.5	78.0	78.0	74.4	74.2
1992	80.5	82.4	83.5	85.3	83.5	82.1	78.9	78.7	78.3	80.9	80.4	77.7	82.2
1993	84.8	89.0	87.0	87.4	88.3	87.5	86.9	86.2	87.7	90.2	86.3	85.9	89.1
1994	87.7	92.2	91.3	91.4	91.2	88.7	87.1	87.7	90.0	92.0	92.6	94.3	93.0
1995	93.8	95.6	96.0	92.9	91.6	90.1	86.8	88.3	93.6	90.3	92.1	90.2	91.7
1996	92.2	92.6	93.8	90.5	89.7	91.3	86.6	87.1	87.7	88.0	87.0	87.9	89.5
1997	85.3	89.3	89.6	89.2	87.9	87.0	85.1	86.4	91.2	86.9	89.6	86.3	89.4
1998	90.0	95.2	93.1	92.5	89.1	86.1	83.0	86.4	83.0	81.0	74.4	74.8	85.7
1999	77.2	79.5	81.7	81.8	81.7	79.7	79.4	82.8	82.3	88.2	89.1	88.5	82.7
2000[2]	89.7	89.4	91.2	92.0	91.3	89.6	85.3	83.5	82.7	81.0	75.1	72.0	85.2

[1] Based on tonnage capability to produce raw steel for a full order book.   [2] Preliminary.   *Sources: American Iron and Steel Institute (AISI); U.S. Geological Survey (USGS)*

Production of Steel Ingots in the United States   In Thousands of Short Tons

Year	Jan.	Feb.	Mar.	Apr.	May	June	July	Aug.	Sept.	Oct.	Nov.	Dec.	Total
1991	7,577	6,608	7,283	7,089	7,076	7,017	7,338	7,386	7,457	7,711	7,461	7,348	87,896
1992	7,754	7,432	8,043	7,875	7,968	7,584	7,542	7,526	7,249	7,742	7,449	7,438	92,949
1993	7,942	7,528	8,148	7,926	8,278	7,937	8,066	8,001	7,878	8,409	7,786	8,008	97,877
1994	8,003	7,598	8,323	8,180	8,437	7,941	7,996	8,053	7,993	8,477	8,256	8,684	100,579
1995	8,918	8,211	9,131	8,548	8,696	8,286	8,308	8,455	8,668	8,685	8,574	8,678	103,142
1996	8,981	8,438	9,136	8,588	8,798	8,661	8,585	8,627	8,407	8,702	8,276	8,689	104,356
1997	8,735	8,266	9,175	8,882	9,048	8,662	8,692	8,818	9,006	9,128	9,116	9,071	107,488
1998	9,510	9,087	9,839	9,524	9,483	8,863	8,832	9,194	8,548	8,681	7,710	8,013	107,643
1999	8,422	7,837	8,854	8,643	8,914	8,413	8,619	8,993	8,650	9,574	9,357	9,604	105,882
2000[1]	9,838	9,170	10,009	9,843	10,097	9,592	9,411	9,213	8,830	8,978	8,054	7,982	111,015

[1] Preliminary.   *Source: American Iron and Steel Institute (AISI)*

Shipments of Steel Products[1] by Market Classifications in the United States   In Thousands of Short Tons

Year	Appliances Utensils & Cutlery	Automotive	Containers, Packaging & Shipping Materials	Construction Including Maint.	Contractors Products	Electrical Equipment	Export	Machinery, Industrial Equipment & Tools	Oil and Gas	Rail Transportaion	Steel for Converting & Processing[2]	Steel Service Center & Distributors	All Other[3]	Total Shipments
1991	1,388	10,015	4,278	9,161	2,306	2,102	4,476	1,982	1,425	999	8,265	19,464	12,985	78,846
1992	1,503	11,092	3,974	9,536	2,694	2,136	2,650	1,951	1,454	1,052	9,226	21,328	13,645	82,241
1993	1,592	12,719	4,355	10,516	2,913	2,213	2,110	2,191	1,526	1,223	9,451	23,714	14,499	89,022
1994	1,736	14,753	4,495	10,935	3,348	2,299	1,710	2,427	1,703	1,248	10,502	24,153	15,775	95,084
1995	1,589	14,622	4,139	11,761	3,337	2,397	4,442	2,310	2,643	1,373	10,440	23,751	14,690	97,494
1996	1,713	14,665	4,101	15,561	[5]	2,401	2,328	2,410	3,254	1,400	10,245	27,124	15,676	100,878
1997	1,635	15,251	4,163	15,885	[5]	2,434	2,610	2,355	3,811	1,410	11,263	27,800	17,241	105,858
1998	1,729	15,842	3,829	15,289	[5]	2,255	2,556	2,147	2,649	1,657	9,975	27,751	16,741	102,420
1999	1,712	15,639	3,768	14,685	[5]	2,260	2,292	1,547	1,544	876	7,599	21,439	32,840	106,201
2000[4]	1,530	14,697	3,684	14,763	[5]	2,039	2,752	1,513	2,268	994	7,753	22,537	35,093	109,624

[1] All grades including carbon, alloy and stainless steel.   [2] Net total after deducting shipments to reporting companines for conversion or resale.

[3] Includes agricultural; bolts, nuts rivets & screws; forgings (other than automotive); shipbuilding & marine equipment; aircraft; mining, quarrying & lumbering; other domestic & commercial equipment machinery; ordnance & other direct military; and shipments of non-reporting companies.

[4] Preliminary.   *Source: American Iron and Steel Institute (AISI)*

Net Shipments of Steel Products[1] in the United States   In Thousands of Short Tons

Year	Cold Finished Bars	Rails & Accessories	Wire Drawn	Tin Mill Products	Plates (Cut & Coils)	Sheet & Strip Galv. (Hot Dipped)	Hot Rolled Bars	Pipe & Tubing	Structural Shapes & Steel Piling	Reinforcing Bars	Hot Rolled Sheets	Cold Rolled Sheets	Carbon	Alloy	Stainless
1991	1,341	486	865	4,041	6,942	6,910	5,431	4,488	5,245	4,859	13,161	11,532	73,480	3,917	1,449
1992	1,458	562	900	3,927	7,102	8,199	5,806	4,198	5,081	4,781	13,361	12,692	76,625	4,101	1,514
1993	1,580	679	802	4,123	7,538	9,712	6,339	4,445	4,973	5,033	14,873	12,758	83,106	4,381	1,534
1994	1,786	631	788	4,137	8,556	10,943	7,088	4,966	5,942	4,929	15,654	13,016	88,505	4,859	1,720
1995	1,782	630	654	3,942	9,043	11,329	6,902	5,437	6,278	5,048	16,978	12,347	90,485	5,115	1,894
1996	1,685	722	652	4,108	8,672	11,456	6,999	5,895	6,140	5,762	17,466	14,089	93,019	5,948	1,912
1997	1,809	875	619	4,057	8,855	12,439	8,153	6,548	6,029	6,188	18,221	13,322	97,509	6,282	2,067
1998	1,780	938	725	3,714	8,864	13,481	8,189	5,409	5,595	5,909	15,715	13,185	94,536	5,847	2,037
1999	1,775	646	611	3,771	8,200	14,870	8,078	4,772	5,995	6,183	17,740	13,874	98,694	5,421	2,086
2000[2]	1,756	783	579	3,742	8,898	14,917	7,901	5,385	7,402	6,893	19,236	14,802	102,141	5,379	2,104

[1] All grades, including carbon, alloy and stainless steel.   [2] Preliminary.   *Source: American Iron and Steel Institute (AISI)*

World Production of Pig Iron (Excludes Ferro-Alloys)   In Thousands of Metric Tons

Year	Belgium	Brazil	China	France	Germany	India	Italy	Japan	Russia[4]	Ukraine[4]	United Kingdom	United States	World Total
1990	9,416	21,360	62,380	14,415	32,058	13,395	11,883	80,229	111,763	----	12,277	50,058	549,000
1991	9,354	22,926	67,650	13,408	30,608	14,176	10,856	79,985	90,900	----	11,883	44,510	528,000
1992	8,533	23,152	75,890	13,051	27,399	15,126	10,462	73,144	45,824	34,663	11,542	47,400	524,000
1993	8,178	23,982	87,390	12,679	26,970	15,674	11,066	73,738	40,871	26,999	11,534	48,200	531,000
1994	8,974	25,177	97,410	13,293	29,923	17,808	11,157	73,776	36,116	21,200	11,943	49,400	544,000
1995	9,199	25,090	105,293	12,860	29,828	18,626	11,684	74,905	39,762	20,000	12,238	50,900	536,000
1996	8,628	23,978	107,225	12,108	30,012	19,864	10,347	74,597	36,061	18,143	12,830	49,400	554,000
1997	8,077	25,013	115,110	13,424	30,939	19,898	11,348	78,519	37,327	20,561	13,057	49,600	581,000
1998[1]	8,730	25,111	118,600	13,603	30,162	20,194	10,704	74,981	34,827	20,840	12,574	48,200	576,000
1999[2]	8,472	25,060	125,390	13,854	27,931	20,139	10,509	74,520	40,033	21,937	12,399	46,300	580,000

[1] Preliminary.   [2] Estimate.   [3] Formerly part of the U.S.S.R.; data not reported separately until 1992.   *Source: U.S. Geological Survey (USGS)*

Production of Pig Iron (Excludes Ferro-Alloys) in the United States   In Thousands of Short Tons

Year	Jan.	Feb.	Mar.	Apr.	May	June	July	Aug.	Sept.	Oct.	Nov.	Dec.	Total
1991	4,077	3,470	4,047	3,830	3,885	3,830	4,179	4,121	4,175	4,251	4,300	4,338	48,503
1992	4,390	4,175	4,524	4,400	4,444	4,232	4,347	4,299	4,065	5,329	4,268	4,306	52,224
1993	4,503	4,503	4,454	4,328	4,555	4,351	4,522	4,504	4,367	4,652	4,218	4,514	53,103
1994	3,970	3,858	3,957	4,099	4,394	4,519	4,518	4,446	4,320	4,564	4,619	4,928	54,426
1995	4,820	4,453	4,916	4,568	4,674	4,499	4,576	4,688	4,727	4,687	4,738	4,762	56,115
1996	4,811	4,476	4,813	4,430	4,556	4,578	4,524	4,498	4,404	4,443	4,307	4,523	54,485
1997	4,489	4,243	4,713	4,440	4,690	4,452	4,420	4,443	4,605	4,662	4,717	4,861	54,680
1998	4,955	4,433	4,881	4,600	4,731	4,299	4,418	4,502	4,170	4,212	3,837	4,119	53,174
1999	4,140	3,802	4,257	4,157	4,352	4,045	4,204	4,280	4,167	4,572	4,447	4,722	51,145
2000[1]	4,571	4,325	4,793	4,741	4,887	4,577	4,454	4,387	4,262	4,138	3,675	3,781	52,591

[1] Preliminary.   *Source: American Iron and Steel Institute*

Salient Statistics of Ferrous Scrap and Pig Iron in the United States   In Thousands of Metric Tons

	Consumption: Ferrous Scrap & Pig Iron Charged To												Stocks -- Dec. 31		
	Mfg. of Pig Iron & Steel Ingots & Castings			Iron Foundries & Misc. Users			Mfg. of Steel	All Uses			Imports of	Exports of	Ferrous Scrap & Pig Iron at Consumers		
Year	Scrap	Pig Iron	Total	Scrap	Pig Iron	Total	Castings (Scrap)	Ferrous Scrap	Pig Iron	Grand Total	Scrap[2]	Scrap[3]	Scrap	Pig Iron	Total Stocks
1990	54,361	49,337	103,698	13,085	835	13,920	1,850	69,296	50,193	119,489	1,324	11,580	4,292	147	4,439
1991	48,778	44,095	92,873	11,126	656	11,782	1,609	61,513	44,765	106,278	1,073	9,502	4,072	190	4,262
1992	50,144	47,263	97,407	11,444	619	12,063	1,640	63,228	47,894	111,122	1,316	9,262	3,752	181	3,933
1993	53,084	48,092	101,176	12,658	676	13,334	1,900	68,000	48,777	116,777	1,390	9,805	3,725	220	3,945
1994	53,801	50,257	104,057	14,000	1,000	15,000	2,000	70,000	51,000	121,000	1,740	8,813	4,100	400	4,500
1995	56,000	51,000	107,000	13,000	1,100	14,100	2,000	72,000	52,000	124,000	2,090	10,400	4,200	620	4,820
1996	56,000	50,000	106,000	13,000	1,100	14,100	2,700	72,000	52,000	124,000	2,600	8,440	5,200	600	5,800
1997	58,000	51,000	109,000	13,000	1,200	14,200	1,800	73,000	52,000	125,000	2,870	8,930	5,500	510	6,010
1998	58,000	49,000	107,000	13,000	1,200	14,200	2,000	73,000	50,000	123,000	3,060	5,570	5,200	560	5,760
1999[1]	56,000	48,000	104,000	13,000	1,100	14,100	1,900	71,000	49,000	120,000	3,670	5,520	5,500	720	6,220

[1] Preliminary.   [2] Includes tinplate and terneplate.   [3] Excludes used rails for rerolling and other uses and ships, boats, and other vessels for scrapping.
Source: U.S. Geological Survey (USGS)

IRON AND STEEL

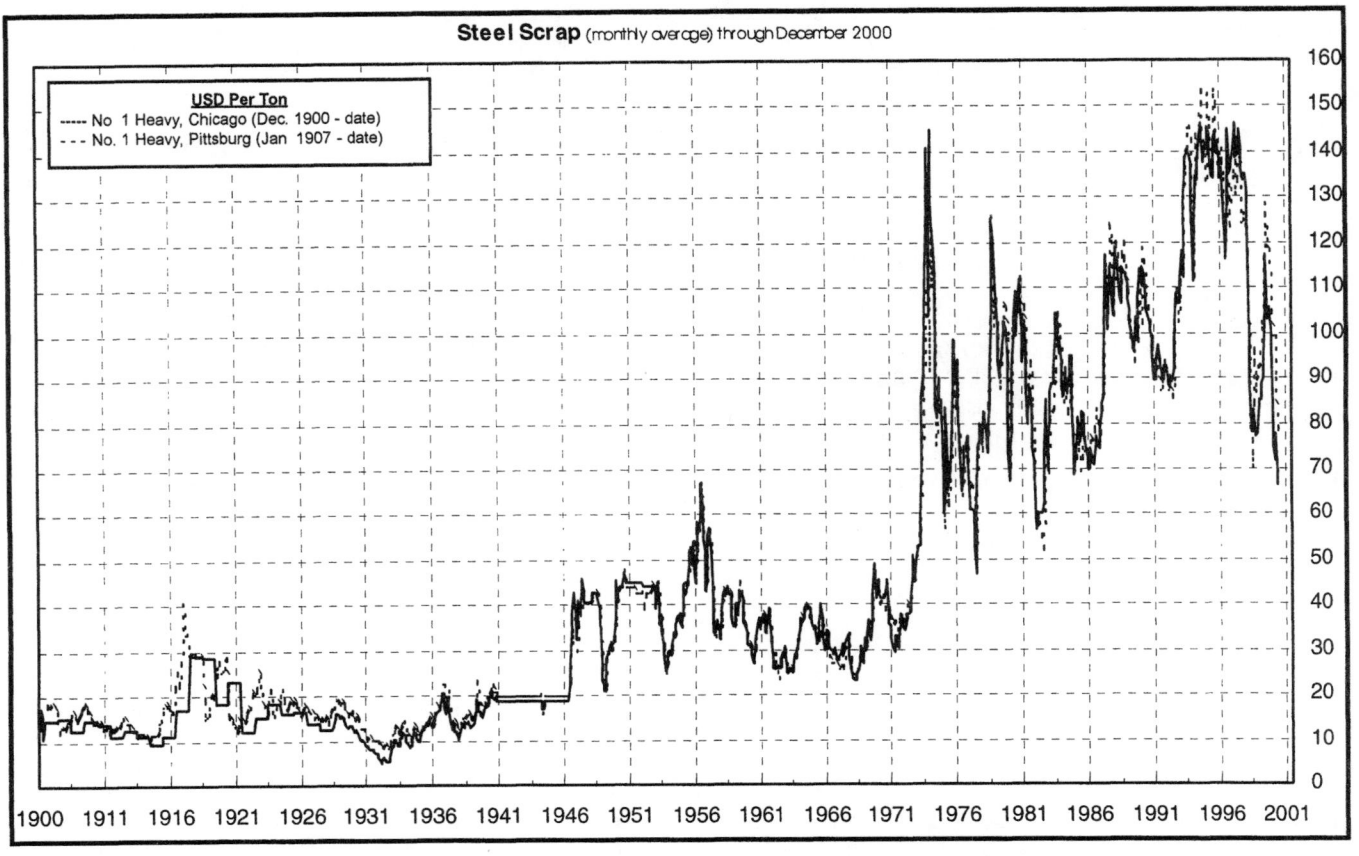

Steel Scrap (monthly average) through December 2000

USD Per Ton
----- No 1 Heavy, Chicago (Dec. 1900 - date)
- - - No. 1 Heavy, Pittsburg (Jan 1907 - date)

Consumption of Pig Iron in the U.S., by Type of Furnace or Equipment   In Thousands of Metric Tons

Year	Open Hearth	Electric	Cupola	Basic Oxygen Process	Air & Other Furnace	Direct Casting	Total
1990	2,072	982	332	47,307	19	387	51,099
1991	997	574	265	42,955	13	106	44,910
1992	----	429	215	47,194	7	49	47,894
1993	----	519	292	47,848	34	84	48,777
1994	----	1,700	520	49,138	4	39	51,401
1995	----	1,700	500	50,000	W	72	52,272
1996	----	2,200	530	49,000	W	42	52,000
1997	----	2,400	400	50,000	W	41	52,000
1998[1]	----	4,000	590	46,000	W	36	50,000
1999[2]	----	3,100	520	45,000	W	W	49,000

[1] Preliminary.   [2] Estimate.   W = Withheld.   *Source: U.S. Geological Survey (USGS)*

Wholesale Price of No. 1 Heavy Melting Steel Scrap in Chicago   In Dollars Per Metric Ton

Year	Jan.	Feb.	Mar.	Apr.	May	June	July	Aug.	Sept.	Oct.	Nov.	Dec.	Average
1991	104.76	100.74	98.00	97.80	93.18	87.50	87.74	94.14	98.50	97.50	91.97	90.50	95.19
1992	90.50	90.50	90.50	90.50	89.70	87.68	87.50	87.55	88.50	85.50	85.50	88.36	88.52
1993	98.34	109.50	109.50	106.50	106.50	111.27	118.50	114.18	113.50	125.88	131.50	138.00	115.26
1994	138.00	138.00	138.00	138.00	123.64	110.50	117.20	133.63	134.50	132.50	137.50	141.50	131.91
1995	152.05	147.50	140.20	141.50	144.50	141.64	141.50	149.76	144.90	141.50	136.50	136.50	143.17
1996	143.41	144.50	139.50	139.50	142.50	139.50	134.50	136.95	140.35	130.89	120.76	120.50	136.07
1997	131.14	143.50	139.70	132.59	136.50	136.50	143.50	146.50	139.60	139.63	142.50	142.50	139.51
1998	144.29	140.39	135.50	133.50	135.30	135.50	131.50	120.88	107.79	85.64	78.71	76.68	118.81
1999	89.66	101.50	90.89	90.50	100.00	104.32	100.98	105.95	106.50	106.50	113.40	120.17	102.49
2000	120.50	111.10	110.50	108.15	101.50	94.59	92.50	92.50	92.50	82.59	72.80	74.20	96.07

Source: American Metal Market (AMM)

World Production of Iron Ore[3] In Thousands of Metric Tons (Gross Weight)

Year	Australia	Brazil	Canada	China	India	Maur-itania	Russia[4]	South Africa	Sweden	Ukraine[4]	United States	Vene-zuela	World Total
1990	110,508	152,300	34,855	168,300	53,700	11,590	236,000	30,291	19,877	----	56,408	20,119	983,000
1991	117,134	151,500	39,307	176,070	56,880	10,246	199,000	29,075	19,328	----	56,761	21,296	955,618
1992	112,101	146,447	33,167	197,600	54,870	8,202	82,100	28,226	19,277	75,700	55,593	18,070	924,993
1993	120,534	150,000	31,830	234,660	57,375	9,360	76,100	29,385	18,728	65,500	55,676	16,871	953,316
1994	128,493	177,331	37,703	240,200	60,473	11,440	73,300	30,489	19,663	51,300	58,454	18,318	991,858
1995	142,936	183,839	38,560	249,350	65,173	11,610	78,300	31,946	19,058	50,400	62,501	18,955	1,034,539
1996	147,100	174,157	34,400	249,550	66,657	11,360	72,100	30,830	20,273	47,600	62,083	18,480	1,017,470
1997	157,766	185,128	37,277	268,000	69,453	11,700	70,900	33,225	21,893	53,000	62,971	18,503	1,069,624
1998[1]	153,964	207,017	37,808	246,900	72,532	11,400	72,343	32,948	20,930	50,758	62,931	16,553	1,062,278
1999[2]	154,979	190,345	34,487	209,000	67,750	11,500	81,311	29,508	18,558	47,540	57,749	17,000	993,638

[1] Preliminary. [2] Estimate. [3] Iron ore, iron ore concentrates and iron ore agglomerates. [4] Formerly part of the U.S.S.R.; data not reported separately until 1992. *Source: U.S. Geological Survey (USGS)*

Salient Statistics of Iron Ore[3] in the United States In Thousands of Metric Tons

Year	Net Import Reliance as a % of Apparent Con-sumption	Production Total	Lake Superior	Other Regions	Ship-ments	Value Million $ (at Mine)	Average Value $ at Mine Per Ton	Stocks Dec. 31 Mines	Con suming Plants	Lake Erie Docks	Imports	Exports	Con-sumption	Value Million $ Imports
1990	21	56,408	54,628	1,780	57,010	1,570.0	27.52	4,795	15,911	2,273	18,054	3,199	76,855	559.5
1991	11	56,096	55,079	1,017	56,775	1,900.0	33.40	4,850	17,612	2,981	13,335	4,045	66,366	436.8
1992	12	55,593	55,018	575	55,600	1,550.0	27.90	3,780	16,100	2,980	12,500	5,060	75,100	396.0
1993	14	55,661	54,814	848	56,300	1,380.0	24.50	2,500	16,500	2,290	14,100	5,060	76,800	419.0
1994	18	58,215	57,848	367	57,600	1,410.0	24.49	2,790	16,300	2,230	17,500	4,980	80,200	499.0
1995	14	60,898	60,462	435	61,100	1,700.0	28.00	4,240	17,100	2,140	17,600	5,270	83,100	491.0
1996	14	62,132	61,748	383	62,200	1,750.0	28.00	4,650	18,800	2,260	18,400	6,260	79,600	556.0
1997	14	63,000	62,600	327	62,800	1,860.0	30.00	4,860	20,200	2,890	18,600	6,340	79,500	551.0
1998[1]	17	62,900	62,591	327	63,200	1,970.0	31.00	6,020	20,500	4,080	16,900	6,000	78,200	517.0
1999[2]	17	57,410	57,410	NA	60,700	1,550.0	26.00	5,710	17,900	2,770	14,300	6,120	75,100	399.0

[1] Preliminary. [2] Estimate. [3] Usable iron ore exclusive of ore containing 5% or more manganese and includes byproduct ore. NA = Not available. *Source: U.S. Geological Survey (USGS)*

U.S. Imports (for Consumption) of Iron Ore[2] In Thousands of Metric Tons

Year	Australia	Brazil	Canada	Chile	Maur-itania	Peru	Sweden	Vene-zuela	Total
1990	14	4,276	9,344	138	666	59	54	3,503	18,054
1991	----	2,481	7,299	103	459	157	51	2,763	13,335
1992	163	2,442	6,834	107	280	70	64	2,540	12,504
1993	254	2,872	7,442	68	206	1	60	3,170	14,097
1994	675	3,610	10,073	134	124	2	45	2,778	17,466
1995	570	4,810	9,050	57	317	54	47	2,500	17,600
1996	511	5,170	9,800	164	275	43	48	2,140	18,400
1997	742	4,970	10,000	228	----	252	149	2,090	18,600
1998	807	5,980	8,520	48	----	126	373	970	16,900
1999[1]	694	5,540	6,860	69	----	63	421	327	14,300

[1] Preliminary. [2] Including agglomerates. *Source: U.S. Geological Survey (USGS)*

Total[1] Iron Ore Stocks in the United States, at End of Month In Thousands of Metric Tons

Year	Jan.	Feb.	Mar.	Apr.	May	June	July	Aug.	Sept.	Oct.	Nov.	Dec.
1991	22,572	22,218	21,316	20,757	21,756	23,174	23,319	24,329	25,148	25,117	25,358	25,445
1992	24,527	23,162	20,922	20,550	21,501	22,492	23,046	21,721	22,735	23,190	23,433	22,856
1993	21,296	20,806	19,235	18,996	19,180	22,036	22,905	21,575	22,629	21,355	21,615	21,341
1994	19,013	17,816	15,950	14,880	15,251	16,592	17,864	18,931	20,554	20,760	21,552	21,339
1995	20,316	19,361	18,193	18,293	19,371	20,905	22,336	23,632	23,414	24,389	24,123	23,576
1996	22,277	20,744	19,779	20,104	23,426	21,822	22,445	23,663	24,116	24,866	25,465	25,701
1997	25,913	25,262	24,745	24,812	25,001	25,620	26,076	26,971	27,562	28,029	28,053	27,912
1998	27,977	26,317	24,039	25,251	25,576	26,197	27,605	29,037	30,301	30,095	30,199	30,624
1999	29,631	28,463	28,614	28,292	29,151	29,021	28,857	27,840	26,506	25,528	25,290	26,371
2000[2]	24,885	24,810	23,556	23,714	23,653	24,233	24,993	26,333	26,815	24,530		

[1] All stocks at mines, furnace yards and at U.S. docks. [2] Preliminary. *Source: U.S. Geological Survey (USGS)*

Lard

Lard production is directly related to commercial hog production. The largest producers of hogs are the largest producers of lard. China is by far the world's largest producer of hogs with 40 percent of world production. In recent year's, China's production of lard has exceeded 2.5 million metric tonnes. The U.S. is the next largest producer of lard with 8 percent of world production, followed by Germany with 7 percent. Other large producers are Russia, Poland, Spain, and Brazil.

The U.S.D.A. reported that U.S. stocks of lard at the beginning of the 1999/00 (October-September) marketing year were 20.8 million pounds, down 49 percent from the 40.4 million pounds at the start of the 1998/99 season.

U.S. lard production in the 1999/00 marketing year was forecast at 1.08 billion pounds, down 3 percent from production in 1998/99. Small amounts of lard are imported.

In the 1999/00 season, imports were estimated at 2 million pounds, up 5 percent from the previous year. Imports have averaged 2 million pounds per year recently. The total supply for the 1999/00 season is estimated at 1.1 billion pounds.

In terms of usage, domestic use of lard in 1999/00 was estimated at 918 million pounds, down 7 percent from 1998/99. Over the last 100 years, U.S. consumption of lard has averaged 904 million pounds per year. Use of lard is trending higher. Lard finds use in baking and frying fats. The emphasis on healthier diets, which are much lower in fats, could limit the use of lard in certain foods. U.S. exports of lard in 1999/00 were 1.55 million pounds, up 11 percent from the previous year. Total use of lard was projected to be 1.08 billion pounds, down 5 percent from the previous year. Projected ending stocks of lard were 25 million pounds, up 20 percent from the previous marketing year.

World Production of Lard   In Thousands of Metric Tons

Year	Brazil	Canada	China	France	Germany	Italy	Japan	Poland	Romania	Spain	United States	Former USSR	World Total
1991-2	165.7	76.9	1,698.4	135.5	411.3	188.0	85.0	303.3	126.8	170.6	447.7	653.6	5,505.3
1992-3	175.5	77.0	1,767.6	142.9	418.2	192.1	85.8	283.6	119.6	185.8	445.0	534.1	5,487.7
1993-4	165.8	83.2	1,707.0	151.3	409.5	189.5	82.4	239.1	115.7	192.8	451.0	465.0	5,390.1
1994-5	181.6	86.3	1,931.8	153.2	404.8	191.3	83.8	267.9	106.9	196.7	471.2	414.0	5,640.7
1995-6	194.3	83.0	2,136.6	154.6	405.6	198.5	76.3	284.9	105.1	206.5	449.3	385.0	5,860.4
1996-7	199.4	83.1	2,400.2	157.3	396.5	197.6	74.1	259.4	96.3	211.8	437.0	359.3	6,048.8
1997-8[1]	210.8	88.1	2,624.8	162.3	413.4	194.0	67.9	266.6	87.4	229.9	478.9	332.6	6,358.6
1998-9[2]	224.0	97.4	2,728.3	169.0	454.1	202.8	66.4	270.9	80.8	260.6	501.7	308.8	6,596.2
1999-00[3]	236.2	105.1	2,823.8	164.6	436.2	197.6	65.0	264.9	81.5	260.1	490.3	303.9	6,675.7

[1] Preliminary.   [2] Estimate.   [3] Forecast.   *Source: The Oil World*

Supply and Distribution of Lard in the United States   In Millions of Pounds

Year	Supply Production	Supply Stocks Oct. 1	Supply Total Supply	Disappearance Domestic	Disappearance Baking & Frying Fats	Disappearance Margarine[2]	Disappearance Exports	Disappearance Total Disappearance	Direct Use	Per Capita (Lbs.)
1991-2	1,016.3	24.1	1,042.9	884.8	299.0	39.0	131.0	1,015.7	423.7	3.3
1992-3	1,011.2	27.2	1,041.5	886.1	274.0	30.0	129.2	1,015.3	438.6	3.5
1993-4	1,014.7	26.2	1,043.6	890.4	251.0	39.0	118.8	1,009.2	573.0	3.4
1994-5	1,052.4	34.4	1,089.0	924.4	332.2	43.0	140.4	1,064.7	561.9	3.4
1995-6	1,012.6	24.3	1,038.8	921.8	295.9	33.0	94.3	1,016.1	593.0	3.5
1996-7	979.0	22.7	1,002.9	879.6	262.0	15.0	103.3	982.9	602.4	3.5
1997-8	1,064.7	19.9	1,086.7	924.6	285.0	17.0	121.8	1,046.4	623.3	3.4
1998-9[1]	1,106.1	40.4	1,148.4	987.6	254.7	15.0	139.9	1,127.5	654.0	3.6
1999-00[2]	1,075.0	20.8	1,097.8	917.8	240.3	13.7	155.0	1,072.8	675.0	3.5

[1] Preliminary.   [2] Forecast.   [3] Includes edible tallow.   NA = not avaliable.   *Source: Economic Research Service, U.S. Department of Agriculture (ERS-USDA)*

Consumption of Lard (Edible and Inedible) in the United States   In Millions of Pounds

Year	Jan.	Feb.	Mar.	Apr.	May	June	July	Aug.	Sept.	Oct.	Nov.	Dec.	Total
1992	33.9	31.6	39.9	40.0	38.7	39.6	42.9	41.1	47.6	46.4	41.0	37.2	479.9
1993	40.1	34.4	45.9	36.8	38.2	38.8	32.6	38.4	41.8	44.0	43.0	40.3	474.3
1994	33.5	33.9	36.2	34.6	35.9	34.4	32.4	37.5	43.4	43.8	44.7	41.7	452.0
1995	37.5	34.7	41.2	36.2	42.2	44.4	34.9	35.9	35.9	40.1	38.9	36.8	458.7
1996	30.5	35.4	36.7	46.9	36.8	31.4	32.6	33.9	30.9	34.5	34.7	33.6	417.9
1997	26.5	30.5	31.0	36.5	39.9	36.2	36.1	35.0	37.4	39.0	41.5	40.4	429.8
1998	34.1	29.9	31.1	29.6	28.5	35.9	33.0	33.0	37.1	37.7	38.9	33.9	402.7
1999	34.6	30.2	28.8	31.1	30.5	32.9	28.9	33.0	29.2	31.2	31.3	30.3	372.1
2000[1]	27.3	25.7	29.1	23.3	30.3	27.6	24.4	31.3	31.1	32.6	29.6	31.7	343.9

[1] Preliminary.   *Source: Bureau of the Census, U.S. Department of Commerce*

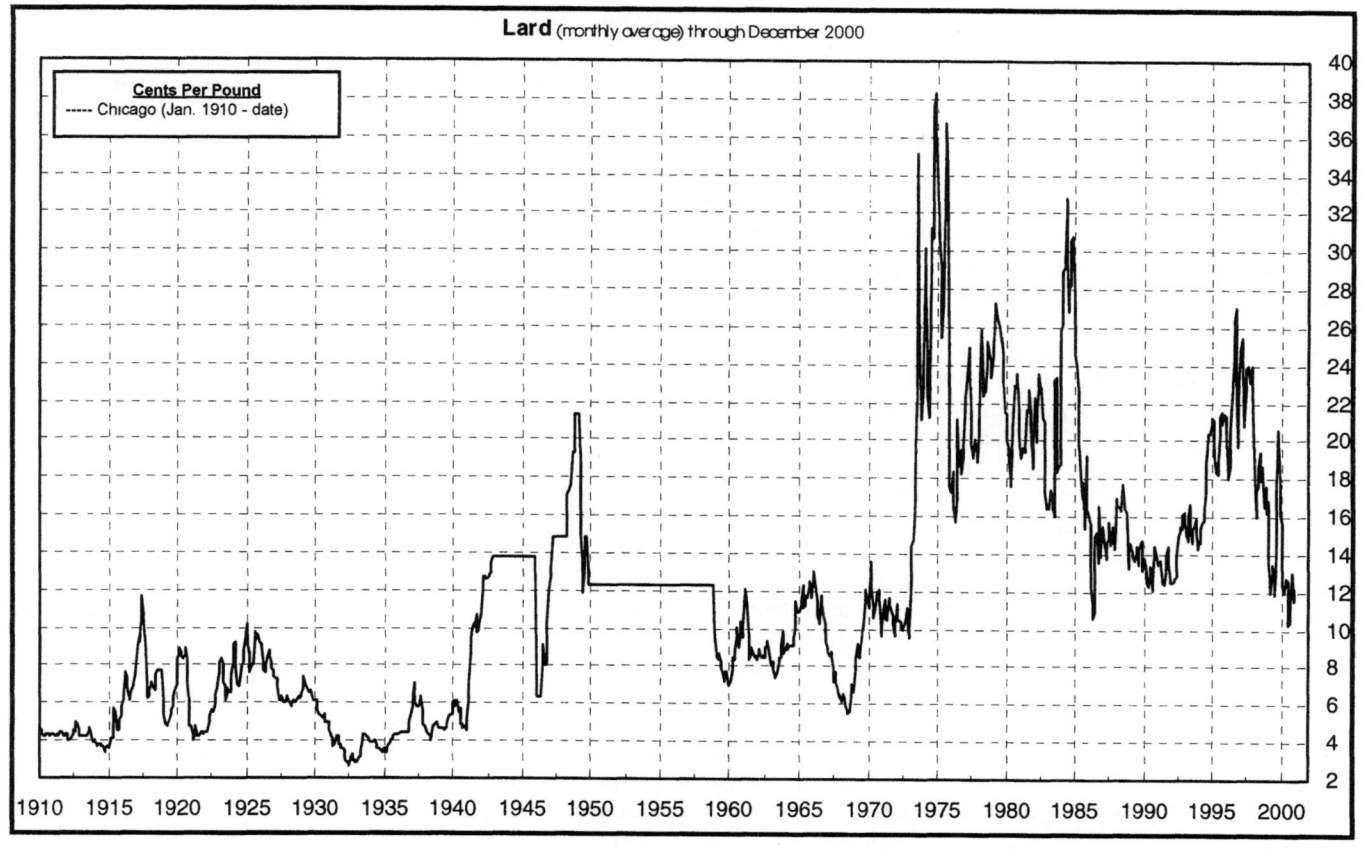

Lard (monthly average) through December 2000

Cents Per Pound
----- Chicago (Jan. 1910 - date)

Average Wholesale Price of Lard, Loose, Tank Cars, in Chicago   In Cents Per Pound

Year	Jan.	Feb.	Mar.	Apr.	May	June	July	Aug.	Sept.	Oct.	Nov.	Dec.	Average
1991	13.50	13.50	13.54	13.63	12.50	12.49	12.44	13.41	13.96	14.42	13.60	12.64	13.30
1992	12.50	12.50	12.57	12.75	12.78	13.93	14.95	15.29	15.49	15.40	16.11	16.25	14.21
1993	15.83	15.03	14.70	16.15	16.67	15.50	14.64	15.42	15.50	15.93	15.26	14.31	15.41
1994	14.50	14.62	15.35	15.74	15.75	16.25	17.24	18.91	20.14	20.39	20.35	20.91	17.51
1995	21.21	21.13	19.25	18.34	18.25	19.02	20.25	21.30	21.48	20.90	21.38	21.35	20.32
1996	20.52	18.17	18.01	18.67	20.47	22.61	24.55	26.30	27.09	23.11	19.70	22.17	21.78
1997	24.93	25.47	24.69	20.82	20.94	22.68	23.83	23.95	23.14	23.41	23.97	22.85	23.39
1998	19.09	16.03	17.36	17.64	18.66	19.38	17.93	18.65	16.58	17.39	17.60	16.27	17.72
1999	16.89	13.91	11.98	13.12	13.43	12.98	11.87	13.89	17.44	20.55	17.74	16.12	14.99
2000	15.66	12.38	11.99	11.96	12.68	12.64	10.32	10.35	11.14	13.01	11.55	12.16	12.15

Source: The Wall Street Journal

United States Cold Storage Holdings of all Lard[1], on First of Month   In Millions of Pounds

Year	Jan.	Feb.	Mar.	Apr.	May	June	July	Aug.	Sept.	Oct.	Nov.	Dec.
1991	----	24.4	----	----	28.3	----	----	24.0	----	----	24.1	----
1992	37.4	27.2	28.9	28.3	26.7	23.2	24.8	29.2	26.9	27.2	22.2	24.8
1993	22.7	25.9	27.2	24.0	22.8	25.8	31.1	27.4	23.6	26.2	24.6	30.1
1994	37.7	38.0	31.8	28.8	25.1	27.4	27.0	25.5	29.7	34.4	34.0	35.8
1995	40.6	50.3	46.4	43.0	36.8	27.1	25.8	22.1	30.2	24.3	19.9	21.6
1996	38.4	38.6	25.8	28.8	21.5	23.2	23.7	30.5	20.7	22.7	20.1	18.8
1997	18.9	16.3	18.5	19.2	18.9	18.7	23.0	23.2	21.5	19.9	21.3	19.7
1998	22.2	30.1	38.3	42.5	41.6	47.6	43.7	44.8	38.8	40.4	34.8	26.3
1999	28.4	30.4	30.6	34.0	27.1	39.9	30.7	25.5	29.4	20.8	19.1	22.8
2000[2]	26.7	27.8	29.2	30.1	20.2	22.5	18.9	19.3	17.3	17.4	16.3	16.8

[1] Stocks in factories and warehouses (except that in hands of retailers).   [2] Preliminary.   *Source: Bureau of the Census, U.S. Department of Commerce*

Lead

Lead is used in a variety of products including batteries, fuel tanks, ammunition, coverings for power and communication cables, cans and containers, solder for pipes and plumbing, as well as construction materials. By far the largest use for lead is in lead-acid batteries, which in the U.S. consume about 90 percent of the lead that is used. Lead and compounds that contain lead are very toxic and there has been an effort to reduce the use of lead. Some of the substitutes for lead include tin, iron, plastic, and bismuth.

The U.S. Geological Survey reported that world mine production of lead in 1999 was 3.04 million metric tonnes compared to 3.10 million tonnes in 1998. The largest producer of lead was Australia with 1999 output of 630,000 tonnes, up 2 percent from the year before. U.S. production of lead was 520,000 tonnes, up 5 percent from a year earlier. In the U.S., there are seven lead mines in Missouri as well as lead mines in Alaska, Colorado, Idaho, and Montana. These produced most of the mined lead. Primary lead was processed at two smelter-refineries in Missouri and a smelter in Montana. Some 68 percent of domestic lead consumption is of secondary lead. Nearly 1.1 million tonnes of secondary lead was produced with nearly all coming from old scrap. About a million tonnes was recovered from used batteries. There were 28 plants in the U.S. that produced secondary lead. Other large producers of lead include China, Peru, Canada, Mexico, and Sweden. World reserves of lead are estimated to be 64 million tonnes.

World mine production (recoverable) of lead in July 2000 was 33,000 tonnes compared to 37,800 tonnes in June. In the first seven months of 2000, mine production was 261,000 tonnes. Data on primary refinery production of lead was not available for year 2000, but for all of 1999 it was 350,0000 tonnes. Secondary refinery production of lead in July 2000 was 88,600 tonnes, with 86,500 tonnes of that reported by smelters and refineries. Some 1,250 tonnes was recovered from copper-base scrap. For the January-July 2000 period, secondary production of lead was 635,000 tonnes. For all of 1999, it was 1.1 million tonnes.

U.S. reported consumption of lead in July 2000 was 127,000 tonnes, down 3 percent from the previous month. In the January-July period, consumption was 919,000 tonnes, while for all of 1999 it was 1.58 million tonnes. In the first seven months of 2000, lead consumed in producing ammunition, shot, and bullets totaled 27,500 tonnes. Lead used in brass and bronze, billet and ingots was 2,290 tonnes. Lead used for cable covering, power and communications, calking lead and building construction was 1,880 tonnes. Lead used in casting metals was 3,350 tonnes, while lead used for solder was 4,190 tonnes. Lead used in storage batteries was 830,000 tonnes.

U.S. imports of refined lead metal in June 2000 were 20,800 tonnes, while in the January-June 2000 period imports were 195,000 tonnes. In 1999, imports totaled 311,000 tonnes. U.S. exports of lead scrap in June 2000 were 6,440 tonnes. In the January-June period exports were 33,400 tonnes, while for all of 1999 exports of scrap were 117,000 tonnes.

World Smelter (Primary and Secondary) Production of Lead — In Thousands of Metric Tons

Year	Australia[3]	Belgium[4]	Canada[3]	China[2]	France	Germany	Italy	Japan	Mexico[3]	Spain	United Kingdom[3]	United States	World Total
1990	229.0	105.8	183.6	296.0	432.7	411.0	166.8	327.4	232.2	110.0	329.4	1,330	5,950
1991	239.4	110.7	212.4	330.0	438.0	362.5	208.2	332.4	161.8	169.0	311.0	1,230	5,770
1992	232.0	116.3	252.9	365.0	284.1	354.3	186.3	330.2	177.0	120.0	346.8	1,220	5,230
1993	243.0	131.1	217.0	412.0	258.7	334.2	182.8	309.5	188.0	123.0	363.8	1,230	5,420
1994	237.0	123.5	251.6	467.9	260.5	331.7	205.9	292.2	171.0	140.0	352.5	1,280	5,360
1995	241.0	122.0	281.4	608.0	296.7	311.2	180.4	287.6	176.0	80.0	320.7	1,390	5,590
1996	228.0	125.0	309.4	706.0	302.8	238.1	209.8	287.4	160.0	86.0	345.6	1,400	5,610
1997	238.0	110.8	271.4	707.0	302.3	329.2	211.6	296.8	178.0	74.9	391.0	1,450	5,830
1998[1]	200.0	120.0	265.5	757.0	306.0	335.0	248.0	302.1	173.0	87.0	350.0	1,450	5,920
1999[2]	275.0	110.0	262.9	859.0	269.0	374.0	215.0	293.5	130.0	85.0	348.0	1,460	6,010

[1] Preliminary. [2] Estimate. [3] Refinded & bullion. [4] Includes scrap. Source: U.S. Geological Survey (USGS)

Consumption of Lead in the United States, by Products — In Metric Tons

Year	Ammunition	Bearing Metals	Pipes, Traps & Bends[2]	Cable Covering	Calking Lead	Casting Metals	Other Metal Products[3]	Total Other Oxides[4]	Sheet Lead	Solder	Storage Battery Grids, Post, etc.	Oxides	Brass and Bronze	Total Consumption
1990	58,210	5,212	9,281	18,253	1,688	14,843	3,812	56,484	21,013	16,490	571,187	448,450	9,943	1,275,226
1991	58,458	3,669	8,975	17,472	1,074	14,141	3,254	59,617	22,334	14,750	591,884	415,233	8,997	1,246,337
1992	64,845	4,785	11,652	15,992	1,045	17,111	3,024	63,225	21,006	13,518	629,147	373,185	9,175	1,236,571
1993	65,100	4,830	5,740	17,165	961	18,500	5,360	63,600	21,200	14,400	677,000	374,000	5,750	1,290,000
1994	62,400	5,560	3,370	16,000	764	18,900	5,330	62,700	21,500	12,200	797,000	425,000	6,320	1,450,000
1995	70,900	6,490	2,210	5,640	935	18,100	5,220	61,700	27,900	16,200	711,000	618,000	5,260	1,560,000
1996	52,100	4,350	1,810	W	767	18,900	5,220	62,100	19,400	9,020	635,000	706,000	5,460	1,540,000
1997	52,400	2,490	1,860	4,930	1,390	34,000	7,570	67,000	19,100	9,580	634,000	761,000	4,410	1,620,000
1998	52,800	2,210	3,130	4,630	1,350	32,600	8,160	53,400	15,500	10,900	685,000	742,000	3,460	1,630,000
1999[1]	58,300	1,570	2,020	2,410	971	34,300	7,130	58,200	15,400	13,100	728,000	744,000	3,940	1,680,000

[1] Preliminary. [2] Including building galvanizing and fishing weights. [3] Including terne metal, type metal, and lead consumerd in foil, collapsible tubes, annealing, plating, [4] Includes paints, glass and ceramic products, and other pigments and chemicals. W = Withheld proprietary data.

Source: U.S. Geological Survey (USGS)

LEAD

Salient Statistics of Lead in the United States — In Thousands of Metric Tons

Year	Net Import Reliance as a % of Apparent Consumption	Production of Refined Lead From Domestic Ores[3]	Foreign Ores[3]	Total Primary	Total Value of Refined Million $	Secondary Lead Recovered As Soft Lead	In Antimonial Lead	In Other Alloys	Total	Total Value of Secondary Million $	Stocks, Dec. 31 Primary	Consumer[4]	Average Price Cents Per Pound New York	London[5]
1990	3	385.6	18.0	403.7	409.5	461.4	425.4	35.6	922.2	935.6	25.5	86.3	46.02	37.05
1991	6	323.9	21.9	345.7	255.2	421.9	426.9	35.8	884.6	652.9	9.1	71.7	33.48	25.30
1992	10	284.0	20.8	304.8	235.9	452.9	424.5	23.1	916.3	709.1	20.5	82.3	35.10	24.50
1993	15	310.7	24.9	335.6	234.4	444.0	417.0	17.0	893.0	625.0	14.3	80.5	31.74	18.42
1994	19	328.0	23.4	351.4	288.0	527.0	371.0	16.1	931.0	763.0	9.3	68.8	37.17	24.83
1995	17	374.0	W	374.0	348.0	584.0	400.0	19.2	1,020.0	951.0	14.2	79.4	42.28	28.08
1996	17	326.0	W	326.0	351.0	625.0	420.0	9.2	1,070.0	1,150.0	8.1	72.1	48.83	31.22
1997	14	343.0	W	343.0	352.0	663.0	411.0	14.2	1,110.0	1,130.0	11.9	89.1	46.54	28.29
1998[1]	21	337.0	W	337.0	336.0	667.0	417.0	16.1	1,120.0	1,110.0	10.9	77.9	45.27	23.96
1999[2]	20	350.0	W	350.0	337.0	635.0	444.0	18.1	1,110.0	1,070.0	12.3	79.5	43.72	22.78

[1] Preliminary. [2] Estimate. [3] And base bullion. [4] Also at secondary smelters. [5] LME data in dollars per metric ton beginning July 1993.
W = Withheld Proprietary data. E = Net exporter. *Source: U.S. Geological Survey (USGS)*

United States Foreign Trade of Lead — In Thousands of Metric Tons

Year	Exports Ore Concentrate	Unwrought Lead[3]	Wrought Lead[4]	Scrap	Ash & Residues	Imports for Consumption Ores, Flue Dust or Fume & Mattes	Base Bullion	Pigs & Bars	Reclaimed Scrap, etc.	Value Million $	General Imports From: Ore, Flue Dust & Matte Australia	Canada	Peru	Pigs & Bars Canada	Mexico	Peru
1990	56.6	57.2	6.8	75.0	13.0	10.7	2.7	90.6	0.3	91.2	1.2	124.3	7.1	70.7	25.0	1.0
1991	88.0	94.4	7.6	72.0	11.0	12.4	0.4	116.5	0.1	82.6	1.0	226.7	3.9	83.6	11.9	0.5
1992	72.3	64.3	5.3	63.2	2.1	5.3	0.2	190.7	0.2	120.6	----	239.9	21.2	124.7	56.1	9.8
1993	41.8	51.4	7.1	54.1	1.7	0.5	----	195.6	0.1	99.4	----	55.7	13.6	130.8	40.3	18.3
1994	38.7	48.2	5.3	88.1	20.6	0.5	0.6	230.8	0.1	146.6	0.5	0.2	----	159.0	31.9	25.6
1995	65.5	48.2	9.0	105.0	8.0	2.6	0.0	264.0	0.1	191.7	1.5	----	0.1	182.0	54.3	22.1
1996	59.7	44.0	16.7	85.3	19.4	6.6	0.0	268.0	0.2	217.0	----	4.4	----	192.0	56.9	17.1
1997	42.2	37.4	15.9	88.4	16.8	17.8	0.0	265.0	0.1	200.3	----	0.8	3.4	186.0	70.4	6.4
1998[1]	72.4	24.1	15.4	99.2	9.0	32.7	0.5	267.0	[6]	191.9	2.4	6.5	18.5	181.0	63.6	11.4
1999[2]	93.5	23.4	13.9	117.0	1.4	12.3	0.1	311.0		196.5				198.0	27.2	6.9

[1] Preliminary. [2] Estimate. [3] And lead alloys. [4] Blocks, pigs, etc. [5] Formerly drosses & flue dust. [6] Less than 1/2 unit. NA = Not avaliable.
Source: U.S. Geological Survey (USGS)

Annual Mine Production of Recoverable Lead in the United States — In Metric Tons

Year	Total	Idaho	Missouri	Montana	Other States	Missouri's % of Total
1990	483,704	W	380,781	W	102,923	79%
1991	465,931	W	351,995	W	113,936	76%
1992	397,923	W	300,589	W	97,334	76%
1993	353,607	W	276,569	W	77,800	78%
1994	363,443	W	290,738	9,940	63,100	80%
1995	386,000	W	359,000	8,350	18,200	93%
1996	426,000	W	397,000	7,970	21,200	93%
1997	448,000	W	412,000	9,230	26,600	92%
1998[1]	481,000	W	439,000	7,310	35,100	91%
1999[2]	503,000	W	464,000	7,950	31,200	92%

[1] Preliminary. [2] Estimate. W = Withheld, included in Other States. NA = Not Avaliable. *Source: U.S. Geological Survey (USGS)*

Mine Production of Recoverable Lead in the United States — In Thousands of Metric Tons

Year	Jan.	Feb.	Mar.	Apr.	May	June	July	Aug.	Sept.	Oct.	Nov.	Dec.	Total
1991	41.5	41.1	41.6	37.8	43.5	36.4	47.5	41.1	36.1	38.9	28.0	26.1	465.9
1992	36.0	34.0	34.0	31.2	31.5	32.4	33.8	32.5	32.5	33.3	30.8	31.7	392.7
1993	33.3	30.5	34.2	30.6	28.5	29.5	25.8	27.5	28.4	27.3	29.5	28.5	355.2
1994	27.6	28.8	33.0	31.3	32.4	29.1	29.4	30.4	31.2	28.0	31.7	29.9	363.4
1995	29.6	30.3	35.2	28.9	32.7	34.8	32.5	33.5	29.9	34.1	31.6	32.1	385.0
1996	36.9	36.4	35.6	35.9	37.5	33.8	35.6	34.1	26.9	35.2	33.6	35.7	426.0
1997	36.7	36.7	37.2	38.6	38.6	35.1	33.4	33.7	34.4	35.4	31.7	32.8	448.0
1998	37.4	35.4	37.8	37.3	35.7	34.7	34.3	35.6	36.1	40.3	37.8	39.2	449.0
1999	41.2	42.1	44.4	43.1	41.7	42.6	47.2	43.6	41.5	41.2	37.8	38.1	504.5
2000[1]	35.1	36.7	43.0	37.5	37.4	37.8	33.0	36.8	36.8	32.4	38.8		442.1

[1] Preliminary. *Source: U.S. Geological Survey (USGS)*

LEAD

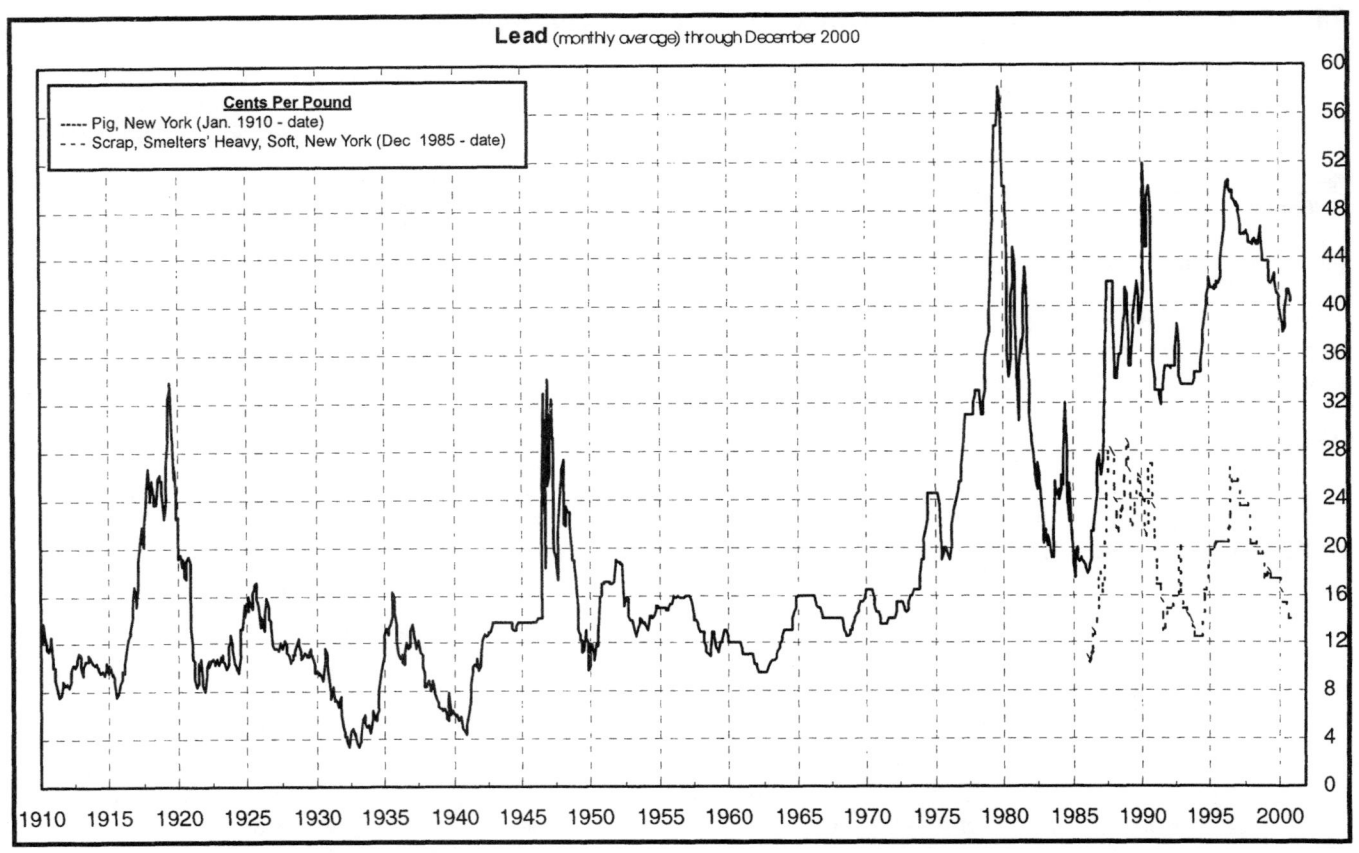

Lead (monthly average) through December 2000

Cents Per Pound
----- Pig, New York (Jan. 1910 - date)
- - - Scrap, Smelters' Heavy, Soft, New York (Dec 1985 - date)

Average Price of Pig Lead, U.S. Primary Producers (Common Corroding)[1]   In Cents Per Pound

Year	Jan.	Feb.	Mar.	Apr.	May	June	July	Aug.	Sept.	Oct.	Nov.	Dec.	Average
1991	34.18	33.00	33.00	33.00	32.00	31.80	33.00	33.00	33.70	35.00	35.00	35.00	33.47
1992	35.00	35.00	35.00	35.00	35.00	35.00	36.91	40.00	40.00	36.64	32.63	32.00	35.68
1993	32.00	32.00	32.00	32.00	32.00	32.00	32.00	32.00	32.00	32.00	32.00	33.00	32.08
1994	34.00	34.00	34.00	34.00	34.00	35.73	37.70	38.00	40.00	42.00	43.70	44.00	37.59
1995	44.00	44.00	42.00	42.00	42.00	42.00	42.00	43.65	44.00	44.00	46.10	48.00	43.65
1996	48.00	49.50	50.96	52.00	52.00	52.00	50.29	49.18	50.00	50.00	50.00	50.00	50.33
1997	50.00	50.00	48.70	48.00	48.00	48.00	48.00	48.00	48.00	48.00	48.00	48.00	48.39
1998	48.00	48.00	48.00	48.00	48.00	48.00	48.00	48.00	48.00	48.00	45.47	45.00	47.54
1999	45.00	45.00	45.00	45.00	45.00	45.00	45.00	45.00	45.00	45.00	45.00	45.00	45.00
2000	45.00	45.00	45.00	45.00	45.00	45.00	45.00	45.00	45.00	45.00	45.00	45.00	45.00

[1] New York Delivery.   Source: American Metal Market (AMM)

Refiners Production[1] of Lead in the United States   In Metric Tons

Year	Jan.	Feb.	Mar.	Apr.	May	June	July	Aug.	Sept.	Oct.	Nov.	Dec.	Total
1991	30,763	30,863	33,771	30,248	27,031	22,371	27,973	28,204	29,411	29,846	26,428	28,813	345,714
1992	29,121	27,691	33,366	27,456	26,742	22,441	24,993	21,587	19,365	22,945	23,674	25,414	304,791
1993	29,627	26,693	30,197	27,578	29,814	28,253	16,734	22,817	32,725	31,220	27,953	31,312	335,014
1994	29,908	30,685	31,420	29,059	31,588	31,707	30,661	27,335	31,185	32,874	29,301	30,447	366,170
1995	32,100	29,100	32,600	32,300	32,600	28,300	31,000	29,300	30,600	34,200	30,100	31,500	374,000
1996	34,700	30,400	30,900	28,600	27,500	21,700	25,500	24,700	25,400	25,300	26,100	25,500	326,000
1997	28,800	28,500	31,900	30,400	30,800	28,700	25,900	28,000	21,600	30,500	29,000	28,700	343,000
1998	29,200	25,900	30,000	29,700	29,500	20,300	28,900	NA	NA	NA	NA	NA	337,000
1999	NA	NA	NA	NA	NA	NA	NA	NA	NA	NA	NA	NA	350,000
2000[2]	NA	NA	NA	NA	NA	NA	NA	NA	NA	NA	NA		

[1] Represents refined lead produced from domestic ores by primary smelters plus small amounts of secondary material passing through these smelters. Includes GSA metal purchased for remelt.   [2] Preliminary.   Source: U.S. Geological Survey (USGS)

Total Stocks of Lead[1] in the United States at Refiners, at End of Month   In Metric Tons

Year	Jan.	Feb.	Mar.	Apr.	May	June	July	Aug.	Sept.	Oct.	Nov.	Dec.
1991	24,177	24,333	26,990	21,261	17,474	16,195	15,362	9,072	6,608	4,091	4,491	9,089
1992	9,774	15,785	21,682	25,220	28,940	26,490	26,634	22,347	17,736	14,971	14,796	20,543
1993	28,069	33,338	34,058	34,306	35,775	32,162	22,753	14,797	15,086	14,408	13,456	14,289
1994	11,964	12,633	12,048	11,445	11,598	10,251	12,368	9,256	8,897	10,659	9,060	9,271
1995	8,200	9,750	11,500	14,500	16,700	16,200	21,300	14,000	12,800	9,820	9,830	14,200
1996	15,000	15,000	15,000	15,000	15,000	19,600	19,900	14,200	12,200	7,060	7,830	8,160
1997	8,460	11,800	21,400	19,900	15,000	10,900	6,530	7,790	5,370	7,310	8,710	11,900
1998	13,000	15,900	18,700	20,900	11,400	11,400	13,700	NA	NA	NA	NA	10,900
1999	NA	NA	NA	NA	NA	NA	NA	NA	NA	NA	NA	NA
2000[2]	NA	NA	NA	NA	NA	NA	NA	NA	NA	NA		

[1] Primary refineries.   [2] Preliminary.   Source: U.S. Geological Survey (USGS)

Total[1] Lead Consumption in the United States   In Thousands of Metric Tons

Year	Jan.	Feb.	Mar.	Apr.	May	June	July	Aug.	Sept.	Oct.	Nov.	Dec.	Total
1991	101.3	105.3	101.2	101.3	98.4	92.4	90.8	101.9	102.7	106.9	102.4	92.7	1,246
1992	102.5	99.3	108.3	98.5	96.0	103.5	94.8	104.8	106.6	105.4	98.2	92.9	1,215
1993	108.9	107.5	112.3	104.6	109.2	113.8	106.8	112.6	117.1	113.2	109.3	102.2	1,357
1994	107.0	115.2	112.8	111.6	113.5	115.2	114.3	115.5	115.9	121.2	118.7	113.0	1,384
1995	119.0	119.0	119.0	109.0	110.0	113.0	115.0	105.0	115.0	116.0	118.0	116.0	1,370
1996	107.0	100.0	106.0	111.0	113.0	106.0	104.0	146.0	140.0	147.0	163.0	143.0	1,530
1997	139.0	138.0	138.0	140.0	137.0	141.0	116.0	119.0	122.0	123.0	117.0	117.0	1,600
1998	116.0	115.0	119.0	128.0	127.0	129.0	128.0	128.0	129.0	129.0	134.0	125.0	1,550
1999	128.0	129.0	130.0	127.0	128.0	130.0	137.0	136.0	141.0	136.0	140.0	133.0	1,595
2000[2]	139.0	139.0	139.0	139.0	140.0	140.0	135.0	141.0	139.0	139.0	136.0		1,665

[1] Represents total consumption of primary & secondary lead as metal, in chemicals, or in alloys.   [2] Preliminary.   Source: U.S. Geological Survey (USGS)

Lead Recovered from Scrap in the United States   In Thousands of Metric Tons (Lead Content)

Year	Jan.	Feb.	Mar.	Apr.	May	June	July	Aug.	Sept.	Oct.	Nov.	Dec.	Total
1991	79.0	74.4	71.0	72.0	72.0	70.7	69.8	70.0	72.3	74.6	70.7	75.9	883.7
1992	76.1	71.5	66.5	71.0	73.3	72.3	71.1	77.7	77.5	79.6	76.9	74.3	888.5
1993	71.1	76.8	71.7	80.2	78.9	72.5	70.3	76.6	76.3	77.0	77.9	79.3	903.6
1994	74.0	76.0	84.2	81.7	81.1	79.0	78.9	79.8	78.4	76.4	81.0	80.4	949.0
1995	82.5	80.8	84.4	72.8	73.7	72.5	79.9	71.5	82.3	80.0	82.3	82.1	945.0
1996	75.7	76.2	84.2	83.7	84.7	80.7	81.2	89.0	92.1	98.8	97.3	93.2	1,100.0
1997	88.0	89.8	91.7	86.0	88.2	85.7	86.7	94.7	97.3	96.2	95.2	91.7	1,110.0
1998	95.0	92.0	92.6	94.1	92.5	89.7	89.3	95.7	94.4	95.0	95.1	90.7	1,110.0
1999	89.5	89.1	88.9	91.0	90.2	91.1	81.3	91.9	91.6	93.5	91.4	93.1	1,082.6
2000[1]	91.0	88.0	91.1	91.4	90.5	91.3	88.6	95.1	94.0	96.0	95.4		1,104.4

[1] Preliminary.   Source: U.S. Geological Survey (USGS)

Domestic Shipments[1] of Lead in the United States, by Refiners   In Thousands of Short Tons

Year	Jan.	Feb.	Mar.	Apr.	May	June	July	Aug.	Sept.	Oct.	Nov.	Dec.	Total
1988	33.5	29.5	39.2	33.0	41.4	44.7	32.0	34.7	33.7	43.0	38.5	35.5	438.7
1989	29.3	28.5	32.2	35.7	45.1	36.4	32.8	41.5	40.0	44.2	40.2	31.1	437.1
1990	39.3	33.9	39.1	33.5	38.4	32.9	32.6	38.9	36.6	38.9	37.9	31.7	433.7
1991	35.4	33.8	34.3	39.8	33.9	26.0	31.8	37.9	35.1	35.7	28.7	26.7	399.2
1992	31.3	23.9	30.4	26.3	25.6	27.2	27.3	28.7	26.3	28.5	26.3	21.7	323.5
1993	24.6	23.6	32.5	30.0	31.3	35.1	28.9	34.0	35.5	35.5	31.7	33.5	376.2
1994	35.9	32.8	35.2	32.7	34.7	36.7	31.6	33.4	34.8	34.3	34.0	33.3	409.3
1995	36.5	30.3	35.1	31.1	33.7	31.9	28.6	40.3	34.9	40.9	33.2	29.8	406.4
1996	37.2	32.4	29.5	30.2	29.4	26.7	27.7	33.5	30.1	33.5	28.1	27.6	366.0
1997[2]	31.5	27.8	24.7	35.2	39.2	36.1	33.4	29.4	26.4	31.5	30.4	28.1	377.8

[1] Includes GSA metal.   [2] Preliminary.   Source: American Metal Market (AMM)

Lumber & Plywood

Lumber prices trended consistently throughout 2000 as there were signs that the rate of growth of the U.S. economy was slowing. Despite the lower prices and slowdown in economic growth, the housing market remained resilient. At the end of year 2000, there remained a lot of questions as to what direction the economy would take in 2001.

U.S. softwood lumber production in August 2000 was 2.9 billion board feet, up 7 percent from July. Total shipments of softwood lumber in August 2000 were 3 billion board feet, up 11 percent from the previous month. Looking at softwood lumber production in August 2000 by regions, the Southern Pine Region produced 1.38 billion board feet with shipments of 1.38 billion board feet. In the January-August 2000 period, production in the Southern Pine Region totaled 11.5 billion board feet. Production in the West Coast Region in August 2000 was 691 million board feet with shipments of 723 million board feet. In the January-August 2000 period, the West Coast Region produced 6 billion board feet of softwood lumber. Production in the Inland Region in August 2000 was 574 million board feet with shipments of 589 million. In the January-August 2000 period softwood lumber production was 4.9 billion board feet. Production in the California Redwood Region in August was 107 million board feet with shipments of 119 million board feet. In the January-August 2000 period, softwood production in the California Redwood Region was 911 million board feet, up 2 percent from 1998. In January-August 2000, total softwood lumber production was 24.8 billion board feet, up less than 1 percent from the same period in 1999. Softwood lumber shipments in the period were 24.6 billion board feet.

Maple flooring production in August 2000 was 2.61 million square feet with shipments of 2.59 million square feet. Orders received for maple flooring were 1.82 million square feet. Gross stocks of maple flooring in August 2000 were 3 million square feet. In July 2000, maple flooring production was 2.22 million square feet with shipments of 2.62 million square feet. Orders received for maple flooring were 1.67 million square feet. In the January-August 2000 period, production of maple flooring was 17.2 million square feet which was up just over 7 percent from the year before. Maple flooring shipments in the first eight months of 2000 were 17.7 million square feet, an increase of 11 percent from the same period in 1999. New orders for maple flooring in January-August 2000 were 15.8 million square feet, up 9 percent from the year before.

Shipments of oak flooring in August 2000 were 48.4 million board feet, an increase of 35 percent from July. Unfilled orders of oak flooring in August 2000 were 13 million board feet, while stocks were 9.3 million board feet. In the January-August 2000 period, shipments of oak flooring were 371.3 million board feet, an increase of 8 percent from a year ago.

Production of structural panels in August were 2.6 billion square feet, an increase of 7 percent from July. Shipments of structural panels in August were 2.62 billion square feet, up 10 percent from the previous month. Orders received for structural panels in August were 2.7 billion square feet, up 10 percent from the previous month. In the January-August 2000 period, production of structural panels was 20.1 billion square feet which was 3 percent more than a year before. Shipments of structural panels in the same period of 2000 were 20.8 billion square feet, an increase of 7 percent from 1999. New orders for structural panel were 20 billion square feet, up 2 percent from 1999. Particleboard shipments in August 2000 were 390 million square feet, down 1 percent from the previous month. In the January-August 2000 period, shipments of particleboard were 3.28 billion square feet, down slightly from 1999.

U.S. exports of softwood logs to Japan in July 2000 were 61.3 billion board feet. In the January-July 2000 period, exports of softwood logs were 508.7 billion board feet. Exports of softwood lumber to Japan in July 2000 were 21.1 billion board feet. In the January-July 2000 period, they were 167 billion board feet. Hardwood log exports in July were 678 million board feet, while in the January-July 2000 period they were 12.7 billion board feet. Exports of hardwood lumber to Japan in July were 4.1 billion board feet, while in the January-July 2000 period they were 33.3 billion board feet. Other markets for U.S. wood products include South Korea, China, Taiwan, and Australia.

Futures Markets

Lumber futures and options are traded on the Chicago Mercantile Exchange.

U.S. Housing Starts: Seasonally Adjusted Annual Rate   In Thousands of Units

Year	Jan.	Feb.	Mar.	Apr.	May	June	July	Aug.	Sept.	Oct.	Nov.	Dec.	Average
1991	798	965	921	1,001	996	1,036	1,063	1,049	1,015	1,079	1,103	1,079	1,009
1992	1,176	1,250	1,297	1,099	1,214	1,145	1,139	1,226	1,186	1,244	1,214	1,227	1,201
1993	1,210	1,210	1,083	1,258	1,260	1,280	1,254	1,300	1,343	1,392	1,376	1,533	1,292
1994	1,272	1,337	1,564	1,465	1,526	1,409	1,439	1,450	1,474	1,450	1,511	1,455	1,446
1995	1,407	1,316	1,249	1,267	1,314	1,281	1,461	1,416	1,369	1,369	1,452	1,431	1,354
1996	1,467	1,491	1,424	1,516	1,504	1,467	1,472	1,557	1,475	1,392	1,489	1,370	1,477
1997	1,355	1,486	1,457	1,492	1,442	1,494	1,437	1,390	1,546	1,520	1,510	1,566	1,474
1998	1,525	1,584	1,567	1,540	1,536	1,641	1,698	1,614	1,582	1,715	1,660	1,792	1,621
1999	1,804	1,738	1,737	1,561	1,649	1,562	1,704	1,657	1,628	1,636	1,663	1,769	1,676
2000[1]	1,744	1,822	1,630	1,652	1,591	1,571	1,527	1,525	1,537	1,528	1,570	1,598	1,608

[1] Preliminary.   Total Privately owned.   Source: American Forest & Paper Association (AF&PA)

World Production of Industrial Roundwood by Selected Countries   In Thousands of Cubic Meters

Year	Austria	Canada	Czech[3] Repulic	Finland	France	Germany	Japan	Poland	Russia[4]	Spain	Sweden	Turkey	United States
1991	12,535	159,039	13,770	31,616	33,754	29,823	27,938	14,334	275,300	12,988	47,600	5,502	388,310
1992	9,255	165,436	8,820	35,279	32,596	29,159	26,934	15,720	164,000	11,624	49,720	8,458	403,100
1993	9,107	169,770	9,706	37,758	29,563	29,357	25,570	15,940	136,030	11,419	50,200	9,408	401,520
1994	11,101	177,346	11,172	44,319	32,442	36,018	24,456	16,711	83,650	12,990	52,100	9,211	410,781
1995	10,746	183,113	11,716	45,799	33,561	36,914	22,897	17,677	83,050	12,997	59,800	10,745	408,948
1996	11,212	183,113	11,882	42,178	30,643	34,538	22,897	18,853	73,005	12,433	52,500	10,229	406,625
1997[1]	11,302	183,113	12,881	47,757	32,596	35,488	NA	20,097	88,410	12,433	56,400	9,773	416,092
1998[2]	10,858	183,113	13,171	49,638	33,070	36,441	NA	21,824	75,690	12,433	54,300	9,979	420,478

[1] Preliminary.   [2] Estimate.   [3] Formerly part of Czechoslovakia; data not reported separately until 1992.   [4] Formerly part of the U.S.S.R.; data not reported separately until 1992.   NA = Not available.   *Source: Food and Agriculture Organization of the United Nations (FAO-UN)*

Lumber Production and Consumption in the United States   In Millions of Board Feet

	Production						Domestic Consumption						
	Softwood						Softwood						
Year	California Redwood	Inland Region	Southern Pine	West Coast	Total	Total Hardwood	Inland Region	Southern Pine	West Coast	Softwood Imports	Total	U.S. Hardwood	Hardwood Imports	Total Lumber
1992	1,571	9,263	14,106	7,948	34,526	11,639	9,107	13,893	6,709	13,381	45,737	10,853	276	56,866
1993	1,354	8,312	14,392	7,319	32,947	11,914	8,129	14,020	6,043	15,260	45,810	10,556	335	56,702
1994	1,474	8,097	15,010	7,902	34,107	12,311	7,856	14,618	6,833	16,380	48,104	11,127	394	59,625
1995	1,305	7,015	14,708	7,452	32,233	12,434	6,956	14,384	6,530	17,396	47,749	11,372	380	59,501
1996	1,371	7,079	15,262	7,745	33,266	NA	7,073	15,112	6,821	18,214	49,883	NA	NA	NA
1997	1,511	7,383	16,113	7,772	34,667	NA	7,180	15,993	7,012	18,002	50,863	NA	NA	NA
1998	1,391	7,298	16,151	7,797	34,677	NA	7,256	15,788	7,502	18,686	52,209	NA	NA	NA
1999	1,325	7,580	16,922	8,625	36,605	NA	7,445	16,525	8,115	19,178	54,262	NA	NA	NA
I	325	1,872	4,055	2,071	8,843	NA	1,839	3,876	1,876	4,270	12,576	NA	NA	NA
II	345	1,884	4,562	2,271	9,628	NA	1,896	4,596	2,197	5,080	14,573	NA	NA	NA
III	345	1,940	4,193	2,156	9,173	NA	1,887	4,109	2,053	5,003	13,820	NA	NA	NA
IV	310	1,884	4,112	2,127	8,961	NA	1,823	3,944	1,989	4,825	13,293	NA	NA	NA
2000[1] I	360	1,994	4,329	2,368	9,618	NA	1,909	4,200	2,181	4,736	13,750	NA	NA	NA
II	340	1,851	4,465	2,319	9,537	NA	1,801	4,390	2,211	5,142	14,312	NA	NA	NA
III	322	1,611	4,089	1,999	8,523	NA	1,600	3,955	1,919	4,914	13,108	NA	NA	NA

[1] Preliminary.   NA = Not available.   *Source: American Forest & Paper Association (AFPA)*

Stocks (Gross) of Softwood Lumber in the United States, on First of Month   In Millions of Board Feet

Year	Jan.	Feb.	Mar.	Apr.	May	June	July	Aug.	Sept.	Oct.	Nov.	Dec.
1991	4,734	4,925	4,949	4,946	4,849	4,600	4,699	4,684	4,793	4,786	4,741	4,710
1992	4,616	4,603	4,567	4,608	4,730	4,731	4,678	4,606	4,418	4,419	4,365	4,263
1993	4,669	4,217	4,166	4,239	4,490	4,618	4,599	4,526	4,418	4,445	4,282	4,298
1994	4,207	4,512	4,656	4,816	4,883	4,649	4,738	4,432	4,349	4,539	4,235	4,294
1995	4,403	4,336	4,344	4,653	4,352	4,663	4,508	4,323	4,342	4,359	4,361	4,335
1996	4,293	4,435	4,459	4,357	4,251	4,153	4,156	4,038	3,918	3,965	3,939	3,906
1997	3,973	4,019	4,113	4,067	3,963	4,017	3,915	3,871	3,875	3,927	3,925	3,865
1998	3,884	3,970	4,048	4,062	4,158	4,084	NA	NA	NA	NA	NA	NA
1999	3,519	3,595	3,688	3,726	3,698	3,581	3,512	3,485	3,533	3,491	3,562	3,536
2000[1]	3,639	3,704	3,811	3,887	3,960	2,738	3,902	3,936	3,878	3,848	3,957	3,875

[1] Preliminary.   NA = Not available.   *Source: American Forest & Paper Association (AFPA)*

Lumber (Softwood)[2] Production in the United States   In Millions of Board Feet

Year	Jan.	Feb.	Mar.	Apr.	May	June	July	Aug.	Sept.	Oct.	Nov.	Dec.	Total
1991	3,534	3,410	3,661	3,958	3,837	3,762	3,664	3,808	3,682	3,933	3,473	3,254	43,976
1992	3,836	3,628	4,121	3,862	3,632	3,911	3,882	3,746	3,736	4,048	3,617	3,425	45,444
1993	3,545	3,596	3,954	3,809	3,555	3,787	3,685	3,930	3,824	4,103	3,883	3,576	45,247
1994	3,839	3,662	4,097	3,735	3,972	4,113	3,785	4,124	4,135	4,145	3,636	3,851	47,094
1995	4,084	3,577	3,931	3,675	3,805	3,897	3,641	3,866	3,757	4,105	3,549	3,297	45,184
1996	2,600	2,606	2,757	2,903	2,833	2,819	2,942	3,077	2,858	3,179	2,758	2,424	33,756
1997	3,012	2,791	2,866	3,149	2,890	3,027	3,097	2,889	2,905	3,094	2,536	2,487	34,743
1998	2,767	2,760	2,928	3,084	2,647	3,051	3,079	2,930	2,953	3,167	2,667	2,754	34,787
1999	2,783	2,921	3,190	3,227	3,071	3,318	3,115	3,054	2,992	3,096	2,954	2,795	36,516
2000[1]	3,020	3,128	3,474	3,058	3,276	3,249	2,730	2,971	2,839	3,041	2,761	2,318	35,865

[1] Preliminary.   [2] Data prior to 1996 are Softwood and Hardwood.   *Source: American Forest & Paper Association (AFPA)*

LUMBER & PLYWOOD

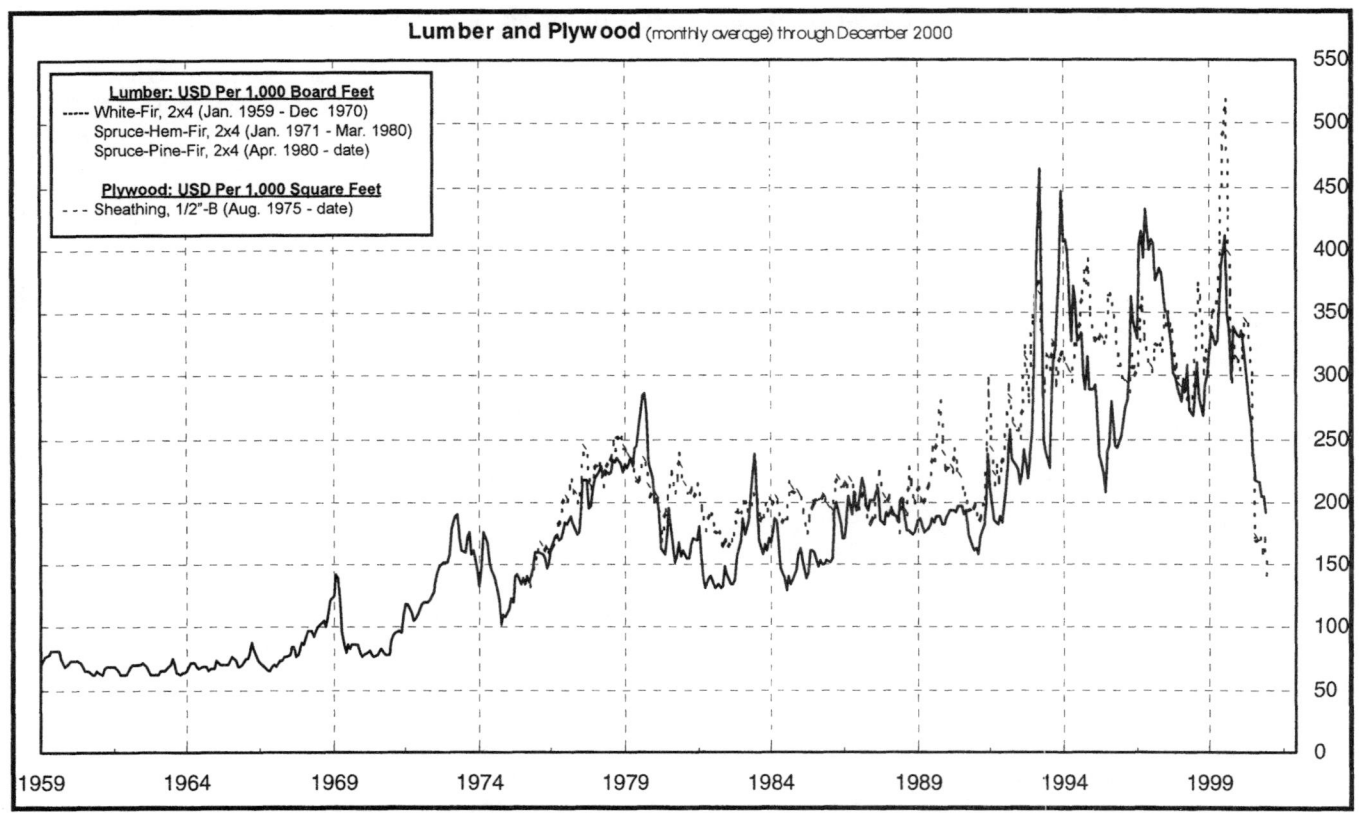

Lumber and Plywood (monthly average) through December 2000

Lumber: USD Per 1,000 Board Feet
- - - White-Fir, 2x4 (Jan. 1959 - Dec 1970)
Spruce-Hem-Fir, 2x4 (Jan. 1971 - Mar. 1980)
Spruce-Pine-Fir, 2x4 (Apr. 1980 - date)

Plywood: USD Per 1,000 Square Feet
- - - Sheathing, 1/2"-B (Aug. 1975 - date)

Lumber (Softwood)[2] Shipments in the United States   In Millions of Board Feet

Year	Jan.	Feb.	Mar.	Apr.	May	June	July	Aug.	Sept.	Oct.	Nov.	Dec.	Total
1991	3,240	3,301	3,617	4,037	4,028	3,764	3,412	3,926	3,676	4,012	3,477	3,370	44,559
1992	3,912	3,693	4,078	3,682	3,565	3,936	3,884	3,878	3,692	4,147	3,745	3,491	45,703
1993	3,575	3,649	3,852	3,563	3,402	3,759	3,721	3,997	3,724	4,211	3,798	3,617	44,868
1994	3,576	3,663	3,912	3,761	4,192	4,091	4,039	4,163	3,914	4,321	3,603	3,696	46,931
1995	3,971	3,584	3,855	3,831	3,765	4,026	3,826	3,870	3,760	4,055	3,478	3,367	45,388
1996	2,460	2,581	2,863	3,002	2,934	2,813	3,058	3,196	2,813	3,206	2,792	2,353	34,071
1997	2,966	2,697	2,890	3,253	2,834	3,126	3,139	2,885	2,852	3,096	2,598	2,461	34,797
1998	2,685	2,685	2,863	3,019	2,684	3,175	3,132	2,963	2,948	3,205	2,703	2,865	34,927
1999	2,689	2,829	3,177	3,227	3,071	3,383	3,141	3,004	3,037	3,021	2,944	2,691	36,214
2000[1]	2,953	3,039	3,394	2,974	3,292	3,309	2,686	3,027	2,871	2,931	2,752	2,418	35,646

[1] Preliminary.   [2] Data prior to 1996 are Softwood and Hardwood.   *Source: American Forest & Paper Association (AFPA)*

Imports and Exports of Lumber in the United States, by Type   In Millions of Board Feet

										Exports[2]				
										Softwood				
		Imports[2]								Pond-				
		Software								erosa/				
		Douglas					Total	Total	Douglas		White	Southern		Total	Total
Year	Cedar	Fir	Hemlock	Pine	Spruce	Total	Hardwood	Lumber	Fir	Hemlock	Pine	Pine	Total	Hardwood	Lumber
1991	700.6	354.1	287.8	55.7	2,248.3	11,741.5	226.2	11,998.2	798.1	497.7	222.9	396.0	2,863.2	934.3	3,858.9
1992	666.4	355.3	300.0	91.4	2,410.5	13,380.5	276.4	13,681.9	735.0	396.7	308.7	440.5	2,650.7	977.2	3,687.1
1993	615.3	327.6	354.9	84.6	3,104.1	15,259.9	335.0	15,625.4	664.9	340.4	273.3	339.6	2,376.4	1,008.9	3,468.9
1994	702.6	336.2	399.2	97.2	2,948.5	16,380.3	394.4	16,787.1	591.9	283.2	157.2	356.7	2,186.6	1,040.9	3,333.4
1995	768.0	395.4	258.1	97.1	2,827.7	17,395.3	379.7	17,786.9	637.9	227.0	106.7	334.6	1,987.5	1,100.5	3,192.5
1996	726.6	264.4	257.1	133.4	1,988.8	18,213.5	396.8	18,640.6	685.4	194.9	96.6	314.5	1,935.3	1,141.0	3,173.4
1997	586.1	263.9	249.8	314.2	1,040.4	18,014.3	464.5	18,505.9	435.8	104.6	122.1	299.3	1,820.0	1,281.4	3,189.0
1998	514.0	417.1	267.8	363.4	848.6	18,685.7	589.4	19,306.1	251.8	39.0	112.9	279.4	1,264.9	1,118.6	2,601.1
1999	590.5	426.0	259.0	448.7	802.8	19,177.8	708.4	19,903.4	248.6	53.6	140.3	326.0	1,430.6	1,241.7	2,867.3
2000[1] I	157.3	90.1	49.4	123.8	186.9	4,736.3	202.9	4,944.0	67.6	19.9	31.4	68.0	361.7	338.0	725.5
II	207.5	111.4	51.3	118.8	202.1	5,141.5	193.8	5,341.6	66.3	13.2	32.9	80.7	354.1	342.0	754.7
III	170.6	137.7	38.2	113.7	232.2	4,913.9	200.1	5,120.6	55.1	12.4	48.2	92.0	371.5	318.6	724.5

[1] Preliminary.   [2] Includes sawed timber, board planks & scantlings, flooring, box shook and railroad ties.

Source: American Forest & Paper Association (AFPA)

Lumber Futures - Chicago Mercantile Exchange (weekly close) as of 29-Dec-2000   USD Per 1,000 Board Feet

Average Open Interest of Random Lumber[1] Futures in Chicago   In Contracts

Year	Jan.	Feb.	Mar.	Apr.	May	June	July	Aug.	Sept.	Oct.	Nov.	Dec.
1991	1,922	2,003	2,023	2,354	2,076	2,601	2,571	2,181	2,276	2,480	2,206	1,606
1992	1,969	2,651	2,743	2,467	1,900	1,774	1,338	1,369	1,507	1,441	1,745	2,155
1993	2,194	2,432	2,163	2,055	2,302	2,658	2,254	2,141	2,011	2,080	2,140	2,721
1994	2,571	2,814	2,638	2,563	1,936	1,838	1,705	1,854	2,102	2,169	1,702	1,967
1995	1,757	1,923	2,142	2,509	2,742	3,252	2,896	2,918	2,809	3,039	2,626	2,940
1996	3,378	4,040	3,752	4,395	5,666	4,972	3,280	5,243	4,743	4,797	4,341	3,691
1997	3,745	3,211	3,048	3,337	2,895	3,137	2,767	3,119	3,267	4,006	3,606	4,068
1998	4,249	3,332	3,394	4,102	4,353	4,773	4,048	4,081	3,466	4,295	3,434	3,893
1999	4,864	5,497	4,698	4,456	4,927	6,405	6,263	4,882	3,457	3,704	2,963	2,868
2000	3,004	3,131	2,728	3,175	3,171	3,218	3,064	3,638	3,845	4,277	4,208	4,405

[1] July 1995 thru March 1996, Lumber and Random Lumber.   *Source: Chicago Mercantile Exchange (CME)*

Volume of Trading of Random Lumber[1] Futures in Chicago   In Contracts

Year	Jan.	Feb.	Mar.	Apr.	May	June	July	Aug.	Sept.	Oct.	Nov.	Dec.	Total
1990	27,416	21,914	20,948	18,362	19,053	16,084	16,465	13,446	8,914	11,839	15,794	11,749	201,984
1991	10,535	13,460	10,326	11,309	15,135	19,029	19,350	14,912	12,214	14,054	10,295	9,902	160,521
1992	17,073	16,778	17,557	13,713	14,059	13,807	12,177	13,043	12,127	11,261	11,514	17,425	170,534
1993	14,915	15,080	14,808	14,661	14,241	15,308	13,287	13,358	12,400	13,248	18,150	18,728	178,184
1994	16,837	15,204	17,323	17,380	14,996	14,348	11,542	13,327	14,856	13,032	10,997	13,121	172,963
1995	12,150	12,909	15,088	12,139	14,536	20,126	13,766	16,919	15,718	18,981	15,551	14,803	182,686
1996	22,954	19,960	20,956	27,094	28,271	26,100	19,302	27,792	31,982	32,042	25,236	22,525	304,214
1997	28,561	20,946	21,071	24,624	18,248	24,797	20,308	18,503	21,736	24,416	15,131	21,977	260,318
1998	19,556	20,339	20,881	24,673	20,519	24,112	21,763	20,453	19,412	19,578	22,002	16,559	249,847
1999	25,962	22,184	28,151	22,618	23,835	30,410	30,791	25,683	24,177	18,125	20,802	15,118	287,856

[1] July 1995 thru March 1996, Lumber and Random Lumber.   *Source: Chicago Mercantile Exchange (CME)*

LUMBER & PLYWOOD

Production of Plywood by Selected Countries   In Thousands of Cubic Meters

Year	Austria	Canada	Finland	France	Germany	Italy	Japan	Poland	Romania	Russia	Spain	Sweden	United States
1994	150	1,834	700	594	397	427	4,865	124	97	890	210	85	17,380
1995	150	1,831	778	559	498	418	4,421	115	83	939	210	108	17,140
1996	150	1,814	869	537	512	402	4,421	109	83	972	210	119	16,975
1997	150	1,828	987	576	392	414	NA	118	81	968	125	113	15,987
1998	150	1,760	992	472	428	420	NA	178	76	1,094	125	114	15,732
1999[1]	150	1,760	1,000	480	400	430	NA	178	70	1,200	125	114	15,504
2000[2]	150	1,760	1,050	480	380	430	NA	185	70	1,335	125	114	15,019

[1] Preliminary.   [2] Estimate.   NA = Not available.   *Source: Food and Agricultural Organization of the United Nations (FAO-UN)*

Imports of Plywood by Selected Countries   In Thousands of Cubic Meters

Year	Austria	Belgium	Canada	Denmark	France	Germany	Italy	Japan	Netherlands	Sweden	Switzerland	United Kingdom	United States
1994	104	267	288	171	234	1,003	257	4,045	560	126	144	1,202	1,547
1995	116	146	353	188	260	1,177	323	4,394	552	112	136	1,127	1,791
1996	115	215	424	167	256	975	295	5,314	522	135	129	1,132	1,930
1997	120	313	428	196	310	1,083	312	5,326	484	184	138	947	1,973
1998	121	487	108	280	325	1,074	380	NA	530	145	143	963	2,150
1999[1]	123	500	125	250	332	1,070	370	NA	500	140	140	960	2,169
2000[2]	123	500	125	250	332	1,100	370	NA	500	140	140	960	2,107

[1] Preliminary.   [2] Estimate.   NA = Not available.   *Source: Food and Agricultural Organization of the United Nations (FAO-UN)*

Exports of Plywood by Selected Countries   In Thousands of Cubic Meters

Year	Austria	Baltic States	Belgium	Canada	Finland	France	Germany	Italy	Netherlands	Poland	Russia	Spain	United States
1994	158	143	134	511	627	193	131	108	102	66	568	67	1,346
1995	130	138	88	818	668	183	149	96	72	60	670	48	1,395
1996	150	187	88	870	794	214	135	117	64	53	612	77	1,384
1997	166	198	101	859	861	223	135	125	50	90	615	69	1,624
1998	180	NA	309	456	831	221	161	157	56	93	736	40	858
1999[1]	190	NA	325	570	850	230	140	130	50	95	800	40	902
2000[2]	190	NA	325	600	900	245	140	130	50	98	900	40	847

[1] Preliminary.   [2] Estimate.   NA = Not available.   *Source: Food and Agricultural Organization of the United Nations (FAO-UN)*

Selected World Prices of Plywood

Year	Jan.	Feb.	Mar.	Apr.	May	June	July	Aug.	Sept.	Oct.	Nov.	Dec.	Average
Southeast Asia, Lauan, Wholesale Price, Spot Tokyo In U.S. Cents Per Sheet[1]													
1996	529.12	548.59	529.22	521.11	535.48	523.62	521.39	538.27	528.50	525.09	526.22	518.62	528.77
1997	500.31	479.63	489.39	485.57	511.91	524.85	512.10	500.68	480.05	454.68	438.61	424.25	483.50
1998	409.19	413.35	387.32	371.74	363.05	349.38	348.29	324.83	349.59	380.46	390.58	417.38	375.43
1999	441.27	420.34	418.38	434.22	426.27	430.68	426.82	441.49	458.03	462.25	468.20	477.41	441.30
2000	456.19	438.49	451.62	454.44	443.40	452.49	443.97	444.25	459.05	451.82			449.57
Canada, Export Unit Value, F.O.B. In Canadian Dollar Per Cubic Meter													
1992	426.14	409.62	373.22	396.94	387.59	395.95	354.61	373.58	385.20	395.29	410.59	353.95	388.56
1993	392.59	396.65	393.73	424.19	515.51	448.76	408.39	435.72	505.58	517.58	494.52	476.08	450.78
1994	442.04	574.74	553.92	553.81	542.95	458.48	472.29	510.01	526.42	454.20	462.90	499.71	504.29
1995	473.77	480.78											477.28
Finland, Export Unit Value, F.O.B. In Markka Per Cubic Meter													
1995	3,681	3,809	3,751	3,897	3,752	3,769	3,771	3,543	3,430	3,370	3,268	2,923	3,579
1996	3,084	2,548	3,129	3,296	3,075	3,225	3,070	3,003	3,245	3,036	3,264	2,900	3,060
1997	3,021	2,943	3,032	3,157	3,174	3,336	3,220	3,222	3,321	3,408	3,465	3,563	3,235
1998	3,488	3,565	3,573	3,774	3,567	3,698	3,542	3,374	3,486	3,474	3,426	3,022	3,505
United Kingdom, Import Unit Value, C.I.F. In Pound Sterling Per Cubic Meter													
1995	232.68	239.77	257.68	264.72	229.18	268.11	256.09	241.61	263.31	285.36	275.38	282.68	258.05
1996	238.86	249.65	224.40	273.23	256.16	275.38	269.36	247.83	253.37	261.66	260.77	293.42	258.67
1997	235.57	234.39	340.66	378.17	274.27	256.75	248.45	276.09	268.64	277.69	270.27	294.06	262.92
1998	188.51	229.59	230.75	237.89	215.24	207.63	209.45	204.69	200.66	206.68	206.01		212.46

[1] Sheet measurement = 1.2cm X 90.0cm X 1.80m.   *Source: Food and Agricultural Organization of the United Nations (FAO-UN)*

Magnesium

Magnesium is one of the most abundant elements found in the Earth's crust and the third most plentiful element found in seawater. Resources from which magnesium may be recovered are virtually unlimited and widespread. Magnesium-bearing brines in the ocean are estimated to be in the billions of tonnes. Magnesium can be recovered from seawater along coastlines where salinity is high. Magnesium is also found in minerals such as dolomite, magnesite, olivine, and brucite.

The U.S. Geological Survey estimated that world primary production of magnesium metal in 1999 was 265,000 metric tonnes excluding production in the United States. In 1998, world production was 369,000 tonnes including U.S. production of 106,000 tonnes. The U.S. is the world's largest producer of magnesium metal. In 1999, other large producers were Canada with 80,0000 tonnes, China with 55,000 tonnes, and Russia with 45,000 tonnes. Other producers include Norway, Israel, and France. World reserves of magnesium metal are considered sufficient for current and future requirements.

Magnesite is used to produce magnesium metal. World production of magnesite in 1999 was estimated to be 2.91 million tonnes, down 6 percent from 1998. U.S. data was withheld from the total. The largest magnesite producer was China with output of 700,000 tonnes in 1999. The next largest producer was North Korea with 1999 output estimated at 460,000 tonnes. Another large producer was Turkey with 1999 output of 300,000 tonnes. Other large producers include Russia, Slovakia, Greece, and Austria. China was the major source for caustic-calcined and dead-burned magnesia.

U.S. imports of magnesium metal in May 2000 were 2,390 tonnes, up 41 percent from the previous month. In the January-May 2000 period, imports of magnesium metal were 9,360 tonnes. For all of 1999, magnesium metal imports were 26,900 tonnes. Imports of magnesium waste and scrap in May 2000 were 775 tonnes compared to 676 tonnes in April. In the first five months of 2000, waste and scrap imports were 3,680 tonnes. For all of 1999, imports were 6,780 tonnes. Imports of magnesium alloys in May 2000 were 5,370 tonnes, up 15 percent from the previous month. In January-May 2000, imports were 24,300 tonnes, while for all of 1999 they were 56,500 tonnes. Imports of magnesium sheet, tubing, ribbons, wire, powder, and other items in May 2000 were 32 tonnes. For all of 1999 they were 593 tonnes. Total imports of magnesium products in 1999 were 90,700 tonnes.

Exports of magnesium metal in January-May 2000 were 2,320 tonnes and for 1999 totaled 4,790 tonnes. Exports of waste and scrap in the first five months of 2000 were 2,080 tonnes and for 1999 totaled 16,500 tonnes. Total exports of magnesium items in 1999 were 29,000 tonnes.

World Production of Magnesium (Primary and Secondary)   In Metric Tons

| | Primary Production | | | | | | | | Secondary Production | | | | |
Year	Brazil	Canada	China	France	Norway	Russia[4]	United States	World Total	Japan	United Kingdom	United States	Former USSR	World Total
1990	8,700	25,300	5,900	14,000	48,222	88,000	139,333	354,000	23,308	900	54,808	7,500	88,100
1991	7,800	35,512	8,600	14,050	44,322	80,000	131,288	342,000	17,158	800	50,543	7,000	77,100
1992	7,300	25,800	10,600	13,660	30,404	40,000	137,000	295,000	12,978	800	57,000	6,500	78,900
1993	9,700	23,000	11,800	10,982	27,300	30,000	132,000	269,000	13,215	1,000	58,900	6,000	80,700
1994	9,700	28,900	24,000	12,280	27,635	35,400	128,000	282,000	19,009	1,000	62,100	5,000	88,700
1995	9,700	48,100	93,600	14,450	28,000	37,500	142,000	395,000	11,767	1,000	65,100	6,000	85,500
1996	9,000	54,000	73,100	14,000	28,000	35,000	133,000	368,000	8,175	1,000	71,200	6,000	88,000
1997	9,000	57,700	75,990	13,740	28,000	39,500	125,000	378,000	10,934	1,000	77,600	NA	91,100
1998[1]	9,000	77,100	70,500	14,000	28,000	41,500	106,000	385,000	7,807	1,000	77,100	NA	87,500
1999[2]	9,000	71,000	83,000	14,000	28,000	35,000	W	277,000	7,500	1,000	87,300	NA	97,400

[1] Preliminary.   [2] Estimate.   [3] Formerly part of the U.S.S.R.; data not reported separately until 1992.   W = Withheld proprietary data.

Source: U.S. Geological Survey (USGS)

Salient Statistics of Magnesium in the United States   In Metric Tons

| | Production | | | | | | | $ Price | Domestic Consumption of Primary Magnesium | | | | | |
| | | Secondary | | | | | | | Castings | Wrought | Total | Aluminum | Other | |
Year	Primary (Ingot)	New Scrap	Old Scrap	Total	Total Exports[3]	Imports for Consumption	Stocks Dec. 31[4]	Per Pound[5]	Structural Products			Alloys	Uses[6]	Total
1990	139,333	23,424	31,384	54,808	51,834	26,755	26,000	1.43-1.63	9,078	10,944	20,022	45,060	31,026	76,086
1991	131,288	23,059	27,484	50,543	55,160	31,863	27,000	1.43	8,857	8,802	17,659	45,809	28,404	74,213
1992	136,947	26,191	30,854	57,045	51,951	11,844	13,000	1.46-1.53	10,223	8,843	19,066	41,003	33,758	74,761
1993	132,144	28,313	30,577	58,890	38,815	37,248	26,000	1.43-1.46	12,543	9,870	22,413	46,498	32,202	78,700
1994	128,000	32,500	29,600	62,100	45,200	29,100	20,030	1.63	15,676	7,690	23,366	61,100	27,900	89,000
1995	142,000	35,400	29,800	65,100	38,300	34,800	21,193	1.93-2.25	15,231	8,510	23,741	60,200	25,100	85,300
1996	133,000	41,100	30,100	71,200	40,500	46,600	25,000	1.70-1.80	16,400	8,080	24,480	52,300	25,500	77,800
1997	125,000	47,000	30,500	77,600	40,500	65,100	23,000	1.60-1.70	20,643	6,840	27,400	50,000	23,000	73,000
1998[1]	106,000	45,200	31,800	77,100	35,400	82,500	27,000	1.52-1.62	27,057	7,100	34,157	52,000	20,900	72,900
1999[2]	W	53,400	33,900	87,300	29,100	90,700	W	1.40-1.55	49,181	9,380	58,561	57,800	14,900	72,700

[1] Preliminary.   [2] Estimate.   [3] Metal & alloys in crude form & scrap.   [4] Estimate of Industry Stocks, metal.   [5] Magnesium ingots (99.8%), f.o.b. Valasco, Texas.   [6] Distributive or sacrificial purposes.   W = Withheld proprietary data.   *Source: U.S. Geological Survey (USGS)*

Manganese

Manganese is primarily used in the steel industry as an alloy. Manganese is essential to iron and steel production by virtue of its sulfur-fixing, deoxidizing, and alloying properties. Manganese increases the metal's hardness so virtually all steel contains some manganese. Steel making accounts for almost all manganese use although there are a variety of other uses for manganese. Manganese is used in aluminum alloys and in oxide form is used in dry cell batteries. Manganese is also used in plant fertilizers and animal feeds. Manganese ore, when converted to a metallic alloy with iron, forms the compound ferromanganese.

The U.S. Geological Survey estimated world mine production of manganese in 1999 at 6.74 million metric tonnes. This represented a decline of 4 percent from 1998. The largest producer of manganese was South Africa with output of 1.27 million tonnes, down 2 percent from the previous year. China was the next largest producer with output of 1.2 million tonnes, the same as in 1998. Production by Gabon was one million tonnes, up nearly 4 percent from 1998. Other large producers of manganese include Australia, Brazil, India, and the Ukraine. World reserves of manganese are estimated to be 689 million tonnes with the largest reserves in South Africa.

U.S. imports of manganese ore in January-July 2000 totaled 293,000 tonnes, gross weight, with a manganese content of 148,000 tonnes. Manganese ore with a content of 47 percent or more manganese totaled 244,000 tonnes, gross weight, with a manganese content of 126,000 tonnes. Imports of manganese ore with a content of 20 percent to 47 percent totaled 48,600 tonnes with a manganese content of 22,200 tonnes. By far, the largest supplier of manganese ore to the U.S. was Gabon followed by Australia, Brazil, and Mexico.

U.S. imports of unwrought manganese metal in the first seven months of 2000 were 9,760 tonnes. Imports of other types of manganese metal were 344 tonnes. The major supplier of manganese metal was South Africa followed by China. U.S. imports of manganese dioxide in January-July 2000 were 31,300 tonnes. The largest supplier was Australia with 16,300 tonnes followed by South Africa and Ireland. Other suppliers were Greece and Belgium. U.S. imports of ferromanganese in the first seven months of 2000 were 199,000 tonnes, gross weight, with a manganese content of 157,000 tonnes. Imports of low-carbon ferromanganese were 11,500 tonnes with a manganese content of 9,900 tonnes. Imports of medium-carbon manganese were 48,700 tonnes, gross weight, with a manganese content of 39,400 tonnes. Imports of high-carbon ferromanganese in the period were 139,000 tonnes with a manganese content of 108,000 tonnes. The major supplier of this type of ferromanganese was South Africa.

World Production of Manganese Ore — In Thousands of Metric Tons (Gross Weight)

Year	Australia[2] 37-53[4]	Brazil 30-50	China 30	Gabon 50-53	Georgia[5] 29-30	Ghana 30-50	Hungary[3] 30-33	India 10-54	Mexico 27-50	Morocco 50-53	South Africa 30-48+	Ukraine[5] 29-30	World Total
1990	1,920	2,300	4,080	2,423	----	247	60	1,385	451	49	4,402	8,500	26,108
1991	1,412	2,000	5,150	1,620	----	320	30	1,401	254	59	3,146	7,240	22,900
1992	1,251	1,703	5,300	1,556	500	276	18	1,810	407	44	2,464	5,819	21,800
1993	2,092	1,837	5,860	1,290	300	295	59	1,655	363	43	2,507	3,800	20,500
1994	1,920	2,199	3,570	1,436	150	270	55	1,632	307	31	2,851	2,979	18,000
1995	2,180	2,398	6,900	1,930	100	217	----	1,764	472	----	3,199	3,200	23,300
1996	2,109	2,506	7,600	1,983	97	448	----	1,797	485	----	3,240	3,070	24,300
1997	2,136	2,124	6,000	1,904	----	437	----	1,596	534	----	3,121	3,040	21,900
1998	1,500	2,149	5,300	2,092	----	537	----	1,557	510	----	3,044	2,226	20,200
1999[1]	1,892	1,644	5,500	2,092	----	541	----	1,500	459	----	3,122	1,986	20,400

[1] Preliminary. [2] Metallurgical Ore. [3] Concentrate. [4] Ranges of percentage of manganese. [5] Formerly part of the U.S.S.R.; data not reported separately until 1992. *Source: U.S. Geological Survey (USGS)*

Salient Statistics of Manganese in the United States — In Thousands of Metric Tons (Gross Weight)

Year	Net Import Reliance as a % of Apparent Consumption	Manganese Ore (35% or More Manganese)				Ferromanganese			Avg. Price Mn. Metallurgical Ore $ Lg. Ton Unit[4]	Silicomanganese	
		Imports for Consumption	Exports	Consumption	Stocks, Dec. 31[3]	Imports for Consumption	Exports	Consumption		Exports	Imports
1990	100	307	70	497	379	380	7	413	3.78	1.8	224.5
1991	100	234	66	473	275	320	15	346	3.72	2.9	258.3
1992	100	247	13	438	276	304	13	339	3.25	9.2	257.2
1993	100	232	16	389	302	347	18	341	2.60	9.4	316.0
1994	100	331	15	449	269	336	11	347	2.40	6.8	273.0
1995	100	394	15	486	309	310	11	348	2.40	7.8	305.0
1996	100	478	32	478	319	374	10	326	2.55	5.3	323.0
1997	100	355	84	510	241	304	12	337	2.44	5.4	306.0
1998[1]	100	332	8	499	163	339	14	290	2.40	6.7	346.0
1999[2]	100	460	4	479	172	312	12	281	2.26	3.7	301.0

[1] Preliminary. [2] Estimate. [3] Including bonded warehouses; excludes Gov't stocks; also excludes small tonnages of dealers' stocks. [4] 46-48% Mn, C.I.F. U.S. Ports. *Source: U.S. Geological Survey (USGS)*

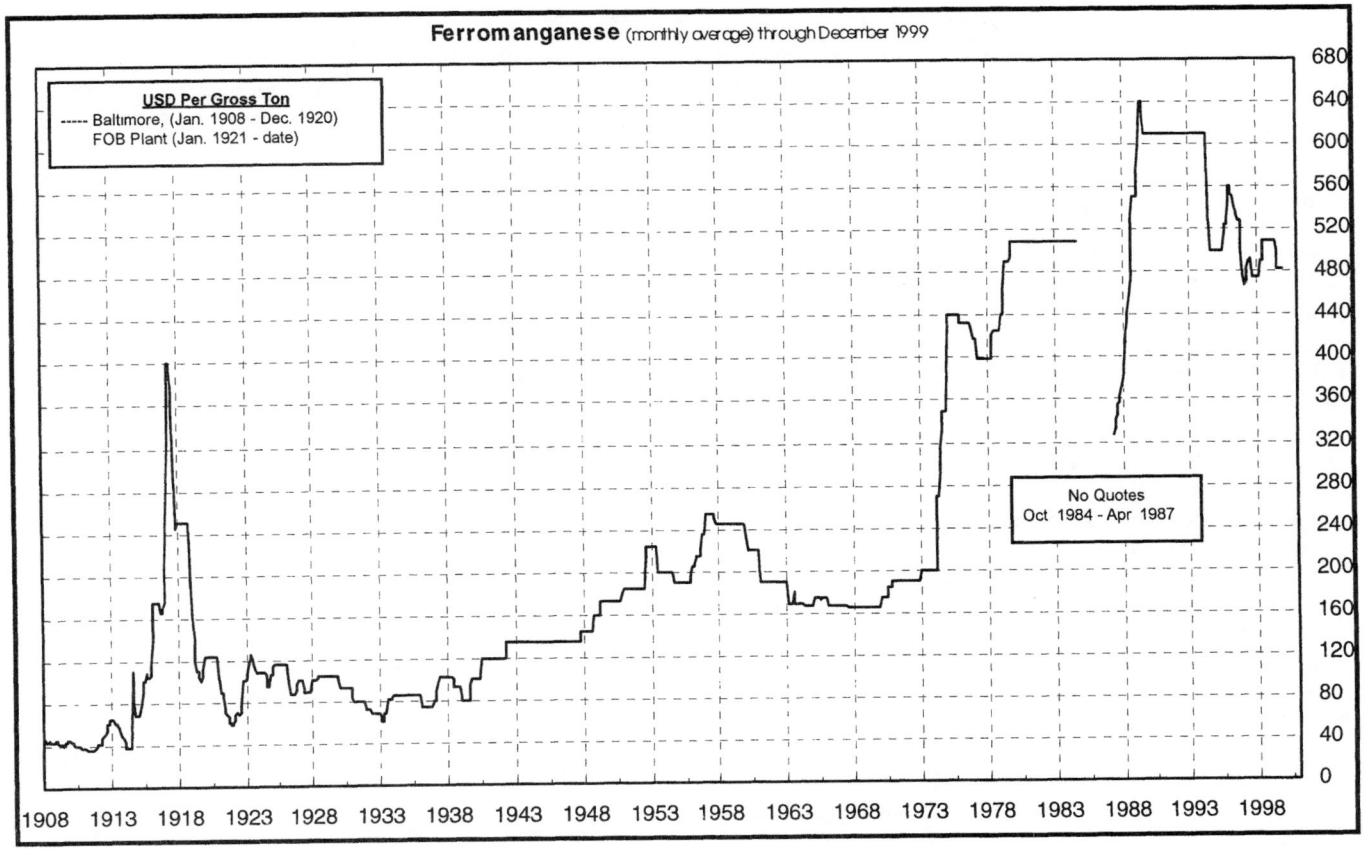

Ferromanganese (monthly average) through December 1999

USD Per Gross Ton
----- Baltimore, (Jan. 1908 - Dec. 1920)
FOB Plant (Jan. 1921 - date)

No Quotes
Oct 1984 - Apr 1987

Imports[3] of Manganese Ore (20% or More Mn) in the United States   In Metric Tons (Mn Content)

Year	Australia	Brazil	Gabon	Mexico	Morocco	South Africa	Total	Customs Value Thous. $
1990	32,544	20,662	67,828	2,732	18	9,958	148,944	40,054
1991	16,485	2,583	79,997	4,673	44	----	117,255	40,332
1992	25,519	15,541	75,354	3,930	56	----	120,400	29,967
1993	30,171	5,573	66,659	7,317	43	6,006	115,770	24,927
1994	23,200	4,530	112,000	13,700	56	7,780	161,000	29,800
1995	31,600	7,080	104,000	23,600	37	13,100	187,000	33,300
1996	48,900	5,640	140,000	16,100	9	20,800	231,000	42,400
1997	16,400	9,100	99,400	30,100	37	----	156,000	30,800
1998[1]	18,700	12,100	94,900	14,600	----	13,800	160,000	27,800
1999[2]	23,500	1	142,000	9,130	----	39,100	224,000	37,200

[1] Preliminary.   [2] Estimate.   [3] Imports for consumption.   *Source: U.S. Geological Survey (USGS)*

Average Price of Ferromanganese   In Dollars Per Gross Ton

Year	Jan.	Feb.	Mar.	Apr.	May	June	July	Aug.	Sept.	Oct.	Nov.	Dec.	Average
1990	610.00	610.00	610.00	610.00	610.00	610.00	610.00	610.00	610.00	610.00	610.00	610.00	610.00
1991	610.00	610.00	610.00	610.00	610.00	610.00	610.00	610.00	610.00	610.00	610.00	610.00	610.00
1992	610.00	610.00	610.00	610.00	610.00	610.00	610.00	610.00	610.00	610.00	610.00	610.00	610.00
1993	610.00	610.00	610.00	610.00	610.00	527.50	500.00	500.00	500.00	500.00	500.00	500.00	548.13
1994	610.00	610.00	610.00	610.00	610.00	527.50	500.00	518.75	525.00	525.00	542.50	560.00	514.27
1995	500.00	500.00	500.00	500.00	500.00	500.00	500.00	518.75	527.50	527.50	501.25	477.50	531.91
1996	560.00	552.50	550.00	550.00	541.00	535.00	533.13	527.50	527.50	527.50	501.25	477.50	480.00
1997	477.50	467.50	470.00	482.50	490.00	490.00	490.00	492.50	475.00	475.00	475.00	475.00	480.00
1998	175.00	175.00	175.00	190.00	190.00	510.00	510.00	510.00	510.00	510.00	510.00	510.00	497.92
1999	510.00	510.00	510.00	510.00	510.00	498.75	482.50	482.50	482.50	482.50	482.50	482.50	495.21

Domestic standard, high carbon, FOB plant, carloads.   *Source: American Metal Market (AMM)*

Meats

U.S. commercial red meat production—the combined total of beef, veal, lamb, and pork—during 2000 totaled a record large 45.7 billion pounds, marginally above 1999's total. However, estimates for 2001 suggest production of 45 billion pounds. Red meat will account for about 55 percent of total U.S. meat production in 2000, and poultry the balance. The combined annual total of 82.7 billion pounds compares with 81.7 billion in 1999, and a forecast of 83 billion in 2001. Beef production in 2000 of 26.8 billion pounds compares with 26.4 billion in 1999. Pork production of 18.9 billion pounds in 2000 compares with 19.3 billion in 1999. Forecasts for total 2001 output are 25.4 billion pounds of beef and 19.4 billion pounds of pork. Poultry production is expected to increase in 2001, to a record 31.6 billion pounds from 30.6 billion in 2000. U.S. veal and lamb production are insignificant.

Worldwide, China is the largest red meat producer at 47 million metric tonnes. Their output is mostly pork with 41.6 million tons in 2000, almost one-third of the world total. The U.S. is second with about one-half of China's total output. However, U.S. beef production is double what China produces. The slide in red meat production in the former U.S.S.R. still shows little sign of abating with 2000 production estimated at 3.3 million tonnes vs. 3.4 million in 1999, and a further drop to 3.2 million likely in 2001.

U.S. per capita beef consumption (retail weight) in 2000 of 69.7 pounds compares with 69 pounds in 1999, and a forecast of only 66 pounds in 2001. Pork use of 52.4 pounds in 2000 compares with 53.8 in 1999, and 53.2 pounds forecast for 2001. The pork industry continues to aggressively advertise pork as a white meat, while the beef industry's advertising focuses on the ease (time-wise) of preparing beef for dinner. For both meats, however, consumer preferences have shifted to foods containing less fat which has benefited poultry at red meat's expense. Per capita retail broiler and turkey consumption totaled a record large 96 pounds in 2000, and is forecast at 98.6 pounds in 2001. Nutritional and advertising factors aside, beef usage in 2000 improved partly due to the strong economy and higher disposable incomes, which in turn helped to increase the restaurant demand for beef. A less buoyant economy in 2001 may adversely impact on beef demand.

Choice steer market prices (basis Nebraska) averaged $68.84/cwt. in 2000 vs. $65.46 in 1999; forecasts for 2001 are for an average between $71.00-$77.00. Hog barrow and gilt prices of $44.51/cwt. in 2000 compare with $34.00 in 1999, and estimates for 2001 of $40.00-$43.00/cwt.

U.S. red meat imports in 2000 of 4.0 billion pounds compares with 3.7 billion in 1999, and forecasts of 4.1 billion in 2001, with beef imports accounting for more than one-half of the totals. U.S. red meat exports, again mostly beef, totaled 3.8 billion pounds in 2000 vs. 3.7 billion in 1999, and a forecast of 3.8 billion pounds in 2001.

World Total Meat Production[3]   In Thousands of Metric Tons

Year	Argentina	Australia	Brazil	Canada	China[4]	France	Germany	Italy	Mexico	Russia	United Kingdom	United States	World Total
1992	2,602	2,810	5,620	2,107	29,406	3,997	4,994	2,648	2,626	6,748	2,297	18,589	116,309
1993	2,630	2,780	5,795	2,052	32,254	3,901	4,796	2,642	2,718	6,260	2,236	18,488	115,852
1994	2,682	2,807	7,030	2,132	36,968	3,868	5,092	2,618	2,852	5,659	2,323	19,361	124,693
1995	2,668	2,644	7,530	2,204	42,653	3,941	5,053	2,602	2,942	4,860	2,359	19,811	129,482
1996	2,636	2,650	7,750	2,226	36,947	3,973	5,161	2,668	2,832	4,487	2,088	19,634	123,100
1997	3,033	2,914	7,590	2,332	42,500	4,046	5,053	2,632	2,875	4,086	2,183	19,667	128,993
1998	2,648	2,973	7,830	2,488	45,982	4,065	5,244	2,595	2,852	3,775	2,367	20,541	134,134
1999	2,890	2,940	8,105	2,800	47,670	4,086	5,532	2,707	2,955	3,544	2,238	20,994	137,352
2000[1]	2,988	2,946	8,400	2,935	49,600	4,054	5,515	2,717	3,020	3,434	2,143	20,980	139,262
2001[2]	2,970	2,285	8,705	3,050	49,000	3,870	5,470	2,590	2,965	3,240	1,793	20,488	134,046

[1] Preliminary.   [2] Forecast.   [3] Data through 2000, includes beef, veal, pork, sheep and goat meat. Beginning 2001, excludes sheep and goat.
[4] Predominately pork production.   *Source: Foreign Agricultural Service, U.S. Department of Agriculture (FAS-USDA)*

Production and Consumption of Red Meats in The United States

	Beef			Veal			Lamb & Mutton			Pork (Excluding Lard)			All Meats		
	Commercial Production	Consumption		Commercial Production	Consumption		Commercial Production	Consumption		Commercial Production	Consumption		Commercial Production	Consumption	
		Total	Per Capita		Total	Per Capita		Total	Per Capita		Total	Per Capita		Total	Per Capita
Year	-- Million Pounds --		Lbs.[4]	- Million Pounds -		Lbs.[4]	- Million Pounds -		Lbs.[4]	-- Million Pounds --		Lbs.[4]	-- Million Pounds --		Lbs.[4]
1992	22,968	24,261	95.0	310	299	1.2	343	388	1.5	17,185	17,475	68.4	40,795	42,437	166.1
1993	22,942	24,006	93.0	267	286	1.1	329	381	1.5	17,030	17,419	67.5	40,568	42,092	163.1
1994	24,278	25,124	96.4	283	290	1.2	304	345	1.3	17,658	17,829	68.4	42,523	43,588	167.3
1995	25,115	25,534	97.0	308	319	1.2	264	338	1.1	17,085	16,826	63.3	42,772	43,017	162.6
1996	25,419	25,863	97.4	378	378	1.4	268	334	1.1	17,117	16,795	63.3	43,182	43,370	163.2
1997	25,490	25,611	95.9	334	333	1.2	260	332	1.1	17,274	16,823	61.4	43,358	43,099	159.6
1998	25,760	26,305	93.3	262	265	1.0	251	360	1.0	19,011	18,309	65.3	45,284	45,239	160.6
1999[1]	26,493	26,932	69.0	235	235	1.0	248	358	1.0	19,308	18,952	54.0	46,284	46,477	125.0
2000[2]	26,882	27,362	70.0	225	225	1.0	232	353	1.0	18,935	18,608	52.0	46,274	46,548	124.0
2001[3]	25,831	26,513	67.0	208	209	1.0	220	354	1.0	19,280	18,916	53.0	46,639	45,992	121.0

[1] Preliminary.   [2] Estimate.   [3] Forecast.   [4] Data through 1998, are for Carcass weight. Beginning 1998, data are for Retail-weight basis.
Source: Economic Research Service, U.S. Department of Agriculture (ERS-USDA)

Total Red Meat Imports[3] (Carcass Weight Equivalent) of Principal Countries · In Thousands of Metric Tons

Year	Canada	France	Germany	Hong Kong	Italy	Japan	Rep. of Korea	Nether-lands	Russia	Singa-pore	United Kingdom	United States	Total
1992	237	1,027	1,338	265	1,231	1,388	187	208	292	147	885	1,424	5,733
1993	292	1,010	1,319	280	1,139	1,480	134	207	227	150	889	1,449	6,118
1994	313	39	190	298	77	1,628	191	35	880	28	217	1,434	6,529
1995	283	39	150	223	37	1,840	239	25	1,084	28	294	1,284	6,465
1996	276	44	139	202	61	1,916	240	31	1,068	38	276	1,249	6,460
1997	311	47	132	238	64	1,727	276	56	1,129	36	293	1,383	6,737
1998	303	44	125	313	57	1,736	173	32	895	31	255	1,555	6,671
1999	325	52	135	329	61	1,885	365	26	1,235	39	256	1,730	7,844
2000[1]	350	53	138	336	67	1,936	408	30	785	38	255	1,873	7,799
2001[2]	360	21	95	349	63	1,890	410	32	900	32	148	1,839	7,618

[1] Preliminary. [2] Forecast. [3] Data through 2000, includes beef, veal, pork, sheep and goat meat. Beginning 2001, excludes sheep and goat.
Source: Foreign Agricultural Service, U.S. Department of Agriculture (FAS-USDA)

Total Red Meat Exports[3] (Carcass Weight Equivalent) of Principal Countries · In Thousands of Metric Tons

Year	Argentina	Australia	Brazil	Canada	China	Denmark	France	India	Ireland	Nether-lands	New Zealand	United States	World Total
1992	301	1,510	470	453	195	1,657	864	110	643	1,491	884	789	7,484
1993	283	1,469	425	494	315	1,272	917	120	672	1,470	858	779	7,290
1994	379	1,495	417	521	256	550	352	138	347	133	934	984	8,138
1995	522	1,374	320	576	328	399	302	206	367	136	864	1,186	8,219
1996	472	1,299	330	658	274	387	290	220	305	195	875	1,294	8,361
1997	439	1,423	354	776	206	531	282	231	271	202	1,001	1,446	9,003
1998	292	1,588	449	848	241	490	214	263	308	150	987	1,545	8,897
1999	347	1,664	631	1,139	164	594	333	284	369	189	850	1,680	9,990
2000[1]	361	1,633	710	1,315	156	575	206	301	289	160	860	1,722	9,661
2001[2]	390	1,255	775	1,425	150	610	185	310	254	150	495	1,711	8,856

[1] Preliminary. [2] Forecast. [3] Data through 2000, includes beef, veal, pork, sheep and goat meat. Beginning 2001, excludes sheep and goat.
Source: Foreign Agricultural Service, U.S. Department of Agriculture (FAS-USDA)

United States Meat Imports by Type of Product · In Metric Tons

Year	Beef and Veal Fresh, Chilled & Frozen	Beef and Veal Canned, Including Sausage	Beef and Veal Other Prepared or Preserved	Lamb, Mutton and Goat, Except Canned	Pork Fresh and Frozen	Pork Canned[2]	Pork Other Prepared or Preserved	Sausage, All Types	Mixed Sausage	Other Meats[3]	Variety Meats, Fresh or Frozen	Total
1990	699,251	57,636	10,939	19,056	233,534	109,313	13,375	3,421	1,874	18,560	11,423	1,178,382
1991	709,997	60,511	12,929	19,100	215,933	82,342	16,948	2,144	1,534	22,979	18,266	1,162,683
1992	728,922	64,303	10,641	23,853	185,672	61,005	16,553	2,453	1,674	19,225	20,059	1,134,360
1993	719,377	59,786	14,559	24,468	207,652	75,434	17,686	2,689	1,368	18,679	25,298	1,166,996
1994	714,450	61,575	13,335	23,276	209,026	75,443	17,577	2,237	1,899	18,724	27,407	1,164,949
1995	641,916	52,012	13,528	29,919	194,386	61,904	15,571	2,553	1,935	19,550	25,972	1,059,246
1996	640,652	53,388	13,616	33,097	183,555	55,247	15,277	2,418	1,639	21,934	32,472	1,053,295
1997	732,933	51,538	12,064	37,871	191,045	56,353	14,632	2,466	1,608	25,852	44,162	1,170,524
1998[1]	822,883	54,288	14,902	51,695	217,192	61,137	14,658	2,861	786	23,669	46,908	1,310,979

[1] Preliminary. [2] Includes canned hams, shoulders and bacon; not specified elsewhere. [3] Mostly mixed luncheon meats.
Source: Foreign Agricultural Service, U.S. Department of Agriculture (FAS-USDA)

United States Meat Exports by Type of Product · In Metric Tons

Year	Beef and Veal Fresh, Chilled & Frozen	Beef and Veal Prepared and Preserved	Lamb and Mutton, Fresh or Frozen	Pork Fresh, Chilled & Frozen	Pork Hams & Shoulders, Cured	Pork Bacon	Other Pork Prepared or Preserved Not Canned	Other Pork Prepared or Preserved Canned	Sausage, Bologna & Frank-furters	Variety Meats, Fresh, Chilled & Frozen	Other Meats[2]	Total
1990	339,925	7,783	2,490	66,756	5,567	4,518	4,310	1,036	14,208	228,623	70,558	745,774
1991	395,830	10,255	3,798	76,378	4,696	5,469	6,180	1,263	24,021	281,034	61,380	870,304
1992	436,534	12,061	3,278	116,582	8,181	7,376	5,812	2,347	22,817	303,700	57,144	975,832
1993	410,635	14,477	3,608	129,041	5,032	7,088	4,761	2,350	34,200	338,408	45,938	995,538
1994	517,458	13,419	3,766	149,414	8,434	12,081	4,472	2,973	46,906	375,029	34,694	1,168,646
1995	581,798	13,651	2,511	228,071	12,066	13,823	6,265	3,613	56,853	447,837	34,113	1,400,601
1996	597,605	14,577	2,478	268,032	9,748	15,843	7,560	5,330	92,503	469,782	42,260	1,525,718
1997	675,994	15,227	2,545	285,805	9,018	12,362	9,230	7,691	122,248	424,724	58,469	1,623,313
1998[1]	696,149	17,950	2,528	355,164	11,742	13,641	9,872	8,445	104,340	447,645	46,681	1,714,157

[1] Preliminary. [2] Includes sausage ingredients, cured (excluding canned); meat and meat products canned; and baby food, canned.
Source: Foreign Agricultural Service, U.S. Department of Agriculture (FAS-USDA)

MEATS

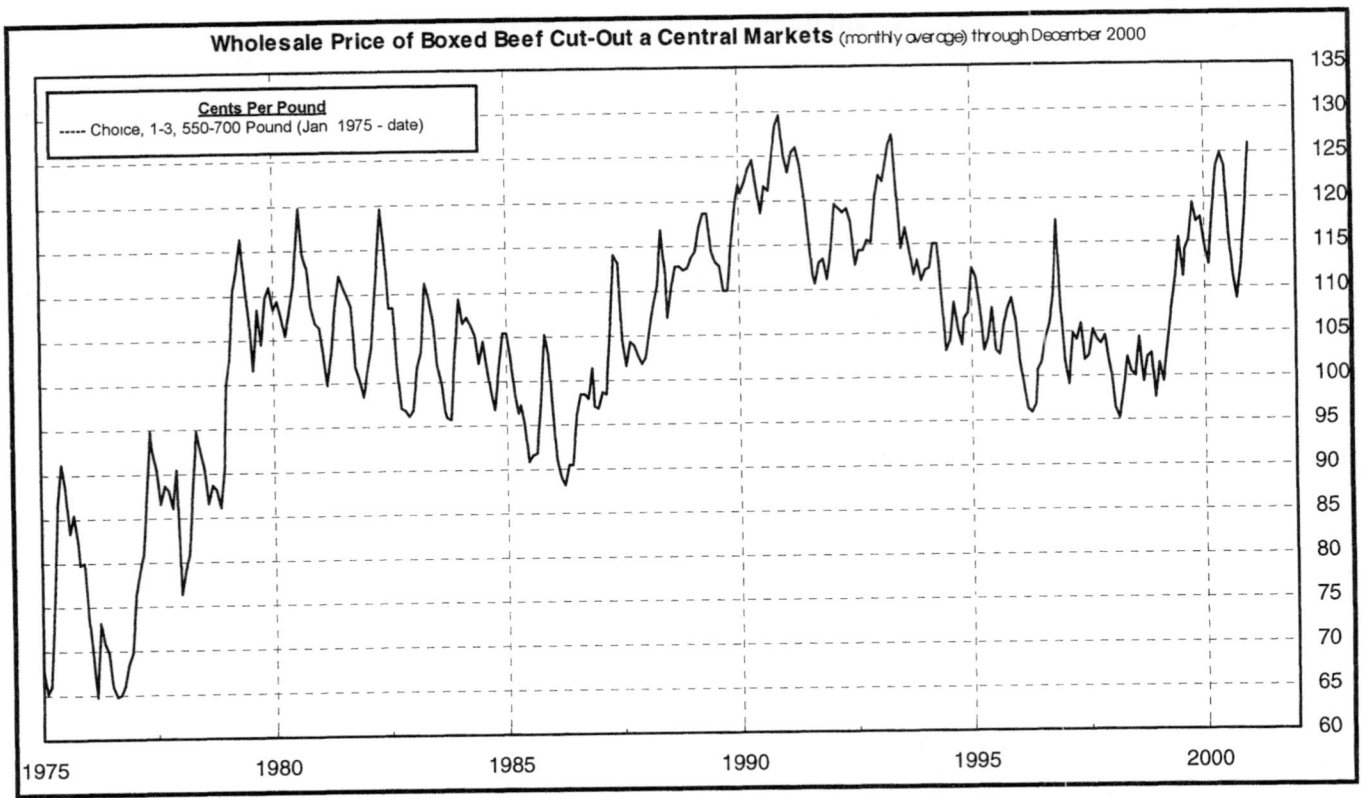

Wholesale Price of Boxed Beef Cut-Out a Central Markets (monthly average) through December 2000

Cents Per Pound
----- Choice, 1-3, 550-700 Pound (Jan 1975 - date)

Exports and Imports of Meats in the United States (Carcass Weight Equivalent)[4] In Millions of Pounds

| | Exports | | | | Imports | | | |
| | Beef | Lamb and | | All | Beef | Lamb and | | All |
Year	and Veal	Mutton	Pork[4]	Meat	and Veal	Mutton	Pork[4]	Meat
1991	1,188	10	290	1,488	2,406	41	775	3,223
1992	1,324	8	420	1,752	2,440	50	645	3,135
1993	1,275	8	446	1,730	2,401	53	740	3,194
1994	1,611	9	549	2,169	2,369	49	743	3,161
1995	1,821	6	787	2,614	2,103	64	664	2,831
1996	1,877	6	970	2,853	2,073	73	618	2,764
1997	2,136	5	1,044	3,185	2,343	83	633	3,059
1998[1]	2,171	6	1,229	3,406	2,642	112	704	3,458
1999[2]	2,374	6	1,272	3,652	2,877	108	822	3,807
2000[3]	2,325	6	1,200	3,531	3,015	114	800	3,929

[1] Preliminary.   [2] Estimate.   [3] Forecast.   [4] Includes meat content of minor meats and of mixed products.   *Source: Economic Research Service, U.S. Department of Agriculture (FAS-USDA)*

Average Wholesale Prices of Meats in the United States   In Cents Per Pound

	Composite						Boxed Beef		Lamb			
	Retail Price						Cut-out,		Carcass,			
						Cow Beef	Choice 1-3,	Pork	Choice-	Pork	Skinned	Pork
	of Beef,		Wholesale		Net Farm	Canner	Central US,	Carcass	Prime,	Loins,	Ham,	Bellies,
	Choice,		Value[4]		Value	& Cutter,	550-700	Cut-out,	East Coast,	Central US,	Central US,	Central US,
Year	Grade 3	of Pork[3]	Beef	Pork	of Pork[5]	Central US	Lbs.	US No. 2	55-65 Lbs.	14-18 Lbs.	20-26 Lbs.[6]	12-14 Lbs.
1992	284.60	198.00	179.60	98.90	67.80	93.85	116.73	58.37	131.66	101.41	67.42	30.39
1993	293.40	197.60	182.50	102.90	72.50	95.43	118.74	62.19	143.97	107.47	67.85	41.62
1994	282.90	198.10	166.70	98.90	62.90	84.39	108.47	57.29	147.62	101.50	58.12	40.00
1995	284.30	194.80	163.90	98.80	66.70	68.22	106.68	59.98	163.45	107.74	58.56	43.04
1996	280.20	220.90	158.10	117.20	84.60	58.18	103.09	72.39	177.58	118.49	72.41	69.97
1997	279.53	231.54	----	----	----	64.30	103.26	70.87	178.99	108.06	62.75	71.41
1998	277.12	239.18	----	----	----	61.33	99.82	52.80	156.75	99.75	44.75	51.94
1999[1]	287.77	241.44	----	----	----	66.51	111.06	53.45	170.29	100.38	45.18	57.12
2000[2]	306.42	258.19	----	----	----	72.57	117.51	64.07	177.78	117.13	52.02	77.46

[1] Preliminary.   [2] Estimate.   [3] Sold as retail cuts (ham, bacon, loin, etc.).   [4] Quantity equivalent to 1 pound of retail cuts.   [5] Portion of gross farm value minus farm by-product allowance.   [6] Prior to 1995, 17-20 pounds.   *Source: Economic Research Service, U.S. Department of Agriculture (ERS-USDA)*

170

Average Wholesale Price of Boxed Beef Cut-Out[1], Choice, at Central Markets   In Cents Per Pound

Year	Jan.	Feb.	Mar.	Apr.	May	June	July	Aug.	Sept.	Oct.	Nov.	Dec.	Average
1991	125.04	123.24	125.45	125.96	123.76	120.61	115.82	111.54	110.61	113.04	113.43	111.18	118.31
1992	114.38	119.65	119.14	118.66	119.18	117.53	112.79	114.36	114.40	115.51	115.26	119.95	116.73
1993	122.69	122.13	124.80	126.12	127.19	120.52	114.48	116.73	114.65	111.52	113.26	110.83	118.74
1994	112.11	112.23	115.03	114.98	108.85	102.92	104.19	108.38	105.49	103.63	106.66	107.22	108.47
1995	112.17	111.12	107.87	103.03	104.21	107.65	103.03	102.55	105.82	107.77	108.88	106.08	106.68
1996	101.71	98.86	96.36	96.01	96.90	100.70	101.53	104.43	105.93	109.10	117.53	108.03	103.09
1997	101.90	98.98	104.87	104.17	105.97	101.83	102.38	105.14	104.06	103.72	104.63	101.50	103.26
1998	100.26	96.27	95.34	98.32	102.09	100.38	99.96	104.28	99.28	102.08	102.61	97.49	99.86
1999	101.37	99.37	103.62	107.55	110.89	115.39	111.14	114.00	115.13	119.21	117.38	117.71	111.05
2000[2]	114.74	112.59	118.42	123.45	124.88	123.30	115.85	111.20	108.68	112.58	118.05	126.41	117.51

[1] Choice 1-3, 550-700 pounds.   [2] Preliminary.   *Source: Economic Research Service, U.S. Department of Agriculture (ERS-USDA)*

Production (Commercial) of All Red Meats in the United States   In Millions of Pounds (Carcass Weight)

Year	Jan.	Feb.	Mar.	Apr.	May	June	July	Aug.	Sept.	Oct.	Nov.	Dec.	Total
1991	3,430	2,954	3,081	3,285	3,291	3,059	3,253	3,425	3,308	3,708	3,324	3,284	39,402
1992	3,623	3,090	3,376	3,259	3,237	3,423	3,441	3,406	3,560	3,656	3,289	3,434	40,794
1993	3,304	3,012	3,396	3,299	3,212	3,481	3,342	3,504	3,516	3,499	3,449	3,554	40,568
1994	3,366	3,126	3,591	3,382	3,431	3,615	3,361	3,756	3,720	3,795	3,666	3,714	42,523
1995	3,560	3,210	3,751	3,304	3,758	3,798	3,424	3,860	3,697	3,795	3,748	3,553	43,458
1996	3,823	3,519	3,512	3,690	3,767	3,439	3,585	3,707	3,396	3,827	3,435	3,432	43,132
1997	3,735	3,278	3,444	3,592	3,571	3,492	3,657	3,619	3,665	4,005	3,453	3,715	43,226
1998	3,836	3,476	3,726	3,701	3,582	3,732	3,781	3,770	3,827	4,033	3,725	3,945	45,134
1999	3,833	3,535	4,016	3,824	3,604	3,940	3,781	3,913	3,933	4,002	3,895	3,862	46,138
2000[1]	3,784	3,767	4,044	3,460	3,878	3,941	3,644	4,113	3,861	4,096	3,919	3,619	46,126

[1] Preliminary.   *Source: Economic Research Service, U.S. Department of Agriculture (ERS-USDA)*

Cold Storage Holdings of All[1] Meats in the United States, at End of Month   In Millions of Pounds

Year	Jan.	Feb.	Mar.	Apr.	May	June	July	Aug.	Sept.	Oct.	Nov.	Dec.
1991	566.2	588.6	606.2	597.7	640.1	614.1	589.7	593.2	592.8	594.7	650.2	644.9
1992	707.9	690.5	725.4	706.8	692.2	665.3	646.0	595.6	613.4	637.8	626.6	615.1
1993	649.4	654.6	652.9	692.0	671.0	660.8	664.2	650.7	671.7	702.4	720.3	726.7
1994	807.7	800.5	842.5	858.0	837.5	822.6	816.2	771.9	788.5	822.7	827.5	802.0
1995	838.7	833.8	834.0	852.7	831.2	820.8	803.6	733.4	711.3	732.3	757.0	749.7
1996	779.5	781.6	729.3	748.6	716.2	687.9	642.7	657.4	678.4	655.5	627.1	621.3
1997	655.9	669.9	719.5	752.5	719.7	742.9	726.3	731.5	728.2	739.1	741.0	722.4
1998	802.8	825.8	816.3	849.3	814.3	771.0	747.2	728.2	738.8	794.9	794.1	821.0
1999	833.0	863.1	883.5	936.4	901.2	843.9	810.4	834.9	746.3	780.3	750.5	748.3
2000[2]	853.1	913.9	934.3	951.3	963.5	926.7	896.2	881.0	871.1	868.0	883.0	836.2

[1] Includes beef and veal, mutton and lamb, pork and products, rendered pork fat, and miscellaneous meats. Excludes lard.   [2] Preliminary.
Source: Economic Research Service, U.S. Department of Agriculture (ERS-USDA)

Cold Storage Holdings of Frozen Beef in the United States, on First of Month   In Millions of Pounds

Year	Jan. 1	Feb. 1	Mar. 1	Apr. 1	May 1	June 1	July 1	Aug. 1	Sept. 1	Oct. 1	Nov. 1	Dec. 1
1991	300.4	298.9	271.3	276.9	265.6	234.7	247.1	273.2	259.4	276.7	298.2	306.3
1992	315.9	329.1	298.9	313.7	302.1	303.5	299.4	294.1	288.9	275.2	291.2	275.9
1993	272.8	286.4	279.9	293.9	276.7	262.1	271.7	285.3	307.5	326.8	344.4	376.3
1994	401.0	430.2	414.4	423.2	399.5	367.9	379.4	388.9	377.2	406.8	410.6	419.5
1995	411.2	420.3	407.7	385.4	392.2	359.1	352.3	359.3	344.9	347.7	381.6	381.4
1996	389.6	367.9	362.6	347.3	335.6	307.4	306.7	291.1	305.2	312.2	295.9	288.1
1997	284.9	290.3	261.7	290.4	285.4	278.7	305.6	302.8	324.6	349.1	351.6	378.2
1998	350.2	331.1	334.9	329.7	335.5	310.2	316.5	303.0	306.7	323.1	358.2	328.2
1999	296.4	301.1	300.1	309.2	316.8	306.7	293.1	292.7	377.9	294.4	322.5	308.9
2000[1]	314.2	350.9	369.0	378.2	396.1	401.1	405.1	391.5	398.8	405.7	404.4	411.8

[1] Preliminary.   *Source: Economic Research Service, U.S. Department of Agriculture (ERS-USDA)*

Mercury

Since 1990, the recovery of mercury from obsolete or recycled items has been the primary source of U.S. mercury production. Domestic mines no longer produce mercury as a primary product. Strict U.S. and foreign environmental policies and the advancement of new technologies have adversely affected both primary and secondary mercury production and usage. U.S. primary mercury production and usage have declined steadily since the 1970's, reflecting the use of substitutes for mercury rather than developing large-scale recycling programs. On a global basis, secondary mercury now accounts for a large part of supply.

Mercury is the only common metal that is liquid at room temperatures. It is highly toxic, and perhaps a greater contaminant than lead because mercury can exist in vapor form. Despite the global efforts to confine mercury it is now believed that airborne mercury, called methyl mercury and formed from the airborne discharge from industrial plants, is as much as three to six times greater than it was in pre-industrial times. In the U.S., prime virgin mercury is produced as a by-product of gold mining operations from fewer than ten mines in California, Nevada, and Utah. The recovery is required to prevent environmental contamination.

World production of mercury is limited to four main countries and a few marginal producers. World production in 1999 of an estimated 1,800 metric tonnes, a record low, compares with 1,970 tonnes in 1998 and over 3,000 tonnes in 1995. (One tonne equals 29+ flasks of 76 pounds each.) Kyrgyzstan, now the world's largest producer, output 620 tonnes in 1999, unchanged from 1998, but nearly twice 1995's production of 380 tonnes. Most of their output is exported, primarily to China. Algeria and China each produced 200 tonnes in 1999, down from about 225 each in 1998. During 1995-97, China's annual mercury production averaged over 700 tonnes. Spain, once the world's largest producer with almost 1,500 tonnes in 1995, produced only 600 tonnes in 1999. World mercury resources are estimated at nearly 600,000 tonnes, mostly in Russia and Spain, with the total viewed as sufficient to last at least a century or more based on declining usage rates.

Mercury is a recoverable metal. U.S. secondary production totaled about 400 tonnes in 1999, unchanged from 1998. EPA restrictions banning landfill disposal and/or transport of mercury-containing wastes has encouraged more efficient recovery methods, especially from fluorescent lamps. The U.S. government has a mercury stockpile of 4,435 tonnes, authorized for disposal but with tight restrictions as to how much, if any, can be sold each year. Reportedly, the goal is to reduce the inventory to zero, but the time frame is uncertain. No disposal was indicated in fiscal 1999.

U.S. industrial consumption of refined mercury reportedly totaled 400 tonnes in both 1999 and 1998. In the mid-1980's, battery production alone consumed 30,000 tonnes. Chlorine and caustic soda manufacture now accounts for the largest domestic use of mercury with 50 percent of the total. Substitutes for mercury include lithium and composite ceramic materials.

U.S. foreign trade in mercury is small. Imports of 62 tonnes in 1999 compare with 128 tonnes in 1998, while exports were 181 tonnes and 63 tonnes, respectively.

Mercury is usually sold in 34.5 kilogram flasks. The average free market price in 1999 of $140/flask compares with $139.84 in 1998.

World Mine Production of Mercury — In Metric Tons (1 tonne = 29.008216 flasks)

Year	Algeria	China	Finland	Kyrgyz-stan[3]	Mexico	Spain	Tajik-istan[3]	Turkey	Ukraine[3]	United States	World Total
1991	431	760	74	----	340	100	----	25	750	58	2,540
1992	476	580	75	350	21	36	100	5	100	64	1,960
1993	459	520	98	1,000	12	64	80	----	50	W	2,390
1994	414	470	83	379	12	393	55	----	50	W	1,960
1995	292	780	90	380	15	1,497	50	----	40	W	3,190
1996	368	510	88	584	15	862	45	----	30	W	2,560
1997	447	830	90	610	15	863	40	----	25	W	2,980
1998[1]	224	230	80	620	15	675	35	----	20	NA	1,970
1999[2]	200	200	80	620	15	600	35	----	NA	NA	1,800

[1] Preliminary. [2] Estimate. [3] Formerly part of the U.S.S.R.; data not reported separately until 1992. W = Withheld to avoid disclosing company proprietary data. NA = Not available. *Source: U.S. Geological Survey (USGS)*

Salient Statistics of Mercury in the United States — In Metric Tons

Year	Priducing Mines	Secondary Production Industrial	Secondary Production Govern-ment[3]	NDS[4] Shipments	Consumer & Dealer Stocks, Dec. 31	Industrial Demand	Exports	Imports
1991	8	165	215	103	313	554	786	56
1992	9	176	103	267	436	621	977	92
1993	9	350	----	543	384	558	389	40
1994	7	466	----	86	469	483	316	129
1995	8	534	----	----	321	436	179	377
1996	6	446	----	----	446	372	45	340
1997	5	389	----	----	203	346	134	164
1998[1]	NA	400	----	----	200	400	63	128
1999[2]	NA	400	----	----	200	400	181	62

[1] Preliminary. [2] Estimate. [3] Secondary mercury shipped from the Department of Energy. [4] National Defense Stockpile. NA = Not available.
Source: U.S. Geological Survey (USGS)

Mercury (monthly average) through December 2000

USD Per 76 Lb. Flask
----- 75 Lb Flask, New York (Dec. 1910 - Dec 1931)
76 Lb Flask, New York (Jan. 1932 - date)

Average Price of Mercury in New York   In Dollars Per Flask of 76 Pounds (34.5 Kilograms)

Year	Jan.	Feb.	Mar.	Apr.	May	June	July	Aug.	Sept.	Oct.	Nov.	Dec.	Average
1991	181.55	169.08	150.36	140.68	129.77	119.75	110.36	102.50	98.00	94.02	127.50	150.12	131.14
1992	162.86	177.24	180.00	180.00	190.63	202.50	202.50	203.45	207.50	207.50	207.50	207.50	194.10
1993	207.50	207.50	207.50	207.50	207.50	201.30	191.00	191.00	185.00	185.00	181.00	175.00	195.57
1994	175.00	175.00	179.78	180.00	180.95	186.64	196.50	200.00	203.10	205.00	217.50	230.71	194.18
1995	235.00	240.00	241.30	250.00	250.00	250.00	250.00	250.00	250.00	250.00	250.00	250.00	247.19
1996	250.00	250.00	261.67	268.33	265.00	265.00	265.00	265.00	265.00	265.00	262.63	235.48	259.84
1997	233.98	232.76	228.88	228.64	220.00	199.05	200.00	198.10	190.83	198.83	191.47	187.00	209.13
1998	187.00	187.00	187.00	187.00	187.00	181.55	175.00	175.00	175.00	175.00	175.00	175.00	180.55
1999	175.00	152.63	150.00	150.00	150.00	150.00	150.00	150.00	150.00	150.00	150.00	150.00	152.09
2000	150.00	157.88	167.50	167.50	167.50	158.23	142.00	142.00	142.00	142.00	142.00	142.00	151.72

Source: American Metal Market (AMM)

Mercury Consumed in the United States   In Metric Tons

Year	Batteries[3]	Chlorine & Caustic Soda	Catalysts, Misc.	Dental Equip.	Electrical Lighting[3]	General Lab Use	Measuring Contraol Instrument	Paints	Wiring Devices & Switches[3]	Other Uses	Total
1988	448	354	86	53	31	26	77	197	176	55	1,503
1989	250	379	40	39	31	18	87	192	141	32	1,212
1990	106	247	29	44	33	32	108	14	70	38	720
1991	18	184	26	41	39	30	90	6	71	49	554
1992	13	209	20	42	55	28	80	-----	82	92	621
1993	10	180	18	35	38	26	65	-----	83	103	558
1994	6	135	25	24	27	24	53	-----	79	110	483
1995	-----	154	-----	32	30	-----	43	-----	84	93	436
1996[1]	-----	136	-----	31	29	-----	41	-----	49	86	372
1997[2]	-----	160	-----	40	29	-----	24	-----	57	36	346

[1] Preliminary.   [2] Estimate.   W = Withheld proprietary data.   *Source: U.S. Geological Survey (USGS)*

Milk

In the second half of the 1990's, U.S. cow milk production set new year-to-year highs, rising from 69.9 million metric tonnes in 1996 to an estimated 76 million tonnes in 2000. The 2000 output estimate is up 2.9 percent from 1999, and makes the U.S. the world's largest milk producer.

The U.S. 2000 milk cow inventory of 9.2 million head was marginally higher than the 1999 inventory. In the mid 1990's, the inventory averaged about 9.4 million head. Milk-per-cow production in 2000 of 1,465 pounds per cow compares with 1,445 pounds in 1999. Favorable milk-feed price relationships during 2000 should help to sustain the expansionary cycle on existing farms and encourage the development of new farms. The year 2000 annual average total of milk cows in the key producing states of 7,849,000 head compares with 7,753,000 in 1999.

As of mid-2000, the U.S. Class 111, 3.5 percent fat (Basic Formula Prices—BFP—before 2000) milk price, was averaging $10.08 per cwt. vs. the 1999 average of $12.43. The wholesale all-milk average price in 1999 of $14.36/cwt. compares with $15.50/cwt. in 1998, and a mid-2000 average of about $12.50/cwt. Retail prices generally show more variance than wholesale values largely due to differences in transportation and marketing costs. The retail fluid milk price index for 1999 was at 107.6 (December 1997=100) and averaged about 108 by late summer 2000.

Politics is deeply imbedded in U.S. milk prices. At issue most of the time is a convoluted Federal milk-pricing system devised in 1937 to insure that fresh milk would be available in all parts of the country with the minimum price that farmers can charge for milk fixed monthly by the U.S.D.A. The country was divided into 31 regions with the set price fixed higher based on the distance the regions were from Wisconsin, effectively making retail prices in the East higher than those in the Midwest. Dairy technology and improved refrigeration have made the old system obsolete, but serious attempts to change the law have generally failed.

The milk industry continues to aggressively advertise milk as a beverage in an effort to bolster U.S. fluid milk consumption, and the effort may be working. Although U.S. fluid milk usage in 2000 of 27.1 million metric tonnes is unchanged from 1999, it compares with the 1995-99 average of 26.8 tonnes. It is believed that one-half of U.S. adults over age 35 have eliminated milk from their diets. Moreover, consumer milk patterns have changed with plain whole milk sales slipping, while low-fat and skim milk sales have increased. About 87 percent of domestic milk output is produced in 22 states, led by California and Wisconsin. Seasonally, milk production is highest during the April-June quarter during which 43 billion pounds were produced in 2000, vs. 42.0 billion a year earlier.

Global year 2000 milk production of a record 390 million metric tonnes compares with 386 million in 1999. Russia is one of the largest producers with 31 million tonnes in 2000, but less than one-half of U.S. output. Germany produced 28 million tonnes in 2000, while France produced 25 million tonnes. The world's milk cow inventory of 127.9 million head in 2000 compares with 128.6 million in 1999, and 135 million in 1995.

Futures Markets

BFP milk futures and options are traded on the New York Board of Trade (NYBOT). Fluid milk futures and options are traded on the Chicago Mercantile Exchange (CME).

World Fluid Milk Production (Cow's Milk)   In Thousands of Metric Tons

Year	Brazil	France	Germany	India	Italy	Nether-lands	New Zealand	Poland	Russia	Ukraine	United Kingdom	United States	World Total
1994	16,700	25,322	27,866	31,000	10,365	10,964	9,719	11,822	42,800	18,138	14,920	69,701	378,408
1995	18,375	25,413	28,621	32,500	10,500	11,294	9,684	11,420	39,300	17,181	14,700	70,440	380,729
1996	19,480	25,083	28,776	33,500	10,800	11,013	10,405	11,690	35,800	16,000	14,640	69,857	364,321
1997	20,600	24,893	28,702	34,500	10,818	10,922	11,500	11,980	34,100	13,650	14,857	70,802	365,609
1998	21,630	24,793	28,378	35,500	10,736	11,000	11,640	12,500	33,000	13,800	14,218	71,373	368,028
1999	21,700	24,892	28,400	36,000	10,444	11,174	11,070	12,068	32,000	13,140	14,584	73,805	371,572
2000[1]	22,134	24,890	28,400	36,250	10,350	10,800	12,835	11,800	31,900	12,200	14,200	76,370	375,676
2001[2]	22,800	24,890	28,400	36,400	10,350	10,500	13,348	12,000	32,000	12,000	14,300	76,975	378,823

[1] Preliminary.   [2] Forecast.   *Source: Foreign Agricultural Service, U.S. Department of Agriculture (FAS-USDA)*

Milk-Feed Price Ratio[1] in the United States   In Pounds

Year	Jan.	Feb.	Mar.	Apr.	May	June	July	Aug.	Sept.	Oct.	Nov.	Dec.	Average
1993	2.96	2.87	2.77	2.79	2.81	2.91	2.78	2.70	2.80	2.79	2.77	2.65	2.80
1994	2.61	2.51	2.52	2.51	2.36	2.42	2.61	2.72	2.81	2.92	2.96	2.81	2.65
1995	2.77	2.73	2.71	2.60	2.52	2.48	2.40	2.50	2.56	2.62	2.69	2.56	2.59
1996	2.59	2.42	2.35	2.17	2.10	2.17	2.19	2.28	2.64	2.98	2.85	2.70	2.45
1997	2.44	2.35	2.27	2.14	2.07	2.12	2.24	2.35	2.44	2.63	2.73	2.80	2.38
1998	2.75	2.77	2.73	2.70	2.58	2.89	3.00	3.60	3.98	4.18	4.22	4.27	3.31
1999	4.09	3.67	3.57	2.97	2.89	3.17	3.61	3.85	4.09	3.96	3.87	3.24	3.58
2000[2]	3.07	2.94	2.90	2.80	2.65	2.94	3.32	3.40	3.31	3.11	3.03	3.05	3.04

[1] Pounds of 16% protein mixed dairy feed equal in value to one pound of whole milk.   [2] Preliminary.   *Source: Economic Research Service, U.S. Department of Agriculture (ERS-USDA)*

Salient Statistics of Milk in the United States   In Millions of Pounds

Year	Number of Milk Cows on Farms[3] (Thousands)	Production Per Cow[4] (Pounds)	Total[4]	Beginning Stocks[5]	Imports	Total Supply	Exports[5]	Fed to Calves	Humans	Total Use	All Milk, Wholesale	Milk, Eligible for Fluid Market	Milk, Manufacturing Grade	Per Capita Consumption[6] (Fluid Milk in Lbs.)
1993	9,581	15,722	150,636	14,214	2,806	167,656	7,894	1,330	148,310	158,086	12.84	12.88	11.80	226
1994	9,494	16,179	153,602	9,570	2,880	166,052	5,725	1,267	152,687	160,292	13.01	13.02	11.85	226
1995	9,466	16,405	155,292	5,760	2,935	163,987	4,321	1,216	153,600	159,819	12.74	12.78	11.78	223
1996	9,372	16,433	154,006	4,168	2,944	161,118	2,061	1,175	152,556	156,404	14.88	14.95	13.38	224
1997	9,252	16,871	156,091	4,714	2,900	163,705	2,094	1,138	154,816	158,048	13.34	13.38	12.18	221
1998[1]	9,154	17,189	157,441	4,887	3,813	166,141	1,408	1,162	157,352	159,922	14.37	14.41	12.78	219
1999[2]	9,156	17,771	162,711	5,302	4,447	172,460	1,303	1,134	163,316	165,753	12.34	12.40	10.52	219

[1] Preliminary.   [2] Estimate.   [3] Average number on farms during year including dry cows, excluding heifers not yet fresh.   [4] Excludes milk sucked by calves.   [5] Government and commercial.   [6] Product pounds of commercial sales and on farm consumption.   *Source: Economic Research Service, U.S. Department of Agriculture (ERS-USDA)*

Utilization of Milk in the United States   In Millions of Pounds (Milk Equivalent)

Year	Butter from Whey Cream	Creamery Butter[2]	Cheese[3]	Cottage Cheese (Creamed)	Canned Milk[4]	Unsweetened	Sweetened	Dry Whole Milk Products	Ice Cream[5]	Other Frozen Dairy Products	Other Manufactured Products[6]	Farm-Churned Butter	Total
1993	4,500	29,493	49,871	557	1,178	244	324	1,130	1,995	12,063	199	428	1,745
1994	4,592	29,127	51,143	524	1,184	205	277	1,227	2,083	13,182	216	394	1,657
1995	4,735	28,388	52,589	494	1,049	203	254	1,262	2,053	13,041	252	346	1,556
1996	4,911	26,187	53,937	461	1,013	242	266	983	2,058	13,190	217	301	1,476
1997	4,939	25,714	55,160	NA	1,208	227	276	898	2,116	13,740	686	256	1,394
1998[1]	5,070	24,248	56,756	NA	1,030	220	186	1,045	2,173	14,323	697	235	1,361

[1] Preliminary.   [2] Excludes whey butter.   [3] American and other.   [4] Includes evaporated and sweetened condensed.   [5] Milk equivalent of butter and condensed milk used in ice cream.   [6] Whole milk equivalent of dry cream, malted milk powder, part-skim milk, dry or concentrated ice cream mix, dehydrated butterfat and other miscellaneous products using milkfat.   *Source: National Agricultural Statistics Service, U.S. Department of Agriculture (NASS-USDA)*

Milk Production[1] in the United States   In Millions of Pounds

Year	Jan.	Feb.	Mar.	Apr.	May	June	July	Aug.	Sept.	Oct.	Nov.	Dec.	Total
1994	12,721	11,662	13,209	13,118	13,719	13,079	13,020	12,837	12,360	12,732	12,330	12,871	153,664
1995	13,147	12,142	13,640	13,343	13,875	13,302	13,152	12,793	12,381	12,716	12,297	12,804	155,423
1996	13,085	12,431	13,537	13,230	13,576	12,832	12,809	12,624	12,241	12,714	12,324	12,928	154,331
1997	13,126	12,141	13,694	13,406	13,902	13,375	13,319	13,059	12,427	12,814	12,362	12,977	156,602
1998	13,282	12,188	13,694	13,510	14,015	13,296	13,162	12,942	12,415	12,956	12,611	13,370	157,441
1999	13,628	12,607	14,270	13,938	14,458	13,633	13,444	13,357	12,970	13,412	13,140	13,854	162,711
2000[2]	14,263	13,606	14,761	14,390	14,791	14,008	14,117	13,798	13,246	13,708	13,212	13,758	167,658

[1] Excludes milk sucked by calves.   [2] Preliminary.   *Source: Economic Research Service, U.S. Department of Agriculture (ERS-USDA)*

Average Price Received by U.S. Farmers for All Milk (Sold to Plants)   In Dollars Per Hundred Pounds (Cwt.)

Year	Jan.	Feb.	Mar.	Apr.	May	June	July	Aug.	Sept.	Oct.	Nov.	Dec.	Average
1994	13.60	13.40	13.50	13.40	12.80	12.60	12.20	12.40	12.80	13.00	13.10	12.80	12.97
1995	12.60	12.60	12.70	12.30	12.30	12.10	12.00	12.40	12.80	13.40	14.00	13.90	12.76
1996	14.00	13.80	13.70	13.90	14.30	14.80	15.40	15.90	16.50	16.40	15.20	14.30	14.85
1997	13.40	13.50	13.50	13.20	12.70	12.20	12.10	12.70	13.10	14.10	14.70	14.80	13.33
1998	14.70	14.70	14.40	14.00	13.30	14.10	14.20	15.50	16.70	17.70	17.80	18.00	15.43
1999	17.40	15.50	15.00	12.60	12.70	13.10	13.80	15.10	15.70	14.90	14.40	12.20	14.37
2000[1]	12.00	11.80	11.90	11.90	12.00	12.20	12.70	12.60	12.80	12.50	12.60	13.10	12.34

[1] Preliminary.   *Source: Economic Research Service, U.S. Department of Agriculture (ERS-USDA)*

Average Farm Price of Milk Eligible for Fluid Market   In Dollars Per Hundred Pounds (Cwt.)

Year	Jan.	Feb.	Mar.	Apr.	May	June	July	Aug.	Sept.	Oct.	Nov.	Dec.	Average
1994	13.60	13.50	13.50	13.50	12.90	12.70	12.20	12.50	12.80	13.10	13.10	12.90	13.03
1995	12.70	12.60	12.60	12.30	12.30	12.20	12.10	12.50	12.80	13.40	14.00	14.00	12.79
1996	14.00	13.90	13.70	13.90	14.30	14.90	15.50	16.00	16.60	16.40	15.30	14.40	14.91
1997	13.40	13.50	13.60	13.20	12.80	12.30	12.20	12.80	13.10	14.10	14.70	14.80	13.38
1998	14.70	14.80	14.50	14.00	13.30	14.10	14.20	15.50	16.80	17.80	17.80	18.10	15.47
1999	17.50	15.60	15.10	12.60	12.80	13.20	13.90	15.00	15.70	15.00	14.50	12.30	14.43
2000[1]	12.00	11.90	12.00	12.00	12.10	12.30	12.70	12.60	12.90	12.60	12.60	13.10	12.40

[1] Preliminary.   *Source: Economic Research Service, U.S. Department of Agriculture (ERS-USDA)*

Molasses

Molasses is a heavy, viscous fluid produced as a by-product of raw sugar refining. Molasses is the syrup remaining from the crystallization of sugar from cane and beet juice. It is separated from the sugar by centrifuging. Blackstrap molasses has had all the sugar removed. About 50 gallons of molasses is produced for each ton of raw sugar refined. Molasses contains about 33 percent sucrose.

U.S. supplies of molasses are about three million metric tonnes per year. Of this total, a third comes from mainland sugar mills, a quarter from beet sugar refiners, and smaller amounts from Hawaiian cane and cane refiners. Beet molasses is used primarily as a livestock feed and a yeast by the pharmaceutical industry. To some extent, an individual country's production of molasses is related to the degree to which it refines sugar. Some countries produce raw sugar and export raw sugar. Other countries produce raw and refined sugar which means they produce more molasses due to refining.

The U.S.D.A. reported in the January 2001 supply/demand for sugar that U.S. sugar production in the 2000/2001 (October-September) season was 8.54 million short tons, raw value, down 6 percent from a year ago. Production of beet sugar was estimated at 4.37 million tons, down 12 percent from a year ago. Cane sugar production was estimated at 4.17 million tons, up 3 percent from a year ago.

In early 2001, U.S. prices for sugarcane molasses were much higher than a year earlier. Domestic supplies were described as light to moderate. The winter of 2000/01 was much colder leading to increased rates of feeding which supported prices. Imports of molasses were limited as some countries, such as Brazil, put a greater emphasis on using sugarcane for ethanol production. In early January 2001, cane blackstrap feed molasses in New Orleans was priced at $55.00 to $60.00 per short ton compared to $32.50 per short ton in January 2000.

World Production of Sugarcane, by Selected Countries   In Thousands of Metric Tons

Crop Year	Australia	Brazil	China	Cuba	India	Indonesia	Mexico	Pakistan	Philippines	South Africa	Thailand	United States	World Total
1990-1	25,140	75,000	57,620	67,500	135,494	28,074	36,000	22,604	18,600	18,083	40,563	24,018	707,497
1991-2	21,306	87,000	67,898	62,000	148,814	28,100	35,300	24,796	22,816	20,078	47,505	26,272	753,303
1992-3	29,400	90,000	73,011	47,150	123,985	32,000	39,700	27,276	23,850	12,955	34,711	26,264	719,671
1993-4	31,951	91,000	63,549	46,000	116,638	33,000	34,100	34,182	22,753	11,244	37,569	26,680	706,433
1994-5	34,860	110,000	60,300	39,000	159,593	30,545	40,134	34,193	18,415	15,683	50,459	25,485	783,373
1995-6	37,378	93,000	65,417	45,500	184,708	30,000	42,300	28,151	22,774	16,750	57,693	25,835	842,937
1996-7[1]	39,878	101,000	68,500	45,000	147,858	28,600	42,000	25,580	23,500	22,512	59,000	24,055	845,645
1997-8[2]	40,878	105,000	69,400	45,500	137,184	29,000		31,600			60,000		

[1] Preliminary.   [2] Estimate.   Source: Economic Research Service, U.S. Department of Agriculture (ERS-USDA)

World Production of Sugarbeet, by Selected Countries   In Thousands of Metric Tons

Year	Belgium-Luxembourg	China	France	Germany	Italy	Poland	Russia	Spain	Turkey	Ukraine	United Kingdom	United States	World Total
1990-1	6,857	14,525	25,520	30,366	11,600	16,721	31,091	7,358	13,986	44,265	8,000	24,959	303,149
1991-2	6,043	16,289	24,403	25,926	11,400	11,412	24,280	6,679	15,474	36,168	7,672	25,485	277,368
1992-3	6,174	15,069	26,491	27,177	14,762	11,052	25,548	7,234	15,563	28,783	9,180	26,438	274,751
1993-4	6,120	11,938	25,514	28,606	10,510	15,621	25,468	8,622	15,463	33,717	8,988	23,813	272,746
1994-5	5,729	12,406	23,943	24,211	11,905	11,630	13,945	8,100	12,757	28,138	8,360	29,024	247,798
1995-6	6,291	13,984	25,121	26,049	12,932	13,309	19,110	7,450	10,989	28,000	8,360	25,460	257,984
1996-7[1]	6,100	13,900	24,400	27,000	11,150	17,460	16,500	7,700	14,383	25,500	8,432	24,104	254,335
1997-8[2]	6,000	14,000	24,500	26,500	12,500	14,000	17,000	6,800	15,100	25,400	8,400	26,134	256,393

[1] Preliminary.   [2] Estimate.   Source: Economic Research Service, U.S. Department of Agriculture (ERS-USDA)

U.S. Annual Average Prices of Molasses, by Types (F.O.B. Tank Car or Truck)   In Dollars Per Short Ton[2]

Year	Blackstrap New Orleans	South Florida	Baltimore	Upper Mississippi	Savannah	California Ports[3]	Houston	Beet Molasses Montana, Wyoming & Nebraska	Red River Valley[4]
1992	61.27	68.36	80.41	92.95	76.70	78.43	63.75	67.81	57.50
1993	55.48	62.36	76.03	89.26	70.00	74.24	57.12	72.63	64.44
1994	65.53	72.23	85.94	91.97	79.23	83.31	69.86	-----	-----
1995	72.00	79.92	86.30	99.11	87.48	90.30	76.37	-----	-----
1996	74.88	83.07	91.27	104.71	92.55	97.11	79.41	-----	-----
1997	58.14	68.00	76.84	90.69	77.51	83.38	62.13	-----	-----
1998	46.35	59.92	63.37	78.00	68.75	69.30	48.85	-----	-----
1999[1]	33.77	49.15	51.06	65.50	56.63	58.32	36.30	-----	-----

[1] Preliminary.   [2] To convert dollars per short ton to cents per gallon divide by 171.   [3] Los Angeles and Stockton.   [4] North Dakota and Minnesota.
Source: Agricultural Marketing Service, U.S. Department of Agriculture (AMS-USDA)

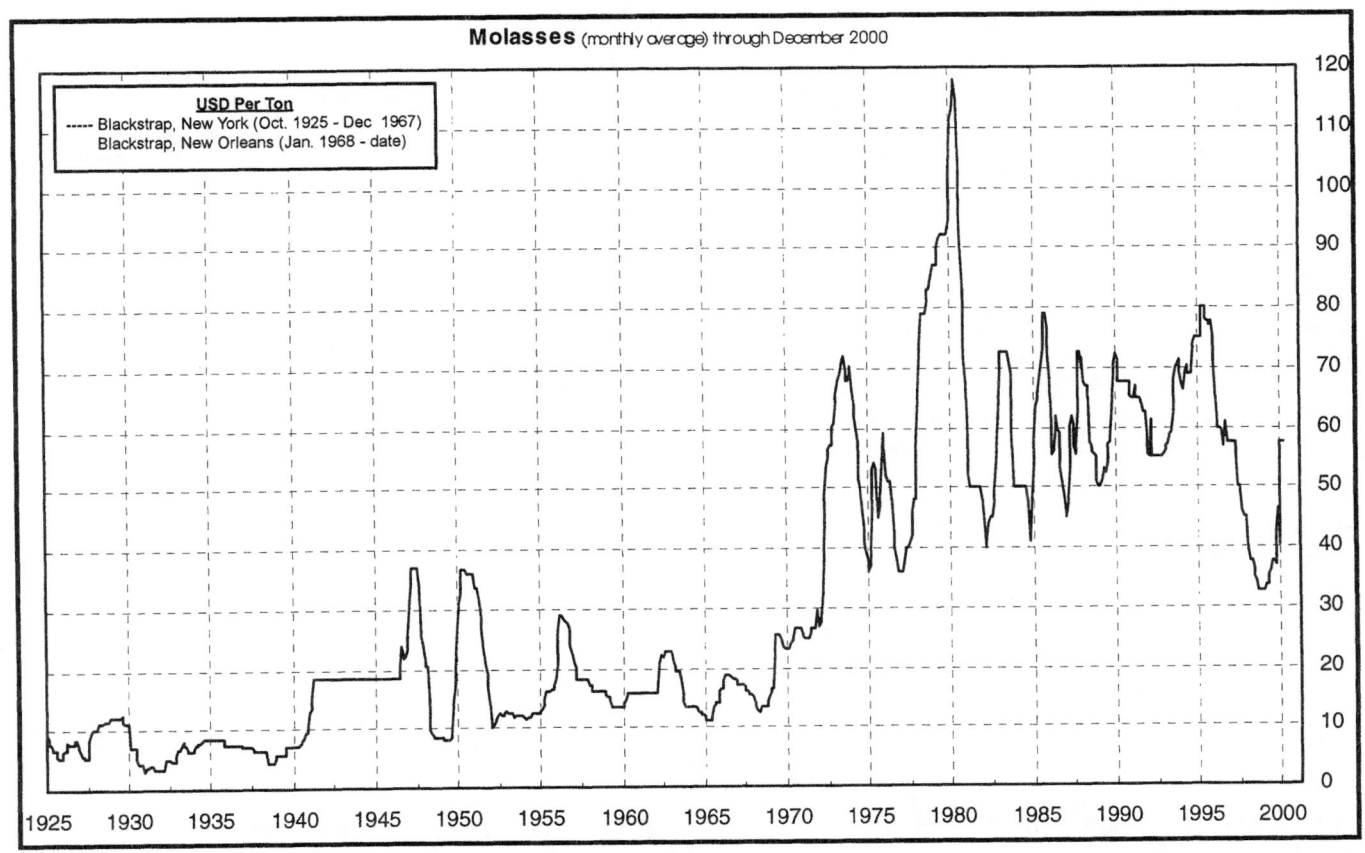

Molasses (monthly average) through December 2000

USD Per Ton
----- Blackstrap, New York (Oct. 1925 - Dec 1967)
Blackstrap, New Orleans (Jan. 1968 - date)

Salient Statistics of Molasses[3] in the United States   In Metric Tons

| | | Production | | | | | Inedible Imports From | | | | | Pro-duction of Edible |
| | | Mainland | | | In Ship-ments | | | | | | Total Molasses | |
Year	Hawaii	Mainland Hills[4]	Refiners Black-strap	Beet	Puerto Rico	From Hawaii	Total Imports	Brazil	Dominican Republic	Mexico	Mainland Exports[5]	U.S. Supply	(1,000 Gallons)
1989	218,009	808,355	122,786	974,179	34,864	169,270	926,870	107,109	147,235	75,634	293,535	2,707,925	1,990
1990	228,968	741,749	105,124	948,820	24,959	214,045	1,078,924	70,986	145,543	88,401	212,263	2,876,399	1,405
1991	188,252	807,652	126,000	1,165,962	27,882	184,337	1,258,637	10,342	137,271	235,244	242,635	3,299,953	1,825
1992	182,849	782,566	123,000	950,312	25,097	183,657	1,115,863	0	127,500	117,722	282,098	2,873,300	1,460
1993	187,915	831,661	113,000	692,465	22,802	190,371	1,040,858	0	163,180	47,596	255,907	2,612,448	1,480
1994	180,884	824,453	114,000	1,200,000	18,531	151,172	1,556,640	0	121,320	197,753	277,098	3,459,167	1,500
1995	146,000	886,826	114,000	1,040,000	16,156	146,000	1,048,726	0	132,983	172,177	274,868	2,960,684	1,500
1996[1]	-----	NA	NA	NA	-----	NA	NA	-----	-----	-----	NA	NA	0
1997[2]	-----	900,000	100,000	1,200,000	-----	100,000	1,583,755	-----	-----	-----	300,000	3,583,755	0

[1] Preliminary.   [2] Estimate.   [3] Feed and industrial molasses.   [4] Includes high-test molasses from frozen cane.   [5] Excluding exports from Hawaii and Puerto Rico.   NA = Not available.   Source: Agricultural Marketing Service, U.S. Department of Agriculture (AMS-USDA)

Wholesale Price of Blackstrap Molasses (Cane) at New Orleans   In Dollars Per Short Ton

Year	Jan.	Feb.	Mar.	Apr.	May	June	July	Aug.	Sept.	Oct.	Nov.	Dec.	Average
1991	67.50	67.50	67.50	67.50	67.50	67.50	67.50	67.50	65.25	65.00	65.00	65.00	67.02
1992	65.00	65.00	65.00	65.00	63.75	62.50	62.50	62.50	58.75	55.31	55.00	55.00	61.27
1993	55.00	55.00	55.00	55.00	55.00	55.00	55.00	55.25	55.31	56.25	56.75	57.19	55.48
1994	57.75	57.50	59.38	62.50	68.00	70.00	70.63	71.25	69.38	67.50	66.25	66.25	65.53
1995	69.00	70.31	68.75	68.75	68.75	69.38	74.25	75.00	75.00	75.00	75.00	75.00	72.00
1996	80.00	80.00	80.00	78.00	77.50	77.50	77.50	77.50	75.00	70.00	65.63	60.75	74.88
1997	60.00	60.00	59.00	56.56	56.88	60.31	57.50	57.50	57.50	57.50	57.50	57.50	58.14
1998	57.50	55.63	51.00	50.00	50.00	46.00	45.00	45.00	45.00	37.50	37.50	37.50	46.35
1999	37.50	36.25	35.00	34.38	32.50	32.50	32.50	32.50	32.50	32.50	33.75	33.75	33.80
2000[1]	35.25	36.11	37.50	37.50	37.50	37.12	42.75	46.25	40.35	57.50	57.50	57.50	43.57

[1] Preliminary.   Source: Agricultural Marketing Service, U.S. Department of Agriculture (AMS-USDA)

Molybdenum

Molybdenum is a silver-gray metal used principally as an alloying agent in cast irons, steels, and superalloys. It is used to enhance strength, toughness, and wear-resistance. There is little substitution for molybdenum as an alloying element in steels and cast irons. Because of the availability and versatility of the metal, new materials are being developed that benefit from the alloying properties. In the form of molybdic acid or ferromolybdenum, it is combined with or added to chromium, manganese, nickel, tungsten, and other alloy metals. Molybdenum also finds use as a refractory metal in chemical applications.

The U.S. Geological Survey reported that world mine production of molybdenum in 1999 was estimated to be 129,000 metric tonnes, down 4 percent from 1998. The largest producer of molybdenum was the U.S. with 1999 production estimated to be 44,100 tonnes, down 17 percent from the previous year. In the U.S., molybdenum ore is produced at three mines in Colorado, New Mexico, and Idaho. Molybdenum is produced as a by-product by mines in Arizona, Montana, New Mexico, and Utah. Other major producers of molybdenum include China, Chile, and Canada.

U.S. production of molybdenum concentrate in the January-July 2000 period was 20,000 tonnes. For all of 1999, production was 43,000 tonnes. Domestic shipments of molybdenum, including metal powder, molybdic oxides, ammonium molybdate, sodium molybdate, and others were 9,550 tonnes in the first seven months of 2000. For all of 1999, shipments were 28,800 tonnes. U.S. gross production of molybdenum products in the first seven months of 2000 was 26,000 tonnes, while for all of 1999 it was 39,800 tonnes. U.S. internal consumption of molybdenum products in January-July 2000 was 13,200 tonnes, while for all of 1999 it was 20,500 tonnes.

U.S. exports of molybdenum ores and concentrates in June 2000 were 2.08 million kilograms, down 20 percent from the previous month. In the January-June 2000 period, exports of ores and concentrates were 13.7 million kilograms. For all of 1999, exports were 27.9 million kilograms. The major export destination was the Netherlands, followed by the U.K. and Belgium. U.S. exports of ferromolybdenum in June 2000 were 85,700 kilograms, up 8 percent from the previous month. In the first half of 2000, exports were 433,000 kilograms, while for all of 1999 they were 913,000 kilograms. The major destination was Canada, followed by Mexico and Japan.

U.S. stocks of molybdenum materials in July 2000 were 1.76 million kilograms. There were 642,000 kilograms of molybdic oxides and 223,000 kilograms of ferromolybdenum.

World Mine Production of Molybdenum   In Metric Tons (Contained Molybdenum)

Year	Bulgaria	Canada[3]	Chile	China	Iran	Kazak-hstan[4]	Mexico	Mongolia	Peru	Russia[4]	United States	Uzbek-isten[4]	World Total
1990	150	11,994	13,830	15,700	542	----	2,000	1,578	2,510	17,000	61,611	----	127,028
1991	120	11,329	14,434	13,200	395	----	1,716	1,716	3,031	16,000	53,364	----	115,000
1992	120	9,405	14,500	19,200	1,320	700	1,458	1,610	3,220	10,800	49,700	700	114,000
1993	120	9,700	14,899	18,300	700	600	1,705	2,050	2,980	10,300	36,800	700	99,200
1994	100	10,250	16,028	21,400	670	100	2,610	2,066	2,765	4,000	46,800	500	108,000
1995	400	9,113	17,889	33,000	560	75	3,883	1,822	3,411	3,000	60,900	400	136,000
1996	400	8,789	17,415	29,600	560	100	4,210	2,201	3,711	2,000	54,900	500	126,000
1997	----	7,612	21,339	33,300	600	100	4,842	1,992	3,835	2,000	60,900	500	139,000
1998[1]	----	7,991	25,298	30,000	600	100	5,949	1,993	4,344	2,000	53,300	500	135,000
1999[2]	----	5,930	27,268	27,900	600	110	6,000	1,750	4,400	2,400	43,000	500	123,000

[1] Preliminary.   [2] Estimate.   [3] Shipments.   [4] Formerly part of the U.S.S.R.; data not reported separately until 1992.
Source: U.S. Geological Survey (USGS)

Salient Statistics of Molybdenum in the United States   In Metric Tons (Contained Molybdenum)

Year	Concentrate Production	Concentrate Shipments Total (Includes Exports)	Concentrate Value Million $	Concentrate For Exports	Concentrate Con-sumption	Imports For Con-sumption	Stocks, Dec. 31[3]	Primary Products[4] Net Production Grand Total	Net Production Molybolic Oxide[5]	Net Production Metal Powder	Price Average Value $ / Kg.[6]	Shipments To Domestic Dest-inations	Shipments Oxide for Exports (Groos Weight)	Con-sumption	Producer Stocks, Dec. 31
1990	61,611	61,580	346.3	41,380	35,455	478	7,672	15,727	15,727	W	7.39	17,983	787	18,060	5,919
1991	53,364	53,607	249.9	22,424	32,998	161	5,291	20,782	18,739	2,043	5.27	19,105	1,571	16,901	9,422
1992	49,700	43,100	189.9	33,439	15,200	831	11,900	13,880	11,916	1,964	4.85	17,300	557	17,200	7,480
1993	36,800	39,200	165.1	28,280	13,800	3,400	11,200	11,989	10,697	1,292	5.13	16,000	1,042	17,700	6,150
1994	46,800	46,000	284.0	14,568	17,200	2,280	5,510	16,000	14,900	1,070	4.60	21,400	2,240	19,100	3,940
1995	60,900	61,700	651.0	18,600	25,500	5,570	5,390	22,900	20,900	1,970	17.50	24,000	2,840	19,900	4,820
1996	54,900	57,900	456.0	19,700	24,500	5,480	2,470	24,100	20,400	1,970	8.30	24,100	1,790	20,900	5,780
1997	60,900	59,100	406.0	20,000	24,300	6,330	3,660	25,900	22,700	2,000	9.46	25,900	1,240	20,000	6,500
1998[1]	53,300	52,100	200.0	----	35,900	6,570	6,270	33,900	31,600	2,270	5.90	38,000	1,100	18,800	7,780
1999[2]	43,000	40,700	203.0	----	34,500	6,390	4,580	19,200	17,400	1,880	5.80	39,000	1,130	17,700	5,340

[1] Preliminary.   [2] Estimate.   [3] At mines & at plants making molybdenum products.   [4] Comprises ferromolybdenum, molybdic oxide, & molybdenum salts & metal.   [5] Includes molybdic oxide briquets, molybdic acid, molybdenum trioxide, all other.   [6] U.S. producer price per kilogram of molybdenum oxide contained in technical-grade molybdic oxide.   W = Withheld proprietary data.   *Source: U.S. Geological Survey (USGS)*

Nickel

Nickel is used in the production of stainless steel and other corrosion-resistant alloys. About one-fifth of the nickel produced in the U.S. is used in plating to provide hard, tarnish-resistant, polishable surfaces. Elemental nickel is used to make nickel-based corrosion resistant alloys. Nickel is used in coins to replace silver, in rechargeable batteries, and in electronic circuitry. Nickel-based alloys are used in wire, bars, sheets, and in tubular forms. Nickel plating techniques, like electroless coating or single-slurry coating, are employed in such applications as turbine blades, helicopter rotors, extrusion dies, and rolled steel strip. By far, the largest use of nickel is in stainless steel production. About two-thirds of the primary nickel consumed in the world goes into stainless steel production.

The U.S. Geological Survey reported that world mine production of nickel in 1999 was 1.14 million metric tonnes, the same as in 1998. The world's largest producer of nickel was Russia with 1999 production estimated at 250,000 tonnes, unchanged from 1998. The next largest producer was Canada with 1999 output of 203,000 tonnes, down 2 percent from 1998. Other large producers include Australia, New Caledonia, Indonesia, Cuba, and China. Estimated world reserves of nickel in 1999 were 46 million tonnes. The largest reserves were located in Australia, Russia, Canada, and New Caledonia. There are extensive deep-sea resources of nickel in manganese crusts and nodules covering large areas of the ocean floor.

U.S. reported consumption of nickel in July 2000 was 9,390 tonnes. In the January-July 2000 period, consumption was 66,500 tonnes. Consumption of nickel in 1999 totaled 105,000 tonnes. In the first seven months of 2000, consumption of nickel for stainless and heat resisting steel was 24,300 tonnes. Steel alloy use, excluding stainless, was 3,460 tonnes. Use of nickel in superalloys was 10,200 tonnes. The other large user was electroplating which took 8,620 tonnes.

U.S. consumption of purchased secondary nickel or scrap in the first seven months of 2000 was 48,200 tonnes. Consumption of ferrous scrap in the period was 40,500 tonnes, while use of nonferrous scrap was 7,630 tonnes. For all of 1999, ferrous scrap use was 53,200 tonnes and nonferrous scrap use was 11,900 tonnes for a total usage of 65,100 tonnes.

U.S. ending stocks of ferrous scrap in July 2000 were 3,520 tonnes, while stocks of nonferrous scrap were 669 tonnes. Total nickel scrap stocks were 4,190 tonnes. In July 2000, stocks of nickel cathodes, pellets, briquets, and powder were 3,600 tonnes. Stocks of ferronickel were 577 tonnes. Stocks of nickel oxide-sinter, salts, and other forms of nickel were 120 tonnes. Total stocks were 4,290 tonnes.

Futures Markets

Nickel is traded on the London Metals Exchange.

World Mine Production of Nickel In Metric Tons (Contained Nickel)

Year	Australia[3]	Botswana	Brazil	Canada	China	Dominican Republic	Greece	Indonesia	New Caledonia	Phillip-pines	Russia	South Africa	World Total
1990	67,000	23,200	24,100	196,225	33,000	28,700	18,500	68,308	85,100	15,818	280,000	29,000	974,000
1991	69,000	23,500	26,400	192,259	31,000	29,062	19,300	71,681	114,492	13,658	245,000	27,700	991,000
1992	57,683	23,000	29,372	186,384	32,800	42,641	17,000	77,600	113,000	13,022	280,000	28,400	1,010,000
1993	64,717	23,000	32,154	188,080	30,700	37,423	12,940	65,757	97,092	7,663	244,000	29,868	926,000
1994	78,962	19,041	27,706	149,886	36,900	50,146	18,821	81,175	97,323	9,895	240,000	30,751	932,000
1995	98,467	18,088	29,124	181,820	41,800	46,523	19,947	88,183	119,905	15,075	251,000	29,803	1,040,000
1996	113,134	21,900	25,245	192,649	43,800	45,168	21,600	87,911	122,486	14,539	230,000	33,861	1,060,000
1997	123,372	19,900	31,936	190,529	46,600	49,152	18,419	71,127	136,467	18,132	260,000	34,830	1,120,000
1998[1]	143,513	21,000	36,764	208,201	48,700	41,600	16,985	74,063	129,200	12,840	250,000	36,411	1,140,000
1999[2]	138,000	23,800	45,800	203,000	51,000	43,000	17,100	83,900	103,000	14,000	250,000	37,900	1,140,000

[1] Preliminary.　[2] Estimate.　[3] Content of nickel sulfate and concentrates.　*Source: U.S. Geological Survey (USGS)*

Salient Statistics of Nickel in the United States In Metric Tons (Contained Nickel)

Year	Net Import Reliance as a % of Apparent Consumption	Production Plant[4]	Production Secondary[5]	Alloy Sheets	Cast Irons	Copper Base Alloys	Electroplating Anodes	Nickel Alloys	Stainless & Heat Resisting Steels	Super Alloys	Chemicals	Apparent Consumption	Stocks, Dec. 31 At Consumers' Plants	Stocks, Dec. 31 At Producer Plants	Primary & Secondary Nickel Exports	Primary & Secondary Nickel Imports	Avg. Price LME[6] $/Lb.
1990	69	3,701	57,367	7,007	2,646	7,594	15,550	16,315	96,120	15,713	1,500	170,042	13,971	8,065	37,057	145,600	4.02
1991	67	7,065	53,521	5,536	1,185	6,938	15,474	16,882	84,292	13,787	1,363	156,663	15,940	11,794	36,902	138,210	3.70
1992	59	8,960	55,871	4,988	1,202	6,313	16,538	15,946	83,460	10,872	51	159,373	17,480	10,140	33,860	128,510	3.18
1993	63	4,880	54,702	4,940	805	6,078	16,611	17,004	87,300	10,783	1,170	158,000	14,430	15,700	33,180	132,710	2.40
1994	64	----	58,590	5,930	499	7,940	15,500	20,500	88,700	11,700	2,670	164,000	11,000	10,200	41,920	133,070	2.88
1995	60	8,290	64,600	9,570	491	8,510	15,600	21,800	103,000	14,100	5,210	181,000	12,300	12,700	51,550	156,930	3.73
1996	59	15,100	59,300	6,240	563	7,300	16,200	19,700	94,000	12,600	5,310	183,000	12,900	13,300	46,700	150,060	3.40
1997	56	16,000	68,400	9,290	654	6,530	15,900	19,400	105,000	19,000	3,720	191,000	16,100	12,600	56,500	158,000	3.14
1998[2]	64	4,290	63,300	8,520	926	6,890	16,400	17,700	93,200	18,600	2,340	186,000	15,800	13,100	43,540	157,920	2.10
1999[3]	63												12,700	10,200			2.73

[1] Exclusive of scrap.　[2] Preliminary.　[3] Estimate.　[4] Smelter & refinery.　[5] From purchased scrap (ferrous & nonferrous).　W = Withheld proprietary data.　NA = Not avaliable.　*Source: U.S. Geological Survey (USGS)*

Oats

Oat prices, basis Chicago futures, have largely traversed a sideways pattern during the past few years but with an overall bearish bias, although the $1.00 per bushel level apparently offered enough support to check the most recent downward pressure.

Within the U.S. and worldwide feed grain complex, oat production is the smallest crop and shows signs of shrinking further. The U.S. 2000/01 crop (June to May) of a near record low 149 million bushels compares with the previous year's 146 million, and 166 million in 1998/99. Production in the first half of the 1990's averaged over 250 million bushels. The U.S. harvested oat acreage in 2000/01 of 2.33 million acres is the smallest on record and compares with 2.45 million in 1999/00. In the first half of the 1990's, harvested acreage averaged almost 5 million acres. Average yield, however, has held steady, averaging 64.4 bushels per acre for the 2000 crop vs. 59.6 bushels for the 1999 crop. North Dakota is generally the largest producing state, followed by Minnesota, Wisconsin, and South Dakota. Imports, mostly from Canada, help complement U.S. supplies and were forecast at 100 million bushels in 2000/01, marginally higher than in 1999/00.

U.S. oat 2000/01 carry-in stocks, as of June 1, 2000, of 76 million bushels compare with 81 million a year earlier. The total domestic supply for 2000/01 of a record low 325 million bushels compares with 326 million in 1999/00. Disappearance was estimated at 250 million bushels, unchanged from 1999/00. Feed and residual usage was forecast at 180 million bushels in 2000/01, the same as in 1999/00. Feed, seed, and industrial usage was placed at 68 million bushels, also unchanged from 1999/00. U.S. oat exports of about 2 million bushels are insignificant. Carryover stocks on May 31, 2001 are forecast at a near record low 75 million bushels. The average farm price for 2000/01 was forecast at $1.05-$1.15 per bushel vs. $1.12 in 1999/00, and $1.96 in 1996/97, the highest farm price of the 1990's.

World oat production in the mid-1990's averaged about 30 million metric tonnes, for 2000/01 the total was 24.6 million as less acreage continues to be allocated to oats. In 2000/01, world acreage of 14.1 million hectares compares with 14.3 million in 1999/00, with an average yield of 1.75 tonnes per hectare vs. 1.73, respectively. Average yields show a wide divergence, from 1 tonne per acre in Russia, to about 4.5 tonnes per acre in Western Europe. Still, Russia is one of the largest producers due to the large acreage devoted to oats. Their 2000/01 crop of 4.5 million tonnes is only marginally higher than the 1999/00 crop, and is only a fraction of the country's production in the mid-1980's. Among the few major producers only Canada has shown steadiness in production during the past decade, averaging about 3.5 to 4.0 million tonnes from 1998/99 forward.

Most of the world's oat production is consumed domestically and world trade is small. In 2000/01, exports were put at 2.0 million tonnes vs. 2.1 million in 1999/00, with Canada accounting for 1.2 million and 1.3 million, respectively. Importing nations are more numerous, but the U.S. is the consistent leader with a 1.75 million tonne forecast for 2000/01, vs. 1.65 million in 1999/00.

Futures Markets

Oat futures and options are traded on the Chicago Board of Trade (CBOT) and the Winnipeg Commodity Exchange (WCE). Oat futures are traded on the Mid-America Commodity Exchange (MidAm).

World Production of Oats   In Thousands of Metric Tons

Year	Argentina	Australia	Canada	China	France	Germany	Italy	Poland	Sweden	Turkey	United States	Ex-USSR	World Total
1991-2	610	1,722	1,794	650	740	1,867	359	1,873	1,426	280	3,539	12,852	33,026
1992-3	600	1,966	2,829	640	700	1,314	333	1,229	807	280	4,271	14,121	33,894
1993-4	436	1,651	3,549	640	713	1,731	372	1,500	1,295	280	3,001	15,004	35,370
1994-5	357	924	3,638	600	681	1,663	355	1,243	991	300	3,322	13,903	32,967
1995-6	260	1,875	2,858	640	617	1,421	301	1,495	947	275	2,338	10,843	28,663
1996-7	310	1,653	4,361	600	622	1,606	350	1,581	1,200	275	2,224	10,430	30,637
1997-8	517	1,634	3,485	400	564	1,599	311	1,630	1,275	280	2,428	11,560	30,903
1998-9[1]	383	1,880	3,958	650	658	1,279	280	1,460	1,136	310	2,409	6,490	25,993
1999-00[2]	553	1,092	3,641	600	550	1,339	346	1,446	1,200	250	2,122	6,195	24,383
2000-1[3]	450	1,250	3,400	600	500	1,100	370	1,275	1,300	250	2,166	6,175	24,483

[1] Preliminary.   [2] Estimate.   [3] Forecast.   Source: Foreign Agricultural Service, U.S. Department of Agriculture (FAS-USDA)

Official Oats Crop Production Reports in the United States   In Thousands of Bushels

Year	July 1	Aug. 1	Sept. 1	Oct. 1	Dec. 1	Final	Year	July 1	Aug. 1	Sept. 1	Oct. 1	Dec. 1	Final
1989	387,593	380,690	380,690	370,693	----	373,587	1995	181,508	186,167	186,167	----	----	162,027
1990	374,457	365,337	365,337	358,288	----	357,654	1996	154,968	157,663	----	----	----	153,245
1991	280,016	259,666	259,666	242,526	----	243,851	1997	182,672	187,127	----	----	----	167,246
1992	256,381	276,381	----	----	----	294,229	1998	183,201	177,211	----	----	----	165,981
1993	262,860	249,830	249,830	208,138	----	206,770	1999	----	162,096	----	----	----	146,218
1994	248,151	247,753	247,753	229,717	----	229,008	2000[1]	151,380	152,745	----	----	----	149,195

[1] Preliminary.   Source: National Agricultural Statistics Service, U.S. Department of Agriculture (NASS-USDA)

Oat Stocks in the United States   In Thousands of Bushels

	On Farms				Off Farms				Total Stocks			
Year	Mar. 1	June 1	Sept. 1	Dec. 1	Mar. 1	June 1	Sept. 1	Dec. 1	Mar. 1	June 1	Sept. 1	Dec. 1
1991	138,600	92,400	173,600	148,100	90,659	78,831	110,487	96,508	229,259	171,231	284,087	244,608
1992	98,150	61,000	199,900	161,200	76,735	66,721	94,717	81,292	174,885	127,721	294,617	242,492
1993	110,250	66,130	161,000	124,200	64,875	47,063	58,004	69,517	175,125	113,193	219,004	193,717
1994	85,050	53,940	144,300	113,400	61,502	51,583	75,551	78,664	146,552	105,523	219,851	192,064
1995	78,400	46,750	107,200	87,200	70,575	53,848	72,967	65,804	148,975	100,598	180,167	153,004
1996	57,350	32,600	93,400	80,650	55,268	33,708	38,716	45,218	112,618	66,308	132,116	125,868
1997	56,200	33,100	107,950	83,200	39,362	33,576	48,972	61,051	95,562	66,676	156,922	144,251
1998	58,800	34,500	110,300	81,500	52,418	39,498	51,502	61,835	111,218	73,998	161,802	143,335
1999	61,700	40,700	97,300	79,800	50,850	40,678	51,151	53,872	112,550	81,378	148,451	133,672
2000[1]	53,300	36,000	101,200	86,900	48,500	40,031	49,177	57,369	101,800	76,031	150,377	144,269

[1] Preliminary.   Source: National Agricultural Statistics Service, U.S. Department of Agriculture (NASS-USDA)

Supply and Utilizationof Oats in the United States   In Millions of Bushels

	Acreage		Yield Per Acre	Pro- duction	Imports	Total Supply	Feed & Residual	Food, Alcohol & Industrial	Seed	Exports	Total Use	Ending Stocks	Farm Price	Findley Loan Rate	Target Price
	Planted	Harvested													
Year	1,000 acres		(Bushels)	In Millions of Bushels									Dollars Per Bushel		
1991-2	8,653	4,816	50.6	243.9	74.8	489.4	265.8	76.6	17.8	1.9	362.1	127.7	1.21	.83	1.45
1992-3	7,943	4,496	65.4	294.2	55.0	476.9	263.1	77.4	17.8	5.7	363.7	113.2	1.32	.88	1.45
1993-4	7,937	3,803	54.4	206.7	106.8	426.7	230.2	73.0	15.0	3.0	321.2	105.5	1.36	.88	1.45
1994-5	6,637	4,008	57.1	228.8	93.2	427.6	242.6	70.0	13.4	1.0	327.0	100.6	1.22	.97	1.45
1995-6	6,225	2,952	54.6	161.1	80.5	342.2	194.9	67.0	12.0	2.1	275.9	66.3	1.67	.97	1.45
1996-7	4,638	2,655	57.7	153.2	97.5	317.1	171.7	63.0	13.1	2.5	250.4	66.7	1.96	1.03	NA
1997-8	5,068	2,813	59.5	167.2	98.4	332.3	184.6	59.0	12.6	2.1	258.3	74.0	1.60	1.11	NA
1998-9	4,892	2,755	60.2	166.0	108.0	347.7	195.6	57.0	12.0	1.7	266.3	81.4	1.10	1.11	NA
1999-00[1]	4,670	2,453	59.6	146.2	99.0	326.0	180.0	56.8	11.2	1.8	250.0	76.0	1.12	1.13	NA
2000-1[2]	4,477	2,324	64.2	149.2	105.0	330.0	175.0			2.0	245.0	85.0	1.05-1.15	1.16	NA

[1] Preliminary.   [2] Forecast.   NA = Not available.   Source: Economic Research Service, U.S. Department of Agriculture (ERS-USDA)

Production of Oats in the United States, by States   In Thousands of Bushels

Year	Illinois	Iowa	Michigan	Minnesota	Nebraska	New York	North Dakota	Ohio	Penn- slyvania	South Dakota	Texas	Wisconsin	Total
1991	6,600	21,250	5,400	22,800	11,880	5,000	10,200	1,292	8,400	38,500	7,200	26,500	243,851
1992	7,930	25,125	8,400	35,000	15,400	7,700	37,400	12,070	13,735	42,900	5,720	34,410	294,229
1993	4,590	9,000	7,150	23,750	6,880	6,510	37,100	9,000	10,000	26,520	5,720	24,150	206,770
1994	5,490	26,660	6,270	24,750	7,500	7,040	33,550	6,720	8,480	31,360	7,420	24,150	206,770
1995	5,360	14,625	5,130	18,000	4,500	5,310	21,600	6,900	9,440	11,500	5,200	25,380	229,008
1996	4,620	12,920	3,600	15,120	7,455	3,850	19,000	5,130	7,560	21,600	5,040	18,700	162,027
1997	5,550	16,790	4,880	17,400	5,850	5,850	18,700	6,660	8,990	14,850	3,400	17,400	153,245
1998	3,920	10,915	4,800	19,530	5,320	6,510	25,200	6,500	8,480	20,100	6,760	20,160	167,246
1999	4,260	11,375	4,875	17,700	4,650	4,760	16,830	7,000	8,480	20,100	6,890	18,300	165,981
2000[1]	4,015	12,060	4,800	22,320	1,890	3,900	19,845	6,840	8,265	13,420	4,300	19,040	149,195

[1] Preliminary.   Source: National Agricultural Statistics Service, U.S. Department of Agriculture (NASS-USDA)

Average Cash Price of No. 2 Heavy White Oats in Toledo   In Dollars Per Bushel

Year	June	July	Aug.	Sept.	Oct.	Nov.	Dec.	Jan.	Feb.	Mar.	Apr.	May	Average
1991-2	1.14	1.24	1.29	1.28	1.31	1.30	1.34	1.41	1.58	1.61	1.48	1.50	1.37
1992-3	1.46	1.47	1.46	1.58	1.54	1.58	1.55	1.54	1.49	1.43	1.53	1.50	1.51
1993-4	1.42	1.50	1.49	1.43	1.41	1.38	1.37	1.43	1.40	1.37	1.37	1.25	1.40
1994-5	1.35	1.26	1.26	1.32	1.35	1.28	1.27	1.34	1.45	1.43	1.48	1.59	1.37
1995-6	1.65	1.76	1.83	1.90	1.76	1.91	2.21	2.14	2.06	2.17	2.32	2.05	1.98
1996-7	NQ	2.45	2.34	2.19	2.02	1.96	1.96	1.99	2.16	2.26	2.12	2.08	2.14
1997-8	2.12	1.79	1.84	1.80	1.77	NQ	NQ	NQ	NQ	NQ	NQ	NQ	1.86
1998-9	NQ	NQ	NQ	NQ	NQ	NQ	NQ	NQ	NQ	NQ	NQ	NQ	NQ
1999-00	NQ	NQ	NQ	NQ	NQ	NQ	NQ	NQ	NQ	NQ	NQ	NQ	NQ
2000-1[1]	NQ	NQ	NQ	NQ	NQ	NQ	NQ	NQ					

[1] Preliminary.   NQ = No quotes.   Source: Economic Research Service, U.S. Department of Agriculture (ERS-USDA)

OATS

Oat Futures - Chicago Board of Trade (weekly close) as of 29-Dec-2000

Cents Per Bushel

Volume of Trading in Oats Futures in Chicago   In Contracts

Year	Jan.	Feb.	Mar.	Apr.	May	June	July	Aug.	Sept.	Oct.	Nov.	Dec.	Total
1991	20,040	30,280	30,320	42,720	20,580	44,940	37,100	41,060	17,860	20,300	34,560	15,200	354,960
1992	31,020	84,020	42,260	47,060	42,020	54,540	22,200	40,160	25,100	16,580	35,220	19,400	459,580
1993	20,480	26,500	26,060	63,140	33,420	43,120	33,300	32,080	26,880	40,780	72,320	37,260	455,340
1994	47,980	57,060	39,800	53,820	34,300	69,760	20,760	39,340	28,840	24,900	56,940	19,680	493,180
1995	13,512	37,014	29,490	45,536	34,116	107,082	29,862	45,677	31,676	38,641	52,321	47,005	511,932
1996	61,451	52,079	34,608	77,395	47,161	34,498	38,960	33,316	30,801	37,579	37,856	16,154	501,858
1997	34,238	51,608	39,607	41,988	27,028	29,632	25,473	26,486	21,241	42,630	38,187	19,214	397,332
1998	21,150	51,247	25,551	65,381	23,490	55,376	29,870	42,156	27,131	31,426	51,172	18,924	442,874
1999	23,747	35,706	43,671	44,974	22,399	40,722	35,812	27,928	17,893	16,155	42,029	20,370	371,406
2000	27,073	43,332	29,707	31,653	38,647	50,461	30,885	42,814	21,846	21,476	48,890	15,406	402,190

Source: Chicago Board of Trade (CBT)

Average Open Interest of Oats in Chicago   In Contracts

Year	Jan.	Feb.	Mar.	Apr.	May	June	July	Aug.	Sept.	Oct.	Nov.	Dec.
1991	11,890	12,832	13,895	15,620	14,223	13,091	11,117	10,894	10,368	11,560	11,257	9,355
1992	9,555	15,499	15,359	15,052	15,329	14,773	12,759	11,100	9,869	9,178	8,781	7,287
1993	7,398	7,739	7,655	11,579	13,357	12,020	10,894	11,381	11,171	14,116	20,057	20,547
1994	21,193	20,137	20,194	19,882	18,312	14,575	11,710	13,923	14,743	16,266	15,354	13,376
1995	13,133	13,231	13,000	15,426	16,054	13,611	11,019	11,348	11,012	11,970	12,542	13,003
1996	13,253	14,095	14,231	14,497	13,897	11,697	11,336	11,803	11,457	11,918	11,150	8,550
1997	8,088	9,650	12,649	11,024	9,830	9,395	8,131	8,606	8,618	10,953	11,816	10,964
1998	12,782	15,368	16,553	17,748	17,441	16,437	14,255	15,052	14,771	16,263	18,466	17,048
1999	17,126	17,019	16,677	15,398	13,491	12,705	11,927	11,670	9,802	10,638	12,754	12,360
2000	15,343	17,521	17,719	18,183	176,686	16,178	15,550	15,225	13,176	13,985	14,377	14,119

Source: Chicago Board of Trade (CBT)

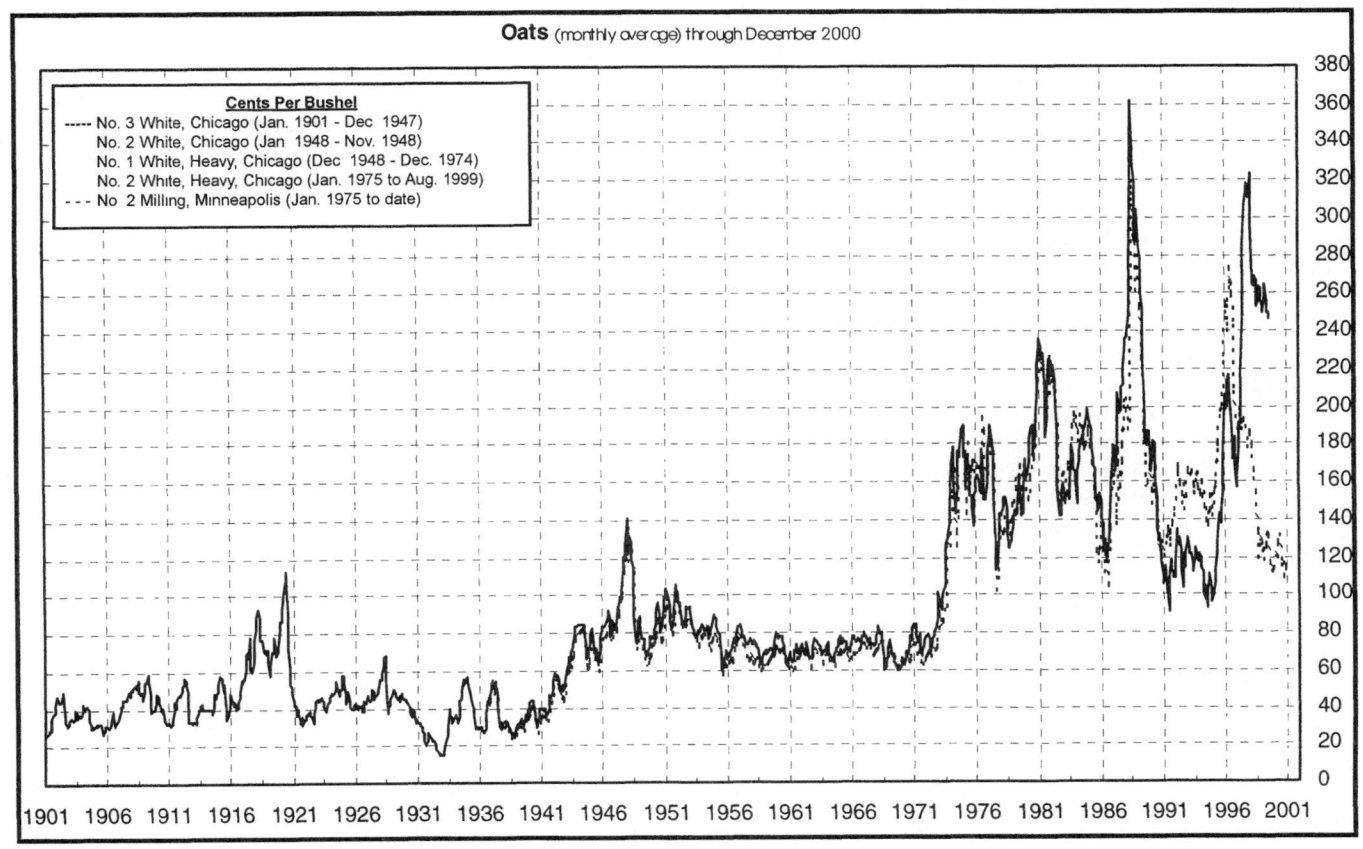

Oats (monthly average) through December 2000

Cents Per Bushel
----- No. 3 White, Chicago (Jan. 1901 - Dec 1947)
No. 2 White, Chicago (Jan 1948 - Nov. 1948)
No. 1 White, Heavy, Chicago (Dec 1948 - Dec. 1974)
No. 2 White, Heavy, Chicago (Jan. 1975 to Aug. 1999)
- - - No 2 Milling, Minneapolis (Jan. 1975 to date)

Average Cash Price of No. 2 Heavy White Oats in Minneapolis   In Dollars Per Bushel

Year	June	July	Aug.	Sept.	Oct.	Nov.	Dec.	Jan.	Feb.	Mar.	Apr.	May	Average
1991-2	1.25	1.33	1.38	1.35	1.41	1.42	1.49	1.50	1.68	1.66	1.57	1.59	1.47
1992-3	1.55	1.49	1.45	1.58	1.52	1.59	1.63	1.66	1.63	1.63	1.66	1.57	1.58
1993-4	1.54	1.63	1.63	1.66	1.56	1.51	1.56	1.57	1.52	1.55	1.46	1.37	1.55
1994-5	1.47	1.36	1.44	1.44	1.44	1.41	NQ	1.46	1.42	1.54	1.62	1.76	1.36
1995-6	1.73	1.92	1.96	2.04	2.11	2.63	2.50	2.40	2.31	2.47	2.56	2.68	2.28
1996-7	2.11	2.48	2.36	2.08	2.06	1.87	1.86	1.89	1.94	1.99	1.88	1.81	2.03
1997-8	1.89	1.76	1.80	1.78	1.75	1.65	1.71	1.68	1.59	1.65	1.54	1.58	1.70
1998-9	1.52	1.42	1.21	1.30	1.29	1.32	1.31	1.33	1.26	1.35	1.36	1.39	1.34
1999-00	1.34	1.25	1.20	1.17	1.20	1.20	1.28	1.21	1.19	1.34	1.45	NQ	1.26
2000-1[1]	NQ	NQ	NQ	NQ	NQ	NQ	NQ	NQ					

[1] Preliminary.   NQ = No quote.   *Source: Economic Research Service, U.S. Department of Agriculture (ERS-USDA)*

Average Price Received by U.S. Farmers for Oats   In Dollars Per Bushel

Year	June	July	Aug.	Sept.	Oct.	Nov.	Dec.	Jan.	Feb.	Mar.	Apr.	May	Average
1991-2	1.08	1.08	1.09	1.12	1.21	1.25	1.25	1.31	1.44	1.44	1.46	1.43	1.21
1992-3	1.38	1.32	1.23	1.28	1.31	1.35	1.36	1.42	1.42	1.43	1.45	1.51	1.32
1993-4	1.43	1.36	1.32	1.31	1.33	1.39	1.42	1.42	1.42	1.39	1.32	1.49	1.36
1994-5	1.31	1.20	1.16	1.18	1.21	1.18	1.18	1.22	1.22	1.33	1.36	1.41	1.22
1995-6	1.38	1.52	1.48	1.43	1.50	1.72	1.91	1.93	1.96	2.04	2.13	2.48	1.46
1996-7	2.17	2.13	2.00	1.83	1.84	1.85	1.72	1.83	1.81	1.91	1.87	1.86	1.96
1997-8	1.81	1.68	1.57	1.47	1.62	1.66	1.57	1.60	1.60	1.64	1.61	1.53	1.61
1998-9	1.39	1.19	1.02	1.07	1.09	1.10	1.19	1.20	1.20	1.20	1.18	1.31	1.18
1999-00	1.22	1.08	.97	1.08	1.06	1.12	1.18	1.20	1.27	1.28	1.35	1.32	1.18
2000-1[1]	1.24	1.07	.94	.94	1.12	1.18	1.14	1.20	1.21				1.12

[1] Preliminary.   *Source: National Agricultural Statistics Service, U.S. Department of Agriculture (NASS-USDA)*

Olive Oil

Like many tree crops, olive and olive oil production trends are very cyclical. The cycle most often seen is a biennial one in which a large tree crop is followed by a smaller crop which in turn is followed by a larger crop. Individual countries can have biennial cycles that run counter to the cycle in another country that is producing the same crop.

An example of this cyclicality can be seen in the production data. The newsletter, *Oil World*, reported that world production of olive oil in the 1992/1993 season was 1.97 million metric tonnes, what appears to be a cyclically large crop. This was followed in the 1993/94 season by the cyclically small crop of 1.88 million tonnes, down 5 percent from the previous year. The 1994/95 world olive oil crop of 1.96 million tonnes increased 5 percent from the previous year. The 1995/96 crop saw a cyclical decline of 19 percent, followed by a production increase of 73 percent in 1996/97.

The world's largest producers of olive oil are Italy, Spain, and Greece. Other large producers include Tunisia, Turkey, Morocco, and Portugal. World production of olive oil in the 1990's averaged close to 2 million tonnes annually.

The world's largest importer of olive oil is the U.S. with average imports in the 1990's of about 140,000 tonnes per year. The U.S. also produces olives in California. The U.S.D.A. reported that olive bearing acreage in 1999 was 35,300 acres, the same as in 1998. Total production of olives in 1999 was 145,000 short tons, up 61 percent from the previous year. Utilization of olives for processing was 144,500 tons, while fresh use was 500 tons. Data on processed utilization was withheld. In 1998, 5 percent of the crop was crushed for oil. In the August 1999 to July 2000 season, U.S. production of canned olives was 196.8 million pounds, up 21 percent from the previous year. Imports in 1999/00 were 155.3 million pounds. Total consumption in 1999/00 was 346 million pounds, with per capita use of 1.26 pounds.

World Production of Olive Oil (Pressed Oil)   In Thousands of Metric Tons

Year	Algeria	Argentina	Greece	Italy	Jordan	Libya	Morocco	Portugal	Spain	Syria	Tunisia	Turkey	World Total
1993-4	21.0	8.5	275.0	451.5	9.5	8.0	45.5	36.1	593.2	71.0	251.0	55.0	1,875.2
1994-5	14.0	10.0	389.8	464.4	15.0	6.5	50.0	36.2	547.0	101.5	106.5	181.5	1,963.6
1995-6	23.0	11.5	362.0	540.0	15.5	4.0	40.0	48.6	320.0	84.0	64.5	45.5	1,598.4
1996-7	46.0	12.0	469.8	317.0	25.5	10.0	121.0	48.8	1,027.5	138.0	288.5	222.0	2,771.6
1997-8	6.5	8.5	405.0	585.0	16.0	6.0	75.0	45.5	1,212.0	78.0	99.0	40.0	2,615.5
1998-9[1]	39.5	7.0	511.0	428.8	23.5	8.0	70.0	41.6	804.0	129.0	231.0	188.0	2,521.2
1999-00[2]	25.0	7.0	378.0	669.6	8.0	7.0	45.0	45.4	667.0	90.0	215.5	77.0	2,273.9
2000-1[3]	31.0	3.0	443.0	445.0	20.0	4.0	40.0	44.0	1,022.0	183.0	163.0	210.0	2,668.0

[1] Preliminary.   [2] Estimate.   [3] Forecast.   *Source: The Oil World*

World Imports and Exports of Olive Oil (Pressed Oil)   In Thousands of Metric Tons

	Imports							Exports					
Year	Australia	Brazil	Italy	Japan	Spain	United States	World Total	Greece	Italy	Spain	Tunisia	Turkey	World Total
1993-4	15.5	18.2	85.8	6.2	46.3	123.9	399.2	8.6	118.2	58.2	166.2	8.7	402.4
1994-5	18.0	23.2	122.6	8.3	68.0	127.6	456.9	9.1	111.4	56.6	141.4	53.2	438.5
1995-6	16.7	18.8	47.0	16.1	26.4	113.6	318.4	7.8	98.0	54.4	33.1	28.9	307.9
1996-7	19.0	26.5	108.1	24.3	35.2	148.1	460.2	10.7	136.8	72.0	101.4	46.6	462.6
1997-8	17.7	28.9	89.4	35.5	28.0	161.0	467.7	14.4	140.2	82.0	126.8	42.2	474.3
1998-9[1]	23.7	23.0	150.4	28.1	76.8	169.9	580.9	20.0	141.6	70.9	174.4	92.1	577.6
1999-00[2]	25.4	24.1	110.0	30.0	45.2	171.0	526.5	18.0	180.0	92.0	130.0	36.7	528.4
2000-1[3]	27.0	28.0	90.0	32.0	15.0	200.0	535.0	19.0	147.0	120.0	115.0	75.0	539.0

[1] Preliminary.   [2] Estimate.   [3] Forecast.   *Source: The Oil World*

World Consumption and Ending Stocks of Olive Oil (Pressed Oil)   In Thousands of Metric Tons

	Consumption							Ending Stocks					
Year	Brazil	Morocco	Syria	Tunisia	Turkey	United States	World Total	Greece	Italy	Spain	Syria	Turkey	World Total
1993-4	18.2	53.5	82.0	66.8	63.4	119.9	2,016.3	32.0	224.4	189.3	19.0	14.0	667.3
1994-5	23.2	46.7	93.4	42.1	71.4	120.8	2,053.5	45.6	133.9	223.0	28.0	71.0	595.8
1995-6	18.8	32.9	98.5	32.4	64.7	110.5	1,884.6	30.9	81.4	88.4	12.0	23.0	320.1
1996-7	26.5	57.2	103.9	89.1	83.4	130.9	2,269.3	115.0	43.6	250.0	50.0	115.0	820.0
1997-8	28.9	61.3	105.6	61.0	82.9	154.8	2,381.5	122.0	196.3	529.0	24.0	35.0	1,047.4
1998-9[1]	23.0	64.5	108.9	60.9	77.0	160.9	2,392.4	190.0	163.6	600.0	45.0	55.0	1,179.5
1999-00[2]	24.1	57.0	114.6	75.3	75.4	167.3	2,464.2	150.0	210.0	490.0	22.0	20.0	987.4
2000-1[3]	28.0	53.0	114.0	70.0	95.0	200.0	2,695.0						

[1] Preliminary.   [2] Estimate.   [3] Forecast.   *Source: The Oil World*

Onions

The U.S.D.A. forecast summer storage onion production, including California, at 50.8 million cwt., down 9 percent from a year ago. Storage onion harvested acres were estimated at 109,370 acres, 10 percent less than in 1999. The California onion crop was expected to be 36,300 acres, down 7 percent from a year ago. California onion production was forecast to be 16.2 million hundredweight or 5 percent less than in 1999.

U.S. fresh onion production in 2000 was forecast by the U.S.D.A. at 5.74 billion pounds, down 3 percent from 1999. The recent peak in onion production was in 1997 when output was 5.96 billion pounds. Imports of fresh onions in 2000 were estimated at 590 pounds, up 1 percent from 1999. The recent high in imports was in 1996 when 625 million pounds

were imported. Fresh onion stocks at the beginning of 2000 were 1.03 billion pounds, down 9 percent from 1999. The total supply of onions in 2000 was 7.36 billion pounds, down 4 percent from the previous year.

For 2000, domestic use of onions was estimated at 5.04 billion pounds, down 1 percent from 1999. In 1997, domestic use of fresh onions was 5.12 billion pounds. Per capita use of fresh onions has been trending higher. In 1980, per capita use was 11.4 pounds, in 1990 it was 15.1 pounds. Usage peaked in 1997 at 19.1 pounds. For 2000, per capita use was estimated at 18.3 pounds, down from 18.6 pounds in 1999. Exports of fresh onions in 2000 were estimated at 675 million pounds. Ending stocks of onions were projected to be 925 million pounds, down 10 percent from 1999.

Salient Statistics of Onions in the United States

Crop Year	Harvested Acres	Yield Per Acre	Production 1,000 Cwt.	Price Per Cwt.	Farm Value $1,000	Jan. 1 Pack Frozen	Annual Pack Frozen	Imports Canned	Exports (Fresh)	Imports (Fresh)	Per Capita[3] Utilization Lbs., Farm Weight -- All	Fresh
						In Millions of Pounds						
1995	164,000	391	64,182	11.10	633,692	51.2	246.8	4.0	662.1	483.7	19.3	18.0
1996	166,210	386	64,106	10.50	604,789	48.8	259.5	3.6	586.3	625.2	19.6	18.7
1997	165,910	414	68,769	12.60	769,974	40.8	230.1	3.8	600.9	576.0	20.0	19.1
1998	171,340	393	67,282	13.80	838,441	42.2	270.9	3.5	628.8	598.5	19.4	18.3
1999[1]	173,400	424	73,562	9.78	635,128	40.3		5.2	667.7	583.9	21.6	18.6
2000[2]	166,170	431	71,604	11.20	732,283	58.3			675.0	590.0	19.4	18.3

[1] Preliminary.   [2] Forecast.   [3] Includes fresh and processing.   *Source: Economic Research Service, U.S. Department of Agiculture (ERS-USDA)*

Production of Onions in the United States   In Thousands of Hundredweight (Cwt.)

Year	Spring				Summer											
	Arizona	California	Texas	Total (All)	California	Colorado	Idaho	Michigan	Minne-sota	New Mexico	New York	Oregon (Malheur)	Texas	Total (All)	Grand Total
1995	672	3,300	3,763	10,110	12,658	6,141	5,481	1,856	125	4,095	4,032	7,134	870	54,072	64,182
1996	760	2,736	4,030	9,290	13,330	5,200	5,590	1,798	114	3,266	2,736	7,080	924	52,079	61,369
1997	746	3,204	1,661	9,087	13,772	5,355	5,658	1,568	180	----	3,660	7,440	----	58,120	68,769
1998	1,175	4,050	2,907	10,356	14,388	6,080	4,640	1,092	150	----	3,750	6,120	----	55,668	66,024
1999	1,635	3,212	3,620	11,222	16,965	5,438	5,530	1,080	118	----	3,528	8,643	----	62,340	73,562
2000[1]	1,376	3,089	4,185	11,200	16,154	4,198	4,810	972	22	----	4,160	6,960	----	60,109	71,309

[1] Preliminary.   *Source: Agricultural Statistics Board, U.S. Department of Agiculture (ASB-USDA)*

Cold Storage Stocks of Frozen Onions in the United States, on First of Month   In Thousands of Pounds

Year	Jan.	Feb.	Mar.	Apr.	May	June	July	Aug.	Sept.	Oct.	Nov.	Dec.
1995	37,472	36,240	35,402	33,906	30,071	30,790	31,309	32,175	32,081	33,594	36,360	34,877
1996	35,354	35,819	31,784	32,782	27,670	29,200	27,511	27,536	27,659	30,288	27,889	32,261
1997	30,481	29,255	32,227	31,811	29,693	28,061	29,314	28,520	27,336	26,908	29,831	30,513
1998	31,187	28,724	27,710	24,428	23,443	22,787	22,179	21,468	18,755	24,553	27,070	25,965
1999	24,596	24,665	27,280	27,972	33,113	35,809	35,605	33,171	31,675	31,338	35,573	41,677
2000[1]	41,236	40,730	44,029	45,874	52,691	55,340	53,537	42,910	40,792	34,318	37,408	39,909

[1] Preliminary.   *Source: National Agricultural Statistics Service, U.S. Department of Agiculture (NASS-USDA)*

F.O.B. Price Received by Growers for Onions in the United States   In Dollars Per Hundred Pounds (Cwt.)

Year	Jan.	Feb.	Mar.	Apr.	May	June	July	Aug.	Sept.	Oct.	Nov.	Dec.	Season Average
1995	13.50	17.50	17.90	20.00	14.60	10.50	13.70	9.67	10.00	9.89	9.52	10.00	11.10
1996	10.70	10.10	8.11	8.86	9.54	11.10	12.10	12.60	12.70	11.50	10.40	10.20	10.50
1997	9.71	7.91	8.15	14.80	13.20	16.40	14.20	13.40	10.10	9.00	10.30	10.90	12.60
1998	11.00	14.60	20.10	18.90	15.80	13.90	19.10	14.00	12.90	12.70	13.90	15.90	13.80
1999	16.10	13.00	10.00	14.10	13.00	14.40	16.10	13.40	9.80	8.17	8.82	6.35	9.78
2000[1]	6.79	5.63	6.67	16.60	16.60	14.80	17.40	14.60	11.70	11.00	10.60	11.60	

[1] Preliminary.   *Source: Economic Research Service, U.S. Department of Agiculture (ERS-USDA)*

Oranges and Orange Juice

The world's largest producers of orange and frozen concentrated orange juice (FCOJ) are Brazil and the United States. Brazilian production is concentrated in Sao Paulo where about 95 percent of the citrus trees are grown. Brazil has emerged as the largest producer of oranges and FCOJ, passing Florida several years ago. The domestic market in Brazil prefers fresh oranges that are squeezed for juice. Other oranges are processed for FCOJ and sent to export markets in the U.S., Europe, and Asia. Other countries that produce oranges include Spain and Mexico.

In the U.S., oranges for processing are grown primarily in Florida. Other states that produce oranges for both processing and the fresh market include Texas, California, and Arizona. The U.S.D.A. reported that U.S. bearing acreage of Early, Midseason, and Navel oranges in the 1999/2000 (December-November) season was 444,200 acres, down 3 percent from the previous season. Acreage of Valencia oranges was 373,400, about unchanged from the season before. Total orange acreage in the U.S. in 1999/00 was 817,600 acres. Acreage planted to oranges in Florida in 1999/00 was 602,100, down 2 percent from a year earlier. Valencia acreage was 295,400. Orange acreage in California was 119,500, down 1 percent from the previous year. Acreage in Arizona was 6,900, the same as in 1998/99. Texas orange acreage was 9,100, the same as the previous year.

The U.S.D.A.'s December 2000 crop production report for citrus fruit indicated that U.S. orange production in the 2000/01 season was 291.1 million boxes, down 4 percent from the 1999/00 season. Production in 1999/00 was estimated at 229 million boxes, down 2 percent from 1999/00. The Early, Midseason, and navel orange crop was 127 million boxes, down 5 percent from the previous year. The Valencia crop was 102 million boxes, up 3 percent from the previous year. The FCOJ yield was 1.55 gallons per box.

The state of Florida reported that in the week ended December 25, 2000, the Navel orange harvest was 227,000 boxes, down from 413,000 boxes the previous week. The Early and Midseason orange harvest for the week December 25, 2000, was 7.34 million boxes compared to 7.07 million the previous week.

The Florida Citrus Processors Association reported that cumulative season movement of FCOJ in the week ended December 16, 2000, was 49 million gallons, up 3 percent from a year ago. Cumulative imports of FCOJ were 11.3 million gallons, 85 percent more than in 1999/00. The inventory of FCOJ was 108.1 million gallons, up 19 percent from a year earlier.

Futures Markets

Frozen concentrated orange juice futures and options are traded on the NYCE Division of the New York Board of Trade (NYBOT).

World Production of Oranges   In Thousands of Metric Tons

Year	Argentina	Australia	Brazil	Egypt	Greece	Italy	Mexico	Morocco	South Africa	Spain	Turkey	United States	World Total
1989-90	750	458	12,036	1,397	932	2,067	1,900	775	697	2,400	740	7,083	33,361
1990-1	600	485	12,362	1,574	819	1,760	2,300	1,103	648	2,590	735	7,222	33,938
1991-2	640	595	14,974	1,694	820	1,842	2,100	780	680	2,651	830	8,175	38,193
1992-3	660	578	14,484	1,771	1,042	2,111	2,913	874	712	2,926	820	10,074	41,582
1993-4	746	651	13,710	1,324	854	2,100	3,174	916	739	2,509	840	9,462	39,595
1994-5	712	416	16,520	1,513	865	1,710	3,500	657	770	2,644	920	10,641	43,539
1995-6	703	589	16,973	1,360	838	1,770	2,600	870	850	2,440	880	10,454	43,066
1996-7[1]	640	543	16,450	1,360	850	1,770	2,600	870	850	2,440	880	10,747	42,932
1997-8[2]	841	556	18,972	1,613	946	2,100	3,917	774	895	2,200	890	11,605	48,296
1998-9[3]	921	421	15,912	1,350	985	2,057	3,920	1,131	961	2,744	740	12,495	46,796

[1] Preliminary. [2] Estimate. [3] Forecast. NA = Not available. Source: Foreign Agricultural Service, U.S. Department of Agriculture (FAS-USDA)

Salient Statistics of Oranges & Orange Juice in the United States

	Production[4]			Farm Price $ Per	Farm Value	Florida Crop Processed				Frozen Concentrated Orange Juice - Florida			
	California	Florida	Total U.S.			Frozen Concentrates	Chilled Products	Total Processed	Yield Per Box Gallons[5]	Carry-in	Pack	Total Supply	Total Season Movement
Year	Million Boxes			Box	Million $	Million Boxes				In Millions of Gallons (42 Deg. Brix)			
1990-1	25.6	151.6	179.0	8.70	1,584.7	100.4	38.2	151.6	1.5	40.0	221.2	261.2	229.2
1991-2	67.4	139.8	209.6	7.43	1,545.2	90.6	37.0	139.8	1.6	31.8	211.7	243.5	212.6
1992-3	66.8	186.6	255.8	5.77	1,489.9	128.3	47.2	186.6	1.6	31.0	292.0	322.9	269.4
1993-4	63.6	174.4	240.5	6.37	1,541.3	111.7	51.0	174.4	1.6	53.5	261.7	315.2	256.6
1994-5	56.0	205.5	263.6	6.08	1,624.1	144.7	54.8	199.8	1.5	58.6	274.2	332.8	290.4
1995-6	58.0	203.3	263.9	6.85	1,821.6	132.9	64.5	197.7	1.5	42.4	284.5	326.9	285.7
1996-7	64.0	226.2	293.0	6.16	1,836.7	153.8	65.7	220.4	1.6	41.2	301.7	342.9	273.9
1997-8[1]	69.0	244.0	315.5	6.13	1,965.4	160.9	74.8	236.6	1.6	69.7	298.8	368.4	263.8
1998-9[2]	36.0	186.0	224.6	7.45	1,700.5	97.2	80.1	178.1	1.6	104.7	108.4	213.1	209.1
1999-00[3]	67.0	233.0	302.8	5.76	1,752.9	134.2	90.1	226.7	1.5				

[1] Preliminary. [2] Estimate. [3] Forecast. [4] Fruit ripened on trees, but destroyed prior to picking not included. [5] 42 deg. Brix equivalent.
Source: Economic Research Service, U.S. Department of Agriculture (ERS-USDA); Florida Department of Citrus

Frozen Concentrate Orange Juice - New York Board of Trade (weekly close) as 29-Dec-2000   Cents Per Pound

Average Open Interest of Frozen Concentrated Orange Juice Futures in New York   In Contracts

Year	Jan.	Feb.	Mar.	Apr.	May	June	July	Aug.	Sept.	Oct.	Nov.	Dec.
1991	6,773	6,457	5,739	6,255	5,762	6,338	5,653	6,556	9,854	11,924	9,877	9,101
1992	9,095	10,033	9,872	11,309	10,791	9,776	10,109	12,132	11,910	14,224	16,669	17,455
1993	17,733	18,199	19,030	20,210	18,525	19,267	20,000	18,899	18,287	18,825	18,422	20,367
1994	17,544	18,137	19,073	21,607	21,450	23,530	24,829	21,874	22,739	23,385	26,859	26,413
1995	27,439	25,885	26,407	30,172	27,057	26,844	23,537	17,881	20,918	22,460	26,303	24,202
1996	22,943	21,670	25,232	23,788	21,724	20,934	20,159	19,834	18,029	18,000	22,513	26,405
1997	29,171	26,929	26,331	28,955	29,868	33,639	31,799	34,339	36,057	40,365	41,811	46,169
1998	38,885	37,893	36,843	33,146	35,749	32,608	25,503	26,394	28,017	26,506	21,984	24,562
1999	25,917	28,965	28,707	31,199	26,669	28,362	28,087	30,021	28,922	27,498	26,893	25,887
2000	23,727	24,647	19,684	22,475	23,456	27,087	27,386	30,272	30,090	32,328	30,192	30,757

Source: New York Board of Trade (NYBOT)

Volume of Trading of Frozen Concentrated Orange Juice Futures in New York   In Contracts

Year	Jan.	Feb.	Mar.	Apr.	May	June	July	Aug.	Sept.	Oct.	Nov.	Dec.	Total
1991	35,037	28,221	17,298	17,116	17,991	20,956	14,905	20,187	26,412	42,016	23,228	24,171	287,076
1992	30,508	28,177	21,371	31,725	21,253	22,473	21,877	27,208	26,912	29,604	33,133	44,979	339,230
1993	43,634	46,067	58,298	52,554	53,566	60,330	49,415	52,381	56,838	63,808	44,167	58,073	640,131
1994	46,166	51,123	43,075	55,955	48,236	60,110	37,069	55,711	52,209	73,155	54,978	76,037	653,824
1995	50,875	66,370	51,292	78,288	32,607	80,165	41,357	67,528	38,781	64,904	45,688	71,077	688,932
1996	59,666	82,057	46,272	65,752	62,247	44,827	40,884	58,346	44,239	40,680	39,291	70,676	654,937
1997	84,982	89,875	66,340	82,772	62,890	78,690	47,242	118,286	55,081	108,413	100,941	134,349	1,029,861
1998	96,020	81,554	66,235	101,651	70,909	79,319	48,844	85,544	81,187	98,639	29,541	75,171	914,614
1999	64,149	92,868	40,027	92,522	49,180	78,627	48,177	99,531	49,323	71,914	42,532	68,734	797,584
2000	45,680	78,532	33,617	71,024	50,475	80,372	46,548	67,312	38,485	64,831	45,966	89,362	712,204

Source: New York Board of Trade (NYBOT)

ORANGES AND ORANGE JUICE

Cold Storage Stocks of Orange Juice Concentrate in the U.S., on First of Month   In Millions of Pounds

Year	Jan.	Feb.	Mar.	Apr.	May	June	July	Aug.	Sept.	Oct.	Nov.	Dec.
1991	1,031.6	1,195.8	1,199.5	1,236.9	1,363.2	1,304.7	1,110.6	1,007.5	876.9	765.2	617.3	655.4
1992	828.4	1,130.7	1,150.0	1,102.9	1,269.3	1,294.8	1,143.8	978.0	874.9	741.9	665.5	638.0
1993	892.9	1,135.9	1,282.8	1,297.5	1,440.9	1,462.3	1,351.8	1,147.0	1,029.6	875.7	813.3	890.9
1994	955.5	1,248.9	1,429.0	1,273.8	1,499.6	1,615.2	1,521.8	1,449.1	1,257.5	1,119.6	1,026.1	1,055.9
1995	1,353.1	1,704.0	1,685.1	1,773.3	1,864.6	1,833.8	1,631.6	1,424.1	1,233.7	1,038.3	830.3	897.7
1996	1,050.6	1,295.4	1,353.0	1,322.3	1,443.9	1,596.9	1,535.0	1,423.6	1,238.6	965.6	732.7	691.0
1997	1,069.4	1,522.6	1,677.6	1,752.9	1,993.4	2,176.0	1,977.7	1,761.8	1,571.8	1,287.8	1,140.9	1,214.4
1998	1,503.4	1,945.9	2,029.7	2,025.0	2,487.0	2,627.5	2,457.7	2,249.0	2,025.1	1,803.9	1,470.7	1,540.2
1999	1,791.9	1,999.4	2,204.2	2,191.3	2,485.7	2,115.6	1,969.7	1,823.0	1,618.5	1,443.4	1,182.0	1,102.7
2000[1]	1,330.7	1,540.6	1,632.7	1,857.9	1,812.5	1,965.6	2,037.9	1,843.7	1,457.7	1,346.6	1,169.4	1,202.0

[1] Preliminary.   Source: Agricultural Statistics Board, U.S. Department of Agriculture (ASB-USDA)

Retail and Nonretail Sales of Orange Juice in the United States   In Millions of SSE Gallons

Year	Retail Sales	% Change[2]	Nonretail Sales	% Change[2]	Apparent Consumption	% Change[2]	Per Capita Consumption	% Change[2]
1987-8	667	-4.9%	432	12.2%	1,229	-1.1%	5.0	-2.0%
1988-9	690	3.4%	401	-7.2%	1,238	.7%	5.0	0
1989-90	628	-9.0%	317	-20.9%	1,079	-12.8%	4.3	-14.0%
1990-1	701	11.6%	296	-6.6%	1,146	6.2%	4.5	4.7%
1991-2	689	-1.7%	268	-9.5%	1,112	-3.0%	4.3	-4.4%
1992-3	748	8.6%	371	38.4%	1,328	19.4%	5.1	18.6%
1993-4	740	-1.1%	-----	-----	1,368	3.0%	5.2	2.0%
1994-5	740	0	-----	-----	1,355	-1.0%	5.1	-1.9%
1995-6[1]	718	-2.9%	-----	-----	1,363	.6%	4.9	-3.9%
1996-7[1]	700	-2.5%	-----	-----	1,320	-3.1%	NA	NA

[1] Estimate.   [2] Percentage change from previous period.   Source: Florida Department of Citrus

Producer Price Index of Frozen Orange Juice Concentrate   1982 = 100

Year	Jan.	Feb.	Mar.	Apr.	May	June	July	Aug.	Sept.	Oct.	Nov.	Dec.	Average
1991	114.4	114.4	111.7	111.7	111.0	111.0	111.0	107.2	107.4	116.0	127.3	131.5	114.6
1992	135.1	134.7	134.7	134.3	126.2	118.5	115.5	114.5	112.5	106.5	104.2	98.8	119.6
1993	91.6	88.8	88.2	89.0	89.3	97.5	104.5	104.5	104.7	104.7	107.9	107.9	98.2
1994	107.9	104.8	104.2	104.2	102.7	101.2	100.2	100.1	99.9	99.8	100.7	100.5	102.2
1995	107.4	105.4	107.6	107.6	109.1	109.1	109.1	105.3	101.0	101.6	106.1	107.3	106.4
1996	109.4	112.5	117.2	119.5	119.5	119.5	115.3	113.6	113.6	112.8	112.8	108.8	114.5
1997	106.9	106.9	106.0	107.6	107.7	107.3	105.3	105.8	102.7	101.4	95.0	94.2	103.9
1998	94.9	101.2	104.1	103.2	108.8	109.1	109.5	109.6	109.5	110.2	119.1	121.2	108.4
1999	119.7	118.6	118.0	115.5	113.3	113.2	112.5	111.3	112.4	112.5	113.1	112.4	114.4
2000[1]	110.0	108.9	108.0	107.1	106.9	106.6	105.4	104.8	101.5	100.4	99.5	98.6	104.7

[1] Preliminary.   Source: Bureau of Labor Statistics, U.S. Department of Labor (BLS)

Average Price of Oranges (Equivalent On-Tree) Received by Growers in the U.S.   In Dollars Per Box

Year	Jan.	Feb.	Mar.	Apr.	May	June	July	Aug.	Sept.	Oct.	Nov.	Dec.	Average
1991	5.64	6.28	6.94	7.09	7.95	19.43	17.40	18.45	21.39	9.87	6.27	5.79	11.04
1992	5.90	6.02	5.81	6.14	6.16	4.26	1.85	1.02	1.05	2.43	4.10	3.67	4.03
1993	3.37	3.21	3.41	4.00	4.03	4.09	5.02	7.25	11.85	11.40	6.15	4.00	5.65
1994	3.76	3.90	4.66	4.83	5.04	4.94	4.08	4.24	3.44	2.92	3.44	3.43	4.06
1995	3.43	3.59	4.22	4.61	4.90	5.63	7.44	7.30	7.26	7.90	3.57	3.55	5.28
1996	3.97	4.39	5.20	6.11	6.63	6.72	6.97	8.15	13.70	10.94	4.17	3.52	6.71
1997	3.59	3.67	4.82	4.68	4.74	4.62	6.48	7.45	7.15	4.48	3.09	3.14	4.83
1998	3.14	3.55	5.05	5.44	5.70	6.05	6.77	5.56	6.03	6.38	5.37	4.99	5.34
1999	4.98	5.71	6.03	6.09	7.40	9.90	7.54	11.48	10.41	9.88	4.29	3.56	7.27
2000[1]	3.55	3.43	3.54	4.14	4.60	4.43	3.07	2.17	0.93	1.09	3.16	2.94	3.09

[1] Preliminary.   Source: Economic Research Service, U.S. Department of Agriculture (ERS-USDA)

Palm Oil

Palm oil is the world's second largest vegetable oil crop, but ranks first in foreign trade. In recent years, palm oil has hardened its relative statistical positions against the major vegetable oils. Palm oil is a tropical oil, but competes directly with other cooking oils such as soybean and sunflower oils that are grown in more temperate climates.

Almost one-half of the world's palm oil production comes from Malaysia and about one-third from Indonesia. However, it is expected that Indonesia can close the gap against Malaysia in approximately ten years, assuming no unsettling political or economic developments that hamper the anticipated new investment in palm oil plantations.

Palm oil production in 2000/01 (October/September) is forecast to reach a record 22.1 million metric tonnes vs. 21.1 million in 1999/00. Two-thirds of the world's production is exported. Estimated consumption of a record 22.1 million tonnes in 2000/01 compares with 20.6 million in 1999/00, and annual usage of 16 million tonnes in the mid 1990's. Palm oil exports go mostly to Europe, the world's largest importer of crude vegetable oils. World palm oil stocks were estimated to be 2.90 million tonnes at year-end 2000/01 (September 2001) vs. 2.80 million a year earlier.

Malaysia's 2000/01 production is forecast at a record 11.1 million tonnes vs. 10.5 million in 1999/00. Ten years ago production averaged only 6 million tonnes in Malaysia. Malaysia's exports are estimated at a record 9.1 million tonnes vs. 8.8 million in 1999/00. Carryover stocks are also increasing and are forecast to total a record 1.4 million tonnes at yearend 2000/01 vs. 1.3 million a year earlier.

Indonesia's estimated crop in 2000/01 of 6.8 million tonnes compares with 6.5 million in 1999/00. Palm kernel production is likewise concentrated in Southeast Asia. The 2000/01 world crop of 6.4 million tonnes compares with 6.2 million in 1999/00.

World palm oil crop prices tend to have wide year-to-year variance. During the 1990's, a high of $651 per metric tonne, basis Malaysia, FOB, was set in 1994/95. The 1999/00 average of $309 per metric tonne was the lowest average of the past decade and compares with $486 in 1998/99.

Futures Markets

Crude Palm Oil is traded on the Commodity and Monetary Exchange of Malaysia.

World Palm Oil Statistics   In Thousands of Metric Tons

Crop Year	Colombia	Indonesia	Ivory Coast	Malaysia	Nigeria	Thailand	World Total	China	Pakistan	World Total	Indonesia	Malaysia	World Total
				Production					*Imports*			*Exports*	
1994-5	391	4,144	282	7,771	661	346	15,073	1,786	1,215	10,674	1,904	6,728	10,573
1995-6	393	4,587	277	8,264	667	369	16,152	1,178	1,166	10,558	2,082	6,896	10,582
1996-7	440	5,078	250	9,000	678	386	17,487	1,851	1,020	11,729	2,419	7,794	11,875
1997-8	439	5,086	276	8,509	688	363	17,018	1,490	1,210	11,866	2,301	7,847	11,630
1998-9[1]	465	5,920	281	9,759	713	458	19,307	1,433	1,053	12,846	3,118	8,482	13,090
1999-00[2]	502	6,704	288	10,432	735	502	20,956	1,329	1,090	14,823	3,758	9,175	14,649
2000-1[3]	517	7,256	287	11,170	748	525	22,397	1,510	1,150	15,949	4,182	10,050	15,940

[1] Preliminary.   [2] Estimate.   [3] Forecast.   *Source: The Oil World*

Supply and Distribution of Palm Oil in the United States   In Thousands of Metric Tons

Year Beginning Oct. 1	Stocks Oct. 1	Imports	Total Supply	Edible Products	Inedible Products	Total End Products	Total Disappearance	Exports	U.S. Import Value[4]	Malaysia, F.O.B., RBD	Palm Kernal Oil, Malaysia, C.I.F. Rotterdam
					Consumption					*Prices*	
				--- In Millions of Pounds ---					--- U.S. $ Per Metric Ton ---		
1994-5	16.4	98.7	115.1	38.1	113.6	151.7	101.8	5.9	538	647	680
1995-6	7.4	106.9	114.3	6.7	103.9	110.6	91.1	9.2	511	545	729
1996-7	14.0	146.4	160.4	0	91.8	91.8	134.8	4.2	432	544	680
1997-8[1]	21.4	128.0	149.4	0	93.8	93.8	155.0	4.4	464	640	653
1998-9[2]	29.0	128.8	157.8	0	72.4	72.4	173.0	5.2	----	514	725
1999-00[3]	34.0	160.0	194.0		55.0	55.0	202.0	4.9		371	

[1] Preliminary.   [2] Estimate.   [3] Forecast.   [4] Market value in the foreign country, excluding import duties, ocean freight and marine insurance.
Sources: The Oil World; Economic Research Service, U.S. Department of Agriculture (ERS-USDA)

Average Wholesale Palm Oil Prices, CIF, Bulk, U.S. Ports   In Cents Per Pound

Year	Jan.	Feb.	Mar.	Apr.	May	June	July	Aug.	Sept.	Oct.	Nov.	Dec.	Average
1994	21.91	21.67	21.72	23.08	26.27	28.94	27.44	30.18	32.15	31.93	34.95	36.83	28.09
1995	34.26	33.82	36.18	35.56	32.80	33.06	33.68	32.59	30.86	31.45	31.96	30.00	33.02
1996	27.08	26.52	26.33	27.52	28.57	25.43	24.78	24.46	27.24	26.13	26.95	27.45	26.54
1997	28.68	29.25	28.00	28.18	28.93	27.25	26.17	25.55	25.37	27.33	27.28	25.05	27.25
1998	29.30	29.59	30.53	32.10	31.11	31.42	32.33	33.14	33.14	33.06	33.30	34.00	31.92
1999	31.06	28.58	25.52	25.52	24.50	21.30	18.15	18.70	21.00	20.00	20.00	20.00	22.86
2000	18.65	17.66	17.73	18.21	18.12	16.52	16.85	16.23	15.90	13.19			16.91

Source: Economic Research Service, U.S. Department of Agriculture (ERS-USDA)

Paper

The paper and paperboard industries are affected by a number of economic factors. The overall strength of the economy increases the amount of paper consumed. The supply of paper is affected by the amount of production capacity in the industry. Increases in production capacity lead to lower prices. In 2000 and into 2001, paper and paperboard production capacity are expected to slow.

One factor that affected the industry was the Asian economic crisis which acted to restrain new capacity from coming to the market. One interesting issue for the industry was what the impact of the Internet and e-commerce would be on paper demand. In part, the Internet can replace paper products like newspapers and catalogs. At the same time, Internet firms need to advertise in print media leading to more paper demand.

The United States is by far the world's largest producer of paper and paperboard. U.S. production has been averaging about 85 million metric tonnes per year. Other large producers of paper and paperboard are Japan, Canada, Germany, Finland, and Sweden. The largest producer of newsprint is Canada, with the U.S. the second largest producer and Japan the third. Other large newsprint producers are Sweden, Germany, Finland, South Korea, Russia, China, and France.

Production of Paper and Paperboard by Selected Countries   In Thousands of Metric Tons

Year	Austria	Canada	Finland	France	Germany	Italy	Japan	Nether-lands	Russia	Spain	Sweden	United Kingdom	United States
1993	3300	17,528	9,990	7,975	13,034	6,019	27,764	2,855	4,459	3,348	8,781	5,406	77,167
1994	3603	18,349	10,909	8,701	14,457	6,705	28,527	3,011	3,412	3,503	9,284	5,829	80,948
1995	3599	18,713	10,942	8,619	14,827	6,810	59,664	2,967	4,073	3,684	9,159	6,093	85,526
1996	3653	17,472	10,441	8,556	14,733	6,954	30,014	2,987	3,224	3,684	9,018	6,188	81,971
1997	3816	17,976	12,149	9,143	15,953	8,032		3,159	3,342	3,684	9,756	6,479	76,449
1998[1]	4009	17,541	12,703	9,058	16,311	8,246		3,180	3,540	3,684	9,879	6,477	75,812

[1] Preliminary.   Source: Food and Agriculture Organization of the United Nations (FAO-UN)

Production of Newsprint by Selected Countries (Monthly Average)   In Thousands of Metric Tons

Year	Australia	Brazil	Canada	China	Finland	France	Germany	India	Japan	Rep. of Korea	Russia	Sweden	United States
1994	33.5	21.9	776.8	60.1	120.5	70.3	124.9	22.9	247.7	72.8	86.5	201.3	582.0
1995	37.4	23.5	768.8	72.1	118.8	74.2	143.8	26.3	258.2	79.0	121.4	195.5	529.3
1996	36.5	23.1	751.3	79.6	110.6	65.2	131.0	24.8	261.7	108.7	103.8	190.2	525.3
1997	34.0	22.1	767.1	68.7	122.5	65.3	134.8	23.3	266.0	132.7	99.8	200.9	545.3
1998	33.9	22.7	718.6	70.8	123.6	75.7	148.0	28.8	272.0	141.7		206.9	
1999[1]	31.8	20.2	767.0	93.4	124.2			32.4	274.6	144.8		208.2	
2000[2]	32.5	21.9	774.3	117.3	112.6			47.1	283.7	151.9		211.2	

[1] Preliminary.   [2] Estimate.   Source: United Nations

Index Price of Paperboard   1982 = 100

Year	Jan.	Feb.	Mar.	Apr.	May	June	July	Aug.	Sept.	Oct.	Nov.	Dec.	Average
1994	130.2	130.1	131.1	133.4	133.1	133.5	137.8	143.5	146.9	153.6	156.0	156.7	140.5
1995	165.3	171.2	172.3	183.8	188.2	188.4	189.9	190.6	190.3	188.8	185.7	182.2	183.1
1996	175.7	172.6	166.6	161.8	154.0	150.6	148.0	145.5	145.6	146.6	146.9	147.6	155.1
1997	147.1	144.2	139.7	137.2	136.8	137.5	137.8	143.8	148.4	150.1	154.4	156.1	144.4
1998	155.9	156.1	156.0	155.2	154.2	153.7	152.2	150.9	149.0	146.9	144.7	143.6	151.6
1999	142.2	142.3	146.4	148.1	149.3	149.5	154.5	158.6	161.0	162.1	162.2	162.3	153.2
2000[1]	163.1	163.6	173.6	176.6	180.4	180.3	180.9	181.2	180.9	179.5	180.1	179.4	176.6

[1] Preliminary.   Source: Bureau of Labor Statistics, U.S. Department of Commerce (BLS) (0914)

Index Price of Wood Pulp, Bleached Suphate Softwood   1982 = 100

Year	Jan.	Feb.	Mar.	Apr.	May	June	July	Aug.	Sept.	Oct.	Nov.	Dec.	Average
1994	106.7	106.9	109.6	113.5	113.4	118.0	119.4	124.3	130.3	137.1	141.4	142.2	121.9
1995	150.9	153.0	187.5	193.0	202.4	215.2	217.8	223.3	218.8	223.3	217.0	212.7	201.2
1996	195.0	175.4	155.5	123.5	111.1	120.1	126.9	129.0	129.4	130.3	129.3	131.5	138.1
1997	129.6	125.9	123.9	119.0	121.8	123.9	130.9	134.4	135.7	135.7	136.8	136.2	129.5
1998	132.0	131.3	127.8	118.7	118.0	122.8	125.7	122.8	117.2	113.7	111.9	111.4	121.1
1999[1]	103.2	102.6	102.4	100.8	101.1	102.3	112.5	115.6	117.9	117.1	121.2	126.5	110.3
2000[1]	No data available for this year.												

[1] Preliminary.   Source: Bureau of Labor Statistics, U.S. Department of Commerce (BLS) (0911-0211)

Index Price of Shipping Sack Paper[2]   1982 = 100

Year	Jan.	Feb.	Mar.	Apr.	May	June	July	Aug.	Sept.	Oct.	Nov.	Dec.	Average
1994	151.3	150.9	154.3	154.5	159.3	163.9	169.9	170.3	176.6	178.2	184.9	185.5	166.6
1995	190.4	204.5	209.5	212.0	221.5	224.2	224.2	224.2	224.0	223.4	212.8	207.3	214.8
1996	205.2	202.2	201.5	194.7	194.3	193.1	189.9	185.7	183.0	183.0	185.8	185.8	192.0
1997	185.8	186.4	186.7	186.5	184.3	184.1	183.9	188.1	182.0	188.5	196.9	197.6	187.6
1998	197.1	197.2	197.2	197.2	196.3	196.3	194.4	194.4	194.4	194.4	194.4	194.4	195.6
1999[1]	194.4	194.4	194.4	199.7	201.7	203.2	203.2	207.8	208.4	208.0	208.4	208.4	202.7

2000[1]   No data available for this year.

[1] Preliminary.   [2] Unbleached kraft.   *Source: Bureau of Labor Statistics, U.S. Department of Commerce (BLS) (0913-0307)*

Producer Price Index of Standard Newsprint   1982 = 100

Year	Jan.	Feb.	Mar.	Apr.	May	June	July	Aug.	Sept.	Oct.	Nov.	Dec.	Average
1994	109.9	109.5	110.7	110.6	112.2	113.8	116.9	116.9	121.7	123.8	126.8	127.3	116.7
1995	135.8	134.6	140.1	147.4	152.3	164.8	166.1	166.1	174.5	186.2	186.2	186.2	161.8
1996	186.2	186.2	185.2	182.7	173.5	164.4	157.4	148.7	145.7	133.1	127.3	123.1	159.5
1997	121.1	120.9	123.1	128.6	135.9	137.2	138.6	139.4	139.4	139.4	141.3	141.8	133.9
1998	142.2	142.5	141.8	142.3	140.0	140.3	143.4	143.1	144.6	147.6	147.6	145.0	143.4
1999	143.0	135.9	128.1	125.0	117.8	117.7	110.3	111.7	111.4	NA	NA	NA	122.3
2000[1]	117.2	116.8	116.5	118.3	123.1	127.1	127.6	130.7	131.5	138.9	140.8	139.1	127.3

[1] Preliminary.   NA = Not available.   *Source: Bureau of Labor Statistics, U.S. Department of Commerce (BLS) (0913-02)*

Index Price of Coated Printing Paper, No. 3   1982 = 100

Year	Jan.	Feb.	Mar.	Apr.	May	June	July	Aug.	Sept.	Oct.	Nov.	Dec.	Average
1994	122.0	122.1	121.8	122.2	121.6	121.6	121.6	125.2	130.7	131.7	132.9	136.3	125.8
1995	139.5	145.8	150.2	153.1	147.7	152.0	159.3	159.3	160.4	160.3	160.3	160.3	154.0
1996	160.2	159.7	159.4	159.2	155.6	153.5	153.0	152.5	152.2	151.8	151.9	152.9	155.2
1997	152.7	153.1	152.9	153.2	153.2	154.6	154.5	154.5	153.2	153.3	153.2	153.3	153.5
1998	153.8	154.7	154.2	154.2	154.1	154.0	154.0	153.8	151.9	151.5	151.5	151.9	153.3
1999[1]	151.1	150.8	149.4	149.4	152.4	152.0							150.9

2000[1]   No data available for this year.

[1] Preliminary.   *Source: Bureau of Labor Statistics, U.S. Department of Commerce (BLS) (0913-0113)*

International Paper Prices--Export Unit Value

Year	Jan.	Feb.	Mar.	Apr.	May	June	July	Aug.	Sept.	Oct.	Nov.	Dec.	Average
NEWSPRINT - Finland In Markka Per Metric Ton													
1995	2,563	2,589	2,577	2,614	2,598	2,667	3,037	3,122	3,172	3,187	3,214	3,191	2,885
1996	3,320	3,412	3,438	3,463	3,442	3,362	3,265	3,110	3,010	3,709	2,899	2,841	3,207
1997	2,741	2,662	2,669	2,667	2,701	2,602	2,642	2,709	2,736	2,697	2,706	2,755	2,694
1998	2,852	2,843	2,858	2,896	2,890	2,839	2,858	2,870	2,847	2,809	2,755	2,748	2,838
PRINTING AND WRITING - Finland In Markka Per Metric Ton													
1995	3,816	3,897	3,905	4,066	4,165	4,284	4,473	4,416	4,439	4,555	4,569	4,400	4,235
1996	4,556	4,555	4,503	4,374	4,265	4,069	3,871	3,743	3,644	3,644	3,667	3,654	4,027
1997	3,620	3,579	3,648	3,651	3,698	3,656	3,620	3,649	3,725	3,738	3,799	3,803	3,687
1998	4,029	4,068	4,097	4,155	4,104	4,070	4,060	4,042	4,003	3,951	3,884	3,841	4,029

Source: Food and Agricultural Organization of the United Nations (FAO-UN)

International Paper Prices--Import Unit Value

Year	Jan.	Feb.	Mar.	Apr.	May	June	July	Aug.	Sept.	Oct.	Nov.	Dec.	Average
NEWSPRINT - United Kingdom In British Pounds Per Metric Ton													
1995	344	353	348	363	376	384	428	465	470	473	469	241	393
1996	498	534	529	514	518	513	504	476	461	412	435	427	485
1997	439	400	394	380	372	380	200	385	374	368	373	377	370
1998	379	367	367	370	357	361	360	357	364	360	359		364
PRINTING AND WRITING - United Kingdom In British Pounds Per Metric Ton													
1995	613	571	611	617	643	619	670	698	718	713	675	684	653
1996	709	776	683	639	661	635	607	919	664	631	629	684	686
1997	606	561	580	561	554	530	555	549	594	559	602	565	568
1998	535	540	540	530	550	516	514	494	532	511	513		525

Source: Food and Agricultural Organization of the United Nations (FAO-UN)

Peanuts and Peanut Oil

World raw peanut (groundnut) production in 2000/01 reached a record high, but remains fourth in production among the world's major oilseeds. The 2000/01 crop of 30.6 million metric tonnes compares with 29.1 million tonnes in 1999/00. On a shelled basis, the totals would be about 25 percent lower. However, within the major oilseeds complex for which world acreage has generally increased, the acreage allocated to peanuts in recent years of around 21 million hectare has shown little change.

China produced a near record large 12.5 million tonnes in 2000/01 vs. 12.6 million in 1999/00. India produced 7.2 million tonnes in 2000/01 compared to 5.5 million the previous year. The two countries combined now produce nearly two-thirds of the world's crop with the U.S. a distant third with 2000/01 production of 1.57 million tonnes. India's peanut acreage in 2000/01 is nearly twice that of China with 7.5 million hectare planted vs. 4.5 million in China, but India's average yield is only one-third of China's yield at 0.96 tonnes per hectare vs. 2.78 tonnes per hectare in China. Generally, the U.S. has the highest world yield.

Foreign trade and world carryover in peanuts is small as most of the crops are consumed locally. World imports during 2000/01 of 1.44 million tonnes were marginally under 1999/00. The world's peanut crush is among the smallest of the major oilseeds at 14.6 million tonnes in 2000/01 vs. 13.7 million in 1999/00, each about one-tenth of the soybean crush. More of the world's peanut crop is allocated to meal production than oil. Meal production totaled 5.7 million tonnes in 2000/01 vs. 5.3 million in 1999/00. Production approximately equaled consumption in both years. Peanut oil production in 2000/01 of 4.4 million tonnes compares with 4.2 million in 1999/00. Foreign trade in peanut meal and oil is small and carryover stocks are generally insignificant.

The average world peanut oilseed price in 1999/00 (October/September) of $820 per metric tonne, basis Rotterdam, compares with $847 in 1998/99, and a 1988/89-1997/98 average of $1003 per tonne. Rotterdam meal prices in 1999/00 were not available at press time, but in the first half of 1998/99 averaged $104 per metric tonne vs. the ten-year average of $164. Oil prices of $744 per tonne compare with $801 and $778, respectively. In the U.S., the average price for peanut meal, basis southeast mills FOB, during 1999/00 averaged $122 per tonne vs. $110 in 1998/99, and the ten-year average of $162. Peanut oil prices averaged $781 per tonne, $876 and $765, respectively.

In the U.S., the 2000/01 crop (October/September) of 3.51 billion pounds compares with 3.83 billion in 1999/00. Production apparently peaked in the first half of the 1990's when average crop size totaled 4.1 billion pounds. U.S. peanut production is largely concentrated in the Southeastern states. Peanuts are also grown in the Southern Plains States where irrigation may be needed and production costs run higher. The average yield for the 2000 crop was put at a higher than initially expected 2,517 pounds per acre vs. 2,667 pounds in 1999, while the acreage harvested of 1.39 million acres compares with 1.44 million, respectively. Georgia is the largest producing state with at least one-third of total production (1.4 billion pounds in 2000), followed by Texas, North Carolina, and Alabama. Georgia's harvested acreage in 2000 of 507,000 acres compares with 544,000 in 1999, but average yield increased to 2,800 pounds per acre from 2,575 pounds, which more than offset the smaller acreage.

Total supplies in 2000/01 of 4.9 billion pounds compares with 5.4 billion for 1999/00, and includes an estimated October 1, 2000, carry-in of 1.2 billion pounds vs. 1.4 billion a year earlier. U.S. peanut imports are generally small, 179 million pounds in 2000/01. Imports, however, have seen wide swings at times and were as low as 2 million pounds per year in the early 1990's.

Total U.S. peanut disappearance in 2000/01 of 3.9 billion pounds compares with 4.2 billion in 1999/00. The crush was forecast at 650 million pounds vs. 713 million, and exports at 590 million pounds vs. 727 million, respectively. Most exports go to Canada, followed by the Netherlands, and U.K. The October 1, 2001, carryover is forecast at 1.0 billion pounds. As a direct food, 2.3 billion pounds were forecast for usage in 2000/01 vs. 2.2 billion in 1999/00. Peanut use as a direct foodstuff showed little growth during the past decade, apparently reflecting reduced demand for peanut butter and a drop in snack peanut based candies.

World Production of Peanuts (in the Shell)   In Thousands of Metric Tons

Year	Argentina	Burma	China	India	Indonesia	Nigeria	Senegal	South Africa	Sudan	Thailand	United States	Zaire	World Total
1991-2	400	440	6,300	7,065	890	220	724	114	400	160	2,235	380	22,138
1992-3	210	433	5,953	8,854	913	250	579	172	390	162	1,943	380	23,082
1993-4	209	389	8,420	7,760	865	250	620	190	390	165	1,539	380	23,996
1994-5	280	445	9,682	8,255	880	250	720	105	390	165	1,927	380	26,278
1995-6	460	500	10,200	7,400	1,060	1,580	830	190	370	150	1,570	580	28,400
1996-7	300	590	10,140	9,020	990	330	650	140	370	150	1,660	570	28,530
1997-8	630	560	9,650	7,580	990	1,250	510	100	370	150	1,610	570	27,530
1998-9	340	540	11,890	7,450	930	1,430	540	140	370	150	1,800	410	29,820
1999-00[1]	430	560	12,640	5,500	990	1,450	650	160	370	160	1,740	420	29,150
2000-1[2]	370	560	13,000	6,100	1,000	1,470	680	230	370	160	1,490	420	29,950

[1] Preliminary.   [2] Estimate.   *Source: Foreign Agricultural Service, U.S. Department of Agriculture (FAS-USDA)*

Salient Statistics of Peanuts in the United States

Crop Year	Agreage Planted	Acreage Harvested for Nuts	Average Yield Per Acre	Pro- duction	Season Farm Price	Farm Value Million	Exports Unshelled	Exports Shelled	Imports Unshelled	Imports Shelled
	----- 1,000 Acres -----		In Lbs.	1,000 Lbs.	Cents/Lb.	Dollars				
1991-2	2,039.2	2,015.7	2,444	4,926,570	28.3	1,392.0	997,000	630,000	5,000	27,000
1992-3	1,686.6	1,669.1	2,567	4,284,416	30.0	1,285.4	951,000	611,250	2,000	2,000
1993-4	1,733.5	1,689.8	2,008	3,392,415	30.4	1,030.9	555,000	352,500	2,000	1,420
1994-5	1,641.0	1,618.5	2,624	4,247,455	28.9	1,229.0	878,000	583,142	74,000	55,385
1995-6	1,537.5	1,517.0	2,282	3,461,475	29.3	1,013.3	826,000	564,021	153,000	108,303
1996-7	1,401.5	1,380.0	2,653	3,661,205	28.1	1,029.8	668,000	440,438	127,000	95,041
1997-8	1,434.0	1,413.8	2,503	3,539,380	28.3	1,001.6	682,000	455,264	141,000	101,792
1998-9	1,521.0	1,467.0	2,702	3,963,440	28.4	1,126.0	562,000	----	155,000	----
1999-00[1]	1,534.5	1,436.0	2,667	3,829,490	25.4	973.0	727,000	----	178,000	----
2000-1[2]	1,543.0	1,315.5	2,499	3,287,600	27.8	977.0	590,000	----	179,000	----

[1] Preliminary. [2] Estimate. *Source: Economic Research Service, U.S. Department of Agriculture (ERS-USDA)*

Supply and Disposition of Peanuts (Farmer's Stock Basis) & Support Program in the United States

Crop Year	Pro- duction	Imports	Stocks Aug. 1	Total	Exports	Crushed fior Oil	Seed, Loss & Residual	Food	Total Disap- pearance	Support Price	Addi- tional	Quantity Mil. Lbs.	% of Pro- duction
	In Millions of Pounds									Cents per Lb.			
1992-3	4,284	2	1,055	5,341	951	891	227	2,122	3,991	33.37	6.6	436	10.2
1993-4	3,392	2	1,350	4,744	553	670	372	2,088	3,683	33.37	6.6	324	9.6
1994-5	4,247	74	1,061	5,382	878	982	316	2,009	4,184	33.92	6.6	820	19.3
1995-6	3,461	153	1,198	4,812	826	999	238	1,993	4,054	33.92	6.6	818	24.0
1996-7	3,661	127	758	4,546	668	692	363	2,029	3,750	30.50	6.6	320	8.7
1997-8	3,539	141	795	4,475	682	544	303	2,099	3,627	30.50	6.6	417	11.8
1998-9	3,963	155	848	4,966	562	460	374	2,153	3,574	30.50	8.8	----	----
1999-00[1]	3,829	178	1,392	5,399	727	713	322	2,233	4,166	30.50	8.8	----	----
2000-1[2]	3,513	179	1,233	4,925	590	650	415	2,270	3,925	30.50	6.6	----	----

[1] Preliminary. [2] Estimate. *Source: Economic Research Service, U.S. Department of Agriculture (ERS-USDA)*

Production of Peanuts (Harvested for Nuts) in the United States, by States In Thousands of Pounds

Year	Alabama	Florida	Georgia	New Mexico	North Carolina	Okla homa	South Carolina	Texas	Virgina	Total
1991	638,485	279,660	2,228,550	51,075	461,700	243,800	33,600	682,500	307,200	4,926,570
1992	591,180	202,510	1,820,465	58,236	406,980	236,180	32,500	680,150	256,215	4,284,416
1993	473,220	194,880	1,383,545	56,680	299,585	233,580	24,500	550,175	176,250	3,392,415
1994	446,220	207,480	1,862,630	51,660	485,465	261,000	36,250	605,570	291,180	4,247,455
1995	483,360	193,590	1,414,880	43,000	347,040	201,880	30,800	540,000	206,925	3,461,475
1996	449,805	236,160	1,433,770	37,950	367,500	195,210	32,550	689,000	219,260	3,661,205
1997	372,490	228,060	1,333,830	46,710	329,640	184,800	30,450	822,150	191,250	3,539,380
1998	432,415	233,100	1,511,655	62,040	397,155	159,750	28,175	917,900	221,250	3,963,440
1999	448,050	260,380	1,400,800	61,600	298,840	189,600	25,300	926,800	218,120	3,829,490
2000[1]	272,640	205,110	1,339,250	60,000	356,700	130,650	34,500	675,000	213,750	3,287,600

[1] Preliminary. *Source: Agricultural Statistics Board, U.S. Department of Agriculture (ASB-USDA)*

Supply and Reported Uses of Shelled Peanuts and Products in the United States In Thousands of Pounds

Crop Year Beginning Aug. 1	Stocks, Aug. 1 Edible	Stocks, Aug. 1 Oil Stock[2]	Production Edible	Production Oil Stock[2]	Candy[3]	Snacks[4]	Sandwich Spread	Butter[5]	Other Products	Total	Shelled Peanuts Crushed[6]	Crude Oil Pro- duction	Cake & Meal Pro- duction
1991-2	386,155	65,950	2,538,398	616,170	327,617	346,255	----	886,367	34,173	1,594,412	828,986	356,276	459,457
1992-3	871,207	57,829	2,376,782	533,641	328,324	352,775	----	797,910	24,981	1,503,990	669,942	285,904	377,301
1993-4	679,639	42,054	1,748,734	425,710	362,418	348,867	----	727,006	36,301	1,474,592	503,674	212,216	292,093
1994-5	752,814	57,188	1,741,824	511,635	349,630	301,548	----	709,823	36,854	1,397,855	738,221	314,189	415,394
1995-6	370,431	58,188	1,253,451	491,818	350,663	277,089	----	728,076	32,015	1,387,843	751,281	320,909	420,919
1996-7	498,954	126,318	1,692,581	305,674	360,846	290,102	----	727,531	33,825	1,412,304	520,413	220,877	294,590
1997-8	509,476	41,000	1,694,016	290,882	351,017	306,908	----	760,230	35,471	1,453,626	409,249	175,853	228,276
1998-9	788,877	16,454	2,186,629	286,060	380,177	349,806	----	744,706	22,131	1,496,820	345,825	145,254	192,425
1999-00[1]	778,671	70,391	2,606,657	450,369	354,774	394,227	----	772,104	20,180	1,541,285	536,164	228,839	291,491

[1] Preliminary. [2] Includes straight run oil stock peanuts. [3] Includes peanut butter made by manufacturers for own use in candy. [4] Formerly titled Salted Peanuts. [5] Includes peanut butter made by manufacturers for own use in cookies and sandwiches, but excludes peanut butter used in candy. [6] All crushings regardless of grade. *Source: National Agricultural Statistics Service, U.S. Department of Agriculture (NASS-USDA)*

PEANUTS AND PEANUT OIL

Shelled Peanuts (Raw Basis) Used in Primary Products, by Type　In Thousands of Pounds

	Virginia				Runner				Spanish			
Year	Candy[2]	Snack Peanuts	Peanut Butter[3]	Total	Candy[2]	Snack Peanuts	Peanut Butter[3]	Total	Candy[2]	Snack Peanuts	Peanut Butter[3]	Total
1991-2	51,312	142,514	89,045	297,570	244,815	180,609	759,747	1,203,233	31,490	23,132	37,575	93,609
1992-3	49,223	124,875	92,355	275,895	259,498	203,732	674,962	1,152,775	19,603	24,168	30,593	75,320
1993-4	44,889	99,381	63,270	222,641	298,325	227,286	365,047	1,179,396	19,204	22,200	28,689	72,555
1994-5	26,857	97,389	51,354	190,916	302,697	185,377	644,711	1,152,110	20,076	18,782	13,758	54,829
1995-6	25,176	93,041	71,310	203,183	304,285	169,142	634,350	1,123,719	21,202	14,906	22,416	60,941
1996-7	24,158	91,882	64,274	193,166	318,924	176,851	634,387	1,149,347	17,764	21,369	28,870	69,791
1997-8	48,428	80,309	59,228	182,100	302,791	206,718	676,839	1,206,946	19,798	19,581	24,163	64,580
1998-9	36,178	99,401	57,864	196,935	321,838	234,486	670,705	1,244,748	22,161	15,919	16,137	55,137
1999-00[1]	23,233	100,354	73,926	200,775	315,236	278,448	690,564	1,300,186	16,305	15,425	7,614	40,324

[1] Preliminary.　[2] Includes peanut butter made by manufacturers for own use in candy.　[3] Includes peanut butter made by manufacturers for own use in cookies and sandwiches, but excludes peanut butter used in candy.　*Source: National Agricultural Statistics Service, U.S. Department of Agriculture (NASS-USDA)*

Production, Consumption, Stocks and Foreign Trade of Peanut Oil in the U.S.　In Millions of Pounds

Crop Year Beginning Aug. 1	Production		Consumption		Stocks Dec. 31		Imports for Consumption	Exports
	Crude	Refined	In Refining	In End Products	Crude	Refined		
1992-3	285.9	181.1	188.4	182.1	46.2	5.3	0	59.0
1993-4	212.2	155.2	163.7	149.1	6.5	3.9	11.0	61.0
1994-5	319.9	120.0	126.1	118.9	5.0	2.8	5.0	21.5
1995-6	329.0	125.7	129.9	126.0	19.9	2.8	3.2	47.8
1996-7	233.9	133.5	138.9	138.4	85.6	2.8	5.0	13.0
1997-8	144.3	104.0	111.6	121.6	42.6	3.0	5.0	35.0
1998-9	172.9	118.3	123.7	180.1	47.2	3.8		
1999-00[1]	262.9	195.9	238.9	236.1	19.7	1.7		
2000-1[2]	246.0	258.3	277.6					

[1] Preliminary.　[2] Forecast.　*Source: Bureau of the Census, U.S. Department of Commerce*

Production of Crude Peanut Oil in the United States　In Millions of Pounds

Year	Jan.	Feb.	Mar.	Apr.	May	June	July	Aug.	Sept.	Oct.	Nov.	Dec.	Total
1991	----	70.8	----	----	71.1	----	----	59.5	----	----	60.1	----	261.5
1992	28.0	26.8	42.5	40.9	39.8	40.6	37.3	31.3	35.1	24.2	19.2	15.6	381.3
1993	16.9	17.0	24.1	28.8	23.3	29.0	25.6	22.5	3.6	8.6	16.4	14.6	230.4
1994	18.1	18.3	21.2	18.7	25.6	15.4	21.7	16.8	17.2	11.9	18.4	24.2	227.5
1995	27.9	28.6	42.7	36.9	39.2	29.2	26.9	26.3	17.4	13.2	19.5	24.3	332.0
1996	29.2	31.9	36.8	36.8	36.7	33.3	31.4	31.5	27.1	21.1	20.6	21.8	358.2
1997	19.9	16.1	18.8	17.9	13.3	15.9	9.9	12.1	6.1	12.2	11.6	14.0	167.7
1998	16.4	14.5	14.3	13.0	10.8	10.0	9.5	6.3	5.8	6.9	13.6	13.9	134.9
1999	16.2	18.2	15.8	18.2	16.4	20.7	20.8	17.8	16.3	13.5	16.9	22.7	213.6
2000[1]	28.2	27.2	25.6	23.9	23.1	25.5	22.3	28.9	20.1	25.2	16.4	15.1	281.5

[1] Preliminary.　NA = Not available.　*Source: Bureau of the Census, U.S. Department of Commerce*

Average Price of Peanut Meal 50% Southeast Mills　In Dollars Per Short Ton

Year	Oct.	Nov.	Dec.	Jan.	Feb.	Mar.	Apr.	May	June	July	Aug.	Sept.	Average
1991-2	----	----	----	----	----	----	----	----	----	----	----	----	154.50
1992-3	163.33	170.00	173.13	180.00	175.83	165.00	161.50	165.63	171.25	200.00	213.75	210.63	172.90
1993-4	196.00	197.00	200.00	209.00	207.50	198.75	191.00	187.50	163.75	164.00	153.75	114.80	194.91
1994-5	151.25	147.50	127.00	105.00	107.50	119.00	125.00	123.75	134.00	138.75	136.25	142.00	128.94
1995-6	132.50	175.00	204.00	220.00	215.00	210.00	210.00	212.00	210.00	224.25	227.00	192.80	202.70
1996-7	170.00	146.13	172.67	221.00	228.13	225.00	233.75	222.00	235.00	220.00	213.00	210.00	232.00
1997-8	210.00	210.00	210.00	210.00	210.00	210.00	210.00	210.00	210.00	210.00	207.50	205.00	209.60
1998-9	161.00	100.00	103.75	105.00	102.50	91.25	94.50	93.75	100.00	100.00	105.00	102.50	104.94
1999-00	98.00	103.00	103.00	104.00	104.75	110.00	115.00	115.00	119.60	118.00	118.00	118.00	108.15
2000-1[1]	118.00	118.00	118.00	142.50	120.00								123.30

[1] Preliminary.　*Source: Agricultural Marketing Service, U.S. Department of Agriculture (AMS-USDA)*

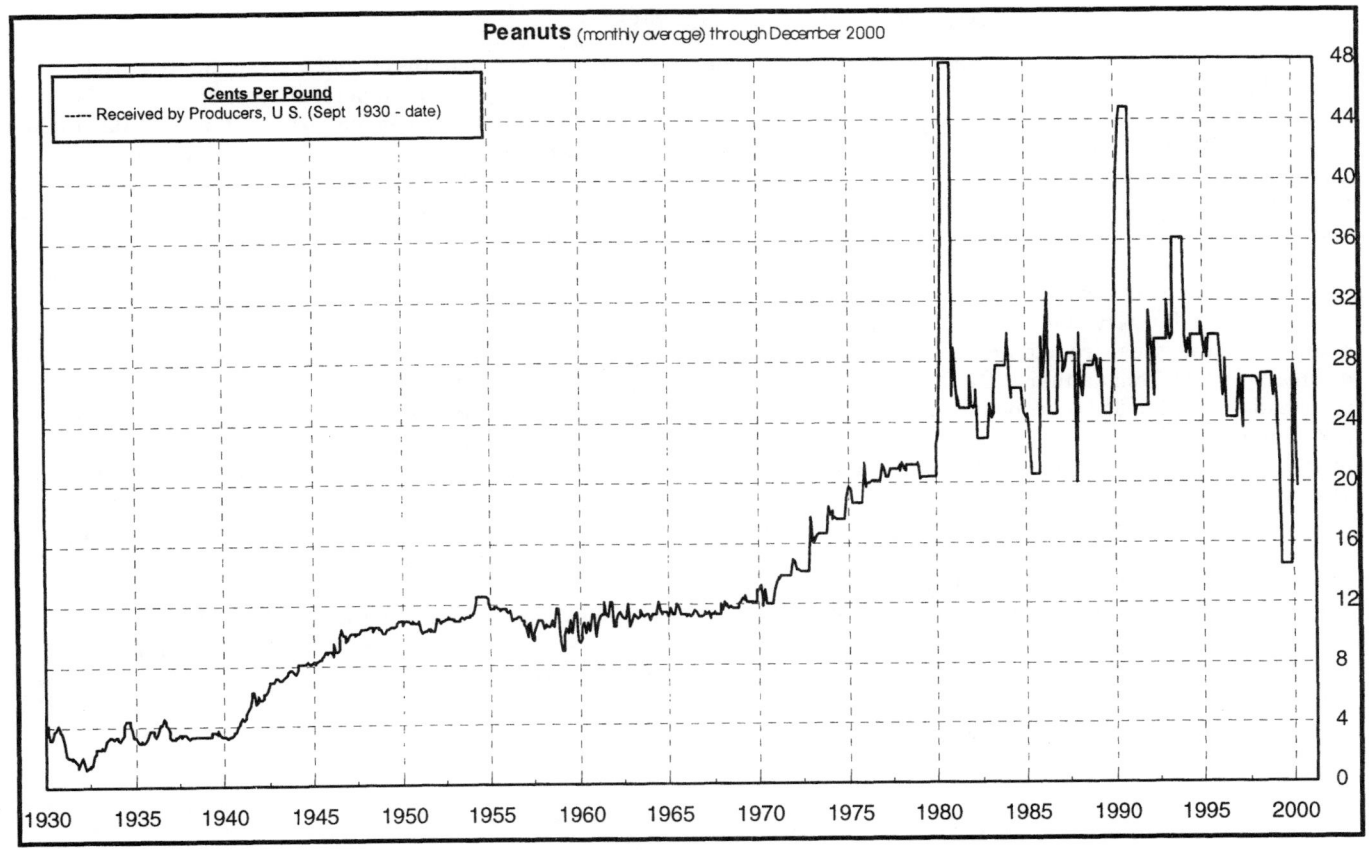

Peanuts (monthly average) through December 2000

Cents Per Pound
----- Received by Producers, U.S. (Sept 1930 - date)

Average Price Received by Producers for Peanuts (in the Shell) in the U.S.   In Cents Per Pound

Year	Aug.	Sept.	Oct.	Nov.	Dec.	Jan.	Feb.	Mar.	Apr.	May	June	July	Average[1]
1991-2	30.4	29.3	28.1	24.4	25.1	NQ	NQ	NQ	NQ	NQ	NQ	NQ	28.3
1992-3	NQ	31.3	29.9	28.2	25.7	29.5	NQ	NQ	NQ	NQ	NQ	NQ	30.0
1993-4	NQ	32.0	30.0	29.5	29.7	36.1	NQ	NQ	NQ	NQ	NQ	NQ	30.4
1994-5	NQ	30.6	28.6	25.9	25.8	25.7	NQ	NQ	NQ	NQ	NQ	NQ	27.9
1995-6	30.6	29.7	28.6	29.5	28.3	29.8	NQ	NQ	NQ	NQ	NQ	NQ	29.4
1996-7	NQ	27.6	25.8	27.1	28.1	24.3	NQ	NQ	NQ	NQ	NQ	NQ	26.6
1997-8	23.3	27.1	25.4	25.0	30.7	24.7	NQ	NQ	NQ	NQ	NQ	NQ	26.0
1998-9	NQ	26.8	26.3	24.6	27.2	NQ	NQ	NQ	NQ	NQ	NQ	NQ	26.2
1999-00	25.7	27.0	25.4	24.1	21.8	14.9	NQ	NQ	NQ	NQ	NQ	NQ	23.2
2000-1[2]	NQ	27.7	26.5	23.1	25.3	29.6							26.4

[1] Weighted average by sales.   [2] Preliminarly.   NQ = No quote.   *Source: National Agricultural Statistics Service,*
U.S. Department of Agriculture (NASS-USDA)

Average Price of Domestic Crude Peanut Oil (in Tanks) F.O.B. Southeast Mills   In Cents Per Pound

Year	Oct.	Nov.	Dec.	Jan.	Feb.	Mar.	Apr.	May	June	July	Aug.	Sept.	Average
1991-2	34.33	27.67	23.50	23.50	23.63	23.17	25.00	27.88	25.60	26.19	23.88	22.00	25.53
1992-3	23.63	25.58	30.30	30.88	27.17	26.00	27.50	30.00	30.20	33.00	39.50	35.93	29.97
1993-4	40.20	43.33	43.17	46.10	46.12	44.50	43.40	44.25	43.75	44.00	45.00	43.10	43.91
1994-5	46.00	50.88	53.80	50.25	41.83	41.00	41.25	40.25	39.00	39.13	41.50	41.30	43.85
1995-6	42.50	41.63	39.20	37.25	36.00	36.60	39.25	42.80	43.00	43.00	42.60	40.80	40.39
1996-7	41.50	39.20	40.75	43.50	43.88	44.75	45.00	46.20	47.88	48.06	48.00	47.25	44.66
1997-8	49.63	51.00	51.25	51.60	51.00	51.00	50.00	47.20	45.50	44.00	43.75	43.88	48.32
1998-9	45.40	45.00	44.25	44.00	39.75	34.75	35.20	35.00	37.75	39.00	38.75	38.00	39.74
1999-00	40.40	41.00	35.40	33.00	32.50	31.60	33.00	36.25	36.00	35.63	35.00	34.90	35.39
2000-1[1]	34.63	35.50	36.40	37.25	37.00								36.16

[1] Preliminary.   *Source: Agricultural Marketing Service, U.S. Department of Agriculture (AMS-USDA)*

Pepper

Pepper prices decreased in calendar year 2000. The price of black pepper (Malabar-Lampong-Brazilian) in January 2000 was reported to be $2.60 per pound (New York spot price). By June 2000, the price had increased to $2.65, but by December 2000 the price had declined substantially to $1.45 per pound. For the year 2000, the average black pepper price was about $2.27, down 11 percent from the 1999 average.

The price of white pepper (Muntok) underwent a similar decline. In January 2000, the price averaged $2.95 per pound. In June, the price had dropped to $2.42 per pound, down 18 percent from January. By December, the average price had dropped to $1.50 per pound, down 49 percent from the January level. For calendar 2000, white pepper prices averaged about $2.27 per pound, down 32 percent from the average price in 1999.

The International Pepper Community (IPC) reported that the market would see a good supply of the spice because of a good harvest in Brazil. India is the largest producer of pepper. Other large producers include Vietnam, Indonesia, Brazil, and Malaysia. The IPC reported that in the January-August 2000 period, Brazilian exports of pepper were 5,233 metric tonnes, which was down 18 percent from the same period in 1999. Pepper exports by Indonesia in the first eight months of 2000 were estimated to be 34,215 tonnes, an increase of 86 percent from the same period in 1999. In 2000, Indonesia exported just over 14,000 tonnes of black pepper and over 20,000 tonnes of white pepper. Indonesia is the largest pepper producer after India. The IPC reported that pepper exports by Malaysia in January-August 2000 were 16,136 tonnes, some 5 percent more than in the same period of 1999. Pepper exports by Vietnam in the first eight months of 2000 were 35,300 tonnes, up 27 percent from the same period in 1999. Pepper exports by Sri Lanka in January-August 2000 were 3,227 tonnes, up 42 percent from 1999.

Pepper exports by India in the first eight months of 2000 were 17,100 tonnes, down 33 percent from the previous year. India's pepper production in the 1999/2000 season has been estimated at about 57,000 tonnes. Because of heavy rains in some production areas, the new 2000/01 crop could reach as much as 70,000 tonnes. In part of India, where there have been production increases, pepper is grown on coffee plantations along with coffee. While the average pepper yield in India is only 300 kilograms per hectare compared to 610 kilograms in the rest of the world, the yield and quality on these Indian plantations is higher than in other parts of the world.

World Exports of Pepper (Black and White) and Prices in the United States   In Metric Tons

| | Exports (In Metric Tons) | | | | | | | | New York Spot Prices (Cents Per Pound) | | | | |
| | | | | | | | | | Indonesian | | Indian | | |
Year	Brazil	India	Indo-nesia	Mada-gascar	Malay-sia	Mexico	Sri Lanka	Vietnam	Lampong Black	Muntok White	Brazilian Black	Malabar Black	Telli-cherry[2]
1990	28,014	34,429	47,675	1,222	27,706	2,663	2,609	1,288	99.1	90.3	97.1	97.1	139.1
1991	47,553	18,735	49,667	1,844	25,458	1,861	2,058	16,252	71.1	70.1	67.1	67.1	117.8
1992	26,277	22,684	62,136	1,948	22,919	3,636	2,143	22,347	56.1	70.8	54.7	54.7	86.1
1993	26,254	47,677	27,684	2,001	16,737	2,430	5,032	20,138	62.5	114.6	62.3	62.3	84.0
1994	22,231	36,536	36,036	2,066	23,275	2,615	1,850	16,000	95.3	151.9	95.0	95.0	110.7
1995	22,158	25,270	57,781	1,274	14,869	3,085	2,082	17,900	116.8	182.3	116.8	116.8	150.9
1996	24,178	47,211	36,849	1,570	28,124	4,200	2,612	25,300	114.8	178.9	114.8	114.8	140.0
1997[1]	13,962	40,000	33,386	894	29,000	4,210	3,485	23,000	206.7	304.6	206.7	206.7	225.8
1998[1]									239.5	356.5	239.5	239.5	286.6
1999[1]									254.5	334.9	254.5	254.5	296.3

[1] Preliminary.   [2] Extra bold.   *Source: Foreign Agricultural Service, U.S. Department of Agriculture (FAS-USDA)*

United States Imports of Unground Pepper from Specified Countries   In Metric Tons

| | Black Pepper | | | | | | | White Pepper | | | | | |
Year	Brazil	India	Indo-nesia	Malay-sia	Singa-pore	Sri Lanka	Total	Brazil	China	Indo-nesia	Malay-sia	Singa-pore	Total
1990	8,778	6,679	8,444	6,768	457	644	32,980	17	15	5,506	24	86	5,721
1991	15,069	2,308	11,330	8,154	391	396	38,860	2	7	4,938	37	96	5,174
1992	6,601	9,892	20,768	2,073	52	310	40,590	51	2	5,089	29	261	5,544
1993	4,580	21,985	7,666	209	----	539	35,969	322	114	4,304	137	363	5,481
1994	8,215	21,097	11,877	829	90	386	43,011	312	756	3,974	228	302	6,102
1995	3,165	10,836	19,630	268	30	327	34,465	414	280	4,037	164	211	5,266
1996	4,267	18,350	17,213	1,084	101	411	41,602	519	54	4,370	150	391	5,765
1997	4,328	23,404	13,610	2,203	678	285	45,319	75	522	3,755	199	750	5,751
1998	5,806	15,540	13,045	422	185	578	36,508	32	108	4,571	195	203	5,393
1999[1]	7,093	24,931	8,429	2,392	525	441	47,591	32	451	5,202	420	342	6,789

[1] Preliminary.   *Source: Foreign Agricultural Service, U.S. Department of Agriculture (FAS-USDA)*

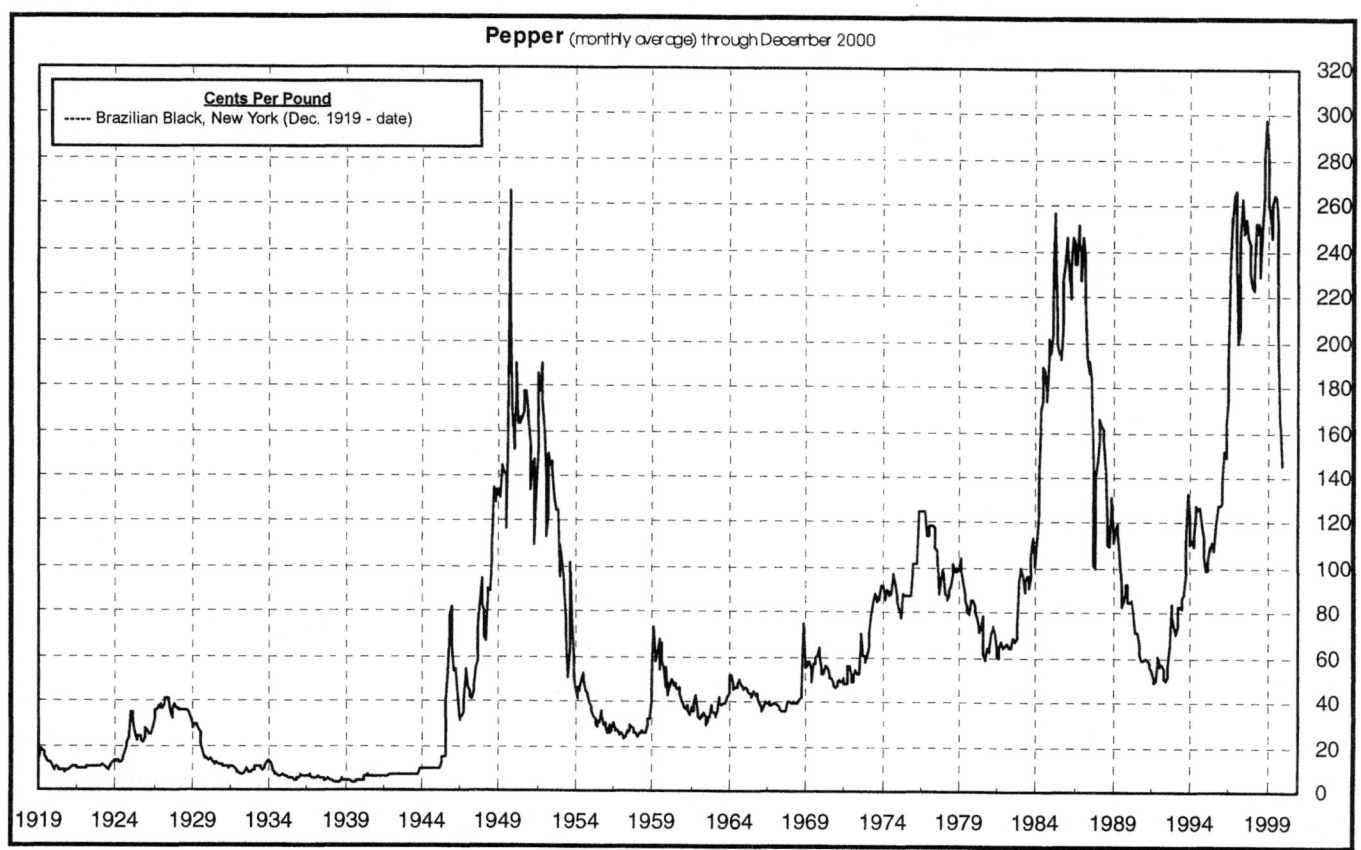

Pepper (monthly average) through December 2000

Cents Per Pound
----- Brazilian Black, New York (Dec. 1919 - date)

Average Black Pepper in New York (Brazilian)   In Cents Per Pound

Year	Jan.	Feb.	Mar.	Apr.	May	June	July	Aug.	Sept.	Oct.	Nov.	Dec.	Average
1991	79.0	78.5	78.6	74.5	66.8	70.0	68.8	61.6	59.5	56.8	55.8	55.0	67.1
1992	55.6	54.5	56.0	55.3	54.0	54.0	50.8	49.0	50.0	57.8	61.0	58.0	54.7
1993	56.0	56.5	54.3	51.2	50.0	51.5	55.8	64.8	84.0	79.0	74.2	70.8	62.3
1994	69.3	74.3	82.0	82.8	82.0	86.5	87.8	97.8	112.2	131.5	123.5	110.4	95.0
1995	111.0	110.0	114.2	124.8	127.3	126.0	127.0	126.3	118.2	113.5	104.8	99.0	116.8
1996	99.3	103.3	109.2	108.3	111.2	109.5	108.0	119.8	126.5	127.5	127.6	128.0	114.8
1997	138.6	151.8	149.0	161.8	173.4	193.8	229.5	255.0	251.3	264.8	266.3	245.0	206.7
1998	199.4	205.5	243.8	262.8	262.8	247.5	253.0	253.8	246.3	243.0	231.3	225.0	239.5
1999	222.5	225.8	252.5	248.0	252.5	250.0	229.0	249.3	263.8	282.0	297.5	281.0	254.5
2000	260.0	256.3	246.0	260.0	265.0	265.0	263.8	252.5	205.0	167.5	147.5	145.0	227.8

Source: Foreign Agricultural Service, U.S. Department of Agriculture (FAS-USDA)

Average White Pepper in New York (Indonesian)[1]   In Cents Per Pound

Year	Jan.	Feb.	Mar.	Apr.	May	June	July	Aug.	Sept.	Oct.	Nov.	Dec.	Average
1991	77.0	72.5	71.4	70.0	67.4	66.0	66.3	63.2	67.0	70.8	78.6	71.5	70.1
1992	70.0	70.0	70.0	70.0	68.0	65.0	64.2	65.0	72.7	79.2	78.5	77.4	70.8
1993	79.0	89.0	85.3	84.0	81.3	87.3	97.0	121.5	181.3	172.6	154.7	142.4	114.6
1994	144.5	139.5	141.3	140.8	137.0	143.3	143.4	156.3	159.2	167.5	176.5	173.0	151.9
1995	179.5	175.8	168.0	181.3	195.0	184.2	187.5	190.8	191.0	182.0	178.5	174.2	182.3
1996	174.5	177.5	181.6	179.5	172.6	164.8	154.0	169.6	181.5	193.5	191.8	205.8	178.9
1997	256.0	264.5	255.0	250.0	241.0	248.8	280.3	324.0	332.5	362.0	433.8	407.5	304.6
1998	348.0	346.3	362.5	390.0	393.0	358.8	354.0	356.3	348.8	340.0	340.0	340.0	356.5
1999	361.3	355.0	365.0	355.0	352.5	335.0	310.0	313.8	325.0	327.0	316.3	303.0	334.9
2000	295.0	293.8	264.0	253.8	246.3	242.0	226.3	227.5	205.0	171.3	150.0	150.0	227.1

[1] Muntok White.   *Source: Foreign Agricultural Service, U.S. Department of Agriculture (FAS-USDA)*

Petroleum

The year 2000 featured much higher prices for all of the various components of the energy complex compared to the previous year. Prices for crude oil, gasoline, heating oil, and natural gas all moved substantially higher during the year.

There were a number of fundamental factors at work in the market that conspired to drive energy prices higher. One was the low prices that were seen in the winter of 1998/99 when crude oil was trading around $10.00 per barrel. That low price reduced the incentive to look for more oil and some producing wells were shut down. That was followed by the Organization of Oil Exporting Countries (OPEC) meeting and resolving to reduce their output of petroleum. While these types of agreements had been made in the past, OPEC members had displayed a history of ignoring agreed upon quota levels which in effect negated the agreements. However, in 2000, it appeared that there was more agreement and unanimity on the part of OPEC members to stay within assigned quotas. The second bullish factor was the strength in the U.S. economy which is heavily dependent upon petroleum. Finally, the winter of 2000/01 began much colder than normal in the U.S. increasing demand for heating oil and therefore crude oil. In the period from late 1998 to October 2000, light crude oil prices increased from about $10.00 per barrel to over $35.00 per barrel. Prices began to decline late in 2000 in response to increased production of crude oil and slowdowns in the U.S and other important global economy's.

The U.S. Energy Information Administration reported that U.S. domestic field production of crude oil in September 2000 was 5.79 million barrels per day, down from 5.81 million barrels in August 2000. A year earlier production was 5.8 million barrels per day. In the January-September 2000 period, crude oil production averaged 5.83 million barrels, down 1 percent from the same period in 1999 and 7 percent less than in 1998. U.S. field production of crude oil has been in a downtrend for several years. In 1985, production averaged 8.97 million barrels per day. By 1995, that had declined 27 percent to 6.56 million barrels. For all of 1999, crude oil production had declined to 5.88 million barrels.

U.S. production of natural gas plant liquids in September 2000 averaged 1.92 million barrels per day, down from 1.94 million barrels in August 2000. The previous year production averaged 1.92 million barrels per day. In the January-September 2000 period, production of natural gas plant liquids averaged 1.95 million barrels, up 7 percent from the same period in 1999 and 10 percent higher than in the 1998 period. For all of 1999, production averaged 1.85 million barrels per day. Total petroleum products supplied in September 2000 averaged 20 million barrels per day, up almost 3 percent from the previous year. In January-September 2000, petroleum products supplied averaged 19.4 million barrels, about the same as in 1999, but up 3 percent from 1998. U.S. stocks of petroleum products and crude oil in September 2000 were 1.53 billion barrels, down 6 percent from the previous year.

U.S. imports of crude oil in September 2000 were 9.2 million barrels per day. This was up 8 percent from September 1999. In the January-September 2000 period, imports averaged just over 8.9 million barrels per day. In the same period in 1999, imports averaged 8.9 million barrels, while in 1998 they averaged 8.7 million barrels. U.S. imports of crude oil have been increasing for many years. In 1985, imports averaged only 3.2 million barrels per day, while in 1995 they averaged 7.2 million barrels, an increase of 125 percent. For all of 1999, imports averaged 8.7 million barrels per day.

Field production of petroleum in Alaska in September 2000 averaged 893,000 barrels per day, down from 914,000 barrels per day in August 2000. In September 1999, production had averaged 933,000 barrels. In the January-September 2000 period, production averaged 965,000 barrels per day. This was down 8 percent from the same period in 1999, and some 18 percent lower than in 1998. Alaskan oil production has been trending lower for several years. In 1985, production averaged 1.83 million barrels per day. By 1995, production had fallen to 1.48 million barrels per day, and by 1999 it was down to 1.05 million barrels per day.

Futures Markets

Futures and options on light sweet crude oil are traded on the New York Mercantile Exchange (NYMEX). Other energy products traded there include heating oil, unleaded gasoline, propane, and natural gas. London's International Petroleum Exchange (IPE) trades Brent crude oil futures and options. The IPE also trades gasoil, natural gas, and fuel oil. The Singapore International Monetary Exchange Ltd. (SIMEX) trades Brent crude oil futures.

World Production of Crude Petroleum In Thousands of Barrels Per Day

Year	Canada	China	Indo-nesia	Iran	Kuwait	Mexico	Nigeria	Russia[3]	Saudi Arabia	United Kingdom	United States	Vene-zuela	World Total
1991	1,548	2,835	1,592	3,312	190	2,680	1,892	9,992	8,115	1,797	7,417	2,375	60,207
1992	1,605	2,845	1,504	3,429	1,058	2,669	1,943	7,632	8,332	1,825	7,171	2,371	60,213
1993	1,679	2,890	1,511	3,540	1,852	2,673	1,960	6,730	8,198	1,915	6,847	2,450	60,236
1994	1,746	2,939	1,510	3,618	2,025	2,685	1,931	6,135	8,120	2,375	6,662	2,588	60,991
1995	1,805	2,990	1,503	3,643	2,057	2,618	1,993	5,995	8,231	2,489	6,560	2,750	62,335
1996	1,837	3,131	1,547	3,686	2,062	2,855	2,188	5,850	8,218	2,568	6,465	3,053	63,711
1997	1,893	3,200	1,546	3,664	2,083	3,023	2,317	5,920	8,562	2,517	6,452	3,315	65,690
1998	1,981	3,198	1,518	3,634	2,085	3,070	2,153	2,854	8,389	2,616	6,252	3,167	66,962
1999[1]	1,907	3,206	1,504	3,557	1,898	2,906	2,130	6,079	7,833	2,684	5,881	2,826	65,678
2000[2]	1,973	3,252	1,467	3,701	2,119	3,009	2,133	6,452	8,367	2,485	5,835	2,926	68,016

Includes lease condensate.   [1] Preliminary.   [2] Estimate.   [3] Formerly part of the U.S.S.R.; data not reported separately until 1992.

Source: Energy Information Administration, U.S. Department of Energy (EIA-DOE)

Refiner Sales Prices of Residual Fuel Oil   In Cents Per Gallon

Year	Jan.	Feb.	Mar.	Apr.	May	June	July	Aug.	Sept.	Oct.	Nov.	Dec.	Average
1995	39.1	37.1	38.3	36.8	40.4	39.9	36.8	35.5	36.4	35.3	36.6	44.7	38.3
1996	49.9	42.8	47.1	48.3	45.0	40.4	41.4	42.0	42.8	47.9	49.1	51.4	45.7
1997	46.2	43.7	39.6	37.6	36.6	39.4	38.5	39.4	40.1	44.6	46.5	38.7	41.5
1998	35.2	30.7	29.4	32.9	31.9	29.3	30.7	26.9	29.9	31.0	27.3	24.0	29.9
1999	27.6	21.9	27.2	30.7	34.9	34.8	38.2	44.5	48.1	47.7	48.9	51.5	36.9
2000[1]	57.2	61.1	53.2	52.3	58.9	65.8	65.1	61.5	71.9	73.7	71.3		62.9

Sulfur 1% or less, excluding taxes.   [1] Preliminary.   *Source: Energy Information Administration, U.S. Department of Energy (EIA-DOE)*

Refiner Sales Prices of No. 2 Fuel Oil   In Cents Per Gallon

Year	Jan.	Feb.	Mar.	Apr.	May	June	July	Aug.	Sept.	Oct.	Nov.	Dec.	Average
1995	49.4	49.1	48.1	50.4	52.4	49.3	48.1	51.0	52.0	50.5	53.4	57.3	51.1
1996	56.8	58.9	62.8	67.5	61.1	53.7	57.1	62.1	68.7	72.7	71.4	71.2	63.9
1997	69.8	64.5	57.7	58.6	58.8	54.5	53.8	55.3	54.3	59.0	58.4	53.4	58.9
1998	48.9	47.7	44.9	44.9	43.4	39.9	38.8	36.9	41.8	41.2	38.9	34.6	42.2
1999	36.3	33.0	39.7	44.5	43.7	44.2	51.4	56.3	60.9	61.3	66.1	67.6	49.2
2000[1]	82.8	91.8	79.6	76.4	78.4	80.3	81.0	88.3	100.9	98.8	100.4		87.2

Excluding taxes.   [1] Preliminary.   *Source: Energy Information Administration, U.S. Department of Energy (EIA-DOE)*

Refiner Sales Prices of No. 2 Diesel Fuel   In Cents Per Gallon

Year	Jan.	Feb.	Mar.	Apr.	May	June	July	Aug.	Sept.	Oct.	Nov.	Dec.	Average
1995	50.1	50.6	51.2	54.8	55.9	52.6	51.4	54.2	55.7	54.6	56.3	57.6	53.8
1996	56.2	57.9	61.9	70.1	67.0	59.1	60.0	64.9	71.7	75.4	73.2	71.0	65.9
1997	69.9	67.8	62.5	61.7	60.7	56.5	55.8	58.9	57.8	61.7	61.5	55.0	60.6
1998	49.6	48.3	45.8	48.2	47.0	43.6	42.6	41.4	45.6	45.5	41.4	35.6	44.4
1999	36.5	35.5	43.6	48.7	47.8	50.3	56.6	61.4	65.0	65.1	69.9	70.6	54.7
2000[1]	77.4	85.2	85.2	79.9	81.6	82.5	83.5	92.1	105.0	104.0	103.2		89.1

Excluding taxes.   [1] Preliminary.   *Source: Energy Information Administration, U.S. Department of Energy (EIA-DOE)*

Refiner Sales Prices of Kerosine-Type Jet Fuel   In Cents Per Gallon

Year	Jan.	Feb.	Mar.	Apr.	May	June	July	Aug.	Sept.	Oct.	Nov.	Dec.	Average
1995	52.3	52.1	50.1	52.6	54.7	53.1	51.3	53.1	55.2	54.1	56.3	58.6	53.9
1996	60.3	57.2	59.6	65.3	62.2	57.5	59.6	64.5	71.6	73.6	72.2	73.0	64.6
1997	73.5	71.4	61.8	60.5	59.4	58.1	56.8	59.4	58.8	61.3	61.3	55.6	61.2
1998	53.4	50.2	45.7	46.6	46.9	43.5	43.8	42.9	44.6	45.8	43.1	36.5	45.0
1999	36.9	35.0	39.3	46.9	47.2	49.3	53.6	59.0	62.5	63.5	66.6	72.0	53.8
2000[1]	79.8	83.6	83.6	77.7	78.0	79.9	83.6	88.0	105.2	104.5	105.1		88.1

Excluding taxes.   [1] Preliminary.   *Source: Energy Information Administration, U.S. Department of Energy (EIA-DOE)*

Refiner Sales Prices of Propane   In Cents Per Gallon

Year	Jan.	Feb.	Mar.	Apr.	May	June	July	Aug.	Sept.	Oct.	Nov.	Dec.	Average
1995	35.6	34.5	34.3	33.0	33.2	32.6	32.1	33.2	33.8	34.4	34.7	37.9	34.4
1996	41.6	44.1	41.1	37.8	36.2	36.2	36.9	38.9	45.3	51.1	58.0	67.7	46.1
1997	59.9	44.7	41.3	37.7	36.9	36.4	35.9	37.5	39.5	41.1	39.6	37.5	41.6
1998	35.4	33.1	31.2	30.3	29.3	26.6	25.7	25.7	26.3	27.6	27.7	25.7	28.8
1999	26.5	26.2	26.9	28.6	29.0	29.6	34.6	38.3	41.5	43.7	42.6	41.7	34.3
2000[1]	49.2	60.3	52.8	48.8	49.4	53.8	54.9	60.2	66.0	64.3	63.2		56.6

Consumer Grade, Excluding taxes.   [1] Preliminary.   *Source: Energy Information Administration, U.S. Department of Energy (EIA-DOE)*

Supply and Disposition of Crude Oil in the United States   In Thousands of Barrels Per Day

	Supply						Stock		Disposition		Ending Stocks		
	-- Field Production --		Imports			Unaccounted for Crude Oil	Withdrawal[3]		Refinery				Other
Yearly Average	Total Domestic	Alaskan	Total	SPR[2]	Other		SPR[2]	Other	Inputs	Exports	Total	SPR[2]	Primary
	In Thousands of Barrels Per Day										In Millions of Barrels		
1993	6,847	1,582	6,787	15	6,772	168	34	47	13,613	98	922	587	335
1994	6,662	1,559	7,063	12	7,051	266	13	5	13,866	99	929	592	337
1995	6,560	1,484	7,230	0	7,230	193	0	-93	13,973	95	895	592	303
1996	6,465	1,393	7,508	0	7,508	215	-71	-53	14,195	110	850	566	284
1997	6,452	1,296	8,225	0	8,225	145	-7	57	14,662	108	868	563	305
1998	6,252	1,175	8,706	0	8,706	115	22	52	14,889	110	895	571	324
1999	5,881	1,050	8,731	8	8,722	191	-11	-107	14,804	118	852	567	284
2000[1]	5,834	970	8,932	8	8,924	301	-73	12	15,078	50	829	541	289

[1] Preliminary.   [2] Strategic Petroleum Reserve.   [3] A negative number indicates a decrease in stocks and a positive number indicates an increase.
Note: Crude oil includes lease condensate. Stocks of Alaskan crude oil in transit were included beginning in January 1981.
Source: Energy Information Administration, U.S. Department of Energy (EIA-DOE)

PETROLEUM

Crude Petroleum Refinery Operations Ratio[1] in the United States   In Percent of Capacity

Year	Jan.	Feb.	Mar.	Apr.	May	June	July	Aug.	Sept.	Oct.	Nov.	Dec.	Average
1991	83.0	84.0	83.0	85.0	87.0	90.0	89.0	89.0	88.0	83.0	84.0	87.0	86.0
1992	83.0	81.0	85.0	86.0	89.0	92.0	92.0	89.0	91.0	89.0	90.0	88.0	87.9
1993	87.0	87.0	89.0	91.0	93.0	95.0	95.0	93.0	93.0	92.0	92.0	91.0	91.5
1994	89.8	88.7	87.6	92.4	95.4	95.8	95.5	96.4	94.4	89.8	92.7	92.6	92.6
1995	89.6	87.9	86.7	90.5	94.0	95.6	94.0	94.0	95.6	90.5	92.1	93.3	92.0
1996	90.6	89.1	90.6	93.7	94.4	95.4	93.9	95.0	95.5	94.6	94.7	94.3	93.5
1997	89.3	87.3	90.7	92.6	97.3	97.7	97.1	98.6	99.7	96.7	95.6	97.2	95.0
1998	93.3	91.3	94.4	96.4	97.1	98.9	99.2	99.8	95.0	89.7	94.7	95.1	95.4
1999	90.4	90.0	90.9	94.6	93.9	93.5	94.9	95.5	94.1	91.1	92.0	90.4	92.7
2000[2]	85.7	86.4	89.8	92.6	94.7	96.2	96.9	95.9	94.3	92.4	92.7		92.5

[1] Based on the ration of the daily average crude runs to stills to the rated capacity of refineries per day.   [2] Preliminary.
Source: Energy Information Administration, U.S. Department of Energy (EIA-DOE)

Crude Oil Refinery Inputs in the United States   In Thousands of Barrels Per Day

Year	Jan.	Feb.	Mar.	Apr.	May	June	July	Aug.	Sept.	Oct.	Nov.	Dec.	Average
1991	12,735	13,046	12,839	13,042	13,539	13,918	13,703	13,800	13,694	12,896	12,929	13,465	13,301
1992	12,923	12,486	13,083	13,260	13,679	14,059	13,953	13,426	13,714	13,584	13,547	13,194	13,411
1993	12,938	12,865	13,200	13,538	13,829	14,129	14,136	13,844	13,841	13,729	13,686	13,571	13,613
1994	13,286	13,130	12,985	13,809	14,272	14,351	14,344	14,491	14,234	13,529	13,968	13,951	13,866
1995	13,604	13,365	13,480	13,817	14,303	14,553	14,403	14,276	14,402	13,598	13,833	14,011	13,973
1996	13,708	13,529	13,755	14,263	14,401	14,535	14,319	14,423	14,483	14,276	14,276	14,194	14,181
1997	13,632	13,425	14,047	14,283	15,083	15,139	14,958	15,217	15,297	14,790	14,654	14,898	14,626
1998	14,313	14,034	14,590	14,961	15,104	15,368	15,496	15,660	14,854	14,001	14,769	14,832	14,837
1999	14,483	14,430	14,495	15,039	14,946	14,943	15,232	15,280	15,107	14,590	14,704	14,420	14,807
2000[1]	13,789	14,046	14,629	15,059	15,512	15,680	15,825	15,645	15,408	15,035	15,027	15,244	15,078

[1] Preliminary.   *Source: Energy Information Administration, U.S. Department of Energy (EIA-DOE)*

Production of Major Refined Petroleum Products in Continental United States   In Millions of Barrels

Year	Asphalt	Aviation Gasoline	Fuel Oil Distillate	Fuel Oil Residual	Gasoline	Jet Fuel	Kerosene	Natural Gas Plant Liquids	Lubricants	Liquified Gasses Total	at L.P.G.[2]	at L.P.G.[3]
1991	156.8	8.0	1,081.0	341.1	2,554	525.0	14.0	639.2	57.0	683.1	487.5	195.6
1992	153.0	7.9	1,088.4	326.1	2,591	512.0	14.8	668.0	57.5	721.9	499.7	222.2
1993	165.6	7.9	1,139.7	303.9	2,644	518.8	17.5	631.2	58.4	849.4	633.5	215.9
1994	164.8	7.9	1,169.7	301.4	2,621	528.4	21.1	630.2	62.1	734.2	511.1	223.2
1995	170.4	7.8	1,151.7	287.6	2,722	516.8	19.2	643.2	63.7	759.9	521.1	238.8
1996	167.8	7.3	1,213.6	265.5	2,769	554.5	22.8	669.8	63.3	789.1	546.7	242.5
1997	177.0	7.2	1,238.0	258.3	2,826	567.3	23.9	663.3	65.9	799.4	547.3	252.2
1998	179.7	7.3	1,248.6	278.0	2,865	554.6	28.6	639.9	67.2	771.2	526.3	244.9
1999	184.3	7.5	1,240.8	254.8	2,896	571.3	24.4	675.1	66.8	811.0	564.5	246.5
2000[1]	180.6	6.2	1,189.9	234.3	2,664	536.6	20.4	649.4	60.9	788.0	545.5	242.5

[1] Preliminary.   [2] Gas processing plants.   [3] Refineries.   *Source: Energy Information Administration, U.S. Department of Energy (EIA-DOE)*

Stocks of Petroleum and Products in the United States on January 1   In Millions of Barrels

Year	Crude Petroleum	Strategic Reserve	Total	Asphalt	Aviation Gasoline	Fuel Oil Distillate	Fuel Oil Residual	Finished Gasoline	Jet Fuel	Kerosene	Liduified Gases[2]	Lubricants	Motor Gasoline Total	Motor Gasoline Finished[3]
1991	908.4	585.7	566.8	18.7	1.7	132.2	48.6	182.4	52.1	5.6	97.9	12.4	220	181
1992	893.1	568.5	576.7	22.3	1.6	143.5	49.9	183.3	48.8	5.8	92.3	12.3	219	182
1993	892.9	574.7	549.1	17.7	1.6	140.6	42.6	179.1	43.1	5.7	88.7	13.3	216	178
1994	922.5	587.1	465.8	19.1	1.8	140.9	44.2	185.7	40.4	4.1	106.6	11.8	226	187
1995	928.9	591.7	468.0	18.6	2.3	145.2	41.9	175.9	46.8	8.0	108.0	11.5	215	176
1996	895.0	591.6	401.2	26.3	2.2	106.3	34.8	162.8	38.4	4.0	99.2	11.7	206	161
1997	868.1	565.8	452.6	22.3	1.7	139.0	40.4	166.1	43.9	7.3	89.5	13.2	203	157
1998	868.1	563.4	451.6	22.1	1.7	138.4	40.5	166.4	44.0	7.3	95.2	12.9	166	166
1999	851.7	567.2	407.1	16.9	1.6	125.5	35.8	154.1	40.5	4.9	89.3	11.8	172	154
2000[1]	836.7	547.5	415.7	21.4	1.4	121.1	38.9	157.4	42.3	5.3	114.6	11.2	193	157

[1] Preliminary.   [2] Includes ethane & ethylene at plants and refineries.   [3] Includes oxygenated.   *Source: Energy Information Administration, U.S. Department of Energy (EIA-DOE)*

Stocks of Crude Petroleum in the United States, on First of Month   In Millions of Barrels

Year	Jan.	Feb.	Mar.	Apr.	May	June	July	Aug.	Sept.	Oct.	Nov.	Dec.
1991	908.4	905.3	912.8	905.3	907.2	924.3	915.3	910.6	913.8	909.1	910.7	912.0
1992	893.1	909.7	914.8	907.1	916.5	912.0	894.6	902.2	898.3	893.5	906.2	899.4
1993	892.9	902.0	908.1	914.7	930.4	935.0	935.1	935.2	919.6	906.4	916.5	924.1
1994	922.5	925.3	922.6	932.6	930.6	922.7	919.6	924.2	920.2	927.0	934.9	938.0
1995	922.2	920.8	931.0	929.4	924.1	919.6	907.3	899.5	897.5	902.8	910.6	894.9
1996	894.9	894.7	892.9	888.8	889.7	889.7	898.9	891.3	890.8	875.8	881.5	869.1
1997	849.7	865.9	862.1	877.6	883.9	890.5	885.3	873.0	864.2	866.6	879.3	886.9
1998	868.1	884.3	885.7	899.8	914.6	916.1	896.4	902.6	893.5	873.0	897.4	906.2
1999	894.4	896.6	897.4	908.0	902.3	914.8	902.8	906.0	889.1	878.0	875.7	866.2
2000[1]	851.6	854.5	858.0	866.3	872.5	868.9	863.2	855.9	861.9	850.5	845.3	836.7

[1] Preliminary.   Source: Energy Information Administration; U.S. Department of Energy (EIA-DOE)

Production of Crude Petroleum in the United States   In Thousands of Barrels Per Day

Year	Jan.	Feb.	Mar.	Apr.	May	June	July	Aug.	Sept.	Oct.	Nov.	Dec.	Average
1991	7,500	7,637	7,546	7,509	7,409	7,320	7,347	7,316	7,368	7,437	7,328	7,299	7,417
1992	7,361	7,389	7,348	7,293	7,169	7,167	7,131	6,922	7,030	7,126	7,024	7,103	7,171
1993	6,961	6,943	6,974	6,881	6,847	6,795	6,688	6,758	6,712	6,839	6,912	6,858	6,847
1994	6,817	6,770	6,746	6,612	6,688	6,611	6,501	6,544	6,609	6,658	6,628	6,760	6,662
1995	6,682	6,794	6,600	6,604	6,629	6,579	6,449	6,447	6,416	6,421	6,585	6,530	6,560
1996	6,495	6,577	6,571	6,444	6,394	6,458	6,338	6,360	6,482	6,481	6,476	6,506	6,465
1997	6,402	6,514	6,452	6,441	6,474	6,442	6,409	6,347	6,486	6,467	6,459	6,531	6,452
1998	6,541	6,476	6,408	6,483	6,347	6,267	6,194	6,203	5,789	6,143	6,140	6,043	6,252
1999	5,963	5,966	5,883	5,887	5,875	5,760	5,798	5,780	5,804	5,947	5,960	5,959	5,881
2000[1]	5,833	5,889	5,873	5,850	5,836	5,824	5,792	5,813	5,767	5,820	5,868	5,839	5,834

[1] Preliminary.   Source: Energy Information Administration, U.S. Department of Energy (EIA-DOE)

U.S. Foreign Trade of Petroleum and Products   In Thousands of Barrels Per Day

	Exports			Imports					Exports			Imports			
Year	Total[2]	Petroleum Products	Crude	Petroleum Products	Distillate Fuel Oil	Residual Fuel Oil	Net Imports[3]	Year	Total[2]	Petroleum Products	Crude	Petroleum Products	Distillate Fuel Oil	Residual Fuel Oil	Net Imports[3]
1981	595	367	4,396	1,599	173	800	5,401	1991	1,001	885	5,782	1,844	205	453	6,626
1982	815	579	3,488	1,325	93	776	4,298	1992	950	861	6,083	1,805	216	375	6,938
1983	739	575	3,329	1,722	174	699	4,312	1993	1,003	904	6,787	1,833	184	373	7,618
1984	722	541	3,426	2,011	272	681	4,715	1994	942	843	7,063	1,933	203	314	8,054
1985	781	577	3,201	1,866	200	510	4,286	1995	949	855	7,230	1,605	193	187	7,886
1986	785	631	4,178	2,045	247	669	5,439	1996	981	871	7,508	1,971	230	248	8,498
1987	764	613	4,674	2,004	255	565	5,914	1997	1,003	896	8,225	1,936	228	194	9,158
1988	815	661	5,107	2,295	302	644	6,587	1998	945	835	8,706	2,002	210	275	9,764
1989	859	717	5,843	2,217	306	629	7,202	1999	940	822	8,731	2,122	250	237	9,912
1990	857	748	5,894	2,123	278	504	7,161	2000[1]	1,040	912	8,932	2,161	277	267	10,053

[1] Preliminary.   [2] Includes crude oil.   [3] Equals imports minus exports.   Source: Energy Information Administration, U.S. Department of Energy (EIA-DOE)

Domestic First Purchase Price of Crude Petroleum at Wells[1]   In Dollars Per Barrel

Year	Jan.	Feb.	Mar.	Apr.	May	June	July	Aug.	Sept.	Oct.	Nov.	Dec	Average
1991	19.60	16.28	15.13	16.16	16.44	15.58	16.36	16.60	16.71	17.72	17.12	14.68	16.54
1992	13.99	14.04	14.12	15.36	16.38	17.96	17.80	17.07	17.20	17.16	16.00	14.94	15.99
1993	14.70	15.53	15.94	16.15	16.03	15.06	13.83	13.75	13.39	13.72	12.45	10.38	14.25
1994	10.49	10.71	10.94	12.31	14.02	14.93	15.34	14.50	13.62	13.84	14.14	13.43	13.19
1995	14.00	14.69	14.68	15.84	15.85	15.02	14.01	14.13	14.49	13.68	14.03	15.02	14.62
1996	15.43	15.54	17.63	19.58	17.94	16.94	17.63	18.29	19.93	21.09	20.20	21.34	18.46
1997	21.76	19.38	17.85	16.64	17.24	15.90	15.91	16.21	16.44	17.68	16.84	15.06	17.24
1998	13.48	12.16	11.53	11.64	11.49	10.00	10.46	10.18	11.28	11.32	9.65	8.05	10.88
1999	8.59	8.58	10.75	12.84	13.84	14.34	16.13	17.58	20.10	19.71	21.35	22.55	15.56
2000[2]	23.53	25.48	26.19	23.19	25.46	27.88	26.83	28.13	29.71	29.63	30.26		26.94

[1] Buyers posted prices.   [2] Preliminary.   Source: Energy Information Administration, U.S. Department of Energy (EIA-DOE)

PETROLEUM

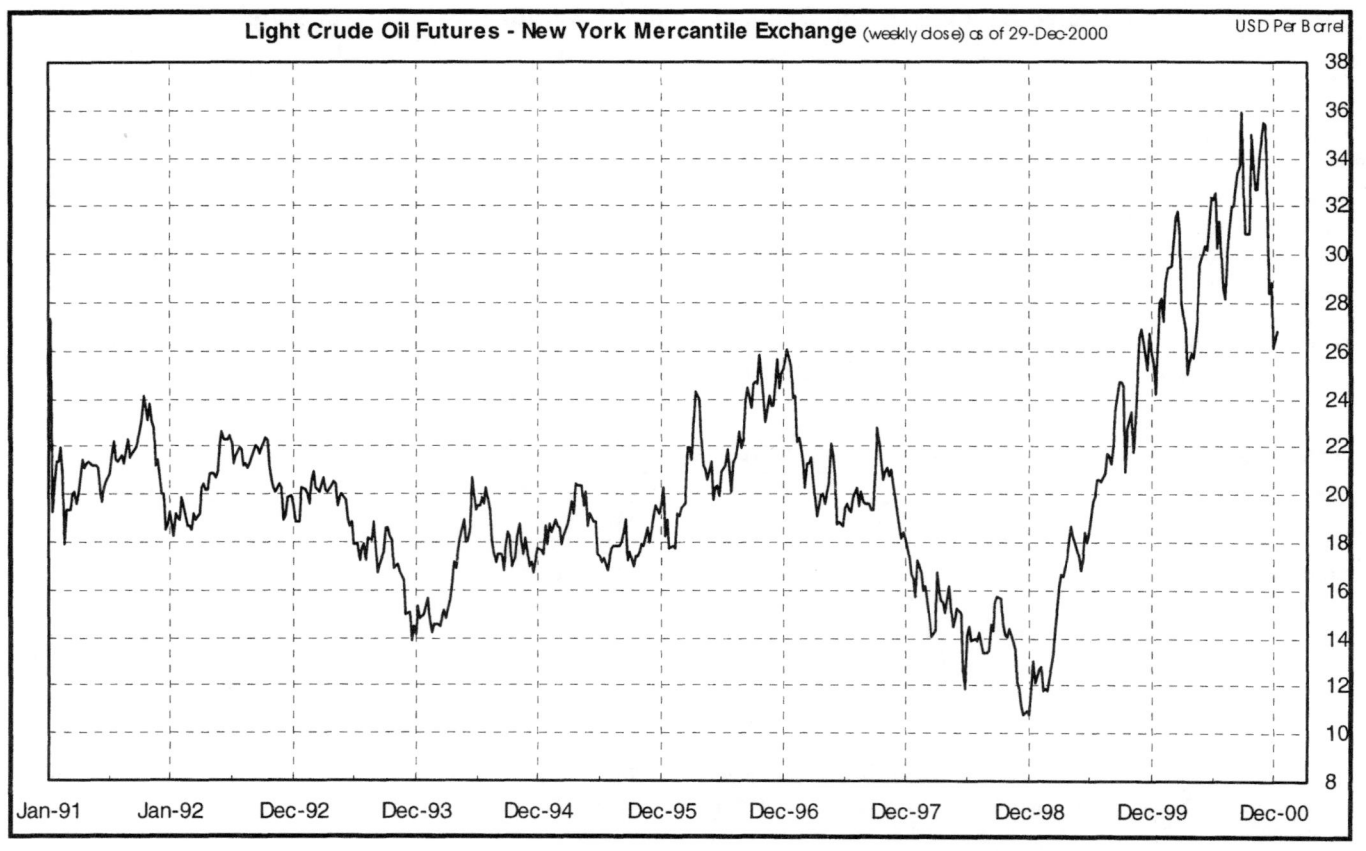

Light Crude Oil Futures - New York Mercantile Exchange (weekly close) as of 29-Dec-2000   USD Per Barrel

Volume of Trading of Crude Oil Futures in New York   In Thousands of Contracts

Year	Jan.	Feb.	Mar.	Apr.	May	June	July	Aug.	Sept.	Oct.	Nov.	Dec.	Total
1991	1,996.9	1,477.5	1,605.3	1,884.5	1,740.6	1,410.7	1,674.8	1,597.9	1,543.0	2,063.7	2,051.1	1,959.8	21,005.9
1992	2,096.6	1,629.9	1,619.8	1,888.6	1,884.7	2,005.7	1,796.3	1,530.9	1,540.7	1,796.8	1,542.1	1,777.5	21,109.6
1993	2,138.9	1,783.6	1,812.7	1,531.4	1,641.5	2,018.5	2,616.2	2,200.3	2,679.5	1,945.2	2,378.4	2,122.4	24,868.6
1994	2,295.6	1,933.0	2,227.7	2,381.7	2,602.3	2,575.8	2,186.5	2,543.6	1,897.5	2,194.5	2,195.9	1,778.2	26,812.3
1995	2,133.5	1,657.3	2,289.8	2,220.1	2,408.9	2,172.4	1,749.3	1,793.8	1,968.0	1,834.6	1,739.1	1,647.2	23,614.0
1996	2,260.1	1,928.3	2,399.3	2,489.9	2,161.3	1,601.7	1,732.1	1,657.0	1,912.6	2,098.0	1,643.1	1,604.3	23,487.8
1997	1,949.9	1,973.7	2,086.6	2,033.7	2,134.9	2,098.6	2,221.4	2,053.7	2,027.5	2,574.0	1,770.2	1,847.2	24,771.4
1998	2,468.3	2,208.3	2,902.8	2,451.1	2,603.6	3,079.5	2,375.0	2,066.7	2,617.8	2,592.4	2,552.9	2,577.3	30,495.6
1999	2,533.6	2,326.0	3,767.7	3,166.8	3,037.9	3,306.8	3,471.3	3,354.8	3,388.4	3,571.2	3,465.1	2,470.4	37,860.1
2000	3,139.0	3,076.6	3,380.2	2,578.9	3,001.8	3,232.2	2,749.7	3,149.3	3,712.0	3,418.0	2,824.5	2,620.5	36,882.7

Source: New York Mercantile Exchange (NYMEX)

Average Open Interest of Crude Oil Futures in New York   In Contracts

Year	Jan.	Feb.	Mar.	Apr.	May	June	July	Aug.	Sept.	Oct.	Nov.	Dec.
1991	249,759	272,396	285,417	303,942	286,159	277,587	278,704	267,186	264,223	298,434	292,889	284,453
1992	310,763	331,050	316,544	340,315	335,545	364,155	331,972	316,066	314,446	301,381	308,467	330,134
1993	352,316	369,180	385,768	381,954	384,309	396,832	423,041	428,418	404,172	397,121	404,046	427,756
1994	427,705	438,929	424,462	410,974	427,071	414,257	409,251	396,657	395,194	413,206	388,932	391,151
1995	373,798	379,329	353,805	364,929	350,826	346,051	357,718	343,636	342,360	334,170	329,786	348,954
1996	389,935	400,236	427,306	460,841	424,994	376,164	367,405	364,458	395,358	410,387	385,415	368,331
1997	365,522	384,737	408,751	409,719	401,663	397,245	411,292	424,529	405,389	419,821	404,597	424,333
1998	424,810	445,167	468,438	463,961	450,611	467,998	476,516	486,499	486,047	481,657	487,175	501,591
1999	501,655	524,677	581,072	611,727	594,032	582,058	601,212	584,962	622,257	595,743	564,488	531,567
2000	512,049	519,090	513,359	467,259	453,042	462,476	432,571	416,934	461,298	478,242	479,008	438,118

Source: New York Mercantile Exchange (NYMEX)

Plastics

Plastics are one of the most used materials in the U.S. for industrial and commercial purposes. The most important developments in the plastics industry have occurred since 1910. The period 1930-40 saw the initial commercial development of the major thermoplastics used today. These include polyvinyl chloride, low density polyethylene, polystyrene, and polymethyl methacrylate. World War II brought plastics into great demand as substitutes for material that was in short supply, such as natural rubber. In the U.S., the production of synthetic rubbers led to the development of more plastics materials. New materials that have been developed are competing with older plastics and other materials like wood. The demand for plastics continues to increase.

U.S. plastic resin sales in 1999 were 85 billion pounds, dry weight basis, up nearly 7 percent from 1998. Of the total sales, plastic resin sales for the packaging industry in 1999 were 21.3 billion pounds, up 9 percent from the previous year. Sales to the packaging industry are 25 percent of total resin sales. Sales to the building and construction industries were 19.1 billion pounds, 22 percent of the total resin sales and up 11 percent from 1998. Consumer and institutional markets took 11.8 billion pounds or 5 percent more than in 1998. This was 14 percent of the total resin sales. The transportation market took 3.8 billion pounds of plastic resin, about unchanged from the previous year. The furniture and furnishings market took 3.6 billion pounds of plastic resins, down 10 percent from the previous year. The electrical and electronic market took 3.3 billion pounds, up 10 percent from 1998. The adhesives, inks, and coatings market took 2.1 billion pounds of plastics resins in 1999, up 5 percent from 1998. The industrial machinery market took one billion pounds, up 12 percent from 1998. Other markets in 1999 took 10.4 billion pounds of plastic resins, up 9 percent from 1998. Exports of plastic resins in 1999 were 8.6 billion pounds, up 2 percent from a year ago.

Thermoset resin production in 1999 was 8 billion pounds (dry weight), up almost 8 percent from 1998. Sales of thermoset resins in 1999 were up 3 percent from 1998. Production of epoxy resins in 1999 were 657 million pounds, up 3 percent from the previous year. Sales of epoxy resins were 632 million pounds, up 2 percent from the previous year. Production of phenolic resins were 4.4 billion pounds, up over 11 percent from 1998, while sales of phenolic resins were 4 billion pounds, up 3 percent from the year before.

Thermoplastic resin production in 1999 was 76 billion pounds, up 7 percent. Polypropylene production was 15.5 billion pounds, up 12 percent. Polyvinyl chloride production in 1999 was 14.9 billion pounds, up 3 percent from 1998.

Plastics Production by Resin in the United States   In Millions of Pounds

Year	Thermosets				Thermoplastics											
	Polyester Unsaturated	Phenlic	Epoxy	Total Thermosets	Thermoplastic Polyester	Polyvinyl Chloride	Polystyrene	Polypropylene	Nylon	Low Density Polyethylene[1]	High Density Polyethylene	Total Thermoplastics	Total Selected Plastics	Other Plastics	Total Plastics
1990	1,221	2,946	499	6,364	1,879	9,096	5,021	8,310	558	11,148	8,337	45,646	52,010	9,950	61,960
1991	1,075	2,658	497	5,909	2,115	9,164	4,954	8,330	576	11,582	9,213	47,146	53,055	9,731	62,786
1992	1,175	2,923	457	6,335	2,413	9,989	5,096	8,421	668	11,917	9,808	49,751	56,086	10,285	66,371
1993	1,264	3,078	512	6,868	2,549	10,257	5,382	8,628	768	12,067	9,941	51,159	58,027	10,777	68,854
1994	1,468	3,229	601	7,513	3,196	11,712	5,848	9,539	943	12,600	11,117	56,794	64,307	11,664	75,971
1995	1,577	3,204	632	7,519	3,785	12,295	5,656	10,890	1,020	12,886	11,211	59,331	66,850	11,834	78,684
1996	1,557	3,476	662	8,129	4,031	13,220	6,065	11,991	1,103	14,145	12,373	64,526	72,655	11,640	84,295
1997	1,621	3,734	654	8,647	4,260	14,084	6,380	13,320	1,222	14,579	12,557	67,872	76,519	12,287	88,806
1998	1,713	3,940	639	9,163	4,423	14,502	6,237	13,825	1,285	14,805	12,924	71,209	78,659	13,026	91,685
1999	2,691	4,388	657	8,030	4,846	14,912	6,471	15,493	1,349	15,807	13,864	75,964	83,994	13,467	97,461

[1] Includes LDPE and LLDPE.   *Source: The Society of the Plastics Industry, Inc. (SPI)*

Total Resin Sales and Captive Use by Important Markets   In Millions of Pounds (Dry Weight Basis)

Year	Adhesive, Inks & Coatings	Building & Construction	Consumer & Industrial	Electrical & Electronics	Exports	Furniture & Furnishings	Industrial & Machinary	Packaging	Transportation	Other	Total
1990	1,373	11,803	5,861	3,165	[1]	2,190	636	16,568	2,504	11,811	55,910
1991	1,391	10,650	5,689	2,896	7,418	2,255	587	16,723	2,328	6,616	56,553
1992	1,723	11,876	6,093	2,766	6,950	2,559	617	18,284	2,817	6,877	60,562
1993	1,572	12,885	6,015	2,981	6,632	2,759	768	19,569	3,221	7,234	63,636
1994	1,789	14,715	9,266	3,325	6,889	3,118	836	19,551	3,795	7,515	70,799
1995	1,795	13,551	8,921	2,872	7,162	3,189	805	17,107	3,376	7,421	66,200
1996	1,833	15,413	9,662	3,022	7,997	3,468	965	18,691	3,469	8,701	73,221
1997	2,019	16,273	10,505	3,021	8,839	3,721	938	19,192	3,603	8,884	76,995
1998	2,038	17,217	11,184	3,036	8,397	3,995	933	19,454	3,788	9,460	79,501
1999	2,065	19,072	11,802	3,256	8,622	3,587	1,043	21,270	3,836	10,446	84,999

[1] Included in other.   *Source: The Society of the Plastics Industry, Inc. (SPI)*

PLASTICS

Average Producer Price Index of Plastic Resins and Materials (066) in the United States   (1982 = 100)

Year	Jan.	Feb.	Mar.	Apr.	May	June	July	Aug.	Sept.	Oct.	Nov.	Dec.	Average
1994	115.0	114.7	114.5	116.5	117.7	119.1	119.6	121.5	126.3	131.9	134.1	138.1	122.4
1995	142.5	144.1	145.9	148.5	149.0	148.9	147.0	144.8	142.7	139.2	135.8	132.2	143.4
1996	129.9	128.4	128.4	127.7	130.6	132.1	133.2	135.2	137.9	138.0	138.0	137.7	133.1
1997	137.0	137.5	138.7	138.9	139.1	139.6	139.3	137.4	136.0	135.9	134.6	133.9	137.3
1998	134.0	132.2	131.0	130.7	128.8	126.8	125.0	123.7	119.6	118.6	117.1	115.9	125.3
1999	115.9	115.8	117.3	118.6	122.1	123.1	127.9	130.0	133.8	135.6	135.8	134.3	125.8
2000[1]	133.2	135.7	139.4	143.7	147.4	147.8	146.4	146.3	142.4	142.1	140.4	136.4	141.8

[1] Preliminary.   *Source: Bureau of Labor Statistics, U.S. Department of Commerce (BLS)*

Average Producer Price Index of Thermoplastic Resins (0662) in the United States   (1982 = 100)

Year	Jan.	Feb.	Mar.	Apr.	May	June	July	Aug.	Sept.	Oct.	Nov.	Dec.	Average
1994	113.0	112.7	112.5	115.0	116.2	117.9	118.4	120.1	125.4	131.6	133.9	138.4	121.3
1995	143.1	145.0	147.1	150.3	151.0	151.2	148.7	146.2	143.7	139.6	135.5	131.1	144.4
1996	128.4	126.7	126.8	125.9	129.4	131.1	132.5	134.8	137.8	137.9	137.9	137.6	132.2
1997	136.7	137.3	138.6	138.8	139.0	139.7	139.3	137.0	135.5	135.3	133.8	133.0	137.0
1998	133.0	130.7	129.5	129.2	127.0	124.7	122.5	121.0	116.4	115.3	113.7	112.2	122.9
1999	112.3	112.5	114.4	116.1	120.4	121.6	127.5	129.9	134.5	136.7	137.0	135.2	124.9
2000[1]	133.8	136.0	140.4	145.2	149.3	149.6	147.6	147.4	142.7	141.8	139.6	134.7	142.3

[1] Preliminary.   *Source: Bureau of Labor Statistics, U.S. Department of Commerce (BLS)*

Average Producer Price Index of PE Resin, Low, Film & Sheeting (0662-0301) in the United States

Year	Jan.	Feb.	Mar.	Apr.	May	June	July	Aug.	Sept.	Oct.	Nov.	Dec.	Average
1993	NA	151.4	145.6	141.8	135.5	137.1	132.2	136.6	129.2	128.4	127.6	127.4	135.7
1994	121.6	119.4	119.3	120.8	127.6	134.5	136.3	140.8	146.6	155.4	172.8	182.2	139.8
1995	188.5	196.0	202.0	210.6	215.4	211.1	205.7	194.4	185.0	173.4	167.5	157.4	192.3
1996	146.4	139.9	137.6	139.5	147.6	158.8	166.0	165.3	190.1	195.2	195.9	196.6	164.9
1997	191.8	189.0	189.7	193.8	196.8	199.4	197.9	201.0	190.2	185.1	182.5	177.2	191.2
1998	181.3	181.0	168.7	NA	159.1	162.9	158.0	152.8	NA	NA	NA	NA	166.3
1999[1]	No data available for this year.												

1982=100.   [1] Preliminary.   NA = Not available.   *Source: Bureau of Labor Statistics, U.S. Department of Commerce (BLS)*

Average Producer Price Index of Styrene Plastics Materials (0662-06) in the United States   (1982 = 100)

Year	Jan.	Feb.	Mar.	Apr.	May	June	July	Aug.	Sept.	Oct.	Nov.	Dec.	Average
1994	105.8	104.1	104.1	108.1	108.3	109.2	110.4	110.6	116.0	123.3	125.3	126.2	112.6
1995	129.0	127.0	132.5	134.7	135.9	137.5	135.1	133.2	132.1	130.1	127.9	126.1	131.8
1996	125.7	123.5	125.0	118.3	120.1	122.7	123.4	123.3	123.6	122.8	122.0	120.9	122.6
1997	120.6	123.1	123.0	121.6	121.6	121.6	122.7	117.7	118.0	116.5	113.5	113.7	119.5
1998	113.3	113.9	115.5	114.9	114.1	112.8	111.3	111.2	107.6	107.9	107.1	106.3	111.3
1999	103.5	102.4	103.5	104.7	103.0	102.3	103.1	101.5	101.4	99.8	99.4	100.5	102.1
2000[1]	103.0	104.3	110.5	113.0	116.2	116.9	118.5	116.5	115.0	113.7	112.9	111.3	112.7

[1] Preliminary.   *Source: Bureau of Labor Statistics, U.S. Department of Commerce (BLS)*

Average Producer Price Index of Thermosetting Resins (0663) in the United States   (1982 = 100)

Year	Jan.	Feb.	Mar.	Apr.	May	June	July	Aug.	Sept.	Oct.	Nov.	Dec.	Average
1994	128.2	128.1	128.1	127.8	128.7	129.1	129.7	132.1	134.9	137.7	140.1	141.5	132.2
1995	144.3	145.1	145.4	145.2	144.7	143.5	144.0	143.5	142.9	142.3	142.4	142.1	143.8
1996	141.8	141.9	141.2	141.3	141.4	141.2	140.6	141.5	141.7	142.0	142.0	142.2	141.6
1997	142.1	142.3	142.7	143.1	143.2	143.0	142.8	142.9	143.0	143.1	142.9	142.9	142.8
1998	143.6	144.0	143.2	142.9	142.6	142.7	142.5	142.2	141.2	140.9	140.1	140.3	142.2
1999	139.9	138.1	137.7	137.4	136.9	136.5	136.2	136.5	136.5	136.5	136.3	136.2	137.0
2000[1]	136.8	141.1	141.3	142.8	144.9	146.0	147.6	147.8	147.5	150.5	151.0	151.8	145.7

[1] Preliminary.   *Source: Bureau of Labor Statistics, U.S. Department of Commerce (BLS)*

Average Producer Price Index of Phenolic & Tar Acid Resins (0663-02) in the United States   (1982 = 100)

Year	Jan.	Feb.	Mar.	Apr.	May	June	July	Aug.	Sept.	Oct.	Nov.	Dec.	Average
1993	128.5	130.3	130.5	131.4	133.7	134.1	133.9	132.8	133.1	132.1	132.0	132.9	132.1
1994	133.0	130.9	129.7	131.3	134.1	135.9	139.2	143.7	147.2	154.7	161.0	161.5	141.9
1995	164.6	166.4	165.1	162.5	158.6	153.5	152.0	148.5	147.7	146.2	143.2	142.6	154.2
1996	142.7	142.6	141.9	142.2	143.1	143.4	143.2	147.2	148.7	149.1	149.8	150.5	145.4
1997	150.5	151.2	150.9	152.7	152.9	152.6	151.9	152.7	153.1	152.5	151.9	151.8	152.0
1998	153.1	154.9	153.0	151.0	148.7	148.8	148.5	149.0	142.8	141.7	140.6	138.6	147.6
1999[1]	No data available for this year.												

[1] Preliminary.   *Source: Bureau of Labor Statistics, U.S. Department of Commerce (BLS)*

Platinum-Group Metals

The year 2000 proved to be a very interesting one for the platinum-group metals. New multi-year high prices were recorded for platinum and palladium. In December 2000, platinum reached a new 13-year high and continued to move higher through early 2001. Much more impressive were the gains posted by palladium, a component in catalytic converters. In early 2001, palladium prices reached over $1,000 per ounce on concerns about the ability of Russian to deliver on contracted sales of the metal. There remains strong demand by the automobile industry for palladium for pollution control devices. Given the general uncertainty over the size of Russian palladium supplies and delivery schedules, prices have moved relentlessly higher. With platinum prices trading well under palladium, there may be more substitution of platinum for palladium in pollution control devices.

Among the platinum-group metals, platinum finds use and value as a precious metal as well as an industrial metal. Palladium is more of an industrial metal finding use in pollution-control devices in the automotive industry. Other platinum-group metals include rhodium, ruthenium, iridium, and osmium.

The U.S. Geological Survey reported that world mine production of platinum in 1999 was estimated to be 150,000 kilograms, up 3 percent from 1998. The largest producer of platinum by far was South Africa with 1999 production estimated at 120,000 kilograms, up nearly 3 percent from the year before. The next largest producer was Russia with estimated production of 17,500 kilograms, up 3 percent from the previous year. Platinum production by Canada in 1999 was 7,300 kilograms, down 4 percent from the previous year. U.S. mine production of platinum in 1999 was estimated at 3,200 kilograms, down slightly from 1998. The U.S. has only one active platinum-group mine located in Montana. Some small quantities of platinum group metals are recovered in copper refining. World reserves of platinum-group metals are estimated at 71 million kilograms. The largest reserves are held by South Africa and are estimated to be 63 million kilograms. It is expected that world production of these metals will increase because of new projects in the U.S. and Canada.

Most platinum-group metals are consumed by the automotive industry. The metals are used as oxidation catalysts in air pollution abatement devices that remove odors, vapors, and carbon monoxide. In the U.S., about 110,000 kilograms of these metals are used by the automotive industry to manufacture catalysts. It is of interest to note that previous to this year palladium prices were less than platinum, and palladium was substituted for platinum in catalytic converters. Palladium is less resistant than platinum to poisoning by sulfur and lead. This season, palladium prices have surged ahead of platinum leading to the idea that there will be substitution of platinum for palladium. The platinum-group metals also find use as chemical catalysts. Platinum alloys find use in jewelry, while both platinum and palladium are used in dentistry. The metals are also used in medicine and cancer chemotherapy. Platinum also finds use in the manufacture of computer storage disks.

Iridium is used in process catalysts and it has also found use in some auto catalysts. Iridium and ruthenium are used in the production of polyvinyl chloride. Rhodium finds use in the automotive industry in pollution control devices. Palladium has replaced rhodium to some extent though whether that continues at these prices is a question. As the standards for allowable levels of pollution are lowered, the use of palladium increases. Some pollution control devices which had used platinum-rhodium have been replaced by palladium.

U.S. mine production of platinum in 1999 was estimated at 3,200 kilograms. Production has doubled since 1995. In addition to mine production, an estimated 70 tonnes of platinum-group metals were recovered from old and new scrap in 1999. Despite the fact that the U.S. is a large producer of platinum, it is a much larger importer. In 1999, imports for consumption were estimated to be 75,300 kilograms, down 23 percent from 1998. U.S. imports of platinum sponge in June 2000 were 5,000 kilograms, down 9 percent from the previous month. For 1999, imports of platinum sponge were 78,300 kilograms. The major supplier was South Africa.

U.S. imports of platinum grain and nuggets in June 2000 were 532 kilograms. For all of 1999, imports were 6,100 kilograms. Imports of platinum waste and scrap in June were 127 kilograms. In the first half of 2000, imports were 10,400 kilograms, while for all of 1999 they were 19,700 kilograms. U.S. exports of unwrought platinum and other forms of platinum in June 2000 were 4,960 kilograms. In the first half of 2000, exports were 16,300 kilograms, while for all of 1999 they were 19,400 kilograms. The major export destination was the United Kingdom.

U.S. imports of unwrought palladium in June 2000 were 12,600 kilograms. The major suppliers were Russia, South Africa, and Switzerland. Imports in the first half of 2000 were 73,600 kilograms, and for all of 1999 they were 165,000 kilograms. Other palladium imports in June were 2,340 kilograms. In 1999, they totaled 24,100 kilograms. Imports of unwrought and other forms of iridium in June 2000 were 71 kilograms, most of which came from South Africa. In the first half of 2000, imports were 1,320 kilograms, while for all of 1999 they were 2,260 kilograms. There were no imports of unwrought osmium in 2000, but in 1999 imports were 23 kilograms. Imports of unwrought ruthenium in June 2000 were 712 kilograms, most of which was supplied by South Africa, the United Kingdom, and Germany. In the first half of 2000, imports were 8,300 kilograms, while for all of 1999 they were 11,400 kilograms. Imports of unwrought and other forms of rhodium in June 2000 were 1,240 kilograms. The major suppliers were South Africa, the United Kingdom, and Austria. Rhodium imports in January-June 2000 were 9,960 kilograms, while for all of 1999 they were 10,500 kilograms.

Futures Markets

Platinum and palladium futures and options are traded on the New York Mercantile Exchange (NYMEX). In Japan, platinum and palladium futures are listed on the Tokyo Commodity Exchange (TOCOM).

PLATINUM-GROUP METALS

World Mine Production of Platinum   In Kilograms

Year	Aust-ralia	Canada	Colom-bia[3]	Finland	Japan	Russia[4]	Serbia/Montenegro[5]	South Africa	United States	Zimbabwe	World Total
1991	100	4,680	1,600	60	988	30,000	22	88,900	1,500	19	128,000
1992	100	4,800	1,956	60	629	28,000	19	94,900	1,650	9	132,000
1993	100	5,000	1,722	60	661	20,000	10	109,000	2,050	4	139,000
1994	100	6,000	1,084	60	691	15,000	10	114,000	1,960	7	139,000
1995	100	5,945	973	60	730	27,000	10	102,000	1,590	7	139,000
1996	100	5,155	672	60	816	25,000	10	105,000	1,840	100	139,000
1997	100	4,813	409	60	693	25,000	10	115,861	2,610	345	150,000
1998[1]	100	5,640	437	60	533	25,000	10	116,483	3,240	2,730	154,000
1999[2]	100	5,442	440	50	750	27,000	5	131,000	2,920	2,000	169,000

[1] Preliminary. [2] Estimate. [3] Placer platinum. [4] Formerly part of the U.S.S.R.; data not reported separately until 1992. [5] Formerly part of Yugoslavia; data not reported separately until 1992. *Source: U.S. Geological Survey (USGS)*

World Mine Production of Palladium and Other Group Metals   In Kilograms

	Palladium										Other Group Metals		
Year	Aust-ralia	Canada	Finland	Japan	Russia[3]	Serbia/Montenegro[4]	South Africa	United States	Zimbabwe	World Total	Russia[3]	South Africa	World Total
1991	400	6,440	100	1,050	82,000	155	38,000	5,200	30	133,000	9,500	16,000	26,100
1992	400	5,800	100	986	70,000	130	41,000	5,440	19	124,000	6,000	17,000	24,300
1993	400	6,000	100	1,183	50,000	72	48,000	6,780	11	113,000	4,000	19,000	24,400
1994	400	7,000	100	1,277	40,000	50	47,800	6,440	17	103,000	3,000	22,100	27,100
1995	400	9,319	95	2,174	85,000	50	51,000	5,260	17	153,000	3,600	29,797	34,200
1996	400	8,082	182	2,182	80,000	50	52,600	6,100	120	150,000	3,500	30,363	34,800
1997	400	7,545	180	1,899	80,000	50	55,675	8,430	245	154,000	3,500	24,930	29,100
1998[1]	400	8,905	180	4,151	80,000	50	56,608	10,600	1,855	163,000	3,500	27,052	31,500
1999[2]	400	8,592	150	5,500	85,000	25	63,600	9,800	1,000	174,000	3,700	30,300	34,800

[1] Preliminary. [2] Estimate. [3] Formerly part of the U.S.S.R.; data not reported separately until 1992. [4] Formerly part of Yugoslavia; data not reported separately until 1992. *Source: U.S. Geological Survey (USGS)*

Platinum-Group Metals Sold to Consuming Industries in the United States   In Kilograms

	Automotive		Chemical		Electrical		Medical		Dental & Decorative		Petroleum		All Platinum-Group Metals			
Year	Platinum	Other[3]	Platinum	Other[3]	Platinum	Other[3]	Platinum	Other[3]	Platinum	Other[3]	Platinum	Other[3]	Platinum	Palladium	Other[3]	Total
1991	18,643	5,338	861	1,749	3,910	14,428	598	4,918	626	500	3,163	181	31,112	25,747	5,738	62,597
1992	20,503	5,860	1,716	2,297	2,922	15,738	640	5,386	881	1,417	1,036	790	31,095	28,935	6,816	66,846
1993	19,446	10,124	2,364	3,121	2,125	12,699	687	5,562	1,024	1,422	1,204	709	29,879	26,840	8,544	65,063
1994	21,756	11,413	3,104	1,889	2,790	7,961	902	5,092	1,345	824	1,581	422	34,044	21,509	7,387	62,940
1995	27,990	12,440	2,022	2,395	4,510	18,225	778	6,158	1,337	1,431	3,421	871	43,524	45,188	----	88,712
1996	28,550	19,282	2,115	2,457	4,541	17,665	778	6,285	1,493	1,493	3,514	902	44,489	45,157	----	89,646
1997	28,923	20,402	2,239	2,426	4,945	19,997	840	6,376	2,115	1,617	3,390	871	46,184	50,227	----	96,411
1998[1]	29,483	26,528	2,301	2,488	5,194	20,215	902	6,376	2,333	1,617	3,390	809	47,396	61,827	----	109,223
1999[2]	31,100	29,390	2,364	2,519	5,443	21,148	933	6,065	2,644	1,679	3,514	NA	49,844	64,470	----	114,314

[1] Preliminary. [2] Estimate. [3] Includes Palladium, iridium, osmium, rhodium, and ruthenium. *Sources: U.S. Geological Survey (USGS); American Metal Market (AMM)*

Salient Statistics of Platinum and Allied Metals[3] in the United States   In Kilograms

	Net Import Reliance as a % of Apparent Con-sumption	Mine Production		Refinery Pro-duction (Secon-dary)	Refiner, Importer & Dealer Stocks as of Dec. 31				Imports for Consumption		Exports		Apparent Con-sumption
Year		Platinum	Palladium		Total Refined	Platinum	Palladium	Other[4]	Total	Refined	Total	Refined	Total	
1991	90	1,730	6,050	72,349	72,564	10,349	12,263	1,701	24,313	121,741	125,661	27,401	39,624	111,798
1992	87	1,650	5,440	64,309	64,309	14,187	10,641	2,118	26,946	129,419	132,006	31,060	57,830	109,469
1993	89	2,050	6,780	65,792	65,792	10,263	8,324	176	18,763	148,790	153,165	43,798	78,486	123,273
1994	91	1,960	6,440	63,000	63,000	10,304	9,345	123	19,772	167,681	170,907	46,259	88,561	127,000
1995	----	1,590	5,260	NA	NA	----	----	----	----	214,143	220,613	41,825	50,575	----
1996	84	1,840	6,100	NA	NA	----	----	----	----	248,860	255,880	39,709	48,836	----
1997	84	2,610	8,430	NA	NA	----	----	----	----	253,114	258,424	67,656	81,249	----
1998[1]	94	3,240	10,600	NA	NA	----	----	----	----	297,961	303,351	52,715	73,162	----
1999[2]		2,920	9,800	28,400	28,400	----	----	----	----					

[1] Preliminary. [2] Estimate. [3] Includes platinum, palladium, iridium, osmium, rhodium, and ruthenium. [4] Includes iridium, osmium, rhodium, and ruthenium. W = Withheld proprietary data. *Source: U.S. Geological Survey (USGS)*

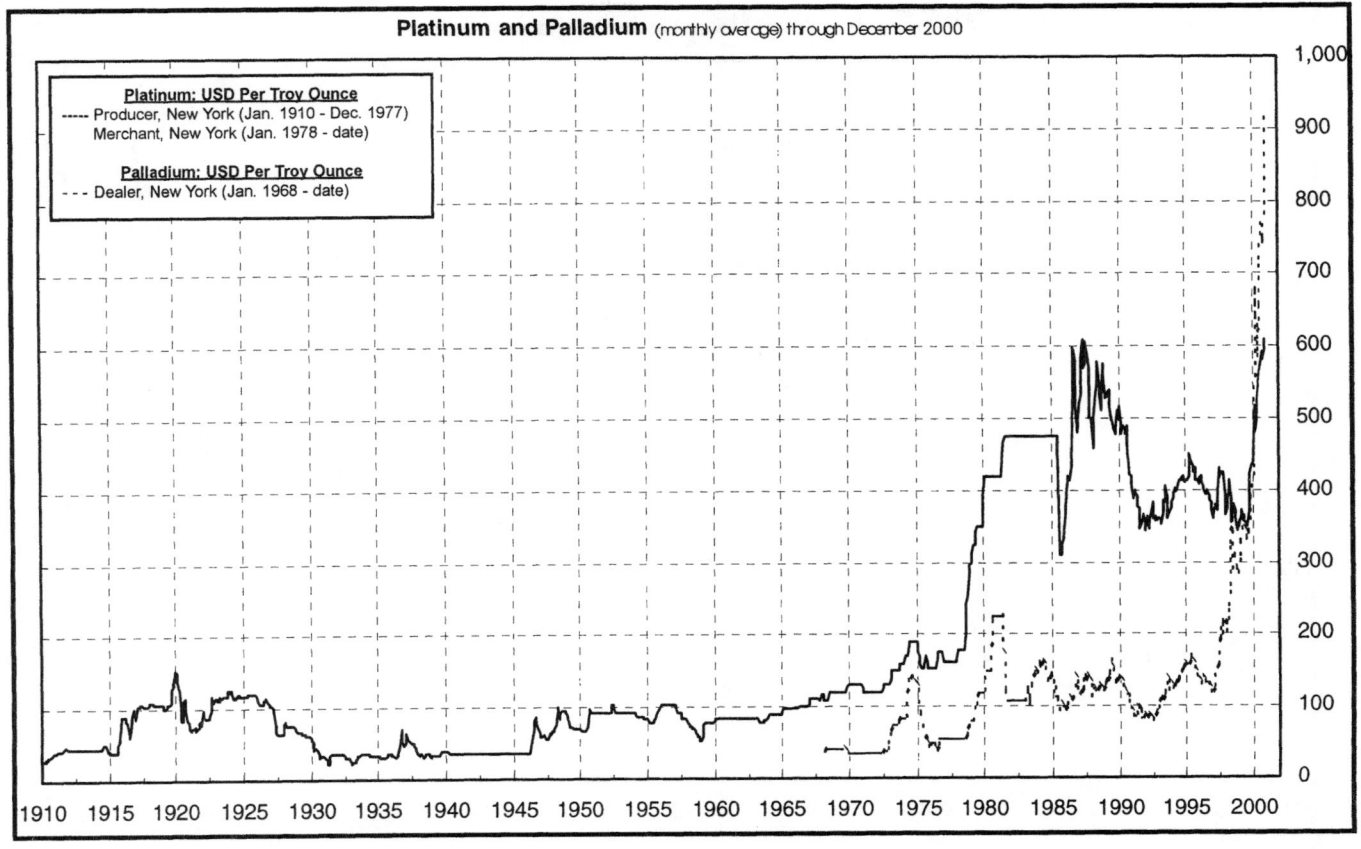

Platinum and Palladium (monthly average) through December 2000

Platinum: USD Per Troy Ounce
----- Producer, New York (Jan. 1910 - Dec. 1977)
Merchant, New York (Jan. 1978 - date)

Palladium: USD Per Troy Ounce
- - - Dealer, New York (Jan. 1968 - date)

Average Merchant's Price of Platinum in the United States — In Dollars Per Troy Ounce

Year	Jan.	Feb.	Mar.	Apr.	May	June	July	Aug.	Sept.	Oct.	Nov.	Dec.	Average
1991	408.92	385.53	403.12	398.16	373.06	374.25	375.38	351.68	348.01	362.52	364.01	356.65	375.11
1992	341.88	362.97	356.84	347.73	354.75	368.17	378.89	360.20	361.60	359.75	355.81	361.98	359.21
1993	359.99	361.53	349.31	365.98	385.50	384.54	401.10	394.69	365.29	369.19	376.98	383.85	374.75
1994	390.30	393.95	398.29	400.38	395.41	401.42	408.25	411.91	415.93	421.11	415.73	408.83	405.13
1995	414.27	415.22	415.37	446.24	439.02	436.58	435.21	425.61	430.31	414.49	413.55	410.17	424.67
1996	416.59	421.45	412.39	405.71	402.86	393.18	392.00	400.97	391.43	385.53	383.92	372.80	398.24
1997	360.13	362.35	382.82	371.18	385.20	427.12	410.25	423.48	424.00	428.59	397.03	369.50	395.14
1998	373.45	390.56	396.18	413.14	392.00	357.38	378.20	372.24	361.56	347.27	349.29	352.35	373.64
1999	353.93	364.24	370.14	357.27	355.65	355.73	349.29	350.06	370.71	421.19	433.52	439.55	376.77
2000	440.20	515.90	479.46	498.11	525.00	557.73	562.05	576.52	590.95	579.75	593.97	610.26	544.16

[1] Preliminary.   *Source: American Metal Market (AMM)*

Average Dealer[1] Price of Palladium in the United States — In Dollars Per Troy Ounce

Year	Jan.	Feb.	Mar.	Apr.	May	June	July	Aug.	Sept.	Oct.	Nov.	Dec.	Average
1991	86.61	85.11	86.44	95.25	96.61	97.39	95.57	84.55	82.49	81.87	85.96	82.72	88.38
1992	82.96	86.04	84.50	83.71	82.90	80.98	86.49	86.04	90.67	95.07	95.01	104.88	88.27
1993	110.39	112.57	106.22	113.79	119.94	125.36	139.74	137.37	121.95	130.04	123.62	125.60	122.22
1994	124.40	130.92	132.43	133.22	135.76	137.03	145.28	151.83	152.99	154.90	158.10	153.80	142.56
1995	156.67	157.53	161.18	170.91	160.87	158.59	156.27	138.81	143.76	137.36	135.57	132.37	150.83
1996	131.59	142.10	140.67	138.05	134.36	132.95	134.55	128.82	123.10	119.39	119.30	119.90	130.40
1997	124.73	141.26	139.55	143.73	173.38	209.47	195.73	221.57	200.38	214.21	217.05	202.64	181.98
1998	229.70	239.68	265.73	326.67	360.55	291.50	310.82	290.62	288.81	283.45	284.00	306.05	289.80
1999	328.58	356.16	357.70	364.52	333.25	341.73	338.90	344.95	367.43	391.95	405.57	430.62	363.45
2000[2]	458.42	637.40	679.39	587.05	586.23	656.86	721.16	769.26	739.60	748.45	792.55	928.55	692.08

[1] Based on wholesale quantities, prompt delivery.   [2] Preliminary.   *Source: U.S. Geological Survey (USGS)*

PLATINUM-GROUP METALS

Platinum Futures - New York Mercantile Exchange (weekly close) as of 29-Dec-2000

USD Per Troy Ounce

Volume of Trading of Platinum Futures in New York   In Contracts

Year	Jan.	Feb.	Mar.	Apr.	May	June	July	Aug.	Sept.	Oct.	Nov.	Dec.	Total
1991	50,807	42,327	72,663	42,995	51,059	55,650	40,589	45,742	55,812	44,867	41,870	60,265	598,600
1992	47,875	38,332	54,104	29,294	37,660	81,984	60,973	50,632	51,797	28,500	42,300	53,800	577,300
1993	29,400	55,555	61,425	50,603	65,778	72,535	59,751	56,399	58,552	36,965	43,998	60,269	651,222
1994	48,259	65,297	94,426	62,600	65,140	88,300	84,182	75,409	92,439	60,878	77,264	81,611	895,805
1995	61,400	38,594	131,294	69,892	60,382	75,353	53,422	62,451	98,837	55,919	56,339	82,810	846,693
1996	80,545	70,260	86,258	54,151	47,929	88,806	53,312	53,654	90,140	47,116	41,970	88,327	802,468
1997	60,515	83,325	86,242	57,719	67,000	72,481	37,836	36,391	62,462	46,188	28,913	58,625	698,597
1998	38,198	35,538	65,871	36,169	36,208	47,464	35,223	27,505	58,302	44,381	42,658	60,752	528,629
1999	37,700	53,698	68,350	36,900	26,507	75,444	57,536	36,115	102,196	30,637	32,176	40,009	597,268
2000	33,226	31,352	35,013	28,057	22,741	47,197	16,527	14,739	36,643	12,122	12,662	30,645	320,924

Source: New York Mercantile Exchange (NYMEX)

Average Open Interest of Platinum Futures in New York   In Contracts

Year	Jan.	Feb.	Mar.	Apr.	May	June	July	Aug.	Sept.	Oct.	Nov.	Dec.
1991	15,497	16,043	16,083	14,334	15,779	18,273	17,503	19,214	18,611	15,933	13,579	14,533
1992	15,464	14,231	14,272	14,130	15,353	19,070	20,402	18,444	17,574	14,079	13,532	14,282
1993	11,889	14,315	12,990	15,490	19,641	17,919	20,931	18,892	16,883	15,690	16,658	19,633
1994	18,779	19,655	21,673	22,834	21,880	22,835	24,804	25,049	24,245	24,159	26,287	26,661
1995	23,285	23,058	23,470	23,657	20,984	21,533	20,801	25,288	23,489	24,498	22,137	21,534
1996	23,130	21,535	23,156	25,081	26,343	27,720	25,861	25,455	28,511	28,305	27,423	29,143
1997	25,890	26,092	22,364	16,568	18,933	18,440	13,280	14,180	13,639	13,466	12,396	13,501
1998	10,791	10,932	13,220	13,559	12,048	11,471	10,607	9,733	11,950	14,601	15,709	13,289
1999	12,311	14,481	16,493	11,471	12,256	12,436	14,703	13,777	15,014	14,892	13,402	12,017
2000	10,858	10,952	9,218	8,484	9,057	10,585	9,566	9,731	9,716	8,106	8,163	8,507

Source: New York Mercantile Exchange (NYMEX)

Volume of Trading of Palladium Futures in New York　In Contracts

Year	Jan.	Feb.	Mar.	Apr.	May	June	July	Aug.	Sept.	Oct.	Nov.	Dec.	Total
1991	5,017	10,542	5,380	7,245	10,521	4,447	5,230	10,114	2,914	5,668	8,150	2,971	78,199
1992	7,217	7,323	3,429	2,833	8,011	2,881	4,965	6,752	5,066	5,359	6,461	7,912	68,209
1993	7,708	14,461	8,057	10,034	12,190	7,368	7,043	13,356	6,977	9,220	12,477	4,790	113,681
1994	8,250	14,953	6,067	6,676	15,481	6,514	9,024	21,741	15,690	9,603	21,384	8,390	143,773
1995	10,684	17,092	21,001	12,775	17,413	9,615	11,816	18,948	9,754	9,320	16,662	11,633	166,713
1996	13,725	33,519	11,931	16,416	27,467	8,989	9,896	23,740	10,721	8,149	28,870	12,187	205,610
1997	13,908	43,160	22,796	21,604	36,422	17,647	18,097	18,751	8,331	13,094	13,143	11,763	238,716
1998	11,506	17,786	18,678	14,042	17,942	7,370	4,241	8,737	6,214	4,962	12,839	6,933	131,250
1999	3,092	11,614	4,082	7,097	8,890	3,411	5,053	6,868	5,826	3,722	10,670	5,069	75,394
2000	4,584	13,976	2,803	1,833	7,034	2,622	3,120	5,169	2,523	2,460	3,041	1,601	50,766

Source: New York Mercantile Exchange (NYMEX)

Average Open Interest of Palladium Futures in New York　In Contracts

Year	Jan.	Feb.	Mar.	Apr.	May	June	July	Aug.	Sept.	Oct.	Nov.	Dec.
1991	4,658	4,559	4,319	4,686	4,559	4,302	4,454	4,429	4,429	4,384	4,337	4,042
1992	3,984	4,071	4,101	4,206	4,137	3,852	3,762	3,362	3,041	2,982	2,901	3,246
1993	3,718	4,213	4,365	4,897	5,312	4,513	4,655	5,080	4,360	4,495	4,472	4,484
1994	4,626	4,995	4,672	4,303	5,116	4,530	5,807	6,851	6,625	6,511	7,726	6,917
1995	7,484	7,579	7,102	7,231	6,519	6,413	6,739	6,852	5,950	6,120	6,486	6,090
1996	6,365	7,539	6,682	7,099	8,713	8,143	7,977	8,805	8,129	7,971	8,227	7,727
1997	8,291	10,946	10,528	9,759	9,947	7,072	5,538	4,973	3,822	4,282	4,291	4,030
1998	4,062	4,873	5,220	5,369	4,371	4,219	4,166	3,488	2,959	3,048	2,938	2,700
1999	2,846	3,234	2,957	3,015	2,796	2,757	2,823	2,496	2,755	3,210	3,301	3,045
2000	3,129	3,101	2,367	2,359	2,628	2,015	2,118	1,974	1,757	1,905	1,859	1,837

Source: New York Mercantile Exchange (NYMEX)

Pork Bellies

Pork belly futures, once one of the more active Chicago markets, have a history of wide price variations and calendar 2000 was no exception. Prices, basis the nearest futures contract, rose 30 cents per pound in the first few months of the year, briefly pushing through $1.00, a 5-year high, before collapsing into mid-summer and dropping to 60 cents when the February 2001 contract became the nearest future. Towards year-end, futures were basically unchanged from a year earlier.

Pork bellies, more commonly known as bacon, are obtained from the underside of a hog. A hog has two bellies, generally weighing about 8-18 pounds, depending on the hog's commercial slaughter weight. Slaughter weights now average about 255 pounds per head, equal to a dressed weight of about 190 pounds. Bellies account for about 12 percent of a hog's live weight, but represent a somewhat larger percentage of the total cutout value of the realized pork products. Frozen bellies, deliverable against futures, generally weigh between 12-14 pounds.

There are definitive seasonalities for pork bellies. Bellies are storable and the movement into cold storage builds early in the calendar year, peaking about mid-year. Net withdrawals from storage then carry stocks to a low around October. The cycle then starts again. Retail bacon demand also follows a time-worn trend; peaking in the summer when consumer preference shifts to lighter foods, and tapering off to a low during the winter months. While demand patterns would suggest the highest prices in the summer and the lowest in the winter, just the opposite is not unusual. Such contra-seasonal price moves can be partially attributed to supply logistics, notably, the availability of frozen storage stocks deliverable against futures at exchange (CME) approved warehouses. When stocks prove either too large or too small, the underlying demand fundamentals for bacon can be relegated to the backburner as a market making variable. The fact that no contract months are traded between August and the following February adds to the mid-summer futures price distortion, as seen in 2000.

Belly prices (cash and futures) are sensitive to the inventory in cold storage, and to the weekly net movement in and out of storage which afford some insight to demand, although a better measure is the weekly quantity of bellies being sliced into bacon. Higher prices tend to encourage placing more supplies into storage by discouraging retail bacon demand. Bacon is not a necessary foodstuff, but demand can be buoyed by favorable consumer disposable income. On the flip side, however, dietary standards have changed dramatically in recent years that do not favor the consumption of high fat and salt content food—like bacon.

The U.S. economy was strong in the 1990's and into 2000, as was consumer demand for bacon, notwithstanding nutritional concerns. Retail prices were strong in the late 1990's, averaging $2.60/lb. vs. below $2.00 in the mid-1990s. In mid-2000, retail prices were holding near $3.20/lb. although wholesale prices showed slippage late in the year.

U.S. foreign trade in bacon as a processed product is small. Imports are largely from Denmark and exports go to Eastern Europe.

Futures Markets

Frozen pork belly futures and options are traded on the Chicago Mercantile Exchange (CME).

Average Retail Price of Bacon, Sliced   In Dollars Per Pound

Year	Jan.	Feb.	Mar.	Apr.	May	June	July	Aug.	Sept.	Oct.	Nov.	Dec.	Average
1991	2.26	2.30	2.32	2.27	2.31	2.31	2.31	2.22	2.16	2.12	2.07	1.99	2.22
1992	1.96	1.95	1.92	1.92	1.90	1.93	1.95	1.94	1.93	1.89	1.85	1.86	1.92
1993	1.87	1.84	1.80	1.89	1.91	1.95	2.00	1.95	1.98	1.99	2.01	2.02	1.93
1994	2.04	2.02	2.02	2.06	1.99	1.99	2.00	1.99	1.97	1.97	1.92	1.89	1.99
1995	1.93	1.93	1.91	1.89	1.92	1.90	1.91	1.97	2.04	2.12	2.16	2.17	1.99
1996	2.14	2.20	2.20	2.24	2.35	2.49	2.54	2.68	2.81	2.72	2.66	2.64	2.47
1997	2.66	2.65	2.66	2.66	2.63	2.69	2.72	2.76	2.75	2.73	2.67	2.61	2.68
1998	2.64	2.62	2.54	2.44	2.44	2.46	2.52	2.51	2.58	2.57	2.62	2.58	2.54
1999	2.52	2.52	2.51	2.45	2.47	2.50	2.50	2.93	2.58	2.57	2.66	2.75	2.58
2000[1]	2.75	2.87	2.93	2.95	3.01	3.13	3.17	3.20	3.21	3.07	3.05	3.03	3.03

[1] Preliminary.   Source: Economic Research Service, U.S. Department of Agriculture (ERS-USDA)

Frozen Pork Belly Storage Stocks in the United States, on First of Month   In Thousands of Pounds

Year	Jan.	Feb.	Mar.	Apr.	May	June	July	Aug.	Sept.	Oct.	Nov.	Dec.
1991	46,998	48,750	54,529	68,094	80,382	79,936	72,032	45,915	29,832	15,944	25,558	48,311
1992	71,318	76,894	75,925	85,095	96,653	92,677	78,646	54,544	26,854	21,973	26,044	49,970
1993	70,576	65,280	65,919	66,064	79,430	77,903	70,251	46,630	20,811	10,964	14,345	33,563
1994	53,168	55,999	54,921	63,099	72,230	79,018	73,583	57,747	30,636	18,260	22,656	40,725
1995	61,073	62,776	64,228	78,975	78,539	77,919	67,607	47,055	17,435	6,255	13,478	37,092
1996	47,587	46,498	46,381	47,655	57,174	63,522	56,767	28,533	18,996	12,702	16,206	30,943
1997	37,930	38,030	44,277	54,767	54,015	55,274	52,274	33,657	18,346	11,148	14,408	25,365
1998	44,763	55,249	55,368	54,441	58,600	59,462	52,010	31,433	14,786	9,452	16,440	41,711
1999	72,657	82,605	93,323	106,194	109,521	108,257	93,383	69,675	34,814	19,273	22,489	26,170
2000[1]	40,300	43,802	49,983	60,527	63,461	68,292	60,097	50,515	33,005	21,341	20,589	38,674

[1] Preliminary.   Source: National Agricultural Statistics Service, U.S. Department of Agriculture (NASS-USDA)

PORK BELLIES

Weekly Pork Belly Storage Movement

1999 Week Ending		In	Out	On Hand	Net Move- ment	2000 Week Ending		In	Out	On Hand	Net Move- ment
		Stocks[1] In Thousands of Pounds						Stocks[1] In Thousands of Pounds			
Jan.	2	3,167	117	38,129	3,050	Jan.	1	3,988	31	17,214	3,957
	9	2,620	785	39,964	1,835		8	1,955	0	19,169	1,955
	16	1,248	302	40,910	946		15	520	511	19,178	9
	23	1,452	415	41,947	1,037		22	916	499	19,595	417
	30	1,245	226	42,966	1,019		29	406	308	19,693	98
Feb.	6	1,083	211	43,838	872	Feb.	5	2,120	765	21,048	1,355
	13	511	200	44,149	311		12	417	309	21,156	108
	20	2,633	85	46,697	2,548		19	441	448	21,149	-7
	27	2,687	160	49,224	2,527		26	1,026	320	21,855	706
Mar.	6	2,336	128	51,432	2,208	Mar.	4	2,394	0	24,249	2,394
	13	1,121	122	52,432	999		11	1,574	79	25,744	1,495
	20	2,067	124	54,375	1,944		18	2,095	47	27,792	2,048
	27	1,260	148	55,487	1,112		25	946	409	28,329	537
Apr.	3	1,143	874	55,756	269	Apr.	1	965	101	29,193	864
	10	1,151	39	56,868	1,112		8	208	207	29,194	1
	17	968	49	57,787	919		15	753	233	29,714	520
	24	382	208	57,961	174		22	1,413	111	31,017	1,302
May	1	1,169	311	58,819	858		29	1,387	167	32,237	1,220
	8	626	459	58,986	167	May	6	2,446	4	34,679	2,442
	15	330	293	59,023	37		13	1,009	480	35,208	529
	22	445	1,084	58,384	-639		20	1,237	8	36,437	1,229
	29	325	667	58,042	-342		27	823	166	37,094	657
June	5	163	1,335	56,870	-1,172	June	3	1,363	415	38,042	948
	12	85	1,527	55,420	-1,442		10	583	290	38,335	293
	19	0	2,706	52,722	-2,706		17	193	847	37,681	-654
	26	126	2,110	50,738	-1,984		24	356	2,118	35,919	-1,762
July	3	83	2,739	48,083	-2,656	July	1	246	2,928	33,237	-2,682
	10	244	1,788	46,539	-1,544		8	1,124	732	33,629	392
	17	353	3,568	43,324	-3,215		15	43	2,331	31,341	-2,288
	24	52	2,717	40,659	-2,665		22	310	1,787	29,864	-1,477
	31	48	5,391	34,845	-5,343		29	84	1,639	28,309	-1,555
Aug.	7	66	4,468	30,443	-4,402	Aug.	5	55	1,524	26,840	-1,469
	14	0	4,163	26,280	-4,163		12	0	2,981	23,859	-2,981
	21	44	3,208	23,116	-3,164		19	167	2,666	21,360	-2,499
	28	165	3,411	19,870	-3,246		26	307	2,447	19,220	-2,140
Sept.	4	15	2,855	17,030	-2,840	Sept.	2	15	2,855	-17,030	-2,840
	11	7	2,080	14,957	-2,073		9	1,510	1,972	18,262	-462
	18	212	2,591	12,578	-2,379		16	675	886	18,051	-211
	25	301	1,832	11,047	-1,531		23	871	2,351	16,571	-1,480
Oct.	2	14	1,215	9,846	-1,201		30	128	1,621	15,078	-1,493
	9	108	1,209	8,745	-1,101	Oct.	7	42	1,800	13,320	-1,758
	16	72	1,333	7,484	-1,261		14	833	524	13,629	309
	23	110	231	7,363	-121		21	1,509	905	14,233	604
	30	33	66	7,330	-33		28	135	754	13,614	-619
Nov.	6	88	93	7,325	-5	Nov.	4	693	593	13,714	100
	13	592	440	7,477	152		11	4,224	770	17,168	3,454
	20	532	684	7,325	-152		18	3,001	809	19,360	2,192
	27	543	91	7,778	452		25	3,930	1,474	1,817	2,456
Dec.	4	885	210	8,452	675	Dec.	2	2,724	396	24,145	2,328
	11	1,226	98	9,580	1,128		9	4,407	1,004	27,548	3,403
	18	1,273	231	10,622	1,042		16	4,089	828	30,809	3,261
	25	2,851	216	13,257	2,635		23	2,382	322	32,869	2,060
							30	987	73	33,783	914

[1] 57 Chicago and Outside Combined Chicago Mercantile Exchange approved warehouses.   *Source: Chicago Mercantile Exchange (CME)*

PORK BELLIES

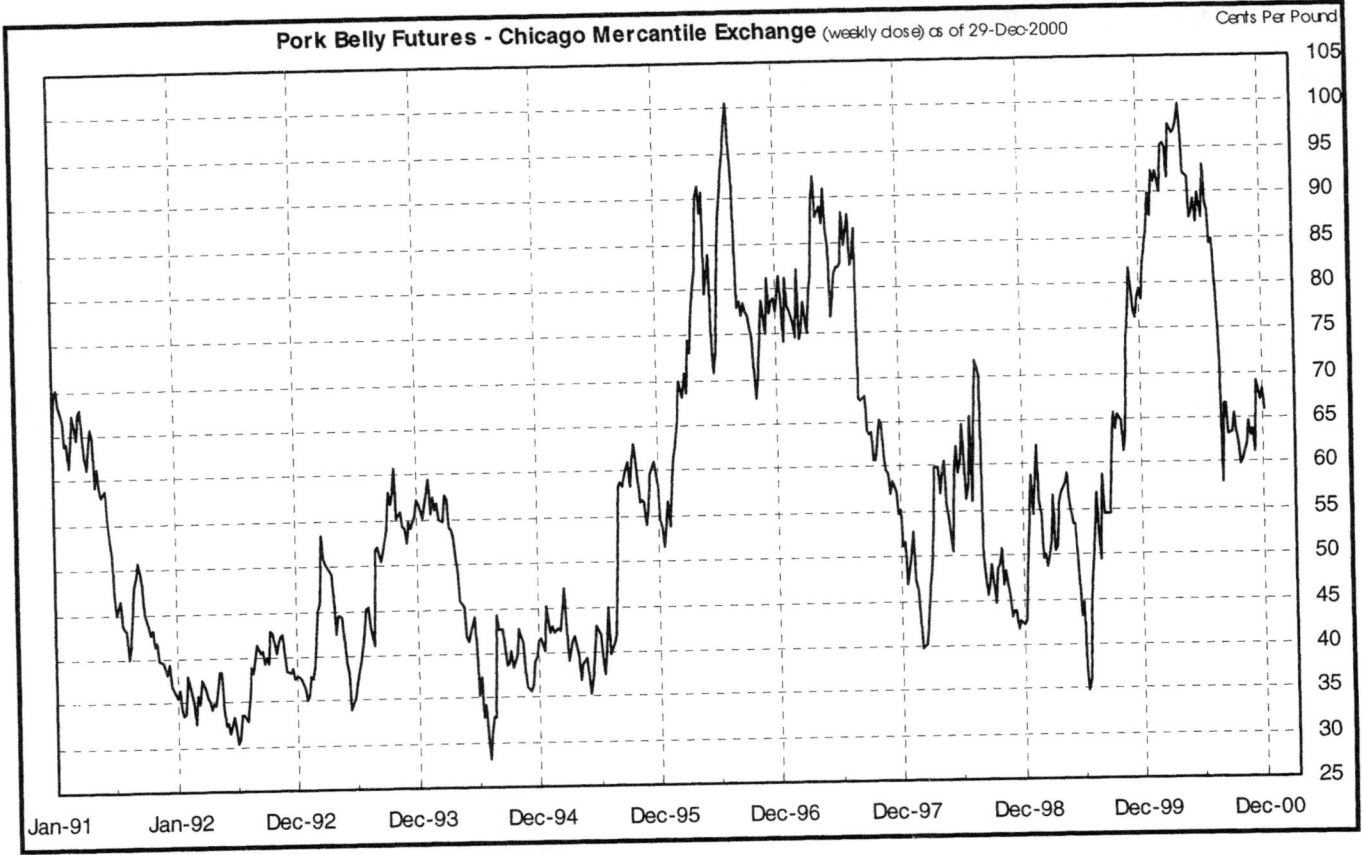

Pork Belly Futures - Chicago Mercantile Exchange (weekly close) as of 29-Dec-2000   Cents Per Pound

Average Open Interest of Pork Belly Futures in Chicago   In Contracts

Year	Jan.	Feb.	Mar.	Apr.	May	June	July	Aug.	Sept.	Oct.	Nov.	Dec.
1991	11,777	10,187	9,776	11,509	10,436	10,111	7,356	6,176	7,532	10,813	13,173	12,844
1992	12,521	12,195	11,901	12,345	12,497	13,598	12,623	7,149	6,540	7,033	9,251	10,953
1993	10,623	9,244	8,283	8,626	10,096	11,092	9,031	5,427	4,644	7,241	8,701	9,121
1994	11,053	10,426	9,375	9,894	8,092	8,248	7,836	7,841	8,398	10,072	10,141	10,216
1995	10,294	9,080	7,809	7,367	8,017	7,036	5,666	4,271	6,246	7,007	7,103	7,282
1996	7,094	8,028	10,521	10,753	10,018	8,136	6,432	6,296	6,056	6,395	6,050	6,480
1997	7,504	7,930	7,260	7,165	8,950	7,203	5,905	4,791	5,242	7,520	8,302	9,009
1998	9,187	9,145	9,082	7,825	6,786	5,406	4,185	3,493	2,933	3,841	4,987	7,085
1999	7,217	6,192	4,623	5,113	6,030	6,639	5,003	2,415	2,320	3,206	4,011	4,868
2000	5,872	6,011	6,320	6,563	5,836	5,306	3,650	1,877	1,860	2,093	2,409	2,610

Source: Chicago Mercantile Exchange (CME)

Volume of Trading of Pork Belly Futures in Chicago   In Contracts

Year	Jan.	Feb.	Mar.	Apr.	May	June	July	Aug.	Sept.	Oct.	Nov.	Dec.	Total
1991	106,078	89,975	88,056	111,195	119,773	96,273	74,255	59,176	65,604	80,707	63,331	50,773	1,005,196
1992	80,697	79,700	67,470	57,565	73,137	73,081	78,588	54,663	39,839	64,248	60,724	54,440	784,152
1993	77,380	62,871	63,988	62,403	62,400	70,124	65,496	42,613	37,992	47,780	60,163	49,099	698,799
1994	60,316	67,250	58,183	53,839	56,575	58,424	50,450	47,626	38,375	45,525	49,280	47,803	633,646
1995	62,994	54,330	59,324	43,501	49,453	53,571	45,869	36,623	31,112	35,444	47,061	42,631	561,913
1996	48,563	56,623	61,669	61,703	61,868	55,337	55,121	45,399	39,182	48,973	42,709	35,502	612,649
1997	60,761	53,604	56,750	76,072	62,190	54,043	55,043	36,153	31,154	44,277	31,663	33,609	595,319
1998	41,894	50,105	47,249	61,910	36,058	48,913	41,133	33,832	24,006	30,538	30,093	35,521	481,252
1999	39,925	36,293	33,322	31,558	31,321	45,030	36,513	23,536	16,544	20,392	28,920	24,955	368,309
2000	37,650	38,943	39,061	31,464	40,311	31,229	25,051	17,875	10,711	11,854	11,737	13,690	309,576

Source: Chicago Mercantile Exchange (CME)

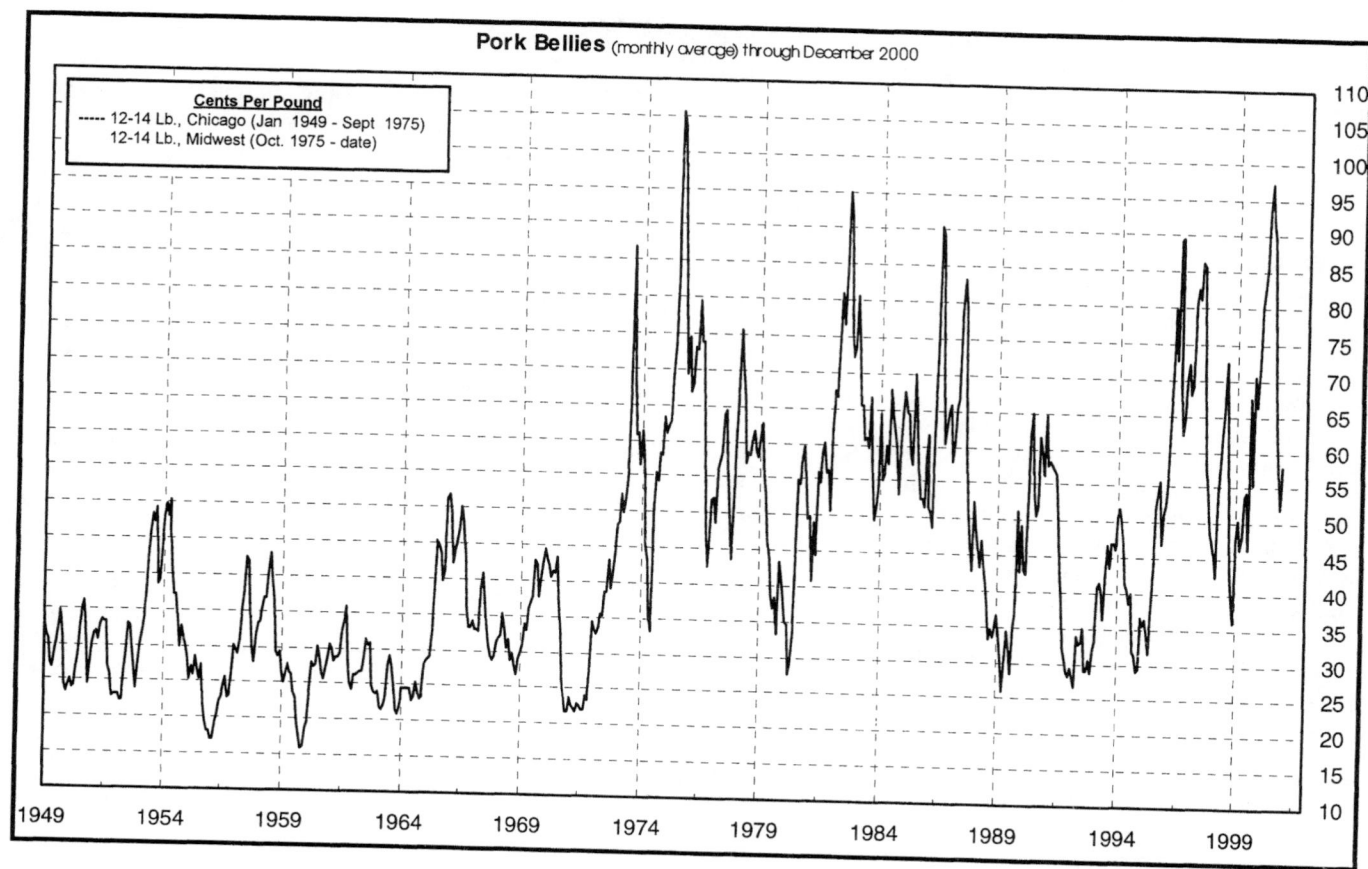

Pork Bellies (monthly average) through December 2000

Cents Per Pound
- 12-14 Lb., Chicago (Jan 1949 - Sept 1975)
- 12-14 Lb., Midwest (Oct. 1975 - date)

Average Price of Pork Bellies (12-14 Pounds) Midwest   In Cents Per Pound

Year	Jan.	Feb.	Mar.	Apr.	May	June	July	Aug.	Sept.	Oct.	Nov.	Dec.	Average
1991	64.11	57.20	58.52	57.25	57.50	56.48	50.40	42.01	38.97	32.26	30.04	28.79	47.79
1992	28.05	29.44	28.01	26.93	34.09	32.78	32.77	35.13	29.09	29.13	30.48	28.80	30.39
1993	31.97	33.22	41.28	41.19	39.86	36.24	44.51	46.68	43.82	47.25	47.21	46.21	41.62
1994	50.63	51.66	49.68	46.84	41.40	40.39	38.64	39.60	31.50	31.33	29.09	29.29	40.00
1995	36.03	35.80	36.30	33.83	31.70	37.94	43.10	52.42	54.43	56.20	47.28	51.45	43.04
1996	52.33	56.33	64.50	69.86	79.50	72.64	89.49	88.40	68.12	63.07	65.27	70.07	69.97
1997	72.04	68.42	59.05	80.54	82.58	80.68	86.70	85.43	72.25	57.97	53.77	47.52	70.58
1998	43.00	45.89	42.28	54.65	57.87	63.10	68.46	72.99	57.49	42.05	39.13	36.31	51.94
1999	48.80	50.76	46.51	49.23	53.76	53.41	47.78	67.29	57.87	70.83	67.81	71.37	57.12
2000[1]	80.45	82.40	85.00	93.70	97.85	91.99	90.38	75.64	63.94	57.83	51.97	58.36	77.46

[1] Preliminary.   Source: Economic Research Service, U.S. Department of Agriculture (ERS-USDA)

Average Price of Pork Loins (12-14 lbs.)[2] Central, U.S.   In Cents Per Pound

Year	Jan.	Feb.	Mar.	Apr.	May	June	July	Aug.	Sept.	Oct.	Nov.	Dec.	Average
1991	107.67	109.13	110.33	104.81	120.48	123.49	121.73	117.54	105.85	100.87	88.63	90.19	108.39
1992	96.89	99.13	94.10	98.65	108.94	113.94	108.22	111.18	102.98	96.98	89.64	96.22	101.41
1993	98.22	100.05	100.61	107.61	111.16	122.28	113.40	116.73	116.74	111.85	98.68	92.33	107.47
1994	103.90	110.75	100.45	101.89	103.99	103.84	109.79	112.86	105.34	95.65	80.00	89.50	101.50
1995	96.94	102.20	95.30	93.33	103.50	118.81	124.65	127.98	117.63	108.23	93.94	110.39	107.74
1996	110.00	116.43	120.49	119.70	131.61	115.73	126.16	118.18	112.28	115.40	115.39	120.45	118.49
1997	112.50	109.50	106.58	117.16	125.68	116.28	122.53	119.28	112.07	99.68	85.99	79.44	108.89
1998	76.50	103.03	104.56	102.51	130.64	113.13	106.51	105.90	97.23	99.63	79.90	72.49	99.34
1999	105.82	92.35	83.47	99.35	107.44	97.62	105.72	111.55	104.99	98.98	94.64	102.75	100.39
2000[1]	99.29	110.66	110.06	127.48	115.38	132.53	131.73	120.45	119.22	119.90	104.19	114.68	117.13

[1] Preliminary.   Source: Economic Research Service, U.S. Department of Agriculture (ERS-USDA)

Potatoes

Potatoes are the largest vegetable crop grown in the U.S. with production in 2000 of a record large 509 million cwt. vs. the previous year's 478 million and the prior record large 1996 crop of 499 million. Planted acreage in 2000 of 1.38 million acres was only marginally higher than in 1999, but the average yield jumped to a record high 376 cwt. per acre from 359 cwt. per acre in 1999. The value of the 1999 crop of $2.75 billion was 4 percent higher than the 1998 crop value and 5 percent above the 1997 crop. The average price per cwt. of $5.77 compares with $5.56 for the 1998 crop and $5.64 in 1997.

Total 1999 consumption (sales) trailed the 1996 record of 452 million cwt., but at 437 million cwt. bested the 1998 total consumption of 435 million. Non-sales (i.e. seed use, shrinkage, and loss) in 1999 of 41 million cwt. were unchanged from 1998 and compare to 38 million in 1997 and 47 million in 1996. Total domestic foodstock usage of 274 million cwt. in 1999 compares with 281 million in 1998 and the record large 284 million in 1996; included in the 1999 total was 140 million cwt. allocated to frozen french fry production vs. 143 million in 1998, and tablestock usage of 134 million cwt. vs. 125 million, respectively. Since the mid-1990's, the U.S. consumer's affinity for deep-fried processed potatoes has slackened apparently due to nutritional concerns. Frozen french fry production totaled over 145 million cwt. in 1996. Some of the slack from reduced french fry production has been offset by increases in fresh potato usage over the past few years.

Potatoes are grown in all fifty states. The crop, however, is divided into four, but not necessarily distinct, seasonal groups based on harvest time. The fall crop, consisting of about two dozen states, accounts for 85-90 percent of total production and is usually harvested from September through November. The winter crop is the smallest and harvested only in Florida and California from January into March. The spring and summer crops tend to be fairly close in size. The seasonal disparities reflect major differences in planted acreage and realized yield, which is consistently higher in the fall producing states. The marketing season follows the harvest, but the movement of the fall crop can extend into the following July with supplies drawn from storage. The inventoried fall crop can serve as a supply buffer in the event the spring and summer crops are short. However, large fall stocks can also prove a depressant on prices should earlier crops prove large. Generally, about one-third of farm marketing's occur during September and October.

Idaho is the nation's largest producer with a 1999 fall crop of 133 million cwt. vs. 138 million in 1998. The record for Idaho production of 143 million cwt. was set in 1996. Washington's crop, a distant second, of 95 million cwt. compares with 93 million in 1998 and 95 million in 1996. As usual, Washington's average yield was the nation's highest, 560 cwt. per acre in 1999 compared to Idaho's average of 339 cwt. Maine, once the largest producing fall state, produced 17.8 million cwt. in 1999 vs. 18 million in 1998 and 21.2 million in 1996, with an average yield per acre in both 1999 and 1998 of 282 cwt. Maine's decline largely reflects the wide variety of potatoes grown in the state—about 80—whereas in Idaho production is focused on one type of baking potato, the Russet Burbank, which has enhanced marketing consistency and consumer preference.

About 57 percent of the 1999 crop was processed, either into frozen products or as a direct consumer food, such as potato chips vs. 59 percent of the 1998 crop. Frozen french fries account for about 29 percent of the nation's total potato crop in 1999 with chips accounting for 11 percent (53 million cwt.) and dehydrated potatoes another 11 percent (52 million cwt.). Generally, about 1 percent of the total crop is used for seed at 4.3 million cwt. in 1999. Nearly 36 million cwt. were considered lost, mostly owing to shrinkage.

Foreign trade in U.S. potatoes is small. Japan imports processed potatoes, mostly french fries, while Canada exports fresh potatoes which are used mostly for seed.

Futures Markets

Potato futures and options are traded on the London International Financial Futures and Options Exchange (LIFFE).

Salient Statistics of Potatoes in the United States

	Acreage		Yield Per Harvested Acre	Farm Disposition				Farm Price	Value of		Stocks on Jan. 1	Foreign Trade[5] (Fresh) Domestic		Consumption[5] Per Capita In Pounds	
				Total Pro-	Used Where Grown				Pro-						
Crop Year	Planted	Harvested		duction	Seed & Feed	Shrinkage & Loss	Sold[2]	Price	duction[3]	Sales	Jan. 1	Exports	Imports	Fresh	Total
	1,000 Acres		Cwt.	In Thousands of Cwt.				$/Cwt.	Million $		1,000 Cwt.	Millions of Lbs.		In Pounds	
1991	1,408	1,374	304	417,622	5,995	32,429	379,198	4.96	2,043	1,880	211,005	341,682	437,349	50.4	134.5
1992	1,339	1,315	323	425,367	5,925	33,807	385,637	5.52	2,336	2,129	215,990	537,939	273,515	48.6	130.7
1993	1,385	1,317	326	428,693	5,931	30,152	392,610	6.17	2,637	2,424	217,300	539,345	541,382	50.6	137.8
1994	1,416	1,380	339	467,054	5,878	37,166	424,010	5.58	2,590	2,367	238,560	655,026	405,899	50.2	138.3
1995	1,398	1,372	323	443,606	5,745	29,530	408,331	6.77	2,992	2,762	223,550	583,938	458,926	49.9	138.8
1996	1,455	1,426	350	499,254	6,221	41,222	451,190	4.91	2,425	2,220	261,320	564,010	690,768	50.7	147.2
1997	1,384	1,354	345	467,091	5,475	32,183	429,433	5.64	2,623	2,421	246,550	670,270	512,321	49.4	144.0
1998	1,417	1,388	343	475,771	5,766	35,454	434,551	5.56	2,635	2,416	246,230	650,917	737,223	47.9	140.8
1999	1,377	1,332	359	478,216	5,538	35,562	437,116	5.77	2,746	2,522	238,160	598,574	610,538	49.2	139.8
2000[1]	1,387	1,352	382	515,964				4.95	2,540					50.8	146.2

[1] Preliminary. [2] For all purposes, including food, seed processing & livestock feed. [3] Farm weight basis, excluding canned and frozen potatoes.

Source: Economic Research Service, U.S. Department of Agriculture (ERS-USDA)

Cold Storage Stocks of All Frozen Potatoes in the United States, on First of Month   In Millions of Pounds

Year	Jan.	Feb.	Mar.	Apr.	May	June	July	Aug.	Sept.	Oct.	Nov.	Dec.
1991	975.8	993.3	988.9	1,041.5	1,052.3	1,167.2	1,216.5	935.5	880.1	985.5	1,148.0	1,037.2
1992	980.8	996.5	1,036.3	1,082.7	1,077.6	1,137.3	1,131.4	966.4	948.7	949.1	1,067.1	1,038.7
1993	963.2	971.2	1,028.2	1,046.6	912.7	979.5	989.8	932.8	902.8	1,019.5	1,184.7	1,130.7
1994	1,006.4	1,019.9	1,057.1	1,054.4	1,050.5	1,118.9	1,099.9	979.8	1,028.2	1,108.7	1,189.0	1,163.5
1995	1,096.6	1,156.0	1,179.9	1,169.0	1,138.0	1,125.4	1,116.5	992.4	992.6	1,145.3	1,225.6	1,174.5
1996	1,123.7	1,147.2	1,172.5	1,164.6	1,112.1	1,076.4	1,059.7	907.1	957.8	1,124.9	1,225.2	1,146.3
1997	1,098.4	1,111.5	1,180.1	1,177.1	1,195.8	1,213.3	1,271.4	1,214.3	1,130.8	1,270.0	1,354.7	1,313.5
1998	1,163.5	1,147.2	1,235.7	1,278.3	1,225.1	1,282.8	1,316.5	1,234.7	1,204.5	1,266.8	1,341.0	1,290.5
1999	1,151.3	1,219.7	1,272.9	1,278.8	1,236.2	1,255.5	1,234.1	1,142.3	1,169.8	1,235.5	1,307.8	1,254.5
2000[1]	1,165.4	1,140.9	1,270.1	1,283.4	1,239.4	1,250.4	1,186.3	1,180.3	1,185.7	1,291.5	1,351.5	1,285.9

[1] Preliminary.   *Source: Agricultural Statistics Board, U.S. Department of Agriculture (ASB-USDA)*

Potato Crop Production Estimates, Stocks and Disappearance in the United States   In Millions of Cwt.

	Crop Production Estimates			Total Storage Stocks[2]							Fall Crop (1,000 Cwt.)			
	Total Crop			Fall Crop			Following Year				Production	Disappearance (Sold)	Dec. 1 Stocks	Average Price $/Cwt.	Value of Sales $ 1,000
Year	Oct. 1	Nov. 1	Dec. 1	Oct. 1	Nov. 1	Dec. 1	Jan. 1	Feb. 1	Mar. 1	Apr. 1	May 1				
1991	----	417.6	----	----	379.5	242.1	211.0	178.5	145.8	108.9	69.1	363,541	334,893	242,070	4.16	1,393,749
1992	----	425.4	----	----	372.4	246.8	216.0	184.6	152.8	115.8	75.0	368,516	341,209	246,820	5.17	1,762,984
1993	----	428.7	----	----	372.4	249.4	217.3	185.5	153.4	115.2	72.9	376,954	353,052	249,710	5.65	1,981,017
1994	----	467.9	----	----	412.4	273.3	238.6	202.5	169.6	129.8	87.6	410,839	380,818	273,290	5.06	1,914,311
1995	----	444.8	----	----	402.4	256.7	223.6	189.4	156.0	115.9	75.9	394,785	370,679	256,710	6.43	2,372,983
1996	----	491.5	----	----	447.9	295.1	261.3	226.1	189.2	147.6	103.2	443,704	408,247	295,100	4.35	1,772,037
1997	----	459.4	----	----	417.5	278.8	246.6	212.6	175.9	134.2	92.8	413,513	387,089	278,830	5.20	2,011,004
1998	----	471.0	----	----	429.0	280.9	246.2	209.6	173.7	131.2	87.9	423,170	392,922	280,910	5.07	1,994,030
1999	----	481.5	----	----	435.6	275.1	239.9	207.2	169.3	128.4	86.9	420,567	390,210	275,100	5.29	2,064,564
2000[1]	----	509.4	----	----	463.4	309.5	273.0	235.1	198.3			461,827		309,520		

[1] Preliminary.   [2] Held by growers and local dealers in the fall producing areas.   *Source: Agricultural Statistics Board, U.S. Department of Agriculture*

Production of Potatoes by Seasonal Groups in the United States   In Thousands of Cwt.

	Winter	Spring		Summer			Fall								
Year	Total	California	Florida	Total	New Mexico	Virginia	Total	Colorado	Idaho	Maine	Minnesota	North Dakota	Oregon	Washington	Wisconsin	Total
1991	2,609	8,284	6,600	20,636	3,450	1,485	22,647	23,800	122,175	18,170	17,160	30,030	22,170	75,435	23,275	371,730
1992	2,998	7,238	7,750	21,535	952	1,980	21,309	22,110	127,050	24,300	16,080	27,690	21,075	69,300	25,160	379,525
1993	2,552	7,508	6,068	19,654	1,290	1,760	14,922	25,270	126,192	19,890	14,780	21,090	23,103	88,500	22,588	385,935
1994	2,372	7,790	8,588	22,646	1,088	1,425	17,381	25,795	138,801	18,375	20,035	28,200	27,514	88,920	25,740	419,645
1995	2,473	6,230	7,830	20,193	1,344	2,040	17,931	23,808	132,657	17,160	20,790	25,410	24,788	80,850	26,000	403,009
1996	3,273	7,538	7,765	22,417	1,404	1,463	19,176	29,175	142,800	21,175	24,600	28,820	30,124	94,990	33,150	454,388
1997	3,431	8,073	7,150	22,299	1,248	1,268	18,171	24,993	140,314	19,080	20,440	22,000	27,319	88,160	30,175	423,190
1998	2,980	6,198	7,358	21,121	962	1,380	18,933	25,360	138,000	18,060	21,170	28,670	26,229	93,225	30,895	432,737
1999	4,070	7,600	8,820	25,327	1,247	1,050	18,972	25,762	133,330	17,813	18,020	26,400	28,020	95,200	34,000	429,847
2000[1]	4,960	7,426	6,343	21,921	1,050	1,260	18,504	27,972	152,320	17,920	21,600	26,950	27,200	103,250	33,800	463,408

[1] Preliminary.   *Source: Agricultural Statistics Board, U.S. Department of Agriculture (ASB-USDA)*

Production of Potatoes by Seasonal Groups in the United States   In Thousands of Cwt.

	Winter	Spring		Summer			Fall								
Year	Total	California	Florida	Total	New Mexico	Virginia	Total	Colorado	Idaho	Maine	Minnesota	North Dakota	Oregon	Washington	Wisconsin	Total
1991	2,609	8,284	6,600	20,636	3,450	1,485	22,647	23,800	122,175	18,170	17,160	30,030	22,170	75,435	23,275	371,730
1992	2,998	7,238	7,750	21,535	952	1,980	21,309	22,110	127,050	24,300	16,080	27,690	21,075	69,300	25,160	379,525
1993	2,552	7,508	6,068	19,654	1,290	1,760	14,922	25,270	126,192	19,890	14,780	21,090	23,103	88,500	22,588	385,935
1994	2,372	7,790	8,588	22,646	1,088	1,425	17,381	25,795	138,801	18,375	20,035	28,200	27,514	88,920	25,740	419,645
1995	2,473	6,230	7,830	20,193	1,344	2,040	17,931	23,808	132,657	17,160	20,790	25,410	24,788	80,850	26,000	403,009
1996	3,273	7,538	7,765	22,417	1,404	1,463	19,176	29,175	142,800	21,175	24,600	28,820	30,124	94,990	33,150	454,388
1997	3,431	8,073	7,150	22,299	1,248	1,268	18,171	24,993	140,314	19,080	20,440	22,000	27,319	88,160	30,175	423,190
1998	2,980	6,198	7,358	21,121	962	1,380	18,933	25,360	138,000	18,060	21,170	28,670	26,229	93,225	30,895	432,737
1999	4,070	7,600	8,820	25,327	1,247	1,050	18,972	25,762	133,330	17,813	18,020	26,400	28,020	95,200	34,000	429,847
2000[1]	4,960	7,426	6,343	21,921	1,050	1,260	18,504	27,972	152,320	17,920	21,600	26,950	27,200	103,250	33,800	463,408

[1] Preliminary.   *Source: Agricultural Statistics Board, U.S. Department of Agriculture (ASB-USDA)*

POTATOES

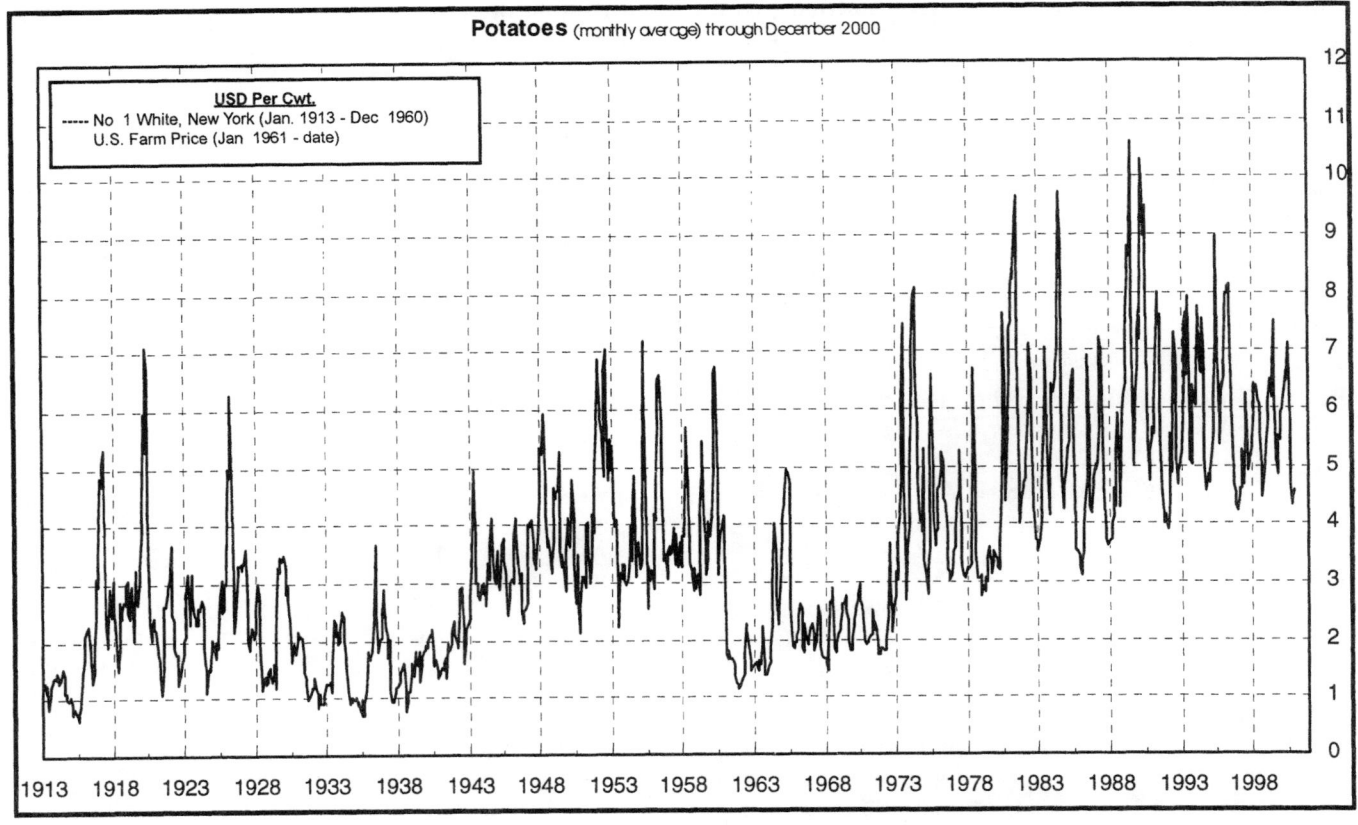

Per Capita Utilization of Potatoes in the United States   In Pounds (Farm Weight)

Year	Total	Fresh	Freezing	Chips & Shoe-string	Dehy-drating	Canning	Total
				Processing			
1991	134.5	50.4	51.2	17.3	13.9	1.7	84.1
1992	130.6	48.6	50.1	17.2	12.9	1.8	82.0
1993	137.7	50.5	53.9	17.8	13.8	1.7	87.2
1994	138.3	50.2	56.3	16.7	13.4	1.7	88.1
1995	138.8	49.9	56.9	16.6	13.4	2.0	88.9
1996	147.2	50.7	61.1	16.7	16.9	1.8	96.5
1997	141.4	48.5	59.3	15.9	15.9	1.8	92.9
1998	140.9	47.8	59.7	14.9	16.9	1.6	93.1
1999[1]	141.9	48.3	62.5	15.7	13.6	1.8	93.6
2000[2]	143.8	47.4	62.8	15.5	16.4	1.7	96.4

[1] Preliminary.   [2] Forecast.   Source: Agricultural Statistics Board, U.S. Department of Agriculture (ASB-USDA)

Average Price Received by Farmers for Potatoes in the United States   In Dollars Per Cwt.

Year	Jan.	Feb.	Mar.	Apr.	May	June	July	Aug.	Sept.	Oct.	Nov.	Dec.	Season Average
1991	5.66	5.53	6.15	7.03	7.98	7.51	7.95	5.39	4.51	4.06	3.99	4.29	4.96
1992	4.07	4.08	4.64	5.16	4.43	4.71	7.00	6.64	4.89	4.55	4.90	5.06	5.52
1993	5.15	5.29	6.06	7.19	7.18	6.45	7.61	6.05	5.12	4.96	6.40	6.12	6.17
1994	6.02	6.43	7.67	6.69	6.59	6.67	7.50	6.28	5.04	4.58	4.75	4.87	5.58
1995	4.88	4.90	5.39	5.54	5.77	6.97	8.66	6.69	5.76	6.30	6.42	6.29	6.77
1996	6.65	6.92	7.51	7.83	8.09	8.14	8.02	5.59	4.93	4.76	4.43	4.32	4.91
1997	4.23	4.50	4.60	4.61	5.26	4.66	5.52	6.26	5.09	4.93	5.13	5.29	5.64
1998	5.40	5.94	6.41	6.27	6.39	6.13	6.03	5.55	4.91	4.43	4.81	5.03	5.56
1999	5.32	5.75	6.12	6.50	6.18	6.51	7.51	6.38	5.09	4.86	5.52	5.44	5.84
2000[1]	5.91	5.92	6.33	6.29	6.62	6.47	7.12	5.77	4.69	4.33	4.40	4.61	

[1] Preliminary.   Source: Agricultural Statistics Board, U.S. Department of Agriculture (ASB-USDA)

Potatoes Processed[1] in the United States, Eight States   In Thousands of Cwt.

States	Storage Season	to Dec. 1	to Jan. 1	to Feb. 1	to Mar. 1	to Apr. 1	to May 1	to June 1	Entire Season
Idaho and	1991-2	22,980	28,910	35,700	42,840	50,260	57,290	----	78,690
Oregon-	1992-3	22,180	29,080	35,710	42,800	50,090	57,090	----	80,570
Malheur	1993-4	24,090	30,540	37,150	44,720	53,070	61,440	----	85,780
Co	1994-5	26,620	34,230	42,330	49,890	57,990	66,680	----	90,300
	1995-6	27,310	35,040	43,260	51,530	59,060	66,690	----	89,250
	1996-7	31,060	38,210	45,420	54,640	62,570	70,720	----	96,970
	1997-8	26,880	33,950	41,050	49,470	57,620	65,750	----	91,450
	1998-9	27,510	34,700	42,670	51,210	60,040	68,550	76,410	92,860
	1999-00	27,970	34,490	40,790	49,220	57,820	66,080	74,110	88,210
	2000-1	29,290	35,720	43,470	50,580				
Maine[2]	1991-2	2,015	2,450	3,050	3,350	3,900	4,445	----	5,210
	1992-3	1,195	1,630	2,205	2,720	3,390	4,020	----	5,055
	1993-4	1,350	1,720	2,210	2,505	2,890	3,275	----	4,555
	1994-5	1,505	1,840	2,265	2,540	2,985	3,330	----	4,770
	1995-6	1,455	1,850	2,430	2,850	3,435	3,965	----	5,725
	1996-7	1,790	2,115	2,820	3,280	3,820	4,420	----	6,495
	1997-8	1,250	1,720	2,265	2,735	3,355	3,900	----	5,870
	1998-9	1,430	1,935	2,530	2,985	3,595	4,180	4,705	5,945
	1999-00	1,270	1,700	2,385	3,070	3,765	4,560	5,150	6,670
	2000-1	1,845	2,475	3,105	3,695				
Wash. &	1991-2	26,345	30,570	35,320	41,320	47,120	52,605	----	65,210
Oregon-	1992-3	26,840	31,550	35,950	41,670	46,530	51,630	----	63,510
Other	1993-4	28,260	33,350	39,010	45,020	51,290	57,180	----	70,690
	1994-5	28,670	33,480	39,120	46,070	52,940	59,540	----	76,780
	1995-6	30,000	35,170	39,460	45,280	51,730	57,360	----	70,250
	1996-7	31,670	36,660	41,700	48,740	55,570	62,320	----	80,970
	1997-8	28,580	33,990	38,690	46,400	53,720	59,780	----	76,930
	1998-9	33,630	38,890	45,650	53,290	60,930	67,180	74,190	83,730
	1999-00	33,320	39,620	45,500	53,350	61,080	67,230	74,840	83,210
	2000-1	34,770	40,970	47,720	55,250				
Other	1991-2	7,515	9,350	11,580	13,585	15,685	17,935	----	24,990
States[3]	1992-3	7,140	9,220	11,265	13,305	15,550	17,555	----	25,070
	1993-4	7,605	9,515	11,605	13,720	16,080	18,705	----	25,690
	1994-5	9,725	13,110	15,630	18,260	21,115	24,060	----	32,260
	1995-6	12,650	15,630	18,815	21,985	25,510	28,610	----	33,580
	1996-7	13,720	17,000	20,645	24,085	27,650	30,830	----	43,100
	1997-8	11,645	13,960	17,115	19,905	23,515	26,365	----	37,842
	1998-9	11,570	14,465	18,030	20,850	24,850	28,190	31,365	39,865
	1999-00	12,455	15,035	17,950	20,855	24,305	27,220	30,410	36,435
	2000-1	12,650	16,235	18,625	22,030				
Total	1991-2	58,855	71,280	85,650	101,095	116,965	132,275	----	174,100
	1992-3	57,355	71,480	85,130	100,495	115,560	130,295	----	174,205
	1993-4	61,305	75,125	89,975	105,965	123,330	140,600	----	186,715
	1994-5	66,520	82,660	99,345	116,760	135,030	153,610	----	204,110
	1995-6	71,415	87,690	103,965	121,645	139,735	156,625	----	198,805
	1996-7	78,240	93,985	110,585	130,745	149,610	168,290	----	227,535
	1997-8	68,355	83,620	99,120	118,510	138,210	155,795	----	212,092
	1998-9	74,140	89,990	108,880	128,335	149,415	168,100	186,670	222,400
	1999-00	75,015	90,845	106,625	126,495	146,970	165,090	184,510	222,400
	1999-00	75,015	90,845	106,625	126,495	146,970	165,090	184,510	222,400

[1] Total quantity received and used for processing regardless of the state in which the potatoes were produced. Excludes quantities used for potato chips in Maine, Michigan, Minnesota, North Dakota or Wisconsin. [2] Includes Maine grown potatoes only. [3] Michigan, Minnesota, North Dakota and Wisconsin. *Source: National Agricultural Statistics Service, U.S. Department of Agriculture (NASS-USDA)*

Rayon and Other Synthetic Fibers

World Cellulosic Fiber Production — In Thousands of Metric Tons

Year	Austria	Brazil	China	Czech Republic	Finland	Germany	India	Japan	Taiwan	United Kingdom	United States	Ex-USSR	World Total
1991	120.0	53.0	242.0	33.5	47.4	118.0	215.4	266.4	149.1	63.0	220.7	401.7	2,433
1992	128.3	54.2	249.1	39.3	56.0	139.9	219.9	254.4	139.3	65.0	224.5	292.3	2,327
1993	131.2	56.7	276.2	41.0	56.5	125.1	238.9	244.4	130.8	67.2	244.5	258.3	2,089
1994	134.3	58.6	336.0	33.7	58.5	138.1	239.7	218.9	149.3	67.0	225.0	189.8	2,308
1995	139.4	53.1	435.0	35.0	57.5	143.5	262.1	212.7	139.6	67.1	226.0	188.4	2,423
1996	145.0	34.4	432.0	31.4	49.8	143.6	251.9	198.2	144.7	62.3	213.1	127.3	2,270
1997	145.0	36.4	450.0	27.3	62.0	155.0	242.4	184.1	148.4	70.0	208.1	401.2	2,314
1998	----	29.2	451.5	26.9	----	----	264.4	164.5	142.6	----	165.5	----	2,172
1999[1]	----	34.6	472.1	17.6	----	----	247.7	135.5	143.7	----	134.7	----	2,118
2000[2]	----	38.6	580.0	45.5	----	----	385.7	221.4	163.9	----	196.9	----	2,960

[1] Preliminary. [2] Producing capacity. Source: Fiber Economics Bureau, Inc. (FEB)

World Noncellulosic Fiber Production (Except Olefin) — In Thousands of Metric Tons

Year	Brazil	China	West Germany	India	Italy/Malta	Japan	Rep. of Korea	Mexico	Spain	Taiwan[3]	United States[4]	Ex-USSR	World Total
1991	219.1	1,488.9	797.0	439.6	564.6	1,429.8	1,365.2	395.3	241.1	1,841.4	2,902.9	804.8	15,273
1992	220.2	1,733.7	817.3	530.5	589.9	1,448.8	1,451.4	425.3	257.0	2,042.6	2,980.6	744.8	16,161
1993	233.3	1,871.9	758.8	608.9	551.6	1,365.1	1,592.0	406.5	240.3	2,121.0	3,039.0	669.8	16,585
1994	243.2	2,119.0	807.6	681.1	599.9	1,394.0	1,825.0	484.4	273.6	2,301.5	3,250.3	658.1	17,939
1995	227.4	2,283.7	771.3	738.0	551.3	1,400.0	1,858.2	516.6	252.3	2,410.5	3,238.9	636.1	18,377
1996	229.6	2,729.6	----	916.4	----	1,399.0	2,025.2	584.6	----	2,561.0	3,284.1	1,359.8	19,765
1997	248.3	3,527.2	----	1,240.7	----	1,433.6	2,403.3	612.7	----	2,932.4	3,420.0	----	22,401
1998	268.6	4,413.7	----	1,361.4	----	1,363.6	2,446.0	591.1	----	3,112.4	3,301.1	----	23,383
1999[1]	300.7	5,237.9	----	1,430.6	----	1,291.4	2,592.8	587.7	----	2,926.8	3,239.5	----	24,455
2000[2]	379.9	6,496.0	----	1,775.1	----	1,788.8	3,037.6	776.0	----	4,032.7	3,962.1	----	31,230

[1] Preliminary. [2] Producing capacity. [3] Beginning 1995; data for S. Korea and Taiwan. [4] Beginning 1995; data for USA and Canada.
Source: Fiber Economics Bureau, Inc. (FEB)

World Production of Synthetic Fibers — In Thousands of Metric Tons

	Noncellulosic Fiber Production (Except Olefin)							Glass Fiber Production						Cigarette
	By Fibers				World Total									
Year	Acrylic & Mod-acrylic	Nylon & Aramid	Polyester	Other Fibers[3]	Yarn & Monofil-aments	Staple, Tow & Fiberfill	Total	Europe	Japan	Other Americas	United States	Total	China	Ex-USSR	Tow Pro-duction
---	---	---	---	---	---	---	---	---	---	---	---	---	---	---	---
1991	2,385	3,605	9,116	167	7,241	8,032	15,273	441	293	75	650	1,561	65	133	480
1992	2,365	3,723	9,916	155	7,971	8,188	16,159	442	307	83	700	1,652	75	84	475
1993	2,314	3,684	10,411	178	8,399	8,188	16,587	508	312	86	794	1,865	77	69	482
1994	2,543	3,706	11,468	222	9,087	8,852	17,939	545	313	87	959	2,235	78	54	536
1995	2,446	3,740	11,945	247	9,684	8,693	18,377	567	318	96	981	2,308	85	55	550
1996	2,604	3,858	13,047	256	10,529	9,236	19,765	585	316	94	996	2,387	98	54	584
1997	2,705	4,029	15,409	257	12,096	10,304	22,401	610	328	100	1,007	2,431	75	55	582
1998	2,671	3,875	16,567	270	13,051	10,333	23,383	660	300	96	1,018	2,416	60	30	554
1999[1]	2,543	3,912	17,769	285	13,717	10,792	24,509	660	300	96	1,126	2,524	60	30	529
2000[2]	3,297	5,416	22,103	415	17,755	13,475	31,230	700	320	100	1,223	2,728	80	35	-----

[1] Preliminary. [2] Producing capacity. [3] Alginate, azion, spandex, saran, etc. Source: Fiber Economics Bureau, Inc. (FEB)

Artificial (Cellulosic) Fiber Distribution in the United States — In Millions of Pounds

	Yarn & Monofilament					Staple & Tow					Glass Fiber
	Producers' Shipments				Domestic Con-sumption	Producers' Shipments				Domestic Con-sumption	Ship-ments
Year	Domestic	Exports	Total	Imports		Domestic	Exports	Total	Imports		
1991	179.9	32.3	212.2	30.8	210.7	255.5	8.1	263.6	92.0	347.5	1,488.5
1992	182.9	35.1	218.0	32.1	215.0	260.7	6.9	267.6	85.6	346.3	1,629.7
1993	196.5	31.5	228.0	40.4	236.9	273.6	10.3	283.9	89.5	363.1	1,780.6
1994	190.3	32.9	223.2	32.9	223.2	252.3	30.7	283.0	65.7	318.0	2,114.0
1995	169.3	41.5	210.8	34.0	203.3	259.8	28.7	288.5	40.8	300.6	2,163.0
1996	169.0	49.6	218.6	39.3	208.3	225.3	20.0	245.3	35.3	260.6	2,196.0
1997	145.9	41.2	187.1	42.9	188.8	205.3	60.1	265.4	51.6	256.9	2,275.0
1998	111.2	32.7	143.9	38.1	149.3	184.4	31.4	215.8	47.4	231.8	
1999[1]	87.6	30.4	118.0	28.2	115.9	168.8	29.9	198.7	47.5	216.3	

[1] Preliminary. Source: Fiber Economice Bureau, Inc. (FEB)

218

RAYON AND OTHER SYNTHETIC FIBERS

Man-Made Fiber Production in the United States   In Millions of Pounds

	-- Artificial (Cellulosic) Fibers --			---------------------------------- Synthetic (Noncellulosic) Fibers ----------------------------------										
	-- Rayon & Acetate --							-------------------- Staple & Tow --------------------					Total	
	Filament Yarn & Monofil-	Staple	Total Cellu-	--------- Yarn & Monofilament ---------			Total			Acrylic & Mod-		Total	Total Noncel-	Manu- factured	Total Glass
Year	ament	& Tow	losic	Nylon	Polyester	Olefin	Yarn	Nylon	Polyester	acrylic	Olefin	Staple	lulosic	Fibers	Fiber
1991	213	273	486	1,667	1,208	1,408	4,282	869	2,202	454	459	3,984	8,266	8,752	1,818
1992	220	275	495	1,651	1,270	1,528	4,449	904	2,308	439	474	4,125	8,573	9,068	1,953
1993	227	278	505	1,700	1,284	1,659	4,643	959	2,274	433	483	4,149	8,791	9,296	2,061
1994	225	273	498	1,805	1,492	1,870	5,167	935	2,366	442	549	4,292	9,459	9,957	2,159
1995	208	290	498	1,829	1,597	1,907	5,333	874	2,290	432	521	4,117	9,450	9,948	2,282
1996	219	245	464	1,920	1,560	1,957	5,437	875	2,259	478	465	4,078	9,515	9,979	2,326
1997	187	266	453	2,005	1,642	2,058	5,704	793	2,454	440	629	4,317	10,012	10,465	2,408
1998	144	216	360	2,060	1,536	2,181	5,776	804	2,319	355	701	4,179	9,955	10,314	2,490
1999[1]	115	199	314	1,874	1,593	2,281	5,747	793	2,283	329	796	4,201	9,949	10,263	2,570
2000[2]	114	231	345	1,833	1,553	2,363	5,748	712	2,275	340	815	4,143	9,891	10,236	2,738

[1] Preliminary.   [2] Estimate.   *Source: Fiber Economics Bureau, Inc. (FEB)*

Domestic Distribution of Synethic (Noncellulosic) Fibers in the United States   In Millions of Pounds

	---------------------------------- Yarn & Monofilament ----------------------------------						-- Staple & Tow --							Dome-
	-------------------- Producers' Shipments --------------------					Dome-	----------------------- Producers' Shipments -----------------------						stic
	-------------- Domestic --------------					stic	----------------- Domestic -----------------						Con-
		Poly-					Con-		Poly-	Acrylic & Mod-					sump-
Year	Nylon	ester	Olefin	Total	Exports	Total Imports	sumption	Nylon	ester	acrylic	Olefin	Total	Exports	Total Imports	tion
1991	1,493.9	1,114.0	1,380.6	3,988.5	246.9	4,235.4	174.8 4,163.3	835.0	2,127.9	319.2	437.5	3,719.6	277.8	3,997.4	263.1 3,982.7
1992	1,570.1	1,229.6	1,496.1	4,295.8	194.8	4,490.6	209.3 4,505.1	891.7	2,202.1	322.3	441.0	3,857.1	267.2	4,124.3	397.7 4,255.0
1993	1,612.7	1,228.4	1,631.5	4,472.6	174.6	4,647.2	295.8 4,768.4	907.9	2,157.8	333.0	468.2	3,866.9	297.1	4,164.0	509.0 4,375.9
1994	1,700.0	1,402.8	1,838.2	4,941.0	204.9	5,145.9	377.7 5,318.7	911.7	2,221.3	319.6	489.0	3,941.6	390.9	4,332.5	622.9 4,564.5
1995	1,741.4	1,439.8	1,870.3	5,051.5	259.0	5,310.5	393.6 5,445.1	828.5	2,100.4	266.1	458.0	3,653.0	398.7	4,051.7	624.9 4,277.9
1996	1,801.2	1,428.7	1,954.4	5,183.1	250.7	5,434.6	482.0 5,665.9	843.8	2,015.8	287.9	514.9	3,662.4	465.2	4,127.6	607.7 4,270.1
1997	1,877.1	1,530.3	2,015.4	5,422.8	238.5	5,661.3	589.0 6,011.8	757.2	2,249.7	288.6	541.9	3,837.4	391.9	4,229.3	672.8 4,510.2
1998	1,940.8	1,427.0	2,141.8	5,509.6	226.8	5,736.4	637.3 6,146.9	766.2	2,105.0	267.3	596.4	3,734.9	340.2	4,075.1	777.4 4,512.3
1999[1]	1,931.7	1,464.4	2,182.9	5,579.0	252.2	5,831.2	719.2 6,298.2	759.3	2,077.8	232.5	680.0	3,749.5	337.9	4,087.4	788.0 4,537.5

[1] Preliminary.   *Source: Fiber Economice Bureau, Inc. (FEB)*

Mill Consumption of Fiber & Products and Per Capita Consumption in the U.S.   In Millions of Pounds

| | -------- Cellulosic Fibers -------- | | | | ---- Noncellulosic Fibers ---- | | | Total Manu- | | | | | Per Capita[4] Mill Consumption (Lbs.) | | | | |
| | Yarn & | | | Total | | | Total | factured | | | Other | Grand | Man- made | | | Other | Total All |
Year	Monofil- ament	Staple & Tow	Net Waste	Cellu- losic	Noncellu- losic	Net Waste	Noncellu- losic	Fibers[2]	Cotton	Wool	Fibers[3]	Total	Fibers[2]	Cotton	Wool	Fibers[3]	Fibers
1991	210.7	347.5	-1.7	556.5	8,146.0	158.7	8,304.7	8,861.2	4,347.5	172.6	78.6	13,459.9	39.1	24.6	1.2	2.5	67.4
1992	215.0	346.3	-3.6	557.7	8,760.1	181.1	8,941.2	9,498.9	4,714.7	171.5	76.7	14,461.8	41.5	27.6	1.2	2.5	72.9
1993	236.9	363.1	-5.6	594.4	9,144.3	189.8	9,334.1	9,928.5	4,921.9	179.5	74.0	15,103.9	43.2	29.2	1.3	2.7	76.4
1994	223.2	318.0	-21.4	519.8	9,883.2	102.4	9,985.6	10,505.5	5,191.6	171.9	54.8	15,923.8	44.5	30.2	1.4	2.7	78.8
1995	203.3	300.6	-22.7	481.2	10,011.6	76.3	10,087.9	10,569.1	5,199.9	161.8	65.6	15,996.4	44.7	30.2	1.4	2.5	78.8
1996	208.2	260.7	-12.8	456.1	9,926.5	99.8	10,026.3	10,482.4	5,191.9	164.4	46.0	15,884.7	44.0	29.6	1.4	1.8	76.8
1997	188.8	256.9	-18.4	427.3	10,347.0	100.4	10,447.4	10,874.7	5,419.5	164.4	43.0	16,501.6	45.9	32.4	1.4	2.0	81.7
1998	149.3	231.8	-18.5	362.6	10,659.2	163.8	10,823.0	11,183.9	5,224.8	125.7	44.6	16,579.0	47.8	34.4	1.3	1.8	85.4
1999[1]	115.9	216.3	-13.3	318.9	10,883.9	176.9	11,060.8	11,377.3	4,996.4	88.5	41.2	16,503.4	49.4	35.4	1.1	2.3	88.2

[1] Preliminary.   [2] Excludes Glass Fiber.   [3] Includes silk, linen, jute and sisal & others.   [4] Mill consumption plus inports less exports of semimanufactured and unmanufactured products.   *Source: Fiber Economics Bureau, Inc. (FEB)*

Producer Price Index of Grey Synthetic Broadwovens   (1982 = 100)

Year	Jan.	Feb.	Mar.	Apr.	May	June	July	Aug.	Sept.	Oct.	Nov.	Dec.	Average
1989	114.3	112.0	112.2	112.2	112.1	113.1	114.7	115.0	115.0	115.8	115.9	115.3	114.0
1990	115.6	115.7	115.6	115.7	115.5	115.6	115.7	115.2	115.3	115.6	115.8	116.1	115.6
1991	115.7	114.7	114.4	114.1	114.3	113.9	114.8	116.4	116.5	116.5	116.8	118.2	115.5
1992	119.0	119.9	120.3	120.9	121.8	122.0	122.6	122.0	121.7	120.8	119.4	119.9	120.9
1993	119.6	119.1	119.1	119.2	117.1	118.4	118.0	118.0	116.9	117.3	115.2	114.5	117.7
1994	113.5	112.8	112.9	113.2	113.2	113.3	113.1	113.3	114.1	111.8	112.9	113.8	113.2
1995	114.8	116.8	116.7	116.3	116.6	117.1	115.4	114.8	116.9	116.4	114.7	116.2	116.1
1996	114.3	114.1	116.9	117.9	116.8	115.7	116.1	117.1	116.9	117.2	116.6	117.0	116.4
1997	117.9	118.3	118.3	117.9	118.4	119.0	118.8	118.5	119.4	118.7	117.6	119.6	118.5
1998[1]	120.1	120.4	119.7	120.2	119.8	119.7	118.0	118.1	116.7	114.2	115.1	115.0	118.1

[1] Preliminary.   *Source: Bureau of Labor Statistics, U.S. Department of Commerce (BLS) (0337-03)*

Rice

Most of the world's rice, the second most popular food-stuff after wheat, is consumed where it is produced. Global milled rice trade in calendar 2001 of an estimated 24.6 million metric tonnes compares with 22.4 million in 2000, and the record high 27.3 million tonnes in 1998. U.S. 2001 exports are estimated at 2.75 million tonnes, unchanged from 2000. The U.S. ranks among the top exporters.

Asia accounts for most of the world's exports, with Thailand the largest exporter at a near record 6.6 million tonnes in 2001 vs. 6 million in 2000. China's exports of 3.4 million tonnes compares with 3.2 million, respectively. Importing nations are numerous, but only four nations are forecast to import one million tonnes or more in 2001. Indonesia is consistently the largest importer with 3 million tonnes in 2001 vs. 2 million in 2000, and 6.1 million tonnes in 1998. On a regional basis, the Middle East tends to be the largest importer. For U.S. rice exports the Western hemisphere is the primary destination and is generally higher priced than Asian rice. Low quality rice, an extremely price sensitive sector and dominated by Asian sellers, constitutes a major portion of total rice imports.

World rice stocks have increased despite higher exports and consumption. Carry-over stocks for the 2000/01 marketing year of almost 63 million tonnes compare with 60 million tonnes in 1999/00, and close to 50 million in the mid 1990's. However, some reduction in carryover is likely by year-end 2000/01. China generally holds 40-50 percent of carryover supplies and India 20 percent.

World rough rice production in 2000/01 of a near record high 591 million tonnes (397 million milled) compares with 598 million (402 million milled) in 1999/00. World consumption of a record high 401 million tonnes (milled) compares with 400 million in 1999/00.

China is both the largest producer and consumer with about one-third each of the world's total, while India ranks second. China's production could quicken in the years ahead reflecting a possible change in traditional planting methods that used a single rice variety which is often susceptible to rice blast fungus, to using a mixture of rice varieties that offer resistance to the disease. The effect has nearly doubled average yield.

Estimated U.S. rice production in 2000/01 (August-July) of 192.2 million cwt. compares with the record 206 million cwt. in 1999/00, the decline reflecting a cut in acreage that more than offset higher yields. Domestic usage was put at a record high 123 million cwt. in 2000/01 vs. 122.6 million in 1999/00. Carry-in stocks for the 2000/01 season totaled 27.5 million cwt. and are forecast to dip to 27.1 million during the year.

The U.S. average farm price in 2000/01 was forecast at $5.75-$6.25 per cwt. vs. $6.11 in 1999/00.

Futures Markets

Rough rice futures and options are traded on the Chicago Board of Trade (CBOT).

World Rice Supply and Distribution   In Thousands of Metric Tons

							--------------- Imports ---------------			---------- Utilization ----------			--------- Ending Stocks ---------		
Year	Brazil	Indonesia	European Union	Iran	Saudi Arabia	Unac-counted	Total	China	India	Total	China	India	Total
1995-6	770	1,029	1,680	1,344	638	1,776	18,618	130,000	79,203	371,401	21,732	11,000	50,429
1996-7	849	808	1,758	973	814	1,621	17,116	132,134	80,707	379,606	25,556	9,500	51,194
1997-8	1,400	6,081	1,733	475	660	1,304	24,679	135,850	78,252	383,294	26,723	10,500	54,725
1998-9[1]	975	3,900	1,635	1,027	775	1,498	25,959	136,000	81,160	388,607	27,289	12,000	60,283
1999-00[2]	650	1,800	1,585	1,100	750	1,277	21,342	137,000	82,500	400,484	26,225	16,400	64,739
2000-1[3]	725	1,800	1,575	1,400	800	1,093	22,886	136,750	84,000	402,656	23,025	19,650	62,674

[1] Preliminary.   [2] Estimate.   [3] Forecast.   Source: Foreign Agricultural Service, U.S. Department of Agriculture (FAS-USDA)

World Production of Rough Rice   In Thousands of Metric Tons

Year	Bangla-desh	Brazil	Burma	China	India	Indonesia	Japan	Rep. of Korea	Pakistan	Philip-pines	Thailand	Vietnam	World Total
1995-6	26,533	10,026	17,000	185,214	119,442	51,100	13,435	6,386	5,951	11,174	21,800	26,792	551,323
1996-7	28,326	9,504	15,517	195,100	121,980	49,360	12,930	7,123	6,461	11,177	20,700	27,277	563,701
1997-8	28,296	8,551	15,345	200,700	123,822	49,237	12,532	7,365	6,500	9,982	23,500	28,930	574,235
1998-9[1]	29,784	11,582	16,034	198,714	129,013	50,400	11,201	6,800	7,012	10,268	23,620	30,467	585,748
1999-00[2]	32,298	11,534	17,000	198,480	134,233	52,919	11,470	7,017	7,735	11,957	25,000	31,435	604,218
2000-1[3]	31,953	10,882	16,897	190,000	132,763	53,000	11,863	7,067	6,451	12,128	25,152	31,970	591,777

[1] Preliminary.   [2] Estimate.   [3] Forecast.   Source: Foreign Agricultural Service, U.S. Department of Agriculture (FAS-USDA)

World Exports of Rice (Milled Basis)   In Thousands of Metric Tons

Year	Argentina	Australia	Burma	China	European Union	Guyana	India	Pakistan	Thailand	Uruguay	Vietnam	United States	World Total
1996-7	500	669	15	938	1,408	262	2,105	1,834	5,216	645	3,327	2,488	20,047
1997-8	525	690	94	3,734	1,415	286	3,300	2,099	6,367	576	3,776	2,772	27,004
1998-9	654	675	57	2,708	1,314	250	3,350	1,837	6,679	745	4,555	2,730	26,943
1999-00[1]	500	575	300	3,200	1,253	300	1,400	1,850	6,300	685	3,200	2,796	24,051
2000-1[2]	200	625	250	3,200	1,219	275	1,300	1,800	6,300	685	3,800	2,522	24,089
2001-2[3]	250	625	250	3,400		275	1,800	1,800	6,600	700	4,000	2,750	24,568

[1] Preliminary.   [2] Estimate.   [3] Forecast.   Source: Foreign Agricultural Service, U.S. Department of Agriculture (FAS-USDA)

RICE

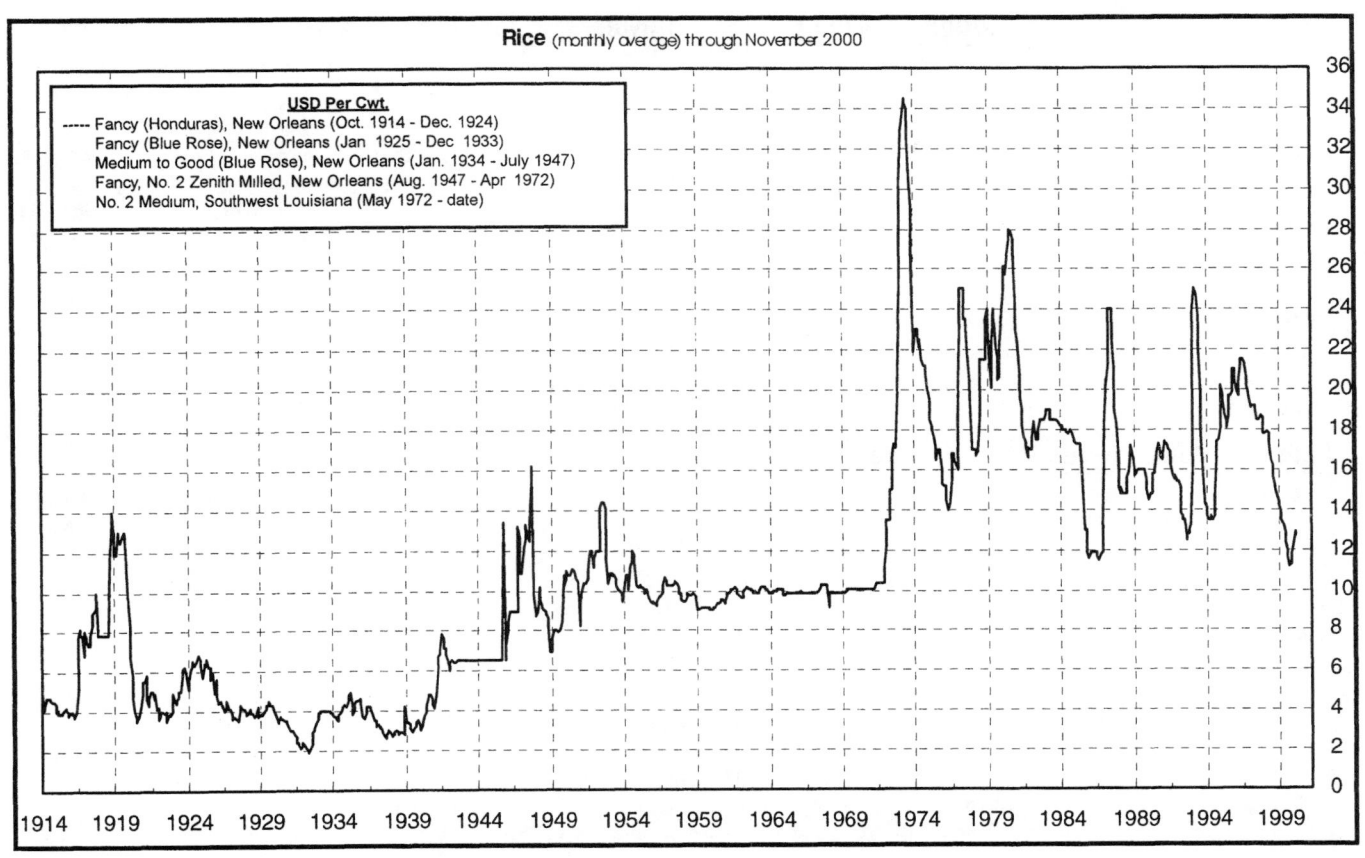

Rice (monthly average) through November 2000

USD Per Cwt.
- - - - Fancy (Honduras), New Orleans (Oct. 1914 - Dec. 1924)
Fancy (Blue Rose), New Orleans (Jan 1925 - Dec 1933)
Medium to Good (Blue Rose), New Orleans (Jan. 1934 - July 1947)
Fancy, No. 2 Zenith Milled, New Orleans (Aug. 1947 - Apr 1972)
No. 2 Medium, Southwest Louisiana (May 1972 - date)

Average Wholesale Price of Rice No. 2 (Medium)[1] Southwest Louisiana   In Dollars Per Cwt. Bagged

Year	Aug.	Sept.	Oct.	Nov.	Dec.	Jan.	Feb.	Mar.	Apr.	May	June	July	Average
1991-2	15.85	16.00	16.00	16.00	16.00	16.00	15.90	15.50	15.50	15.15	14.50	14.50	15.60
1992-3	14.50	14.00	14.50	14.15	13.40	13.40	13.00	12.80	12.40	11.94	12.00	12.00	13.15
1993-4	12.25	12.45	15.65	21.95	24.00	24.00	23.88	23.80	24.00	23.70	22.00	20.00	20.65
1994-5	18.30	15.88	15.00	15.00	14.00	13.80	14.16	14.38	14.38	14.70	14.75	14.55	14.91
1995-6	15.44	17.50	20.25	20.13	20.00	20.00	19.88	19.25	19.13	19.38	19.40	19.50	19.15
1996-7	19.50	19.50	19.25	19.25	19.00	18.81	19.19	19.25	19.25	19.25	18.40	19.00	19.14
1997-8	18.25	18.35	18.63	19.00	19.00	19.00	19.00	18.20	18.00	18.13	18.50	18.50	18.55
1998-9	18.35	18.75	19.00	19.00	20.00	20.00	20.00	20.00	20.00	20.00	20.00	20.00	19.59
1999-00	18.60	17.50	14.88	14.70	14.67	14.35	14.00	13.83	13.75	13.40	12.50	12.63	14.57
2000-1[2]	12.34	12.48	12.41	12.38									12.40

[1] U.S. No. 2 -- broken not to exceed 4%.   [2] Preliminary.   Source: Economic Research Service, U.S. Department of Agriculture (ERS-USDA)

Average Price Received by Farmers for Rice (Rough) in the United States   In Dollars Per Cwt.

Year	Aug.	Sept.	Oct.	Nov.	Dec.	Jan.	Feb.	Mar.	Apr.	May	June	July	Average[2]
1991-2	7.16	7.67	7.65	7.84	7.98	7.84	7.97	7.78	7.46	7.18	6.97	6.99	7.58
1992-3	6.60	6.41	6.40	6.42	6.39	6.36	6.06	5.64	5.52	5.24	5.02	4.92	5.89
1993-4	5.19	5.21	6.10	8.06	8.91	8.98	10.10	10.20	9.93	10.00	8.88	7.80	7.98
1994-5	6.87	6.89	6.47	6.53	6.56	6.78	6.71	6.64	6.70	6.75	7.03	7.17	6.78
1995-6	7.64	7.95	8.77	9.12	9.36	9.33	9.10	9.31	9.34	9.69	9.74	9.68	9.15
1996-7	10.10	10.00	9.66	9.41	9.82	9.95	10.10	10.20	10.30	10.20	9.90	10.00	9.96
1997-8	9.94	9.92	10.00	9.82	9.77	9.57	9.75	9.67	9.40	9.38	9.58	9.58	9.70
1998-9	8.95	9.35	9.25	8.98	9.06	9.05	8.97	8.86	8.54	8.16	8.20	8.15	8.83
1999-00	7.62	6.88	6.23	6.11	6.19	6.03	5.98	5.82	5.86	5.56	5.59	5.47	6.11
2000-1[1]	5.60	5.72	5.61	5.63	5.60	5.84	5.69						5.67

[1] Preliminary.   [2] Weighted average by sales.   Source: Economic Research Service, U.S. Department of Agriculture (ERS-USDA)

RICE

Salient Statistics of Rice, Rough & Milled (Rough Equivalent) in the United States   In Millions of Cwt.

Crop Year Beginning Aug. 1	Supply				Disappearance								Government Support Program					
	Stocks Aug. 1	Pro-duction	Imports	Total Supply	Domestic				Resi-dual	Exports	Total Disap-pearance	CCC Stocks July 31	Put Under Price Support	Loan Rate ($ Per Cwt.)				
														Rough[3]			All Classes	Milled Long
					Food	Brewers	Seed	Total						Long	Medium			
1995-6	31.3	173.9	7.7	212.8	78.0	15.6	3.5	104.5	8.5	83.2	187.8	0	100.9	6.68	6.12		6.50	10.69
1996-7	25.0	171.6	10.5	207.1	81.0	15.8	3.9	101.6	2.0	78.3	179.9	0	68.9	6.68	6.17		6.50	10.77
1997-8	27.2	183.0	9.2	219.4	84.2	16.0	4.1	103.3	.2	88.2	191.5	0	67.6	6.67	6.14		6.50	10.69
1998-9	27.9	184.4	10.5	222.9	87.3	16.0	4.4	114.0	11.4	86.8	200.8	0	80.2	6.67	6.14		6.50	10.71
1999-00[1]	22.1	206.0	10.0	238.1	90.1	16.0	4.0	121.4	6.5	89.2	210.6	0	107.6	6.67	6.12		6.50	10.66
2000-1[2]	27.5	192.4	10.3	230.2	119.0	[4]	3.9	122.9	[4]	80.0	202.9	0		6.66	6.12		6.50	10.71

[1] Preliminary.   [2] Forecast.   [3] Loan rate for each class of rice is the sum of the whole kernels' loan rate weighted by its milling yield (average 56%) and the broken kernels' loan rate weighted by its milling yield (average 12%).   Source: Economic Research Service, U.S. Department of Agriculture (ERS)

Acreage, Yield, Production and Prices of Rice in the United States

Crop Year	Acreage Harvested (1,000 Acres)		Yield Per Harvested Acre (In Lbs.)		Production 1,000 Cwt.			Value of Pro-duction $1,000	Wholesale Prices ($ Per Cwt.)		Milled Rice, Average C.I.F. at Rotterdam		
	Southern States	California	United States	California	United States	Southern States	California	United States	Arkan-sas[2]	Hous-ton[3]	U.S. No. 2[4]	Thai "A"[5]	Thai "B"[5]
											$ Per Metric Ton		
1995-6	2,628	465	3,093	7,600	5,621	138,519	35,352	173,871	1,587,236	19.10	19.15	404	----	407
1996-7	2,304	500	2,804	7,490	6,120	134,140	37,459	171,599	1,690,270	19.02	20.95	428	----	380
1997-8	2,587	516	3,103	8,250	5,897	140,446	42,546	182,992	1,756,136	18.14	19.61	417	----	345
1998-9	2,799	458	3,257	6,850	5,663	153,057	31,386	184,443	1,686,580	19.04	18.05	368	----	333
1999-00	3,007	505	3,512	7,270	5,866	169,337	36,690	206,027	1,257,071	15.01	15.33	272	----	278
2000-1[1]	2,537	548	3,085	7,900	6,212	148,894	43,292	192,186				267	----	240

[1] Preliminary.   [2] F.O.B. mills, Arkansas, medium.   [3] Houston, Texas (long grain).   [4] Milled, 4%, container, FAS.   [5] SWR, 100%, bulk.
NA = Not available.   Source: Economic Research Service, U.S. Department of Agriculture (ERS-USDA)

U.S. Exports of Milled Rice, by Country of Destination   In Thousands of Metric Tons

Year Beginning October	Canada	Haiti	Iran	Ivory Coast	Jamaica	Mexico	Nether-lands	Peru	Saudi Arabia	South Africa	Switzer-land	United Kingdom	Total
1991-2	143.7	116.9	11.6	73.4	46.3	157.0	67.7	43.6	179.6	136.6	94.2	59.8	2,279
1992-3	146.0	152.9	184.3	107.3	39.4	241.5	120.9	61.6	223.5	122.1	71.2	72.2	2,710
1993-4	141.3	57.2	60.4	34.2	53.8	234.0	92.8	47.0	180.5	110.9	64.8	82.4	2,433
1994-5	160.0	210.2	240.6	92.0	88.5	309.6	170.3	81.8	176.1	106.1	91.2	58.7	3,763
1995-6	172.1	149.6	24.5	61.3	63.1	359.1	113.9	97.8	141.5	169.9	80.3	85.4	2,826
1996-7[1]	162.9	178.7	-----	35.6	27.4	381.3	54.0	35.1	150.9	108.5	64.2	101.0	2,560

[1] Preliminary.   Source: Economic Research Service, U.S. Department of Agriculture (ERS-USDA)

U.S. Rice Exports by Export Program   In Thousands of Metric Tons

Fiscal Year	PL 480	Section 416	CCC Credit Pro-grams[2]	CCC African Relief Exports	EEP[3]	Export Pro-grams[4]	Exports Outside Specified Export Programs	Total U.S. Rice Exports	% Export Programs as a Share of Total Exports
1995	196	0	321	0	113	463	3,300	3,763	12
1996	182	0	141	0	23	353	2,473	2,826	12
1997	116	0	80	0	0	298	2,262	2,560	12
1998	184	0	499	0	0	694	2,616	3,310	21
1999	536	0	192	0	0	777	2,299	3,076	25
2000[1]	221	141	225	0	0	626	2,673	3,299	19

[1] Preliminary.   [2] May not completely reflect exports made under these programs.   [3] Sales not shipments.   [4] adjusted for estimated overlap between CCC export credit and EEP shipments.   Source: Economice Research Service, U.S. Department of Agriculture (ERS-USDA)

Production of Rice (Rough) in the United States, by Type and Variety   In Thousands of Cwt.

Year	Long Grain	Medium Grain	Short Grain	Total	Year	Long Grain	Medium Grain	Short Grain	Total
1991	109,137	47,567	753	157,457	1996	113,629	56,901	1,069	171,599
1992	128,015	50,633	1,010	179,658	1997	124,485	57,091	1,416	182,992
1993	103,064	51,873	1,173	156,110	1998	139,328	43,404	1,711	184,443
1994	133,445	63,390	944	197,779	1999	151,863	50,540	3,624	206,027
1995	121,730	51,241	900	173,871	2000[1]	130,446	59,313	2,427	192,186

[1] Preliminary.   Source: National Agricultural Statistics Service, U.S. Department of Agriculture (NASS-USDA)

Rubber

According to the International Rubber Study Group, world production of natural rubber in 1999 was 6.84 million metric tonnes. That represented an increase of 2 percent from 1998. Estates production of natural rubber in 1999 was 1.61 million tonnes, unchanged from 1998. Smallholdings production of rubber was 5.23 million tonnes, up 3 percent from 1998. In the January-April 2000 period, world production of natural rubber was 2.19 million tonnes. Estates production of rubber in the same period was 530,000 tonnes and smallholdings production was 1.66 million tonnes.

World consumption of natural rubber in 1999 was 6.70 million tonnes, up 2 percent from 1998. In the January-April 2000 period, consumption of natural rubber was 2.41 million tonnes. Producer stocks of natural rubber at the end of April 2000 were 730,000 tonnes, down 12 percent from the year before. Producer stocks at the end of 1999 were 880,000 tonnes. Consumer reported stocks of rubber at the end of April 2000 were 369,000 tonnes, up 4 percent from a year ago. At the end of 1999, stocks were 399,000 tonnes. Consumer total stocks of rubber in April 2000 were 810,000 tonnes, up 7 percent from the year before. Stocks afloat in April 2000 were 520,000 tonnes, down 9 percent from a year earlier. At the end of 1999, rubber stocks afloat were 590,000 tonnes. World stocks of natural rubber in April 2000 were 2.06 million tonnes, down 5 percent from the year before.

World production of synthetic rubber in 1999 was 10.2 million tonnes, up 3 percent from 1998. Production of synthetic rubber in the January-April 2000 period was 3.48 million tonnes. Global consumption of synthetic rubber in 1999 was 10.1 million tonnes, up 2 percent from the previous year. In the first four months of 2000, world consumption of synthetic rubber was 3.50 million tonnes.

Reported world stocks of synthetic rubber at the end of April 2000 were 1.12 million tonnes. At the end of April 1999, stocks were 1.10 million tonnes. Russian Federation stocks of synthetic rubber in April 2000 were 220,000 tonnes. A year earlier stocks were the same size. China's stocks of synthetic rubber at the end of April 2000 were 100,000 tonnes, unchanged from the previous year. Stocks elsewhere in April 2000 were 690,000 tonnes, down 3 percent from the year before. Synthetic rubber stocks afloat were 290,000 tonnes in April, up 4 percent from the year before. Total world stocks of synthetic rubber in April 2000 were 2.42 million tonnes, about the same as the year before. Stocks at the end of 1999 were 2.44 million tonnes.

U.S. consumption of natural and synthetic rubber in 1999 was 3.19 million tonnes, down 9 percent from 1998. In the first four months of 2000, U.S. consumption of natural and synthetic rubber was 1.17 million tonnes. China's consumption of natural and synthetic rubber in 1999 was 2.11 million tonnes, up 15 percent from the year before. Japan's consumption in 1999 was 1.87 million tonnes, up 2 percent from the previous year. Russian Federation consumption of rubber in 1999 was 435,500 tonnes, up 20 percent from the previous year. Consumption of rubber by Germany was 829,000 tonnes, up 2 percent from the previous year. Other large users of rubber are India, France, and South Korea.

The U.S. stockpile of rubber held in the National Stockpile Center in April 2000 was 69,200 tonnes, down 2 percent from the previous year. Stocks of natural rubber held by India were 181,000 tonnes, while stocks held by Japan were 84,300 tonnes. U.S. reported stocks of synthetic rubber in April 2000 were 428,000 tonnes, up 6 percent from the year before. Stocks of synthetic rubber in Japan were 357,400 tonnes in April, while stocks in France were 239,900 tonnes.

The major producers of natural rubber are Thailand, Indonesia, and Malaysia. Thailand's production of natural rubber in 1999 was 2.27 million tonnes, up 2 percent from a year ago. Production of natural rubber in Malaysia in 1999 was 768,900 tonnes, down 13 percent from the previous year. Indonesia's production of natural rubber in 1999 was 1.69 million tonnes, down 2 percent from the year before. Production of rubber by India was 618,700 tonnes, up 4 percent. Natural rubber production by China in 1999 was 460,000 tonnes, up 2 percent from 1998.

Futures Markets

Natural Rubber and Rubber Index futures are traded on the Osaka Mercantile Exchange (OME). Rubber futures are traded on the Shanghai Metal Exchange (SME) and the Tokyo Commodity Exchange (TOCOM).

U.S. Imports of Natural Rubber (Includes Latex & Guayule)   In Thousands of Metric Tons

Year	Jan.	Feb.	Mar.	Apr.	May	June	July	Aug.	Sept.	Oct.	Nov.	Dec.	Total
1991	59.9	54.1	69.5	90.9	59.6	56.7	53.4	52.4	65.5	74.4	71.3	68.9	776.2
1992	77.5	75.2	84.7	64.7	79.0	73.8	80.5	77.2	73.9	81.3	68.1	77.5	913.4
1993	95.3	79.9	93.9	86.3	74.1	81.2	83.6	77.8	69.2	73.4	86.0	86.9	987.6
1994	87.5	74.7	102.6	78.9	88.3	77.8	66.7	85.0	78.8	89.3	70.0	76.0	975.6
1995	81.7	86.9	102.3	90.2	94.1	93.4	78.0	81.0	81.5	89.2	79.1	68.7	1,026.1
1996	105.4	86.1	82.2	90.6	65.1	70.4	79.0	81.0	82.1	113.6	73.5	85.0	1,014.0
1997	94.2	92.0	93.9	88.2	93.0	65.1	76.8	90.1	87.5	86.8	87.6	89.0	1,044.2
1998	104.4	76.6	102.8	81.0	98.0	92.9	96.4	100.8	123.2	104.8	87.6	89.0	1,176.8
1999	91.8	90.7	93.4	101.6	84.8	80.0	76.6	112.2	88.7	127.5	84.5	111.4	1,116.3
2000[1]	127.4	88.2	114.1	107.9	114.9	120.1	65.9	91.3					1,244.7

[1] Preliminary.   Source: International Rubber Study Group (IRSG)

RUBBER

World Production[1] of Rubber   In Thousands of Metric Tons

	-- Natural --								-------------------------------- Synthetic --------------------------------				
Year	China	India	Indo-nesia	Malaysia	Sri Lanka	Thailand	Vietnam	World Total	Ger-many	Japan	United States	Russia[3]	World Total
1990	264.2	323.5	1,262.0	1,291.0	113.1	1,275.3	103.0	5,080	524.5	1,425.8	2,114.5	2,277.0	9,890
1991	296.4	360.2	1,284.0	1,255.7	103.9	1,341.2	87.0	5,160	504.4	1,377.3	2,050.0	2,125.3	9,290
1992	309.3	383.0	1,387.0	1,173.2	106.1	1,531.0	114.0	5,440	544.7	1,389.9	2,300.0	1,610.5	9,300
1993	326.1	428.1	1,300.5	1,074.3	104.2	1,553.4	114.0	5,310	569.7	1,309.8	2,180.0	1,102.5	8,600
1994	374.0	464.0	1,358.5	1,100.6	105.3	1,717.9	156.0	5,720	621.6	1,349.0	2,390.0	631.9	8,870
1995	424.0	499.6	1,454.5	1,089.3	105.7	1,804.8	154.0	6,040	480.0	1,497.6	2,530.0	836.9	9,480
1996	430.0	540.1	1,527.0	1,082.5	112.5	1,970.4	218.0	6,390	548.1	1,519.9	2,486.0	775.1	9,760
1997	444.0	580.3	1,504.8	971.1	105.8	2,032.7	209.0	6,390	555.1	1,591.5	2,589.0	724.9	10,070
1998	450.0	591.1	1,714.0	885.7	95.7	2,215.9	199.7	6,680	619.0	1,520.1	2,600.0	621.0	9,900
1999[2]	460.0	620.1	1,599.2	768.9	96.6	2,265.5	230.0	6,760	720.1	1,576.7	2,354.0	737.0	10,230

[1] Including rubber in the form of latex.   [2] Preliminary.   [3] Formerly part of the U.S.S.R., data reported separately until 1992.
Source: International Rubber Study Group (IRSG)

World Consumption of Natural and Synthetic Rubber   In Thousands of Metric Tons

	-- Natural --							-------------------------------- Synthetic --------------------------------					
Year	Brazil	France	Ger-many	Japan	United Kingdom	United States	World Total	France	Ger-many	Japan	United Kingdom	United States	World Total
1990	124.1	179.0	208.7	677.0	136.0	807.5	5,210	351.0	511.0	1,133.0	223.0	1,820.8	9,660
1991	122.8	183.0	210.7	689.5	119.0	755.8	5,060	342.0	502.0	1,118.5	201.0	1,768.1	9,220
1992	123.4	179.0	212.8	685.4	124.5	910.2	5,320	365.4	506.0	1,080.6	231.0	1,959.6	9,360
1993	131.7	168.5	174.9	631.0	119.0	966.7	5,430	314.7	488.0	1,022.0	211.0	2,001.0	8,630
1994	144.7	179.8	186.4	639.8	135.0	1,001.7	5,650	400.1	512.2	1,026.2	220.0	2,117.6	8,820
1995	155.2	176.0	211.7	692.0	118.0	1,003.9	5,950	430.2	426.4	1,085.0	226.0	2,172.0	9,270
1996	155.0	182.2	193.0	714.5	111.0	1,001.7	6,100	436.1	478.0	1,124.5	230.0	2,186.6	9,590
1997	160.0	192.3	212.0	713.0	119.0	1,044.1	6,460	416.2	501.0	1,163.0	235.0	2,322.7	10,000
1998	160.0	223.0	247.0	707.3	139.0	1,157.4	6,550	451.4	569.0	1,115.7	177.0	2,354.4	9,890
1999[1]	170.0	252.7	226.0	734.2	130.0	1,117.0	6,680	434.3	604.0	1,132.9	189.0	2,113.0	10,160

[1] Preliminary.   *Source: International Rubber Study Group (IRSG)*

World Stocks[1] of Natural & Synthetic Rubber (by Countries) on January 1   In Thousands of Metric Tons

	Total	------------------------------- In Producing Countries -------------------------------							------ In Consuming Countries (Reported Stocks) ------				
Year	Synthetic	Africa	Indo-nesia	Malaysia	Sri Lanka	Thai-land	Vietnam	Total Natural	Brazil	India	Japan	United States	Total
1991	980	18.2	110	190.3	29.8	83.7	11.0	490	11.9	92.9	91.6	94.3	291
1992	963	18.4	110	196.1	17.3	89.3	9.0	500	6.0	106.0	92.7	109.4	443
1993	1,004	19.6	110	187.2	16.0	89.0	12.0	560	17.0	90.9	82.9	108.0	442
1994	949	21.6	110	159.2	17.2	115.6	12.0	570	25.0	96.4	85.4	71.3	410
1995	915	17.0	110	187.0	16.5	96.5	19.0	480	17.0	94.1	72.9	45.2	363
1996	988	21.0	110	175.6	17.0	113.0	20.0	490	13.0	127.4	77.1	67.1	414
1997	1,057	20.5	70	190.3	17.6	147.7	28.0	510	16.0	123.4	86.8	79.3	430
1998	1,070	25.5	40	209.5	17.9	159.4	28.0	510	14.0	157.0	87.2	57.2	386
1999	1,118	27.6	30	234.2	18.6	209.5	21.0	730	35.0	194.0	58.0	70.4	428
2000[1]	1,104	27.4	33	236.6	18.7	250.8	9.0	870	34.0	215.1	79.1	46.0	443

[1] Preliminary.   *Source: International Rubber Study Group (IRSG)*

Net Exports of Natural Rubber from Producing Areas   In Thousands of Metric Tons

Year	Cam-bodia	Guat-emala[4]	Indo-nesia	Liberia	Malaysia	Nigeria	Sri Lanka	Thai-land	Vietnam	Other Africa[2]	Other Asia[3]	World Total
1990	28.0	13.4	1,077.3	19.0	1,185.6	81.2	86.7	1,150.8	75.9	118.0	37.6	3,940
1991	21.0	14.3	1,220.0	32.0	1,041.2	63.0	76.4	1,231.9	62.9	126.0	44.0	3,890
1992	20.0	15.7	1,268.1	30.0	939.1	70.4	78.6	1,412.9	80.9	135.0	25.9	4,010
1993	21.0	16.9	1,214.3	45.0	769.8	79.7	69.6	1,396.8	96.7	136.0	32.6	3,880
1994	32.0	22.3	1,244.8	10.0	782.1	49.6	69.1	1,605.0	135.5	145.0	28.9	4,230
1995	30.0	23.2	1,323.8	13.0	777.5	99.2	68.2	1,635.5	138.1	140.0	31.1	4,320
1996	31.0	29.2	1,434.3	30.0	709.8	48.8	72.1	1,763.0	194.5	167.0	41.0	4,540
1997	32.0	28.3	1,403.8	67.2	586.8	53.0	61.4	1,837.1	194.2	186.0	38.0	4,500
1998	33.0	25.2	1,641.2	75.0	424.9	74.0	41.4	1,839.4	190.6	182.0	39.0	4,580
1999[1]	34.0	32.0	1,585.1	85.0	435.5	38.0	42.7	1,657.0	218.0	205.0	40.2	4,600

[1] Preliminary.   [2] Includes Cameroon, Cote d'Ivoire, Gabon, Ghana and Zaire.   [3] Includes Myanmar, Papua New Guinea and the Philippines.
Source: International Rubber Study Group (IRSG)

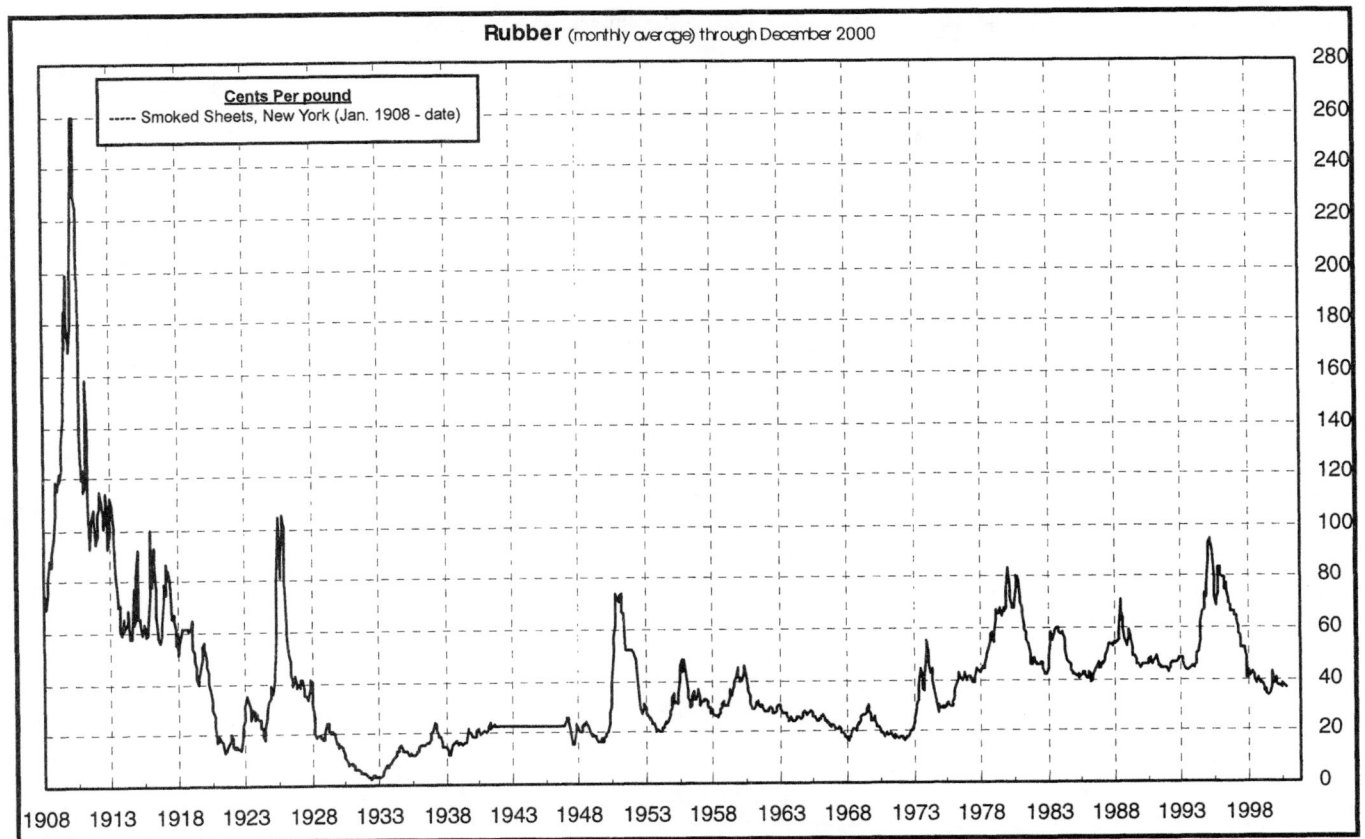

Rubber (monthly average) through December 2000

Cents Per pound
----- Smoked Sheets, New York (Jan. 1908 - date)

Average Spot Crude Rubber Prices (Smoked Sheets1) in New York   In Cents Per Pound

Year	Jan.	Feb.	Mar.	Apr.	May	June	July	Aug.	Sept.	Oct.	Nov.	Dec.	Average
1991	47.47	48.92	48.09	45.92	45.17	45.26	44.59	44.45	44.25	44.52	44.75	44.16	45.63
1992	43.11	43.95	44.50	45.86	46.41	46.57	46.78	47.05	46.86	47.83	48.00	48.03	46.25
1993	48.51	48.30	46.41	44.15	43.78	43.78	43.30	43.85	44.54	44.23	44.90	44.70	45.04
1994	44.92	46.11	49.62	50.83	51.43	55.13	62.49	66.35	67.15	73.51	71.76	77.35	59.72
1995	85.68	92.61	94.15	93.43	89.50	80.57	72.13	68.54	70.70	73.59	83.19	83.39	82.29
1996	80.25	79.90	79.76	75.08	76.99	75.10	71.03	69.13	68.75	66.32	66.32	66.14	72.90
1997	65.06	64.76	63.53	59.97	57.71	57.30	51.96	52.45	51.89	51.36	47.99	40.53	55.38
1998	40.21	43.96	41.70	41.23	42.65	41.28	40.03	38.58	38.62	40.26	39.96	38.20	40.56
1999	38.99	38.58	36.34	34.98	35.75	34.64	33.60	33.63	34.45	37.58	42.57	38.88	36.67
2000	38.16	40.36	38.17	37.80	37.76	37.07	36.65	37.90	37.35	37.61	37.02	36.90	37.73

[1] No. 1, ribbed, plantation rubber.   *Source: The Wall Street Journal*

Natural Rubber Prices in London   In British Pounds Per Metric Ton

Year	Jan.	Feb.	Mar.	Apr.	May	June	July	Aug.	Sept.	Oct.	Nov.	Dec.	Average
Buyers' Price RSS 1 (CIF)													
1997	777.6	783.6	800.9	731.3	715.1	699.6	605.9	604.1	592.5	573.9	525.9	461.4	654.3
1998	464.6	516.9	470.7	473.3	487.0	461.5	473.8	456.6	469.3	490.2	487.7	464.6	476.1
1999	495.8	463.3	430.0	414.4	442.4	435.7	410.2	404.5	419.9	455.4	509.8	484.7	446.4
2000	462.0	518.2	487.6	496.0	500.5	501.8	494.5	529.5	526.2	537.4	518.4		506.6
Buyers' Prices RSS 3 (CIF)													
1997	762.2	769.4	788.7	721.3	708.9	696.9	588.7	592.1	575.8	553.0	490.1	411.4	636.5
1998	416.0	500.3	445.5	465.6	480.7	451.0	466.3	439.1	454.3	478.0	467.1	430.0	457.6
1999	466.4	451.6	417.9	394.0	418.8	425.3	391.1	384.8	398.6	439.0	489.5	453.3	427.1
2000	440.0	498.5	464.8	481.0	483.0	479.3	472.0	509.5	507.3	519.9	498.4		486.7
Sellers' Prices SMR 20 (CIF)													
1997	767.5	769.4	765.0	697.5	663.1	653.8	597.0	600.0	580.6	567.5	530.0	468.3	640.7
1998	477.5	539.4	485.0	487.0	495.0	438.8	417.0	396.3	403.0	416.9	409.4	401.0	445.6
1999	414.4	411.9	380.5	375.0	396.9	393.5	373.8	388.8	417.0	453.1	518.8	480.0	415.8
2000	471.9	504.4	472.5	466.3	465.0	447.5	435.0	477.0	478.1	486.3	487.0		471.9

Source: International Rubber Study Group (IRSG)

RUBBER

Consumption of Natural Rubber in the United States   In Thousands of Metric Tons

Year	Jan.	Feb.	Mar.	Apr.	May	June	July	Aug.	Sept.	Oct.	Nov.	Dec.	Total
1991	60.0	60.0	65.0	65.0	65.0	60.0	55.0	55.0	65.0	70.0	65.0	66.0	755.8
1992	83.4	63.3	85.9	66.9	80.6	78.6	82.6	79.5	70.2	84.6	64.4	70.2	910.2
1993	96.3	76.0	93.4	93.4	67.9	76.8	77.3	84.9	72.0	73.6	82.9	72.2	966.7
1994	92.8	84.9	93.1	82.7	89.6	84.6	76.2	87.8	74.8	90.1	66.4	78.7	1,001.7
1995	70.5	75.8	98.4	90.3	92.2	93.3	85.0	82.7	83.1	89.9	81.4	61.3	1,003.9
1996	102.5	85.8	81.2	87.9	65.6	76.7	81.9	88.1	83.3	108.4	72.1	68.2	1,001.7
1997	94.2	92.0	93.9	88.2	93.0	65.1	76.8	90.1	87.5	86.8	87.5	89.0	1,044.1
1998	104.4	76.6	102.7	81.0	98.0	92.9	96.4	91.7	119.1	104.8	78.4	111.4	1,157.4
1999	90.0	90.0	90.0	86.0	86.0	86.0	90.0	90.0	90.0	98.0	98.0	99.0	1,093.0
2000[1]	110.0	110.0	110.0	114.0	114.0	114.0	80.0	80.0					1,248.0

[1] Preliminary.   Source: International Rubber Study Group (IRSG)

Stocks of Natural Rubber in the United States, on First of Month   In Thousands of Metric Tons

Year	Jan.	Feb.	Mar.	Apr.	May	June	July	Aug.	Sept.	Oct.	Nov.	Dec.
1991	94.3	94.0	88.0	93.0	119.0	113.0	110.0	108.0	106.0	106.0	110.0	117.0
1992	109.4	103.6	112.7	110.4	107.5	105.9	101.1	99.0	96.7	100.3	97.0	100.7
1993	108.0	49.4	53.3	53.7	46.7	52.9	57.3	63.6	56.5	53.7	53.4	56.5
1994	71.3	65.9	55.7	65.2	61.4	60.0	53.2	43.8	41.0	45.0	44.2	47.8
1995	45.2	56.4	67.5	71.4	71.2	72.6	73.0	66.0	64.4	62.8	62.1	59.8
1996	67.1	70.0	70.3	71.2	73.9	73.4	67.1	64.2	57.2	56.0	61.1	62.4
1997	79.3	74.2	74.2	76.9	77.5	62.2	55.2	53.6	52.1	51.2	52.4	55.2
1998	57.2	61.2	65.5	63.5	60.9	66.7	53.6	57.9	54.7	58.3	58.9	66.5
1999	70.4	68.0	66.0	64.0	62.0	60.0	58.0	56.0	54.0	52.0	50.0	48.0
2000[1]	46.0	69.2	69.2	69.2	69.2	69.2	69.2	69.2	69.2			

[1] Preliminary.   Source: International Rubber Study Group (IRSG)

Stocks of Synthetic Rubber in the United States, on First of Month   In Thousands of Metric Tons

Year	Jan.	Feb.	Mar.	Apr.	May	June	July	Aug.	Sept.	Oct.	Nov.	Dec.
1991	403.7	406.0	403.0	404.0	402.0	388.0	394.0	385.0	356.0	334.0	330.0	325.0
1992	403.7	386.0	381.2	383.9	393.2	389.2	372.8	382.7	382.1	375.1	378.6	401.1
1993	406.9	345.9	345.7	346.0	340.5	351.8	342.1	341.6	333.6	326.4	319.9	321.4
1994	331.1	313.3	313.3	307.9	306.0	314.2	302.5	323.2	318.5	304.6	299.4	299.5
1995	305.4	307.4	302.8	293.5	319.4	315.6	325.9	349.2	355.7	354.6	347.0	351.5
1996	366.2	355.3	342.0	354.8	365.4	360.0	367.0	377.3	366.0	362.8	354.1	370.6
1997	400.5	400.4	408.4	412.7	411.9	403.5	393.1	376.9	378.4	364.4	365.2	377.7
1998	377.7	382.2	375.7	379.5	387.5	402.8	394.6	406.8	394.2	398.7	395.7	396.5
1999	409.3	404.0	404.0	406.0	399.0	420.0	410.0	419.0	413.0	390.0	391.0	389.0
2000[1]	406.0	416.0	413.0	402.0	409.0	421.0	417.0	423.0	423.0			

[1] Preliminary.   Source: International Rubber Study Group (IRSG)

Production of Synthetic Rubber in the United States   In Thousands of Metric Tons

Year	Jan.	Feb.	Mar.	Apr.	May	June	July	Aug.	Sept.	Oct.	Nov.	Dec.	Total
1991	168.0	163.0	184.0	174.0	173.0	159.0	154.0	133.0	159.0	159.0	173.0	164.0	2,050
1992	180.0	190.0	200.0	210.0	200.0	190.0	190.0	200.0	210.0	200.0	195.0	175.0	2,300
1993	120.0	160.0	220.0	190.0	200.0	180.0	190.0	180.0	180.0	180.0	190.0	180.0	2,180
1994	180.0	180.0	210.0	200.0	210.0	200.0	200.0	210.0	190.0	210.0	200.0	200.0	2,390
1995	220.0	200.0	210.0	210.0	240.0	220.0	210.0	230.0	210.0	200.0	200.0	190.0	2,530
1996	200.0	190.0	220.0	210.0	200.0	210.0	200.0	210.0	200.0	210.0	220.0	216.0	2,486
1997	220.0	200.0	220.0	230.0	220.0	200.0	220.0	220.0	230.0	210.0	210.0	203.0	2,589
1998	230.0	200.0	230.0	220.0	240.0	210.0	220.0	210.0	230.0	210.0	200.0	210.0	2,610
1999	200.0	181.0	209.0	195.0	205.0	190.0	199.0	192.0	180.0	204.0	197.0	202.0	2,354
2000[1]	202.0	202.0	214.0	193.0	216.0	202.0	198.0	190.0					2,426

[1] Preliminary.   Source: International Rubber Study Group (IRSG)

Consumption of Synthetic Rubber in the United States   In Thousands of Metric Tons

Year	Jan.	Feb.	Mar.	Apr.	May	June	July	Aug.	Sept.	Oct.	Nov.	Dec.	Total
1991	145.0	140.0	160.0	150.0	160.0	135.0	140.0	140.0	160.0	140.0	150.0	149.0	1,768
1992	167.8	159.5	174.7	158.9	162.6	184.2	154.5	177.7	180.2	171.5	155.1	148.2	1,960
1993	161.3	154.4	189.4	172.8	164.5	173.6	166.0	173.9	162.0	169.4	155.1	148.2	2,001
1994	177.7	160.8	191.8	173.0	173.5	187.5	164.9	187.1	176.0	178.8	175.7	151.4	2,118
1995	188.6	182.2	194.3	179.1	212.7	188.7	160.0	190.7	182.4	178.1	169.7	170.8	2,172
1996	188.0	173.7	186.9	176.8	184.9	178.5	177.0	197.3	182.9	201.0	177.8	145.5	2,187
1997	191.7	181.4	190.0	187.9	192.2	187.7	205.9	208.0	204.2	203.0	181.9	165.5	2,323
1998	196.5	192.5	214.8	194.4	199.8	201.4	192.0	204.5	202.2	200.3	181.2	188.8	2,354
1999	164.0	166.0	195.0	178.0	170.0	186.0	177.0	176.0	191.0	171.0	178.0	174.8	2,113
2000[1]	179.0	183.0	197.0	170.0	185.0	192.0	176.0	176.0				161.0	2,187

[1] Preliminary.   Source: International Rubber Study Group (IRSG)

U.S. Exports of Synthetic Rubber   In Thousands of Metric Tons

Year	Jan.	Feb.	Mar.	Apr.	May	June	July	Aug.	Sept.	Oct.	Nov.	Dec.	Total
1991	43.8	46.1	44.0	45.2	47.9	40.4	42.8	43.2	43.1	46.3	47.3	42.2	532.3
1992	52.3	55.1	51.3	59.1	58.2	51.6	46.5	52.8	58.0	51.4	48.1	39.7	624.1
1993	47.1	34.1	57.7	47.4	52.4	46.9	46.9	43.8	48.8	46.6	49.0	41.9	562.6
1994	48.8	46.4	55.4	57.0	52.4	49.6	50.2	62.8	60.7	59.9	56.9	55.0	655.1
1995	54.9	51.6	62.7	55.6	58.6	58.6	50.0	54.9	53.0	60.4	53.9	52.6	666.8
1996	61.1	57.7	64.0	68.0	48.2	66.8	62.3	57.1	63.9	65.2	58.6	58.6	731.5
1997	63.1	58.2	57.5	74.2	66.9	61.6	64.1	70.0	65.6	65.6	63.0	58.7	768.5
1998	61.1	60.8	62.8	59.8	66.9	61.8	60.1	64.4	63.7	62.3	59.2	59.2	742.1
1999	57.6	63.3	65.0	70.5	64.7	66.0	61.5	68.2	65.1	79.0	70.2	65.7	796.8
2000[1]	64.3	73.4	83.8	70.2	73.2	72.3	72.4	67.3					865.4

[1] Preliminary.   Source: International Rubber Study Group (IRSG)

Production of Tyres (Car and Truck) in the United States   In Thousands of Units

Year	First Quarter	Second Quarter	Third Quarter	Fourth Quarter	Total	Year	First Quarter	Second Quarter	Third Quarter	Fourth Quarter	Total
1982	47,304	45,602	42,656	42,938	178,500	1991	51,296	52,796	49,183	51,115	202,391
1983	45,859	47,451	45,370	47,353	186,923	1992	57,890	57,319	57,554	57,487	230,250
1984	53,369	53,588	50,957	51,463	209,375	1993	61,809	60,752	57,702	57,184	237,447
1985	54,460	49,385	46,468	46,610	196,923	1994	63,586	63,331	57,018	59,442	243,696
1986	49,240	45,687	46,855	48,507	190,289	1995	63,800	63,800	63,800	63,754	255,521
1987	51,205	50,210	49,723	51,839	202,978	1996	64,000	64,000	64,000	63,700	255,723
1988	54,677	52,986	51,195	52,493	211,351	1997	----	----	----	----	263,860
1989	56,716	56,626	50,086	49,444	212,870	1998	----	----	----	----	270,905
1990	55,915	53,856	51,163	49,729	210,663	1999[1]	----	----	----	----	267,652

[1] Preliminary.   [2] Estimate.   Source: International Rubber Study Group IRSG

U.S. Foreign Trade of Tyres (Car and Truck)   In Thousands of Units

Year	Imports First Quarter	Second Quarter	Third Quarter	Fourth Quarter	Total	Exports First Quarter	Second Quarter	Third Quarter	Fourth Quarter	Total
1991	12,011	13,008	11,320	10,158	46,497	6,407	6,388	6,623	6,342	25,760
1992	10,760	12,496	11,850	12,285	47,391	6,243	6,475	7,125	6,646	26,489
1993	11,519	13,045	12,688	13,036	50,288	7,266	6,930	7,163	7,133	28,492
1994	13,809	15,352	14,906	14,774	58,841	7,444	8,035	7,945	8,678	32,102
1995	14,883	14,977	13,762	12,718	56,340	8,438	8,502	8,478	9,174	34,592
1996	13,163	13,864	12,543	13,186	52,756	8,244	10,013	8,672	9,401	36,330
1997	13,359	14,487	15,314	16,064	59,224	9,466	11,386	10,456	11,085	42,393
1998	17,046	17,728	18,016	19,346	72,136	12,840	10,678	10,018	10,372	43,908
1999[1]	19,471	22,280	22,180	23,769	87,700	9,874	9,580	10,480	10,387	40,321
2000[2]	24,200				96,800	11,200				44,800

[1] Preliminary.   [2] Estimate.   Source: International Rubber Study Group (IRSG)

Rye

In the U.S., rye is a minor crop with annual production now roughly one-half of what it was throughout the 1980's. Still, there is a relatively large variation in recent year-to-year production ranging from a high of 12.2 million bushels in 1998 to a record low 8.2 million in 1997. Production in 2000 of 8.6 million bushels compares with 11 million in 1999. The U.S. is a net importer of rye, importing at times almost one-half of domestic production. The major producing states in 2000 were the Dakotas, Oklahoma, and Georgia, accounting for more than one-half of total production (June/May). Although average yield appears to have steadied in recent years at 29 bushels per acre, the area planted to rye continues to slip with only 1.33 million acres in 2000 vs. 1.58 million in 1999.

In the U.S., rye is used as an animal feed and as an ingredient in bread and some whiskeys. About one-third of the total supply is used as a feedstuff, an equal quantity as a foodstuff, and the balance as seed and for whisky. U.S. rye exports are minimal, generally about one million metric tonnes. Carryover stocks are also small with 40,000 tonnes at the end of 1999/00, and forecast to be the same on May 31, 2001. The contraction in U.S. supply/demand reflects a seemingly deep rooted lack of interest towards the grain by producers and consumers alike.

On a world basis, the slippage in production is also evident, although for a time in the mid-1990's production appeared to have stabilized in the 20-25 million metric tonne range vs. a mid-1980's average of more than 30 million

tonnes. World production in 2000/01 of a record low 19.5 million tonnes compares with 19.7 million in 1999/00. Average yield in 2000/01 was forecast at 1.93 metric tonnes per hectare vs. 1.97 in 1999/00. World 2000/01 acreage was estimated at 10.11 million hectares vs. 10.02 the previous year.

Eastern Europe is the major producing area with almost one-half of the world's crop. Individually, Poland vies with Germany for the title of largest producer. Poland produced 4.1 million tonnes in 2000/01 vs. 5.2 million in 1999/00, with Germany at 4.2 million tonnes and 4.3 million, respectively. Canada, whose output is not much larger than that of the U.S., exports most of its crop to the U.S. Canada's 2000/01 exports are forecast at 75,000 tonnes, the same as in 1999/00.

World trade in 2000/01 (October/September) of 2.0 million metric tonnes compares with 2.4 million in 1999/00, but percentagewise is well above the paltry 662,000 tonnes in 1997/98. Importing nations show wide year-to-year variance. China's 2000/01 imports of 100,000 tonnes are unchanged from 1999/00, but compare with only 11,000 tonnes in 1996/97. South Korea's 2000/01 imports of 350,000 tonnes compare with 450,000 in 1999/00, and only 4,000 in 1997/98. The largest exporter is the European Union with 1.7 million tonnes in 2000/01, down 400,000 tonnes from a year earlier. Russia's exports in 2000/01 of 100,000 tonnes are twice the 1999/00 total and well above the 1996/97-1998/99 average of 7,000 tonnes.

World Production of Rye   In Thousands of Metric Tons

Year	Austria	Canada	Czech Republic[5]	Denmark	France	Germany	Poland	Russia[4]	Spain	Turkey	Ukraine[4]	United States	World Total
1991-2	350	339	484	395	210	3,324	5,899	ÑÑ	242	240	14,061	248	27,359
1992-3	278	265	255	308	205	2,422	3,981	13,890	230	240	1,160	304	28,656
1993-4	290	320	300	323	190	2,984	5,000	9,150	300	230	1,180	263	26,090
1994-5	320	400	280	380	180	3,450	5,300	6,000	220	250	940	290	21,890
1995-6	310	310	260	500	200	4,520	6,290	4,100	170	260	1,210	260	21,890
1996-7	150	310	200	340	230	4,210	5,650	5,900	300	250	1,100	230	22,230
1997-8	210	320	260	450	210	4,580	5,300	7,500	210	240	1,350	210	24,390
1998-9[1]	240	400	260	540	220	4,780	5,660	3,300	210	240	1,140	310	20,310
1999-00[2]	220	390	200	240	180	4,330	5,180	4,800	220	250	900	280	19,690
2000-1[3]	170	260	150	330	170	4,150	4,100	5,400	240	250	1,000	220	19,440

[1] Preliminary.   [2] Estimate.   [3] Forecast.   [4] Formerly part of the U.S.S.R.; data not reported separately until 1992.   [5] Formerly part of Czechoslovakia; data not reported separately until 1992.   *Source: Foreign Agricultural Service, U.S. Department of Agriculture (FAS-USDA)*

Production of Rye in the United States   In Thousands of Bushels

Year	Georgia	Kansas	Michigan	Minnesota	Nebraska	North Dakota	Oklahoma	Pennsylvania	South Carolina	South Dakota	Texas	Wisconsin	Total
1991	1,300	115	360	648	1,000	992	665	297	630	1,152	228	435	9,761
1992	1,560	130	496	720	1,040	1,496	798	720	675	1,666	280	330	11,952
1993	1,380	693	420	667	500	1,050	660	340	380	1,600	363	260	10,340
1994	1,890	325	442	810	546	700	945	320	600	1,485	435	875	11,341
1995	1,155	400	544	609	480	726	810	330	440	1,650	380	480	10,064
1996	1,820	150	351	480	323	528	975	216	520	1,476	190	384	8,936
1997	1,430	300	450	400	240	513	1,080	400	250	728	330	432	8,132
1998	1,050	375	420	837	288	2,562	1,540	495	400	1,400	400	360	12,161
1999	1,050	300	756	775	405	1,517	1,045	600	500	1,012	450	384	11,038
2000[1]	1,170	[2]	[2]	[2]	[2]	704	1,470	[2]	[2]	779	[2]	[2]	8,619

[1] Preliminary.   [2] Estimates not published beginning in 2000.   *Source: Agricultural Statistics Board, U.S. Department of Agriculture (ASB-USDA)*

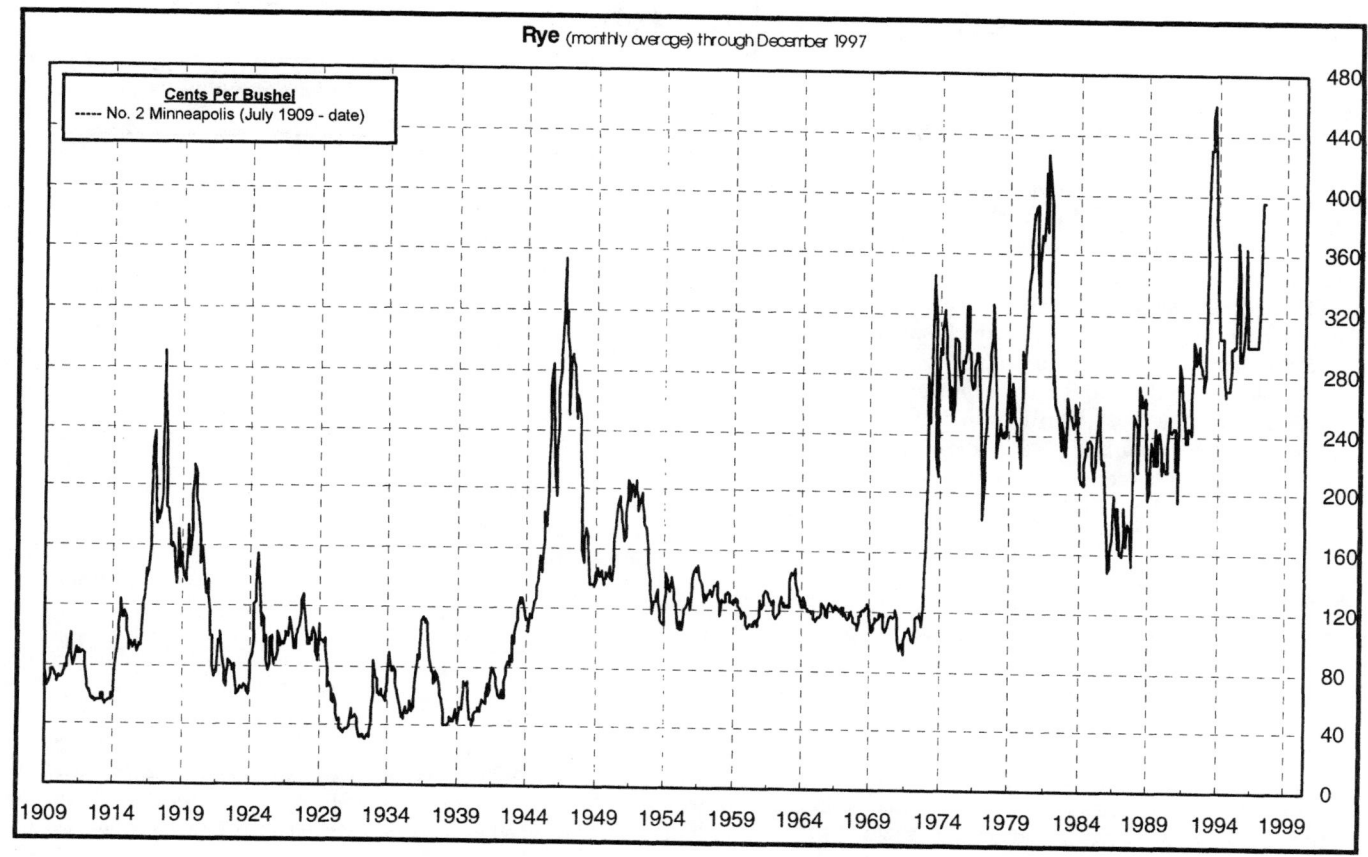

Rye (monthly average) through December 1997

Cents Per Bushel
----- No. 2 Minneapolis (July 1909 - date)

Salient Statistics of Rye in the United States   In Thousands of Bushels

| Crop Year Beginning June 1 | Supply | | | | Disappearance | | | | | | Acreage | | | Yield Per |
| | Stocks June 1 | Pro- duction | Imports | Total Supply | Domestic Use | | | | | Exports | Total Disap- pearance | Planted | Harvested for Grain | Harvested Acre Bushels |
					Food	Industry	Seed	Feed & Residual	Total		----- 1,000 Acres -----			
1991-2	3,327	9,761	4,542	17,630	3,500	2,000	3,000	7,528	16,028	53	16,081	1,671	396	24.6
1992-3	1,523	11,952	3,099	16,100	3,419	2,000	3,000	6,065	14,484	14	14,498	1,582	406	29.4
1993-4	1,555	10,340	4,607	16,502	3,538	2,000	3,000	6,977	15,515	16	15,531	1,493	381	27.1
1994-5	971	11,341	4,386	16,698	3,312	2,000	3,000	6,900	15,212	35	15,247	1,613	407	27.9
1995-6	1,451	10,064	3,760	15,275	3,318	2,000	3,000	6,018	14,336	41	14,377	1,602	385	26.1
1996-7	898	8,936	4,327	14,161	3,459	2,000	3,000	4,916	13,375	32	13,407	1,457	345	25.9
1997-8	754	8,132	5,562	14,448	3,298	3,000	2,000	5,306	13,604	80	13,684	1,400	316	25.7
1998-9[1]	764	12,161	3,322	16,247	3,639	3,000	3,000	4,392	14,031	33	14,064	1,566	418	29.1
1999-00[2]	2,400	11,038	4,000	17,438	3,300	3,000	3,000	5,900	15,200	300	15,500	1,582	383	28.8
2000-1[3]		8,619										1,335	302	28.5

[1] Preliminary.   [2] Estimate.   [3] Forecast   Source: Economic Research Service, U.S. Department of Agriculture (ERS-USDA)

Average Price of Cash Rye No. 2 in Minneapolis   In Cents Per Bushel

Year	July	Aug.	Sept.	Oct.	Nov.	Dec.	Jan.	Feb.	Mar.	Apr.	May	June	Average
1991-2	216	238	195	288	288	279	251	263	235	235	235	245	247
1992-3	245	241	267	295	303	298	288	290	300	289	285	282	282
1993-4	280	270	280	354	387	427	430	430	452	460	400	383	372
1994-5	360	336	305	305	305	305	285	267	270	270	270	270	296
1995-6	287	298	299	300	300	350	368	346	290	290	290	304	310
1996-7	325	364	314	300	300	300	300	300	300	300	300	300	309
1997-8	300	327	395	395	395	395	NQ	NQ	NQ	NQ	NQ	NQ	382
1998-9	NQ	NQ	NQ	NQ	NQ	NQ	NQ	NQ	NQ	NQ	NQ	NQ	NQ
1999-00	NQ	NQ	NQ	NQ	NQ	NQ	NQ	NQ	NQ	NQ	NQ	NQ	NQ
2000-1[1]	NQ	NQ	NQ	NQ	NQ	NQ	NQ	NQ					

[1] Preliminary.   NQ = No quote.   Source: Agricultural Marketing Service, U.S. Department of Agriculture (AMS-USDA)

Salt

Salt, or sodium chloride, is a basic commodity with many uses. Salt is added to food to enhance flavor and is used to remove ice in winter. Salt is used in the manufacture of caustic soda and as a feedstock for chlorine. Salt is produced by a number of methods including solar evaporation, vacuum pan, mined as rock salt, and taken from the ocean as brine. There are no economic substitutes or alternates for salt. Calcium chloride or calcium magnesium acetate, hydrochloric acid, and potassium chloride can be substituted for salt in deicing, certain chemical processes, and food flavoring, although at a higher cost.

The U.S. Geological Survey reported that U.S. salt production in 1999 was 41.4 million metric tonnes, up slightly from the 1998 output of 41.2 million tonnes. A rock salt mine in Michigan reopened and a new mine in New York opened in 1999 that would act to replace some production lost in a previous New York mine closing. There were 31 companies involved in salt production in 1999, operating 69 plants in 15 states.

The estimated percentage of salt sold or used by type in 1999 was salt in brine, 51 percent; rock salt, 32 percent; vacuum pan, 9 percent; and solar salt, 8 percent.

Reported consumption of salt in 1999 was 48.9 million tonnes, up 11 percent from the previous year. The chemical industry consumed about 50 percent of the total salt sales with salt brine representing about 89 percent of the type of slat used for feedstock. The main consuming sectors in the chemical industry were chlorine and caustic soda manufacturing. Salt for highway deicing accounted for 21 percent of U.S. demand. U.S. imports for consumption in 1999 were 8.8 million tonnes. The major suppliers of salt to the U.S. were Canada, Chile, and Mexico.

World production of salt in 1999 was estimated at 200 million tonnes, up 8 percent from 1998. The U.S. was the largest producer with 21 percent of the world total, next was China at 31.0 million tonnes, Germany with 15.2 million tonnes, and Canada with 13.4 million tonnes. Other large producers were India, Mexico, France, and the U.K.

World Production of All Salt   In Thousands of Metric Tons

Year	Australia	Canada	China	France	Germany	India	Italy	Mexico	Poland	Spain	United Kingdom	United States	World Total
1992	7,693	11,171	28,100	6,116	12,709	9,503	3,821	7,395	3,887	3,610	6,101	36,100	183,000
1993	7,737	10,900	29,500	6,980	12,688	9,503	3,730	7,490	3,817	3,410	6,790	39,300	187,000
1994	7,685	11,700	29,746	7,536	13,099	9,503	3,953	7,458	4,074	4,932	7,000	40,100	192,000
1995	8,148	10,957	29,780	7,539	15,224	12,544	3,552	7,670	4,214	4,776	6,650	42,200	199,000
1996	7,905	12,248	29,035	7,860	15,907	14,466	3,541	8,508	4,163	4,000	6,610	42,300	203,000
1997	8,801	13,264	30,830	7,085	15,787	14,251	3,510	7,933	3,859	4,000	6,600	41,500	206,000
1998[1]	8,879	13,296	22,420	7,000	15,700	11,964	3,600	8,412	4,005	3,500	6,600	41,300	198,000
1999[2]	10,003	12,481	28,124	7,000	15,700	14,453	3,600	8,500	4,000	3,200	5,800	45,000	209,000

[1] Preliminary.   [2] Estimate.   *Source: U.S. Geological Survey (USGS)*

Salient Statistics of the Salt Industry in the United States   In Thousands of Metric Tons

Year	Net Import Reliance as a % of Apparent Consumption	Average Value FOB Mine Vacuum & Open Pan $ Per Ton	Production Total	Production Open & Vacuum Pan	Production Solar	Production Rock	Production Brine	Sold or Used Producers Open & Vacuum Pan	Sold or Used Producers Rock Salt	Sold or Used Producers Brine	Total Salt	Value[3] Million $	Imports for Consumption	Exports Total	Exports To Canada	Apparent Consumption
1992	11	113.20	36,016	3,811	3,221	11,411	17,574	3,763	10,910	34,784	34,784	802.6	5,394	992	718	39,186
1993	12	111.97	39,200	3,864	2,960	14,253	18,100	3,850	13,401	18,100	38,200	904.0	5,868	688	499	43,400
1994	18	115.35	40,100	3,960	3,020	15,100	18,000	3,930	14,900	18,000	39,700	990.0	9,630	742	573	48,600
1995	14	118.63	42,100	3,950	3,540	14,000	20,600	3,920	13,000	20,500	40,800	1,000.0	7,090	670	558	47,200
1996	19	120.54	42,200	3,920	3,270	13,500	21,500	3,900	14,500	21,500	42,900	1,060.0	10,600	869	710	52,600
1997	17	119.61	41,400	3,980	3,170	12,900	21,400	3,990	12,200	21,400	40,600	993.0	9,160	748	624	49,000
1998[1]	17	114.93	41,200	4,040	3,190	12,900	21,100	4,040	12,700	21,100	40,800	986.0	8,770	731	533	48,800
1999[2]	16	112.49	44,900	4,190	3,580	14,400	22,700	4,190	14,700	22,700	44,400	1,110.0	8,870	892	730	52,400

[1] Preliminary.   [2] Estimate.   [3] Values are f.o.b. mine or refinery & do not include cost of cooperage or containers.   *Source: U.S. Geological Survey*

Salt Sold or Used by Producers in the U.S. by Classes & Consumers or Uses   In Thousands of Metric Tons

Year	Chemical[2]	Tanning Leather	Textile & Dyeing	Meat Packers	Canning	Baking	Agricultural Distribution	Feed Dealers	Feed Manufacturers	Rubber	Oil	Paper & Pulp	Metal Processing	Water Treatment	Grocery Stores	Water Conditioning Distrib.	Ice Control and/or Stabilization
1992	18,538	67	271	389	252	161	553	1,020	392	34	1,208	230	217	435	849	899	7,814
1993	19,273	67	313	418	322	152	808	1,120	476	37	1,220	110	216	419	823	527	13,600
1994	18,400	82	304	410	342	157	842	1,070	478	33	1,290	150	239	440	934	505	16,400
1995	21,100	74	290	410	332	155	726	1,040	407	67	2,420	152	236	413	847	563	12,900
1996	22,400	83	288	407	336	169	661	1,150	403	71	2,430	122	199	534	855	719	17,700
1997	22,400	78	273	416	334	167	307	1,110	683	68	2,440	107	177	471	800	624	15,000
1998	22,000	93	250	440	275	219	362	1,190	536	68	2,320	115	170	531	800	598	9,490
1999[1]	22,400	103	235	405	225	234	254	1,210	533	72	2,430	112	153	899	831	600	15,300

[1] Preliminary.   [2] Chloralkali producers and other chemical.   *Source: U.S. Geological Survey (USGS)*

Sheep & Lambs

The well entrenched contraction in U.S. sheep inventory shows no signs of abating. The mid-2000 total of all sheep and lambs of 8.5 million head compares with 9 million in mid-1999, and nearly 20 million ten years earlier. Of the 2000 total, the breeding sheep inventory declined to 5.03 million head vs. 5.35 million in 1999. The 2000 lamb crop of 4.53 million head compares with 4.72 million in 1999.

The largest sheep producing states include Texas, South Dakota, and Wyoming. Commercial 2000 U.S. lamb production (through October) of 189 million pounds compares with 198 million in the like 1999 period. The U.S. is a net importer of lamb, almost all from Australia and New Zealand, totaling 61.7 million pounds through the first eight months of 2000 vs. 58.5 million in the like 1999 period.

However, the U.S. imports live sheep from Canada. Per capita retail usage of lamb in the U.S. totals one pound.

Choice wholesale lamb prices in the second half of 2000 of $80.00/cwt. compare with $75.00/cwt. in late 1999, basis San Angelo, Texas. East Coast choice 55 pound lamb prices of $182.00/cwt. compare with over $161.00/cwt., respectively.

Although demand for sheep meat is low in the U.S., foreign demand is higher, especially in those countries with large sheep herds utilized for wool production from which there is a derived demand for meat. Thus, the price of wool is a key factor in determining the availability of sheep meat. World sheep numbers increased during the late 1990's due largely to gains in China and India which more than offset declines in Australia and New Zealand.

World Sheep and Goat Numbers in Specified Countries on January 1   In Thousands of Head

Year	Argentina	Australia	China	India	Kazakhstan	New Zealand	Romania	Russia	South Africa	Spain	Turkey	United Kingdom	World Total
1991	27,552	173,982	210,021	160,207	35,700	57,852	14,062	58,200	37,585	24,037	45,000	30,147	962,853
1992	25,706	161,073	206,210	161,084	34,556	55,162	13,879	55,255	36,076	24,625	44,700	28,932	931,903
1993	24,500	140,542	207,329	162,155	34,420	52,568	12,079	51,368	35,770	24,615	44,600	29,493	900,400
1994	23,500	120,900	217,314	169,569	34,208	50,298	12,276	43,700	33,800	23,872	44,000	29,333	881,258
1995	21,626	121,100	240,528	171,626	25,132	50,135	12,119	34,500	33,385	23,058	43,000	29,484	874,912
1996	17,956	121,200	279,535	173,519	19,600	48,816	11,086	28,336	35,145	21,322	42,400	28,797	897,009
1997	17,295	120,228	236,961	175,976	13,742	47,394	10,317	23,519	35,830	23,981	41,100	28,256	842,179
1998	15,232	117,494	255,055	178,462	10,896	46,970	9,747	20,697	36,821	24,857	39,500	30,027	853,061
1999[1]	13,953	117,091	268,143	180,130	9,556	46,150	9,167	18,213	34,910	24,199	37,300	31,080	857,109
2000[2]	13,800	117,191	271,130	180,885	9,000	45,800	8,700	15,698	35,000	23,700	34,400	30,800	852,745

[1] Preliminary.   [2] Forecast.   Source: Foreign Agricultural Service, U.S. Department of Agriculture (FAS-USDA)

Salient Statistics of Sheep & Lambs in the United States (Average Live Weight)   In Thousands of Head

Year	Inventory, Jan. 1 Without New Crop Lambs	Inventory, Jan. 1 With New Crop Lambs	Lamb Crop	Total Supply	Marketings[3] Sheep	Marketings[3] Lambs	Slaughter Farm	Slaughter Commercial	Slaughter Total[4]	Net Exports	Total Disappearance	Production (Live Weight) Mil. Lbs.	Farm Value Jan. 1 All Million $	Farm Value Jan. 1 $ Per Head
1992	10,797	11,507	7,225	18,732	1,923	7,007	87	5,496	5,585	770	7,595	746.0	660.7	61.2
1993	10,201	10,906	6,379	17,285	1,952	6,752	74	5,182	5,268	750	7,180	688.6	714.2	70.6
1994	9,836	9,714	5,897	15,611	1,536	6,384	76	4,938	5,008	760	6,742	630.0	681.4	69.9
1995	8,989	8,886	5,606	14,492	990	6,228	69	4,560	4,628	680	5,807	599.4	663.4	74.7
1996	8,465	8,461	5,282	13,743	1,024	6,023	65	4,184	4,249	264	5,488	565.7	732.2	86.5
1997	8,024	8,024	5,356	13,380	1,011	5,709	62	3,907	3,969	----	5,946	591.3	761.7	96.0
1998	7,825	7,825	5,007	12,832	977	5,510	73	3,804	3,861	----	----	555.7	797.8	102.0
1999[1]	7,215	7,215	4,733	11,948	----	----	----	3,701	----	----	----	----	637.6	88.0
2000[2]	7,032	7,032	4,622	11,654	----	----	----	3,455	----	----	----	----	668.1	95.0

[1] Preliminary.   [2] Estimate.   [3] Excludes interfarm sales.   [4] Includes all commercial and farm.   Source: Economic Research Service, U.S. Department of Agriculture (ERS-USDA)

Sheep and Lambs[3] on Farms in the United States on January 1   In Thousands of Head

Year	California	Colorado	Idaho	Iowa	Minnesota	Montana	New Mexico	Ohio	South Dakota	Texas	Utah	Wyoming	Total
1993	995	685	250	320	245	554	405	190	591	2,000	490	885	10,500
1994	1,120	647	266	267	231	534	340	198	550	1,895	442	813	9,742
1995	1,060	545	270	294	190	490	315	162	530	1,700	445	790	8,886
1996	1,000	535	273	345	185	465	265	153	500	1,650	395	680	8,461
1997	960	575	285	285	180	432	235	130	450	1,400	375	720	7,937
1998	800	575	285	265	165	415	290	135	420	1,530	420	710	7,825
1999	810	440	265	260	175	380	275	125	420	1,350	400	630	7,215
2000[1]	800	440	275	265	165	370	290	134	420	1,200	400	570	7,032
2001[2]	840	420	275	270	170	360	255	142	420	1,100	390	530	6,915

[1] Preliminary.   [2] Estimate.   [3] Includes sheep & lambs on feed for market and stock sheep & lambs.   Source: Economic Research Service, U.S. Department of Agriculture (ERS-USDA)

SHEEP & LAMBS

Average Wholesale Price of Slaughter Lambs (Choice) at San Angelo Texas   In Dollars Per Cwt.

Year	Jan.	Feb.	Mar.	Apr.	May	June	July	Aug.	Sept.	Oct.	Nov.	Dec.	Average
1992	58.56	57.69	66.55	74.63	68.88	64.50	58.17	52.38	53.61	52.81	56.93	67.25	61.00
1993	69.88	73.38	75.50	71.25	62.50	57.75	57.00	58.97	66.08	63.75	65.69	68.44	65.85
1994	56.67	62.31	61.19	51.25	60.94	66.92	75.33	79.50	76.08	69.96	73.60	67.50	66.77
1995	65.38	75.08	73.75	68.58	77.20	81.63	83.70	87.00	80.00	75.50	72.00	70.50	75.86
1996	74.44	85.63	84.07	83.10	86.17	97.50	92.67	83.75	84.40	82.58	80.00	88.88	85.27
1997	94.63	100.81	97.50	95.50	83.17	83.25	78.94	90.25	85.45	82.75	80.33	83.52	88.01
1998	74.38	74.31	71.50	63.00	73.00	91.21	82.21	82.05	69.50	67.20	63.33	71.44	73.59
1999	69.31	67.88	68.54	70.50	82.70	81.06	77.29	81.17	77.00	74.81	78.00	83.29	75.96
2000[1]	73.71	76.83	78.17	78.25	89.65	78.30	84.17	82.20	82.00	77.50	76.70	75.33	79.40

[1] Preliminary.   Source: Economic Research Service, U.S. Department of Agriculture (ERS-USDA)

Federally Inspected Slaughter of Sheep & Lambs in the United States   In Thousands of Head

Year	Jan.	Feb.	Mar.	Apr.	May	June	July	Aug.	Sept.	Oct.	Nov.	Dec.	Total
1992	468	422	481	503	374	419	427	400	470	452	413	460	5,289
1993	380	384	476	461	396	462	394	413	410	391	403	430	5,000
1994	383	409	515	402	418	377	302	382	384	381	393	411	4,756
1995	373	363	456	420	355	347	296	355	344	356	364	358	4,388
1996	352	353	403	374	313	271	313	315	313	365	324	336	4,032
1997	294	317	386	321	308	293	295	288	310	324	299	337	3,771
1998	301	300	377	367	270	283	269	263	295	312	290	344	3,671
1999	260	291	411	295	260	259	253	283	294	293	317	341	3,557
2000[1]	271	284	334	330	248	247	229	269	257	266	286	287	3,308

[1] Preliminary.   Source: Economic Research Service, U.S. Department of Agriculture (ERS-USDA)

Cold Storage Holdings of Lamb and Mutton in the U.S., on First of Month   In Thousands of Pounds

Year	Jan.	Feb.	Mar.	Apr.	May	June	July	Aug.	Sept.	Oct.	Nov.	Dec.
1992	6,296	7,255	6,670	8,455	8,580	9,870	10,968	11,711	9,314	8,751	8,520	8,406
1993	7,864	6,343	6,620	6,661	11,064	11,181	13,152	13,495	12,241	12,615	11,843	10,161
1994	8,372	9,198	9,507	11,194	11,505	11,368	12,124	12,026	11,016	9,261	8,946	8,796
1995	10,913	11,621	10,825	12,679	14,934	13,992	12,306	10,679	10,240	7,412	7,503	7,846
1996	7,606	9,794	13,017	12,247	13,649	12,187	13,726	13,164	14,645	11,249	10,494	9,788
1997	8,899	9,473	9,862	11,163	13,027	15,220	16,594	18,535	19,383	16,119	16,894	16,534
1998	13,741	13,920	15,284	16,226	16,306	16,666	16,040	16,188	14,530	12,253	12,558	11,914
1999	11,721	10,452	12,134	12,374	13,146	12,313	12,459	11,975	12,240	9,815	9,210	9,446
2000[1]	8,740	10,394	10,335	11,437	13,345	13,137	13,984	13,557	14,042	12,867	12,195	12,486

[1] Preliminary.   Source: Economic Research Service, U.S. Department of Agriculture (ERS-USDA)

Average Price Received by Farmers for Sheep in the United States   In Dollars Per Cwt.

Year	Jan.	Feb.	Mar.	Apr.	May	June	July	Aug.	Sept.	Oct.	Nov.	Dec.	Average
1992	28.10	29.80	31.60	28.30	23.10	22.60	24.00	25.80	25.00	25.30	25.50	33.20	26.86
1993	33.10	35.20	36.10	27.30	29.10	28.90	29.00	28.50	25.80	24.60	25.70	30.30	29.47
1994	35.10	37.00	34.30	29.60	29.30	33.60	30.10	29.40	27.90	27.30	30.50	34.70	31.57
1995	32.80	37.50	31.90	29.50	27.90	28.30	28.60	27.00	26.00	24.50	23.80	26.00	28.65
1996	34.40	33.80	34.00	27.30	25.30	26.60	30.50	29.10	30.20	28.80	29.80	34.20	30.33
1997	41.80	41.30	42.50	37.50	34.00	36.60	39.40	38.40	33.90	35.80	38.90	37.70	38.15
1998	42.00	39.60	41.00	34.40	30.30	30.20	29.40	28.30	26.80	26.10	26.40	30.10	32.05
1999	32.40	30.20	32.70	31.80	31.50	28.90	32.00	29.80	29.20	26.40	30.20	33.40	30.71
2000[1]	36.80	39.50	38.80	35.00	30.50	30.00	34.20	30.70	30.30	29.50	33.60	36.20	33.76

[1] Preliminary.   Source: Economic Research Service, U.S. Department of Agriculture (ERS-USDA)

Average Price Received by Farmers for Lambs in the United States   In Dollars Per Cwt.

Year	Jan.	Feb.	Mar.	Apr.	May	June	July	Aug.	Sept.	Oct.	Nov.	Dec.	Average
1992	53.50	55.20	63.40	69.30	68.80	65.60	62.20	55.90	56.70	55.40	58.20	65.20	60.78
1993	67.30	72.70	76.00	68.10	61.50	55.70	53.90	59.20	64.50	64.50	65.80	66.00	64.60
1994	60.60	59.40	58.60	54.50	54.50	63.00	72.80	75.50	71.20	68.00	70.60	69.10	64.82
1995	67.50	70.40	74.80	74.60	80.40	85.70	85.70	85.60	82.70	77.60	77.10	76.50	78.22
1996	76.10	84.30	86.60	85.90	90.30	100.70	98.30	89.10	88.50	87.00	84.60	88.20	88.30
1997	94.60	99.80	99.70	96.40	90.80	86.50	81.10	92.70	90.20	87.20	83.10	83.90	90.50
1998	78.40	75.00	70.10	66.00	63.00	88.90	81.30	80.10	71.80	67.60	62.60	64.70	72.46
1999	68.20	67.20	67.40	67.40	82.80	81.30	77.00	80.30	75.30	72.60	76.30	77.60	74.45
2000[1]	70.90	72.00	80.20	82.60	96.40	89.70	87.00	83.60	80.80	76.80	71.50	71.80	80.28

[1] Preliminary.   Source: Economic Research Service, U.S. Department of Agriculture (ERS-USDA)

232

Silk

Silk is the cloth and thread made from silkworms. The fiber used in commercial silk production is produced primarily by the mulberry silkworm. Silk is produced in a number of countries where the requirement is primarily a favorable climate and adequate labor. A primary requirement of silk production is an adequate number of mulberry trees. The mulberry leaf-feeding silkworm thrives on mulberry leaves. The silkworm, which is a caterpillar, has been domesticated for thousands of years. The silkworm spins a cocoon made of silk fiber. In a matter of a few days, one silkworm can spin a cocoon of unbroken thread as much as 600 meters in length. The process of collecting the silk fiber is called reeling. Reeling is the bringing together of two or more cocoons to form them into one continuous strand of silk.

World production of silk has seen little trend. Between 1988 and 1991, production averaged 83,600 metric tonnes. Increased production by China allowed world production to increase in 1992-1995 to 110,000 tonnes per year. That was followed by a decline in silk production in China, and in the 1996-1997 period world production averaged 83,500 tonnes. By far, the world's largest producer of silk is China. Production by China is about 60 percent of the world total. The next largest producer of silk is India with production averaging about 15,000 tonnes per year. Other large producers

of silk include North Korea, Japan, Brazil, Uzbekistan, Thailand, Vietnam, and Turkmenistan.

China, the world's largest exporter of silk, has been trying to reduce its surplus production capacity. While China produces and exports the most silk, it has a large amount of excess capacity in terms of the number of spindles devoted to silk. In Thailand, in late 2000, a group of textile firms stopped construction of a silk production zone in the central part of the country. The reason construction was halted was because of slow growth in the textile industry. Uzbekistan has been making an effort to increase production of silk. Uzbekistan had been a large producer of silk in the late 1980's and early 1990's.

The major exporters of silk are China, Hong Kong, Brazil, North Korea, and Japan. Among the major importers are Japan, India, Italy, Hong Kong, South Korea, and France. Japan imports about 20 percent of the world's silk exports. China exports about one-half of the world's silk.

Futures Markets

Raw silk is traded on the Kansai Agricultural Commodities Exchange (KANEX). Dried cocoons are traded on the Chuba Commodity Exchange (CCE). Raw silk and dried cocoons are traded on the Yokohama Commodity Exchange.

World Production of Raw Silk   In Metric Tons

Year	Brazil	China	India	Iran	Japan	North Korea	South Korea	Kyrgy-zstan[3]	Thailand	Turkmen-istan[3]	Uzbek-istan[3]	Viet Nam	World Total
1988	1,900	42,041	10,255	900	6,862	3,800	1,355	-----	1,250	-----	4,300	420	73,866
1989	1,697	50,244	10,500	537	6,078	4,000	1,400	-----	1,250	-----	3,900	400	80,745
1990	1,693	55,003	11,000	537	6,000	4,200	971	-----	1,250	-----	4,094	500	85,987
1991	2,077	60,002	14,000	537	5,527	4,400	837	-----	1,300	-----	4,100	500	93,880
1992	2,296	70,302	15,000	537	5,085	4,500	870	1,200	1,300	600	2,200	500	105,220
1993	2,450	76,801	14,168	480	4,254	4,600	683	1,000	1,500	500	2,000	550	109,790
1994	2,450	84,001	14,500	600	2,400	4,700	700	1,000	1,600	500	2,000	600	115,796
1995	2,450	80,001	15,000	600	2,400	4,700	700	1,000	1,600	500	2,000	650	112,350
1996[1]	2,000	51,000	16,000	1,000	3,000	5,000	-----	1,000	1,000	1,000	2,000	1,000	84,000
1997[2]	2,000	51,000	16,000	1,000	3,000	5,000	-----	1,000	1,000	1,000	2,000	1,000	83,000

[1] Preliminary.   [2] Estimate.   [3] Formerly part of the U.S.S.R.; data not reported separately until 1992.   *Source: Food and Agricultural Organization of the United Nations (FAO-UN)*

World Trade of Silk by Selected Countries   In Metric Tons

	Imports							Exports					
Year	France	Hong Kong	India	Italy	Japan	South Korea	World Total	Brazil	China	Hong Kong	Japan	North Korea	World Total
1988	771	7,489	1,411	8,094	10,259	4,851	39,216	670	20,168	8,553	442	1,200	37,276
1989	1,012	6,362	1,400	7,740	8,512	3,763	35,968	534	19,314	6,748	417	1,100	39,064
1990	796	3,928	1,647	4,775	7,111	3,204	27,322	1,064	13,066	4,102	380	1,200	27,977
1991	579	4,347	2,100	5,297	6,933	3,519	29,623	2,052	15,178	4,186	405	900	29,188
1992	693	4,400	2,843	4,337	5,137	3,627	28,239	1,552	13,474	4,358	701	800	26,433
1993	1,001	5,475	4,977	5,634	5,982	4,494	36,086	1,495	15,652	7,204	904	1,200	35,634
1994	1,047	6,165	5,750	9,235	5,772	4,128	44,136	1,739	21,004	6,149	1,265	1,400	41,998
1995	663	4,775	4,276	5,612	4,331	3,513	37,854	966	16,788	5,176	925	1,000	40,633
1996	675	3,978	2,980	4,400	6,098	3,737	36,629	1,071	15,791	4,165	946	1,000	38,650
1997[1]	582	4,320	4,204	5,482	4,229	2,796	46,802	905	14,382	4,501	936	1,000	37,468

[1] Preliminary.   *Source: Food and Agricultural Organization of the United Nations (FAO-UN)*

Silver

Silver prices spent most of the year 2000 moving sideways to lower. The market was reacting to a perceived supply glut along with sluggish consumption prospects. What made the decline interesting was the fact that other metals that silver typically would mirror moved higher. Despite this, the price trend in silver remained lower. In late 2000, gold prices moved somewhat higher while silver moved lower allowing the gold-silver ratio to increase further. There were expectations in the market of more selling by Russian and Chinese producers though increased sales at such low prices are somewhat suspect. One seller of silver has been the U.S. Government. The National Defense Stockpile has been selling silver for some time. Over the past 17 years, from 1982 to 1999, the Government has reduced the quantity of silver in the stockpile by 80 percent from 4,300 metric tonnes down to 815 tonnes. The remainder of the National Defense Stockpile will be moved to the U.S. Mint for use in coins. After all of its stocks are used the U.S. Mint will have to buy silver on the open market.

The U.S. Geological Survey reported that world mine production of silver in 1999 was estimated at 15,900 tonnes, down 3 percent from 1998 when production was estimated at 16,400 tonnes. The U.S. is a major producer of silver with 1999 mine production of 1,860 tonnes, down 10 percent from a year ago. The largest producer of silver in 1999 was Mexico with output of 2,700 tonnes, about 1 percent more than in 1998. Silver production by Peru in 1999 was estimated at 1,900 tonnes, about the same as in 1998. Australia's production was 1,500 tonnes, up 2 percent from 1998, while Canada produced 1,100 tonnes. China is also a large producer.

World reserves of silver are estimated at 280,000 tonnes which includes silver that is recoverable from base metal ores. Approximately two-thirds of the world's silver resources are associated with copper, lead, and zinc deposits which are often in deep mines. Another one-third of the silver resources are found in gold deposits.

Use of silver in photographic applications accounts for about 28 percent of consumption. In conventional photography silver halide film is used. The new digital technologies convert images into electronic form and do not use silver. There are advantages and disadvantages in both methods. Digital cameras are expensive and the picture quality in not as good. Silver finds use in many other products including jewelry and coins. Silver is used for reflecting surfaces though aluminum and rhodium can be substituted. Silver is also used in surgical plates and pins though tantalum can be used as a substitute for silver. Stainless steel is also a replacement for silver in table flatware. U.S. apparent consumption of silver in 1999 was estimated to be 4,500 tonnes, up 5 percent from 1998.

In the U.S., the largest producing state is Nevada. About one-half of domestic silver production is found with precious metal ores. The other half is recovered as a by-product of processing copper, lead, and zinc ores. There were 22 principal refiners of commercial-grade silver in 2000. There were about 30 fabricators of silver which accounted for 90 percent of the silver used in arts and industry. On the industrial side, silver finds use in electrical products, catalysts, brazing alloys, dental products, and bearings. U.S. primary refinery production of silver in 1999 was 2,300 tonnes, while secondary production was 1,700 tonnes.

U.S. mine production of silver in July 2000 was estimated at 156,000 kilograms, down 7 percent from the previous month. In the January-July 2000 period, production totaled 1.19 million kilograms. Production by Nevada in July 2000 was 56,700 kilograms and in the January-July 2000 period production was 440,000 kilograms. Silver production in Idaho in July 2000 was 34,200 kilograms. In the first seven months of 2000, Idaho silver production was 240,000 kilograms.

U.S. imports for consumption of silver bullion in June 2000 were 222,000 kilograms. The major suppliers of silver bullion were Canada, Mexico, and the United Kingdom. For all of 1999, imports of silver bullion were 2.66 million kilograms. Imports of silver powder in June 2000 were 40,100 kilograms with the major suppliers being Canada, Japan, and Germany. U.S. exports of silver nitrate (gross weight) in June 2000 were 24,500 kilograms. In January-June 2000, total exports were 108,000 kilograms.

Futures Markets

Silver futures are traded on the New York Mercantile Exchange, COMEX Division (COMEX), the Chicago Board of Trade (CBOT), the Mid America Commodity Exchange (MidAm), the London Metals Exchange (LME), and the Tokyo Commodity Exchange (TOCOM). Options are traded on the Amsterdam Exchanges (AEX) and the COMEX.

World Mine Production of Silver   In Thousands of Kilograms In Metric Tons

Year	Australia	Bolivia	Canada[3]	Chile	China	Kazakhstan[4]	Rep. of Korea	Mexico	Peru	Poland	Sweden	United States	World Total[2]
1990	1,173	311	1,501	655	130	2,500	238	2,425	1,930	832	243	2,121	16,600
1991	1,180	376	1,339	678	150	2,200	265	2,295	1,927	899	239	1,860	15,600
1992	1,218	282	1,220	1,029	800	500	333	2,098	1,614	798	210	1,800	14,900
1993	1,092	333	896	970	840	500	215	2,136	1,671	767	255	1,640	14,100
1994	1,045	352	768	983	810	506	257	2,215	1,768	1,064	276	1,490	14,000
1995	939	425	1,285	1,041	910	489	299	2,324	1,929	1,001	268	1,560	14,900
1996	1,013	384	1,309	1,047	1,140	468	254	2,528	1,970	935	272	1,570	15,000
1997	1,106	387	1,224	1,091	1,300	465	268	2,679	1,998	1,029	304	2,180	16,100
1998[1]	1,474	404	1,196	1,340	1,400	470	339	2,686	2,025	1,100	299	2,060	17,000
1999[2]	1,720	422	1,246	1,780	1,400	575	489	2,338	2,217	1,100	300	1,950	17,700

[1] Preliminary.   [2] Estimate.   [3] Shipments.   [4] Formerly part of the U.S.S.R.; data not reported separately until 1992.
Source: U.S. Geological Survey (USGS)

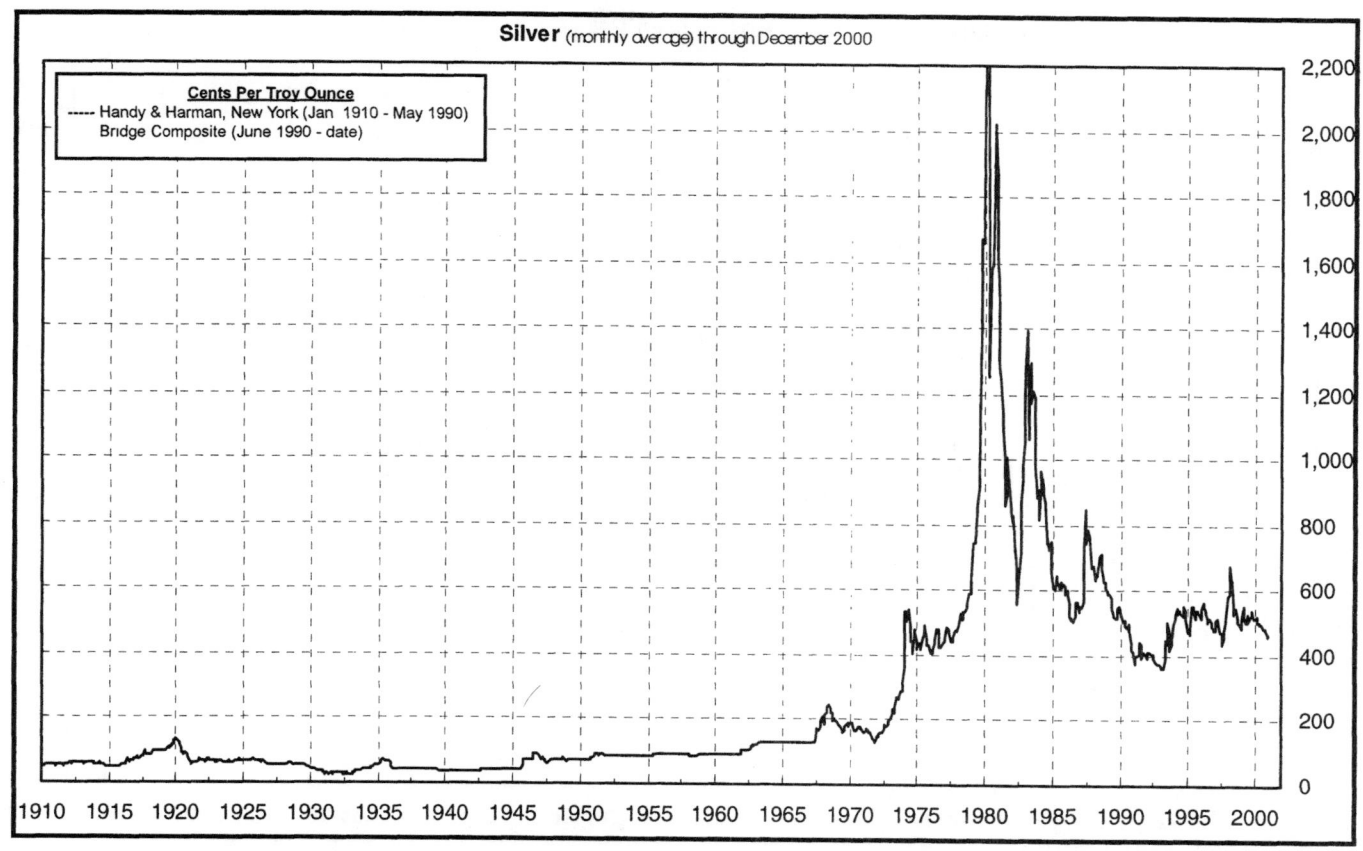

Silver (monthly average) through December 2000

Cents Per Troy Ounce
----- Handy & Harman, New York (Jan 1910 - May 1990)
Bridge Composite (June 1990 - date)

Average Price of Silver in New York (Handy & Harman)   In Cents Per Troy Ounce (.999 Fine)

Year	Jan.	Feb.	Mar.	Apr.	May	June	July	Aug.	Sept.	Oct.	Nov.	Dec.	Average
1991	402.82	372.34	396.90	397.07	404.07	438.85	430.38	393.80	403.60	410.22	406.05	390.90	403.92
1992	412.08	413.71	410.36	403.00	406.83	405.64	394.89	379.67	376.33	373.66	376.32	370.98	393.62
1993	367.93	364.39	364.80	396.36	445.02	437.50	503.74	480.61	417.19	433.45	450.25	496.83	429.84
1994	513.14	527.24	545.11	530.87	543.64	539.34	528.65	519.54	552.88	544.10	519.60	476.88	528.42
1995	476.36	469.53	464.83	552.42	555.25	535.27	517.58	539.59	540.78	534.48	529.30	514.75	519.18
1996	547.03	562.75	551.38	540.14	536.02	513.58	502.95	510.50	501.57	492.76	481.69	480.14	518.34
1997	483.70	508.76	519.88	476.41	475.80	474.60	435.96	451.36	472.69	501.15	507.30	571.53	489.07
1998	584.58	672.61	617.18	628.86	558.65	526.05	546.82	516.45	502.67	500.18	498.39	476.85	552.68
1999	511.61	554.55	519.85	509.21	529.83	507.73	522.81	529.36	527.86	541.67	519.20	521.95	524.75
2000	523.47	529.65	510.15	510.37	504.30	505.20	501.82	492.76	494.50	488.14	471.93	466.40	499.89

Source: American Metal Market (AMM)

Average Price of Silver in London (Spot Fix)   In Pence Per Troy Ounce (.999 Fine)

Year	Jan.	Feb.	Mar.	Apr.	May	June	July	Aug.	Sept.	Oct.	Nov.	Dec.	Average
1990	317.67	311.77	312.45	309.08	302.29	287.85	269.56	263.50	255.45	225.76	212.45	210.97	273.23
1991	209.50	190.10	216.00	227.61	234.43	266.86	263.97	235.06	234.22	238.90	229.09	228.03	231.15
1992	227.68	233.21	238.36	230.72	225.02	219.32	206.74	197.03	203.89	226.06	246.94	240.01	224.58
1993	240.39	254.41	249.55	256.16	287.61	289.42	335.27	324.64	276.85	285.48	306.07	332.78	286.55
1994	344.48	354.77	364.74	358.95	360.86	353.28	341.86	336.67	353.15	339.73	326.64	306.49	345.14
1995	302.80	300.36	290.35	341.95	248.74	336.31	323.80	343.72	348.99	340.29	339.90	336.05	329.44
1996	359.20	367.64	362.03	392.85	354.25	334.68	325.81	330.93	322.98	310.78	290.51	289.77	336.79
1997	287.63	311.95	323.99	293.08	291.43	289.16	272.73	280.36	295.67	308.69	300.76	348.90	300.36
1998	359.62	416.55	375.76	378.77	339.42	319.05	331.87	317.74	297.40	295.41	298.72	291.77	335.17
1999	312.69	340.46	320.27	315.12	326.80	315.51	328.86	327.98	322.20	326.42	317.53	319.87	322.75

Source: American Metal Market (AMM)

SILVER

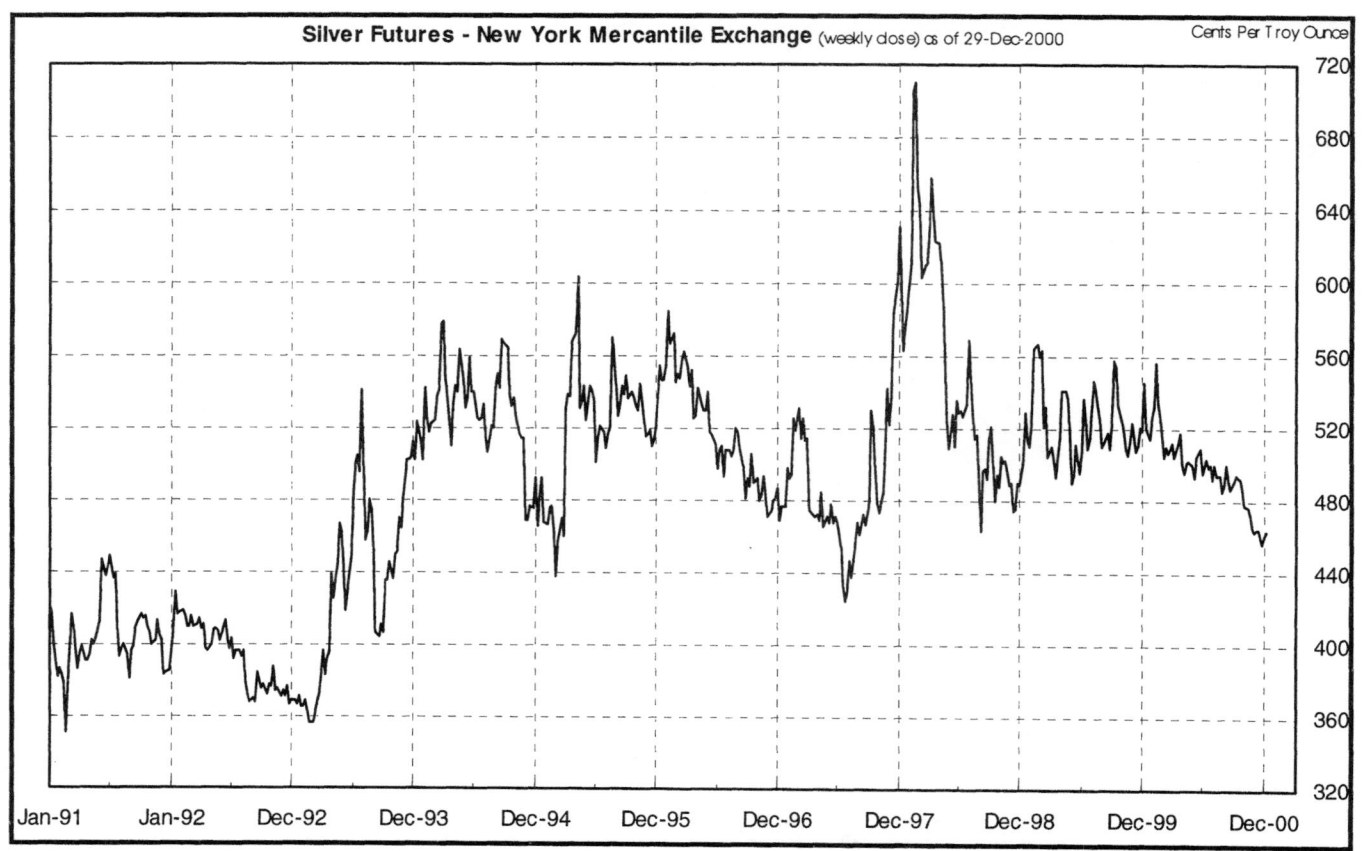

Average Open Interest of Silver Futures in New York (COMEX) In Contracts

Year	Jan.	Feb.	Mar.	Apr.	May	June	July	Aug.	Sept.	Oct.	Nov.	Dec.
1991	91,685	101,352	99,564	99,791	94,921	105,646	97,554	95,536	87,079	90,791	89,765	91,390
1992	97,179	93,352	88,445	96,427	87,355	84,002	80,879	81,695	74,265	72,090	77,633	72,296
1993	80,155	86,241	87,127	100,985	105,931	102,539	107,537	109,427	93,891	93,316	101,576	110,029
1994	112,584	116,652	112,745	119,314	121,296	126,255	122,138	118,081	113,261	117,224	126,666	134,099
1995	132,158	139,806	132,317	129,063	112,723	108,941	101,842	111,251	95,433	101,763	105,453	95,551
1996	99,316	107,667	92,186	101,011	99,529	110,247	105,627	103,618	93,448	95,809	93,238	83,879
1997	91,385	94,539	90,531	97,434	87,510	90,145	96,777	89,250	79,344	100,464	96,695	93,761
1998	95,717	108,284	91,730	83,045	79,451	91,563	78,353	82,530	74,848	74,451	76,440	78,716
1999	77,946	97,593	82,435	82,824	78,745	78,943	78,151	86,601	77,490	86,577	80,564	70,275
2000	76,187	81,398	75,765	76,213	75,001	76,466	75,199	91,083	73,441	78,222	83,142	73,644

Source: New York Mercantile Exchange (NYMEX), COMEX Division

Volume of Trading of Silver Futures in New York (COMEX) In Contracts

Year	Jan.	Feb.	Mar.	Apr.	May	June	July	Aug.	Sept.	Oct.	Nov.	Dec.	Total
1991	309,841	420,092	446,491	395,957	255,548	547,495	344,683	320,639	268,660	252,983	349,698	242,617	4,154,704
1992	408,179	320,226	229,010	322,364	184,825	295,358	197,946	266,347	173,165	125,537	355,728	127,654	3,016,339
1993	167,201	315,916	242,974	476,554	433,460	523,961	503,935	531,772	428,366	338,189	520,591	373,005	4,855,924
1994	489,055	555,136	484,134	585,058	516,396	729,414	339,298	535,722	377,540	455,049	589,220	348,323	5,994,345
1995	390,453	501,454	541,807	592,620	500,522	476,481	280,651	655,854	344,182	272,362	447,095	179,755	5,183,236
1996	415,801	583,767	368,175	547,629	334,973	549,631	296,905	460,686	316,366	321,781	415,441	259,653	4,870,808
1997	401,995	530,514	360,871	493,999	280,536	472,306	340,245	425,471	335,400	430,397	488,024	333,762	4,893,520
1998	352,688	550,800	368,127	360,130	310,130	393,971	278,774	367,257	283,475	280,066	319,216	229,982	4,094,616
1999	315,165	550,271	355,559	424,822	274,002	373,662	288,480	422,653	328,907	318,256	344,289	161,434	4,157,500
2000	258,053	425,910	231,336	318,752	216,938	407,455	175,235	370,739	146,007	149,252	303,673	113,667	3,117,017

Source: New York Mercantile Exchange (NYMEX), COMEX division

Mine Production of Recoverable Silver in the United States   In Metric Tons

Year	Arizona	Idaho	Montana	Nevada	Total	Year	Arizona	Idaho	Montana	Nevada	Total
1988	152	340	192	608	1,661	1994	183	158	71	602	1,390
1989	171	439	194	625	2,007	1995	220	182	76	766	1,640
1990	173	442	220	646	2,125	1996	189	234	11	596	1,570
1991	148	337	222	578	1,848	1997	190	341	W	878	2,180
1992	153	255	195	586	1,740	1998	211	447	W	670	2,060
1993	157	190	125	713	1,610	1999[1]	183	416	W	597	1,950

[1] Preliminary.   W = Withheld proprietary data.   Source: U.S. Geological Survey (USGS)

Consumption of Silver in the United States, by End Use   In Millions of Troy Ounces

Year	Brazing Alloy & Solders	Catalysts	Batteries	Mirrors	Electrical Contacts-Conductors	Photo-graphic Materials	Silver-plate	Jewelry	Sterling Ware	Total Net Industrial Con-sumption	Coinage	Total Con-sumption
1990	2.8	3.0	3.0	1.2	23.3	67.0	2.8	2.0	3.5	121.6	9.4	131.0
1991	5.6	3.3	3.1	1.1	18.3	60.0	2.8	2.0	3.5	118.7	9.1	127.8
1992	7.1	3.8	3.1	1.2	18.3	64.4	2.9	3.0	3.9	118.9	8.1	127.0
1993	7.2	4.0	3.3	1.3	18.8	65.0	3.0	3.3	4.0	121.1	8.9	130.0
1994	7.5	4.2	3.6	1.5	19.5	71.0	3.1	3.7	4.2	130.1	8.1	138.2
1995	7.7	4.9	4.1	1.7	20.9	72.9	3.5	4.1	4.4	136.2	7.5	143.7
1996	8.2	5.5	4.5	2.1	22.3	78.3	3.9	4.4	4.8	146.7	5.0	151.7
1997	8.9	5.7	4.8	2.4	26.5	84.6	4.1	4.9	5.1	160.5	5.3	165.8
1998	9.3	5.9	4.9	2.6	28.4	91.0	4.5	5.5	5.7	172.3	5.6	177.9
1999[1]	9.1	5.9	5.0	2.6	29.2	96.0	4.4	5.7	5.8	178.5	10.0	188.5

[1] Preliminary.   Source: The Silver Institute

Commodity Exchange, Inc. (COMEX) Warehouse of Stocks of Silver   In Thousands of Troy Ounces

Year	Jan. 1	Feb. 1	Mar. 1	Apr. 1	May 1	June 1	July 1	Aug. 1	Sept. 1	Oct. 1	Nov. 1	Dec. 1
1991	266,206	263,832	257,851	263,563	263,686	266,087	276,961	270,804	269,661	265,874	262,835	270,734
1992	271,692	278,990	270,449	262,239	267,003	267,818	271,259	273,743	278,575	278,526	280,712	275,156
1993	272,824	273,629	271,856	265,580	270,800	273,947	277,228	278,745	276,819	275,370	277,666	263,138
1994	251,685	250,730	239,374	240,187	233,950	236,459	246,291	249,417	255,198	259,634	265,710	258,618
1995	260,708	264,045	235,114	211,028	189,668	184,570	181,269	175,764	156,544	156,529	156,110	156,932
1996	159,695	143,426	151,336	139,059	141,789	150,141	168,079	155,441	151,283	141,673	129,911	148,451
1997	204,051	195,450	193,381	191,676	189,498	201,682	184,691	169,079	164,296	138,775	133,470	128,252
1998	110,437	103,778	89,458	86,926	89,715	89,628	85,911	79,136	78,681	73,142	133,470	128,252
1999	76,301	75,017	78,135	79,664	79,415	76,976	73,973	77,592	80,126	73,142	74,260	76,818
2000	75,984	73,326	95,594	104,053	102,589	99,053	102,713	101,786	97,133	99,552	95,387	95,717

Source: New York Mercantile Exchange (NYMEX), COMEX Division

Production[2] of Refined Silver in the United States, from All Sources   In Metric Tons

Year	Jan.	Feb.	Mar.	Apr.	May	June	July	Aug.	Sept.	Oct.	Nov.	Dec.	Total
1991	273	209	229	228	285	236	220	254	263	259	250	268	2,973
1992	414	388	396	375	408	295	366	350	323	393	331	364	4,403
1993	359	406	374	357	315	266	293	275	292	293	261	303	3,794
1994	278	327	319	307	209	371	239	288	273	254	297	281	3,443
1995	279	273	340	281	381	355	331	404	364	340	384	351	4,083
1996	373	299	332	321	327	316	354	314	333	344	304	403	4,020
1997	343	262	296	331	250	326	292	344	331	281	340	382	3,778
1998	338	486	426	372	377	374	394	324	463	443	469	447	4,860
1999	424	420	441	356	368	394	404	316	354	371	364	396	4,608
2000[1]	435	1,175	566	399	427	390	360	402	393				6,063

[1] Preliminary.   [2] Through 1991; output of commercial bars .999 fine, including U.S. Mint purchases of crude. Production is from both foreign and domestic silver. Beginning 1992; U.S. mine production of recoverable silver plus imports of refined silver.   Source: U.S. Geological Survey (USGS)

SILVER

U.S. Exports of Refined Silver to Selected Countries   In Thousands of Troy Ounces

Year	Canada	France	Germany	Hong Kong	Japan	Singapore	South Korea	Switzerland	United Arab Emirates	United Kingdom	Uruguay	Other Countries	World Total
1990	2,586	64	749	----	16,568	1,005	298	74	----	2,060	152	108	23,664
1991	736	22	350	755	6,519	1,593	2,823	8	3,462	8,628	259	73	25,318
1992	2,177	44	140	497	4,554	2,126	2	70	6,922	10,856	671	47	29,274
1993	4,910	2	34	1,002	3,414	2,500	1,492	38	4,403	3,673	530	44	22,673
1994	3,138	2	8	456	10,385	16	2,701	14	4,823	4,212	1,489	14	27,889
1995	1,665	431	2	2	5,819	2,209	2,932	1,177	10,288	63,980	939	5	90,462
1996	489	2	2	646	4,662	3,601	383	2,413	15,850	35,366	624	40	93,346
1997	903	2	2	797	6,044	2	547	5,305	16,751	62,694	402	17	96,038
1998	485	2,206	347	----	579	208	----	20	3,569	60,444	621	9	72,479
1999[1]	11	2	1	----	585	37	----	----	4,249	7,719	----	20	15,455

[1] Preliminary.   [2] Included in other countries, if any.   Source: American Bureau of Metal Statistics, Inc. (ABMS)

U.S. Imports of Silver From Selected Countries   In Thousands of Troy Ounces

Year	Canada	Mexico	Other Countries	Total	Canada	Chile	Mexico	Peru	Uruguay	Other Countries	Total
1990	12	189	2	203	33,518	1,671	40,204	8,141	2,265	942	86,741
1991	42	277	29	348	25,389	6,640	34,448	13,748	2	973	81,198
1992	646	126	42	814	24,937	2,002	40,230	16,841	400	1,162	85,572
1993	299	836	12	1,147	28,622	1,058	27,241	12,709	2	559	70,189
1994	369	3,805	97	4,271	28,678	1,923	22,135	12,663	2	742	66,141
1995	338	6,655	243	7,236	27,649	2,003	31,957	13,728	2	9,197	84,534
1996	256	4,662	----	4,918	35,365	1,874	30,285	12,153	2	3,122	82,799
1997	7	4,437	85	4,529	29,385	608	28,774	8,873	2	376	68,016
1998	24	5,851	419	6,294	34,722	813	41,152	9,388	2	3,931	90,006
1999[1]	11	335	1	347	42,952	1,048	33,050	5,433	2	2,562	85,045

[1] Preliminary.   [2] Included in other countries, if any.   Source: American Bureau of Metal Statistics, Inc. (ABMS)

World Silver Consumption[1]   In Millions of Troy Ounces

Year	Industrial Uses										Coinage							Grand Total
	Canada	France	Germany	India	Italy	Japan	Mexico	United Kingdom	United States	World Total	Austria	Canada	France	Germany	Mexico	United States	World Total	
1990	4.6	24.1	51.7	46.8	51.4	106.9	12.9	24.6	121.6	684.6	.5	1.9	2.1	2.6	1.2	9.4	32.1	716.7
1991	3.8	26.0	52.2	44.8	56.5	108.8	13.5	25.0	119.8	677.8	.6	.9	2.3	5.7	1.6	10.8	29.2	707.0
1992	1.5	28.8	49.3	58.1	60.1	104.9	14.2	26.3	127.1	681.1	.5	.8	2.1	5.6	8.7	8.5	33.5	714.6
1993	1.6	28.1	45.7	108.8	56.3	105.5	14.9	27.7	131.6	739.1	.5	1.2	2.1	2.8	17.1	9.2	41.5	780.6
1994	1.6	27.2	45.7	93.9	51.6	108.4	14.6	30.4	140.4	722.4	.5	1.5	1.0	7.1	13.0	9.5	43.8	766.2
1995	2.0	30.0	43.6	101.3	49.5	112.7	16.9	31.6	148.7	752.7	.5	.7	1.2	2.4	.6	9.0	24.7	777.4
1996	2.0	26.9	41.0	122.2	51.7	112.1	20.3	33.8	155.0	785.8	.5	.7	.3	4.6	.5	7.1	23.3	809.1
1997	2.2	28.3	42.3	122.9	56.1	119.9	23.3	34.9	166.3	828.2	.4	.6	.3	3.7	.4	6.5	28.5	856.7
1998	2.3	28.3	38.4	104.3	56.0	112.8	22.0	38.6	181.8	809.9	.3	1.1	.3	8.4	.2	7.0	26.1	836.0
1999[2]	2.1	26.2	35.1	109.0	62.0	125.2	23.0	39.3	193.9	850.4	.3	1.4	.3	5.4	.4	11.2	27.0	877.4

[1] Non-communist areas only.   [2] Preliminary.   Source: The Silver Institute

Soybean Meal

Soybean meal prices, basis Chicago futures, slowly strengthened during 2000 following a basically flat market in 1999. Prices started the year in the vicinity of $150 per ton and towards year-end were near $200. The price action, however, was nearly opposite that seen in soybean oil.

The world supply/demand statistics for soybean meal have shown persistent growth during the past decade and that trend is likely to persist due to the expansion in global poultry numbers. Soybean meal, a high protein feed used in formulating livestock and poultry rations, is obtained from the processing (crush) of soybeans and is the world's top protein meal with about 60-65 percent of total meal production (112 million short tons in 2000/01 out of a total of 172 million). Cottonseed and rapeseed meals account for a combined total of about 20 percent of protein meal production. The U.S. is the largest producer followed by Brazil and Argentina.

World soybean meal production in the mid-1990's averaged about 90 million metric tonnes. In 2000/01, a record large 112 million metric tonnes were produced, of which the U.S. produced a record 34.8 million tonnes, a shade below initial estimates. Brazil's production reached a record 17.1 million tonnes vs. 16.6 million in 1999/00. Argentina's production of 14.5 million tonnes in 2000/01 was higher than expected and compared to 14.0 million tonnes in 1999/00.

Part of the growth in meal production has been indirectly derived from the strong worldwide demand for vegetable oils, but again the primary reason is that more countries have increasing livestock numbers and a burgeoning need for high protein feed; a fact underscored by the sharp expansion in the world's soybean meal trade. Significantly, many of the recent gains in foreign trade have come from developing nations in Latin America and Asia.

World soybean meal consumption in 2000/01 of a record large 112.6 million tonnes compares with 109.7 million in 1999/00. The U.S. is the largest single consumer with about 28 million tonnes annually in recent years, but the European Union and Asia run a close second and third with 27 million and 29 million tonnes, respectively, in 2000/01. Asia's usage was particularly strong during the past decade reflecting the growth in the region's poultry production. China's 2000/01 consumption of a record 13.5 million tonnes compares with an annual average of less than 10 million prior to 1996/97. Despite China's surging demand imports

have dropped, totaling only 1 million tonnes in 2000/01 vs. a record large 4.2 million in 1997/98. Still, early in the 1990's, China was a net exporter of soybean meal. France in 2000/01 was the largest single importer with almost 4.0 million tonnes, about 10 percent of the world total. Exports are dominated by Argentina and Brazil with a combined 24 million tonnes in 2000/01, out of a 39.6 million tonne total.

World carryover at the end of the 2000/01 season is forecast at 3.9 million tonnes, marginally lower than both initial estimates and the year earlier total of 4.1 million tonnes. As usual, Argentina and Brazil account for at least one-third of the carryover.

U.S. soybean meal production (October-September) in 2000/01 of a record 38 million short tons compares with 37.6 million in 1999/00. Total 2000/01 supplies of 38.4 million tons compares with 38 million in 1999/00, including a small carry-in at the start of each crop year of about 300,000 tons. Total supplies in the early 1990's averaged near 30 million tons. Domestic usage climbed steadily in the 1990's and is expected to total a record high 31 million tons in 2000/01 vs. 30.5 million in 1999/00, also due to increases in poultry production. It now appears that poultry demand controls the U.S. soybean crush, and not the soybean oil factor. Cattle accounts for little soybean meal use, hogs somewhat more.

U.S. soybean meal exports in 2000/01 were forecast at 7.1 million short tons vs. 7.3 million in 1999/00, and a record large 9.3 million in 1997/98. The decline reflects lower demand from China and increased competition from Brazil and Argentina, but a contributing factor in 2000/01 is weaker demand from the European Union.

U.S. soybean meal wholesale prices, basis 44 percent protein, Decatur, Illinois, in 1999/2000 averaged $176 per short ton vs. $145 in 1998/99, and the 1988/89-1997/98 average of $193 per ton. Rotterdam prices tend to average about $4 per ton higher and Brazilian prices about $6 above U.S. prices.

Futures Markets

Soybean meal futures and options are traded on the Chicago Board of Trade (CBOT). A smaller futures contract is traded on the Mid-America Commodity Exchange (MidAm).

World Supply and Distribution of Soybean Meal   In Thousands of Metric Tons

Year Beginning Oct. 1	Production					Exports			Imports		Consumption			Ending Stocks		
	Brazil	China	European Union	United States	Total	Brazil	United States	Total	France	Total	European Union	United States	Total	Brazil	United States	Total
1991-2	11,556	2,745	10,536	27,062	72,837	8,136	6,313	27,928	3,546	27,681	21,174	20,860	72,529	467	209	2,927
1992-3	13,161	3,634	10,991	27,546	77,497	9,301	5,673	29,025	3,500	27,980	22,249	21,981	76,050	526	185	3,329
1993-4	14,726	6,160	9,855	27,682	81,304	10,519	4,867	30,105	3,798	29,508	22,862	22,927	80,996	434	136	3,040
1994-5	16,977	6,958	11,825	30,182	89,346	11,471	6,092	32,389	3,792	31,502	25,068	24,081	87,770	640	203	3,729
1995-6	15,841	6,051	11,387	29,508	87,986	10,900	5,446	32,218	3,343	32,692	23,462	24,140	88,705	381	193	3,484
1996-7	14,863	5,963	11,987	31,035	89,654	9,800	6,344	32,576	3,266	34,397	22,334	24,785	91,866	344	191	3,093
1997-8	17,235	6,717	12,866	34,633	103,793	10,850	8,464	41,446	3,647	37,590	24,740	26,213	100,091	332	198	2,939
1998-9	17,000	10,023	12,912	34,285	107,903	10,150	6,461	38,881	4,106	39,341	27,655	27,812	107,357	457	300	3,945
1999-00[1]	16,255	11,815	12,015	34,131	108,555	9,300	6,651	38,445	4,070	39,240	26,823	27,559	109,875	402	266	3,420
2000-1[2]	17,475	13,150	12,719	34,670	114,041	10,200	6,623	40,013	4,187	40,285	27,871	28,122	114,280	477	250	3,453

[1] Preliminary.   [2] Forecast.   *Source: Foreign Agricultural Service, U.S. Department of Agriculture (FAS-USDA)*

SOYBEAN MEAL

Soybean Meal Futures - Chicago Board of Trade (weekly close) as of 29-Dec-2000

Average Open Interest of Soybean Meal Futures in Chicago   In Contracts

Year	Jan.	Feb.	Mar.	Apr.	May	June	July	Aug.	Sept.	Oct.	Nov.	Dec.
1991	62,172	60,017	56,179	59,107	49,973	57,068	55,629	54,342	67,765	68,627	68,263	71,900
1992	67,575	56,453	55,370	59,528	57,204	60,519	66,315	66,861	66,648	72,403	73,255	72,881
1993	63,178	70,384	64,550	66,121	78,386	74,191	91,435	73,770	75,267	77,065	83,802	85,039
1994	87,612	91,142	82,193	89,453	85,553	81,721	84,461	82,691	85,508	94,483	101,030	98,717
1995	97,661	101,253	101,846	99,898	90,237	86,090	83,712	74,233	79,450	85,290	103,824	110,193
1996	95,903	90,010	87,468	101,204	91,453	88,641	77,961	80,727	93,373	88,969	90,007	84,399
1997	86,204	97,618	107,763	111,413	113,848	110,780	114,372	108,923	111,447	118,409	125,201	116,760
1998	114,243	122,979	131,390	137,251	136,212	136,216	126,108	139,239	140,904	141,426	134,095	122,788
1999	123,041	130,473	121,435	112,155	104,176	108,134	116,464	121,202	120,462	112,426	117,523	104,246
2000	115,285	124,822	120,157	123,957	123,691	112,425	105,230	94,469	105,240	103,263	120,164	127,529

Source: Chicago Board of Trade (CBT)

Volume of Trading of Soybean Meal Futures in Chicago   In Contracts

Year	Jan.	Feb.	Mar.	Apr.	May	June	July	Aug.	Sept.	Oct.	Nov.	Dec.	Total[1]
1991	323,403	281,772	310,004	429,281	296,782	412,475	484,290	463,616	394,712	410,790	351,607	339,555	4,498.3
1992	368,714	290,492	312,556	312,187	388,097	380,975	425,995	333,639	327,556	320,176	327,854	357,156	4,145.4
1993	295,555	273,673	346,607	323,253	356,757	518,212	575,510	460,550	402,399	315,643	469,343	380,593	4,718.1
1994	405,590	339,834	330,694	380,736	467,223	456,279	384,508	354,372	366,263	317,438	370,377	420,500	4,593.8
1995	283,623	307,477	404,387	410,860	532,694	479,589	610,833	491,775	481,949	449,009	523,440	625,606	5,601.2
1996	496,414	442,937	435,764	655,984	439,212	442,370	507,240	490,349	425,850	581,126	491,917	452,139	5,861.3
1997	479,001	481,841	509,515	576,564	581,886	569,760	579,748	452,188	531,299	589,542	561,133	512,471	6,424.9
1998	458,519	454,310	449,806	592,614	499,468	749,765	675,104	536,650	504,088	553,224	521,231	559,067	6,553.8
1999	420,240	509,348	476,104	477,102	390,527	646,806	710,110	597,026	568,859	511,503	572,194	447,078	6,326.9
2000	455,335	537,527	556,010	467,698	566,607	606,190	488,172	469,017	484,617	483,174	690,313	513,328	6,318.0

[1] In thousands of contracts.   *Source: Chicago Board of Trade (CBT)*

SOYBEAN MEAL

Supply and Distribution of Soybean Meal in the United States   In Thousands of Short Tons

Year Beginning Oct. 1	For Stocks Oct. 1	Pro- duction	Total Supply	Domestic	Exports	Total	$ Per Ton Decatur 48% Protein Solvent	Decatur 44% Protein Solvent	Brazil FOB 45-46% Protein	Rotter- dam CIF
1991-2	285	29,831	30,183	23,008	6,945	29,953	189.20	194	184	203
1992-3	230	30,364	30,687	24,251	6,232	30,483	193.75	201	185	207
1993-4	204	30,514	30,788	25,282	5,356	30,638	192.86	199	182	202
1994-5	150	33,269	33,483	26,542	6,717	33,260	162.55	167	172	184
1995-6	223	32,527	32,826	26,611	6,002	32,613	236.00	248	256	256
1996-7	212	34,211	34,525	27,321	6,994	34,316	270.90	286	289	278
1997-8	210	38,176	38,442	28,894	9,330	38,224	185.54	193	201	197
1998-9[1]	218	37,797	38,114	30,662	7,122	37,784	138.50	145	150	150
1999-00[2]	330	37,632	38,012	30,459	7,260	37,719	137.70	176	182	180
2000-1[3]	293	38,017	38,375	31,000	7,100	38,100	160-180	192	205	209

[1] Preliminary.   [2] Estimate.   [3] Forecast.   Source: Economic Research Service, U.S. Department of Agriculture (ERS-USDA)

U.S. Exports of Soybean Cake & Meal by Country of Destination   In Thousands of Metric Tons

Year	Algeria	Australia	Canada	Dominican Republic	Italy	Japan	Mexico	Nether- lands	Philip- pines	Russia[2]	Spain	Vene- zuela	Total
1990	373.5	28.2	555.5	130.5	146.4	20.8	253.0	229.7	200.7	1,568.4	19.6	332.2	4,826
1991	323.5	99.4	651.2	142.6	33.5	24.1	303.6	339.8	150.4	2,271.0	5.5	405.9	5,536
1992	237.8	75.9	582.5	146.7	93.4	167.2	454.4	420.0	434.8	765.1	92.3	473.8	6,236
1993	266.1	90.6	646.7	200.8	91.5	208.7	187.8	580.8	295.7	697.1	203.8	425.0	5,536
1994	248.3	247.0	706.3	209.2	27.1	76.9	367.5	465.6	257.9	159.5	92.6	258.9	4,825
1995	216.7	190.2	798.7	219.2	70.2	246.7	340.0	751.6	593.4	11.1	127.7	181.4	5,890
1996	203.4	156.2	687.3	260.7	85.9	225.5	292.2	453.5	423.2	5.1	51.8	274.9	5,860
1997	250.8	134.1	651.6	261.1	284.1	263.0	142.1	451.2	483.1	8.3	329.1	336.7	6,994
1998	263.2	135.5	774.7	221.2	217.6	265.7	127.8	274.6	758.7	----	296.2	446.2	8,035
1999[1]	213.2	166.8	790.8	308.9	51.5	208.9	304.3	197.6	860.5	----	60.1	357.8	6,634

[1] Preliminary.   [2] Formerly part of the U.S.S.R.; data not reported separately until 1992.   Source: The Oil World

Production of Soybean Cake & Meal[2] in the United States   In Thousands of Short Tons

Year	Oct.	Nov.	Dec.	Jan.	Feb.	Mar.	Apr.	May	June	July	Aug.	Sept.	Total	Yield in lbs.
1990-1	2,508.8	2,513.2	2,431.5	-----	7,082.0	-----	-----	6,640.8	-----	-----	7,148.9	-----	28,325	47.47
1991-2	-----	7,920.4	-----	2,665.5	2,393.8	2,544.4	2,411.3	2,262.5	2,372.4	2,434.2	2,429.0	2,397.3	29,831	47.51
1992-3	2,698.1	2,697.3	2,763.4	2,781.2	2,430.4	2,691.3	2,519.1	2,536.3	2,373.0	2,324.1	2,188.3	2,361.8	30,364	47.54
1993-4	2,707.1	2,714.8	2,696.7	2,632.3	2,458.1	2,696.3	2,510.0	2,446.4	2,330.7	2,398.0	2,406.6	2,517.1	30,514	47.62
1994-5	2,812.5	2,903.5	3,027.8	3,007.5	2,755.0	3,048.5	2,829.8	2,697.9	2,492.1	2,565.4	2,589.8	2,535.8	33,269	47.33
1995-6	2,893.2	2,948.9	2,972.3	2,945.2	2,652.1	2,757.5	2,683.1	2,534.6	2,566.2	2,656.3	2,513.4	2,404.1	32,527	47.69
1996-7	2,992.8	3,151.8	3,263.8	3,251.7	2,966.8	3,089.1	2,709.1	2,618.1	2,573.2	2,517.4	2,465.2	2,611.0	34,211	47.36
1997-8	3,344.0	3,390.6	3,624.2	3,592.1	3,279.2	3,484.0	3,172.5	2,956.7	2,795.2	2,941.5	2,665.6	2,930.7	37,176	47.41
1998-9	3,365.1	3,368.4	3,422.4	3,214.4	3,027.7	3,302.7	3,044.2	3,024.4	2,844.0	3,011.9	3,003.5	3,167.8	37,797	47.25
1999-00[1]	3,573.4	3,400.4	3,413.5	3,345.9	2,994.3	3,126.1	2,893.2	2,918.5	2,847.4	3,107.8	2,914.1	3,088.6	37,623	47.76

[1] Preliminary.   [2] At oil mills; including millfeed and lecithin.   Sources: Economic Research Service, U.S. Department of Agriculture (ERS-USDA)

Stocks (at Oil Mills)[2] of Soybean Cake & Meal in the U.S., on First of Month   In Thousands of Short Tons

Year	Oct.	Nov.	Dec.	Jan.	Feb.	Mar.	Apr.	May	June	July	Aug.	Sept.
1990-1	318.3	290.9	313.6	-----	455.8	-----	-----	527.8	-----	-----	425.0	-----
1991-2	-----	285.0	-----	281.0	258.3	291.3	315.6	310.4	310.2	274.7	260.5	209.9
1992-3	230.0	307.9	411.3	360.8	440.0	420.5	336.9	268.5	328.4	257.3	386.1	353.8
1993-4	204.4	375.1	282.3	290.1	230.0	283.1	277.3	333.0	325.2	254.3	267.5	144.9
1994-5	149.6	240.9	231.6	241.1	197.7	227.1	173.1	382.7	337.6	222.6	252.0	203.8
1995-6	223.4	196.9	241.3	394.8	302.2	229.9	369.3	382.1	306.8	406.2	298.8	218.3
1996-7	212.4	200.2	291.8	254.4	263.0	198.5	322.6	280.1	256.5	317.3	303.2	257.4
1997-8	206.6	218.2	412.2	262.0	269.3	280.7	238.0	210.4	290.2	193.1	205.3	187.2
1998-9	218.1	271.9	352.3	313.9	380.5	436.4	341.0	316.0	447.7	284.2	394.8	279.4
1999-00[1]	330.2	467.6	460.2	436.5	508.1	487.6	354.1	443.6	344.1	260.2	305.8	225.9

[1] Preliminary.   [2] Including millfeed and lecithin.   Source: Economic Research Service, U.S. Department of Agriculture (ERS-USDA)

SOYBEAN MEAL

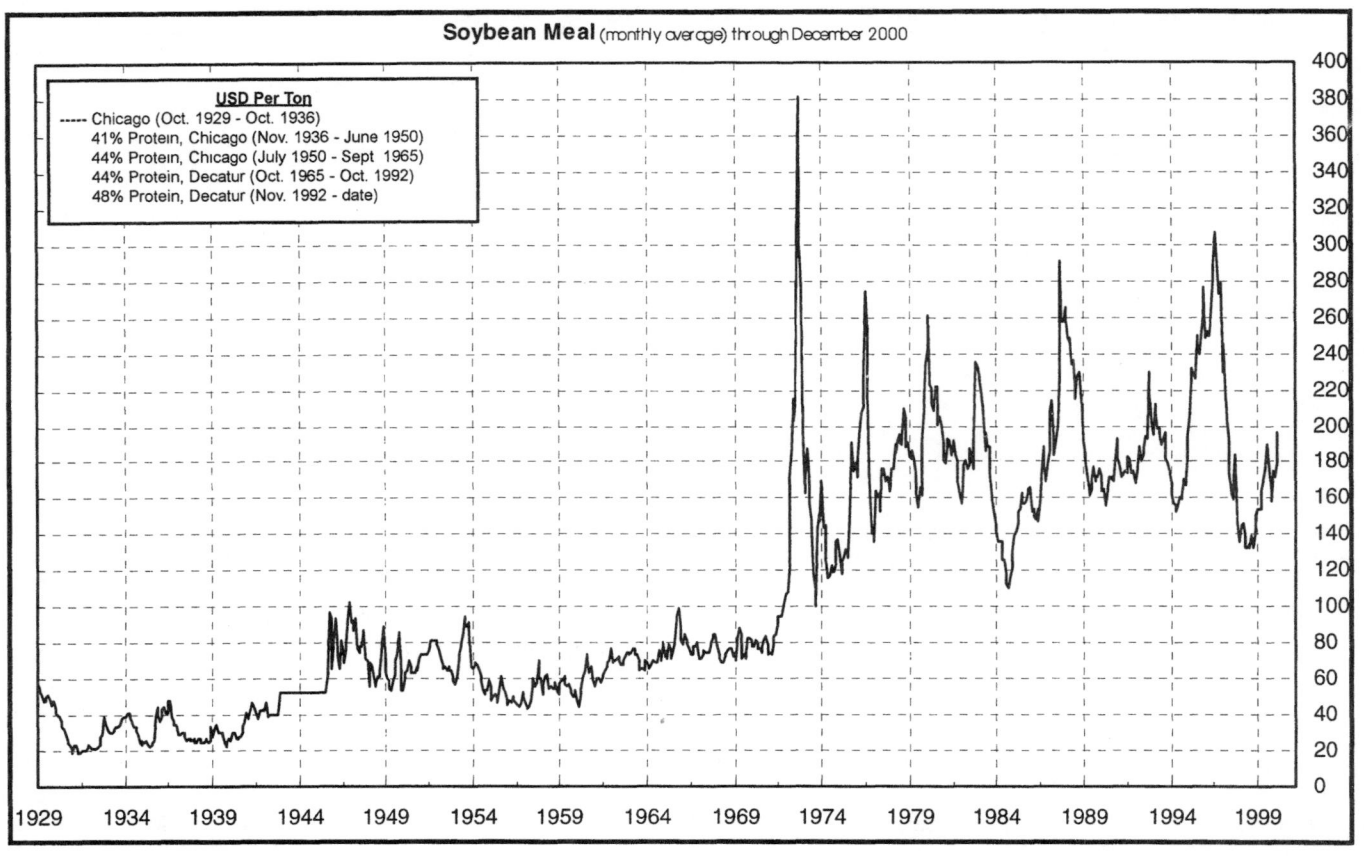

Soybean Meal (monthly average) through December 2000

USD Per Ton
----- Chicago (Oct. 1929 - Oct. 1936)
41% Protein, Chicago (Nov. 1936 - June 1950)
44% Protein, Chicago (July 1950 - Sept. 1965)
44% Protein, Decatur (Oct. 1965 - Oct. 1992)
48% Protein, Decatur (Nov. 1992 - date)

Average Price of Soybean Meal (44% Solvent) in Decatur Illinois   In Dollars Per Short Ton -- Bulk

Year	Oct.	Nov.	Dec.	Jan.	Feb.	Mar.	Apr.	May	June	July	Aug.	Sept.	Average
1990-1	172.5	163.8	164.8	153.7	163.5	165.8	171.5	171.0	171.1	169.7	177.6	191.9	169.7
1991-2	183.0	178.0	170.7	172.7	174.3	174.2	174.8	182.8	181.7	173.9	174.4	175.1	176.3
1992-3	168.6	170.9	176.4	175.6	167.5	172.4	175.6	181.7	181.3	217.6	206.9	186.5	181.8
1993-4	180.6	195.7	192.5	185.9	184.4	182.0	176.4	191.1	183.0	168.1	165.6	162.5	180.7
1994-5	156.4	150.9	145.4	145.1	149.4	145.7	151.0	148.1	149.1	160.1	157.5	171.8	152.5
1995-6	183.4	194.1	213.6	220.5	216.7	215.7	237.9	232.3	227.9	242.3	251.1	265.5	225.1
1996-7	238.0	242.7	240.9	240.7	253.6	270.4	277.7	296.0	275.9	261.5	261.6	265.7	260.4
1997-8	216.0	231.6	214.9	193.1	182.1	165.3	152.8	150.3	157.8	173.3	135.7	126.9	175.0
1998-9	129.4	139.3	139.6	131.0	124.4	127.2	128.6	127.0	131.7	125.7	135.9	144.1	132.0
1999-00	147.2	148.1	145.4	155.0	163.6	166.6	168.1	180.1	170.2	156.8	151.4	166.9	160.0

Source: Economic Research Service, U.S. Department of Agriculture (ERS-USDA)

Average Price of Soybean Meal (48% Solvent) in Decatur Illinois   In Dollars Per Short Ton -- Bulk

Year	Oct.	Nov.	Dec.	Jan.	Feb.	Mar.	Apr.	May	June	July	Aug.	Sept.	Average
1991-2	196.30	190.25	183.10	184.00	185.40	185.90	187.20	195.25	203.90	186.25	186.00	187.00	189.20
1992-3	180.60	181.90	187.60	188.75	179.90	183.60	187.40	193.25	193.10	229.90	219.10	199.90	193.75
1993-4	194.50	209.40	206.00	198.30	198.40	195.40	188.90	193.75	195.50	181.10	178.60	174.50	192.86
1994-5	168.50	161.00	156.90	156.40	151.30	156.90	161.90	159.10	160.40	170.45	166.70	180.99	162.55
1995-6	193.90	204.10	223.60	232.00	228.30	226.57	249.30	244.30	238.80	252.50	261.20	276.40	235.90
1996-7	248.50	251.50	250.60	249.20	262.40	280.50	288.60	306.40	287.90	273.60	273.30	278.30	270.90
1997-8	229.30	245.30	222.50	202.85	192.75	174.20	162.50	160.00	168.55	183.40	146.25	135.80	185.28
1998-9	135.70	144.45	146.40	138.80	132.30	133.00	134.50	133.20	139.10	132.70	141.70	150.65	138.54
1999-00	153.57	154.70	154.00	163.41	170.85	175.50	177.53	189.34	177.45	163.38	157.48	174.60	167.65
2000-1	171.52	179.95	195.65	183.17	166.08								179.27

Source: Economic Research Service, U.S. Department of Agriculture (ERS-USDA)

Soybean Oil

The world's supply/demand situation for soybean oil has shown a decade long progression of new year-to-year record highs. World production in 2000/01 of a record 25.4 million metric tonnes compares with the previous year's 24.8 million. The U.S., the world's largest soybean oil producer, generally accounts for about one-third of total production, producing nearly twice that of Brazil, the second largest producer. Of the important edible vegetable oils, soybean oil is the world's largest with almost 30 percent of total vegetable oil production in 2000/01, followed by palm oil and rapeseed oil. World usage of soybean oil in 2000/01 of a record 25.7 million tonnes compares with 24.3 million in 1999/00. World carryover stocks at the end of 2000/01 were estimated at 2.25 million tonnes vs. 2.44 million a year earlier, with more than one-third of the total in the U.S. The U.S. is the world's largest consumer using almost one-third of the total new supply, 8.3 million tonnes in 2000/01, followed by China with 3.4 million tonnes in 2000/01.

Global soybean oil exports in 2000/01 were estimated at a near record 7.6 million tonnes vs. the previous year's 7.3 million and 8.1 million in 1998/99. Argentina is the largest exporter with 3.1 million tonnes in 2000/01. Importing nations are numerous with Asia, collectively, the largest importer with 3.12 million tonnes in 2000/01 vs. 2.6 million in 1999/00. Next is the Middle East at about 2 million tonnes in each year.

The U.S. soybean oil crop year begins October 1. Production in 2000/01 of a record high 18.3 billion pounds compares with 17.7 billion in 1999/00. In the mid-1990's, production averaged about 15 billion pounds. The oil content of U.S. soybeans correlates directly with temperatures and sunshine during the pod-filling stages. Carry-in stocks on October 1, 2000 were estimated at 1.8 billion pounds vs. 1.5 billion a year earlier. The U.S. supply for 2000/01 of a record high 20.1 billion pounds compares with 19.4 billion in 1999/00. Disappearance in 2000/01 of a near record 18.3 billion pounds compares with 17.6 billion in 1999/00. Soybean oil stocks were forecast to build during 2000/01, lifting the September 30, 2001 carryover to 1.85 billion pounds, the highest since year-end 1995/96.

Domestic soybean oil use in 2000/01 is forecast at a record high 16.5 billion pounds vs. 16.2 billion in 1999/00 as domestic prices prove competitive to other fats and oils. However, U.S. exports have shown an irregular trend in recent years estimated at 1.8 billion pounds in 2000/01 vs. 1.4 billion 1999/00, but well under the record high 3.1 billion pounds in 1997/98.

Crude soybean oil prices (basis Decatur) in 1999/00 averaged 16.3 cents per pound and are forecast during 2000/01 to range between 15-18 cents per pound.

Futures Markets

Soybean oil futures and options are traded on the Chicago Board of Trade (CBOT). A smaller contract trades on the MidAmerica Commodity Exchange (MidAm).

World Supply and Demand of Soybean Oil   In Thousands of Metric Tons

Year Beginning Oct. 1	Production Brazil	Production European Union	Production United States	Production Total	Exports Brazil	Exports United States	Exports Total	Imports India	Imports Total	Consumption Brazil	Consumption European Union	Consumption India	Consumption United States	Consumption Total	Stocks[3] United States	Stocks[3] Total
1991-2	2,760	2,356	6,507	16,783	710	746	4,502	65	3,754	2,156	1,592	425	5,555	15,702	1,016	2,005
1992-3	3,154	2,545	6,250	17,466	771	663	4,268	42	3,792	2,342	2,002	562	5,903	17,169	705	1,826
1993-4	3,522	2,232	6,328	18,243	1,556	695	5,064	41	4,717	2,399	1,831	711	5,869	18,347	500	1,375
1994-5	4,061	2,672	7,082	20,188	1,643	1,217	6,287	60	5,978	2,500	1,927	555	5,857	19,227	516	2,027
1995-6	3,749	2,567	6,913	19,899	1,320	450	5,285	60	5,252	2,630	1,960	772	6,108	19,622	914	2,271
1996-7	3,521	2,685	7,145	20,349	1,075	922	6,013	49	5,947	2,676	1,871	706	6,471	20,613	690	1,941
1997-8	4,096	2,914	8,229	23,607	1,418	1,397	8,072	236	6,688	2,827	1,799	1,095	6,922	22,211	627	1,953
1998-9	4,040	2,926	8,202	24,780	1,463	1,076	8,229	833	7,953	2,816	1,830	1,805	7,101	24,529	689	1,928
1999-00[1]	3,850	2,727	8,085	24,709	1,220	624	7,352	770	7,202	2,950	1,643	1,562	7,283	24,398	905	2,089
2000-1[2]	4,137	2,880	8,244	25,937	1,320	703	7,379	780	7,546	3,060	1,758	1,635	7,461	25,809	1,021	2,084

[1] Preliminary.   [2] Forecast.   [3] End of season.   Source: Foreign Agricultural Service, U.S. Department of Agriculture (FAS-USDA)

Supply and Distribution of Soybean Oil in the United States   In Millions of Pounds

Year Beginning Oct. 1	Production	Imports	Stocks Oct. 1	Exports	Total Domestic	Food Shortening	Food Margarine	Food Cooking & Salad Oils	Food Other Edible	Total Food	Non-Food Paint & Varnish	Non-Food Resins & Plastics	Total Non-Food	Total Disappearance
1991-2	14,345	1	1,786	1,648	12,245	4,091	1,911	4,961	148	11,112	46	98	301	13,893
1992-3	13,778	10	2,239	1,419	13,054	4,465	1,970	4,717	254	11,505	38	95	296	14,473
1993-4	13,951	68	1,555	1,529	12,942	4,773	1,840	4,999	221	11,832	46	115	304	14,471
1994-5	15,613	17	1,103	2,680	12,916	4,714	1,693	5,546	222	12,175	49	124	287	15,597
1995-6	15,240	95	1,137	992	13,465	4,702	1,699	5,317	159	11,877	48	119	297	14,457
1996-7	15,752	53	2,015	2,033	14,267	4,578	1,667	6,119	68	12,432	51	132	333	16,300
1997-8	18,143	60	1,520	3,079	15,262	4,688	1,623	6,188	78	12,576	49	128	490	18,341
1998-9	18,078	83	1,382	2,372	15,652	4,842	1,590	6,191	120	12,743	37	117	576	18,024
1999-00[1]	17,826	83	1,520	1,375	16,059	4,956	1,590	6,481	128	13,156	65	96	586	17,433
2000-1[2]	18,160	90	1,995	1,650	16,450						73	91	596	18,100

[1] Preliminary.   [2] Forecast.   Source: Economic Research Service, U.S. Department of Agriculture (ERS-USDA)

SOYBEAN OIL

Stocks of Crude Soybean Oil in the United States, at End of Month   In Millions of Pounds

Crop Year	Oct.	Nov.	Dec.	Jan.	Feb.	Mar.	Apr.	May	June	July	Aug.	Sept.
1995-6	990.4	908.9	1,154.3	1,237.4	1,264.2	1,366.6	1,490.1	1,531.7	1,672.4	1,951.4	1,874.3	1,799.3
1996-7	1,796.5	1,711.6	1,805.1	1,928.5	1,982.6	1,938.2	1,929.9	1,919.4	1,917.8	1,760.3	1,492.8	1,321.1
1997-8	1,307.0	1,303.6	1,439.8	1,518.8	1,459.1	1,498.6	1,533.3	1,577.6	1,451.7	1,535.9	1,240.1	1,167.4
1998-9	1,195.0	1,142.0	1,041.1	1,066.2	1,209.5	1,318.6	1,462.0	1,499.5	1,411.8	1,441.8	1,417.8	1,316.1
1999-00	1,378.3	1,422.9	1,516.5	1,742.4	1,829.7	1,847.2	1,847.5	1,760.3	1,802.9	1,903.7	1,831.3	1,773.4
2000-1[1]	1,873.6	1,961.8	2,035.0	2,177.3								

[1] Preliminary.   Source: Bureau of the Census, U.S. Department of Commerce

Stocks of Refined Soybean Oil in the United States, at End of Month   In Millions of Pounds

Crop Year	Oct.	Nov.	Dec.	Jan.	Feb.	Mar.	Apr.	May	June	July	Aug.	Sept.
1995-6	205.5	223.1	254.6	275.2	257.2	287.0	257.3	227.2	216.1	205.1	217.1	216.1
1996-7	196.4	186.8	222.0	243.8	220.6	233.1	233.9	223.9	220.1	217.8	207.1	199.0
1997-8	218.6	221.9	239.8	269.1	252.1	264.0	324.3	279.4	260.9	243.2	213.0	215.0
1998-9	221.7	264.4	246.5	246.7	296.1	289.0	254.2	267.8	235.6	229.4	213.0	203.4
1999-00	238.1	240.7	250.0	271.3	270.1	245.6	251.8	231.6	225.5	216.7	186.3	222.0
2000-1[1]	187.2	205.7	263.1	263.5								

[1] Preliminary.   Source: Bureau of the Census, U.S. Department of Commerce

U.S. Exports of Soybean Oil[1], by Country of Destination   In Metric Tons

Year Beginning Oct. 1	Canada	Ecuador	Ethiopia	Haiti	India	Mexico	Morocco	Pakistan	Panama	Peru	Turkey	Venezuela	Total
1988-9	5,364	30,930	8,960	2,846	28,127	17,730	80,023	453,067	6,695	5,778	0	29,055	753,576
1989-90	5,443	26,314	22,858	1,688	16,391	4,435	77,985	309,502	3,174	5,206	0	8,198	613,902
1990-1	3,790	20,832	14,948	4,946	13,544	11,087	73,255	66,209	8,123	6,566	16,460	0	353,959
1991-2	11,153	528	19,619	4,737	67,577	23,383	127,602	250	11,143	32,696	81,976	13	747,465
1992-3	28,585	17	8,272	6,753	49,452	44,194	57,995	-----	641	36,340	58,436	0	643,796
1993-4	4,401	0	24,509	1,747	46,846	18,499	31,563	72,204	248	24,081	34,920	26	693,697
1994-5	24,886	12,698	8,391	49,793	28,949	58,623	29,053	25,500	13,342	8,692	5,750	2,016	1,215,804
1995-6	43,912	1,155	4,546	15,041	20,841	46,643	-----	-----	9,512	35,999	1,960	1,877	449,876
1996-7[2]	60,318	6,587	19,492	36,436	26,675	81,901	46,682	-----	3,623	37,726	6,952	517	923,871

[1] Crude & Refined oil combined as such.   [2] Preliminary.   Source: Economic Research Service, U.S. Department of Agriculture (ERS-USDA)

Production of Crude Soybean Oil in the United States   In Millions of Pounds

Year	Oct.	Nov.	Dec.	Jan.	Feb.	Mar.	Apr.	May	June	July	Aug.	Sept.	Total
1991-2	-----	3,772	-----	1,270	1,147	1,228	1,167	1,096	1,152	1,177	1,179	1,158	14,345
1992-3	1,238	1,200	1,239	1,247	1,102	1,216	1,148	1,152	1,083	1,070	1,006	1,078	13,778
1993-4	1,241	1,228	1,218	1,192	1,122	1,231	1,155	1,123	1,070	1,099	1,104	1,168	13,951
1994-5	1,328	1,342	1,403	1,400	1,289	1,419	1,333	1,275	1,183	1,205	1,228	1,208	15,613
1995-6	1,354	1,360	1,382	1,360	1,236	1,292	1,259	1,197	1,221	1,263	1,171	1,139	15,234
1996-7	1,401	1,430	1,473	1,474	1,348	1,413	1,254	1,216	1,196	1,176	1,141	1,231	15,752
1997-8	1,591	1,580	1,689	1,684	1,558	1,655	1,526	1,418	1,337	1,410	1,286	1,410	18,143
1998-9	1,598	1,598	1,611	1,528	1,439	1,587	1,453	1,450	1,383	1,451	1,452	1,528	18,078
1999-00[1]	1,687	1,597	1,599	1,576	1,416	1,484	1,363	1,399	1,362	1,482	1,393	1,468	17,826

[1] Preliminary.   Source: Economic Research Service, U.S. Department of Agriculture (ERS-USDA)

Production of Refined Soybean Oil in the United States   In Millions of Pounds

Year	Oct.	Nov.	Dec.	Jan.	Feb.	Mar.	Apr.	May	June	July	Aug.	Sept.	Total
1992-3	1,095.6	999.4	951.0	960.1	935.4	1,054.9	1,039.7	950.6	1,042.8	978.2	1,066.7	1,109.7	12,184
1993-4	1,094.3	1,053.5	1,030.8	960.1	945.5	1,056.6	1,018.5	1,012.0	1,017.3	968.0	1,107.2	1,044.6	12,308
1994-5	1,123.0	1,079.2	1,060.6	1,002.5	968.2	1,063.6	1,010.4	1,077.0	993.5	940.9	1,076.8	1,039.8	12,435
1995-6	1,119.2	1,088.8	1,018.5	979.9	934.3	1,042.6	997.3	1,009.3	962.8	971.9	1,115.8	1,058.7	12,299
1996-7	1,111.7	1,064.1	1,025.7	969.8	931.5	1,057.1	1,023.7	1,026.2	984.8	1,019.1	1,094.3	1,072.5	12,381
1997-8	1,173.9	1,156.3	1,110.1	1,092.6	1,047.4	1,148.2	1,094.8	1,140.7	1,053.1	1,083.9	1,173.4	1,114.5	13,389
1998-9	1,200.6	1,108.8	1,042.2	1,016.7	976.7	1,138.2	1,073.2	1,087.7	1,060.7	1,058.6	1,122.6	1,116.2	13,002
1999-00	1,201.1	1,195.2	1,150.4	1,056.9	1,045.1	1,173.7	1,109.6	1,141.4	1,063.8	1,080.2	1,176.0	1,177.7	13,571
2000-1[1]	1,260.3	1,159.7	1,093.4	1,089.6									13,809

[1] Preliminary.   Source: Bureau of the Census, U.S. Department of Commerce

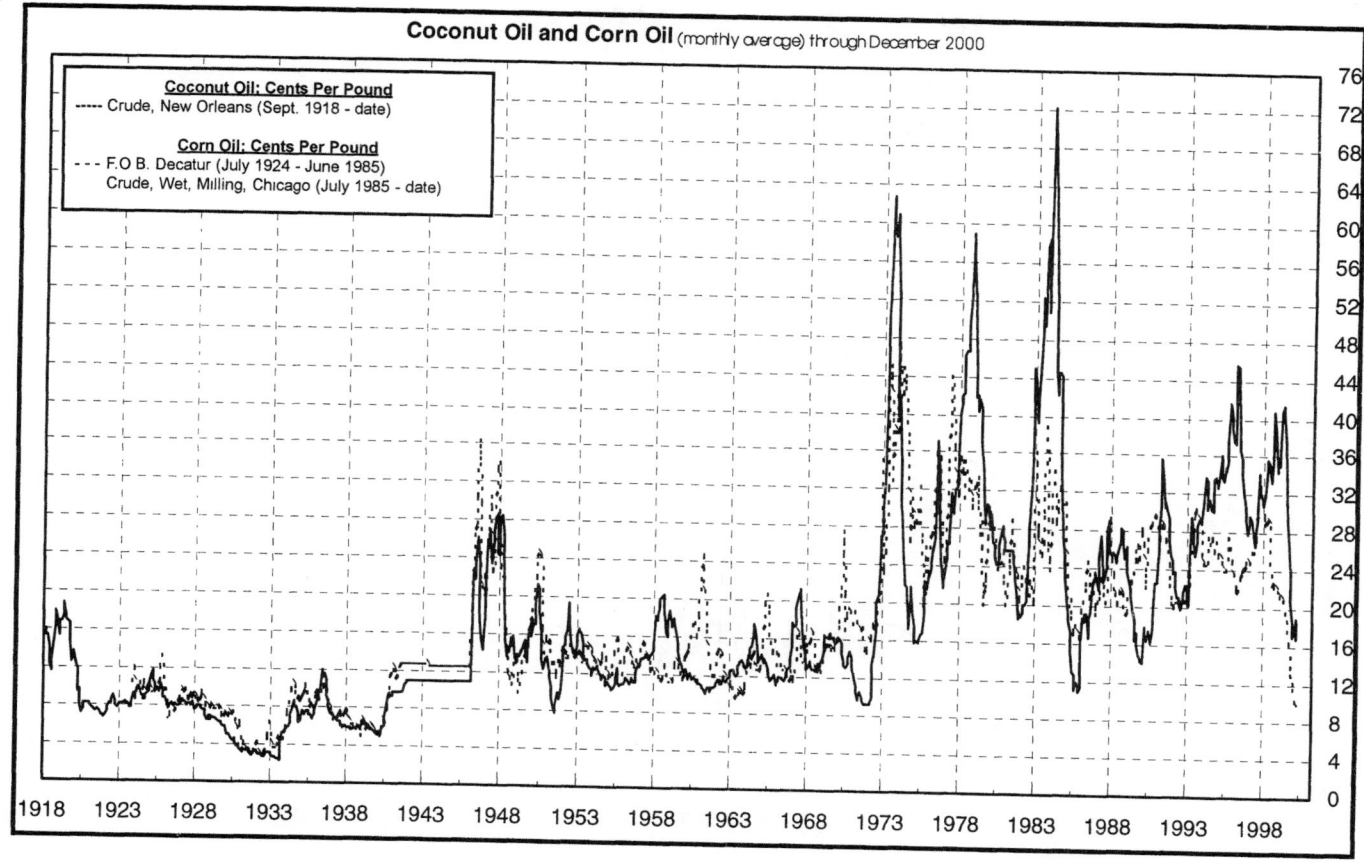

Coconut Oil and Corn Oil (monthly average) through December 2000

Coconut Oil: Cents Per Pound
----- Crude, New Orleans (Sept. 1918 - date)

Corn Oil: Cents Per Pound
--- F.O B. Decatur (July 1924 - June 1985)
Crude, Wet, Milling, Chicago (July 1985 - date)

Consumption of Soybean Oil in End Products in the United States   In Millions of Pounds

Year	Jan.	Feb.	Mar.	Apr.	May	June	July	Aug.	Sept.	Oct.	Nov.	Dec.	Total
1991	-----	2,690.3	-----	-----	2,831.8	-----	-----	2,837.7	-----	-----	2,907.8	-----	11,268
1992	880.4	867.0	1,010.1	947.9	956.7	962.1	935.5	932.4	1,019.8	1,061.7	951.8	946.1	11,472
1993	934.5	942.2	1,092.6	1,044.6	981.2	1,036.0	1,019.3	1,097.3	1,103.3	1,123.6	1,092.1	1,029.2	12,496
1994	924.5	939.1	1,084.7	1,040.6	1,001.4	1,023.8	974.9	1,119.2	1,075.4	1,123.3	1,103.4	1,063.8	12,474
1995	991.1	950.0	1,093.8	1,006.2	1,077.3	1,020.8	948.7	1,046.1	1,042.3	1,092.0	1,067.7	1,002.6	12,339
1996	964.9	927.4	1,026.4	999.8	1,020.6	946.2	959.9	1,123.3	1,042.8	1,137.1	1,080.9	1,093.1	12,322
1997	1,086.0	979.7	1,104.9	1,060.4	1,034.1	995.2	991.4	1,126.1	1,067.8	1,128.5	1,080.9	1,093.1	12,762
1998	1,045.8	1,020.2	1,129.7	1,066.5	1,101.6	1,070.1	1,062.2	1,123.4	1,122.0	1,231.5	1,100.0	1,087.8	13,180
1999	1,031.5	979.0	1,156.1	1,087.7	1,091.9	1,079.5	1,082.9	1,185.0	1,185.7	1,183.0	1,150.2	1,057.0	13,397
2000[1]	1,096.6	1,050.5	1,217.9	1,158.9	1,183.6	1,102.9	1,121.1	1,226.4	1,163.6	1,306.1	1,139.7	1,079.6	13,847

[1] Preliminary.   Source: Bureau of the Census, U.S. Department of Commerce

U.S. Exports of Soybean Oil (Crude and Refined)   In Millions of Pounds

Year	Jan.	Feb.	Mar.	Apr.	May	June	July	Aug.	Sept.	Oct.	Nov.	Dec.	Total
1991	-----	71.8	-----	-----	132.3	-----	-----	434.8	-----	-----	336.1	-----	975
1992	140.0	171.9	134.6	155.4	69.1	129.1	163.7	205.2	142.5	169.5	113.2	91.6	1,686
1993	146.8	188.0	143.3	61.1	154.8	75.4	59.9	116.0	99.7	190.4	88.6	200.2	1,524
1994	120.4	144.6	94.4	46.1	111.6	36.1	57.7	184.6	254.0	154.8	303.2	305.9	1,813
1995	217.4	367.6	564.2	236.2	90.8	160.4	91.0	109.4	79.4	69.3	205.4	95.9	2,287
1996	189.1	97.0	68.0	75.3	63.9	16.1	27.1	28.0	56.7	121.0	303.8	213.3	1,259
1997	190.7	239.2	301.1	84.9	28.9	44.9	144.1	212.9	152.1	217.2	424.0	199.7	2,240
1998	449.4	387.6	268.6	191.1	148.1	204.7	161.8	316.0	108.9	189.6	343.5	376.7	3,146
1999	246.1	231.1	130.8	230.8	91.3	135.0	111.7	91.2	196.2	209.1	114.9	157.6	1,946
2000[1]	98.4	152.1	161.3	91.6	48.2	111.0	104.6	56.8	68.0				1,189

[1] Preliminary.   Source: Economic Research Service, U.S. Department of Agriculture (ERS-USDA)

SOYBEAN OIL

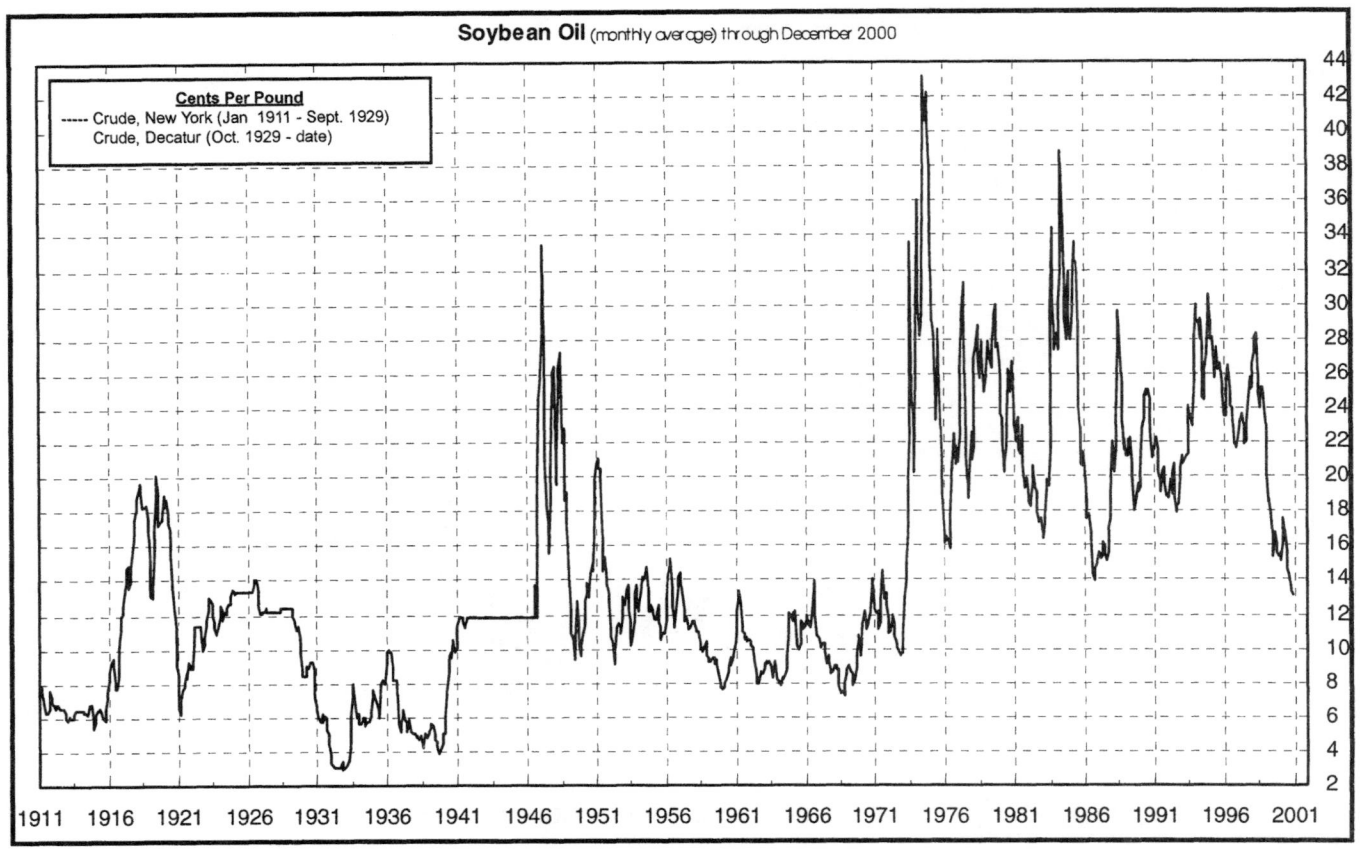

Soybean Oil (monthly average) through December 2000

Cents Per Pound
----- Crude, New York (Jan 1911 - Sept. 1929)
Crude, Decatur (Oct. 1929 - date)

Stocks of Soybean Oil (Crude & Refined) at Factories and Warehouses in the U.S.   In Millions of Pounds

Year	Oct. 1	Nov. 1	Dec. 1	Jan. 1	Feb. 1	Mar. 1	Apr. 1	May 1	June 1	July 1	Aug. 1	Sept. 1
1990-1	1,305.0	1,216.0	1,320.0	-----	1,463.8	-----	-----	1,874.6	-----	-----	1,853.1	-----
1991-2	-----	1,786.3	-----	2,217.0	2,159.0	2,402.0	2,400.0	2,423.0	2,433.0	2,426.5	2,421.0	2,363.0
1992-3	2,239.4	2,076.4	2,110.8	2,280.1	2,410.1	2,336.8	2,246.1	2,297.9	2,240.8	2,174.0	2,060.7	1,719.8
1993-4	1,554.8	1,452.7	1,399.6	1,406.9	1,414.6	1,400.9	1,402.2	1,553.3	1,566.8	1,553.8	1,570.9	1,339.4
1994-5	1,103.1	1,055.5	1,026.9	1,055.2	1,116.8	1,128.8	1,059.5	1,089.6	1,130.4	1,111.6	1,142.0	1,100.0
1995-6	1,136.7	1,195.9	1,132.0	1,408.9	1,512.6	1,521.5	1,653.5	1,747.4	1,758.9	1,888.5	2,156.5	2,091.4
1996-7	2,015.4	1,992.9	1,898.4	2,027.1	2,172.3	2,203.2	2,171.3	2,163.8	2,143.2	2,137.9	1,978.1	1,699.9
1997-8	1,520.2	1,525.6	1,525.5	1,679.6	1,787.9	1,711.2	1,762.6	1,857.6	1,857.0	1,712.6	1,779.1	1,453.2
1998-9	1,382.4	1,416.8	1,406.5	1,312.9	1,505.6	1,607.6	1,716.2	1,640.5	1,767.3	1,647.4	1,671.2	1,630.8
1999-00[1]	1,519.6	1,616.4	1,663.6	1,791.1	2,013.7	2,099.8	2,092.7	2,099.2	1,991.9	2,028.3	2,120.4	2,018.1

[1] Preliminary.   *Source: Economic Research Service, U.S. Department of Agriculture (ERS-USDA)*

Average Price of Crude Domestic Soybean Oil (in Tank Cars) F.O.B. Decatur   In Cents Per Pound

Year	Oct.	Nov.	Dec.	Jan.	Feb.	Mar.	Apr.	May	June	July	Aug.	Sept.	Average
1991-2	19.57	18.78	18.99	18.77	18.88	19.74	19.00	20.15	20.71	18.82	17.87	18.28	19.10
1992-3	18.36	20.10	20.52	21.23	20.72	21.00	21.24	21.15	21.30	24.13	23.47	23.61	21.40
1993-4	22.98	25.37	28.09	29.91	28.84	29.03	27.94	29.10	27.60	24.53	24.51	26.11	27.00
1994-5	27.06	29.84	30.61	29.01	28.15	28.33	27.16	26.00	26.78	27.60	26.56	26.26	27.51
1995-6	26.56	25.41	24.76	23.69	23.65	23.60	25.82	26.50	24.95	24.10	23.99	23.92	24.70
1996-7	21.95	21.80	21.60	22.45	22.41	23.29	23.17	23.68	22.97	21.89	22.06	22.88	22.50
1997-8	24.31	25.73	25.08	25.09	26.51	27.09	28.10	28.28	25.83	24.88	23.99	25.13	25.84
1998-9	25.20	25.20	24.00	22.90	20.00	19.50	18.80	17.85	16.50	15.30	16.50	16.80	19.88
1999-00	16.08	15.63	15.30	15.63	15.09	16.21	17.52	16.75	15.65	14.70	14.34	14.24	15.60
2000-1[1]	13.50	13.37	13.12	12.53	12.38								12.98

[1] Preliminary.   *Source: Economic Research Service, U.S. Department of Agriculture (ERS-USDA)*

Soybean Oil Futures - Chicago Board of Trade (weekly close) as of 29-Dec-2000

Average Open Interest of Soybean Oil Futures in Chicago   In Contracts

Year	Jan.	Feb.	Mar.	Apr.	May	June	July	Aug.	Sept.	Oct.	Nov.	Dec.
1991	72,987	71,607	76,800	70,361	70,954	73,870	73,864	70,058	66,128	61,227	69,657	63,901
1992	68,619	73,919	75,508	68,749	65,084	71,507	64,450	72,569	70,228	65,243	76,168	76,908
1993	73,683	68,887	66,803	68,598	65,814	73,892	83,730	72,746	64,927	62,348	80,136	94,990
1994	97,198	99,640	100,334	98,659	97,595	83,165	93,994	88,196	81,735	86,901	108,327	114,928
1995	101,171	103,856	97,715	87,300	76,175	75,171	81,650	77,064	70,410	71,652	85,241	84,138
1996	87,214	85,611	87,859	95,954	95,422	86,366	81,440	80,090	83,211	98,514	97,496	86,119
1997	89,112	89,348	102,388	101,191	101,544	104,433	105,346	95,282	94,521	107,471	119,877	106,406
1998	105,798	121,657	142,100	160,004	159,248	139,934	117,487	112,177	115,879	115,260	110,386	104,738
1999	115,407	131,875	136,967	133,404	131,993	147,749	157,999	147,280	146,239	155,768	163,439	144,798
2000	131,948	135,196	143,699	155,114	134,093	140,582	134,392	135,506	136,590	135,584	142,712	134,873

Source: Chicago Board of Trade (CBT)

Volume of Trading of Soybean Oil Futures in Chicago   In Contracts

Year	Jan.	Feb.	Mar.	Apr.	May	June	July	Aug.	Sept.	Oct.	Nov.	Dec.	Total[1]
1991	330,215	259,353	354,973	342,117	264,569	322,897	433,757	399,802	303,184	340,553	297,865	369,259	4,018.5
1992	344,204	293,729	399,754	255,848	381,807	352,349	413,086	298,001	425,859	346,755	365,760	405,526	4,282.7
1993	341,366	267,022	378,389	306,092	261,620	434,704	513,329	444,559	449,338	302,084	465,173	448,553	4,612.2
1994	442,026	401,580	366,007	391,175	442,419	378,177	397,483	357,896	415,407	476,936	516,724	477,358	5,063.2
1995	424,387	363,695	464,413	355,884	457,682	418,182	377,355	330,507	303,893	317,201	431,711	366,426	4,611.3
1996	354,602	355,220	375,237	443,408	376,716	423,089	512,563	449,014	425,850	414,018	396,233	454,327	4,980.3
1997	473,290	381,921	503,998	445,848	389,741	439,626	442,846	375,122	417,970	413,722	489,541	511,369	5,285.0
1998	443,562	556,982	497,887	673,091	624,518	648,098	629,642	491,155	558,032	383,844	450,073	540,379	6,498.3
1999	367,303	555,097	520,622	463,236	350,850	489,184	516,205	552,198	523,376	395,243	497,090	433,491	5,663.9
2000	424,232	451,677	483,212	438,526	451,162	533,376	422,418	456,195	436,841	378,419	507,044	386,801	5,369.9

[1] In thousands of contracts.   *Source: Chicago Board of Trade (CBT)*

Soybeans

The soybean market, basis Chicago futures, experienced some sharp price swings during calendar 2000, but towards year-end prices were fairly close to year earlier levels around $5.00 per bushel. On balance, the year's trend finished with a moderate bullish bias, notwithstanding a sharp May to July break that carried from a high of $5.84/bu. to a low of $4.48/bu., basis November 2000 futures. The market's action might be reflective of a broad base building trading range following a protracted three-year decline that carried from about $9.00/bu. down to $4.00/bu. in mid-1999.

The 2000/2001 world soybean production of a record large 166.2 million metric tonnes compares with 157.2 million in 1999/00. In the early 1990's, production averaged less than 120 million tonnes, suggesting that the growth trend accelerated during the second half of the decade and appears likely to remain so into the new century. Although the 2000/01 U.S. crop of a record large 2.77 billion bushels (77 million metric tonnes) proved to be about 46 million bushels less than expected, it still topped the 1999/00 crop by 125 million bushels. The U.S. produces nearly half of the world's soybeans and Brazil, the second largest producer, about a fifth. Soybean production is expanding in a number of countries, but the U.S. ranking is well entrenched. A key question zeroes in on China and Argentina, the latter becoming the third largest global producer during the past few years, which until 1996/97 had been China. In 2000/01, China's near record large crop of 15 million tonnes compares with the Argentine's record large 22.6 million. The odds would seem to favor a stronger percentile growth in China than seen in the late 1990's, in line with their expanding poultry flocks and the derived need for high protein soybean meal. However, as China's economy becomes more market sensitive, growers apparently have switched to higher priced crops, with more soybean acreage moved into corn and cotton production. It is possible that China's soybean acreage has peaked at around 9 million hectare, suggesting that further production gains will be dependent upon higher average yields, which have yet to be realized, estimated at 1.61 tonnes per hectare in 2000/01 vs. 1.75 tonnes in 1999/00.

Brazil's soybean crop is sown right at the tail-end of the U.S. crop's harvest period. In 2000/01, Brazilian production was forecast at a record large 33.5 million tonnes vs. 32 million in 1999/00. Brazil's bean acreage, however, of 13.4 million hectare was unchanged from 1999/00, whereas Argentina's acreage increased to 9.3 million hectare from 8.6 million. The average yield in both countries is about the same at 2.45 tonnes per hectare. However, unlike Brazil, Argentine soybean farmers have significantly lower production costs and a better transportation structure. Brazil's crop year encompasses February to January; Argentina's is April to March.

World soybean trade in 2000/01, of 45 million tonnes, compares with 1999/00's record large 46.9 million. The U.S. now accounts for almost 60 percent of world exports, a somewhat lower percentage than in the mid-1990's; 26 million tonnes in 2000/01 vs. 26.4 million in 1999/00. Brazil's exports of 9.9 million tonnes in 2000/01, compare with 11.2 million in 1999/00, and about 3.5 million in the mid-1990's. Argentina's exports totaled 4.4 million tonnes in 2000/01, vs. 4.8 million in 1999/00, but compare with the 1996-98

average of less than 3 million. Importing nations are more numerous; collectively, Asia is now the largest importer at almost 20 million tonnes in 2000/01, with China and Japan accounting for about 12 million tonnes. The European Union, formerly the largest importing bloc, is forecast to import 16.6 million tonnes in 2000/01, about unchanged from 1999/00, with Germany taking 3.7 million and the Netherlands 5 million, the same totals as the previous year.

The ending 2000/01 world bean carryover, of a lower than expected 23.4 million tonnes, compares with 23.8 million in 1999/00. The U.S., Brazil, and Argentina together accounted for about 20 million tonnes at the end of both crop years.

U.S. farmers harvested a record large 73 million acres of soybeans in 2000, vs. 72.4 million in 1999. The average yield of a near record 38 bushels per acre was lower than expected, but still topped the previous season's 36.6 bushels, and the record 38.9 bushels in 1998. Iowa is the largest producing state with 453 million bushels in 2000, with Illinois a close second, followed by Minnesota and Indiana.

The U.S. soybean crop year begins September 1. Carryover stocks on August 31, 2000, of 288 million bushels, lifted total 2000/01 supplies to almost 3.1 billion bushels, vs. 3.0 billion in 1999/00. Total disappearance in 2000/01 was forecast at 2.7 billion bushels, of which at least 1.6 billion will be crushed, 0.9 billion exported, and about 167 million allocated to seed and residual usage, with any late revisions expected to lift the crush and/or exports. Carryover as of August 31, 2001, is forecast at 320 million bushels. Projected carryover, as a percentage of usage in 2000/01, was estimated at about 12 percent.

U.S. soybean exports have seen a strong shift in regional demand during the past two years. The traditional European market has come to represent a smaller share of U.S. exports, while Asia and Mexico have increased their importance to U.S. exporters. Asia's share is expected to increase due to the area's improved economy's and the shift away from importing meal in favor of processing soybeans.

Historically, when a more positive soybean usage outlook takes hold it's apt to show in early calendar year prices. Demand bull years in soybeans generally show counterseasonal strength in January and February, however, if total usage holds neutral and/or weakens, then prices, manifested chiefly in futures, tend to witness what is referred to as the "February break." If the latter develops, it's not unusual for prices to penetrate the harvest lows of the previous October-December quarter.

The U.S.D.A.'s average price received by farmers in 2000/01 was forecast at $4.40-$5.00 per bushel vs. $4.65 in 1999/00. The highest farm price during the past decade was $7.35 in 1996/97, and the lowest was $5.56 in 1992/93.

Futures Markets

Soybean futures are traded on the Bolsa de Mercadorias & Futuros (BM&F), the Mercado a Termino de Buenos Aires (MAT), the Dalian Commodity Exchange in China, the Tokyo Grain Exchange (TGE), the Chicago Board of Trade (CBOT), and the Mid-America Commodity Exchange (MidAm). Options are traded on the MAT, the TGE, the CBOT, and the MidAm.

World Production of Soybeans   In Thousands of Metric Tons

Crop Year[4]	Argentina	Bolivia	Brazil	Canada	China	India	Indonesia	Mexico	Paraguay	Thailand	United States	Ex-USSR	World Total
1991-2	11,150	308	19,300	1,460	9,710	2,492	1,750	718	1,300	435	54,065	759	107,336
1992-3	11,350	513	22,500	1,455	10,300	3,106	1,700	572	1,750	480	59,612	581	117,382
1993-4	12,400	735	24,700	1,851	15,310	4,000	1,565	497	1,800	480	50,885	557	117,769
1994-5	12,500	810	25,900	2,251	16,000	3,236	1,680	523	2,200	450	68,444	451	137,697
1995-6	12,430	900	24,150	2,293	13,500	4,476	1,517	190	2,400	368	59,174	320	124,915
1996-7	11,200	1,040	27,300	2,165	13,220	4,100	1,460	61	2,771	360	64,780	299	132,217
1997-8	19,500	1,071	32,500	2,738	14,728	5,350	1,306	189	2,988	338	73,176	298	158,063
1998-9[1]	20,000	960	31,300	2,737	15,152	6,000	1,300	143	3,000	335	74,598	333	159,832
1999-00[2]	20,700	1,200	32,500	2,776	14,290	5,200	1,360	124	2,900	330	72,224	333	157,675
2000-1[3]	23,500	1,200	34,500	2,703	15,400	5,500	1,420	110	3,100	330	75,579	388	167,345

[1] Preliminary.   [2] Estimate.   [3] Forecast.   [4] Spilt year includes Northern Hemisphere crops harvested in the late months of the first year shown combined with Southern Hemisphere crops harvested in the early months of the following year.   Sources: Oil World; Foreign Agricultural Service, U.S. Department of Agriculture (FAS-USDA)

World Crushings and EndingStocks of Soybeans   In Thousands of Metric Tons

Year	Argentina	Brazil	China	Germany	India	Japan	Mexico	Netherlands	United States	World Total	Brazil	United States	World Total
	Crushings										Ending Stocks		
1991-2	7,900	14,721	3,389	2,885	2,232	3,554	2,600	3,565	34,128	91,614	831	7,578	11,389
1992-3	8,667	16,765	4,486	3,107	2,810	3,785	2,670	3,721	34,808	97,967	832	7,955	11,388
1993-4	8,718	18,736	7,605	2,781	3,600	3,700	2,640	3,582	34,716	102,051	651	5,691	9,045
1994-5	9,280	21,599	8,590	3,286	2,750	3,760	2,330	3,991	38,242	112,556	710	9,112	12,878
1995-6	9,927	20,154	7,470	3,242	4,046	3,700	2,436	3,940	37,273	110,827	825	4,993	8,508
1996-7	10,423	18,910	7,500	3,686	3,650	3,810	2,690	3,980	39,080	112,813	475	3,588	7,815
1997-8	16,782	21,900	8,450	3,950	4,770	3,720	3,600	4,205	43,464	130,190	560	5,438	12,179
1998-9[1]	16,800	21,600	12,607	4,071	5,400	3,700	3,950	4,263	43,262	135,795	470	9,484	14,653
1999-00[2]	17,000	20,660	14,870	3,497	4,400	3,730	4,100	4,260	42,968	136,439	430	7,829	14,647
2000-1[3]	18,200	22,200	16,559	3,900	4,750	3,720	4,200	4,335	43,681	143,534	590	8,722	14,354

[1] Preliminary.   [2] Estimate.   [3] Forecast.   Sources: Oil World; Foreign Agricultural Service, U.S. Department of Agriculture (FAS-USDA)

World Imports and Exports of Soybeans   In Thousands of Metric Tons

Year	China	Germany	Japan	Mexico	Netherlands	Taiwan	World Total	Argentina	Brazil	Canada	Paraguay	United States	World Total
	Imports							Exports					
1991-2	136	3,026	4,672	2,100	4,054	2,453	28,849	2,921	3,826	252	830	18,614	28,086
1992-3	150	3,308	4,866	2,136	4,257	2,506	29,951	2,274	4,184	211	1,250	20,972	29,804
1993-4	125	2,785	4,855	2,200	4,137	2,500	29,062	2,957	5,395	489	1,200	16,006	27,982
1994-5	155	3,363	4,837	1,867	4,624	2,598	32,663	2,614	3,492	542	1,450	22,867	32,251
1995-6	795	3,249	4,776	2,401	4,300	2,646	32,921	2,014	3,633	599	1,600	23,108	31,966
1996-7	2,274	3,681	5,043	2,720	4,450	2,632	37,330	750	8,328	478	2,150	24,110	37,044
1997-8	2,940	4,000	4,873	3,479	4,875	2,387	39,436	3,231	9,336	769	2,390	23,760	41,046
1998-9[1]	3,850	4,095	4,807	3,764	5,007	2,150	40,539	3,200	8,973	876	2,300	21,898	38,681
1999-00[2]	10,100	3,500	4,900	3,950	5,000	2,300	47,660	4,100	11,000	900	2,200	26,492	46,100
2000-1[3]	7,800	3,903	4,750	4,150	5,060	2,350	46,424	4,800	10,900	900	2,400	26,535	46,852

[1] Preliminary.   [2] Estimate.   [3] Forecast.   Sources: Oil World; Foreign Agricultural Service, U.S. Department of Agriculture (FAS-USDA)

Supply and Distribution of Soybeans in the United States   In Millions of Bushels

Crop Year Beginning Sept. 1	Farms	Mills, Elevators[3]	Total	Production	Total Supply	Crushings	Exports	Seed, Feed & Residual	Total Distribution
	Supply					Distribution			
	Stocks, Sept. 1								
1991-2	118.4	210.6	329.0	1,986.5	2,319.0	1,253.5	683.9	103.1	2,040.6
1992-3	105.0	173.4	278.4	2,190.4	2,470.8	1,279.0	769.6	130.0	2,178.6
1993-4	125.0	167.3	292.3	1,869.7	2,168.4	1,275.6	589.1	95.6	1,959.3
1994-5	59.1	150.0	209.1	2,514.9	2,729.5	1,405.2	838.1	151.4	2,394.7
1995-6	105.1	229.7	334.8	2,174.3	2,513.5	1,369.5	851.2	109.3	2,330.1
1996-7	59.5	123.9	183.5	2,380.3	2,572.6	1,437.0	881.8	123.0	2,440.8
1997-8	43.6	88.2	131.8	2,688.8	2,825.6	1,597.0	870.4	158.4	2,625.8
1998-9	84.3	115.5	199.8	2,741.0	2,944.0	1,590.0	805.0	201.0	2,595.0
1999-00[1]	145.0	203.5	348.5	2,654.0	3,006.0	1,579.0	973.0	164.0	2,716.0
2000-1[2]	112.5	177.7	290.2	2,770.0	3,063.0	1,590.0	975.0	168.0	2,718.0

[1] Preliminary.   [2] Estimate.   [3] Also warehouses.   Source: Economic Research Service, U.S. Department of Agriculture (ERS-USDA)

SOYBEANS

Salient Statistics & Official Crop Production Reports of Soybeans in the U.S.   In Millions of Bushels

Year	Planted ---- 1,000	vested Acres ----	Acreage Har-Yield Per Acre (Bu.)	Farm Price ($ / Bu.)	Farm Value (Million Dollars)	Yield of Oil	Yield of Meal	Aug. 1	Crop Production Reports In Thousands of Bushels Sept. 1	Oct. 1	Nov. 1	Dec. 1	Final
1991-2	59,180	58,011	34.2	5.58	11,092	11.42	47.51	1,868,825	1,816,825	1,933,570	1,961,840	----	1,986,539
1992-3	59,180	58,233	37.6	5.56	12,168	10.84	47.54	2,079,487	----	----	----	----	2,190,354
1993-4	60,135	57,347	32.6	6.40	11,950	10.87	47.62	1,902,023	1,909,188	1,890,808	1,833,788	----	1,870,958
1994-5	61,670	60,859	41.4	5.48	13,756	11.08	47.33	2,282,367	2,316,077	2,458,087	2,522,527	----	2,516,694
1995-6	62,575	61,624	35.3	6.72	14,737	11.15	47.69	2,245,901	2,284,551	2,190,661	2,182,991	----	2,176,814
1996-7	64,205	63,409	37.6	7.35	17,440	10.91	47.37	2,299,675	2,269,505	2,346,220	2,402,610	----	2,380,274
1997-8	70,005	69,110	38.9	6.47	17,373	11.26	47.40	2,744,451	2,745,891	2,721,843	2,736,115	----	2,688,750
1998-9	72,025	70,441	38.9	4.93	13,494	11.30	47.25	2,824,744	2,908,604	2,768,919	2,762,609	----	2,741,014
1999-00[1]	73,730	72,446	36.6	4.63	12,205	11.33	47.76	2,869,519	2,778,392	2,696,272	2,672,972	----	2,642,908
2000-1[2]	74,496	72,718	38.1		13,073			2,988,669	2,899,571	2,822,821	2,777,036	----	2,769,665

[1] Preliminary.   [2] Forecast.   Source: National Agricultural Statistics Service, U.S. Department of Agriculture (NASS-USDA)

Stocks of Soybeans in the United States   In Thousands of Bushels

Year	---- On Farms ---- Mar. 1	Jun. 1	Sept. 1	Dec. 1	---- Off Farms[1] ---- Mar. 1	Jun. 1	Sept. 1	Dec. 1	---- Total Stocks ---- Mar. 1	Jun. 1	Sept. 1	Dec. 1
1991	555,500	336,500	118,400	810,000	634,619	387,022	210,642	968,957	1,190,119	723,522	329,042	1,778,957
1992	505,000	279,000	105,000	876,100	672,343	416,671	173,437	959,885	1,177,343	695,671	278,437	1,835,985
1993	576,900	319,800	124,970	697,400	638,667	363,613	167,314	876,220	1,215,567	683,413	292,284	1,573,620
1994	425,700	195,000	59,080	985,800	595,917	360,260	150,037	1,116,156	1,021,617	555,260	209,117	2,101,956
1995	635,300	348,800	105,130	861,500	734,898	443,072	229,684	971,929	1,370,198	791,872	334,814	1,833,429
1996	512,000	234,100	59,523	935,100	678,356	388,701	123,935	889,984	1,190,356	622,801	183,458	1,825,084
1997	514,000	216,000	43,600	1,048,000	541,912	283,890	88,233	951,417	1,055,912	499,890	131,833	1,999,417
1998	637,000	318,000	84,300	1,187,000	565,922	275,654	115,499	999,440	1,202,922	593,654	199,799	2,186,440
1999	815,000	458,000	145,000	1,150,000	642,338	390,573	203,482	1,032,666	1,457,338	848,573	348,482	2,182,666
2000	730,000	370,000	112,500	1,217,000	665,986	404,425	177,662	1,022,092	1,395,986	774,425	290,162	2,236,092

[1] Includes stocks at mills, elevators, warehouses, terminals and processors.   NA = Not avaliable.   Source: National Agricultural Statistics Service, U.S. Department of Agriculture (NASS-USDA)

Commercial Stocks of Soybeans in the United States, on First of Month   In Millions of Bushels

Year	Jan.	Feb.	Mar.	Apr.	May	June	July	Aug.	Sept.	Oct.	Nov.	Dec.
1991	90.2	78.1	70.5	56.2	43.5	35.5	33.3	25.5	25.3	29.7	80.6	84.0
1992	76.0	75.9	67.1	67.8	58.5	57.2	51.7	32.1	18.6	59.0	75.1	79.9
1993	71.5	63.5	54.5	48.5	44.0	32.1	26.6	24.4	15.8	9.6	52.3	60.2
1994	62.6	65.3	54.4	46.3	40.7	34.7	29.9	24.3	19.8	11.5	68.1	83.4
1995	80.7	72.5	67.8	63.5	51.8	50.8	44.3	35.7	33.6	23.0	60.8	61.7
1996	57.2	57.2	59.2	54.7	56.2	44.9	36.9	32.7	12.0	5.3	55.2	50.6
1997	32.6	28.8	22.9	26.0	29.2	24.7	14.3	12.8	6.3	4.5	50.2	49.4
1998	35.3	31.2	22.9	18.4	14.5	14.2	10.2	9.7	8.7	18.6	43.5	40.6
1999	39.1	31.5	29.0	28.7	25.0	18.9	16.1	17.3	14.1	19.5	46.9	42.3
2000	34.1	28.3	30.0	23.9	23.8	20.6	17.0	12.3	8.6	15.5	38.2	37.9

Source: Livestock Division, U.S. Department of Agriculture (LD-USDA)

Stocks of Soybeans at Mills in the United States, on First of Month   In Millions of Bushels

Year	Jan.	Feb.	Mar.	Apr.	May	June	July	Aug.	Sept.	Oct.	Nov.	Dec.
1990-1	45.2	34.5	130.1	130.7	-----	106.5	-----	-----	78.5	-----	-----	61.2
1991-2	-----	-----	67.0	-----	126.9	121.4	109.6	94.7	79.8	73.5	65.7	56.2
1992-3	43.8	46.3	132.3	137.4	119.1	111.2	97.2	90.1	83.6	67.7	67.1	55.3
1993-4	42.0	28.0	108.6	114.9	120.9	126.1	118.5	119.7	98.7	97.8	90.0	63.5
1994-5	47.9	46.8	114.1	124.3	108.0	114.7	114.3	112.6	94.1	81.2	69.1	55.1
1995-6	52.8	54.2	125.6	129.1	120.0	123.3	121.9	110.6	104.2	92.5	70.4	57.4
1996-7	40.7	23.4	101.1	117.4	106.0	112.6	122.2	104.9	89.2	78.2	64.0	43.6
1997-8	28.3	37.0	126.4	124.3	110.3	98.7	93.4	72.0	56.9	41.0	42.5	44.1
1998-9	32.8	66.5	175.0	154.3	131.0	109.6	102.5	93.7	80.5	56.9	55.5	48.1
1999-00[1]	41.7	70.8	162.9	144.7	144.2	140.5	138.5	129.9	98.7	78.9	78.4	52.1

[1] Preliminary.   Source: Economic Research Service, U.S. Department of Agriculture (ERS-USDA)

250

Production of Soybeans for Beans in the United States, by State — In Millions of Bushels

Year	Arkansas	Illinois	Indiana	Iowa	Kentucky	Michigan	Minnesota	Mississippi	Missouri	Nebraska	Ohio	Tennessee	Total
1991	89.6	341.3	171.6	349.5	36.7	52.8	195.3	46.8	135.1	82.4	135.7	31.5	1,986.5
1992	104.3	405.5	194.4	359.5	42.2	47.5	172.8	59.5	161.5	103.3	147.2	33.3	2,190.4
1993	92.3	387.0	223.1	257.3	38.0	54.7	115.0	42.9	118.8	90.0	156.2	32.2	1,871.0
1994	115.6	429.1	215.3	442.9	42.4	57.0	224.0	57.0	173.3	134.4	173.6	38.3	2,516.7
1995	88.4	378.3	196.7	407.4	41.4	59.6	234.9	37.8	132.8	101.0	153.1	34.6	2,176.8
1996	112.0	398.9	203.7	415.8	44.8	46.7	224.2	54.3	149.9	135.5	157.2	38.5	2,380.3
1997	109.8	427.9	230.6	478.4	42.1	71.6	255.5	64.2	174.6	143.8	191.0	40.8	2,688.8
1998	85.0	464.2	231.0	496.8	36.0	73.7	285.6	48.0	170.0	165.0	193.2	35.1	2,741.0
1999	92.4	443.1	216.5	478.4	24.4	77.6	289.8	44.7	147.1	180.6	162.0	22.8	2,653.8
2000[1]	83.2	459.8	259.0	459.2	46.0	74.9	293.2	34.8	175.0	173.9	186.5	28.8	2,769.7

[1] Preliminary.   Source: Agricultural Statistics Board, U.S. Department of Agriculture (ASB-USDA)

United States Exports of Soybeans — In Millions of Bushels

Year	Sept.	Oct.	Nov.	Dec.	Jan.	Feb.	Mar.	Apr.	May	June	July	Aug.	Total
1990-1	27.9	29.8	62.8	55.8	-----	190.1	-----	-----	117.7	-----	73.9	-----	557.9
1991-2	26.8	-----	235.6	-----	73.8	90.6	63.3	56.6	28.3	27.3	42.6	39.2	683.9
1992-3	50.1	98.0	84.2	73.6	89.1	104.7	79.7	48.7	34.6	39.4	42.7	24.6	769.5
1993-4	30.1	73.6	72.4	73.9	71.0	67.8	53.6	34.8	27.5	26.7	17.1	40.7	589.1
1994-5	42.3	99.9	78.5	104.2	89.3	91.4	83.1	80.7	45.2	35.5	41.2	46.7	838.1
1995-6	70.7	77.4	65.5	89.6	106.2	82.9	93.5	52.9	42.1	51.8	46.0	52.6	851.2
1996-7	41.6	95.8	152.4	121.6	106.5	105.7	68.2	58.8	43.0	32.4	23.2	36.5	885.9
1997-8	42.6	174.3	150.4	121.2	91.1	94.8	56.9	36.7	27.3	24.7	27.9	26.6	874.3
1998-9	27.9	135.6	106.3	90.4	84.3	66.8	72.4	52.5	37.8	36.4	36.7	57.5	804.7
1999-00[1]	69.4	122.8	104.5	109.1	104.0	103.1	109.7	50.6	45.6	46.0	50.3	58.4	973.4

[1] Preliminary.   Source: Economic Research Service, U.S. Department of Agriculture (ERS-USDA)

Spread Between Value of Products and Soybean Price in the United States — In Cents Per Bushel

Year	Sept.	Oct.	Nov.	Dec.	Jan.	Feb.	Mar.	Apr.	May	June	July	Aug.	Average
1990-1	99	77	58	64	63	73	79	75	72	74	91	99	77
1991-2	118	120	94	82	74	74	75	78	87	104	80	83	89
1992-3	98	93	87	93	94	77	77	79	82	84	120	97	90
1993-4	95	108	105	92	93	99	88	85	89	88	94	118	96
1994-5	146	167	143	137	130	109	114	109	86	102	87	90	118
1995-6	88	107	82	88	82	77	79	94	73	76	77	71	82
1996-7	109	117	126	115	94	95	86	80	107	96	123	151	108
1997-8	207	127	140	112	80	76	55	56	56	55	77	68	92
1998-9	74	68	50	56	51	49	49	51	49	53	63	59	56
1999-00	64	76	79	79	94	78	91	93	101	99	85	76	84

Source: Economic Research Service, U.S. Department of Agriculture (ERS-USDA)

Soybean Crushed (Factory Consumption) in the United States — In Millions of Bushels

Year	Sept.	Oct.	Nov.	Dec.	Jan.	Feb.	Mar.	Apr.	May	June	July	Aug.	Total
1990-1	92.1	106.1	106.0	102.7	-----	297.9	-----	-----	280.1	-----	202.5	-----	1,187
1991-2	98.9	-----	333.3	-----	112.0	100.8	107.2	101.6	95.2	100.0	102.3	102.3	1,254
1992-3	101.2	113.9	113.1	116.2	116.8	102.2	113.0	105.9	106.5	99.9	98.0	92.2	1,279
1993-4	98.4	113.7	114.4	114.1	110.7	103.3	113.3	105.6	103.0	97.2	101.0	101.0	1,276
1994-5	105.9	119.3	122.5	128.5	127.3	116.5	128.1	119.4	114.2	105.6	108.4	109.5	1,405
1995-6	107.4	120.6	123.4	125.1	122.8	111.2	115.5	112.1	106.3	107.5	111.9	105.7	1,370
1996-7	100.9	127.0	133.1	138.1	137.3	125.1	130.1	114.8	110.7	108.9	106.1	103.8	1,436
1997-8	110.8	142.2	142.8	153.1	151.8	138.3	147.0	134.0	123.9	117.5	123.8	111.9	1,597
1998-9	123.9	142.4	143.0	144.6	136.4	127.6	140.0	128.4	128.0	121.2	127.3	126.9	1,590
1999-00[1]	133.8	150.2	142.8	143.0	139.8	125.3	130.6	121.0	122.4	118.0	129.8	122.2	1,579

One Bushel = 60 Pounds.   [1] Preliminary.   Source: Economic Research Service, U.S. Department of Agriculture (ERS-USDA)

SOYBEANS

Soybean Futures - Chicago Board of Trade (weekly close) as of 29-Dec-2000   Cents Per Bushel

Average Open Interest of Soybean Futures in Chicago   In Contracts

Year	Jan.	Feb.	Mar.	Apr.	May	June	July	Aug.	Sept.	Oct.	Nov.	Dec.
1991	109,311	110,421	110,318	106,995	102,369	103,362	91,449	86,132	98,050	114,206	112,407	112,782
1992	114,871	118,317	132,639	121,171	121,398	137,896	116,208	106,830	104,115	125,734	118,877	114,261
1993	121,726	126,682	126,681	138,155	137,821	142,721	199,681	183,422	163,647	159,641	161,170	168,694
1994	177,648	167,217	156,059	147,569	145,798	150,203	132,010	121,126	126,947	147,198	137,187	136,351
1995	138,345	138,794	137,843	138,624	133,533	143,119	143,671	135,584	144,409	167,200	174,775	194,021
1996	198,731	199,150	192,927	207,284	191,989	179,548	180,817	182,324	196,361	178,872	155,937	152,966
1997	157,728	176,242	189,352	188,617	186,792	159,720	141,658	133,732	150,606	172,098	148,760	150,201
1998	135,340	142,778	147,900	152,732	143,994	149,563	133,532	140,236	158,627	163,759	143,814	146,463
1999	152,757	166,003	162,690	166,565	164,777	163,663	157,433	134,105	146,087	174,583	164,306	153,693
2000	149,468	172,494	174,465	195,189	193,500	167,678	140,894	126,952	149,074	183,734	168,023	177,324

Source: Chicago Board of Trade (CBT)

Volume of Trading of Soybean Futures in Chicago   In Thousands of Contracts

Year	Jan.	Feb.	Mar.	Apr.	May	June	July	Aug.	Sept.	Oct.	Nov.	Dec.	Total
1991	745.0	620.8	715.4	808.0	684.4	776.2	992.4	943.2	662.4	876.2	571.2	619.0	8,974
1992	804.4	738.4	688.0	558.8	873.8	1,054.6	933.2	630.8	572.2	867.4	613.2	665.4	9,000
1993	683.4	624.6	675.8	761.2	778.0	1,287.0	1,643.2	1,180.0	925.0	962.2	1,188.0	941.4	11,649
1994	1,134.6	898.5	922.0	919.3	1,158.4	1,197.0	892.4	688.4	622.6	857.0	825.8	633.2	10,749
1995	614.0	572.0	799.6	698.3	949.4	1,050.8	1,196.7	817.0	800.2	1,127.8	840.4	1,145.4	10,612
1996	1,302.6	1,122.9	1,009.4	1,683.2	1,149.3	989.5	1,295.9	989.8	1,050.2	1,002.7	1,695.6	940.1	14,231
1997	1,119.8	1,254.2	1,405.9	1,585.5	1,391.1	1,355.6	1,217.4	835.0	852.3	1,505.8	1,010.7	1,006.6	14,540
1998	875.7	971.2	935.9	1,116.2	973.6	1,378.8	1,286.3	884.5	864.4	1,264.6	867.0	1,012.9	12,431
1999	871.1	1,025.3	1,440.1	963.5	823.6	1,149.5	1,502.5	1,669.8	903.0	1,158.6	839.4	872.3	12,482
2000	1,071.9	1,099.3	1,191.6	1,079.1	1,321.6	1,302.0	883.4	801.4	860.9	1,188.8	932.5	895.3	12,628

Source: Chicago Board of Trade

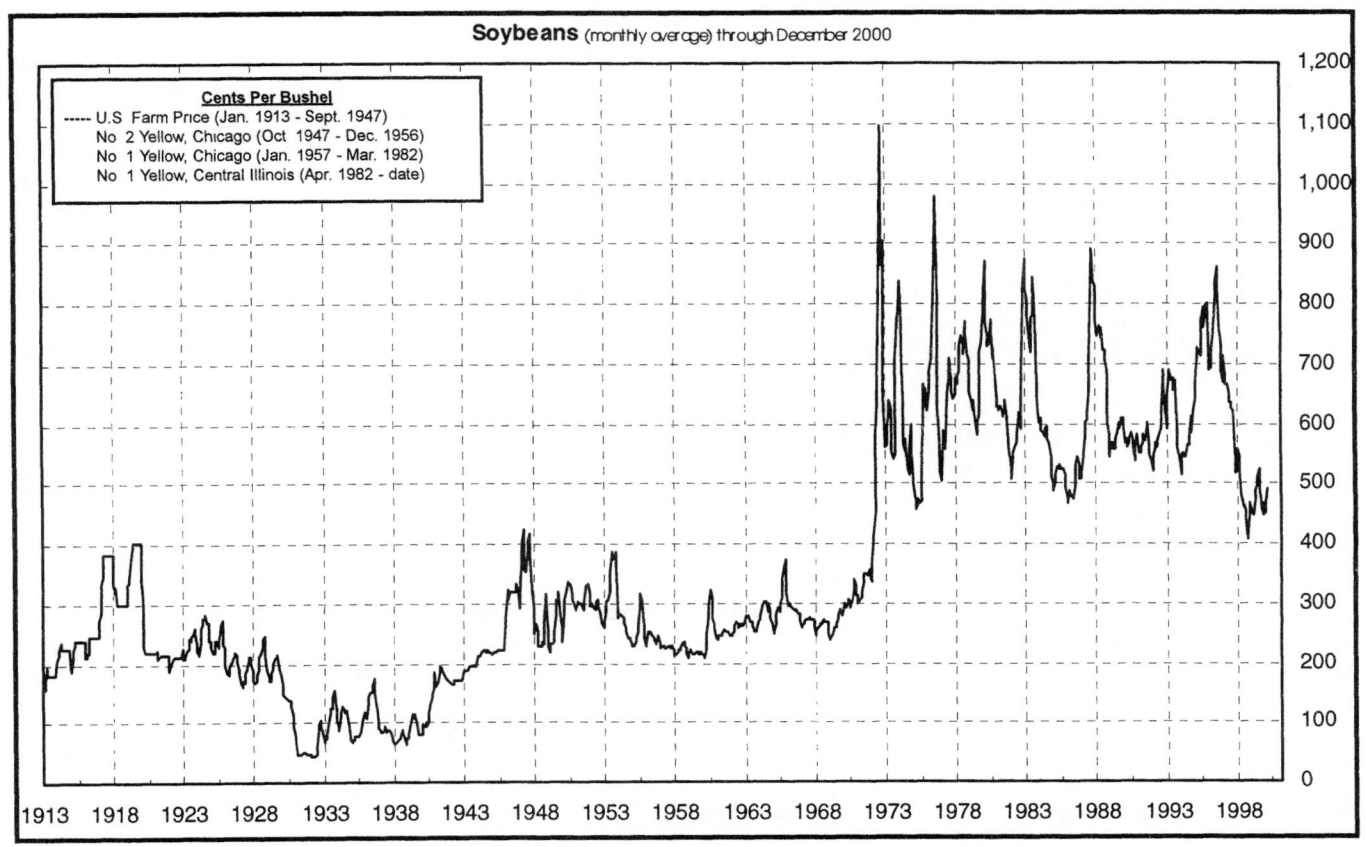

Soybeans (monthly average) through December 2000

Cents Per Bushel
----- U.S Farm Price (Jan. 1913 - Sept. 1947)
No 2 Yellow, Chicago (Oct 1947 - Dec. 1956)
No 1 Yellow, Chicago (Jan. 1957 - Mar. 1982)
No 1 Yellow, Central Illinois (Apr. 1982 - date)

Average Cash Price of No. 1 Yellow Soybeans at Illinois Processor — In Cents Per Bushel

Year	Sept.	Oct.	Nov.	Dec.	Jan.	Feb.	Mar.	Apr.	May	June	July	Aug.	Average
1990-1	628	614	587	591	576	585	592	601	589	583	554	578	590
1991-2	598	568	571	568	577	581	593	585	609	619	580	564	584
1992-3	554	535	560	572	582	575	587	597	607	606	689	679	595
1993-4	643	606	664	694	701	686	692	670	689	685	603	576	659
1994-5	557	531	566	567	558	560	574	578	580	577	623	602	573
1995-6	632	656	686	717	737	730	726	791	808	778	795	816	739
1996-7	820	711	704	708	737	769	833	854	878	837	769	741	780
1997-8	703	684	727	699	679	680	662	649	649	640	642	556	664
1998-9	533	536	572	558	532	490	475	480	468	462	425	465	500
1999-00[1]	485	470	464	460	473	500	513	529	542	510	474	463	490

[1] Preliminary.   *Source: Economic Research Service, U.S. Department of Agriculture (ERS-USDA)*

Average Price Received by Farmers for Soybeans in the United States — In Cents Per Bushel

Year	Sept.	Oct.	Nov.	Dec.	Jan.	Feb.	Mar.	Apr.	May	June	July	Aug.	Average
1991-2	564	548	548	545	554	559	567	566	587	594	559	540	558
1992-3	536	526	536	546	558	556	565	573	581	590	656	656	556
1993-4	621	601	632	664	672	671	673	657	677	672	592	558	640
1994-5	547	530	536	541	547	540	551	555	556	568	590	583	548
1995-6	598	615	640	676	677	701	700	743	769	741	762	782	672
1996-7	779	694	690	691	713	738	797	823	840	816	752	725	735
1997-8	672	650	685	671	669	657	640	626	626	616	614	543	647
1998-9	525	518	540	537	532	480	461	463	451	444	420	439	493
1999-00	457	448	445	443	462	479	491	500	519	493	453	445	463
2000-1[1]	457	445	455	478	468	437							457

[1] Preliminary.   *Source: Economic Research Service, U.S. Department of Agriculture (ERS-USDA)*

Stock Index Futures, U.S.

The U.S. equity markets began the twenty-first century with a deep rooted optimism that the market strength of the late 1990's would carry into calendar 2000; and it did through the first quarter of the year. However, by year-end investor psychology had reversed to pessimism owing to a number of diverse reasons, but perhaps most important was that the markets failed to show any sustainable recovery following periods of weakness. This was not the scenario seen in the 1990's when price declines were seen as buying opportunities. In 2000, recoveries became viewed as chances to move capital into investments other than equities. For the year, about $2.7 trillion in shareholder value was lost.

Ironically, it was the high-tech oriented NASDAQ index that led the decline as it had previously led the advance that had propelled overall equity values to historic highs. The NASDAQ composite index in 2000 dropped 39.3 percent, its worst annual loss ever. More dramatic was the 50 percent collapse in the composite index after it reached the record intraday high of 5132.52 on March 10, 2000, closing the year at 2470.52. However, it should be remembered that only a small number of stocks account for nearly 50 percent of the NASDAQ's value and that in 1999 the index registered an 85 percent gain. The bellwether price weighted Dow-Jones 30 industrial index, which now includes some NASDAQ stocks, lost 6.18 percent in 2000 vs. a gain of 25 percent in 1999. 2000 was the Dow's worst year since 1981, when it fell 9.2 percent. The market capitalization weighted S&P 500 index fell 10.14 percent vs. a gain of nearly 20 percent in 1999; the Wilshire 5000 lost 11.85 percent, the Russell 2000 was down 4.2 percent and the value line "A" lost nearly 9 percent. However, there were some gains, notably the Dow-Jones Utility index which rose by 45 percent. Trading volume continued at a record pace with the New York Stock Exchange trading about 263 billion shares

vs. 203 billion in 1999, while the NASDAQ's volume topped 433 billion shares vs. 262 billion in 1999. As has been the case since the mid-1990's, market volatility was the rule rather than the exception, partially reflecting burgeoning computer driven day trading that tends to feed upon itself. The weakness in 2000 also reflected a return to evaluating corporate earnings, realized and projected, and assessing a seemingly rational price/earning ratio. This was not the case in the late 1990's when the traditional analytical parameters were relegated to the backburner.

The U.S. economy grew robustly for a time in early 2000, but warning signs were falling into place that the buoyancy was slipping. A tightening federal reserve policy with a series of interest rate increases likely contributed to the slippage, but consumer confidence held strong, at least into late 2000, and unemployment at 4 percent was a 30-year low. Higher oil prices unsettled the markets but the effect appeared to have little lasting impact. In either case, the damage witnessed in the equity markets in 2000 ran deep, suggesting that the overall approach towards the market in 2001 will be more cautious, although the long-term uptrend that took hold in the 1990's, while battered in 2000, is still in place and mainstream America is apt to continue viewing stocks as the best investment.

Futures Markets

The Chicago Mercantile Exchange (CME) IOM division trades index futures and options on the S&P 500, the S&P MidCap 400, the NASDAQ 100, and the Russell 2000. The Chicago Board of Trade (CBOT) lists futures and options on the Dow-Jones 30 industrial index. New York Stock Exchange Composite index futures and options are traded on the New York Board of Trade (NYBOT).

Dow Jones Industrial Average (30 Stocks)

Year	Jan.	Feb.	Mar.	Apr.	May	June	July	Aug.	Sept.	Oct.	Nov.	Dec.	Average
1991	2,587.6	2,863.0	2,920.1	2,925.5	2,928.4	2,968.1	2,978.2	3,006.1	3,010.4	3,019.7	2,986.1	2,958.6	2,929.3
1992	3,227.1	3,257.3	3,247.4	3,294.1	3,376.8	3,337.8	3,329.4	3,307.4	3,293.9	3,198.7	3,238.5	3,303.1	3,284.3
1993	3,277.7	3,367.3	3,440.7	3,423.6	3,478.2	3,513.8	3,529.4	3,597.0	3,592.3	3,625.8	3,674.7	3,744.1	3,522.1
1994	3,868.4	3,905.6	3,817.0	3,661.5	3,708.0	3,737.6	3,718.3	3,797.5	3,880.6	3,868.1	3,792.5	3,770.3	3,793.8
1995	3,872.5	3,953.7	4,062.8	4,230.7	4,391.6	4,510.8	4,684.8	4,639.3	4,746.8	4,760.5	4,935.8	5,136.1	4,493.8
1996	5,179.4	5,518.7	5,612.2	5,579.9	5,616.7	5,671.5	5,496.3	5,685.5	5,804.0	5,995.1	6,318.4	6,435.9	5,742.8
1997	6,707.0	6,917.5	6,901.1	6,657.5	7,242.4	7,599.6	7,990.7	7,948.4	7,866.6	7,875.8	7,677.4	7,909.8	7,441.1
1998	7,808.4	8,323.6	8,709.5	9,037.4	9,080.1	8,873.0	9,097.1	8,478.5	7,909.8	8,164.3	9,005.8	9,018.7	8,625.5
1999	9,345.9	9,323.0	9,753.6	10,443.5	10,853.9	10,704.0	11,052.2	10,935.5	10,714.0	10,396.9	10,809.8	11,246.4	10,464.9
2000	11,281.3	10,541.9	10,483.4	10,944.4	10,580.3	10,582.9	10,663.0	11,014.5	10,967.9	10,441.0	10,666.1	10,652.4	10,734.9

Average.   Source: New York Stock Exchange (NYSE)

Dow Jones Transportation Average (20 Stocks)

Year	Jan.	Feb.	Mar.	Apr.	May	June	July	Aug.	Sept.	Oct.	Nov.	Dec.	Average
1991	962.2	1,110.4	1,113.5	1,138.8	1,167.6	1,205.2	1,204.7	1,204.7	1,182.3	1,241.5	1,237.1	1,233.3	1,166.8
1992	1,378.7	1,412.2	1,409.0	1,356.9	1,380.4	1,333.3	1,303.1	1,254.6	1,275.2	1,286.1	1,375.9	1,430.2	1,349.6
1993	1,488.1	1,533.2	1,541.6	1,619.7	1,583.4	1,533.9	1,553.7	1,631.6	1,623.9	1,660.5	1,732.6	1,763.2	1,605.5
1994	1,812.1	1,810.4	1,719.9	1,614.7	1,602.2	1,619.2	1,596.2	1,602.8	1,553.7	1,485.8	1,473.7	1,415.3	1,608.8
1995	1,515.8	1,547.2	1,584.6	1,648.9	1,646.2	1,699.3	1,852.1	1,883.9	1,961.4	1,922.9	2,008.3	2,029.5	1,775.0
1996	1,932.7	2,030.0	2,136.0	2,180.0	2,229.1	2,213.4	2,053.1	2,060.4	2,050.8	2,100.1	2,224.3	2,273.9	2,123.7
1997	2,295.0	2,341.4	2,427.8	2,464.0	2,635.1	2,711.4	2,858.0	2,925.8	3,086.0	3,239.9	3,155.7	3,233.5	2,781.1
1998	3,275.8	3,456.8	3,521.5	3,586.5	3,401.9	3,373.2	3,459.3	3,021.1	2,763.0	2,647.8	2,953.4	3,027.6	3,207.3
1999	3,172.0	3,188.3	3,296.4	3,477.7	3,628.2	3,396.1	3,423.7	3,207.0	3,006.2	2,928.7	2,988.7	2,902.1	3,217.9
2000	2,812.2	2,483.4	2,534.5	2,823.9	2,813.2	2,717.2	2,822.3	2,835.6	2,641.5	2,491.0	2,792.3	2,822.9	2,715.8

Average.   Source: New York Stock Exchange (NYSE)

Dow Jones 30 Industrials Index (weekly close) as of 29-Dec-2000

Index Value

Dow Jones Public Utilities Average (15 Stocks)

Year	Jan.	Feb.	Mar.	Apr.	May	June	July	Aug.	Sept.	Oct.	Nov.	Dec.	Average
1991	205.3	213.7	213.2	214.4	211.2	204.6	199.6	204.4	208.0	213.6	216.7	219.3	210.3
1992	215.7	206.8	204.4	206.1	213.2	212.5	219.1	220.2	220.0	217.2	217.7	220.2	214.4
1993	222.0	234.2	240.0	242.1	237.8	241.5	246.5	252.0	253.0	243.1	227.1	227.1	238.9
1994	222.3	215.6	207.0	196.5	185.5	182.9	181.8	188.9	179.6	179.9	177.7	181.0	191.6
1995	186.9	194.0	187.9	192.7	197.6	204.5	202.5	202.8	207.2	216.4	215.3	221.4	202.4
1996	228.4	228.6	216.3	209.5	211.2	210.0	212.8	214.8	217.2	222.3	234.0	232.1	219.8
1997	235.8	230.5	223.7	213.8	222.1	223.5	232.0	231.9	238.9	242.9	249.2	263.9	234.0
1998	265.6	267.9	279.0	285.4	281.2	291.1	289.3	279.4	289.1	307.0	308.1	309.0	287.7
1999	307.4	293.9	299.4	299.9	320.5	327.8	319.9	317.3	306.8	298.8	294.9	277.4	305.3
2000	300.6	302.3	285.4	307.0	325.2	322.2	325.0	355.6	384.2	386.9	392.5	394.9	340.2

Average.   *Source: New York Stock Exchange (NYSE)*

Standard & Poor's 500 Composite Price Index

Year	Jan.	Feb.	Mar.	Apr.	May	June	July	Aug.	Sept.	Oct.	Nov.	Dec.	Average
1991	325.5	362.3	372.3	379.7	378.0	378.3	380.2	389.4	387.2	386.9	385.9	388.5	376.2
1992	416.1	412.6	407.4	407.4	414.8	408.3	415.1	417.9	418.5	412.5	422.8	435.6	415.7
1993	435.2	441.7	450.2	443.1	445.3	448.1	447.3	454.1	459.2	463.9	462.9	466.0	451.4
1994	473.0	471.6	463.8	447.2	451.0	454.8	451.4	464.2	467.0	463.8	461.0	455.2	460.3
1995	465.3	481.9	493.2	507.9	523.8	539.4	557.4	559.1	578.8	582.9	595.5	614.6	541.6
1996	614.4	649.5	647.1	547.2	661.2	668.5	644.1	662.7	674.9	701.5	735.7	743.3	662.5
1997	766.1	798.4	792.2	763.9	833.1	876.3	925.3	927.7	937.0	951.2	938.9	962.4	872.7
1998	963.4	1,023.7	1,076.8	1,112.2	1,108.4	1,108.4	1,156.6	1,074.6	1,020.7	1,032.5	1,144.5	1,190.0	1,084.3
1999	1,248.7	1,246.6	1,281.7	1,334.8	1,332.1	1,322.6	1,381.0	1,327.5	1,318.2	1,300.0	1,391.0	1,428.7	1,326.1
2000	1,425.6	1,388.9	1,442.2	1,461.4	1,418.5	1,462.0	1,473.0	1,485.5	1,468.0	1,390.1	1,375.0	1,330.9	1,426.8

Average.   *Source: Index and Option Market (IOM), division of the Chicago Mercantile Exchange (CME)*

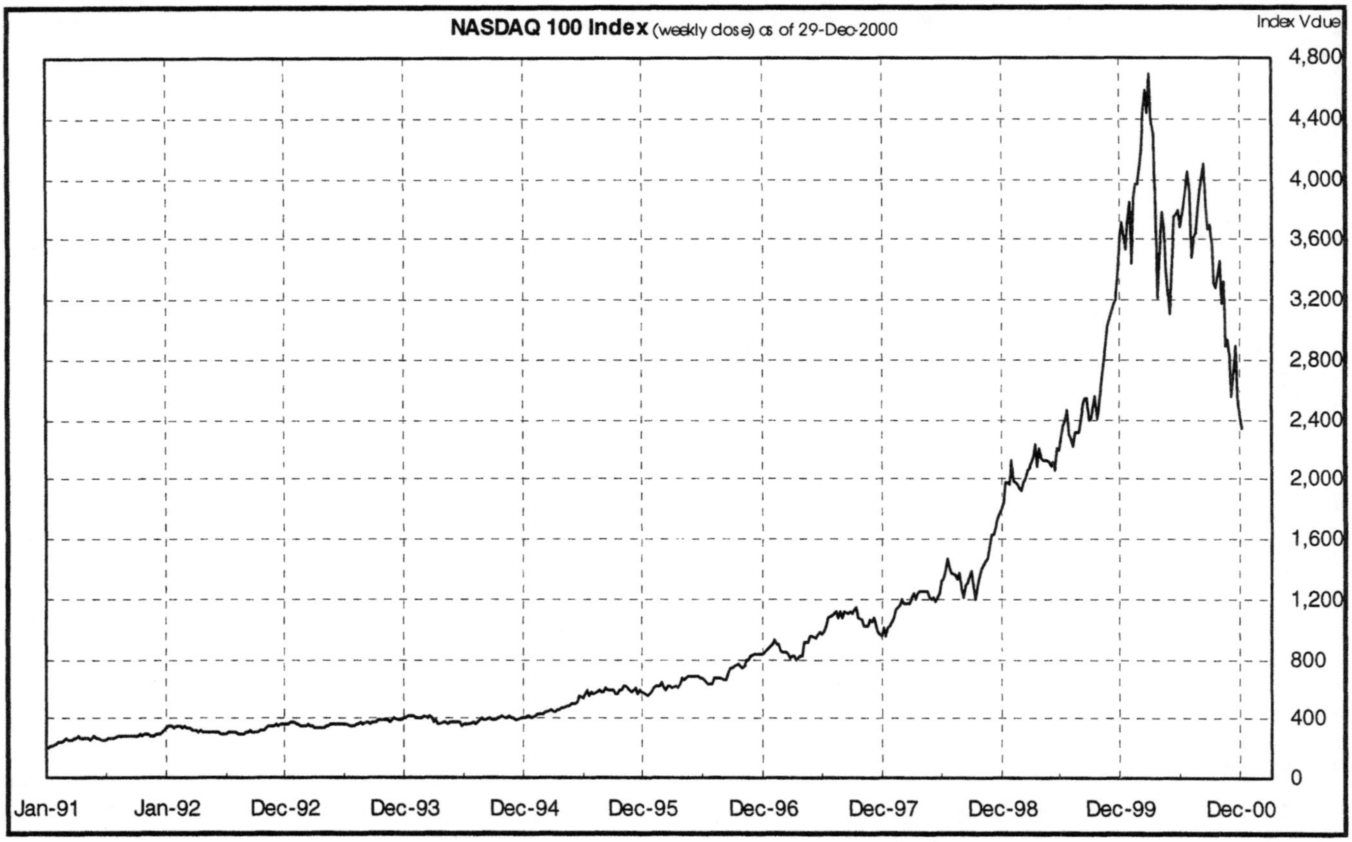

STOCK INDEX FUTURES, U.S.

NASDAQ 100 Index (weekly close) as of 29-Dec-2000

Index Value

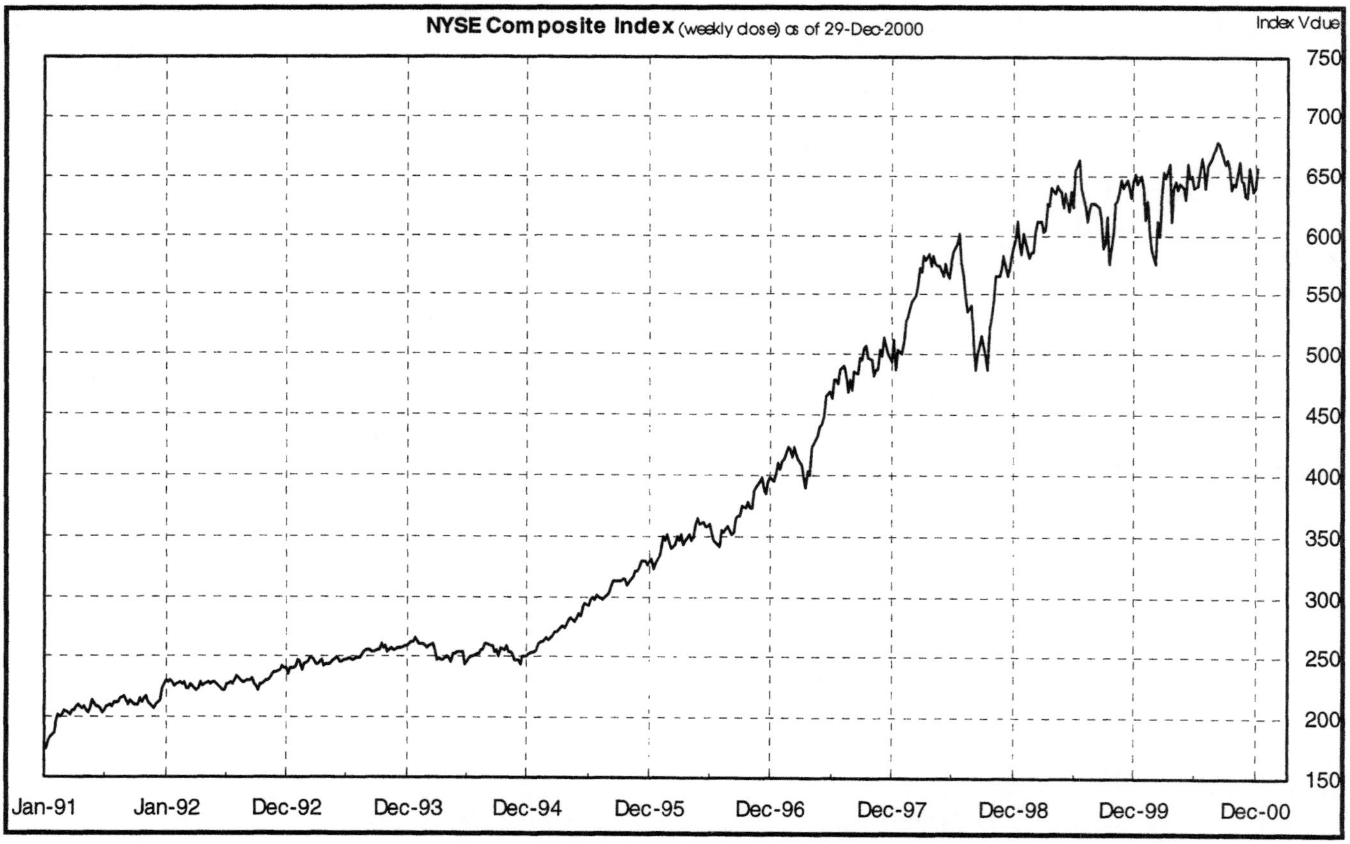

NYSE Composite Index (weekly close) as of 29-Dec-2000

Index Value

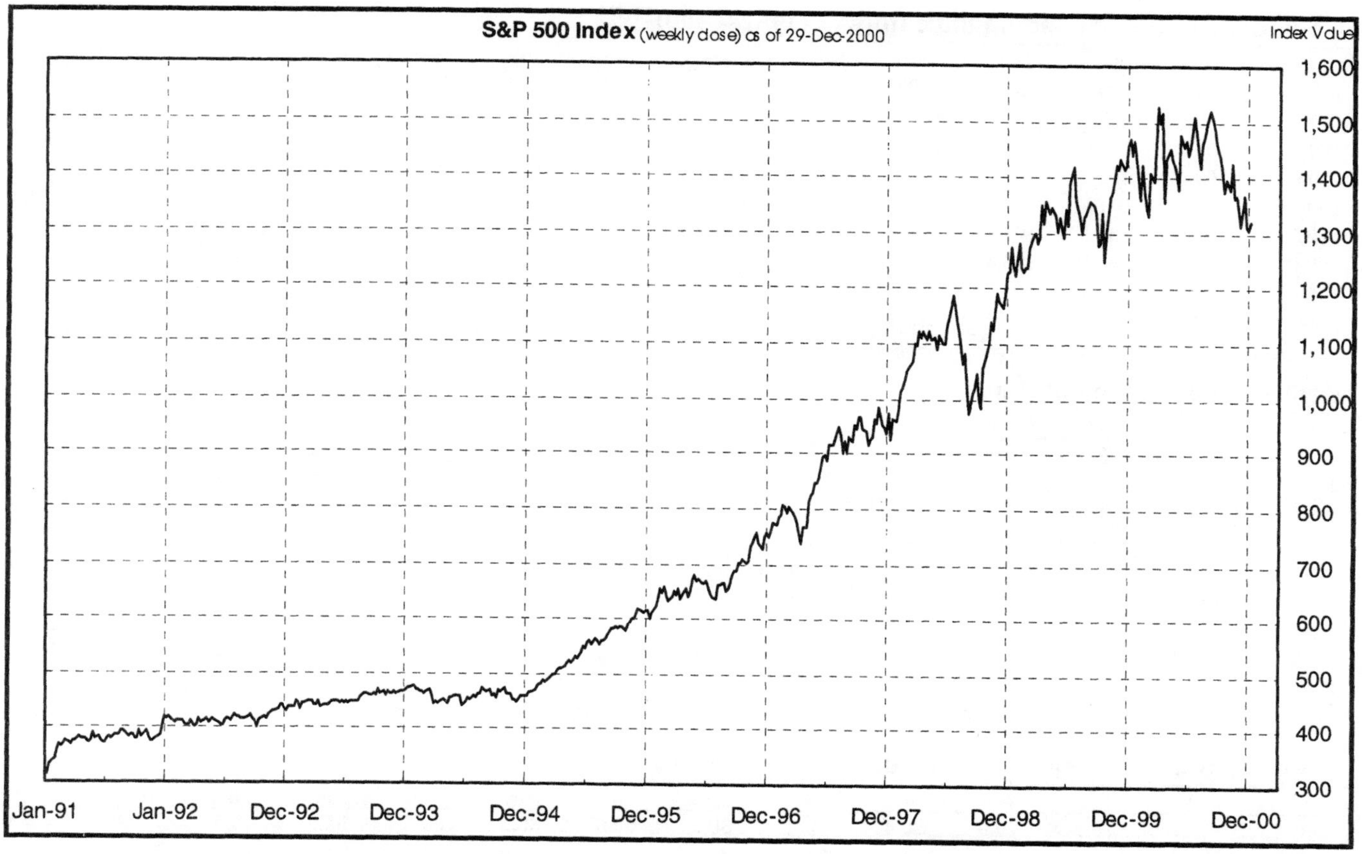
S&P 500 Index (weekly close) as of 29-Dec-2000
Index Value
1,600
1,500
1,400
1,300
1,200
1,100
1,000
900
800
700
600
500
400
300
Jan-91
Jan-92
Dec-92
Dec-93
Dec-94
Dec-95
Dec-96
Dec-97
Dec-98
Dec-99
Dec-00

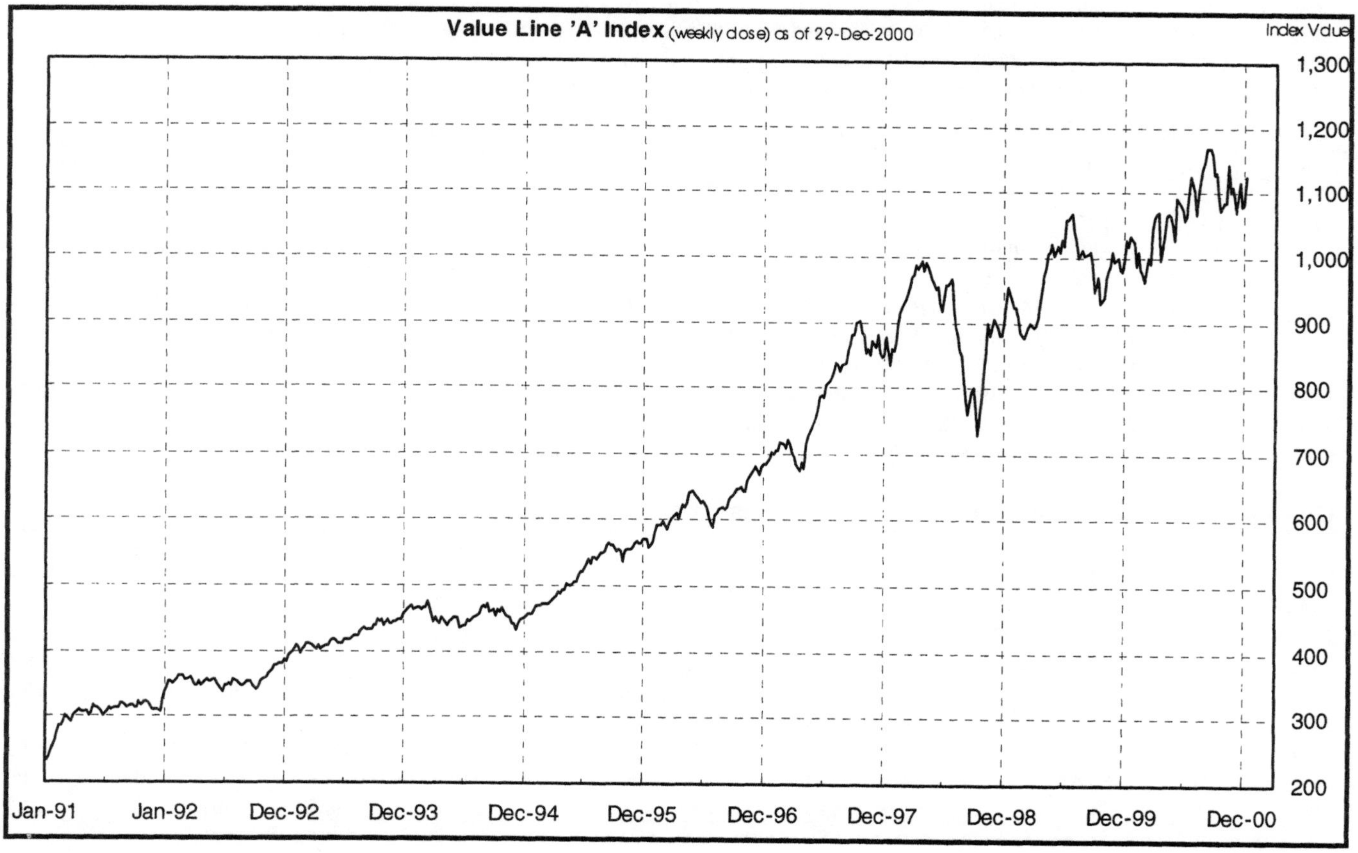
Value Line 'A' Index (weekly close) as of 29-Dec-2000
Index Value
1,300
1,200
1,100
1,000
900
800
700
600
500
400
300
200
Jan-91
Jan-92
Dec-92
Dec-93
Dec-94
Dec-95
Dec-96
Dec-97
Dec-98
Dec-99
Dec-00

STOCK INDEX FUTURES, U.S.

Composite Index of Leading Indicators   (1992 = 100)

Year	Jan.	Feb.	Mar.	Apr.	May	June	July	Aug.	Sept.	Oct.	Nov.	Dec.	Average
1992	99.4	99.7	99.9	99.9	100.0	99.9	99.9	99.9	99.9	100.1	100.4	101.0	100.0
1993	100.7	100.7	100.1	100.4	100.2	100.3	100.1	100.3	100.4	100.5	100.8	101.2	100.5
1994	101.2	101.0	101.5	101.4	101.4	101.4	101.2	101.5	101.4	101.5	101.6	101.6	101.4
1995	101.5	101.1	100.7	100.6	100.4	100.5	100.7	101.0	101.1	100.9	100.9	101.2	100.9
1996	100.5	101.4	101.6	101.8	102.1	102.3	102.3	102.4	102.5	102.5	102.5	102.6	102.0
1997	102.8	103.3	103.4	103.3	103.6	103.6	103.9	104.0	104.3	104.4	104.7	104.6	103.8
1998	104.8	105.2	105.4	105.4	105.4	105.2	105.6	105.6	105.6	105.7	106.2	106.4	105.5
1999	104.5	104.7	104.8	104.7	105.0	105.3	105.6	105.5	105.4	105.5	105.7	110.3	105.6
2000[1]	110.6	110.2	110.4	110.4	110.2	110.1	109.8	109.7	109.8	109.4	109.0	108.3	109.8

[1] Preliminary.   Source: Bureau of Economic Analysis, U.S. Department of Commerce (BEA)

Civilian Unemployment Rate

Year	Jan.	Feb.	Mar.	Apr.	May	June	July	Aug.	Sept.	Oct.	Nov.	Dec.	Average
1992	7.3	7.4	7.4	7.4	7.6	7.8	7.7	7.6	7.6	7.3	7.4	7.4	7.5
1993	7.3	7.1	7.0	7.1	7.1	7.0	6.9	6.8	6.7	6.8	6.6	6.5	6.9
1994	6.7	6.6	6.5	6.4	6.0	6.1	6.1	6.1	5.9	5.8	5.6	5.4	6.1
1995	5.6	5.5	5.4	5.7	5.6	5.6	5.7	5.7	5.7	5.5	5.6	5.6	5.6
1996	5.7	5.5	5.5	5.5	5.5	5.3	5.4	5.2	5.2	5.2	5.3	5.3	5.4
1997	5.4	5.3	5.2	4.9	4.8	5.0	4.9	4.9	4.9	4.8	4.6	4.7	5.0
1998	4.6	4.6	4.7	4.3	4.4	4.5	4.5	4.5	4.5	4.5	4.4	4.3	4.5
1999	4.3	4.4	4.2	4.3	4.2	4.3	4.3	4.2	4.2	4.1	4.1	4.1	4.2
2000[1]	4.0	4.1	4.1	3.9	4.1	4.0	4.0	4.1	3.9	3.9	4.0	4.0	4.0

[1] Preliminary.   Source: Bureau of Economic Analysis, U.S. Department of Commerce (BEA)

Capacity Utilization Rates (Total Industry)   In Percent

Year	Jan.	Feb.	Mar.	Apr.	May	June	July	Aug.	Sept.	Oct.	Nov.	Dec.	Average
1992	79.0	79.4	79.9	80.4	80.6	80.2	80.6	80.2	80.5	81.0	81.3	81.2	80.4
1993	81.4	81.7	81.6	81.7	81.2	81.2	81.3	81.0	81.7	81.8	82.1	82.5	81.6
1994	82.6	82.8	83.2	83.3	83.7	83.9	84.1	83.9	83.8	84.1	84.4	84.9	83.9
1995	84.9	84.5	84.3	83.9	83.7	83.6	83.4	83.8	83.9	83.3	83.2	83.0	83.4
1996	82.4	83.2	82.6	83.1	83.2	83.5	83.2	83.2	83.1	83.0	82.5	82.5	82.4
1997	82.4	82.6	82.5	82.6	82.4	82.3	82.6	82.8	82.7	83.4	83.4	83.4	82.9
1998	83.0	82.6	82.6	82.6	82.6	81.5	81.1	82.0	81.3	81.5	80.9	80.6	81.8
1999	80.4	80.4	80.5	80.4	80.5	80.5	80.7	80.7	80.6	81.0	81.5	81.7	80.6
2000[1]	81.9	82.0	82.2	82.5	82.7	82.7	82.3	82.6	82.4	81.9	81.4	80.6	82.1

[1] Preliminary.   Source: Bureau of Economic Analysis, U.S. Department of Commerce (BEA)

Manufacturers New Orders, Durable Goods   In Billions of Constant Dollars

Year	Jan.	Feb.	Mar.	Apr.	May	June	July	Aug.	Sept.	Oct.	Nov.	Dec.	Average
1992	122.15	122.14	124.63	127.60	125.65	128.77	125.51	123.79	125.86	128.69	125.49	135.19	126.29
1993	129.56	133.47	128.50	130.20	126.93	131.29	128.27	128.99	130.31	133.01	135.60	136.82	131.08
1994	142.23	138.88	140.91	141.21	142.61	146.15	142.60	145.92	146.93	145.72	149.89	152.88	144.66
1995	153.42	151.82	151.72	146.32	149.74	148.21	147.45	152.12	156.78	154.37	154.09	158.89	154.10
1996	158.86	155.10	157.67	156.01	162.59	162.67	168.25	162.76	170.45	170.59	169.34	166.02	163.48
1997	171.73	174.80	170.02	173.13	177.05	176.93	175.82	181.08	181.15	181.33	189.71	181.44	177.03
1998	184.33	183.87	184.17	187.35	181.58	182.22	186.22	190.39	193.18	189.33	190.21	197.11	194.42
1999	211.18	203.31	209.39	204.68	206.78	207.27	216.02	218.02	214.83	212.77	215.34	229.47	212.67
2000[1]	225.14	221.12	230.44	217.17	232.76	254.20	220.74	227.27	232.41	217.47	222.56		227.39

[1] Preliminary.   Source: Bureau of Economic Analysis, U.S. Department of Commerce (BEA)

Change in Manufacturing and Trade Inventories   In Billions of Dollars

Year	Jan.	Feb.	Mar.	Apr.	May	June	July	Aug.	Sept.	Oct.	Nov.	Dec.	Average
1992	-60.6	-0.3	13.8	28.3	-22.3	53.6	28.4	21.4	-8.4	4.6	11.8	23.9	7.9
1993	34.9	31.8	66.7	43.7	12.9	25.6	7.3	39.0	34.8	27.2	63.2	1.6	32.4
1994	15.3	45.1	-8.1	42.1	114.2	56.3	60.8	98.6	60.3	71.8	65.3	64.5	57.2
1995	127.4	78.5	100.6	97.6	54.4	48.1	42.9	50.6	51.4	61.8	24.1	-39.7	58.5
1996	66.2	14.2	-27.7	61.5	-8.4	80.3	123.6	-272.1	90.6	143.4	86.1	72.0	19.9
1997	107.0	103.4	76.3	56.2	25.2	76.8	20.9	19.1	91.5	55.2	43.1	28.2	47.1
1998	27.8	86.1	85.7	38.5	5.5	11.4	-91.6	47.9	67.6	36.3	51.0		34.0
1999	10.4	36.8	66.7	31.2	44.4	61.6	67.2	42.5	58.0	50.4	121.1	70.9	50.6
2000[1]	76.7	66.1	39.6	74.6	122.4	120.7	58.7	102.3	24.6	96.8	67.9		77.3

[1] Preliminary.   Source: Bureau of Economic Analysis, U.S. Department of Commerce (BEA)

Comparison of International Stock Price Indexes   (1990 = 100)

Year	Jan.	Feb.	Mar.	Apr.	May	June	July	Aug.	Sept.	Oct.	Nov.	Dec.	Average
United States
1995	141.4	146.5	150.5	154.7	160.3	163.7	168.9	168.9	175.7	174.8	182.0	185.1	164.4
1996	191.2	192.5	194.0	196.6	201.1	201.6	192.4	196.0	206.6	212.0	227.6	222.7	202.9
1997	236.3	237.7	227.6	240.9	255.0	266.1	286.8	270.4	284.7	274.9	287.2	291.7	263.3
1998	294.7	315.4	331.2	334.2	327.9	340.8	336.9	287.7	305.7	330.2	349.8	369.5	327.0
1999	384.6	372.2	386.7	401.3	391.3	412.6	399.4	396.9	385.6	409.7	417.5	441.6	400.0
2000[1]	419.2	410.7	450.5	436.6	427.0	437.2	430.1	456.2	431.8	429.7	395.3		429.5
Canada
1995	117.4	120.6	126.1	125.1	130.0	132.3	134.9	132.0	132.4	130.3	136.2	137.8	129.6
1996	145.2	144.2	145.3	150.4	153.4	147.4	144.1	150.3	154.7	163.7	175.9	173.2	154.0
1997	178.6	180.0	171.0	174.7	186.6	188.2	201.0	193.3	205.8	200.0	190.4	195.8	188.8
1998	195.8	207.3	220.9	224.0	221.9	215.3	202.6	161.7	164.0	181.5	185.4	189.6	197.5
1999	196.7	184.5	192.9	205.0	200.0	204.9	207.0	203.8	203.4	212.1	219.9	245.9	206.3
2000[1]	247.9	266.8	276.6	273.2	270.4	298.0	304.2	328.8	303.3	281.8	257.8		282.6
France
1995	98.9	97.8	102.3	105.6	107.2	102.3	105.6	103.6	98.4	99.8	100.6	103.0	102.1
1996	111.2	109.5	112.5	118.1	116.1	116.9	109.8	108.4	117.4	117.8	127.4	127.4	116.0
1997	138.5	143.5	146.2	145.2	142.2	157.3	169.2	152.4	165.5	150.7	157.3	165.0	152.8
1998	174.5	188.3	213.3	213.5	222.4	231.3	229.8	200.9	176.0	193.8	211.5	216.9	206.0
1999	233.9	225.2	231.0	242.4	239.4	249.6	241.1	252.5	252.6	269.0	293.9	327.8	254.9
2000[1]	311.4	340.6	345.9	353.2	353.6	354.7	360.0	364.5	344.8	352.0	326.2		346.1
Germany[2]
1995	103.8	108.2	98.6	103.5	106.6	106.6	112.8	113.7	111.4	109.3	111.9	114.0	108.4
1996	123.7	123.2	123.3	123.0	124.4	126.3	122.1	125.6	130.4	130.6	139.0	139.7	153.2
1997	147.0	157.8	167.8	167.1	172.2	183.8	209.6	184.1	195.3	177.8	186.0	196.3	221.4
1998	204.9	217.5	234.9	302.0	329.3	348.7	347.3	285.8	264.6	276.2	297.0	295.8	299.1
1999	305.1	290.4	288.8	318.9	299.8	318.0	301.6	311.6	304.5	326.7	348.6	411.4	318.8
2000[1]	404.2	452.0	449.3	438.4	420.4	407.9	425.1	426.7	401.9	418.5	376.8		420.1
Italy
1995	102.8	97.5	93.3	99.8	98.8	94.9	98.8	99.0	96.1	90.5	86.1	91.8	95.8
1996	96.5	94.5	90.4	102.4	104.1	102.4	93.4	93.2	99.0	94.0	102.4	103.7	98.0
1997	119.8	115.4	115.3	119.5	117.9	130.0	144.5	136.6	155.0	144.6	149.4	164.0	134.3
1998	184.0	194.3	239.3	220.9	236.1	222.1	240.5	208.1	184.6	194.1	223.7	231.5	214.9
1999	231.7	234.1	245.4	245.9	237.1	237.5	221.5	230.4	231.0	226.5	241.3	282.8	238.8
2000[1]	276.8	330.7	308.7	303.1	307.1	309.0	308.5	320.5	307.2	318.8	316.3		309.7
Japan
1995	64.7	59.2	56.0	58.3	53.6	50.4	57.9	62.9	62.1	61.2	65.0	68.9	60.0
1996	72.2	69.8	74.3	76.5	76.2	78.2	71.8	70.0	74.8	71.0	72.9	67.2	72.9
1997	63.6	64.4	62.5	66.4	69.6	71.5	70.5	63.2	62.1	57.1	57.7	52.9	63.5
1998	57.7	58.4	57.3	54.3	54.4	54.9	56.8	48.9	46.5	47.1	51.6	48.0	53.0
1999	50.3	49.8	54.9	57.9	55.9	60.8	62.0	60.5	61.1	62.2	64.4	65.7	58.8
2000[1]	67.8	69.2	70.6	62.4	56.7	60.4	54.6	58.5	54.6	50.4	50.8		59.6
United Kingdom
1995	136.8	137.4	142.1	145.8	150.8	150.0	157.3	158.8	160.2	160.2	165.2	166.6	152.6
1996	170.2	170.0	170.3	176.9	174.2	171.5	169.6	177.0	179.7	180.8	183.4	186.0	175.8
1997	192.8	194.7	194.0	197.3	203.3	201.8	212.0	210.3	226.8	211.9	211.4	222.7	206.6
1998	234.3	247.9	257.0	257.6	258.9	253.4	252.6	225.5	216.6	231.4	242.7	247.0	243.7
1999	249.0	261.0	267.4	279.8	266.9	272.2	270.2	271.5	261.1	268.3	285.2	299.5	271.0
2000[1]	274.9	276.2	287.3	277.3	278.7	279.9	282.9	296.3	279.8	284.4	272.1		280.9

[1] Preliminary.   [2] Federal Republic of Germany.   Not Seasonally Adjusted.   Source: Economic and Statistics Administration, U.S. Department of Commerce (ESA)

Corporate Profits After Tax -- Quarterly   In Billions of Dollars

Year	First Quarter	Second Quarter	Third Quarter	Fourth Quarter	Average	Year	First Quarter	Second Quarter	Third Quarter	Fourth Quarter	Average
1989	219.3	206.7	196.9	204.4	206.8	1995	401.0	405.9	411.8	418.8	409.4
1990	221.7	232.2	233.9	237.1	231.2	1996	438.7	450.0	447.5	454.0	454.1
1991	240.7	236.4	238.6	247.6	240.8	1997	467.2	475.3	504.7	487.1	488.3
1992	267.2	275.2	240.4	270.6	263.4	1998	479.2	481.8	477.3	472.5	541.7
1993	282.5	296.1	298.4	324.0	300.3	1999	570.1	581.4	564.8	599.9	589.1
1994	312.1	342.5	361.6	377.7	348.5	2000[1]	634.4	650.4	654.4		646.4

[1] Preliminary.   Source: Bureau of Economic Analysis, U.S. Department of Commerce (BEA)

STOCK INDEX FUTURES, U.S.

Productivity: Index of Output per Hour, All Persons, Nonfarm Business -- Quarterly   (1992 = 100)

Year	First Quarter	Second Quarter	Third Quarter	Fourth Quarter	Average	Year	First Quarter	Second Quarter	Third Quarter	Fourth Quarter	Average
1989	95.5	95.7	96.0	96.1	95.8	1995	100.5	100.9	101.3	101.1	100.7
1990	96.4	96.7	96.4	95.5	96.3	1996	101.5	101.7	102.0	102.4	103.7
1991	96.1	96.8	97.4	97.6	97.0	1997	103.4	104.0	105.6	105.9	107.2
1992	99.3	99.9	99.7	101.1	100.0	1998	106.6	106.6	107.3	111.5	110.2
1993	100.1	99.7	100.1	100.8	100.2	1999	112.2	112.4	113.6	115.8	113.5
1994	100.2	100.5	101.0	101.2	100.7	2000[1]	116.3	118.1	119.1		117.8

[1] Preliminary.   Source: Bureau of Economic Analysis, U.S. Department of Commerce (BEA)

Consumer Confidence, The Conference Board   (1985 = 100)

Year	Jan.	Feb.	Mar.	Apr.	May	June	July	Aug.	Sept.	Oct.	Nov.	Dec.	Average
1992	50.2	47.3	56.5	65.1	71.9	72.6	61.2	59.0	57.3	54.6	65.6	78.1	61.6
1993	76.7	68.5	63.2	67.6	61.9	58.6	59.2	59.3	63.8	60.5	71.9	79.8	65.9
1994	82.6	79.9	86.7	92.1	88.9	92.5	91.3	90.4	89.5	89.1	100.4	103.4	90.6
1995	101.4	99.4	100.2	104.6	102.0	94.6	101.4	102.4	97.3	96.3	101.6	99.2	100.0
1996	88.4	98.0	98.4	104.8	103.5	100.1	107.0	112.0	111.8	107.3	109.5	114.2	104.6
1997	118.7	118.9	118.5	118.5	127.9	129.9	126.3	127.6	130.2	123.4	128.1	136.2	125.4
1998	128.3	137.4	133.8	137.2	136.3	138.2	137.2	133.1	126.4	119.3	126.4	126.7	131.7
1999	128.9	133.1	134.0	135.5	137.7	139.0	136.2	136.0	134.2	130.5	137.0	141.7	135.3
2000[1]	144.7	140.8	137.1	137.7	144.7	139.2	143.0	140.8	142.5	135.8	132.6	128.3	138.9

[1] Preliminary.   Source: The Conference Board (TCB) Copyrighted.

Average Open Interest of NYSE Composite Stock Index Futures in New York   In Contracts

Year	Jan.	Feb.	Mar.	Apr.	May	June	July	Aug.	Sept.	Oct.	Nov.	Dec.
1992	5,216	5,290	5,469	4,575	4,867	5,858	6,491	7,049	6,647	6,034	6,430	5,890
1993	5,033	5,083	4,113	3,613	4,222	4,340	3,714	4,178	3,997	4,315	4,721	4,539
1994	4,653	4,471	4,823	3,720	3,839	3,969	3,903	3,982	4,142	4,494	4,244	4,617
1995	3,695	4,159	4,113	3,476	3,396	3,254	3,205	3,029	2,966	2,683	3,125	3,403
1996	3,644	4,139	3,245	2,822	2,839	2,547	2,492	2,526	2,759	2,798	2,649	3,050
1997	3,126	3,232	3,194	2,801	3,154	2,744	2,316	2,823	2,780	2,384	3,005	4,354
1998	4,803	5,216	5,252	4,754	4,888	5,990	10,154	12,249	10,574	8,554	7,977	9,806
1999	8,299	8,661	5,457	4,050	4,169	3,849	3,419	3,882	3,730	3,958	4,447	4,260
2000	3,653	3,715	3,747	3,285	2,533	2,597	2,452	2,793	2,463	1,690	1,943	2,406

Source: New York Futures Exchange (NYFE)

Average Open Interest of Value Line Stock Index Futures in Kansas City   In Contracts

Year	Jan.	Feb.	Mar.	Apr.	May	June	July	Aug.	Sept.	Oct.	Nov.	Dec.
1992	276	277	279	304	375	543	485	592	477	355	425	398
1993	330	393	382	375	497	449	387	455	413	359	519	534
1994	432	501	530	566	648	593	575	583	573	1,111	1,041	845
1995	678	792	951	1,108	1,132	972	839	1,042	966	980	1,193	1,138
1996	1,238	1,580	1,949	1,804	1,669	1,576	1,611	1,813	1,818	1,466	1,641	1,958
1997	1,459	1,354	1,338	1,448	1,326	1,686	2,160	2,523	1,980	1,477	1,213	1,675
1998	1,739	1,442	1,433	1,498	1,549	1,390	697	839	667	696	914	780
1999	746	738	699	725	900	967	515	503	381	314	300	283
2000	273	284	246	135	155	148	155	216	179	182	181	185

Source: Kansas City Board of Trade (KCBT)

Average Open Interest of S & P 500 Stock Index Futures in Chicago   In Contracts

Year	Jan.	Feb.	Mar.	Apr.	May	June	July	Aug.	Sept.	Oct.	Nov.	Dec.
1992	294,868	286,026	283,884	273,982	283,514	299,924	306,070	327,226	336,526	340,130	356,684	359,884
1993	329,228	347,382	357,878	348,554	365,792	380,106	364,378	382,622	416,780	390,218	402,748	392,350
1994	376,450	391,648	420,130	401,636	438,218	599,134	434,056	455,742	475,868	461,188	487,162	502,740
1995	427,004	442,628	445,584	420,104	443,296	453,364	420,024	422,608	417,812	402,794	441,780	447,528
1996	406,400	428,058	419,688	368,620	399,070	407,914	369,248	382,266	413,944	374,726	416,102	448,382
1997	393,086	396,528	417,542	377,100	392,034	417,006	372,274	392,812	423,449	391,922	402,044	417,717
1998	394,410	408,851	417,721	365,746	371,732	412,739	370,410	385,820	434,838	405,395	421,928	435,907
1999	399,093	406,516	410,164	381,402	391,035	400,503	372,455	385,809	408,176	394,316	408,751	416,425
2000	369,295	374,365	400,089	379,651	383,677	409,448	380,118	391,867	416,600	413,912	447,245	498,049

Source: Index and Option Market (IOM), division of the Chicago Mercantile Exchange (CME)

Average Open Interest of S & P 400 Midcap Stock Index Futures in Chicago   In Contracts

Year	Jan.	Feb.	Mar.	Apr.	May	June	July	Aug.	Sept.	Oct.	Nov.	Dec.
1992	-----	2,776	3,060	3,017	3,712	4,476	4,073	4,350	4,762	4,355	5,778	6,883
1993	7,197	9,048	9,095	8,759	8,640	9,336	8,731	10,183	10,728	12,955	13,343	13,261
1994	13,183	11,999	12,748	10,801	10,829	11,902	11,970	12,369	15,002	13,702	13,896	14,494
1995	13,787	13,355	11,130	9,275	9,329	9,929	11,198	11,708	13,107	11,702	12,341	12,863
1996	11,088	10,474	11,375	8,700	9,254	10,403	9,763	10,867	11,168	9,641	10,596	11,107
1997	11,215	11,825	11,258	9,721	10,807	10,877	11,292	12,346	13,505	11,595	11,874	13,329
1998	12,688	13,319	14,363	14,130	13,352	13,940	12,964	13,589	14,893	16,645	16,768	17,569
1999	16,191	16,309	14,573	12,154	12,705	14,422	14,263	13,496	13,182	12,699	13,933	14,902
2000	12,810	13,119	13,965	12,495	13,355	14,040	12,957	13,162	15,026	16,143	16,510	17,479

Source: Index and Option Market (IOM), division of the Chicago Mercantile Exchange (CME)

Average Open Interest of NASDAQ 100 Index Futures in Chicago   In Contracts

Year	Jan.	Feb.	Mar.	Apr.	May	June	July	Aug.	Sept.	Oct.	Nov.	Dec.
1996	-----	-----	-----	1,364	3,336	6,182	5,977	4,737	7,957	10,999	10,465	8,897
1997	6,610	7,064	8,073	7,627	7,587	8,270	6,346	8,255	8,444	6,235	8,831	8,210
1998	6,918	8,184	9,314	7,652	8,833	11,128	9,991	9,507	9,233	8,187	9,176	10,838
1999	10,669	14,766	19,786	21,286	23,028	26,938	21,646	22,765	21,808	19,946	23,429	27,876
2000	27,242	34,555	37,795	36,512	37,578	35,314	29,974	32,922	34,754	35,559	44,022	48,757

Source: Index and Option Market (IOM), division of the Chicago Mercantile Exchange (CME)

Average Open Interest of Dow Jones Industrials Index Futures in Chicago   In Contracts

Year	Jan.	Feb.	Mar.	Apr.	May	June	July	Aug.	Sept.	Oct.	Nov.	Dec.
1997	-----	-----	-----	-----	-----	-----	-----	-----	-----	5,249	11,542	15,952
1998	14,853	15,558	14,421	13,846	14,464	16,226	15,707	17,586	18,569	17,416	17,795	17,597
1999	16,794	19,401	19,807	20,492	25,890	22,198	21,556	25,333	23,977	24,847	22,342	17,299
2000	13,713	16,331	20,443	18,157	19,253	17,394	14,367	15,748	14,840	15,087	19,113	20,966

Source: Chicago Board of Trade (CBT)

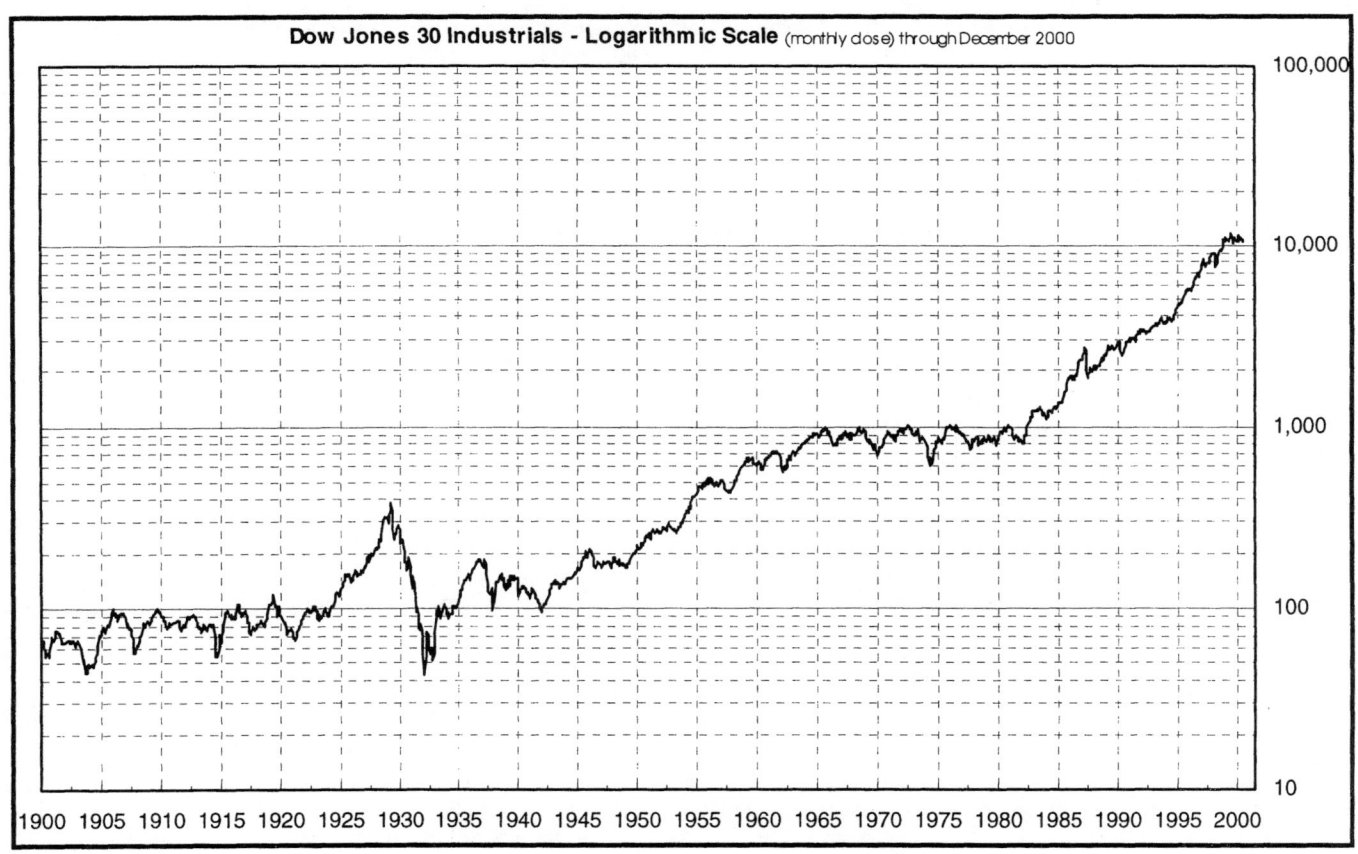

Dow Jones 30 Industrials - Logarithmic Scale (monthly close) through December 2000

Stock Index Futures, Worldwide

The world's equity markets as a group, excluding the United States, during 2000 posted their worst performance in a decade, led by the sharpest drop in Japan's market since 1990. One leading international equity index fell 16.3 percent in dollar terms during 2000, the sharpest decline since 1990, and compares with a 13.6 percent fall in a U.S. composite equity index. Moreover, throughout the world, the sell-off accelerated late in the year in line with the plunge in the U.S. markets. However, there were sharp variations among the six dozen or so major indices that are now tracked worldwide. Among the variables that weighed on world markets in 2000 were (1) the scaling back of global and U.S. real economic growth estimates, (2) simmering problems in emerging world stock markets, (3) high oil prices, and (4) the tendency of foreign equity markets to take their lead from the U.S. Among the few markets that finished with gains in 2000 China led the pack, as Shanghai's "B" share index (stocks priced in dollars and available to foreigners) surged 136 percent vs. a gain of 32 percent in 1999. China's economy grew by 8 percent in 2000, buoyed by strong exports and record government spending. The Chinese GDP topped $1 trillion for the first time. No other major Asian equity market was up in 2000 in dollar terms, largely due to the global decline in telecommunication stocks.

In Europe, many of the major markets declined in dollar terms, including Britain, where the weak Pound added to losses for the year of 14.2 percent in the FTSE 100-share index. The FTSE's loss for the year was only the third in its 17-year history. Germany's DAX index lost 16.5 percent and France's CAC-40 index fell about 7 percent. However, the Swiss market registered a 6 percent gain, largely because its currency is outside of Europe's unified currency, the Euro. In Ireland, which is part of the Euro alliance, stocks bucked the downward Euro trend and rose 7 percent.

In other countries, Japan's Nikkei 225 index was down almost 30 percent in 2000, South Korea's composite was off 50 percent, Australia's All Ordinaries index was down 14 percent, Hong Kong's Hang Seng index fell 11 percent, and Taiwan's market dropped 47 percent. The stock markets in Brazil, Argentina, and Mexico were each down about 20 percent for the year. Canada's Toronto Stock Exchange managed a 4.4 percent gain in U.S. dollar terms.

Aside from the percentile swings, perhaps of greater importance in 2000 was the burgeoning growth in electronic trading platforms that caused a number of exchanges to look for merger partners in an effort to remain competitive and cut costs. The odds are that coming years will see further consolidation and/or electronic link-ups, but in 2000 the trend was set back, if only briefly, by the collapse of a planned merger between the London and Frankfurt stock exchanges. Despite a surge in the number of seemingly well financed world equity markets, the capitalization of the U.S. markets remains dominant and are not likely to lose that position any time soon.

As usual, the world economic setting was sharply divided. However, a subtle change seemed to take hold in 2000 that could set the tone for the world markets in this century's first decade. In the 1980's, Japan and its Nikkei index attracted the most attention, in the 1990's, it was the U.S. markets, but the focus may now be on Europe. Capital is still flowing out of that region, but the rate slowed in 2000, totaling a hefty 106 billion Euro through October, but 22 percent less than the year earlier outflow. Moreover, the two-year pessimism towards the Euro lifted somewhat during 2000, in turn helping to improve liquidity in European capital markets. As of early 2001, the Euro currency was used in 12 of the 15 European Union nations. Perhaps more importantly, Europe's central bank apparently sees little reason to change monetary policy, whereas in the U.S. interest rates are apt to trend lower to ward off a possible recession, while Japan's economy appears stalled if not headed lower.

In the Japanese equity market during the past twenty years one of the striking features has been a very high price/ earnings ratio, averaging around 50 vs. an average P/E in the U.S. of about 21, and in Europe averaging 17-25. In 2000, the high Japanese valuations were apparently one reason for the Nikkei's slide as more traditional western sized P/E ratios were seen as appropriate, a market approach that may take greater hold over the longer term. Japanese leaders frequently talk of maintaining stock market values with public funds, but often fail to address concerns about the nation's future growth; not an unreasonable aversion in view of Japan's $6 trillion government debt and a creaky banking system.

Cyclically, the U.S. economy's unprecedented decade long expansionary phase carried into 2000, and U.S. equity markets, paced by the high tech NASDAQ, reached record highs in the first quarter of the year. However, the optimism had finally outdistanced reality during 2000 and while the economy remained strong, cracks appeared that finally burst the speculative bubble; the NASDAQ index falling 39.3 percent for the year, but from its record March high down 50 percent by year-end. The wealth effect that the equity markets had filtered into the U.S. economy during the 1990's, and the optimistic psychology that went with it, were beginning to slip as the year 2000 progressed. A series of Federal Reserve interest rate increases from mid-1999 and into 2000 did more than slow the markets and economy, by year-end attitudes had reversed and fears of recession were taking hold. While the U.S. equity markets were long overdue for a correction, the public's underlying bias towards equities, although shaken by year-end 2000, was still positive. The odds favor less volatile markets in 2001, with underlying strength paced by the so-called "old economy" stocks, while the high-tech stocks in the U.S. and abroad are approached with considerably more caution.

Futures Markets

Futures and option trading on stock indices expanded rapidly in recent years, taking their place alongside debt instruments futures and options as the most successful exchange traded contracts. Nearly every global futures exchange lists a variety of stock index contracts, primarily on those indices based on their domestic stock markets. In 2001 look for growth in new single-stock futures and futures options. The list of stock indices traded worldwide has grown too large for this space, but is available in the worldwide futures exchange volume tables in the front section of this Yearbook.

262

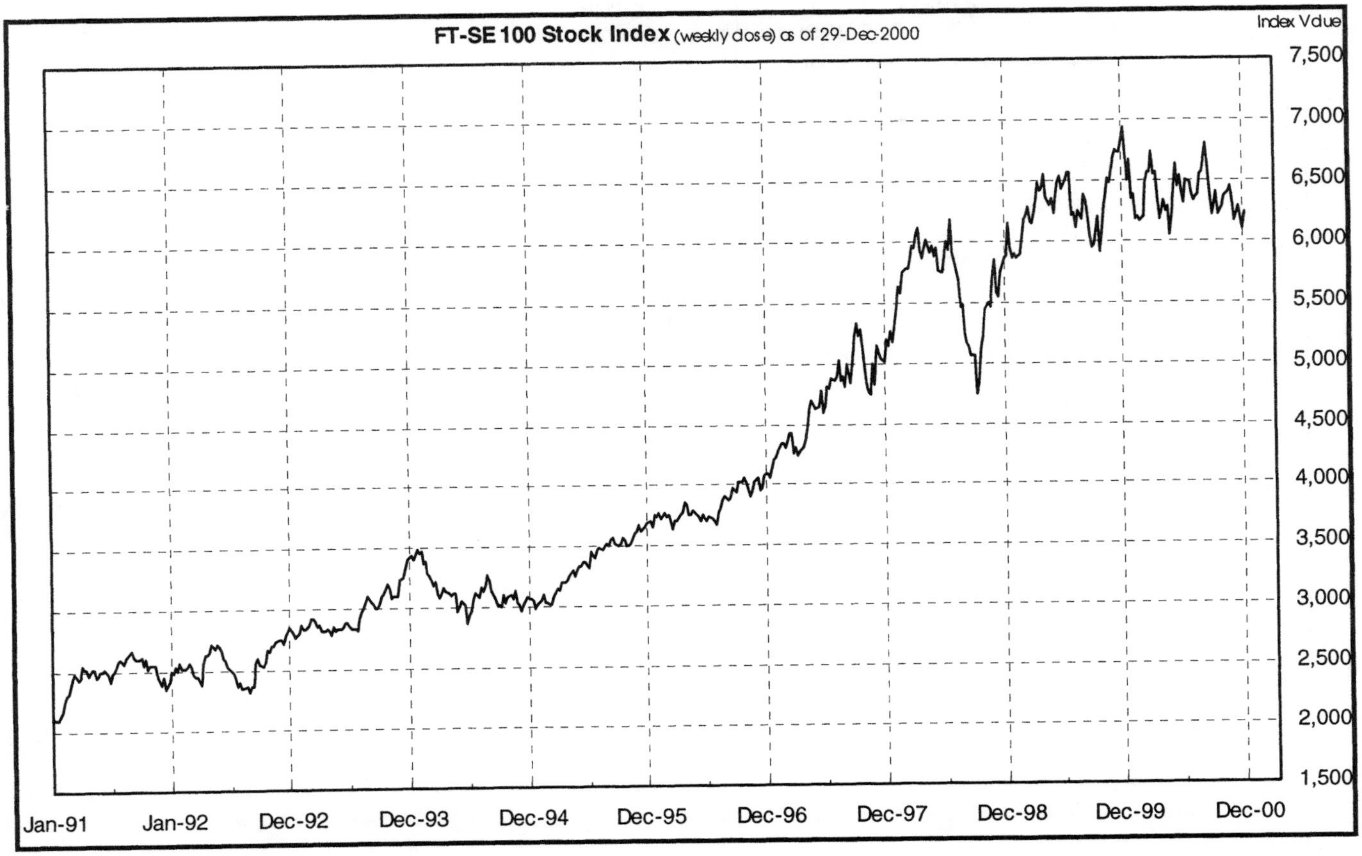

FT-SE 100 Stock Index (weekly close) as of 29-Dec-2000

Index Value

7,500
7,000
6,500
6,000
5,500
5,000
4,500
4,000
3,500
3,000
2,500
2,000
1,500

Jan-91　Jan-92　Dec-92　Dec-93　Dec-94　Dec-95　Dec-96　Dec-97　Dec-98　Dec-99　Dec-00

Toronto 35 Stock Index (weekly close) as of 29-Dec-2000

Index Value

640
600
560
520
480
440
400
360
320
280
240
200
160
120

Jan-91　Jan-92　Dec-92　Dec-93　Dec-94　Dec-95　Dec-96　Dec-97　Dec-98　Dec-99　Dec-00

STOCK INDEX FUTURES, WORLDWIDE

CAC-40 Stock Index (weekly close) as of 29-Dec-2000

Index Value

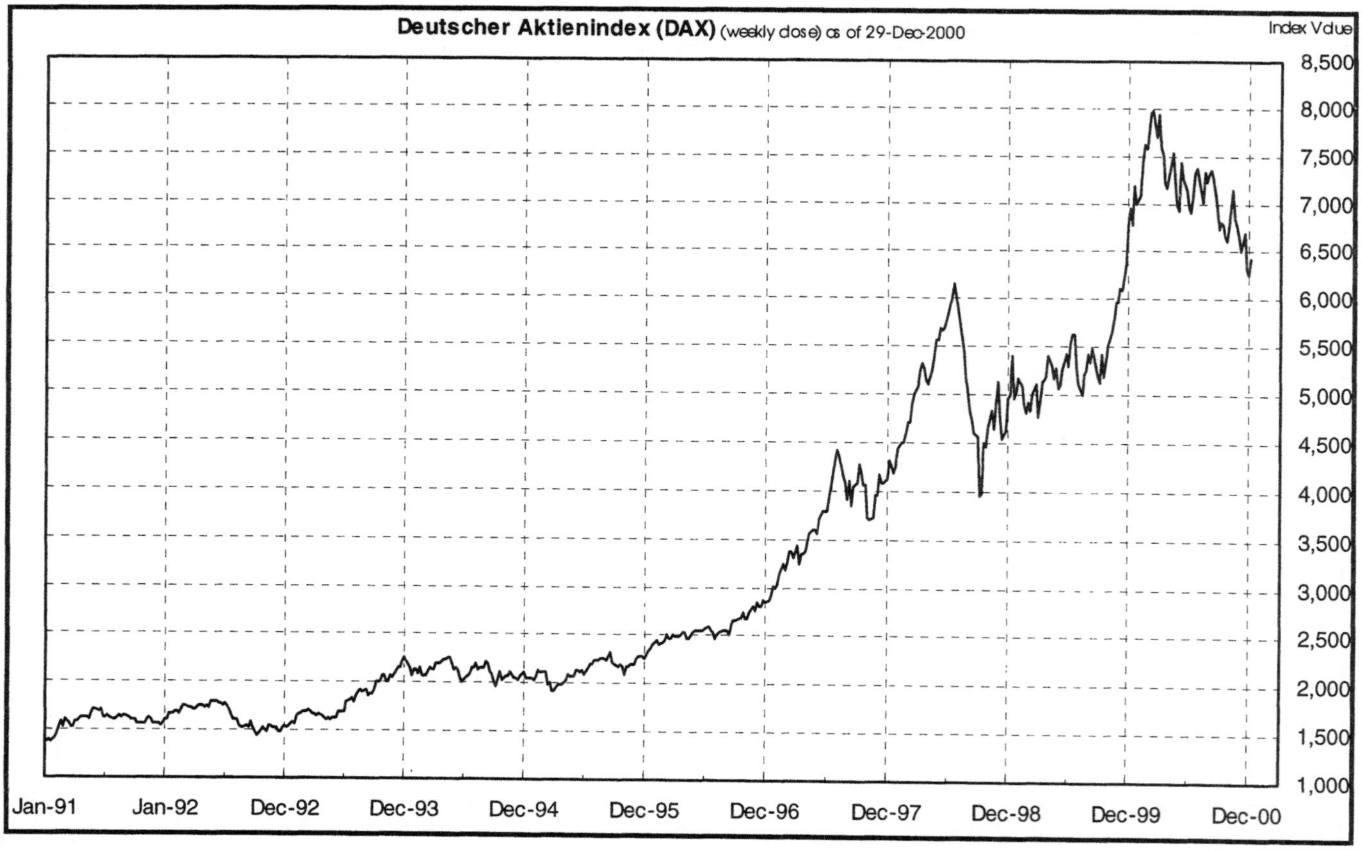

Deutscher Aktienindex (DAX) (weekly close) as of 29-Dec-2000

Index Value

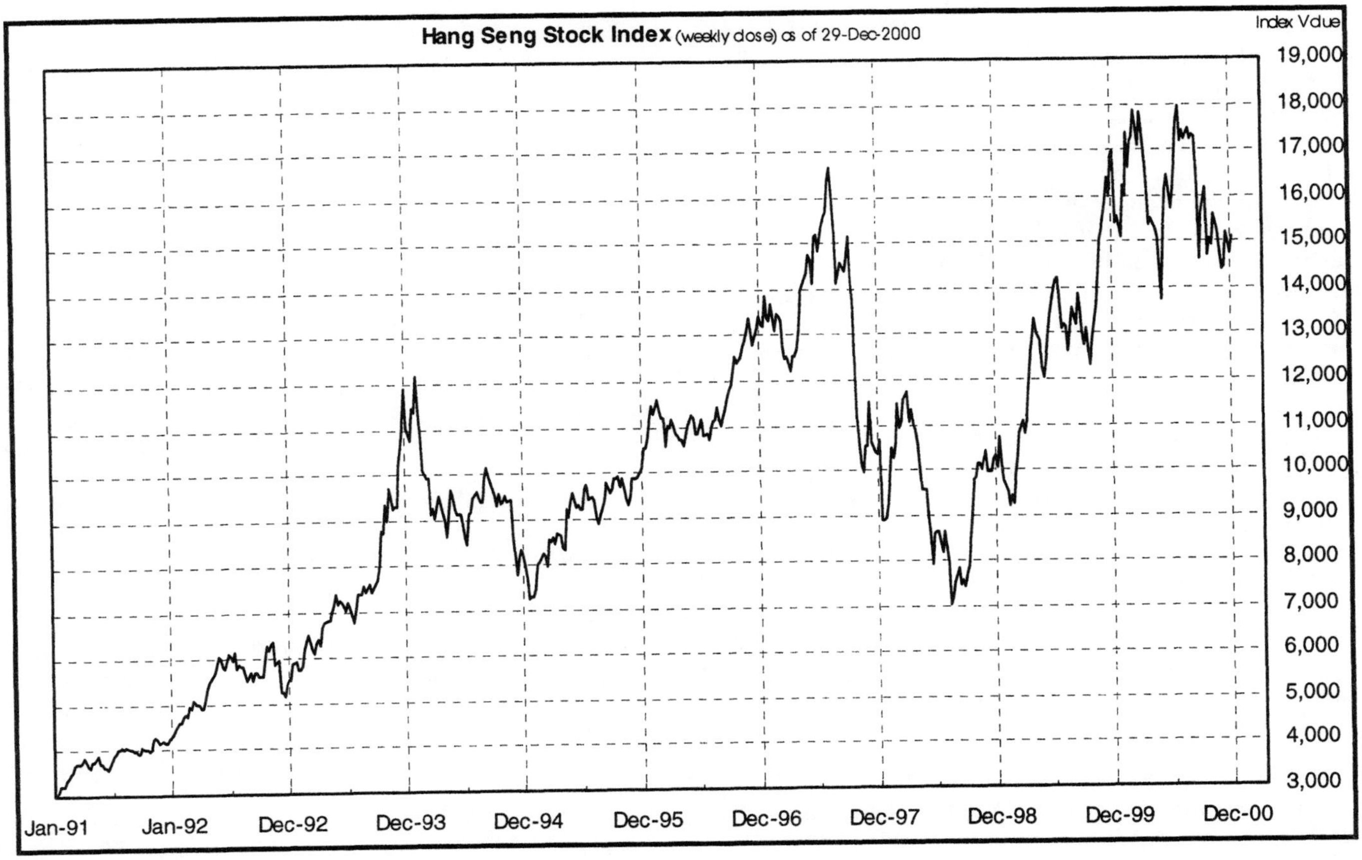

Hang Seng Stock Index (weekly close) as of 29-Dec-2000

Index Value

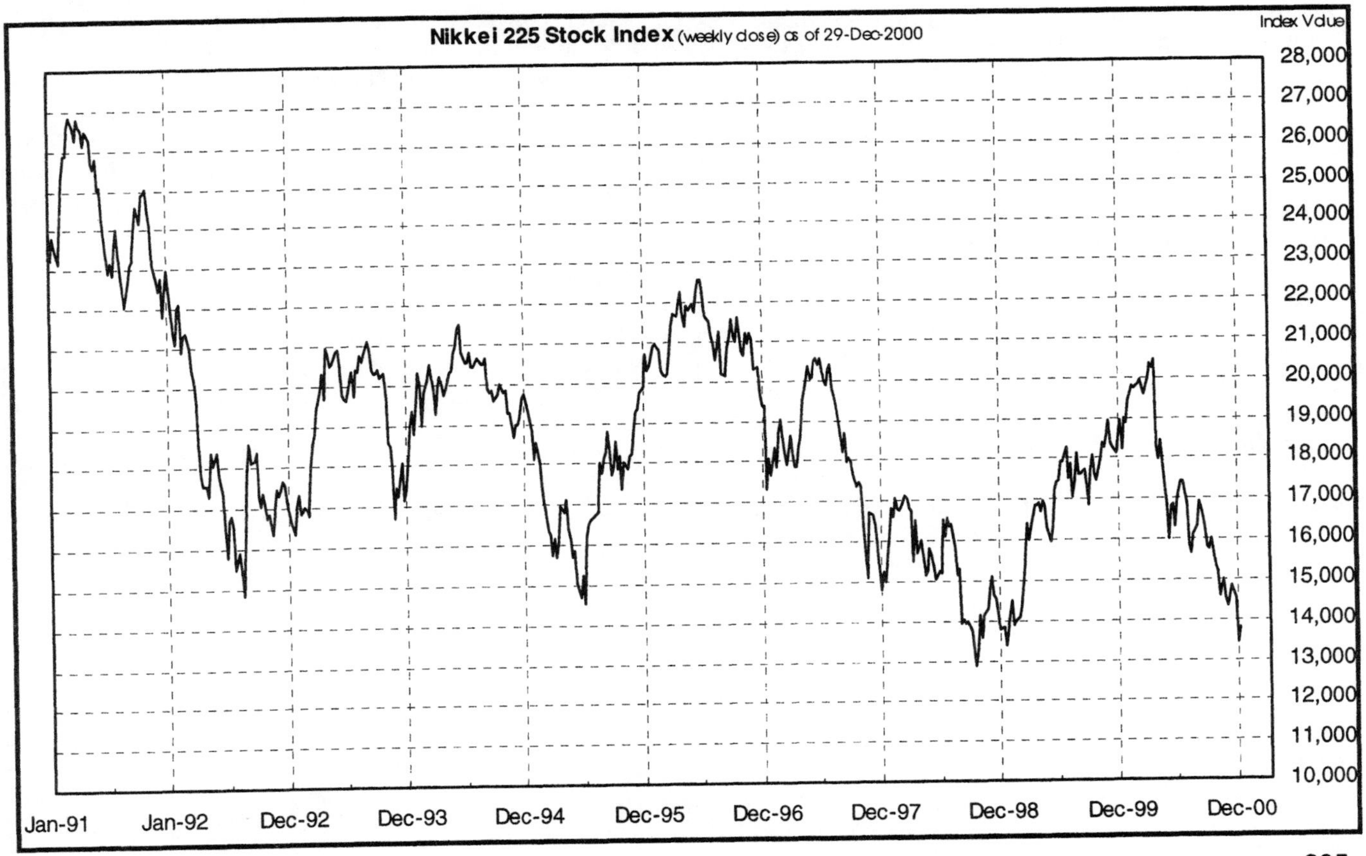

Nikkei 225 Stock Index (weekly close) as of 29-Dec-2000

Index Value

Sugar

A salient feature of the world sugar market is that global stocks of sugar have been increasing. World production of sugar has been exceeding world consumption leading to a progressive buildup in stockpiles. Part of the reason for this is that Brazil has been producing larger and larger crops. Stocks of sugar in some countries have risen to excessive levels. India, already a large producer of sugar, is estimated to be holding some 10 million metric tonnes of sugar. In an attempt to reduce this massive stockpile, India has tried to export sugar though without much success so far. One problem in sugar is that production is not very responsive to price. Low prices have not reduced output very much. Beet sugar is an annual crop that is planted each year. If there is price responsiveness it is on the part of the beet producing countries. Another problem is that governments in many countries act to insulate both growers and the industry from market prices. This leads to production increases even when prices are low. Cane sugar, which is not planted every year, is not very responsive to price. One effect of low prices is that the crops are not as well cared for. Less fertilizer and pesticide usage result in lower production. It is usually weather which reduces the amount of sugar that is produced, as was the case in the 2000/2001 season.

As the next season approaches, the first crops to be harvested are in the Southern Hemisphere where the largest producers are Brazil and Australia. Both countries are large producers of cane sugar and dominant exporters. Brazil exports sugar to Russia and Africa, while Australia is a major supplier to Asia. Any production problems in these countries will likely lead to prices moving higher and that is what happened in 2000. By March 2000, it was already apparent that both countries would see production declines. Brazil's huge Center-South cane crop was damaged by an intense drought. In Australia, a cyclone damaged the cane.

The U.S.D.A. estimated that Brazilian sugar cane production would decline by 20 million tonnes leading to raw sugar production of some 15.4 million tonnes. Production in the previous year had been 20.1 million tonnes, a decline of 23 percent. More important for the market was the fact that sugar exports would decline to just over 6 million tonnes, down 45 percent from the previous season. For Australia, the U.S.D.A. forecast 2000/01 sugar production at 4.6 million tonnes, down 16 percent from the previous year. The decline in these two important crops was the most positive fundamental development in the 2000/01 season. As the 2001/02 season approaches, the new cane crops in these countries are being watched closely. In Brazil, the drought has ended. It is widely expected that it will take two seasons for the cane to fully recover. The 2001/02 cane crop is expected to increase by about 5 percent. For Australia, the weather remains a problem as there has been severe flooding which has led to some disease problems. The new crop in Australia looks like it will be smaller than initially expected.

In November 2000, the U.S.D.A. released its second estimate of the world sugar supply/demand situation. World production was estimated at 124.5 million tonnes, raw value, slightly higher than the May estimate but some 6 percent less than the 1999/00 season total of 133.1 million tonnes. The U.S.D.A. attributed the decline to the drought-damaged Brazilian crop. Production by the European Union was estimated to be 17.6 million tonnes. Global consumption of sugar was estimated to be 128.7 million tonnes, down 800,000 tonnes from the previous estimate but some 1.7 million tonnes more than in 1999/00. As a result, the U.S.D.A. expects the 2000/01 season to be one in which there is a production deficit, that is global production of sugar will be less than consumption. The 2000/01 deficit is expected to be 4.2 million tonnes. For the 1999/00 season, the U.S.D.A. had estimated a production surplus of 6.1 million tonnes. World stocks of sugar at the end of the 2000/01 season are estimated to be 30.9 million tonnes, down 6 percent from the year before. The world ending stocks-to-use ratio for 2000/01 calculates to be 0.24, while in 1999/00 it was 0.26. The U.S.D.A. estimated world sugar exports in 2000/01 at 32.8 million tonnes, down 13 percent from the previous year.

The U.S.D.A. in the December supply/demand report estimated 2000/01 (October-September) season U.S. sugar production at 8.67 million short tons, raw value, down 4 percent from the 1999/00 crop of 9 million tons. Beet sugar production was estimated at 4.45 million tonnes, down 11 percent from the previous season. Cane sugar production was forecast at 4.22 million tons, up 4 percent from the year before. U.S. sugar imports in 2000/01 were forecast to be 1.79 million tons, up 9 percent from the previous season. Imports under the Tariff Rate Quota were 1.275 million tons, up 13 percent from 1999/00. Countries with large quota allocations include the Dominican Republic, Brazil, the Philippines, and Australia. U.S. domestic deliveries of sugar were estimated to be 10.4 million tons with ending stocks at 2.1 million tons, down 5 percent from 1999/00.

Futures Markets

Sugar futures are traded on the Bolsa de Mercadorias & Futures (BM&F), Chubu Commodity Exchange (C-COM) Kansai Commodities Exchange (KANEX), the Tokyo Grain Exchange (TGE), the London International Financial Futures and Options Exchange (LIFFE), and the CSCE Division of the New York Board of Trade (NYBOT) Options are traded on the KANEX, the TGE, the LIFFE and the NYBOT.

World Production, Supply & Stocks/Consumption Ratio of Sugar   In 1000's of Metric Tons (Raw Value)

Marketing Year	Beginning Stocks	Production	Imports	Total Supply	Exports	Domestic Consumption	Ending Stocks	Stocks/ Consumption Percentage
1991-2	21,011	116,527	30,831	168,369	30,831	114,029	23,509	20.7
1992-3	23,509	112,099	28,937	164,545	28,937	114,037	21,571	18.9
1993-4	21,570	109,731	29,565	160,866	29,565	112,054	19,247	17.2
1994-5	19,288	115,920	31,317	167,553	30,289	113,716	22,520	19.8
1995-6	22,520	122,229	32,182	174,894	34,219	116,275	26,437	22.7
1996-7	26,437	122,546	32,772	178,711	35,816	119,476	26,463	22.1
1997-8	26,463	124,939	32,653	181,282	35,426	122,778	25,851	21.1
1998-9	25,851	130,425	34,469	189,270	35,944	124,067	30,734	24.8
1999-00[1]	30,734	134,528	35,519	197,043	39,257	126,829	34,695	27.4
2000-1[2]	34,695	124,472	33,243	192,831	32,822	128,715	30,873	24.0

[1] Preliminary.   [2] Forecast.   *Source: Foreign Agricultural Service, U.S. Department of Agriculture (FAS-USDA)*

World Production of Sugar (Centrifugal Sugar-Raw Value)   In Thousands of Metric Tons

Year	Australia	Brazil	China	Cuba	France	Germany	India	Indonesia	Mexico	Thailand	United States	Ukraine	World Total
1991-2	3,192	9,200	8,492	7,030	4,413	4,250	15,249	2,250	3,500	5,062	6,627	4,178	116,527
1992-3	4,367	9,800	8,300	4,280	4,723	4,401	12,447	2,300	4,330	3,750	7,111	3,965	112,099
1993-4	4,412	9,930	6,505	4,000	4,725	4,736	11,704	2,480	3,780	3,975	6,945	4,188	109,731
1994-5	5,196	12,500	6,299	3,300	4,363	3,991	16,410	2,450	4,556	5,448	7,191	3,600	115,920
1995-6	5,049	13,700	6,686	4,450	4,564	4,159	18,225	2,090	4,660	6,223	6,686	3,800	122,229
1996-7	5,659	14,650	7,789	4,200	4,594	4,558	14,616	2,094	4,835	6,013	6,536	2,935	122,546
1997-8	5,567	15,700	8,631	3,200	----	----	14,592	2,190	5,490	4,245	7,276	2,032	124,939
1998-9	4,997	18,300	8,969	3,780	----	----	17,436	1,492	4,985	5,386	7,597	2,000	130,425
1999-00[1]	5,481	20,100	7,203	4,100	----	----	20,112	1,600	4,977	5,721	8,203	1,720	134,528
2000-1[2]	4,600	15,400	8,079	4,000	----	----	17,803	1,500	4,987	5,600	7,662	1,650	124,472

[1] Preliminary.   [2] Forecast.   *Source: Foreign Agricultural Service, U.S. Department of Agriculture (FAS-USDA)*

World Stocks of Centrifugal Sugar at Beginning of Marketing Year   In Thousands of Metric Tons (Raw Value)

Year	Australia	Brazil	China	Cuba	France	Germany	India	Iran	Mexico	Philippines	United Kingdom	United States	World Total
1991-2	189	757	1,350	500	689	428	3,563	275	1,505	242	228	1,371	21,011
1992-3	163	950	2,002	500	589	340	5,245	300	910	515	281	1,340	23,509
1993-4	125	880	1,508	130	701	358	3,502	400	1,040	679	416	1,546	21,570
1994-5	125	455	1,168	170	784	511	2,776	400	575	412	450	1,213	19,288
1995-6	152	710	3,215	400	437	271	5,990	270	601	100	453	1,126	22,520
1996-7	101	510	2,684	400	684	331	8,455	300	714	511	457	1,354	26,437
1997-8	228	860	2,784	300	----	----	6,979	480	634	345	----	1,350	26,463
1998-9	253	560	2,515	290	----	----	5,850	590	670	183	----	1,523	25,851
1999-00[1]	183	1,010	2,548	150	----	----	7,374	365	665	454	----	1,487	30,734
2000-1[2]	531	710	1,101	420	----	----	10,676	640	585	460	----	2,020	34,695

[1] Preliminary.   [2] Forecast.   *Source: Foreign Agricultural Service, U.S. Department of Agriculture (FAS-USDA)*

Centrifugal Sugar (Raw Value) Imported into Selected Countries   In Thousands of Metric Tons

Year	Algeria	Canada	China	France	Iran	Rep. of Korea	Malaysia	Morocco	Nigeria	Russia	United Kingdom	United States	World Total
1991-2	980	961	1,230	398	825	1,258	921	380	560	3,850	1,442	2,071	30,831
1992-3	980	1,095	506	487	780	1,233	900	408	430	3,500	1,352	1,827	28,937
1993-4	990	1,219	1,469	156	950	1,258	958	417	510	3,150	1,363	1,604	29,565
1994-5	990	1,020	4,110	361	800	1,345	1,030	455	490	2,700	1,261	1,664	31,317
1995-6	1,000	1,174	1,775	523	940	1,411	1,120	477	542	3,200	1,361	2,536	32,182
1996-7	920	1,057	1,014	553	1,350	1,497	1,166	513	555	3,600	1,260	2,517	32,772
1997-8	925	1,061	420	----	1,200	1,424	1,065	586	660	4,210	----	1,962	32,653
1998-9	940	1,110	517	----	900	1,403	1,186	561	700	5,400	----	1,655	34,469
1999-00[1]	1,000	1,130	555	----	1,500	1,440	1,280	457	825	5,170	----	1,491	35,519
2000-1[2]	900	1,170	1,000	----	1,300	1,460	1,310	465	700	3,820	----	1,624	33,243

[1] Preliminary.   [2] Forecast.   *Source: Foreign Agricultural Service, U.S. Department of Agriculture (FAS-USDA)*

SUGAR

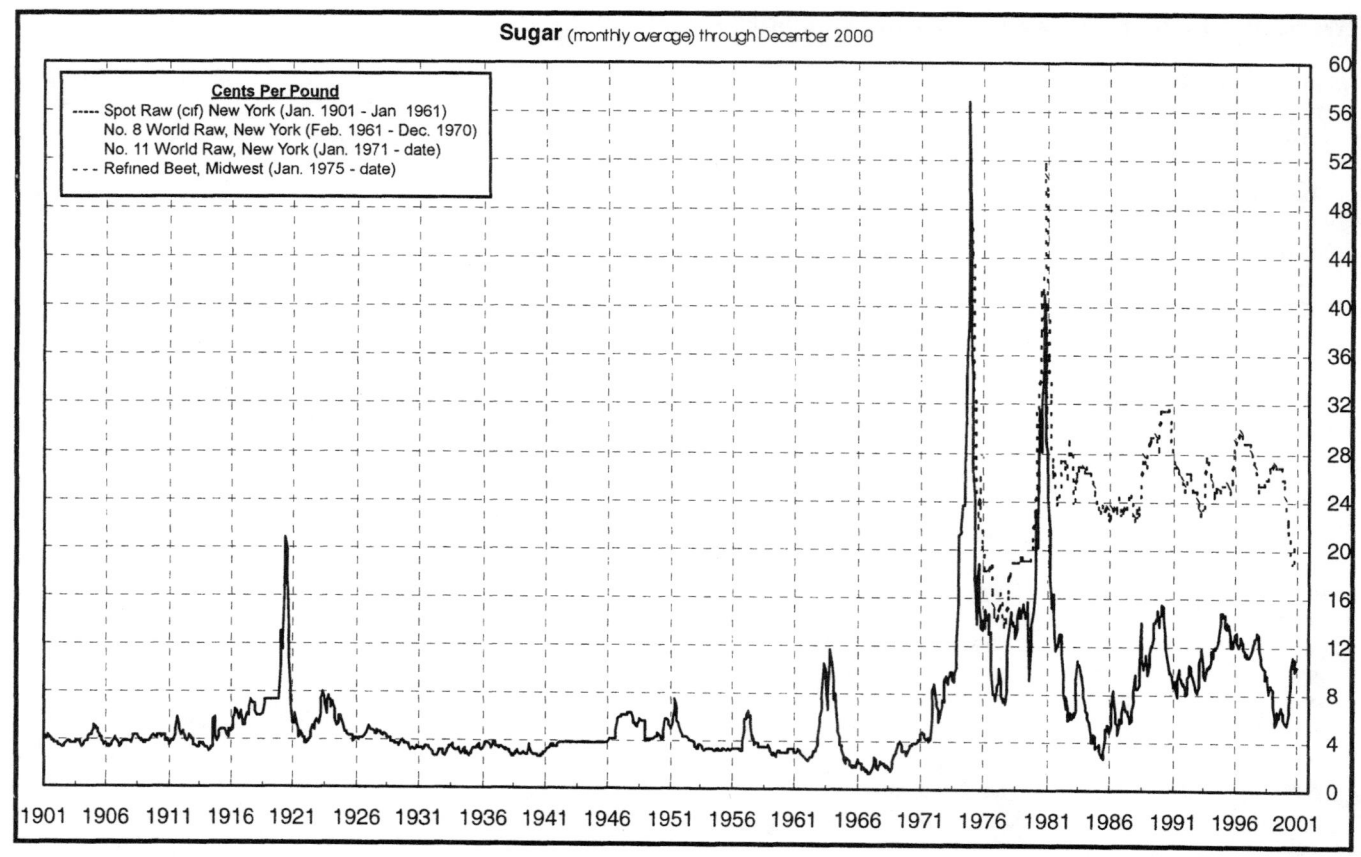

Sugar (monthly average) through December 2000

Cents Per Pound
----- Spot Raw (cif) New York (Jan. 1901 - Jan. 1961)
      No. 8 World Raw, New York (Feb. 1961 - Dec. 1970)
      No. 11 World Raw, New York (Jan. 1971 - date)
- - - Refined Beet, Midwest (Jan. 1975 - date)

Centrifugal Sugar (Raw Value) Exported From Selected Countries · In Thousands of Metric Tons

Year	Aus-tralia	Brazil	Cuba	Dominican Republic	France	Ger-many	Mau-ritius	Mexico	South Africa	Swazi-land	Thai-land	United Kingdom	Total
1991-2	2,345	1,607	6,100	344	2,682	1,557	590	50	969	474	3,657	368	30,831
1992-3	3,476	2,425	3,800	327	2,822	1,607	621	0	123	409	2,332	300	28,937
1993-4	3,663	2,861	3,300	346	2,636	1,785	590	0	27	395	2,718	410	29,565
1994-5	4,321	4,300	2,600	295	3,004	1,417	508	235	369	296	3,809	263	30,289
1995-6	4,242	5,800	3,800	325	2,735	1,180	560	587	399	307	4,537	327	34,219
1996-7	4,564	5,800	3,600	364	2,730	1,430	593	750	1,056	293	4,194	388	35,816
1997-8	4,554	7,200	2,500	270	----	----	644	1,224	1,160	272	2,839	----	35,426
1998-9	4,076	8,750	3,200	191	----	----	550	590	1,355	300	3,352	----	35,944
1999-00[1]	4,141	11,300	3,100	185	----	----	320	575	1,410	250	4,100	----	39,257
2000-1[2]	3,349	6,200	3,500	185	----	----	650	540	1,450	350	3,800	----	32,822

[1] Preliminary. [2] Estimate. [3] Forecast. *Source: Foreign Agricultural Service, U.S. Department of Agriculture (FAS-USDA)*

Average Wholesale Price of Refined Beet Sugar[1]--Midwest Market · In Cents Per Pound

Year	Jan.	Feb.	Mar.	Apr.	May	June	July	Aug.	Sept.	Oct.	Nov.	Dec.	Average
1991	26.88	26.50	26.50	26.13	26.00	25.75	25.50	25.50	25.00	24.94	24.60	24.50	25.65
1992	25.40	26.50	26.50	26.50	26.40	26.00	25.00	25.00	25.00	24.90	24.13	23.90	25.44
1993	23.25	23.00	23.00	23.50	23.50	23.50	25.50	27.75	27.50	27.50	27.25	26.50	25.15
1994	25.75	25.50	25.50	24.50	24.75	25.25	25.00	25.00	24.70	25.00	25.38	26.50	25.15
1995	25.50	25.50	25.50	25.50	25.13	25.10	24.75	24.75	25.50	25.75	28.13	28.85	25.83
1996	28.69	29.00	29.50	29.50	29.70	29.50	29.50	29.00	29.00	29.00	29.00	29.00	29.20
1997	29.00	29.00	28.13	28.00	28.00	27.50	27.00	26.65	26.38	24.90	25.00	25.50	27.09
1998	25.50	25.50	25.50	25.50	26.00	26.00	26.00	26.00	26.50	26.90	27.00	27.00	26.12
1999	27.20	27.13	27.00	27.00	27.00	27.00	27.00	27.00	27.00	26.00	26.00	25.20	26.71
2000[2]	23.38	22.25	21.50	21.00	19.75	19.00	19.00	19.00	20.70	21.25	21.00	21.80	20.80

[1] These are f.o.b. basis prices in bulk, not delivered prices. [2] Preliminary. *Source: Economic Research Service, U.S. Department of Agriculture (ERS)*

Average Price of World Raw Sugar[1]   In Cents Per Pound

Year	Jan.	Feb.	Mar.	Apr.	May	June	July	Aug.	Sept.	Oct.	Nov.	Dec.	Average
1991	8.88	8.57	9.22	8.55	7.88	9.37	10.26	9.45	9.39	9.10	8.79	9.03	9.04
1992	8.43	8.06	8.22	9.53	9.62	10.52	10.30	9.78	9.28	8.66	8.54	8.15	9.09
1993	8.27	8.61	10.75	11.30	11.87	10.35	9.60	9.30	9.52	10.27	10.10	10.47	10.03
1994	10.29	10.80	11.71	11.10	11.79	12.04	11.73	12.05	12.62	12.75	13.88	14.76	12.13
1995	14.87	14.43	14.58	13.63	13.49	13.99	13.46	13.75	12.72	11.94	11.96	12.40	13.44
1996	12.57	12.97	13.07	12.43	11.94	12.54	12.83	12.33	11.87	11.65	11.29	11.38	12.24
1997	11.13	11.06	11.17	11.50	11.54	12.02	12.13	12.54	12.65	12.86	13.19	12.90	12.06
1998	11.71	11.06	10.66	10.27	10.17	9.33	9.70	9.50	8.21	8.24	8.73	8.59	9.68
1999	8.40	7.05	6.11	5.44	5.83	6.67	6.11	6.39	6.98	6.90	6.54	6.00	6.54
2000[2]	5.64	5.51	5.54	6.48	7.33	8.72	10.18	11.14	10.35	10.96	10.02	10.23	8.51

[1] Contract No. 11, f.o.b. stowed Caribbean port, including Brazil, bulk spot price.   [2] Preliminary.   *Source: Economic Research Service, U.S. Department of Agriculture (ERS-USDA)*

Average Price of Raw Sugar in New York (C.I.F., Duty/Free Paid, Contract #12/#14)   In Cents Per Pound

Year	Jan.	Feb.	Mar.	Apr.	May	June	July	Aug.	Sept.	Oct.	Nov.	Dec.	Average
1991	21.86	21.42	21.46	21.23	21.29	21.42	21.25	21.83	22.06	21.76	21.75	21.50	21.57
1992	21.38	21.56	21.36	21.38	21.04	20.92	21.10	21.34	21.55	21.61	21.39	21.11	21.31
1993	20.76	21.16	21.56	21.76	21.36	21.42	21.89	21.85	21.97	21.80	21.87	22.00	21.62
1994	22.00	21.95	21.95	22.08	22.18	22.44	22.72	21.84	21.78	21.58	21.57	22.35	22.04
1995	22.65	22.69	22.46	22.76	23.10	23.09	24.47	23.18	23.21	22.67	22.60	22.63	22.96
1996	22.39	22.68	22.57	22.71	22.62	22.48	21.80	22.51	22.38	22.37	22.12	22.14	22.40
1997	21.88	22.07	21.81	21.79	21.70	21.62	22.04	22.21	22.30	22.27	21.90	21.93	21.96
1998	21.85	21.79	21.74	22.14	22.31	22.42	22.66	22.19	21.92	21.67	21.83	22.19	22.06
1999	22.41	22.38	22.55	22.57	22.65	22.61	22.61	21.24	20.10	19.50	17.45	17.87	21.16
2000[1]	17.70	17.24	18.46	19.43	19.12	19.31	17.64	18.12	18.97	21.15	21.39	20.56	19.09

[1] Preliminary.   *Source: Economic Research Service, U.S. Department of Agriculture (ERS-USDA)*

Supply and Utilization of Sugar (Cane and Beet) in the United States   In 1,000's of Short Tons (Raw Value)

	Supply								Utilization			Domestic Disappearance		
	Production			Offshore Receipts						Net Changes in Invisible Stocks	Refining Loss Adjustment	In Polyhydric Alcohol[4]		
Year	Cane	Beet	Total	Foreign	Territories	Total	Beginning Stocks	Total Supply	Total Use	Exports				Total	Per Capita
1992-3	3,446	4,392	7,838	2,039	0	2,039	1,477	11,354	9,650	405	48	0	15	9,034	64.7
1993-4	3,565	4,090	7,655	1,772	0	1,772	1,704	11,131	9,794	454	7	0	15	9,175	64.9
1994-5	3,434	4,493	7,927	1,853	0	1,853	1,337	11,117	9,876	502	37	0	10	9,239	64.3
1995-6	3,454	3,916	7,370	2,777	0	2,777	1,241	11,388	9,896	385	-43	0	13	9,441	65.1
1996-7	3,191	4,013	7,205	2,774	0	2,774	1,492	11,471	9,983	211	30	0	21	9,564	65.7
1997-8	3,631	4,389	8,020	2,163	0	2,163	1,488	11,671	9,992	179	-2	0	20	9,672	65.5
1998-9[1]	3,951	4,423	8,374	1,824	0	1,824	1,679	11,877	10,238	230	-58	0	25	9,872	66.5
1999-00[2]	4,065	4,976	9,041	1,636	0	1,636	1,639	12,316	10,098	124	-137	0	32	9,993	66.1
2000-1[3]	4,168	4,370	8,538	1,790	0	1,790	2,219	12,547	10,560	175	0	0	35	10,225	67.2

[1] Preliminary.   [2] Estimate.   [3] Forecast.   [4] Includes feed use.   Source: Economic Research Service, U.S. Department of Agriculture (ERS-USDA)

Sugar Cane for Sugar & Seed and Production of Cane Sugar and Molasses in the United States

			Production					Farm Value		Sugar Production				Molasses Made	
	Acreage Harvested 1,000 Acres	Yield of Cane Per Harvested Acre Net Tons	for Sugar	for Seed	Total	Sugar Yield Per Acre Short Tons	Farm Price $ Per Ton	of Cane Used for Sugar	of Cane Used for Sugar & Seed	Raw Value		Refined Basis 1,000 Tons		Edible	Total[3]
Year			1,000 Tons					1,000 Dollars		Total 1,000 Tons	Per Ton of Cane in Lbs.			1,000 Gallons	
1992	906.4	32.7	28,873	1,490	30,363	3.79	28.1	811,350	852,235	3,373	234	3,152		1,460	194,247
1993	923.9	32.8	29,652	1,449	31,101	3.82	28.5	846,132	886,285	3,482	235	3,255		1,480	198,167
1994	936.8	33.0	29,405	1,524	30,929	3.96	29.2	857,438	900,827	3,595	----	3,308		----	193,628
1995	932.3	33.0	29,155	1,641	30,796	3.90	29.5	859,604	906,956	3,489	----	----		----	195,429
1996	888.9	33.1	27,687	1,777	29,464	----	28.3	784,113	833,297	----	----	----		----	----
1997	914.0	34.7	30,003	1,706	31,709	----	28.1	842,840	890,257	----	----	----		----	----
1998	947.1	36.6	32,743	1,964	34,707	----	27.3	893,049	944,562	----	----	----		----	----
1999[1]	993.3	35.5	33,577	1,722	35,299	----	25.6	859,175	901,900	----	----	----		----	----
2000[2]	1,037.0	35.0	34,484	1,862	36,346	----	----	----	----	----	----	----		----	----

[1] Preliminary.   [2] Estimate.   [3] Excludes edible molasses.   *Source: Economic Research Service, U.S. Department of Agriculture (ERS-USDA)*

SUGAR

U.S. Sugar Beets, Beet Sugar, Pulp & Molasses Produced from Beets and Raw Sugar Spot Prices

Year of Harvest	Acreage Planted	Acreage Harvested	Yield Per Harvested Acre Ton	Pro-duction 1,000 Tons	Sugar Yield Per Acre Sh. Tons	Price[3] Dollars	Farm Value $1,000	Equiv-alent Raw Value[4]	Refined Basis	World[5] Refined #5	CSCE #11 World	CSCE N.Y. Duty Paid	Wholesale List Price HFCS (42%) Midwest
	----- 1,000 Acres -----							-- 1,000 Short Tons --		------ In Cents Per Pound ------			
1991	1,427	1,387	20.3	28,203	2.68	38.50	1,085,728	3,729	3,485	13.41	9.04	21.57	20.93
1992	1,437	1,412	20.6	29,143	3.10	41.10	1,206,480	4,386	4,099	12.39	9.09	21.31	20.70
1993	1,438	1,409	18.6	26,249	2.87	39.00	1,023,687	4,047	3,792	12.79	10.03	21.62	18.83
1994	1,476	1,443	22.1	31,853	3.17	38.80	1,234,470	4,578	4,090	15.66	12.13	22.04	20.17
1995	1,445	1,420	19.8	28,065	2.78	38.10	1,070,663	3,944	----	17.99	13.44	22.96	15.63
1996	1,368	1,323	20.2	26,680	3.06	45.40	1,211,001	3,900	----	16.64	12.24	22.40	14.46
1997	1,459	1,428	20.9	29,886	3.00	38.80	1,160,029	----	----	14.33	12.06	21.96	10.70
1998	1,498	1,451	22.4	32,499	----	36.40	1,181,494	----	----	11.59	9.68	22.06	10.58
1999[1]	1,561	1,527	21.9	33,420	----	37.20	1,242,895	----	----	9.10	6.54	21.16	11.71
2000[2]	1,564	1,378	23.6	32,521	----	----	----	----	----	9.97	8.51	19.09	11.32

[1] Preliminary. [2] Estimate. [3] Includes support payments, but excludes Government sugar beet payments. [4] Refined sugar multiplied by factor of 1.07. [5] F.O.B. Europe. *Source: Economic Research Service, U.S. Department of Agriculture (ERS-USDA)*

Sugar Deliveries and Stocks in the United States   In Thousands of Short Tons (Raw Value)

Year	Quota Allocation	Actual Imports	Cane Sugar Refineries	Beet Sugar Factories	Importers of Direct Con-sumption Sugar	Mainland Cane Sugar Mills[3]	Total Deliveries	Total Domestic Con-sumption	Cane Sugar Re-fineries[4]	Beet Sugar Factories	CCC	Refiners' Raw	Mainland Cane Mills	Total
1991	1,526.7	1,477.0	4,786	3,713	30	11	8,540	9,499	168	1,327	0	371	812	2,729
1992	3,958.4	3,926.6	4,808	3,966	52	11	8,936	9,638	194	1,336	0	619	890	3,039
1993	5	5	4,781	4,087	52	15	9,064	9,577	183	1,640	0	507	895	3,225
1994	5	5	4,929	4,170	78	12	9,321	9,177	218	1,696	0	438	1,160	3,512
1995	2,413.2	2,308.0	4,808	4,486	44	15	9,451	9,337	192	1,600	6	448	906	3,139
1996	2,339.1	----	5,539	3,923	33	14	9,619	9,496	195	1,383	0	334	996	2,908
1997	----	----	5,553	3,997	27	----	9,755	9,578	196	1,520	0	323	1,156	3,195
1998	----	----	5,347	4,313	24	----	9,851	9,684	212	1,535	0	322	1,308	3,377
1999[1]	----	----	5,419	4,536	41	----	10,167	9,996	255	1,499	0	332	1,335	3,422
2000[2]	----	----	----	----	----	----	----	----	208	1,554	0	356	1,737	3,855

[1] Preliminary. [2] Estimate. [3] Sugar for direct consumption only. [4] Refined. [5] Combined with 1992. *Source: Economic Research Service, U.S. Department of Agriculture (ERS-USDA)*

Sugar, Refined--Deliveries to End User in the United States   In Thousands of Short Tons

Year	Bakery & Cereal Products	Beverages	Confec-tionery[2]	Hotels, Restaurant & Insti-tutions	Ice Cream & Dairy Products	Canned, Bottled & Frozen Foods	All Other Food Uses	Retail Grocers[3]	Whole-sale Grocers[4]	Non-food Uses	Non-industrial Uses	Industrial Uses	Total Deliveries
1990	1,608	228	1,279	108	462	332	642	1,077	2,130	109	3,391	4,660	8,051
1991	1,632	204	1,277	100	439	331	623	1,182	2,079	88	3,469	4,594	8,063
1992	1,719	164	1,246	101	429	315	649	1,230	2,104	69	3,668	4,591	8,259
1993	1,785	158	1,292	108	424	336	725	1,235	2,075	85	3,589	4,805	8,394
1994	1,952	156	1,313	93	453	322	704	1,269	2,039	77	3,598	4,977	8,575
1995	1,905	169	1,372	103	452	279	863	1,236	2,173	64	3,701	5,103	8,804
1996	1,993	196	1,335	80	445	318	849	1,263	2,241	66	3,759	5,202	8,962
1997	2,161	158	1,350	78	436	308	793	1,281	2,283	66	3,828	5,272	9,100
1998	2,301	165	1,336	79	438	331	907	1,230	2,223	76	3,761	5,556	9,317
1999[1]	2,312	179	1,361	72	499	346	862	1,263	2,257	71	3,804	5,630	9,434

[1] Preliminary. [2] And related products. [3] Chain stores, supermarkets. [4] Jobbers, sugar dealers. *Source: Economic Research Service, U.S. Department of Agriculture (ERS-USDA)*

Deliveries[1] of All Sugar by Primary Distributors in the U.S., by Quarters   In Thousands of Short Tons

Year	First Quarter	Second Quarter	Third Quarter	Fourth Quarter	Total	Year	First Quarter	Second Quarter	Third Quarter	Fourth Quarter	Total
1989	1,923	2,051	2,181	2,185	8,340	1995	2,105	2,311	2,542	2,379	9,337
1990	1,837	1,911	2,154	2,149	8,051	1996	2,191	2,355	2,519	2,445	9,496
1991	1,878	1,955	2,173	2,057	8,063	1997	2,143	2,401	2,591	2,443	9,578
1992	1,985	2,178	2,390	2,273	8,826	1998	2,233	2,428	2,565	2,458	9,684
1993	2,039	2,172	2,432	2,277	8,920	1999	2,208	2,553	2,655	2,580	9,996
1994	2,121	2,265	2,532	2,260	9,177	2000[2]	2,318	2,484	2,611		9,884

Raw Value. [1] Includes for domestic consumption and for export. [2] Preliminary. *Source: Economic Research Service, U.S. Department of Agriculture (ERS-USDA)*

Sugar #11 Futures - New York Board of Trade (weekly close) as of 29-Dec-2000 — Cents Per Pound

Average Open Interest of World Sugar No. 11 Futures in New York   In Contracts

Year	Jan.	Feb.	Mar.	Apr.	May	June	July	Aug.	Sept.	Oct.	Nov.	Dec.
1991	124,637	129,361	114,432	115,704	110,142	105,607	106,406	107,852	102,546	91,649	90,976	93,827
1992	96,255	105,166	93,774	109,137	95,101	106,310	96,038	87,089	77,740	69,023	74,292	93,039
1993	91,426	105,147	123,023	115,400	112,085	101,843	94,296	94,932	91,312	92,832	96,246	99,592
1994	108,936	123,148	137,582	115,060	117,030	126,843	106,749	118,057	141,361	140,011	171,843	191,801
1995	186,893	167,451	149,027	152,600	127,978	121,877	114,027	119,787	114,069	119,561	140,008	157,779
1996	156,047	159,563	150,093	142,773	137,897	148,447	144,527	153,845	153,202	144,830	150,866	150,573
1997	155,156	147,198	143,623	166,143	150,480	175,139	165,884	197,331	187,477	158,065	200,486	201,922
1998	206,100	212,072	183,472	182,770	171,555	186,978	149,536	152,754	155,076	138,762	139,896	148,983
1999	165,717	176,465	168,624	188,324	196,864	177,266	142,416	151,621	189,606	161,760	167,549	175,125
2000	191,464	199,031	193,554	187,810	201,756	200,973	172,361	171,808	160,809	154,101	148,035	145,760

Source: New York Board of Trade (NYBOT)

Volume of Trading of World Sugar No. 11 Futures in New York   In Contracts

Year	Jan.	Feb.	Mar.	Apr.	May	June	July	Aug.	Sept.	Oct.	Nov.	Dec.	Total
1991	313,915	510,163	388,672	477,954	286,120	534,639	309,836	352,351	366,007	240,812	253,201	234,876	4,268,546
1992	376,704	395,793	255,501	583,535	246,360	454,854	264,528	275,677	334,962	163,263	168,470	147,844	3,667,481
1993	330,474	481,506	507,370	518,292	415,283	390,261	255,581	307,181	368,194	222,082	272,579	217,142	4,285,945
1994	289,593	486,222	360,787	472,388	407,343	443,002	252,012	349,079	471,899	316,330	484,943	387,620	4,719,218
1995	591,861	489,274	472,519	478,757	352,000	485,131	298,756	402,358	360,086	246,584	278,906	254,850	4,711,082
1996	550,780	544,514	341,940	526,255	384,302	496,745	279,707	290,732	562,082	264,290	203,921	306,584	4,751,852
1997	436,935	493,199	268,343	618,176	308,563	575,264	400,150	427,082	580,551	440,208	323,286	413,214	5,284,971
1998	601,378	688,036	431,818	551,628	364,203	686,997	294,354	370,179	527,270	303,951	358,096	346,201	5,524,111
1999	683,891	543,477	452,485	688,181	361,895	762,271	346,534	408,289	657,572	344,434	405,495	256,775	5,911,299
2000	422,527	609,793	501,115	617,633	523,939	717,700	376,769	420,611	622,350	507,562	371,824	242,027	5,933,850

Source: New York Board of Trade (NYBOT)

Sulfur

Elemental sulfur is used in the synthesis of sulfur compounds. With its derivative product, sulfuric acid, sulfur is an important industrial raw material. Sulfuric acid is the major end use of sulfur. More sulfuric acid is produced in the U.S. than any other chemical. Sulfur finds use in the construction industry where it is added to concrete to aide corrosion resistance. The U.S. Geological Survey reported that elemental sulfur and the by-product sulfuric acid were produced at 149 operations in 30 States, Puerto Rico, and the Virgin Islands. Elemental sulfur was produced at two mines in 1999, although one has since been closed. Sulfuric acid was recovered at 11 nonferrous smelters.

World production of sulfur in 1999 was estimated to be 55.99 million metric tonnes, down 3 percent from 1998. The U.S. was the largest producer with output of 11.1 million tonnes, down 4 percent from the previous year. Canada produced 9.5 million tonnes in 1999, while other large pro-

ducers included China, Russia, Japan, and Mexico. World reserves of sulfur are estimated at 1.4 billion tonnes.

U.S. production of sulfur from petroleum in August 2000 was 559,000 tonnes. In the January-August 2000 period, sulfur production from petroleum totaled 4.16 million tonnes, while for all of 1999 it was 6.21 million tonnes. Production of sulfur from natural gas in August 2000 was 259,000 tonnes. In the first eight months of 2000, production was 2.19 million tonnes and for all of 1999 it was 3.79 million tonnes. In January-August 2000, total U.S. sulfur production was 6.34 million tonnes.

U.S. consumption of sulfur in July 2000 was 884,000 tonnes. In the January-July 2000 period, consumption totaled 6.51 million tonnes. For all of 1999, consumption was 11.7 million tonnes. U.S. imports of sulfur in the first seven months of 2000 totaled 1.44 million tonnes. In 1999, imports were 2.58 million tonnes.

World Production of Sulfur (All Forms)   In Thousands of Metric Tons

Year	Canada	China	France	Germany	Iraq	Japan	Mexico	Poland	Russia	Saudi Arabia	Spain	United States	World Total
1992	7,487	5,900	1,150	1,160	350	2,745	2,300	3,134	3,500	2,370	885	10,700	50,700
1993	8,430	6,360	1,260	1,260	450	2,922	906	2,120	3,720	2,400	768	11,100	51,600
1994	8,850	7,020	1,180	1,005	475	2,900	1,177	2,325	3,650	1,630	694	11,500	53,400
1995	8,953	7,030	1,170	1,110	475	3,110	1,241	2,591	3,840	2,400	786	11,800	54,000
1996	9,490	7,260	1,090	1,110	475	3,150	1,280	1,916	3,800	2,300	943	11,800	55,200
1997	9,480	7,640	1,060	1,160	450	3,380	1,340	1,976	3,750	2,400	967	12,000	57,100
1998[1]	9,694	6,150	1,110	1,180	450	3,430	1,387	1,666	4,650	2,300	993	11,600	56,700
1999[2]	10,116	5,690	1,100	1,190	----	3,460	1,310	1,510	5,270	2,400	955	11,300	57,100

[1] Preliminary.   [2] Estimate.   Source: U.S. Geological Survey (USGS)

Salient Statistics of Sulfur in the United States   In Thousands of Metric Tons (Sulfur Content)

	Production of											Sales Value of Shipments		
	Elemental Sulfur				By-product Sulfuric Acid	Other Sulfuric Acid Compounds	Pro-duction (All Forms)	Imports Sulfuric Acid[4]	Exports Sulfuric Acid[4]	Producer Stocks Dec. 31[5]	Apparent Con-sumption (All Forms)	F.O.B. Mine/Plant		
	Native - Sulfur[3] -	Recovered										Frasch	Recovered	Average
Year	Frasch	Petroleum & Coke	Natural Gas	Total								$ Per Metric Ton		
1992	2,320	4,524	2,524	7,048	1,292	3	10,700	2,725	139	809	13,400	58.15	44.47	48.14
1993	1,900	4,820	2,905	7,725	1,430	3	11,100	2,440	145	1,382	12,600	51.60	25.06	31.86
1994	2,960	4,930	2,240	7,160	1,380	0	11,500	2,130	140	1,160	13,100	W	W	30.08
1995	3,150	5,040	2,210	7,250	1,400	0	11,800	1,920	170	583	14,300	W	W	44.46
1996	2,900	5,370	2,100	7,480	1,430	0	11,800	2,070	117	646	13,600	W	W	34.11
1997	2,820	5,230	2,420	7,650	1,550	0	12,000	2,010	118	761	13,900	W	W	36.06
1998[1]	1,800	6,060	2,160	8,220	1,610	0	11,600	2,040	155	283	14,100	W	W	29.14
1999[2]	1,780	6,210	2,010	8,220	1,320	0	11,300	1,370	155	451	13,400	W	W	37.81

[1] Preliminary.   [2] Estimate.   [3] Or sulfur ore; Withheld included in natural gas.   [4] Basis 100% H2SO4, sulfur equivalent.   [5] Frasch & recovered.
[6] Data 1996 to date includes Frasch.   W = Withheld proprietary data.   Source: U.S. Geological Survey (USGS)

Sulfur Consumption & Foreign Trade of the United States   In Thousands of Metric Tons (Sulfur Content)

	Consumption			Sulfuric Acid Sold or Used, by End Use[2]						Foreign Trade				
	Native Sulfur Frasch	Re-covered Sulfur	Total Elemental Form	Total Sulfuric Acid	Pulpmills & Paper Product	Inorganic Chem-icals[3]	Synthetic Rubber & Plastic	Pho-sphatic Fertilizers	Petro-leum Refining[4]	Exports			Imports	
										Frasch	Re-covered	Value 1,000 $	Frasch	Re-covered	Value 1,000 $
Year														
1992	3,083	8,368	11,451	12,340	296	617	278	8,300	385	362	604	69,662	845	1,877	129,894
1993	1,331	9,046	10,377	11,886	304	549	259	7,906	388	246	656	39,726	100	2,070	49,800
1994	W	11,100	11,100	11,300	295	448	256	8,040	236	----	899	48,400	----	1,650	62,000
1995	W	12,300	12,300	11,500	319	170	245	8,200	479	----	906	66,200	----	2,510	143,000
1996	W	11,500	11,500	10,900	343	152	270	7,380	525	----	855	51,700	----	1,960	70,200
1997	W	11,800	11,800	10,700	334	232	85	7,000	610	----	703	36,000	----	2,060	64,900
1998	W	11,900	11,900	10,600	134	174	69	7,590	632	----	889	35,400	----	2,270	58,400
1999[1]	W	11,700	11,700	10,400	138	174	68	7,770	508	----	685	35,800	----	2,580	51,600

[1] Preliminary.   [2] Sulfur equivalent.   [3] Including inorganic pigments, paints & allied products, and other inorganic chemicals & products.
[4] Including other petroleum and coal products.   W = Withheld proprietary data.   NA = Not available.   Source: U.S. Geological Survey (USGS)

Sunflowerseed, Meal and Oil

World sunflowerseed production has shown relatively little variation in recent years, but its ranking as the world's fifth major oilseed crop seems secure. However, unlike soybeans for which most of the crop is crushed for meal, sunflowerseed has nearly equal amounts of meal and oil produced. The U.S. produces only about 6 percent of global sunflowerseed production, but has a larger role in world trade.

World production in 2000/01 of 23.8 million metric tonnes fell short of initial forecasts and compares with the record large 1999/00 crop of 26.3 million tonnes. Argentina is the largest single producer with 4.8 million tonnes in 2000/01 vs. the previous year's near record of 6.1 million tonnes. The Russian Federation (FSU-12) remains the largest producer with 6.8 million tonnes in 2000/01 vs. 7.3 million in 1999/00. The world sunflowerseed crush for 2000/01 is forecast at 21.8 million tonnes vs. 23.6 million in 1999/00.

Sunflowerseed is the third largest oilseed in foreign trade, but only a fraction of the total trade in soybeans. 2000/01 total world exports of 2.65 million tonnes compares with 3.5 million in 1999/00. World stocks have generally averaged about one million tonnes, but at year-end 2000/01 are estimated to be 800,000 tonnes.

Sunflower meal production in 2000/01 of 9.65 million tonnes compares with 10.7 million in 1999/00; sunflower oil production of 8.7 million tonnes compares with 9.5 million, respectively.

The acreage planted to sunflowerseed production in the U.S. tends to show an irregular year-to-year pattern as does average yield. The acreage planted for the 2000/01 of 3 million acres compares with a near record large 3.6 million in 1999/00. Average yield for the 1999 crop year was 1262 pounds per acre and in 1998 was 1510 pounds per acre. Production (September/August) in 2000/01 of 1.7 million metric tonnes compares with 2.0 million in 1999/00. The Dakotas are the largest producing states with about two-thirds of total U.S. production.

U.S. sunflower meal production in 2000/01 (Oct./Dec.) of 463,000 tonnes compares with 544,000 in 1999/00. Total disappearance in both years equaled supply, leaving carryover unchanged at 5,000 tonnes. Sunflower oil 2000/01 production of 406,000 tonnes compares to 460,000 in 1999/00. However, unlike meal, most U.S. sunflower oil production is exported with 306,000 tonnes in 2000/01 vs. 324,000 tonnes in 1999/00. U.S. exports of sunflower seed were 159,000 tonnes in 2000/01 vs. 211,000 in 1999/00.

The 2000/01 U.S. sunflower oil price was forecast at $362-432 per metric tonne vs. $385 in 1999/00, basis average crude Minneapolis. The sunflower meal price was forecast to range from $71-103 per metric tonne vs. $77, basis 28 percent protein, respectively. Abroad, the 1999/00 average sunflowerseed oil price of $413/tonne compares with $560/tonne in 1998/99, basis Rotterdam. For meal, the 1999/00 average of $102/tonne compares with $76, respectively.

World Production of Sunflowerseed   In Thousands of Metric Tons

Crop Year	Argentina	Bulgaria	China	France	Hungary	India	Romania	South Africa	Spain	Turkey	United States	Ex-USSR	World Total
1991-2	3,800	434	1,420	2,570	797	1,194	612	174	900	650	1,639	5,621	21,658
1992-3	3,100	578	1,472	2,110	756	1,185	618	364	1,343	980	1,163	5,645	21,135
1993-4	3,850	440	1,282	1,640	700	1,400	696	390	1,215	700	1,167	5,251	20,600
1994-5	5,900	595	1,370	2,050	665	1,204	767	450	979	600	2,193	4,356	23,342
1995-6	5,600	650	1,270	1,900	730	1,400	933	755	575	750	1,819	7,368	25,720
1996-7	5,400	490	1,325	2,000	800	1,315	1,180	450	1,138	545	1,614	5,268	23,800
1997-8	5,500	500	1,176	1,940	545	1,150	858	562	1,373	650	1,668	5,368	23,206
1998-9	7,100	500	930	1,680	706	1,200	970	1,109	1,097	650	2,392	5,548	26,128
1999-00[1]	6,100	570	1,300	1,910	795	1,300	1,100	531	579	800	1,969	7,262	26,404
2000-1[2]	4,400	400	1,300	1,850	450	1,200	700	630	1,200	575	1,684	7,814	24,167

[1] Preliminary.   [2] Forecast.   Source: Economic Research Service, U.S. Department of Agriculture (ERS-USDA)

World Imports and Exports of Sunflowerseed   In Thousands of Metric Tons

Crop Year	Imports						Exports						
	France	Germany	Netherlands	Spain	Turkey	World Total	Argentina	France	Hungary	Ex-USSR	United States	Uraguay	World Total
1991-2	7	320	434	134	104	2,481	300	1,075	75	360	144	----	2,214
1992-3	36	278	428	92	50	1,984	200	663	80	366	118	----	1,837
1993-4	194	331	427	170	100	2,615	580	516	250	755	99	----	2,545
1994-5	109	279	543	472	550	3,287	884	628	260	708	287	----	3,173
1995-6	300	366	617	681	500	3,972	550	480	249	1,750	224	----	3,647
1996-7	395	484	658	531	360	4,215	100	825	220	2,481	149	----	4,167
1997-8	220	345	563	524	583	4,063	453	911	155	1,825	189	----	3,930
1998-9	406	474	524	764	595	4,365	910	499	145	1,863	260	----	4,272
1999-00[1]	140	370	550	749	520	3,554	550	475	253	1,523	199	----	3,726
2000-1[2]	240	385	465	400	565	3,480	350	500	125	1,917	204	----	3,512

[1] Preliminary.   [2] Forecast.   Source: Economic Research Service, U.S. Department of Agriculture (ERS-USDA)

SUNFLOWERSEED, MEAL AND OIL

Sunflowerseed Statistics in the United States   In Thousands of Metric Tons

Crop Year Beginning Sept. 1	Harvested Acres 1,000	Harvested Yield Per Cwt.	Farm Price $ Per Metric Ton	Value of Production Million $	Supply Stocks, Sept. 1	Supply Production	Supply Imports	Supply Total	Disappearance Crush	Disappearance Exports	Disappearance Non-oil Use & Seed	Disappearance Total
1991-2	2,673	13.52	192	316.8	85	1,639	75	1,799	952	144	444	1,540
1992-3	2,043	12.55	215	249.8	262	1,163	47	1,472	923	118	362	1,403
1993-4	2,486	10.35	284	331.8	69	1,167	24	1,260	661	99	429	1,189
1994-5	3,430	14.10	236	517.4	71	2,193	42	2,306	1,313	287	603	2,203
1995-6	3,368	11.90	254	461.1	103	1,819	21	1,943	915	224	599	1,738
1996-7	2,479	14.36	258	416.4	205	1,614	18	1,837	844	149	648	1,641
1997-8	2,792	13.17	256	426.5	196	1,668	29	1,893	1,061	189	551	1,801
1998-9	3,492	15.10	225	537.0	92	2,392	34	2,518	1,178	260	849	2,287
1999-00[1]	3,441	12.62	166	340.0	231	1,969	41	2,241	1,139	199	680	2,018
2000-1[2]	2,629	12.63	130-152	241.4	223	1,684	36	1,943	932	204	712	1,848

[1] Preliminary.   [2] Forecast.   *Source: Economic Research Service, U.S. Department of Agriculture (ERS-USDA)*

World Production of Sunflowerseed Oil and Meal   In Thousands of Metric Tons

Year	Sunflowerseed Oil Argentina	France	Spain	Turkey	Ex-USSR	World Total	Sunflowerseed Meal Argentina	France	Spain	Turkey	United States	Ex-USSR	World Total
1991-2	1,400	605	380	299	1,883	7,836	1,470	785	425	271	498	1,821	8,828
1992-3	1,112	548	430	420	1,747	7,336	1,197	722	470	380	440	1,817	8,551
1993-4	1,280	478	440	319	1,542	7,083	1,393	642	550	289	327	1,521	8,340
1994-5	1,980	590	455	445	1,287	8,247	2,129	703	485	408	653	1,221	9,527
1995-6	2,000	593	470	482	1,920	9,018	2,100	720	485	430	458	1,805	10,198
1996-7	2,070	588	540	410	1,161	8,588	2,174	742	570	370	440	1,166	10,070
1997-8	1,990	566	525	506	1,292	8,258	2,092	707	550	463	494	1,232	9,545
1998-9	2,450	577	588	512	1,364	9,186	2,573	720	615	460	617	1,351	10,499
1999-00[1]	2,220	585	504	535	1,944	9,325	2,332	740	525	492	549	1,973	10,720
2000-1[2]	1,610	635	588	462	2,170	8,714	1,690	800	615	423	463	2,204	10,027

[1] Preliminary.   [2] Forecast.   *Source: Economic Research Service, U.S. Department of Agriculture (ERS-USDA)*

Sunflower Oil Statistics in the United States   In Thousands of Metric Tons

Crop Year Beginning Oct. 1	Supply Stocks, Oct. 1	Supply Production	Supply Total[3]	Disappearance Exports	Disappearance Domestic	Disappearance Total	Minneapolis, Crude $ Per Metric Ton
1991-2	21	413	438	239	154	393	476
1992-3	45	331	376	266	85	351	558
1993-4	25	263	291	204	58	262	683
1994-5	29	528	558	444	77	521	622
1995-6	37	390	428	285	76	361	560
1996-7	67	381	458	322	94	416	497
1997-8	42	435	480	370	83	453	608
1998-9	27	534	563	363	145	508	446
1999-00[1]	55	474	531	286	165	451	364
2000-1[2]	80	401	483	272	159	431	342-408

[1] Preliminary.   [2] Forecast.   [3] Includes imports.   *Source: Economic Research Service, U.S. Department of Agriculture (ERS-USDA)*

Sunflower Meal Statistics in the United States   In Thousands of Metric Tons

Crop Year Beginning Oct. 1	Supply Stocks, Oct. 1	Supply Production	Supply Total[3]	Disappearance Exports	Disappearance Domestic	Disappearance Total	28% Protein $ Per Metric Ton
1991-2	5	498	510	54	450	504	85
1992-3	6	440	451	48	401	449	98
1993-4	2	327	333	37	291	328	104
1994-5	5	653	658	89	564	653	72
1995-6	5	458	463	25	433	458	136
1996-7	5	440	445	21	419	440	122
1997-8	5	494	499	13	481	494	90
1998-9	5	617	622	41	576	617	72
1999-00[1]	5	549	554	19	530	549	83
2000-1[2]	5	454	459	14	440	454	61-83

[1] Preliminary.   [2] Forecast.   [3] Includes imports.   *Source: Economic Research Service, U.S. Department of Agriculture (ERS-USDA)*

Tall Oil

Tall oil is a product of the paper and pulping industry. Crude tall oil is the major by-product of the kraft or sulfate processing of pinewood. Crude tall oil starts as tall oil soap which is separated from recovered black liquor in the kraft pulping process. The tall oil soap is acidified to yield crude tall oil. The resulting tall oil is then fractionated to produce fatty acids, rosin, and pitch. Crude tall oil contains 40-50 percent fatty acids such as oleic and linoleic acids; 5-10 percent sterols, alcohols, and other neutral components. The demand is for the tall oil rosin and fatty acids which are used to produce adhesives, coatings, and ink resins. The products find use in lubricants, soaps, linoleum, flotation and waterproofing agents, paints, varnishes, and drying oils.

Since tall oil and its production are derived from the paper and pulping industry, the amount of tall oil produced is related in part to the pulp industry and in part to the U.S. economy. Crude tall oil production has declined in recent years due to declines in pulp and paper production. Younger pine trees produced on farms have a lower tall oil yield.

U.S. production of tall oil in January 2000 was reported by the U.S. Department of Commerce to be 101.3 million pounds, down 14 percent from the year before. In recent years, U.S. annual production of crude tall oil has been 1.35 billion pounds. Annual consumption of tall oil in inedible products is 1.16 billion pounds. Stocks of crude tall oil in May 2000 were 132 million pounds, down 20 percent from a year earlier. Refined tall oil stocks in May 2000 were 9.9 million pounds, down 33 percent from a year ago.

Consumption of Tall Oil in Inedible Products in the United States   In Millions of Pounds

Year	Jan.	Feb.	Mar.	Apr.	May	June	July	Aug.	Sept.	Oct.	Nov.	Dec.	Total
1993	68.6	64.8	73.1	68.1	76.3	68.8	79.0	78.1	78.0	75.4	78.4	83.2	892
1994	117.4	98.8	124.0	118.4	115.0	118.8	106.8	114.9	119.8	113.7	101.9	113.0	1,363
1995	99.8	93.6	96.9	95.8	87.3	96.5	93.1	102.3	89.4	91.6	100.5	88.9	1,136
1996	93.1	103.4	89.2	104.1	100.5	96.6	85.4	100.7	94.9	111.5	101.4	98.8	1,180
1997	111.5	89.0	91.0	99.5	97.0	105.8	103.7	94.4	84.7	87.2	87.3	88.4	1,139
1998	86.7	114.4	113.2	120.0	108.0	101.8	117.2	114.8	120.3	111.6	119.0	121.0	1,348
1999	99.4	115.1	111.0	114.0	99.9	109.2	119.1	113.0	103.9	108.4	106.4	102.2	1,302
2000[1]	91.7	88.1	106.4	97.5	90.9	98.8	91.8	106.6	94.9	93.7	89.4	96.2	1,146

[1] Preliminary.   *Source: Bureau of the Census, U.S. Department of Commerce*

Production of Crude Tall Oil in the United States   In Millions of Pounds

Year	Oct.	Nov.	Dec.	Jan.	Feb.	Mar.	Apr.	May	June	July	Aug.	Sept.	Total
1993-4	107.5	120.7	124.6	127.0	115.4	148.1	131.0	119.1	109.1	108.7	110.8	117.4	1,322.0
1994-5	111.1	114.5	115.1	108.3	108.1	123.0	111.1	116.5	118.2	116.4	119.2	102.9	1,261.6
1995-6	109.8	105.2	105.2	115.5	123.3	126.9	108.9	120.3	120.3	120.5	124.9	112.9	1,281.0
1996-7	119.2	113.9	114.5	119.9	125.1	125.1	118.5	116.6	116.4	135.0	132.9	130.8	1,337.2
1997-8	122.7	115.4	135.4	137.7	126.6	127.5	132.3	131.2	131.1	132.0	120.2	121.1	1,540.6
1998-9	118.4	113.4	119.3	118.0	115.2	134.6	121.0	103.8	100.7	103.2	103.5	113.6	1,364.8
1999-00	93.8	101.6	107.8	101.3	104.6	115.2	95.4	91.8	99.5	94.5	97.0	86.5	1,202.6
2000-1[1]	92.3	91.6	81.4	94.7									1,079.9

[1] Preliminary.   *Source: Bureau of the Census, U.S. Department of Commerce*

Stocks of Crude Tall Oil in the United States, on First of Month   In Millions of Pounds

Year	Oct.	Nov.	Dec.	Jan.	Feb.	Mar.	Apr.	May	June	July	Aug.	Sept.
1993-4	132.8	124.0	113.0	103.7	109.5	109.7	118.2	124.4	112.6	105.3	101.1	97.5
1994-5	86.3	82.7	94.1	104.1	107.6	117.2	123.4	132.1	118.1	132.3	134.7	135.0
1995-6	120.9	117.5	112.9	100.7	105.7	120.3	146.0	131.8	127.0	130.5	138.7	147.3
1996-7	172.3	192.1	167.4	182.4	173.0	196.0	200.8	220.6	187.3	237.5	248.5	242.2
1997-8	208.6	187.9	209.7	202.1	202.8	219.4	256.8	254.1	239.1	259.1	278.4	245.2
1998-9	268.7	219.8	200.3	197.5	164.8	156.9	163.3	177.5	183.0	180.7	183.6	152.7
1999-00	146.8	130.9	135.3	121.5	131.8	153.5	136.6	138.5	154.6	130.5	136.7	117.1
2000-11	110.5	102.4	105.4	117.0	113.2							

[1] Preliminary.   *Source: Bureau of the Census, U.S. Department of Commerce*

Stocks of Refined Tall Oil in the United States, on First of Month   In Millions of Pounds

Year	Oct.	Nov.	Dec.	Jan.	Feb.	Mar.	Apr.	May	June	July	Aug.	Sept.
1993-4	7.0	7.5	8.5	10.7	13.7	13.5	13.5	12.0	10.2	9.7	11.6	10.9
1994-5	12.0	14.4	16.3	13.5	15.4	14.1	11.7	10.8	10.2	10.0	9.9	8.9
1995-6	10.1	11.6	7.9	6.0	7.9	9.7	8.5	10.4	8.5	6.0	6.1	7.2
1996-7	8.3	7.0	7.5	8.9	6.5	26.5	17.4	31.7	20.9	32.0	13.2	16.6
1997-8	32.3	25.6	34.9	21.4	30.4	17.0	14.2	13.0	13.1	15.1	14.7	15.3
1998-9	15.1	14.9	17.0	12.5	14.8	9.9	7.2	7.6	7.2	7.3	6.3	7.0
1999-00	7.5	7.0	8.5	9.1	9.8	11.0	9.8	13.7	10.4	7.8	11.9	8.2
2000-1[1]	9.6	9.0	9.9	10.2	10.6							

[1] Preliminary.   *Source: Bureau of the Census, U.S. Department of Commerce*

Tallow and Greases

Production of tallow and greases is directly related to the number of cattle produced. Those countries that are the large cattle producers are also the largest producers of tallow. World production of tallow and greases (edible and inedible) has averaged just over 8 million metric tonnes since 1991. Prices are responsive to changes in production. In the 1996/1997 (October-September) season, U.S. tallow production declined by 10 percent. Prices moved higher and during the season averaged over 21 cents per pound in Chicago for edible, loose tallow. Prices since have dropped back into the teens. There are substitutes for tallow such as palm stearin and when prices move sharply higher, cheaper substitutes are likely to be used.

The U.S.D.A. estimated that global production of tallow and greases (edible and inedible) in 1999 was 8.3 million tonnes, about the same as the year before. The largest producer of tallow and greases was the U.S. with 44 percent of the world total. The next largest producer was Brazil with some 6 percent of the global output. Australia's share of the market was 5 percent. Other large producers of tallow and greases included Russia, Canada, and Argentina. Between 1990 and 1999, U.S. production averaged 3.6 million tonnes.

The U.S.D.A. estimated that U.S. stocks of edible tallow at the beginning of the 1999/2000 season were 43 million pounds, down 7 percent from a year ago. U.S. production of edible tallow in February 2000 was 143 million pounds. In the October 1999 to February 2000 period, edible tallow production totaled 692 million pounds. A year earlier in the same period, production was 629 million pounds.

Imports of tallow are minor and appear to be declining. In the 1998/99 season, imports were 3 million pounds, while the previous year they were 2 million pounds. In the period between 1990/91 and 1994/95, imports of tallow averaged 12 million pounds per season. In the first five months of the 1999/00 season, imports totaled 5 million pounds.

In January 2000, domestic use of edible tallow was estimated to be 111 million pounds. Tallow finds widespread use in the baking and cooking industries. In the 1998/99 season, domestic use of tallow was 1.36 billion pounds. The months with the highest rates of edible tallow use are May through August.

The U.S. exports more tallow than it imports. Exports in January 2000 were estimated to be 15 million pounds. In the first four months of the 1999/00 season, tallow exports totaled 80 million pounds. For all of 1998/99, exports of tallow were 322 million pounds. Ending stocks of tallow in the U.S. in February 2000 were estimated to be 40 million pounds. A year earlier they were 44 million pounds.

World Production of Tallow and Greases (Edible and Inedible)   In Thousands of Metric Tons

Year	Argentina	Australia	Brazil	Canada	France	Germany	Rep. of Korea	Netherlands	New Zealand	Russia	United Kingdom	United States	World Total
1991	285	530	340	193	185	270	85	150	132	386	230	3,180	6,968
1992	268	472	336	212	275	197	121	150	134	352	225	3,309	7,077
1993	260	526	429	209	240	178	115	163	145	706	212	3,650	8,492
1994	250	446	435	213	206	167	120	159	135	437	215	3,851	8,258
1995	248	423	46	217	220	166	118	158	147	377	230	3,756	8,312
1996	240	397	467	242	220	168	198	161	155	400	165	3,581	8,184
1997	265	456	460	250	220	167	209	200	161	340	160	3,467	8,342
1998	220	560	467	265	220	166	235	190	150	340	170	3,694	8,374
1999[1]	235	565	480	285	220	165	230	168	135	330	180	3,855	8,584
2000[2]	230	540	505	290	220	165	230	192	142	310	195	3,562	8,312

[1] Preliminary.   [2] Forecast.   Source: Foreign Agricultural Service, U.S. Department of Agriculture (FAS-USDA)

Salient Statistics of Tallow and Greases (Inedible) in the United States   In Millions of Pounds

Year	Production (Supply)	Stocks, Jan. 1 (Supply)	Total (Supply)	Exports	Soap (Consumption)	Feed (Consumption)	Total (Consumption)	Edible, (Loose) Chicago (Wholesale Prices, Cents/Lb.)	Inedible, No. 1 Chicago (Wholesale Prices, Cents/Lb.)
1991	5,759	357	6,116	1,936	392	1,748	2,949	14.3	13.3
1992	5,768	349	6,117	2,276	334	1,954	3,050	15.5	14.4
1993	6,621	309	6,930	2,117	300	1,995	3,018	16.2	14.9
1994	6,364	320	6,684	3,039	301	2,183	3,246	18.4	17.4
1995	6,481	350	6,831	2,486	264	2,071	2,334	21.4	19.2
1996	6,242	373	6,615	1,807	245	2,389	2,634	22.0	20.1
1997	6,249	266	6,515	775	245	2,401	2,646	23.5	20.8
1998	6,644	339	6,983	1,041	228	2,533	2,761	19.1	17.5
1999[1]	7,079	437	7,516	877	229	2,847	3,076	15.1	13.0
2000[2]	7,035	405	7,440	805	146	2,727	2,849	11.6	10.0

[1] Preliminary.   [2] Estimate.   Sources: Economic Research Service, U.S. Department of Agriculture (ERS-USDA); Bureau of the Census, U.S. Department of Commerce

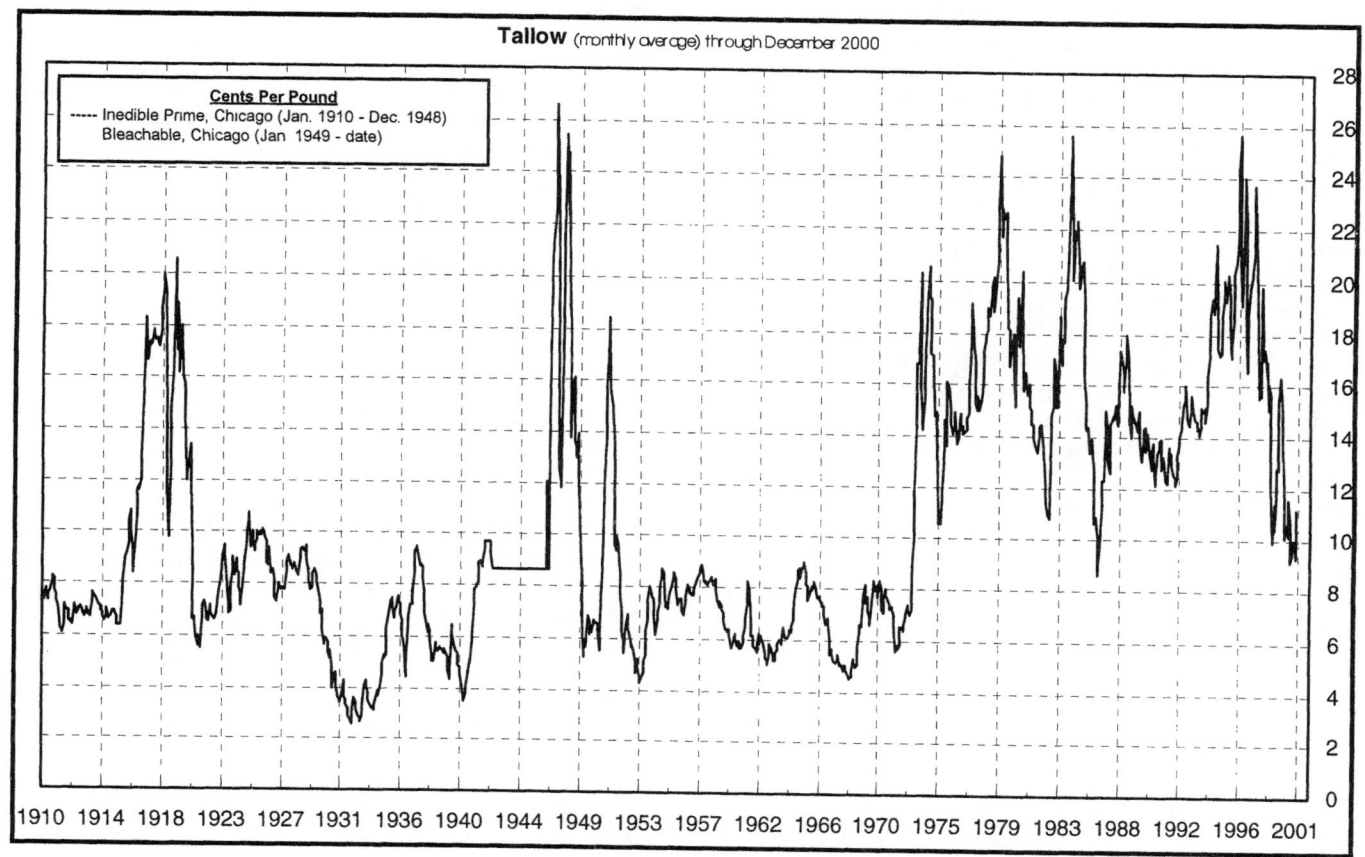

Tallow (monthly average) through December 2000

Cents Per Pound
----- Inedible Prime, Chicago (Jan. 1910 - Dec. 1948)
Bleachable, Chicago (Jan 1949 - date)

Supply and Disappearance of Edible Tallow in the United States   In Millions of Pounds, Rendered Basis

Year	Stocks Jan. 1	Production	Total	Domestic	Exports	Total	Diret Use	Baking or Frying Fats	Per Capita (Lbs.)
	----- Supply -----			----- Disappearance -----					
1990	38	1,207	1,251	963	252	1,214	154	637	3.9
1991	37	1,251	1,299	975	285	1,261	367	460	3.9
1992	39	1,527	1,571	1,205	333	1,538	610	427	4.7
1993	33	1,425	1,470	1,127	310	1,437	412	404	4.4
1994	33	1,510	1,606	1,275	295	1,570	639	405	4.9
1995	36	1,536	1,590	1,268	279	1,548	533	374	4.9
1996	43	1,520	1,568	1,317	218	1,535	602	320	5.0
1997	33	1,416	1,455	1,223	185	1,408	585	312	4.6
1998[1]	47	1,537	1,586	1,301	246	1,547	868	259	4.8
1999[2]	39	1,729	1,775	1,425	317	1,742	998	262	5.3

[1] Preliminary.   [2] Forecast.   *Sources: Economic Research Service, U.S. Department of Agriculture (ERS-USDA); Bureau of the Census, U.S. Department of Commerce*

Wholesale Price of Tallow, Inedible, No. 1 Packers (Prime), Delivered, Chicago   In Cents Per Pound

Year	Jan.	Feb.	Mar.	Apr.	May	June	July	Aug.	Sept.	Oct.	Nov.	Dec.	Average
1991	13.88	14.28	14.43	14.80	13.02	12.36	12.96	14.00	13.50	13.68	13.08	12.50	13.54
1992	12.25	12.63	12.68	13.25	13.75	13.98	14.75	15.42	15.25	15.94	16.75	16.13	14.40
1993	15.36	14.70	15.24	16.15	15.41	14.51	14.36	14.53	14.66	14.62	14.69	14.63	14.91
1994	15.00	15.00	15.22	15.19	15.25	15.63	16.67	18.64	19.50	19.78	20.38	22.48	17.40
1995	21.75	18.86	18.00	17.75	17.50	17.89	19.61	19.81	19.53	19.46	19.75	20.08	19.17
1996	19.45	17.00	17.03	17.54	19.37	19.50	20.98	22.40	25.98	21.05	19.65	21.63	20.13
1997	23.40	22.88	19.35	17.39	18.09	19.64	19.65	20.10	20.88	22.13	22.88	22.60	20.75
1998	18.20	16.88	17.58	17.70	20.35	19.63	17.31	17.57	16.69	16.98	16.90	16.70	17.71
1999	16.30	12.53	11.18	11.38	10.40	11.49	11.50	11.69	14.38	16.37	14.95	13.88	13.00
2000[1]	11.89	10.14	10.67	10.21	11.60	10.74	9.19	9.48	10.07	10.05	9.35	11.23	10.39

[1] Preliminary.   *Sources: Economic Research Service, U.S. Department of Agriculture (ERS-USDA)*

Tea

Tea is produced in a number of countries around the world. It is usually grown on plantations. The tea plant is an evergreen shrub which can grow 15-30 feet tall in its natural state, though on a plantation it is kept to a height of about five feet. It thrives in tropical climates with plenty of rain. It does well at higher altitudes though it can be grown at sea level. Most commercial production of tea takes place near the equator.

Tea is usually classified in three classes. The first is black tea or fermented tea, the second is green tea or unfermented tea, and the third is oolong tea or semifermented. All of these teas are differentiated in processing, the tea leaves used are all the same. Black tea is made by taking tea leaves and fermenting them under damp clothes, then drying the leaves until they are black. The fermentation reduces astringency and changes flavor. Green tea is steamed in a boiler with fermentation before drying the leaves. Oolong teas are partially fermented. After drying, teas are graded with orange pekoe being the highest quality.

World production of tea has been increasing about one percent per year for the last decade. World production as estimated by the Food and Agricultural Organization of the United Nations is about 2.7 million metric tonnes. In 1990, production was about 2.5 million tonnes. The world's largest producer of tea is India with about 29 percent of the world total. India produced mostly black tea and has been putting more emphasis on producing higher quality teas.

In late 2000, a trade body in India asked planters to temporarily stop production due to a decline in prices, a decline in quality, and excess production. India's production has exceeded the government target. The tea season in India ends in January and the new season starts in April. Of concern is the amount of poor quality tea being produced. While India is the largest producer of tea it is not the largest exporter. Most of the tea produced is consumed domestically.

China is the next largest producer of tea with about 23 percent of global output. Green tea is produced for the domestic market and black tea is exported. The third largest tea producer is Sri Lanka with about 10 percent of the world market. Despite years of civil strife, Sri Lanka continues to increase its tea production.

Tea production is increasing in Africa. The largest producer is Kenya with about 8 percent of the world market. Kenya's crop has been in excess of 200,000 tonnes. The crop was damaged by frost early in 2000 and a drought. The weather appears to have improved with needed rains, heat, and sun helping the crop. Africa's second largest tea producer is Malawi with about 1 percent of the world output. Kenyan tea is considered to be of high quality along with the teas from Rwanda, Burundi, and Tanzania.

The U.S. is a major importer of mostly black tea. U.S. per capita consumption is just over nine gallons. The U.S. also exports a small amount of tea. The Department of Commerce reported that in September 2000, exports were 459 metric tonnes compared to 335 tonnes in August.

World Tea Production, in Major Producing Countries   In Thousands of Metric Tons

Year	Argentina	Bangladesh	China	India	Indonesia	Iran	Japan	Kenya	Malawi	Sri Lanka	Turkey	Ex-USSR[2]	World Total
1988	44.0	43.6	545.0	700.0	133.8	55.6	89.8	164.0	40.2	228.2	166.4	118.0	2,490
1989	48.0	39.1	535.0	688.1	141.4	46.0	90.5	180.6	39.5	208.0	141.6	119.2	2,444
1990	50.0	45.9	540.0	720.3	145.2	44.0	89.9	197.0	39.1	234.1	126.7	123.2	2,528
1991	40.0	45.2	542.0	741.7	133.4	45.0	87.9	203.6	40.5	241.6	135.3	110.0	2,541
1992	43.0	46.0	580.0	704.0	163.0	55.0	92.0	188.0	28.0	179.0	144.0	57.0	2,439
1993	55.0	55.0	621.0	758.0	165.0	57.0	92.0	211.0	39.0	232.0	117.0	81.0	2,643
1994	50.0	51.0	613.0	744.0	136.0	56.0	86.0	209.0	35.0	242.0	134.0	66.0	2,615
1995	47.0	52.0	609.0	753.0	154.0	54.0	85.0	245.0	34.0	246.0	103.0	44.0	2,613
1996	47.0	48.0	617.0	780.0	159.0	62.0	89.0	257.0	37.0	258.0	115.0	38.0	2,701
1997[1]	48.0	53.0	633.0	785.0	162.0	62.0	91.0	221.0	38.0	277.0	121.0	38.0	2,734

[1] Preliminary.   [2] Mostly Georgia and Azerbaijan.   *Sources: Foreign Agricultural Service, U.S. Department of Agriculture (FAS-USDA); Food and Agriculture Organization of the United Nations (FAO-UN)*

World Tea Exports from Producing Countries   In Metric Tons

Year	Argentina	Bangladesh	Brazil	China	India	Indonesia	Kenya	Malawi	P. New Guinea	Sri Lanka	Vietnam	Zimbabwe	World Total
1988	34,258	26,187	9,686	198,289	200,956	92,687	138,201	36,961	5,834	219,710	14,800	14,190	1,039,313
1989	43,335	23,426	9,400	204,584	211,622	114,709	163,188	39,891	5,439	203,763	15,016	12,768	1,121,251
1990	45,966	26,970	7,976	195,471	209,085	110,964	169,586	43,039	5,375	215,251	24,698	11,507	1,141,026
1991	36,029	26,860	7,347	190,188	215,144	110,207	175,625	41,185	3,747	212,017	7,953	11,304	1,206,282
1992	36,530	24,990	8,211	180,834	166,359	121,243	172,053	37,056	5,638	181,259	12,967	6,088	1,130,355
1993	44,258	29,620	8,335	206,659	153,159	123,925	199,379	35,264	6,441	134,742	21,200	8,065	1,193,144
1994	43,355	29,040	8,377	184,071	150,874	84,916	176,962	38,670	3,400	115,097	23,500	9,688	1,078,460
1995	41,175	26,445	7,252	169,788	158,333	79,227	258,564	32,600	4,200	178,005	18,800	9,156	1,179,705
1996[1]	35,042	26,600	3,891	173,145	138,360	101,532	260,819	36,700	7,510	218,714	20,800	11,540	1,238,537
1997[2]	56,806	24,300	3,404	205,381	203,000	66,843	199,224	20,000	7,510	267,726	10,000	13,057	1,291,700

[1] Preliminary.   [2] Estimate.   *Source: Food and Agriculture Organization of the United Nations (FAO-UN)*

Tin

Tin is used in the manufacture of coatings for steel containers used to preserve food and beverages. Tin finds use in solder alloys, electroplating, ceramics, and in plastic. Research by the tin industry has focused on the use of tin in more products because of its non-toxic properties compared to other metals. Tin is relatively non-toxic compared with other metals and therefore the use of tin as a replacement for these metals is desirable. Some replacements would be for lead-free solders, tin shotgun pellets to replace lead, and the use of inorganic tin compounds to replace antimony in flame-retardant chemicals. The U.S. Geological Survey estimated that the major uses for tin were: cans and containers, 30 percent; electrical, 20 percent; construction, 10 percent; transportation, 10 percent; other, 30 percent. In 1999, there was no U.S. domestic tin mine production. Outside of imports, tin is only produced by recycling old and new scrap.

World mine production of tin in 1999 was estimated at 210,000 metric tonnes, an increase of 2 percent from the previous year. The largest producer of tin is China with 1999 production estimated at 80,000 tonnes, an increase of 1 percent from 1998. The next largest producer was Indonesia with 1999 production of 42,000 tonnes, an increase of 5 percent from the previous year. The third largest producer was Peru with 1999 production of 27,000 tonnes, up 4 percent from 1998. Mine production of tin in Brazil was 17,000 tonnes, down 6 percent from the previous year. Production by Bolivia was 12,000 tonnes, up 9 percent from 1998. Other large producers include Australia, Malaysia, Russia, and Portugal.

World reserves of tin are estimated to be 7.7 million tonnes. The largest reserves are in China which has an estimated 2.1 million tonnes. Reserves in Brazil and Malaysia are estimated to be 1.2 million tonnes each. Other significant reserves are located in Thailand, Bolivia, Indonesia, and Australia. U.S. resources of tin are located mostly in Alaska and are relatively insignificant compared to the rest of the world.

U.S. production of secondary tin including tin recovered from alloys and tinplate in August 2000 was 900 tonnes, unchanged from July. In the January-August 2000 period, secondary production of tin was 7,200 tonnes, while for all of 1999 it was 10,800 tonnes.

U.S. consumption of primary tin in August 2000 was 3,560 tonnes, up less than 1 percent from July. In the January-August 2000 period, consumption of primary tin was 28,300 tonnes. For all of 1999, consumption was 42,800 tonnes. Consumption of secondary tin in August 2000 was 906 tonnes compared to 858 tonnes in July. For the January-August 2000 period, consumption of secondary tin was 7,170 tonnes and for all of 1999 it was 12,300 tonnes.

U.S. production of tin plate in August 2000 was 157,000 tonnes, gross weight, with a tin content of 795 tonnes. There were 5.1 kilograms of tin per metric tonne of plate. In July 2000, tinplate production was 165,000 tonnes with a tin content of 780 tonnes. There were 4.7 kilograms of tin per tonne of plate. For all of 1999, tinplate production was 1.75 million tonnes with a tin content of 9,080 tonnes. There were 5.2 kilograms of tin per tonne of plate. Shipments of tinplate in August 2000 were 214,000 tonnes, up 18 percent from July. For all of 1999, shipments were 2.37 million tonnes.

U.S. imports of tin metal in July 2000 were 4,030 tonnes, down 5 percent from June. In the January-July 2000 period, imports of tin metal were 27,700 tonnes. For all of 1999 imports were 47,500 tonnes. In 1999, the major supplier of tin metal to the U.S. was China with 13,900 tonnes followed by Peru with 11,000 tonnes. Other large suppliers included Indonesia, Brazil, Chile, and Bolivia. U.S. imports of other tin products in July 2000 were 2,090 tonnes, down 14 percent from June. In the January-July period, imports totaled 9,200 tonnes. For all of 1999, imports were 9,100 tonnes. Imports in 1999 for tin alloys were 3,090 tonnes. Imports of waste and scrap were 2,730 tonnes, while bars and rods were 872 tonnes. U.S. exports of tin metal in July 2000 were 524 tonnes. In the first seven months of 2000, exports were 3,390 tonnes.

U.S. consumption of finished tin products in August 2000 was 3,570 tonnes. In July, consumption was 3,500 tonnes. In the January-August 2000 period, consumption was 28,300 tonnes. For all of 1999, U.S. consumption of finished tin products was 41,300 tonnes. In 1999, consumption of tin solder was 14,000 tonnes, consumption of tinplate was 9,080 tonnes, and tin chemical use was 8,140 tonnes. Consumption of tin in bronze and brass products was 3,170 tonnes.

Futures Markets

Tin futures and options are traded on the London Metals Exchange (LME).

World Mine Production of Tin — In Metric Tons (Contained Tin)

Year	Australia	Bolivia	Brazil	China	Indo-nesia	Malaysia	Nigeria	Peru	Portugal	Russia[3]	Thailand	United Kingdom	World Total
1990	7,377	17,249	39,149	42,000	30,200	28,468	192	5,134	4,780	15,000	14,635	3,400	221,000
1991	5,708	16,830	29,253	42,100	30,061	20,710	217	6,558	8,333	13,500	14,937	2,326	201,000
1992	6,609	16,516	27,000	43,800	29,400	14,339	415	10,044	6,560	15,160	11,484	2,044	191,000
1993	8,057	18,634	26,500	49,100	29,000	10,384	200	14,310	5,334	13,100	6,363	2,232	190,000
1994	7,495	16,169	16,619	54,100	30,610	6,458	278	20,275	4,332	10,460	3,926	1,922	178,000
1995	8,656	14,419	17,317	61,900	46,058	6,402	357	22,331	4,627	9,000	2,201	1,973	201,000
1996	8,828	14,802	19,617	69,600	52,304	5,175	139	27,004	4,637	8,000	1,457	2,103	220,000
1997	10,169	12,898	19,065	67,500	55,175	5,065	150	27,952	2,667	7,500	756	2,396	217,000
1998[1]	10,204	11,308	14,607	70,100	53,959	5,756	200	25,747	3,000	4,500	2,124	376	208,000
1999[2]	10,038	11,300	13,200	61,700	47,754	7,340	200	30,403	3,000	4,500	2,722	----	198,000

[1] Preliminary. [2] Estimate. [3] Formerly part of the U.S.S.R.; data reported separately until 1992. *Source: U.S. Geological Survey (USGS)*

TIN

World Smelter Production of Primary Tin   In Metric Tons

Year	Australia	Bolivia	Brazil	China	Indo-nesia	Japan	Malaysia	Mexico	Russia[2]	South Africa	Spain	Thailand	World Total
1990	312	12,567	37,580	35,000	30,389	816	49,067	5,004	16,000	1,140	600	15,512	246,000
1991	340	14,663	25,776	36,400	30,415	716	42,722	2,262	13,000	1,042	600	11,255	205,000
1992	240	14,393	27,000	39,600	31,915	821	45,598	2,590	15,200	592	600	10,679	194,000
1993	222	14,541	26,900	52,100	30,415	804	40,079	1,640	13,400	452	500	8,099	215,000
1994	315	15,285	20,400	67,800	31,100	706	37,990	768	11,500	43	500	7,759	216,000
1995	570	17,709	16,787	67,700	38,628	630	39,433	770	9,500	----	500	8,243	223,000
1996	460	16,733	18,361	71,500	39,000	524	38,051	1,234	9,000	----	150	10,981	228,000
1997	605	16,853	17,525	67,700	52,658	507	38,400	1,188	6,700	----	150	11,986	244,000
1998	655	11,102	17,500	79,300	53,401	500	27,900	102	3,000	----	100	15,353	246,000
1999[1]	585	11,000	13,200	92,300	49,105	600	35,800	500	2,800	----	50	17,306	269,000

[1] Preliminary.   [2] Formerly part of the U.S.S.R.; data not separately until 1992.   Source: U.S. Geological Survey (USGS)

United States Foreign Trade of Tin   In Metric Tons

		Concentrates[2] (Ore)			Imports for Consumption								
								Unwrought Tin Metal					
Year	Exports (Metal)	Total All Ore	Bolivia	Peru	Total All Metal	Bolivia	Brazil	China	Indo-nesia	Malaysia	Singa-pore	Thailand	United Kingdom
1990	658	----	----	----	33,810	8,472	6,535	4,339	4,695	3,873	40	60	227
1991	970	1	1	----	29,102	8,912	4,489	5,281	4,425	1,751	100	----	344
1992	1,890	----	----	----	27,314	4,623	8,167	5,389	3,854	2,799	320	427	----
1993	2,600	----	----	----	33,682	8,027	11,366	4,202	5,678	846	220	----	6
1994	2,560	----	----	----	32,400	7,260	9,990	3,230	6,620	1,390	142	----	666
1995	2,790	----	----	----	33,200	6,630	8,070	5,610	7,230	3,810	40	----	97
1996	3,670	----	----	----	30,200	6,290	9,460	2,760	7,550	965	120	----	243
1997	4,660	57	----	----	40,600	6,680	8,610	4,710	7,610	1,640	120	600	20
1998	5,020	----	----	----	44,000	5,160	4,710	9,870	7,880	1,870	822	540	790
1999[1]	6,770	----	----	----	47,500	3,850	4,700	13,900	7,930	944	60	20	60

[1] Preliminary.   [2] Tin content.   Source: U.S. Geological Survey (USGS)

Consumption (Total) of Tin (Pig) in the United States   In Metric Tons

Year	Jan.	Feb.	Mar.	Apr.	May	June	July	Aug.	Sept.	Oct.	Nov.	Dec.	Total
1991	4,100	3,900	4,100	4,300	4,100	4,200	3,900	4,100	4,000	4,300	4,100	4,000	49,000
1992	3,800	3,800	3,800	3,800	3,700	3,800	3,800	3,500	3,600	3,600	3,400	3,300	45,090
1993	3,400	3,500	3,600	3,600	3,500	3,600	3,500	3,600	3,500	3,500	3,500	3,400	47,107
1994	3,500	3,700	3,700	3,600	3,600	3,700	3,500	3,400	2,500	3,600	3,600	3,400	42,700
1995	3,500	3,600	3,680	3,726	3,877	3,833	3,544	3,895	3,825	3,823	3,735	3,770	44,808
1996	3,862	3,938	3,940	3,878	3,894	3,976	3,926	3,996	3,687	3,779	3,908	3,730	48,800
1997	4,953	4,025	4,023	4,067	3,999	4,079	3,936	3,912	4,050	4,098	3,964	4,250	44,350
1998	4,410	4,493	4,445	4,508	4,388	4,483	4,273	4,300	4,404	4,402	4,348	4,268	52,720
1999	4,660	4,667	4,790	4,790	4,760	4,700	4,254	4,396	4,340	4,316	4,275	4,227	55,100
2000[1]	4,362	4,466	4,430	4,377	4,466	4,470	4,398	4,476	4,397	4,460	4,244	4,148	52,694

[1] Preliminary.   Source: U.S. Geological Survey (USGS)

Tin Stocks (Pig-Industrial) in the United States, on First of Month   In Metric Tons

Year	Jan.	Feb.	Mar.	Apr.	May	June	July	Aug.	Sept.	Oct.	Nov.	Dec.
1991	6,337	6,677	6,688	6,177	5,993	5,991	6,348	6,739	6,544	8,544	6,616	6,347
1992	3,024	3,022	3,369	2,844	2,877	2,901	2,651	3,111	3,321	3,454	3,654	3,178
1993	3,221	3,572	4,450	4,483	3,898	3,609	4,648	4,652	4,561	3,709	3,262	3,535
1994	3,651	4,635	3,775	3,967	3,471	3,470	3,825	3,027	2,891	2,980	2,844	2,908
1995	2,741	3,931	3,850	2,780	3,000	3,080	3,210	3,910	3,800	3,880	4,380	4,290
1996	4,580	6,000	5,200	4,390	4,880	5,590	5,760	5,640	4,790	4,580	4,810	6,810
1997	4,670	5,100	5,610	5,600	5,070	5,270	5,180	5,650	5,590	5,420	5,290	5,590
1998	6,100	5,570	5,390	5,840	6,170	5,940	5,830	5,580	6,660	6,270	5,880	5,710
1999	5,620	8,120	7,770	7,760	7,760	7,510	7,750	7,560	7,870	7,790	8,390	8,800
2000[1]	8,300	8,330	7,960	7,580	7,810	7,930	8,090	8,240	7,820	8,210	7,200	7,970

[1] Preliminary.   Source: U.S. Geological Survey (USGS)

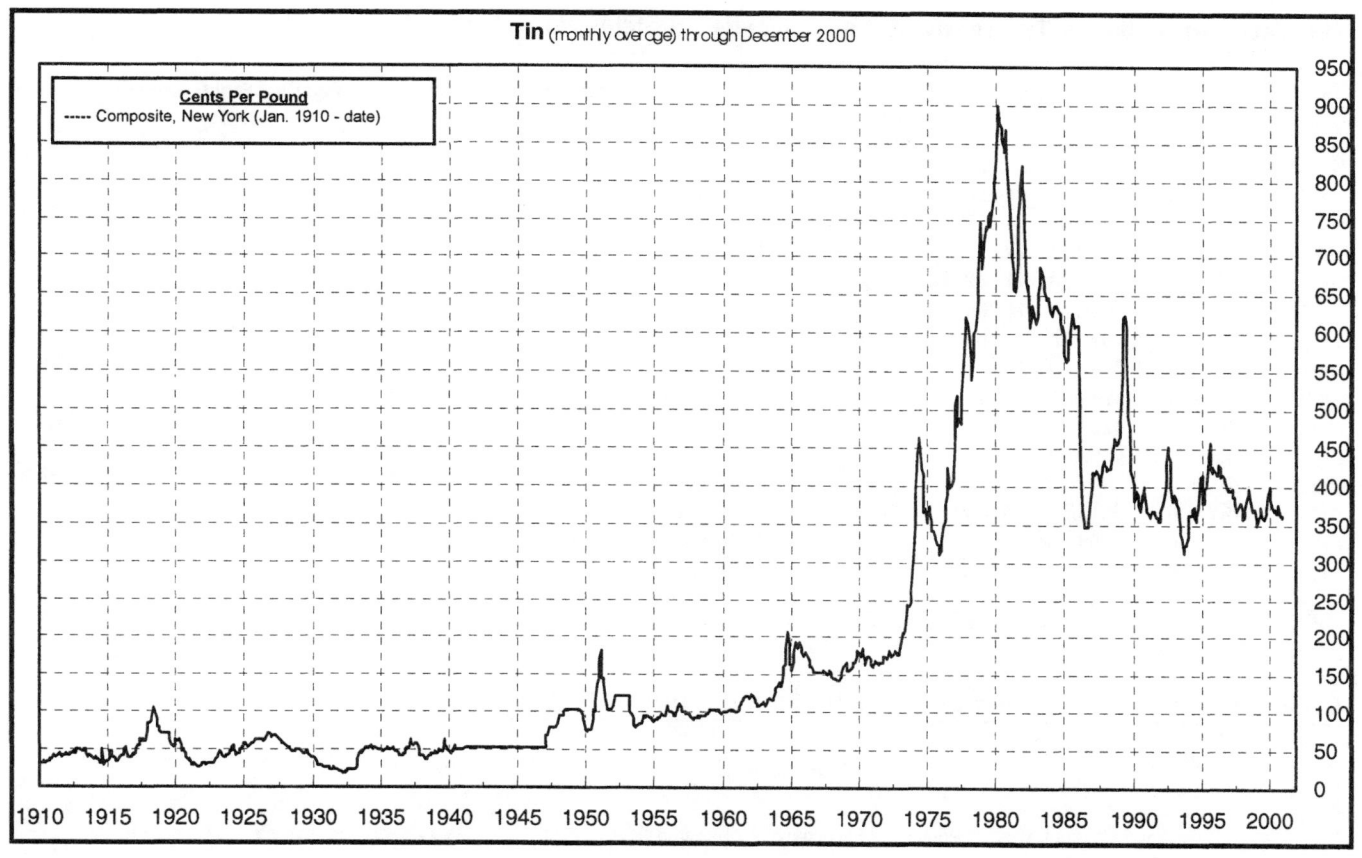

Tin (monthly average) through December 2000

Cents Per Pound
----- Composite, New York (Jan. 1910 - date)

Average Price of Ex-Dock Tin in New York[1]   In Cents Per Pound

Year	Jan.	Feb.	Mar.	Apr.	May	June	July	Aug.	Sept.	Oct.	Nov.	Dec.	Average
1991	269.97	268.00	264.51	265.78	271.78	272.30	270.55	269.02	265.86	264.50	262.26	262.05	267.22
1992	261.30	267.79	267.52	277.20	290.05	313.07	331.10	322.19	315.66	291.60	268.54	271.76	289.82
1993	280.40	280.91	277.43	275.67	269.62	255.35	252.31	230.17	213.22	220.02	224.88	236.90	251.41
1994	249.55	267.55	261.20	258.49	264.18	264.45	254.83	249.18	255.10	262.46	293.72	284.99	263.81
1995	374.77	260.25	266.45	288.00	283.62	314.33	316.06	331.64	304.12	297.77	304.47	300.28	303.48
1996	299.55	297.45	296.68	308.49	306.71	296.20	298.47	291.30	292.13	285.11	285.87	280.61	294.88
1997	281.91	281.34	281.51	274.36	274.23	267.31	261.03	259.85	262.56	266.77	268.33	262.61	270.15
1998	249.39	252.65	262.36	271.65	279.50	284.27	268.87	270.98	260.79	259.17	261.82	251.75	264.43
1999	244.46	251.04	255.13	256.97	269.42	253.64	251.09	251.32	256.38	260.70	278.24	274.51	258.73
2000	283.63	271.70	263.42	259.59	259.70	260.16	257.77	255.92	262.54	254.56	253.64	252.19	261.24

Source: American Metal Market (AMM)

Average Price of Tin (Straights) in New York   In Cents Per Pound

Year	Jan.	Feb.	Mar.	Apr.	May	June	July	Aug.	Sept.	Oct.	Nov.	Dec.	Average
1991	368.22	364.86	360.89	362.04	368.33	368.95	367.07	365.06	361.19	358.63	355.35	354.27	362.91
1992	367.89	375.70	375.25	386.88	402.70	431.63	453.05	441.89	434.02	398.27	380.41	380.89	402.38
1993	390.01	384.48	378.36	374.06	369.82	347.55	339.79	330.63	310.94	322.67	322.26	326.72	349.77
1994	334.38	362.81	361.86	363.65	371.63	372.59	360.45	353.85	362.48	371.82	411.63	401.31	369.04
1995	415.05	379.08	378.61	395.99	399.17	433.75	438.04	458.66	423.71	417.23	425.41	419.75	415.37
1996	418.68	415.65	414.71	429.34	427.24	413.65	416.63	409.12	407.79	400.25	400.65	394.46	412.35
1997	396.18	395.50	395.64	386.52	386.58	377.83	369.97	369.01	372.45	377.39	378.00	371.35	381.37
1998	356.97	359.76	370.96	381.99	392.16	397.36	377.72	380.02	368.89	366.87	370.49	357.69	373.41
1999	348.77	356.50	361.11	363.01	372.62	359.05	359.96	357.35	366.06	370.68	392.04	288.77	357.99
2000	400.90	384.13	372.50	368.42	370.13	370.81	366.49	364.65	375.25	363.54	362.94	360.68	371.70

Source: Wall Street Journal (WSJ)

TIN

Tin Plate Production & Tin Recovered in the United States   In Metric Tons

	Tinplate Waste		Tin Content (Tonne)	Tin Per Tonne of Plate (Kilograms)	Tin Metal	Bronze & Brass	Solder	Type Metal	Babbitt	Anti-monial Lead	Chemical Com-pounds	Misc.[2]	Grand Total
Year	---- Gross Weight ----												
1986	120,186	2,068,246	8,660	4.2	1,134	7,996	3,676	197	66	891	W	17	13,977
1987	141,842	2,302,173	10,357	4.5	1,353	10,245	3,765	66	77	623	W	30	16,159
1988	149,054	2,375,809	11,582	4.9	578	9,939	3,619	70	112	902	W	29	15,249
1989	153,542	2,263,769	11,764	5.2	569	10,305	3,225	46	116	952	W	W	15,213
1990	156,419	2,467,205	11,750	4.8	186	13,312	2,876	46	28	739	W	4	17,187
1991	166,647	2,468,769	11,482	4.7	234	11,719	W	44	24	928	W	2,705	12,949
1992	195,760	1,620,007	9,821	6.1	137	12,761	W	47	78	704	W	181	13,727
1993	196,874	1,625,132	9,945	6.0	112	10,670	W	43	51	796	W	W	11,672
1994	188,921	1,528,303	9,396	6.1	NA	NA	NA	NA	NA	NA	NA	NA	NA
1995	205,000	1,660,000	9,600	5.8	W	11,200	W	39	W	335	W	W	11,600
1996	181,100	1,551,000	9,617	6.2	W	11,400	W	37	34	171	W	W	11,600
1997	157,000	2,010,000	9,300	4.6	W	12,200	W	W	W	149	W	W	12,300
1998	W	1,700,000	8,900	5.2	NA	NA	NA	NA	NA	NA	NA	NA	NA
1999[1]	W	1,750,000	9,080		NA	NA	NA	NA	NA	NA	NA	NA	NA

Header spanning notes: ------ Tin Content of Tinplate Produced ------ / -------- Tinplate (All Forms) -------- / -------------------- Tin Recovered from Scrap by Form of Recovery --------------------

[1] Preliminary.   [2] Includes foil, terne metal, cable lead, and items indicated by symbol W.   W = Withheld Proprietary data.
Source: U.S. Geological Survey (USGS)

Consumption of Primary and Secondary Tin in the United States   In Metric Tons

Year	Net Import Reliance as a % of Apparent Consumption[2]	Industry Stocks Jan. 1[2]	Primary	Secondary	Scrap	Total	Available Supply	Stocks Dec. 31 (Total Available Less Total Processed)	Total Processed	Consumed in Manu-facturing Products
1986	74	9,336	35,475	11,636	6,346	53,457	62,793	18,915	43,878	43,524
1987	74	9,876	38,401	11,707	6,635	56,743	66,619	21,887	44,731	44,219
1988	78	10,217	39,421	12,472	6,707	58,600	68,817	23,586	46,232	45,602
1989	77	9,242	37,760	10,901	8,168	56,829	66,071	19,184	46,887	46,463
1990	71	13,551	38,473	9,501	6,534	54,508	68,059	22,578	45,481	45,165
1991	74	12,502	36,126	1,622	8,370	46,118	58,620	13,540	45,080	44,805
1992	80	12,038	34,327	2,279	8,412	45,018	57,056	11,669	45,387	45,120
1993	84	8,556	37,700	3,280	8,768	49,700	58,300	11,566	46,700	46,600
1994	83	9,540	35,400	4,210	4,940	44,500	54,100	11,600	42,500	42,200
1995	84	8,480	39,400	5,020	6,240	50,600	59,100	13,000	46,100	46,000
1996	83	9,300	39,200	2,750	6,140	48,100	57,300	12,500	44,900	44,700
1997	85	9,180	39,000	2,360	6,010	47,300	56,500	11,900	44,600	44,400
1998	NA	9,280	39,900	2,490	6,240	48,600	57,900	12,000	45,800	45,700
1999[1]	NA	9,290	40,800	2,790	6,380	50,000	59,300	11,900	47,400	47,300

Header spanning note: --------------------- Net Receipts ---------------------

[1] Preliminary.   [2] Includes tin in transit in the U.S.   *Source: U.S. Geological Survey (USGS)*

Consumption of Tin in the United States, by Finished Products   In Metric Tons (Contained Tin)

Year	Tinplate[2]	Solder	Babbitt	Bronze & Brass	Tinning	Chem-icals[3]	Tin Powder	Bar Tin & Anodes	White Metal	Other	Total	Total Primary	Total Secondary
1986	8,660	15,810	1,324	3,502	1,437	W	1,002	449	1,134	10,204	43,522	33,324	10,198
1987	10,357	15,240	1,060	3,559	1,398	W	W	703	1,175	10,704	44,219	35,620	8,599
1988	11,582	15,288	926	3,934	1,406	W	W	557	1,131	10,777	45,601	37,529	8,072
1989	11,764	16,370	794	3,693	1,505	W	711	619	1,074	9,926	46,456	36,603	9,853
1990	11,750	16,443	763	3,166	1,707	6,275	563	603	1,045	2,850	45,165	36,770	8,395
1991	11,482	16,296	941	2,896	1,465	6,564	539	436	868	3,318	44,805	35,138	9,667
1992	9,821	18,461	916	2,916	1,275	6,301	573	919	974	2,964	45,090	34,983	10,137
1993	9,650	19,000	823	3,093	1,249	6,446	608	946	789	3,927	46,600	34,600	11,900
1994	9,480	15,100	831	3,080	1,230	5,740	625	1,190	992	3,990	42,200	33,700	8,530
1995	9,670	17,700	871	2,830	1,110	7,060	W	1,200	965	4,550	46,000	35,200	10,800
1996	9,340	15,600	851	2,760	2,050	7,520	573	1,150	1,340	3,230	44,700	36,500	8,180
1997	9,350	15,900	909	3,160	1,210	8,170	W	684	754	3,980	44,400	36,200	8,250
1998	8,900	16,900	1,020	3,610	1,100	8,180	W	704	778	4,260	45,700	37,100	8,620
1999[1]	9,150	18,700	1,610	3,410	862	8,220	W	718	892	3,620	47,300	38,400	8,890

Header spanning note: ------------ Total ------------

[1] Preliminary.   [2] Includes small quantity of secondary pig tin and tin acquired in chemicals.   [3] Including tin oxide.   W = Withheld proprietary data.
Source: U.S. Geological Survey (USGS)

Titanium

Titanium is a metal known for its corrosion resistance and its strength. It has a density that is half that of steel. Titanium occurs in a number of materials but primarily in ilmenite, leucoxene, and rutile. With its properties of high strength and lightweight, titanium is ideal as a construction material for engines and air frames. Pure titanium metal is called "sponge" because of its porous cellular form. Titanium sponge is processed to form an ingot, which is then processed by mills to make plate sheet tubing. Due to its strength-to-weight properties, titanium is finding use in products like golf clubs and bicycles. Titanium is used in the automotive industry as well as in pollution control devices and in chemical processing. About 95 percent of titanium is consumed in the form of titanium dioxide, a white pigment used in paints, paper, and plastic.

The U.S. Geological Survey reported that 1999 world mine production of titanium was 4.01 million metric tonnes vs. 4.26 million tonnes in 1998. Australia was the largest reported producer with 1999 output of 1.32 million tonnes, down 16 percent from 1998. Production by South Africa was 1.04 million tonnes, about the same as in 1998. Other producers include Norway, India, and the Ukraine. World reserves of titanium are estimated to be 370 million tonnes.

U.S. production of titanium sponge in the second quarter of 2000 was withheld. Production of titanium ingot in the second quarter of 2000 was 9,180 tonnes, down 5 percent from the first quarter of 2000. Titanium ingot production in the first half of 2000 was 18,800 tonnes, while for all of 1999 it was 40,700 tonnes. Titanium mill products production in second quarter 2000 was 6,080 tonnes, down 6 percent from the first quarter. In the first half of 2000, mill products production was 12,600 tonnes, while for all of 1999 it was 24,200 tonnes.

U.S. consumption of titanium sponge in the second quarter of 2000 was 4,440 tonnes, while for the first six months of 2000 it was 8,580 tonnes. For all of 1999, titanium sponge consumption was 18,100 tonnes. Consumption of titanium scrap in the second quarter of 2000 was 4,620 tonnes and in the first half of 2000 totaled 9,600 tonnes. For all of 1999, it was 21,900 tonnes. Consumption of titanium ingot in second quarter 2000 was 5,680 tonnes. In the first half of 2000, ingot consumption was 13,800 tonnes, while for all of 1999 it was 30,800 tonnes. Total titanium product consumption in the first half of 2000 was 32,000 tonnes.

U.S. imports of titanium products in the first half of 2000 were 8,580 tonnes and for all of 1999 imports were 17,400 tonnes. Government stocks of titanium sponge in June 2000 were 30,600 tonnes, while industry stocks were 7,640 tonnes.

Average Prices of Titanium in the United States

Year	Ilmenite F.O.B. Australian Ports	Slag, 85% TiO2 F.O.B. Richards Bay, South Africa	Rutile Large Lots Bulk, F.O.B. U.S. East Coast	Rutile Bagged F.O.B. Australian Ports	Average Price of Grade A Titanium Sponge, F.O.B. Shipping Point	Titanium Metal Sponge	Titanium Dioxide Pigments, F.O.B. U.S. Plants	
	Dollars Per Metric Ton					Dollars Per Pound		
1990	69-77	285-310	550-580	693-770	5.31	4.75	.99	1.01
1991	68-76	295-325	606-650	515-545	5.25	4.75	.99	.99
1992	58-62	310	510-520	380-414	3.96	3.50-4.00	.99	.92-.95
1993	61-64	330	NA	370-400	3.75	3.50-4.00	.99	.92-.95
1994	74-80	334	410-430	450-480	3.96	3.75-4.25	.94-.96	.92-.94
1995	81-85	349	550-650	650-800	4.06	4.25-4.50	.92-.96	.99-1.03
1996	82-92	353	525-600	700-800	----	4.25-4.50	1.06-1.08	1.08-1.10
1997	68-81	391	500-550	650-710	----	4.25-4.50	1.01-1.03	1.04-1.06
1998[1]	72-77	386	470-530	570-620	----	4.25-4.50	.96-.98	.97-.99
1999[2]	90-103	406	435-510	500-530	----	3.70-4.80	.92-.94	.99-1.02

[1] Preliminary.　[2] Estimate.　NA = Not available.　Source: U.S. Geological Survey (USGS)

Salient Statistics of Titanium in the United States　In Metric Tons

Year	Titanium Dioxide Pigment Production	Imports[3]	Apparent Consumption	Ilmenite Imports[3]	Ilmenite Consumption	Titanium Slag Imports[3]	Titanium Slag Consumption	Rutile[4] Imports[3]	Rutile[4] Consumption	Ores & Concentrates	Scrap	Dioxide & Pigments	Ingots, Billets, Etc.
1990	978,659	147,592	925,447	345,907	688,948	373,623	390,537	274,605	369,454	18,765	5,487	202,288	2,371
1991	991,976	166,094	935,829	213,886	738,089	408,302	341,379	240,120	368,643	26,912	4,568	211,854	1,700
1992	1,137,038	169,260	999,930	294,585	684,882	537,118	539,323	317,399	460,969	34,665	2,770	270,422	1,455
1993	1,161,561	171,939	1,028,311	301,000	693,940	476,000	545,809	371,481	464,825	15,202	3,893	261,000	1,511
1994	1,250,000	176,000	1,090,000	808,000	W	472,000	583,000	332,000	510,000	19,000	4,120	313,000	1,559
1995	1,250,000	183,000	1,130,000	861,000	1,410,000	388,000	582,000	318,000	480,000	32,300	3,420	306,000	2,560
1996	1,230,000	167,000	1,070,000	939,000	1,400,000	421,000	----	324,000	398,000	15,500	3,410	292,000	3,130
1997	1,340,000	194,000	1,130,000	952,000	1,520,000	----	----	336,000	489,000	23,800	5,500	362,000	3,860
1998[1]	1,330,000	200,000	1,140,000	1,010,000	1,300,000	----	----	387,000	421,000	59,700	7,010	356,000	3,780
1999[2]	1,350,000	225,000	1,160,000	1,070,000	1,280,000	----	----	344,000	494,000	9,380	8,130	344,000	3,390

[1] Preliminary.　[2] Estimate.　[3] For consumption.　[4] Natural and synthetic.　[5] 1994 to date includes Slag.　W = Withheld proprietary data.
Source: U.S. Geological Survey (USGS)

TITANIUM

World Produciton of Titanium Illmenite Concentrates — In Thousands of Metric Tons

Year	Aus-tralia[2]	Brazil	China	India	Malaysia	Norway	Sierra Leone	Sri Lanka	Thailand	Ukraine[3]	World Total	Titaniferous Slag[4] Canada	Titaniferous Slag[4] South Africa
1986	1,252	75.5	140.0	140.0	414.9	803.6	-----	129.9	13.50	450	4,705	850	435
1987	1,509	169.3	140.0	140.0	509.2	852.3	5.6	128.5	27.10	455	3,937	925	650
1988	1,622	142.2	150.0	229.7	486.3	898.0	42.1	74.3	18.30	460	4,033	1,025	400
1989	1,714	144.2	150.0	240.7	533.7	929.8	62.3	101.4	16.99	460	4,353	1,040	725
1990	1,621	114.1	150.0	280.0	530.2	814.5	54.6	66.4	10.67	430	4,072	1,046	840
1991	1,381	69.1	150.0	311.5	336.3	625.0	60.4	60.9	17.08	400	3,360	701	808
1992	1,806	76.6	150.0	300.0	337.7	708.0	60.3	33.3	2.97	450	3,920	753	884
1993	1,804	90.6	155.0	320.0	279.0	713.0	62.9	76.9	20.82	450	3,990	653	892
1994	1,817	97.4	155.0	300.0	116.7	826.4	47.4	60.4	1.68	530	3,970	764	744
1995	2,011	102.1	160.0	290.0	151.7	833.2	----	49.7	.03	359	4,010	815	990
1996	2,061	98.0	165.0	330.0	244.6	746.6	----	62.8	----	250	4,010	825	1,000
1997	2,265	97.2	170.0	332.0	167.5	750.0	----	18.0	----	250	4,070	850	1,100
1998	2,409	103.0	175.0	378.0	124.7	590.0	----	34.1	----	250	4,140	950	1,100
1999[1]	2,022	103.0	180.0	378.0	127.7	590.0	----	35.0	----	250	3,780	950	1,100

[1] Preliminary. [2] Includes leucoxene. [3] Formerly part of the U.S.S.R.; data not reported separately until 1992. [4] Approximately 10% of total production is ilmenite. Beginning in 1988, 25% of Norway's ilmenite production was used to produce slag containing 75% TiO2.   NA = Not available.
Source: U.S. Geological Survey (USGS)

World Production of Titanium Rutile Concentrates — In Metric Tons

Year	Australia	Brazil	India	Sierre Leone	South Africa	Sri Lanka	Thailand	Ukraine[2]	World Total
1986	215,774	495	7,000	97,100	55,000	8,443	48	10,000	393,860
1987	246,263	324	7,000	113,300	55,000	7,200	92	10,000	439,179
1988	230,637	1,514	5,000	126,358	55,000	5,255	128	10,000	433,892
1989	243,000	2,613	9,931	128,198	60,000	5,589	150	10,000	459,331
1990	245,000	1,814	11,000	144,284	64,056	5,460	NA	9,500	481,114
1991	201,000	1,094	13,635	154,800	77,000	3,085	76	9,000	460,000
1992	183,000	1,798	10,000	148,990	84,000	2,741	281	60,000	491,000
1993	186,000	1,744	13,900	152,000	85,000	2,643	87	60,000	501,000
1994	233,000	1,911	14,000	137,000	78,000	2,410	49	80,000	545,000
1995	195,000	1,985	14,000	----	90,000	2,697	----	112,000	416,000
1996	180,000	2,018	15,000	----	115,000	3,532	----	50,000	366,000
1997	214,000	1,742	14,000	----	123,000	2,970	----	50,000	406,000
1998	241,000	1,800	16,000	----	130,000	1,930	----	50,000	441,000
1999[1]	190,000	1,800	16,000	----	130,000	2,000	----	50,000	390,000

[1] Preliminary. [2] Formerly part of the U.S.S.R.; data not reported separately until 1992. NA = Not available.
Source: U.S. Geological Survey (USGS)

World Production of Titanium Sponge Metal & U.S. Consumption of Titanium Concentrates

Year	Production of Titanium (In Metric Tons) — Sponge Metal[2] China	Japan	Russia[3]	United Kingdom	United States	Total	U.S. Consumption — Ilmenite (TiO$_2$ Content) Pigments	Misc.	Total	Rutile (TiO$_2$ Content) — Welding Rod Coatings	Pigments	Misc.	Total
1986	1,814	16,330	43,546	1,361	15,876	78,926	463,643	1,501	465,144	6,956	221,518	52,199	280,673
1987	1,814	10,074	44,453	1,361	17,849	75,298	420,099	1,648	421,747	3,781	246,448	51,309	301,538
1988	2,000	16,500	46,000	1,500	24,000	88,000	429,736	590	430,326	3,737	262,998	64,641	331,376
1989	2,000	21,000	46,000	1,500	25,225	95,725	419,329	414	419,743	3,603	271,208	71,178	345,989
1990	2,000	25,630	47,000	1,500	24,679	101,000	445,502	726	446,228	4,047	271,637	71,373	347,057
1991	2,000	18,945	20,000	2,000	13,366	56,000	476,145	495	476,640	6,931	286,741	42,200	335,872
1992	2,000	14,554	20,000	2,000	W	38,554	425,876	647	426,523	W	405,875	32,553	438,428
1993	2,000	14,400	20,000	1,000	27,938	37,000	434,097	451	434,548	W	405,784	30,223	436,007
1994	2,000	14,400	12,000	----	29,510	33,000	W	637	W	W	460,000	18,500	478,500
1995	2,000	16,000	12,000	----	W	35,000	1,010,000	[4]	1,010,000	W	417,000	22,300	439,300
1996	2,000	21,100	18,000	----	W	51,000	1,010,000	[4]	1,010,000	W	341,000	24,200	365,000
1997	2,000	24,100	20,000	----	W	58,000	1,410,000	[4]	1,410,000	W	406,000	27,600	434,000
1998	----	----	----	----	----	----	1,290,000	14,000	1,300,000	W	384,000	37,300	421,000
1999[1]	----	----	----	----	----	----	1,270,000	13,400	1,280,000	W	469,000	25,800	494,000

[1] Preliminary. [2] Unconsolidated metal in various forms. [3] Formerly part of the U.S.S.R.; data not reported separately until 1993. [4] Included in Pigments. NA = Not available. W = Withheld proprietary data. *Source: U.S. Geological Survey (USGS)*

Tobacco

The U.S.D.A. in November 2000 forecast the 2000 U.S. tobacco crop at 1.13 billion pounds, down 12 percent from 1999. The national average tobacco yield was 2,289 pounds per acre or some 15 percent more than in 1999. As of early November, tobacco acreage for the 2000 marketing year was estimated to have declined 24 percent from 1999 to 492,300 acres. The decline in acreage was somewhat offset by the increased yield of 2,289 pounds per acre. The yield in 1999 was the lowest in 15 years due to poor weather for the burley tobacco crop and flooding problems with the flue-cured tobacco crop. This year the weather was much better than a year ago though there was some disease that adversely affected cigar tobacco production. Some 94 percent of the U.S. tobacco leaf production was used for cigarette production. Cigar tobacco leaf, which is also used in smoking and chewing tobacco, was only 1 percent of production. Other types of tobacco, dark-air and fire-cured leaf totaled 5 percent of production.

The burley tobacco crop was smaller than a year ago due to lower acreage because of a lower marketing quota. Total production and carryover of burley tobacco was expected to exceed the marketings allowed. Actual marketings of burley tobacco are likely to be less which would mean there will be large stocks of tobacco. Additionally, because of a decline in domestic use of burley tobacco, beginning stocks are higher. The flue-cured tobacco crop was estimated by the U.S.D.A. in September 2000 at 597 million pounds. That was 9 percent less than in 1999. On-farm stocks of flue-cured tobacco were estimated at 43 million pounds. Due to the quota on flue-cured tobacco, marketings are expected to be 570 million pounds which is less than the size of the crop. Stocks of flue-cured tobacco at the start of the season were 1.2 billion pounds, about 4 percent less than in 1999. Adding in the crop, the total supply of flue-cured tobacco in 2000 is estimated at 1.79 billion pounds. Use of flue-cured tobacco in the 1999/2000 season was 699 million pounds and in 2000/01 that was expected to decline due to lower cigarette production and exports.

The U.S.D.A. reported that U.S. cigarette production declined in 1999, continuing a trend that has been in place. Production data indicate that cigarette output in 1999 fell 73 billion pieces from 1998. Cigarette production in 2000 was 536 billion pieces. Taxable removals in 1999 were 430 billion pieces, down 6 percent from 1998. Tax-exempt removals were down 50 million pieces to 150 million. Ciga-

rette consumption continues to decline because of changes in social acceptance as well as higher prices. Litigation against the tobacco industry continues and that is helping to increase cigarette prices leading to lower consumption. Cigarette prices increased in late 1998 and early 1999. U.S. cigarette consumption in 1999 was 435 billion pieces. Consumption in 2000 was expected to decline but by a smaller amount. Consumers may be adapting to higher prices. In 2000, the Federal excise tax on cigarettes increased by 10 cents per pack of 20 cigarettes. Cigarette manufacturers increased wholesale cigarette prices twice in 2000 which resulted in the wholesale price increasing 10 percent. The consumer price index for cigarettes showed the retail price increased 9 percent between July 1999 and July 2000.

World production of unmanufactured tobacco in calendar 2000 was estimated by the U.S.D.A. to be 2.02 million metric tonnes, dry weight, down 3 percent from a year ago. In 1997, world production was 3.61 million tonnes. The world's largest producer of tobacco was India with 599,400 tonnes, up 2 percent from a year ago. The next largest producer was Brazil with 2000 production estimated at 493,100 tonnes, down 1 percent from last season. Tobacco production by Turkey was 197,260 tonnes, down 9 percent from 1999. Indonesia's crop was forecast at 157,353 tonnes, up 18 percent from a year ago.

World consumption of unmanufactured tobacco in 2000 was forecast at 2.39 million tonnes, down 4 percent from last year. India was the largest user of tobacco with 2000 consumption estimated at 470,310 tonnes, down 2 percent from a year ago. U.S. consumption was estimated at 470,310 tonnes, down 2 percent from a year ago. Consumption in the Russian Federation was 276,600 tonnes, up 4 percent from 1999. Consumption by Japan was 183,000 tonnes, down 1 percent from a year ago. Global stocks of tobacco in 2000 were forecast to be 6.18 million tonnes, down 4 percent from a year ago.

World cigarette production in 2000 was estimated to be 5.57 trillion pieces, up less than 2 percent from 1999. The largest producer of cigarettes is China with estimated production of 1.67 trillion pieces. Cigarette production by the European Union in 2000 was estimated to be almost 759 billion pieces. Germany is the largest producer in the European Union. Production by Japan was 265 billion pieces, while Indonesia produced 229 billion pieces.

World Production of Leaf Tobacco   In Metric Tons

Year	Brazil	Canada	China	Greece	India	Indo-nesia	Italy	Japan	Pakistan	Turkey	United States	Zim-babwe	World Total
1990	435,000	63,057	2,627,500	134,368	564,400	158,865	214,846	80,542	68,040	295,599	737,710	139,803	7,106,502
1991	422,000	78,704	3,030,700	165,650	555,900	164,850	193,296	69,897	80,806	239,405	754,949	178,107	7,262,539
1992	577,000	71,775	3,499,000	196,500	584,400	145,420	150,784	79,366	107,980	331,786	780,944	211,394	8,160,788
1993	608,000	86,094	3,451,000	148,000	580,600	152,800	135,698	67,430	105,966	338,068	731,914	235,286	8,261,069
1994	442,000	71,500	2,238,000	135,400	528,000	160,000	131,010	79,503	100,351	187,733	717,990	177,816	6,391,977
1995	398,000	79,287	2,317,700	131,875	587,100	171,400	124,492	78,212	80,917	204,900	575,380	209,042	6,376,704
1996	439,000	65,320	3,076,000	131,000	562,750	177,000	130,590	66,031	80,760	229,400	688,258	207,767	6,962,473
1997	576,600	71,110	4,251,000	132,450	623,700	184,300	140,634	68,504	86,279	310,850	810,154	192,144	8,822,851
1998[1]	447,000	69,300	2,966,000	132,200	633,200	202,000	136,944	67,100	92,728	260,750	696,116	223,977	7,470,332
1999[2]	569,000	64,864	2,380,000	130,500	648,600	210,000	132,500	63,960	98,500	238,600	635,029	192,025	6,842,322

[1] Preliminary.   [2] Estimate.   *Source: Foreign Agricultural Service, U.S. Department of Agriculture (FAS-USDA)*

TOBACCO

Production and Consumption of Tobacco Products in the United States

Year	Cigarettes (Billions)	Cigars[3] (Millions)	Chewing Tobacco Plug	Twist	Loose-leaf	Total	Smoking Tobacco	Snuff[4]	Consumption Cigarettes (Number)	Cigars[3] (Number)	Cigarettes (Pounds)	Cigars[3]	Smoking Tobacco	Chewing Tobacco	Total Products
			In Millions of Pounds						Number		In Pounds				
1991	694.5	1,740	6.7	1.2	64.3	72.2	15.7	54.3	2,727	25.1	4.83	.41	.18	.80	5.54
1992	718.5	1,741	5.9	1.2	61.6	68.7	14.9	57.5	2,647	24.5	4.62	.40	.18	.75	5.30
1993	661.0	1,795	5.3	1.1	58.0	64.4	13.7	59.1	2,543	23.4	4.70	.38	.17	.70	5.39
1994	725.5	1,942	4.6	1.1	56.8	62.5	13.4	15.1	2,524	25.3	4.23	.41	.16	.67	4.90
1995	746.5	2,058	4.1	1.1	57.7	62.9	12.2	60.2	2,505	27.5	4.22	.45	.13	.67	4.67
1996	754.5	2,413	3.9	1.1	56.0	61.1	12.0	61.5	2,482	32.7	4.20	.54	.12	.64	4.70
1997	719.6	2,324	3.5	1.0	53.7	58.1	11.4	64.3	2,423	36.9	4.10	.53	.12	.64	4.55
1998	679.7	2,751	3.1	1.0	49.2	53.3	12.5	65.5	2,320	37.8	3.90	.53	.12	.64	4.49
1999[1]	606.6	2,938	2.8	0.9	47.2	50.9	14.7	67.0	2,136	39.0	3.60	.53	.12	.64	4.49
2000[2]	610.0	2,800	2.6	0.8	45.5	48.9	13.5	70.6	2,054	39.2	3.40	.64	.14	.51	4.90

[1] Preliminary. [2] Estimate. [3] Large cigars and cigarillos. [4] Includes loose-leaf. [5] Consumption of tax-paid tobacco products. Unstemmed processing weight. [6] 18 years and older. Source: Economic Research Service, U.S. Department of Agriculture (ERS)

Production of Tobacco in the United States, by States   In Thousands of Pounds

Year	Florida	Georgia	Indiana	Kentucky	Maryland	North Carolina	Ohio	Pennsvania	South Carolina	Tennessee	Virginia	Wisconsin	Total
1991	15,312	80,600	18,920	479,794	12,900	634,655	22,776	20,765	111,180	121,524	116,849	15,191	1,664,372
1992	19,575	100,980	18,900	524,378	11,931	609,873	21,840	20,840	112,320	146,556	111,459	13,100	1,721,671
1993	18,673	96,320	17,415	455,080	12,255	608,415	18,900	18,260	110,760	139,423	99,544	6,643	1,613,319
1994	16,575	80,660	15,265	453,687	12,750	599,853	18,360	18,360	108,100	132,289	106,092	5,866	1,582,896
1995	17,676	84,000	13,601	328,581	11,475	484,599	15,015	15,685	105,000	92,907	81,269	6,220	1,268,538
1996	20,100	113,620	14,972	395,542	10,000	585,542	12,640	16,817	117,810	109,888	103,543	5,162	1,518,704
1997	19,053	89,225	18,690	497,928	12,000	731,199	22,230	17,020	126,360	114,292	117,576	5,690	1,787,399
1998	17,102	90,200	17,000	443,628	9,100	551,730	17,934	15,720	92,250	111,100	95,898	4,230	1,479,867
1999	15,312	64,020	11,700	408,492	9,100	448,980	17,052	11,170	78,000	122,601	88,855	2,818	1,292,692
2000[1]	11,475	69,130	7,980	299,530	9,000	419,710	13,200	10,170	81,260	105,398	64,130	2,020	1,099,884

[1] Preliminary. Source: Agricultural Statistics Board, U.S. Department of Agriculture (ASB-USDA)

Salient Statistics of Tobacco in the United States

Year	Acres Harvested 1,000 Acres	Yield Per Acre Pounds	Production Million Pounds	Farm Price Cents/Lb.	Farm Value Million $	Tobacco Exports[2]	Imports[3]	U.S. Exports of Cigarettes Millions	Cigars & Cheroots	All Tobacco	Smoking Tobacco	Stocks of Tobacco[5] All Tobacco	Fire Cured[6]	Cigar Filler[7]	Maryland
						Million Pounds		Millions		In Millions of Pounds					
1991	763.4	2,179	1,664	177.3	2,951	511.0	502.2	179,200	70	499	63.2	2,232	66.7	25.6	12.1
1992	784.4	2,195	1,722	177.7	3,059	528.8	881.0	205,600	76	574	59.1	2,280	61.6	26.7	9.4
1993	746.4	2,161	1,613	175.3	2,830	529.7	706.1	195,476	67	458	62.5	2,412	64.0	26.7	7.5
1994	671.1	2,359	1,583	177.4	2,779	442.1	537.5	220,200	74	434	77.0	2,588	69.7	24.1	8.4
1995	663.1	1,913	1,269	182.0	2,305	432.6	623.3	231,100	94	462	91.8	2,541	80.5	20.5	11.7
1996	733.1	2,072	1,519	188.2	2,854	533.1	717.2	243,900	67	486	110.4	2,225	80.2	17.9	15.0
1997	836.2	2,137	1,787	180.2	3,217	450.1	565.8	217,000	86	487	118.2	2,031	83.3	13.2	18.7
1998	717.6	2,062	1,480	182.8	2,701	461.9	529.6	201,300	93	467	142.5	2,250	84.8	13.0	20.6
1999	647.2	1,997	1,293	182.8	2,356	390.3	480.3	151,400	84	423	151.1	2,301	86.7	11.4	16.0
2000[1]	485.7	2,264	1,100	187.2	2,056	255.0	417.5	14,550	93	408	145.5	2,388	87.8	9.5	16.0

[1] Preliminary. [2] Domestic. [3] For consumption. [4] In bulk. [5] Flue-cured and cigar wrapper, year beginning July 1; for all other types, October 1. [6] Kentucky-Tennessee types 22-23. [7] Types 41-46. Source: Economic Research Service, U.S. Department of Agriculture (ERS-USDA)

Tobacco Production in the United States, by Types   In Thousands of Pounds (Farm-Sale Weight)

Year	11-14	21	22	23	31	32	35-36	37	41	41-61	51	54	55	61
1991	911,887	3,563	20,620	8,704	658,181	19,920	8,776	156	13,735	32,587	1,433	9,799	5,392	2,228
1992	906,025	2,567	23,736	10,486	719,552	18,771	10,332	124	14,000	30,098	1,484	8,460	4,640	1,514
1993	886,908	1,872	26,985	12,060	633,838	18,335	11,123	104	12,180	22,094	1,694	4,690	1,953	1,577
1994	869,920	2,403	31,723	14,205	612,398	19,770	11,797	124	11,340	20,680	1,808	4,180	1,686	1,666
1995	746,616	1,540	26,609	11,041	436,343	17,935	8,488	79	9,225	19,887	2,441	4,513	1,707	2,001
1996	908,345	1,738	29,461	13,029	520,483	16,545	8,550	112	10,272	20,441	2,901	3,610	1,552	2,106
1997	1,047,438	1,968	27,952	12,342	648,633	18,240	8,196	119	10,780	22,511	3,637	4,194	1,496	2,404
1998	812,797	2,340	25,922	11,573	582,336	15,370	9,663	122	9,450	19,744	3,633	3,270	960	2,431
1999	656,752	2,672	24,773	10,630	555,185	14,350	11,640	155	5,920	16,535	4,169	2,252	566	3,628
2000[1]	613,115	2,210	30,890	14,240	401,352	14,130	14,308	170	5,040	9,469	729	1,606	414	1,680

[1] Preliminary. Source: Agricultural Statistics Board, U.S. Department of Agriculture (ASB-USDA)

U.S. Exports of Unmanufactured Tobacco   In Millions of Pounds (Declared Weight)

Year	Australia	Belgium-Luxem.	Denmark	France	Germany	Italy	Japan	Nether-lands	Sweden	Switzer-land	Thailand	United Kingdom	Total
1991	7.7	11.0	14.8	6.5	82.8	19.9	83.1	42.8	8.3	14.8	19.5	18.9	499.3
1992	6.9	21.4	15.6	4.2	93.3	19.0	131.0	49.9	8.8	7.5	16.9	24.3	574.4
1993	5.7	12.8	15.5	4.3	52.1	7.3	124.7	38.1	8.1	6.1	17.8	20.8	458.0
1994	6.4	12.3	14.9	3.1	54.1	11.3	126.2	30.9	7.3	6.0	19.0	14.7	433.9
1995	4.8	17.9	14.6	3.9	70.7	14.8	106.9	39.2	3.0	14.4	19.0	14.2	461.8
1996	5.6	39.7	15.1	3.2	60.1	17.3	88.7	40.4	3.7	14.9	15.9	34.4	485.5
1997	4.2	38.9	15.5	7.0	72.2	18.3	80.5	30.2	5.3	11.4	21.3	18.2	487.4
1998	5.0	25.2	14.8	6.6	84.6	13.6	85.3	43.9	2.6	10.3	14.2	15.6	466.3
1999	16.1	2.0	3.9	9.0	5.6	71.9	11.7	14.9	1.3	23.0	.8	15.5	417.5
2000[1]	2.9	8.6	11.0	3.7	72.9	12.3	47.4	18.6	2.7	8.5	5.8	6.4	308.5

[1] Preliminary.   Source: Economic Research Service, U.S. Department of Agriculture (ERS-USDA)

U.S. Salient Statistics for Flue-Cured Tobacco (Types 11-14) in the United States   In Millions of Pounds

Crop Year	Acres Harvested 1,000	Yield Per Acre Pounds	Mar-ketings	Stocks July 1	Total Supply	Exports	Domestic Disap-pearance	Total Disap-pearance	Farm Price Cents/Lb.	Placed Under Gov't Loan Million Lb.	Price Support Level Cents/Lb.	Loan Stocks Nov. 30	Uncom-mitted
1991-2	402.6	2,265	883	1,216	2,098	403	471	875	172.3	49.9	152.8	153.7	174.5
1992-3	401.5	2,257	901	1,224	2,125	420	509	929	172.6	81.8	156.0	223.6	129.0
1993-4	400.1	2,217	892	1,196	2,087	359	433	792	168.1	204.9	157.7	330.5	317.5
1994-5	359.5	2,420	807	1,295	2,102	346	569	915	169.8	97.7	158.3	298.5	396.5
1995-6	386.2	1,933	854	1,187	2,041	345	531	875	179.4	12.0	159.7	157.6	62.3
1996-7	422.2	2,151	897	1,166	2,064	391	555	947	183.4	1.8	160.1	181.0	.0
1997-8	458.3	2,285	1,014	1,117	2,130	334	541	877	172.0	195.5	162.1		.0
1998-9	368.8	2,204	813	1,253	2,068	341	492	834	175.5	82.4	162.8		
1999-00[1]	303.8	2,162	647	1,234	1,888	262	437	699	173.6				
2000-1[2]	250.0	2,452	613	1,189	1,737	290	435	725	179.0				

[1] Preliminary.   [2] Estimate.   Source: Economic Research Service, U.S. Department of Agriculture (ERS-USDA)

Salient Statistics for Burley Tobacco (Type 31) in the United States   In Millions of Pounds

Crop Year	Acres Harvested 1,000	Yield Per Acre Pounds	Mar-ketings	Stocks Oct. 1	Total Supply	Exports	Domestic Disap-pearance	Total Disap-pearance	Farm Price Cents/Lb.	Gross Sales[3]	Price Support Level Cents/Lb.	Loan Stocks Nov. 30	Uncom-mitted
1991-2	312.0	2,110	657	765	1,422	209	407	616	178.8	501.5	158.4	62.3	32.8
1992-3	332.7	2,163	700	807	1,507	183	385	568	181.5	502.4	164.9	131.2	71.7
1993-4	299.7	2,115	627	939	1,566	152	399	552	181.6	492.4	168.3	178.8	141.9
1994-5	266.3	2,300	568	1,014	1,582	155	468	623	184.1	455.7	171.4	345.2	380.8
1995-6	234.2	1,863	483	959	1,441	165	386	551	185.5	341.6	172.5	212.5	50.8
1996-7	268.3	1,940	516	890	1,407	192	446	656	192.2	422.6	173.7	216.8	27.1
1997-8	335.0	1,934	628	751	1,379	189	379	548	188.5	337.9	176.0		24.1
1998-9	307.1	1,896	582	832	1,422	190	349	520	190.3	431.6	177.8		
1999-00[1]	303.6	1,829	555	901	1,453	139	273	413	182.8	356.6			
2000-1[2]	198.4	2,023	401	1,040	1,450	125	345	470	NA	169.7			

[1] Preliminary.   [2] Estimate.   [3] Before Christmas holidays.   Source: Economic Research Service, U.S. Department of Agriculture (ERS-USDA)

Exports of Tobacco from the United States (Quantity and Value)   In Metric Tons

Year	Flue-Cured	Value 1,000 USD	Burley	Value 1,000 USD	Total	Value 1,000 USD	Manu-factured	Value 1,000 USD
1991	115,481	776,654	61,852	441,223	226,463	1,427,630	NA	4,574,086
1992	146,100	983,478	64,481	483,743	260,526	1,650,559	58,115	4,509,395
1993	111,636	752,646	51,892	389,964	207,747	1,306,067	49,669	4,253,286
1994	107,411	749,305	49,859	380,993	196,792	1,302,744	63,837	5,367,220
1995	123,040	866,208	47,129	365,206	209,481	1,399,863	77,135	5,221,487
1996	112,797	786,473	52,202	380,012	222,316	1,390,311	83,383	5,238,340
1997	116,457	832,381	56,803	454,849	221,510	1,553,314	85,734	4,956,392
1998	110,435	776,640	50,167	409,773	211,930	1,458,877	----	4,517,500
1999[1]	86,838	611,054	49,398	404,564	191,975	1,311,643	----	3,232,862
2000[2]	65,062	482,255	35,248	293,566	148,476	991,484	----	3,296,719

[1] Preliminary.   [2] Forecast.   NA = Not available.   Source: Foreign Agricultural Service, U.S. Department of Agriculture (FAS-USDA)

Tung Oil

Tung oil is a yellow drying oil produced from the seed of the tung tree. The seeds or nuts of the tung tree are harvested and pressed yielding tung oil. Tung oil finds the most use as an industrial lubricant and drying agent. It finds use in paints and varnishes as well as in soaps, inks, and electrical insulators. Tung oil is poisonous, containing glycerol esters of unsaturated acids. It is the most powerful drying agent known. It finds use as a substitute for linseed oil in paints, varnishes, and linoleum. It is also used as a waterproofing agent. As such, it finds use in many industrialized countries.

Production of tung oil in very concentrated. The three largest producers are China, Argentina, and Paraguay with smaller producers being Madagascar, Malawi, and Brazil.

Production in recent years has been estimated at about 45,000 metric tonnes. China produces tung oil from trees grown in the southern part of the country. Chinese production is about 75 percent of the world total. Paraguay produces about 18 percent of the world supply.

China is the largest exporter of tung oil with shipments over 20,000 tonnes. The major markets have been Japan and the European Union. The major suppliers to the U.S. are Argentina and Paraguay. U.S. consumption of tung oil has been about 15 million pounds per year according to the U.S. Department of Commerce. U.S. stocks at the beginning of 2000 had fallen to one million pounds, down 50 percent from the previous year.

World Tung Oil Trade   In Metric Tons

| | Imports | | | | | | | | Exports | | | | |
Year	Germany	Hong Kong	Japan	Nether-lands	South Korea	Taiwan	United States	World Total	Argen-tina	China	Hong Kong	Para-guay	World Total
1993	777	5,222	6,549	1,427	3,490	3,595	4,270	30,834	2,497	16,990	6,004	2,295	30,074
1994	912	7,843	8,628	1,663	4,594	7,454	5,401	43,082	2,415	30,582	6,476	4,603	45,182
1995	825	3,671	8,429	2,174	7,200	5,777	4,427	38,234	4,319	25,620	3,838	4,587	39,816
1996	863	1,247	3,619	1,253	7,317	4,244	3,944	27,250	2,427	18,205	1,266	3,156	27,068
1997	733	1,404	6,807	1,076	6,700	5,931	6,264	34,877	3,976	25,260	991	4,260	37,010
1998[1]	601	1,101	3,813	944	6,000	5,730	3,880	28,406	2,205	21,265	552	2,161	28,407
1999[2]	499	500	2,455	1,100	6,000	6,699	5,822	29,057	1,425	20,800	471	2,500	27,868

[1] Preliminary.   [2] Estimate.   Source: The Oil World

Consumption of Tung Oil in Inedible Products in the United States   In Thousands of Pounds

Year	Jan.	Feb.	Mar.	Apr.	May	June	July	Aug.	Sept.	Oct.	Nov.	Dec.	Total
1994	608	592	635	1,408	1,558	840	861	910	480	392	660	382	9,326
1995	427	503	976	1,389	1,437	1,387	1,886	2,830	2,549	2,645	2,455	2,126	20,610
1996	1,724	1,427	1,730	1,750	1,498	1,813	2,214	2,024	1,431	2,045	1,908	2,081	21,645
1997	934	1,922	2,720	2,170	1,335	2,034	2,618	1,262	1,267	1,099	857	1,157	19,375
1998	935	1,146	1,342	1,103	1,536	1,255	1,248	1,172	1,214	1,216	1,037	1,112	14,316
1999	862	797	967	1,071	2,137	1,140	1,519	1,043	1,012	933	962	937	13,380
2000[1]	1,065	1,083	1,064	1,193	1,159	1,176	1,107	1,224	733	711	700	648	11,863

[1] Preliminary.   Source: Bureau of the Census, U.S. Department of Commerce

Stocks of Tung Oil at Factories & Warehouses in the U.S., on First of Month   In Thousands of Pounds

Year	Jan.	Feb.	Mar.	Apr.	May	June	July	Aug.	Sept.	Oct.	Nov.	Dec.
1994	1,551	2,053	1,507	2,049	2,091	2,591	2,148	1,562	820	2,455	1,712	1,909
1995	1,764	1,490	1,055	3,193	2,554	2,551	2,369	2,116	2,038	2,361	2,210	2,048
1996	2,013	1,635	2,232	3,018	2,386	2,532	2,641	2,381	2,670	2,525	2,459	2,834
1997	2,373	2,754	3,417	2,808	2,134	2,230	2,230	1,561	2,525	2,535	2,311	2,326
1998	2,484	3,116	4,548	3,949	3,357	3,300	2,435	2,409	3,578	2,523	2,501	2,272
1999	2,010	3,427	5,427	3,740	3,078	2,788	2,710	2,346	2,047	1,959	1,359	1,002
2000[1]	691	910	611	2,555	2,254	1,982	1,658	1,381	1,262	1,217	1,011	827

[1] Preliminary.   Source: Bureau of the Census, U.S. Department of Commerce

Average Price of Tung Oil (Imported, Drums) F.O.B. in New York   In Cents Per Pound

Year	Jan.	Feb.	Mar.	Apr.	May	June	July	Aug.	Sept.	Oct.	Nov.	Dec.	Average
1994	93.00	79.25	78.00	78.00	78.00	78.00	78.00	78.00	78.00	74.40	60.00	60.00	76.05
1995	60.00	60.00	60.00	60.00	60.00	60.00	60.00	60.00	60.00	60.00	60.00	60.00	60.00
1996	60.00	60.00	64.00	64.00	64.00	64.00	64.00	64.00	64.00	64.00	64.00	64.00	63.33
1997	74.00	92.00	92.00	103.00	103.00	103.00	103.00	108.00	110.00	110.00	110.00	110.00	101.50
1998	110.00	110.00	110.00	110.00	100.00	100.00	100.00	100.00	100.00	100.00	100.00	100.00	103.33
1999	100.00	100.00	100.00	100.00	100.00	74.00	74.00	74.00	74.00	74.00	74.00	74.00	84.83
2000[1]	59.00	59.00	59.00	59.00	59.00	59.00	59.00	59.00	59.00	59.00			59.00

[1] Preliminary.   Source: Economic Research Service, U.S. Department of Agriculture (ERS-USDA)

Tungsten

Tungsten has a wide range of industrial uses. Tungsten has a high melting point, high density, good corrosion resistance, excellent wear-resistance, and excellent cutting properties. Most tungsten is used to produce tungsten carbide which is used in the production of cemented carbides. Cemented carbides are also called hardmetals and are used in mining, metal working, and construction. Tungsten is used to make dies, bearings, superalloys for turbine blades as well as armor-piercing metal projectiles. Tungsten metal wires, electrodes, and contacts are used in electrical, heating, welding, and lighting applications.

The U.S. Geological Survey indicated that 1999 world mine production of tungsten was 31,300 metric tonnes, down 3 percent from the previous year. The largest producer by far was China with output of 24,700 tonnes or 79 percent of the world total. Other producers include Russia, Austria, North Korea, and Portugal. There was no mine production in the U.S. in 1999. The world reserves of tungsten are estimated to be two million tonnes.

U.S. reported consumption of ferrotungsten in August 2000 was 37 tonnes. In the January-August 2000 period, consumption totaled 330 tonnes. For all of 1999, consumption was 473 tonnes. Consumption of tungsten metal powder in August 2000 was 175 tonnes, while in the first eight months of 2000 it was 1,340 tonnes. For 1999, consumption was 1,500 tonnes. Tungsten powder consumption in August 2000 was 485 tonnes. In January-August 2000, it was 3,920 tonnes and in 1999 it totaled 5,930 tonnes. Tungsten scrap consumption in January-August 2000 was 246 tonnes.

World Concentrate Production of Tungsten   In Metric Tons (Contained Tungsten[3])

Year	Australia	Austria	Bolivia	Brazil	Burma	China	Kazak-hstan	Mongolia	Peru	Portugal	Rep. of Korea	Russia	World Total
1993	23	105	287	245	524	21,600	350	250	388	768	----	8,000	34,300
1994	11	----	462	196	544	27,000	122	----	259	59	----	4,000	34,000
1995	----	738	655	98	531	27,400	249	34	728	875	----	5,400	38,500
1996	----	1,413	582	99	334	26,500	----	17	332	776	----	3,000	34,800
1997	----	1,400	513	40	272	25,000	----	26	280	1,036	----	3,000	33,200
1998[1]	----	1,423	497	----	178	24,700	----	35	76	831	----	3,000	32,000
1999[2]	----	1,610	334	----	87	24,000	----	16	----	450	----	3,500	31,000

[1] Preliminary.   [2] Estimate.   [3] Conversion Factors: WO3 to W, multiply by 0.7931; 60% WO3 to W, multiply by 0.4758.
Source: U.S. Geological Survey (USGS)

Salient Statistics of Tungsten in the United States   In Metric Tons (Contained Tungsten)

Year	Net Import Reliance as a % of Apparent Consumption	Total Consumption	Tool	Steel Stainless & Heat Assisting	Alloy Steel[3]	Super-alloys	Cutting & Wear Resistant Materials	Products Made from Metal Powder	Miscellaneous	Chemical and Ceramic	Exports	Imports for Consumption	Stocks at End of Year Concentrates Consumers	Producers
1993	81	2,870	388	43	40	282	5,064	1,434	2	37	63	1,721	592	44
1994	95	3,630	529	20	19	300	5,920	1,200	W	108	44	2,960	756	44
1995	90	5,890	265	W	18	215	6,590	1,200	3,600	W	5	4,660	627	44
1996	89	5,260	434	107	177	371	5,960	687	0	97	18	4,190	569	44
1997	84	6,590	361	151	277	366	6,280	828	151	123	12	4,850	658	44
1998[1]	78	3,210	[4]	532	219	333	6,640	1,270	532	97	10	4,750	514	W
1999[2]	81	2,100	W	486	189	306	5,910	1,410	----	93	26	2,870	W	W

[1] Preliminary.   [2] Estimate.   [3] Other than tool.   [4] Included with stainless & heat assisting.   W = Withheld proprietary data; included with Miscellaneous.   *Source: U.S. Geological Survey*

Average Price of Tungsten at European Market (London)   In Dollars Per Metric Ton

Year	Jan.	Feb.	Mar.	Apr.	May	June	July	Aug.	Sept.	Oct.	Nov.	Dec.	Average
1995	56.00	60.00	64.00	64.00	65.00	66.00	67.00	66.00	66.00	66.00	66.00	62.50	64.04
1996	56.00	54.00	56.00	57.00	57.00	57.00	53.50	50.00	50.00	47.50	45.00	48.00	52.58
1997	48.00	49.00	50.00	50.00	50.00	50.00	50.00	43.00	43.00	43.00	46.00	46.00	47.33
1998	46.00	46.00	46.00	46.00	46.00	46.00	45.00	43.00	43.00	43.00	43.00	43.00	40.00
1999	37.38	38.50	38.50	38.50	38.50	38.50	38.50	40.36	43.00	43.00	43.00	43.00	40.25

65% WO3 Basis, C.I.F., combined wolframite and scheelite quotations; data thru 1970 are for 60% WO3.   *Source: U.S. Geological Survey (USGS)*

Average Price of Tungsten at U.S. Ports (Including Duty)   In Dollars Per Short Ton

Year	Jan.	Feb.	Mar.	Apr.	May	June	July	Aug.	Sept.	Oct.	Nov.	Dec.	Average
1995	44.00	44.00	44.00	44.00	55.00	65.00	65.00	62.50	60.00	60.00	60.00	60.00	55.29
1996	60.00	60.00	60.00	60.00	60.00	60.00	60.00	60.00	60.00	60.00	60.00	60.00	60.00
1997	60.00	60.00	60.00	60.00	60.00	60.00	60.00	60.00	60.00	55.00	50.00	50.00	57.92
1998	64.00	64.00	64.00	64.00	64.00	62.44	57.00	57.00	57.00	57.00	54.43	49.88	57.19
1999	49.50	49.50	49.50	49.50	48.57	48.75	49.16	50.88	51.50	54.44	54.75	54.75	52.00

U.S. Spot Quotations, 65% WO3, Basis C.I.F.   *Source: U.S. Geological Survey (USGS)*

Turkeys

U.S. federally inspected turkey production rose to a record high 5.45 billion pounds in 2000, based on the 4 percent gain during the first eight months of the year. A further rise to 5.6 billion pounds is forecast for 2001. Production in the mid-1990's averaged about 5 billion pounds. On the demand side, to help iron out the pronounced year-end holiday seasonality for whole birds, the industry in recent years shifted a larger proportion of retail sales to prepackaged turkey parts. The additional processing required to cut up and package turkey cuts, such as breasts and legs, increased the supply of edible trimmings which processors sell in several forms, including mechanically deboned turkey (MDT). A strong market for the latter is exports; also, as a relatively low-cost meat protein MDT can be readily incorporated into sausage and other meat products.

Despite the record high output and effort to broaden domestic demand, U.S. per capita ready-to-cook retail weight turkey consumption has so far failed to match the record high 18.5 pounds in 1996. Usage in 2000, of 18.1 pounds compares with 17.9 pounds in 1999 and a forecast 18.2 pounds in 2001. The October-December period still accounts for more than one-third of total domestic use followed by a sharp usage drop in the January-March period. Traditionally, November is the highest slaughter month with about 25 million birds. Prices, basis 8-16 pound hens in New York, follow a similar pattern, peaking generally in the fourth quarter and trending lower during the first quarter. Heavier turkeys, 14-22 pounds, are classified as toms. However, with the industry's new marketing approach and changes in consumer food tastes, shifts in the traditional seasonalities are taking root and many grocery chains now use turkeys as a loss leader in an effort to broaden same store purchases of other holiday related foodstuffs.

An estimated 273 million turkeys were raised in the U.S. in 2000, almost unchanged from 1999. Six states account for about two-thirds of the turkeys produced with North Carolina generally the largest producer, 44 million in 2000, followed by Minnesota with 43 million birds.

U.S. turkey exports of 426 million pounds in 2000 compare with 379 million in 1999. Exports are forecast to be 420 million in 2001. Mexico remains the largest importer with at least one-half of the total followed by China, Hong Kong and Russia. Russian imports are generally lower priced turkey parts.

Wholesale Eastern turkey prices in 2000 averaged 71.00 cents per pound vs. 69.00 cents in 1999 and forecasts of 65.00-71.00 cents in 2001.

Production and Consumption of Turkey Meat, by Selected Countries — In Thousands of Metric Tons (RTC)

| | Production | | | | | | | Consumption | | | | | | |
Year	Canada	France	Germany	Italy	United Kingdom	United States	World Total	Canada	France	Germany	Italy	United Kingdom	United States	World Total
1992	132	558	159	269	226	2,167	3,916	129	354	272	268	210	2,072	3,761
1993	128	532	169	266	267	2,176	3,935	126	331	280	256	264	2,075	3,801
1994	133	568	180	269	266	2,239	4,055	128	330	295	245	271	2,110	3,894
1995	141	650	206	294	289	2,299	4,292	126	353	327	262	287	2,133	4,121
1996	146	671	217	315	293	2,450	4,552	123	352	361	277	298	2,225	4,382
1997	142	708	243	338	293	2,455	4,702	126	332	386	295	277	2,141	4,364
1998	139	725	256	361	268	2,366	4,635	130	360	396	302	276	2,214	4,494
1999	139	691	271	343	264	2,372	4,613	136	395	410	310	255	2,223	4,535
2000[1]	140	705	272	330	265	2,441	4,602	122	380	412	303	250	2,262	4,395
2001[2]	141	715	272	350	268	2,507	4,635	123	374	412	317	250	2,293	4,355

[1] Preliminary.   [2] Forecast.   Source: Foreign Agricultural Service, U.S. Department of Agriculture (FAS-USDA)

Salient Statistics of Turkeys in the United States

| | | | Liveweight | | Value of Production | | Beginning Stocks | | Ready-to-Cook Basis | | | | | Wholesale Ready-to-Cook | |
| | | | | | | | | | Consumption | | Production Costs | | | | |
Year	Poults Placed[3] ---- In Thousands ----	Number Raised[4] ---- In Thousands ----	Produced Mil. Lbs.	Price Cents/Lb.	of Production Million $	Production	Beginning Stocks	Exports	Total	Per Capita Lbs.	Feed	Total	Production Costs	3-Region Weighted Average Price[5]
1990	304,863	282,445	6,043.2	39.6	2,393.4	4,514	236	54	5,390	17.6	23.40	37.10	62.60	62.35
1991	308,083	284,910	6,114.6	38.5	2,353.0	4,603	306	122	4,523	17.9	22.72	36.42	61.83	60.79
1992	307,823	289,880	6,355.3	37.7	2,396.4	4,777	264	202	4,568	17.9	23.06	36.76	62.25	60.48
1993	308,871	287,650	6,432.6	39.0	2,509.1	4,798	272	244	4,577	17.7	22.20	35.86	61.12	62.83
1994	317,468	286,585	6,540.3	40.4	2,643.1	4,937	249	280	4,652	17.8	24.00	37.70	63.40	65.90
1995	320,882	292,356	6,761.3	41.0	2,769.4	5,069	254	348	4,705	17.9	21.90	35.60	60.80	66.20
1996	325,375	302,713	7,222.8	43.3	3,124.5	5,466	271	438	4,907	18.5	31.60	45.30	72.90	66.80
1997	305,612	301,251	7,225.1	39.9	2,884.4	5,478	328	606	4,720	17.6	28.20	41.90	68.70	63.80
1998[1]	297,798	285,204	7,050.9	38.0	2,679.3	5,281	415	446	4,880	18.1	22.96	36.66	62.12	62.15
1999[2]	297,387	272,994	6,947.2	40.8	2,835.4	5,278	304	400	4,868	17.8	19.00	32.70	57.17	67.81

[1] Preliminary.   [2] Estimate.   [3] Poults placed for slaughter by hatcheries.   [4] Turkeys place August 1-July 31.   [5] Regions include central, eastern and western. Central region receives twice the weight of the other regions in calculating the average.   Source: Economic Research Service, U.S. Department of Agriculture (ERS-USDA)

Turkey-Feed Price Ratio in the United States   In Pounds[1]

Year	Jan.	Feb.	Mar.	Apr.	May	June	July	Aug.	Sept.	Oct.	Nov.	Dec.	Average
1991	6.0	6.3	6.4	6.5	6.7	6.9	7.2	7.1	7.0	6.5	6.4	6.5	6.6
1992	6.0	5.8	6.0	6.0	6.0	6.1	6.5	6.8	6.7	7.1	7.2	7.1	6.4
1993	6.3	6.4	6.6	6.5	6.6	6.7	6.4	6.4	6.9	7.2	6.7	6.0	6.5
1994	5.4	5.4	5.5	5.8	5.9	6.1	6.9	7.4	7.4	7.9	7.9	7.3	6.6
1995	6.8	6.4	6.5	6.4	6.3	6.3	6.0	6.3	6.4	6.4	6.5	5.7	6.3
1996	5.3	5.2	5.1	4.8	4.6	4.9	4.9	4.8	5.3	6.2	6.4	6.1	5.3
1997	5.4	5.1	5.0	5.1	5.3	5.6	6.0	5.9	6.1	6.2	6.2	5.8	5.7
1998	5.4	5.2	5.4	5.7	5.8	6.1	6.5	7.6	8.1	8.3	8.2	7.5	6.7
1999	6.5	7.1	7.5	7.8	8.2	8.7	9.7	9.5	9.6	10.0	9.9	9.2	8.6
2000[2]	7.6	7.2	7.6	7.8	7.7	8.5	9.5	9.9	10.0	10.0	9.8	8.1	8.6

[1] Pounds of feed equal in value to one pound of turkey, liveweight.   [2] Preliminary.   [3] New data series due to NASS switching to basing ration costs on raw ingredient prices (corn and soybeans) rather than commercial feed prices.   *Source: Economic Research Service, U.S. Department of Agriculture (ERS-USDA)*

Average Price Received by Farmers for Turkeys in the United States (Liveweight)   In Cents Per Pound

Year	Jan.	Feb.	Mar.	Apr.	May	June	July	Aug.	Sept.	Oct.	Nov.	Dec.	Average
1991	33.6	35.1	37.0	37.6	38.3	38.7	39.1	40.1	40.2	37.0	37.0	38.1	37.7
1992	36.3	35.5	37.0	37.0	37.7	37.7	37.9	37.8	37.5	38.5	39.4	39.3	37.6
1993	35.6	35.7	37.6	37.6	37.7	37.6	38.7	39.6	41.1	43.2	42.7	40.8	39.0
1994	37.0	37.3	38.4	39.2	39.9	40.3	40.6	42.1	43.1	44.5	44.3	42.2	40.7
1995	39.3	37.2	38.3	38.3	38.4	39.3	39.6	41.9	43.6	45.2	47.3	44.0	41.0
1996	40.9	42.4	41.8	42.2	43.2	44.4	45.0	44.3	44.2	45.1	45.5	43.2	43.5
1997	38.6	36.4	37.8	39.7	41.3	41.6	41.1	41.0	41.1	41.0	41.9	38.7	40.0
1998	35.5	34.0	34.6	35.7	35.5	35.9	37.5	38.6	40.2	42.7	43.8	40.3	37.9
1999	34.8	35.7	37.0	38.7	39.4	41.3	42.0	43.0	44.3	45.3	45.3	42.2	40.8
2000[1]	36.4	35.7	38.2	39.8	40.4	41.6	41.9	42.9	44.5	45.9	47.0	40.5	41.2

[1] Preliminary.   *Source: Economic Research Service, U.S. Department of Agriculture (ERS-USDA)*

Average Wholesale Price of Turkeys[1] (Hens, 8-16 Lbs.) in New York   In Cents Per Pound

Year	Jan.	Feb.	Mar.	Apr.	May	June	July	Aug.	Sept.	Oct.	Nov.	Dec.	Average
1991	53.49	55.76	59.10	60.32	62.32	62.68	63.41	64.66	64.38	60.52	63.07	65.18	61.24
1992	58.74	55.00	58.77	60.00	60.03	59.46	57.02	57.80	61.02	63.92	65.57	65.14	60.21
1993	58.05	56.83	58.41	58.98	58.81	58.35	59.76	63.43	66.73	71.28	71.76	68.20	62.55
1994	60.09	59.32	60.98	61.58	63.14	64.61	65.26	66.39	68.98	73.13	74.01	70.35	65.65
1995	60.71	58.54	60.04	60.05	60.57	62.76	64.78	68.52	72.92	76.73	80.31	70.35	66.36
1996	64.60	64.65	65.07	64.82	65.39	65.85	65.66	64.94	64.16	69.09	73.58	70.05	66.49
1997	59.71	57.84	59.30	62.93	66.64	68.60	68.59	68.20	67.89	67.33	70.07	62.18	64.94
1998	55.65	54.04	55.49	55.49	58.68	58.14	58.68	63.17	65.65	71.52	72.95	69.00	61.54
1999	57.67	58.84	61.69	63.02	65.55	68.89	71.62	73.57	76.28	79.30	78.99	72.39	68.98
2000[2]	61.58	61.84	65.35	67.38	69.18	70.36	71.55	73.61	76.53	78.74	79.58	70.31	70.50

[1] Ready-to-cook.   [2] Preliminary.   *Source: Economic Research Service, U.S. Department of Agriculture (ERS-USDA)*

Certified Federally Inspected Turkey Slaughter in the U.S. (RTC Weights)   In Millions of Pounds

Year	Jan	Feb.	Mar.	Apr.	May	June	July	Aug.	Sept.	Oct.	Nov.	Dec.	Total
1991	365.6	322.0	329.7	375.8	398.2	380.7	402.2	421.8	404.8	482.0	419.2	349.9	4,652
1992	362.9	331.7	361.3	385.2	374.2	435.0	451.8	411.9	431.3	467.6	423.0	393.1	4,829
1993	354.1	322.7	382.9	391.9	378.7	446.7	419.3	426.9	436.0	451.4	461.8	375.3	4,848
1994	347.8	342.0	400.9	380.6	415.6	457.9	405.6	483.6	447.7	459.1	453.9	397.5	4,992
1995	386.3	368.9	433.1	369.6	441.4	478.4	409.1	447.3	419.5	480.2	463.0	394.4	5,091
1996	412.4	426.5	422.3	430.9	483.0	454.7	484.8	476.6	440.9	518.1	465.9	406.1	5,422
1997	439.7	389.5	399.6	448.8	465.8	481.4	488.8	453.0	457.6	510.0	450.6	457.9	5,443
1998	430.5	407.7	437.8	444.0	419.1	454.2	456.0	409.9	425.3	470.5	459.5	428.2	5,243
1999	408.9	361.0	428.8	435.8	438.6	452.4	434.7	464.3	451.3	468.7	487.6	425.4	5,257
2000[1]	396.9	414.5	466.0	411.9	488.7	478.3	422.5	480.4	418.2	491.5	478.8	395.5	5,343

[1] Preliminary.   *Source: Economic Research Service, U.S. Department of Agriculture (ERS-USDA)*

TURKEYS

Per Capita Consumption of Turkeys in the United States   In Pounds

Year	First Quarter	Second Quarter	Third Quarter	Fourth Quarter	Total	Year	First Quarter	Second Quarter	Third Quarter	Fourth Quarter	Total
1990	3.5	3.6	4.2	6.2	17.6	1996	3.7	3.9	4.6	6.2	18.5
1991	3.7	4.0	4.1	6.4	18.0	1997	3.5	4.0	4.2	6.0	17.6
1992	3.4	3.8	4.2	6.5	18.0	1998	3.9	3.9	4.2	6.0	18.1
1993	3.5	3.7	3.9	6.5	17.7	1999	3.8	3.8	4.4	5.8	18.0
1994	3.6	3.9	4.4	6.2	17.8	2000[1]	3.7	4.2	4.3	5.5	17.8
1995	3.6	3.9	4.2	6.2	17.9	2001[2]	3.9	4.0	4.3	5.9	18.1

[1] Preliminary.   [2] Estimate.   *Source: Economic Research Service, U.S. Department of Agriculture (ERS-USDA)*

Storage Stocks of Turkeys (Frozen) in the United States on First of Month   In Millions of Pounds

Year	Jan.	Feb.	Mar.	Apr.	May	June	July	Aug.	Sept.	Oct.	Nov.	Dec.
1991	306.4	302.5	342.2	370.0	408.5	453.4	503.1	571.3	625.8	667.2	653.0	305.5
1992	264.1	325.5	354.1	392.3	430.2	486.8	580.1	662.1	684.2	734.4	714.7	320.5
1993	271.7	314.7	359.8	359.2	424.4	474.0	556.1	624.2	678.6	713.8	683.6	290.6
1994	249.1	279.8	304.8	346.5	399.1	461.4	539.2	588.1	623.4	648.6	636.2	280.7
1995	254.4	312.9	359.5	432.1	466.2	536.3	598.8	651.1	678.2	686.0	644.2	270.1
1996	271.3	339.2	423.1	445.4	514.5	587.4	679.7	718.2	723.2	721.0	658.3	347.8
1997	328.0	401.0	446.4	496.5	543.3	611.8	667.9	714.3	742.0	770.7	736.6	438.6
1998	415.1	497.6	512.7	527.0	579.7	614.1	656.5	701.8	706.8	699.5	658.7	310.4
1999	304.3	363.8	375.6	374.9	455.4	494.3	556.1	599.0	580.3	596.4	494.5	252.3
2000[1]	254.3	319.4	353.9	387.5	413.3	477.0	503.6	524.1	524.8	527.8	478.0	260.8

[1] Preliminary.   *Source: Economic Research Service, U.S. Department of Agriculture (ERS-USDA)*

Average Retail[2] Price of Turkeys (Whole frozen) in the United States   In Cents Per Pound

Year	Jan.	Feb.	Mar.	Apr.	May	June	July	Aug.	Sept.	Oct.	Nov.	Dec.	Average
1991	62.3	63.1	66.6	66.8	69.7	70.0	70.3	72.2	72.8	69.1	70.8	73.9	69.0
1992	67.9	65.8	68.1	68.7	69.2	69.0	65.7	68.1	69.6	72.3	74.0	74.9	69.5
1993	67.9	67.2	67.9	68.8	68.4	68.2	67.1	72.1	74.9	78.4	80.1	75.0	71.3
1994	70.3	69.4	70.6	70.9	72.0	72.6	72.8	74.8	77.3	79.9	83.3	77.3	74.3
1995	69.5	67.1	68.5	68.6	70.1	72.5	74.2	77.8	81.6	84.9	86.5	77.5	74.9
1996	103.5	104.7	106.9	101.4	104.3	104.1	104.4	108.6	106.5	107.4	98.1	102.0	104.3
1997	106.3	106.7	104.7	103.2	104.5	107.8	107.4	109.2	108.9	106.2	97.6	98.2	105.1
1998	103.4	100.1	99.6	97.2	95.7	99.1	100.8	102.4	105.2	102.5	93.4	95.4	99.6
1999	96.9	100.1	98.4	93.6	97.5	100.5	103.1	101.5	101.8	102.5	96.4	97.6	99.2
2000[1]	101.3	102.5	101.5	99.7	102.9	106.5	109.5	104.5	104.4	106.7	98.1	99.4	103.1

[1] Preliminary.   [2] Data prior to 1996 are prices to selected retailers.   *Source: Economic Research Service, U.S. Department of Agriculture (ERS-USDA)*

Average Retail-to-Consumer Price Spread of Turkeys (Whole) in the United States   In Cents Per Pound

Year	Jan.	Feb.	Mar.	Apr.	May	June	July	Aug.	Sept.	Oct.	Nov.	Dec.	Average
1991	37.1	38.1	31.2	33.7	30.9	32.0	32.6	31.2	30.3	34.9	20.8	17.5	30.9
1992	28.2	29.2	27.0	29.4	29.6	29.5	33.3	32.5	31.4	27.2	15.4	18.1	27.6
1993	30.0	31.7	32.6	31.9	32.3	34.5	35.8	29.7	27.7	25.0	13.6	20.4	28.8
1994	27.5	29.7	28.1	25.1	27.1	28.8	28.7	27.6	27.1	25.5	13.9	20.3	25.8
1995	28.5	32.0	33.7	32.1	32.7	32.8	30.8	28.2	27.0	20.1	10.6	21.2	27.5
1996	30.4	30.7	33.6	28.0	29.3	28.0	27.9	32.1	30.3	28.9	18.0	26.6	28.7
1997	38.3	40.7	37.5	32.0	29.6	32.0	32.0	34.5	34.3	31.9	20.0	26.9	32.5
1998	38.8	37.2	35.2	31.2	29.4	30.7	29.6	29.0	29.3	21.3	10.3	19.0	28.4
1999	29.9	32.7	28.6	21.3	22.5	22.6	23.2	29.1	18.5	17.6	12.0	19.6	23.1
2000[1]	32.1	33.9	29.1	25.9	27.6	29.5	30.9	23.7	21.1	21.7	13.4	23.1	26.0

[1] Preliminary.   *Source: Economic Research Service, U.S. Department of Agriculture (ERS-USDA)*

Uranium

The U.S. Energy Information Administration reported that in 1999, U.S. uranium mine production was 4.55 million pounds, while uranium concentrate production was 4.6 million pounds. U.S. mine production of uranium in 1999 was down 5 percent from 1998. Production of uranium has been trending lower for a number of years. In 1990, mine production was 5.88 million pounds. In 1999, there were a number of sources of uranium. These included three underground mines, six in-situ leaching sites, and five other sites.

Uranium concentrate production in 1999 was 4.61 million pounds, down 2 percent from 1998. Uranium concentrate production in the U.S. has been trending lower. In 1990, concentrate production was 8.89 million pounds. Total uranium concentrate shipped from mills and plants in 1999 was 5.53 million pounds which was up 14 percent from 1998. Total uranium ore fed to mills for processing in 1999 was 1.26 million pounds. Actual uranium concentrate produced at mills in 1999 was 970,000 pounds. Other processing of uranium from in-situ leaching and as a by-product of phosphate processing resulted in 3.7 million pounds of concentrate, down 15 percent from a year ago.

In 1999, total exploration and development expenditures were $8.97 million, a decline of 59 percent from 1998. Surface drilling (exploration and development) expenditures were $7.89 million. In 1999, there were 265 holes drilled in surface drilling exploration. This represented a decline of 81 percent from 1998. In surface drilling exploration and development, there were 3,176 holes drilled, down 52 percent from a year ago. There were no acres acquired for land exploration in 1999. The total acreage held for land exploration in 1999 was 807,000 acres.

U.S. utilities in 1999 received from U.S. producers 5.16 million pounds of uranium, down 20 percent from the year before. Utilities received 10.4 million pounds of uranium from U.S. brokers and traders, down 1 percent from 1998. From foreign suppliers, U.S. utilities received 26.8 million pounds of uranium. In 1999, U.S. utilities purchased 47.95 million pounds of uranium, up 12 percent from 1998. U.S. utilities in 1999 purchased 11.5 million pounds of U.S.-origin uranium and 36.5 million pounds of foreign-origin uranium. The purchases of U.S.-origin were up 59 percent from 1998, while foreign-origin uranium purchases were up 3 percent. Of the foreign-origin uranium purchases in 1999 of 36.5 million pounds, 12.5 million pounds were from Canada and 7.3 million pounds were from Australia. Purchases from Russia were 6.3 million pounds. Other large suppliers were South Africa, Uzbekistan, and the Ukraine.

Deliveries of uranium feed for enrichment to U.S. enrichers in 1999 totaled 25.1 million pounds, about the same as in 1998. The major supplier in 1999 was Canada with 10.6 million pounds. Deliveries of uranium for enrichment by Russia in 1999 were 6.1 million pounds, while deliveries by Australia were 3 million pounds. Other large suppliers were South Africa and Uzbekistan.

World Production of Uranium Oxide (U_3O_8) Concentrate — In Short Tons (Uranium Content)

Year	Australia	Canada	China	Czech Rep. & Slovakia	France	Gabon	Germany	Namibia	Niger	South Africa	United States	Ex-USSR	World Total
1990	4,589	11,400	1,039	2,600	3,661	922	3,864	4,030	3,682	3,169	4,443	18,199	64,642
1991	4,909	10,609	1,039	2,340	3,204	882	1,569	3,185	3,853	2,248	3,975	13,650	53,458
1992	3,032	12,087	1,039	2,040	2,755	702	325	2,199	3,855	2,449	2,822	11,205	46,124
1993	2,949	11,990	1,300	911	2,220	769	195	2,168	3,786	2,261	2,587	10,491	43,027
1994	3,050	11,950	-----	-----	1,700	750	-----	2,500	3,800	2,250	1,950	-----	41,750
1995	4,900	13,600	-----	-----	1,250	800	-----	2,600	3,750	1,850	3,050	-----	43,050
1996	6,450	15,250	-----	-----	1,200	750	-----	3,150	4,300	2,200	3,150	-----	46,650
1997	7,150	15,650	-----	-----	940	600	-----	3,770	4,500	1,065	2,900	-----	46,550
1998[1]	6,350	14,200	-----	-----	660	950	-----	3,590	4,850	1,250	2,435	-----	44,110
1999[2]	7,875	10,680	-----	-----	450	380	-----	3,495	3,790	1,195	2,325	-----	39,640

[1] Preliminary. [2] Estimate. *Source: American Bureau of Metal Statistics, Inc. (ABMS)*

Commercial and U.S. Government Stocks of Uranium, End of Year — In Millions of Pounds U_3O_8 Equivalent

Year	Utility Natural Uranium	Utility Enriched Uranium[1]	Domestic Supplier Natural Uranium	Domestic Supplier Enriched Uranium[1]	Total Commercial Stocks	DOE Owned & USEC Held Natural Uranium	DOE Owned & USEC Held Enriched Uranium[1]
1992	66.5	25.5	19.1	6.1	117.3	45.8	23.1
1993	57.9	23.3	19.1	5.4	105.7	52.4	26.9
1994	42.4	23.0	17.4	4.1	86.9	57.2	28.0
1995	41.2	17.5	13.2	.5	72.5	82.0	28.8
1996	42.2	23.9	13.0	1.0	80.0	83.2	25.3
1997	47.1	18.8	10.3	30.1	106.2	53.2	0
1998	42.1	23.7	35.0	35.7	136.5	24.5	0
1999	44.7	13.5	29.5	39.4	127.0	53.1	0

[1] Includes amount reported as UF_6 at enrichment suppliers.   DOE = Department of Energy   USEC = U.S. Energy Commission

Source: Energy Information Administration, U.S. Department of Energy (EIA-DOE)

URANIUM

Reported Average Price Settlements for Purchases by U.S. Utilities and Domestic Suppliers   In $/Pound

Year of Delivery	Contract Price	Market Price[1]	Price & Cost Floor	Total	Contract & Market	Year of Delivery	Contract Price	Market Price[1]	Price & Cost Floor	Total	Contract & Market
	------- Averages of Reported Prices -------						------- Averages of Reported Prices -------				
1990	17.94	9.18	19.40	11.65	15.70	1995	10.58	10.19	17.86	12.05	10.79
1991	13.94	9.04	21.84	12.62	13.66	1996	13.40	13.66	16.13	14.91	13.72
1992	13.16	8.65	18.35	13.89	13.45	1997	13.33	11.20	14.52	12.11	13.13
1993	14.96	9.57	14.87	11.03	13.14	1998	12.53	9.33	13.50	10.31	12.37
1994	10.68	9.76	20.03	10.57	10.63	1999	12.72	9.52	14.75	11.16	12.57

[1] No floor.   Note: Price excludes uranium delivered *under litigation settlements. Price is given in year-of-delivery dollars.*
Source: Energy Information Administration, U.S. Department of Energy (EIA-DOE)

Uranium Industry Statistics in the United States   In Millions of Pounds U_3O_8

Year	Production Mine	Production Concentrate	Concentrate Shipments	Exploration	Employment Mining	Employment Milling	Employment Processing	Employment Total	Deliveries to U.S. Utilities[1]	Average Price Delivered Uranium $/Lb. U_3O_8	Imports	Avg. Price Delivered Uranium Imports $/Lb. U_3O_8	Exports
1990	5.9	8.885	12.957	73	664	304	293	1,335	20.5	15.70	26.6	12.55	2.0
1991	5.2	7.952	8.437	52	411	191	361	1,016	26.8	13.66	23.1	15.55	3.5
1992	1.0	5.645	6.853	51	219	129	283	682	23.4	13.45	45.4	11.34	2.8
1993	2.0	3.063	3.374	36	133	65	145	871	15.5	13.14	41.9	10.53	3.0
1994	2.5	3.352	6.319	41	157	105	149	980	38.3	10.40	36.6	8.95	17.7
1995	3.5	6.000	5.500	27	226	121	161	1,107	43.4	11.25	41.3	10.20	9.8
1996	4.7	6.300	6.000	27	333	155	175	1,118	47.3	14.12	45.4	13.15	11.5
1997	4.7	5.600	5.800	30	413	175	175	1,097	42.0	12.88	43.0	11.81	17.0
1998	4.8	4.700	4.900	30	518	160	203	1,120	42.7	12.14	43.7	11.19	15.1
1999	4.5	4.600	5.500	7	310	201	132	848	47.9	11.63	47.6	10.55	85.1

[1] From suppliers under domestic purchases.   Source: Energy Information Administration, U.S. Department of Energy (EIA-DOE)

Month-End Uranium (U_3O_8) Transaction Values[1]   In Dollars Per Pound

Year	Jan.	Feb.	Mar.	Apr.	May	June	July	Aug.	Sept.	Oct.	Nov.	Dec.	Average
1990	9.25	9.05	8.75	8.65	8.55	8.80	9.75	10.80	11.40	10.10	9.30	9.15	9.46
1991	9.40	9.45	9.35	9.30	9.30	9.20	9.15	8.95	8.70	8.35	7.45	7.50	8.84
1992	7.55	7.80	7.95	7.90	7.85	7.80	7.75	7.85	7.95	8.40	8.55	8.75	8.01
1993[2]	8.80	8.60	8.80	9.20	8.70	8.90	8.20	8.80	9.05	8.45	8.60	8.71	8.74
1994	8.58	8.45	8.25	8.25	8.23	8.25	8.23	8.15	8.13	8.10	8.13	8.25	8.25
1995	8.30	8.45	8.65	8.78	9.18	9.48	9.50	9.83	9.83	9.83	9.95	10.05	9.32
1996	10.20	10.48	10.93	11.70	13.03	13.25	14.93	15.18	15.40	15.53	15.48	15.38	13.45
1997	15.33	15.08	14.85	14.75	14.43	10.95	10.68	10.45	10.55	10.48	10.43	10.53	12.37
1998	10.63	10.63	10.60	10.05	10.00	9.80	9.80	9.73	9.55	9.35	9.25	9.05	9.87
1999	9.03	9.08	9.20	9.20	9.53	9.48	9.48	9.40	9.35	9.23	9.18	9.13	9.27

[1] Transaction value is a weighed average price of recent natural uranium sales transactions, based on prices paid on transactions closed within the previous three-month period for which delivery is scheduled within one year of the transaction date; at least 10 transactions involving a sum total of at least 2 million pounds of U_3O_8 equivalent.   [2] Beginning December 1993; data represents average of Unrestricted and Restricted.
Source: American Metal Market (AMM)

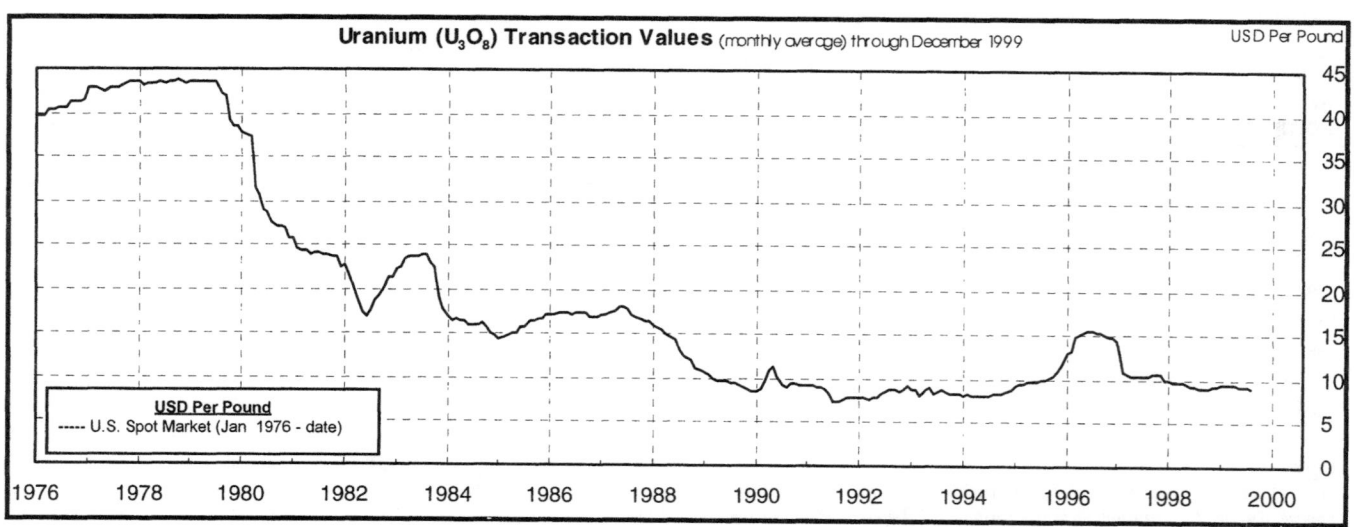

Uranium (U_3O_8) Transaction Values (monthly average) through December 1999   USD Per Pound

USD Per Pound
----- U.S. Spot Market (Jan 1976 - date)

Vanadium

Vanadium is used in the production of carbon and alloy plates and steel, pipe steels, and structured bars. Vanadium is also used as an oxidation catalyst, in tool production to provide strength and toughness, and in the production of aerospace titanium alloys. Vanadium pentoxide is used in dyeing and painting applications. There are substitutes for vanadium in some applications. Platinum and nickel are substitutes in chemical processes, but there are no substitutes for aerospace titanium alloys.

Vanadium occurs in deposits of titanferous magnetite, phosphate rock, and in uraniferous sandstone and siltstone. Vanadium is also found in bauxite materials. In the U.S. in 1999, almost all vanadium production came from industrial waste streams including vanadium-bearing ferrophosphorus slag, iron slag, fly ash, petroleum residues, and spent catalysts. These materials were processed to produce vanadium pentoxide, ferrovanadium, and vanadium metal.

The U.S. Geological Survey reported that seven countries recovered vanadium from ores, concentrates, slag, or petroleum residues. World mine production of vanadium in 1999 was estimated at 40,000 metric tonnes, down 4 percent from the previous year. The largest producer of vanadium was South Africa with 160,000 tonnes followed by China with 14,000. The other large producer is Russia. Production in China, Russia, and South Africa is primarily a by-product of the iron and steel industry. Japan and the U.S. recover significant quantities of vanadium from petroleum residues. Recycling of vanadium is negligible.

U.S. consumption of ferrovanadium in August 2000 was 263,000 kilograms, contained vanadium, a decline of 11 percent from July. For all of 1999, consumption of ferrovanadium was 3.49 million kilograms. Consumption of other vanadium-containing products like vanadium metal, vanadium pentoxide, and vanadium alloys in August 2000 was 33,800 kilograms, down 11 percent from July. For all of 1999, consumption of these products was 337,000 kilograms. U.S. stocks of ferrovanadium in August 2000 were 254,000 kilograms compared to stocks at the end of 1999 of 354,000 kilograms. Stocks of vanadium-aluminum alloy in August 2000 were 10,900 kilograms. Stocks of other vanadium materials were 8,190 kilograms in August 2000 and 14,000 kilograms at the end of 1999.

U.S. imports for consumption of aluminum-vanadium master alloy in the January-July 2000 period were 16,300 kilograms, while for all of 1999 they were 1.21 million kilograms. Vanadium metal imports in the first seven months of 2000 were 39,200 kilograms, while for all of 1999 they were 30,400 kilograms. Imports of ferrovanadium in January-July 2000 were 1.57 million kilograms. Vanadium pentoxide imports were 735,000 kilograms in the same period.

World Production of Vanadium   In Metric Tons (Contained Vanadium)

| | | | From Ores, Concentrates and Slag | | | | From Petroleum Residues, Ash, Spent Catalysts | | | |
| | | | Republic of South Africa | | | | | | | |
Year	China[3]	Russia[4]	Content of Pentoxide & Vanadate Products	Content of Vanadiferous Slag Products	Total	Total[5]	Japan[4]	United States[7]	Total	World Total
1990	4,500	9,000	7,100	10,000	17,106	33,900	700	2,308	3,008	36,900
1991	4,500	8,500	6,500	8,460	14,962	31,700	404	2,250	2,650	34,300
1992	4,700	11,000	6,300	7,730	14,285	31,600	245	1,347	1,590	33,200
1993	5,000	12,800	6,650	8,400	15,051	33,900	252	2,867	3,120	37,000
1994	5,400	11,900	6,050	9,600	16,350	34,700	252	2,740	2,990	37,700
1995	13,700	11,000	6,500	9,000	16,297	42,100	245	1,990	2,240	44,400
1996	14,000	11,000	----	----	14,770	40,900	245	3,730	3,980	45,800
1997	15,000	9,000	----	----	15,590	40,700	245	----	----	----
1998[1]	15,500	9,000	----	----	18,868	44,500	245	----	----	----
1999[2]	16,000	9,000	----	----	16,000	42,000	245	----	----	----

[1] Preliminary.   [2] Estimate.   [3] In vanadiferous slag product.   [4] Formerly part of the U.S.S.R.: data not reported separately until 1992.   [5] Excludes U.S. production.   [6] In vanadium pentoxide product.   [7] In vanadium pentoxide and ferrovanadium products.   Source: U.S. Geological Survey(USGS)

Salient Statistics of Vanadium in the United States   In Metric Tons (Contained Vanadium)

Year	Consumer & Producer Stocks, Dec. 31	Tool Steel	Cast Irons	High Strength, Low Alloy	Stainless & Heat Resisting	Super- alloys	Carbon	Full Alloy	Total	Average $ Per Lb. V2O5	Vanadium Pent- oxide Anhydride	Oxides & Hydr- oxides	Ferro- Vana- dium	Ores, Vanadium Slag, Re- sidues	Pent- oxide Anhydride	Oxides & Hydr- oxides	Ferro- Vana- dium
1990	1,082	421	18	1,122	38	42	994	814	4,081	4.21	819	976	271	3,826	83	217	244
1991	935	242	15	919	37	14	919	739	3,293	2.85	700	1,110	94	882	133	110	420
1992	1,084	453	17	989	28	13	1,262	828	4,079	2.28	26	1,113	213	838	206	103	592
1993	900	373	21	981	33	13	1,413	789	3,973	1.45	126	895	219	1,454	70	19	1,630
1994	1,110	424	31	979	26	16	1,680	777	4,290	1.55	335	1,050	374	1,900	294	3	1,910
1995	1,100	443	40	1,070	32	20	1,870	833	4,640	4.63	229	1,010	340	2,530	547	36	1,950
1996	1,070	433	W	890	22	16	1,820	1,030	4,200	3.11	241	2,670	479	2,270	485	11	1,880
1997	1,000	481	W	944	20	24	1,800	908	4,730	7.40-11.00	614	385	446	2,950	711	126	1,840
1998[1]	336	269	W	950	42	20	1,650	891	4,380	5.25-15.50	681	232	579	2,400	847	33	1,620
1999[2]	368	344	W	949	82	15	1,240	802	3,830	4.35-6.25	747	70	213	1,650	208	----	1,930

[1] Preliminary.   [2] Estimate.   W = Withheld proprietary data.   Source: U.S. Geological Survey (USGS)

Vegetables

The U.S.D.A. reported that the area for harvest of 13 selected fresh market vegetables during the 2000 fall quarter was forecast at 177,650 acres, down 5 percent from 1999. Acreage reductions were seen in bell peppers, carrots, celery, cucumbers, head lettuce, and tomatoes. This more than offset increased harvested acreage in broccoli, cabbage, cauliflower, snap beans, and sweet corn. Acreage of escarole/endive and eggplant were unchanged. Acreage forecast for the melon harvest was 14,900 acres, down 16 percent from 1999. Cantaloupe acreage was forecast at 8,900 acres, down 22 percent from 1999. Honeydew acreage was forecast at 5,100 acres, down 4 percent from a year ago. Watermelon acreage of 900 acres was down 10 percent from a year ago.

U.S. production of fresh tomatoes in year 2000 was forecast to be 3.63 billion pounds, an increase of 2 percent from 1999. Imports of fresh tomatoes were forecast at 1.6 billion pounds, down 2 percent from 1999. Exports of fresh tomatoes in 2000 were estimated to be 335 million pounds with domestic use of 4.89 billion pounds. Per capita use is estimated at 177.8 pounds, unchanged from 1999.

U.S. production of fresh onions in 2000 was forecast to be 5.74 billion pounds, down 3 percent from 1999. Imports were estimated to be 590 million pounds, while exports were 675 million pounds. Domestic use of onions was forecast to be 5.04 billion pounds, down 1 percent from 1999. Per capita use of onions in 2000 was estimated to be 18.3 pounds.

Production of head lettuce in 2000 was forecast to be 7.1 billion pounds, down 2 per cent from the previous year. Imports were 25 million pounds, while exports were 400 million pounds. Domestic use was estimated at 6.73 billion pounds, down 3 percent from 1999. Per capita use of lettuce is estimated to be 24.4 pounds. U.S. imports of fresh lettuce in May 2000 were 1.24 million pounds. For all of 1999 imports were 57.3 million pounds.

Index of Prices Received by Growers for Commercial Vegetables[1] in the United States

Year	Jan.	Feb.	Mar.	Apr.	May	June	July	Aug.	Sept.	Oct.	Nov.	Dec.	Average
1995	120	116	148	174	155	121	98	102	117	97	98	101	121
1996	94	111	147	122	103	116	99	116	102	109	112	96	111
1997	111	105	118	113	106	112	112	122	119	145	122	136	118
1998	120	114	123	153	126	107	119	112	111	131	113	117	121
1999	105	111	119	129	118	110	104	105	104	97	99	97	108
2000[2]	97	87	106	140	135	117	118	127	142	124	141		121

Not seasonally adjusted.   1990-92=100.   [1] Includes fresh and processing vegetables.   [2] Preliminary.   *Source: National Agricultural Statistics Service, U.S. Department of Agriculture (NASS-USDA)*

Index of Prices Received by Growers for Fresh Vegetables (0113-02) in the United States

Year	Jan.	Feb.	Mar.	Apr.	May	June	July	Aug.	Sept.	Oct.	Nov.	Dec.	Average
1995	163.5	149.2	159.2	199.1	167.2	127.2	107.3	94.8	152.9	116.0	115.8	125.5	139.8
1996	133.9	119.4	202.5	155.6	108.2	96.6	108.8	97.2	91.3	106.0	131.5	99.3	120.9
1997	105.2	126.2	150.4	109.6	103.2	112.2	115.7	125.2	121.8	143.1	124.7	118.5	121.3
1998	133.1	136.6	148.2	162.9	123.2	106.5	153.7	114.9	135.0	161.9	131.2	148.1	137.9
1999	131.9	93.1	117.4	144.4	111.3	125.8	103.4	113.7	117.5	101.6	100.9	151.6	117.7
2000[1]	111.3	100.5	122.3	126.8	152.0	128.1	127.2	136.7	155.9	165.0	174.5	121.7	135.1

Not seasonally adjusted.   1990-92=100.   [1] Preliminary.   *Source: National Agricultural Statistics Service, U.S. Department of Agriculture (NASS)*

Producer Price Index of Canned[1] Processed Vegetables (0244) in the United States   1982 = 100

Year	Jan.	Feb.	Mar.	Apr.	May	June	July	Aug.	Sept.	Oct.	Nov.	Dec.	Average
1995	112.6	114.3	114.7	112.9	115.6	117.5	118.2	117.5	117.6	117.8	118.4	119.6	116.4
1996	120.4	119.8	120.4	120.4	120.8	121.0	122.6	122.1	121.9	121.8	121.9	121.8	121.2
1997	121.5	121.1	120.5	120.1	119.8	119.9	119.1	119.3	119.3	120.2	120.3	120.7	120.1
1998	121.2	121.9	121.8	121.8	121.9	121.9	122.0	122.0	120.0	119.6	120.0	120.0	121.2
1999	120.6	120.6	120.9	120.9	121.0	121.0	120.8	120.9	120.7	120.7	121.3	121.3	120.9
2000[2]	121.3	120.8	121.2	120.9	121.2	121.5	121.1	120.9	121.1	121.1	121.7	121.5	121.1

Not seasonally adjusted.   [1] Includes canned vegetables and juices, including hominy and mushrooms.   [2] Preliminary.   *Source: Bureau of Labor Statistics, U.S. Department of Labor (BLS)*

Producer Price Index of Frozen Processed Vegetables (0245) in the United States   1982 = 100

Year	Jan.	Feb.	Mar.	Apr.	May	June	July	Aug.	Sept.	Oct.	Nov.	Dec.	Average
1995	125.1	124.7	124.9	125.1	124.3	123.6	123.2	123.6	124.4	124.6	123.7	124.0	124.3
1996	125.1	124.8	124.6	124.9	125.0	125.4	125.5	125.8	126.0	125.7	125.8	126.0	125.4
1997	125.9	125.7	125.6	125.6	125.7	125.7	126.9	125.6	125.7	126.6	125.5	125.3	125.8
1998	125.2	126.0	124.8	125.7	125.0	124.6	125.5	125.6	125.3	125.6	125.5	125.2	125.3
1999	125.8	126.6	125.6	126.7	125.9	126.0	126.8	126.1	126.0	126.4	125.5	125.3	126.1
2000[1]	125.4	126.2	125.7	126.3	126.3	124.9	125.9	126.4	126.2	126.6	125.8	126.7	126.1

Not seasonally adjusted.   [1] Preliminary.   *Source: Bureau of Labor Statistics, U.S. Department of Labor (BLS)*

Per Capita Use of Selected Commercially Produced Fresh and Processing Vegetables in the U.S.
In Pounds, farm weight basis

Crop	1990	1991	1992	1993	1994	1995	1996	1997	1998	1999[9]	2000[10]
Asparagus, all	1.0	1.0	1.0	1.0	.9	1.0	.9	1.0	1.1	1.2	1.2
Fresh	.6	.6	.6	.6	.6	.6	.6	.7	.8	.9	.9
Canning	.3	.3	.3	.3	.2	.3	.2	.2	.2	.2	.2
Freezing	.1	.1	.1	.1	.1	.1	.1	.1	.1	.1	.1
Snap Beans, all	6.7	7.0	7.2	7.3	7.4	7.0	7.3	6.9	7.5	7.7	7.6
Fresh	1.1	1.1	1.5	1.5	1.6	1.7	1.5	1.4	1.7	1.9	1.7
Canning	3.7	4.1	4.0	4.0	3.8	3.6	3.9	3.7	3.8	3.8	3.9
Freezing	1.9	1.8	1.7	1.8	2.0	1.7	1.9	1.8	2.0	2.0	2.0
Broccoli, all[1]	5.6	5.4	5.8	5.7	6.8	7.0	7.2	7.4	7.3	8.2	8.0
Fresh	3.4	3.1	3.4	3.4	4.5	4.4	4.6	5.1	5.2	6.0	5.7
Freezing	2.2	2.3	2.4	2.3	2.3	2.6	2.6	2.3	2.1	2.2	2.3
Carrots, all[2]	11.9	11.2	12.3	14.8	17.1	15.6	17.2	18.5	17.8	17.6	17.9
Fresh	8.3	7.7	8.3	10.9	12.8	11.3	12.6	14.4	13.5	13.6	13.7
Canning	1.3	1.1	1.7	1.1	1.5	1.7	1.7	1.5	1.5	1.5	1.5
Freezing	2.3	2.4	2.3	2.8	2.8	2.6	2.9	2.6	2.8	2.5	2.7
Cauliflower, All[1]	3.0	2.6	2.5	2.8	2.6	2.3	2.2	2.2	2.3	2.5	2.3
Fresh	2.2	2.0	1.8	2.1	2.0	1.7	1.7	1.8	1.5	2.1	1.7
Freezing	.8	.6	.7	.7	.6	.6	.5	.4	.8	.4	.6
Celery, fresh	7.2	6.8	7.4	7.3	7.4	6.9	6.4	6.1	6.0	6.2	6.3
Sweet Corn, all[3]	26.3	26.4	27.8	28.0	27.6	28.9	29.5	27.9	28.9	29.7	29.6
Fresh	6.7	5.9	6.9	7.0	8.2	7.9	8.5	8.4	9.5	9.8	9.8
Canning	11.0	11.1	11.9	11.2	10.2	10.5	10.5	9.3	9.4	9.3	9.5
Freezing	8.6	9.4	9.0	9.8	9.2	10.5	10.5	10.2	10.0	10.6	10.3
Cucumbers, all	9.7	9.7	9.6	9.7	10.2	10.8	10.1	11.8	10.7	11.1	11.7
Fresh	4.7	4.6	5.0	5.3	5.4	5.7	6.0	6.5	6.6	6.9	6.9
Pickles	5.0	5.1	4.6	4.4	4.8	5.1	4.1	5.3	4.1	4.2	4.8
Melons, all	24.6	23.4	25.4	24.7	25.7	26.4	29.3	28.8	27.8	30.5	30.2
Watermelon	13.3	12.8	14.8	14.3	15.2	15.4	16.8	15.8	14.6	15.8	15.6
Cantaloupe	9.2	8.7	8.5	8.7	8.5	9.1	10.4	10.7	10.9	11.9	11.9
Honeydew	2.1	1.9	2.1	1.7	2.0	1.9	2.1	2.3	2.3	2.8	2.7
Lettuce, Head	27.8	26.1	25.9	24.6	25.3	22.5	21.9	24.3	22.0	25.3	24.0
Onions, all	17.1	17.3	17.6	19.3	18.1	19.3	19.6	20.0	19.4	21.3	19.4
Fresh	15.1	15.7	16.2	17.3	17.1	18.0	18.7	19.1	18.3	18.9	18.3
Green peas, all[4]	4.2	4.2	4.1	3.5	3.7	3.7	3.4	3.6	3.4	3.5	3.5
Canning	2.0	1.9	2.1	1.6	1.5	1.6	1.5	1.5	1.5	1.4	1.4
Freezing	2.2	2.3	2.0	1.9	2.2	2.1	1.9	2.1	1.9	2.1	2.1
Tomatoes, all	90.9	92.8	89.2	92.8	93.5	92.7	91.9	91.0	93.6	90.5	92.2
Fresh	15.5	15.4	15.5	16.4	16.4	17.1	17.7	17.1	17.9	17.7	17.7
Canning	75.4	77.4	73.7	76.4	77.1	75.6	74.2	73.9	75.7	72.8	74.5
Subtotal, all[8]	268.1	268.2	272.5	280.1	285.0	280.8	286.0	289.2	288.8	295.9	294.4
Fresh	138.5	134.3	141.6	146.3	153.3	149.3	156.1	161.6	158.6	166.7	163.9
Canning	107.3	110.8	108.8	109.6	108.6	107.2	105.5	104.3	106.5	103.6	106.2
Freezing	20.3	21.5	20.7	22.2	22.1	23.0	23.5	22.4	22.6	23.2	23.2
Potatoes, all	124.1	134.5	130.7	137.8	138.3	138.8	147.3	141.4	140.8	141.9	142.4
Fresh	46.8	50.4	48.6	50.6	50.2	49.9	50.7	48.5	47.8	48.3	47.4
Processing	77.3	84.1	82.1	87.2	88.1	88.9	96.6	92.9	93.0	93.6	95.0
Sweetpotatoes, all	4.6	4.0	4.3	3.9	4.7	4.5	4.6	4.5	4.1	4.0	4.4
Total, all items	407.5	418.2	419.3	433.2	440.4	436.3	450.0	447.2	445.4	454.2	454.1

[1] All production for processing broccoli and cauliflower is for freezing. [2] Industry allocation suggests that 27 percent of processing carrot production is for canning and 73 percent is for freezing. [3] On-cob basis. [4] In-shell basis. [5] Includes artichokes, brussels sprouts, eggplant, endive/escarole, garlic, radishes, and spinach. [6] Includes beets, chile peppers (1980-94, all uses), and spinach. [7] Includes green lima beans, spinach, and miscellaneous freezing vegetables. [8] Fresh, canning, and freezing data do not add to the total because onions for dehydrating are included in the total.
[9] Preliminary. [10] Forecast. Source: Economic Research Service, U.S. Department of Agriculture (ERS-USDA)

VEGETABLES

Average Price Received by Growers for Broccoli in the United States   In Dollars Per Cwt.

Year	Jan.	Feb.	Mar.	Apr.	May	June	July	Aug.	Sept.	Oct.	Nov.	Dec.	Season Average
1993	32.60	28.10	28.60	23.70	22.30	26.80	24.50	20.00	36.60	22.40	24.20	30.00	26.60
1994	23.50	21.40	19.50	21.80	27.10	21.10	21.60	18.50	38.60	37.00	57.70	46.00	27.50
1995	24.70	34.30	54.40	34.00	26.50	27.30	19.50	31.30	27.70	23.60	20.80	26.90	29.30
1996	34.60	22.00	30.90	25.20	28.20	30.60	24.10	24.10	23.90	24.30	31.10	28.60	27.10
1997	36.80	27.80	25.90	24.20	23.10	30.30	27.50	23.30	31.20	40.70	27.00	30.20	29.10
1998	33.80	26.80	30.70	40.70	27.10	29.60	23.30	27.60	29.20	32.80	29.70	35.00	30.20
1999	27.10	20.10	21.70	20.30	18.60	23.10	18.70	27.40	29.30	23.00	22.50	20.90	23.00
2000[1]	22.60	20.20	26.80	23.30	44.30	30.00	31.50	25.20	27.70	34.10	50.40		

[1] Preliminary.   *Source: National Agricultural Statistics Service, U.S. Department of Agriculture (NASS-USDA)*

Average Price Received by Growers for Carrots in the United States   In Dollars Per Cwt.

Year	Jan.	Feb.	Mar.	Apr.	May	June	July	Aug.	Sept.	Oct.	Nov.	Dec.	Season Average
1993	18.00	13.20	11.20	12.70	11.20	10.20	9.04	10.10	9.98	10.30	11.00	10.90	11.90
1994	10.70	10.50	11.50	10.30	12.10	12.10	13.50	16.10	15.30	15.30	15.10	15.70	12.90
1995	19.20	16.90	18.70	19.40	19.20	15.20	15.00	16.10	16.10	15.30	15.50	13.00	16.70
1996	12.60	13.80	15.90	15.70	12.00	11.00	10.50	14.50	12.60	12.00	16.00	17.20	13.40
1997	15.00	14.70	13.40	12.60	12.60	12.60	12.60	13.10	12.70	12.10	12.50	16.80	12.90
1998	14.00	13.00	13.00	12.60	12.00	11.90	10.60	10.80	10.60	10.90	11.50	11.00	12.00
1999	16.60	20.10	21.80	26.80	25.20	21.90	15.70	12.60	10.10	10.60	11.60	11.30	17.00
2000[1]	8.87	11.60	11.80	12.30	13.40	14.60	15.50	14.70	13.80	13.90	14.70		

[1] Preliminary.   *Source: National Agricultural Statistics Service, U.S. Department of Agriculture (NASS-USDA)*

Average Price Received by Growers for Cauliflower in the United States   In Dollars Per Cwt.

Year	Jan.	Feb.	Mar.	Apr.	May	June	July	Aug.	Sept.	Oct.	Nov.	Dec.	Season Average
1993	34.30	29.10	24.70	44.90	26.90	37.00	28.30	29.30	38.70	27.40	21.60	30.90	31.20
1994	24.80	24.90	23.10	20.80	32.20	29.10	31.40	24.30	34.00	31.30	42.50	29.80	28.80
1995	31.40	31.50	53.90	68.40	47.70	37.60	26.70	34.20	25.40	21.10	22.60	33.20	34.70
1996	35.20	36.10	52.80	37.00	37.70	35.70	24.30	27.20	23.80	29.20	30.00	31.10	33.00
1997	30.40	34.70	32.90	27.90	20.70	31.20	38.90	23.40	34.60	47.10	27.60	36.20	32.30
1998	39.10	43.20	49.10	44.70	35.50	26.40	23.20	26.10	32.30	25.90	41.40	47.20	34.50
1999	29.40	31.10	42.60	46.30	23.40	25.50	19.60	25.30	21.60	22.20	25.00	29.80	28.30
2000[1]	23.10	30.20	31.70	34.80	46.00	31.20	37.20	24.00	24.80	21.60	71.20		

[1] Preliminary.   *Source: National Agricultural Statistics Service, U.S. Department of Agriculture (NASS-USDA)*

Average Price Received by Growers for Celery in the United States   In Dollars Per Cwt.

Year	Jan.	Feb.	Mar.	Apr.	May	June	July	Aug.	Sept.	Oct.	Nov.	Dec.	Season Average
1993	24.00	35.60	27.40	16.50	14.40	9.45	9.41	11.80	14.20	13.30	11.50	11.10	14.80
1994	11.40	8.85	7.78	8.34	13.50	8.92	12.40	14.90	12.60	12.00	13.90	25.50	12.50
1995	24.30	26.00	20.60	33.30	24.50	14.40	11.50	10.50	16.50	13.20	12.90	11.40	16.30
1996	7.90	8.50	12.20	11.60	8.90	11.50	11.50	10.30	11.60	9.79	12.40	13.40	10.50
1997	16.20	16.20	12.30	10.50	15.40	9.89	19.30	17.00	14.30	13.40	18.40	19.10	14.70
1998	11.20	11.40	16.40	13.80	15.40	12.40	10.80	10.50	10.60	10.50	11.90	14.00	12.30
1999	9.51	8.47	8.35	10.20	12.80	18.30	14.10	10.50	11.00	9.43	13.60	14.00	11.70
2000[1]	19.20	16.00	12.90	21.20	25.60	29.10	18.60	21.80	16.80	13.90	19.50		

[1] Preliminary.   *Source: National Agricultural Statistics Service, U.S. Department of Agriculture (NASS-USDA)*

Average Price Received by Growers for Sweet Corn in the United States   In Dollars Per Cwt.

Year	Jan.	Feb.	Mar.	Apr.	May	June	July	Aug.	Sept.	Oct.	Nov.	Dec.	Season Average
1993	23.30	39.20	25.20	23.50	20.60	17.70	18.50	16.80	14.70	22.10	16.60	24.30	17.80
1994	26.80	17.60	26.40	17.90	20.40	20.20	19.10	11.90	15.30	19.70	19.90	26.00	17.20
1995	25.00	44.70	27.80	16.60	24.50	18.80	18.60	17.10	18.50	20.70	24.00	23.30	18.30
1996	29.90	30.20	28.90	21.90	17.50	14.00	18.90	17.40	16.70	17.90	19.40	17.70	16.90
1997	29.00	25.80	33.90	26.10	21.20	17.10	18.60	18.00	16.60	15.20	18.90	19.90	16.90
1998	18.70	31.60	24.20	19.60	17.10	14.00	16.40	16.40	18.10	25.40	23.80	19.80	17.20
1999	19.60	23.30	21.80	18.90	18.00	15.60	15.80	16.40	16.00	17.20	29.50	29.50	16.80
2000[1]	28.60	21.40	18.80	15.60	14.30	13.60	17.70	19.70	21.00	18.20	16.70		

[1] Preliminary.   *Source: National Agricultural Statistics Service, U.S. Department of Agriculture (NASS-USDA)*

Average Price Received by Growers for Head Lettuce in the United States   In Dollars Per Cwt.

Year	Jan.	Feb.	Mar.	Apr.	May	June	July	Aug.	Sept.	Oct.	Nov.	Dec.	Season Average
1991	10.20	6.63	10.40	9.00	23.10	9.51	6.70	8.32	11.30	10.80	21.40	9.66	11.40
1992	7.23	6.75	11.90	9.91	11.20	9.84	13.00	19.90	21.00	13.60	9.63	16.30	12.50
1993	10.80	18.70	14.30	37.80	12.60	11.50	18.80	14.90	16.80	12.20	10.50	8.28	16.00
1994	7.91	11.80	9.71	11.70	11.40	13.80	10.60	10.90	17.30	22.10	22.40	37.20	13.30
1995	13.40	9.32	27.00	48.20	47.00	15.60	12.60	15.20	25.60	13.30	11.50	16.10	23.50
1996	11.30	14.90	16.50	13.20	13.30	15.20	12.70	23.50	13.70	15.40	17.70	8.87	14.70
1997	14.90	9.58	13.50	15.70	10.40	14.90	17.10	22.80	22.30	34.80	22.20	25.10	17.50
1998	19.00	10.90	12.50	27.20	14.30	11.80	15.50	16.40	14.00	21.10	10.80	12.50	16.10
1999	10.30	15.50	16.50	20.50	14.00	11.40	12.70	11.90	13.10	13.10	11.20	12.00	13.30
2000[1]	14.60	9.28	14.00	22.90	23.50	13.40	15.00	19.20	29.40	16.10	18.00		

[1] Preliminary. Source: National Agricultural Statistics Service, U.S. Department of Agriculture (NASS-USDA)

Average Price Received by Growers for Tomatoes in the United States   In Dollars Per Cwt.

Year	Jan.	Feb.	Mar.	Apr.	May	June	July	Aug.	Sept.	Oct.	Nov.	Dec.	Season Average
1991	23.10	31.60	44.00	49.30	56.10	59.50	30.50	21.90	21.20	20.50	23.90	15.40	31.70
1992	40.50	76.00	80.70	32.40	16.70	21.90	28.30	23.50	29.30	60.10	39.10	34.30	35.80
1993	38.30	21.90	21.20	45.20	58.10	22.90	23.30	32.70	29.80	19.40	31.60	57.60	31.70
1994	41.50	19.30	24.50	16.50	20.60	31.30	26.90	30.60	22.70	28.50	31.20	37.40	27.40
1995	41.10	29.80	37.10	20.50	14.70	35.70	24.40	19.60	19.50	22.50	33.10	25.00	25.50
1996	18.40	40.00	81.70	50.50	24.40	24.20	26.00	22.10	23.40	28.30	29.70	30.40	28.10
1997	32.10	45.90	57.40	24.90	32.20	30.30	29.20	27.60	25.90	26.50	43.60	40.80	31.70
1998	26.40	44.00	34.00	37.20	36.50	29.00	40.90	25.10	28.30	43.00	42.10	42.20	35.20
1999	33.50	23.40	22.30	23.70	22.20	32.20	25.70	25.70	26.50	21.30	25.90	29.50	25.90
2000[1]	22.50	23.50	30.00	40.50	27.40	24.70	23.50	30.70	27.80	42.60	48.50		

[1] Preliminary. Source: National Agricultural Statistics Service, U.S. Department of Agriculture (NASS-USDA)

Frozen Vegetables: January 1 and July 1 Cold Storage Holdings in the U.S.   In Thousands of Pounds

Crop	1996 July 1	1997 Jan. 1	1997 July 1	1998 Jan. 1	1998 July 1	1999 Jan. 1	1999 July 1	2000 Jan. 1	2000 July 1	2001[1] Jan. 1
Asparagus	14,001	8,353	12,276	6,908	11,766	6,162	15,712	12,076	15,494	11,359
Lima Beans	33,350	60,696	28,015	72,221	37,659	75,469	38,390	71,993	29,220	46,930
Snap Beans	80,224	202,648	95,868	230,661	91,266	213,400	82,525	186,390	64,964	175,959
Broccoli	150,883	120,972	108,411	112,311	108,673	113,752	189,160	157,375	135,209	107,960
Brussels sprouts	9,533	16,314	7,975	19,926	7,485	18,745	15,145	25,649	14,913	19,632
Carrots	177,248	283,770	162,153	300,870	163,176	256,623	162,569	307,197	180,217	295,376
Cauliflower	38,355	54,376	32,785	58,512	38,028	5,298	32,894	57,812	37,597	44,974
Corn, Sweet[2]	215,553	494,308	203,740	532,645	228,765	673,315	255,389	585,866	226,980	570,912
Mixed vegetables	67,031	54,208	50,755	45,744	79,375	53,020	46,699	51,537	47,855	46,312
Okra	23,902	28,576	18,711	52,230	63,950	46,567	51,951	39,837	53,942	47,217
Onions	38,342	40,790	37,817	42,218	33,598	40,348	49,002	58,262	65,818	54,905
Black-eyed peas	3,529	9,795	2,952	9,344	6,654	8,039	5,598	6,517	3,517	4,438
Green peas	163,293	224,134	137,615	219,533	230,233	277,858	226,888	276,154	254,497	295,784
Peas and carrots	8,340	6,731	6,840	5,760	7,154	10,285	10,062	11,314	7,512	7,770
Spinach	86,281	46,890	104,073	67,092	10,369	69,232	142,617	73,349	99,820	50,765
Squash	44,785	58,749	48,184	75,397	64,966	70,272	49,942	58,254	41,097	42,572
Southern greens	32,363	26,936	16,681	20,771	37,660	32,765	39,455	26,944	36,237	38,934
Other vegetables	235,880	314,640	253,158	285,670	251,391	301,595	243,759	272,866	280,841	340,043
Total	1,422,893	2,185,704	1,317,049	2,303,007	1,539,168	2,317,745	1,657,757	2,279,392	1,595,730	2,201,842
Potatoes	1,057,470	1,131,642	1,271,316	1,163,547	1,316,450	1,151,294	1,234,126	1,165,389	1,186,310	1,189,663
Grand total	2,480,363	3,317,346	2,588,365	3,466,554	2,855,618	3,469,039	2,891,883	3,444,781	2,782,040	3,391,505

[1] Preliminary. [2] Cut-basis with cob corn converted to cut-basis using a factor of 0.4706. Source: National Agricultural Statistics Service, U.S. Department of Agriculture (NASS-USDA)

Wheat

U.S. wheat prices traded within a $0.50 per bushel range during calendar 2000, showing even less decisiveness than the 1999 trading range, basis Chicago futures. On balance, the bias was mildly positive as year-end prices were moderately higher than a year earlier, notwithstanding a July through September break that carried prices down about $0.35.

World wheat production in 2000/01 of 577 million metric tonnes compares with 584 million in 1999/00, and the record large 1997/98 crop of 610 million tonnes. Production in the mid-1990's averaged about 540 million tonnes. Global usage in 2000/01 of a record high 597 million tonnes compares with 594 million in 1999/00. For the third consecutive season a draw on world carryover stocks will be necessary; the projected ending 2000/01 carryover of a lower than expected 110 million tonnes compares with 127 million a year earlier, and the record high 139 million of three years ago. Still, carryover supplies appear adequate, certainly relative to the 108 million tonnes at year-end 1995/96, the lowest since the 1970's. The 2000/01 world stocks-to-usage ratio of 18 percent compares with 21 percent a year earlier.

Since the late 1980's, China has been the world's largest single wheat producer with nearly 20 percent of total production at 102 million metric tonnes in 2000/01 vs. 114 million in 1999/00. China appears to be allocating less acreage to wheat with 27 million hectare harvested in 2000/01 (the lowest total in years) vs. 28.9 million in 1999/00. However, muting the significance of the lower acreage, average yield has improved in recent years to 3.8 tonnes per hectare in 2000/01 vs. 3.9 tonnes in 1999/00, and a mid-1990's average of 3.5 tonnes. China's 2000/01 domestic wheat usage was forecast at 114 million tonnes vs. the record large 117 million in 1999/00. Despite the supply/demand imbalance, China's 2000/01 imports of only 2 million tonnes pale relative to earlier in the 1990's when imports over 10 million tonnes were not unusual. World prices, however, are still highly sensitive to news, real or otherwise, of possible Chinese import needs, but any resultant higher prices tend to quickly brake their apparent interest. China's carryover stocks have dropped sharply in the past few years although the marketplace tends to view the government's official totals as suspect. The ending 2000/01 carryover of 14.7 million tonnes compares with 25.2 million a year earlier and 33.5 million at year-end 1997/98.

The overall persistent decline during the 1990's of the former U.S.S.R.'s wheat production may have run its course. 2000/01 production estimates in the key republics were: Russia, 36.5 million tonnes vs. 31 million in 1999/00; Kazakstan at 9 million vs. 11 million; and the Ukraine at 11 million vs. 13 million, respectively. However, any major improvements in average yield throughout the region remain elusive. The Russian Federation was once the world's largest importer. Now, Russia's 2000/01 imports of 2.5 million tonnes compare to 4.8 million in 1999/00 and 14 million tonnes early in the 1990's. The decline is directly attributable to a chronic lack of foreign exchange and/or credit. The decline in consumption among the Russian republics shows signs of slowing. Russia's usage is estimated at 37 million tonnes in 2000/01 vs. 35.5 million in 1999/00, and

more than 50 million on average in the early 1990's. The Ukraine's 2000/01 forecast usage of 12 million tonnes is marginally lower than in 1999/00, and compares with the early 1990's average of more than 20 million tonnes.

The 2000/01 world wheat trade is forecast at a near record large 105 million tonnes vs. 108 million in 1999/00. Four countries generally account for about two-thirds of total exports: Argentina, Australia, Canada, and the U.S., with the European Union supplying much of the balance. The U.S., the largest exporter, is forecast to ship 30.5 million tonnes in 2000/01 vs. 29.5 million in 1999/00. Canadian 1999/00 exports were forecast at 18 million tonnes vs. 19.4 million in 1999/00. E.U. exports of 16 million tonnes were about unchanged. Australian exports of 16.5 million tonnes in 2000/01 compare with 17.1 million in 1999/00, and a mid-1990's average of less than 10 million. Importing nations are scattered. Among those expected to take at least 6 million tonnes in 2000/01 are Brazil, Egypt, and Iran.

The U.S. 2000/01 wheat crop (June/May) of 2.22 billion bushels compares with 2.30 million in 1999/00. The decline reflects an average yield of 41.9 bushels per acre vs. 42.7, and a drop in harvested acreage to 53 million acres from 53.9 million, respectively. Winter wheat accounts for more than one-half of U.S. production with Kansas the largest producing state. North Dakota is the largest spring wheat and durum producing state. The 2000/01 durum wheat crop of 110 million bushels compares with 100 million in 1999/00. Spring wheat production was put at 550 million bushels vs. 502 million, respectively.

The U.S. imports some wheat, mostly from Canada. Carry-in stocks as of June 1, 2000, of 950 million bushels compare with 946 million a year earlier. The U.S. wheat supply for 2000/01 of 3.27 billion bushels compares with 3.34 billion in 1999/00. Total usage in 2000/01 of 2.38 billion bushels compares with 2.39 billion in 1999/00. Exports generally account for almost one-half the total disappearance. Food use takes about three-quarters of domestic usage, feed about 20 percent, and seed the balance. If the 2000/01 supply/demand estimates are realized, ending stocks on May 31, 2001 would fall to 862 million bushels, lowering the stock to use ratio down to 36 percent vs. 40 percent a year earlier. This ratio is often used to forecast prices; the smaller it is the greater the likelihood for higher prices as the crop year progresses.

The 2000/01 average price received by farmers was forecast to range from $2.45 to $2.75 a bushel vs. $2.48 in 1999/00.

Futures Markets

Wheat futures and options are traded on the Mercado a Termino de Buenos Aires (MAT), Sydney Futures Exchange (SFE), London International Financial Futures and Options Exchange (LIFFE), Marche a Terme International de France (MATIF), Budapest Commodity Exchange (BCE), the Chicago Board of Trade (CBOT), the Kansas City Board of Trade (KCBT), the Minneapolis Grain Exchange (MGE), the Mid-America Commodity Exchange (MidAm), and the Winnipeg Commodity Exchange (WCE).

World Production of Wheat   In Thousands of Metric Tons

Year	Argentina	Australia	Canada	China	France	Germany	India	Pakistan	Russia	Turkey	United Kingdom	United States	World Total
1991-2	9,880	10,557	31,946	96,000	34,594	16,610	55,134	14,565	38,900	16,500	14,400	53,891	542,919
1992-3	9,800	16,184	29,871	101,590	32,777	15,542	55,690	15,684	46,170	15,500	14,000	67,135	562,407
1993-4	9,700	16,479	27,232	106,390	29,253	15,767	57,210	16,157	43,500	16,500	12,890	65,220	558,740
1994-5	11,300	8,903	23,122	99,300	30,549	16,481	59,840	15,212	32,100	14,700	13,314	63,167	524,072
1995-6	8,600	16,504	25,037	102,215	30,862	17,763	65,470	17,002	30,100	15,500	14,310	59,404	538,531
1996-7	15,900	23,702	29,801	110,570	35,940	18,922	62,097	16,907	34,900	16,000	16,102	61,980	582,801
1997-8	14,800	19,417	24,280	123,289	33,764	19,827	69,350	16,650	44,200	16,000	15,018	67,534	609,439
1998-9[1]	12,400	22,108	24,076	109,726	39,793	20,188	66,350	18,694	27,000	18,000	15,470	69,327	588,391
1999-00[2]	15,500	25,012	26,850	113,880	37,009	19,615	70,780	17,854	31,000	16,500	14,870	62,569	587,247
2000-1[3]	16,500	19,500	26,800	102,000	37,500	21,600	74,300	21,000	36,500	17,500	16,800	60,512	580,347

[1] Preliminary.   [2] Estimate.   [3] Forecast.   *Source: Foreign Agricultural Service, U.S. Department of Agriculture (FAS-USDA)*

World Supply and Demand of Wheat   In Millions of Metric Tons/Hectares

Crop Year	Area Harvested	Yield	Production	World Trade	Utilization Total	Ending Stocks	Stocks as a % of Utilization
1991-2	222.5	2.44	542.9	111.2	555.5	132.5	23.8
1992-3	222.9	2.52	562.4	113.0	550.3	144.5	26.3
1993-4	222.0	2.52	558.7	101.6	561.6	141.6	25.2
1994-5	214.5	2.44	524.0	101.4	547.4	118.2	21.6
1995-6	218.7	2.46	538.4	99.5	548.2	108.4	19.8
1996-7	230.0	2.53	581.9	103.8	576.9	113.4	19.7
1997-8	228.0	2.67	609.2	104.0	583.9	138.7	23.8
1998-9[1]	224.7	2.62	588.2	102.0	590.1	136.8	23.2
1999-00[2]	216.8	2.71	587.9	112.4	598.7	126.0	21.0
2000-1[3]	215.4	2.69	579.5	106.8	596.6	108.9	18.3

[1] Preliminary.   [2] Estimate.   [3] Forecast.   *Source: Foreign Agricultural Service, U.S. Department of Agriculture (FAS-USDA)*

Salient Statistics of Wheat in the United States

Crop Year	Planting Intentions	Acreage Harvested — Winter	Spring	All	Average - All Yield Per Acre in Bushels	Value of Production $1,000	Foreign Trade[5] Domestic Exports[2]	Imports[3]	Per Capita[4] Consumption Flour	Cereal
	← 1,000 Acres →						← In Millions of Bushels →		← In Pounds →	
1991-2	69,881	39,506	18,297	57,803	34.3	5,954,912	1,282.3	40.7	137.0	4.5
1992-3	72,219	42,123	20,638	62,761	39.3	8,009,711	1,353.6	69.4	139.0	4.7
1993-4	72,168	43,811	18,901	62,712	38.2	7,647,527	1,227.8	108.9	143.0	5.0
1994-5	70,349	41,335	20,415	61,770	37.6	7,968,237	1,188.3	91.9	144.0	5.2
1995-6	69,132	40,972	19,973	60,945	35.8	9,787,213	1,241.1	67.9	142.0	5.4
1996-7	75,105	39,574	23,245	62,819	36.3	9,782,238	1,001.5	92.3	149.0	5.4
1997-8	70,412	41,340	21,500	62,840	39.5	8,286,741	1,040.4	94.9	150.0	5.4
1998-9	65,821	40,126	18,876	59,002	43.2	6,780,623	1,042.2	103.0	146.0	5.4
1999-00	62,714	35,486	18,337	53,823	42.7	5,593,989	1,089.5	94.5	----	----
2000-1[1]	62,529	35,022	18,006	56,028	41.9	5,970,197	1,100.0	95.0	----	----

[1] Preliminary.   [2] Includes flour milled from imported wheat.   [3] Total wheat, flour & other products.   [4] Civilian only.   [5] Year beginning June.
Source: Economic Research Service, U.S. Department of Agriculture (ERS-USDA)

Supply and Distribution of Wheat in the United States   In Millions of Bushels

Crop Year Beginning June 1	Supply — Stocks, June 1 On Farms	Mills, Elevators[3]	Totl Stocks	Production	Imports[4]	Total Supply	Domestic Disappearance — Food	Seed	Feed & Residual[5]	Total	Exports[4]	Total Disappearance
1991-2	341.2	524.7	868.1	1,980.1	40.7	2,889.0	789.5	97.7	244.5	1,131.7	1,282.3	2,413.9
1992-3	144.6	327.2	475.0	2,466.8	70.0	3,011.8	834.8	99.1	193.6	1,127.5	1,353.6	2,481.2
1993-4	183.8	345.3	530.7	2,396.4	108.8	3,035.9	871.7	96.3	271.7	1,239.7	1,227.8	2,467.4
1994-5	175.3	393.2	568.5	2,321.0	91.9	2,981.4	853.0	89.0	344.5	1,286.6	1,188.3	2,474.8
1995-6	163.4	343.2	506.6	2,182.7	67.9	2,757.2	882.9	103.5	153.7	1,140.1	1,241.1	2,381.2
1996-7	74.6	301.4	376.0	2,277.4	92.3	2,745.7	890.8	102.3	307.6	1,300.7	1,001.4	2,302.1
1997-8	154.6	289.0	443.6	2,481.5	94.9	3,020.0	914.1	92.6	250.5	1,257.1	1,040.4	2,297.5
1998-9	224.2	498.3	722.5	2,547.3	103.0	3,372.8	907.3	80.7	396.6	1,384.5	1,042.4	2,426.9
1999-00[1]	277.7	668.2	945.9	2,299.0	94.5	3,339.4	924.7	91.6	283.8	1,300.1	1,089.5	2,389.7
2000-1[2]	226.8	723.0	949.7	2,223.4	95.0	3,268.2	945.0	84.0	300.0	1,329.0	1,100.0	2,429.0

[1] Preliminary.   [2] Estimate.   [3] Also warehouses and all off-farm storage not otherwise designated, including flour mills.   [4] Imports & exports are for wheat, including flour & other products in terms of wheat.   [5] Mostly feed use.   *Source: Economic Research Service, U.S. Department of Agriculture*

WHEAT

Stocks, Production and Exports of Wheat in the United States, by Class   In Millions of Bushels

Year Beginning June 1	Hard Spring Stocks June 1	Hard Spring Pro-duction	Hard Spring Exports[3]	Durum[2] Stocks June 1	Durum[2] Pro-duction	Durum[2] Exports[3]	Hard Winter Stocks June 1	Hard Winter Pro-duction	Hard Winter Exports[3]	Soft Red Winter Stocks June 1	Soft Red Winter Pro-duction	Soft Red Winter Exports[3]	White Stocks June 1	White Pro-duction	White Exports[3]
1991-2	279	431	380	62	104	45	360	901	559	80	325	105	87	219	193
1992-3	131	707	438	55	100	47	194	967	464	41	427	210	54	266	195
1993-4	171	512	266	49	71	54	204	1,066	486	43	401	173	64	347	249
1994-5	201	515	292	28	97	40	227	971	422	45	434	212	67	304	222
1995-6	193	475	230	26	102	39	194	825	384	37	456	250	57	325	238
1996-7	106	631	300	25	116	38	154	759	286	35	420	140	55	352	237
1997-8	166	491	240	31	88	57	143	1,098	358	45	472	180	59	332	205
1998-9	220	486	247	26	138	40	307	1,180	453	80	443	105	90	301	198
1999-00	233	448	230	55	99	44	435	1,051	486	136	454	170	87	247	160
2000-1[1]	218	499	235	50	110	50	458	844	430	133	471	185	91	301	200

[1] Preliminary.   [2] Includes Red Durum.   [3] Includes four made from U.S. wheat & shipments to territories.   *Source: Economic Research Service, U.S. Department of Agriculture (ERS-USDA)*

Seeded Acreage, Yield and Production of all Wheat in the United States

Year	Seeded Acreage -- 1,000 Acres Winter	Other Spring	Durum	All	Yield Per Harvested Acre (Bushels) Winter	Other Spring	Durum	All	Production (1,000,000 Bushels) Winter	Other Spring	Durum	All
1991	51,024	15,604	3,253	69,881	34.7	33.4	32.5	34.3	1,371.6	504.6	104.0	1,980.1
1992	50,922	18,750	2,547	72,219	38.2	41.8	39.7	39.3	1,609.3	757.6	99.9	2,466.8
1993	51,587	18,340	2,241	72,168	40.2	33.7	33.6	38.2	1,760.1	565.8	70.5	2,396.4
1994	49,197	18,329	2,823	70,349	40.2	31.8	35.6	37.6	1,661.9	562.3	96.7	2,321.0
1995	48,686	17,010	3,436	69,132	37.7	32.2	30.5	35.8	1,544.7	535.7	102.3	2,182.6
1996	51,445	20,030	3,630	75,105	37.1	35.1	32.6	36.3	1,469.6	691.7	116.1	2,277.4
1997	47,985	19,117	3,310	70,412	44.6	29.9	27.6	39.5	1,845.5	548.2	87.8	2,481.5
1998	46,449	15,567	3,805	65,821	46.9	34.9	37.0	43.2	1,880.7	528.5	138.1	2,547.3
1999	43,331	15,348	4,035	62,714	47.8	34.1	27.8	42.7	1,696.6	503.1	99.3	2,299.0
2000[1]	43,348	15,244	3,937	62,529	44.6	38.2	30.7	41.9	1,562.7	550.9	109.8	2,223.4

[1] Preliminary.   *Source: Economic Research Service, U.S. Department of Agriculture (ERS-USDA)*

Production of Winter Wheat in the United States, by State   In Thousands of Bushels

Year	Colorado	Idaho	Illinois	Kansas	Missouri	Montana	Neb-raska	Ohio	Okla-homa	Oregon	Texas	Wash-ington	Total
1991	71,300	49,000	44,800	363,000	48,000	76,000	67,200	52,920	135,000	41,600	84,000	40,600	1,371,617
1992	70,500	55,250	62,100	363,800	64,800	65,250	55,500	59,095	168,150	42,900	129,200	102,000	1,609,284
1993	94,350	67,150	68,200	388,500	53,200	102,900	73,500	52,520	156,600	61,060	118,400	162,500	1,760,143
1994	76,500	56,880	50,400	433,200	50,400	64,750	71,400	68,440	143,100	55,680	75,400	124,200	1,661,943
1995	102,600	58,520	68,110	286,000	47,970	54,800	86,100	73,810	109,200	57,750	75,600	133,300	1,544,653
1996	70,400	68,800	41,800	255,200	48,750	61,380	73,500	51,870	93,100	58,680	75,400	164,500	1,469,618
1997	86,400	68,800	66,490	501,400	58,320	55,100	70,300	68,670	169,600	53,790	118,900	141,900	1,845,528
1998	99,450	63,140	57,600	494,900	57,500	48,750	82,800	74,240	198,900	52,930	136,500	136,500	1,880,733
1999	103,200	53,960	60,600	432,400	44,160	36,860	81,600	72,100	150,500	29,610	122,400	96,860	1,696,580
2000[1]	68,150	65,700	52,440	347,800	49,400	44,550	59,400	79,920	142,800	45,260	66,000	131,400	1,562,733

[1] Preliminary.   *Source: Crop Reporting Board, U.S. Department of Agriculture (CRB-USDA)*

Official Winter Wheat Crop Production Reports in the United States   In Thousands of Bushels

Crop Year	May 1	June 1	July 1	August 1	September 1	Current December	Final
1991-2	1,495,943	1,449,418	1,361,316	1,371,946	1,372,182	-----	1,372,617
1992-3	1,618,017	1,618,017	1,573,901	1,600,931	-----	-----	1,609,284
1993-4	1,807,657	1,824,062	1,821,345	1,788,005	1,788,005	-----	1,760,143
1994-5	1,657,938	1,674,563	1,658,426	1,670,436	1,670,436	-----	1,661,043
1995-6	1,638,211	1,608,396	1,529,950	1,552,230	1,552,230	-----	1,544,653
1996-7	1,363,851	1,369,861	1,484,836	1,494,716	-----	-----	1,477,058
1997-8	1,561,470	1,603,580	1,780,554	1,855,474	-----	-----	1,845,528
1998-9	1,706,784	1,743,294	1,898,719	1,914,359	-----	-----	1,880,733
1999-00	1,614,799	1,611,559	1,673,222	1,688,582	-----	-----	1,696,580
2000-1[1]	1,648,805	1,621,966	1,588,376	1,594,321	-----	-----	1,562,733

[1] Preliminary.   *Source: Crop Reporting Board, U.S. Department of Agriculture (CRB-USDA)*

Production of All Spring Wheat in the United States, by State   In Thousands of Bushels

| | | Durum Wheat | | | | | Other Spring Wheat | | | | | | |
Year	Arizona	California	Montana	North Dakota	South Dakota	Total Durum	Idaho	Minnesota	Montana	North Dakota	Oregon	South Dakota	Washington	Total Other
1991	3,705	3,360	5,907	88,350	1,675	103,957	32,660	64,170	81,600	212,350	2,300	49,000	58,000	504,565
1992	3,740	5,115	4,851	81,700	990	99,906	44,840	137,500	79,050	382,200	4,900	85,000	17,640	757,608
1993	4,500	3,800	3,534	57,970	432	70,476	43,200	69,750	99,900	274,350	3,900	54,540	15,080	565,821
1994	8,554	5,605	5,340	76,375	598	96,747	43,400	70,000	100,500	278,775	2,900	51,480	9,800	562,291
1995	8,514	6,800	7,950	77,760	896	102,280	44,800	70,400	133,000	221,400	5,928	33,600	20,470	535,658
1996	14,760	13,800	7,000	79,380	720	116,090	50,400	105,000	106,600	313,500	6,405	83,250	18,170	691,680
1997	8,010	13,680	7,540	57,860	513	87,783	45,030	75,200	118,900	210,000	6,600	63,000	23,220	548,155
1998	15,120	15,750	12,040	94,400	624	138,119	39,270	78,720	108,000	211,200	4,560	59,200	20,925	528,469
1999	7,275	8,925	9,450	72,000	1,512	99,322	50,560	78,000	108,000	168,000	5,049	59,850	27,280	503,108
2000[1]	8,075	9,700	13,160	78,300	468	109,805	42,750	95,550	77,500	230,400	5,750	60,040	33,480	550,902

[1] Preliminary.   Source: Crop Reporting Board, U.S. Department of Agriculture (CRB-USDA)

Grindings of Wheat by Mills in the United States   In Millions of Bushels (60 Pounds Each)

Year	July	Aug.	Sept.	Oct.	Nov.	Dec.	Jan.	Feb.	Mar.	Apr.	May	June	Total
1991-2	65.3	71.2	67.7	72.2	73.5	65.6	65.7	66.0	65.6	67.3	67.0	67.2	814.3
1992-3	70.0	77.3	71.9	77.9	71.9	65.5	68.1	70.0	76.2	72.0	69.6	67.9	858.2
1993-4	69.2	75.2	74.1	75.8	77.0	76.3	70.0	68.3	81.1	73.0	73.0	70.6	883.8
1994-5	68.9	78.7	76.3	77.9	75.9	71.1	69.0	65.2	76.9	66.6	74.7	71.9	873.1
1995-6	69.8	77.8	74.2	78.4	74.8	70.0	70.1	72.4	72.1	69.4	72.6	67.7	869.1
1996-7	73.6	77.4	75.1	82.7	73.7	71.3	69.6	66.9	70.3	73.2	72.5	72.2	878.6
1997-8	76.4	75.8	78.4	82.7	75.3	74.8	-----	215.5	-----	-----	216.6	-----	895.5
1998-9	-----	224.7	-----	-----	238.6	-----	-----	213.5	-----	-----	228.0	-----	904.9
1999-00	-----	234.0	-----	-----	242.2	-----	-----	223.2	-----	-----	224.4	-----	923.7
2000-1[1]	-----	242.7	-----	-----	245.5	-----	-----			-----	-----	-----	976.5

[1] Preliminary.   Source: Bureau of the Census, U.S. Department of Commerce

Wheat Stocks in the United States   In Millions of Bushels

| | On Farms | | | | Off Farms | | | | Total Stocks | | | |
Year	Mar. 1	June 1	Sept. 1	Dec. 1	Mar. 1	June 1	Sept. 1	Dec. 1	Mar. 1	June 1	Sept. 1	Dec. 1
1991	532.9	341.2	828.0	564.8	863.3	524.7	1,212.7	877.3	1,396.3	865.9	2,040.7	1,442.1
1992	275.6	144.6	979.4	672.0	611.7	327.2	1,128.2	918.5	887.2	471.9	2,107.6	1,590.5
1993	378.0	183.8	987.0	653.1	670.3	346.8	1,145.6	932.6	1,048.3	530.7	2,132.6	1,585.7
1994	363.2	175.3	859.8	575.6	664.8	393.2	1,209.7	920.6	1,028.0	568.5	2,069.5	1,491.1
1995	335.3	163.4	743.6	477.0	633.8	343.2	1,137.5	861.3	969.1	506.6	1,881.1	1,338.3
1996	220.6	74.6	824.5	584.2	602.9	301.4	899.7	634.7	823.5	376.0	1,724.2	1,218.8
1997	320.8	154.6	794.4	604.0	501.1	289.0	1,282.0	1,015.2	821.8	443.6	2,076.3	1,619.2
1998	399.9	224.2	885.7	680.2	766.6	498.3	1,499.6	1,215.5	1,166.6	722.5	2,385.3	1,895.7
1999	471.2	277.7	888.1	647.4	979.2	668.2	1,557.0	1,236.3	1,450.4	945.9	2,445.0	1,883.7
2000[1]	424.7	226.8	808.4	623.4	991.8	723.0	1,544.3	1,178.4	1,416.5	949.7	2,352.7	1,801.8

[1] Preliminary.   Source: National Agricultural Statistics Service, U.S. Department of Agriculture (NASS-USDA)

Wheat Supply and Distribution in Canada, Australia and Argentina   In Millions of Metric Tons

| | Canada (Year Beginning Aug. 1) | | | | | Australia (Year Beginning Oct. 1) | | | | | Argentina (Year Beginning Dec. 1) | | | | |
| | Supply | | | Disappearance | | Supply | | | Disappearance | | Supply | | | Disappearance | |
Crop Year	Stocks Aug. 1	New Crop	Total Supply	Domestic	Exports[3]	Stocks Oct. 1	New Crop	Total Supply	Domestic	Exports[3]	Stocks Dec. 1	New Crop	Total Supply	Domestic	Exports[3]
1991-2	10.3	31.9	42.2	7.8	24.5	2.8	10.6	13.4	3.4	7.1	.8	9.9	10.7	4.6	5.8
1992-3	10.1	29.9	40.0	8.1	19.7	2.9	16.2	19.1	4.2	9.9	.3	9.8	10.1	4.3	5.9
1993-4	12.2	27.2	39.4	9.3	19.1	5.0	16.5	21.5	4.1	13.7	0	9.7	9.7	4.3	5.0
1994-5	11.1	23.1	34.2	7.8	20.9	3.7	8.9	12.7	3.9	6.4	.4	11.3	11.7	4.3	7.3
1995-6	5.7	25.0	30.7	7.8	16.3	2.4	16.5	18.9	3.7	13.3	.2	8.6	8.8	4.2	4.5
1996-7	6.7	29.8	36.5	8.2	19.5	1.5	22.9	24.4	3.3	19.2	.2	15.9	16.1	5.1	10.2
1997-8	9.0	24.3	33.3	7.3	20.1	2.4	19.2	21.6	5.0	15.3	.8	14.8	15.6	4.5	10.7
1998-9	6.0	24.1	30.1	8.1	14.7	1.3	21.5	22.8	4.5	16.5	.4	12.4	12.8	4.1	8.4
1999-00[1]	7.4	26.9	34.3	7.9	19.2	1.9	25.0	26.9	5.0	17.8	.3	15.5	15.8	4.1	11.6
2000-1[2]	7.4	26.8	34.2	8.2	19.0	4.1	20.5	24.6	5.6	15.5	.2	16.5	16.7	4.5	12.0

[1] Preliminary.   [2] Forecast.   [3] Including flour.   Source: Foreign Agricultural Service, U.S. Department of Agriculture (FAS-USDA)

WHEAT

Quarterly Supply and Disappearance of Wheat in the United States   In Millions of Bushels

Crop Year Beginning June 1	Beginning Stocks	Production	Imports[3]	Total Supply	Food	Seed	Feed & Residual[7]	Total	Exports[3]	Total Disappearance	Gov't Owned[4]	Privately Owned[5]	Total Stocks
1990-1	536.5	2,729.8	36.4	3,302.6	789.8	92.9	482.4	1,365.1	1,069.5	2,434.6	162.7	705.4	868.1
June-Aug.	536.5	2,729.8	8.0	3,274.2	194.1	1.7	399.7	595.5	267.7	863.2	104.6	2,306.5	2,411.1
Sept.-Nov.	2,409.5	-----	13.4	2,424.5	210.6	62.9	-38.3	235.2	279.4	514.6	129.9	1,780.0	1,909.9
Dec.-Feb.	1,908.0	-----	7.8	1,917.7	191.0	2.1	101.5	294.6	225.5	520.1	152.5	1,245.2	1,397.7
Mar.-May	1,396.0	-----	7.2	1,404.9	194.1	26.3	19.5	239.9	296.9	536.8	162.7	705.4	868.1
1991-2	868.1	1,980.1	40.7	2,889.0	789.5	97.2	244.5	1,131.2	1,282.3	2,413.5	152.0	323.0	475.0
June-Aug.	868.1	1,980.1	7.8	2,856.1	189.4	1.2	359.1	549.7	251.7	801.4	162.8	1,891.9	2,054.7
Sept.-Nov.	2,054.7	-----	7.3	2,062.0	213.0	62.2	-26.9	248.3	365.9	614.2	160.7	1,287.1	1,447.8
Dec.-Feb.	1,447.8	-----	10.7	1,458.5	192.9	2.4	-.5	194.8	371.7	566.5	156.9	735.1	892.0
Mar.-May	892.0	-----	14.9	906.9	194.2	31.9	-87.3	138.8	293.0	431.8	152.0	323.0	475.0
1992-3	475.0	2,466.8	70.0	3,011.8	834.3	99.1	194.2	1,127.6	1,353.6	2,481.2	150.0	380.7	530.7
June-Aug.	475.0	2,466.8	20.1	2,962.0	212.1	1.4	345.3	558.8	282.6	841.4	151.6	1,969.0	2,120.6
Sept.-Nov.	2,120.6	-----	16.4	2,137.0	218.8	63.4	-81.9	200.3	345.0	545.3	151.1	1,440.6	1,591.7
Dec.-Feb.	1,591.7	-----	17.4	1,609.1	196.7	2.6	5.2	204.5	356.3	560.8	150.4	897.9	1,048.3
Mar.-May	1,048.3	-----	16.1	1,064.4	206.7	31.7	-74.4	164.0	369.7	533.7	150.0	380.7	530.7
1993-4	530.7	2,396.4	108.8	3,035.9	871.7	96.3	271.7	1,239.7	1,227.8	2,467.4	150.3	418.2	568.5
June-Aug.	530.7	2,396.4	14.6	2,941.7	211.3	1.3	295.8	508.4	300.7	809.1	149.9	1,982.7	2,132.6
Sept.-Nov.	2,132.6	-----	30.1	2,162.7	225.3	60.9	-38.5	247.7	329.2	577.0	150.3	1,435.4	1,585.7
Dec.-Feb.	1,585.7	-----	26.9	1,612.6	211.0	2.3	39.0	252.3	332.3	584.6	150.4	877.6	1,028.0
Mar.-May	1,028.0	-----	37.2	1,065.2	224.1	31.8	-24.7	231.2	265.5	496.7	150.3	418.2	568.5
1994-5	568.5	2,321.0	92.0	2,981.4	852.5	89.2	344.9	1,286.6	1,188.3	2,474.9	142.1	364.5	506.6
June-Aug.	568.5	2,321.0	30.7	2,920.2	213.2	1.6	376.3	591.1	259.6	850.7	146.4	1,923.1	2,069.5
Sept.-Nov.	2,069.5	-----	21.4	2,090.9	229.3	61.1	-28.8	261.6	338.2	599.8	142.8	1,348.3	1,491.1
Dec.-Feb.	1,491.1	-----	17.7	1,508.8	201.5	2.2	25.6	229.3	310.4	539.7	142.3	826.8	969.1
Mar.-May	969.1	-----	22.2	991.2	208.5	24.3	-28.2	204.6	280.1	484.7	142.1	364.5	506.6
1995-6	506.6	2,182.6	67.9	2,757.1	882.9	104.1	153.0	1,139.9	1,241.1	2,381.1	118.2	257.8	376.0
June-Aug.	506.6	2,182.6	22.7	2,711.9	215.3	8.0	305.0	528.3	302.5	830.8	141.5	1,739.6	1,881.1
Sept.-Nov.	1,881.1	-----	16.3	1,897.4	232.2	64.9	-98.7	198.3	360.8	559.1	141.2	1,197.1	1,338.3
Dec.-Feb.	1,338.3	-----	11.8	1,350.0	215.8	3.0	13.3	232.1	294.5	526.6	137.5	686.0	823.5
Mar.-May	823.5	-----	17.2	840.7	219.6	28.2	-66.5	181.3	283.4	464.6	118.2	257.8	376.0
1996-7	376.0	2,277.4	92.3	2,745.7	890.7	102.3	307.6	1,300.6	1,001.5	2,302.1	93.0	350.6	443.6
June-Aug.	376.0	2,277.4	14.9	2,668.3	223.7	8.7	377.5	610.0	334.1	944.1	109.5	1,614.7	1,724.2
Sept.-Nov.	1,724.2	-----	20.7	1,744.9	233.8	59.9	-76.0	217.8	308.3	526.1	96.1	1,122.7	1,218.8
Dec.-Feb.	1,218.8	-----	27.1	1,245.9	212.7	1.8	30.3	244.7	179.3	424.1	95.3	726.5	821.8
Mar.-May	821.8	-----	29.7	851.6	220.5	31.8	-24.2	228.1	179.8	407.9	93.0	350.6	443.6
1997-8	443.6	2,481.5	94.9	3,020.0	914.1	92.5	250.5	1,257.1	1,040.4	2,297.5	94.2	628.3	722.5
June-Aug.	443.6	2,481.5	22.7	2,947.8	227.9	3.1	352.2	583.2	288.2	871.4	93.2	1,983.1	2,076.3
Sept.-Nov.	2,076.3	-----	22.8	2,099.1	238.7	58.6	-113.4	183.9	296.0	479.9	93.1	1,526.1	1,619.2
Dec.-Feb.	1,619.2	-----	23.8	1,643.0	219.2	2.1	.3	221.6	254.9	476.4	93.0	1,073.6	1,166.6
Mar.-May	1,166.6	-----	25.7	1,192.2	228.3	28.7	11.4	268.4	201.3	469.8	94.2	628.3	722.5
1998-9	722.5	2,547.3	103.0	3,372.8	907.3	80.7	396.6	1,384.5	1,042.4	2,426.9	127.9	818.0	945.9
June-Aug.	722.5	2,547.3	24.4	3,294.2	225.7	1.0	424.9	651.6	257.3	908.9	99.8	2,285.5	2,385.3
Sept.-Nov.	2,385.3	-----	23.9	2,409.2	240.7	55.0	-73.9	221.8	291.8	513.6	126.6	1,769.1	1,895.7
Dec.-Feb.	1,895.7	-----	27.7	1,923.4	212.7	1.4	12.0	226.2	246.8	473.0	124.2	1,326.2	1,450.4
Mar.-May	1,450.4	-----	27.0	1,477.4	228.1	23.2	33.6	284.9	246.6	531.5	127.9	818.0	945.9
1999-00[1]	946.0	2,299.0	95.0	3,339.0	925.0	92.0	284.0	1,301.0	1,090.0	2,391.0	100.0	897.4	950.0
June-Aug.	946.0	2,299.0	31.0	3,276.0	230.0	6.0	270.0	506.0	324.0	830.0	132.2	2,312.8	2,445.0
Sept.-Nov.	2,445.0	-----	19.0	2,465.0	241.0	55.0	-8.0	288.0	291.0	579.0	115.0	1,764.0	1,886.0
Dec.-Feb.	1,886.0	-----	19.0	1,905.0	221.0	2.0	31.0	254.0	236.0	490.0			1,415.0
Mar.-May	1,412.0	-----	25.0	1,440.0	232.0	28.0	-9.0	251.0	239.0	490.0			950.0
2000-1[2]	950.0	2,223.0	95.0	3,268.0	945.0	84.0	300.0	1,329.0	1,100.0	2,429.0			839.0
June-Aug.	950.0	2,223.0	20.0	3,194.0	237.0	1.0	317.0	555.0	286.0	841.0			2,353.0
Sept.-Nov.	2,353.0	----	25.0	2,378.0	249.0	51.0	-17.0	283.0	293.0	576.0			1,802.0

[1] Preliminary.   [2] Forecast.   [3] Imports & exports include flour and other products expressed in wheat equivalent.   [4] Uncommitted, Government only.
[5] Includes total loans.   [6] Less than 50,000 bushels.   [7] Includes alcoholic beverages.   *Source: Economic Research Service,*
U.S. Department of Agriculture (ERS-USDA)

Wheat Government Loan Program Data in the United States   Loan Rates (Cents Per Bushel)

| | | | | Farm Loan Prices | | | | | | Stocks Ending May 31 | | | | |
| | | | | | | | Placed | | Acquired by CCC | | | Total | ---- Outstanding ---- | | |
Crop Year Beginning June 1	National Average	Target Rate	Corn Belt (Soft Red Winter)	Central & Southern Plains (Hard Winter)	Northern Plains (Spring & Durum)	Pacific Northwest (White)	Under Loan	% of Production	Under Program	Total Stocks	CCC Stocks	CCC Loans	Farmer-Owned Reserve	"Free"
									In Millions of Bushels					
1992-3	221	400	232	220	221	237	240	9.8	0.1	531	150	47	28	353
1993-4	245	400	251	243	245	269	258	14.7	0.3	569	150	0	6	413
1994-5	258	400	253	257	258	271	231	10.0	0	507	142	0	0	365
1995-6	258	400	254	258	258	276	114	5.2	0	376	118	13	0	258
1996-7	258	NA	253	257	258	271	194	8.1	0	444	93	72	0	351
1997-8	258	NA	253	257	258	271	248		0	723	94	134	0	629
1998-9[1]	258	NA	253	257	258	271			0	946	128	140	0	818
1999-00[2]	258	NA							0	950	104	50	0	846

[1] Preliminary.   [2] Estimate.   [3] The national average loan rate at the farm as a percentage of the parity-priced wheat at the beginning of the marketing year.   [4] Beginning with the 1996-7 marketing year, target prices are no longer applicable.   NA = Not avaliable.   *Source: Agricultural Marketing Service, U.S. Department of Agriculture (AMS-USDA)*

Exports of Wheat (Only)[2] from the United States   In Thousands of Bushels

Year	June	July	Aug.	Sept.	Oct.	Nov.	Dec.	Jan.	Feb.	Mar.	Apr.	May	Total
1992-3	75,045	96,382	99,290	92,723	132,232	108,235	111,389	111,584	118,607	118,782	126,845	104,540	1,295,653
1993-4	85,874	103,836	100,516	104,732	100,618	112,667	121,900	109,389	87,250	96,873	71,575	82,838	1,178,068
1994-5	73,364	66,314	103,941	117,555	101,450	107,549	104,139	93,735	97,478	98,876	85,251	75,006	1,124,658
1995-6	78,355	88,649	119,797	131,424	117,679	105,535	99,175	96,085	91,876	108,800	90,373	78,303	1,206,051
1996-7	73,715	108,437	145,840	125,910	98,302	75,245	50,979	63,431	59,039	55,936	69,821	47,640	974,295
1997-8	65,654	92,465	123,141	119,029	89,331	79,528	80,906	97,090	68,972	63,914	64,623	68,359	1,013,012
1998-9	67,372	86,605	96,664	90,507	109,168	81,913	96,486	73,017	63,794	65,522	86,066	85,057	1,002,171
1999-00	90,594	110,814	107,168	91,438	96,154	89,211	84,460	71,763	64,198	68,836	73,815	87,789	1,036,240
2000-1[1]	88,581	82,739	104,944	113,785	82,716	86,034							1,117,598

[1] Preliminary.   [2] Grains.   *Source: Economic Research Service, U.S. Department of Agriculture (ERS-USDA)*

United States Wheat and Wheat Flour Imports and Exports   In Thousands of Bushels

| | | Imports | | | | | | Exports | | | | | |
| | --------- Wheat --------- | | | | | | Foreign Donations | | | | CCC | Export Exhance- | Total U.S. |
Crop Year Beginning June 1	Suitable for Milling	Unfit for Human Con-sumption	Grain	Flour & Products[2]	Total	P.L. 480	Sec. 416	Aid[3]	Total Con-cessional	Export Credit	ment Programs	Wheat Exports
			--- Wheat Equivalent ---				In Thousands of Metric Tons					
1991-2	30,924	----	31,019	9,675	40,694	2,286	0	0	2,416	13,334	21,111	34,322
1992-3	56,859	----	56,859	13,142	70,001	2,043	891	NA	4,001	8,538	21,806	36,081
1993-4	91,287	----	91,288	17,529	108,817	2,801	0	NA	3,527	5,874	18,157	31,145
1994-5	70,561	----	70,562	21,386	91,946	1,491	0	NA	1,948	4,202	18,073	32,088
1995-6	47,753	----	47,753	20,180	67,933	1,530	0	NA	1,530	5,662	570	33,708
1996-7	71,727	----	71,727	20,605	92,333	1,009	0	NA	1,155	4,844	0	24,526
1997-8	73,245	----	73,245	21,556	94,801	1,453	0	NA	1,727	4,550	0	25,791
1998-9[1]	79,766	----	79,765	23,238	103,004	556	4,682	NA	5,333	3,500	0	28,806

[1] Preliminary.   [2] Includes macaroni, semolina & similar products.   [3] Shipment mostly under the Commodity Import Program, financed with foreign aid funds.   NA = Not available.   *Source: Economic Research Service, U.S. Department of Agriculture (ERS-USDA)*

Comparative Average Cash Wheat Prices   In Dollars Per Bushel

| | | --- Minneapolis --- | | | | | | | -------- Export Prices[2] (U.S. $ Per Metric Ton) -------- | | | | |
Crop Year Beginning June 1	Received by U.S. Farmers	No. 2 Soft Red Winter, Chicago	No. 1 Hard Red Ordinary Protein, Kansas City	No. 2 Soft Red Winter, St. Louis	No. 1 Dark Northern Spring 14%	No. 1 Hard Amber Durum	No. 1 Soft White, Portland, Oregon	No. 2 Western White Pacific Northwest	No. 2 Soft White, Toledo	Aust-ralian Standard	Canada Vancouver No. 1 CWRS 13 1/2%	Argentina F.O.B. B.A.	U.S. Gulf No. 2 Hard Winter	Rotterdam C.I.F. U.S. No. 2 Hard Winter
1993-4	3.26	3.22	3.60	3.23	5.02	5.76	3.53	3.12	3.16	154	192	131	141	200
1994-5	3.45	3.52	3.97	3.62	4.26	5.98	4.16	3.75	3.37	162	199	131	150	210
1995-6	4.55	4.83	5.49	4.82	5.72	7.03	5.27	4.74	4.41	198	204	178	177	221
1996-7	4.30	3.92	4.88	4.10	4.97	5.59	4.54	4.26	3.71	229	230	218	207	235
1997-8	3.38	3.29	3.71	3.43	4.31	5.97	3.81	3.41	3.12	192	181	157	160	166
1998-9	2.65	2.46	3.08	2.40	3.83	4.06	3.02	2.64	2.27	154	163	120	126	132
1999-00	2.48		2.87	2.39	3.65	4.23	3.02			145	152	114	112	
2000-1[1]	2.65		3.20	2.31	3.53	4.48	2.84							

[1] Preliminary.   [2] Calendar year.   NA = Not available.   *Source: Economic Research Service, U.S. Department of Agriculture (ERS-USDA)*

WHEAT

Wheat (monthly average) through December 2000

Cents Per Bushel
----- No. 2 Red, Chicago (Jan. 1901 - Mar. 1982)
No. 2 Soft, Red, St. Louis (Apr. 1982 - date)

Average Price of No. 2 Soft Red Winter (30 Days) Wheat in Chicago   In Dollars Per Bushel

Year	June	July	Aug.	Sept.	Oct.	Nov.	Dec.	Jan.	Feb.	Mar.	Apr.	May	Average
1990-1	3.26	3.04	2.83	2.62	2.62	2.41	2.52	2.50	2.53	2.76	2.80	2.83	2.73
1991-2	2.86	2.79	2.97	3.24	3.50	3.57	3.79	4.12	4.15	3.71	3.53	3.68	3.49
1992-3	3.60	3.39	3.09	3.24	3.39	3.60	3.59	3.77	3.67	3.58	3.72	3.19	3.49
1993-4	2.82	3.03	3.12	2.99	3.02	3.29	3.53	3.67	3.48	3.28	3.19	3.15	3.22
1994-5	3.21	3.14	3.37	3.75	3.83	3.63	3.76	3.68	3.55	3.39	3.40	3.56	3.52
1995-6	3.91	4.41	4.28	4.53	4.72	4.85	5.04	4.92	5.10	4.99	5.65	5.57	4.83
1996-7	4.94	4.64	4.49	4.33	3.96	3.57	3.54	3.47	3.29	3.49	3.77	3.57	3.92
1997-8	3.38	3.30	3.52	3.49	3.51	3.44	3.31	3.27	3.26	3.25	2.91	2.87	3.29
1998-9	2.72	2.51	2.39	2.32	2.56	2.58	2.49	2.46	2.28	2.63	2.31	2.24	2.46
1999-00[1]	2.20	1.94	2.09	2.12	1.98	1.96	2.12	2.34	2.38				2.13

[1] Preliminary.   Source: Economic Research Service, U.S. Department of Agriculture (ERS-USDA)

Average Price[1] Received by Farmers for Wheat in the United States   In Dollars Per Bushel

Year	June	July	Aug.	Sept.	Oct.	Nov.	Dec.	Jan.	Feb.	Mar.	Apr.	May	Average
1991-2	2.55	2.50	2.63	2.80	3.07	3.25	3.44	3.54	3.78	3.72	3.65	3.64	3.00
1992-3	3.43	3.15	3.01	3.20	3.21	3.29	3.31	3.37	3.33	3.30	3.26	3.11	3.24
1993-4	2.84	2.85	2.96	3.10	3.25	3.47	3.63	3.58	3.60	3.70	3.56	3.43	3.26
1994-5	3.21	3.04	3.25	3.57	3.76	3.75	3.74	3.69	3.61	3.52	3.48	3.66	3.45
1995-6	3.84	4.10	4.26	4.53	4.72	4.81	4.88	4.83	4.98	5.07	5.32	5.73	4.55
1996-7	5.25	4.73	4.58	4.37	4.18	4.14	4.06	4.03	3.88	3.93	4.11	4.09	4.28
1997-8	3.52	3.23	3.56	3.67	3.55	3.50	3.45	3.33	3.27	3.32	3.15	3.06	3.38
1998-9	2.77	2.56	2.39	2.41	2.79	2.97	2.87	2.80	2.74	2.65	2.62	2.53	2.68
1999-00	2.50	2.22	2.53	2.58	2.57	2.66	2.52	2.51	2.54	2.59	2.57	2.59	2.53
2000-1[2]	2.50	2.32	2.41	2.44	2.68	2.83	2.87	2.88					2.62

[1] Includes an allowance for unredeemed loans and purchases.   [2] Preliminary.   Source: Economic Research Service, U.S. Department of Agriculture

Average Price of No. 1 Hard Red Winter (Ordinary Protein) Wheat in Kansas City   In Dollars Per Bushel

Year	June	July	Aug.	Sept.	Oct.	Nov.	Dec.	Jan.	Feb.	Mar.	Apr.	May	Average
1991-2	2.99	2.91	3.10	3.31	3.64	3.76	4.06	4.66	4.51	4.33	4.02	3.90	3.77
1992-3	3.91	3.52	3.27	3.56	3.60	3.78	3.81	3.97	3.75	3.74	3.59	3.51	3.67
1993-4	3.33	3.38	3.34	3.37	3.52	3.39	4.15	4.00	3.80	3.64	3.63	3.65	3.60
1994-5	3.60	3.48	3.70	4.05	4.31	4.24	4.27	4.06	3.98	3.87	3.86	4.22	3.97
1995-6	4.72	4.98	4.76	5.00	5.28	5.34	5.51	5.40	5.67	5.63	6.60	7.02	5.49
1996-7	6.12	5.34	5.01	4.70	4.76	4.78	4.70	4.61	4.52	4.58	4.78	4.61	4.88
1997-8	4.08	3.57	3.84	3.86	3.88	3.87	3.72	3.61	3.64	3.61	3.39	3.41	3.71
1998-9	3.16	3.02	2.74	2.81	3.30	3.42	3.31	3.27	3.05	3.02	2.94	2.89	3.08
1999-00	2.93	2.68	2.85	2.92	2.80	2.89	2.81	2.90	2.94	2.91	2.84	2.95	2.87
2000-1[1]	3.07	2.97	2.89	3.13	3.41	3.45	3.47						3.20

[1] Preliminary.   *Source: Economic Research Service, U.S. Department of Agriculture (ERS-USDA)*

Average Price of No. 1 Dark Northern Spring (14% Protein) Wheat in Minneapolis   In Dollars Per Bushel

Year	June	July	Aug.	Sept.	Oct.	Nov.	Dec.	Jan.	Feb.	Mar.	Apr.	May	Average
1991-2	3.04	2.94	3.10	3.21	3.68	3.78	4.11	4.36	4.56	4.36	4.28	4.44	3.82
1992-3	4.42	4.04	3.65	3.79	3.85	3.94	3.88	4.05	3.87	3.87	3.80	3.71	3.91
1993-4	3.96	4.80	4.88	4.90	5.17	5.50	5.45	5.32	5.29	4.94	4.99	5.05	5.02
1994-5	4.20	4.14	4.00	4.27	4.40	4.41	4.37	4.21	4.09	4.11	4.30	4.61	4.26
1995-6	4.89	5.52	5.06	5.27	5.52	5.63	5.80	5.62	5.82	5.81	6.53	7.14	5.72
1996-7	6.73	6.04	5.29	4.63	4.69	4.64	4.51	4.62	4.45	4.62	4.78	4.58	4.97
1997-8	4.44	4.36	4.49	4.36	4.35	4.42	4.27	4.12	4.15	4.26	4.29	4.24	4.31
1998-9	4.01	3.89	3.58	3.53	4.03	4.15	3.97	3.92	3.78	3.79	3.65	3.61	3.83
1999-00	3.73	3.68	3.58	3.55	3.70	3.78	3.64	3.37	3.59	3.65	3.69	3.80	3.65
2000-1[1]	3.78	3.50	3.29	3.17	3.69	3.77	3.52						3.53

[1] Preliminary.   *Source: Economic Research Service, U.S. Department of Agriculture (ERS-USDA)*

Average Farm Prices of Winter Wheat in the United States   In Dollars Per Bushel

Year	June	July	Aug.	Sept.	Oct.	Nov.	Dec.	Jan.	Feb.	Mar.	Apr.	May	Average
1993-4	2.72	2.76	2.83	2.88	3.00	3.21	3.43	3.41	3.36	3.26	3.24	3.17	3.11
1994-5	3.09	2.99	3.23	3.57	3.79	3.76	3.75	3.67	3.61	3.47	3.45	3.65	3.50
1995-6	3.77	4.05	4.22	4.47	4.70	4.78	4.88	4.80	5.01	5.06	5.39	5.81	4.75
1996-7	5.14	4.67	4.52	4.28	4.07	4.05	4.04	4.02	3.90	3.98	4.14	4.14	4.25
1997-8	3.42	3.16	3.39	3.47	3.42	3.31	3.25	3.16	3.16	3.15	2.94	2.90	3.23
1998-9	2.68	2.47	2.25	2.29	2.66	2.76	2.68	2.70	2.55	2.53	2.48	2.34	2.53
1999-00	2.32	2.12	2.35	2.46	2.47	2.42	2.27	2.32	2.37	2.37	2.32	2.44	2.35
2000-1[1]	2.43	2.23	2.31	2.37	2.63	2.70	2.76	2.82					2.53

[1] Preliminary.   *Source: National Agricultural Statistics Service, U.S. Department of Agriculture (NASS-USDA)*

Average Farm Prices of Durum Wheat in the United States   In Dollars Per Bushel

Year	June	July	Aug.	Sept.	Oct.	Nov.	Dec.	Jan.	Feb.	Mar.	Apr.	May	Average
1993-4	3.18	3.26	3.43	3.92	4.23	4.91	4.92	4.97	5.36	5.71	5.70	4.93	4.54
1994-5	4.59	4.32	4.30	4.51	4.89	4.88	4.67	4.61	4.68	4.61	4.48	4.82	4.61
1995-6	5.20	5.29	5.33	5.87	5.80	5.78	5.75	5.66	5.72	5.73	5.63	5.62	5.62
1996-7	5.58	5.13	5.03	4.69	4.78	4.56	4.59	4.47	4.31	4.32	4.40	4.50	4.70
1997-8	4.21	4.61	5.23	5.35	5.09	5.25	5.17	5.02	4.71	4.68	4.45	4.29	4.84
1998-9	3.98	3.39	3.23	3.03	3.04	3.08	3.05	3.20	2.84	2.82	2.80	2.84	3.11
1999-00	2.93	2.89	2.76	2.29	2.30	2.64	2.96	2.90	2.88	2.63	2.89	3.02	2.76
2000-1[1]	2.71	2.90	2.33	2.32	2.42	2.97	3.03	3.09					2.72

[1] Preliminary.   *Source: National Agricultural Statistics Service, U.S. Department of Agriculture (NASS-USDA)*

Average Farm Prices of Other Spring Wheat in the United States   In Dollars Per Bushel

Year	June	July	Aug.	Sept.	Oct.	Nov.	Dec.	Jan.	Feb.	Mar.	Apr.	May	Average
1993-4	3.21	3.50	3.51	3.37	3.50	3.67	3.75	3.69	3.68	3.64	3.68	3.63	3.57
1994-5	3.51	3.28	3.19	3.38	3.52	3.51	3.56	3.50	3.40	3.38	3.34	3.53	3.43
1995-6	3.78	4.26	4.19	4.27	4.45	4.61	4.72	4.66	4.81	4.88	5.21	5.67	4.63
1996-7	5.48	5.30	4.63	4.41	4.23	4.11	4.01	3.95	3.80	3.83	4.04	3.94	4.31
1997-8	3.74	3.66	3.75	3.64	3.49	3.55	3.51	3.45	3.34	3.42	3.41	3.31	3.52
1998-9	3.22	3.08	2.69	2.62	3.04	3.23	3.19	3.12	3.09	3.00	2.95	2.92	3.01
1999-00	3.01	2.93	2.86	2.86	2.79	2.94	2.87	2.82	2.82	2.85	2.89	2.92	2.88
2000-1[1]	2.90	2.74	2.59	2.59	2.80	2.97	2.98	2.99					2.82

[1] Preliminary.   *Source: National Agricultural Statistics Service, U.S. Department of Agriculture (NASS-USDA)*

WHEAT

Wheat Futures - Chicago Board of Trade (weekly close) as 29-Dec-2000

Cents Per Bushel

Average Open Interest of Wheat Futures in Chicago   In Contracts

Year	Jan.	Feb.	Mar.	Apr.	May	June	July	Aug.	Sept.	Oct.	Nov.	Dec.
1991	48,597	51,520	55,922	53,668	53,030	58,997	54,946	52,283	55,220	61,257	57,679	51,845
1992	61,484	70,152	58,957	53,706	50,978	50,340	60,116	62,071	50,093	54,564	57,693	49,263
1993	50,329	47,858	44,885	48,354	51,353	55,829	58,705	64,335	58,603	61,496	62,877	50,523
1994	53,912	48,013	45,110	47,430	44,552	54,622	57,151	65,388	73,200	78,419	70,815	67,150
1995	66,715	67,768	55,973	55,612	67,875	90,208	101,351	90,800	91,505	103,987	102,475	99,422
1996	102,718	104,807	91,378	98,260	93,378	81,211	69,222	66,128	65,561	65,639	60,810	58,533
1997	63,388	71,304	76,747	85,516	84,721	83,675	92,815	105,320	104,587	108,480	101,089	90,386
1998	96,870	99,103	97,585	114,193	115,199	116,008	121,794	127,240	125,747	131,322	130,186	116,249
1999	119,096	131,961	118,503	117,905	111,541	117,075	120,365	129,748	128,403	135,884	140,798	124,063
2000	127,419	135,316	123,980	128,462	130,938	133,527	139,194	144,953	141,803	150,592	153,287	134,997

Source: Chicago Board of Trade (CBT)

Volume of Trading of Wheat Futures in Chicago   In Contracts

Year	Jan.	Feb.	Mar.	Apr.	May	June	July	Aug.	Sept.	Oct.	Nov.	Dec.	Total
1991	198,340	182,158	291,762	268,560	234,880	391,134	286,097	271,625	187,232	300,628	271,927	262,501	3,146,844
1992	366,736	460,354	318,810	236,063	290,148	303,044	304,217	283,379	250,003	220,502	257,017	188,541	3,498,814
1993	246,125	237,936	277,632	217,898	173,607	268,206	366,414	266,893	202,308	256,329	310,464	195,817	3,019,629
1994	288,321	211,703	187,617	244,544	300,324	370,135	272,492	330,758	343,548	398,041	354,975	318,173	3,620,631
1995	353,603	302,950	316,330	279,099	345,455	598,762	507,876	527,716	436,145	472,794	454,352	359,985	4,955,067
1996	628,340	510,138	455,981	660,722	531,979	512,883	452,690	345,626	305,448	362,047	359,005	261,108	5,385,967
1997	312,680	373,411	368,547	567,099	422,935	469,158	470,992	493,225	401,277	405,978	432,621	340,722	5,058,645
1998	363,511	473,114	452,186	514,557	432,167	601,149	401,508	490,242	475,766	543,680	539,488	394,201	5,681,569
1999	426,524	597,448	710,375	559,211	444,696	674,580	523,516	665,897	536,014	437,689	613,633	380,442	6,570,025
2000	467,050	691,068	522,394	490,694	627,722	759,371	461,068	572,879	388,237	466,328	596,581	364,139	6,407,531

Source: Chicago Board of Trade (CBT)

Commercial Stocks of Domestic Wheat[1] in the United States, on First of Month   In Millions of Bushels

Year	July	Aug.	Sept.	Oct.	Nov.	Dec.	Jan.	Feb.	Mar.	Apr.	May	June
1991-2	244.8	275.5	296.9	308.2	271.0	264.8	249.8	227.0	205.2	180.7	170.9	209.1
1992-3	269.6	290.5	202.5	228.2	231.9	202.7	185.5	169.5	153.3	132.6	112.9	87.0
1993-4	102.9	145.1	171.8	194.9	199.3	174.9	169.5	168.3	162.2	143.8	127.3	111.3
1994-5	145.7	203.9	243.0	269.7	268.6	238.2	199.5	181.0	162.5	150.2	108.7	91.8
1995-6	92.3	161.7	201.1	234.3	228.3	200.2	178.7	170.8	156.6	137.7	107.6	87.2
1996-7	86.3	112.9	128.0	145.3	117.2	94.9	89.0	80.4	77.0	75.6	68.1	64.6
1997-8	80.1	186.3	235.2	268.1	258.1	231.4	196.8	178.1	170.6	158.0	146.4	145.7
1998-9	209.8	265.0	314.9	325.6	307.3	291.3	272.9	265.7	256.8	251.5	236.7	218.3
1999-00	248.6	294.9	335.8	354.0	334.6	301.5	277.4	273.7	267.8	266.3	247.6	240.3
2000-1	285.5	310.3	335.3	335.5	306.2	286.6	263.7	251.7	243.2			

[1] Domestic wheat in storage in public and private elevators in 39 markets and wheat afloat in vessels or barges at lake and seaboard ports, the first Saturday of the month.   *Source: Livestock Division, U.S. Department of Agriculture (LD-USDA)*

Stocks of Wheat Flour Held by Mills in the United States   In Thousands of Sacks -- 100 Pounds

Year	Jan. 1	April 1	July 1	Oct. 1	Year	Jan. 1	April 1	July 1	Oct. 1
1989	4,800	4,423	5,116	5,489	1994	5,611	5,904	5,834	6,020
1990	5,207	5,072	5,818	7,980	1996	6,869	6,927	6,400	6,350
1991	8,051	5,474	8,115	6,336	1997	6,671	6,040	5,820	6,330
1992	5,660	5,210	5,841	5,864	1998	6,343	6,245	6,210	7,345
1993	5,487	4,863	6,197	5,882	1999	7,544	5,920	5,697	4,265
1994	5,611	5,904	5,834	6,020	2000[1]	5,099	5,215	5,064	5,240

[1] Preliminary.   *Source: Bureau of the Census, U.S. Department of Commerce*

Average Producer Price Index of Wheat Flour (Spring)   June 1983 = 100

Year	Jan.	Feb.	Mar.	Apr.	May	June	July	Aug.	Sept.	Oct.	Nov.	Dec.	Average
1991	88.7	90.2	92.0	93.0	94.0	93.7	91.3	94.1	96.3	100.1	97.5	102.7	94.5
1992	109.7	116.4	111.5	110.3	109.2	111.0	104.9	99.6	104.1	104.4	104.7	103.5	107.4
1993	107.5	108.1	107.2	108.4	105.2	104.7	103.7	107.2	102.1	107.3	108.4	112.5	106.9
1994	111.8	110.5	108.9	107.9	109.4	106.4	100.8	101.2	109.1	112.0	110.9	111.4	108.4
1995	110.7	108.5	107.9	109.8	113.5	118.6	127.4	126.7	129.5	132.6	132.3	133.5	120.9
1996	130.4	138.0	136.6	137.6	160.1	146.8	138.0	127.0	121.5	125.7	121.7	121.4	133.7
1997	119.4	119.3	116.6	121.8	120.8	117.4	112.1	113.5	115.1	112.6	111.5	111.1	115.9
1998	106.8	108.1	111.5	110.1	109.9	106.4	105.5	101.8	100.9	106.6	107.8	104.8	106.7
1999	104.8	102.7	105.0	100.5	102.2	102.7	100.7	103.5	101.4	99.8	101.4	96.8	101.8
2000[2]	99.9	99.9	100.2	99.4	100.1	101.7	100.2	100.4	101.2	106.0	104.7	103.6	101.4

[1] Standard patent.   [2] Preliminary.   *Source: Bureau of Labor Statistics, U.S. Department of Commerce (BLS) (0212-0301)*

World Wheat Flour Production (Monthly Average)   In Thousands of Metric Tons

Year	Australia	France	Germany	Hungary	India	Japan	Kazakhstan	Rep. of Korea	Mexico	Poland	Russia	Turkey	United Kingdom
1991	112.7	464.8	341.1	97.7	398.0	389.8	167.8	130.4	207.3	128.6	----	111.1	320.0
1992	113.9	465.2	327.0	106.9	400.0	389.0	161.0	129.4	223.3	167.1	----	112.2	320.0
1993	116.3	480.6	336.4	75.0	399.4	399.3	155.3	129.5	214.0	113.4	449.5	122.1	331.0
1994	116.9	470.8	378.8	62.9	400.0	387.2	157.0	132.6	219.8	150.5	348.0	104.9	337.0
1995	112.6	473.1	382.3	84.0	400.0	389.3	131.0	139.9	210.7	156.9	274.6	119.7	341.0
1996	123.8	450.0	394.2	75.1	400.0	389.6	132.7	141.2	215.9	164.1	309.7	132.1	353.5
1997	129.7	----	404.8	77.7	412.5	388.1	127.3	145.9	216.0	115.9	361.9	159.1	354.5
1998	146.8	----	407.5	70.1	403.6	382.0	129.8	143.5	213.2	116.8	347.8	152.6	355.5
1999[1]	----	----	423.6	69.1	182.2	389.4	84.6	152.8	202.8	125.0	360.0	156.6	----
2000[2]	----	----	404.7	76.3	200.5	373.9	77.0	155.0	199.8	126.3	367.5	163.5	----

[1] Preliminary.   [2] Estimate. NA = Not available.   *Source: United Nations (UN)*

WHEAT

Production of Wheat Flour in the United States   In Millions of Sacks (100 Pounds Each)

Year	July	Aug.	Sept.	Oct.	Nov.	Dec.	Jan.	Feb.	Mar.	Apr.	May	June	Total
1992-3	31.1	34.2	31.9	34.6	32.2	29.2	30.6	31.3	34.1	32.0	31.0	30.3	382.4
1993-4	30.7	33.3	32.9	33.5	34.0	33.8	30.9	30.2	35.9	32.3	32.2	31.1	390.8
1994-5	30.5	34.9	34.2	35.0	33.7	31.7	30.9	29.4	34.5	29.9	33.5	32.3	390.4
1995-6	31.0	34.5	33.0	35.1	33.4	31.2	31.6	32.3	32.2	31.2	33.2	30.6	389.3
1996-7	33.9	35.6	34.6	37.5	33.1	32.0	31.3	30.0	31.8	33.1	32.6	32.5	397.9
1997-8	34.0	34.3	35.1	37.2	33.8	33.5	-----	96.0	-----	-----	96.2	-----	400.1
1998-9	-----	100.2	-----	-----	106.5	-----	-----	96.1	-----	-----	103.5	-----	406.3
1999-00	-----	104.2	-----	-----	108.2	-----	-----	99.5	-----	-----	100.1	-----	412.0
2000-1[1]	-----	107.4	-----	-----	108.1	-----	-----	-----	-----	-----	-----	-----	430.9

[1] Preliminary.   Source: Bureau of the Census, U.S. Department of Commerce

United States Wheat Flour Exports (Grain Equivalent[2])   In Thousands of Bushels

Year	June	July	Aug.	Sept.	Oct.	Nov.	Dec.	Jan.	Feb.	Mar.	Apr.	May	Total
1992-3	3,257	5,284	2,856	2,325	3,840	4,641	3,903	2,325	7,744	5,832	7,499	5,285	54,791
1993-4	4,408	3,793	1,811	3,642	3,840	3,416	3,170	5,838	4,390	6,099	4,198	3,368	47,973
1994-5	2,922	6,824	5,636	3,407	3,105	4,721	4,734	2,805	7,085	7,617	6,945	6,005	61,806
1995-6	2,822	5,018	7,520	2,249	2,080	1,221	3,458	808	2,537	1,230	2,415	1,830	33,188
1996-7	2,005	2,008	1,669	3,133	2,496	2,748	2,240	1,344	1,897	2,490	1,253	2,086	25,369
1997-8	1,731	2,849	1,621	3,101	2,518	1,631	3,118	1,403	2,723	1,280	1,257	925	24,157
1998-9	1,971	1,740	2,027	2,914	3,812	2,354	6,472	2,551	3,341	4,126	3,105	1,948	36,361
1999-00	5,900	5,085	3,673	6,503	4,576	2,332	6,566	2,924	6,108	2,615	3,193	1,286	50,761
2000-1[1]	3,620	3,805	1,623	3,174	4,165	2,332							37,438

[1] Preliminary.   [2] Includes meal, groats and durum.   Source: Economic Research Service, U.S. Department of Agriculture (ERS-USDA)

Supply and Distribution of Wheat Flour in the United States

Year	Wheat Ground - 1,000 Bu. -	Millfeed Production - 1,000 Tons -	Flour Production[2]	Flour & Product Imports	Total Supply	Exports Flour	Exports Products	Domestic Disappear-ance	Total Population July 1 - Millions -	Per Capita Disappear-ance - Pounds -
			------------------------------ In 1,000 Cwt. ------------------------------							
1992	833,339	6,707	370,829	4,749	375,578	20,194	787	354,680	255.4	138.9
1993	871,408	6,963	387,419	5,786	393,205	22,731	687	369,976	258.1	143.4
1994	884,707	7,186	392,519	8,425	400,944	23,801	811	376,594	260.6	144.5
1995	869,296	7,144	388,689	8,918	397,607	23,615	857	373,135	263.0	141.9
1996	878,070	7,042	397,776	8,574	406,350	10,651	881	394,818	265.5	148.7
1997	885,843	6,886	404,143	8,684	412,827	11,038	1,167	400,622	268.0	149.5
1998	895,369	6,955	398,914	9,766	408,680	12,574	1,353	394,753	270.6	145.9
1999	917,797	7,040	411,968	9,305	416,354	21,367	1,610	393,377	273.1	144.0
2000[1]	935,747	7,248	415,093							

[1] Preliminary.   [2] Commercial production of wheat flour, whole wheat, industrial and durum flour and farina reported by Bureau of Census.
Source: Economic Research Service, U.S. Department of Agriculture (ERS-USDA)

Wheat and Flour -- Price Relationships at Milling Centers in the United States   In Dollars

Crop Year (June-May)	At Kansas City Cost of Wheat to Produce 100 lb. Flour[1]	At Kansas City Bakery Flour 100 lb. Flour[2]	At Kansas City By-Products Obtained 100 lb. Flour[3]	At Kansas City Total Products Actual	At Kansas City Total Products Over Cost of Wheat	At Minneapolis Cost of Wheat to Produce 100 lb. Flour[1]	At Minneapolis Bakery Flour 100 lb. Flour[2]	At Minneapolis By-Products Obtained 100 lb. Flour[3]	At Minneapolis Total Products Actual	At Minneapolis Total Products Over Cost of Wheat
1991-2	8.58	9.53	1.26	10.79	2.21	8.71	9.39	1.16	10.55	1.84
1992-3	8.53	9.65	1.28	10.93	2.40	8.91	10.12	1.15	11.27	2.37
1993-4	10.03	10.34	1.46	11.79	1.77	11.45	12.50	1.28	13.77	2.33
1994-5	9.25	10.50	1.21	11.71	2.46	9.71	11.01	1.04	12.05	2.34
1995-6	12.97	13.35	1.93	15.28	2.31	13.04	13.03	1.68	14.71	1.67
1996-7	11.22	11.89	1.92	13.81	2.60	11.32	11.68	1.87	13.54	2.22
1997-8	9.03	9.99	1.43	11.41	2.38	9.83	10.62	1.34	11.96	2.12
1998-9	7.91	9.06	1.09	10.15	2.23	8.76	9.80	1.02	10.82	2.06
1999-00	7.78	8.81	.97	9.78	2.00	8.24	9.23	.94	10.17	1.94
June-Aug.	7.62	8.88	.80	9.68	2.06	8.35	9.20	.86	10.06	1.71
Sept.-Nov.	7.84	8.85	1.01	9.86	2.02	8.30	9.37	.92	10.29	1.99
Dec.-Feb.	7.87	8.70	1.09	9.79	1.93	8.06	9.13	1.04	10.17	2.11

[1] Based on 73% extraction rate, cost of 2.28 bushels: At Kansas City, No. 1 hard winter 13% protein; and at Minneapolis, No. 1 dark northern spring, 14% protein.   [2] quoted as mid-month bakers' standard patent at Kansas City and spring standard patent at Minneapolis, bulk basis.   [3] Assumed 50-50 millfeed distribution between bran and shorts or middlings, bulk basis.   Source: Agricultural Marketing Service, U.S. Department of Agriculture (AMS-USDA)

Wool

The protracted slide in world wool production during the 1990's is likely to persist into the next decade owing to the well entrenched contraction in world sheep numbers which total less than 900 million head vs. more than 1 billion head 10 years ago. Notwithstanding the reduction in new supply, worldwide demand for wool has also fallen due to changing consumer attitudes which favor casual dress that uses more cotton and man-made fibers than wool.

China now accounts for at least one-fifth of the world's sheep inventory with more than 200 million head, nearly twice their early 1990's total. In contrast, New Zealand's sheep herd of 46.5 million head is the lowest since the 1960's, and in Australia the estimated January 1, 2000 inventory number of 117 million head compares with more than 175 million a decade ago. Russia's sheep inventory in 2000 of 18 million head has fallen nearly 75 percent since the early 1990's. A drop in U.S. sheep numbers also persists; the 2000 inventory of about 7 million head is one-half the number on hand in the late 1980's. U.S. shorn wool production (tops and noils) is now insignificant at 46.5 million pounds in 1999 vs. 49.3 million in 1998. In the early 1980's, U.S. production averaged about 105 million pounds.

In line with the world's declining wool production and usage foreign trade has also fallen. Australia remains the largest exporter followed by New Zealand. The two nations combine to account for 75 percent of world exports. Importing nations are numerous, but China leads followed by Japan, the U.K., Italy, and France. U.S. raw wool imports (clean) through the first ten months of 2000 totaled 36 million pounds vs. 38 million a year ago. Australian wool accounts for most of U.S. imports. The U.S. also imports a relatively small quantity of wool tops with 4.8 million pounds for the year 2000 through October. However, the U.S. exports raw wool: the January-September 2000 total of 3.9 million pounds (clean) compares with 4.3 million a year earlier, and wool top exports during the same period of 5.1 million pounds compares with 5.8 million, respectively.

Global wool prices are a function of origin and grade. South African wool tends to be more expensive than Australian wool, while Australian wool is more expensive than New Zealand wool. U.S. clean wool prices (56's) were weak in the late 1990's, with little relief seen into late 2000. The early fall 2000 price of $0.50 per pound compares with $0.45 a year earlier, while U.S. 60's grade averaged $0.77 per pound in September 2000 vs. Australian 60's at $1.37; the latter in the mid-1990's averaged near $3.00 per pound.

Futures Markets

Wool futures are traded on the Sydney Futures Exchange (SFE). Wool yarn futures are traded on the Chubu Commodity Exchange (CCE), the Osaka Mercantile Exchange (OME), and the Tokyo Commodity Exchange (TOCOM).

World Production of Wool   In Metric Tons--Degreased

Year	Argentina	Australia	China	Kazakhstan[3]	New Zealand	Pakistan	Romania	Russia[3]	South Africa	United Kingdom	United States	Uruguay	Total
1989	87,600	622,000	120,111	-----	302,800	34,800	20,900	284,400	46,500	52,765	21,665	60,000	2,011,693
1990	85,800	724,000	122,400	64,750	233,000	28,200	26,500	136,050	49,500	53,358	21,140	58,100	2,029,209
1991	75,400	699,000	123,000	62,640	227,000	28,900	19,196	122,700	51,000	51,055	20,830	56,500	1,953,339
1992	74,200	574,000	121,500	63,000	221,000	29,600	16,800	107,400	48,500	50,876	19,980	50,700	1,780,613
1993	58,000	557,000	122,000	56,800	193,000	30,300	15,600	95,000	45,000	48,329	18,520	49,410	1,688,806
1994	48,000	570,000	130,000	55,000	214,000	31,000	17,000	73,000	40,000	47,000	16,000	50,000	1,693,000
1995	44,000	475,000	141,000	35,000	214,000	32,000	16,000	56,000	35,000	48,000	15,000	46,000	1,512,000
1996[1]	39,000	447,000	152,000	25,000	199,000	32,000	16,000	46,000	38,000	46,000	14,000	43,000	1,449,000
1997[2]	39,000	447,000	153,000	25,000	200,000	33,000	13,000	42,000	38,000	46,000	14,000	48,000	1,450,000

[1] Preliminary.   [2] Estimate.   [3] Formerly part of the U.S.S.R.; data not reported separately until 1990.   *Source: Food and Agriculture Organization of the United Nations (FAO-UN)*

Production of Wool Goods[1] in the United States   In Millions of Yards

Year	First Quarter	Second Quarter	Third Quarter	Fourth Quarter	Total	Year	First Quarter	Second Quarter	Third Quarter	Fourth Quarter	Total
1991	38.0	48.7	41.4	41.5	169.6	1996	44.8	43.6	30.8	32.8	152.0
1992	45.7	47.2	43.9	39.5	176.3	1997	42.7	49.7	42.3	40.5	175.2
1993	48.4	48.9	43.9	42.8	184.0	1998	38.8	37.5	29.6	26.3	132.2
1994	49.1	51.1	39.4	39.0	178.6	1999	25.0	20.9	17.4	14.6	77.9
1995	46.8	45.9	35.2	34.3	162.2	2000[2]	17.9	18.0	13.4	17.0	66.3

[1] Woolen and worsted woven goods, except woven felts.   [2] Preliminary.   *Source: Bureau of the Census, U.S. Department of Commerce*

Consumption of Apparel Wool in the United States   In Millions of Pounds--Clean Basis

Year	First Quarter	Second Quarter	Third Quarter	Fourth Quarter	Total	Year	First Quarter	Second Quarter	Third Quarter	Fourth Quarter	Total
1991	31.6	37.1	34.6	33.9	137.2	1996	39.1	36.2	27.4	26.8	129.5
1992	36.4	35.1	33.6	31.1	136.1	1997	33.1	33.8	30.6	32.8	130.4
1993	35.5	35.9	35.5	34.4	141.4	1998	29.3	29.6	21.9	17.5	98.4
1994	36.3	35.6	32.7	34.0	138.6	1999	17.3	16.8	15.8	13.6	63.5
1995	36.3	35.5	29.4	28.1	129.3	2000[2]	17.1	15.7	14.1	13.4	60.3

[1] Woolen and worsted woven goods, except woven felts.   [2] Preliminary.   *Source: Bureau of the Census, U.S. Department of Commerce*

WOOL

Salient Statistics of Wool in the United States

								---------------- Raw Wool (Clean Content) ----------------							
	Sheep & Lambs Shorn[4]	Weight Per Fleece	Shorn Wool Pro- duction	Price Per	Value of Pro- duction	Payment Support	Rate	Total Wool Pro- duction	Domestic Pro- duction	Exports Domestic Wool	Dutiable Imports for Consump- tion[3] 48's & Finer	Total New Supply[2]	Duty Free Imports (Not Finer than 46's)	Mill -- Consumption -- Apparel	Carpet
Year	-1,000's-	-In Lbs.-	1,000 Lbs.	Lb.	1,000 $	--Cents Per Lb.--		------------------------------ In Thousands of Pounds ------------------------------							
1991	11,009	7.97	87,740	55.0	47,178	188	133.0	87,740	46,327	3,867	68,242	128,868	18,166	137,187	14,352
1992	10,521	7.88	82,943	74.0	60,162	197	123.0	82,943	43,794	3,413	65,457	129,640	23,802	136,143	14,695
1993	9,976	7.77	77,535	51.0	39,077	204	153.0	77,535	40,938	2,529	76,001	138,286	21,876	141,380	15,431
1994	8,877	7.73	68,577	78.0	52,377	209	131.0	68,577	36,209	2,863	64,889	122,880	24,645	138,563	14,739
1995	8,138	7.80	63,513	104.0	64,277	212	108.0	63,513	33,535	6,042	63,781	116,313	25,039	129,299	12,667
1996	7,279	7.79	56,669	70.0	39,659	----	----	56,159	29,921	5,715	54,063	99,575	20,971	129,525	12,311
1997	7,032	7.70	53,889	84.0	45,172	----	----	53,578	28,630	4,732	51,484	100,344	24,295	130,386	13,576
1998	6,428	7.70	49,255	60.0	29,415	----	----	49,239	30,321	1,700	45,760	102,528	23,121	98,373	16,331
1999[1]	6,150	7.60	46,549	38.0	17,852	----	----		25,000	3,000	21,251		20,645	63,535	13,950

[1] Preliminary. [2] Production minus exports plus imports; stocks not taken into consideration. [3] Apparel wool includes all dutiable wool; carpet wool includes all duty-free wool. [4] Includes sheep shorn at commercial feeding yards. *Source: Economic Research Service, U.S. Department of Agriculture (ERS-USDA)*

Shorn Wool Prices

	U.S. Farm Price Shorn Wool Greasy Basis[1]	-------------- Australian Offering Price, Clean[2] --------------						---------- Graded Territory Shorn Wool, Clean Basis[4] ----------				
		Grade 70's Type 61	Grade 64's Type 63	Grade 64/70's Type 62	Grade 60/62's Type 64A	Grade 58's-56's 433-34	Market Indicator[3]	64's Staple 2 3/4" & up	60's Staple 3" & up	58's Staple 3 1/4" & up	56's Staple 3 1/4" & up	54's Staple 3 1/2" & up
Year	-Cents/Lb.-	-------------------- In Dollars Per Pound --------------------					-Cents/Kg.-	---------------- In Dollars Per Pound ----------------				
1991	55.0	3.56	2.32	2.70	1.87	1.68	627	1.99	1.31	1.14	1.03	.93
1992	74.0	2.58	2.32	2.17	2.10	1.94	557	2.04	1.61	1.47	1.35	1.23
1993	51.0	2.08	1.70	1.84	1.49	1.44	488	1.37	1.13	1.05	.99	.94
1994	78.0	3.72	2.43	3.01	1.96	1.86	547	2.12	1.50	1.26	1.27	1.21
1995	104.0	3.22	2.81	3.01	2.49	2.33	888	2.49	1.93	1.77	1.63	1.53
1996	70.0	2.81	2.34	2.54	1.96	1.84	619	1.93	1.54	1.43	1.31	1.22
1997	84.0	3.56	2.57	2.90	2.06	1.95	615	2.38	1.78	1.64	1.43	1.14
1998	60.0	2.70	1.94	2.02	1.74	1.60	663	1.62	1.31	1.21	1.06	.94
1999	38.0	2.63	1.58	1.76	1.46	1.33	527	1.10	.85	.74	.66	.59

[1] Annual weighted average. [2] F.O.B. Australian Wool Corporation South Carolina warehouse in bond. [3] Index of prices of all wool sold in Australia for the crop year July-June. [4] Wool principally produced in Texas and the Rocky Mountain States. *Source: Economic Research Service, U.S. Department of Agriculture (ERS-USDA)*

Average Wool Prices[1] --Australian-- 64's, Type 62, Duty Paid--U.S. Mills   In Cents Per Pound

Year	Jan.	Feb.	Mar.	Apr.	May	June	July	Aug.	Sept.	Oct.	Nov.	Dec.	Average
1991	334	335	209	221	271	286	NA	248	229	215	274	270	263
1992	259	270	277	264	268	246	NA	224	210	192	195	193	236
1993	186	176	170	158	179	169	167	154	153	171	175	176	170
1994	204	216	205	223	249	258	243	248	259	256	273	297	244
1995	281	297	302	302	307	308	292	284	266	236	242	237	280
1996	240	237	238	234	242	245	236	234	228	220	225	232	234
1997	234	261	254	261	279	287	NA	270	262	250	245	240	258
1998	218	225	247	205	214	179	NA	144	144	140	156	147	184
1999	158	150	157	156	150	149	152	148	139	139	143	137	148
2000	154	146	144	156	156	154	155	151	149	146	140	148	150

[1] Raw, clean basis. NA = Not available. *Source: Economic Research Service, U.S. Department of Agriculture (ERS-USDA)*

Average Wool Prices --Domestic[1]-- Graded Territory, 64's, Staple 2 3/4 & Up--U.S. Mills In Cents Per Pound

Year	Jan.	Feb.	Mar.	Apr.	May	June	July	Aug.	Sept.	Oct.	Nov.	Dec.	Average
1991	217	210	163	167	203	230	230	167	156	148	148	155	183
1992	163	203	195	196	199	218	210	188	210	193	168	168	193
1993	158	148	132	127	135	140	138	140	130	129	133	133	137
1994	140	150	170	201	226	230	230	235	250	238	238	252	213
1995	245	252	265	288	295	285	261	250	235	185	208	192	247
1996	188	192	197	197	195	192	192	192	192	192	190	190	192
1997	190	190	208	228	248	255	255	255	255	255	260	260	238
1998	236	195	195	188	177	170	170	150	115	115	115	115	162
1999	115	115	115	110	117	122	116	110	105	100	110	95	111
2000	95	95	101	110	125	125	125	120	107	105	105	97	109

[1] Raw, shorn, clean basis. *Source: Economic Research Service, U.S. Department of Agriculture (ERS-USDA)*

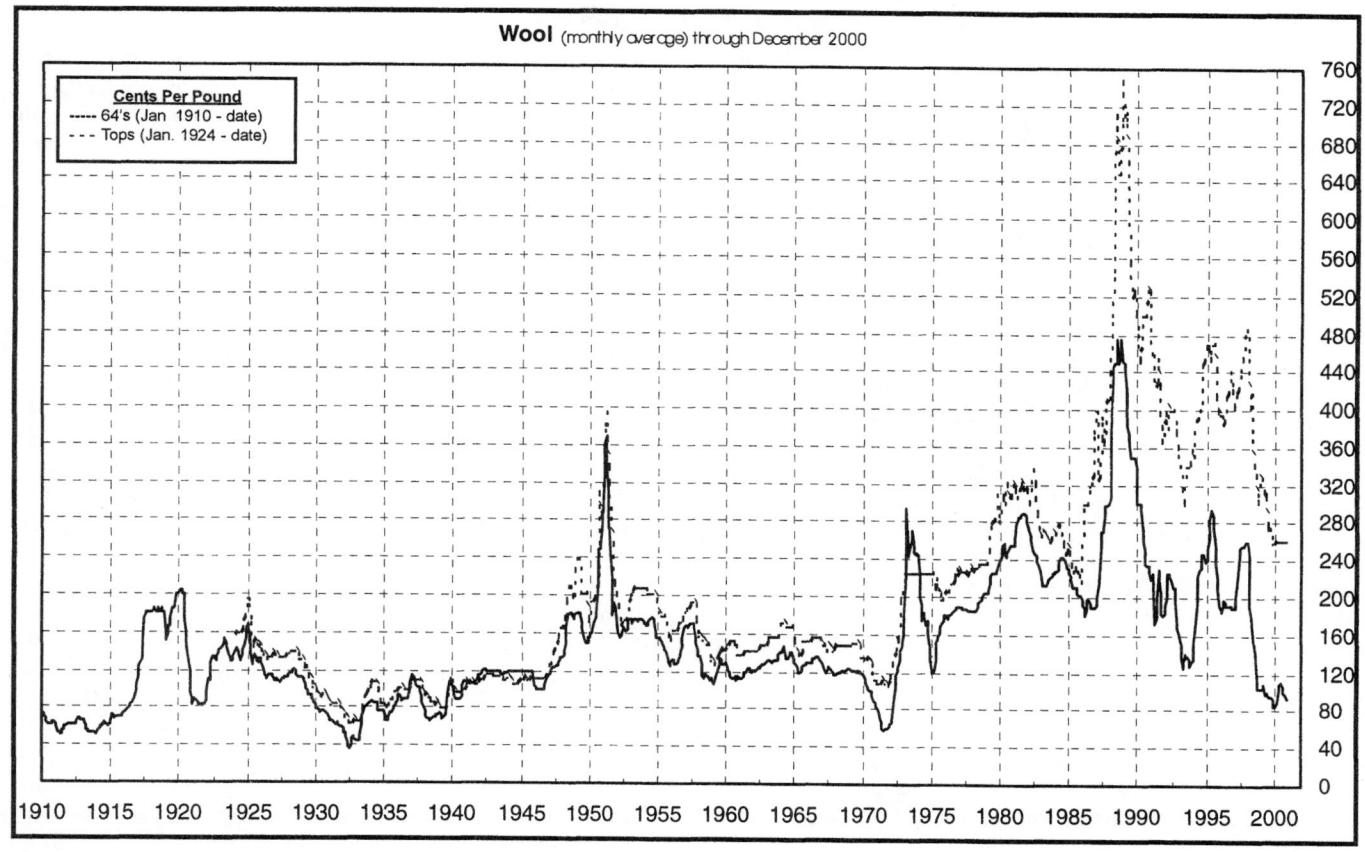

Wool (monthly average) through December 2000

Cents Per Pound
----- 64's (Jan 1910 - date)
- - - Tops (Jan. 1924 - date)

Wool: Mill Consumption, by Grades in the U.S., Scoured Basis   In Millions of Pounds

| | Apparel Class[1] | | | | | | | |
| | Woolen System | | | Worsted System | | | | |
Year	60's & Finer	Coarser Than 60's	Total	60's & Finer	Coarser Than 60's	Total	All Total	Carpet Wool[2]
1990	26,173	24,941	51,114	50,630	18,878	69,508	120,622	12,124
1991	31,961	26,599	58,560	56,521	22,106	78,627	137,187	14,352
1992	33,878	25,600	59,478	58,495	18,170	76,665	136,143	14,695
1993	40,895	26,624	67,519	58,834	15,027	73,861	141,380	15,431
1994	35,960	26,038	61,998	59,599	16,966	76,565	138,563	14,739
1995	30,211	27,089	57,300	54,980	17,019	71,999	129,299	12,667
1996	42,141	27,575	69,716	46,057	13,752	59,809	129,525	12,311
1997	49,038	21,303	70,341	48,153	11,892	60,045	130,386	13,576
1998[3]	31,258	15,079	46,337	42,243	9,793	52,036	98,373	16,331
1999[4]	18,379	10,772	29,151	27,429	6,955	34,384	63,535	13,950

[1] Domestic & duty-paid foreign.   [2] Duty-free foreign.   [3] Preliminary.   [4] Estimate.   Source: Economic Research Service, U.S. Department of Agriculture (ERS-USDA)

United States Imports[1] of Unmanufactured Wool (Clean Yield)   In Millions of Pounds

Year	Jan.	Feb.	Mar.	Apr.	May	June	July	Aug.	Sept.	Oct.	Nov.	Dec.	Total
1991	10.7	6.9	5.4	5.5	7.3	8.1	9.2	7.0	4.4	7.8	5.1	9.0	86.4
1992	10.2	8.1	7.3	10.6	8.8	6.2	6.9	5.0	3.9	5.5	9.1	7.8	89.4
1993	7.8	8.7	8.5	9.3	11.0	9.6	9.7	8.7	5.7	7.7	7.2	8.4	102.2
1994	10.0	7.7	7.7	12.7	7.5	7.7	6.9	6.5	4.1	5.7	8.1	7.0	91.7
1995	10.4	7.7	10.8	6.0	11.5	5.2	7.3	7.3	4.9	7.9	7.7	4.1	90.6
1996	9.6	9.1	8.8	5.6	7.0	5.9	5.3	6.6	3.1	4.6	4.6	5.1	75.3
1997	5.1	5.8	5.8	6.6	5.8	4.2	4.9	4.2	4.8	8.5	7.3	8.6	71.5
1998	8.8	5.4	5.4	7.2	5.9	5.5	5.7	4.4	3.3	7.3	4.9	4.3	68.0
1999	6.2	3.6	3.9	7.9	3.5	3.0	3.7	3.1	2.6	3.8	2.8	2.5	46.3
2000[2]	4.9	3.8	3.8	4.6	5.1	2.7	3.2	3.7	4.3	3.2	3.5	2.4	45.0

[1] For consumption.   [2] Preliminary.   Source: Economic Research Service, U.S. Department of Agriculture (ERS-USDA)

Zinc

Zinc is utilized as a protective coating for other metals, such as iron and steel, in a process known as galvanizing. Zinc also finds use as an alloy with copper to make brass and as an alloying compound with aluminum and magnesium. There are a number of substitutes for zinc in chemical, electronic, and pigment uses. Aluminum, steel, and plastic substitute for galvanized sheet. Aluminum alloys can replace brass.

The U.S. Geological Survey reported that world mine production of zinc in 1999 was 7.64 million metric tonnes, up 1 percent from the year before. Production by Australia in 1999 was 1.1 million tonnes, up 4 percent from the previous year. Canada produced 1.1 million tonnes of zinc, up 4 percent from 1998. China was the next largest producer with mine output of 1.05 million tonnes, down 5 percent from the previous year. U.S. zinc production in 1999 was 810,000 tonnes, up 7 percent from the previous year. U.S. production at a mine in Alaska increased to offset the closure of a mine in Tennessee and a mine in Colorado. The U.S. is the largest importer of zinc metal and the largest exporter of zinc concentrates. Other major producers of zinc are Peru and Mexico.

The world reserves of zinc are estimated to be 190 million tonnes. The largest reserves are estimated to be in Australia with 34 million tonnes followed by China with 33 million tonnes. U.S. reserves are estimated to be 25 million tonnes. Other large reserves are in Canada, Peru, and Mexico.

U.S. mine production of zinc (recoverable zinc) in August 2000 was 69,000 tonnes, up 1 percent from the previous month and 6 percent more than in June. In the January-August 2000 period, mine production was 527,000 tonnes. For all of 1999, mine production was 808,000 tonnes (recoverable zinc). Smelter production of zinc (refined) in August 2000 was 30,800 tonnes, the same output as in July and just under the June output. In the January-August 2000 period, smelter production of zinc was 254,000 tonnes, while for all of 1999 it was 356,000 tonnes. U.S. production of zinc oxide in August 2000 was 9,290 tonnes, the same as in the previous two months. In the January-August 2000 period, zinc oxide production was 75,400 tonnes, while for all of 1999 it was 123,000 tonnes. U.S. shipments of refined zinc in August 2000 were 30,800 tonnes. In January-

August 2000, shipments were 255,000 tonnes, while for all of 1999 they were 355,000 tonnes. Stocks of refined zinc in August 2000 were 8,460 tonnes, while at the end of 1999 they were 9,960 tonnes.

Zinc oxide shipments in August 2000 were 9,310 tonnes compared to 9,290 tonnes in July. In the January-August 2000 period, shipments were 74,900 tonnes, while for all of 1999 they were 125,000 tonnes. In the January-August 2000 period, zinc oxide shipments to the rubber industry were 47,900 tonnes, while the chemical industry took 16,500 tonnes. Shipments to the ceramics industry were 3,710 tonnes, while the paint industry took 2,600 tonnes. U.S. stocks of zinc oxide in August 2000 were 3,740 tonnes, while stocks at the end of 1999 were 3,250 tonnes.

U.S. apparent consumption of refined zinc in August 2000 was 105,000 tonnes, up 10 percent from July. In the January-August 2000 period, consumption was 902,000 tonnes. Of the total, sheet and strip galvanizing took 357,000 tonnes, while other galvanizing uses took 131,000 tonnes. Refined zinc used in brass and bronze was 128,000 tonnes. Use of refined zinc in zinc-base alloy was 165,000 tonnes, while other uses were 121,000 tonnes. U.S. consumption of zinc ore (zinc content) in August 2000 was 82 tonnes, the same as in the previous two months. In the January-August 2000 period, zinc ore consumption was 668 tonnes, while for all of 1999 it was 986 tonnes. Consumption of zinc-base scrap (zinc content) in August 2000 was 15,900 tonnes, while for the first eight months of 2000 it was 139,000 tonnes. For all of 1999, zinc-base scrap consumption was 191,000 tonnes. Copper-base scrap (zinc content) consumption in August 2000 was 17,200 tonnes. In January-August 2000, it was 136,000 tonnes and in 1999 it was 207,000 tonnes.

U.S. imports for consumption of refined (slab) zinc in July 2000 were 66,900 tonnes. In January-August 2000, they were 551,000 tonnes. Zinc oxide imports in July 2000 were 4,870 tonnes. Zinc ore and concentrate (zinc content) imports in July 2000 were 2,950 tonnes.

Futures Markets

Zinc futures and options are traded on the London Metals Exchange (LME).

Salient Statistics of Zinc in the United States   In Metric Tons

Year	Slab Zinc Production — Primary	Slab Zinc Production — Secondary	Mine Production (Recovered)	Imports for Consumption — Slab Zinc	Imports for Consumption — Ore (Zinc Content)	Exports — Slab Zinc	Exports — Ore (Zinc Content)	Consumption — Slab Zinc	Consumption — Consumed as Ore	Consumption — All Classes[3]	Net Import Reliance as a % of Consumption	High-Grade, Price -Cents/Lb.-
1990	262,704	95,708	515,355	631,742	46,684	1,238	220,446	992,000	2,178	1,240,000	41	74.59
1991	253,276	124,078	517,804	549,137	45,419	1,253	381,416	931,000	2,098	1,160,000	24	52.77
1992	272,000	128,000	523,430	644,482	44,523	565	307,114	1,050,000	2,400	1,290,000	33	58.38
1993	240,000	141,000	488,374	723,563	33,093	1,410	311,278	1,120,000	2,200	1,340,000	36	46.15
1994	216,600	139,000	570,000	793,000	27,374	6,310	389,000	1,180,000	2,400	1,400,000	35	49.26
1995	232,000	131,000	603,000	856,000	10,300	3,080	424,000	1,230,000	2,400	1,460,000	35	55.83
1996	226,000	140,000	586,000	827,000	15,100	1,970	425,000	1,210,000	1,400	1,450,000	33	51.11
1997	226,000	141,000	592,000	876,000	49,600	3,630	461,000	1,260,000	----	1,490,000	35	64.56
1998[1]	234,000	134,000	709,000	879,000	46,300	2,330	552,000	1,290,000	----	1,580,000	35	51.43
1999[2]	241,000	131,000	808,000	966,000	74,600	1,880	531,000	1,340,000	----	1,610,000	30	53.48

[1] Preliminary. [2] Estimate. [3] Based on apparent consumption of slab zinc plus zinc content of ores and concentrates and secondary materials used to make zinc dust and chemicals. *Source: U.S. Geological Survey (USGS)*

World Smelter Production of Zinc[3] In Thousands of Metric Tons

Year	Australia	Belgium	Canada	France	Germany	Italy	Japan	Kazakhstan[4]	Mexico	Poland	Spain	United States	World Total
1990	308.5	356.5	591.8	263.1	350.3	264.4	731.6	890.0	199.3	132.2	252.7	358.4	7,178
1991	326.5	384.2	660.6	299.6	345.7	263.8	778.7	800.0	189.1	126.0	262.2	376.0	7,310
1992	333.0	310.6	671.7	318.7	383.1	252.6	780.6	260.0	151.6	134.6	351.9	399.0	7,260
1993	321.0	299.6	659.9	310.0	380.9	182.0	744.6	263.0	209.9	149.1	341.6	382.0	7,360
1994	328.0	306.2	691.0	306.0	359.9	203.6	713.0	172.4	209.2	154.4	294.7	356.0	7,330
1995	325.0	301.1	720.3	300.0	322.5	180.4	711.1	169.2	222.7	162.7	358.0	363.0	7,370
1996	331.0	234.4	715.6	324.3	327.0	269.0	642.3	190.0	221.7	163.1	360.8	366.0	7,560
1997	317.0	244.0	703.8	346.0	251.7	227.7	650.2	189.0	231.4	171.0	364.2	367.0	7,870
1998[1]	322.0	205.0	745.1	321.0	334.0	231.6	652.7	241.6	230.3	175.0	360.0	368.0	8,120
1999[2]	348.0	232.4	784.8	340.0	330.0	152.8	565.0	247.0	220.0	178.0	375.0	371.0	8,400

[1] Preliminary. [2] Estimate. [3] Secondary metal included. [4] Formerly part of the U.S.S.R.; data not reported separately until 1992.
Source: U.S. Geological Survey (USGS)

Consumption (Reported) of Slab Zinc in the United States, by Industries and Grades In Metric Tons

Year	Total	Galvanizers	Brass Products	Zinc-Base Alloy[3]	Zinc Oxide	Other	Special High Grade	High Grade	Remelt and Other	Prime Western
1990	801,969	388,421	104,276	171,771	67,532	69,969	445,427	92,424	78,265	210,373
1991	764,038	364,629	97,952	169,883	64,035	67,539	421,316	91,468	57,786	189,930
1992	814,228	396,480	112,990	165,598	71,224	67,936	414,661	119,660	56,185	223,723
1993	1,035,000	532,400	139,500	222,000	63,448	141,100	403,696	116,500	71,202	182,309
1994	859,000	395,000	107,000	196,000	68,300	92,400	486,000	112,000	68,400	192,000
1995	1,240,000	390,000	91,500	194,000	70,900	90,800	135,000	98,200	54,400	251,000
1996	788,000	398,000	87,400	142,000	[4]	161,000	385,000	111,000	54,000	238,000
1997	672,000	347,000	76,800	107,000	[4]	141,000	319,000	88,700	57,200	207,000
1998[1]	647,000	320,000	60,300	122,000	[4]	145,000	331,000	72,800	51,700	192,000
1999[2]	614,000	308,000	78,200	105,000	[4]	124,000	317,000	58,400	55,400	184,000

[1] Preliminary. [2] Estimated. [3] Die casters. [4] Included in other. Source: U.S. Geological Survey (USGS)

United States Foreign Trade of Zinc In Metric Tons

Year	Ores[1]	Blocks, Pigs, Slabs	Sheets, Plates, Other	Waste & Scrap	Dross, Ashes, Fume	Dust, Powder & Flakes	Total Value $1,000	Blocks, Pigs, Anodes, etc. Unwrought	Wrought & Alloys Unwrought Alloys	Sheets, Plates & Strips	Angles, Bars, Rods, etc.	Waste & Scrap	Dust (Blue Powder)	Zinc Ore & Concentrates
1990	46,684	631,742	929	31,720	6,411	8,834	1,049,940	1,238	4,566	11,881	3,731	109,316	8,701	220,446
1991	45,419	549,137	539	31,596	6,483	15,424	687,879	1,253	4,224	10,385	6,151	96,314	5,737	381,416
1992	44,523	644,482	171	31,176	11,813	17,051	910,289	5,886	----	----	----	82,088	5,889	307,114
1993	33,093	723,563	135	38,079	11,862	16,218	799,999	8,765	----	----	----	46,385	6,727	311,278
1994	27,374	793,482	475	51,676	12,152	11,954	878,100	13,220	----	----	----	58,297	6,603	389,488
1995	10,300	856,000	332	42,300	10,900	11,700	1,018,620	----	----	----	----	55,900	8,840	424,000
1996	15,100	827,000	16,900	31,900	14,500	10,300	1,001,800	----	----	----	----	45,500	11,100	425,000
1997	49,600	876,000	19,200	29,600	----	11,700	1,340,390	----	----	----	----	46,100	9,980	461,000
1998[2]	46,300	879,000	16,900	29,200	----	17,600	1,098,690	----	----	----	----	35,000	5,530	552,000
1999[3]	74,600	966,000	22,600	26,600	----	21,300	1,167,190	----	----	----	----	28,200	5,050	531,000

[1] Zinc content. [2] Preliminary. [3] Estimate. NA = Not available. Source: U.S. Geological Survey (USGS)

Mine Production of Recoverable Zinc in the United States In Thousands of Metric Tons

Year	Jan.	Feb.	Mar.	Apr.	May	June	July	Aug.	Sept.	Oct.	Nov.	Dec.	Total
1991	45.5	41.9	43.8	45.5	49.4	36.9	43.0	47.4	49.5	39.0	33.4	38.0	517.8
1992	41.5	48.8	47.7	40.3	40.7	40.4	46.2	49.1	47.6	36.2	40.4	42.2	520.1
1993	48.0	42.5	46.4	39.5	43.0	40.7	33.5	32.1	35.9	41.8	41.4	43.4	488.3
1994	43.2	40.2	48.4	44.0	47.9	47.1	52.5	47.1	50.1	41.6	46.0	48.0	557.0
1995	49.8	48.1	52.8	45.6	54.5	50.0	50.2	55.0	48.1	52.0	47.8	48.1	601.0
1996	52.4	48.9	49.7	45.5	50.7	49.9	53.7	48.1	46.8	43.4	43.1	42.6	600.0
1997	46.2	45.7	45.8	47.9	49.7	45.3	45.9	49.8	53.0	47.6	44.2	48.4	574.0
1998	50.1	48.3	56.5	56.2	56.7	55.0	59.5	57.2	60.1	55.7	62.0	61.9	722.0
1999	61.4	57.6	63.0	67.0	61.7	62.8	68.2	72.1	60.8	67.8	61.2	65.9	808.0
2000[1]	64.4	56.6	68.5	64.5	70.2	65.3	68.1	71.4	59.6	62.3	63.5	61.9	776.3

[1] Preliminary. Source: U.S. Geological Survey (USGS)

ZINC

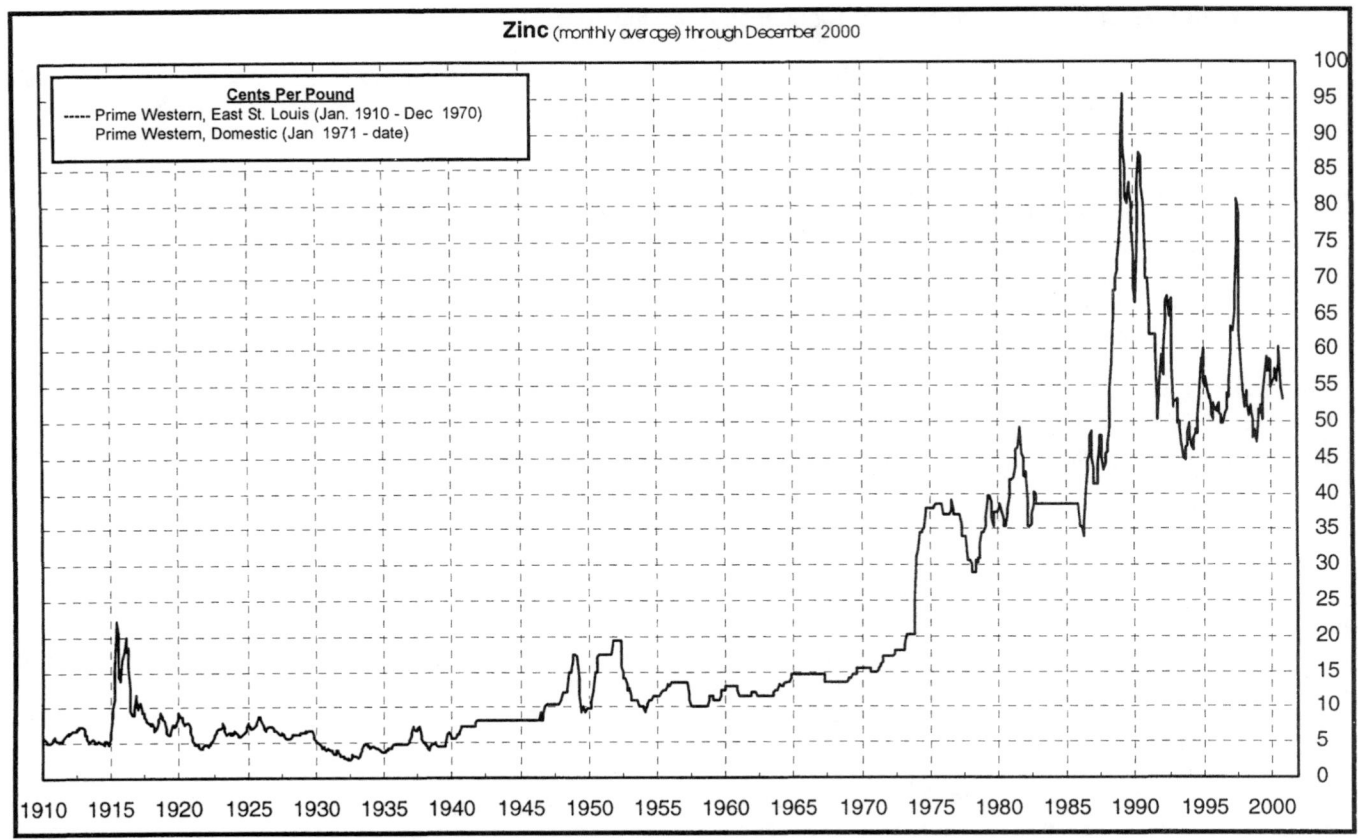

Zinc (monthly average) through December 2000

Consumption of Slab Zinc by Fabricators in the United States   In Thousands of Metric Tons

Year	Jan.	Feb.	Mar.	Apr.	May	June	July	Aug.	Sept.	Oct.	Nov.	Dec.	Average
1991	80.0	69.0	65.9	67.8	68.3	68.8	73.6	78.0	79.3	85.9	84.2	82.0	764.0
1992	93.8	77.2	85.0	89.9	76.0	76.9	47.2	53.8	52.2	53.5	50.3	47.6	814.2
1993	50.9	49.2	55.8	59.2	60.8	55.7	44.6	49.1	47.0	52.7	50.9	51.0	774.0
1994	50.8	53.7	55.7	58.5	58.7	52.7	48.0	53.2	53.6	53.9	52.5	45.0	623.0
1995	51.3	57.8	56.3	57.9	53.4	58.0	44.0	44.0	58.8	57.0	56.0	54.5	838.0
1996	56.3	55.6	59.3	55.7	56.3	55.9	48.9	48.1	54.4	56.4	54.2	53.1	788.0
1997	47.2	43.1	48.6	50.1	48.1	45.3	45.1	45.5	50.9	49.6	44.3	46.2	588.0
1998	46.3	45.2	47.4	44.8	45.4	49.0	46.0	45.0	45.9	45.9	40.5	43.9	647.0
1999	40.5	45.4	43.8	40.3	42.5	47.1	37.8	40.1	42.0	42.8	41.1	39.7	614.0
2000[1]	41.8	44.6	47.7	45.6	44.4	49.1	42.0	43.3	42.6	47.5	43.8	40.3	532.7

[1] Preliminary.   *Source: U.S. Geological Survey (USGS)*

Average Price of Zinc, Prime Western Slab (Delivered U.S. Basis)   In Cents Per Pound

Year	Jan.	Feb.	Mar.	Apr.	May	June	July	Aug.	Sept.	Oct.	Nov.	Dec.	Total
1991	70.00	64.53	62.00	62.00	62.00	62.00	62.00	NQ	NQ	50.44	54.85	59.22	60.90
1992	57.62	56.40	60.19	64.12	66.83	67.29	64.57	66.47	67.12	57.84	52.16	52.71	61.11
1993	52.70	53.18	49.72	50.07	49.27	46.75	46.90	45.08	44.54	46.21	46.54	48.69	48.30
1994	49.64	48.29	46.70	46.16	47.66	48.42	48.81	48.26	50.55	53.81	58.64	57.41	50.36
1995	60.11	55.44	54.84	56.08	54.61	53.08	53.75	52.00	50.77	50.42	52.52	51.60	53.77
1996	51.38	51.86	52.66	51.03	50.76	49.75	49.86	50.86	51.22	51.76	53.81	53.39	51.53
1997	55.64	59.82	63.28	62.62	65.65	67.78	75.29	80.89	78.96	62.55	57.83	54.45	65.40
1998	55.43	51.86	51.98	54.31	52.77	50.78	52.23	51.64	50.29	47.63	48.74	48.44	51.23
1999	47.29	51.11	51.68	51.07	52.20	50.35	53.73	56.28	59.12	57.07	56.91	58.75	53.84
2000	58.44	54.67	55.60	56.14	57.44	55.67	56.52	58.04	60.53	54.67	53.07	53.00	56.15

NQ = No Quote.   *Source: American Metal Market (AMM)*